Psalms

Volume 1

Allan Harman's commentary is the fruit of a lifetime's study of the Psalter and provides a well-informed, reliable guide to the vast literature on the subject. The extensive introduction is itself worth its weight in gold while the Scripture text is opened up in a clear, careful and devout way.

Philip H Eveson,
Former principal of London Theological Seminary and lecturer in Old Testament exegesis, theology and preaching

Harman's Commentary on the Psalms is a solid exposition of the Psalms. The focus is on the original meaning of the psalms with clear explanations of the message of each psalm through an analysis of structure, key words, and the flow of the psalm. And yet, the meaning of the psalms for God's people today is also emphasized by showing important connections to the New Testament. The reader will discover the rich treasures in the Psalms through the use of this commentary.

Richard P. Belcher, Jr.
Professor of Old Testament, Reformed Theological Seminary, Charlotte, North Carolina

Allan Harman writes as a Christian scholar, with academic precision and devotional warmth. The unique character of this commentary is undoubtedly due to the method of its preparation (revealed in the author's "Foreword"). After completing careful exegesis of each Psalm, Allan brought the fruits of his study into the service of family worship in his own home. The result is a commentary that is both academically solid and devotionally rich. This commentary will be a worthy resource for the pastor and student in the study as well as the layman seeking personal edification.

Michael LeFebvre
Pastor, Christ Church Reformed Presbyterian Church, Indianapolis, Indiana

Psalms

Volume 1

Psalms 1-72

A Mentor Commentary

Allan Harman

MENTOR

To Mairi

Allan Harman is Research Professor of Old Testament at the Presbyterian Theological College in Melbourne, Australia. He has taught graduate courses at Ontario Theological Seminary, Toronto and Reformed Theological Seminary, Jackson, Mississippi.

ISBN 978-1-84550-737-4

(Volume 2 ISBN 978-1-84550-738-1)

10 9 8 7 6 5 4 3 2 1

Published in 2011
in the
Mentor Imprint
by
Christian Focus Publications,
Geanies House, Fearn, Tain,
Ross-shire, IV20 1TW, Great Britain
www.christianfocus.com

Cover design by Daniel van Straaten
Printed and bound by MPG Books, UK

Contents

BOOK 2

Abbreviations

ASV — *American Standard Version.*
AV — *Authorised (King James) Version.*
BASOR — *Bulletin of the American Schools of Oriental Research.*
BBR — *Bulletin for Biblical Research.*
BDB — Brown, Driver, and Briggs, *eds., A Hebrew and English Lexicon of the Old Testament.* (Oxford: Clarendon Press, 1975 reprint).
BHS — *Biblia Hebraica Stuttgartensia (Stuttgart: Deutsche Bibelstiftung, 1967/77).*
Bib — *Biblica.*
BS — *Bibliotheca Sacra.*
c. — Latin, around, about.
CJT — *Canadian Journal of Theology.*
CHAL — *A Concise Hebrew and Aramaic Lexicon of the Old Testament (Grand Rapids: Eerdmans, 1988).*
DCH — *Dictionary of Classical Hebrew,* ed. David J.A. Clines, 7 vols. (Sheffield: Sheffield Academic Press, 1993-)
DIHG~S — J. C. L. Gibson, *Davidson's Introductory Hebrew Grammar~Syntax,* 4th ed. (Edinburgh: T. & T. Clark, 1994).
DOTT — *Documents from Old Testament Times.*
EBC — *Expositor's Bible Commentary.*
ESV — *English Standard Version.* Wheaton: Good News Publishers, 2001.
EQ — *Evangelical Quarterly.*
ET — *Expository Times.*
GKC — *Gesenius' Hebrew Grammar*, 2nd ed., Gesenius, Kautzsch, Cowley eds. (Oxford: Clarendon Press), 1966.
HALOT — *The Hebrew and Aramaic Lexicon of the Old Testament* (Leiden: Brill, 2000).
Heb. — Hebrew.
IBHS — *An Introduction to Biblical Hebrew Syntax,* Bruce K. Waltke and M. O'Connor (Winona Lake: Eisenbrauns, 1990).
IBS — *Irish Biblical Studies.*
IDB — *Interpreter's Dictionary of the Bible,* 4 vols. (Nashville: Abingdon Press, 1962).
ISBE — *International Standard Bible Encyclopaedia.* 4 vols. (Grand Rapids: Eerdmans, 1979).
JANES — *Journal of the Ancient Near Eastern Society.*
JB — *Jerusalem Bible.*
JBL — *Journal of Biblical Literature.*
JETS — *Journal of the Evangelical Theological Society.*
JNSL — *Journal of North West Semitic Languages.*
JSOT — *Journal for the Study of the Old Testament.*

JSS	*Journal of Semitic Studies.*
JTS	*Journal of Theological Studies.*
lit.	literally.
LXX	The Septuagint, the oldest and most important Greek translation of the Old Testament made in Egypt about 250 BC.
mg.	margin.
MT	Massoretic text, the Hebrew text of the Old Testament that became recognised as authoritative after the fall of Jerusalem in 70 AD.
NASB	*New American Standard Bible*: Updated Edition. Anaheim, CA: Foundation Publications, 1997.
NEB	*The New English Bible.* New York: Oxford University Press, 1976.
NICOT	*New International Commentary on the Old Testament.*
NIDOTTE	*New International Dictionary of Old Testament Theology and Exegesis,* ed. Willem A. VanGemeren, 5 vols. (Grand Rapids: Zondervan, 1997).
NIV	*New International Version.* Colorado Springs: International Bible Society, 1984.
NKJV	*New King James Version.* Nashville: Thomas Nelson, 1982.
NLT	*New Living Translation.* Wheaton: Tyndale House, 1996.
NRSV	*New Revised Standard Version.* Nashville: Thomas Nelson, 1989.
OTS	*Oudtestamentische Studiën.*
part.	participle.
pass.	passive.
PEQ	*Palestine Exploration Quarterly.*
PTR	*Princeton Theological Review.*
REB	*The Revised English Bible.* Oxford University Press, 1989.
RSV	*Revised Standard Version.*
RTR	*Reformed Theological Review.*
RV	*Revised Version.*
SJT	*Scottish Journal of Theology.*
TB	*Tyndale Bulletin.*
TS	*Theological Studies.*
TDOT	*Theological Dictionary of the Old Testament,* 15 vols. (Grand Rapids: Zondervan, 1997).
TWOT	*Theological Wordbook of the Old Testament,* 2 vols. (Chicago: Moody Press, 1980).
VT	*Vetus Testamentum.*
WTJ	*Westminster Theological Journal.*
×	The number of occurrences of a word in a particular verse or section is marked by this multiplication sign, e.g. 2×.
ZAW	*Zeitschrift für die alttestamentliche Wissenschaft.*
ZPEB	*Zondervan Pictorial Encyclopedia of the Bible,* 5 vols. (Grand Rapids: Zondervan Publishing House, 1975).

GLOSSARY

acrostic	In an acrostic poem the first letter of each verse or stanza follows an alphabetic sequence.
Dead Sea Scrolls	About 800 scrolls containing all or part of Old Testament books discovered at or near Qumran, on the north-western side of the Dead Sea.
fixed pair	The term 'fixed pair' refers to words that regularly occur in parallel expressions in Hebrew, e.g., head/skull, earth/dust, mouth/lip.
ellipsis (or, gapping)	This occurs when a normal element of a sentence is missing and has to be understood from the context.
hapax legomenon	A word occurring only once (pl. *hapax legomena*).
hendiadys	lit. 'one through two [words]', the presentation of one idea by two expressions, e.g., 'with might and main'.
homonym	A word having the same sound as another, but with a different meaning and origin. In the text, these Hebrew words are marked by the addition of a Roman numeral as listed in the *Dictionary of Classical Hebrew*, e.g., *rav* II.
inclusio	A literary device by which a repeated theme both introduces and concludes a passage, so marking it as a separate section.
K^{e}tiv	A massoretic marginal note to the Hebrew text meaning 'that which is written' (see also Q^{e}re).
maqqef	A short horizontal stroke linking two Hebrew words.

Massoretes	Groups of Jewish scholars (AD 600-1000) who produced the final form of the OT text, adding the vocalisation, accents, and various notations.
Q^ere	A massoretic marginal note to the Hebrew text meaning 'that which is to be read' (in place of 'that which is written', the K^etiv).
Qumran	See above, 'Dead Sea Scrolls'.
targum	An Aramaic translation or paraphrase of some part of the Old Testament. They were oral at first but were later written. The earliest examples (found at Qumran) are from the second century BC.
theophany	A visible appearance of God.
Vulgate	The Latin version of the Bible produced by Jerome in the period AD 380-405, which became the official Bible of the Roman Catholic Church at the Council of Trent in 1546.

Notes on Hebrew

Verbal Themes

Qal	Qal
Ni.	Nif'al
Pi.	Pi'el
Pu.	Pu'al
Hi.	Hif'il
Ho.	Hof'al
Hitp.	Hitpa'el

Grammatical Expressions

absol. inf.	Absolute infinitive: a verbal form normally placed before another form of the verb in order to emphasise it.
cognate accusative	The use of a noun as the object of a verb which comes from the same root, e.g., 'They dreaded [with] dread' (Ps. 14:5).
coh.	cohortative: indirect imperative forms in the 1st person singular and plural, e.g., 'Let me (us) send'.
constr.	construct: a noun, usually in a shortened form, placed before another noun and with a close semantic relation to it, covering all the nuances of the English *of*.
enclitic *mem*	A final *mem* added to words in poetry. This is a rare survival of an archaic form that has no obvious function.
imper.	imperative
imperfect	A verbal conjugation in Hebrew that identifies a situation as fluid or in motion.
inf.	infinitive

interrogative marker: The use of h^a prefixed to a sentence to change it into a question.

jussive: 3rd person forms of the indirect imperative, e.g., 'Let him (them) send'.

m.: masculine

part.: participle

pass.: passive

perfect: A verbal conjugation in Hebrew that identifies a situation as static or at rest.

pers.: person

pl.: plural

s.: singular

vav consecutive: The use of the conjunction *vav* ('and') and a verbal form to indicate a simple action that has arisen out of something that has gone before.

Transliteration of Consonants

alef	ʾ
bet	b/v
gimel	g
dalet	d
he	h
vav	v
zayin	z
chet	ch (as in German *ich*, or Scottish *loch*)
tet	t
yod	y
kaf	k
lamed	l
mem	m
nun	n

samek	s
ayin	ʿ
peh	p/f
tsadeh	ts
qof	q
resh	r
sin	s
shin	sh
taw	t

Note:

1. Long vowels are marked with a circumflex, e.g. *â, ê, î, ô, û*.
2. Hebrew words are normally accented on the final syllable. However, there is a group of nouns in which the stress is placed on the first of a pair of vowels, resulting in next-to-last syllable stress. This is marked by the use of an acute, e.g. *régel* (foot). The acute is also used with a small number of other nouns that do not have the stress on the final syllable, e.g. *shâmáyim* (heavens).

Foreword

To be able to work twice through the Psalms in preparing commentaries has been a special privilege for me. I thank Christian Focus Publications for the invitation to enlarge my earlier commentary (published in 1998). I have expanded the exegesis, and in doing so I have maintained my method as a commentator that I have explained in the foreword to *Isaiah: A Covenant to be Kept for the Sake of the Church* (Fearn: Christian Focus Publications, 2005). My aim has been to explain the Hebrew text without entering into debate with others. Footnotes have been added to expand on some matters requiring further detail, or to direct the reader's attention to sources of grammatical or lexicographical information. While I have referred to Hebrew quite often, I hope I have done it in a way that still makes it easy for those without a knowledge of the language to feel at home in using this commentary.

It has been encouraging to hear from those who have used my earlier volume and to know that it has served the purpose for which it was written. In the years since its publication I have read widely on the Psalms, and I thank those who have contributed to my thinking, even though there is no express acknowledgement of them in the text.

Once more I have to thank my wife Mairi, who has either read the manuscript, or listened to me reading it, as we worked through the Psalter in our evening devotions. She has partnered me in the work of the Gospel and her help and encouragement continues to be integral to my writing ministry.

Allan M. Harman

Approaching the Psalms

1. SINGING GOD'S PRAISE

1.1 Introducing God's Songs

Songs of praise to God do not only occur in the Book of Psalms. Scattered through various books of the Old Testament are songs sung by the believing community of Israel. The list includes songs such as:

- The Song of the Sea (Exod. 15:1-18) which was composed to celebrate the LORD's deliverance of his people from their bondage in Egypt, and recorded following their dramatic passage through the sea.
- The Song of Moses (Deut. 32:1-43) which was taught to the children of Israel by Moses as a review and a farewell.
- The Song of Deborah and Barak (Judg. 5:1-31) in which they give thanks for the righteous and protective acts of the Lord which had just been manifested in their midst (Judg. 4).
- The Song of Hannah (1 Sam. 2:1-10), a song of thanksgiving with a recognition that life and death come from the Lord.
- 2 Samuel 22:2-51 (appearing also as Ps. 18), a song of joy by David in God as his rock and deliverer.
- Hezekiah's Song (Isa. 38:9-20), composed after his recovery from illness, and in which he sings of God's faithfulness to him (vv. 18-19).

These and various other songs have many similarities with the Book of Psalms. Their language is the same, and they use the same kind of style. In singing both *to* God and *about* him, they do so in a way we quickly recognise as being like the psalmists. It helps to look at some general features of these songs of praise before we come specifically to the Psalter.

1.2 Singing Doxologies

Praise is addressed to God primarily because it is a special way of extolling who he is and what he does. Often we think of using what we call 'doxologies' at the beginning or end of a service of worship. However, every hymn addressed to God is really a doxology, for in using it we are proclaiming to God what we know of his person and work. Thus we say to God: 'You are the one whose glory is over all the earth' (Ps. 108:5), or 'You are my King and my God, who decrees victories for Jacob. Through you we push back our enemies; through your name we trample our foes' (Ps. 44:4-5).

Singing in this way in front of others, or joining with them in communal songs of praise, also involves an element of confession. In addressing God in words or song we are telling others what we know of him, and also confessing that he is the God whom we have come to honour and trust. Singing the Lord's songs then can be an acknowledgment of an allegiance to him.

1.3 Praise and the Wonderful Deeds of the LORD

The songs of praise in the Old Testament focus attention on what God has done. They are often long recitals of the great deeds of God. This is particularly so of the 'historical psalms' such as 78, 105, 106, and 136, while in many other psalms there are references to historical incidents. The psalmist, in Psalm 77, speaks of calling to mind the deeds of the LORD and remembering God's wonders of old (vv. 11-12). The use of the word 'wonder' is important in psalms like this, because it translates a Hebrew word which has the idea that it is something that only God can do. Telling out the 'wonders of the LORD' means to proclaim the great things God has done for the salvation of his people.

1.4 Praise and Commitment to God's Covenant

The praises of Israel have to be seen in the wider context of Israel's commitment to the Lord. There was a bond or covenant between God and Israel, and they were solemnly pledged to be the Lord's people. In all their worship they acknowledged the relationship, and numerous features of their life were said to be 'to the Lord' (e.g. the Passover, Exod. 12:11, 27, 48; the Sabbath, Exod. 16:23; the year of Jubilee, Deut. 15:2; the Nazirite, Num. 6:2). In singing to the Lord the people were in a verbal way paying their tribute to their great king and Saviour. It was another way of reaffirming the oath they had taken to him. This comes out strikingly in David's words, 'The Lord lives, blessed be my Rock' (Ps. 18:46). It is clear from Jeremiah 5:2 that the phrase 'as the Lord lives' was part of an oath formula. Here it appears in conjunction with a doxology to God.

Another way to see this same commitment is in regard to God's law. There are psalms such as Psalm 119 in which there is constant reference to God's word, or statutes, or testimonies. In other words, the praise of God's law is once again submission to God's covenant requirements.[1] From the same perspective we can see that the laments, especially of a communal nature, are saying that the people have departed from God's covenant pattern for them.

1.5 Praise and Promise for the Future

Believers are able to sing contemporaneously with glorified believers in heaven. There is a union between saints on earth and saints in heaven (Heb. 12:22-24). They sing a song on earth that echoes that of saints above. Believers still living have access to the heavenly Zion of which they have become citizens. They are 'Blest inhabitants of Zion, Washed in the Redeemer's blood' (John Newton, 'Glorious things of thee are spoken'), and so can sing in unison with the great company in heaven of redeemed sinners and angels who together sing praise to the Lamb who was slain (Rev. 5:12-13; 7:9-12).

---

[1] A valuable discussion on 'The Concept of the Word of God as Seen in Psalm 119' can be found in John P. Milton, *The Psalms* (Rock Island, Illinois: Augustana Book Concern, 1954), pp. 99-127.

Having learned of the grace of God in salvation, Old Testament psalmists also realised that it had implications for the future. The kingdom of God had not come to full expression. The Gentiles were hardly yet touched with the blessings of God, but they would yet experience the blessing of the Lord (Ps. 67). There are songs which express longing for the extension of God's kingdom, so that Messiah will reign from the River (i.e. the Euphrates) to the uttermost ends of the earth (Ps. 72:11), and all ends of the earth will turn to the Lord, and all families of the nations will bow down before Him (Ps. 22:27).

The fact that God has often intervened in human history and does great and wonderful things encourages his people to sing of coming events. Believers have the confidence that the LORD will keep them and ultimately bring them into his glory (Ps. 73:24). At the end the LORD will come to judge the world in righteousness (Ps. 96:13). He has established a throne from which he will judge the world (Ps. 9:8), but he will vindicate his own people (Ps. 135:14).

2. THE USE OF POETRY

2.1 Poetry and Music

Jewish and Christian worship make extensive use of religious poetry. Such poetry involves two distinct features:

(a) It is a style of writing that is different from the normal style of narrative prose. For example, compare the account of God's covenant with David as recorded in 2 Samuel 7 with the poetical expression of it in Psalm 89; or Genesis 1 with Psalm 8. The same ideas can be conveyed in prose and poetry, but poetry contains music in words and this attracts us and is more memorable.

(b) This religious poetry is not only *said*, but it is *sung*, and such singing forms an important part of religious expression. Naturally we do not have examples directly from biblical times but there are many examples of synagogue music. Some of these are carried over into Christian worship, as, for example, the tune Leoni sung to the hymn, 'The God of Abraham Praise'.

Music, like language, has its origin in the fact that man is a creature of God, and in making music man is imitating God himself. He has been created in God's image, and his ability to use both words and music is a result of his being a unique image bearer. Music is not given for pure entertainment but as a thing of beauty that directs attention to God's works of creation (creativity) and providence (order). When music and religious poetry are brought together in harmony there is a special appeal to the human mind and emotions. In itself music is not identical to language but it has some of the same abilities as poetical language to appeal to the imagination and to touch human emotions.

Creativity in language and music are brought together in psalmody and hymnody. A message is conveyed in both words and music which combine to produce an effect upon the hearer, which in turn heightens religious understanding and experience.

2.2 Characteristics of Poetry

The poetry of the Old Testament shares some features with Western poetry, but in other respects it is quite different. Some of the features in common are:

(a) The normal patterns of word order can be varied in poetry. The impact of normal word order is important as we can often predict what the end of a sentence will be. However, an unusual pattern has the effect of pressing on our attention the idea being presented.

(b) The language of poetry is often much more conservative than popular speech, and unusual words are frequently used. Some words are even invented to fit a particular context. We have only to glance at an older hymn book (and some modern ones) to see examples which would be very strange in ordinary conversation: 'inly', 'Bethlem', 'sage', 'Christly', 'illuming', 'wert', 'cloys', 'lays', 'supernal', 'pent', 'till moons shall *wax* ...', 'riven', 'assuage', 'transport of delight'. It also retains words that have dropped out of everyday use, and thereby fossilises them in poetic form. For example, in modern Scripture in song you will still find words like 'thee', 'thine', 'thou', 'realm', 'diadem', and many others.

(c) It uses many features of style such as playing on the initial sound in words (alliteration) or sound in other syllables (assonance). Poetry also uses similes (in which there is a comparison) and metaphors (in which something is said to be something else, e.g. the LORD is a rock). Metaphors are very important because they ensure that our minds are involved because we have to work out the meanings of the words of the poem. They also appeal to our imagination which is attracted by the total idea. Moreover, metaphors often touch our emotions for they appeal to our senses. Hence, because they combine an idea with a feeling, they express much more to us than the bare idea expressed without a metaphor.

(d) There is no sharp dividing line between prose and poetry, for sometimes elevated prose will contain features which are normally characteristic of poetry. There are distinctive characteristics of both prose and poetry, and many examples of literature share features from both. The distinction between poetry and prose may be one of degree, rather than an absolute division. For Old Testament poetry this can be illustrated by the following diagram:

Parallelism
Figurative language
Non-predictable word order

Prose ⟷ Poetry

Narrative sequence
Non-figurative language
Predictable word order

2.3 The Distinctiveness of Old Testament Poetry

Other features of Old Testament poetry are quite different because they are part of Hebrew and therefore of Near Eastern poetic style. The most important feature of Old Testament poetry is the use of phrases in a parallel way. Thus the psalmist says:

> The eyes of the Lord are on the righteous,
> and his ears are attentive to their cry (Ps. 34:15).

There is a correspondence between the two phrases which may be similar as in this one, or which may express opposites as in Psalm 1:6:

> For the Lord watches over the way of the righteous,
> but the way of the wicked will perish.

Perhaps the most common pattern is where the second phrase adds something more to the expression. The poet introduces an idea, and then focuses more specifically on it in the following phrase. We can express this by calling the two phrases A and B. The pattern is:

> A, and what's more,
> B.

For example, Psalm 6 commences with the words:

> O Lord, do not rebuke me in your anger
> or discipline me in your wrath.

The psalm opens with a plea to God not to speak words of rebuke to him (A), but then in the second part of the verse (B), the psalmist asks that no action ('discipline') will be taken against him. The phrases are clearly not identical, but show a progression of thought.

Hebrew poetry also uses a range of devices to draw attention to the ideas. These include features that are very stilted if we attempt to bring them over into English translations. For example, many poems in the Old Testament use acrostics, in which the letters of the alphabet appear in order at the beginning of lines. This can be done where a single line follows (Ps. 34) or where several lines follow (Pss. 9-10), or as in Psalm 119, in which every line of the twenty-two sections starts with the appropriate letter of the Hebrew alphabet.[2] This explains why in English translations of this psalm the Hebrew letters are actually printed in the text (see also the NIV footnote). For native Hebrew speakers these devices would attract attention and make an appeal to the reader or listener. Also, they may have been useful for memorisation. They can be likened to embroidery, which takes so many hours to do, but the result is a beautiful piece of work that attracts and delights.[3]

2.4 Sung Praise in Old Testament Worship

From earliest times music was employed (Gen. 4:21) and songs of praise feature in the Pentateuch (Exod. 15:1-18, 21; Deut. 32) and the early historical books (Judg. 5; 1 Sam. 2). Music and religious poetry are inseparably connected from the time of David onwards. When the ark of the covenant was brought to Jerusalem David instructed the leaders of the Levites to appoint singers of joyful songs, who were to be accompanied with lyres, harps and cymbals (1 Chron. 15:16). For service in the house of God he appointed the sons of Asaph, Heman, and Jeduthun to a ministry of singing (1 Chron. 25:1ff.; singing is called 'prophesying' in the Hebrew of this passage). On the day in which the ark was brought to Jerusalem David committed to Asaph and his associates a song which is a combination of several psalms (cf. 1 Chron. 16:8-36 with Pss. 105:1-15; 96; 106:1, 47-48), and to this song the people responded with 'Amen, Hallelujah'. Over 80 per cent of the

---

[2] Cf. the attempt by Edward H. Sugden, *The Psalms of David: Translated into English Verse in accordance with the Metres and Strophic Structure of the Hebrew* (Melbourne: MacMillan & Co., 1924), to reproduce the alphabetic patterns in his translations.

[3] For readers who want to carry on further reflection on this subject, an excellent and stimulating starting point is the discussion by Leland Ryken, '"I Have Used Similitudes": The Poetry of the Bible', *BS* (1990), pp. 259-69.

Psalms come from the period of David or later, and over 40 per cent are attributed to David himself. There was song in the temple especially when sacrifices were being offered, and at times the people responded with refrains (2 Chron. 7:3; Ezra 3:11).

2.5 Printing Biblical Poetry

Translation and printing of biblical poetry involves difficulties, as the effort to reproduce in English the complexities of a totally different type of poetry forces many choices to be made. The older translations, such as the Authorised Version, simply printed the Psalms in the same way as the prose passages. Recent translations (e.g. NIV, ESV) have attempted to print the poetic parts of the Bible in a different way to prose. This alerts the reader to the fact that the translators consider these passages are poetical. While they have not necessarily carried over many aspects of Hebrew poetry, yet at least the form in which they are printed prepares the reader for dealing with poetry, not prose. Poems have formal qualities (cf. the reference above to alphabetical psalms) and sometimes these can be brought out in a way that catches the reader's eye. Consider this rendering of Psalm 117 by the Elizabethan poetess, Mary Sidney Herbert (1561-1621):

P raise him that aye
R emains the same:
A ll tongues display
I ehovah's fame,
S ing all that share
T his earthly ball:
H is mercies are
E xposed to all
L ike as the word
O nce he doth give,
R olled in record,
D oth time outlive.

While the poems of the Old Testament are part of divinely inspired Scripture, yet human activity is entailed both in the composition as well as in the translation and printing.[4] Continued effort has to be devoted to translation *and* format so that as much as possible of the original Hebrew poems are conveyed in modern printed English.[5] Communication of the content of the Psalms to generation after generation requires constant endeavour to accurately translate and intelligently convey its message to modern readers and listeners.[6]

3. INTRODUCING THE PSALTER

3.1 The Titles

The Hebrew Bible simply calls the Book of Psalms in Hebrew *tᵉhillîm*, 'Praises'. The Greek translation of the Old Testament (commonly referred to as the LXX), produced by about 200 BC, called them 'Psalmoi', and it is from this word that ultimately we get our English word 'Psalms'. In the New Testament the collection of Psalms is called 'the Book of Psalms' (Luke 20:42; Acts 1:20) and from that expression we get our general descriptive title for the book. One early manuscript of the LXX translation has the title 'Psalterion'. This was the word used

---

[4] This was stated clearly by B. B. Warfield in his discussion, 'The Divine and the Human in the Bible', *Selected Shorter Writings of Benjamin B. Warfield*, ed. John E. Meeter (Phillipsburg: Presbyterian and Reformed, 1973), 2, p. 547: 'The whole of Scripture is the product of divine activities which enter it, however, not by superseding the activities of the human authors, but confluently with them; so that the Scriptures are the joint product of divine and human activities, both of which penetrate them at every point, working harmoniously together to the production of a writing which is not divine here and human there, but at once divine and human in every part, every word, every particular.' See also the discussion on this and other points in D. G. Hart, 'The Divine and the Human in the Seminary Curriculum,' *WTJ* 65 (2003), pp. 36-41.

[5] While alphabetic poetry cannot be imitated in translation (apart from noting the twenty-two sections in Psalm 119), yet other features can be shown, e.g. some chiastic patterns, or the refrains in psalms such as 42-43, 46, and 99.

[6] Further helpful discussions are by Keith R. Crim, 'Translating the Poetry of the Bible', *BT* (January 1972), pp. 102-09; and, William A. Smalley, 'Restructuring Translations of the Psalms as Poetry', in Matthew Black and William A. Smalley, edd., *On Language, Culture, and Religion: In Honor of Eugene A. Nida* (The Hague: Moulton, 1974), pp. 337-71.

for an instrument like a zither, and from this Greek word we get another English title for the Psalms, 'the Psalter'.

Many of the individual psalms have titles given to them. These titles may not have originally been part of the psalms, but they are certainly very early. This is shown by the way in which songs outside the Book of Psalms have titles, such as David's psalms of thanksgiving (2 Sam. 22:1), Hezekiah's song (Isa. 38:9) and Habakkuk's psalm (Hab. 3:1, 19b). Also, the fact that the translators of the Old Testament into Greek had difficulties with the titles when they came to translate them suggests their antiquity. The titles can be grouped according to the type of information they contain. Some merely designate the type of psalm in question (e.g. hymn or song, 32, 83, 145), while others contain musical information (e.g., 4 and 5) or an indication of special use (e.g. 30, 'For the dedication of the Temple'; 92, 'For the Sabbath Day'). Many of the titles relate to a person or groups of people (e.g. David, 3; Solomon, 72; Moses, 90) or give information relating the particular psalm to a historical situation particularly with reference to David (e.g. 18, 56, 60, and 63).[7]

3.2 Difficulties in Approaching the Psalms

The greatest difficulty we face is our familiarity with the Book of Psalms. For many Christian people the Psalms, or particular well-loved psalms, are the parts of the Bible that they know best. In many branches of the Christian tradition the Psalms are said or sung in a distinctive and traditional manner. Thus in Anglican churches usually the Psalms are read or chanted. In Reformed churches, originating either on the Continent or in Scotland, the Psalms for long formed either the major part of sung praise or in many cases the exclusive content of praise. Others are known because they are now part of the paraphrased poetry of a hymn book. Simply because they

---

[7] For full listings of the titles, see W. VanGemeren, 'The Psalms', *The Expositor's Bible Commentary* (Grand Rapids: Zondervan, 1991), 5, pp. 33-39; or, C. Hassell Bullock, *Encountering the Psalms: A Literary and Theological Introduction* (Grand Rapids: Baker Academic, 2001), pp. 24-30. An excellent discussion on the antiquity of the titles can be found in Roger T. Beckwith, 'The Early History of the Psalter', *TB* 46.1 (May 1995), pp. 10-17.

are used so much does not necessarily mean that they are understood better than other parts of the Bible. A fresh look at the Psalms will bring us to a deeper appreciation of their content and meaning.

The Psalter is also a difficult book to study because it has an accumulation of problems that we do not face in the same way elsewhere in the Old Testament. For example, when we come to another book of the Old Testament, such as a historical book like Joshua, or a prophetical book like Ezekiel, we are able to put it in a distinct historical setting. When we are faced with the Psalter we have a tremendous range of historical settings, so that each psalm has to be interpreted individually. Moreover, we are not just dealing with one type of literature in the Psalms. While we can go to historical, prophetical, and poetical parts of the Old Testament in general, in the Psalter we have all these represented and more. For the Psalter, though, the absence of historical context for a particular psalm makes our task harder as we try to date the period from which it came, to see if the historical background helps us to interpret it better.

3.3 The Creed of Israel

The Book of Psalms brings together the faith of Israel into one book. The format in which it appears is new, but not the content. All the themes of the book are held together by the fact that it is the confession of Israel, for it is Israel's creed, sung not signed. That is to say, it expresses for us what believers in Israel of old knew and felt about the Lord in whom they trusted. It is a word from the heart, not the formal expression of a carefully composed creedal statement to which they could have added their signature. The unity that it possesses is the unity which that faith gives to the whole book.

The Psalter is also important because it is virtually a theology of the Old Testament. Even without the other books that make up our Old Testament we could produce from the Psalms all the essential material from which we could write the theology. It contains long historical psalms which recount the history of God's people, while other psalms, as we know either by their titles or their contents, show us how the church in the Old Testament times reacted to particular situations. Their faith was on trial, and the songs they sang expressed their deepest religious convictions.

The theology of the Psalms, moreover, is popular theology. That is to say, it is not the theology or philosophy of a group of expert theologians discussing matters and formulating their conclusions in a very abstract way. The concreteness of the Psalms strikes us as we read them, as well as how down-to-earth they are. They display how life in response to God was lived in ancient Israel, and how believers 'through each perplexing path of life' ('O God of Bethel', Scottish Paraphrase 2) put their trust in him. When we read other parts of the Old Testament we have to balance them with the underlying ideas about God contained in the Psalter, for it gives us what people were thinking and feeling in relation to their religious experiences. This is also another reason why the Psalms appeal to the broad Christian community. While many Christians feel they need special help to understand, for example, the Book of Leviticus, they are able to approach and appropriate the Psalms for themselves.

As we will see later, the groupings of Psalms may well reflect some aspects of theological significance. That is to say, the way in which the Psalms are brought together in the one bundle, may well have significance in that psalms with similar meanings are often placed in close proximity. Psalms 3 and 4 have similarities and are placed together, while Psalms 9 and 10 may well have originally been a single composition, for together they form in Hebrew a single acrostic poem. Other psalms, such as Psalms 42 and 43 and Psalms 142 and 143, are also brought together because of common themes.

It is also important to see the first two psalms as setting the pattern for the whole book. Psalm 1 contains the basic distinction between the righteous and the wicked and speaks of the blessedness or happiness of the person who delights in the LORD and his law (vv. 1-4). Jesus, in the Sermon on the Mount, also uses the idea of blessedness, when he expounds the same basic principles even more fully and carries on the teaching concerning the two ways (Matt. 5–7). The second psalm carries on the theme of the two ways by emphasising how nations set themselves against the LORD and his anointed, which came to pass at the crucifixion (see the quotation from this psalm in Acts 4:25-26). Both psalms refer to 'the way' (1:1; 2:12). The anointed king of Psalm 2 transcends any of David's successors, and the presentation of this figure points to Jesus as the appointed Son and Servant (see Matt. 3:17; 17:5; 2 Pet. 1:17).

3.4 The Prayer Book of the Bible

At times the Book of Psalms has been called the prayer book of the Bible. Although this suggests that all the psalms are addressed to God, there are some which are not (e.g., 1, 2, 32, 45, etc.). It is better to think of the Psalms as showing us the true nature of prayer, and how believers can respond to the great saving acts of God. To what God does in an objective way, his people give their subjective response in the meditation and prayers of the Psalter.

The Psalms help us to understand the true nature of prayer because of their main characteristics.

(a) When men pray to God using human words, the prayer can only be the response to God's words to them. Thus when the psalmists are praying to God, they are praying back to him what he had spoken. They also appeal to God to remember the word that he has given (Ps. 119:49). The whole principle of meditation rests upon the fact that God has both spoken and acted.

(b) The focus of attention is God himself. This holds true even when the psalmists are praying concerning their own needs. So many of the psalms are declarations of God's gracious character, and they are therefore basically songs of praise. It is not surprising, therefore, that the Jews called the whole book *tᵉhillîm* ('praises'). The very act of prayer to God is a recognition of who he is, and in coming to him in this way we are proclaiming that we acknowledge that he is precisely who he claims to be.

(c) The Psalms also teach us that a mark of true prayer is humility before God. The descriptions we have of human sin and guilt in the Psalms are not accidental. Rather, these descriptions go to the very heart of prayer with the recognition that we have no right to stand our ground before a holy God (Ps. 24:3), for none living is righteous in his sight (Ps. 143:2). We are reminded that those who pray come as humble servants, waiting till the LORD shows mercy (Ps. 123:2). The constant references in the Psalms to the need for God's intervention are another aspect of the psalmists' humility before him. They know that in need or in deliverance the glory is to be given to God's name on account of his love and faithfulness (Ps. 115:1).

4. THE PSALMS AND SPIRITUAL LIFE

4.1 The Psalms – The Most Comprehensive Book of the Old Testament

The Book of Psalms is very different from every other Old Testament book. To use the illustration of Athanasius (AD *c*. 295-373), all the other books are like gardens that grow only one kind of fruit. However, the Book of Psalms, in addition to growing its own special fruit, also grows some from all the other gardens. Thus it includes history and prophecy as well as praise and prayer. As Luther expressed it: 'You may rightly call the Psalter a Bible in miniature.'

There is no other Old Testament book that has such a historical range. Psalm 90 is attributed to Moses, while the bulk of the book comes from the period of David and Solomon. There are psalms such as Psalm 74, 79, and 80 which are clearly written after the destruction of Jerusalem, and in them the psalmists recount something of the destruction of Jerusalem (74:3-8; 79:1-4; 80:4-6, 8-16) and appeal to God to again visit his people and restore them. Psalm 137 pictures the exiles being mocked in their captivity in Babylon, while Psalm 126 rejoices in what the LORD has done in restoring the people to their own land.

In the Psalms we have a representative sample of the faith of Israel over centuries. This helps us to see how enduring was the commitment of the people to the LORD, and how their trust in him sustained them during periods of testing. Clearly too the psalmists saw the responsibility of parents and elders to pass on the faith to coming generations. They wanted succeeding generations not only to know about the great deeds of the LORD, but also to put their trust in him for themselves (78:7). Generations yet unborn had to be told about the LORD and his righteousness, so that they too would serve him (22:30-31). Children were encouraged to learn of the fear of the LORD and to know that his eyes were on the righteous (34:11-16).

4.2 The Psalms – The Most Personal Book of the Old Testament
The Psalter is markedly different from the rest of the Old Testament in other ways as well. The human authors normally write in the third person about events, even those concerning themselves. We see this illustrated by the way in which Moses reports the conflict between himself and Aaron and Miriam (Num. 12:1-16), or in the manner in which Amos speaks in the third person in connection with his own conflict with Jeroboam and Amaziah (Amos 7:10-17). There are brief biographical elements in some of the prophets such as Isaiah (6:1-13) and Jeremiah (1:4-19), but in the main the Old Testament is written in the third person.

However, the Psalter uses the first person throughout. It speaks of 'I' or 'we', which points out straight away that they are expressions of personal religious life. The Psalms are not abstract writing about theology, or anything approaching a philosophical discussion of religious themes. They are really an expression of the knowledge about God and his ways that is rooted in personal experience of a vital relationship with him. If knowledge of God was revealed for all in Israel to profit from it, then that knowledge should be grasped and used by all. The Psalms articulate that theology for ancient Israel, and so we see in them the popular religious feeling of redeemed sinners.

Another amazing feature of the Psalms is that they portray all the varied experiences and emotions of the human heart, with all its ups and downs. They describe real life in which the psalmists bare their souls for others to see and express their deepest emotions and longings. We not only see them at the heights of joy, but they express their honest feelings of despair and doubt.

4.3 Identification with the Psalmist

The Psalms also provoke a response in us because of our similar spiritual experiences. They are in themselves a response to God and truths concerning him. They stimulate us as we pass through similar experiences and find that we can identify with the psalmists in their days. Their words become our words, and we find that we can take over their expression of religious faith and use it as if it were our own.

This also means that the Psalms serve as a mirror of the soul. Calvin expressed it like this: 'I am in the habit of calling this book, not inappropriately, "The Anatomy of all the parts of the soul," for not an affection will no one find in himself, an image of which is not reflected in this mirror'.[8] Here Calvin is echoing the words of Athanasius who said: 'It seems to me, moreover, that because the Psalms thus serve him who sings them as a mirror, wherein he sees himself and his own soul, he cannot help but render them in such a manner that their words go home with equal force to those who hear him sing, and stir them also to a like reaction.' The Psalms both serve as a suitable means for us to express our own feelings, and also stimulate us further as we crystallise our thoughts regarding

[8] This comes in Calvin's Preface to his commentary on the *Psalms: A Commentary on the Psalms of David* (Oxford: D. A. Talboys, 1840), I, p. vi. James A. De Young further elaborates on the impact of the Psalms on Calvin in his article, '"An Anatomy of All Parts of the Soul": Insights into Calvin's Spirituality from His Psalms Commentary', in W. H. Neusner, ed., *Calvinus Sacrae Scripturae Professor: Calvin as Confessor of Holy Scripture* (Grand Rapids: Eerdmans, 1994), pp. 1-14. I have discussed the broader question of the place of the Psalms for life in the Reformed community in 'The Psalms and Reformed Spirituality', *RTR* 53, 2 (1994), pp. 53-62.

God's dealings with us. In this way, the Psalms not only speak to us, but they also speak for us.

The variety of experiences described by the psalmists also meets us in our needs. Whatever the situation in which we are, we can turn to the Psalms knowing that something appropriate for us will be found there. This is why Martin Luther gained such comfort in the Psalms during his own spiritual agony, for he discovered in them his own innermost feelings. If Luther was mad, then so was the psalmist; if Luther was hungry and thirsty for God, then so was the psalmist! He said that in the Psalms 'everyone, in whatever state he is, finds words that fit his case and suit him exactly, as though they were put there for his sake alone ... Then he becomes sure that he is in the communion of saints.'

The emotional element of poetry and song enables us to express with power and feeling our response to God in the words of the Psalms. The Psalms are directed towards the emotions of men and women, because they are the expressions of human beings as they passed through crises in their lives. One of the ways in which we can classify the Psalms is by the emotion expressed in them. Thus we can think of songs of joy, or cries of despair, or laments of abandonment, or the calm peace of confident trust. Emotions are grounded in our faith, and thus our present relationship with God will affect our emotions. The Psalms help us to see how Old Testament believers wrestled with their emotional response to situations, and how their changed understanding of God and his ways impelled them to action.

4.4 The Faith of the Psalmists

We must not make any distinction between the faith of Old Testament believers and believers in the New Testament period in respect to trust in God and his word. The same principle applies even to us today. When the New Testament writers wish to illustrate the nature of faith they appeal to Old Testament examples (Rom. 4; Gal. 3; Heb. 11; James 2). Those believers are part of the great cloud of witnesses whose testimony should stimulate us to run with patience looking unto Jesus (Heb. 12:2). While they did not have the fullness of New Testament revelation, yet they responded to what God had revealed up to their day, and they believed it.

When we turn to the Psalms we see frequent expressions of trust in the Lord. Those whose trust is in him display an entire self-commitment to him, coupled with obedience to his word and commands. A wide variety of language is used to describe this relationship. The people of God are said to act in certain ways including 'believe', 'trust', 'take refuge in', 'rely upon', 'wait for', and 'wait patiently for'. Some of these expressions are used in contrast to putting trust in substitutes like military weapons, princes, idols, or even man himself (44:6; 146:3; 135:15-18; 52:7). The words of Psalm 62:8 express the basic message of the Psalms regarding faith: 'Trust in him at all times, O people.'

In all their experiences the psalmists were relying on the character of God as he had made himself known. There was no special word of revelation to help them in their time of need. Because there was no personal message they had to rely simply on God's love and mercy revealed previously. In times of great perplexity, it was knowledge of God's existing revelation which broke through and brought light into a dark situation. Thus in Psalm 73 the psalmist was in turmoil about the prosperity of the wicked until he came into God's house and then understood their end (73:16-17). In the Book of Psalms faith is like faith elsewhere in the Bible; it is reliance on God and his character as revealed in earlier periods of the Old Testament.

5. DEVELOPMENT OF THE PSALTER

5.1 The Groupings

Clearly the Psalms have been arranged in some order, but certainly this is not chronological. While we do have psalms from the period of the exile or later (such as 126 or 137) coming towards the end of the Psalter, they do not come at the very end. The most that can be said is that the psalms of David appear predominantly in the first half of the Psalter, though just after a song of the exile (137) a psalm of David follows (138). Neither is the arrangement by author or by content, though some sections do bring together psalms by a particular author or link by theme. However, this is not done consistently throughout the whole book.

What is apparent is that, whereas the Psalms have been brought together into a complete book, there are actually five separate books that make the whole. Jewish tradition accepted that the division into five was in imitation of the five books of Moses (Genesis to Deuteronomy), with Psalter readings linked to the appropriate Pentateuchal passages for reading in the synagague.[9] This division can be set out in a table like this:

The Complete Psalter

Book 1	Psalms 1-41
Book 2	Psalms 42-72
Book 3	Psalms 73-89
Book 4	Psalms 90-106
Book 5	Psalms 107-150

Each of these divisions ends with a doxology. Thus the first book ends with the words of Psalm 41:13:

> Praise be to the LORD, the God of Israel,
> from everlasting to everlasting.
> Amen and Amen.

Similar doxologies occur at the end of Books 2, 3, 4 (72:18-19; 89:52; 106:48). There is no doxology of that kind to end the final book, but the whole of Psalm 150 is a doxology, which fittingly concludes the whole Psalter with the call: 'Let everything that has breath praise the LORD. Praise the LORD.'

This division is old, because the Greek translation (LXX) contains it. The doxology that ends the fourth book is also quoted in 1 Chronicles 16:36 in connection with the ark of the covenant being brought into Jerusalem.

---

[9] *Midrash Tehillim* on Psalm 1:5.

5.2 The Development of the Psalter[10]

The gradual development of the Psalter is shown by several facts:

(a) In addition to the doxology at the end of the third book there is also a note, 'This concludes the prayers of David son of Jesse' (72:20). As psalms of David do come later than this (cf. 108-110, 138-145) it seems that Psalm 72 must have been the ending of an earlier collection later incorporated in the present Psalter.

(b) There are various psalms or portions that are repeated in the Psalter. They are:

Psalm 14	=	Psalm 53
Psalm 40:13-17	=	Psalm 70
Psalm 57:7-11	=	Psalm 108:1-5
Psalm 60:5-12	=	Psalm 108:6-13

Duplication is not unknown in the prophetical books where the same passage can occur in two different prophets (cf. Isaiah 2:2-4 with Micah 4:1-3) but very rare within the same book. Here it suggests that collections of psalms were in use prior to the present full Psalter.

(c) Within the Psalter there are clearly defined blocks of material, which appear to have been collected together prior to their being brought into the full Psalter. There are various smaller groups but the main subsidiary collections can be seen from the following table:

Groups of Songs within the Psalter

Davidic Collections	3-41; 51-72; 138-145
Korahite Collections	42-49; 84-85; 87-88

[10] For a fine survey of the information relating to this topic, see R. Dean Anderson, 'The Division and the Order of the Psalms', *WTJ* 56 (1994), pp. 219-41. Leslie McFall, 'The Evidence for a Logical Arrangement of the Psalter', *WTJ* 62 (2000), 223-56, is an extremely detailed discussion with valuable charts. He argues that the present shape of the Psalter is a result of a hierarchical order of sorting, according to authorship, the use of divine names, placing of psalms according to genre, and grouping according to the continuity of thought.

Elohistic Collection (using the name Elohim in reference to God)	42-83
Asaphite Collection	73-83
Kingship Psalms	93-100
Praise Psalms	103-107
Songs of Ascent (used on pilgrimage to Jerusalem or on return from exile)	120-134
Hallelujah Psalms (beginning or ending with 'Hallelujah')	104-106; 111-118; 146-150

(d) The use of the names for God in the Psalter also suggests stages in development. Psalms 1-41 (Book 1) mainly use the covenant name *Yahweh* (taken into English as 'Jehovah'), with *Elohîm* only occurring rarely. In Psalms 42-72 (Book 2) the main word for God is *Elohîm*, while in Book 4 only *Yahweh* is used. The preference for one name for God over another comes out very clearly in the duplicate psalms. Whereas Psalm 14 uses the name *Yahweh*, its duplicate, Psalm 53, has *Elohîm* instead (there are some other minor alterations as well).[11] The Jews felt great reverence for the name Yahweh and did not even pronounce it, substituting the word 'Lord' instead, and this usage carried over into the New Testament.

(e) Certain facts, however, suggest that there was an earlier division into three books, two of which were later subdivided to create the present five. The difference in size among the five books has often been noted, with two of them being much shorter than the other three. Books 3 and 4 only have seventeen psalms each, whereas Book 2

[11] Discussions in regard to literary features in the Psalms must also take into account the use of divine names, and some implications for the connection between the books that comprise the Psalter may follow. See Ronald Youngblood, 'Divine Names in the Book of Psalms: Literary Structures and Number Patterns', *JANES* 19 (1989), pp. 171-181; Gerald H. Wilson, 'The Use of Royal Psalms at the "Seams" of the Hebrew Psalter', *JSOT* 35 (1986), p. 87. For a convenient tabulation of the usage of divine names in the Psalter, see L. McFall, 'A Logical Arrangement of the Psalter', pp. 248-49.

has thirty-one, Book 1 has forty-one, and Book 5 has the largest number, forty-four. The contents, the use of the divine names, and the psalm titles point to this threefold division, with Book 1 having forty-one psalms, Books 2-3 having forty-eight, and Books 4-5 having sixty-one. This explanation helps to solve other difficulties, including the odd separation of the Hallelujah psalms between Books 4 and 5. The present situation, with three of these psalms coming in Book 4 (104-106) but the majority in Book 5 (111-13, 115-17, 135, 146-150) is explicable if they all originally came in the same book.[12]

Clearly the Psalter is a collection of songs which was brought together over centuries, and finally some time after the return from Exile were put into its present form. It has often been called 'the hymn book of the second temple', that is to say, the book used for song in the restored temple in Jerusalem (completed in 516 BC) and which remained in use until the destruction of Jerusalem in AD 70. While definitive proof of this is lacking, the evidence certainly points to the use of the Psalter in the Jewish observances before and after Christ, and the continuing use of the Psalms in early Christian worship (Matt. 26:30; 1 Cor. 14:26; James 5:13). The Psalter should not be compared to the building of a magnificent palace, but rather to the development over centuries of a cathedral. It bears the marks of various styles, distinctive development in stages, and yet an overall beauty as a whole book of the Bible.

There is another movement in the Psalter and that is towards a climax of praise. With all the varied moods of the human heart being apparent in earlier songs, it is clear that towards the end of the Psalter the exultant joy of God's people come to the fore. The final songs (Pss. 144-150) are all ones of joyous praise that culminate in the call: 'Let everything that has breath praise the Lord. Praise the Lord' (Ps. 150:6). The emphasis on praise towards the end of the Psalter seems deliberate, and this movement may well be the reason why the whole book was called *t^ehillîm, songs of praise.*

---

[12] For full discussion of this argument for an original three books, see Roger T. Beckwith, 'The Early History of the Psalter'.

5.3 The Message of the Five Books

While it is certainly possible to interpret individual psalms, or trace their use in Old Testament worship, or their use in the New Testament, yet the question remains: 'Is there a point behind the whole Psalter?' Or, to state the question another way: 'What place does the Psalter as a whole have within Old Testament biblical theology?'

Older commentators discussed the structure of the Psalter and the reasons behind its development.[13] In more recent times the debate on this matter has been vigorous, though no consensus has been reached.[14] It has been noted that there is a progression from lament to praise in the Psalter, with its final form emphasising that the LORD is king.[15] This progression from obedience to God's Word (Ps. 1) to universal praise of him (Ps. 150) has been proposed as the main theme of the Psalms,[16] though the stress on the Davidic covenant has also been proposed as the main theme.[17] Another view that has been advanced is that eschatology dominates the Psalter, not

---

[13] For examples, see E. W. Hengstenberg, *Commentary on the Psalms* (Edinburgh: T. & T. Clark, 1869), III, Appendix, pp. i-liv; F. Delitzsch, *Psalms* (Edinburgh: T. & T. Clark, 1871), I, pp. 19-30; J. J. S. Perowne, *The Book of Psalms; A New Translation, with Introductions and Notes Explanatory and Critical*, 6th ed. (London: George Bell & Sons, 1886), I, pp. 70-83; A. F. Kirkpatrick, *The Book of Psalms* (Cambridge: CUP, 1903), pp. xiii-xviii, l-lix.

[14] The recent discussion was provoked by the work of Gerald H. Wilson, *The Editing of the Hebrew Psalter* (Chico, CA: Scholars Press, 1985). He gives a summary of his position in 'The Structure of the Psalter,' in *Interpreting the Psalms: Issues and Approaches*, edd. Philip S. Johnston and David G. Firth (Leicester: Apollos, 2005), pp. 229-46. His other contributions on this topic are listed in his volume *Psalms 1* (The NIV Application Commentary, Grand Rapids:, Zondervan, 2002), p. 88. For help in orientation to the debate regarding the structure of the Psalter, see the article by David M. Howard Jr.; 'Recent Trends in Psalms Study', in David W. Baker, and Bill T. Arnold, edd., *The Face of Old Testament Studies: A Survey of Contemporary Approaches* (Leicester: Apollos, 1999), pp. 329-44; and his abbreviated, but more recent discussion, in *Interpreting the Psalms*, pp. 23-29.

[15] This is G. H. Wilson's position, ibid., p. 249.

[16] For this view, see Walter Brueggemann, 'Bounded by Obedience and Praise: The Psalms as Canon', *JSOT* 50 (1991), pp. 63-92.

[17] J. H. Walton, building on Wilson's work, has suggested this in his discussion, 'Psalms: A Cantata about the Davidic Covenant', *JETS* 34 (1991), pp. 21-31.

only in that this dominates the content, but that it is part of the purposeful shaping of the arrangement of the 150 psalms.[18]

While various single themes have been proposed, none of them seem to be satisfactory explanations of the evidence. All hypotheses depend upon the selection of psalms around which a proposed common theme is based.[19] While evident connections between adjacent psalms exist, and even between books (the so-called 'seams' connecting them to each other), yet no evidence points to a systematic ordering of the entire content of the Psalter. This means that we should not try and state a single overarching theme but rather recognise that the Psalter reflects the breadth of theological reflection in Israel.[20]

5.4 The Numbering of the Psalms and Verses

The decision to make the Psalter comprise 150 songs seems to have been deliberate, and this number is confirmed both by the LXX and the major psalms scroll from cave 11 at Qumran. The latter contains an idealised note relating to David's songs, which says that he wrote 3,600 psalms and 450 songs. These numbers are divisible by 150, and 3,600 is 150 multiplied by 24, the number of courses of Levites appointed to sing the psalms at the temple (1 Chron. 25:9–31).[21]

While the verse enumeration does not affect our understanding of the Psalms, it does affect our use of the Bible and also commentaries on the text. There is a difference

---

[18] For this approach, see David Mitchell, *The Message of the Psalter: An Eschatological Programme to the Book of Psalms* (Sheffield: JSOT, 1997). Mitchell also interacts with the views of Gerald H. Wilson in his essay, 'Lord, Remember David: G. H. Wilson and the Message of the Psalter', *VT* LVI (2006), pp. 526-47.

[19] This is the conclusion of S. Jonathan Murphy, 'Is the Psalter a Book with a Single Message?' *BS* 165 (2008), pp. 283-93.

[20] For discussions that demonstrate the breadth of the theology embraced within the Psalter, see Robert B. Chisholm, Jr, 'A Theology of the Psalms', in Roy B. Zuck, ed., *A Biblical Theology of the Old Testament* (Chicago: Moody Press, 1991), pp. 257-304; and, Paul R. House, 'The God Who Rules (Psalms)', in his book, *Old Testament Theology* (Downers Grove: IVP, 1998), pp. 402-23.

[21] R. T. Beckwith, 'The Early History of the Psalter', p. 22. The other Qumran manuscripts of the Psalms have variations in content and order, but it must be remembered that the Qumran sect was not within mainstream Judaism, and some of its manuscripts were assembled as part of a liturgical manual.

between the numbering of verses in the printed Hebrew Bible and most English versions. The reason for this is that in the Hebrew Bibles the titles of the Psalms are often regarded as a verse, and therefore the numbering of what we regard as the first verse will be v. 2. This means that for many psalms the Hebrew text shows one more verse than corresponding English versions. Quite a few commentaries, especially those working from the Hebrew text, follow this system.

There is also a difference in the numbering of the Psalms themselves. The explanation for this lies in differences between the Hebrew Bible and the way in which the Psalms have come over into English. The Greek Bible subdivided two of the psalms (116 and 147) and twice joined two of them together (9/10 and 114/115). The Greek Bible also contains an additional psalm (151) that has never been reckoned by others as part of the Psalter. It is specifically noted that this psalm is 'outside of the number'.[22] The table below shows the two systems of numbering the psalms.

The Numbering of the Psalms

Hebrew and Protestant Bibles	Greek and Roman Catholic Bibles
1-8	1-8
9	9
10	
11-113	10-112
114	113
115	
	114
116	115
117-146	116-145
	146
147	147
148-150	148-150
	151 (Greek)

[22] The full inscription in the LXX is: 'This psalm is a genuine one of David, though outside the number (*exôthen tou arithmou*), when he fought alone with Goliad.'

6. THE PSALMS AND GOD'S COVENANT

6.1 God and Covenant

The Bible speaks of God's relationship with his people as being a covenant. This relationship is the concept that gives unity to the whole of the biblical revelation. A covenant is a bond between God and man, and it is given by a sovereign God as an expression of his grace. In a formal way he expresses the relationship that exists between himself and his people. The central core of the covenant is that God promises, 'I will be your God and you shall be my people.' There is a progressive unfolding of this covenant throughout the Old Testament in various stages. The arrangement entered into by God at creation (Gen. 1-2) is reaffirmed after the flood (Gen. 6:18; 9:1-7). The call of Abraham is followed by a formal covenant arrangement (Gen. 12, 15, 17) which is supplemented by the covenant at Sinai (Exod. 20–23) following the Exodus from Egypt. After the introduction of kingship there is a special covenant in which the Davidic family is chosen (2 Sam. 7). Finally the Old Testament speaks about a new covenant which will come to pass (Jer. 31:31-34; and see Hebrews 8:7-13; 10:11-16).

From archaeological discoveries we know that God used a form of covenant that was familiar to the people. Kings who conquered another nation forced them to enter into a covenant bond, in which they pledged themselves to serve him as their overlord. Many of the expressions used in the Old Testament of the covenant relationships can be paralleled from extra-biblical sources. The treaties or covenants from these sources follow a formalised pattern that has many similarities to the biblical covenants. The language they employed in connection with them and various aspects of the ceremony of entering into a covenant or of enforcing one have their counterpart in the Old Testament.

6.2 Covenant in the Psalms

The word 'covenant' is not common in the Psalms, occurring only twenty-one times (25:10, 14; 44:17; 50:5, 16; 55:20; 74:20;

78:10, 37; 83:5 (NIV, 'alliance'); 89:3, 28, 34, 39; 103:18; 105:8, 10; 106:45; 111:5, 9; 132:12).[23] This is very similar to its use in the prophetical books of the Old Testament where it does not appear frequently. However, in both there are many other indications of the presence of the whole idea of covenant that underlies all the expressions of religious faith and feeling.

The Psalms contain many references to the earlier parts of the Old Testament and especially to the relationships between God and the patriarchs and with the people of Israel after they had been redeemed from Egypt. There is also reference to the covenant with David which is set out in 2 Samuel 7. A summary of the references is as follows:

Covenant with Abraham	105:1-22
Exodus and the Sinai Covenant	50:4-6, 16; 66:5-12; 78:12-53; 80:8-11; 81:1-16; 86:5; 99:7; 103:7; 105:23-4; 106:1-33; 114; 135:4, 8-9
Covenant with David	78:65-72; 89:1-52; 132:1-18

A series of other expressions also draws attention to the covenant relationship. Many of these expressions echo passages from the Pentateuch which speak of God and his people. Attention can be focussed on a few of these terms.

(a) Israel is often spoken of as the people of God (29:11; 81:11; 100:3). They were the inheritance of the Lord and often this phrase is used in conjunction with reference to them as God's people (28:9; 78:62, 71; 94:5; 106:4–5). The phrase, 'I will be your God and you shall be my people,' is echoed in passages like Psalm 95:7 which declares: 'for he is our God and we are the people of his pasture, the flock under his care.'

---

[23] For covenantal language in the Psalter, the best listing I have found is in the unpublished Cambridge Ph.D. thesis of J. A. Thompson, *The Vocabulary of Covenant in the Old Testament* (1963). Parts of his research appeared in his booklet, *The Ancient Near Eastern Treaties and the Old Testament* (London: Tyndale Press, 1964), and in his commentary, *Deuteronomy: An Introduction and Commentary* (London: Inter-Varsity Press, 1974).

(b) The fact that God had chosen Israel to be his covenant people is emphasised in the Psalter. The word 'choose' is first used in Deuteronomy to describe Israel as God's choice (Deut. 7:6). The Psalms use it when recalling the wonder of God's election of Israel, and link it with other words that also point to the same sovereign choice. For example, 33:12 speaks of Israel being chosen as God's inheritance, while 135:4 says that he chose Israel as his 'special possession' (*s^e^gullâh*). This latter word is a rare one, being used to denote the utterly special position that Israel occupied before God (Exod. 19:5; Deut. 7:6; 14:2; Mal. 3:17).

(c) A variety of other terms associated with the covenant also make their appearance in the Psalter. The repeated use of the word 'servant' recalls how this expression is used of an inferior submitting to a great king. Thus King Ahaz sent word to the king of Assyria and said: 'I am your servant and your son' (2 Kings 16:7). Reference is also made to the oath by which the covenant was sworn, and to such features as the ark of the covenant. There is constant reference to God's faithfulness, which is not just expressing trust in God's character in general but in the specific form in which he revealed it in the covenant relationship. He was the God who even in the Ten Words declared that he would show his 'steadfast love to the thousandth generation of those who love him and who keep his commandments' (Exod. 20:6; Deut. 5:10).

6.3 The Covenant Relationship

The Psalms are not just individual expressions of religious understanding but rather they are distinctly expressions of faith which came out of a community of faith. The sphere from which the songs of Israel came was the covenant community, bound in common allegiance to the Lord. Some of the Psalms are clearly communal because they use the first person plural ('we', 'our'), but even the majority, which use the first person singular ('I', 'my'), stem from a common commitment to the God of Israel.

The Psalms also show how vital the covenant relationship was, for the various songs put into poetry the depth of such a relationship with God. The faith of the psalmists is built upon God's word to his people, not upon individual personal promises from God. Knowledge of God's character and his works provided the common basis upon which individuals could live. The singers knew that God was concerned with their personal lives and with the good of each one of his covenant children. Psalm 84 puts it like this: 'For the LORD God is a sun and a shield; the LORD bestows favour and honour; no good things does he withhold from those whose walk is blameless. O LORD Almighty, blessed is the man who trusts in you' (vv. 11-12; notice the connection with passages such as Gen. 15:1; 17:1). It is not surprising that they wanted to sing and rejoice in this relationship, for those who feared the LORD lacked no good thing (Ps. 34:9).

The central feature is God's kingship over his people. As covenant servants the people had to reaffirm in various ways their allegiance to the LORD. They paid their tribute of praise to him in extolling his creation or his great acts of redemption. In speaking of the majesty of his person they were offering spiritual sacrifices of praise to their king. When they sang of the beauties of God's law, this was another affirmation of the manner in which they were submitting to his claims upon them. The Psalter, therefore, served the broad purpose of reminding the people that they were God's people, the people who made up his flock (Ps. 100:4). It also assisted them in maintaining a right relationship with him.

God's presence with his people in their history and also with them as individuals is reaffirmed in the Psalms. The long historical psalms in particular are recitals of the ways in which God's power had been shown in the life of Israel. At important times Israel had to repeat summaries of what God had done for her (see the declaration at the time of bringing the firstfruits [Deut. 26:3-10] and at the time of covenant renewal [Josh. 24:16-18]).

Finally, the Psalter emphasises the grace of God in forgiving and restoring an erring covenant people. Thus one psalmist can say to God: 'You were to Israel a forgiving God, though you punished their misdeeds' (Ps. 99:8). This was simply a re-affirmation of the declaration that God had made of himself when he proclaimed his own name to Moses on the occasion of the second giving of the tablets of stone (Exod. 34:6-7). David says that 'all the ways of the Lord are loving and faithful for those who keep the demands of his covenant'. Then on the basis of God's covenant he pleads: 'For the sake of your name, O Lord, forgive my iniquity, though it is great' (Ps. 25:10-11). A covenant God was true to his word of promise and would forgive and restore.

7. SPECIAL TYPES OF PSALMS

7.1 Identifying Types

In English we have various types of literature, just as we have various types of spoken language. To illustrate the latter first of all, we know that there are different styles in keeping with different occasions. Thus when a bridegroom stands up to speak at his wedding we can often predict the style his speech will take and some of the standard expressions that will be used. There is an expected format to the speech and we are almost disappointed if it does not occur. Other types of speeches to think about could be a politician conceding an election defeat or a speech presenting a gift to a fellow-employee on his retirement.

The same thing holds true concerning written English. We adopt a particular style depending on the complete set of circumstances that has led to our writing. A letter written to one's mother will be quite different from a formal letter to one's solicitors concerning some property matter. The form in which a newspaper report on a traffic accident is written will be quite different from the style of the same paper's editorial. A variety of situations demand a known and predictable style.

We very quickly identify particular forms of writing, and subconsciously read them with that in mind. This is important because our mental approach to the form will often determine our attitude to the text. If, for example, we recognise a particular piece as a novel, we know we can read it quickly and even miss out some parts without affecting the flow of the story. However, if we try that with other pieces of writing, for example, a set of instructions on how to construct an unassembled piece of furniture, we could run into great difficulty and create problems for ourselves.

So it is when we come to the Psalms. There are various types of psalms and we have to recognise the differences. Look at these three quotations from successive psalms:

> O LORD my God, I take refuge in you;
> save and deliver me from all who pursue me,
> or they will tear me like a lion and rip me in pieces with
> no one to rescue me (Ps. 7:1-2).

> O LORD, our Lord,
> how majestic is your name in all the earth!
> You have set your glory above the heavens (Ps. 8:1).

> I will praise you, O Lord,
> with all my heart;
> I will tell of all your wonders.
> I will be glad and rejoice in you;
> I will sing praise to your name,
> O Most High (Ps. 9:1-2).

They are all quite different and are indicative of different styles. The first is from a lament in which an individual is asking God for protection as he faces false accusations from his enemies. The second comes from a hymn of praise, and particularly one that is praising God for his creation. The third example is from a hymn in which there is mention of rejoicing and exaltation of God's name. As we note the different types of psalms it helps us to recognise other psalms of a similar nature and to read them accordingly.

There are several benefits to be gained by looking at the psalms in this way. It means above all else that we are viewing them as whole units, rather than just individual verses. That is to say, we are considering them as a total piece of literary composition and reading them in that light. We come to them knowing that they are not like a telephone directory, in which there is no necessary connection between successive entries. Any connection that might appear is quite accidental, not by design. In the Psalms, however, the connection is there simply because each psalm is a poem which holds together as a unit, and therefore we must interpret it in that way. To extract a single verse and isolate it from its context in the psalm is to distort the meaning. Thus a phrase such as 'I will fear no evil' (Ps. 23:4) should not be taken out of that psalm and used as an isolated encouragement. Its meaning can only be seen in the light of the whole psalm and the certainty of God's care as a shepherd of his people. Similarly the opening verse of Psalm 89, 'I will sing of the Lord's great love forever; with my mouth I will make your faithfulness known throughout all generations', is not an isolated promise concerning God's faithfulness. It comes in a psalm that is putting into poetry the covenant which God made with David (see 2 Sam. 7). To extract the one verse and apply its teaching without reference to the setting in the psalm is to teach contrary to the express message of the psalm itself. This principle of interpreting a verse within the unit of which it forms a part applies, of course, to the whole of the Bible.

This type of approach also lets us ask questions regarding the function of any particular song. From the books of Chronicles we know that particular songs were appropriate to special occasions such as the bringing of the ark of the covenant into Jerusalem (1 Chron. 16:7-36, and cf. Pss. 96; 105:1-5; and 106:1, 47, 48), or for use at the dedication of the temple (2 Chron. 5-7 and especially cf. 5:13 and 7:3, 6 with Ps. 136). If we can find out something about the function that a particular psalm fulfilled, we will be helped to understand it better. Sometimes this may be apparent from within the psalm itself, or the title may show how the psalm was used. Clearly the Psalms were meant for singing, and many were used in appropriate settings during the religious life of the people. We can compare this to the way in which modern Christian hymn books not only list hymns according to content but also show the appropriate hymns for particular occasions (e.g. Easter,

Pentecost, Christmas, Baptism, the Lord's Supper, Harvest Thanksgiving).

A word of warning is also needed. This method of listing psalms according to type should be used as a valuable tool to help our understanding but should not be pressed to an extreme. There is the constant danger that a psalm will be classified according to a specific type, and in so doing its individual distinctiveness may be overlooked. The characteristics of a particular psalm have to be taken seriously so that common features of a group do not cause us to overlook important variations. Any classification has to be fluid, and certain groups of psalms overlap in their characteristics. An outline of some of the major Psalm types follows.

7.2 Hymns

A hymn is a song that extols the glory and greatness of God. Many psalms come into this category, for the Psalter contains a great number of songs of joy in the LORD. Typical examples are 92, 103, 113, and 117. Songs other than those in the Psalter also come into this category. The Song of Moses and the Song of Miriam (Exod. 15:1-18, 21) are good examples, as are Hannah's Song (1 Sam. 2:1-10) and Hezekiah's Song (Isa. 38:10-20).

Nearly all of them share some common features, including initial and concluding calls to worship and reasons why God is to be praised. It is this latter feature that takes the greatest space, for the psalmists draw attention to the concrete things that God has done and which call forth a response of praise.

The hymns have a definite structure like this:

A. Introduction: Call to Worship

Usually the hymn commences with a call to worship in the form of an imperative in the second person plural. Sometimes it can be a form in which the person calls upon his own soul to praise the LORD, such as in 103 and 104, 'Praise the LORD, O my soul.'

B. Main Section: The Reasons for Praise

Often this section is introduced by a clause beginning with the word 'for', followed by the explanation of the motives behind the praise. Sometimes this is disguised in English translation for the Hebrew word which is normally used (*kî*) can be translated by more than one English word (e.g., in 8:3 it is translated by 'when': *when I look up into the heavens ...*). If this 'for' is omitted in the Hebrew, there will be other words which serve the same function, such as can be seen in 103:3-5 or 104:2-4.

C. Call to Worship: A Repetition of the Opening Call
Frequently the same sort of call resounds again at the end of the song.

A good example of the hymn is Psalm 117, the shortest song in the book.

A. Praise the LORD, all you nations;
Extol him, all you peoples.

B. For great is his love towards us
and the faithfulness of the LORD endures for ever.

C. Praise the LORD.

Martin Luther wrote a long commentary on this shortest of all psalms because he thought that these two verses were basic to our understanding of the love of God. They stress the covenant love of the LORD to his people and the missionary vision of reaching out to the nations.

Three major topics provide the motive for praise of the LORD in these psalms. First, there is a group of psalms (66:1-12; 100; 114; 149) that praise God for the fact that he created (or redeemed) Israel. They have much in common with songs outside the Psalter such as Exodus 15:1-8, Deuteronomy 32:1-43, Habakkuk 3:2-19, and Isaiah 52:7-10. Secondly, another group of psalms sing the praise of God as creator of the world, either in a brief form such as in Psalm 8, or much more extensively as in Psalm 104. In this latter psalm even the order of Genesis 1 is preserved as the psalmist describes poetically the wonder of God's creation (104:2-4 = Gen. 1:6-8; 104:5-9 = Gen. 1:9-10; 104:10-13 = implied in Gen. 1:6-10; 104:19-23 = Gen. 1:14-18; 104:24-26 = Gen. 1:20-22; 104:27-30 = Gen. 1:24-30). Thirdly, the final group of hymns sing of God as the creator and covenant God who is the ruler of history (33; 103; 113; 117; 145; 146; 147; 150).

7.3 Laments

Laments form the largest group of psalms in the Psalter. They are cries of distress, either by an individual (e.g. 3, 7, 13, 17, 26) or by the community as a whole (e.g. 12, 44, 60, 74). Enemies are mentioned but rarely are they identified clearly. The term 'laments', however, is rather misleading, as it suggests that these psalms are full of sadness and are completely pessimistic in spirit. That is not altogether true as many of them contain strong affirmations of trust in the LORD. Other terms such as 'complaint', 'confidence in distress', or 'appeal for help' may be closer to the mark in describing them, because they are appeals to God to come and intervene in particular situations and to bring his deliverance. In this way they are songs of praise, however muted, because the psalmists know of God's power to help. Some of them, after pleading for help, contain both an expression of confidence in God's power to aid and a concluding song of praise.

As with other types of psalms, the lamentations have similarities with various parts of the Old Testament outside the Psalter. Job even cursed the day he was born and wonders why it was that he did not perish at birth (Job 3:1-26). The Book of Jeremiah contains several long laments by the prophet (11:18–12:6; 15:10-21; 17:14-18; 18:19-23; 20:7-13; 20:14-18).

The question arises as to why so many psalms are of this kind, as they far outnumber any other type of psalm. What they emphasise is the reality of religious experience, and the fact that believers do not always have periods of great joy. In this way these psalms are so realistic of the experiences of God's people. They pass through times when events overwhelm them, as they are not immune to the changing situations of human life. Suffering is a part of human life, and the Psalms both show us how believers suffered and also how they reacted.[24]

There is a considerable amount of individual variation, depending upon the particular situation of the psalmist. The psalms that have been designated as the penitential psalms since the early Christian centuries are also included in this grouping (6, 32, 38, 51, 102, 130, 143). The following features are characteristic of this type of psalm, though not all may necessarily be present or there may be variation in order:

A. Address to God

This can be very brief or at other times expanded into a longer form.

B. Complaint

The form of complaint varies depending on whether it is a song of the community, who mainly complain about famine or attack by enemies, or an individual complaining from sickness or from fear. The penitential psalms refer to the psalmist's awareness of sin and his plea for forgiveness.

C. Confession of Trust

In the midst of complaints the psalmists often express confidence in God as the one who can help, and frequently they introduce this with words like 'but' or 'nevertheless'.

D. Petition

Appeal is made to God to come and help in the particular situation that the psalmist is facing. At times reasons are given why this should happen.

E. Words of Assurance

The psalmist expresses certainty that his prayer is heard and that God will come to his aid.

---

[24] I have amplified this point in *Suffering in the Psalms* (Han Sang Dong Memorial Lecture, Kosin University, Pusan, 1998).

F. Vow of Praise

In the confidence that God has heard, the psalmist pledges himself to call on God's name and to tell what God has done for him.

A good example is Psalm 13, which has this pattern:

A. How long, O LORD? Will you forget me for ever?
How long will you hide your face from me? (v. 1)

B. How long must I wrestle with my thoughts
and every day have sorrow in my heart?
How long will my enemy triumph over me? (v. 2)

C. But I trust in your unfailing love;
my heart rejoices in your salvation (v. 5).

D. Look on me and answer, O LORD my God.
Give light to my eyes, or I will sleep in death;
my enemy will say, 'I have overcome him,'
and my foes will rejoice when I fall (v. 3–4).

E. I will sing to the LORD, for he has been good to me (v. 6).

The setting of some of these psalms of complaint suggests that they may have been said or sung at the temple in conjunction with some form of sacrificial offering. When Hannah prayed in the tabernacle in Shiloh, Eli watched her praying and accused her of drunkenness. In reply she spoke of how she was pouring out her heart before God. She said: 'I have been praying here out of my great anguish and grief.' Eli then responded: 'Go in peace, and may the God of Israel grant what you have asked of him' (1 Sam. 1:9-17). It may have been customary to give such a benediction in response to similar complaints, including many of the complaints recorded in the Psalter. There is often an abrupt change in mood in the psalm, with the indication in some that a similar declaration by the LORD's servant has been made. Thus Psalm 85 has a series of petitions by the psalmist followed by the words:

I will listen to what God the Lord will say;
he promises peace to his people, his saints –
but let them not return to folly (85:8).

An assurance like that could well have been made to the psalmist by the person, like Eli, ministering at the altar, and this may explain the more joyful note at the end of the psalm.

7.4 Thanksgiving Psalms

When they respond to God's answer to a cry of need, the psalmists extol him for the answered prayer. The psalms in this group (such as 18, 32, 34) are characterised by praise of the Lord and a testimony to God's goodness, often in the form of a description of God's salvation.

There is a close connection between the thanksgiving psalms and both the psalms of lamentation and the hymns of praise. The lamentations often have a concluding song of praise. In comparison with them the thanksgiving psalms expand that type of song considerably. There is also the difference that in the complaints the song of praise is in *anticipation* of the deliverance of the Lord, while in the thanksgiving psalms the praise is for the deliverance that has *already come*.

The comparison with the hymns is also helpful to see the essential difference between them and the thanksgiving psalms. There are two ways in which God is praised in the psalms. He is praised in general terms simply for what he is in himself or as he is manifested in his creation. On the other hand, he is praised for specific acts of deliverance. In the first case the praise is describing something wonderful about God, while in the second case there is a declaration of what he has done.

Like the laments, the songs of thanksgiving come in two forms. There are several which are a form of thanksgiving by the whole community. The most specific is 124, which rejoices in a deliverance that God brought to his people. Other community thanksgiving songs are 65, 67, 75, 107, and 136. The more common form, however, is the individual song of thanksgiving in which an individual gives a testimony to what the LORD has done in his life. These are typical examples:

> You have granted him the desire of his heart,
> and have not withheld the request of his lips (21:2).
>
> O LORD, you brought me up from the grave;
> you spared me from going down into the pit (30:3).
>
> He put a new song in my mouth,
> a hymn of praise to our God (40:3).
>
> Come and listen, all you who fear God;
> let me tell you what he has done for me (66:16).

The pattern that the individual thanksgivings take is as follows:

A. Address to God
There is direct address to God, frequently brief but sometimes more extended.

B. Description of the Psalmist's Experiences
Usually this includes an account of the trouble which the psalmist faced, an indication of his cry for help, and then finally the deliverance which God has provided for him.

C. Testimony to the LORD
The psalm finishes with a proclamation of the goodness of the LORD. There may also be other features such as a request for future help.

Psalm 116 provides an excellent illustration of this pattern:

A. Address to God
The psalmist calls to the LORD (vv. 1-2), and gives the reason why he is praising him (notice the clause beginning with *for*).

B. Description of the Psalmist's Experiences
Verse 3 gives the circumstances that the psalmist faced, followed by his cry for help (v. 4). As he thinks over what has happened he expresses his confidence in the Lord, who is gracious and righteous (vv. 5-7).

C. Testimony to the Lord
The psalmist rejoices in what God has done for him.

> For you, O Lord, have delivered my soul from death,
> my eyes from tears,
> my feet from stumbling,
> that I may walk before the Lord
> in the land of the living (vv. 8-9).

The psalm ends with the psalmist pledging himself to the Lord and making his vows in the presence of the congregation (referred to in verses 14 and 18). He is the Lord's servant (v. 16), and he ends his song with a 'Hallelujah' (v. 19).

Since the Psalms are so personal in their authorship, clearly there is blessing in our personal appropriation of them.

7.5 Wisdom Psalms
Within the Old Testament there are several books that collectively are often called 'the Wisdom books'. They include Job, Proverbs, and Ecclesiastes, and are so-called because their main emphasis is not on the great facts of God's redemption, but with the practical outworking of life that is lived in the fear of the Lord. This phrase, 'the fear of the Lord', occurs both in the Book of Proverbs and in the Psalms (e.g., Prov. 1:7; 8:13; 14:26; 15:33; Pss. 19:9; 34:11; 111:10). It does not describe the abject fear of a slave before a master, but rather the devotion of a loving heart towards one's sovereign Lord. The wisdom literature shows how such a fear displays itself in practical life, so that it is really 'godliness in working clothes'.

Much of the wisdom literature appears in the form of proverbs. These proverbs are marked out by the following characteristics:

(a) Proverbs are brief, usually consisting of fewer than twenty-five words. The best proverbs are often the shortest, such as 'like father, like son'. The brevity comes from a desire to put the wisdom saying into as short a form as possible, and also as an aid to memorisation. Sometimes there is a repetition of a word or sound which is a further help to the memory.

(b) Proverbs use figurative language. They are dealing with truth, but they put it in a form that is easy to grasp and retain. They take an experience from everyday life and use it to teach a lesson. Because they paint pictures the vividness of the proverb is retained in spite of repeated use.

(c) Proverbs have many different applications. They do not refer to just one situation in life. Rather, their general nature enables them to be applied in a variety of situations. Thus the proverb, 'like father, like son' may be applied to a relationship between a teacher and a pupil, or even between a mother and a daughter.

(d) Proverbs express general truths. They are not promises of God that apply without exception. Rather, they are generalisations based on human experience, and there may well be exceptions to the general truths contained in them.

There are several psalms that fit into the general pattern of the wisdom literature, while parts of other psalms reflect something of the same approach to life or share in matters of style and form. Among the former are 37, 49, and 73, while psalms such as 25, 34, 78, 111, 112, 127, and 128 have features that resemble wisdom literature. Of these Psalm 78 starts with the words:

> O my people, hear my teaching;
> listen to the words of my mouth.
> I will open my mouth in parables, I will utter things hidden
> from of old (Ps. 78:1-2).

Several features in this opening are typical of wisdom literature, such as the call to hear and the words 'teaching', 'parables' and 'hidden things'.

In contrast to other types of psalms, these wisdom psalms do not display a structure that remains constant to them all.

Rather, they are distinguished by characteristics that mark them out as distinctive. These characteristics include:

(a) the knowledge that the fear of the Lord is the beginning of wisdom

(b) a concern for the practical issues of life

(c) a clear distinction between the two ways which face us in life, so that a clear distinction is drawn between the righteous and the wicked

(d) a struggle with the problem of why the wicked seem to prosper as compared with the righteous

(e) hints that the final solution lies in the life to come.

The first of the major wisdom psalms is Psalm 37, whose eleventh verse ('But the meek will inherit the land and enjoy great peace') was picked up by Christ and appears as the third beatitude (Matt. 5:5). The psalm is an acrostic, with each second verse commencing with another letter of the Hebrew alphabet. The teaching of this psalm has come over into English through John Wesley's translation of Paul Gerhardt's hymn 'Put thou thy trust in God' (Gerhardt's hymn 'Befehl du deine Wege' is also an acrostic, with each of its twelve verses commencing with a successive word from Psalm 37:5, 'Commit your way to the Lord ...'). The psalm points to the source of true wisdom and blessedness and encourages readers to follow the way of the Lord.

The second of these psalms which are strongly in the wisdom type is Psalm 73. It presents teaching very similar to Job and Ecclesiastes and it is clearly a teaching poem. When faced with the arrogance of the wicked and their prosperity, the psalmist did not understand the situation until he went into the sanctuary of God. There in the temple he realised what was to be their ultimate outcome (vv. 16-17).

7.6 Psalms of Trust

The Psalms are full of expressions of confidence in the God of Israel, though many do not clarify with certainty the precise situation that provoked the expression of trust. Some of them are the songs of an individual (e.g. 4, 11, 16, 23, 27, 62, 73, and 91); others are communal in nature (e.g. 90, 115, 123, 125, and 126). This group of psalms share in specific ways several features in common:[25]

(a) while their structure is not the same they share a common content

(b) in the face of enemies there is calm trust in the LORD

(c) their declarations have a ring of certainty about them, and in none of them is this feature omitted

(d) they use a variety of metaphors to describe God ('refuge', 'rock', 'shepherd', 'help').

7.7 Kingship Psalms

There is a group of psalms which all speak of God as king (29, 47, 93, 95-99). These psalms (with which some others may be associated (e.g. 24, 110) have among their characteristics:

a) the assertion that the LORD ('Yahweh') reigns

b) that this rule was from of old

c) that this rule is not only over Israel but over the whole world

d) in Zion, the God of Israel is extolled as universal king.

Some of the terms used of Israel's God are borrowed from the common Semitic background. Thus, he is called 'the Great King' (48:2), a term that was appropriated by human kings in the ancient Near East (cf. its use in reference to the king of Assyria in 2 Kings 18:19//Isa. 36:4). This use is accompanied by assertions of the ways in which God is superior to human rulers. Their kingdoms were limited earthly ones; his kingdom is universal and eternal (see section 10. The Kingship of God, for fuller discussion).

8. PSALMS OF REMEMBRANCE

8.1 Israel's Historical Faith

Another special group of psalms require more extended discussion. The faith of Israel was rooted in the events of

---

[25] Excellent tables depicting the characteristics of both types of psalms of trust are given by C. Hassell Bullock, *Encountering the Psalms*, pp. 167, 169.

Old Testament history. God acted in the world and especially he redeemed his people from their bondage and slavery in Egypt. It was a real world to which God came and the events were calendar events in human history. Thus the happenings in the Old Testament are not fictitious accounts composed to teach a certain message, but the record of actual events. There are serious consequences for any professing Christian to maintain that these events were fictitious. If we accept that the historical confession of Israel's faith does not have its roots in history, then we deprive the Christian faith of its foundation.

Israel expressed her faith over and over again in the Old Testament and in doing so recounted the historical developments of the nation. Some of these opportunities were provided in the annual ceremonies, especially the Passover. In this annual commemoration the children of Israel were reminded of the origin of the nation at the momentous time of the Exodus. When their children asked them, 'What does this ceremony mean to you?' they were to reply: 'It is the Passover sacrifice to the LORD, who passed over the houses of the Israelites in Egypt and spared our homes when he struck down the Egyptians' (Exod. 12:25-27). This was one way in which parents were to teach their children the historical facts that were the basis for the Passover. This was developed over the centuries into the Passover Haggadah that is still used to the present day. Jewish people still confess in the Passover ceremony that not only their forefathers *but they themselves* were brought out of Egypt.

> "It was not alone our fathers whom the Holy One, blessed be He, redeemed, but also us whom He redeemed with them, as it is said, 'And us He brought out thence that He might lead us to, and give us, the land which He swore to our fathers.'"

Similar communal aspects of a confession of faith occur in the declaration required in the presentation of the firstfruits. When Israel came into Canaan at the time of presenting the firstfruits, a man had to confess that his father (Jacob) was a wandering Aramean who had gone down into Egypt and become a great nation. The confession continued:

> "But the Egyptians ill-treated us and made us suffer, putting us to hard labour. Then we cried out to the LORD, the God of our fathers, and the LORD heard our voice and saw the misery, toil and oppression. So the LORD brought us out of Egypt with a mighty hand and a stretched out arm, with great terror and with miraculous signs and wonders. He brought us to this place and gave us this land, a land flowing with milk and honey; and now I bring the firstfruits of the soil that you, O LORD, have given me" (Deut. 26:6-10).

This confession was not a private one, for it was performed by all Israelites as they brought the firstfruits to the sanctuary. It was, therefore, a very public acknowledgment and reminder of the great events of the Exodus from Egypt. Moreover, the Israelite had to make the confession not just for himself but for others as well. He identified himself as part of the total community of Israel ('the Egyptians ill-treated *us*', '*we* cried out', 'the LORD heard *our* voice', 'he brought *us*'). The central intent of it was to bring praise to the God of Israel who had done such wonderful things for his people. It sets a pattern of recounting the distress of the people but then extolling the great deeds of the LORD.

It is important to note that the people even sang their history at the command of the LORD himself. Moses was told to write down a song that the LORD would give him, and to teach it to the people. They were to sing this song so that it might be a witness against them. Moses did as he was instructed (Deut. 31:19, 22). In this act he was joined by Joshua, so that the outgoing leader of the people was acting in conjunction with the incoming leader (Deut. 32:44). It was really the covenant commitment expressed in the form of a song, with the warning that the departure from God's requirements would result in his judgments coming upon the nation. The importance of the song of Moses is highlighted by the way in which, in Revelation 15:3-4, 'the song of Moses the servant of God' is linked with 'the song of the Lamb'.

8.2 The Purpose of the Historical Psalms

There are a group of psalms (especially 78, 105, 106, 114, 135, 136) which are essentially story-telling psalms. The story is not like those in English that begin with 'Once upon a time', for these songs are proclaiming the great deeds of the LORD. They are story-telling in the sense that they are narrative psalms which recount the history of Israel.

Just as the confession on the occasion of the presenting of the firstfruits was intended to be praise of God, so also with the narrative psalms. They were intended to teach the people the events of their history and to point them to the significance of those events so that they would praise the LORD. This is especially true of psalms such as 105 and 106 which both end with a song of praise to the LORD.

Within them there is a pattern of declaring the distress in which God's people were found at particular times, and then of proclaiming the deliverance which God afforded them.

> But he brought his people out like a flock;
> he led them like sheep through the desert. (Ps. 78:52)

> For he remembered his holy promise
> given to his servant Abraham.
> He brought out his people with rejoicing,
> his chosen ones with shouts of joy. (Ps. 105:42-43)

The historical songs of Israel were clearly to magnify the deeds of the Lord and remind the people whenever they were used that their God alone was the deliverer of his people. Because many of them recount numerous historical incidents, they are generally much longer than most psalms (with the exception of Psalm 119).

8.3 The Stories of the Lord

The main historical psalms are these:

Psalm 78: A summary of the history of Israel that recounts the story from the Exodus until the time of David and the choice of Jerusalem.

Psalm 105: An account of Israel's history from the Exodus till the occupation of Canaan and surrounding territory.

Psalm 106: Another narrative of Israel's history, but carrying the story further on to tell of the sins of the people after they came into Canaan.

Psalm 135: A song which includes references to God as creator, and one whose power was shown in Egypt and in giving Israel the land of Canaan as an inheritance.

Psalm 136: Another song which refers to creation, and then recounts the history of Israel in antiphonal form.

The narrative style is also displayed in many more psalms, which are not totally given over to historical remembrance. Using the Pentateuch (Genesis to Deuteronomy) as a guide, we can reconstruct from the Psalms the history from the time of Abraham up till the time of occupation of Canaan and later. The events include:

Israel, the offspring of Abraham	105:6
Israel went into Egypt	105:16-25
God delivered from their oppression	77:15; 81:6
He inflicted plagues on Egypt	78:44-51; 105:27-36; 135:8-9; 136:10
He led them through the sea	77:16-20; 78:13, 53; 114:3, 5
He guided them in the wilderness	68:7-10; 78:14-16; 105:39-42; 106:13-33; 114:8
Canaan was their heritage	44:2; 47:4; 60:7-8; 135:10-12; 136:17-22.

However, what is different about these references and the major story-telling psalms is that in the latter there is a chronological record of the events of Israel's history.

8.4 The Faithfulness of God

The historical psalms hark back to the great salvation of God seen in the redemption from Egypt. They record his great deeds in order that his people might have their faith strengthened, and that the record of past deliverance would serve as a model of hope for the believing community. Just as God had acted in this way before, so would he act again to save his people.

Ultimately this idea of hope for the future is based on the faithfulness of God. The fundamental theme of Israel's praise in this group of psalms is the fact that God is utterly faithful to his word of promise. There is frequent mention of the fact that God has remembered his covenant:

> He remembered that they were but flesh,
> a passing breeze that does not return (Ps. 78:39).
>
> For he remembered his holy promise
> given to his servant Abraham (Ps. 105:42).
>
> For their sake he remembered his covenant
> and out of his great love he relented (Ps. 106:45).
>
> He remembered us in our low estate (Ps. 136:23).

God's relationship with his covenant people is characterised by his utter steadfastness. He has spoken a word and he will perform it. There was no variableness with him, but complete integrity towards his people. The New Testament reinforces this Old Testament teaching. As Christians we will be kept 'strong to the end', so that we 'will be blameless on the day of the Lord Jesus Christ. God, who has called you into fellowship with his Son Jesus Christ our Lord, is faithful' (1 Cor. 1:8-9).

9. GOD IN THE PSALMS

9.1 Reverence in Worship

Any teaching of the Psalter has to be considered in relation to the fact that they are songs of worship. The presentation of teaching about God and his ways is given in the context of worship of him. Thus all the Psalms are God-centred because they are prayers *to* him or songs *about* him. Our response in studying the Psalms should be one of worship, and our love to him should be deepened through understanding better their message. 'How is my love for God is kindled by the Psalms,' exclaimed Augustine.

The Book of Psalms is a tremendous testimony to the living God, and its use throughout centuries by the Christian church has had a far greater influence than is often realised. In the liturgies of the Christian church the language of the Psalter features very prominently, and the thought of the Psalter has been influential either through its direct use or through hymnology based on Psalter passages. Much of our Christian understanding of God and our relationship with him is based on the Psalter.

In their focus on God the Psalms show us how vital he was in the life of Israel. Our knowledge of that relationship comes largely from the Psalms and when God's attributes are being set forth, it is in the context of prayer and praise. We should not think, though, that the type of understanding of God revealed in the Psalms was universal in Israel. The fact that the prophets had to direct condemnatory speeches against the people shows a different picture.

9.2 The Majestic God

The Psalms are full of praise of God, and this praise takes two forms. In some passages the psalmists simply declare God's praise, but in many of them they describe who the LORD is and what he has done. Thus the opening and closing of Psalm 103 voices praise to God:

> Praise the LORD, O my soul;
> all my inmost being, praise his holy name. (v. 1)
> Praise the LORD, all his works everywhere in his dominion.
> Praise the LORD, O my soul. (v. 22)

In between these two exclamations of praise is the main body of the psalm, which contains descriptions of God and his works like this:

> who forgives all my sins
> and heals all my diseases;
> who redeems my life from the pit
> and crowns me with love and compassion;
> who satisfies my desires with good things,
> so that my youth is renewed like the eagle's. (vv. 3-5)

The language of praise is accompanied by content, which tells us things about the God who was being worshipped. The Psalms are not empty liturgy but are full of words that direct attention to the glorious person of the living God.

The picture that the Psalms present of God is that of a sovereign God before whom all must come in worship. The greatness of God is stressed in various ways including the use of a distinctive name. He is said to be *Elyon*, the Most High. This word occurs almost only in poetical passages in the Old Testament, and most of these are in the Psalms (eighteen occurrences out of thirty). At times it is used in parallelism with *Elohîm* ('God') or *Shaddai* ('the Almighty'), but other times by itself. Psalm 47, one of the songs of the sons of Korah, provides a good example of its usage:

> Clap your hands, all you nations;
>   Shout to God with cries of joy.
> How awesome is the LORD Most High,
>   the great King over all the earth! (vv. 1-2)

God's character is stressed at times in contrast to the heathen gods, who are only lifeless idols. When the nations say, 'Where is their God?', Israel can reply, 'Our God is in heaven, and he does whatsoever pleases him' (115:1-3). The response which is called for when one is confronted with the greatness of God is to bow down in worship before him (96:6-7).

But though God is so high, yet he stoops to make himself known to men. 'He made known his ways to Moses, his deeds to the people of Israel' (103:7). The same psalm goes on to liken God to a father who has compassion on his children, and who knows their frailty (vv. 13-16). In him David also found a substitute father and mother (27:10). The picture of God presented in the Psalms is of one involved in the life of his children so that he is a shepherd for them (23:1; 80:1); or like a bird who protects her young under her wings (91:1, 4); or a judge who dispenses justice (50:4, 6); or a warrior who is a shield to them (18:1). The great wonder is that the God who calls the stars by name is the same God who heals the broken-hearted and binds up their wounds (147:3-4).

9.3 God the Creator

The doctrine of creation as set out in Genesis 1 is reaffirmed in the Psalter. God had only to speak the word and the world came into being:

> By the word of the LORD the heavens were made,
> their starry host by the breath of his mouth …
> For he spoke, and it came to be;
> he commanded, and it stood firm. (33:6, 9)

Genesis 1 is turned into a prayer in Psalm 8, and man's role as vice-regent is again set forth. All of creation has been placed under him, and God has made him ruler over everything which has been created (8:5-10). Psalm 104 comprises a long song in praise of creation, in which there are many echoes of Genesis 1.

Throughout the Psalter the creation is depicted as God's handiwork, not something divine in itself or originating by itself. Hence there is no worship of nature, only worship of the creator. He is the God who has shown his power in the creation of the world. The inference is drawn from this that because God is so powerful, then he will care for his own. There is a formula in use in the Psalms that joins together the thought of the Lord as the maker of heaven and earth with the idea of blessing for his people. This formula may well go back very early in the Old Testament, for Melchizedek blessed Abram saying, 'Blessed be Abram by God Most High, Creator of heaven and earth' (Gen. 14:19). By the right of creation the Lord controls the world, and is therefore able to bring blessing and protection to Israel (115:12-15; 121:2; 124:8; 134:3; 146:5-6).

There are also hymns of praise to God as the creator who sustains all his creatures, animals as well as mankind. A group of psalms (104:24-30; 136:25; 145:12-16) speak of God as opening his hand to provide for the needs of his creatures, and they even speak of his 'steadfast love' for them. This term occurs so often of God's covenant love for his own people, but it can be applied to his gracious concern for all his creatures (33:5; 119:64; 136:25). This usage of covenant terminology may surprise us, yet God made a covenant not just with Noah but with all living creatures (Gen. 9:9-16). The scope of God's concern is as extensive as his creation in its entirety.

9.4 The Compassionate God

Special attention needs to be given to this aspect. The very fact that the psalmists come in prayer to God is a recognition of their need of him and his forgiving grace. They come because they know of his righteousness, and how they have offended against him. David, in his cry for mercy in Psalm 51, recognises that his sins against Uriah and Bathsheba were horrendous in the sight of God, and includes them in his utmost confession to the Holy One of Israel: 'Against you, you only, have I sinned and done what is evil in your sight' (51:4). Repeatedly the psalmists confess the sinfulness of man in the strongest terms. Men are sinful right from their mother's womb (51:5; 58:3), and all their actions are corrupt and vile (14:1). In the New Testament, when Paul comes to convince his readers of the universal sinfulness of men, he does so by citing from six psalms and one passage from Isaiah (Rom. 3:10-18), and even his conclusion in that passage echoes a psalm: 'Therefore no one will be declared righteous in his sight by observing the law' (Rom. 3:20; cf. Ps. 143:2b).

The Psalms do not only paint the extent of sin. They also point to the grace of God shown in the forgiveness of sins. There is a group of psalms that Luther once called 'the Pauline Psalms' (32, 51, 103, 130, 143) because they teach the same truths which Paul has in his epistles. He said of these psalms: 'They all teach that the forgiveness of sins comes, without the law and without works, to the man who believes ... and when David sings, "There is forgiveness with you, that you may be feared," this is just what Paul says, "God has concluded them all in unbelief, that he might have mercy upon all" (Rom. 11.32). Thus no man may boast of his own righteousness. That word, 'That you may be feared', dusts away all merit, and teaches us to uncover our heads before God, and confess, *it is mere forgiveness, not merit at all; remission, not satisfaction*. We are brought into a relationship with God in which we enjoy the forgiveness of sins solely by the free grace of God. The teaching that we are forgiven by faith alone is one which is imbedded in the Psalms: 'Blessed are they whose transgressions are forgiven, whose sins are covered. Blessed is the man whose sin the Lord will never count against him' (Rom. 4:7-8, quoting Ps. 32:1-2). God will not despise a broken and a contrite heart (51:17), and those who come to him will find that their cry for mercy will be answered by his declaration of forgiveness (130:1-4).

The God who forgives sin is the one who works in the hearts of the penitent. Many of the Psalms reveal the profound spiritual experiences through which the writers went and they lay the foundation for truths that the New Testament develops more fully. Profound sorrow for sin accompanied confession to God (38:18), and there is a recognition of the need for a profound spiritual change. Psalm 51 highlights this in the case of David, who pleaded for a clean heart and an internal change by the work of the Holy Spirit (v. 10). This experience is described more fully in the New Testament in terms of the new birth (John 3:5, 6; 2 Cor. 5:17; Gal. 6:15). Those who experienced it could sing for joy because God gives his forgiven children a new song to sing, 'a hymn of praise to our God' (Ps. 40:3).

10. THE KINGSHIP OF GOD

10.1 The Idea of Kingship

The idea of God's kingship is central to the Bible. It appears from the beginning of Genesis, even though the actual words 'king' and 'kingdom' do not appear till later. The basic idea underlying the Bible's presentation of the relationship between God and humans is that the creator God is a sovereign who exercises his rule over his world and over his human creatures in particular. The kingdom of God is concerned with God's people, in God's place, and under God's rule. Living under God's covenant rule, they were directed in their response to God by the various commandments he gave them. As loyal servants they yielded obedience to him as their master.

At the time of the Exodus from Egypt the children of Israel were brought into a formal relationship with God and with one another by the formation of the nation of Israel. At Mount Sinai God entered into a covenant with them, which regulated the life of the nation. By this covenant God set the conditions under which his people would live. He initiated the covenant and he was sovereign in the relationship.

As noted earlier, the pattern that the covenant at Sinai takes has been shown to be similar to other covenants in the ancient Near East. Countries, especially when one had been conquered by another, had to enter into a political treaty which noted their subservience. The king of the more powerful country (the conqueror) initiated a new relationship with the less powerful (the conquered). The great king set out his demands on his new subjects, and in turn promised to defend them if they were attacked. In the Book of Exodus God is the great king who establishes a new form of covenant relationship with his people Israel.

When God redeemed his people from Egypt, Moses and the people sang a song extolling his triumph. The song tells of the LORD's power over Pharaoh (15:1-7), the sea (15:8-12), and the nations generally (15:13-18). The LORD is a mighty warrior who saves (v. 2), destroys the enemy (v. 6), does wonders (v. 11), guides his redeemed people (v. 13), and who reigns for ever and ever (v. 18). This last verse is important because it speaks of the eternal reign of the LORD: *The LORD will reign for ever and ever.* The fitting outcome of the victor's conquest is that he rules his people. How that takes place is spelled out in detail later in Exodus. The people have become a royal priesthood and a holy nation (19:6). Everyone in Israel was to be a priest to God, while the nation as a whole was to be consecrated to God. The detailed laws that follow in Exodus and Leviticus show how the king desired his subjects to live under his authority. Specific details were given of the structures in life which were to regulate their lives. The kingdom of God from the period of Moses can be set out in the following diagram:

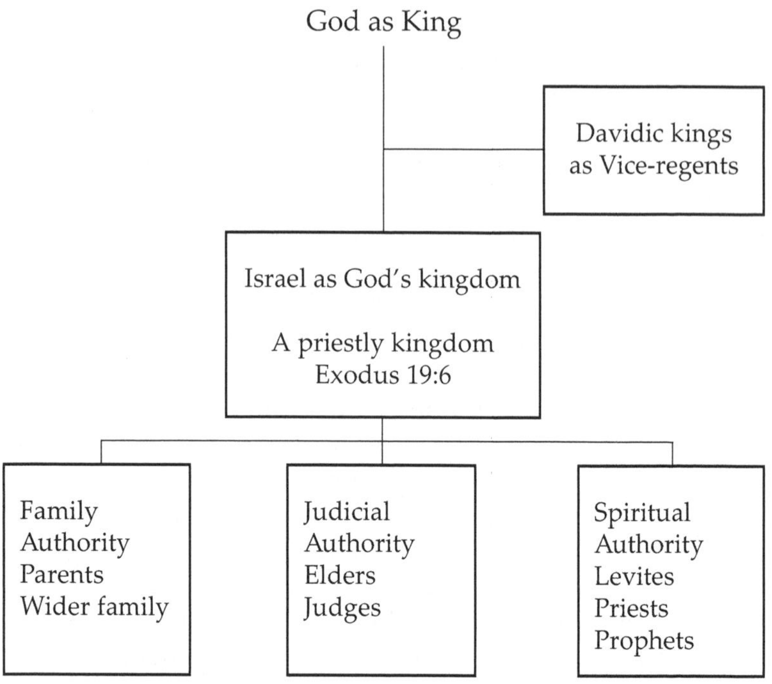

This form of government, which is often called 'a theocracy', continued until the appointment of the first king of Israel in the person of Saul. When David succeeded Saul, God entered into a special covenant with David, adopting the Davidic family and appointing them as his vice-regents. During the period of the monarchy God was still the ultimate king, but the Davidic kings were to display his rule among men, and they were also to point to the coming of Jesus as the final king.

10.2 The LORD's Kingship in the Psalms

It is hardly surprising that the central fact of Israel's faith, that the LORD was their king, should be so prominent in the songs of the people. They proclaim him as their own Lord and call upon others to acknowledge him also (96:10).

The Psalms speak of God as the one who is king forever and ever (10:16). He is seated on his heavenly throne (11:4; 29:10) and as the creator is clearly the 'king from of old' (74:12). Thus he is rightly king over all the earth (47:2, 7) and all nations are to be told, 'The Lord reigns' (96:10).

But more particularly he is the king of Israel, and many of the psalms which speak in this way of him link his kingship with Zion (Jerusalem). Zion is called 'the city of the Great King' (48:2) and the declaration is made that he is 'great in Zion' (99:2). It is striking the number of times that God is called 'the Great King' or reference is made to his greatness. Several psalms proclaiming his kingship are grouped together in the Psalter (93, 95–100). These psalms use the expression, 'The Lord reigns' (or, 'is king'). This recalls the shout that went up when Absalom assumed the kingship: 'Absalom reigns in Hebron' (2 Sam. 15:10). When used of the Lord this acclamation has something of a dynamic ring about it, rather like the triumphant Easter hymn, 'Jesus Christ is risen today, Alleluia!'

God is also the king who made Israel his own flock, and he calls them 'my people' (50:7, 81:8, 11). He created Israel, and the people can say, 'We are his people, the sheep of his pasture' (100:3). The Lord chose 'Jacob to be his own, Israel to be his treasured possession' (135:4, and cf. Exod. 19:6).

Some psalms also fix attention on the final outcome of human history, when the Lord will be seen to be king of all nations. He will come to judge 'the world in righteousness and the peoples in his truth' (96:13). Because he reigns, even the distant isles can be called upon to rejoice (97:1). It is as if the psalmist is picturing the result after the final judgment when God's universal dominion will be established.

10.3 The Davidic Kingship

There are also many psalms that speak of the kingship of the line of David. They show how the covenant with David (2 Sam. 7) was understood in Israel. If we follow the titles of the psalms, David himself calls God 'my king' (5:3), and recognises that his own authority came from God. Two of the psalms (89 and 132) are expositions of the covenant that God made with David (2 Sam. 7), and they show the special place that the Davidic kingship occupied in Israel. David himself grasped the significance of God's promise affecting the future and destiny of the human race.[26] In psalms such as 18, 20, and 21 David acknowledges that his strength comes from God and that his victories are really God's victories.

The king also speaks of the people as not his own, but as God's people. He can appeal to God in these terms for them: 'Save your people and bless your inheritance; be their shepherd and carry them for ever' (28:9). The evildoers are described as crushing 'your people, O LORD; they oppress your inheritance' (94:5).

This attitude of the king also helps us to explain some of the difficult passages in the Psalter in which there is appeal to God to destroy the enemies. The contexts make it clear that the enemies were not primarily personal enemies but really they were enemies of God. Thus in Psalm 5 David prays for his enemies to be banished for their sins, and he gives as the reason, 'for they have rebelled *against you*' (5:10; for a fuller discussion of these passages, see section 12 on the imprecatory psalms in this introduction).

10.4 Our Response to the Kingship of God

Two important aspects come out of the Psalter in relation to the impact that the teaching about God as king should have upon us.

First, our response should be one of worship. Repeatedly in the kingship psalms the thought of worship appears, especially because God is not only king, but is also a holy God.

> Come, let us bow down in worship,
> let us kneel before the LORD. (95:6)

> Ascribe to the LORD the glory due to his name;
> bring an offering and come into his courts.

---

[26] The significance of David's words in 2 Samuel 7:18-21 is brought out by Walter Kaiser in 'The Blessing of David: The Charter for Humanity', in John H. Skilton, ed., *The Law and the Prophets: Old Testament Studies in Honor of Oswald T. Allis* (Nutley, NJ: Presbyterian and Reformed Publishing Co., 1974), pp. 298-318; and, W. J. Dumbrell, *Covenant and Creation: An Old Testament Covenantal Theology* (Exeter: Paternoster Press, 1984), pp. 151-52.

Worship the LORD in the splendour of his holiness;
tremble before him, all the earth.
Say among the nations, 'The LORD reigns' (96:8-10).

Exalt the LORD our God and worship at his footstool; he is holy.
Exalt the LORD our God and worship at his holy mountain,
for the LORD our God is holy (99:5, 9).

In a similar way the message of Revelation 19 concludes with the mighty shout: 'Hallelujah! For our Lord God Almighty reigns. Let us rejoice and be glad and give him glory!' John in response to this fell at the angelic messenger's feet, but the angel said: 'Do not do it! Worship God!' (Rev. 19:6-10). A knowledge of God as king should bring us to his footstool in worship.

Secondly, the thought of the kingship of God should be a stimulus to us in regard to missionary work. The Psalms present to us a picture of the nations of the world being subject to our God. God is so great that the nations must come and worship before him. This picture is not just a vision of the future, but something that stirs the psalmists with a real missionary urge. They call upon the world at large to come and worship the LORD (57:8-11; 66:1-4; 67:2-5; 96:3, 7-13; 99:2-3; 100:1-3; 108:3; 113:3-4; 117:1-2; 145:21). There is an eagerness about their longing to see all nations bowing before the king and being subject to his rule. The vision of the ultimate kingdom of God impels them with a real missionary spirit.

11. GOD'S LAW IN THE PSALMS

11.1 A Sovereign and His Laws

The laws of the Old Testament are not abstract moral laws, but the requirements of a covenant God. They are the personal demands of a personal, sovereign God upon his subjects. God spoke his law on Mount Sinai and then it was given in written form, both as the tablets of stone and also as the book of the covenant (Exod. 24:7) and the Book of Deuteronomy (Deut. 31:9). The personal character of the law is emphasised by the exhortations that occur so often, encouraging Israel to keep the law and to be holy because the Lord was holy (Lev. 20:26).

The way in which the law was given to Israel places stress on the fact that it was given to a redeemed people. They had been brought out of slavery in Egypt by the Lord, who had shown great favour and grace to them in their need. There could be no thought that salvation was going to be based on their obedience to God's law. Even at Mount Sinai the people had sinned against him and provoked him to anger. They had not, and could not have, merited God's favour (Deut. 7:7-8; 9:4-6).

Israel was taught that God's covenant was unchangeable. The promises to the patriarchs, Abraham, Isaac, and Jacob could not be broken (see, for example, Exodus 3:15-17). This meant also that the basic requirements of the covenant, God's law, were also unchangeable. The psalmists say that God remembered his covenant (105:42; 106:45). Moreover he brought his people into the land of Canaan so 'that they might keep his precepts and observe his laws' (105:45).

To enforce his law upon the people, God promised blessings if they obeyed. Following an initial experience of God's grace when they were redeemed from slavery, further obedience would result in greater experience of God's grace. God's choice of Israel came first, and then as the people obeyed God a fuller appropriation of the blessings of salvation would become theirs.

The opposite truth was that curses were expressed against the people if they were unfaithful to God's covenant (for the curses, see especially Leviticus 26 and Deuteronomy 28). The Psalms reflect both these aspects, since blessings are pronounced on those who walk in the way of the Lord (1:1; 119:1), and often judgments are expressed against those who have gone their own way (14:3).

11.2 God's Law in the Psalms

We saw earlier that the Psalter came out of the covenant community. Hence it is quite understandable that a community that sang about God as their great king would also sing about his law. In Psalm 81 God challenges his people to listen to his warning, and says:

> You shall have no foreign god among you;
> you shall not bow down to an alien god.
> I am the LORD your God, who brought you up out of Egypt
> (vv. 9-10).

These words, of course, are taken from, or echo, the opening of the Decalogue, and contain parts of the preface and the first two commandments (Exod. 20:2-4). They are used to reassert the claims which the Redeemer God had upon his people. They had to own him as their God, and not yield obedience or worship to any other.

There is a group of psalms that concentrate on God's law, and they focus particular attention on the blessings that come to those who obey them. They make God's law the object of thanks and praise, and they teach us especially the blessings of the law. Three of them in particular stand out because of their emphasis of walking in the way of God's law.

(a) Psalm 1 sets the pattern for the whole Psalter, as we have already seen (section 3.3). It opens with the word of blessing on those whose delight is in the law of the Lord. The contrast with the wicked is brought out in a very striking way:

[positive] 1. Blessed is the man who does not walk ...
Rather . . .
Result

[negative] 2. Not so the wicked! . . .
Rather . . .
Result

3. Summary
For the LORD . . .

(b) The thought of this psalm is extended in Psalm 19, which first of all refers to the declaration of God's glory in his creation (vv. 1-6) before it goes on to speak of the preciousness of God's law. The language used about the law is deliberate and most revealing. A variety of nouns is employed to describe God's revealed will ('law', 'testimony', 'precepts', 'commandments', and 'ordinances'). The adjectives used in reference to them highlight the nature of God's law ('perfect', 'sure', 'right', 'pure', 'clean', 'true'), while the succession of verbs (e.g. 'reviving', 'making wise', 'giving joy', 'giving light', 'enduring') tell of the impact which God's law has upon his children.

(c) The high point of praise of the law comes in Psalm 119, which is the longest song in the Book. It is an acrostic psalm divided into twenty-two sections, with every verse in each section beginning with the same letter of the Hebrew alphabet. This is not a sudden outpouring of the heart such as other psalms are, for it is not the sort of poem which could be composed quickly. The psalm is a beautiful work of art singing the praise of God's law, for every verse but three (vv. 84, 121, 122) contains a virtual synonym for 'law' ('word', 'statutes', 'testimonies', etc.). The psalmist rings the changes on these words to portray how wonderful God's law is, and to show yet again how it serves as a lamp to the feet and as a light to the path (119:105).

11.3 The Response to God's Law

God's law was clearly precious to the psalmists. This contrasts with the modern view of law which may respect God's demands and try to obey them but hardly thinks of them as exhilarating. But that is precisely the way believers in the Old Testament period considered God's laws.

> The ordinances of the LORD are sure
>   and altogether righteous.
> They are more precious than gold,
>   than much pure gold;
> they are sweeter than honey,
>   than honey from the comb. (19:9-10)

> How sweet are your promises to my taste,
>   sweeter than honey to my mouth! (119:103)

> Because I love your commands
>   more than gold, more than pure gold,
> and because I consider all your precepts right,
>   I hate every wrong path. (119:127-128)

God's law directed the ways of his people. At the time of renewing the covenant just before entry into the land of Canaan Moses said: 'What other nation is so great as to have such righteous decrees and laws as this body of laws which I am setting before you today? ... Teach them to your children and to their children after them' (Deut. 4:8-9). Thus the psalmists can ask for God to teach his way (25:4-5; 119:33) and also make mention of God's command to teach succeeding generations (78:5-8). In pleading for forgiveness David promised that if this was granted he would then 'teach transgressors your ways, and sinners will turn back to you' (51:13).

God's law was the object of meditation. As the children of Israel went into the promised land, they did so with Joshua's words ringing in their ears: 'Do not let this Book of the Law depart from your mouth; meditate upon it day and night, so that you may be careful to do everything written in it' (Josh.1:8). The Psalms show us how the people had taken this command to heart and practised it.

> Blessed is the man
> whose delight is in the law of the LORD
> and on his law he meditates day and night. (1:2)

> I will remember the deeds of the LORD;
> yes, I will remember your miracles of long ago.
> I will meditate on all your works
> and consider all your mighty deeds. (77:11-12)

> I meditate on your precepts and consider your ways. (119:15)

Meditation, according to the Psalter, consists of three things. It is firstly grounded in the *truth* of God. God has spoken in his word, and that word is to be hidden in the heart (119:1). Meditation stimulates thought about his word and heightens the meaning of a passage. Secondly, meditation is a response to the *love* of God. Faith in God is evidence of a personal relationship with him, and love to him is stimulated by meditation upon his word. Thirdly, meditation is really an aspect of *praise* of God. It is worship of the living God and consists of adoration of God and his works. In meditating on his word our attention is directed to God himself.[27]

12. THE PROBLEM SONGS

12.1 Introduction

One group of psalms stands out above all others because of the difficulties they have created for Christian people. These psalms are often called 'the imprecatory psalms'. The word *imprecation* comes from a Latin word *imprecatio,* which describes calling down harm on someone. Thus the English word is used in this connection to describe the psalms in which curses are expressed on others. Often it is not a whole psalm in question but only some verses from it.[28] The psalms in which these passages mainly occur are 55, 59, 69, 79, 109, and 137.

The problem which they present is of reconciling the curses and prayers for destruction of the wicked with the teaching of the New Testament. For some the problem is so acute that they assert that no New Testament Christian can use or approve of the imprecations in the psalms. This kind of judgment is often made without realising the full picture that has to be taken into consideration.

There are some facts we have to remember before we look at the solutions to the problem.

Firstly, this is not just a pressing problem for those who use the Psalter as a song book in worship. It is just as real a problem for those who merely want to read the Psalms in private devotions or in public worship.

Secondly, the fact that there are other portions of the Bible which contain similar curses must be borne in mind. These occur in passages such as Jeremiah 15:5; 17:18; 18:21-23; 20:12; Nehemiah 6:14 and 13:29. They also occur in New Testament

---

[27] A very helpful introduction to meditation is Edmund Clowney, *Christian Meditation* (Nutley, NJ: Craig Press, 1978).

[28] The total number of verses containing imprecations is around a hundred, and these are spread over thirty-two psalms. A listing of the passages is given in John N. Day, 'The Imprecatory Psalms and Christian Ethics', *BS* 159 (2002), pp. 166-86.

passages such as Acts 8:20; 2 Timothy 4:14; Galatians 1:9; 5:12; and Revelation 6:10.

Thirdly, Christ quoted freely from the Psalms. He used the messianic psalms most frequently, but then quoted most often from the psalms with curses in them. Thus in his lament over Jerusalem he referred to dashing the little ones to the ground, taking the words from Psalm 137:9 (in the LXX version). He also repeatedly used Psalm 69 (see John 2:17; 15:25). The fact that these psalms were endorsed and appropriated by our Lord does not explain their difficulty, but it should warn us not to judge them rashly.

Fourthly, some of these psalms are expressly referred to in the New Testament as having been given by inspiration as the psalmists spoke under the guidance of the Holy Spirit. In the case of Psalm 109 the apostle Peter quoted from it and said 'which the Holy Spirit spoke long ago through the mouth of David concerning Judas' (Acts 1:16).

12.2 Suggested Solutions

Various solutions to the problem have been proposed, and some of these can be reviewed.

An obvious solution which some have adopted is simply to leave these psalms alone and to pretend they are not there. This is done by avoiding any use or recognition of them. This presents us with the problem that the curses often come in psalms with other wonderful sayings, to which we wish to cling. Also, these psalms and many others were part and parcel of our Lord's use of the Old Testament. The problem has to be faced, not avoided.

It has been claimed that the Psalter belongs to the Old Testament dispensation, not the New Testament dispensation of grace, and therefore it teaches a lower morality than the New Testament with its injunction to love one's enemies (Matt. 5:44-45). But this would make Scripture contradict itself, for the Old Testament does not teach hatred towards one's enemies (Exod. 23:4, 5; Lev. 19:17, 18). Also, when Paul was condemning the sin of a revengeful spirit, he does so by quoting in Romans 12:18-20 from two Old Testament passages (Deut. 32:35; Prov. 25:21, 22).

Others have suggested that these psalms merely predict the doom of the wicked but are not to be understood as desiring their destruction. While there is an element of truth in this explanation, yet it does not explain many of the cases which go far beyond mere prediction. They ask God to carry out the destruction of the wicked (see, for example, 55:9 and 59:12-13).

Another view has been that the curses are to be understood in a figurative or spiritual sense. Thus the enemies spoken of are really temptations, and when we use these psalms we are praying that our temptations may be put to death or removed from us. But the persons spoken about give every appearance of having been real persons, not just some desires or emotions we may have.

Some have the idea that the imprecations are cries stemming from personal vindictiveness and they are seeking personal vengeance. Such utterances were wrong, but because of the circumstances in which the psalmists were placed they may to some extent be excused for speaking such curses. This theory does not fit the facts, as they show that in David's history there is no such spirit of vindictiveness. The real answer is deeper.

12.3 The Curses of the Covenant

Earlier we saw that the Psalms have to be placed in their true setting within God's covenant. It is striking that the cursing psalms strongly emphasise the relationship between Israel and the LORD. They stress the kingship of God over his people, and appeal to the God who is enthroned for ever to hear the cry of his people and to afflict their enemies (55:19). The relationship to God is stressed by use of the term 'servant' (69:17; 109:28) and also by the claim of the community to be God's people (79:13).

In almost all the imprecatory psalms the context is one of judgment. The appeal is to God to act as judge, and to be the vindicator of his people. In Psalm 109, for example, there is explicit reference to blessing and cursing (109:17-19, 28). This seems to be a clear allusion back to Genesis 12:3:

'I will bless those who bless you, and whoever curses you I will curse, and all peoples on earth will be blessed through you.' Psalm 137 is different because there is no reference to a judicial procedure. However, two passages from the prophets (Hos. 13:16; Isa. 13:16) provide the background for the curse in this imprecatory psalm. The psalmist speaks a word of cursing against the arch-enemy of Israel, Babylon, in language which is clearly reminiscent of these two prophets. In particular Isaiah 13:16 had already prophesied the downfall of Babylon. This link between prophets and psalmists should also serve as a reminder that there is a prophetic dimension to the Psalter. Just as the prophets deliver divine oracles, so do the psalmists.[29] The New Testament confirms this conjunction by referring to David as a prophet (Acts 2:30), and also understanding passages from the Psalms as prophecies concerning Jesus.[30]

The imprecatory psalms also show that the enemies were indeed God's enemies, not just the enemies of the psalmists. Thus Psalm 5 calls on God to declare the wicked guilty because, he says, 'they have rebelled against *you*' (5:10). Similarly Psalm 79 asks God to repay 'the reproaches they have hurled at *you*, O Lord' (v. 12). Even Psalm 137 must be understood to imply that the enemies are the enemies of the Lord. It is Babylon as the opponent of Israel who is in view. Just as Jeremiah cried: 'Do to her as she has done to others' (Jer. 50:15), so the psalmist was asking for divine visitation on her.

The concept of cursing was central to the whole idea of covenant, both within and without the Bible. In the extra-biblical treaties a person entering into a treaty was obliged to treat the other party's enemies as his enemies. The principle was, as one Hittite treaty puts it, 'with my friend you shall be friend, and with my enemy you shall

[29] These oracles are found in 2:6-9; 12:5; 46:10; 50:5-23; 60:6-8; 68:22-23; 81:6-16; 82:2-7; 89:3-4, 19-37; 90:3; 91:14-16; 95:8-11; 105:15; 110:1, 4; and 132:11-18.

[30] For a very helpful discussion on these aspects, see Alex Luc, 'Interpreting the Curses in the Psalms', *JETS* 42/3 (September 1999), pp. 400-05.

be enemy'.[31] In the Old Testament itself the word 'curse' could be employed as a virtual synonym for 'covenant' (Deut. 29:14, 18).[32] When the prophets speak judgment against Israel, they echo the curses of the covenant from passages such as Leviticus 26 and Deuteronomy 27 and 28. Rebels, whether within the covenant nation or outside, came under the same curses. In this respect the curses in the Psalter are typical of the covenantal approach of the Old Testament both in regard to relationships between men and relationships between God and humanity.

Finally, we should remember that the Bible consistently marks a sharp distinction between those who are for God and those who are against him. There is a final judgment day coming when the Son of Man will separate the sheep from the goats (Matt. 25:31-33). The picture the New Testament gives us of heaven is that nothing sinful or unclean will ever enter it (Rev. 21:27). As elsewhere in the Bible, the psalmists are looking at life from the perspective that is going to prevail at the last day. In appealing for God's vindication they are virtually asking for God's final judgment to be advanced in time and made a reality here and now.[33]

13. A CHRISTIAN READING OF THE PSALMS

13.1 An Open Song Book

The Psalter grew up over a long period of time. In its early development it was an open songbook of God's people, in

---

[31] J. B. Pritchard, ed., *Ancient Near Eastern Texts Relating to the Old Testament*, 3rd ed. (Princeton: Princeton University Press, 1991), p. 204.

[32] *DCH*, 1, pp. 272-73, gives as one of the meanings of *'âlâh*, 'covenant stipulation' or 'sometimes perh. used collectively, '**covenant**', citing Deut. 29:11, 13, 18 [Eng. enumeration 12, 14, 19]. Both 'oath' and 'covenant' are listed as synonyms. This lies behind the decision of the NIV translators to use 'oath' in these verses.

[33] I have discussed more fully the imprecatory psalms in 'The Continuity of the Covenant Curses in the Imprecations of the Psalms', *RTR* 54, 2 (1995), pp. 65-72. For wider discussions, including Christian use of the imprecations, see J. Carl Laney, 'A Fresh Look at the Imprecatory Psalms,' *BS* 138 (January-March 1981), pp. 35-45; reprinted in *The Bib Sac Reader: Commemorating Fifty Years of Publication of Dallas Theological Seminary 1934-1983* (Chicago: Moody Press, 1983), pp. 115-125; Alex Luc, 'Interpreting the Curses of the Psalms'; John N. Day, 'The Imprecatory Psalms and Christian Ethics'.

the sense that it was being added to by the addition of new psalms. Moreover, it was in constant use by individuals and the collective group of believers as it was growing. There must have been many other songs which were composed, but these we have were especially written under the influence of the Holy Spirit and brought together as the special songbook of the Old Testament church.

The Psalter is an open songbook in another sense as well. While the Psalms come out of the individual experiences of their authors, yet they often lack precise indications which would enable us to say exactly what those experiences were. Thus to say that the Lord has delivered our eyes from tears does not specify anything more than that the Lord has removed our sorrow or grief. It does not tell us the details of the experience which caused such sorrow. This is in marked contrast to other Old Testament songs such as the Song of the Sea (Exod. 15) or the Song of Deborah (Judg. 5). The lack of specific details is important, however, as it enables us to identify all the more closely with the Psalms. Because they are general in character we can use them so readily and apply them to our own specific need.

The New Testament sets a pattern of use of the Psalms for Christians in that it appropriates them and uses them for believers passing through similar experiences. Their pastoral use and application were realised, and when in trouble New Testament Christians found comfort in them. Thus when Paul is describing his deliverance on the occasion of his preliminary hearing he says he 'was delivered from the lion's mouth' (2 Tim. 4:17). This is an apparent reference to Psalm 22:21, and may indicate that he had used that lament in prayer at the time of his hearing. In the letter of the Hebrews the writer quotes a word from the Psalms that had relevance for his experience and for his readers: 'The Lord is my helper; I will not be afraid. What can man do to me?' (Heb. 13:6; cf. Ps. 118:6). These and many other quotations and allusions are applied on the principle given by Paul in Romans 15:4: 'For everything that was written in the past was written to teach us, so that through endurance and the encouragement of the

Scriptures we might have hope.' He has just quoted from a psalm (69:9) and his readers are encouraged to place their trust in the Lord, for the Old Testament Scriptures gave ample evidence of his faithfulness.

13.2 The Psalms and the New Testament

We cannot read the Psalms today as believers in the Old Testament read them, for we live *after* the coming of Christ. Jesus himself was brought up in a Jewish environment in which the Psalms were extensively used. Augustine said of Jesus, *iste cantator psalmorum*, 'He, the singer of the psalms.' On occasions of pilgrimage to Jerusalem (Luke 2:41-51), such as at the Passover, he would have been part of the community who sang from the Psalter. During the washing of his feet he quoted from Psalm 41:10 (John 13:18), while on the Cross he used several phrases from the Psalms ('My God, My God, why have you forsaken me?', Ps. 22:1; 'It is done', cf. Ps. 22:31 ['he has done it']; 'Father, into your hands I commend my spirit', Ps. 31:5).

Moreover, Jesus is the focus of both Old and New Testaments, and in his own ministry he gave indications of how we are to understand the Old Testament (including the Psalms) in reference to himself. Twice following his resurrection he spoke of how the Old Testament pointed to himself as the promised Messiah. To Cleopas and his friend he began with Moses and all the prophets and 'explained to them what was said in all the Scriptures concerning himself' (Luke 24:27). Then to the assembled disciples in Jerusalem Jesus appeared and said: 'Everything must be fulfilled that is written about me in the Law of Moses, the Prophets and the Psalms' (Luke 24:44). Clearly Jesus expounded the Psalms to the disciples and explained them in terms of his own coming and work.

Jesus' use of the Psalms also explains the extensive use of the Psalms throughout the New Testament. There are about 360 quotations from the Old Testament in the New, and of these about one-third are from the Book of Psalms. Many appear in the early sermons of the apostles as recorded in the

Book of Acts. Peter uses Psalms 110 and 16 in his speech on the day of Pentecost (Acts 2:25-28, 34), while in his speech to the rulers he quotes Psalm 118:22 (Acts 4:11). When Paul spoke in the synagogue at Pisidian Antioch he quoted from Psalm 2 and like Peter also used Psalm 16 (Acts 13:33-35). Clearly the apostles preached and taught on the basis of the instruction that they had received, and Jesus had assured them that the Holy Spirit would bring to their remembrance the things he had spoken (John 14:26). Hence the meaning and intent of Jesus' words, including his use of passages from the Psalms and other Old Testament books, is developed in the New Testament writings. The New Testament epistles are replete with quotations and allusions to the Psalms.[34]

13.3 Messianic Element[35]

What Jesus himself and his apostles saw in the Psalms his followers also wish to see. In our discussion on the messianic element in the Psalms we must be guided by the way in which the New Testament uses and applies specific psalms. Some writers have taken the position that there are no psalms that directly prophesy of the Messiah. This would be strange as messianic prophecies occur in many other places in the Old Testament, and the closest parallel to many psalms are the eschatological parts of the prophetical books.[36] It is also difficult to uphold this

---

[34] I have examined the Pauline usage in 'Aspects of Paul's Use of the Psalm', *WTJ* 32, 1 (1969), pp. 1-23.

[35] The comments on individual psalms should be consulted for exegesis of particular passages that contain messianic teaching. Further, and fuller, discussion of the messianic element in the Psalter can be found in Derek Kidner, *Psalms 1–72: An Introduction and Commentary on Books I and II of the Psalms* (London: Inter-Varsity Press, 1973), pp. 18-25. See also David Starling, 'The Messianic Hope in the Psalms', *RTR* 58, 3 (1999), pp. 121-34.

[36] This is the point made explicitly by Geerhardus Vos: 'So far as the content [of the Psalter] objectively considered is concerned, the difference from prophecy is not perhaps sufficiently pronounced to justify separate treatment. The general scheme is in both essentially the same'. 'Eschatology of the Psalter', Appendix to *The Pauline Eschatology* (Grand Rapids: Eerdmans, 1972), pp. 331-32. The discussion first appeared in the *PTR 18* (1920), pp. 1-43.

position when we consider the words of quite a few of the Psalms, for they speak of a king in a way which goes far beyond anything that a king in David's line could ever be.[37] The inadequacies of human kings helped to create expectation of a far greater ruler to come.

It is probably best to view the messianic psalms under several categories. Most of the messianic psalms take their starting point from the promise to David in 2 Samuel 7, which involved both a direct promise to David and the prospect of a continuing royal dynasty. A significant group comprises those that refer to this promise, yet speaks of the enduring nature of David's kingdom in such a way as points to the ultimate messianic kingdom. Psalms 89 and 132 expound 2 Samuel 7, while many other psalms, including 18, 21, and 61, celebrate the grace that God showed to David and family. The past deliverances of David formed the basis on which he looked ahead so confidently to the exaltation of the Lord among the nations (Ps. 18:46-50).

Another group of psalms comprises those which are directly related to the coming of the Messiah. While a song like Psalm 2 may be couched in language that echoes 2 Samuel 7, yet the words used point with distinctiveness to the one in whom the promise would find its final fulfilment. The king spoken about is both the Lord's *anointed* and also his *son*. The way in which Paul used this psalm in his speech in Pisidian Antioch confirms this understanding of Psalm 2 (Acts 13:32-33). From the vision of David and his kingdom, the eye was directed to a greater son of David who would ultimately be lord of all, having the ends of the earth as his possession (Ps. 2:8). Psalm 110 points to a promised son of David who would have priesthood, not by ancestry, but by divine appointment (110:5).

Other psalms take their starting point from Solomon's kingdom, and yet point far beyond it. Thus while a psalm

---

[37] Cf. the comments made by Franz Delitzsch on Psalm 22: 'In Ps. xxii., however, David descends, with his complaint, into a depth that lies beyond the depth of his affliction, and rises, with his hopes, to a height that lies far beyond the height of the reward of his affliction'. *Commentary on the Psalms* I, p. 306.

such as Psalm 45 was probably composed on the occasion of a royal wedding, yet the eyes of the inspired psalmist were suddenly lifted up to see the glory of the messianic ruler who is even called 'God' (v. 6). Psalm 72 presents us with the true prince of peace whose kingdom is going to far transcend the limits of the Davidic/Solomonic empire. His kingdom is going to extend from the River (i.e., the Euphrates) outwards! This same reference to Messiah's rule occurs in another messianic passage in Zechariah 9:10.

The final group of messianic psalms are those which are typically messianic. That is to say, their primary reference is not to Jesus, but he is the one who fulfils the descriptions which they give. They are psalms of righteous people; he is the *only* righteous one. The idea of a righteous person undergoing suffering and putting his trust in God is fully realised in the life and ministry of Jesus. These psalms include 6, 16, 22, 35, 40, 41, 69, 70, 71, 102, and 109. In this sense many of the Psalms (or perhaps all) are messianic. Some of this group of psalms had in view not only David but also his descendants (102, 109), and in this way a link is formed with the psalms specifically based on 2 Samuel 7.

14. USING THE PSALMS TODAY

14.1 The Psalms and Spiritual Life

As we have seen in earlier discussion, the Book of Psalms serves two great purposes, which can be expressed in these statements:

The Psalms speak *to us.*
The Psalms speak *for us.*

Each of these aspects is important and has practical consequences for us today. The Psalter came from God and it leads to God. We receive blessing as we read and use the Psalms and as we are instructed by them. They speak *to* our hearts and minister spiritual truths to our minds and consciences. But they also speak *for* us, as we utilise them in praise and prayer as if we were their author. They come out of real life situations and because they are facing the variety of human needs, we are able to respond to God by using their words as our own.

14.2 Personal Devotions

Christians today need the richness of the Psalter to aid them in their spiritual life. It is *the* devotional book of the Bible, and as such continues to be our devotional book and our guide. In using it we are ministered to by the thoughts and prayers it contains, and in turn we mouth our praise and adoration of God and our petitions in its words. Very often the Book of Psalms has been published along with the New Testament so that Christians can have ready access to it for their devotional use.

The Christian church right down throughout the centuries has found spiritual nourishment in the Book of Psalms. It was common in the early church for the whole Psalter to be memorised by those who were seeking to become pastors. Jerome (*c.* 347–420) tells that in his time it was common to hear the Psalms being sung in the fields and in the gardens. The same phenomenon occurred at the time of the Reformation, when the Psalms again became so prominent in the life of the church. The Reformation movement is the reason why the reading and chanting of the Psalms became customary in Anglican churches, while metrical Psalters became central in the worship of Dutch and Scottish churches. The Psalms should fill a central place, not only in the life of individuals, but also in the collective worship of the church.

The word of Christ must dwell in us richly. Paul, in writing to the Colossian Christians, says: 'Let the peace of Christ rule in your hearts, since as members of one body you were called to peace. And be thankful. Let the word of Christ dwell in you richly as you teach and admonish one another with all wisdom, and as you sing psalms, hymns and spiritual songs with gratitude in your hearts to God' (Col. 3:15–16). The various types of Christian songs, including psalms, are regarded as 'Christ's word'. It is to take up its abode in our hearts and it is to be used as we teach and admonish each other. That indwelling word builds us up in our faith and it counsels us, and it also forms part of our praise and thanksgiving to God (Col. 3:15–17).

14.3 Praise[38]

The Psalms have been and can be used in various ways in our worship. Chanting of prose psalms has a long history, though it is frequently associated with Anglican worship. It has the advantage of allowing the words to be dominant, and it usually only requires a restricted number of chants to be known. Many in our cultural setting prefer a greater variety of tunes to be used in worship than is normally the case with chanting.

'Scripture in Song' is a modern phenomenon, whereby small passages of Scripture are set to music. This has meant that many Christian people are singing portions of psalms, and it is good to hear this use of God's Word. The disadvantage is that the selections are taken out of their context in the Psalms, and often they are interpreted by users of 'Scripture in Song' in a way that is not supported by the context in the particular psalm. We need to remember that the Psalms are poetic pieces *as a whole*, and that simply to select a verse or two can distort their essential message.

The Reformation, which in significant respects brought a revolution in worship, in other ways continued the practices of the pre-Reformation church though in a new form. The use of the Psalms not only continued but took on a new role as their use was popularised in the Reformation movement. Luther wrote in 1523: 'I plan after the example of the prophets and ancient fathers of the Church to make German psalms for the people, that is to say, spiritual songs, so that the Word of God may dwell among the people by means of song also.' To this he added that the words were to be 'all quite plain and common, such as the common people may understand, yet pure and skilfully handled.' Calvin also regarded music as a gift of God and encouraged the use of the full Psalter, and he himself attempted to translate some of them into French,

[38] A modern survey of the use of the Psalms in Christian worship can be found in John D. Witvliet, *The Biblical Psalms in Christian Worship: A Brief Introduction and Guide to Resources* (Grand Rapids: Eerdmans, 2007), pp. 45-134.

though the work of Clement Marot (1497-1544) and Theodore Beza (1519-1605) was much more extensive and influential. Wherever the Protestant Reformation reached, the Psalms were used in worship, and they became so popular that even Roman Catholics were known to sing them.

This tradition of Psalm singing continues to this day.[39] The Scottish Metrical Psalter of 1650 has been widely used, and has often been used alongside modern revisions or alternative versions. The Irish Presbyterian Church undertook a light revision and added twenty-seven additional versions in 1880. The United Presbyterian Church of North America produced complete Psalters in 1871 and 1912 which have been widely used, especially in the United States. *The Book of Psalms with Music* (1950) and *The Book of Psalms for Singing* (1973) of the Reformed Presbyterian Church of North America have also been extensively used. The Presbyterian Church of America produced the *Trinity Psalter* (1994) with metrical settings of all 150 Psalms. In Australia, *The Complete Book of Psalms for Singing* (Presbyterian Church of Eastern Australia, Melbourne, 1991), was intentionally a version of *all* the Psalms, and not just a selection of songs *from* the Psalms. Similarly the Free Church of Scotland has issued a complete new Psalter which is being used quite widely. In modern English Anglicanism there has been renewed interest in the Psalter and *Psalm Praise* (1973) and the later *Psalms for Today* and *Songs from the Psalms* are representative of this approach. The variety of versions available testifies to the abiding character of the Psalter as *the* songbook of the Church and one which has helped to give vitality to the worship of Christians in many countries and situations.

The Psalter has also been most influential in serving as a model for the church's hymnology, and often individual psalms have been used extensively as the basis of many hymns. There are hymns from the Reformation period such as Luther's 'A mighty fortress is our God' (based on Psalm 46), but it is especially from the period of Isaac Watts (1674–1748)

[39] For a good, though not complete, list of resources for metrical psalmody, see Witvliet, *ibid.*, pp. 106-14.

and Charles Wesley (1707-1788) that the attempt was made to use the content of the Psalms but to infuse distinctively New Testament teaching into them. Watts in particular carried this too far, but some of his hymns based on psalms remain in constant use today (e.g. 'Jesus shall reign' from Psalm 72, and 'O God our help in ages past' from Psalm 90). Wesley makes no claim that his hymns are translations of psalms, but rather they are Christian hymns based on the Psalms, just as he based other hymns on other parts of the Bible or on Christian writings. Thus his hymn 'O for a heart to praise my God' uses the ideas of Psalm 51, while 'Jesu, mighty to deliver' is Psalm 70 expanded as a Christian song of praise. Many other hymns clearly reflect the influence and pattern of the Psalter, and this is good for the Church.

14.4 Preaching

As part of God's Word, the Psalms are to be preached. They form a section of Holy Scripture that is not duplicated elsewhere. No other part presents so vividly the varied emotions of the human heart, and they show how believers in the Old Testament time put their trust in their covenant God even in times of deep distress. This being so, it is a contradiction to preach in a passionless way on passages from the Psalter, for we must respond to the feelings expressed in them and mediate their teaching to the experiential needs of Christians today. The Psalms are part of the things 'written for our instruction, that through endurance and through the encouragement of the Scriptures we might have hope' (Rom. 15:4). They form an important part of the Scriptures that were God-breathed, and accordingly 'profitable for teaching, for reproof, for correction, and for training in righteousness, that the man of God may be competent, equipped for every good work' (2 Tim. 3:16-17). The Psalms were very important in the ministry of Jesus and his apostles, and they should be in our ministries as well.[40]

[40] I have developed this whole subject in 'Preaching from the Psalms' in *Preaching the Word: Essays in Honour of Professor Tom Wilkinson*, ed. Stewart Gill (*RTR* Supplement 3; Melbourne, 2009), pp. 30-41.

14.5 Epilogue

Study of the Psalms should never be an end in itself. The purpose should be to direct us back to the Psalms with fuller understanding and greater interest. The use of them should be a vital part of our spiritual growth, as we use them to pray to God and as they speak to us. In turn that study should provoke us to use them all the more in praise to God and adoration of him and his works. Our song should be like the one which ends the Psalter:

> Praise the LORD . . .
> Let everything that has breath
>   praise the LORD.
> Praise the LORD. (Ps. 150:1, 6)

Suggestions for Further Reading

Commentaries

J. A. Alexander, *The Psalms Translated and Explained* (Darlington: Evangelical Press, 1975).

J. M. Boice, *Psalms,* 3 vols (Grand Rapids: Baker Books, 1994, 1996, 1998).

John Calvin, *Commentary on the Psalms* (Grand Rapids: Baker Book House, 1979).

P. C. Craigie, *Psalms 1–50,* 2nd ed, with 2004 Supplement by Marvin Tate (Waco: Word, 2004).

Geoffrey W. Grogan, *Psalms,* The Two Horizons Commentary (Grand Rapids: Eerdmans, 2008).

E. W. Hengstenberg, *Commentary on the Psalms,* 3 vols (Edinburgh: T. & T. Clark, 1869).

Walter C. Kaiser, *The Journey Isn't Over: The Pilgrim Psalms* [Pss. 120-134] *for Life's Challenges and Joys* (Grand Rapids: Baker Book House, 1993).

F. D. Kidner, *Psalms: An Introduction and Commentary,* 2 vols (London: Inter-Varsity Press, 1973).

H. C. Leupold, *Exposition of the Psalms* (Grand Rapids: Baker Book House, 1969).

J. J. Stewart Perowne, *The Psalms,* 2 vols (London: George Bell and Sons, 1886).

O. Palmer Robertson, *Psalms in Congregational Celebration* (Darlington: Evangelical Press, 1995).

W. VanGemeren, 'The Psalms', in *The Expositor's Bible Commentary* (Grand Rapids: Zondervan 1991), vol. 5, pp. 3-880.

E. J. Young, *The Way Everlasting: A Study in Psalm 139* (Edinburgh: Banner of Truth Trust, 1997).

General

James E. Adams, *War Psalms of the Prince of Peace: Lessons from the Imprecatory Psalms* (Nutley, NJ: Presbyterian and Reformed, 1991).

R. Dean Anderson, Jr., 'The Division and Order of the Psalms', *Westminster Theological Journal* 56,2 (Fall, 1994), pp. 219-41.

J. Calvin Beisner, *Psalms of Promise: Celebrating the Majesty and Faithfulness of God*, 2nd ed. (Nutley, NJ: Presbyterian and Reformed, 1994).

C. Hassell Bullock, *Encountering the Book of Psalms: A Literary and Theological Introduction* (Grand Rapids: Baker Academic, 2001).

C. Hassell Bullock, *An Introduction to the Old Testament Poetic Books* (Chicago: Moody Press, 1988), 'The Book of Psalms', pp. 111-45.

Robert B. Chisholm, Jr., 'A Theology of the Psalms', Roy B. Zuck, ed., *A Biblical Theology of the Old Testament* (Chicago: Moody Press, 1991), pp. 257-304.

Raymond B. Dillard and Tremper Longman III, *An Introduction to the Old Testament* (Grand Rapids: Zondervan, 1994), 'Psalms', pp. 211-34.

Geoffrey W. Grogan, *Prayer, Praise and Prophecy* (Fearn: Mentor, 2001).

Philip S. Johnston and David G. Firth, edd., *Interpreting the Psalms: Issues and Approaches* (Leicester: Apollos, 2005).

Tremper Longman III, *How to Read the Psalms* (Downers Grove: Intervarsity Press, 1988).

J. B. Payne, 'Book of Psalms', *Zondervan Pictorial Bible Encyclopedia*, vol. 4, pp. 934-47.

N. H. Ridderbos and P. C. Craigie, 'Psalms' in *The International Standard Bible Encyclopedia*, fully revised, vol. 3, pp. 1029-40.

Harry Upritchard, *A Son Promised: Christ in the Psalms* (Darlington: Evangelical Press, 1994).

Bruce K. Waltke, 'A Canonical Approach to the Psalms', in *Tradition and Testament: Essays in Honor of Charles Lee Feinberg*, edd. Paul Feinberg and John Feinberg (Chicago: Moody Press, 1981).

Bruce K. Waltke, 'Psalms, Theology of', in *New International Dictionary of Old Testament Theology and Exegesis*, vol. 4, pp. 1100–1115.

John D. Witvliet, *The Biblical Psalms in Christian Worship: A Brief Introduction and Guide to Resources* (Grand Rapids: Eerdmans, 2007).

Book 1

Psalm 1

The manner in which the Book of Psalms opens is important. The first two psalms are keys to the whole Psalter because they are not strictly prayers but declarations. The first prayer is actually Psalm 3. Taken together, Psalms 1 and 2 help us understand the whole book, and their interconnection is shown by a chiastic structure in that Psalm 1 opens with the idea of blessing (*'ashᵉrê hâ'îsh*, 'Blessed is the man') while Psalm 2 closes with it (*'ashᵉrê kol-chôsê bô*, 'Blessed are all who take refuge in him'). A link also exists in thought between the righteous person of Psalm 1 and the messianic king in Psalm 2. The king in Israel had to have a copy of the 'law' for himself (*tôrâh*, Deut. 17:18), and hence he should have been the one in Israel who exemplified most clearly the character of the righteous, delighting in the law and being guided by his daily meditation upon it (Ps. 1:2).[1] The absence of a superscription before Psalm 2 also points to a connection between the two.[2]

The opening and closing of the Psalter are also important (see Introduction, for a discussion of the structure of the Psalter). It opens here in Psalm 1 with a call for obedient service,

---

[1] Some manuscript evidence exists pointing to the fact that Psalms 1 and 2 were regarded as a single psalm. While the majority of Greek manuscripts in Acts 13:33 quote from Ps. 2 and refer to it as 'the second psalm', yet the Western text calls it 'the first psalm'. The early church fathers, Justin Martyr (AD *c*. 100-165) and Origen (AD *c*.185-254), both knew them as a single entity.

[2] The only other psalms in Book 1 without a superscription are Psalms 10 and 33. For fuller discussion on the links between Psalms 1 and 2, and their role as the opening of the whole psalter, see P. D. Miller, 'The Beginning of the Psalter', in J. Clinton McCann, ed., *The Shape and Shaping of the Psalter* (Sheffield: JSOT Supplement Series 159, 1993), pp. 83-92.

while it closes in Psalm 150 with a call for universal praise.[3] It commences with the challenge of walking diligently in the ways of the LORD, while it closes with universal adoration of him.

This first key starts by contrasting the two ways in which people can go. As the opening song of the whole collection it is intended to challenge readers as to their commitment to the LORD and to his law. It points to two 'ways', just as Jesus did in the Sermon on the Mount (Matt. 7:13-14).

1. Near to God *(vv. 1-3)*

The book opens with a pronouncement of blessing. **Blessed is the man.** In Hebrew there are two words for blessing, one used by God when he is expressing a benediction (*bâruch*), and the other used here (*'ash^e^rê*) by men when referring to other men. To merit the word **blessed** used here, man has to do something, or, as in this case, not do something, for which he can be commended. Here the character of the blessed man is defined by three negative terms — **who does not walk in the counsel of the wicked or stand in the way of sinners or sit in the seat of the mockers** (*v. 1*). With mounting emphasis the psalmist describes the character of those whose trust is in the LORD. They do not look to ungodly men as a source of wisdom; their path is not that taken by sinners; their company is not with those who mock God or who are self-satisfied and proud.

On the contrary, the blessed man is marked out because **his delight is in law of the LORD, and on his law he meditates day and night** (*v. 2*). God's instruction forms the basis of his conduct and the treasure of his heart. The word 'law' (*tôrâh*) does not mean a list of rules and the appropriate punishments, but the fullness of God's 'teaching' for his children. This instruction, which included the history of God's dealings with his people, was to be passed on from generation to generation (see Ps. 78:1-8). In the Old Testament the references to God's *tôrâh* are almost universally positive,

[3] See the discussion by W. Brueggeman *JSOT* 50 (1991), 'Bounded by Obedience and Praise', pp. 63-91.

so that it is to be both obeyed and loved (Ps. 119:97, 113, 163, 165). It was to be the object of reverence and devotion. The Hebrew word translated 'meditates' (*hâgâh*) implies something more than silent reflection. It means to whisper or to murmur, a use that may point to the fact that reading was usually done aloud in biblical times. It also seems to be taking up and using in a new context the words of God to Joshua: 'Do not let this Book of the Law depart from your mouth; meditate upon it day and night, so that you may be careful to do everything written in it. Then you will be prosperous and successful' (Josh. 1:8).[4]

He is like a tree planted by streams of water, which yields its fruit in season and whose leaf does not wither. Whatever he does prospers (*v.* 3). The result of such meditation is that the blessed man is like a transplanted tree, set alongside an irrigation canal.[5] The thought of being transplanted recalls the imagery of God transplanting a little vine from Egypt into Canaan, where it became a great tree (Ps. 80:8-16). It may also reflect the situation prevailing when the whole Psalter was brought to completion, soon after the experience in exile, in which they knew so much about the irrigation canals of Babylon. In its well-watered position the tree brings forth its fruit, and its bountiful location ensures that it will not fade. So it is with the believing child of God who endures to the end (Phil. 1:6) and who brings forth fruits of righteousness (Gal. 5:16-26).

---

[4] The command, 'meditate upon it day and night' (*v^e^hâgîtâ bô yômâm vâlay^e^lâh*) in Josh. 1:8, is replaced by a statement in Ps. 1:2, 'and on his law he meditates day and night' (*ûv^e^tôrâtô yehgeh yômâm vâlay^e^lâh*). The comparison is also closer than the NIV suggests as 'then you will be prosperous' is really 'then your way shall prosper', which in Hebrew contains the words 'way' (*dérek*) and 'shall prosper' (*yatslîach*), both occurring in Ps. 1. See verses 1 and 3.

[5] The Hebrew verb used (*shâtal*) can mean either 'plant' or 'transplant'. All its ten occurrences in the Old Testament are metaphorical and all relate either to Israel or the righteous Israelite. What God [trans]plants thrives for ever. Jer. 17:8 contains almost the same phrase as Ps. 1:3, declaring that the 'blessed man' 'will be like a tree planted by the water', though the application is different. Here it is that such a person will bring forth fruit, whereas in Jer. 17 it is that the tree will put forth roots towards the water.

2. Far from God *(vv. 4-6)*
How different are those whose trust is not in the LORD! The lines of demarcation between God's children and the children of the world are clearly drawn. **Not so the wicked! They are like chaff that the wind blows away** (*v. 4*). The contrast is clear.[6] Instead of being like a living tree, the wicked are as unstable as chaff. They are without root and without fruit. **Therefore the wicked will not stand in the judgment, nor sinners in the assembly of the righteous** (*v. 5*). Such people will not be able to stand their ground at God's judgment seat, neither have they any right to be among God's people. The combination of the Hebrew verb 'rise' (*qûm*) with the noun 'judgment' (*mishpât*) points to God's final judgment. Their experience will be one of exclusion from the company of God's people on earth, and exclusion from the presence of God in eternity.

The final verse of the psalm sums up the contrast. **For the LORD watches over the way of the righteous, but the way of the wicked will perish** (*v. 6*). The way of the righteous is overseen constantly by the LORD, whereas the way of the ungodly has no future. It is going to perish utterly. This is a poetic form of the challenge of Moses to the children of Israel in Deuteronomy 30:11-20. By implication the psalmist echoes Moses' command: 'Now choose life, so that you and your children may live.'

---

[6] The contrast is marked by the words 'not so' (*ʿal kên*), which when appearing at the beginning of a sentence, signify emphasis, or, as here, contrast.

Psalm 2

Psalm 2, like Psalm 1, is a key to the Book of Psalms, and it is linked to the first by two words, 'plot' (in Ps. 1:2 translated as 'meditate') and 'blessed'. Here in this psalm the focus is on the ungodly and specifically on the Gentile nations who reject the LORD's rule. The only solution to their situation is to accept the rule of God's chosen Messiah, and then they will know the blessedness of trusting in him (v. 12). Just as Psalm 1 begins with the word 'blessed' (v. 1), so Psalm 2 ends with this word. It is possible that these two psalms were in fact regarded as one.[1] This psalm is structured around four clearly defined stanzas (cf. the division of Isa. 52:13–53:12 into five stanzas).

1. Rebellious Nations (*vv. 1-3*)

Why do the nations rage and the peoples plot in vain? The kings of the earth take their stand and the rulers gather together against the LORD and his Anointed One (*vv. 1-2*).[2] The opening **why?** is not so much indicating the seeking of information as an expression of astonishment that the Gentile nations would act in this way. **In vain** translates a Hebrew noun (*rîq*) that means 'emptiness' or worthlessness'.[3]

---

[1] See f.n. 1 on Psalm 1.

[2] The Hebrew verbal aspects in these verses (perf./imperf., imperf./perf.) appear to be used almost interchangeably. For a fine discussion on the question of tense in Hebrew, see P. C. Craigie, *Psalms 1-50: Second Edition with 2004 Supplement by Marvin Tate,* 'Excursus II: The Translation of Tenses in Hebrew Poetry' (Word Biblical Commentary; Waco: Word, 2004), pp. 110-13.

[3] The word *rîq* here is not a Hebrew adverb but a noun forming an accusative of relation.

Whereas the godly meditate on God's word (Ps. 1:2), the ungodly rulers of the Gentile nations meditate in the sense of pondering over plots that they can make, but their plans have no real substance to them. Isaiah presents a similar picture of the turmoil among nations in the Assyrian period, and also has the assurance that God is able to intervene with his devastating rebuke (Isa. 17:12-14). The word 'anointed' (*mâshîach*) is the Hebrew word from which we get the English word 'messiah'. It can be used for any anointed servant of God, including Cyrus of Persia (Isa. 45:1), or can even be applied to the Antichrist (Dan. 9:25, 26).[4] The expression of rebellion mounts to a climax with the words **against the LORD and his Anointed One**. Ultimately the hostility that the nations show is directed against God himself, and not only against him, but also against his chosen servant, whose appointment is spoken of later in this psalm (*vv. 6-9*). What these kings and rulers did not realise is that their plans are useless in God's sight.

When they take their stand and gather together they make a declaration of their independence: **'Let us break their chains,' they say, 'and throw off their fetters'** (*v. 3*). Sinful men never want to walk within the limitations that God places on his creatures. In their arrogance they proclaim their supposed freedom, and they claim to be master of their own destinies. Their spirit is typified in Ernest Henley's poem, *Invictus*:

> It matters not how strait the gate,
> How charged with punishments the scroll.
> I am the master of my fate;
> I am the captain of my soul.

The suffix on the words 'chains' and 'fetters' is a poetic form (*-mô*) that can be substituted for many of the regular forms. Here the context favours translating '*his* chains' and '*his* fetters'.[5] The nations are set against the LORD, and hence they desire to be loosed from any restraint he places upon them.

---

[4] For a discussion of the Hebrew *mâshîach* in Daniel 9, see my commentary on *Daniel* (Darlington: Evangelical Press, 2007), pp. 239-44.

[5] See *GKC* §91 b, f.

2. Divine Rule (*vv.* 4-6)
In contrast to the feverish activity described in verse 1, the Lord is able to view the plottings of men from his heavenly throne. **The One enthroned in heaven laughs; the Lord scoffs at them** (*v.* 4). The description of God and his kingship uses a common expression for his heavenly rule. He 'dwells in the heavens' (*yôshêv bashshâmayim*; cf. also Pss. 29:10; 113:5), whereas for his temporary manifestations a different verb is used (*shâkan*; cf. the description of him sitting 'between the cherubim', 1 Sam. 4:4; 2 Sam. 6:2; 2 Kings 19:15; Ps. 99:1). He does not laugh to ridicule them, but because he views their planning from his sovereign security, and because he knows that *his* day is coming (Ps. 37:13, *kî yâvo' yômô*), the day of his final judgment. Almost the same expression as here involving the two verbs 'to laugh' and 'to mock' (*sâchaq, lâʿag*) occurs also in Psalm 59:8.

Then he rebukes them in his anger and terrifies them in his wrath, saying, 'I have installed[6] my King on Zion, my holy hill' (*vv.* 5-6). When the Lord does speak, it will be in anger for he will terrify them. The thought is stated in a typical pattern of chiastic parallelism: 'speak in anger/in wrath terrify.' By far the most occurrences of the verb 'terrify' (*bâhal*) occur in contexts like this involving the idea of divine judgment. The NIV inserts the word 'saying' to smooth out the translation. In Hebrew it is simply 'and I', or better, 'yet I' (*va'ᵃnî*). The declaration he makes concerns the place of his king, against whom the heathen rulers have been plotting. Kingship in Israel was an institution that God had given for his people (see Deut. 17:14-20). God's displeasure at the people's request for a king (1 Sam. 8:5) was not because the concept was wrong in itself but because of the type of king being envisioned, and the reasons for making the request were a denial of the covenantal relationship with him (for the introduction of kingship, see 1 Sam. 8-12). From the

---

[6] The use of the Hebrew verb *nâsak* is interesting, for it is not the usual verb for anointing. It is employed most often in reference to pouring out a libation, and here it may continue to have that basic meaning: 'consecrate [with a libation]', (*DCH*, V, p. 699), or, 'I have poured out (my libation in the consecration of) my king' (*NIDOTTE*, 3, p. 114).

time that David captured the fortress of Zion (2 Sam. 5:7) it became the centre of both religious and political life in Israel, and there was never any question thereafter for devout Israelites as to where worship was to be offered at the tabernacle/temple. Jeroboam's attempt after the division of the kingdom to have the people worship at Dan and Bethel was a deliberate strategy to stop them worshipping at Zion, God's holy hill (1 Kings 12:26-27).[7] Each Davidic ruler typified the coming of the final messianic king who is spoken of here.

3. God's Declaration to His Son (*vv. 7-9*)
The third stanza commences with the messianic king speaking of his own appointment. The references to the LORD's anointed in verse 2 and the one called 'my king' in verse 6 are now taken a step further, as New Testament references to this passage confirm. The anointed king declares: **'I will proclaim the decree of the LORD: He said to me, "You are my Son; today I have become your Father"'** (*v. 7*). Elsewhere in the Psalms the LORD's decree refers to the establishment of his orderly rule in the universe (Ps. 148:6). Here it is used of a sovereign appointment of his son.[8] The words are echoed at Jesus' baptism (Matt. 3:17) and at the transfiguration (Matt. 17:5). Paul also uses the words in reference to the resurrection (Acts 13:33). Jesus later entered another stage of his sonship when through the Spirit of holiness he was 'declared with power to be the Son of God by his resurrection from the dead' (Rom. 1:4).

Ask of me, and I will make the nations your inheritance, the ends of the earth your possession. You will rule them[9]

---

[7]The term 'mountain of God' is used exclusively of Mt Sinai, whereas the term here, 'holy mountain', always refers to Zion (see Pss. 3:4; 43:3; 87:1-2; Isa. 27:13; Zech. 8:3). For discussion of the theology of Zion, see *NIDOTTE*, 4, pp. 1314-21.

[8] The Hebrew expression is unusual: 'I will proclaim to (*'el*) the decree of the LORD.' See the prepositional usage with this noun in *DCH*, III, pp. 301-02 and the translation, 'I will proclaim *concerning* the LORD's decree.'

[9] The MT has *tᵉroʾêm*, 'you will break them'. The LXX reading is *poimaneis* = *tirʿêm*, 'you will shepherd them'. The Hebrew manuscript evidence is uniformly in favour of the former, and it also best suits the context.

with an iron sceptre; you will dash them to pieces like pottery (*vv. 8-9*). The command to ask of the LORD was given to Solomon at Gibeon (1 Kings 3:5), but now it is said to a far greater than Solomon. Just as the kingly rule in Psalm 72 extends to the ends of the earth, so here also. Messiah's rule is one that ensures that the nations become his inheritance and the ends of the earth his possession. Rebellious kings ('them' in verse 9) have already been mentioned in verse 2. They will find that his sceptre is not just a symbolic staff, but an iron sceptre which is able to shatter them in pieces. The word 'sceptre' (*shêvet*) can denote both an instrument of punishment and a mark of authority, and so here the two ideas of smiting and ruling are brought into conjunction.

4. A Call to Allegiance (*vv. 10-12*)

A sovereign call now goes to these kings. **Therefore, you kings, be wise; be warned, you rulers of the earth** (*v. 10*). It opens with a Hebrew expression that often denotes a new stage in an argument, though continuing the same subject matter (*veʿattâh*, lit., 'and now'). Earthly rulers can only find blessing for themselves and their subjects when they are subservient to the claims of God's messiah. The implication is that the wisdom and the warning come from the LORD, a point made explicitly in the wisdom books of the Old Testament with repeated use of these two verbs.

Serve the LORD with fear and rejoice with trembling (*v. 11*), is the call that goes to them. They must become his vassals (for so the word *serve* implies). The expression 'rejoice' with trembling may seem odd because it combines two seemingly opposite emotions, but no really satisfactory alternative translations have emerged. Furthermore, the rulers have to **Kiss the Son, lest he be angry and you be destroyed in your way, for his wrath can flare up in a moment. Blessed are all who take refuge in him** (*v. 12*). The word used here in the Hebrew text for son is not the usual word (*ben*), but an Aramaic form (*bar*). Clearly the early versions had difficulty with this verse, and rendered *bar* with words suggesting they understood it to be *bor* ('pure') or *bad* ('clean'). However, *bar* as 'son' is attested in the Old Testament.[10] Numerous suggestions have been made for emending the text, but the traditional MT text is strongly attested and should be maintained. Three explanatory comments should be made. First, Aramaic was the common language for much of the ancient Near East over many centuries, and it was spoken from about the ninth century BC. Hence, the Davidic/Solomonic empire would have had Aramaic speakers within it. Secondly, the use of the usual Hebrew word would have resulted in an awkward conjunction of *ben pen*, and so to avoid the dissonance *bar pen* may have been used instead.[11] Thirdly, the choice of the Aramaic word may have been done deliberately to bring greater force to the message to Gentile kings, who presumably would have been Aramaic speakers.[12] To 'kiss' was a sign of homage and submission (cf. 1 Sam. 10:1; 1 Kings 19:18; Hosea 13:2) and it is appropriate that such a word is used to call for an act of homage before the LORD's anointed king. The 'son' seems to be the subject of the next verb. If rulers do not submit to his claims, then his anger will burn against them and they will be destroyed. Just as the first Psalm commenced with the concept of blessing, so this second Psalm finishes on the same reassuring note. All who take refuge in the LORD will find true blessing and satisfaction in him. The expression used here, 'all who take refuge in him' (*kol-chôsê wô*),[13] points on the one hand to the insecurity of those who are depending on their own power, but on the other hand to the security of those whose trust is in the LORD. He is the only refuge from the storm of God's anger.

In addition to the quotations of this psalm in the New Testament already noted above, it is important to realise how often it is alluded to in the Book of Revelation (see e.g.,

---

[10] *DCH*, II, p. 257.

[11] This was first suggested by Delitzsch in his *Commentary on the Psalms*, I. p. 98.

[12] As proposed by P. C. Craigie, *Psalms 1-50*, p. 64. Craigie's whole note on the crux is worth consulting. For another good note on it, see Willem VanGemeren, 'Psalms', p. 72.

[13] Grammatically, these three words taken together are the equivalent of a single noun. See *IBHS*, p. 155.

2:27; 12:5; 19:15). Christians see in Psalm 2 the picture of the messianic king who is ruling now in the world, and who is going to rule until he subdues all other rulers, and delivers the kingdom to the Father (1 Cor. 15:24). The Book of Revelation shows us the ultimate picture of Christ ruling with an iron sceptre, and bearing the name 'King of Kings, and Lord of Lords' (Rev. 19:15-16).

Psalm 3

A psalm of David. When he fled from his son Absalom.

For the context of this psalm, we have to look back to the account in 2 Samuel 15-18 in reference to Absalom's conspiracy against his father David. Absalom had plotted the rebellion and won over the hearts of many in the country (2 Sam. 15:1-6). When the rebellion became known to David he fled, and the historical narrative gives a graphic picture of the king weeping as he went up the Mount of Olives, barefooted and with his head uncovered (2 Sam. 15:30).[1] Here David makes his appeal to God. This is the first of a collection of Davidic psalms that constitute Psalms 3-41.[2]

1. A Forlorn Cry (*vv. 1*-2)

O Lord, how many are my foes! How many rise up against me! Many are saying of me, 'God will not deliver him.' *Selah* (*vv. 1*-2). This is the first prayer of the Book of Psalms, and the threefold mention of 'many' attracts attention straight away. David feels the pressure that has been put on him by his numerous opponents, and cries out to his covenantal God. The verb 'rise up' can be used of rebellions or of the enemies who arise against Israel (see Deut. 28:7), but it also has a wider

[1] The NIV has 'his [David's] head was covered'. Two homonyms may well have existed, one meaning 'cover' and the other 'uncover'. Ezek. 24:17, 23 suggest that uncovering the head was an appropriate action when mourning, and the context in 2 Sam. 17 supports this. See R. P Gordon, *1 & 2 Samuel: A Commentary* (Exeter: Paternoster Press, 1986), p. 271.

[2] Other psalms attributed to David, or are linked by the title to some aspect of David's life, are Pss. 51-65, 68-70 (Book 2); Ps. 86 (Book 3); Pss. 101 and 103 (Book 4); Pss. 108-10, 122, 124, 131, 138-145 (Book 5). See the discussion on the structure of the Psalter in the Introduction.

connotation of any opposition coming against someone. Here the context suggests enemies within Israel. Not only did David recognise the extent of opposition against him, but he also knew that numerous others were talking *about* him. What they were saying touched the very honour of God himself, for they were claiming that there was no salvation with God. 'Selah', which appears seventy-one times in the Psalter (and three times in Hab. 3), comes in here for the first time. It generally occurs in psalms that are divided into three sections, and always comes at the end of a section, sometimes of all three. It is a technical term that probably denotes louder musical accompaniment, or alternatively, simply identifies the end of a stanza without any indication being given of what was said or sung in the interval between stanzas.[3]

2. Certain Protection (*vv. 3-4*)
In spite of the opposition against him, David knew how sure was the LORD's protection. **But** [on the contrary] **you are a shield around me, O LORD, my Glorious One, who lifts up my head. To the LORD I cry aloud, and he answers me from his holy hill.** ***Selah*** (*vv.* 3-4). The opening words of this section are a marked contrast to what the enemies have been saying. The LORD is indeed the protector, for he is David's shield (*mâgên*). The expression goes back to Genesis 15:1, where God reassures Abraham that he will safeguard him from danger. In the context there the military metaphor is plain, especially as in 14:20 mention has been made by Melchizedek that the LORD had delivered Abram (*miggên*). 'Shield' is often used in the Psalms along with another term descriptive of God's power: 'my strength and my shield' (Ps. 28:7); 'our help and our shield' (Ps. 33:20); 'a sun and a shield' (Ps. 84:11). He knew that his 'Glorious One' (see Pss. 4:2; 106:20 for the similar use of this title; Rom. 1:23, '[they] exchanged the glory of the immortal God for images made to look like mortal man' draws upon this

[3] See the discussion by N. H. Snaith, 'Selah', *VT* 2 (1952), pp. 43-56. Snaith draws attention to 1 Chron. 16:41 and proposes that *selah* marked the break where the Levites came in with the words: 'Give thanks to the LORD for he is good, for his mercy endures for ever'. A good discussion can also be found in P. C. Craigie, *Psalms 1-50,* pp. 76-7, 'Excursus I, The Meaning of SELAH (סלה) in the Psalms'.

OT usage) would lift him up out of the dust. 'To lift up the head' denotes placing someone in a position of honour, and it is a term rich in theological meaning for it speaks of the redemptive presence of God. David's cry was constantly to the LORD, and he had received repeated answers. These had come from God's holy hill, mount Zion, to which site David had brought the ark of the LORD (see comment on 2:6). The bringing of the ark to it, and the subsequent building of the temple, brought to fulfilment what had been foreshadowed long before in the Song of the Sea. The intention was expressed that God would bring his people in 'and plant them on the mountain of your inheritance – the place, O LORD, you made for your dwelling, the sanctuary, O LORD, your hands established' (Exod. 15:17).

3. Sure Deliverance (*vv. 5-8*)

Quiet sleep was possible for David because his salvation was from the LORD. **I lie down and sleep; I wake again, because the LORD sustains me** (*v. 5*). Moreover, the fact that Absalom had so many followers was not the point. Because the LORD was his shield, David could rest securely at night, and the support he received meant that 'God's hand is his pillow'.[4] The verb 'sustains' (*sâmak*) is often used in the Psalms with God as the subject. He is the one who upholds the righteous (cf., in addition to this verse, Pss. 37:17, 24; 119:116; 145:14).

I will not fear the tens of thousands, drawn up against me on every side (*v. 6*). We know from the historical record that the majority of the people had followed Absalom (2 Sam. 15:13; 17:11; 18:7), but David makes a confident appeal to his protector. The reference to 'the tens of thousands' is an assertion of God's ability to deliver in the face of innumerable enemies.

It is not only the enemies who arise (see v. 1), but also the LORD. **Arise, O LORD! Deliver me, O my God! Strike all my enemies on the jaw; break the teeth of the wicked** (*v. 7*). This is a typical anthropomorphic expression (one describing God in human terms), calling on him to bring help quickly as he had done in the past. The word 'arise' (*qûm*) is used in military contexts in which the idea of anticipated victory by the LORD is present (cf. Judg. 7:15). It

---

[4] F. Delitzsch, *Psalms*, I, p. 107.

is a neutral term in English, but in Hebrew it conveys the idea that God's saving power is going to be demonstrated. Moses used it whenever the ark of the covenant was being moved (Num. 10:35), for Israel's battles were in reality part of the LORD's holy war. When the imperative 'arise' is used here and elsewhere in the Psalms it points to a confident expectation of victory (cf. 7:6; 9:19; 17:13).[5] The outcome of the appeal to God is expressed in metaphorical terms of 'smiting' the cheekbone and 'breaking' the teeth of the enemies. These parallel expressions are descriptive of complete victory. The use of these two verbs (*nâkâh,* Hi., *shâvar,* Pi.) may be significant, for the former is used of God's destruction of the living creatures by the flood (Gen. 8:21), and of his smiting Egypt as he rescued his people (Exod. 3:20; 12:12, 29).The latter conveys the concept of intense breaking of something, so that 'smashing to smithereens'[6] the teeth of the wicked represents the removal of all power. Though the verbs 'strike' and 'break' are strictly perfect forms in the Hebrew text, yet here the context demands that they be treated as supplicatory, and hence English imperatives are in order.[7] The conclusion of the psalm is a confident expression of trust on and hope in the LORD.

From the LORD comes deliverance. May your blessing be on your people. ***Selah*** **(*v. 8*).** The word 'deliverance' in Hebrew is *yᵉshûʿa,* from which the word 'Jesus' comes. David knew that this was not only a personal truth, but one that applied to all the people. Hence he prays for the LORD's blessing to be granted to the nation as a whole. Personal problems did not outweigh his spiritual vision for the people. A psalm that commenced with mention of overwhelming opposition ends on the note of victory achieved by the LORD. When that happens, it achieves blessing for his people.

---

[5] J. T. Willis, 'Qûmâh YHWH', *JNSL* 16 (1990), pp. 207-21 suggests that the use of this imperative in military contexts means 'swing into action', a colloquial translation but an effective one.

[6] The translation is that of Victor Hamilton, *TWOT*, II, p. 901.

[7] For discussion on the so-called 'precatory perfect', see *IBHS*, pp. 494-95, and *DIHG~S*, pp. 69-70. The first editions of NIV translated these verbs as English past tenses ('you struck down', 'you have broken'), but this was corrected in the 1984 edition. The usage is most common in Psalms and Lamentations, and rare elsewhere.

Psalm 4

For the director of music. With stringed instruments.
A psalm of David.

There are various connections between Psalms 3 and 4. Jointly they give us morning and evening prayers, even to the extent of repeated key words as the following table shows:

Psalm 3	Psalm 4
3:1 Lord, how many are my *foes* (*tsâr*)	4:1b from my *distress* (*tsâr)*
3:2 *Many (rabbîm)* are *saying (*'*om*^e^*rîm*) of me	4:6 *Many (rabbîm)* are *saying* (*'om*^e^*rîm*)
3:3b my *Glorious One* (*kevôdî*)	4:2b my *glory* (*kevôdî*)
3:4 To the Lord I *cry aloud* (*qârâ'*) and he *answers* (*'ânâh*) me	4:1a *Answer* (*'ânâh*) me when *I call* (*qârâ'*) to you
	4:3bThe Lord hears when I *call* (*qârâ'*) to him.
3:5 I *lie down*(*shâkav*) and *sleep* (*shânâh*)	4:8a I will *lie down* (*shâkav*) and *sleep* (*shânâh*)
	4:4a on your beds (*mishkâv*)

1. A Cry in Need (*v. 1*)
David appeals to his righteous God, i.e., the God who does right, and who keeps his covenantal word. **Answer me when I call to you, O my righteous God. Give me relief from my distress; be merciful to me and hear my prayer** (*v. 1*). Whenever he calls, he wants God to respond. This response is not something that God is obliged to give, but it is an expression of his grace (cf. Ps. 69:16, 'out of the goodness of your love'). He desires relief by having his distress removed far from him.

There is the recognition of his need for undeserved grace in order that God may hear and answer his prayer.

2. A Description of His Enemies (*vv. 2-6*)

How long, O men, will you turn my glory into shame? How long will you love delusions and seek false gods? ***Selah*** **Know that the LORD has set apart the godly for himself; the LORD will hear when I call to him** (*vv. 2-3*). Now David speaks to his enemies and accuses them of forsaking the true God and seeking after false gods. 'Glory' is here a title for God as in Psalm 106:20. To turn glory to shame (*k^e^limmâh*) denotes an entire change in condition so that honour is replaced by disgrace.[1] The action of men is ever the same, for, as Paul says, sinful men always want to exchange the glory of the immortal God for man-made images (Rom. 1:21-23). Moreover, such turning from the living God means that love for him is replaced by love for what is but empty show, while the people have been searching for substitute 'gods' that ultimately prove to be false.[2] But godly ones, like David, are set apart by the LORD, who discriminates between them and those who seek other gods. Anyone who shows covenantal commitment (*chésed*) is a godly one (*châsîd*), and can assuredly say that God will answer one's prayers. It is frequently asserted in the Psalms that God hears the cries of his people and responds to them (cf. Pss. 6:9; 22:24; 61:5; 116:1).

The enemies are then encouraged to consider their evil deeds. **In your anger do not sin; when you are on your beds, search your hearts and be silent** (*v. 4*). The Hebrew verb rendered by 'in your anger' conveys the idea of trembling. David wants his enemies to be deeply moved before the LORD, and not to continue in their sin. Rather, they should heed his words and in the quietness of the night reflect upon their ways. Paul uses this verse in Ephesians 4:26, following exactly

---

[1] The English word 'calumny' may well derive from the Hebrew word *k^e^limmâh*.

[2] Though Jerry Shepherd, *NIDOTTE*, 4, p. 1107, is critical of the NIV rendering 'false gods', yet the context points to things of shame being loved and sought. Hence the NIV rendering is close to the mark.

the LXX rendering. He is urging the 'new man' (Eph. 4:24) not to sin if anger is present.[3] **Selah** adds emphasis to this call.

Offer right sacrifices and trust in the LORD (*v. 5*). They need to be like the righteous and put their trust in the LORD. Those who do that will also bring the proper and appropriate offerings to the sanctuary. The phrase 'right sacrifices' is first used in Deuteronomy 33:19, and here it probably notes that they would need to make an offering for their past sin.

Many are asking, 'Who can show us any good?' Let the light of your face shine upon us, O LORD (*v. 6*). Spectators, who had seen all that had happened to David, now speak. They desire to share in blessing, and pray for themselves in terms of the Aaronic benediction, merging two of its expressions (Num. 6:24-26; cf. also Pss. 31:16; 80:3, 7, 19). The translation 'let the light of your face shine on us' obscures the fact that in the MT text the clause commences with an imperative *n^esâh*, often taken to be from the common verb *nâsâ'*. However, two of the consonants are different, and it is possible that it may be an emphatic form of the verb *nûs*, 'to flee', giving a rendering like the NEB, 'the light of your presence has fled from us'.[4] This is the only occurrence in the Old Testament of the phrase 'the light of your face'. 'Light' is predicated of God in the Old Testament, and he gives it to individuals ('the LORD is my light', Ps. 27:1) and to the nation of Israel ('the light of Israel', Isa. 10:17). 'Light' is virtually equivalent to 'salvation' or 'deliverance'.

3. An Evening Prayer (*vv. 7-8*)

You have filled my heart with greater joy than when their grain and new wine abound. I will lie down and sleep in peace, for you alone, O LORD, make me dwell in safety (*vv. 7-8*). God provides for his servants, like David, joy in

---

[3] For the interpretation of Eph. 4:26, see Peter T. O'Brien, *The Letter to the Ephesians* (Pillar New Testament Commentary: Leicester: Apollos, 1999), pp. 339-40.

[4] For other possible solutions to the problem, see *DCH*, V, p. 759. The conjunction of the verb 'show' in the preceding clause with the idea of light probably points to something like the traditional rendering, though the LXX renders the verb by the Greek verb *sêmeioô*, 'to mark' or 'note'.

the midst of distress. His enemies could have their festive occasions at harvest, but God-given joy was something far greater. Christians are called to rejoice in sufferings (1 Pet. 4:13), and believing in Christ brings 'inexpressible and glorious joy' (1 Pet. 1:8). Peaceful sleep comes because God is his protector. The emphasis at the end of verse 8 is definitely on the LORD: 'Indeed, it is you LORD, you alone ...' The contrast with the false gods of verse 2 is plain. Only in the LORD is there safety.

Psalm 5

For the director of music. For Flutes. A psalm of David.

This psalm is clearly an appeal for help, but no precise indication is given of the circumstances that lay behind it. Throughout the psalm, in almost every verse, there is mention of the words which the psalmist was addressing to God, and also some indication of the evil with which he was contending. It begins with the address to God, and ends with acclamation of him.

1. A Cry to the King (*vv. 1-3*)
Give ear to my words, O Lord, consider my sighing. Listen to my cry for help, my King and my God, for to you I pray (*vv. 1-2*). Now there is an urgent appeal to God, though the psalmist had for long been sighing in his affliction. The word for 'sighing' (Hebrew *hâgîg*) only appears here and in Psalm 39:3 in the Psalter. It is connected with the word for 'murmuring' or 'meditating' (see Pss. 1:2; 2:1), which at times appears in association with verbs like 'cry out' (*zâʿaq*, Jer. 48:31) or 'wail' (*yâlal*, Hi., Isa. 16:7). There is both inaudible prayer to God as well as direct and loud appeals. However, there is confidence in the psalmist's approach, as he is coming to his king and his God. From the time of the Exodus onwards God was regarded as the king of Israel (see Exod. 15:18), and in particular the Davidic kingship was intended as a reflection of the divine rule. Recognition of God as king was not just communal; individual believers saw themselves as his subjects and could address him directly as 'my king'.

Morning by morning, O Lord, you hear my voice; morning by morning I lay my requests before you and wait

in expectation (*v. 3*). Just as there were morning sacrifices, so prayers were directed to the LORD at that time. This was part of the threefold pattern of daily prayer (cf. Dan. 6:10). The language of sacrifice is carried over here, for 'lay my requests' represents the verb used of laying in order the wood (Lev. 1:7) or the victim for sacrifice (Lev. 1:8; 6:12). The psalmist then waits expectantly for God's answer.

2. God and Evildoers (*vv. 4-8*)

You are not a God who takes pleasure in evil; with you the wicked cannot dwell (*v. 4*). Emphasis in the Hebrew text comes on the negative assertion, 'But *not a God taking delight are you* ...' God does not delight in wickedness, and with him is no haven for wicked men because his holiness is to them a consuming fire (Isa. 33:14). Those coming to his holy hill must receive righteousness from God (cf. Pss. 15:1-5 and 24:1-6).

The arrogant cannot stand in your presence; you hate all who do wrong. You destroy those who tell lies; bloodthirsty and deceitful men the LORD abhors (*vv. 5-6*). Those who reject the wisdom of the LORD and live by their own folly cannot stand their ground before him. Here the wicked are characterised as liars, murderers, and deceivers. God's attitude towards them is one of abhorrence and hate, and their ultimate destiny is destruction. Those who have these characteristics will never abide in God's holy presence (Rev. 22:12-15).

But I, by your great mercy, will come into your house; in reverence will I bow down toward your holy temple. Lead me, O LORD, in your righteousness because of my enemies – make straight your way before me (*vv. 7-8*). The opening words of verse 7 provide a contrast with the commencement of verse 4. The psalmist is not shut out from God's presence or God's house. He goes there on one ground only—God's abundant covenantal love to him, and he can enter therefore into the holy place. The Epistle to the Hebrews points to the fact that because Jesus has gone before us into heaven we have an anchor for the soul in the inner sanctuary of God (Heb. 6:19-20). The psalmist prays for assistance from the LORD that he might walk in 'paths of righteousness' (cf. Ps. 23:3) and along a straight way. That is to say, he wants to walk according to the LORD's commands and the precepts he has given. This prayer is made because he does not wish to give his enemies cause to gloat over any deviation from the prescribed way.[1]

3. God and Judgment (*vv. 9-10*)

Not a word from their mouth can be trusted; their heart is filled with destruction. Their throat is an open grave; with their tongue they speak deceit (*v. 9*). After reference to the character of the holy God and the righteous worshipper comes the character of the evildoer. Here the concentration falls on the sins of the tongue (cf. James 3:6-12), and Paul uses the words of the second part of verse 9 as he sets out the universal sinfulness of the human race in his list of quotations from the Old Testament in Romans 3 (see *v.* 13a). The psalmist is accusing his enemies of treachery because there is no sincerity or truth in their speech. 'Throat' is not so much the organ for swallowing as the organ of speech as in Psalms 115:7 and 149:6. This agrees with the context where the emphasis is on speech, with the mouth as the instrument of speech, of the heart as its source, and of the tongue. The comparison with an open grave reflects on the corruption that comes to expression in speech.[2]

Declare them guilty, O God! Let their intrigues be their downfall. Banish them for their many sins, for they have rebelled against you (*v. 10*). The expression 'declare them guilty' is one word in Hebrew. It comes from the root *ʾâsham,* which is used of the sacrifice for sins of inadvertence. Here

---

[1] The word 'enemy' (*shôrêr*) is not the usual Hebrew word. It only occurs six times, all in the Psalms (in addition to this verse, see 27:11; 54:5; 56:2; 59:10; 92:11). Ps. 27:11 contains the closest parallel to this verse, for it is a prayer for guidance in right living and the exact phrase, 'because of my enemies' (*l^{e}maʿan shôr^{e}rây*) occurs in both. The NIV is inconsistent in its translation of this word, using 'enemy' here and synonyms twice ('oppressor', 27:11; 'adversary', 92:11) but using 'slanderer' three times (54:5; 56:2; 59:10). For the argument for using 'slanderer' consistently, see M. Dahood, *Psalms II: 51-100* (New York: Doubleday & Co., 1974), pp. 25-26.

[2] The same combination, 'an open grave' (*qéver pâtûach*), occurs in Jer. 5:16.

it means 'make guilty' or even 'punish'. Guilt must lead to atonement, or alternatively to destruction. The wicked may think they are so clever in their plotting, but they can be caught out by their own secret scheming. The desired punishment is banishment, using the same verb (*nâdach,* Hi.) that is used in Deuteronomy 30:1 of banishment from Canaan. Covenantal overtones may well be present. That David was not asking for personal vengeance is made clear by the closing words of verse 10: 'they have rebelled *against you.*' As a loyal covenantal servant he asks God to exercise his judgment on his rebel subjects. For fuller discussion of the psalms of cursing, see the Introduction.

4. Protection and Joy (*vv. 11-12*)

But let all who take refuge in you be glad; let them ever sing for joy. Spread your protection over them, that those who love your name may rejoice in you (*v. 11*). The character of God's people as those who take refuge in the LORD is illustrated in this very psalm by David's own trustful attitude. Those who live under God's protection can sing for joy because he provides the screen that overshadows them. Probably the idea is that of the mother bird protecting her young with her wings (cf. Ps. 91:4). Another description of the righteous is that they love God's name, i.e. his character. He had revealed himself as the redeemer of Israel, and the sanctuary of which the psalmist had already spoken (v. 7) was the place where God had made his name dwell (Deut. 12:5).

For surely, O LORD, you bless the righteous; you surround them with your favour as with a shield (*v. 12*). The idea of protection is carried on from the preceding verse. God surrounds his people with a protective shield so that they are safe from the enemy. Moreover, it remains true that blessing from the LORD is the portion of his believing children. It is something that comes through his grace (cf. verse 4 and comment).

Psalm 6

For the director of music. With stringed instruments. According to sheminith. A psalm of David.

Though an individual composition, yet this psalm was intended for corporate singing. The term *sheminith* in the title is difficult, as the literal meaning is 'an eighth'. If this means an octave, then it is possible that the term indicates that it should be accompanied at a lower octave, in keeping with the solemn note of the psalm, or sung by the male voices. While it has been suggested that it could refer to an instrument with eight strings, the fact that it occurs in 1 Chronicles 15:21 along with the verb 'to play on a stringed instrument' (*nâtsach* Pi.) points to it as referring to the range of voice.[1] This psalm is a complaint to God, and exhibits not only appeal to him but also confidence in the midst of distress. It should be compared to other similar appeals in the Psalter and to Hezekiah's prayer after his illness (Isa. 38:10-20). Traditionally, this psalm was the first of the seven penitential psalms (Pss. 6, 32, 38, 51, 102, 130, 143), a collection known to Augustine, and mentioned by Cassiodorus (AD *c.* 584).

1. A Cry to a Gracious God (*vv. 1-3*)
O LORD, do not rebuke me in your anger or discipline me in your wrath. Be merciful to me, LORD, for I am faint; O LORD, heal me, for my bones are in agony. My soul is in anguish. How long, O LORD, how long? (*vv. 1-3*). Each section of the psalm opens with an imperative, and the first two follow on with a question. The psalmist does not confess any sin here, as compared with Psalm 38, which opens with almost the same

[1] See *DCH*, V, p. 736. *Sheminith* also occurs in the title of Ps. 12.

words. Hence the opening request may mean: 'Don't be angry with my raising this matter with you in prayer'. However, he is very conscious that he has brought himself under God's wrath, and he goes on to plead for God's intervention in his case. He desires mercy for he is languishing. Death stares him in the face, and he knows that it is God alone who can deliver him. The full extent of his trouble is disclosed by the reference to both bones and soul. In body and spirit he is greatly troubled. This is not a reference to two distinct entities but is rather a way in which the psalmist refers to himself (cf. the use of 'soul' and 'body' in Pss. 31:9; 63:1). While the prophets often speak of healing in the sense of restoration of the nation, in the Psalms, as here, the use of the verb (*râfâ'*) relates to literal, physical healing. The unfinished question 'how long?' appears about thirty times in the Bible, and of these about sixteen are in the psalms. It is very characteristic of the laments. The NIV translation repeats the expression 'how long', but this is unnecessary and the Hebrew text only has it once. In his distress he breaks off in the midst of the sentence, and the conclusion is implied from the preceding verse: 'O LORD, how long until *you have mercy and heal me*?' During his last painful illness, Calvin uttered no word of complaint, but raising his eyes heavenward he would say in Latin, '*Usquequo Domine*' ('Lord, how long?')

2. His Need Described (*vv.* 4-7)

Turn, O LORD, and deliver me; save me because of your unfailing love (*v.* 4). His appeal is that he feels that God has been absent from him (a frequent experience of distressed believers), and he wants him to turn from his anger. The verb used here for 'turn' or 'return' (*shûv*) is often used in the sense of God turning (or not turning) from his anger.[2] The 'how long?' of the previous verse now becomes an urgent request for deliverance. The basis of his call is God's unfailing covenantal love.

---

[2] The negative form occurs eight times in Amos 1-2, 'do not return [it].' While many translations assume that 'it' is punishment, a more likely explanation is that 'it' is God's anger. See *NIDOTTE*, 4, p. 58.

No one remembers you when he is dead. Who praises you from the grave? (*v. 5*) This verse finds its parallel (or perhaps its echo) in Hezekiah's prayer (Isa. 38:18). It is the living who are the testimony to God's power and grace, not those who are already dead. The Hebrew word translated 'grave' is *sh^{e}'ôl*. Its translation raises theological as well as linguistic questions. Some versions prefer to simply transliterate the Hebrew word ('Sheol'), but it is better to decide what it means and render accordingly. The context here points to some word that will parallel 'dead', and 'grave' is appropriate.[3]

I am worn out from groaning; all night long I flood my bed with weeping and drench my couch with tears. My eyes grow weak with sorrow; they fail because of all my foes (*vv. 6-7*). At the very centre of the psalm a thematic line describes the psalmist's condition: 'I am worn out from groaning.'[4] The distressing condition is not specified. All we know is that the night hours were particularly difficult for him. Because of physical illness and also the sense of separation from God he wept so copiously that it seemed as if he flooded his bed with tears. No hesitation was felt in the ancient Near East to expressing sorrow and grief by tears and groaning. Moses' eyes had not failed even near his death (Deut. 34:7), but David's eyes failed because of his grief and also because of his enemies. His friends may well have forsaken him at this time, and so appear as if they were enemies.

3. A Prayer Heard (*vv. 8-10*)

Away from me, all you who do evil, for the LORD has heard my weeping. The LORD has heard my cry for mercy; the LORD

---

[3] For an excellent general discussion on the translation of *sh^{e}'ôl* and explanation of the position adopted by the NIV translators, see R. Laird Harris, 'Why Hebrew Sh^{e}'ôl Was Translated "Grave"', *The Making of a Contemporary Translation: New International Version*, ed. Kenneth Barker (London: Hodder & Stoughton, 1987), pp. 75-92. Every time the NIV renders the Hebrew *sh^{e}'ôl* by 'grave' a footnote is inserted, thus enabling readers to judge the suitability of the word in the biblical context.

[4] This same device of placing a key line in the centre of a psalm can also be seen in other psalms. See, for example, 8:4; 23:4; 42:8; 48:8; 71:14; 76:7; 97:7; 141:5.

accepts my prayer. May all my enemies be ashamed and dismayed; may they turn back in sudden disgrace (*vv. 8-10*). The sudden change in tone is surprising. This may indicate either that the psalmist reached an understanding of God's help, or that a priest ministered a word of encouragement, such as Eli gave to Hannah (1 Sam. 1:17). Probably the former is the case, and twice he says that God has heard him. This leads on to the triumphant declaration in verse 9. The tenses are important here: the LORD *has heard* my cry, the LORD *will accept* my prayer. The final verse has a lot of music in the Hebrew text, in that there is repetition of words and sounds. This helps to reinforce the message.[5] Presumably the evildoers and his enemies are the same people, and he longs to see them put to shame. Early in the psalm his bones and soul had been 'disturbed' (vv. 2-3). Now he uses the same verb of his enemies in verse 10 ('dismayed'), while his desire for them is expressed ('turn back') by using the same verb he has used earlier of God's seeming return to him ('turn', verse 4). He knows that when he is restored, then his enemies will be put to shame.

[5] The NIV obscures some of the repetition by rendering the same verb (*yēvoshû*) by two different English verbs, 'ashamed' and 'in disgrace'. NKJV is better: 'Let all my enemies be ashamed … and be ashamed suddenly'.

Psalm 7

A shiggaion of David, which he sang to the Lord concerning Cush, a Benjamite

In the midst of distress David calls on the Lord. Though his situation is serious, yet at the end of the psalm he is singing praise to his God. The precise details of the incident(s) concerning Cush are unrecorded in the biblical history. We do know, however, that David faced many problems from the Benjamites (see 1 Sam. 24, 26; 2 Sam. 16:5; 20:1), and since Cush was from Benjamin it may be that he was a supporter of Saul. David protests his innocence in the face of false accusations and asks God to arise to help him. *Shiggaion* in the title is only used here in the Psalter, though the plural form occurs in Habakkuk 3:1 (*shigyonôt*). It probably was a word meaning 'a lamentation', though because of its infrequency it cannot be defined with precision. The vocabulary of the psalm stresses the appeal to the heavenly king and judge. The word 'righteousness' (*tsédek*) occurs twice (vv. 8, 17) while 'righteous [person]' (*tsâdîk*) occurs three times (vv. 9 twice, 11). The verb 'to judge' (*shâfat*) or derivatives are used three times (vv. 6, 8, 11), while 'execute justice' (*dîn*) is also employed (v. 8). This vocabulary points to a situation in which David is appealing for divine intervention so that he can be delivered from his enemies.

1. God – A Safe Refuge (*vv. 1-2*)

O Lord my God, I take refuge in you; save and deliver me from all who pursue me, or they will tear me like a lion and rip me to pieces with no-one to rescue me (*vv. 1-2*). David starts with a confident assertion of his hope. He appeals to his God, saying, 'In you [alone] I take refuge.' While the verb 'to take refuge' (*châsâh*) can be used literally of shelter from natural elements (Job 24:8; Isa. 4:6; 25:4), yet its most common use is figurative as here. In the midst of all their troubles, God's children know where their help is to be found, and they turn to the LORD. They can confidently sing:

> All my hope on God is founded;
> He doth still my trust renew.
> Me through change and chance He guideth,
> Only God and only true.
> God unknown,
> He alone
> Calls my heart to be His own.
> (Joachim Neander 1650-1680)

Though David's problem seems to have been slander, he feels that he is being torn apart like a lion's victim. The verb 'pursue' points to the intensity of the attacks on David, so that it is virtually equivalent to 'persecute'. Hence he asks for salvation from his God, for if that does not come, there will be no other salvation ('deliver' and 'to rescue' in these verses are from the same Hebrew verb, *nâtsal*).[1]

2. God — A Just Vindicator (*vv. 3-9*)

O LORD my God, if I have done this and there is guilt on my hands — if I have done evil to him who is at peace with me or without cause have robbed my foe — then let my enemy pursue and overtake me; let him trample my life to the ground and make me sleep in the dust. Selah (*vv. 3-5*). Again, David addresses God in the same terms as in verse 1 ('O LORD my God') before proceeding to express a self-cursing oath. We meet protestations of innocence like this on the part of psalmists quite often (cf. e.g. Pss. 17:3; 18:20-24; 26:1). These should not be taken as claims to sinlessness. Rather they testify to a practical and relevant life of

---

[1] The final phrase, 'no one to rescue me', is the translation of an idiomatic expression in Hebrew (*v*^e*'ên matstsîl*) in which the conjunction and a negative particle precede a participle. The negative virtually becomes an adverb, and with the participle forms a compound expression, 'without deliverer'. For further discussion, see *GKC* § 150 *l* and *NIDOTTE*, 4, pp. 1034-35.

obedience as over against their wicked oppressors. They affirm that their lifestyle shows devotion to God, and therefore they are worthy recipients of his protection. The threefold repetition of 'if' (Hebrew *'im;* NIV renders 'if ... and ... if') stresses in a cumulative way the protestation of innocence against the charges. The main accusation seems to have been that he has not been faithful to a covenantal partner ('him who is at peace with me', 'my ally').[2] If that was true, he invites death, with his enemy permitted to pursue[3] him and crush him to the dust.[4]

Arise, O Lord, in your anger; rise up against the rage of my enemies. Awake, my God, decree justice. Let the assembled peoples gather around you. Rule over them from on high; let the Lord judge the peoples (*vv. 6-8a*). Following Moses' example (Num. 10:35), David requests God to take action against his foes, using three synonymous expressions, 'arise', 'rise up', and 'awake'. He follows with another plea, wanting God to intervene in his case and administer his just laws.[5] These terms relate both to military and judicial action. He pictures a judgment scene in which God has gathered the nations on earth before him, and then from on high he carries out his judgment. The psalmist is happy to rest in that judgment. The same verb (*dîn*) is used similarly of righteous

---

[2] I think that Craigie is correct in taking 'him who is at peace with me' (*shôlᵉmî*) as 'my ally', following a view already found in *BDB*, p. 1023. However, Craigie has to accept emendation of the second clause of verse 5 to obtain his translation of 'and rescued *his adversary* empty-handed', though no manuscript evidence can be cited. See, P. C. Craigie, *Psalms 1-50*, p. 98.

[3] The MT has a very odd vocalisation of this verb, *yiradof,* which is neither the Qal nor the Piel form of the verb. Probably the explanation in *GKC* § 63 *n*, that it is simply a form derived from the regular Qal form *yirdof,* is the best one.

[4] The psalmist refers to himself in these verses using three different nouns: 'my soul', 'my life', 'my glory'. The first two are common, but the use of 'glory' is unusual. However, because of the usage here and in passages such as Gen. 49:6 and Ps. 30:12, it is correct to note that this is a form of self-reference in the Old Testament. For further discussion, see C. John Collins in *NIDOTTE*, 2, p. 583, and also the entry in *DCH*, IV, p. 353.

[5] The verb 'decree' (*tsivvîtâ*) is strictly perfect in form, but it is one of a number of cases restricted to Hebrew poetry in which a perfect occurs but 'where the translation as though it were a juss. or an imper. is either demanded or makes better sense': *DIHG~S*, p. 69, §60 (c).

divine action against the nations in Psalms 9:8 and 96:10. The NIV rendering 'rule' involves an emendation of the MT (a change from *shûvâh*, 'return' to *shêvâh*, 'sit [enthroned]'). The fact that the song of the ark in Numbers 10:35-36 contains both the imperatives 'arise' (*qûmâh*) and 'return' (*shûvâh*) suggests that the MT should stand. God is depicted as arising to execute judgment and then returning to his throne on high (cf. also Ps. 68:1, 18).

Judge me, O LORD, according to my righteousness, according to my integrity, O Most High. O righteous God, who searches minds and hearts, bring to an end the violence of the wicked and make the righteous secure (*vv. 8b-9*). The psalmist now comes back to his own need, and the prayer here is the central one for the whole psalm. As over against his enemies he stands in integrity before the LORD, who alone can search the inner recesses of the heart (cf. Ps. 17:3; Jer. 11:20; 17:10; 20:12; Rev. 2:23). The NIV's title for God in verse 9, 'O Most High', is a translation of what traditionally has been taken to be an Hebrew preposition with suffix (*ʿalây*) that means 'on' or 'over me'. Some confusion may have existed between the preposition *ʿal* and an abbreviated divine name, *ʿal* or *ʿalî*, 'Most High', and here NIV may be correct in accepting that this is an epithet for God.[6] Repetition of the idea of righteousness marks the confidence of the psalmist before God's judgment. He knows that the righteous God, who establishes the righteous, will confirm his righteousness in the face of his opponents.

3. God — A Certain Saviour (*vv. 10-16*)

My shield is God Most High, who saves the upright in heart. God is a righteous judge, a God who expresses his wrath every day. If he does not relent, he will sharpen his sword, he will bend and string his bow. He has prepared his deadly weapons; he makes ready his flaming arrows (*vv. 10-13*). The military language is carried on first of all by referring to

[6] For discussion on this question, see *TWOT*, 2, pp. 669-70. P. C. Craigie, *Psalms 1-50*, p. 98, accepts that the word *ʿalây* is the divine name in verse 8, but not in verse 10. For M. Dahood's innovative discussion on this matter, see 'The Divine Name "eli" in the Psalms', *TS* 14 (1953), pp. 454-57.

God as his shield,[7] the protector of the upright in heart. As in verse 8, the NIV takes the Hebrew word *ʿal* to be an epithet for God in combination with *ʾelohîm*, 'God Most High'. This is the best explanation of a difficult expression. He is the divine warrior who protects his people (for the word 'shield', see the comment on 3:5). Then the military metaphor is continued by reference to God getting his weapons (sword, bow, and flaming arrows) ready to attack. God is 'sifting out the hearts of men before His judgment seat', and he has 'loosed the fatal lightning of His terrible swift sword' (Julia Ward Howe, 'Mine eyes have seen the glory').

He who is pregnant with evil and conceives trouble gives birth to disillusionment. He who digs a hole and scoops it out falls into the pit he has made. The trouble he causes recoils on him; his violence comes down on his own head (*vv. 14-16*). The main idea expressed in these verses appears in other contexts in the Old Testament wisdom literature (see, for example, Ps. 34:21 and Job 4:8). It also appears in the New Testament in Galatians 6:7-8. The metaphor of a pregnant woman is taken over and applied to the sinner plotting against the righteous. He conceives the plan, only to find that it does not eventuate. Like a hunter who digs a trap for an animal, he falls into it himself. Whatever action he takes, he discovers that it comes back on himself. This last thought is often alluded to in the Old Testament (cf. e.g. Ps. 37:14-15; Prov. 26:27).

4. God — Worthy of Praise (*v. 17*)

I will give thanks to the LORD because of his righteousness and will sing praise to the name of the LORD Most High. No mention is made of the ultimate outcome of the distress. While the psalmist wanted immediate action to free him from his troubles (see vv. 6-9), yet he may have been disappointed that the answer did not come speedily. But what was most important (and we need to learn the lesson as well) is that he was given a new perspective on the problem by taking it to

[7] M. Dahood has argued that the word 'shield' (*mâgên*) means 'sovereign', but the evidence is not persuasive. For criticism of this idea, see P. C. Craigie, *Psalms 1-50*, p. 71.

God in prayer. He could rest in the confidence that God would deal justly and would vindicate him. No wonder that he can sing a doxology to the LORD! That praise was in honour of God's righteousness. Here, the additional name for God is the 'Most High' (*ʿelyôn*). This title for God occurs thirty-one times in the Old Testament, of which eighteen are in the Psalter. It emphasises the majesty of God, and it mainly appears in contexts in which universal claims are made in connection with Israel's God.[8] It was clearly an early title for God (see its use in Gen. 14:18, 19, 20, 22). In confidence David sings praise to the name of his God.[9] That does not mean simple repetition of God's name, but praise for the revelation that God has made of his nature. He is indeed a saviour and a righteous judge.

---

[8] See the extended note, 'Yahweh is El Elyon', in W. VanGemeren, 'Psalms', pp. 123-24.

[9] The form of the verb 'I will sing' (*'azammᵉrâh*) is cohortative ('let me sing'), not the regular imperfect. Thus the implication may be that the psalmist is among other singers in a public setting for worship. See Samuel Terrien, *The Psalms: Strophic Structure and Theological Commentary* (Grand Rapids: Eerdmans, 2003), p. 122.

Psalm 8

For the director of music. According to the gittith.
A psalm of David.

Creation is the focus of this hymn of praise. It is the latter part of Genesis 1 turned into a song. Biblical Hebrew has no word for 'thank you', but it manages to express thanks in a way rather like many of our English expressions are used when a gift is received ('It's the very thing I wanted!'; 'How beautiful it is!'). As psalmists and prophets understand more of God's character and works, they extol them. The expressions of delight in God's works, as here in verse 1, are themselves a mode of thanking him for them. Here a joyful song praises God's creative activity. The term *gittith* in the title may indicate a musical instrument (a Gittite lyre) or a bright melody to which it was sung. All three psalms that have this word in the title (Pss. 8, 81, and 84) are joyful songs of thanksgiving. *Gittith* is probably from the name of the town Gath in the south-west of Israel.

1. God's Majesty (*vv. 1-2*)

The psalm opens with a declaration of the majesty of God's name. **O Lord, our Lord, how majestic is your name in all the earth! You have set your glory above the heavens. From the lips of children and infants you have ordained praise because of your enemies, to silence the foe and the avenger** (*vv. 1-2*). God is addressed by the use of the covenantal name, Lord, to which is added 'our Lord', using the common word for 'Lord' (*ʾâdôn*).[1]

---

[1] Here the word for 'lord' is plural in form, as is usual when it applies to the God of Israel, though it takes singular agreement ('*your* name'). This is an honorific usage, probably modelled on the word for 'God' (*ʾelohîm*). The singular form is used of God only in the phrase 'the God of all the earth'. For discussion on this grammatical point, see *IBHS*, pp. 122-23; *DIHG~S*, p. 19.

The pronoun 'our' most probably relates to Israel, rather than to mankind. The NIV rendering of the second part of verse 1 is possible, but it omits the particle *ʾasher* that commences the clause and takes the verb *tenâh* as a past tense ('you have set'). The clause is difficult as both the syntax and the verb are anomalous. Possibly the particle links the two clauses together by carrying forward the idea of God's majesty, even though 'splendour' (*ʾaddîr*) in the first clause is replaced by 'majesty' (*hôd*) in the second. The verb is either an imperative with an emphatic ending ('set'), or a perfect ('you have set').[2] God's character is seen in the created world, and to believing eyes the whole world manifests God's glory.

Heaven above is softer blue,
Earth around is sweeter green;
Something lives in every hue,
Christless eyes have never seen.
(George Wade Robinson, 'Loved with everlasting love')

There is a fuller explanation of God's glory in creation in verse 3. Even the young children can be used by God to establish his 'strength',[3] and such praise is able to quieten that of his enemies. God is able to use the weak things of this world to confound the mighty (1 Cor. 1:27). Jesus quoted verse 2 in Matthew 21:16 when rebuking the authorities who wanted him to quieten the children shouting his praise when he entered Jerusalem. The quotation is from the LXX version and confirms the place of even little children in offering acceptable praise.

2. Man's Insignificance (*vv. 3-5*)

When I consider your heavens, the work of your fingers, the moon and the stars, which you have set in place, what is man that you are mindful of him, the son of man that you

[2] Many other suggestions have been made over the years. Mitchell Dahood, *The Psalms I, 1-50,* (Anchor Bible: Garden City, NY: Doubleday & Co., 1965). p. 49, proposed that the particle and the verb be taken together as a single word, giving the verbal form 'I will worship' (*ʾashâretannâh*). Though this suggestion was taken up by P. C. Craigie, *Psalms 1-50,* p. 105, yet it gives a form not otherwise attested in the Old Testament.

[3] The word *ʿoz* primarily refers to 'strength' or 'might'. However, it occurs in several passages in which ascribing strength to God implies praise of him for his overwhelming majesty.

care for him? (*vv.* 3-4). In comparison with the majesty of all creation, which is an expression of the majesty of God (cf. '*your* heavens, the work of *your* fingers'), man's position seems so very insignificant. The words chosen for 'man' in this verse (Hebrew *ᵓᵉnôsh* and *ben ᵓâdâm*) seem to be deliberately chosen to highlight his frailty. The expected answer to the question the psalmist asks has to be, 'Nothing!'

You have made him a little lower than the heavenly beings and crowned him with glory and honour (*v.* 5). It is better to follow the NIV margin and insert 'than god' instead of 'than the heavenly beings'. The Massoretic Hebrew text has 'God' (*ᵓᵉlohîm*). Though the translation 'heavenly beings' does occur in some of the early translations, yet that is probably due to a theological reason. Versions such as the LXX, the Syriac, and the Targums were probably trying to avoid the idea that man was invested with such great dignity. However, man occupies a special position in creation, in that he alone of all the creatures was made in the image and likeness of God (Gen. 1:26-27; 5:1). Because of his creation he has to reflect God's glory in a special way as he rules as his vice-regent, and God's attitude to mankind continues to be, in spite of man's sinfulness, one of favour and blessing. The reference to God's action is not just to the past, but his abiding bestowal of 'glory and honour'.

3. Man's Role in Creation (*vv.* 6-8)

You made him ruler over the works of your hands; you put everything under his feet: all flocks and herds, and the beasts of the field, the birds of the air, and the fish of the sea, all that swim the paths of the seas (*vv.* 6-8). Man was given dominion over the rest of creation (Gen. 1:28-30; 9:1-3), and these verses show how comprehensive this rule was. At the apex of creation (note the distinctiveness of the account of man's creation in Gen. 1:26-30 as compared with the preceding narrative) man's rule extended over all the rest of creation, a fact reaffirmed after the flood (Gen. 9:2-3). The words 'you put everything under his feet' find their fullest meaning in Jesus' dominion through his resurrection and exaltation (1 Cor. 15:27; Eph. 1:22; Heb. 2:6-8). What is pictured here of man in respect to creation is yet to have its fullest significance in the great re-creation that will follow the return of Christ.

4. God's Praise Renewed (*v. 9*)

O LORD, our Lord, how majestic is your name in all the earth! Just as the psalm begins, so it ends. It started on the note of praise. Then the reasons for praise were unfolded, and finally the psalm ends with more praise. This is a pattern often followed with psalms of thanksgiving. Either the opening is repeated, or given at the end with some slight variation (cf. Ps. 117:1, 2).

Psalm 9

For the director of music. To the tune of 'The Death of the Son'. A psalm of David

Psalms 9 and 10 form a unit, as they together comprise an acrostic (see Introduction), and in early versions such as the LXX and the Vulgate they are a single entity. The acrostic pattern is not complete, as several letters of the Hebrew alphabet are missing and some letters are not in the usual order. Psalm 9 employs the Hebrew letters Alef–Kaf, though Dalet is missing in verses 5-6. Lamed–Taw are found in Psalm 10, though Mem and Nun are reversed in verses 3-6, while Ayin and Pe are similarly reversed in verses 7-9.[1] The use of an acrostic clearly appealed to some poets, and it must also have brought responsive appreciation from hearers or readers. Acrostics may well have served a teaching purpose in that they were a device to assist in memorising a poem. The emphasis on Psalm 9 is on praise of God who governs the whole world, while in Psalm 10 the main focus is an appeal to God in distress caused by personal enemies. Thoughts and words also bind the two psalms together:

Psalm 9	**Psalm 10**
The LORD is … a stronghold *in times of trouble* (v. 9)	Why do you hide yourself *in times of trouble* (v. 1)
He does not *forget* the cry of the afflicted (v. 12)	He says to himself, 'God has *forgotten*' (v. 11)

[1] For recent discussion on the acrostic psalms, see D. N. Freedman and J. C. Geoghegan, 'Alphabetic Acrostic Psalms' in D. N. Freedman, *Psalm 119: The Exaltation of the Torah* (Winona Lake, Ind.: Eisenbrauns 1999), pp. 13-19.

Psalm 9	Psalm 10
O LORD, see how my enemies *pursue* me (v. 13)	In his pride the wicked does not *pursue* him (v. 4)
	Why does he say in his heart, 'He won't *pursue* [me]' (v. 13)
Their feet are caught in the *net* they have hidden (v. 15)	He catches the helpless and drags them off in his *net* (v. 9)
Let the *nations* be judged in your presence; ... let the *nations* know they are but men (vv. 19-20)	The LORD is king for ever and ever; the *nations* will perish from his land (v. 16)

On balance it seems best to assume that the two psalms, while having certain similarities, were written independently, and brought together at this point in the Psalter because of common ideas and words.

The inscription, 'For the director of music. To [the tune of] "The Death of the Son", A psalm of David', contains commonly used words, but the phrase 'To the death of the son' does not occur elsewhere in the Psalter. This involves dividing one word in the MT (*ʿalmût*) into two (*ʿal mût*). Various suggestions have been made,[2] but no consensus has emerged. Perhaps an old explanation going back as far as Grotius (1583-1645) should be again considered. He proposed that a transposition of letters had taken place with the words 'of the son' (*labên*) and that the true reading should be *nâvâl*, Nabal. Hengstenberg refined this suggestion further, by taking *nâvâl*, not as a proper name, but as the noun 'a fool'.[3] This gives a translation 'on the dying of a fool' which suits the context (see especially

[2] See a summary in W. VanGemeren, 'Psalms', pp. 116-17.
[3] E. W. Hengstenberg, *Commentary on the Psalms*, pp. 141-42.

verses 3, 5, 6, 12, 17) and also can be supported by David's words regarding Abner, 'Died Abner as the fool dies?' (*hakk*[e]*môt nâvâl yâmût ʾavnêr*, 2 Sam. 3:33).

1. A Song of Thanksgiving (*vv. 1-2*)

I will praise you, O Lord, with all my heart; I will tell of all your wonders; I will be glad and rejoice in you; I will sing praise to your name, O Most High (*vv. 1-2*). These verses contain several terms that concentrate on praise, and probably public praise in the sanctuary: *praise, tell, be glad, praise, sing praise.* To the opening one is added, *with all my heart,* to indicate the depth of his 'praise'. The 'wonders' were the deeds that the Lord alone could and did perform, such as the great redemptive acts connected with the Exodus (see the first use of the word in Exod. 3:20). It is a word used especially in the Psalms (twenty-four occurrences out of forty-one), and often with the same verb as here (*sappêr,* 'count, recount'). The 'name' is a reference not to a title for Lord but the revelation he had made of himself. The psalmist sings praise to his covenant God (*Lord*) and to his exalted sovereign (*Most High*). Similar language is used at the opening of Psalm 75.

2. Acknowledgment of Personal Help (*vv. 3-6*)

My enemies turn back; they stumble and perish before you. For you have upheld my right and my cause; you have sat on your throne, judging righteously. You have rebuked the nations and destroyed the wicked; you have blotted out their name forever and ever. Endless ruin has overtaken the enemy, you have uprooted their cities; even the memory of them has perished (*vv. 3-6*). These verses refer back to historical incidents that are the foundation of praise. God had intervened, and the psalmist's enemies had turned back from their evil plans. They perished before the righteous God. The verb 'to stumble' often occurs in the poetical books in this metaphorical sense of being brought to ruin.

Along with verse 8, these verses contain very significant declarations joining together the concepts of God as judge and his acting in righteousness (*tsédek*). An accumulation of related terms occurs, relating to both personal and national levels of judgment: 'right' (*mishpât*), 'cause' (*dîn*), 'to judge' (*shâfat*), and 'justice' (*mêshârîm*). Judgment had been executed on the psalmist's behalf by God, who from his kingly throne executed his just decrees. Even the Gentile nations had felt God's 'rebuke', using a word elsewhere applied to dramatic actions of God such as the flood (cf. Ps. 106:9; Isa. 54:9). Nations had been blotted out before him so that no recollection of them remained. The use of the verb 'blot out' (*mâchâh*) is important, as it almost always has theological significance.[4] It is first used of the blotting out by the flood (Gen. 7:22-23), and also both in threats to Israel (Deut. 9:14; 29:20) and to describe the reality of God's judgment against Jerusalem (2 Kings 21:13). Here the application is to enemy nations that have been blotted out and brought to ruin. The duration of this is stressed by the use of 'for ever and ever' and 'endless'. Not being remembered at the time of death is the fate of evildoers and Israel's enemies (Exod. 17:14; Deut. 25:19; Ps. 34:16), while the righteous are remembered for ever (Ps. 112:6; Prov. 10:7).

3. The Rule of the King/Shepherd (*vv. 7-10*)

The thought of God as judge leads on to statements concerning his general rule and his protective care. **The LORD reigns forever; he has established his throne for judgment** (*v. 7*). In contrast to the enemies whose names are blotted eternally, the LORD sits enthroned for ever. Here the picture seems to move to the scene at the end of time, when all shall appear before the LORD's throne of judgment.

An action of judgment occurred in the past (v. 5), but future judgment is still in store. **He will judge the world in righteousness; he will govern the peoples with justice** (*v. 8*). Unlike human judges, God judges righteously. His administration will not be marred by the flawed justice of human systems. The whole of the inhabited world (Heb., *têvêl*) will be subject to his rule. This verse is used again in the later Royal Psalms to describe the end-time judgment of the divine king (Pss. 96:13; 98:9).

[4] See W. C. Kaiser's note in *TWOT*, 1, pp. 498-99.

The LORD is a refuge for the oppressed, a stronghold in times of trouble. Those who know your name will trust in you, for you, LORD, have never forsaken those who seek you (*vv. 9-10*). For any afflicted persons, there is the assurance that God is a 'refuge' or 'stronghold' (in the NIV translation these words render the same Hebrew word [*misgâv*] that occurs twice in verse 9). The main idea of the Hebrew word is a place with high fortifications (cf. Isa. 25:12), but it never occurs as a synonym for a Canaanite high place (Hebrew *bâmâh*). 'In times of trouble' the oppressed find refuge with the LORD (cf. the use of the identical expression in 10:1 and a similar one in 37:39). 'Oppressed' is a synonym for 'afflicted' in verse 12. The character of those who take refuge is described as 'those who know your name'. Unlike the names of the wicked that are blotted out (v. 5), God's name is the revelation of his person. Those who love him have come to a personal knowledge of him, and therefore they put their confidence in him. The verb 'to trust' (*bâtach)* is one of the most frequent ways employed in the Old Testament and especially in the Psalms to denote the confidence that comes through reliance on God.[5]

None of those who seek God ever find themselves left in the lurch. The verb 'to seek' appears often in the Psalms, especially in the general sense of asking help or assistance from the LORD (cf. Ps. 14:2). Verse 10 is also significant, for after speaking of God in the third person in verses 1-9, the change is made to the second person: 'those who know *your name,*' 'for *you*, O LORD', 'those who seek *you*'. This has the effect of drawing attention to the personal relationship that David enjoyed with his God. Such expressions regarding God's character towards his believing community were rooted in the psalmist's own experience of God's grace and power.

4. A Doxology (*vv. 11-12*)

Sing praises to the LORD, enthroned in Zion; proclaim among the nations what he has done. For he who avenges blood remembers; he does not ignore the cry of the afflicted

[5] For discussion of the wider use of this verb and other related ones, see G. J. Wenham, *Faith in the Old Testament* (TSF, n.d.); O. Adutwum, '*BATACH* in the Book of Psalms', *IBS* 15 (1993), pp. 28-38.

(*vv. 11-12*). The psalmist returns now to the theme of praise found at the beginning of the psalm (vv. 1-2). The call is most probably to the assembled people at the sanctuary, as the psalmist wants all who hear to join with him in praising God for his goodness and righteous acts. The LORD who is enthroned on Zion (the presence of the ark in Jerusalem is intended) is to be praised, and his deeds declared to the Gentile nations. Just as God sat on a heavenly throne (v. 7), so he dwelt in an earthly way in the tabernacle which was in Zion by his own appointment (see Ps. 132:13-14). Proclamation of God's deeds is to take place among the Gentile nations. 'The deeds' are clearly the same as 'the wonders' in verse 1, even though different Hebrew words are used. What his deeds consist of is made clear in verse 12. God was the one who would avenge those who took (or attempted to take) the life of others (cf. Gen. 4:10; 9:5). His sovereign deliverance of his people would be proclaimed as his 'wonders'. God's faithfulness is asserted in the phrase 'he does not ignore (lit. 'forget') the cry of the afflicted'. Not till later in the Psalms is there fuller expression of this wish that all the nations might know the LORD's deeds (cf. Pss. 18:49; 57:9, and also the Introduction).

5. An Appeal for Help (*vv. 13-14*)
The tone of the psalm changes at this point to become more like a lament, with appeals to God for his mercy and deliverance. These appeals are going to be repeated in a different form at the end of the psalm (vv. 19-20). **O LORD, see how my enemies persecute me! Have mercy and lift me up from the gates of death, that I may declare your praises in the gates of the Daughter of Zion and there rejoice in your salvation** (*vv. 13-14*). Stemming out of the assurance that God is the avenger, given in the preceding verse, the psalmist appeals in respect to his own case. Statements of God's character often form the basis for individual prayer. The NIV does not follow the word order of the MT, which puts the appeal for mercy at the beginning. It is better to follow the RSV and the NASB, which render: 'Be gracious to me. Behold ...,' and this highlights the appeal for mercy. David's persecution

by his enemies had reached the point where he felt he had reached the gates of death itself. Death is looked at as if it was a territory, or a city with doors (cf. Rev. 1:18, 'the keys of death and Hades'). The psalmist wants mercy to be shown to him so that he, in turn, can declare God's praises. The highest desire he had is not just his own deliverance but the opportunity to praise his deliverer. Those delivered by God desire to declare the praises of him who called them out of darkness into his marvellous light (1 Pet. 2:9). 'The Daughter of Zion' is a personification of Jerusalem as a young girl, perhaps better rendered as 'Daughter Zion'. 'Daughter' is used of other cities and countries (cf. 'daughter of Tyre' [Ps. 45:12], 'daughter of Babylon' [Ps. 137:8], 'daughter of Edom' [Lam. 4:21]). Here it is a personification of Zion, and the phrase also serves to emphasise the father/daughter relationship between God and the city he had chosen (see Pss. 2:6 and 132:13-14). There, surrounded by the inhabitants of Jerusalem, he longs to sing and rejoice in God's salvation.

6. The Wicked Ensnared (*vv. 15-18*)

The nations have fallen into the pit they have dug; their feet are caught up in the net they have hidden. The LORD is known by his justice; the wicked are ensnared by the work of their hands. ***Higgaion Selah*** (*vv. 15-16*). Attention now comes back to the nations (see verse 5). The outcome for the wicked is described in terms of them falling into their own pit, being caught in the net they have set, or being trapped in their own snares. What they wanted to do to Israel has become their own portion. They were to know the consequences of their own plotting, not on others, but on themselves (cf. Pss. 5:10; 7:14-16). The work of their own hands turns on them. The reference to the LORD's justice picks up the theme of verse 4. The opening of verse 16 makes it plain that God's hand was also in this. 'The wicked' (synonymous with 'nations' in verses 5, 15, 17 and 19) are subjects of God's justice, which turns their plots against themselves.

The meaning of 'higgaion' is uncertain, but it may come from a Hebrew root that means 'to murmur', 'sigh', 'meditate'.[6] It also occurs in Psalm 92:4 of lyre music, but the same derivation would fit that context as well. Hence, here it probably denotes that the last part of the psalm is to be rendered softly in keeping with the solemnity of the subject. For 'Selah', see the comments on Psalm 3:2.

7. The Destiny of the Wicked (*vv. 17-18*)

The wicked return to the grave, all the nations that forget God. But the needy will not always be forgotten, nor the hope of the afflicted ever perish (*vv. 17-18*). Those who forget God return to Sheol (see comment on Ps. 6:5). Earlier in this psalm there is mention of 'forgetting' (v. 12, NIV 'ignore'). Here it means people who do not think about the true God and serve him, but rather strive against his people. The verdict expressed against them may not mean immediate judgment and death, but that which is treasured up for them in the future (see verse 20). The verb 'to forget' appears again in verse 18, but with what a great contrast! God will never forget his poor and afflicted ones. He will never allow their hope to perish. Their expectation is based on God's sure word to his children.

8. A Final Appeal (*vv. 19-20*)

Arise, O LORD, let not man triumph; let the nations be judged in your presence. Strike them with terror, O LORD; let the nations know they are but men (*vv. 19-20*). It is clear that the opposition to the righteous (and especially to the psalmist himself) was still present, and therefore he asks for God's speedy help (for 'arise' cf. Ps. 7:6). The language used here goes back to Moses' words in Numbers 10:35 when the ark was being moved: 'Rise up, O LORD! May your enemies be scattered; may your foes flee before you' (cf. also Ps. 68:1-2). The psalmist does not want frail man to be able to rejoice in triumph. The Hebrew word used for man carries with it implications of human frailty and weakness, especially in

---

[6] See P. C. Craigie, *Psalms 1-50*, p. 116.

contrast, as here, to God's power (Hebrew *ʾenôsh* as compared with the more common *ʾâdâm*). What was needed was a fresh demonstration of God's power such as had been shown at the Exodus. The word 'terror' implies this, for it is used in Deuteronomy 4:34 of God's awesome deeds when he brought Israel out of Egypt. By a repetition of such divine action the nations would truly know their own frailty and insignificance before the LORD. An appearance of God would fill his enemies with apprehension as they realised that they could not stand before him.

Psalm 10

Almost all the psalms in the first book (Psalms 1-41) have a title. The only exceptions are 1, 2, 10, and 33. The fact that a title is missing for this psalm is another indication that it is to be considered in conjunction with Psalm 9, whose title also covers this psalm. The note of appeal to God is much more prominent here, though at the end of the psalm there is an affirmation that God the king is also a prayer-hearing God. Though the word 'nations' appears in verse 16, yet the thrust of the complaint is against an individual oppressor *within* Israel. The fact that the word used for the 'wicked' (Heb., *râshaʿ*) almost always appears in the singular supports this position. The one exception is in verse 2b, where the NIV translation has to be emended to read 'caught in the schemes *they* have devised'. The use of the plural is understandable in this verse, as it is describing the more general setting before concentrating on the individual problem of persecution.

The style of this complaint is marked out, not only by the use of standard expressions, but also by the repetition of them. These include:

the wicked [man]	verses 2, 3, 4, 13, 15 (2×)
says to himself	verses 6, 11, 13
schemes, evil thoughts	verses 2, 4
lie in wait, ambush	verses 8-9 (twice the verb *ʾârav* and once the derived noun *maʾªrâv*)
weak, afflicted	verses 2, 9 (2×), 12, 17

in secret, hide	verses 8, 9 (the noun *mistâr*), 11 (the verb *sâtar*)
to seize	verse 9 (2×)

The effect of this repetition is to heighten the appreciation of the reader for the heart-rending situation in which David found himself. He states and restates the agony of one who was persecuted without cause and without cessation.

1. A Heartfelt Cry (*vv. 1-2*)

Why, O Lord, do you stand far off? Why do you hide yourself in times of trouble? (*v. 1*) The psalmist is in deep trouble and turns to the one who is a stronghold at such times (see 9:9). The introductory word is 'Why?'This speaks of the hurt and disappointment he feels, but it also includes the idea of expectation of God's help. There is also the note of puzzlement at the treatment believers receive from persecutors. Later Psalms 37 and 73 help to provide the answer to that puzzle. No indication is given that it was because of the psalmist's sin that God had placed himself afar off (contrast Jer. 23:23). The idea that God conceals himself from troubled believers occurs elsewhere (see Ps. 55:1 and Lam. 3:56), though such concealment is a figment of their imagination.

In his arrogance the wicked man hunts down the weak, who are caught in the schemes he devises (*v. 2*). This short statement of the situation is explained more fully later in the psalm (see especially vv. 7-10). The imagery of hunting is frequently employed in Hebrew poetry as by analogy the readers or hearers could transfer the concepts easily into their own situation. In the second clause of this verse the subject of the verb 'caught' is 'they'. While this could refer to the wicked being caught in their own snares, more probably the NIV is correct to take it as meaning the poor are entrapped. However, the verb 'devise' is plural as well, so that the translation has to be 'caught in the schemes *they* devise'. This provides the general statement, before individual specification of the attitude and actions of the wicked person follow.

2. The Pride of the Wicked (*vv. 3-6*)
He boasts of the cravings of his heart; he blesses the greedy and reviles the LORD. In his pride the wicked does not seek him; in all his thoughts there is no room for God (*vv. 3-4*). It is part of the routine of sinners to glorify themselves. Right from the time of the first sin they have wanted to elevate themselves to be as God (Gen. 3:5). They can extol the very longings that ultimately come to expression in outward transgression. Sin also causes wrong understanding of the deeds of other sinners, as well as of God's character. Hence the sinner praises greedy and ruthless men, while God is blasphemed. He makes no attempt to seek after God and shuts him out of all his thoughts. Part of the nature of sinful man is to suppress the knowledge he has of the truth and to fail to glorify God and give thanks to him (Rom. 1:18-21).

His ways are always prosperous; he is haughty and your laws are far from him; he sneers at all his enemies. He says to himself, 'Nothing will shake me; I'll always be happy and never have trouble' (*vv. 5-6*). The wicked enjoy prosperity, but it makes them even more arrogant. They live in seeming freedom from divine judgment (it is better to take the Hebrew word *mishpât* as 'judgment' rather than the NIV 'law'). Towards their enemies they show contempt and make the boastful claim that they will always stand firm. Such arrogance will continue into the future, as though the wicked person could control it as well as the present circumstances. The second part of verse 6 is difficult to translate and interpret, and an awkward verse division complicates it further. A literal rendering is: 'which (*ᵓᵃsher*) not in evil'. The NKJV ('I shall never be in adversity') or ESV ('I shall not meet adversity') are closest to the MT. The NIV translation accepts an emendation of the text, with *ᵓᵃsher* being revocalised as *ᵓosher*, 'happiness'.[1] It is part of the wicked man's arrogance to claim exemption from trouble and from judgment. He considers himself unassailable.

[1] This is followed in *DCH*, I, p. 436: 'in happiness, not in misfortune'. The only time the word *ᵓosher* appears with certainty in the MT is Gen. 30:13 where Leah says, 'How happy I am!'

3. The Character of the Wicked (*vv. 7-11*)
A description of sinful man now follows, with emphasis on his role as an oppressor. Some commentators take 'curse' with the preceding verse, in order to allow the letter *pe* to begin verse 7,[2] and so supply another letter of the alphabet to try and complete the acrostic pattern. However, the pattern is still incomplete even if that is done, and hence this suggestion does not carry much weight.[3] **His mouth is full of curses and lies and threats; trouble and evil are under his tongue. He lies in wait near the villages; from ambush he murders the innocent, watching in secret for his victims** (*vv. 7-8*). The description at the start of verse 7 of sinful man (with a tongue that is always speaking lies) is taken over by Paul from the LXX and used in his description of the utter sinfulness of man without Christ (Rom. 3:14).[4] Continually the wicked pour out their evil words against others, with the mouth being ready with its arsenal of deadly weapons. In addition to words, they act with violence against others. There is no reason to suggest anything other than a literal understanding of the description here. They act like lions in attacking their prey. Similar imagery occurs quite frequently in the Psalter (cf. Pss. 17:12; 37:32; 56:6; 59:3; 64:4).

He lies in wait like a lion in cover; he lies in wait to catch the helpless; he catches the helpless and drags them off in his net. His victims are crushed, they collapse; they fall under his strength. He says to himself, 'God has forgotten; he covers his face and never sees' (*vv. 9-11*). The spiritual conditions behind these verses are unknown to us. However, we have enough evidence from the prophets to confirm the accuracy of the description given here. There were clearly

---

[2] See, for example, P. C. Craigie, *Psalms 1-50*, p. 122. His translation, 'I won't slip throughout all generations. Happiness without misfortune – so has he sworn', in addition takes *ʾâlâh* not as 'curse' but as the verb 'he has sworn'.

[3] See the excellent note by Craigie, 'Excursus III: Acrostic Psalms', ibid., pp. 128-31.

[4] Paul does not quote the LXX precisely, and even it differs from the MT, mainly in that in place of 'deceits' the LXX has 'bitterness'. This appears to be caused by the LXX translators taking the Hebrew word *mirmôt* as coming from the verb *mârar*, 'to be bitter', rather than from *râmâh*, 'to deceive'.

many occasions when force was used against the poor and needy in Israel (see Hos. 4:2; 6:8-9; Isa. 1:15-17, 21-23; Jer. 7:9; Ezek. 22:2-5). Sheer brute force had been used and the helpless were felled. In addition, the wicked have been deceitful and cunning as they set traps for the righteous. In verse 11 the thought of verse 6 is taken up and developed further. The inner thoughts of the wicked are exposed, for what has taken place outwardly is only the expression of inward godlessness. The wicked are depicted as claiming that, as God does not see them, they can act sinfully with great boldness. Jesus, in his teaching, developed the whole concept of inner sin coming to expression in outward actions (see Matt. 5:21-30; Mark 7:20-23).

4. A Call to God (*vv. 12-13*)

Arise, LORD! Lift up your hand, O God. Do not forget the helpless. Why does the wicked man revile God? Why does he say to himself, 'He won't call me to account'? (*vv. 12-13*). The appeal to God is urgent. This is emphasised by the call to him to 'arise'. This is the fourth time in the first ten psalms that the words 'Arise, LORD' are used (see the comment on 3:7; note the other occurrences in 7:6 and 9:19).[5] The urgency is also stressed by the use of three different names for God in these verses. He is first of all addressed as covenant LORD (Heb., *yhwh*), then as God (Heb., *ʾêl*), and finally by another word for God (Heb., *ʾᵉlohîm*). To lift up the hand clearly means to punish (cf. v. 15; see also 2 Sam. 18:28), or to put it positively, to rescue his afflicted ones (as in Ps. 138:7). Those who reviled God thought that he would not seek them out. They had already declared themselves as atheists (vv. 4,11), and now they proudly boast that they will be left alone to carry out their evil deeds.[6] Sinners ever need to be reminded that ultimately

---

[5] The expression also appears in 17:13 and 132:8, while 'Arise, O God' is used in 74:22 and 82:8.

[6] The NIV rendering 'He won't call me to account' follows the LXX and the Syriac in reading the verb as the 3 pers. sing., but the MT has 2 pers. sing., lit. '*you* will not seek me'. Probably the rendering should be indirect speech in English: 'Why does he say to himself that you won't call me to account?' The Hebrew verb here (*dârash*) is rightly translated 'call to account' as one of its uses conveys this sense of demanding or requiring something. It is then a quasi-legal term.

they will be called to account before the judgment seat of God (2 Cor. 5:10).

5. A Song of Confidence (*vv. 14-18*)

How different were things in reality! **But you, O God, do see trouble and grief; you consider it to take in hand. The victim commits himself to you; you are the helper of the fatherless. Break the arm of the wicked and evil man; call him to account for his wickedness that would not be found out** (*vv. 14-15*). The opening words in the NIV ('But you, O God') are good, in that they bring out the emphasis of the MT on the fact that God had indeed seen what was happening. The same effect can be gained by rendering: 'You have seen the trouble and vexation, yes you have!'[7] God saw everything that happened, in contrast to the claim that he neither saw (v. 11) nor punished (v. 13). The orphan is singled out as representative of that group for whom the LORD ever showed great care (Exod. 22:22-24; Mal. 3:5). Here the orphan represents helplessness and desertion. Those in need have the reassurance that God sees their trouble and that he acts as their helper. In verse 15 the psalmist asks God to break the powerful arm of the wicked so that he cannot continue in his evil way. God is said to seek out the wicked for punishment (Heb., lit. 'you seek [to punish] his wickedness. Surely you can find it!').

The LORD is King for ever and ever; the nations will perish from his land. You hear, O LORD, the desire of the afflicted; you encourage them, and you listen to their cry, defending the fatherless and the oppressed, in order that man, who is of the earth, may terrify no more (*vv. 16-18*). The psalmist ends with a song of complete confidence in the LORD, and he was so certain of being heard by him that he describes the result of his prayers as a present reality. He recognises that the LORD exercises his kingship over the whole land, and will even destroy the enemies from it. That thought is remarkable, because in the psalm the enemies are opponents *within* Israel. However, the concept of judgment on the enemies reminds

---

[7] This is the translation in Craigie, *Psalms 1-50*, p. 121.

him that God will also deal with the external enemies of Israel. Verse 17 contains the assurance that the prayers he has already expressed for the afflicted are indeed heard by God (notice the variety of terms the psalmist uses for the needy: *weak,* verse 2; *innocent,* verse 8; *helpless,* verse 12; *fatherless,* verses 14 and 18; *afflicted,* verse 17; *oppressed,* verse 18). What God does is to make the heart firm (NIV 'encourage'; for the negative use of this expression, see Ps. 78:8). Man, who boasts of his might, is but frail man (Heb., *ʾenôsh,* cf. Ps. 9:19) who will no longer be able to terrify others. He is 'of the earth', a mere earthling who cannot stand before the judge of all. This psalm reminds us that under persecution and oppression we must turn to God for relief. Our pattern is Jesus who, 'when they hurled their insults at him, he did not retaliate; when he suffered, he made no threats. Instead, he entrusted himself to him who judges justly' (1 Pet. 2: 23-24). The same epistle counsels us that if we suffer we are to commit ourselves to our faithful creator and continue to do good (1 Pet. 4:19).

Psalm 11

For the director of music. Of David.

This is a song of confidence, probably composed when David fled from Absalom, though David had previously fled several times (see 1 Sam. 19:1-3, 12; 20:1; 21:1, 10; 22:1, 3; 23:13; 24:1-2; 26:1; 27:1). He knew very well what it was to be a fugitive. If the psalm does come from the time of Absalom's revolt, then verse 1 may contain the advice his friends were giving him. They were telling him to flee for safety as he had done when Saul was persecuting him to 'the Crags of the Wild Goats' (1 Sam. 24:2). But he knew that his protection was only with the Lord. While the opening verse speaks of David's trust, the remainder of the psalm is in the third person and has application to the broader situation in life in which the character of the righteous and the wicked is displayed. It is a continuation of the theme of Psalm 1, marking the sharp distinction in God's sight of these two groups in society (see the sharp contrasts in verses 5-7).

1. The Needy Situation Described (*vv. 1-3*)

In the Lord I take refuge. How then can you say to me: 'Flee like a bird to your mountain (*v. 1*). The Psalm opens and closes on a confident note: 'In the Lord I take refuge … the Lord is righteous.' The opening words give the basic theme of the psalm – confident trust in the Lord, using a verb (*châsah*) and its cognates that form an important part of the devotional vocabulary of Israel. In his critical situation friends were giving David advice. They were suggesting he should fly or escape like a bird to a mountain hideout. The verb is plural, so perhaps his friends and associates were intended to flee as well. The designation, 'your mountain', has been taken by some to indicate the well-known retreat that David had previously used.[1] But the imagery is simply that of birds seeking shelter in the nooks and crannies of hills, a well-known and apposite illustration.

For look, the wicked bend their bows; they set their arrows against the strings to shoot from the shadows at the upright in heart (*v.* 2). Elsewhere the wicked are also described as bending the bow (Ps. 37:14). The thought of the bird fleeing is carried over from verse 1, and now the imagery is of a hunter going out after the birds with his bow. The language of fleeing to the mountains to escape may well be a reflection of the advice to Lot (Gen. 19:17; and see v. 6 later in this psalm). The godless are ready to shoot their arrows at the upright without being seen, taking their aim from some concealed hiding place (cf. Ps. 10:8-9).

When the foundations are being destroyed what can the righteous do?' (*v.* 3). There was so much upheaval that even the foundational principles of society were being shaken. There was no truth or justice any more. The final sentence could refer to the past: 'What has the righteous done?' i.e., to deserve this. Yet it is better to follow the NIV and take it as a question of despair: 'What can the righteous do?' In times when justice and righteousness no longer reign supreme in society, what can the upright do? The answer follows in the second section of the psalm.

2. The Source of Confidence (*vv.* 4-7)

The question of despair asked by the psalmist's friends now finds its answer. **The LORD is in his holy temple; the LORD is on his heavenly throne. He observes the sons of men; his eyes**

---

[1] Several awkward things confront the reader in this verse: (1) the switch from 1st pers. in 'I take refuge' to the 2nd plural masc., 'you say' (2) the consonantal text gives the verb 'flee' as 2nd pers. masc. plural imperative, while the Q^{e}re reading has it as 2nd pers. fem. sing. (3) the last two words (*har^{e}kem tsippôr*, lit. 'your (masc. plur.) mountain [like] a bird') are often emended to *har k^{e}mo tsippôr*, ' [to] a hill like a bird'. While the interchange between singular and plural may be difficult, it is best to stay with the MT rather than attempting to emend the text.

examine them. The LORD examines the righteous, but the wicked and those who love violence his soul hates (*vv. 4-5*). Normally there is a spoken prayer after an expression of great need, but one is lacking here. Rather the psalmist points to the LORD on high, seated on his judgment throne. There was the visible presence of God in the tabernacle, but he was also the exalted heavenly ruler. From heaven he saw all that happened, and with penetrating gaze, he was able to test the works of all mankind. The verb translated 'examine' (*bâchan*) is often used of testing metals by fire and is a favourite word in Jeremiah (Jer. 11:20; 17:10; 20:12). While it is similar in meaning to 'put to the test' (*nâsâh*) and 'refine' (*tsâraf*), yet it seems to point to knowledge gained intuitively, and is therefore the most apt of the three in relation to spiritual realities.[2] Even the actions in darkness (v. 2) were open to his sight. The LORD examines the righteous, but his soul hates the wicked and those who love violence. Both righteous and unrighteous come under God's judging eye (cf. Paul's words, 'we must all appear before the judgment seat of Christ', 2 Cor. 5:10), though God's attitude is quite different with each of the two. His innermost being ('his soul') hates the violent man, presumably an indication that the psalmist's enemies were of this kind.

On the wicked he will rain fiery coals and burning sulphur; a scorching wind will be their lot (*v. 6*). The thought of fire used for testing metals changes in verse 6 to become a picture of the fiery judgment. For believers the fire will test the quality of their work (1 Cor. 3:13), while for unbelievers the fire will come as the exterminator of evil. 'Fiery coals and burning sulphur' remind us of what happened to Sodom (Gen. 19:24), and also point forward from the psalmist's time to another sulphur rain that will be poured out on Gog (Ezek. 38:22). A similar fate will be the lot of the wicked in general. The reference to the scorching wind is a description of the east wind that blows over Israel, bringing with it the desert heat.

For the LORD is righteous, he loves justice; upright men will see his face (*v. 7*). How differently God will act towards

---

[2] See the comments by B. K. Waltke, *TWOT*, 1, p. 100.

the righteous! He himself is righteous and he loves justice, i.e. the righteous deeds done by his people. The phrase 'loves justice' could mean that God loves to do righteous deeds, but this is less likely in the context. The final outcome is that the upright in heart will see God's presence manifested in his saving deliverance of them. It is possible that the vision of God here is the ultimate vision of him that every believer will have after death (see the two important passages for this concept, Psalm 17:15; Job 19:26-27). The psalmist returns at the end of the psalm to the same confession he made at the beginning.

Psalm 12

For the director of music. According to sheminith.
A psalm of David.

Psalms like this one show us the contrasts in spiritual life within Israel. So many had turned away from obedience to the Lord that it seemed that the godly had disappeared altogether. Psalm 120 is similar in that it depicts the godly living within Israel as though they were among barbarians. The other contrast in the psalm is between the lying words of the ungodly and the sure words of the Lord. The word *sheminith* has already occurred in the title of Psalm 6 (see comment).

1. The Vain Speech of the Ungodly (*vv. 1-4*)

Help, Lord, for the godly are no more; the faithful have vanished from among men (*v. 1*). The opening word is a cry of desperation. The Hebrew word used (*hôshîʿâh*) is normally followed by an object: 'help *me*.' Here, and also in the Hebrew text of Psalm 118:25, the shout is never finished. It is like a drowning person calling out, 'Help.' The Hebrew verb is the one from which the names Joshua and Jesus come. The urgency of the request concerns the apparent disappearance of the faithful from the land. They are described by use of the words for covenantal loyalty (Heb., *châsîd*) and faithful (Heb., *ʾemûnîm*; cf. the fanatical Israeli group *Gush Emunim, assembly of the faithful*). The spiritual division of society into two contrasting groups was recognised later by Elijah (1 Kings 19:9-18), and manifested particularly in Jesus' rejection by his own (John 1:10-11).

Everyone lies to his neighbour; their flattering lips speak with deception (*v. 2*). Life was marked by deceit, so that everyone spoke against his neighbour. No society or church fellowship can continue if this is the case (cf. Eph. 4:25). With double hearts (Heb., *a heart and [still another] heart*) they spoke, so that their words did not agree with reality.

May the LORD cut off all flattering lips and every boastful tongue that says, 'We will triumph with our tongues; we own our lips – who is our master?' (*vv. 3-4*). The psalmist adds to his cry for help (v. 1) an appeal for the LORD to intervene by cutting off all deceivers and those who boast in their arrogance. The verb 'cut off' goes back to the threat in Genesis 17:14 that any unfaithful covenantal person will be 'cut off'. Rather than cutting a covenant with the LORD, they will be cut off, i.e. executed. The fact that synonyms include 'die' and 'be destroyed' confirms that this is the meaning of the term. These people are described further as proud boasters.[1] Their lips are at their service and they challenge anyone to prevail against them. Later, the prophets had to rebuke the people for the sins of the tongue (Hos. 4:1-2; Jer. 12:6), while the New Testament reaffirms how the tongue is a fire, corrupting the whole person (James 3:6).

2. The Sure Speech of the LORD (*vv. 5-8*)

'Because of the oppression of the weak and the groaning of the needy, I will now arise,' says the LORD. 'I will protect them from those who malign them' (*v. 5*). Prayer was made and speedily answered. No indication is given of how the LORD's words came to the psalmist. It could have been by the ministry of a priest, just as Eli ministered God's word to Hannah (1 Sam. 1:17). The answer is more direct than English translations are able to convey. The cry of help in verse 1 (*hôshî'âh*) is followed now by an assurance that the LORD is going to bring salvation (*yêsha'*, from the same root, *yâsha'*) for him. God hears the cry of the weak and needy and arises

---

[1] The NIV alternative reading, 'our lips are our ploughshares', is based on a suggestion by Dahood that instead of reading *'ittânû* ('with us'), *'ittênû* ('our ploughshares') should be the emended vocalisation. For Dahood's viewpoint, see his *Psalms I: 1-50*, pp. 73-74. However, the MT text, 'our lips are with us', makes good sense and it should be retained.

to help (cf. Pss. 7:6; 9:19; Isa. 33:10). He is the deliverer of the oppressed (Pss. 72:12; 103:6).

The second part of verse 5 is uncertain. The Hebrew text says, 'I will bring (lit. set, put) salvation to him who puffs for it.' Various attempts have been made to emend the text but without any certainty. Most probably, the meaning is that God will provide deliverance to those who pant with intense desire for it. The NASB rendering is good: 'I will set him in the safety for which he longs', or the NLT, 'Now I will rise up to rescue them as they have longed for me to do'.[2]

And the words of the LORD are flawless, like silver refined in a furnace of clay, purified seven times (*v. 6*). The contrast with the words of the deceivers is so clear. The LORD's words are pure, i.e. they have been purified like silver in the furnace, and so they stand forever (cf. the use of the same expression for the law of the LORD in 19:9). The reference to 'seven times' simply denotes the completeness of the process. The LORD's words contain no dross, and so can be relied upon. The implication is that the words of the deceivers are all dross!

O LORD, you will keep us safe and protect us from such people forever (*v. 7*). The message from the LORD has brought reassurance to the psalmist. In the MT text the two verbs in this verse have different suffixes. 'Keep us safe' has a third person masculine plural suffix ('keep *them* safe'), while 'protect' has a first person plural suffix ('protect *us*'). The early versions and a number of Hebrew manuscripts make both first person plural, and this is the way in which most English versions render the verse. Protection will be provided from 'such people' (the Hebrew has 'from this generation'; cf. Jesus' words in Matt. 17:17, 'O unbelieving and perverse generation'). 'Generation' is used in the broad sense of a type of people who share the same mindset, a group bound together by common interests.

---

[2] P. C. Craigie, *Psalms 1-50*, p. 136, chooses to follow the lead of the LXX and Syriac and renders: 'I shall appear in radiance to him', though he admits that 'the emendation is by no means certain'. For suggestions that appeal to Ugaritic, see D. Pardee, '*Ypḥ*, "Witness in Hebrew and Ugaritic', *VT* 28 (1978), pp. 204-13, and P. D. Miller Jr., '*Yâpîah* in Psalm XII 6', *VT* 29 (1979), pp. 495-501.

The wicked freely strut about when what is vile is honoured among men (*v. 8*). The psalm returns in its conclusion to its opening ideas. The ungodly are still parading around and 'among men' (*b^e^nê 'âdâm,* repeated from verse 1) and what is vile is still highly regarded. The end of the psalm is a reminder that believers have to persevere in prayer, even as wickedness continues or even abounds. Our pattern has to be that of Jesus who suffered at the hands of liars (John 8:44-47) and who 'offered up prayers and petitions with loud cries and tears to the one who could save him from death, and he was heard because of his reverent submission' (Heb. 5:7).

Psalm 13

For the director of music. A Psalm of David.

This short psalm has all the characteristics and structure of a lament or appeal for help. It moves from the desolation of the opening verses, with the sense of God's abandonment, to the strong confidence in his abiding mercy in the closing ones. Like other similar psalms no clue is offered as to the reason for the abrupt change in mind and heart (cf. comments on Psalm 6:8-10). The content of the psalm reminds the reader that as many as the LORD loves he rebukes and chastens (Rev. 3:19), and a sense of desolation does not necessarily mean that God has removed from them his favour and steadfast love.

1. A Cry of Distress (*vv. 1-2*)

How long, O LORD? Will you forget me forever? How long will you hide your face from me? How long must I wrestle with my thoughts and every day have sorrow in my heart? How long will my enemy triumph over me? (vv. 1-2). The fourfold cry, 'How long?' dominates the opening stanzas. The psalmist feels himself forgotten by God, and even suggests that God does not remember him as his covenantal servant. While the NIV translation of the Hebrew word *nétsach* as 'forever' is possible, yet it appears here without a preposition such as *l*ᵉ or *ʿad*. In some instances it can be used as a superlative, 'utterly', and this makes excellent sense here: 'Will you utterly forget me?'[1] The thought of 'forever' is alien to the context, as the concluding section of the psalm shows. 'How long?' is a phrase of urgency, even of desperation. God can reach

[1] For this meaning, see *DCH*, V, pp. 739-40.

the end of divine endurance as he did with Israel: 'How long will these people treat me with contempt? How long will they refuse to believe in me, in spite of all the miraculous signs I have performed among them? I will strike them down with a plague and destroy them ...' When Moses pleaded God's covenantal mercy he relented and forgave the people (Num. 14:10-25). Here we have the same link made between 'How long?' and God's covenantal mercy (v. 5). The personal feelings that predominate in a situation like this are inward thoughts. These thoughts may be of sorrow, yet the word used here (*ʿêtsâh*) is not the normal word for 'thoughts' but rather for 'plans' or 'advice'. The idea may be that the psalmist, in his hour of need, is thinking up possible ways to escape from his difficulties and evade his tormentors. Sorrowful thoughts occur all the time as the psalmist faces his foes, that seemingly include illness and death (see verse 3). He is faced with a continuous battle as his enemies rise up against him.

2. A Plea to the LORD (*vv. 3-4*)

Look on me and answer, O LORD my God. Give light to my eyes, or I will sleep in death; my enemy will say, 'I have overcome him,' and my foes will rejoice when I fall (*vv. 3-4*). In his opening lament the psalmist has spoken of God hiding his face (v. 1). Now his plea is for the LORD to 'look' (i.e. to consider, scrutinise) and to answer his questions. Illness is understood as a darkening of the eyes. Hence the psalmist prays for light to dawn on him so that he will not experience death. There is a tender note in the way he makes his plea. He says, 'O LORD *my* God.' The pronoun 'my' injects an affectionate aspect into the prayer and also a note of believing confidence. Those who approach God in prayer 'must believe that he exists and that he rewards those who earnestly seek him' (Heb. 11:6). The metaphor of death as sleep developed in many languages because of the similarities between a dead person and one who is sleeping. Here the psalmist prays that God will let his eyes see ('give light to my eyes') lest he sleep in death. If his God does not answer him he will die, and all his foes will then take joy in gloating over what has happened to him (cf. Ps. 38:16). They will claim that they have prevailed and rejoice in his downfall.

3. A Certain Confidence (*vv. 5-6*)

A marked difference exists between the psalmist's foes and himself, and the opening of verse 5 sets them over against each other. **But I,** he says, **trust in your unfailing love; my heart rejoices in your salvation. I will sing to the LORD, for he has been good to me** (*vv. 5-6*). His confidence is in the covenantal love of the LORD that expresses itself in his deliverance. This is one of the passages in the Old Testament in which 'unfailing love' (*chésed*) is parallel with 'salvation' (*y^eshû^ʿâh*). If a distinction is to be made between them, then 'unfailing love' is displayed in God's acts of 'salvation'.[2] Hence the psalmist can overflow with loving praise and he asks God to let his heart rejoice when that salvation appears. This understanding of verse 5 (that his deliverance is yet in the future) is confirmed by the Hebrew idiom in the final verse, which means that he will sing praise 'as soon as he has dealt bountifully with me'. Deliverance, though yet to come, is acknowledged and praised in believing trust. Believers can always look forward in anticipation of God's deliverances, and they can be filled with 'an inexpressible and glorious joy' as they await on the return of Christ the ultimate salvation of their souls (1 Pet. 1:8-9).

---

[2] See Gordon R. Clark, *The Word Hesed in the Hebrew Bible* (Sheffield: JSOT Press, 1993), pp. 156-58. He makes the further point that while God's people experienced and were aware of both 'unfailing love' and 'salvation', the Gentile nations only saw the demonstration of 'salvation'.

Psalm 14

For the director of music. Of David.

Psalms 14 and 53, while not exactly identical, are so close that one is basically a replica of the other. The main differences lie in the use of divine names (Ps. 14 uses Lord [*yhwh*] four times; Ps. 53 consistently uses God, [*ʾelohîm*]), the addition of a title to Psalm 53, slight verbal differences in the opening verses, and more major differences in the closing verses (Ps. 14:5-6 = Ps. 53:5). The verbal changes in general involve the change of a common word for a more unusual one, though no indication exists in the text as to the reason behind the changes.[1] Most probably Psalm 14 is the earlier version, but the importance of its teaching must have been recognised and an alternative version used as well in worship. Finally, both forms were incorporated into the present Psalter.

The content of Psalm 14 is very similar to Psalm 12, for while speaking of universal sinfulness, both also contrast the way of the wicked with the way of the righteous. Further amplification is given of the condition of 'the sons of men' (see references in psalms that immediately precede: 11:4, 12:1, 8), and the repetition of the phrase 'there is no-one who does good' (v. 1) in verse 4, with the additional phrase, 'not even one', highlights human depravity.

The style of the psalm is closest to Psalms 1 and 2, or to the wisdom literature, especially illustrated by the Book of

[1] There is a good note in E. W. Hengstenberg, *Commentary on the Psalms*, I, pp. 205-07, on the differences between Psalms 14 and 53. He argues that 'these alterations (with the exception of the "all" in ver. 4) have all the same character, – everywhere, in Ps. liii., is the rare, the uncommon, the strong, and the elevated, substituted for the common and the simple' (p. 205).

Proverbs. Psalm 14 is not concerned with intellectual atheism. Its focus is rather on the person who is a practical atheist because he has renounced the covenant and therefore the covenantal God. The New Testament points more fully than the Old Testament to the ultimate wisdom of God which is found in Jesus Christ (1 Cor. 1:23-25).

1. A Description of the Fool (*vv. 1-3*)

The fool says in his heart, 'There is no God'. They are corrupt, their deeds are vile; there is no one who does good (*v. 1*). The Hebrew word for fool or folly (*nâvâl*) marked out those who had renounced their allegiance to the covenantal God and consequently to one another. It was used, for example, of the nation in Isaiah 9:15-17, and English expressions like 'outcast' or 'sacrilegious person' may convey better the meaning.[2] The fool lacks the wisdom with which the fear of the LORD begins. He not only says but lives as if 'there is no God'.

The second part of verse 1 clearly shows the normal character of such fools. Their actions are corrupt and an abomination to the LORD. They do not do what is good. This may imply more than general goodness, and specifically, failure to follow covenantal commitments.

The LORD looks down from heaven on the sons of men to see if there are any who understand, any who seek God. All have turned aside, they have together become corrupt; there is no one who does good, not even one (*vv. 2-3*). An anthropomorphic description (one in terms of human characteristics) is given of God's actions to emphasise how he sees all people. He looks out for those who 'understand' (*maskîl*). The Hebrew word stands in contrast to 'fool' in verse 1, and is a synonym for 'wise', 'spiritually understanding'. Another expression for the godly is used at the end of verse 2. They 'seek God,' i.e. they approach the face of God in prayer.

The divine verdict is given in verse 3. The godless, far from seeking God, have turned aside and they have become corrupt. The words, 'there is no one who does good,' are repeated from verse 1, with the addition of the emphatic,

[2] See *DCH*, V, pp. 593-94.

'not even one'. Almost certainly there is an allusion here to Genesis 6:5-12, where the account is given of how God looked on the earth and saw how great was the corruption, 'for all the people on earth had corrupted their ways' (Gen. 6:12). While different verbs meaning 'to see' are used, the same verb for 'to be corrupted' (*shâchat*, Hi.) occurs in both passages, and also the extent of the corruption (Gen. 6:12, *kol-bâsâr*; Ps. 14:3, *hakkol*) is stated in similar terms. Paul takes over words from verses 2 and 3 to give further confirmation to his assertion that none are righteous before God (Rom. 3:10-12). In the course of time the passage in Romans 3:10-18 was included in the text of the LXX in Psalm 14, and even appears in some Hebrew manuscripts, having been translated into Hebrew.

2. The Oppression of the Righteous (*vv. 4-6*)

Will evildoers never learn—those who devour my people as men eat bread and who do not call on the LORD? (*v. 4*). It becomes clear that not everyone has turned aside from the LORD, for there are those whom the psalmist can call 'my people'. They are the objects of oppression on the part of 'fools', or, as they are called here, 'evildoers'. Their problem is that they do not have spiritual knowledge, or more specifically, they do not understand their responsibility to their covenantal lord.[3] As a consequence they have spurned him and this shows in that they 'do not call on the LORD'. This last phrase can be used in the Old Testament in the sense of proclaiming the LORD (cf. what God himself did for Moses, Exod. 33:19), but it also means, as here, to use God's name in prayer (Gen. 4:26). The character of the righteous is such that they depend upon God and his grace, and demonstrate it by their prayerful attitude.

There they are, overwhelmed with dread, for God is present in the company of the righteous. You evildoers frustrate the plans of the poor, but the LORD is their refuge (*vv. 5-6*). These are difficult verses to interpret. In both of them

[3] For the argument that the verb 'know' (Heb., *yâdaʿ*) has covenantal connotations, see H. B. Huffmon, 'The Treaty Background on Hebrew YADA', *BASOR* 181, pp. 31-37.

there is a contrast between the evildoers in the first part of the verse, and the righteous in the second. There does not seem to be any direct connection between the two clauses other than direct contrast. The evildoers live in fear as a result of their folly (lit. 'they feared a fear'),[4] and they oppress the poor. On the other hand, the righteous have God in their midst, in their assembly.[5] They also have the assurance that while they are being oppressed, the LORD is their refuge.

3. A Prayer for Deliverance (*v. 7*)

Oh, that salvation for Israel would come out of Zion! When the LORD restores the fortunes of his people, let Jacob rejoice and Israel be glad! (v. 7). The psalmist longs for the coming salvation of the LORD. Clearly the psalm dates from a time when Zion was the religious centre (i.e. after David's bringing of the ark there). The words 'restoring the fortunes' need not be a reference to the pending return from exile. Rather, the Hebrew phrase (lit. *restores the captivity*) can be taken in a general way as speaking of a real change in the people's circumstances. Salvation would come from the LORD. Every saving action of God in the Old Testament was a precursor of the far fuller salvation that Jesus would bring. It is not surprising that the psalm ends on a note of joy, for salvation brings forth a song from the people of God. When the ultimate redemption is completed, a great multitude will sing: 'Salvation belongs to our God who sits on the throne, and to the Lamb' (Rev. 7:10).

---

[4] For this usage, called a cognate accusative, see *GKC* §117p. The effect of this is to strengthen the idea of the verb.

[5] Hebrew has two words that are identical in orthography and pronunciation (*dôr*), one meaning 'generation' and the other 'assembly'. The NIV rendering is preferable here, especially since the word is preceded by the preposition 'in' (*b^{e}dôr*). Cf. ESV, 'with the generation of the righteous'. See *DCH*, II, p. 430.

Psalm 15

A psalm of David.

Psalm 15 and Psalm 24 have much in common. They both ask about coming into the presence of the LORD at his holy hill, and they both answer in a similar way. The character of the godly worshipper is set out clearly. Both psalms probably originated with the removal of the ark of the covenant to Jerusalem by David (2 Sam. 6). It is possible that the opening questions were asked by the worshippers as they approached the sanctuary, and then the priests answered with the appropriate responses that specify the character of true worshippers.

The concerns in the opening part of this psalm are reflected elsewhere in the Old Testament. Passages such as Jeremiah 7:1-7 and Ezekiel 18:5-9 show that the prophets expressed the same requirements on worshippers as the psalmists (see especially the reference in Jeremiah 7:2 to entering into the gates of the LORD's house). The closest parallel, however, to Psalm 15:1 is Isaiah 33:14-16, where the questions bear a close resemblance: 'Who of us can dwell with the consuming fire? Who of us can dwell with everlasting burning?' Both verbs for 'dwell' used in the opening questions in the psalm (*gûr* and *shâkan*) occur in Isaiah 33:14, 16, while the answer given mentions six characteristics: righteous walk, upright speech, no extortion, no bribes, no participation in plotting murder, and rejection of planned evil deeds. The general principle being stated in all these passages is that personal character will determine one's destiny. It is not the person who says 'Lord, Lord' who will enter the kingdom of heaven, but the one who does God's will (Matt. 7:21-23).

1. The Question Asked (*v. 1*)

LORD, who may dwell in your sanctuary? Who may live on your holy hill? The two clauses are clearly used in parallel with one another. Two different verbs are used ('dwell', 'live') and two different descriptions of God's dwelling place are given ('sanctuary', 'holy hill'). The Hebrew word for 'sanctuary' is *ʾōhel*, 'tent', which, while strictly the outer covering of the 'tabernacle' (*mishkân*), is often used as synonymous with it. The mountain of the LORD has been spoken of in the Song of Moses (Exod. 15:17). When David captured Mount Zion (2 Sam. 5:7) he took up residence there and made it the dwelling place for the ark of the LORD. From that point onwards there was never any question as to where the central place of worship should be. The worshipper now asks who can sojourn as the LORD's guest. The verb 'sojourn' (*gûr*) does not only imply temporary dwelling as Psalm 61:4 shows: 'I long to dwell in your tent *for ever*'. To 'live' or 'dwell' (*shâkan*) is a verb used of living in a tent and from it one of the names for the tabernacle was derived (*mishkân*). The principle underlying the tabernacle in the Old Testament came to its fullest expression in Jesus taking upon himself human flesh: 'The Word became flesh and dwelt (lit. 'tabernacled') among us' (John 1:14).

2. The Answers Provided (*vv. 2-5a*)

The answer comes in a pattern of two sets of positive conditions, with two corresponding sets of negative conditions.

Positive	**Negative**
Verse 2a	Verse 3a
Verse 2b	Verse 3b
Verse 2c	Verse 3c

Positive	**Negative**
Verse 4a	Verse 5a
Verse 4b	Verse 5b
Verse 4c	

He whose walk is blameless and who does what is righteous, who speaks the truth from his heart (*v. 2*). The first group of positive conditions does not include sacrificial requirements, nor do any of the others. The concentration is on moral characteristics. The first one, walking blamelessly (*tâmîm*), is virtually a synonym for being godly, and speaks of the wholeness of the person. It is a term that is used of a person's close relationship with the LORD, and is very close in meaning to 'upright' (*yâshâr*) and 'righteous' (*tsâdîq*). The second one starts to be more specific, demanding righteous actions, while the third one asks for truthful speech.

The relationship with the LORD has to be demonstrated in deeds and words ... **and has no slander on his tongue, who does his neighbour no wrong and casts no slur on his fellow man** (*v. 3*). The negative conditions now follow. The first one implies no wrong use of his tongue. Literally it is, 'he has not spied with [or possibly, tripped over] his tongue.' The idea of spying is clearly carried over here in regard to stealthy behaviour in the area of speech. Nor has he done any harm to his neighbour, or made fun of the faults or situations of his friends (or possibly relations). The Hebrew word *qârôv* can refer to nearness (both geographical and temporal), but also for nearness in human relationships (cf. its use in 2 Sam. 19:42 [Heb. 43]).[1]

... **who despises a vile man but honours those who fear the LORD, who keeps his oath even when it hurts,** (*v. 4*). The second set of positive conditions included honouring those who fear God and despising those who are rejected by God. The NIV 'vile man' is too weak a translation of the Hebrew word *nimʾâs* (Ni. part. of *mâʾas*). Something closer to 'rejected' or 'reprobate' is needed. 'The fear of the Lord' is a standard Old Testament expression, occurring twenty-one times, mostly in wisdom literature. It is a multifaceted concept, but in passages such as this it designates those who walk uprightly. This group in Israel comprised those who served the LORD with devotion and formed part of the worshipping community (cf. its use in parallel with *qâhâl râv,*

[1] The use of this word in Isa. 33:13 provides another link between that context and Ps. 15.

'great congregation', in Psalm 22:25).[2] Thus spiritual attitudes are important in the worshipper. The third condition in this verse is difficult to translate and interpret. The NIV rendering is one possibility. It could also mean 'he has sworn to do no wrong and does not alter', i.e. he keeps his pledged word without any change.

... who lends his money without usury and does not accept a bribe against the innocent (*v. 5a*). The final two conditions are negative and both relate to money. They are activities that strike at the very heart of societal life. It was forbidden for an Israelite to lend with interest to a fellow Israelite (Lev. 25:36-37; Deut. 23:19). It was, however, permissible to lend with interest to a foreigner (Deut. 23:20). To take interest from a fellow Israelite who was in financial difficulties would only compound the situation. Just as God had shown mercy and compassion to his people, so they in turn had to act compassionately to those in need (see Lev. 25:35-37). Also, no bribe could be taken to ensure the conviction of the innocent (cf. Exod. 23:8; Deut. 16:19). Perverted justice was no justice at all. The exemplar for true justice was God himself, 'the righteous judge' (Pss. 7:11; 67:4). Passages in the prophetical books such as Isaiah 33:14-16 and Micah 6:6-8 may well be building upon these conditions given in verses 2-5a.

3. The Promise (v. 5b)

He who does these things will never be shaken. The final word in the psalm is one of reassurance. The person who fulfils its conditions will not be moved, i.e. be removed from the house of the LORD and from the LORD's presence. The answer to the opening question in verse 1 in effect is: 'Whoever does these things shall dwell in his sanctuary for ever'.

---

[2] 'The fear of the LORD' has two dimensions to it. On the one hand, there is a vertical dimension involving both general and special revelation. On the other hand, there is a horizontal dimension involving emotional responses as diverse as awe and love. See the discussion by Bruce Waltke, 'The Fear of the Lord: The Foundation for a Relationship with God', in J. I. Packer and L. Wilkinson, *Alive to God: Studies in Spirituality presented to James Houston* (Downers Grove: Inter-Varsity Press, 1992), pp. 17-33. Other full discussions are provided by John Murray, *Principles of Conduct: Aspects of Biblical Ethics* (London: Tyndale Press, 1957), pp. 229-42, and Henri Blocher, 'The Fear of the Lord as the "Principle" of Wisdom', *TB* 28 (1977), pp. 3-28.

Psalm 16

A miktam of David.

The title attributes the psalm to David, and both Peter and Paul in the New Testament confirm this (Acts 2:25-32; 13:36). The word *miktâm* occurs here and in the titles of five other psalms (56, 57, 58, 59, 60). Only here and in Psalm 58 is there omission of details linking this particular psalm with incidents in David's life. The explanations of *miktâm* vary. Some have thought that it is a musical term whose meaning is now lost. In rabbinical sources the most common explanation was that it was formed by a prefix *mi-* together with the word *kétem*, 'gold', and meant a golden piece or one artistic in form or character. The oldest interpretation is that of the LXX, which translated it as *stêlographia*, an inscription on a pillar or monument. This is assuming that it comes from a verb meaning 'to inscribe', and therefore a *miktâm* is a song that is to be inscribed on a tablet or some similar surface.[1]

This is a song of confidence. While the psalm commences with a cry for help, it is quickly silenced by the sense of God's favour and the hope to which he looks forward. The psalm was probably written while David was an outlaw, when he was alienated from his property and exposed to false gods.

[1] *DCH*, V, p. 276, identifies this tentatively as designating a particular type or kind of psalm, especially in relation to writing on a tablet. Some want to read *miktâm* in the heading of Hezekiah's song in Isaiah 38:9, but the manuscript evidence overwhelmingly supports the reading *miktâv*, 'writing'. This heading is unique in the Old Testament in that it is the only case in which a poem within a *narrative* section has such a heading. See my discussion in *Isaiah: A Covenant to be Kept for the Sake of the Church* (Fearn: Christian Focus Publications, 2005), pp. 256-57.

He repudiates the thought of yielding allegiance to such gods, for his trust is firmly placed in Israel's Saviour.

The most difficult part of the psalm is verses 2-4a. Several perplexing points of translation have to be faced, and also the place of this section within the psalm as a whole.

1. An Opening Prayer (*v. 1*)

Keep me safe, O God, for in you I take refuge. As no details are given of any particular crisis in David's life it is best to take this appeal at the beginning of the psalm to be for God's continuing protection. Those who have already experienced this protection know how to pray, for, like David, they have taken refuge in him. This request is a favourite with him (see Pss. 7:1 and 11:1). The New Testament expands this concept. The Lord Jesus prayed that the believing community given to him should be 'kept' (John 17:11), while the assurance is given that the believer is 'preserved in Christ Jesus' (Jude 1).

2. The Words of an Idol Worshipper (*vv. 2-4a*)

I said to the LORD, 'You are my Lord; apart from you I have no good thing'. As for the saints who are in the land, they are the glorious ones in whom is all my delight. The sorrows of those will increase who run after other gods. There are problems in giving a good English translation of these verses and fitting them satisfactorily into the psalm as a whole.[2] The verb at the beginning of verse 2 is not first person singular (as given in the NIV, '*I* said'), but second person singular ('*you* (fem.) said').[3] The following comments assume that the words are those of an idol worshipper who claimed allegiance to the LORD but who followed other gods. He tried to maintain a

[2] The note in A. F. Kirkpatrick, *The Book of Psalms*, pp. 74-75 remains an excellent summary of different approaches to these verses, supplemented by the footnotes in *BHS*, p. 1097. See also R. Bratcher and W. Reyburn, *A Translator's Handbook to the Book of Psalms* (New York: UBS, 1991), p. 140-41.

[3] Though many manuscripts do have *'âmartî*, 'I said', the harder reading is *'âmart*, 'you (fem. sing.) said'. The object addressed has then to be 'my soul' (as expressly supplied in Pss. 42:6 and 43:5). This would result in a translation very near to the NIV rendering. If the MT consonantal text is retained but the vocalisation changed to *'âmartâ*, then the verb is 2nd pers. masc., 'you (m.) have said'.

spoken commitment to the Lord ('my Lord') and a claim that all his goodness was to be found in him ('apart from you I have no good thing'). However, the reality was that he followed foreign gods, calling them in verse 3 'holy ones' and 'mighty ones'. Because of the parallelism between 'to the Lord' and 'to the holy ones', it is best to assume that the verb 'to say' is understood at the commencement of verse 3: '[You have said] to the holy ones'.[4] His real pleasure was solely in these heathen deities. The psalmist gives his verdict on all those who follow this example (v. 4a). The word rendered 'run' in the NIV is better taken as meaning 'acquire' or 'exchange' (cf. Ps. 106:20; Jer. 2:11).[5] Those who exchange the true God for idols will always increase their sorrows. This may be an allusion to the fertility rites practised in the heathen religions (cf. Isa. 57:7-8).

3. A Song of Confidence (*vv. 4b-6*)

I will not pour out their libations of blood or take up their names on my lips (*v. 4b*). Heathen worship holds no attraction for a true believer. David says emphatically that he will not share in their false sacrifices, nor even take their names on his lips. He will shun any association that might link him with such false beliefs.

Lord, you have assigned me my portion and my cup; you have made my lot secure. The boundary lines have fallen for me in pleasant places; surely I have a delightful inheritance (*vv. 5-6*). Here is the reaffirmation of the blessings that the Lord had given him, and which stand in such contrast to the sorrows that the idol worshipper experiences (v. 4a). 'Portion and cup' refers to the overflowing bounty that God had given him. The imagery is related to that concerning God's provision for the Levites (Num. 18:20; Deut. 10:9; 18:1-2). His allocated territory was certain, and the places where the lines had been marked for him were pleasant. He is not speaking

---

[4] This is the viewpoint of P. C. Craigie, *Psalms 1-50*, p. 155.

[5] See *DCH*, V, p. 167. While there is evidence pointing to a verb *mâhâr*, 'to acquire', there is none confirming the suggestion in *DCH*, that this may be a verb 'to serve'.

of an earthly inheritance, such as the tribes received, but of God's gift of himself.

3. The Reward of Confidence (*vv. 7-11*)

The psalmist breaks into a song of thanksgiving for the wisdom that has come to him from the LORD. **I will praise the LORD, who counsels me; even at night my heart instructs me. I have set the LORD always before me. Because he is at my right hand, I will not be shaken** (*vv. 7-8*). The NIV rendering 'praise' is an unnecessary alteration as the Hebrew verb is 'to bless' (*ʾavârêk*, 'I will bless'), though in this type of context 'bless', with God as the object, is not significantly different from the verb 'to praise' (*hâlal* Pi.). 'At night time' (or possibly the plural form in Hebrew, *lêlôt*, denotes dark nights) he considers and meditates on this instruction. True meditation is never with a blank mind, but is based on God's revealed word. 'Heart' is literally the kidneys, which the Hebrew people considered as the seat of the emotions.

Verse 8 gives further expression to the thought of refuge in verse 1. The LORD is always before his eyes, and he is ever at his right hand. There is no 'he' in the MT, but the context demands that 'the LORD' continues as the subject. The right hand is the position that is mentioned as the place of the helper (Pss. 109:31; 121:5). Because the LORD is with him, he knows assuredly that he will not be moved.

Safety with the LORD produces a further song of praise from David. **Therefore my heart is glad and my tongue rejoices; my body also will rest secure, because you will not abandon me to the grave, nor will you let your Holy One see decay** (*vv. 9-10*). Various synonyms, for 'I' (in addition to 'kidneys' in the previous verse) appear in these verses: 'my heart', 'my glory' (the NIV follows the LXX text and reads 'my tongue'),[6] 'my flesh', and 'my soul' (NIV 'me'). David is not separating soul from body, but simply indicating that the whole person

[6] Though the LXX has *hê glôssa mou* ('my tongue'), no Hebrew text has this reading. A different suggestion, that *kevôdî*, 'my glory', be revocalised as *kevêdî*, 'my liver', has greater merit, as this would add 'liver' to the accumulation of references to bodily parts. See R. L. Harris in *TWOT*, 1, p. 427.

is living securely. The verbs in this verse are awkward (the first, a perfect; the second, a *vav* consecutive; the third, an imperfect), but in the context the NIV rendering is perfectly legitimate.[7] Verse 10 occupies a special place in biblical thought because it is quoted in reference to Jesus' resurrection. David is asserting that the LORD will not abandon his life to Sheol, nor let his faithful one (i.e. David) see corruption. He knows that his prayer of verse 1 ('help me') is answered and that he will not die, or alternatively, that he will be preserved from a premature death. But David also speaks prophetically by the Holy Spirit and looks to the resurrection of the Messiah. His eye is on one of his descendants (see Acts. 2:27) and his words have a far deeper meaning than the surface reading of them would suggest. They pointed to the fact that the Christ would not be abandoned in the grave nor his body see corruption (Acts 2:31).

You have made known to me the path of life; you will fill me with joy in your presence, with eternal pleasures at your right hand (*v. 11*). This final verse uses words and ideas already employed earlier in the psalm ('make known', 'life', 'joy', 'your presence', 'pleasure', 'evermore'). He wants to experience God's leading in the path through life (cf. 'the path of the righteous', Prov. 4:18; and 'the path of peace', Luke 1:79). Fullness of joy is to be found where the LORD reveals his presence (cf. Pss. 4:7; 21:6), and the pleasant places and things (see v. 6) from the LORD's hand will last right through life. Hence 'lasting pleasures' would be a preferable translation to the NIV's 'eternal pleasures'.

---

[7] Two Hebrew manuscripts read the impf. *yismach* instead of *sâmach* in the opening clause, but this seems to be an attempt to conform the text to what was perceived as the more normal verbal aspect.

Psalm 17

A prayer of David.

A psalm such as this shows how strongly the covenantal hope supported troubled and persecuted believers in the Old Testament period. The psalmist calls on God and asks for a further display of covenantal mercy, such as God showed in acts of deliverance at the time of the Exodus. There is dependence upon words from the Song of the Sea (Exod. 15:1-18) and also from the Song of Moses (Deut. 32). There are also many points of connection between Psalms 16 and 17. Some of these are: the prayer, 'keep me' (16:1; 17:8); communion with God at night (16:7; 17:3); the use of the Hebrew word *'ēl* for God in prayer (16:1; 17:6); the reference to the right hand of God (16:8; 17:7, 14); and the pleasures of God's presence (16:11; 17:15). The two psalms may well form a pair composed near the end of David's life.

1. A Prayer from an Innocent Person (*vv. 1-5*)

Hear, O Lord, my righteous plea; listen to my cry. Give ear to my prayer – it does not rise from deceitful lips. May my vindication come from you; may your eyes see what is right (*vv. 1-2*). The request that David makes is given in three forms: 'hear', 'listen', and 'give ear'. Likewise his description of his plea is threefold: '[my] righteous [plea]'; 'my cry'; and 'my prayer'. The varied language draws attention immediately to the intensity of his requests and the deep need in which he found himself. He disclaims any deceitfulness on his part. This type of protestation of innocence is common to the Psalter (cf. 18:20-24; 26:1). These should not be understood as self-righteous claims to sinless perfection. They are affirmations that the writers were essentially devoted to God, that they were innocent of the slanderous accusations of their enemies, and hence they were worthy of God's protection. The psalmist knows that right judgment will come from the LORD[1] and he is quite prepared to leave his life open before his all-seeing eye. He is willing to have sentence passed by his judge.

Though you probe my heart and examine me at night, though you test me, you will find nothing; I have resolved that my mouth will not sin (*v.* 3). David claims that all of God's testing, however probing it may be (two of the terms, 'probe' [*bâchan*] and 'test' [*tsâraf*], are from metallurgy), will find no dross in his life. He knew the dangers of the sins of the tongue, as he was the victim of accusations. Yet he set himself to refrain from transgressing with his mouth. The final clause in the verse has received various explanations, though the overall meaning is clear enough.[2]

As for the deeds of men – by the word of your lips I have kept myself from the ways of the violent. My steps have held to your paths; my feet have not slipped (*vv.* 4-5). The psalmist isolates himself from the wicked for, in contrast to them, he has kept to God's word and his steps have followed his paths. Attention to the divine revelation has kept him in a right way. His enemies were clearly violent in action as well as in word. By following God's directions he had shunned their way of life and had not deviated from God's paths. The idea of following certain paths is often tied in with the concept of the feet slipping (for examples, see Pss. 38:16; 94:18). When the verb 'to slip' is preceded by a negative, it conveys the idea of absolute certainly and dependability.

---

[1] The Hebrew word *mishpât* has many nuances, but most common is the use here to denote a judgment issued by a court, or by God as the great judge over all. While the translation 'judgment' would have been acceptable, yet the NIV 'vindication' respects the context where the idea of a favourable judgment is present.

[2] The MT has the word *zammotî*, which seems to be an irregular inf. of the verb *zâmam*, plus suff. 1 sing. This gives a translation: 'my thoughts do not extend beyond my mouth'. The NIV follows the LXX which presupposes a verbal form *zimmâtî*, 'I have determined'.

2. A Fresh Appeal in the Face of Danger (*vv. 6-12*)
From pressing dangers the psalmist turns again to God. **I call on you, O God, for you will answer me; give ear to me and hear my prayer** (*v. 6*). The 'I' with which this verse begins is emphatic. He has just described himself in the previous verses and he now calls urgently to his God, whom he knows will answer. Many times the psalmists refer to calling upon God, and then receiving answers. God also invites his people to call on him, and promises an answer (Ps. 91:15). Certainty about this encourages expectancy. The second half of the verse is virtually an abbreviated form of verse 1. 'Give ear to me' corresponds to 'give ear to my prayer', while 'hear my prayer' is parallel to 'hear ... my righteous plea'.

Show the wonder of your great love, you who save by your right hand those who take refuge in you from their foes. Keep me as the apple of your eye; hide me in the shadow of your wings from the wicked who assail me, from my mortal enemies who surround me (*vv. 7-9*). The basis of his appeal is the covenantal bond (*chasâdekâ*, 'your gracious acts of commitment'),[3] which he wants to be revealed as wonderful.[4] He longs for a fresh manifestation of God's power and redeeming mercy as was shown during the Exodus. The language here echoes that in the Song of the Sea (Exod. 15:6-7, 11-13). Historical recollection often forms the basis for present prayer in the Psalms. David knew that God saved those who take their refuge in him. The expression 'the LORD's right hand', used three times in the Song of the Sea (vv. 6 [2×] and 12), denotes his omnipotence and power to rescue his people from their enemies. It forms the theme of praise in many psalms (cf. 18:35; 44:3; 48:10; 98:1).

---

[3] The singular, 'your mercy', is more common, but the plural form as in this verse, 'your mercies', does occur (see for example, Pss. 89:2; 107:7; Isa. 63:7). I have tried in the translation above to bring out the force of the plural by using the expression 'gracious acts of commitment', because the appeal is to the great acts of God in redeeming his people.

[4] It is hard to be sure whether the verb that commences this verse is the Hi. of *pâlâh* or *pâlâ'*. NIV deviates from the MT (*hiflêh*, 'treat with distinction'), but is following the well-attested variant verbal form (*haflê'*, 'do wonders'). See P. C. Craigie, *Psalms 1-50*, p. 160.

Allusion to the Exodus continues in verse 8. God found Israel in the wilderness and guarded her as the apple of his eye (Deut. 32:10). The idiom for 'apple of the eye' used there of the people as a whole is taken over here, when an individual Israelite prays for himself. The thought of being protected under the LORD's wings is probably taken from Deuteronomy 32:11, whence the imagery of the eagle is introduced. God provides protection from all the dangers (cf., for use of the idea of God's wings, Pss. 36:7; 57:1; 61:4; 63:7; 91:4). The danger is from enemies (also called 'the wicked') who attack his life. They come against him with murderous intent.

They close up their callous hearts, and their mouths speak with arrogance. They have tracked me down, they now surround me, with eyes alert, to throw me to the ground. They are like a lion hungry for prey, like a great lion crouching in cover (*vv. 10-12*). A fuller description is given of these enemies. They shut up their hearts. The Hebrew text says 'they shut up their fat'. Probably this is another reference to Deuteronomy 32 and specifically to God's Jeshurun (Israel), who grew fat and kicked (Deut. 32:15).[5] The idea of rebelliousness carries over here, for the enemies will not bow before God's majesty and they attack his servant David. He felt surrounded on every side (v. 11) for they were waiting for their chance to overthrow him. The most threatening enemy is singled out in verse 12 (cf. with the use of the plural in verses 10-11), or perhaps the leader of the band. He is likened to a crouching lion which is ready to leap out at his prey from his secret hiding place. The words 'lion' and 'young lion' (not 'great lion' as in NIV) are often used in parallel (see Amos 3:4; Isa. 31:4). It is not surprising that the New Testament depicts the devil as a roaring lion (1 Pet. 5:8).

3. Another Urgent Prayer (*vv. 13-15*)

Rise up, O LORD, confront them, bring them down; rescue me from the wicked by your sword (*v. 13*). The military language,

---

[5] The word 'Jeshurun' only occurs in Deut. 32:15; 33:5, 26, and in Isa. 44:2. It could be a diminutive, 'my little upright one', but no example exists in biblical Hebrew of a diminutive ending in – *un*. As a derivative of the root *yâshar* it probably means to be upright, so marking Israel off from the surrounding nations as the nation to which God's law was given. Cf. Deut. 4:5-8.

already noted in Psalms 3:7; 7:6; 10:12, is again used by David. He appeals with urgency to his divine protector to come as a warrior ('your sword') and subdue his enemy, delivering him from his enemy, rescuing him from his clutches.

O LORD, by your hand save me from such men, from men of this world whose reward is in this life. You still the hunger of those you cherish; their sons have plenty, and they store up wealth for their children (*v. 14*). The enemies are described as being 'men of this world' who will only know rewards in this life. They will know nothing of having the LORD as their portion, which is the condition of the righteous (Ps. 16:5). The New Testament speaks of the same type of people who belong to the world (John 15:19), who are people of this world (Luke 16:8), and whose mind is on earthly things (Phil. 3:19). From such men David seeks rescue by God's hand (cf. the use of 'right hand' in verse 7).

The final part of this verse speaks of God's blessings on his cherished ones. They have plenty to eat, they have many children (taking 'sons' as the object of the verb), and are able even to pass on their superabundance to their children. However, such people may have an abundance of earthly riches, but they are not rich towards God (Luke 12:21).

And I – in righteousness I will see your face; when I awake, I will be satisfied with seeing your likeness (*v. 15*). The contrast with the worldly men of verse 14 is most obvious. Any satisfaction they get has to be in this life. For David, there was the prospect of satisfaction beyond the grave, because he gives us in this verse a glimpse of eternity. The language is similar to that used by Moses when speaking of his relationship with the LORD (Num. 12:8). David grasps something, however tenuous, of a doctrine of resurrection, which is spoken of elsewhere as an awaking from sleep (see Isa. 26:19; Dan. 12:2). The Greek LXX translation clearly read the verse in this way in pre-Christian time for it added the words 'in the vision of your glory'. God's actual presence would then be his joy and satisfaction. It is the pure in heart who will see God (Matt. 5:8).

Psalm 18

For the director of music. Of David the servant of the LORD. He sang to the LORD the words of this song when the LORD delivered him from the hand of all his enemies and from the hand of Saul. He said:

This psalm is tied into historical circumstances both by its title and by the fact that it occurs in a duplicate form in 2 Samuel 22:1-51. Because of its length, as the longest hymn in the Psalter, and also because of questions relating to its parallel in 2 Samuel, several comments need to be made before proceeding to its exegesis.

1. The essential text is the same in the two songs, though there are numerous minor differences. These should not be exaggerated, however, for the general spirit of the two songs remains identical. Numerous discussions already exist noting the differences, with extensive notes on Hebrew vocabulary, grammar and textual questions.[1]

2. In spite of all that has been written on this subject, it is impossible to assert with confidence which is the earlier song, or whether both come from the same author. The two texts confront the reader without sufficient clues to come to definitive answers on questions relating to the origin and transmission of these songs.

3. The heading of both Psalm 18 and 2 Samuel 22 place the songs in a historical context – 'when the LORD delivered him [David] from the hand of all his enemies and from the hand of Saul'. In the texts explicit reference to David only occurs at the end (Ps. 18:50; 2 Sam. 22:51). In 2 Samuel, the song follows an account of Saul's death and then a summary of various

[1] For detailed listing of the variations in the Hebrew text, see F. Delitzsch, *Psalms*, I, pp. 269-78; F. M. Cross and D. N. Freedman, 'A Royal Song of Thanksgiving: 2 Samuel 22 = Psalm 18', *JBL* 72, 1 (1953), pp. 15-34; P. C. Craigie, *Psalms 1-50*, pp. 168-71.

campaigns against the Philistines (2 Sam. 21:15-22). It is quite possible that this song was utilised in celebratory worship after a series of incidents in which David was delivered by the LORD. The real enemy, in any case, was death and the grave (Ps. 18:5-6).

4. In form it is similar to victory songs like Exodus 15:1-18 and Judges 5, though the details of any specific victory are not given. David achieved many victories, and this song seems to be a royal thanksgiving psalm when he looks back on all that the LORD did for him. The pictorial language makes it a graphic description of God's help, and how God preserved David for, and established him in, his kingship.

5. A strong connection exists between this song and that of Hannah (1 Sam. 2:1-10). The central theme of Hannah's song is expanded in this one. Each finishes with reference to the LORD's support of his anointed king. The difference in Psalm 18 is that it post-dates the covenant with David (2 Sam. 7) and hence the reference to David's successors ('to David and his descendants for ever', verse 50).

6. The pattern of the psalm is straightforward. It starts and finishes with reference to God as the rock of Israel (vv. 1-2 and 46-50), having therefore a prologue and an epilogue. The centre of the psalm is composed of two main passages, verses 3-30 and 31-45.

1. An Introductory Song of Praise (*vv. 1-2*)

I love you, O LORD, my strength (*v. 1*). The psalm begins with an unusual verb for 'love' (Hebrew *râcham*, Qal 1 sing.), which in the form used here occurs nowhere else in the Old Testament. While not the most common usage, the verb is applied to a mother's love for her baby (Isa. 49:15), or of a father's love for his children (Ps. 103:13). Much more frequent is another form of the verb (Hebrew Pi.) that occurs over thirty times with God as the subject. David expresses his heartfelt love to the LORD (cf. Ps. 116:1 where the more common verb *'âhav* occurs) and confesses that he is his 'strength', i.e. his strong helper. This is the first of eight titles for God that are clustered together, all with the personal suffix 'my'. This fact points to the faith from which David speaks and of the bond between himself and the LORD.

The LORD is my rock, my fortress and my deliverer; my God is my rock, in whom I take refuge. He is my shield and the horn of my salvation, my stronghold (*v.* 2). The first two titles point to the majesty of God as David's hiding place. He has his refuge in the cliff (Hebrew uses a different word for 'rock' later in the verse) and it is a fortress for him. Linked with those first two titles, the third one could be expected to be 'a place of refuge', but the vowels in the Hebrew text make it the participle 'my deliverer' (Hebrew *m*[e]*falêt* instead of *miflât*). 'Rock' is an old title for God (Deut. 32:4, 15, 18, 31, 37), stressing God's permanence and the security he affords those who trust in him. To call him 'my shield' immediately brings to mind God's words to Abraham (Gen. 15:1), a passage in which Abraham is reassured of God's protection.[2] 'Horn' is descriptive of power in battle (and only here is it a title for God), and finally 'stronghold' completes the list by giving added emphasis to God's protective care for his servant.

2. The Account of God's Salvation (vv. 3-19)

The two major sections of the psalm are introduced with a note of praise that is in essence a summary of their main theme (vv. 3 and 30).

a) *Praise for Redeeming Grace* (*v.* 3) **I call to the LORD, who is worthy of praise, and I am saved from my enemies.** God is worthy of praise (the Hebrew word, *m*[e]*hullâl*, comes from the same root as 'Hallelujah'), and David expresses his settled conviction that he can call on God and he will answer. He knows, and what follows in this psalm is a testimony to the fact, that God can save him from his enemies.

---

[2] It is possible that the Hebrew consonants in this word 'shield' (*m-g-n*) may denote a 'donor' or 'giver'. If this meaning applies here, it would suggest that the LORD was to reward Abraham greatly. See M. Kessler, 'The "Shield" of Abraham?' *VT* 14 (1964), pp. 494-97; G. Rendsburg, 'Notes on Genesis XV', *VT* 42 (1992), pp. 266-72. The biblical passages listed in *DCH*, V, p. 134, should also be noted.

b) *A Divine Appearance* (*vv. 4-19*) The dangers that David has faced are described, before a description is given of God's saving work. **The cords of death entangled me; the torrents of destruction overwhelmed me. The cords of the grave coiled around me; the snares of death confronted me** (*vv. 4-5*). Death came very near to David. He felt tied by its cords and terrified by its torrents. The Hebrew text says 'torrents of Belial'. 'Belial' occurs in Deuteronomy 13:13 and 15:9. Various derivations of 'Belial' have been suggested. Jerome held that it meant 'without a yoke', and hence signified 'lawless'. Another common interpretation is that it means 'without profit', 'worthless'. In more recent times it has been proposed that it is an abstract noun meaning 'destructiveness'. This last definition certainly fits the context here, where 'torrents of destruction' is paralleled by 'the cords of Sheol' and 'the snares of the grave'.[3] The cords of Sheol (NIV 'grave') were pulling David there and he felt entrapped by death. David must have felt his life to be in danger for many years, and in this poetic description he expresses his feelings in the face of constant deadly situations.

In my distress I called to the LORD; I cried to my God for help. From his temple he heard my voice; my cry came before him, into his ears (*v. 6*). The prayer of faith comes from his lips. He says, 'my God' (cf. v. 2). In his need he knew to turn to the God with whom he had a living relationship, and to him he makes his heartfelt cry. God heard from his 'temple', a word that describes both the place where God is honoured and worshipped, and where he sits enthroned in majesty (cf. Isa. 6:1-7). The psalmist was assured that when he 'cried for help' his 'cry' had come to the LORD's ears (the verb and the noun come from the same Hebrew root, *sh-v-ʿ*). The description of his rescue that follows is given in poetic terms as a theophany, i.e. a visible manifestation of God. God came to him in a way similar to his coming to Sinai of old (Exod. 19:16-19), or to

---

[3] For literature on the subject, see the references in *DCH*, II, pp. 608-9, especially J. A. Emerton, 'Sheol and the Sons of Belial', *VT* 37 (1987), pp. 214-18.

Elijah on his visit there (1 Kings 19:11-12).[4] Similar descriptions of a theophany are given in Psalms 68:7-8 and 77:14-20. God's great acts of salvation are pictured in similar terms by psalmist and prophet alike (Ps. 97; Hab. 3).[5] The psalmist makes the connection between his experience and that of the children of Israel in days long past. He is the second Moses who has seen God's great redemptive work as at the Red Sea (see v. 16).

The earth trembled and quaked, and the foundations of the mountains shook; they trembled because he was angry. Smoke rose from his nostrils; consuming fire came from his mouth, burning coals blazed out of it (*vv. 7-8*). First, there is an earthquake, and in Hebrew poetical style the first two verbs are similar in sound (*vattig'ash vattir'ash hâ'ârets*), the assonance adding to the overall effect. The first of these verbs is repeated at the end of the verse (*vayitgâ'ashû*). The expression, 'the foundation of the mountains,' is borrowed from Deuteronomy 32:22. God had heard his servant's cry and was ready to do battle with those who were attacking him. His anger was aroused and he was preparing to come as he had done at Mount Sinai. The description points to a powerful sense of God's presence. The divine warrior comes to display his wrath against his, and the psalmist's, enemies.

He parted the heavens and came down; dark clouds were under his feet. He mounted the cherubim and flew; he soared on the wings of the wind. He made darkness his covering, his canopy around him—the dark rain clouds of the sky (*vv. 9-11*). The theophany moves on from the earthquake to the picture of dark clouds enveloping the earth (cf. Deut. 5:22). The heavens are described as though they were a curtain that could be split to allow God to come down. He brought storm clouds down, while he himself flew on cherubim. Because

---

[4] The English versions fail to mark the connection between Moses' and Elijah's experience at Mt Sinai by translating the opening of 1 Kings 19:9 as 'and there he came to *a* cave'. The MT has '*the* cave', which seems to point to the cleft of the rock in which Moses was placed as the glory of the LORD passed by.

[5] For some apposite comment on how this psalm and other similar poetic passages far surpass narrative description, see Elmer Martens, *God's Design: A Focus on Old Testament Theology* (Grand Rapids: Baker Books, 1994), p. 164.

of the parallelism in verses 9-10 'cherubim' may here be a poetic term for clouds. In the midst of the storm the LORD was there, controlling all the forces at his disposal. He comes with majesty to bring deliverance.

Out of the brightness of his presence clouds advanced, with hailstones and bolts of lightning. The LORD thundered from heaven; the voice of the Most High resounded. He shot his arrows and scattered the enemies, great bolts of lightning and routed them. The valleys of the sea were exposed and the foundations of the earth laid bare at your rebuke, O LORD, at the blast of breath from your nostrils (*vv. 12-15*). The storm now breaks. Thunder and lightning come from the LORD's presence. The light that streams from the LORD becomes a consuming fire for his enemies. The bolts of lightning are likened to a warrior's arrows with which he attacks and routs the enemies. The representation of the LORD's voice as being thunder is common in the Old Testament (cf. Ps. 29:3-4; Job 37:2-5; Joel 3:16). The use of the divine title 'Most High' in verse 13 serves to designate how exalted he is over all, including the enemies. The NIV translation deviates from the MT at the end of verse 13 in that it omits the repeated words 'with hailstones and bolts of lightning'. Though some Hebrew manuscripts and the LXX do not repeat these words, yet the repetition reinforces the idea of God's dramatic intervention in human affairs as if it had the suddenness and power of a mighty storm.[6] Earth experiences turmoil as God's breath pours forth as a storm. Even the very foundations of the earth are uncovered as the storm blows upon it. The language in verse 15 is reminiscent of that in the Song of the Sea in Exodus 15:8.

He reached down from on high and took hold of me; he drew me out of deep waters. He rescued me from my powerful enemy, from my foes, who were too strong for me. They confronted me in the day of my disaster, but the LORD was my support. He brought me out into a spacious place;

---

[6] The repetition is retained in other modern versions such as RSV, NASB, NKJV, and ESV. The fact that the repetition does not occur in 2 Samuel is not decisive, as the two passages are not identical at many points.

he rescued me because he delighted in me (*vv. 16-19*). The hand of the LORD was then stretched out to save David. The figurative language describes a divine arm that reaches down to rescue David from the overwhelming flood. At the end of verse 16 the theophany ceases and the description then reverts to an ordinary one. The LORD delivered him from his powerful enemy. This is probably a reference to Saul, while the plural 'my foes' may very well include Saul's henchmen. When he was confronted by them he found that the LORD was his 'support'. In the context the Hebrew word used (*mishʿân*) suggests not only support or stay but also provider. He found that the LORD brought him out of his narrow and confined situation into a place where there was so much liberty. To be in 'a spacious place' denotes freedom from the restraints and oppression that he had experienced earlier. Hence this song may come from a later time in David's life when he could look back on the troubles he endured in years past. God's delight in his servant was because he was indeed his anointed kingly servant. He was the man after God's own heart (1 Sam. 13:14), the man of his choice. This was no arrogant boast for he was the man with whom God had made a covenant promising him an enduring dynasty (2 Sam. 7, and cf. also the wording of verse 50 of this psalm). The following verses that deal with David's integrity before the LORD point to his life and obedience as being also part of the reason for God's delight in him.

c) *The Goodness of God* (*vv. 20-30*) **The LORD has dealt with me according to my righteousness; according to the cleanness of my hands he has rewarded me** (*v. 20*). David is not claiming sinless perfection (see the comments on Psalm 17:1) but is asserting his own integrity before the LORD (cf. Paul's words in Acts 24:16, 'a conscience void of offence toward God and men'). He was walking in righteousness and his hands were clean. According to his character God had rewarded him. Even the king was not exempt from showing obedience to the LORD's commands. That is why it was stipulated that the king had to have a copy of the law for himself (Deut. 17:18).

For I have kept the ways of the LORD; I have not done evil by turning from my God. All his laws are before me; I have not turned away from his decrees (*vv. 21-22*). He had not turned aside from the ways of the LORD, but had guarded his steps carefully. Never had he acted rebelliously and departed from his God. This is an unusual use of the verb 'to commit wrongdoing' (*râsha*ʿ), but in the context it clearly does mean turning away from God to commit evil deeds. The judgments and ordinances of the LORD were constantly before him, as if placarded before his eyes. At no time had he turned away from God's commands and consciously set his requirements aside (cf. Ps. 101:2).

I have been blameless before him and have kept myself from sin. The LORD has rewarded me according to my righteousness, according to the cleanness of my hands in his sight (*vv. 23-24*). The word 'blameless' should not be read as if it meant 'sinless'. It speaks rather of the legal obedience of a covenantal servant, and it reappears later in this psalm in verses 25, 30, and 32. It denotes the wholehearted dedication of a person to a sanctified life. The repeated reference to guarding is a reminder of the watch that the Bible teaches believers to have over their lives ('Keep yourself pure', 1 Tim. 5:22; 'keep oneself from being polluted by the world,' James 1:27). Verse 24 repeats the thought of verse 20. Such repetition of the opening thought of a section at its close was a typical poetic device that calls attention to a major idea or theme.

To the faithful you show yourself faithful, to the blameless you show yourself blameless, to the pure you show yourself pure, but to the crooked you show yourself shrewd. You save the humble but bring low those whose eyes are haughty (*vv. 25-27*). These verses confirm what has been already said of God's character and his way of dealing with his servants. To the faithful covenant servant (*châsîd*) God shows himself merciful (*châsad*, Hitp.).[7] To the man of integrity, he acts with integrity towards him. To the pure, God responds with a demonstration of his own purity. Other Old

---

[7] It is only here and in 2 Samuel 22:26 that the verb occurs, as over against the 246 times that the noun *chésed* appears in the Old Testament.

Testament passages give the full doctrine. God dealt with Israel in terms of his covenant and thus not according to their sins (Ps. 103:10; cf. also Ps. 143:2).

After these assertions about the godly, one assertion is dedicated to the ungodly with an introduction that sets it over against what has preceded ('*but,* to the crooked ...'). It may not seem good to call God 'shrewd' (*pâtal,* Hitp.). The Hebrew word can have a more neutral meaning closer to 'inscrutable'. David is saying that God will deal with the person who mocks him over his covenantal dealings, just as he has already described God's dealings with his own personal enemies. This section of the psalm points to the way in which God deals with a person according to his/her character. It is only divine grace that makes the difference in God's attitude to the godly and the ungodly, and that, therefore, determines the abiding destiny of both at the final judgment (Rev. 22:11).

You save the humble but bring low those whose eyes are haughty. You, O Lord, keep my lamp burning; my God turns my darkness into light (*vv. 27-28*). A summary statement is given in verse 27 that ties the themes together about which David has been speaking. God shows his gracious character in delivering the afflicted, whereas the proud and arrogant are humbled by him. 'He mocks proud mockers but gives grace to the humble' (Prov. 3:34), words that are quoted by Peter with the added instruction: 'Humble yourselves, therefore, under God's mighty hand, that he may lift you up in due time' (1 Pet. 5:6). David goes on to describe his deliverance in terms of God providing a lamp for him, and giving him light in his darkness. A special application of the idea of David's lamp is made in 1 Kings 11:36 when God promised, through Ahijah the prophet, that David would always have a lamp. The same promise is repeated in 1 Kings 15:4 and 2 Kings 8:19.[8]

With your help I can advance against a troop; with my God I can scale a wall. As for God, his way is perfect; the

[8] Cf. also the words of David's men when David was rescued when in danger from a Philistine: 'Never again will you go out with us to battle, so that the lamp of Israel will not be extinguished' (2 Sam. 21:17). For further information on the varied Old Testament use of the word 'lamp' (Hebrew *nêr*), see *TDOT,* X, pp. 14-24.

word of the LORD is flawless. He is a shield for all who take refuge in him (*vv. 29-30*). Now David returns to the theme of the opening of the psalm and specifically to God's help for him in his battles. With confidence he could attack an enemy troop (or possibly, following NIV margin, 'can run through a barricade'), or leap over a wall. The thoughts that have preceded lead David to praise his God. He extols the LORD's ways, i.e. his actions, his dealings with David, and proclaims them as complete. Along with his actions his word is mentioned. It has been tested (the word comes from metal-working), and almost the same language is used of God's spoken word in Psalm 119:140. The final statement in this section is virtually a brief summary of verse 2. For all who, like David, put their confidence in the LORD and trust him as their refuge, he proves to be a shield.

3. The Character of God (*vv. 31-45*)

David as king had good reason to praise the LORD for the help he provided him. He does so in words extolling him as the only God, and the one who so blessed him during his military campaigns.

a) *Praise for Redeeming Grace (vv. 31-32).* **For who is God besides the LORD? And who is the Rock except our God? It is God who arms me with strength and makes my way perfect** (*vv. 31-32*). As with the section beginning at verse 3, this section also commences on a note of praise that virtually summarises the section. It is a statement of the creed of Israel with its implicit monotheism.[9] The rhetorical questions are an important way of emphasising that there was no other God except the LORD (cf. the way Isaiah, in particular, uses similar language and style in chaps. 40-48). The style here is typical of hymnic sections of the Old Testament, especially when descriptions of God's character and work are given. As in Isaiah 40:21-22, three clauses follow the questions, each beginning with a participle:

[9] This is a counterpart to the Islamic claim, 'There is no God but Allah', and preceding it by many centuries. Even the New Testament contains assertions that pre-date the Islamic one. See particularly, 1 Corinthians 8:4, 'there is no God but one.'

31 For who is God besides the LORD?
And who is the Rock except our God?
32 It is God
the one who arms me (*ham^{e}ʾazz^{e}rênî*) with strength
who makes (*m^{e}shavveh*) my feet like the feet of a deer;
who trains (*m^{e}lammêd*) my hands for battle.

The use of this pattern helps to draw attention to the concepts, as David explains why God is incomparable.[10]

The language concerning God as a 'rock' has already been used by David in verse 2, in dependence on Deuteronomy 32. This is one of many references to Deuteronomy throughout this song. The word for God (Hebrew *ʾ^{e}lôah*) is a relatively uncommon word, but it seems to be employed to give variation in the use of the divine names.[11] God had indeed strengthened David for his battles and made his way perfect. This last expression must here mean that God had so assisted David that his life turned out well and especially that his kingship was a fulfilment of God's purposes.

He makes my feet like the feet of a deer; he enables me to stand on the heights. He trains my hands for battle; my arms can bend a bow of bronze (*vv.* 33-34). Like a swift and sure-footed deer he was able to escape his enemies and stand upon the heights, i.e. upon mountain strongholds he had captured. Almost the same expression comes at the conclusion of the Book of Habakkuk (Hab. 3:19). God gave to David the physical strength he needed to engage in battle. This line from verse 34 is used again in Psalm 144:1. So strong was David that he could even use a bow that required considerably more than normal strength.

You give me your shield of victory, and your right hand sustains me; you stoop down to make me great. You broaden the path beneath me, so that my ankles do not turn

---

[10] A further grammatical point reinforces the use of the participles. Following the first two, the Hebrew text uses *imperfect* forms: *vayyittên* … *yaʿ^{a}mîdênî*, that have the sense of present time, 'and makes my way' and 'he enables me to stand'. For this grammatical point, see DIHG-S, § 113(e).

[11] The word *ʾelôah* occurs 57× in the Old Testament, mainly in the Book of Job (41×). It appears in early poetry (Deut. 32:15, 17), but then seems to have dropped out of use until the time of the exile and after. For further information, see *TWOT*, 1, pp. 43-44.

(*vv.* 35-36). David recognises that it was not his own strength that won him victories. God had provided for him a 'shield' (see comment on verse 2 and the footnote) and constantly supported his servant (cf. the use of 'right hand' in Ps. 16:8). The last part of verse 35 is a remarkable anthropomorphic expression, for David says that God's condescension has made him great. God had stooped to David and taken a humble shepherd boy and made him king. All of God's acts of mercy to his children and expressions of his condescension came to fullest expression in Jesus' coming in human flesh. David's path was made plain and broad before him so that he was able to go along it without impediment and also he did not suffer any injury.

b) *Complete Victory (vv. 37-42).* **I pursued my enemies and overtook them; I did not turn back till they were destroyed. I crushed them so that they could not rise; they fell beneath my feet** (*vv. 37-38*). In a psalm of thanksgiving for his victories, David now details some of the events surrounding them. He had pursued his enemies and did not turn back till his mission was completed. His armies had so smitten the enemies that they were unable to arise, and hence they were in subjection under his feet.

You armed me with strength for battle; you made my adversaries bow at my feet. You made my enemies turn their backs in flight, and I destroyed my foes (*vv. 39-40*). Once again David acknowledges that his victories did not come from his own strength or from that of his army. It was the LORD who had girded him for war (see verse 32 for the earlier use of the same idiom and using the same verb, *'âzar*, Pi.), and his opponents have been made to prostrate themselves before him. The word used for his 'adversaries' can mean opponents in general, though it could also designate rebellious subjects (see its use in Deut. 28:7 for enemies of Israel). Verse 40 contains a Hebrew idiom that is not brought out in the NIV translation. The meaning is that God gave the enemies into his hands so that he could put his foot on their necks. This was the sign of victory in the Near East. The AV rendering is correct: 'Thou hast also given me the necks of my enemies.'

An illustration of the practice is provided by Joshua's action regarding the kings of Jerusalem, Hebron, Jarmuth, Lachish, and Eglon (Josh. 10:22-24; cf. also the prophecy concerning Judah that his hand would be on the neck of his enemies, Gen. 49:8).

They cried for help, but there was no one to save them—to the LORD, but he did not answer. I beat them as fine as dust borne on the wind; I poured them out like mud in the streets (*vv. 41-42*). In their distress David's enemies prayed – presumably to their own gods – but no saviour appeared on the scene. In their extremity they prayed to the LORD.[12] While it is possible that the enemies were Saul and his supporters, the fact that they prayed to Israel's God does not necessarily mean that the enemies were people within Israel. At times of crisis heathen people used the name of the LORD in prayer (see Jonah 1:14). There was no answer from the LORD and David continued his attack until they were destroyed. The metaphors concerning 'dust' and 'mud' depict the definitive nature of David's victories.

c) *Kingdom Extension (vv. 43-45).* **You have delivered me from the attacks of the people; you have made me the head of nations; people I did not know are subject to me. As soon as they hear me, they obey me; foreigners cringe before me. They all lose heart; they come trembling from their strongholds** (*vv. 43-45*). David's victories had not only been internal to Israel but external as well. He subdued surrounding nations and so became their head. This meant that he was sovereign over them, hence the saying they were subject to him, i.e. they became his servants. It is not clear if the foreigners in verses 44-45 are those subdued through further foreign victories or those already conquered. Probably the former is correct. Kings like Tou of Hamath heard of David's victories and quickly made peace with him (2 Sam. 8:9-10). The accounts of David's battles were enough to cause them to come trembling from their strongholds. When David was succeeded by his

---

[12] The Hebrew text has *ʿal yhwh,* whereas 2 Samuel 22:42 has *ʾel yhwh.* No emendation is needed as the prepositions *ʾel* and *ʿal* were often used interchangeably.

son Solomon the territorial boundaries of Israel extended to the promised limits for the land (1 Kings 4:20-21, 25).

4. David's Doxology to the LORD (*vv. 46-50*)

Having reviewed his past victories, David now sings a triumphal song: **The LORD lives! Praise be to my Rock! Exalted be God my Saviour!** (*v. 46*). That truth was so evident from his past experience, for not only does the LORD live but he reveals that to his own believing people. This parallels the familiar words in the Psalter, 'the LORD reigns' (cf. Pss. 97:1; 99:1). It may also be a deliberate counter-assertion to the Canaanite cry regarding Baal, who, when he supposedly returned from the dead, was greeted with the words, 'For Baal the Mighty is alive, for the Prince, the Lord of the earth exists'.[13] Seeing that this is a statement it is probably best to take the following words as a statement too: 'My rock is worthy to be praised!' Likewise the third phrase: 'God my Saviour is exalted!' All three statements stem from David's own experience of the LORD.

He is the God who avenges me, who subdues nations under me, who saves me from my enemies. You exalted me above my foes; from violent men you rescued me (*vv. 47-48*). Vengeance is something that belongs to the LORD (Deut. 32:35), and room must be left for God's wrath (Rom. 12:19). The MT has the plural 'vengeances' denoting the judicial acts by which the LORD had vindicated David. Here he acknowledges that God had indeed avenged him, and that he had brought foreign nations under his sovereignty.[14] God was his Saviour who had also exalted him over all his enemies, and had not allowed those who attacked him with malicious intent to prevail.

Therefore I will praise you among the nations, O LORD; I will sing praises to your name (*v. 49*). Assuming that such foreign nations were brought under his authority, David

---

[13] *DOTT*, p. 131.

[14] For 'subdue', the MT has *vayadbêr*, whereas 2 Samuel 22:49 has *ûmôrîd*. Emendation is not necessary as this is probably *d-v-r* II, 'to destroy', 'to subdue'. See *DCH*, II, p. 396; Craigie's comments, *Psalms*, p. 171; and Dahood, *Psalms 1-50*, I, p. 118.

says that he will praise the Lord among the Gentiles. No attempt is made at self-aggrandisement. Rather, he wants to make public proclamation of what the Lord has done for him. Quotations from Deuteronomy 32:43, Psalm 117:1, and Isaiah 11:10 are used along with this verse in Romans 15:9-12 to show that participation of the Gentiles in gospel blessings was anticipated in the Old Testament.

He gives his king great victories; he shows unfailing kindness to his anointed, to David and his descendants forever (v. 50). The final verse of the psalm changes from first person ('I') to third person ('his anointed, 'David'). This could be a later addition by another inspired poet, or else David referred to himself in this way. Two things are said about the Lord. First, he had given and was still giving great victories to David. This may be another pointer to the fact that the psalm was composed much earlier than its position in 2 Samuel would suggest. Secondly, the Lord shows covenantal mercy to his anointed.[15] It cannot be doubted that 'his anointed' is defined by the word 'David' which follows. David was the anointed king to whom great promises were given concerning his seed (see 2 Sam. 7: 8-16). The mention of 'seed' points even to Christ in whom the promises to David's house find their ultimate fulfilment (Luke 1:30-33; Rom. 1:2-4). David, in his varied experiences set out in this song of thanksgiving, is a pointer to Jesus who bears the name 'Christ', 'anointed one'.

[15] The idiom here is 'to show covenantal mercy to' someone (*ʿoseh chésed l^{e}*). The phrase itself, and the use of the participle *ʿoseh* in particular, points to the enduring nature of the Lord's commitment to David and his descendants.

Psalm 19

For the director of music. A psalm of David.

God has manifested himself clearly. His great power is seen in the created world around us. But the revelation that comes from that display of his power is not in words. For revelation in words, we have to turn to the Scriptures, which are indeed the Word of God. Both forms of revelation are celebrated in this nineteenth psalm, though the focus is more on the wonder and beauty of God's Word. It begins with reference to the demonstration of God's power in the natural world before changing to the perfection of his law. That change is marked by the use of the covenantal name for God – 'LORD' (*yhwh*), used seven times in the second major section, while in the first it is absent. Instead, the general name 'God' (*'ēl*) is used in verse 1, followed by the appropriate personal pronouns in the following verses. The point is clearly that while natural revelation points to God, yet true knowledge only comes through the divinely given law. Sin causes distortion, and it is only through the aid of God's Spirit that we can see clearly God's revelation of himself in nature (cf. Paul's teaching in Romans 1:18-23).

1. God's Glory in Nature (*vv. 1-6*)
The beautifully balanced opening sentence sets the theme for the first section. **The heavens declare the glory of God; the skies proclaim the work of his hands** (*v. 1*). The first part of the verse has the subject ('the heavens'), the verb ('declare'), and the object ('the glory'). Then in typical Hebrew poetic style it has parallel expressions in the second half with the word order reversed (object, verb, subject). The created world

declares in an ongoing way the glory of God. Its testimony is never finished.

The second verse continues the same idea and does so with similar poetic artistry. **Day after day they pour forth speech; night after night they display knowledge** (*v.* 2). Day by day the message of creation bubbles forth.[1] Night by night the majesty of the stars is a witness to the creator. Creation cannot contain itself, but constantly proclaims the glory of God. The heavenly bodies are not divine (Deut. 4:19; 17:3), nor do they have control over human destiny.[2]

There is no speech or language where their voice is not heard. Their voice goes out into all the earth, their words to the ends of the world (*vv. 3-4a*). Nowhere in the world is isolated from this message, for it penetrates everywhere. The voice of creation is a universal messenger. The NIV deviates from the MT to follow the lead of the LXX and the Latin Vulgate in reading *qôlâm*, 'their voice', instead of *qavvâm*, 'their measuring line'. The MT text makes good sense, though, as it asserts that the measuring line of the heavens is over the whole earth, a truth confirmed by the following words.[3] The voice (or call) of the heavens and earth has gone to the uttermost part. This is a proclamation or a summons from God to mankind. Nonetheless this is a muted message for it cannot say anything about God's grace or the way of approach that he has provided to his throne.

In the heavens he has pitched a tent for the sun, which is like a bridegroom coming forth from his pavilion, like a

---

[1] The verb 'bubble forth' (*nâva'*, Hi.) is an uncommon verb, only used once of water bubbling forth (Prov. 18:4). However, it is also used as here in the figurative sense of God's praise coming forth in a stream in Psalms 78:2, 119:171, and 145:7.

[2] Cf. the comments of Derek Kidner on Genesis 1:16-18: 'Sun, moon and stars are God's good gifts. . . . As *signs* (14) they will speak for God, not fate (Jer. 10:2; cf. Mt. 2:9; Lk. 21:25, 28), for they *rule* (16, 18) only as lightbearers, not as powers. In these few simple sentences the lie is given to a superstition as old as Babylon and as modern as a newspaper-horoscope': *Genesis: An Introduction and Commentary* (London: Tyndale Press, 1967), p. 49.

[3] The Hebrew text simply says '*their* line', just as it says 'in *them*' in verse 4b. In both cases the pronouns refer back to 'the heavens' and 'the firmament' in verse 1.

champion rejoicing to run his course. It rises at one end of the heavens and makes its circuit to the other; nothing is hidden from its heat (*vv. 4b-6*). The picture is enlarged with a description of the sky as the tent that God has provided for the sun. Despite all its glory, the sun is still a created thing, set in its place by God. Just as the bridegroom comes out from under his canopy, or the virile athlete runs his race, so the sun comes forth to run its daily course. It covers a daily circuit, and from the standpoint of human observation it goes from one edge of the heavens to the other. Its heat penetrates everywhere. The description of the sun is clearly based on Middle Eastern experience. How many receive the message of creation? Paul says in effect: 'Very few.' For although men 'knew God, they neither glorified him as God nor gave thanks to him, but their thinking became futile and their foolish hearts were darkened' (Rom. 1:21). It is only a believer who can truly see in creation the hand of God, and give him praise for the wonder of his works.

2. God's Glory in His Word (*vv. 7-10*)

The last clause in verse 6 serves as a bridge between the first and second parts of the psalm. Just as the sunshine reveals everything, so does God's Word search our hearts. It is 'sharper than any double-edged sword, it penetrates even to dividing soul and spirit, joints and marrow; it judges the thoughts and attitudes of the heart' (Heb 4:12).

The law of the LORD is perfect, reviving the soul. The statutes of the LORD are trustworthy, making wise the simple. The precepts of the LORD are right, giving joy to the heart. The commands of the LORD are radiant, giving light to the eyes. The fear of the LORD is pure, enduring forever. The ordinances of the LORD are sure and altogether righteous (*vv. 7-9*).

There are several noteworthy things about these verses. First, instead of the word 'God' (Hebrew *ʾēl*) used when speaking of creation, the psalmist now uses the covenantal name LORD (Hebrew *yhwh*) when speaking of the Scripture. Secondly, he uses six parallel expressions to describe the

Scriptures ('law', 'statutes', 'precepts', 'commands', 'fear', and 'ordinances'). While each name adds something more to the description, yet together they form a multifaceted picture of God's Word. Thirdly, we have a balancing list of six attributes ('perfect', 'trustworthy', 'right', 'radiant', 'pure', and 'sure'). Fourthly, accompanying each title is a descriptive phrase telling what the Scripture does ('reviving the soul', 'making wise the simple', 'giving joy to the heart', 'giving light to the eyes', 'enduring forever', 'altogether righteous').

The description starts in verse 7 with the revelation of the LORD being referred to as his perfect law. That is, it was divine instruction that brought refreshment in weakness or despair. The Hebrew word used here, *tôrâh,* comes from a verb 'to teach' or 'instruct' (*yârâh*). To call it 'perfect' is to say that it is an expression of the pure will of God. Likewise the LORD's statutes are trustworthy, and they bring wisdom to those who lack it, the 'simple'. The psalmist is not indicating a special class of people, for he would certainly include all in the description of 'simple' (cf. our Lord's words in Matthew 11:25). The Hebrew word translated 'simple' (*petî*) has a good sense in the Psalms where it indicates those who lack wisdom but who can gain it by receiving knowledge. In contrast, when used in Proverbs it marks out the 'gullible', who, unless they repent, will be reckoned alongside the fools and mockers.[4]

In verse 8 the psalmist moves on to speak of the righteous precepts that are a source of joy and satisfaction. The verb 'to rejoice' (*sâmach*) is frequently used in the Psalter, with the source of joy being found in God's presence, or else in things emanating from him like his precepts, as here. From another angle they are sincere commands that bring light to the eyes. Spiritual illumination comes through God's own revelation of himself. When David speaks of the fear of the LORD in verse 9 he is not concerned with the inward experience of a believer. As it is in parallel with other terms relating to Scripture it must mean the 'law', which had as one of its purposes to

---

[4] For the contrast in usage between Psalms and Proverbs, see *TWOT*, II, p. 743; Bruce K. Waltke, *The Book of Proverbs: Chapters 1-15, NICOT* (Grand Rapids: Eerdmans, 2004), pp. 111-12.

bring men to fear the Lord (cf. Deut. 4:10; 17:19). The word 'fear' is used elsewhere in this objective sense (Ps. 34:11; Prov. 1:29). Moreover, this 'fear' stands in perpetuity as the abiding manifestation of God. The final concluding statement in verse 9 sums up the character of the law – it is true becomes it comes from God who is true. It is altogether righteous since it comes from the righteous God himself.

They are more precious than gold, than much pure gold; they are sweeter than honey, than honey from the comb (*v. 10*). This section concludes with the assurance of how precious and sweet is God's Word. It is far more valuable than purified gold; it is far sweeter than honey. For those in the ancient world who did not have an abundance of sugar, there was nothing sweeter than honey. Similar expressions about God's law are found in Psalm 119 (gold, 119:72, 127; honey, 119:103).

3. The Response to God's Word (*vv. 11-14*)

By them is your servant warned; in keeping them there is great reward. Who can discern his errors? Forgive my hidden faults (*vv. 11-12*). Now comes the reflection on what has been said about God's precious Word. They brought meaning (or perhaps better, 'enlightenment') to David, as they continue to do to us, and there is great blessing in walking in the pathway of God's commands. David knew that there was no complete and perfect obedience to be given to God's law and therefore he asks concerning his 'errors'. The Hebrew word he uses here (*sh^{e}gî'âh*) is related to the word used for the sins for which atonement could be sought (*sh^{e}gâgâh*, Lev. 4:2, 22, 27). His plea is for forgiveness to blot out even inadvertent sins. There has to be sensitivity of heart before the Lord so that we can pray this prayer with David. A true response to this truth is to seek cleansing even from faults not obvious to our eyes.

Keep your servant also from wilful sins; may they not rule over me. Then will I be blameless, innocent of great transgression (*v. 13*). The danger of sin was present with David. Hence he asks for preservation from presumptuous and wilful sins, which have a tendency to rule over people.

The Hebrew word for 'wilful' is *zêd*, only used here in reference to sins. Usually it is applied to people who are arrogant or impudent. Such sins are like a wild animal waiting to catch its prey, as Cain found out to his cost (Gen. 4:7). They take hold of people and make them their slaves (John 8:34). If kept from such sins David would be heart-whole with the LORD and not guilty of the 'great transgression'. Elsewhere in the Old Testament this phrase commonly refers to adultery (see Gen. 39:9), but here it probably means sin in general.

May the words of my mouth and the meditation of my heart be pleasing in your sight, O LORD, my Rock and my Redeemer (*v. 14*). The psalm opened with the thought of the heavens speaking. It closes with the psalmist asking that *his* words would be pleasing to the LORD. He is referring to the words of this song in particular, and acknowledges that it is his speech and meditation that he desires to be acceptable to his Rock and his Redeemer (for the idea of meditation, see the comment on 1:2). The use of 'rock' ties in closely with the way it has appeared in the previous psalm (see Ps. 18:2, 31, 46). The psalm that began on the note of the glory of all God's creation, closes on the note of a personal relationship with the Saviour.

Psalm 20

For the director of music. A psalm of David.

Before battles it was customary in Israel and Judah to pray to the LORD and to seek an answer from him. Thus Jehoshaphat prayed before his battle with Moab and Ammon, a Levite responded, and then all the people worshipped (2 Chron. 20:5-19). Psalm 20 seems to come from a similar situation and be intended as a song to be sung before a battle. Like Jehoshaphat's prayer, this one seems to be influenced in its thought and language by Solomon's prayer at the dedication of the temple (see especially 2 Chron. 6:18-21). The early part may have been sung by all the people after the king had offered sacrifices. They look forward to rejoicing in his victory (v. 5), and then an individual (probably a Levite) makes a declaration, and finally all the congregation respond in praise. The poetry of this psalm is marked out by repetition of key words that form an important stylistic feature (cf. 'answer(s)', vv. 1, 6, 9; 'name', vv. 1, 5; 'remember', vv. 3, 7; 'fulfil', vv. 4, 5; 'save(s)', vv. 5, 6, 9).[1]

1. A Prayer Before Battle (*vv. 1-5*)

May the LORD answer you when you are in distress; may the name of the God of Jacob protect you (*v. 1*). The psalm begins and ends with similar words (closer in Hebrew than the English translation suggests). 'Answer in the day of ...' is clearly a key term. The appeal is to the LORD, or as he is also described, 'the God of Jacob'.This term occurs again in an

[1] The NIV obscures the repetition by translating some of the Hebrew words with different English words: 'remember' (v. 3), 'trust' (v. 7), 'fulfil' (v. 4), and 'grant' (v. 5).

abbreviated form in Psalm 24:6, and it is common elsewhere in the Psalter (Pss. 46:7,11; 75:9; 76:6; 81:1; 84:8; cf. also Isaiah's term, 'The mighty one of Jacob,' Isa. 49:26; 60:16). 'The name' of the LORD is clearly God himself (cf. Isa. 30:27) through whom enemies were overcome (Ps. 44:5). It is the self-revelation of his character.

May he send you help from the sanctuary and grant you support from Zion (*v. 2*). The date of writing was clearly after the ark was brought to Jerusalem, and the establishment of the sanctuary on Mount Zion. The following verse, with reference to sacrifices, shows that it is the earthly and not the heavenly sanctuary that is meant. The combination of the idea of God's name being associated with the sanctuary and prayer to God at the temple are drawn from Solomon's prayer (1 Kings 8:27-30; 2 Chron. 6:18-21).[2] The people's plea is that when they leave for battle they go with the LORD's help and sustaining power.

May he remember all your sacrifices and accept your burnt offerings Selah (*v. 3*). The sacrifices could be all those of the past, but probably what is meant are those offered on the particular occasion of going into battle (cf. 1 Sam. 7:9; 13:9). The first word for sacrifice (*minchâh*) is a general term that covers many types, while the second is the burnt offering (*ʿôlâh*), in which everything was consumed as a symbol of dedication to God. The use of 'Selah' marks a break after these opening petitions, though the exact significance of its presence is hard to determine (for discussion on this term, see the comments on Ps. 3:2).

May he give you the desire of your heart and make all your plans succeed (*v. 4*). What is intended is that the plans of the king for the battle would come to fruition. His heart's desire and his counsel were that he would overcome the enemy, and for that the people pray: 'May God give it!' The verb translated 'succeed' (*mâlêʾ*, Pi.) is used again at the end of verse 5 (NIV 'May the LORD *grant*').

---

[2] For a detailed discussion on the temple and its significance, see W. A. VanGemeren, 'Appendix: The Ark of the Covenant and the Temple, Symbols of Yahweh's Presence and Rule', 'Psalms', pp. 809-15.

We will shout for joy when you are victorious and will lift up our banners in the name of our God. May the LORD grant all your requests (*v. 5*). The scene moves now to the future when those at present praying will be among those rejoicing in victory. Songs of rejoicing will be heard as the people celebrate God's salvation or victory. Jubilant shouting will mark the outcome of battle. They will also erect or wave banners, possibly the tribal banners under which they camped (Num. 1:52).[3] The final clause in the verse repeats the idea of verse 4 in describing full realisation of the king's requests.

2. God's Declaration of Victory (*v. 6*)

Now I know that the LORD saves his anointed; he answers him from his holy heaven with the saving power of his right hand (*v. 6*). The introductory 'now' (*ʿattâh*) is important, as it is an adverb that often marks a change in narrative and especially in the prophetical books introduces imminent activities of the LORD, either in blessing or cursing (see, for a good example, Isa. 43:1). Here it precedes the declaration that the LORD saves his anointed. The deliverance is still in the future but the assurance is given that the LORD hears and answers the cry of the king. While some have taken 'anointed' to be the future eschatological king, the context points to its use as designating a contemporary king.[4] The LORD answers from his holy throne on high. His 'right hand' describes in anthropomorphic terms God's power and ability to deliver.

3. A Song of Thanksgiving (*vv. 7-9*)

Some trust in chariots and some in horses, but we trust in the name of the LORD our God (*v. 7*). Without trusting in the LORD the use of horses and chariots was useless. There was a constant temptation for God's people to trust in human might or agencies to give deliverance. Even Moses had to learn the lesson in this respect (see Exod. 2:11-14, and Stephen's

---

[3] The parallel expression is 'shout for joy', and hence the idea is that in victory parades banners would be waved as part of the celebration.

[4] See the discussion by G. Vos, 'The Eschatology of the Psalter', in *The Eschatology of the Old Testament*, ed. James T. Dennison Jr. (Nutley, NJ; P. & R. Publishing, 2001), pp. 131-40.

comment in Acts 7:23-29). There could be no trusting in horses, chariots, bows, or swords (Ps. 44:5-7), but only in the LORD himself (see the use of 'name' already in verses 1 and 5) who was their God. Also, since the ideal condition of God's kingdom was to be peace, consequently this was meant to be the condition of Israel as a theocracy at all times. Some in Israel clearly followed the untheocratic principle of trust in human might, against which prophets and psalmists warned.[5]

They are brought to their knees and fall, but we rise up and stand firm (*v. 8*). The outcome of battle, if the LORD was on their side, was that their enemies would be humbled and fall. The word 'fall' often occurs in military contexts as here and denotes falling to death (see the account of Sisera's death in Judg. 5:27: 'At her feet he sank, he fell; there he lay. At her feet he sank, he fell; where he sank, there he fell – dead'). In contrast the Israelites will arise and stand their ground.[6]

O LORD, save the king! Answer us when we call! (*v. 9*) Again the whole congregation joins in singing, as the worshippers repeat the opening intercession. They want God to show his power in delivering the king in battle. This cry of the people lies behind the British expression of loyalty to the sovereign, 'God save the King/Queen!'[7] The New Testament use of 'Hosanna' particularises this cry and does so by way of its use in Psalm 118:25. The psalm that began with the cry of 'answer', finishes on the note of entreaty with the repetition of the word 'answer'.

---

[5] Cf. passages such as Hosea 14:3: 'Assyria cannot save us; we will not mount war-horses,' and Isaiah 31:1: 'Woe to those who go down to Egypt for help, who rely on horses, who trust in the multitude of their chariots and in the great strength of their horsemen, but do not look to the Holy One of Israel, or seek help from the LORD.'

[6] See my discussion of this usage of the verb 'fall' in *NIDOTTE*, 3, p.130.

[7] The LXX rendering is *kurie, sôson basilea sou* ('Lord, save your king') and the Vulgate's *Domine salvum fac regem* is the origin of our familiar 'God save the king!'

Psalm 21

For the director of music. A psalm of David.

This psalm is closely connected in theme with the preceding one. It is a song that recounts past victories which the LORD gave, and which expresses trust that he will do the same yet again for his people. It is also a psalm with strong covenantal overtones. This is best seen in verse 7. On the LORD's part he shows covenantal commitment (*chésed*) to his people; on the people's part (represented by the king) they respond in trust (*bâtach*). The former never altered, but time and again the people had to be challenged in regard to their commitment to the LORD. At the heart of this psalm is this fresh affirmation of the covenantal faith, and this is confirmed by the blessings in verses 2-7, and promised divine protection in verses 8-13. As with the previous psalm, the conclusion returns to the opening theme forming an *inclusio*. Just as the king can rejoice in the LORD's strength (v. 1), so will the people sing of the LORD's strength and might (v. 13).

1. Rejoicing in the LORD's Victories (*vv. 1-7*)
O LORD, the king rejoices in your strength. How great is his joy in the victories you give! (*v. 1*). The people join in a song of praise to the LORD because of the assistance he has provided for the king. The LORD's strength (*ʿoz*) has been manifested in the battles of the past. At the end of the psalm reference is made again to this aspect (v. 13), and though a different noun is used (*g*ᵉ*vûrâh*), it is synonymous in meaning. So much of the history of Israel and Judah was dominated by battles, as the people extended or endeavoured to maintain

their boundaries. All these victories were the LORD's, and the king and people together rejoiced in them.

You have granted him the desire of his heart and have not withheld the request of his lips. *Selah* (*v.* 2). Prayer before battle was customary in Israel (see vv. 1-4 in the previous psalm). Now the people acknowledge that when the king prayed, God answered him. In time of need, the LORD had not refused to listen to the requests that the king made. Though the word for 'victory' (*yᵉshûʿâh*) is singular, the context implies repeated demonstrations of God's saving power.

You welcomed him with rich blessings and placed a crown of pure gold on his head. He asked you for life, and you gave it to him — length of days, for ever and ever (*vv.* 3-4). The blessings of the kingship are described, using the crown as a symbol of all the good things that the LORD bestowed upon the king. It is only a poetical figure to sum up the many gifts that God gave to the Davidic kings. The word used for 'crown' (*ʿᵃṭârâh*) is a general word and one most frequently used in metaphorical expressions like this one.[1] In regard to verse 4 the question can be posed: 'When was the request made, and when was the answer given?' Most probably before going into battle the king asked that his life would be spared. When he came back after the battle he knew that God had prolonged his life in accordance with his prayer. The expression 'length of days, for ever and ever' does not mean eternal life. The expression is used even of heathen kings (Neh. 2:3; Dan. 2:4), and here it means prolonged life extending into the foreseeable future,[2] or possibly continuation of the Davidic line.

Through the victories you gave, his glory is great; you have bestowed on him splendour and majesty. Surely you have granted him eternal blessings and made him glad with the joy of your presence (*vv.* 5-6). After the God-given victories the king received not only life but 'splendour and majesty'

---

[1] In contrast, the word *nêzer* is used both for the royal crown (2 Sam. 1:10; 2 Kings 11:12, Ps. 89:39) and the holy headband of the High Priest (Exod. 29:6; 39:30; Lev. 8:9). The connecting link between these two usages is the idea of consecration to God's service.

[2] Cf. also the use of 'length of days' (*'ôrek yâmîm*) in Psalm 23:6, and see the commentary on that verse.

(*hôd vᵉhâdâr*). These are attributes of God himself (Pss. 96:6; 104:1; 111:3), but the king reflected these characteristics as he occupied the divinely appointed office. As in verse 4 the thought is not of blessings of eternal life, but of long-lasting blessings. Other possible interpretations would be blessings of enduring value, or blessings whose flow to recipients was continuous. While it is not expressly stated, the idea behind the expression is that the king was a mediator of God's blessings to others. The first main part of the psalm comes to climactic expression in the following words:

For the king trusts in the LORD; through the unfailing love of the Most High he will not be shaken (*v. 7*). This is the key verse of the psalm, and the one connecting verses 1-6 with verses 8-13. It is in the third person, not in the second person as is the rest of the psalm. Covenantal love shown by the Most High is the foundation of the whole relationship.[3] If that trust continues, then the king will not be moved or shaken, an expression denoting fixity of purpose and life (cf. its use in Pss. 15:5; 16:8; 46:5; 112:6). The response of the people has to be one of trust in the LORD, just as the king placed his ground of hope in him.

2. Confidence in the LORD's Future Victories (*vv. 8-12*)

Now the focus switches to the future, and to deliverances that the LORD will provide. It is the king who is being addressed. **Your hand will lay hold on all your enemies; your right hand will seize your foes. At the time of your appearing you will make them like a fiery furnace. In his wrath the LORD will swallow them up, and his fire will consume them** (*vv. 8-9*). Just as verses 2-7 described the *blessings* of God on the king, so now verses 8-12 set out the *curses* that the king visits on his enemies. When the king appears (using language which is often used of God himself) he will destroy his enemies with the aid of the LORD. Double parallelism occurs in verse 8: 'your hand'/'your right hand', and 'your enemies'/'your haters' (i.e 'those who hate you'). The same verb (*mâtsâ'*, 'to find') is used twice, probably with the meaning 'to find out, to search for'.

[3] For comment on the 'Most High', see Psalm 7:17.

Just as the contents of a burning oven are destroyed, so shall the enemies perish. This is described as a divine action, even though the king and his forces would accomplish it.

You will destroy their descendants from the earth, their posterity from mankind. Though they plot evil against you and devise wicked schemes, they cannot succeed; for you will make them turn their backs when you aim at them with drawn bow (*vv. 10-12*). The destruction of the enemies would be so complete that they would leave no descendants behind them. This was a curse often expressed in the ancient Near East (cf. Jeremiah 22:30 in reference to King Jehoiachin). The idea is that the lack of descendants would mean that these particular enemies through lack of followers would never be in a position to attack again. However much they devise plans, and scheme against the king, they will not succeed, for the LORD has them on the run, so that their backs are exposed to the pursuing troops.

3. The Prayer of the Congregation (*v. 13*)

Be exalted, O LORD, in your strength; we will sing and praise your might. The psalm ends with a prayer asking for God to reveal his strength and majesty. There are military overtones here in keeping with the subject matter of the psalm (cf. Num. 10:35). The request for God to be exalted is echoed later in the Psalter (see Ps. 57:5, 11). The might of the LORD is to be the subject of praise by the people as a whole ('we'), just as verses 2-7 were such praise regarding the past victories.

Psalm 22

To the director of music.
To the tune of 'The Doe of the Morning'. A psalm of David.

This is a priceless psalm, and in many ways the supreme example in the Psalter of an appeal for help. According to the title, it is a cry from David to the LORD, and there are features in the psalm that point to it being connected with incidents in David's life (see v. 2, which shows that the appeal was made over a considerable period of time). He calls on God in whom 'our fathers put their trust' (v. 4), which seems to be a reference to earlier fathers of the nation, or possibly even to the patriarchs, Abraham, Isaac, and Jacob. It may be, as Calvin claims, that David sums up here various incidents of suffering and persecution in his life.[1]

There are strong connections between this psalm and Jeremiah's writings (cf. Ps. 22:6b with Jer. 49:15; Ps. 22:7a with Jer. 20:7b; Ps. 22:7b with Lam. 2:15 and Jer. 18:16; Ps. 22:9-10 with Jer. 1:5; 15:10; 20:14, 17-18).[2] Yet the fact that it is quoted thirteen times in the New Testament, and nine times alone in the account of Jesus' suffering and death, points to a fuller meaning realised only in our Lord's messianic affliction. Because of this Psalm 22 has even been referred to as 'the Fifth Gospel'.[3] Though the primary reference in the psalm must be to David and his experiences, there is an

[1] John Calvin, *A Commentary on the Psalms of David* (London: Thomas Tegg, 1840), I, p. 232.

[2] For the reference to Jeremiah, see W. L. Holladay, 'The Background of Jeremiah's Self-Understanding, Moses, Samuel, and Psalm 22', *JBL* 83 (1964), pp. 153-64.

[3] See, S. B. Frost, 'Psalm 22: An Exposition', *CJT* 8 (1962), pp. 102-15.

indirect messianic application (see my broader discussion on the messianic element in the Introduction). This explains why in the North African churches in Augustine's time (AD c. 354–430) this psalm was sung at the Easter celebration of the Lord's Supper. Similarly, it has been traditionally associated with communion services of the Scottish churches since the Reformation.

1. Invocation and Call for Help (*v. 1-2*)

The psalm opens with a despairing cry. **My God, my God, why have you forsaken me?** (*v. 1a*). The ultimate expression of desolation is Jesus' use of these words on the cross (Matt. 27:46; the words quoted, *Eloi, Eloi, lama sabachtani*, are the Aramaic equivalent of the Hebrew words here in v. 1). The idea of being forsaken by God occurs several times in the Old Testament, especially in passages in which God accuses his people of sinning against him (Judg. 10:13; 1 Sam. 8:8; 1 Kings 11:33; 2 Kings 22:17). Neither here nor in Psalm 44, which is a communal lament on being forsaken by God, is there any suggestion of sin on the part of the speakers.

Why are you so far from saving me, so far from the words of my groaning? O my God, I cry out by day, but you do not answer, by night, and am not silent (*vv. 1b-2*). Even though the speaker has called God 'my God', yet he feels that salvation is so far away from him. The words of his groaning are addressed to God day and night, and yet no answer seems to come. A sense of abandonment comes over the psalmist, and God's silence troubles him. The word 'far' (*râchôq*) is repeated in verses 11 and 19, which helps to maintain the sense of isolation throughout the psalm.

2. The Basis of Faith (*vv. 3-5*)

Yet you are enthroned as the Holy One; you are the praise of Israel. In you our fathers put their trust; they trusted and you delivered them. They cried to you and were saved; in you they trusted and were not disappointed (*vv. 3-5*). Verse 3 can be translated as the NIV does, or we can adapt slightly the NIV margin and render: 'You the Holy One are enthroned on the praises of Israel.' Whichever option is taken, the idea is present that God is the object of Israel's praise, and he is indeed the Holy One. The Hebrew word for holiness used here (*qâdôsh*) comes from a Semitic root that means 'cut off' or 'separate'. It denotes God's transcendence and his ethical purity. It is used in a threefold refrain in Psalm 99 and also in the threefold call of the seraphim in Isaiah 6:3. The psalmist appeals to Israel's history to show why he is calling upon God with expectancy. The explanation for this is that their forefathers had put their trust in him. Three times the verb 'to trust' is used (Hebrew *bâtach*), and this is one of the great 'faith' words of the Old Testament and the most frequent of them.[4] Those who had called on Israel's God in times of great need had experienced his saving mercy. Their faith was not misplaced. All who trust or take refuge in the LORD will never be put to shame, for he will save them (cf. Ps. 71:1).

3. Lament (*vv. 6-8*)

The psalmist now bemoans his condition, in that he is barely left as a man. **But I am a worm and not a man, scorned by men and despised by the people** (*v. 6*). There are many similarities here to the language of Isaiah, who calls Israel a 'worm' (Isa. 41:14), and who says of the Servant of the LORD that he is so disfigured that people can hardly recognise him as a man (Isa. 52:14; 53:2-3). The use of 'worm' highlights the psalmist's perception of himself, for he is weak and insignificant, while the parallel expressions in the second part of the verse indicate the result of others' perception of him.

All who see me mock me; they hurl insults, shaking their heads: (*v. 7*). All who see his suffering take delight in it. They shake their heads, not in compassion, but out of joy that he has been brought to this condition, and they cast

---

[4] For a helpful discussion on this and other words relating to faith, see G. J. Wenham, *Faith in the Old Testament*.

reproaches in his face. They react to his condition and need with derision.

What they say to him is: '**He trusts in** (Hebrew *gol*, which is an imperative: lit. *roll on*) **the LORD; let the LORD rescue him. Let him deliver him, since he delights in him'** (*v. 8*). Of course, this is said in jest, with no expectation that God would intervene and save his servant. But later in the psalm we see that the prayer of the psalmist was indeed answered, for God did not turn his face away and refuse to listen (v. 24). 'Rescue' and 'deliver' are used as synonyms, while the verb 'delights in' (*châfêts*) is used of God's pleasure in his servants such as David (2 Sam. 22:20) or in their observance of his law (Isa. 56:4).

4. A Confident Appeal (*vv. 9-11*)

All the songs of appeal have as a characteristic an expression of trust in the LORD and commitment to him. It comes here in the words: **Yet you brought me out of the womb; you made me trust in you even at my mother's breast. From birth I was cast upon you; from my mother's womb you have been my God. Do not be far from me, for trouble is near and there is no one to help** (*vv. 9-11*). The words of the mockers are now turned against them, as the psalmist says that from infancy he has been trusting in the LORD. The same verb for 'trust' is used as has already appeared in verses 4-5. The God in whom he trusts is said to be 'my God', echoing the appeal to God in verse 1. Verses 9 and 10 are paired, in that the expressions in verse 9 are paralleled in verse 10, though in reverse order:

> You/brought me/from the womb/you made me
> trust in you/upon my mother's breasts:
> Upon you/I was cast/from the womb/from the
> womb of my mother/my God are you.[5]

---

[5] The two Hebrew words for 'womb' (*béten* and *rêchem*) are synonymous, and are used in parallelism also in Job 3:11; 10:18-19; 31:15; Ps. 58:3; Isa. 46:3, and Jer. 1:5. See Y. Avishur, *Stylistic Studies of Word-Pairs in Biblical and Ancient Semitic Languages* (Neukirchen-Vluyn: Neukirchener 1984), p. 70.

The request, 'Do not be far from me', also echoes verse 1, as he pleads with God to reverse the present seeming separation between them.

5. Another Lament (*vv. 12-18*)
The imagery in these verses is dramatic, for various metaphors are used to describe graphically the ordeals he has been through. **Many bulls surround me; strong bulls of Bashan encircle me. Roaring lions tearing their prey open their mouths wide against me. I am poured out like water, and all my bones are out of joint. My heart has turned to wax; it has melted away within me. My strength is dried up like a potsherd, and my tongue sticks to the roof of my mouth; you lay me in the dust of death. Dogs have surrounded me; a band of evil men has encircled me** (*vv. 12-16a*). Such metaphors are part of biblical poetry, for they serve to engage the mind and to stir emotions. We can feel for the psalmist as he describes his enemies as bulls, lions, and dogs, while he himself has a heart of wax, strength as dry as a potsherd, a tongue stuck to his palate, and he feels as if he is already in the grave. On every side the psalmist is hemmed in by those who seek to kill him. The reference to Bashan is to an area east of the Jordan that was well known for its cattle (cf. Amos 4:1).

They have pierced my hands and my feet (*v. 16b*). This part of verse 16 has for long provided difficulty for commentators as the Hebrew text does not seem to make good sense.[6] It reads literally, 'like a lion, my hands and my feet.' All the early translators into Greek, Latin, Syriac, and Arabic found this verse a problem, and instead of 'like a lion', they all insert a verb: 'they pierced', or 'they bound', or 'they put to shame'. Unless we propose some textual change and read something like, 'My hands and feet are exhausted', we are left with the problems. If so, then the

---

[6] Of the older commentators full notes can be found in E. W. Hengstenberg, *The Psalms*, I, pp. 383-87, F. Delitzsch, *The Psalms*, I, pp. 317-20, and J. J. S. Perowne, *The Book of Psalms:* I, pp. 255-56. For modern bibliography on this psalm as a whole and also the textual problem in verse 16, see Samuel Terrien, *The Psalms*, pp. 226-28.

word normally translated 'lion' may well be a verb 'to bind'. Hence, the translation would be: 'they bound my hands and feet'.[7] The only other alternative would be to understand a verb, e.g. 'like a lion [they maul] my hands and feet', or else assume that the force of the verb in 16a is carried over into 16b: 'they surround me, like a lion, [even] my hands and my feet.' The point of mentioning hands and feet is that 'hands' form the means of defence against the enemy, the feet the means of escape. While the New Testament quotes Psalm 22 so often, yet never once is this verse referred to the crucifixion.[8]

I can count all my bones; people stare and gloat over me. They divide my garments among them and cast lots for my clothing (*vv. 17-18*). The final act of indignity is that the sufferer, who can count all his bones that are out of joint (see v. 14a), is the laughing stock of his persecutors, who strip him of his clothing. The enemies gaze with pleasure on one destined for death; they take pleasure in his humiliation. The dividing-up of the garments is not for gain, but to indicate that all is now finished for the afflicted sufferer. The words of the psalmist come to highest fulfillment in the death of the sufferer *par excellence*, Jesus.

6. A Further Appeal (*vv. 19-21*)

Once more the psalmist cries to his God, commencing with the same language as at the end of his previous appeal in verse 11.

---

[7] Several factors must be considered in assessing proposed alterations to the text. (1) The Hebrew manuscript evidence is almost without exception supportive of the reading 'like a lion'. (2) The word for 'a lion' (*ʾᵃrî*) fits the context as lions have already been mentioned in verse 13 and will again be part of the scene in verse 21, even though a slightly variant form of the word is used in these verses (*ʾaryēh* instead of *ʾᵃrî*). (3) The evidence of the versions, though supporting a verbal form (either *kâʾrû*, 'they pierced', or *kârû*, 'they bound'), is not uniform. (4) Modern emendations, such as given by P. C. Craigie, *Psalms 1-50*, p. 196, involve even greater alteration to the MT.

[8] Another objection to the interpretation that assumes that this verse points to the crucifixion of Jesus is that crucifixion does not appear to have been practised in Israel at the time at which the psalm was composed. Deuteronomy 21:22-23 deals with impalement on a tree after execution. See my comments on these verses in *Deuteronomy: The Commands of a Covenant God* (Fearn: Christian Focus Publications, 2001), p. 201.

But you, O LORD, be not far off; O my Strength, come quickly to help me (*v. 19*). There has been a progression in the psalm in regard to this idea of God being far off. First, there was the recognition of this fact (v. 1); then, the appeal for him to come near, noting there was none to help (v. 11); and, finally, with an added emphasis ('But you' is emphatic), an urgent appeal for God to come quickly. The form of address to God uses the word *ʾeyâlûtî* which is a *hapax legomenon*. The NIV translation 'my strength' is also adopted by many commentators, and it is probably preferable to 'my help' found in the RSV, NRSV, NEB, and REB.[9] While the petitioner is so near to death and in utter despair, yet, like the poet in Psalm 88, he can still direct an appeal to God for deliverance.

Deliver my life from the sword, my precious life from the power of the dogs. Save me from the mouth of the lions; you have heard me from the horns of the wild oxen (*vv. 20-21*). The enemies are again depicted as wild animals ('dogs', 'lions', 'wild oxen'), crowding in on him waiting for his death. But now he knows with assurance that God has heard him (following the NIV margin).[10] This interpretation then regards verses 20 and 21a as forming a triple appeal for deliverance, including deliverance from 'the horns of the wild oxen' ('Save me from the mouth of the lions and from the horns of the wild oxen'). This section of the psalm is then concluded with the words 'you have answered me', which both show the change that has come about since the psalmist said 'you do not answer' (v. 2) and also provide a fitting introduction to the final songs of thanksgiving that conclude the psalm.[11] 'You have answered me' is the transition point leading into the expression of praise for God's deliverance.

---

[9] For fuller information see P. C. Craigie, *Psalms 1-50*, p. 197, and *NIDOTTE*, 1, p. 377.

[10] The MT has *ʿanîtânî*, that appears to be from the verb *ʿânâh* I, 'to answer'. The LXX has *tên tapeinôsin mou*, 'my humiliation', which, while fitting in with the general context, yet is based on a reading that deviates from the MT. The same objection can be made against Samuel Terrien's suggestion (*The Psalms*, p. 233) that the word means 'my wounded flesh', taking the root of the word to be *ʿânâh* III, 'to afflict'.

[11] In interpreting verses 20-21 in this way I am following E. W. Hengstenberg, *The Psalms*, I, pp. 389-90. More recently P. C. Craigie, *The Psalms*, pp. 197, 200 has adopted a similar position.

7. Two Songs of Thanksgiving (*vv. 22-26, 27-31*)
What a contrast between the beginning and end of the psalm! Now that God has heard, the psalmist wants to proclaim God's character ('name' often has this connotation in Hebrew) to his fellow Israelites. The shift from penitent supplication to praise, though sudden, is not without parallel (cf. Ps. 6:8-10). **I will declare your name to my brothers; in the congregation I will praise you. You who fear the LORD, praise him! All you descendants of Jacob, honour him! Revere him, all you descendants of Israel! For he has not despised or disdained the suffering of the afflicted one; he has not hidden his face from him but has listened to his cry for help** (*vv. 22-24*). The reason for this praise is that God has remembered his afflicted one, and answered his call for help. The synonymous expressions for the people of God are important: 'my brothers', 'the congregation', 'you who fear the LORD', 'all you descendants of Jacob/Israel'. The word used for 'congregation' (Hebrew *qâhâl* = Greek *ekklēsia*) refers to the assembled people of God, and denotes an enduring feature of Israel's existence. When called 'the great congregation', this assembly is simply being described as the major gathering of God's people in Old Testament times (see Pss. 22:25; 35:18; 40:9, 10). David even adopts a missionary spirit, as he encourages others to honour and revere the LORD. The words of verse 22 are used in Hebrews 2:12 in reference to Jesus not being ashamed to call believers his brothers. He revealed his Father's will to them, and in turn this resulted in their becoming his brothers.[12] Deliverance by the LORD is the greatest, and most basic, motivation for missionary service. David refers to himself in the third person here, calling himself 'the afflicted one', in order to bring into sharper focus God's mercy to him. Other humans would turn their faces away from the afflicted, but God, who is not a man, has listened and heard his cry. Furthermore, the psalmist unites with other sufferers as they together praise the Lord.

From you comes my praise in the great assembly; before those who fear you, will I fulfil my vows. The poor will eat and

[12] See in particular the discussion of verse 23 in relation to Hebrews 2:12 in S. Kistemaker, *The Psalm Citations in the Epistle to the Hebrews* (Amsterdam: Wed. G. VanSoest N. V., 1961), pp. 83-85.

be satisfied; they who seek the LORD will praise him – may your hearts live forever! (*vv. 25-26*). He acknowledges that from the LORD alone comes the reason for his praise; it is all of his doing. As in verses 22-23, after his deliverance by the LORD, he sings his praise at the sanctuary in the presence of other God-fearers. He also brings a thank-offering that he had vowed during his trouble (Lev. 7:16), and in accordance with the custom in reference to the tithes (Deut. 14:28-29; 26:12) and at the harvest (Deut. 16:11), the widows, orphans, and poor in the community share in the meal. The final phrase in verse 26 may well have been a customary expression used at meals, asking for divine provision always to be the portion of those present at that time. Other similar statements without any introductory comment or explanation, that are in effect exclamations, occur in Psalms 31:14a; 45:6a; and 87:6b.[13]

David widens his vision at the end of this psalm and prophesies that all the nations and even children yet to be born will join in praise to the LORD. **All the ends of the earth will remember and turn to the LORD, and all the families of the nations will bow down before him, for dominion belongs to the LORD and he rules over the nations. All the rich of the earth will feast and worship; all who go down to the dust will kneel before him – those who cannot keep themselves alive** (*vv. 27-29*). In the context the primary meaning is that even far off nations will hear about David's deliverance and turn to the LORD in repentance. Gentile nations will come and bow in subjection to him who has all dominion and authority (cf. Pss. 72:8-11; 96:10-13). Just as direct address to the assembled people occurs in verse 26, so in verse 27 there is direct address to God: 'all the families of the nations will bow down *before you*.' This is the reading of the MT, but NIV and other versions adopt the translation 'before him'. In doing so they are following the LXX and the Syriac versions, which are also supported by Jerome. These verses are part of the missionary vision of the Old Testament, as prophets and psalmists sing of God's kingdom being extended to incorporate Gentile believers. The thought

---

[13] Here the use of the jussive form (*yᵉchî*, 'may [your hearts] live') may be an intentional use in order to vary the verb sequences, addressing directly the persons who have just been spoken of in the preceding context. For the grammar, see *IBHS*, p. 570.

of verse 29 is that rich and poor alike will join in worship of the LORD, sharing together in a communal meal, though this will be an eschatological feast rather than the votive meal mentioned in verse 26.[14] There will be no separation of rich and poor in that day, for the wealthy and those so poor that they are on the brink of the grave will both bow in submission to their Saviour.

Posterity will serve him; future generations will be told about the Lord. They will proclaim his righteousness to a people yet unborn – for he has done it (*vv. 30-31*). Within Israel coming generations will serve the LORD, for generation after generation shall be told about the wonderful deeds of the LORD. Those yet to be born will in their day hear of the LORD's righteousness (cf. Psalm 78:1-7). In this context 'righteousness' has the idea of 'salvation', 'deliverance'. The final words of the psalm stress that salvation is indeed of the LORD alone: 'for he has done [it].' Neither the subject nor the object are expressed in the Hebrew text, but the preceding references to the way in which the Lord heard the cry of the psalmist makes it plain that it is the deliverance by the LORD that is in view. The psalm that began on such a sorrowful note ends with the theme of universal joy in God's redemption.

David's experiences as set out in this psalm are not his alone, but in particular they are a pointer to the coming sufferings of the Lord Jesus. On the Cross our Lord used both its opening words ('My God, My God, why have you forsaken me?') and also its closing words ('It is finished', cf. 'for he has done it'). He is the one who has identified with us in our sufferings, which the writer to the Hebrews stresses in his exposition of the work of Jesus (Heb. 2:10-18; 4:15-16; 5:7-10). Having been made perfect through suffering, he is able to be a merciful and faithful high priest for his people, and even to unite with them in singing praise for God's salvation.

[14] Many commentators and translators think that the opening word of verse 29 should be emended from *'âk^{e}lû* ('they shall eat') to *'ak lô* ('indeed to him', cf. *BHS*, RSV). If this suggestion is followed, then a further emendation is required to change the following verb from being a *vav* consecutive to a simple future by deleting the initial *vav*. As eating has already been mentioned in verse 26, it seems best to retain the MT, avoiding both word division, revocalisation, and deletion.

Psalm 23

A psalm of David.

Probably no psalm is better known nor more universally loved than this one. Because of its lack of details it is impossible to date this psalm, or to link it with any specific event. Its general nature, however, helps us to identify with it as it proclaims the depth of personal relationship between the LORD and a believer. It is steeped in a covenantal setting, and it has many affinities with descriptions of the Exodus experience. It uses the metaphor of the shepherd to speak of God's loving concern for his sheep and the richness of provision he makes for them.

1. The Divine Shepherd (*vv. 1-4*)

The LORD is my shepherd, I shall lack nothing (*v. 1*). The covenantal nature of this psalm is emphasised by the fact that the opening word is the distinctive covenantal name for God. The psalmist makes the declaration that this LORD is his own shepherd. He is appropriating language for himself that applied to the nation as a whole (see Pss. 79:13; 95:7; 100:3; Isa. 40:11; Ezek. 34). In the same way Christian believers can speak in personal terms of Christ's work (cf. Gal. 2:20b: he 'loved *me* and gave himself for *me*'). Just as God saw to it that the children of Israel lacked no good thing after the Exodus, so also the individual believer will lack nothing (cf. Deut. 2:7).

He makes me lie down in green pastures, he leads me beside quiet waters, he restores my soul. He guides me in paths of righteousness for his name's sake (*vv. 2-3*). The function of the shepherd with respect to the flock as a whole is now particularised to his care for the individual sheep. He leads to pasture and to water, and thus brings what seems like new life to the soul. The first part of verse 3 defines further what has already been said in verse 2. All the paths of the LORD are paths of righteousness, and he leads his people in them 'for his name's sake'. The verb 'leads' (*nâhal*) re-echoes the use of the same verb at the Exodus (Exod. 15:13), while 'for his name's sake' (*l^{e}maʿan sh^{e}mô*) is also used of the Exodus experience (Ps. 106:8).

Even though I walk through the valley of the shadow of death, I will fear no evil, for you are with me; your rod and your staff, they comfort me (*v. 4*). The many ravines in Palestine suggest the metaphor of this verse. In all the facets of life, including the most feared ('the valley of shadow of death', or alternatively, 'the valley of deepest darkness'),[1] the shepherd's rod and staff give comfort and assurance. David knew from his pastoral experience how helpful the rod and staff were, and so transfers the idea to God as the great and good shepherd. If God is with believers, then why should they fear? (cf. Rom. 8:31-39).

2. The Gracious Provision (*vv. 5-6*)

You prepare a table before me in the presence of my enemies. You anoint my head with oil; my cup overflows. Surely goodness and love will follow me all the days of my life, and I will dwell in the house of the LORD forever (*vv. 5-6*). The scene changes from food and water for sheep to banquet fare for humans. While it is possible that the psalmist is thinking of the special meals at times of sacrifice, yet it is more probable that he is thinking of the other meal times or special feasts. 'Table' is not to be understood as like Western wooden ones, but a skin or hide spread on the ground, though the verb 'to prepare' (*ʿârak*) implies

---

[1] The Hebrew word in question, *tsalmâvet*, occurs eighteen times, all in poetry. The debate is whether the traditional derivation and the translation, 'valley of the shadow of death,' should be retained, or a derivation sought from the root *ts-l-m*, 'to become dark', and giving a rendering like 'deep darkness'. The traditional rendering has strong support, and the reference to death certainly brings in the emotional element present in situations of fear or danger. For this view, and a summary of other positions, see *NIDOTTE*, 3, pp. 807-10.

thoughtful preparation.[2] The shepherd lavishes his care on his children. He anoints the head, and gives so liberally that it is like an overflowing cup. Oil was used on festive occasions and, along with perfumes, symbolised joy (cf. Ps. 133:2). All this is because of the covenantal relationship.

The psalmist is sure that the blessings of the covenant and God's steadfast love will pursue him to the end of his life. The two Hebrew words used here (*tôv* and *chésed*) have strong covenantal connotations,[3] and together they form a fixed pair.[4] He commits himself to come back constantly to God's house. The Hebrew text has 'I will return', while the commonly accepted English translation (as in NIV) follows the LXX.[5] God's house (the tabernacle or later the temple) will be the constant abode of his people. The final phrase in the Hebrew text is simply 'length of days', that parallels 'all the days of my life' in the first part of the verse. The phrase denotes a long life (cf. Job 12:12), not an eternal life.[6] A lifelong experience of God's tender care brings a commitment to be always found in the LORD's house. This reference to God's house provides a key word that links this and the four following psalms (Pss. 23-27), and it forms a central and unifying theme

---

[2] Victor Hamilton draws attention to the fact that the basic meaning of this verb 'is "to arrange in order" for the sake of accomplishing a useful purpose. It is never used to describe arranging something arbitrarily or haphazardly' (*NIDOTTE*, 3, p. 536). Samuel Terrien points out that the corresponding Arabic word for 'table' continues to mean an animal skin or woven rug thrown on the ground (*The Psalms*, p. 241).

[3] See in particular A. R. Millard, 'For He is Good', *TB*, 1966, pp. 115-17, and the literature he cites. For fuller discussion of the covenantal significance of *tôv* and *tôvâh*, see P. Kalluveettil, *Declaration and Covenant: A Comprehensive Review of Covenant Formulae from the Old Testament and the Ancient Near East* (Rome: Biblical Institute Press, 1982), pp. 42-47.

[4] For further discussion on this point, see M. L. Barré, 'The Formulaic Pair *ṭwb (w) ḥsd* in the Psalter', *ZAW* 98 (1986), pp. 100-05.

[5] I have discussed the interpretation of this verse, including the question of whether the verb is 'to return' or 'to dwell', in 'The Conclusion of Psalm 23', *The Tyndale Paper* (Australia), XXXIV, 1 (March, 1989), pp. 1-8.

[6] It is strange that later Protestant commentators took the Hebrew to mean 'eternal life' when Renaissance and Reformation scholars had correctly understood it to have a temporal connotation. For some examples of the exegesis of Psalm 23 in those periods, see William Yarchin: *History of Biblical Interpretation: A Reader* (Peabody: Hendrikson, 2004), pp. 175-83.

within them. In Psalm 24 the poet asks about the character of the person who comes into the LORD's presence (vv. 3-4), while Psalm 25 has explicit references to covenant (vv. 6, 7, 10, 14). Psalm 26 contains the declaration that the author loves the house where the LORD lives (v. 8), followed in the next psalm by expressions of longing to dwell in the LORD's house (Ps. 27:4) and confidence in the protection the temple affords (Ps. 27:5).

Psalm 24

Of David. A psalm.

From Jewish tradition we know that this psalm was sung every Sabbath morning in the temple when the wine offering was made. The LXX evidence agrees with this as it adds to the title the words, 'for the seventh day of the week'. The psalm opens with an affirmation of the LORD's sovereignty over everything. It moves on to describe the character of the true worshipper, and then ends on the kingship of God as the ark is brought into Jerusalem.

1. The LORD of Creation (*vv. 1-2*)

The earth is the LORD's, and everything in it, the world, and all who live in it; for he founded it upon the seas and established it upon the waters (*vv. 1-2*). The opening words of this psalm are quoted by Paul (1 Cor. 10:26) to show that all foods can be eaten, because they all come from the LORD. The words were very familiar in Jewish circles because they were part of prayers said at mealtimes.[1] Paul was clearly thinking of mealtimes when he uses this quotation as his later comment on partaking of a meal and giving thanks to God make evident (1 Cor. 10:30). He does not draw a conclusion from his use of the quotation, but the reader is expected to understand that even though meat may be offered to idols, because it comes from God, it may be eaten. Central to the psalm's message is that the LORD is not only the God of Israel; he is the God of the whole world. To him it belongs, as well as all who live in it. It is his, because he is the creator of it. The founding of the earth is

[1] Cf. *Berakot* 35a-b.

described in terms reminiscent of other ancient Near Eastern creation accounts. Other passages in the Old Testament use similar language (Pss. 104:5-6; 136:6; Job 38:4-11).

2. The Character of True Worshippers (*vv. 3-6*)

Who may ascend the hill of the LORD? Who may stand in his holy place? (*v. 3*). These questions are very like those in Psalm 15:1. They may well have been asked as the ark was being brought into Jerusalem, but they also clearly have a wider connotation. The psalmist is asking regarding the character of the worshipper who approaches God's dwelling and stands his ground there.[2]

The answer to the questions specifies four characteristics. **He who has clean hands and a pure heart, who does not lift up his soul to an idol or swear by what is false** (*v. 4*). Purity of action and purity of desire are both demanded, which Jesus later spoke of when he said: 'Blessed are the pure in heart, for they will see God' (Matt. 5:8). Likewise there could be no compromise with idolatry. The Hebrew word translated 'idol' (*shâv'*) is simply 'vanity', but this word is applied to false gods in the Old Testament (see Pss. 24:4; 31:6; Jer. 18:15). The phrase clearly refers to an Israelite who is not living a life of obedience to the LORD. The final characteristic describes a life of falsehood by singling out one special form that it takes – false swearing.

He will receive blessing from the LORD and vindication from God his Saviour. Such is the generation of those who seek him, who seek your face, O God of Jacob. ***Selah*** (*vv. 5-6*). What is impossible for sinful man to do is ultimately received as a gift of God. The content of the blessing becomes much clearer in the New Testament, where it is seen as spiritual and eternal gifts (see Matt. 25:34; Gal. 3:14; Eph. 1:3). God the Saviour is also the vindicator of his people, as he lives up to his part of the covenant and faithfully blesses them. 'Seekers' is a common Old Testament expression for true worshippers

---

[2] This comment is based on the fact that the Hebrew verb for 'stand' (*qûm*) can be used in the sense of 'endure', 'survive'. Cf. Nahum 1:6a: 'Who can *endure* his fierce anger?' with the parallel verb being *'âmad*.

who seek the LORD in prayer and who turn to him in their need. The conclusion of verse 6 is awkward in the Hebrew text, as after the words 'who seek your face', it simply says 'Jacob'. The NIV follows the common view that this is probably a case of ellipsis, so that the words 'God of' have to be added to complete the meaning. While this understanding is old (the LXX contains it), yet it would be very unusual if mention of God was omitted. In the context, with the reference being to those who seek God, it makes better sense to take it to be an identification of the true worshippers with their forefather Jacob. He was the one who pled with God: 'I will not let you go unless you bless me' (Gen. 32:26). It makes good sense to understand the comment at the end of the verse to be: '[They are] Jacob.'

3. The Triumph of the King of Glory (*vv. 7-10*)
Lift up your heads, O you gates; be lifted up, you ancient doors, that the King of glory may come in. Who is this King of glory? The LORD strong and mighty, the LORD mighty in battle (*vv. 7-8*). This psalm either dates from the bringing of the ark to Jerusalem (see 2 Sam. 6), or the return of the ark after a victorious battle. In the midst of the people is the ark, 'which is called by the Name, the name of the LORD Almighty, who is enthroned between the cherubim that are on the ark' (2 Sam. 6:2; cf. also Num. 10:35). It represents God himself, and therefore the call goes out for the gates of Zion to receive the LORD. The removal of the ark to Jerusalem marked the end of the battles to obtain possession of the land. The LORD comes as a mighty warrior to his rightful dwelling place.

Lift up your heads, O you gates; lift them up, you ancient doors, that the King of glory may come in. Who is he, this King of glory? The LORD Almighty – he is the King of glory. ***Selah*** (*vv. 9-10*). The words of verse 7 are repeated almost exactly (the only change is from 'be lifted up' to 'lift up'). The final question draws attention to the character of this triumphant king. The king of glory is the LORD Almighty (*yhwh tsᵉvâ'ôt*). This name for God, 'LORD of hosts' or 'LORD Almighty', occurs here for the first of its fifteen appearances in the Psalter. It often carries military overtones, and so designates the LORD of the armies. This would be most fitting here, as the LORD leads his armies into Jerusalem.[3] The procession into the temple is also an occasion to acknowledge afresh the LORD as the glorious king. He is LORD of creation (vv. 1-2) and also the exalted king of salvation (vv. 7-10).

[3] The term 'LORD' or 'God of hosts' (for both forms were used) can have a variety of meanings. 'Hosts' can refer to the angels, the heavenly bodies, the armies of Israel, or even the universe. An excellent summary of the Old Testament usage is provided by J. E. Hartley in *TWOT*, 2, pp. 750-51, and further discussion on its use in the Psalms can be found in J. P. Ross, 'Yahweh Seba'ot in Sam and Ps', *VT* 17 (1967), pp. 76-92.

Psalm 25

Of David.

This beautiful psalm reads well in English, but our translations disguise another aspect of it. In Hebrew it is an acrostic like Psalms 9-10, with each successive verse beginning with the next letter of the Hebrew alphabet.[1] Four of the exceptions are that the letter *vav* is missing, the letter *qôf* is missing, the letter *rêsh* occurs twice in consecutive verses, and after the final letter of the alphabet is used in verse 21, another verse follows introduced by the letter *pê*.[2] This too may be deliberate, because the first letter (*alef*), the middle letter (*lamed*), and the final letter (*pe*) form a Hebrew word that means 'to learn' or 'to teach' (*lâmad*).The theme of teaching is so central to the psalm, with its repeated mention of being taught God's ways. The background of this instruction is God's covenant love, which the psalmist wants to make known.

It has been suggested that the psalm revolves around a chiastic structure that follows this pattern:[3]

[1] For discussion on the acrostic psalms, see the Introduction.

[2] Psalm 34 exhibits some of the same variations of the acrostic pattern, in that the letter *vav* is omitted, and that after the alphabet is completed, the final verse commences with the letter *pê*. Another detail about the pattern in Psalm 25 is that all the verses consist of two clauses, except the opening and closing verses which only have one clause each. Clearly the pattern of the psalm has been carefully conceived.

[3] Nineteenth century scholars suggested this pattern, and it has been revived lately by Samuel Terrien, *The Psalms*, p. 253. Craigie, *The Psalms*, pp. 217-18 discusses it, but considers there is insufficient evidence to sustain it. An alternative pattern is given by David A. Dorsey, *The Literary Structure of the Old Testament: A Commentary on Genesis–Malachi* (Grand Rapids: Baker, 2004), p. 184.

A	vv. 1-3	A plea for help
B	vv. 4-7	Claiming God's mercy
C	vv. 8-10	Covenant love
D	v. 11	Core verse: a plea for pardon
C[1]	vv. 12-14	Meditation on the covenant
B[1]	vv. 15-18	Prayer for deliverance
A[1]	vv. 19-21	Prayer for protection

Verse 11 does seem to be the fulcrum around which the rest of the psalm revolves, but some of the other proposed parallels are not so certain. It is better to simply take it that the psalm can be broken into three sections. In the first one (vv. 1-7) he addresses God in the second person, while changing to the third person in the second section (vv. 8-15). The final section (vv. 16-22) reverts to direct address to God in the second person.

1. Prayer to the LORD (*vv. 1-7*)
To you, O LORD, I lift up my soul; in you I trust, O my God. Do not let me be put to shame, nor let my enemies triumph over me (*vv. 1-2*). A word of prayer is addressed directly to God. The close relationship between the psalmist and his God is indicated by the way in which he addresses him and by the confident appeal he makes. He claims the LORD as '*my* God', that is the language of faith. He couples this with a declaration of trust in him.[4] The themes of trust and confident waiting on God are a feature of this song (see the ideas of waiting for God in vv. 2, 5, and 21, and of taking refuge in God in v. 20). Because of that relationship he can go on to make his appeal to God. What he wants is help against his enemies. Later in the psalm he is going to describe more closely his affliction (vv. 16-18). If there is no help from God, an audience of gloating enemies will rejoice over his downfall. For Christians there is the assurance that by faith in Christ we come to possess a hope that will never disappoint us (Rom. 5:1-5).

---

[4] For the Hebrew usage of 'trust in' (*bâtach b[e]*), see the comment on Psalm 9:10. No great difference exists in meaning between this verb and *châsâh b[e]* that is used in verse 20, though D. J. Wiseman has suggested that *châsâh* may denote 'more precipitate action' (*TWOT*, I, p. 307).

No one whose hope is in you will ever be put to shame, but they will be put to shame who are treacherous without excuse (*v. 3*). In this verse a different word is used to express confidence in the LORD. No one who truly 'waits on' the LORD will find their prayer disregarded, for they are displaying confidence in him. The Hebrew verb used (*qâvah*) is one of several that our English versions translate by the word 'wait', but it is distinctive in that it does not denote passive waiting on God. Rather, it points to prayer that involves action, striving with God in prayer. The root idea is associated with tension, which explains why the noun from it can mean both a cord (Josh. 2:18, 21) and the ground of hope (Job 4:6; Ps. 71:5).[5] On the other hand, those who deal treacherously with God (the verbs 'wait' and 'deal treacherously' stand in contrast with God as the object) will find that there is no deliverance for them. 'Put to shame' tends to suggest in English that the inner state of mind is primarily in view, whereas the Hebrew usage points rather to public disgrace.

Show me your ways, O LORD, teach me your paths; guide me in your truth and teach me, for you are God my Saviour, and my hope is in you all day long (*vv. 4-5*). Two things especially are needed by the psalmist and they are interconnected. He needs enlightenment regarding God's ways, and then he needs God's help to rescue him from his present troubles. In the context God's 'ways' are not the general moral principles to be observed, but rather the ways of deliverance to be provided by him. This is made plain in verse 5 by the clause '*for* (Hebrew *kî*) you are God my Saviour', and also by verse 9, where the 'ways' are those in which God guides as deliverer. He looks for further instruction from the LORD, with the Hebrew root *d-r-k* appearing twice in verses 4-5 (*d^erâkîm* 'ways' and *dârak* Hi. 'lead [me]'). To be 'led in the truth' (Hebrew *^{ʾe}met*) means the truth that belongs to

---

[5] No exact equivalent occurs in the New Testament, though the idea is present in the reference to our Lord being in agony (*agônia*) so that 'he prayed more earnestly' (Luke 22:44). Similarly, Epaphras is described by Paul as 'wrestling in prayer' (*agônizomenos*) for the Colossians (Col. 4:12). For a discussion on the various Hebrew verbs used regarding 'waiting on the Lord', see J. G. S. S. Thomson, 'Wait on the Lord', *ET* 66 (1954), pp. 196-98.

God (cf. the expression in verse 10, 'all the ways of the LORD are loving and *faithful* [Hebrew *ʾᵉmet*]). Appeal to his God involves acknowledgment that he is the God of his salvation or deliverance ('God my Saviour'). The use of this description of God is in reference to his distress. Constantly he looks in trust to his God. The last sentence in verse 7 is usually taken to mean that David was constantly looking to his God, but an alternative interpretation is possible. It is possible to translate 'I wait for your sign [of deliverance] all day long', and this makes very good sense in the context.[6]

Remember, O LORD, your great mercy and love, for they are from of old. Remember not the sins of my youth and my rebellious ways; according to your love remember me, for you are good, O LORD (*vv. 6-7*). There is a threefold use of 'remember' in these verses. He asks for forgiveness of past sins, for God not to remember his sins, and finally for God to remember him as an individual. His past sins troubled him, even the rash sins of youth, and he did not want them held against him. He can pray confidently because he is basing his prayer on the character of God. He is the covenant God who displays covenant love to his people, and acts towards them with generous compassion.

2. The Goodness of the LORD (*vv. 8-15*)

The final statement of verse 7 is amplified at the start of verse 8. **Good and upright is the LORD; therefore he instructs sinners in his ways. He guides the humble in what is right and teaches them his way** (*vv. 8-9*). God is good, and one way in which he shows that goodness is in teaching sinners his ways. He desires that they know his ways and so be guided in true paths. He wants all men to come to a knowledge of the truth (1 Tim. 2:4) and repent of their sinful ways. God's scholars should always be humble, for 'he mocks proud mockers but gives grace to the humble' (Prov. 3:34; also quoted in 1 Pet. 5:5).

---

[6] The Hebrew word translated by the NIV 'is in you' is *ʾôtᶜkâ,* which can be the object marker (*ʾet* with pronominal suffix 2 m.s.) or the noun *ʾôt* (with pronominal suffix 2 m.s.) meaning a 'sign'. I have commented on this word in *Isaiah: A Covenant to be Kept for the Sake of the Church,* pp. 83-84.

All the ways of the LORD are loving and faithful for those who keep the demands of his covenant. For the sake of your name, O LORD, forgive my iniquity, though it is great (*vv. 10-11*). A cluster of terms point to the covenant relationship, and the general demands of God on Israel as a whole are individualised in passages such as this when personal responsibility is the issue. Being in covenant with the LORD always brought with it demands. The same is true of Christians who have to show their love to Jesus by obedience to his commands (Matt. 28:20; John 14:15). Here the psalmist says that God's ways reflect his character in that they are also loving and faithful.[7] The NIV rendering is a little free at the end of verse 10 because the Hebrew text uses two synonyms to describe the formal relationship with the Lord – 'his covenant and his testimonies'. The NLT is better: 'The LORD leads with unfailing love and faithfulness all those who keep his covenant and obey his decrees'. This is a reminder that the relationship binding the believers to the LORD was of a formal nature with a solemn ceremony in which they swore allegiance to him. Because God is both 'good and upright' the psalmist asks for forgiveness. God cannot overlook sin, but in his mercy can forgive. No matter how great the sin, it can be forgiven. He remains today just and the justifier of the person who believes in Jesus (Rom. 3:26).

Who, then, is the man that fears the LORD? He will instruct him in the way chosen for him. He will spend his days in prosperity, and his descendants will inherit the land (*vv. 12-13*). Already the psalmist has described what fearing the LORD involves – including praying, and receiving his instruction. Now he says that that instruction will be in the way of God's will. While the NIV translation 'the way chosen

---

[7] The pair 'unfailing love' (*chésed*) and 'faithfulness' (*ᵓᵉmet*) come together fifty-one times in the Old Testament. The usage suggests that they express a single idea, but this is hard to bring out in English translation. 'Unfailing love' comes near to it, as the meaning of *chésed* seems more dominant than that of 'truth' or 'faithfulness'. On this expression, see Gordon R. Clark, *The Word Hesed in the Hebrew Bible*, pp. 235-55. The New Testament use of 'grace and truth' (John 1:17) echoes this phrase, and both the older Hebrew translation of the New Testament and the modern one retain the two Hebrew words *chésed* and *ᵓᵉmet*.

for him' is possible, it is better to understand it as an active choice the individual makes—'the way he must go', or 'the way he should go'. Such a man will enjoy rest and safety, while his descendants will continue to occupy the land of Canaan. Elsewhere the psalms teach that the wicked will be uprooted from the land and perish (Pss. 1:5; 37:10-11), a repetition of the covenant curse first stated in Leviticus 26:27-35 and then also in Deuteronomy 4:26-27.[8]

The LORD confides in those who fear him; he makes his covenant known to them. My eyes are ever on the LORD, for only he will release my feet from the snare (*vv. 14-15*). The covenant also meant a close bond of friendship with the LORD. There existed a reciprocal relationship in which believers feared the LORD (with a child's, not a slave's, fear) and the LORD disclosed to them more of himself and his covenant.[9] It also meant that in times of trouble, such as the psalmist presently faced, the believer fixed his eyes on the LORD. Only he could deliver from all the traps that the enemies had laid.

3. A Tender Appeal (*vv. 16-22*)

Turn to me and be gracious to me, for I am lonely and afflicted. The troubles of my heart have multiplied; free me from my anguish. Look upon my affliction and my distress and take away all my sins (*vv. 16-18*). Again the psalm returns to direct address to God. The psalmist was facing troubles from within (his own sins) and troubles from without (hatred from his enemies). From both he pleads for release. He senses his loneliness, i.e. he was without a helper, and consequently he makes his appeal for God's graciousness to be shown to him. He feels hemmed in by his troubles and he wants to be taken out of his distress. Knowing that God would forgive for his own name's sake (see verse 11), he asks again for the removal of his sins along with help

---

[8] This teaching is an important aspect of the way in which the concept of 'the land' is dealt with in Deuteronomy. See 6:18; 8:1; 11:8, 21; 16:20; 28:11; 28:58-63; 30:17-20.

[9] The opening word in Hebrew of verse 14 is *sôd*, which can have the meaning of 'secret' (cf. the older English translations, 'the *secret* of the LORD'). However, in this context, as in Psalm 55:14, it means 'trustworthy speech' or 'close fellowship'.

in his troubles. Whereas in verse 16 'affliction' is paralleled with 'loneliness', in verse 18 it is linked with 'distress'. This indicates something of the breadth of meaning that 'affliction' can have, ranging from personal illness to social ostracism.

See how my enemies have increased and how fiercely they hate me! Guard my life and rescue me; let me not be put to shame, for I take refuge in you. May integrity and uprightness protect me, because my hope is in you (*vv. 19-21*). The call for God to 'see' is really a call to help.[10] The trouble surrounding him was not just verbal abuse. He was facing physical danger from the enemies. That is why he asks for God to rescue him, lest his enemies should be able to gloat over him. As his song draws to a close he returns to the theme of trusting in the LORD and also the idea of facing shame or reproach (see vv. 2-3). He had no other helper, for his trust was in the LORD alone. God's character ('integrity and uprightness') was the basis for his plea, and his desire is to reflect in his life God's own character (cf. v. 8). There is no reference to God's answer in the psalm itself, but clearly the praise portion which has preceded (vv. 8-14) suggests an expectancy on the part of the psalmist.

4. A Prayer for the Nation (*v. 22*)

Redeem Israel, O God, from all their troubles! (*v. 22*). This final verse begins with the letter *pe* (like *p* coming after *A–Z* in English). This has led many to think that this verse was added when the psalm began to be used in formal worship situations. The fact that it uses the name 'God' and not 'LORD' also supports this. On the other hand, the references to the covenant in the psalm may well have led into this final verse with reference to all Israel. What was true of the psalmist, was also true of the whole nation, or to put it in another way, the whole psalm was applicable to Israel. If an individual could appeal for help in his personal troubles, why should Israel not appeal for deliverance as well? The call for redemption is equivalent to a call for deliverance (cf. Ps. 3:8, 'Deliverance belongs to the LORD').

[10] The MT begins with a verb whose initial consonant is *rêsh*, whereas the letter expected in the acrostic pattern is *qôf*. Craigie, *Psalms 1-50*, pp. 216-17, emends provisionally by inserting a verb starting with *qôf* and meaning 'meet', but no textual support for this is available.

Psalm 26

Of David.

This psalm does not appear to be an individual complaint to God, for there is no mention of illness or of persecution. Rather, the context from which it comes seems to be worship at the tabernacle. The psalmist renounces connection with ungodly men (vv. 4-5, 9-10), and longs to be in the assembly of the righteous proclaiming the wonderful deeds of the LORD (vv. 6-8, 12). His love is for God's altar (v. 6), God's house (v. 8), and God's people (v. 12). Possibly this song was later used as worshippers came individually to the temple precincts to worship at the LORD's altar.

1. A Confession of Trust *(v. 1)*

Vindicate me, O LORD, for I have led a blameless life; I have trusted in the LORD without wavering. The psalmist expresses his confident trust in the LORD, for he has maintained his confidence without slipping from his ways.[1] His appeal to God is for vindication as he comes to the temple again to worship. He knows that all authority is of God, who is going to preside at the last great judgment (Ps. 96:13). To him he cries again for vindication, since the central issue of his life is his relationship with his God. The combination of the noun 'perfection' (*tôm*) and the verb 'to walk' (*hâlak*) is frequently

[1] The NIV rendering 'without wavering' represents the Hebrew *lô' 'em'âd*, 'I shall not slip.' Those whose trust is in the LORD will not depart from his ways (cf. also Ps. 37:31), whereas those who lack integrity before him are sure to slip (Job 12:5; Ps. 69:23; Prov. 25:19).

used to indicate blameless conduct. The same combination occurs again in verse 11.[2]

2. A Prayer and an Affirmation (*vv. 2-5*)
Stemming from his confession of trust in verse 1, the psalmist moves on to make his request from the LORD. **Test me, O LORD, and try me, examine my heart and my mind; for your love is ever before me, and I walk continually in your truth** (*vv. 2-3*). Here three synonyms are used to describe putting to the test. The first of these ('test') is commonly used of God, and often has a very spiritual connotation. The second ('try') is the general word for testing or refining, while the third ('examine') is the more specific, being a term from metallurgy meaning 'smelt' or 'refine'. The psalmist is so confident of his standing that he is willing to submit to the all-seeing eye of the LORD. His attention was continually fixed on God's covenantal love and his whole conduct (his 'walk') was based on God's truth. The fact that the appeal is based on God's 'love' (Hebrew, *chésed*) is characteristic of hope in times of trouble (see also Psalms 13:5; 17:7; 33:18, 22; 36:7; 143:8; and 147:11).

I do not sit with deceitful men, nor do I consort with hypocrites; I abhor the assembly of evildoers and refuse to sit with the wicked (*vv. 4-5*). Anyone like the psalmist, committed to the LORD and his truth, shuns the association with those who show no love to the LORD. There is no desire to be in constant contact with them as individuals, for they are utterly deceitful.[3]

---

[2] Many, including C. S. Lewis, *Reflections on the Psalms* (London: Geoffrey Bles, 1958), pp. 66-67, misunderstand protests of innocence on the part of the psalmists. Instead of looking at them as holding a position that leads 'straight to "Pharisaism" in the sense which Our Lord's own teaching has given that word', they must be viewed as expressing knowledge that there is 'no condemnation' for them in God's presence. Such a view of their innocence lies behind their confident appeal to their deliverer.

[3] The expression 'deceitful men' (*m^{e}tê shâv'*) employs an unusual word for 'men', which can be used both for those of good or bad character. While *shâv'* can mean 'an idol' (cf. 24:5), here it probably is best to retain a translation like 'deceitful'. This is necessary in the context because of the following word that the NIV translates as 'hypocrites' (*na'^{a}lâmîm*). Most probably this is a Ni. part. of the verb *'âlam*, indicating those who hide themselves and their actions. It parallels, therefore, the other terms used here for deceitful men, evildoers, and the wicked.

Nor will they identify with such people when they gather together, finding them abhorrent because of their wickedness.

3. Approaching the Place of Worship (*vv. 6-8*)

Coming to the temple the psalmist now speaks of the nature of true worship. **I wash my hands in innocence, and go about your altar, O LORD, proclaiming aloud your praise and telling of all your wonderful deeds** (*vv. 6-7*). The idea of washing one's hands probably comes from Exodus 30:17-21, where Aaron and his sons were commanded to wash their hands and feet before they did service at the altar. Here the idea is figurative. Nowhere is such a ceremony of going round the altar commanded in the law, but apparently such an occasion involved singing songs of thanksgiving to the LORD. It may be that the king had a special function at this ceremony. It was an opportunity for praise and proclamation. 'Proclaiming aloud your praise' is more literally to 'proclaim with the voice of thanksgiving' (NASB). While the Hebrew noun for 'thanksgiving' (*tôdâh*) is used in a technical sense in reference to the peace offering called a thank-offering (Lev. 7:12), here it is used in its other more general meaning of a song of praise. To tell of the LORD's wonderful deeds means to recount the great acts of God, especially those associated with his work as saviour and deliverer.[4]

I love the house where you live, O LORD, the place where your glory dwells (*v. 8*). Past association with the place of worship, which is intended especially as the place of God's presence, meant that David could speak of his love for it. It was where God's glory took up an abiding presence, and it is noticeable that God's glory is specially mentioned in connection with the ark of the covenant (see Psalm 24:7; 1 Samuel 4:21; and 1 Kings 8:10-11).

4. Another Prayer (*vv. 9-10*)

Do not take away my soul along with sinners, my life with bloodthirsty men, in whose hands are wicked schemes,

---

[4] The Hebrew verb used here (*sâfar*) in the Qal form means 'to count', while the Piel form means 'to re-count, to tell'. The English verb 'tell' once had two distinct meanings, though the second one (to count) has almost dropped out of use except for the name of a specific bank employee, a teller.

whose right hands are full of bribes (*vv. 9-10*). The thought of entering into God's house immediately suggests the contrast – being with ungodly sinners. Any evildoer who attempted to draw near to God would be destroyed (Ps. 5:4-6). David does not want to be killed by God's judgment along with other ungodly people, and so he prays that God will not take away his life. The sins he mentions were probably intended as a general description of sinful actions, though they could also have been things of which he was unjustly accused.

5. Continuing Trust (*vv. 11-12*)

But I lead a blameless life; redeem me and be merciful to me. My feet stand on level ground; in the great assembly I will praise the LORD (*vv. 11-12*). At the close of the psalm, reference is made back to verse 1, picking up again the theme of integrity before the LORD. Entry into God's presence was not to be determined by merit, but only by grace. Hence the psalmist prays for redemptive mercy to be shown to him. The reference to 'level ground' could be to the floor of the tabernacle, or else the phrase could be a metaphor for uprightness of life. When, by grace, he entered the assembly of God's people, the psalmist would there bless the LORD. The psalm, which began on a note of trust (v. 1), ends here on the note of praise.

Psalm 27

Of David.[1]

This personal appeal to the LORD is made in the face of pressing attacks, though nothing in the psalm enables precise identification of them to take place. There are expressions of a military nature in the psalm that suggest that David is speaking as king. Especially in verse 3 the picture is of a battle situation in which he and his country are facing serious attacks. Yet his trust is in the LORD and he can encourage himself and others to take heart and to wait for him. He knows that the enmity that he is experiencing is not so much against him as against the LORD.

1. Confidence in the LORD (*vv. 1-6*)

The LORD is my light and my salvation – whom shall I fear? The LORD is the stronghold of my life – of whom shall I be afraid? (*v. 1*). David sums up what the LORD was to him in three words – 'light', 'salvation', and 'stronghold'. 'Light' may well have carried overtones of a military nature, for it is used in Psalm 18:28-29 of military victory. 'Salvation', in a context like this, can be virtually equivalent to deliverance and victory. 'Stronghold' notes the safety that the LORD affords, and the protection he was to David and his people. Is it surprising then that, by his two questions, he can assert his complete trust in his deliverer?

[1] The LXX adds *pro tou christhênai*, 'before he was anointed'. This could in effect be a claim that the psalm was composed before David was anointed at Hebron, though it is so indefinite that it could be a reference to some other anointing, for example, of a high priest.

When evil men advance against me to devour my flesh, when my enemies and my foes attack me, they will stumble and fall (*v.* 2). It is not clear if 'devouring the flesh' is to be taken as a metaphor for destruction, thus comparing his enemies with wild animals. It could also refer to personal attacks of a verbal kind, such as false witnesses could make (see verse 12). This latter viewpoint is probably correct, as in Aramaic the phrase 'to eat the flesh' means 'to slander', an interpretation followed by the RSV, 'uttering slanders against me'. Whatever the oppression he was certain of God's intervention and that no attack would succeed. God would ensure that the enemies stumbled and fell.

Though an army besiege me, my heart will not fear; though war break out against me, even then will I be confident (*v.* 3). This verse is an expansion of the idea of verse 1, 'Whom shall I fear?' Even if faced with a siege against Jerusalem, or a bold attack on him, yet the psalmist will trust in what God is to him. He had promised himself as a deliverer, and on that David stakes his confidence. The repetition of words and sounds in the opening of each of the statements in this verse makes them stand out.

ʾim-tachᵃneh ʿâlay machᵃneh … Though an host encamp against me …
ʾim-tâqûm ʿâlay milchâmâh … Though war arises against me …

One thing I ask of the LORD, this is what I seek: that I may dwell in the house of the LORD all the days of my life, to gaze upon the beauty of the LORD and to seek him in his temple (*v.* 4). The opening of verse 4 has no parallel anywhere in the Old Testament. It is a statement of exclusive trust in the LORD. His faith is such that he wants to live continually in God's presence. In particular he wants to see the glory of the LORD symbolised by the ark of the covenant and the associated ceremonies of worship, and to be able to see the LORD at the sanctuary. Such 'seeking' may well have been in connection with the military dangers he faced, when advice from the priest concerning the will of the LORD would be sought. The clause 'that I may dwell in the house of the LORD all the days of my life' is very similar to words in Psalm 23:6, 'that I may return to the house of the LORD for length of days'.[2] 'House' (*báyit*) can designate the temple (see 2 Sam. 7:13; Ps. 122:1), and this is made clear in the context by the use of 'temple' (*hêkâl*) later in the verse. Expressions such as these may well have been part of the standard religious language in Israel. The desire to 'see' God may refer to visionary experience, such as Isaiah experienced (Isa. 6:1), but the verb used can have wider connotations of perception and appreciation. Hence it is probably synonymous with the verb to 'seek'.

For in the day of trouble he will keep me safe in his dwelling; he will hide me in the shelter of his tabernacle and set me high upon a rock (*v. 5*). Confident trust enables the psalmist to express how safe he felt. Probably the references to 'dwelling' and 'tabernacle' are general in character, and are not directed specifically to the dwelling place of the ark.[3] The final words of the verse support this interpretation, because lifting high on a rock suggests safety and protection in general (cf. Ps. 3:3). The expression 'hide me in the shelter' is very striking in Hebrew because both verb and noun come from the same root (*yastirênî bᵉsêter*), rather like saying in English, 'hide me in the hide.'

Then my head will be exalted above the enemies who surround me; at his tabernacle will I sacrifice with shouts of joy; I will sing and make music to the LORD (*v. 6*). The outcome of the LORD's protection is that the psalmist experiences deliverance from his enemies, and with thankful heart he wants to sacrifice and praise the LORD. Sacrifices of thanksgiving would be offered after military victories, and with joyful song the LORD would be praised (for an example, see 1 Sam. 4:6). The idea of a sacrifice of praise goes back to

---

[2] Here the verb is vocalised as *shivtî* ('dwell') as compared with *shavtî* ('return') in Psalm 23:6. No need exists to suggest as *BHS* does, that this expression has been taken over by a copyist and inserted at this point in Psalm 27. There is no grammatical reason to support this, and it is hard to explain why, if this happened, the whole clause was not repeated, i.e. including 'length of days' instead of 'all the days of my life'.

[3] The phrase 'in his dwelling' is the Qᵉre reading (*bᵉsukkô*), whereas the Kᵉtiv reading is 'booth' (*sukkâh*). The Massoretic vocalisation seems to be correct (cf. Psalm 76:2), and gives a good parallel to the following 'tent' (*'ôhel*).

Leviticus 7:12, and this is reflected in the New Testament phrase, 'a sacrifice of praise' (Heb. 13:15). If this psalm was used in later worship situations in the Old Testament church, it may have been that a sacrifice would be offered at this point in its recitation.

2. Prayer for Divine Assistance (*vv. 7-13*)

Hear my voice when I call, O LORD; be merciful to me and answer me (*v. 7*). The flow of thought from the first part of the psalm continues on into the second part, with several key words being repeated. Now the psalmist cries to God to hear his request and to show compassion to him in his need. Praise has turned into prayer. Here he prays in general terms, while later (see v. 11) he becomes more specific. The appeal to God to 'hear the voice' is one of the standard expressions of petition (see other examples in Pss. 64:1; 119:149; 130:2), while the plea for mercy is a repetition of the prayer already uttered in the previous psalm (Ps. 26:11). 'Answer me' is a frequent cry that both acknowledges the supplicant's need and invokes God's favour.

My heart says of you, 'Seek his face!' Your face, LORD, I will seek (*v. 8*). The translation of this verse is difficult, as all the ancient translations show. The main problem is that in Hebrew the imperative 'seek' is second person plural, while the context requires second person singular. The NIV margin provides an alternative that may be the best solution at the moment: 'To you, O my heart, he has said, "Seek my face".'[4] The expressions 'seek God' and 'seek his face' may go back to Deuteronomy 4:29. If so, the psalmist is acting in the spirit of that verse as he indicates that he is indeed seeking admission to God's presence in order to ask a favour.

Do not hide your face from me, do not turn your servant away in anger; you have been my helper. Do not reject me or forsake me, O God my Saviour (*v. 9*). He wants God's presence to be manifest to him, not hidden as when God is

[4] This suggestion still does not solve all the problems, for it presupposes a singular imperative ('seek') whereas the MT has the plural. For discussion of other suggestions, and also possible emendation, see P. C. Craigie, *Psalms 1-50*, p. 230.

angry with his children. He acknowledges that God has been his helper, using a Hebrew expression that suggests God's abiding nature as his helper.[5] What he was in the past, he continues to be to David. The psalmist pleads that his Saviour will not thrust him away in his need.

Though my father and mother forsake me, the LORD will receive me (*v. 10*). This expression is not to be taken literally, as though David's parents are abandoning him. Rather, it expresses the new relationship that David as king has with the LORD. God now fills the role that David's parents previously occupied. The king is adopted as God's son (Ps. 2:7) and therefore is sheltered by him.

Teach me your way, O LORD; lead me in a straight path because of my oppressors. Do not turn me over to the desire of my foes, for false witnesses rise up against me, breathing out violence (*vv. 11-12*). The specific request he makes is for guidance in God's way and for direction in a straight path (cf. the same type of request in Psalm 25:4-5). He wants to be kept in God's paths, though his oppressors are attacking him.[6] He fears their designs on him, for they are speaking lies against him and their purpose is to destroy him.[7] The opponents could well be foreign nations who do not want Israel's king to be walking in the ways of her covenant LORD.

I am still confident of this: I will see the goodness of the LORD in the land of the living (*v. 13*). The commencement of this verse in Hebrew presents a problem, one that was apparent to the Massoretic scholars for they marked it with unusual notation, placing dots both above and below each of the three consonants of the opening word. They also added a note drawing attention to the fact that this is the only

---

[5] The construction consists of the verb *hâyâh* and a substantive with suffix, *ʿezrâtî*, 'my help'. This is used instead of the perfect of the verb *ʿâzar*, 'to help'.

[6] See the footnote on 5:9 for discussion on the word 'oppressors'. This is one of the contexts where the translation 'slanderers' would be appropriate, especially since 'false witnesses' are mentioned in the following verse.

[7] 'The desire of my foes' is an idiomatic Hebrew expression (lit. 'the life of my foes') that occurs again in Psalm 41:2.

occurrence in the Hebrew Bible of this phenomenon.[8] The best explanation of the difficulty is to suggest that verse 13 contains an opening clause that is never finished by the addition of an apodosis. The translation then can be: 'If I did not believe that I would see the goodness of the LORD in the land of the living ...!' The unspoken result is that he would perish. While the NIV and similar translations do not follow exactly the grammatical structure of the Hebrew text, yet they convey faithfully the meaning. The verse is a confident assertion of trust in the LORD and the conviction that David would see his saving power. He knew that he would not be cut off in the midst of his days (Psalm 102:24, lit. 'in the half of my days'). The land of the living is simply the opposite of the land of the dead (see Pss. 52:5 and 116:9, and Isa. 38:11).

3. A Call to Wait (*v. 14*)

Wait for the LORD; be strong and take heart and wait for the LORD (*v. 14*). This final verse appears to be a call to others to follow the psalmist's example, though it is possible that it is addressed to himself as a word of self-encouragement. The repetition of the word 'wait' gives particular force to the idea, emphasising waiting with tenseness or eagerness.[9] From a strong faith in the LORD flows mighty deeds in his name. The 'heart' stands for the centre of the psalmist's whole life. With all of his being he is willing, like Joshua (Deut. 31:7 and Josh. 1:6-7), to serve the LORD.

---

[8] The Massoretic note reads: 'One of 4 occurrences written with a final א and the only occurrence in the Bible of a word with special diacritical points both above and below all consonants, except the consonant *vav*, and this is one of 15 words in the Bible with special diacritical points.' See *The Masorah of Biblia Hebraica Stuttgartensia: Introduction and Annotated Glossary*, Page H. Kelley, Daniel S. Mynatt, and Timothy G. Crawford (Grand Rapids: Eerdmans, 1998), p. 140. The note on this verse by P. C. Craigie, *Psalms 1-50*, p. 230, gives a good summary of the difficulty.

[9] *CHAL*, p. 315. See also the footnote on Psalm 25:3.

Psalm 28

Of David.

While the setting of this psalm seems to be very similar to that of Psalm 26, it also has affinities with both Psalms 23 and 25. The reference to the Lord as the shepherd in the last verse connects it with Psalm 23. Like Psalm 25, it ends with prayer for the Israel of God. The interconnection of Psalms 23-28 suggests that it formed a group of songs linked together by common themes. The period of Absalom's rebellion against David may form the historical background of both this psalm and Psalm 26. The peril of the psalmist, his enemy's hypocrisy, and the mention of the sanctuary, all point in this direction. It is an appeal on behalf of the people and their anointed king (God's anointed one, 'his messiah', v. 8) against enemies from within their own nation. Many of the expressions in the psalm are paralleled elsewhere, forming part of the language of individual and corporate prayer.

1. A General Plea (*vv. 1-2*)

To you I call, O Lord my Rock; do not turn a deaf ear to me. For if you remain silent, I will be like those who have gone down to the pit. Hear my cry for mercy as I call to you for help, as I lift up my hands toward your Most Holy Place (*vv. 1-2*). There is but one 'rock' for the psalmist and that is the Lord (cf. Ps. 18:2). To him he makes his appeal and asks that he will not refuse to listen to him. He doesn't want God to remain deaf to his plea. This would really mean being 'inactive', 'not helping'. If God doesn't intervene, then death stares him in the face. 'To go down to the pit' is an Old Testament expression for death (cf. Psalms 30:3; 88:4; and 143:7).[1] The poet recognises he needs mercy, for his situation is desperate. He has his hands lifted up, as it were, out of the pit, waiting for God to rescue him. Alternatively, here and elsewhere the expression 'to lift up the hands' could be to a posture symbolising being ready to receive from God an answer to prayer. The 'Most Holy Place' (*d*[e]*vîr*) appears to designate the inner sanctuary of the tabernacle/temple, the place that symbolised God's earthly presence.[2]

2. Deliverance from his Enemies (*vv. 3-5*)

Do not drag me away with the wicked, with those who do evil, who speak cordially with their neighbours but harbour malice in their hearts (*v. 3*). The psalmist did not want to be associated with wicked people. He characterises them in three ways. They practise evil, on the surface they speak peacefully to their neighbours, and in their hearts they treasure up evil. 'To practise evil' is a phrase that occurs about twenty times, in Job, the Psalms and Proverbs. It may designate men who were skilled in magic or idolatrous ritual, for the Hebrew word for evil in this phrase (*'âven*) sometimes denotes idolatry (cf. *Beth-aven,* Hos. 5:8; 10:5, 8).

Repay them for their deeds and for their evil work; repay them for what their hands have done and bring back upon them what they deserve. Since they show no regard for the works of the LORD and what his hands have done, he will tear them down

[1] 'Pit' (*bôr*) and *she'ôl* are often synonymous terms, though in Ezekiel 32:18-32 a distinction is made between them. *Bôr* can also mean a cistern, and then by transference of ideas, a prison. The best discussion on the Hebrew terms for death is W. VanGemeren, 'Appendix: Sheol-Grave-Death in the Psalms', 'Psalms', pp. 569-73.

[2] The Hebrew phrase 'toward your Most Holy Place (*'el d*[e]*vîr qodsh*[e]*kâ*) only occurs here. The word *d*[e]*vîr* is never used of the holy of holies in the wilderness tabernacle. It occurs sixteen times, mainly in the descriptions regarding the building of the temple. However, some ambiguity exists regarding its meaning, for while it does denote the holy place, it also seems to be distinguished from it, designating a back or side room of the temple (see 1 Kings 8:6). For further discussion, see Earl S. Kalland in *TWOT* 1, p. 181 (and the literature cited), and G. H. Jones, *1 and 2 Kings* (New Century Bible: London: 1984), 1, pp. 169, 195.

and never build them up again (*vv. 4-5*). Words such as these, calling for vengeance on enemies, seem to some as contradictory to Christian belief in love and forgiveness. However, a much broader view has to be taken of them (see the fuller discussion in the Introduction, p. 72-76). David is asking for the curses of the covenant to be visited on those who are in breach of its requirements.[3] To repay what people deserve is a technical legal expression. The LORD is a God of retribution (Ps. 94:2; Jer. 51:56) who gives to the wicked their due. They have yet to learn that there is a marked contrast between the works of their hands (v. 4) and the works of the LORD's hands (v. 5). The form of the cursing here echoes Deuteronomy 28 and it has many similarities to passages in Jeremiah (cf. verse 5b with Jer. 24:6; 42:10; 45:4). While the psalmists call for retribution now, the prophets in their declarations regarding retribution focus more on the future.

3. Praise for the Deliverer (*vv. 6-9*)
Praise be to the LORD, for he has heard my cry for mercy. The LORD is my strength and my shield; my heart trusts in him, and I am helped. My heart leaps for joy and I will give thanks to him in song (*vv. 6-7*). There is a direct link between the words of thanksgiving and the earlier part of the psalm. He had asked, 'Hear my cry for mercy' (v. 2a). Here he says that the LORD has heard his cry for mercy. He has received the assurance of the LORD's intervention on his behalf (v. 5), and now he praises him for deliverance. This, in concise form, is a song of thanksgiving. It starts with an introduction (v. 6a) and ends with a conclusion (v. 7c, d). It has a confession in verse 7a, and a recounting of the deliverance in verses 6b and 7b. He acknowledges his refuge, and he can sing a jubilant song about the LORD,[4] now and always. Even in his great need he did

---

[3] The general theme of God's retribution as taught in the Old Testament is dealt with by J. Robert Vannoy, 'Retribution, Theology of' in *NIDOTTE*, 4, pp. 1140-49.

[4] The MT, 'and from a song' (*ûmishshîr*), is awkward in the context. Consonantal emendation is unnecessary as here and in Psalm 137:3 the word is *mâshîr*, 'a song'. This means that, as in Ugaritic, biblical Hebrew had two words for 'song', *shîr* and *mâshîr*. Cf. *DCH*, V, p. 522, and the bibliography on p. 883.

not cease to trust in the LORD, and in deliverance the psalmist confesses where his help lies. The combination of 'shield' and another word like 'strength', 'help', or 'sun' is frequent in the Psalms to convey the ideas of God as protector and defender of his people. The use of the military term 'shield' also ties in with the concepts of the divine warrior and the holy war.[5]

The LORD is the strength of his people,[6] a fortress of salvation for his anointed one (*v. 8*). The psalmist's confession continues with the acknowledgment that the LORD is not only his strength, but that of his people in general. What he is to the king in person ('his anointed one'), he is also to the believing community as a whole. A play on words occurs, for the LORD is both the strength (*ʿoz*) of his people and their fortress (*mâʿoz*).

Save your people and bless your inheritance; be their shepherd and carry them forever (*v. 9*). This verse confirms the impression that the setting of the psalm is a time of national danger. David prays for salvation of the people of Israel, and blessing for God's inheritance. The concept of Israel as God's special, chosen heritage (Exod. 34:9; Deut. 4:20) is carried over in New Testament thought (see Eph. 1:3-6). The idea of the loving shepherd is reminiscent of Psalms 23:1; 80:1; 100:3; and Isaiah 40:11.

---

[5] Cf. the comments on Psalm 3:5. For a summary discussion of the concept of the divine warrior, see Tremper Longman III, 'Divine Warrior', *NIDOTTE*, V, p. 545-49.

[6] The NIV 'of his people' involves an alteration of the text from 'for them' (*lâmô*) to 'for his people' (*leʿammô*). But the variant form of the preposition *le* with suffix can indicate 'for *them*' as well as 'for *him*'. The form of suffix in this case is one of a considerable number of occurrences in Hebrew poetry that are certainly archaic and that remain unexplained. On this point, see *IBHS*, p. 189.

Psalm 29

A psalm of David.

This is a mighty song of victory, and an exaltation of the power of the LORD. The sevenfold repetition of 'the voice of the LORD' (*qôl yhwh*) led Delitzsch to call it 'the psalm of the seven thunders'.[1] It has often been pointed out that this psalm has certain similarities to poetry known from Canaanite sources. This does not necessarily imply borrowing poetry and simply changing the name from Baal to the LORD (*yhwh*). It could be a polemical psalm directed against the heathen notions of the Canaanites, and in particular a denial of the place of Baal in the world of nature.[2] The fact that all the geographical references in the psalm are to places outside the area controlled by Israel (Lebanon, Sirion/Hermon, the desert of Kadesh) simply reinforces this point. The LORD is the mighty creator who has all the forces of nature at his control, both within and without Israelite territory. The emphasis on 'the LORD' comes out also in the fact that the name appears eighteen times in this short psalm. It also has similarities to other victory songs such as Exodus 15:1-18 and Judges 5:2-31, which also use storm imagery to describe victory in battle. A Jewish tradition, as early as around 250 BC, associated this psalm with the Feast of Tabernacles. The LXX reflects this in that it adds to the title '[on

[1] F. Delitzsch, *Psalms*, I, p. 367. The phrase 'the seven thunders' comes from Rev. 10:3.

[2] Cf. the conclusion of P. C. Craigie, *Psalms 1-50*, p. 245 on this question of possible borrowing from Canaanite sources: 'it is clear that there are sufficient parallels and similarities to require a Canaanite background to be taken into account in developing the interpretation of this psalm, but it is not clear that those parallels and similarities require one to posit a Canaanite/Phoenician original of Ps. 29.'

the occasion] of the solemn assembly', though in later rabbinic tradition this psalm was linked to the Feast of Weeks.[3]

1. A Call to Praise (*vv. 1-2*)

Ascribe to the LORD, O mighty ones, ascribe to the LORD glory and strength. Ascribe to the LORD the glory due his name; worship the LORD in the splendour of his holiness (*vv. 1-2*). The opening call is for the LORD's glory and strength to be acknowledged, and this is done using two significant features of Hebrew poetry, repetition and development. The pattern of these verses can be set out in diagrammatic form:

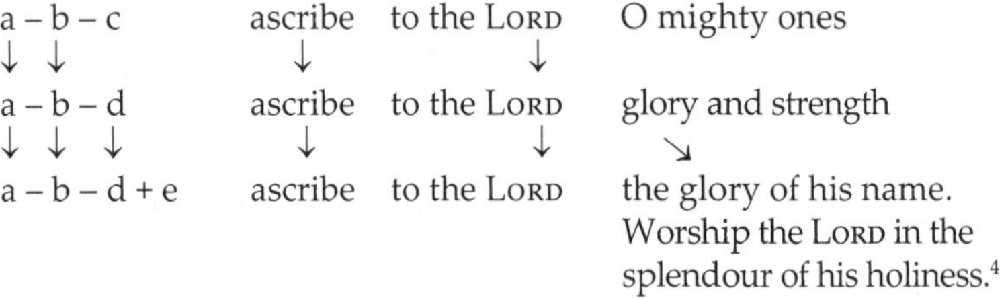

'Glory', when an attribute of God, normally refers to visible beauty of God when he reveals himself, while the word 'strength' is often associated with victory in battles, as is the reference to God's name (see Exod. 15:3, for example). Those addressed are called 'sons of God' (*b^e^nê 'ēlîm*), which here and in Psalm 89:7 most probably denotes the angels.[5] The speaker requests the heavenly host to join in praise of the LORD. What is fittingly his, should be rendered to him in praise and adoration. Even angelic beings have to bow in submission to him.[6] The final phrase of verse 2 could refer to the manner in which the LORD was worshipped (as in NIV translation), or

[3] *Soferim* 18:3.

[4] For this basic structure, see Carroll Stuhlmueller, *Psalms I:1-72* (Collegeville, Minnesota: Michael Glazier, 1983), p. 171.

[5] Extensive bibliography exists in relation to this phrase. See P. C. Craigie, *Psalms 1-50*, p. 241-47; S. Terrien, *The Psalms*, pp. 274-75; *NIDOTTE*, 1, pp. 375-77.

[6] The verb 'to worship' is probably from a root *ch-v-h*, and carries the idea of prostration. It is normally used of communal worship, but it does occur less frequently of individuals. For details on the derivation and meaning, see *TDOT*, IV, pp. 248-56; *TWOT*, I, pp. 269-71.

it could refer to the garments that the servants wore. Some commentators have suggested that it refers to the dress that the priests wore on special occasions (see 2 Chron. 20:21). If that is correct, then a translation like 'the adornment of the king' is quite close in meaning to the NIV translation.[7]

2. The Mighty Voice of the LORD (*vv. 3-9*)

The voice of the LORD is over the waters; the God of glory thunders, the LORD thunders over the mighty waters (*v. 3*). Mention is made seven times of the LORD's voice in this central section of the psalm. Thus it is clearly the focal point, as the psalmist uses the language of the storm to refer to God's power and glory. The picture of the LORD's coming is in terms of the thunderstorms that originate over the Mediterranean (v. 3), then cross the hill country (vv. 5-7) and finally peter out over the eastern desert (v. 8). Over all the mighty waters he reigns supreme, and he speaks as with a clap of thunder. The phrase 'the God of glory' is reminiscent of Psalm 24:7-10 with fourfold mention of 'the king of glory'.[8]

The voice of the LORD is powerful; the voice of the LORD is majestic (*v. 4*). No verbs occur in this verse. Either the verb 'to be' has to be inserted in English (as in the NIV translation), or the verb 'to thunder' carries over from the previous verse. 'Powerful' (*koach*) is virtually the equivalent of 'strength' (*ʿoz*) in verse 1, while 'majestic' (*hâdâr*) is from the same root as 'splendour' (*hadârâh*) in verse 2.

The voice of the LORD breaks the cedars; the LORD breaks in pieces the cedars of Lebanon (*vv. 5*). The reference to Lebanon is interesting, because it marked the border with the Canaanite territory to the north. The cedars of Lebanon were

---

[7] The meaning of this rare word has been a problem even as far back as the time when the LXX was being translated. The LXX has 'court' (*aulê*), but no support for this comes from Hebrew manuscripts. Also, the LXX translation requires an emendation in the next word to make it read 'in *his* holy court'. An association with a Ugaritic word *hdrt*, 'revelation' or 'vision', is unlikely.

[8] Other links with Psalm 24 are the waters (v. 2), the sanctuary (v. 4), and celebration of the LORD's kingship (vv. 7-10).

well known, and they represented the strength of Lebanon itself. But they could be shattered by the majestic voice of the LORD. When he commanded, they split in pieces.

He makes Lebanon skip like a calf, Sirion like a young wild ox. The voice of the LORD strikes with flashes of lightning (*vv. 6-7*). Now Lebanon itself and nearby Sirion come directly into the picture. 'Sirion' is Mount Hermon (see Deut. 3:9), and here it is used as basically synonymous with Lebanon. God's voice makes these great mountains skip like young animals, for the creator has power over his creation.[9] Perhaps an earthquake is in view. The likening of the LORD's voice to lightning is in keeping with Near Eastern ideas, for lightning was often used in visual depictions to denote weaponry used in battle.

The voice of the LORD shakes the desert; the LORD shakes the Desert of Kadesh (*v. 8*). It is hard to know whether a specific desert is in view here, or whether it is just a general reference to the semi-desert steppe country. While the locality could be the Kadesh, situated about 50 miles (80 km) south-west of Beersheba (Kadesh Barnea), more probably it refers to Kadesh on the Orontes, a Hittite capital about 80 miles (128 km) north of Damascus. This places it in geographical proximity to Lebanon and Hermon. Whatever the exact location, the point is that the LORD exercises control over vast territories.

The voice of the LORD twists the oaks and strips the forests bare. And in his temple all cry, 'Glory!' (*v. 9*). This verse presents a contrast between what is happening outside (thunder, lightning, earthquake), and which disturbs the whole natural world, with what is happening in God's sanctuary. It is not clear if this sanctuary is the heavenly one, or the one

---

[9] The NIV translation assumes that the final *mem* on the verb (*vayyardîqêm*) is not the third person plural suffix but an enclitic *mem* (see Glossary for explanation). J. C. L. Gibson, *Canaanite Myths and Legends* (Edinburgh: T. & T. Clark, 1977), p. 150, regards this as one of the two 'reasonably certain survivals in Hebr. poetry' of this phenomenon: *vayyarqîd + m*, 'he made Lebanon skip'. Cf. also his later reference to enclitic *mem* in *DIHG—S*, pp. 24-5. The fullest bibliography on this matter can be found in *DCH*, V, pp. 823-25.

situated in Jerusalem. Perhaps the two were combined in the thought of the people, the earthly sanctuary being made after the fashion of the heavenly one. In the sanctuary there is peace, and a cry of 'Glory' arises. This provides a beautiful ending to this part of the psalm, for there is no parallel expression accompanying it and it calls attention to the way in which the psalm opened with a twofold command to praise (v. 1, 'ascribe to the LORD ... ascribe to the LORD glory and strength').

3. A Concluding Song of Praise (*vv. 10-11*)

The LORD sits enthroned over the flood; the LORD is enthroned as King forever. The LORD gives strength to his people; the LORD blesses his people with peace (*vv. 10-11*). The final verses of the psalm rejoice in the fact that the LORD is the eternal king. There seems to be a reference back to the creation account in Genesis 1 and to the story of the flood, recalling the manner in which God is sovereign over his creation, including the waters. What God is in himself (v. 1), he gives to his people, and having won victory for them he bestows his peace. The psalm that starts with 'glory to God in the highest' ends with 'peace upon earth'.

Psalm 30

A psalm. A song. For the dedication of the temple. Of David.

This song of thanksgiving is a joyful response to what God has done. Wailing has turned to dancing (v. 11), and there is praise to the LORD for the fact that he spared his servant, delivering him from death. The anguish on the part of the psalmist is reflected in the poetry, especially that the rhythmic patterns of the Hebrew text are very irregular. The staccato effect accentuates the distress of heart. The title is ambiguous. The Hebrew word translated 'dedication' (*ch*[a]*nukâh*) could mean 'initiation, commencement of use',[1] while the word 'temple' (*báyit*) is the Hebrew word for 'house' or 'palace'. This may be a Davidic psalm intended for use in his palace, or alternatively for the temple when it was built. It is possible that these words relating to the dedication of the temple were added to the superscription much later after the restoration of the temple following the exile. It is a song that concentrates on the LORD, using that title nine times, and twice he is called 'my God'. It is also much more concrete in its description of the danger from which the psalmist has been delivered than those in many other psalms.

1. A Grateful Song (*vv. 1-5*)
I will exalt you, O LORD, for you lifted me out of the depths and did not let my enemies gloat over me (*v. 1*). The verb

[1] The Jewish Feast of Dedication (Hanukkah) is post-biblical in origin. It commemorates the rededication of the temple in 165 BC by Judas Maccabeus, and later Jewish practice included the singing of Psalm 30 at the feast. The 'Feast of Dedication' is noted in John 10:22. For further details concerning it, see *TDOT*, 5:19-21.

'exalt' in a setting like this has the meaning of praising (cf. Ps. 99:5). The 'depths' from which the psalmist is lifted is clearly sickness, as becomes explicit in the following verses. Had he succumbed to that illness and died as a result of it, then his enemies would have taken great delight. The verb 'to lift' really means 'to draw [water]' and is paralleled by 'you brought me up' in verse 3.[2]

O LORD my God, I called to you for help and you healed me. O LORD, you brought me up from the grave; you spared me from going down into the pit (*vv. 2-3*). The psalmist directed his cry for help to God, and he found that he was restored. The verb 'to cry for help' (*shâvaʿ*) is found more often in the psalms than in any other Old Testament book, and it is usually used in autobiographical settings such as this one. On most occasions it is used, as here, in a psalm of lament. In verse 3 'Sheol' (or the grave) and 'the pit' (*bôr*) are used in parallel to describe death.[3] What was involved in calling on the LORD is spelt out in more detail in verses 8-10.

Sing to the LORD, you saints of his; praise his holy name (*v. 4*). The psalmist wants the whole congregation to share with him in praising the LORD for his deliverance. He calls the members of the congregation 'saints' or 'holy ones'. The word used (*châsîd*) is clearly related to the Hebrew word *chésed*, 'mercy', and 'the holy ones' were probably called this because, having received God's mercy, they also were characterised by it in their lives. 'His holy name' is literally 'his holy memorial', which is an echo of Exodus 3:15, 'This is my name for ever, the name by which I am to be remembered from generation to generation.'

For his anger lasts only a moment, but his favour lasts a lifetime; weeping may remain for a night, but rejoicing comes in the morning (*v. 5*). The first part of this verse has long been recognised as proving difficult to translate. The LXX renders: 'For anger is in his wrath, but life in his favour.' This does not make much sense unless 'anger' is equivalent to

---

[2] This is the only time that the Pi. form of this verb occurs in the Old Testament. The Hebrew word for 'bucket' (*d^elî*) comes from this root (*d-l-h*). Cf. Isaiah 40:15, 'like a drop in a bucket'.

[3] See f.n. 1 on Psalm 28 for discussion on *she'ol* and *bôr*.

'death'. Certainly, the context here shows a contrast between death and life, and the idea that the Hebrew word *réga*ʿ (NIV 'moment') means 'death' has had advocates both among older commentators and those in recent time.[4] This idea receives support, moreover, by the fact that the Hebrew word for 'life (*cháyyîm*) is never used to refer to a 'lifetime'. Rather, it appears in contrast to death. In the second part of the verse, sorrow is depicted as if it was a guest that intruded into our lives. It takes up temporary lodging,[5] but it is eventually replaced by joy. The light of God's love chases away the night of sorrow and gloom.

2. A Detailed Description of His Deliverance (*vv. 6-12*)
When I felt secure, I said, 'I will never be shaken' (*v. 6*). The detailed description of the trouble from which the LORD had delivered him starts here. Looking back on his life before the onset of sickness, the psalmist realises that in his health he had been complacent and self-sufficient. This was something that a member of the covenant community should not have been (see Deut. 8:17-18). Prosperity and safety both came from the LORD.

O LORD, when you favoured me, you made my mountain stand firm; but when you hid your face, I was dismayed (*v. 7*). David has already spoken of 'favour' in verse 5. It is the response of God to repentance and faith on the part of his people. The contrast he presents is between being firmly established by God (as though set firm on a mountain) and trembling when God removes his favour. David was perplexed when God took away the signs of his gracious presence.

The psalmist now recalls his prayer to the LORD at the time of his trouble. **To you, O LORD, I called; to the Lord I cried for mercy: 'What gain is there in my destruction, in my going down into the pit? Will the dust praise you? Will it proclaim your faithfulness?** (*vv. 8-9*). These words show how, when realising his true condition, he turned to the LORD, seeking

---

[4] See in particular, M. Dahood, *Psalms I: 1-50*, pp. 182-83; P. C. Craigie, *Psalms 1-50*, pp. 250-51; E. W. Hengstenberg, *Commentary on the Psalms*, I, pp. 288-89.

[5] The verb is *lîn*, 'to lodge the night'.

mercy from him. His argument was that his death would not be any profit to God. All it would do would be to rob God of an offering of praise and confession.

Hear, O LORD, and be merciful to me; O LORD, be my help (*v. 10*). This is the outcome of the reasoning of the psalmist in the preceding verse. He now knew that his former feelings of self-sufficiency were gone. Instead he recognises that he needs the LORD's mercy if he is to recover from his sickness and join in praising him again. The only helper he has is the LORD. The repetition of the same verb in verses 8 and 10 serves to emphasise the urgency of his appeal (v. 8, 'I cried for mercy'; v. 10, 'be merciful to me').

You turned my wailing into dancing; you removed my sackcloth and clothed me with joy, that my heart may sing to you and not be silent. O LORD my God, I will give you thanks forever (*vv. 11-12*). In an expansion of verse 5b, the psalmist describes the complete reversal in his circumstances. Here the allusions are to the outward signs of sorrow (wailing and wearing of sackcloth) being removed. Instead, he has God-given joy and his whole being (his heart, his soul) is able to sing and praise the LORD.[6] Death would have brought silence. Recovery brings praise. The final verse is a reaffirmation of the praise with which the psalm began. It can be compared with the final verse of Hezekiah's song after he received mercy from the LORD and was spared: 'The LORD will save me, and we will sing with stringed instruments all the days of our lives in the temple of the LORD' (Isa. 38:20).

---

[6] For 'my heart' the Hebrew text has 'glory'. For this as a term of self-reference, see the note on Psalm 7:5. The LXX inserted the personal pronoun 'my', but this is not confirmed from Hebrew manuscripts.

Psalm 31

For the director of music. A psalm of David.

The indications, within the psalm itself, of its setting are not precise enough to allow certainty. Clearly the psalmist faced scheming enemies, who were slandering him. It may even have been a warlike situation, as there are various expressions that suggest the need for defence in the heat of battle. It is typical of songs of complaint in that, while the urgent needs come to the fore, yet there is thankful recognition for the wonderful love of the LORD shown to him. This individual lament falls into two parts (vv. 1-8, 9-24) that are more or less parallel, though the second part is more expansive. In both parts the steadfast love of the LORD sustains the psalmist (see vv. 7 and 16).

1. A Prayer for Deliverance (*vv. 1-8*)

In you, O LORD, I have taken refuge; let me never be put to shame; deliver me in your righteousness (*v. 1*). This opening is very like that of Psalm 71:1-3. The NIV translation captures well the emphasis at the commencement of the psalm. The psalmist points away from himself to the LORD, in whom he had taken refuge.[1] This is accentuated by the fact that there is

---

[1] The verb used here for 'to trust' (*châsâh*) is normally construed with the preposition *b^e^*. It occurs most commonly in the Psalms, and in particular in songs of lament. In them it draws attention to the confident hope of the psalmist, even when circumstances seem so discouraging. The phrase used here, 'in you I trust' (*b^e^kâ châsîtî*), seems to have become a stylised expression, and is often associated with other almost synonymous verbs such as 'trust' (*bâtach*), 'wait for' (*qâvâh*), and 'wait' (*yâchal*). For comment on the expression as a stylised form, see R. C. Culley, *Oral Formulaic Language in the Biblical Psalms* (Toronto: University of Toronto Press, 1967), p. 53; and for general discussion on this verb, *TWOT*, V, pp. 64-75.

no parallel expression to match it, and therefore it stands as an introduction to the whole psalm. In a context such as this 'put to shame' has the idea of being confused and disappointed. 'Righteousness' is not a reference to God's justice, but rather to his power to save. It often has this meaning in prophetical passages such as in Isaiah chapter 40 onwards.

Turn your ear to me, come quickly to my rescue; be my rock of refuge, a strong fortress to save me (*v.* 2). The opening prayer is expanded now, as the psalmist appeals for speedy help. In a pressing situation he asks that God would listen to him, and then hastily answer. 'To turn the ear' is a common expression in the Psalms (cf. Pss. 17:6; 71:2; 86:1; 88:2) and is an appeal to God to pay heed to the supplications of his worshippers. The terms the psalmist uses in the second part of the verse point to a military situation, for he is asking for protection and safety from a fierce enemy.

Since you are my rock and my fortress, for the sake of your name lead and guide me (*v.* 3). After asking for God to be his fortress, he now declares that is exactly what God is to him! That conviction is a fruit of his praying. He calls him 'my rock' and 'my fortress', and requests that for the honour of his name he will take him to a safe place. These metaphors denoting security and protection commonly occur in close proximity to verbs of 'trust'. The reference to 'name's sake' seems to go back to the experiences of the Exodus, when God, for his name's sake redeemed his people from their bondage and showed his mighty power (see Ps. 106:7-8).

Free me from the trap that is set for me, for you are my refuge. Into your hands I commit my spirit; redeem me, O LORD, the God of truth (*vv.* 4-5). For the first time in the psalm specific mention is made of the enemies, and he asks for deliverance from their snares. This is not just a metaphor, but an allusion to real life in the ancient Near East. Drawings exist that show Mesopotamian kings enclosing captured enemies in a net.[2] Again the overtones of the Exodus deliverance are here, with the expression 'free me' being one of the common

[2] J. B. Pritchard, ed., *Ancient Near East: An Anthology of Texts and Pictures* (Princeton: Princeton University Press, 1973), 1, p. 288.

expressions to describe God's bringing his people out of Egypt (see Exod. 13:3, 9, 14, 16; 20:2). He has just declared that God is his rock and fortress, and now he says that God is his refuge.

Verse 5 is well known because of the use of the first part of it by the Lord Jesus upon the Cross: 'Father, into your hands I commit my spirit' (Luke 23:46). Jesus used these words in a similar spirit of trust as the psalmist when he spoke them. Knowing that he had finished the work he had come to do (his 'exodus', Luke 9:31),[3] he committed his life into the Father's hands. This action of Jesus also became a model for his disciples (cf. the case of Stephen, Acts 7:59). The words should not be taken to mean that the psalmist was simply resigning himself to his fate. Rather, they indicate the strong faith of one who has complete confidence in God's ability to save and to keep. 'Redeem' is a further reference to the exodus, and just as God had acted in this way for his people (see Deut. 7:8), so now the psalmist asks for similar redemption for himself from the faithful God ('God of truth').

I hate those who cling to worthless idols; I trust in the LORD (v. 6). The phrase 'who cling to worthless idols' only occurs here and in an almost identical form in Jonah 2:8. It refers to false gods that disappoint their worshippers, who in time of crisis find them impotent to help. Calling them vanities goes back to Deuteronomy 32:21. Later it was to become a favourite expression of Jeremiah to describe the idols (see Jer. 2:5; 8:19; 10:15; 14:22; 16:19). The contrast between those people and the psalmist is made plain in the final clause. The true source of help was the LORD, and the psalmist expresses his trust in him. This was the response that covenant commitment required, and it is just putting in another way the confession the psalmist had made in his opening words (v. 1).

I will be glad and rejoice in your love, for you saw my affliction and knew the anguish of my soul. You have not handed me over to the enemy but have set my feet in

---

[3] In the Greek text of Luke 9:31 the word for 'departure' is *exodos*. This is a significant link in thought between the Old Testament exodus from Egypt and the ministry and the work of Jesus. It is also interesting to consider the way in which Jesus quotes on the cross from a psalm that is replete with exodus terminology.

a spacious place (*vv. 7-8*). God's covenant love (*chésed*) had been the psalmist's stay, and it provoked a spirit of rejoicing, for God had taken note of his servant's pitiable condition, his heartfelt anguish. He records how God had heard his cry and delivered him, putting him into a broad place. This last phrase is a favourite one of David (see Pss. 4:1; 18:19, 36), and it describes the release from oppression into a condition of freedom. He had not been abandoned to the enemy, because the LORD had intervened, and song and joy were but the rightful response to his dealings with David.

2. A Description of Sorrows (*vv. 9-18*)

The central part of the psalm is a description of the psalmist's sorrows and afflictions. **Be merciful to me, O LORD, for I am in distress; my eyes grow weak with sorrow, my soul and my body with grief** (*v. 9*). The appeal he makes for mercy is set over against the oppressive situation in which he lives. Whereas he had pled on the basis of God's righteousness earlier (v. 1), he now pleads on the basis of God's mercy. He sets out in detail before the LORD his misery and anguish, using language that has already appeared in Psalm 6:7.[4] No word for 'grief' occurs in the Hebrew, hence it is better to simply conclude the verse with 'my soul and body [too]'. His whole being is consumed with anguish, so that he feels that all strength is gone.

My life is consumed by anguish and my years by groaning; my strength fails because of my affliction, and my bones grow weak (*v. 10*). It is better to accept the NIV marginal reading of 'guilt' in place of 'affliction', for the Hebrew word *ʿâwôn* can carry ideas both of a misdeed and its punishment. This is the only place in the psalm in which mention is made of the psalmist's own sin. It is a blessing when suffering turns the heart inward to see one's true condition before the LORD. He pictures himself as an old man, stumbling along in his weakened condition, whereas he previously had been so

---

[4] The phrases are almost identical in Psalms 6:7 and 31:9, the only difference being that the former has *mikaʿas*, 'from sorrow', while the latter has *b^{e}kaʿas*, 'in sorrow'. No real difference in meaning is observable.

strong. The expression 'to have one's bones weakened' is a frequent idiom in the Old Testament to describe the reaction to acute pain or emotional distress (cf. Job 33:19, 21; Psalms 6:2; 38:3; Lam. 1:13). Neat parallelism occurs in verses 9 and 10, as the rare verb 'to grow weak' (*'âshash;* it only appears elsewhere in Ps. 6:7) is used near the beginning of verse 9 and at the end of verse 10.

Because of all my enemies, I am the utter contempt of my neighbours; I am a dread to my friends – those who see me on the street flee from me (*v. 11*). He faces problems on every side – enemies assail him, neighbours shun him, even friends turn away from him in public places as if he had a dreadful, infectious disease. The NIV rendering '*utter* contempt' is an attempt to bring out the force of the Hebrew word *me'od* that often translates as 'very' or 'greatly', but here the syntax of the sentence is unusual: 'I am a reproach, and to my neighbours greatly.' Since readers would probably expect a noun parallel to 'reproach' to appear, many attempts have been made to propose emendation. However, the fact that the LXX translates it as *sphodra* ('very [much], exceedingly') certainly points to the MT being correct.[5] This is all because he is facing such opposition from his enemies, and no one wants to associate with him any longer.

I am forgotten by them as though I were dead; I have become like broken pottery (*v. 12*). The hurt of his situation is described in these words. He is so shunned by his acquaintances that it is as if he were dead. The NIV translation fails to bring out clearly the presence of the Hebrew word *millêv* ('from the heart') after the words 'I am forgotten', and the insertion of 'by them', while implied by the context, does not correspond to any words in the MT. Here the NKJV translation is better: 'I am forgotten like a dead man, out of mind.' In the final clause the psalmist thinks of himself as just being a cast-off piece of pottery, broken and of no more use!

---

[5] The note in *BHS* lists four suggestions that have been proposed: *mânôd* ('shaking [of the head]), *mâgôr* ('terror'), *morâ'* ('fear'), and *mâdôn* ('quarrel'). While all are plausible, yet the uniformity of the MT reading suggests that alteration of the text is not an option.

For I hear the slander of many; there is terror on every side; they conspire against me and plot to take my life (*v. 13*). The first part of this verse is like Jeremiah 20:10, though there the expression 'terror on every side' is what the people were saying. The phrase 'terror on every side' (Hebrew *mâgôr missavîb*) is a frequent one in Jeremiah's writing (see Jer. 6:25; 20:3; 46:5; 49:29; Lam. 2:22). Here the picture is simply of back-biting enemies who attack from all sides and who plot together to take his life. The same phrase is used in Psalm 2:2 of the rebellious rulers plotting against the LORD. Not just slander, but death threats come against him.

But I trust in you, O LORD; I say, 'You are my God' (*v. 14*). In the midst of all his afflictions the psalmist can turn to the LORD and make confession of his faith in him. The sudden transition between this and the preceding verse is remarkable. What matters most in his situation is the relationship between himself and the LORD. The pronouns 'I' and 'you' stand next to each other in the Hebrew text before the verb, and emphasise the bond between the psalmist and the LORD: 'But I, upon you I trust …'. In addition to this profession of absolute trust, the psalmist confesses that the LORD is indeed his only God.

My times are in your hands; deliver me from my enemies and from those who pursue me (*v. 15*). By 'times' the psalmist means all the circumstances of life. The same word is used in 1 Chronicles 29:30 of the circumstances of David's lifetime. Because all of his life is in God's control, he can appeal to him to come and rescue him from his present distress. Having made his confession of trust, he is on even surer ground as he renews his cry for deliverance. A sharp contrast exists between committing himself *into* the LORD's hand in the first part of the verse, and praying for deliverance *from* the enemy's hand in the second part.

Let your face shine on your servant; save me in your unfailing love (*v. 16*). The first phrase is an allusion to the priestly blessing in Numbers 6:24-25: 'The LORD bless you and keep you; the LORD make his face shine upon you and be gracious to you.' The psalmist appeals for saving mercy to be shown him in his distress. His request is doubly based on the covenant: he is the LORD's servant (ʿ*avdekâ*), and he pleads on the basis of the LORD's unfailing covenant love (*chasdekâ*).

Let me not be put to shame, O LORD, for I have cried out to you; but let the wicked be put to shame and lie silent in the grave (*v. 17*). The appeal is for a completely different result to come for the psalmist than for his enemies. In regard to them he wants them to be put to shame. In English the idea of shame stresses the inner feelings, whereas in Hebrew thought it is more outward disgrace. 'To lie silent in the grave' is equivalent to saying 'dead'. Those in Sheol are both inactive and silent.[6]

Let their lying lips be silenced, for with pride and contempt they speak arrogantly against the righteous (*v. 18*). The reference to lying lips goes back to the thought of verse 13. In their arrogance the ungodly speak against the righteous, such as the psalmist. He now asks for an end to their slander, so that no longer will the deceitful words of his enemies be a trouble to him.

3. Praise and Thanksgiving (*vv. 19-24*)

The psalm draws to a close with a beautiful acknowledgment of the LORD's mercies and with a call to all God's saints to love him. **How great is your goodness, which you have stored up for those who fear you, which you bestow in the sight of men on those who take refuge in you** (*v. 19*). The psalmist extols the wonderful goodness of God, a goodness (*tûv*) that is promised because of God's covenant with his people.[7] His servants are described by the parallel expressions 'who fear you' and 'who take refuge in you'. The LORD has stored up his love, described in terms of precious things that are set aside (cf. Ps. 119:11 for use of the verb *tsâfan* of treasuring up God's word in the heart). The demonstration of that love to his servants, however, is done publicly. Those who continue to set their trust on the LORD receive blessings from him that are apparent to others.

---

[6] For further information on the Hebrew word *sh*^{e}*'ôl*, see comment on Psalm 6:5.

[7] See f.n. 3 on Ps. 23 in reference to *tûv*.

In the shelter of your presence you hide them from the intrigues of men; in your dwelling you keep them safe from accusing tongues (*v. 20*). God himself is a place of refuge and protection for his people. Just as God stores up love for his people (v. 19), so he stores them up (using the same Hebrew verb) in a secure place, and so protects them against the slander of men. The NIV 'your dwelling' is clearly intended to form the parallel to 'your presence' in the first clause, but the MT simply has 'a shelter' (*sukkâh*). Since the almost identical phrase occurs in Psalm 27:5, it is preferable to translate simply 'You will hide them in a shelter.' This is one particular way in which God's love is shown to them.

Praise be to the LORD, for he showed his wonderful love to me when I was in a besieged city. In my alarm I said, 'I am cut off from your sight!' Yet you heard my cry for mercy when I called to you for help (*vv. 21-22*). The expression 'praise' or 'blessed' often comes at the beginning or at the end of a psalm of thanksgiving (cf. 28:6; 66:20; 144:1). The reason for such ascription of praise to the LORD is because of an unique and sovereign display of his covenant love. 'Showed his wonderful love' attempts to convey in English the idea that God has acted to manifest his love in a way that belongs to him alone. The expression is unique in that it combines a verb that is used of divine action (*pâlâ'*, Hi.) with the common noun (*chésed*) denoting God's affection expressed primarily in the covenant. It is hard to know whether the reference to a besieged city is a true historical allusion (to a city such as Ziklag) or a metaphorical description of the acute distress in which he was. Verse 22 tells the story of his deliverance. The cry for mercy (v. 9) has been heard. When in a state of disquiet ('alarm') he had claimed that he was cut off from God's sight. This is the only occurrence of this particular word for being 'cut off' (*gâraz,* Ni.), but the context makes clear that it is a metaphorical description of being rejected by God. Using other verbs, the Old Testament describes being cut off from God's hand (Ps. 88:5), from God's house (2 Chron. 26:21), and from the land of the living (Isa. 53:8). The reality was, though, that God heard the psalmist's cry for help and responded.

Love the Lord, all his saints! The Lord preserves the faithful, but the proud he pays back in full. Be strong and take heart, all you who hope in the Lord (*vv.* 23-24). An experience of God's mercy leads to a desire to see others sharing in it. He calls on all of God's saints, that is, all who have been objects of his mercy, to respond in love to him. This word for saints (Hebrew *châsîd*) occurs most often in the Psalms, and later it became the word for the orthodox party in Judaism in pre-Christian times (*the Chasidim*). All who firmly rely on the Lord will be guarded by him. On the other hand, those who vaunt themselves in their pride will find that the Lord renders to them just punishment. The final call is to strengthen themselves as they hope in the Lord. 'To hope' is practically synonymous with other expressions such as 'to trust' or 'to wait for'. The ultimate expression of believing trust is set out for the Christian in Romans 8:28-29.

Psalm 32

Of David. A maskil.

This is the first time in the Psalter that the technical term *maskîl* is used in the title.[1] It also occurs in Psalms 42, 44, 45, 52-55, 74, 78, 88, 89, 142, and in 47:7. A difficulty that faces the reader and interpreter of the Psalms is that it is uncertain whether it refers to the content of the psalm in question, or the musical accompaniment. The description of a group of Levites, the Maskilim, who 'showed good understanding of the service of the LORD' (2 Chron. 30:22), may be the best clue as to the meaning of the term. In that context a *maskîl* seems to be a song or a collection of songs for use in worship by a special group of Levites who are called *maskilîm*.[2]

The central theme of this psalm is the free grace of God in forgiving sin. Paul speaks of it as illustrating 'the blessedness of the man to whom God credits righteousness apart from works' (Rom. 4:6). No precise mention is made here of the nature of the sin itself. He clearly had been through a deep experience of knowing God's disfavour and of suffering illness at his hand. But with a fresh experience of God's unfailing mercy, he can sing this song of thanksgiving. This psalm forms another of the penitential psalms of the early church.

1. The Blessing of Pardon (*vv. 1-2*)

The psalm opens on a note of rejoicing because of the free grace of God. **Blessed is he whose transgressions are**

[1] *Maskîl* is a participial formation from the Hi. of the verb *s-k-l*. The root essentially means to have insight and hence success.

[2] See the note by Marvin Tate, *Psalms 51-100* (Word Biblical Commentary: Dallas: Word Books, 1990), p. 33.

forgiven, whose sins are covered. Blessed is the man whose sin the LORD does not count against him and in whose spirit is no deceit (*vv. 1-2*). Three terms for sin are used. 'Transgressions' (*pésha*ʿ) refers to acts of rebellion against God, while 'sins' (*chᵃtâ'âh*) is the broadest term for sin in the Old Testament. It denotes in general a missing of the mark, and hence an offence against God. The third term (ʿ*âwôn*), also translated as 'sin' in the NIV, has the idea of distortion or twisting from the right way. The wonderful thing that the psalmist can sing about is that all three kinds of sin can be forgiven by God. He can remove sin as far as the east is from the west (Ps. 103:12).

The three expressions for sin are paralleled by three expressions for forgiveness: 'taken away' (*nâshâh*, pass. part.), 'covered' (*kâsâh*, pass. part.), and 'not reckoned' (*châshav*). The psalmist, though, is not speaking of forgiveness in general. Rather, he is relating his own experience of the grace of God. For us today the New Testament makes it plain that forgiveness comes through the same free grace of God displayed in the death and resurrection of Jesus. 'He was delivered over to death for our sins and was raised to life for our justification' (Rom. 4:25).

2. A Personal Confession (*vv. 3-5*)

We now have a glimpse back to the period before the psalmist came to repentance and made his confession to the LORD. **When I kept silent, my bones wasted away through my groaning all day long. For day and night your hand was heavy upon me; my strength was sapped as in the heat of summer. Selah** (*vv. 3-4*). The time of silence was the time prior to his confession of guilt. The psalmists repeatedly speak of God being silent, but God also has cause to complain of the silence of his children. The physical effects brought on by his spiritual condition included a wasting of bones and a sapping of strength. The verb used of his bones (*bâlâh*, 'wasted away') is one normally used of clothes wearing out (cf. Josh. 9:13). Other psalms, such as 6:2-7, 102:3-5, and 119:83, also describe the physical effects of spiritual conflict. Constantly[3] he was aware of God's hand upon him, but resisted the promptings of his conscience to turn to the LORD in repentance.

Then I acknowledged my sin to you and did not cover up my iniquity. I said, 'I will confess my transgressions to the LORD' – and you forgave the guilt of my sin. Selah (*v. 5*). The three words for sin already used in verse 1 also appear here, while the phrase 'the guilt of my sin' (lit. 'the iniquity of my sin') is a combination of two of these terms. The silence is broken and the psalmist recounts abruptly his change of heart. When God's Spirit brings true repentance there is no attempt to cover one's sin and guilt. The psalmist had openly confessed his sin, and he knew the reality of God's forgiving mercy. The confession and the forgiveness are simultaneous (cf. 1 John 1:9).

3. Instruction for the Godly (*vv. 6-10*)

Therefore let everyone who is godly pray to you while you may be found; surely when the mighty waters rise, they will not reach him. You are my hiding place; you will protect me from trouble and surround me with songs of deliverance. Selah (*vv. 6-7*). Having experienced forgiveness for himself, the psalmist now wants others to seek the LORD as well. The godly[4] can find God (Isa. 55:6), whereas proud sinners discover that God has withdrawn himself from them (Prov. 1:28; Hos. 5:6).[5] The person, who in faith prays to the

---

[3]The Hebrew expression used here (*yômâm vâlay^e lâh*; lit. 'daily and night') is a standard one to express continuity. At times the words occur in reverse order without any difference in meaning.

[4] The NIV also uses 'saint' as a translation of the Hebrew word *chasîd*. See comment on Psalm 31:23.

[5] The translation 'while you may be found' represents the MT 'at the time of finding only' (*l^e‛êt m^etso᾽ raq*). Three main approaches to a problem text have been taken. (1) As NIV to compare the expression with Isaiah 55:6 and translate accordingly. (2) To emend 'finding' (*m^etso᾽*) to 'distress' (*mâtsôq*), which is followed by NRSV, RSV, NEB, JB. (3) To assume that this is a case of ellipsis, with the omitted object being 'his heart'. Cf. the full phrase 'when he comes to search his heart' in 2 Samuel 7:27. All these proposals still have to deal with the unusual use of *raq* ('only'). Probably it should be taken with the following clause and rendered 'assuredly'.

LORD, will find him, and knows that he keeps his children safe, even when the mighty waters look like overwhelming them. There may be an allusion here back to the flood in Noah's day. A believer will be safe because he has found a sure hiding place with the LORD (cf. 27:5; 31:20). When God protects his people he also gives them a joyful spirit and enables them to sing songs of deliverance (lit. 'songs of escape').

I will instruct you and teach you in the way you should go; I will counsel you and watch over you (*v. 8*). Some have taken these words to be what God said to David. But in the context they appear to be part of David's response to the LORD. Elsewhere he pledged himself to teach sinners the ways of the Lord (Ps. 51:13). Here he assures another godly person that he will both give instruction and also keep a watchful eye upon him. If another believer was caught in a similar set of circumstances to those which had overtaken him, he would be able to instruct him in the ways of the Lord.

Do not be like the horse or the mule, which have no understanding but must be controlled by bit and bridle or they will not come to you (*v. 9*). This could be advice against stubbornness in general, but in the context it may well be suggesting that there should be none of the hesitancy that David had in confessing his sin (see vv. 3-4). A sinner should not be constrained like a rebellious animal to come to the LORD. Out of a sense of need he should make his confession and seek pardon.

Many are the woes of the wicked, but the LORD's unfailing love surrounds the man who trusts in him (*v. 10*). The contrast is drawn between the sinner and the person constantly trusting in the LORD. The one knows many distresses (possibly 'sicknesses', cf. the use of the same Hebrew word in Isa. 53: 3, 'man of sorrows'), whereas the other has the knowledge of God's covenant love. Trust is the abiding characteristic of a believer.

4. A Call to Praise (*v. 11*)

Rejoice in the LORD and be glad, you righteous; sing, all you who are upright in heart! (*v. 11*). The call to praise concludes the psalm. It is very similar to other calls such as Psalm 97:12. It fits in well with the thought of the psalm because of the place 'the righteous' has in it (see especially v. 6). The verb 'sing' (*rânan*) is first used in the Old Testament in connection with a divinely appointed sacrifice (Lev. 9:24). In its later usage it normally denotes joy in connection with God's great saving acts. 'Righteous' and 'upright in heart' are parallel terms describing the condition of those who have received God's mercy.

Psalm 33

This is a hymn of praise to the Lord, and it is his creative work that is especially in focus. It is a short commentary on Genesis 1 (see particularly vv. 6-9), and then the implications of the Lord's mighty power for Israel are applied. The creator of the world is the creator of Israel and he is able to keep and deliver a people whom he chose for his own. Some of the language is drawn from Genesis 1, while other parts are dependent upon the Exodus account, and in particular the poetry of Exodus 15.

The psalm falls into the normal pattern for hymns (see section on hymns in the Introduction), having an introductory call to praise the Lord, followed by the reasons for this, and a conclusion that expresses confident trust in the covenantal love of the Lord. The double use of *chésed* towards the end of the Psalm (vv. 18 and 22) picks up and amplifies the earlier use of the same word in verse 5. This is the last of the psalms in Book 1 that has no title.

The position of this psalm following Psalm 32 may well be deliberate. The theme of praise at the end of Psalm 32 is taken up in a renewed way at the beginning of Psalm 33. Also, the commands in 32:11 and 33:1 are both addressed to 'the righteous' (*tsaddîqîm*), and the repetition of the verb 'sing [joyfully]' (*rânan*) is another link. While Psalm 33 has twenty-two verses (the exact number of letters in the Hebrew alphabet), no acrostic pattern is evident.[1]

---

[1] Eight Hebrew manuscripts actually join Psalms 32 and 33 together. However, this may have happened since Psalm 33 had no title, though the LXX and Qumran both include one.

1. A Call to Praise (*vv. 1-3*)
Praise is something appropriate for the righteous, and so this psalm commences with a call to jubilant song. **Sing joyfully to the LORD, you righteous; it is fitting for the upright to praise him** (*v. 1*). The verb rendered here 'to sing' (Hebrew *rânan* Pi.) is first used in Leviticus 9:24, where a shout of jubilation accompanied a burnt offering. It occurs most frequently in the Psalms and Isaiah, often in parallel with other terms for 'joy', 'rejoicing', and 'praise'. It also occurs in parallel with 'song' (*shîr,* Ps. 59:16) and the verb denoting 'playing an instrument' or 'singing' (*zâmar,* Ps. 98:4). Certainly 'jubilation' seems to be the main connotation, whether by 'music' (cf. 2 Chron. 20:22) or by 'singing' (Ps. 71:23). The word rendered 'fitting' by the NIV occurs again in Psalm 147:1: 'How good it is to sing praises to our God, how pleasant and *fitting* to praise him!' In that context, because of the parallelism, the word seems to suggest that praise is lovely. Such an idea fits in well here too. Praise is to be expected from the righteous, but when rendered it is also lovely. 'Righteous' (*tsaddîqîm*) and 'upright' (*y*[e]*shârîm*) occur as parallel terms to describe the believing community.

Praise the LORD with the harp; make music to him on the ten-stringed lyre. Sing to him a new song; play skilfully, and shout for joy (*vv. 2-3*). The choice of only two instruments is meant to be representative of the whole range of instruments used in ancient Israel (see Ps. 150 for a fuller list). The thought of a 'new song' can be interpreted in two ways. The use of the word 'new' has suggested to some commentators that it designates an eschatological or end-time song, just as 'new heavens and new earth' designate the great physical change that is coming. This would be in agreement with the use of the expression in Psalms 96:1 and 98:1, and it would also suit the use of the same phrase in Revelation 5:9. However, the phrase appears to be sometimes more general in its use (here and in Ps. 149:1), so that it marks out the freshness of praise that is rendered to the LORD.

2. The Reasons for Praise (*vv. 4-19*)

For the word of the LORD is right and true; he is faithful in all he does. The LORD loves righteousness and justice; the earth is full of his unfailing love (*vv. 4-5*). The first reason given for praise concerns the word of the LORD. The use of the word 'for' (Hebrew *kî*) is one of the distinctive characteristics of psalms such as this, as it marks out the things for which praise is to be given to the LORD (see also v. 9). The things that mark out God's Word are those that first of all distinguish him (uprightness, truth, righteousness, justice, and covenant love). Then in the work of creation, as he speaks the word and the world comes into being, his love is seen displayed there. He always acts in a manner consistent with his own character, for God cannot deny himself.

By the word of the LORD were the heavens made, their starry host by the breath of his mouth. He gathers the waters of the sea into jars; he puts the deep into storehouses (*vv. 6-7*). This is the start of a description of the creative work of God, for it was the LORD's word that caused the heavens to come into existence. The word 'host' has a variety of meanings in the Old Testament. It can be used for an army, for the angelic beings, or, as here, for the stars. The NIV correctly identifies its meaning here by adding the word 'starry'. The gathering of the waters (see Gen. 1:9-10) is described in poetical language as if God gathered up all the seas into a heap,[2] or as if he put the deeps (cf. Gen. 1:2) into stores.

Let all the earth fear the LORD; let all the people of the world revere him. For he spoke, and it came to be; he commanded, and it stood firm (*vv. 8-9*). By God's powerful word the world came into being. Since then, as Paul teaches in Romans 1:20, 'God's invisible qualities – his eternal power and divine nature — have been clearly seen, being understood from what has been made, so that men are without any excuse.' God's voice was heard, and creation resulted. It is not expressly called 'creation out of nothing', but that certainly is the implication of what is taught here and elsewhere in the

---

[2] Though early versions such as the LXX imply by their translations that the gathering of the waters of the sea was 'into jars' (NIV and other modern translations), the MT should be retained as it makes good sense and the parallel expression in Exodus 15:8 confirms this.

Old Testament about creation. As this revelation is universal, then everyone in the world should bow in adoration and reverence before him. In a context such as this, 'fear' does not mean 'to be afraid', but rather to 'adore' or 'revere'.

The LORD foils the plans of the nations; he thwarts the purposes of the peoples. But the plans of the LORD stand firm forever, the purposes of his heart through all generations. Blessed is the nation whose God is the LORD, the people he chose for his inheritance (*vv. 10-12*). The second reason for praise comes in verses 10-12. God is not only great in his creative work, but also in the outworking of his providence in history. The Bible ties together very closely the ideas of creation and providence. Nations may plot, but God intervenes to work out his own purposes. Israel was to see various kingdoms rise and fall. Through Isaiah, the LORD told the surrounding nations that their strategies would fail, and their purposes would not stand (Isa. 7:7; 8:10). God's purposes are sure, and his plans continue generation after generation. The contrast is so marked. Human schemes are temporary and fail; the LORD's plans are enduring and successful. After speaking of creation and providence, the psalmist now reaches the point where he speaks of the unique position of Israel. It was part of God's purpose that he chose Israel to be his people, and his inheritance. The truth stated here is reiterated in Psalm 135:4: 'For the LORD has chosen Jacob to be his own, Israel to be his treasured possession.' The verb 'choose' (*bâchar*) in the Old Testament always involves the idea of careful, well thought-out choice, and mostly (as here) it is used to designate the choice that expresses God's eternal purpose. God chose Israel to be his 'inheritance' (see Exodus 34:9 and Deut. 4:20), and how happy should Israel be in knowing that is so! The choice was based, not on any superiority or greatness of Israel, but solely on God's sovereign love (Deut. 7:7-10).

From heaven the LORD looks down and sees all mankind; from his dwelling place he watches all who live on earth – he who forms the hearts of all, who considers everything they do (*vv. 13-15*). The third reason for praise is that God's eye is over all his creation. The fact that it is 'from heaven' that he looks down, emphasises the rule that he has over everything. The LORD can see much more than just the outworking of sinful purposes by men (cf. vv. 10-11). He can even see into the hearts that he has made. He is the creator of those hearts, and this action is described using a word ('form', Hebrew *yâtsar*) that is used in Genesis 2:7, 8, 19 of the original creative work (see also its use in Pss. 74:17 and 94:9; Isa. 45:18; and Jer. 10:16). It is a word that describes the divine potter forming man from the dust of the ground.

No king is saved by the size of his army; no warrior escapes by his great strength. A horse is a vain hope for deliverance; despite all its great strength it cannot save (*vv. 16-17*). The fourth reason for praise is that God's might delivers his people. There is reference to displays of human strength that fail. It is not simply the size of a king's army that guarantees success in battle. Nor does an individual warrior manage to escape by his own ability. The horse was noted for its strength in battle, but Israel was warned not to trust in it for military victories (Isa. 30:15-16; 31:1). The Egyptians had learned at the Exodus that the horse and its rider could be overthrown by the LORD, for the LORD fought for his people (Exod. 15:1-4). The cluster of expressions denoting salvation or deliverance in these verses serves to highlight how vain it is to trust in human or earthly powers.

But the eyes of the LORD are on those who fear him, on those whose hope is in his unfailing love, to deliver them from death and keep them alive in famine (*vv. 18-19*). The contrast is marked by the introductory word at the beginning of verse 18. The 'but' (Hebrew *hinnêh, behold*) marks out the transition to the opposite idea. The LORD does not only look down on all mankind (v. 13), but he has a special interest in the God-fearing community. The parallel description of them (they who fear the LORD and who hope for his covenant love) also occurs in passages such as Psalm 119:74. The verb 'to hope for' (*yâchal,* Pi.) has the idea of expectant looking for something, coupled with the idea of patient waiting. In this case, it is that the God-fearers look to the LORD's covenanted mercy to deliver them in time of trouble. He is able to save from death (from enemies) or to preserve alive in times of famine. This seems to mean more than just to be kept alive. Rather it is preservation to enjoy God's presence and blessing, and to henceforth live in relationship with him.

3. A Declaration of Trust in the LORD (*vv. 20-22*)

A change takes place at this point, as the third person forms in the earlier part of the psalm give way to the first person plural ('we', 'our', 'us'). The conclusion is an affirmation of communal confidence in the LORD. The creator of both the world and Israel is well able to provide protection. **We wait in hope for the LORD; he is our help and our shield** (*v. 20*). Now the song of confidence sounds again from the psalmist. The NIV rendering 'wait in hope' aptly captures the sense of the Hebrew verb used here (*châkâh*), for it denotes eager expectation and confident trust. The assertion that follows about the LORD is taken up as a refrain in Psalm 115, 'He is their help and shield' (vv. 9, 10, 11). Both descriptions of God are fitting in a psalm that has spoken about battle. God supports and strengthens his people, and because he is their protector it is not surprising that he is called their shield.

In him our hearts rejoice, for we trust in his holy name (*v. 21*). After the acknowledgment which has just been made of the LORD's help, the psalmist now shows that the communal response was one of joy. Where there is believing trust in God's character, then there can be songs of joy that extol what he is to his people. The aspect of God's holiness is most important, for he is distinguished from his creatures in his character and his works. His character is the guarantee of blessing for those who trust in him.

May your unfailing love rest upon us, O LORD, even as we put our hope in you (*v. 22*). The psalm concludes with a prayer for covenant mercy to rest upon the believing community. This is putting verse 18b into the form of a prayer. The repetition of the two key words 'unfailing love' and the verb 'to hope' serves to point to the nature of the relationship between the community of Israel and the LORD. The song of joyful trust, evident at the outset of the psalm, continues right through to its close.

Psalm 34

Of David. When he pretended to be insane before Abimelech, who drove him away, and he left.

This is an acrostic psalm, with each verse of it beginning with a letter of the Hebrew alphabet. The only irregularities are that one letter is omitted (*vav*) and that an extra *pe* is added to commence the last verse (see the introductory comment on Psalm 25, as it similarly omits *vav* and has a supernumerary *pe*). Using an acrostic pattern placed certain restrictions on an author, but the thought flows well throughout this psalm. As an acrostic appeals more to the eye than the ear, its use in the Old Testament attests to a cultured and literate community in Israel. Attempts have been made to identify further alphabetical features about this psalm but they are unconvincing.[1]

It is a song of thanksgiving, though it is hard to be certain what the precise situation was in which the psalmist was placed. There is no reason to doubt the accuracy of the title, and to relate the psalm to this specific period of David's life. The word 'Abimelech' (which means, 'my father is king') may well have been a title for the Philistine kings, just as 'Pharaoh' was for the Egyptians. If this was so, then the king referred to would be Achish (1 Sam. 21:10).

A link exists with the previous psalm, in that the words 'But the eyes of the LORD are on those who fear him' (33:18a) are paralleled in this psalm by the words 'The eyes of the LORD are on the righteous' (34:15a). Also, in both psalms the repeated occurrence of the word 'LORD' is striking, with

---

[1] See especially A. R. Ceresko, 'The ABCs of Wisdom in Psalm XXXIV', *VT* 35 (1985), pp. 99-104.

it being used thirteen times in Psalm 33 and fifteen times in Psalm 34. More commonly psalmists intersperse use of the divine name (*yhwh*) with metaphorical expressions. Repetition of other words throughout the psalm also gives a feeling of literary unity to it.[2]

Another feature of this psalm is the presence of expressions that are very typical of wisdom literature in general. These include the invitation to 'taste and see', followed by the declaration, 'Blessed is the man ...' (v. 8). The invitation to the children to come and receive instruction (v. 11) is also redolent of a wisdom setting.

1. An Introductory Hymn (*vv. 1-3*)

I will extol the LORD at all times; his praise will always be on my lips (*v. 1*). As part of his thanksgiving the psalmist pledges himself to bless the LORD always, and to have his praise constantly on his lips. This is a vow that he is making, and he does so to the covenant LORD of Israel. The constant repetition of the name of the LORD is a striking feature throughout the psalm (see vv. 1-4, 6-11, 15-19, 22). So great has been the LORD's mercy to him that he pledges himself to praise him repeatedly. The word 'always' (*tâmîd*) has the idea of constancy, and it is used in other similar expressions (cf. 'my praise shall be continually of you', Ps. 71:6 NKJV).

My soul will boast in the LORD; let the afflicted hear and rejoice (*v. 2*). The experience of joy that David had was one that he wanted others to know as well. He wanted his fellow afflicted ones to listen to this call and also to rejoice in the LORD. Some have thought that he is referring to those who have come to worship at the sanctuary, but this seems too restrictive. Elsewhere the psalmist says that all who swear by God's name will rejoice (Ps. 63:11).

Glorify the LORD with me; let us exalt his name together (*v. 3*). Human praise can never make God any greater than he is, but he desires praise that calls others to magnify his name in public acknowledgment of him. Most probably 'his name'

---

[2] Notice the threefold or more repetition of 'hear', 'deliver', 'fear', 'good', 'evil', and 'righteous'.

is to be understood as the object of the verb 'glorify', for the Hebrew has, 'glorify *for the LORD* with me'. It is common in Hebrew poetry not to repeat the same phrase in both parts of a verse.[3] What is sought is a united song of praise to the LORD.

2. A Testimony to Deliverance (*vv. 4-10*)

Now the psalmist relates his own experience of seeking the LORD and finding him. **I sought the LORD, and he answered me; he delivered me from all my fears. Those who look to him are radiant; their faces are never covered with shame** (*vv. 4-5*). The verb 'sought' often suggests a diligent seeking. His cry had been heard and had received a ready answer from the LORD, and he had found deliverance from the fears that had oppressed him. 'Fears' carries with it the idea of the terror that God's judgment brings (cf. the only other occurrences of the word in Isa. 66:4 and Prov. 10:24). To look to God is the same as seeking him, and those who do look will not do so in vain.[4] None who cry to him will know disappointment. Instead, there is a radiance about their faces as they receive from his hand, as God's face shines on them (cf. the Aaronic blessing in Num. 6:24-26).

This poor man called, and the LORD heard him; he saved him out of all his troubles. The angel of the LORD encamps around those who fear him, and he delivers them (*vv. 6-7*). These verses form a parallel with the preceding pair. Thinking back on his own condition David refers to himself as a poor man who cried to the LORD. That cry was heard and salvation or deliverance resulted. The outcome was that he knew deliverance or salvation was from the LORD. By means of his angel the LORD stations himself around his people as their

---

[3] This feature is a form of ellipsis, or gapping as it is sometimes called. It is much more common in Hebrew poetry than in prose, and in contradistinction to prose it may occur in poetry in the first clause, as here in Psalm 34:2. For further discussion, see *DIHG~S*, pp. 163-64.

[4] A little awkwardness exists in the translation 'Those who look to him', as the subject has not been introduced in the preceding verses. Some Hebrew manuscripts make the verb an imperative (pointing it *habbîtû* instead of the MT *hibbîtû*). The LXX has *proselthate* that presupposes reading something like *g^e^shû*, 'draw near'. Confirmation of the Massoretic vocalisation comes from the following suffix, '*their* faces'.

protector. The language involving 'camping' and 'deliverance' suggests a military situation, but, whatever the precise battles in which David had engaged, the expressions here are general in character. He is reflecting on the fact that those who fear the LORD will find in him a protector and deliverer.

Resulting from his own experience of the LORD the psalmist now calls to others to enter into a similar experience. **Taste and see that the LORD is good; blessed is the man who takes refuge in him** (*v. 8*).'Taste' is used here, as in Proverbs 31:18, of discernment (lit. 'She [the wife] sees [Hebrew *tastes*] that her trading is profitable'). In the early church, because of the invitation to 'taste and see', this verse was appropriated for use at the Lord's Supper.[5] The reference to knowing that the LORD is good fits in well with the psalm as a whole, which, by its constant use of the divine name, emphasises the covenantal character of the relationship. It is significant that 'good' or 'goodness' are terms used in the Old Testament to describe the things promised by a covenant.[6] Peter adapts these words from the LXX version, omitting 'and see' as not essential to his argument (1 Pet. 2:3). The person, who takes refuge in the LORD, will know indeed the blessedness that he bestows on his children. The expression here, 'Blessed is the man ...' (*ʾashᵉrê haggever*), seems just to be a poetic synonym for either *ʾashᵉrê hâʾîsh* (Ps. 1:1) or *ʾashᵉrê ʾâdâm* (Ps. 32:2). The blessing closely resembles that which occurs at the end of Psalm 2.

Fear the LORD, you his saints, for those who fear him lack nothing. The lions may grow weak and hungry, but those who seek the LORD lack no good thing (*vv. 9-10*). The expression, 'the fear of the LORD', is one of the most comprehensive terms that the Old Testament has to describe a true believing attitude to the LORD. It is the devoted reverence of a trusting saint.[7] Those who do trust him will find that he fulfils his word to them and that they will not miss out on any of the good things he has promised in his covenant. Even

---

[5] *Apostolical Constitutions*, 8.13; Cyril, *Catech. Myst.* 5.17.

[6] See note on Psalm 23:6.

[7] For the concept of 'the fear of the LORD', see note on Psalm 15:4.

a powerful animal like the lion may go hungry, but none of God's children will lack food.

3. Instruction Offered (*vv. 11-20*)

Come, my children, listen to me; I will teach you the fear of the LORD. Whoever of you loves life and desires to see many good days, keep your tongue from evil and your lips from speaking lies (*vv. 11-13*). The style now becomes very like the wisdom style of the Book of Proverbs. The children addressed are students or pupils rather than literal sons, and the phrase is commonly used in the Book of Proverbs in this sense (cf. Prov. 1:8; 4:1). Hence the teacher is called a father (2 Kings 2:12; Matt. 23:9). In the Hebrew text verses 12-13 form a question that finds its answer in verses 14 and following (the NASB and NKJV both accurately reflect the MT). The question relates to the fundamental meaning of life. Verses 12-16 are quoted in 1 Peter 3:10-12, to enforce the lesson that we must not repay insult with insult.

Turn from evil and do good; seek peace and pursue it (*v. 14*). The life lived in the fear of the LORD is not just a state of heart and mind, but one that translates into action. It involves shunning evil and seeking good. Moreover, peace is to be sought as a harmonious relationship, and here it is largely relationship with other human beings rather than peace with God. He desires that his children will 'make every effort to do what leads to peace and to mutual edification' (Rom. 14:19). Jew and Gentile can both be brought into peace with one another through the blood of the cross (Eph. 2:14-16).

The eyes of the LORD are on the righteous and his ears are attentive to their cry; the face of the LORD is against those who do evil, to cut off the memory of them from the earth (*vv. 15-16*). The LORD keeps watchful guard over his children, and he is ever willing to heed their cry. The evildoers of verse 16 seem to be the righteous in name only, and against them God will display his anger if they set themselves to follow evil ways. The ultimate result is that they will perish from the earth, and no memory of them will remain. The language used here echoes the threat against covenant rebels of being 'cut off' (Gen. 17:14), and almost identical wording occurs again in Psalm 109:15.

The righteous cry out, and the LORD hears them; he delivers them from all their troubles. The LORD is close to the broken-hearted and saves those who are crushed in spirit (*vv. 17-18*). In the Hebrew text the subject of the verb 'cry out' is simply 'they'. The context at first suggests that the subject should be the evildoers, but as the main thrust of the passage concerns the righteous it is best to follow the NIV and understand the reference as being to them. Verse 17 is then to be understood as stating a general and abiding truth. The LORD ever hears the cry of his people and is ready to free them from their troubles. He is also ready to help. This and other similar expressions are used throughout the Psalms to convey the knowledge that God is able to save his people from whatever trouble they are in (cf. Pss. 25:22; 34:6; 54:7; 81:7). Two synonyms are used in verse 18 to describe the righteous – 'broken-hearted' and 'crushed in spirit'. Both are virtually equivalent to describing them as humble or contrite. The same combination of words occurs in Psalm 51:17. God's promise through the prophet Isaiah was that he would dwell 'with him who is contrite and lowly in spirit, to revive the spirit of the lowly and to revive the heart of the contrite' (Isa. 57:15). The adjective 'near' (*qârôv*) is used to designate closeness of relationship, so that God is near to all who call upon him in truth (Ps. 145:18). The Israelites claimed to be different from other nations in having God so near to them whenever they called on him (Deut. 4:7).

A righteous man may have many troubles, but the LORD delivers him from them all; he protects all his bones, not one of them will be broken (*vv. 19-20*). These verses are very similar in style to the Book of Proverbs, as they both state general truths, not promises to individuals. Trouble is the norm for the life of the righteous, but there is another norm applying as well, which is that God is the deliverer. The third use in this psalm of the same verb to 'deliver (*nâtsal*, Hi.) places emphasis on the truth that God indeed is the one who can rescue his people whatever their circumstances. Verse 20 puts the truth in a pictorial way. God will not allow his people to be brought into an extreme situation of danger, nor allow them to be made objects of derision and shame. When the soldiers came and found Jesus dead they did not break his bones, so that this scripture would be fulfilled (John 19:33-37). That was the highest expression of the idea of verse 20.

4. Concluding Summary (*vv. 21-22*)

Evil will slay the wicked; the foes of the righteous will be condemned. The Lord redeems his servants; no one will be condemned who takes refuge in him (*vv. 21-22*). The psalm ends with a short summary statement. Just as verses 15-16 contained a contrast, so there is another here. Those who give themselves to evil will find that in time they are destroyed by that evil. The enemies of the righteous will perish (taking the Hebrew verb *'âsham* here and in the following verse in this sense). That is to say, they will suffer the appropriate penalty as the consequence of their sin. On the other hand, the Lord redeems his servant. This final verse stands outside the acrostic pattern, just as the last verse of Psalm 25 does too. There is another similarity between these two psalms in that the letter *pe* is introduced to commence the final verse and in both cases it is the verb 'redeem' that is used. Also, the idea of finding refuge in the Lord occurs at the conclusion of both psalms (25:20; 34:22). Whereas the wicked perish, God saves his servants, and none perish who trust in him. All who seek refuge with him will find that they are preserved.

Psalm 35

Of David.

At first glance this appears to be an individual song of complaint. However, on closer examination it seems to be a psalm sung by the king. He appeals to God to intervene in a situation in which some treaty partners have proved false to their commitments. There are various phrases in the psalm that have either a legal or a military connotation. In general it is similar to the much shorter Psalm 20. A striking parallel expression to the opening of the psalm occurs in David's words to Saul: 'May the Lord be our judge and decide between us. May he consider my cause and uphold it; may he vindicate me by delivering me from your hand' (1 Sam. 24:15).

This psalm is composed of three main sections, each of which concludes with a promise of thanksgiving (vv. 10, 18, 28). The opening one (vv. 1-10) sets the tone for the others, and while it may appear different from them, yet definite links are apparent. For example, the thoughts of verses 4 and 17 are clearly connected, while the concept of 'ruin' occurs in both verses 8 and 17. The cluster of terms denoting 'shame' in verse 4 (the verbal roots *bôsh, kâlam, châpar*) recur in verse 26. The links between the second and third sections are closer. Fear of the reproaches of the enemy is mentioned in verses 11, 15, and 20, together with his enemies' glee over his distress in verses 15, 19, and 24-26. In both the second and third parts the enemies are depicted as voracious animals (vv. 15-17, 21, 25).

1. A Request for Help (*vv. 1-10*)

Contend, O Lord, with those who contend with me; fight against those who fight against me (*v. 1*). This verse is very terse in Hebrew. It can be rendered, 'Contend, O LORD, with my contenders, and fight with my fighters'. The Hebrew verb translated 'contend' (*rîv*) often occurs in a legal or covenant setting (cf. Jeremiah 2:9: 'I bring charges', *'ârîv*; Micah 6:1: 'Plead your case before the mountains', *rîv*).[1] The cognate noun ('strife', 'defence') appears in verse 23. The psalmist wants God to fight his legal battles and also to defend him against his attackers. If the attack was caused by a treaty partner who had gone back on a formal agreement, then both battles were in fact identical.

Take up shield and buckler; arise and come to my aid. Brandish spear and javelin against those who pursue me. Say to my soul, 'I am your salvation' (*vv. 2-3*). 'Shield' (*mâgên*) and 'buckler' (*tsinnâh*) were two different types of shields used in battle. The shield was the smaller round one carried by infantry, while the buckler was a larger rectangular shield that protected the whole body. The appeal is for God to enter into battle for the psalmist, lifting up weapons both to defend and to attack. Though 'spear' (*ch^anît*) is a common word, 'javelin' is more problematical. As it is vocalised in the MT (*s^egor*), it appears to be an infinitive from the verb 'to close' (cf. AV, 'and stop *the way*'). Different vocalisation (*seger* or *sâgâr*) yields a translation 'battle axe' or 'javelin'. The psalmist also longs for reassurance from God by means of a declaration that he is his deliverer. The phrase 'I am your salvation' may well be an abbreviated form of a phrase like 'I, the LORD, am your saviour' (Isa. 49:26; 60:16).[2]

May those who seek my life be disgraced and put to shame; may those who plot my ruin be turned back in dismay (*v. 4*). At this point there is a change from direct address to God (vv. 1-3) to indirect appeal in the form of curses on his enemies.

---

[1] This word is not common in the Psalter (for other instances see 43:1; 74:22, 103:9; 119:154). Literature on this topic includes H. B. Huffmon, 'The Covenant Lawsuit and the Prophets', *JBL* 78 (1959), pp. 286-95; J. Limburg, 'The Root RIB and the Prophetic Lawsuit Speeches', *JBL* 88 (1969), pp. 291-301; M. De Roche, 'Yahweh's *rîb* Against Israel: A Re-Assessment of the So-Called "Prophetic Lawsuit" in Pre-exilic Prophets', *JBL* 102 (1983), pp. 563-74.

[2] This suggestion is made by W. VanGemeren, 'The Psalms', p. 287.

Curses such as these are not to be regarded as expressions of personal vindictiveness. They are best taken as expressions of a covenant servant desiring God to deal with his enemies (see section on imprecatory psalms in the Introduction). Here David prays that his enemies will be disgraced (*yêvoshû*) and shamed (*vᵉyikkâlᵉmû*). These two verbs (*bôsh, kâlam*) often occur together in the Old Testament. In English 'shamed' has the idea of inner feelings, whereas the Hebrew verb conveys the idea of public disgrace. His enemies were seeking his life, and he wants them to be put to open shame.

May they be like chaff before the wind, with the angel of the LORD driving them away; may their path be dark and slippery, with the angel of the LORD pursuing them (*vv. 5-6*). The reference to 'chaff before the wind' suggests complete worthlessness (cf. Ps. 1:6). The idea of the angel of the LORD pursuing the enemies probably comes from the role that the angel played in the defeat of the Egyptians (Exod. 14:19-25). In the previous psalm the angel of the LORD was the guardian of his people (Ps. 34:7). Here he is the one who brings destruction on the enemies.

Since they hid their net for me without cause and without cause dug a pit for me, may ruin overtake them by surprise – may the net they hid entangle them, may they fall into the pit, to their ruin (*vv. 7-8*). As often in psalms like this, the psalmist proclaims his innocence. His enemies have acted against him without just cause, with emphasis on this because of the repeated use of 'without cause' (*chinnâm*, 'gratuitously'). Their actions are unprovoked on his part (cf. similar assertions in Pss. 109:3 and 119:161). He feels trapped by their plots, but prays that these plots will turn upon themselves and they will be caught by their own craftiness.

Then my soul will rejoice in the LORD and delight in his salvation. My whole being will exclaim, 'Who is like you, O LORD? You rescue the poor from those too strong for them, the poor and needy from those who rob them' (*vv. 9-10*). The psalmist anticipates that his prayer will be heard and answered. Thus he is able to express his delight in the LORD as his saviour and deliverer (cf. the declaration in verse 3). He is confident that his present situation will be overturned, and that the judgment he has invoked on his enemies will come to pass. The question, 'Who is like you, O LORD?' is typical of victory songs, and it is probably an echo of the one sung after the Exodus: 'Who among the gods is like you, O LORD? Who is like you – majestic in holiness, awesome in glory, working wonders?' (Exod. 15:11). The psalmist is so conscious of his own weakness ('poor and needy'), yet he knows that his salvation rests with the LORD alone.

2. A Description of the Enemies (*vv. 11-18*)

This new section of the psalm sets out the psalmist's innocence in the light of the persecution he is facing. He urges this as a reason why God should intervene and help him. **Ruthless witnesses come forward; they question me on things I know nothing about. They repay me evil for good and leave my soul forlorn** (*vv. 11-12*). The phrase 'ruthless witnesses' is literally 'witnesses of violence' (*ʿêdê châmâs*; cf. Exod. 23:1; Deut. 19:16). The scene is that of an irregular court. He is questioned by these violent men about crimes about which he knows nothing. The expression 'they questioned me' reflects legal terminology, as the verb 'to ask' (*shâʾal*) can be used of questioning a witness in a court of law.[3] The translation 'on things I know nothing about' is a possible interpretation of the MT. The alternative is to take the words (lit. 'who/which I do not know') as denoting the accusers of whom he has no knowledge. Either, they could have been friends whose appearance was so changed that he did not recognise them, or else they used messengers with whom he was unfamiliar. The parallelism with 'ruthless attackers' and the repetition of the same phrase 'those I do not know' in verse 15 suggest that this is the better interpretation.[4] The result of these illegalities is that he is punished for things he has never done, and so is left desolate. He is like a child who has lost his mother.

---

[3] T. H. Gaster, 'Questioning a Witness in a Court of Law', *VT* (1954), p. 25.

[4] This reflects the argumentation of W. VanGemeren, 'Psalms', p. 289.

Yet when they were ill, I put on sackcloth and humbled myself with fasting. When my prayers returned to me unanswered, I went about mourning as though for my friend or brother. I bowed my head in grief as though weeping for my mother (*vv. 13-14*). These verses contain several of the Old Testament terms for mourning. Sackcloth was an outward sign of mourning, and worn against the skin it was very uncomfortable. Fasting was practised in dangerous and sorrowful situations. 'To go about in mourning' is a phrase to describe mourners who show their deep grief by going about without washing, and by wearing soiled clothes. To pray with bowed head (lit. 'my prayer returns to my bosom') like the tax collector did (Luke 18:13) meant that physical posture and inward agony were seen to be united. How different was the psalmist's attitude to his enemies than theirs to him! Even if his enemies had been the closest of family, he could not have shown more grief for them.

But when I stumbled, they gathered in glee; attackers gathered against me when I was unaware. They slandered me without ceasing. Like the ungodly they maliciously mocked; they gnashed their teeth at me (*vv. 15-16*). A very unusual word is used here for attackers (*nêkîm*). It seems to come from a Hebrew verb meaning to strike (*nâkâh*), but in form it should probably be passive ('stricken', 'crippled'). It is used in Isaiah 66:2 of those who are crushed in spirit.[5] If this meaning is taken here, it implies that even those who were in a similar state as the psalmist did not try to console him. Rather, they gloated over his condition, and wounded him further with their bitter words. The NIV translation 'when I was unaware' should be emended to 'whom I did not know', as it is a repetition of the same phrase in verse 11.

While the general meaning is clear, the opening of verse 16 is extremely difficult to interpret. Literally it translates: 'as profane men, mockers for a cake.' While this may mean mockers who do so in pursuit of food, yet various changes

---

[5] Another alternative is to accept Dahood's suggestion that this is an occurrence of the Qal form of this verb that is otherwise unattested. This involves revocalising the word as *nokîm*. See M. Dahood, *Psalms I*, p. 213.

have been proposed.[6] The simplest solution is to take the word rendered 'cake' as meaning 'a circle', so that the meaning is that the psalmist faced mockers who stood in a circle around him. The verb 'to gnash the teeth' only occurs five times in the Old Testament and in each of the passages in the Psalms in which it occurs the context indicates that the machinations of the wicked against the righteous come to naught (see, in addition to v. 16, Pss. 37:12 and 112:10).

Now there is direct appeal to the LORD to step into the situation and deliver him. **O Lord, how long will you look on? Rescue my life from their ravages, my precious life from these lions. I will give you thanks in the great assembly; among throngs of people I will praise you** (*vv. 17-18*). 'How long?' occurs when there is a feeling of utter abandonment (Pss. 13:1; 79:5; 89:46). He wants his life delivered from the present bitter attacks by these evil men. The reference to 'my precious life' may suggest that he is very self-centred, but the word almost invariably is used of those loved by God. Such love by God brought protection (cf. Benjamin, Deut. 33:12). Our attitude to our own lives must be taken in Christian terms, and like Paul we must only view them in relation to God's purpose for us (Acts 20:24). The promise is made that not only will praise be given to God in an individual way, but also in the presence of others as the people of God assemble for worship. The phrase 'the great congregation' seems to be referring to the same assembly as the simple 'the congregation' (for other occurrences of 'the great congregation', see 1 Kings 8:65; 2 Chron. 20:14; 30:13; and Ps. 22:25). This note of thanksgiving is very fitting following on the cries of lament in the preceding verses.

3. A Call for God's Help (*vv. 19-27*)

Direct appeal to the LORD is now made, replacing the curses earlier in the psalm. **Let not those gloat over me who are my enemies without cause; let not those who hate me without reason maliciously wink the eye** (*v. 19*). Once more the innocence of the

[6] For discussion of various proposals, see W. VanGemeren, 'Psalms', p. 290; M. Dahood, *Psalms I*, pp. 212-13; *DCH*, 5, p. 383; A. A. Anderson, *The Book of Psalms I* (London: Marshall, Morgan & Scott, 1972), p. 282.

psalmist is maintained for he is being persecuted 'without cause' and 'without reason'. He does not want such people to be able to gloat (lit. 'rejoice') over his trouble. The Hebrew verb translated 'wink' has the idea of pinching something together. 'Wink' is probably too much associated with merriment in English. It would be better to use an expression like 'narrow the eyes' which may better depict the hostility.

They do not speak peaceably, but devise false accusations against those who live quietly in the land (*v. 20*). Further indication comes here of the treaty or covenant background to the psalm. The term 'peace' was used in international treaties of the ancient Near East to designate the relationship between the parties. Thus Joshua made peace with the Gibeonites, establishing a treaty relationship between Israel and themselves (Josh. 9:15). Clearly the psalmist's enemies were breaching the terms of the treaty, and making false claims against those living in quietness in the land. The phrase 'those who live quietly in the land' only occurs here, apparently designating the congregation of faithful worshippers.[7]

They gape at me and say, 'Aha! Aha! With our own eyes we have seen it.' O LORD, you have seen this; be not silent. Do not be far from me, O Lord (*vv. 21-22*). The enemies make the claim that they have seen something that broke the requirements of the covenant they had made. The cry 'Aha!' is an exclamation of joy over the fact that they have discovered something with which they can accuse the psalmist. But someone else had seen the situation. God had been witness to the treaty, and the psalmist appeals to him to intervene. 'Do not be silent' and 'do not be far from me' are simply ways of asking for God's immediate help to rectify the situation.

Awake, and rise to my defence! Contend for me, my God and Lord. Vindicate me in your righteousness, O LORD my God; do

---

[7] The difficulty in understanding the phrase is not just because it is a *hapax legomenon*. The word in question (*râgêaʿ*) comes from a root *r-g-ʿ* that has two divergent meanings, 'to stir' or 'act in a moment', and 'to be at rest'. Context has to be the determining factor, and in this psalm the phrase seems to designate those who experience the tranquility 'that results from having ceased one's own efforts and from having found security through trust in God' (John N. Oswalt, *NIDOTTE*, 3, p. 1054).

not let them gloat over me (*vv. 23-24*). Legal terminology is used to show the action that is needed by the LORD. The request for God to contend for him, with which the psalm opened, is now repeated. He is asked to 'awake', i.e. to stir himself and to act on behalf of the psalmist, for he seems so distant. God is not hostile but seems so indifferent. The psalmist longs for deliverance, and the phrase 'vindicate me in your righteousness' may refer to victory in battle as much as to legal vindication. The final clause of verse 24 is the same as the first in verse 19.

Do not let them think, 'Aha, just what we wanted!' or say, 'We have swallowed him up' (v. *25*). If God does not intervene, then this would be the consequence. These enemies would be able to think and say, 'We got our wish!' Again the exclamation 'Aha!' denotes joy. With rejoicing they would be able to claim that the psalmist had been destroyed (cf. Ps. 124:3 for the idiom concerning being swallowed).

May all who gloat over my distress be put to shame and confusion; may all who exalt themselves over me be clothed with shame and disgrace. May those who delight in my vindication shout for joy and gladness; may they always say, 'The LORD be exalted, who delights in the well-being of his servant' (*vv. 26-27*). This section of the psalm moves to a close with a contrast between two groups of people. For those who desire his ruin, the psalmist asks again (see v. 4) that they will be covered with shame and disgrace, as though they were wearing it like clothes. On the other hand he longs for his supporters to be able to rejoice in what the LORD has done for him. The covenant theme is continued here with reference to the well-being (lit. 'the peace') of the LORD's servant. Human treaties might promise peace, but it is only the LORD who can give it. True peace is a gift of the Saviour (John 14:27). The response from the psalmist is praise for God's salvation.

My tongue will speak of your righteousness and of your praises all day long (*v. 28*). He will ever speak (the same word as used in Ps. 1:2 for murmuring or meditating) of his deliverance, and make mention of God's praise. It is noticeable that God's praise is closely tied in here and elsewhere with God's acts of deliverance (see Exod. 15:11; and Pss. 78:4 and 106:47).

Psalm 36

For the director of music. Of David the servant of the Lord.

There are features in this psalm that resemble appeals to God, but there are also other features which are more like wisdom psalms such as Psalms 37 or 73. Perhaps it is best to compare it to the first psalm, though it deals with the subject matter in reverse order. In fact, there are four sections in the psalm. It starts with the wicked, progresses to God's covenant love (*chésed*), prays for the continuation of that love, and then reverts to the fate of the wicked. This chiastic pattern is clearer in the Hebrew text, but it can be set out in this fashion:

1. The character of the godless (vv. *1-4*)
Subject: the wicked [*râshâʿ*] (v. *1*)
2. The covenant love of the Lord (vv. *5-9*)
Subject: covenant love [*chésed*] (v. *5*)
3. Continuation of the Lord's love (v. *10*)
Subject: covenant love [*chésed*] (v. *10*)
4. The fate of the wicked (vv. *11-12*)
Subject: the wicked [*râshâʿ*] (v. *11*)

This psalm, along with others such as Psalm 32, shows how wisdom teaching found a congenial place in the worship of Israel. The characteristics of the godly and the ungodly are described graphically, setting out both their way of life and also the attitude of God to them. On the one his favour rests; from the other, his grace is withheld.

1. The Character of the Godless (*vv. 1-4*)
The opening verse is called by the notable nineteenth-century commentator, J. A. Alexander, one of the most difficult verses in the whole book.[1] **An oracle is within my heart concerning the sinfulness of the wicked: There is no fear of God before his eyes** (*v. 1*). The word translated 'oracle' is a technical term (*n*ᵉ*'um*), occurring again in Psalm 110:1. It is used repeatedly in the prophets to introduce a divine proclamation. Here it is either used of the psalmist, as the NIV takes it, or else it refers to the decision the wicked man has made: 'I have resolved in my heart to do evil'.[2] While not without problems, these interpretations at least are trying to interpret and translate the MT without changing it.

The second part of the verse is the psalmist's comment on the character of the wicked man. He has none of the terror inspired by God, and hence God is excluded from the whole horizon of his life. The phrase is not the normal one for the fear of God (*yir'at yhwh*) but one that speaks more of terror (*pachad 'ᵉlôhîm*). Paul quotes these words in Romans 3:18 as giving the cause of all the manifestations of sin he has just listed.

For in his own eyes he flatters himself too much to detect or hate his sin. The words of his mouth are wicked and deceitful; he has ceased to be wise and to do good (*vv. 2-3*). The nature of sin is that it is self-deceptive. Without a true relationship with the LORD the transgressor does not view himself aright, and therefore is unable to acknowledge or come

[1] J. A. Alexander, *The Psalms Translated and Explained* (Edinburgh: Andrew Elliot and James Thin, 1864; republished by Zondervan, n. d.), pp. 155-56.

[2] The phrase *n*ᵉ*'um pesha'* is a *hapax legomenon*. The use of *n*ᵉ*'um* is almost invariably with *yhwh*, designating a word from the LORD given to a prophet and then transmitted to his hearers. But it is not only the opening phrase that is difficult, but also the word 'in my heart' (*libbî*). The fact that a few Hebrew manuscripts have *libbô*, 'his heart', only shows that scribes recognised a problem and sought to overcome it. Older commentators discussed the problem (cf. in addition to Alexander, F. Delitzsch, *Psalms*, II, pp. 1-4; Hengstenberg, *Psalms*, II, pp. 12-14). Good modern discussions can be found in Craigie, *Psalms 1-50*, p. 290, and VanGemeren, 'Psalms', p. 293. Craigie proposes that *n*ᵉ*'um*, 'oracle', should be added to the title, and this is accepted by C. C. Broyles, *Psalms* [NIV International Biblical Commentary] (Peabody, MA; Hendrickson, 1999), pp. 174, 177. However, both Craigie and Broyles proceed to accept the emendation 'his heart'.

to hate his sin. Pride rules his motives and his self-sufficiency creates the inability to feel any sense of sin. His words reveal his true character, and being under the dominion of sin he has ceased acting wisely and doing good.

Even on his bed he plots evil; he commits himself to a sinful course and does not reject what is wrong (*v.* 4). As part of his way of life, the evil man thinks that in the solitude of his own bedroom he can plot evil without God knowing. Instead of thinking about God's goodness while in bed (Ps. 63:6) he is deliberately setting himself to plot further evil for the next day. He sets himself upon a path that is not good, the MT making not-good a single word (*lô'-tôv*).

2. The Covenant Love of the LORD (*vv.* 5-9)

In stark contrast to these descriptions of the wicked is the covenant love (*chésed*) of the LORD. **Your love, O LORD, reaches to the heavens, your faithfulness to the skies** (*v.* 5). The idea of this verse is very similar to the opening of Psalm 89, which is proclaiming the wonder of God's grace shown in his covenant with David (Ps. 89:1-4). Both 'love' and 'faithfulness' describe the unchanging commitment of God, his total dependability in keeping his pledged word. It is beyond human ability to grasp the full extent of this love (cf. Ps. 103:11 and Paul's words in Eph. 3:18-19).

Your righteousness is like the mighty mountains, your justice like the great deep. O LORD, you preserve both man and beast (*v.* 6). Another pair of attributes are ascribed to God, indicating how his character affects both men and animals. Both 'righteousness' and 'justice' are terms that carry on the idea of God's covenant commitment. They are compared to the great, unchanging parts of God's creation in order to demonstrate how unchangeable they are.[3] He will continue to preserve both men and animals. The allusion here is probably to the covenant with Noah, in which God pledged himself

---

[3] In the MT 'like the mighty mountains' is 'like the mountains of God' (*kᵉharê 'êl*). This construction in effect has the force of a superlative in linking a word with a divine name. Most probably the usage arose from the idea that God created the thing in question. See, for further comment, illustration, and literature, *DIHG~S*, p. 46; *IBHS*, pp. 154 n. 33, 268.

never again to cut off all life by means of a flood (Gen. 8:21-22; 9:9-17).

How priceless is your unfailing love! Both high and low among men find refuge in the shadow of your wings (*v. 7*). An exclamation or a doxology is a fitting response to what has just been said. The NIV takes the Hebrew word *'elohîm* to stand for men of high station. It is better to take it in its normal meaning of 'God', and so render: 'How precious is your unfailing love, O God! Men find refuge. ...' This also forms a neat parallel with 'O LORD, you preserve ...' in the previous verse. An expression of God's covenant love is seen in the truth that men can find shelter with him, just as Israel did of old (cf. Deut. 32:10-11 and Ps. 17:7-8).

They feast on the abundance of your house; you give them drink from your river of delights. For with you is the fountain of life; in your light we see light (*vv. 8-9*). God's grace is depicted as feasting or drinking. As people came to the sanctuary they found that God provided richly for them. The idea of feasting may come from the practice of participating in the fellowship meals. Linked with this is the picture of drinking from a cool fountain of water. It may be that 'house' here is God's creation as a whole, from which men and animal alike receive the bounty. All of life is traced back to God as its source. The word 'delights' (pl. *'adânîm*) only occurs three times in the Old Testament, and there may be an illusion to the Garden of Eden, the garden of delight (*'êden*). The imagery is furthered in the Book of Revelation with reference to drinking from the fountain of life (Rev. 21:6). Then the psalmist changes the imagery to light. This statement in verse 9 is similar to the opening verse of Psalm 27 where God is said to be light and salvation. This idea anticipates the gospel message of the New Testament that Jesus is indeed the true light (John 1:4-9; 1 John 1:5-7).

3. The Continuation of the LORD's Love (*v. 10*)

Continue your love to those who know you, your righteousness to the upright in heart (*v. 10*). The verb used at the outset of this verse (*mâshak*) conveys the idea of drawing out or prolonging something. It forms a prayer here that the covenant love of the LORD will be maintained for those in a vital relationship with him. 'To know the LORD' is an expression denoting close fellowship with him, because strangers to him do not have this knowledge (cf. 1 Sam. 2:12; 3:7). The parallel phrase repeats the same idea in variant language, continuing the close connection between covenant love and righteousness (see v. 5). As in Psalm 33:1, 'the upright in heart' is a term that describes the believing community.

4. The Fate of the Wicked (*vv. 11-12*)

May the foot of the proud not come against me, nor the hand of the wicked drive me away (*v. 11*). The thought of the wicked plotting evil ways against the righteous is taken up again from the beginning of the psalm. The psalmist prays for protection against the foot and hand of the wicked that would trample him down or drive him far away from the place of blessing and salvation.

See how the evildoers lie fallen – thrown down, not able to rise! (*v. 12*). Whereas the earlier picture of the wicked in this psalm was one of busyness in their own sinful ways, now their end is depicted with startling brevity. 'There they lie!' exclaims the psalmist. The place or time is not mentioned, making the statement an even greater threat. The person who does not live in the fear of the LORD will ultimately perish.

Psalm 37

Of David.

None of the previous acrostic psalms (9-10, 25, and 34) is as elaborate as this one. Every letter of the Hebrew alphabet is included, and two verses are allocated to each letter. In its general theme the psalm is most closely related to Psalm 73, though it has numerous verses that have parallels in the Book of Proverbs. Many of the statements are in the form of proverbs, which are general assertions of a truth rather than promises to individuals. Twice (in verses 25 and 35) the psalmist refers to his own experience in which he had seen something of the character of both the righteous and the wicked. Its teaching centres on the source of true blessing, and it encourages its readers to follow the ways of the LORD. It concludes on the note of salvation for those who find refuge in him (v. 40). While the alphabetic pattern places constraints on the author, yet there does seem to be some divisions in the psalm.

This psalm was utilised by the Qumran community in pre-Christian times. Considerable parts of a commentary on it have survived (4QPs37), in which the community itself becomes 'those who wait for the LORD' (v. 9), while the wicked are interpreted as their opponents.[1]

1. A Call to Trust in the LORD *(vv. 1-9)*

The opening and close of the psalm are marked by imperatives and prohibitions. **Do not fret because of evil men or be**

---

[1] For further discussion on this document, see J. M. Allegro, 'A Newly Discovered Fragment of Ps 37 from Qumran', *PEQ* LXXXVI (1954), pp. 69-75, and D. Pardee, 'A Restudy of the Commentary on Psalm 37 from Qumran Cave 4', *Revue de Qumran* VIII (1973), pp. 163-94.

envious of those who do wrong; for like the grass they will soon wither, like green plants they will soon die away (*vv. 1-2*). The Hebrew word for 'fret' (*chârâh*) comes from a stem meaning to burn, and it is used here in a reflexive form; 'Do not let yourself burn [with envy]'. It is only in this psalm (vv. 1, 7, 8) and Proverbs 24:19 that this form occurs.[2] The parallel expression points to envy of the ill-doing of the wicked and their short-lived prosperity. The problem faced in this psalm, as in Psalm 73, is the seeming prosperity of the wicked. The psalmist says to his readers, 'Don't be jealous of the wicked, for they are just like grass, which seems to be flourishing and then is gone'. The comparison with the grass is used elsewhere in the Psalms to teach the frailty of all human life (Ps. 103:15).

Trust in the LORD and do good; dwell in the land and enjoy safe pasture. Delight yourself in the LORD and he will give you the desires of your heart (*vv. 3-4*). What was needed was not envy, but trust in the LORD! This command has as its background the possession by Israel of the land of promise. What was needed was continuing commitment to the LORD and the appropriate obedience to his word which would result in them 'doing good'. The references to the land are reminiscent of passages such as Deuteronomy 11, in which 'the land' was a summary of all the blessings promised under the covenant. 'Enjoy safe pasture' is the NIV's attempt to translate a difficult clause in the MT (*rᵉʿêh ʾᵉmûnâh,* lit. 'shepherd faithfulness'). It is preferable to take the word 'faithfulness' as an adverb, 'faithfully', and the resulting translation, 'shepherd faithfully', gives a good parallel to 'dwell in the land'.[3] There was to be enjoyment in the LORD (the verb is a very rare one in the Old Testament), and the assurance is given that he would respond to the prayers of his people.

The theme of verses 3-4 is repeated in alternative language in verses 5-6. **Commit your way to the LORD; trust in him and he will do this: He will make your righteousness shine**

[2] It is a mistake to think that the Hitpael of this verb refers to passionate anger as over against simple anger in the Qal form. The Qal already has intensive force. See the comment by B. K. Waltke, *The Book of Proverbs Chapters 15-31,*(NICOT: Grand Rapids: Eerdmans, 2005), p. 286 n. 59.

[3] For fuller discussion, see W. VanGemeren, 'Psalms', p. 299.

like the dawn, the justice of your cause like the noonday sun (*vv. 5-6*). The call is to commit (lit. 'roll', *gôl*) their way on the LORD (cf. Ps. 22:9). When this expression is compared with Proverbs 16:3 – 'Commit to the LORD whatever you do, and your plans will succeed' – it seems to suggest that heavy demands, like a great burden, are to be rolled onto the LORD. He is able to do whatever is demanded. The New Testament equivalent is to cast all our anxiety upon him because he cares for us (1 Pet. 5:7). The outcome of this trust will be that the cause entrusted to him will flourish just like the appearance of the sun in its glory. NIV takes the Hebrew word *ʾôr* (*light*) as 'dawn', but the parallelism suggests 'sun' is the better rendering.

Be still before the LORD and wait patiently for him; do not fret when men succeed in their ways, when they carry out their wicked schemes (*v. 7*). The situation confronting the readers of this psalm was that the prosperity of wicked men was causing them problems. When they thought about it they were becoming angry and resentful. What they should have done was to be silent before the LORD (cf. the use of the same verb already in Pss. 4:4 and 30:12, and also in Ps. 62:1) and to wait patiently for him to deal with the situation. The command 'Do not fret' is taken up from the opening verse and is repeated in both this and the following verse. Present success of ungodly men is no true indication of God's favour or blessing.

Refrain from anger and turn from wrath; do not fret – it leads only to evil. For evil men will be cut off, but those who hope in the LORD will inherit the land (*vv. 8-9*). Becoming angry about the situation is only to imitate the unrighteous ways of the wicked. Those ways are not to be followed, only forsaken. Inward turmoil over it results in more evil, and places one in danger of God's judgment. 'To be cut off' is used here as in Exodus 30:33, 38 and 31:14 of being put to death. To remain in the good land and enjoy its benefits required true faith and hope in the LORD. This latter expression complements the other expressions already used such as 'trust', and 'commit your way to the Lord'. To hope in the LORD indicates long, patient endurance in waiting on him. The New Testament parallels to it are our Lord's experience in Gethsemane (Luke 22:44: 'in anguish') and the description of Epaphras' prayers (Col. 4:12: 'always wrestling in prayer').

2. The Ruin of the Wicked (*vv. 10-15*)

A little while, and the wicked will be no more; though you look for them, they will not be found. But the meek will inherit the land and enjoy great peace (*vv. 10-11*). The seeming prosperity of the wicked is only an illusion, for they are going to be cut off. When one looks to see where they are (lit. 'you perceive his place'), they are gone. The contrast is that the meek shall abide in the land and enjoy (the same word as translated 'delight' in verse 4) abundant peace. The word 'meek' represents all those who are truly waiting on the LORD. It is often contrasted with the wicked as here in this verse, or with the scoffers (Prov. 16:19). They experience God as their deliverer (Ps. 10:17), receive grace from him (Prov. 3:34), and they know that he is finally going to save them (Pss. 147:6; 149:4). The concept of the land was so central for Old Testament believers that occupation of it could be used to summarise all the blessings that God had promised. Jesus, in the Sermon on the Mount (Matt. 5:5), broadened the concept of the meek inheriting the land. He spoke not just of 'land' but of the world. Then, too, he further developed the idea both by integrating it with his teaching on the kingdom and also by expanding the idea to embrace Jew and Gentile.

The wicked plot against the righteous and gnash their teeth at them; but the Lord laughs at the wicked, for he knows their day is coming (*vv. 12-13*). Those whose hearts are not right with God spend their time scheming against the righteous. In their bitterness they vent their rage by grinding their teeth as they display their anger.[4] In Psalm 2:4 the Lord mocks at the scheming of the hostile kings. Here he mocks at the wicked in general. The reason for this is that he knows that 'his day' is coming. This could refer to the Lord's 'day', but in the context it seems to be the wicked man's day. In effect

---

[4] For the expression 'gnash the teeth', see comment on 35:16.

it amounts to the same thing, for his day will be the final day of judgment.

The wicked draw the sword and bend the bow to bring down the poor and needy, to slay those whose ways are upright. But their swords will pierce their own hearts, and their bows will be broken (*vv. 14-15*). Hostility towards the righteous is the hallmark of the wicked. They plot to use weapons against them, and even to kill them. The verb 'to slay' (*tâvach*) is a very strong word, being used elsewhere normally of the slaughter of animals. However, what they will find is that their own schemes turn against themselves and they are destroyed by their own weapons. This theme, of evil turning back on its practitioners, is dealt with in Psalm 7:14-16 (see commentary; for the same idea, see Jer. 2:19 and 5:24-25).

3. The Blessing of the LORD (*vv. 16-26*)

Better the little that the righteous have than the wealth of many wicked; for the power of the wicked will be broken, but the LORD upholds the righteous (*vv. 16-17*). Money may be part of a happy life but it is not its real basis. The righteous may be poor, but that is better than thinking that wealth is what matters in life. Money in itself is not wrong. It is the love of it that the Bible condemns (1 Tim. 6:10). The wicked will find that their ability to acquire wealth will disappear. The word 'power' is literally 'arms', for often 'arm' (*z^{e}rôʿa*) is used as a symbol for power (see Pss. 77:15 and 89:10). On the other hand, the sustenance of the righteous comes from the LORD. He is the constant provider for his people, and his role is emphasised in the Hebrew text (and all the ancient translations) by placing his name at the end of the verse.

The days of the blameless are known to the LORD, and their inheritance will endure forever. In times of disaster they will not wither; in days of famine they will enjoy plenty (*vv. 18-19*). The whole idea of Canaan as the land that God swore to give to Israel lies behind the words here. Canaan was the inheritance that the LORD provided (Exod. 15:17; Deut. 31:20), and his eyes were 'continually on it from the beginning of the year to the end' (Deut. 11:12). God knew each day of his people's lives, and he so met their needs that even in times of famine they enjoyed abundance. On occasions this was done by extraordinary means, as in the days of Elijah (1 Kings 17:1-6).

But the wicked will perish: The LORD's enemies will be like the beauty of the fields, they will vanish – vanish like smoke (v. 20). The stress here is on the passing nature of the wicked. This is emphasised by the use of two verbs, 'perish' and 'vanish', with the double use of the latter drawing attention to the accomplishment of God's wrath against the wicked. Two illustrations are involved. The first one is that of the beauty of the grass, which then fades. The second is of things being consumed by fire. Both of them draw attention to how fleeting is the existence of the wicked.

The wicked borrow and do not repay, but the righteous give generously; those the LORD blesses will inherit the land, but those he curses will be cut off (*vv. 21-22*). The contrast is between the wicked who borrow so extensively and are unable to pay when the crisis comes, and the righteous, who not only have sufficient for their own needs, but are also able to help others as well. In the Hebrew text of verse 21, two phrases are used both of the wicked and the righteous (borrow/not repay, show mercy/give). It is best to retain this parallelism with a translation such as the NKJV: 'The wicked borrows and does not repay, but the righteous shows mercy and gives.' The introduction of the reference to blessing and cursing in verse 22 recalls the sections in the covenant that list the appropriate blessings and cursings (Deut. 27:1-26; 28:1-6, 15-68). The description of death as a 'cutting off' goes back to the language of instituting a covenant (lit. 'cutting a covenant') and the threat of being cut off because of failure to keep the provisions of the covenant (Gen. 17:14).

The LORD delights in the way of the man whose steps he has made firm; though he stumble, he will not fall, for the LORD upholds him with his hand (*vv. 23-24*). The general principle being stated is that the righteous may experience falls during life, but yet the LORD will uphold them so that they are lifted up again (see the similar teaching in Prov. 24:16). The

LORD's pleasure is shown towards the righteous as they walk in his ways, and he establishes those ways. The righteous are not isolated from trouble, but when it comes, the LORD strengthens their hand (the same verb 'uphold' occurs here as in v. 17).[5]

I was young and now I am old, yet I have never seen the righteous forsaken or their children begging bread. They are always generous and lend freely; their children will be blessed (*vv. 25-26*). The elderly psalmist reflects on his knowledge of life, extending from being a lad (*naʿar*) until he has reached old age (*zâqantî*). While he has seen the righteous passing through difficult times (cf. vv. 7, 12, 14, 16, 19), yet he has never seen them completely forsaken by the LORD. Though they may have periods in life when it seems that the LORD has withdrawn his love, yet that is never final. The righteous are able to show compassion to others and share with them their resources. The lending is not in a commercial sense, for no interest was to be charged on such loans (Exod. 22:25). The final phrase of verse 26 points to the fact that not only will the righteous be provided by the LORD, but their children, in turn, will receive from him.

4. The Marks of the Righteous (*vv. 27-33*)

In the closing parts of the psalm there is a return to the style of the opening, with commands again evident. The theme of dwelling in the promised land continues. **Turn from evil and do good; then you will dwell in the land forever. For the LORD loves the just and will not forsake his faithful ones** (*vv. 27-28a*). Continuity of life in the promised land depended on obedience by the people (see Deut. 11:8-9: 'Observe therefore all the commands I am giving you today … so that you may live long in the land that the LORD swore

---

[5] Ambiguity is present in both of these verses. The verb 'he delights' could have either 'the LORD' or 'the righteous man' as the subject. Then at the conclusion of verse 24, 'his hand' could be either the direct object of the verb ('he upholds his hand', i.e. the hand of the righteous man), or it could be as the NIV translates, 'the LORD upholds by his hand.' These ambiguities explain the difference in rendering by various English versions.

to your forefathers to give them and their descendants …').[6] Following the LORD meant that they had to turn from evil and do good, which is a reference to living in a morally good way (1 Kings 8:36). The Hebrew text of verse 28a says that the LORD loves 'justice', but it seems best to take this as meaning 'the just' as in Proverbs 2:8. To those who are just and who are his loyal servants (*chasîdîm*, see on 4:3; 12:1; 18:25), there is the promise that God will never forsake them (Deut. 31:6, quoted in Heb. 13:5).

They will be protected forever, but the offspring of the wicked will be cut off; the righteous will inherit the land and dwell in it forever (*vv. 28b-29*). Verse 28b commences the section of the acrostic beginning with the letter *ayin*, though here and in verse 39 the conjunction *vav* must be disregarded.[7] The contrast is between the just and the wicked and their respective descendants. The seed (NIV 'children') of the righteous will be blessed (v. 26), whereas the seed (NIV 'offspring') of the wicked will be destroyed. This is a repetition in other words of what has already been stated in verses 9 and 22. The psalmist builds here on the concept of the land being an inheritance for Israel. God's covenant people had to maintain their inheritance by obedience to his demands. This is the fourth time that the psalmist has mentioned inheriting the land, and the variety of expressions used to designate the persons involved shows how close in meaning several of the phrases are ('those who hope in the LORD', v. 9; 'the meek', v. 11; 'those who the LORD blesses,' v. 22; 'the righteous', v. 29). The idea of this statement forms the background for Jesus' words in the Sermon on the Mount: 'Blessed are the meek, for they will inherit the earth' (Matt. 5:5).

---

[6] 'In the land' is not in the MT but it is clearly implied in the context (see vv. 22 and 29). Also, as this section of the psalm reverts to the themes of the early verses, it is certainly in parallel with verse 3, 'Trust in the LORD and do good; dwell in the land …'

[7] The alternative to this is textual change. Craigie, *Psalms 1-50*, p. 296 says that the initial word needed for a strophe beginning with *ayin* 'was presumably dropped accidentally'. However, taking this approach requires further emendation to give a translation such as 'the wicked are destroyed for ever' that has some support from the LXX.

The mouth of the righteous man utters wisdom, and his tongue speaks what is just. The law of his God is in his heart; his feet do not slip (*vv. 30-31*). Again, there is a parallel with a saying in the Book of Proverbs (see Prov. 10:31). The righteous person ponders over God's wisdom and speaks about it. The word 'utters' is translated as meditate in Psalm 1:2, but it can also mean 'speak' (see on Ps. 35:28). Here meditation and speech are linked together, for the righteous man has God's law in his heart, and thus he speaks of what is wise and just. His steps do not slip because he has God's instruction as his guide.

The wicked lie in wait for the righteous, seeking their very lives; but the Lord will not leave them in their power or let them be condemned when brought to trial (*vv. 32-33*).[8] These two verses have the ring of the courthouse about them. Hence it may well be that 'seeking their very lives' (Hebrew lit. 'seeking to kill him') refers to action in a court to secure a verdict of guilty, one which amounted to 'legal' murder. The 'lying in wait' would then be giving false evidence against the righteous. But while men may condemn, God will acquit. The righteous judgment of God is here contrasted (as in 1 Cor. 4:3) with human judgment. Tertullian (AD *c.* 160-240), one of the great theologians of the early church, said: 'If we are condemned by the world, we will be acquitted by God.' The righteous will not be forsaken at this time of trial, but rather find vindication from the Lord.

5. Salvation from the Lord (*vv. 34-40*)

Wait for the Lord and keep his way. He will exalt you to inherit the land; when the wicked are cut off, you will see it (*v. 34*). The final verses of the psalm sum up its message, repeating ideas already seen in verses 7, 9, and 11. The psalmist issues a call for patient and expectant waiting for the Lord, which is coupled with following his paths.

[8] The NIV turns the singular forms of the MT into plurals in these verses. While the meaning is preserved, yet it is preferable to retain the singular: 'The mouth of the righteous speaks wisdom, and his tongue talks of justice. The law of his God is in his heart; none of his steps shall slide' (NKJV).

'The way of the LORD' is an expression that goes back to God's words concerning Abraham and his descendants (Gen. 18:19). David, at the end of his life, instructed his son Solomon to 'observe what the LORD your God requires: Walk in his ways, and keep his decrees and commands' (1 Kings 2:3). To 'exalt' in this context is practically equivalent to deliver (cf. Ps. 27:6). Once more the land of Canaan comes into focus here. When the wicked come to destruction, the righteous are going to be observers (for the same idea, see Pss. 52:6 and 91:8).

I have seen a wicked and ruthless man flourishing like a green tree in its native soil, but he soon passed away and was no more; though I looked for him, he could not be found (*vv. 35-36*). In the psalmist's own experience he had seen wicked and tyrannical men. They seemed to be like indigenous trees, well rooted and luxuriant. But when he next looked they were gone, and no searching could locate them. This is using the same illustration as in Psalm 1, but in the opposite way.

Consider the blameless, observe the upright; there is a future for the man of peace. But all sinners will be destroyed; the future of the wicked will be cut off (*vv. 37-38*). Another imperative follows. 'Consider' is the Hebrew verb 'to keep' or 'guard'. It is used here in the sense of 'regard', or 'pay attention to'. The object of this attention is the righteous man, called here 'the blameless' (see on Pss. 15:2 and 18:23) and 'the upright'. His final end (NIV 'future') is one of well-being and prosperity. His character and his destiny stand in marked contrast to the man of violence (v. 35). All transgressors will be destroyed, for at the end they will be cut off by the LORD.

The psalm ends with a summary of its entire message. **The salvation of the righteous comes from the LORD; he is their stronghold in time of trouble. The LORD helps them and delivers them; he delivers them from the wicked and saves them, because they take refuge in him** (*vv. 39-40*). The source of salvation is the LORD, who is a refuge in time of trouble. He sustains and delivers. The verb 'deliver' used (Hebrew *pâlat*) is almost exclusively a Psalter word. It is often used as here in a word of testimony regarding God's deliverances, and also it frequently has as its parallel the verb 'help'. The final words are important because they explain the reason for God's deliverances. The righteous have taken refuge with him, and hence he saves them.

Psalm 38

A psalm of David. A petition.

The title of this psalm does not provide much help in trying to put it into a historical setting. The description, 'a petition', is literally 'to bring to remembrance'. Some suggest a link with the memorial offering of Leviticus 2:2 and 24:7. The Aramaic Targum ties the psalm in with the daily memorial offering (Lev. 6:8-13), while the Greek Septuagint associates it with the Sabbath memorial offering (Lev. 24:5-9). It is better to think of the title as a later description of a psalm used by sufferers to bring their plight to God's remembrance. The situation the psalmist faced is twofold. On the one hand, he is suffering inwardly, but on the other hand he also has numerous enemies who are venting their hatred against him. These enemies are not mentioned in the early part, but from verse 12 onwards they dominate the text. Many affinities exist with Psalm 6, except that no recorded answer to the appeal for help occurs here.

The descriptions in the psalm are noteworthy because of the clusters of terms that are employed. God's attitude is described by words like 'anger', 'wrath', 'arrows', 'hand', and 'indignation'. The psalmist feels the pain in his 'flesh', 'bones', 'head', 'wounds', 'loins', 'heart', and 'eyes'. He describes his condition as being 'weighed down', 'bowed down', 'mourning', 'crushed' and 'sighing'.

Another feature of this psalm is that while it is not an acrostic, yet it is a poem of twenty-two lines, thus matching the number of letters in the Hebrew alphabet. The restriction of following the alphabetic sequence is gone, yet the use of twenty-two lines seems to be characteristic of laments.[1]

1. A Cry for Help (*v. 1*)

O LORD, do not rebuke me in your anger or discipline me in your wrath (*v. 1*). The opening of the psalm is almost identical to Psalm 6:1, though different words are used for 'anger', *kétsef* replacing *ʾaf*. Comparison of the contexts in which these two words are used suggests that little difference in meaning exists between them. The psalmist knows that God will punish sin, but he asks God not to display his anger as he brings his case before him. He approaches the one who is 'the compassionate and gracious God, slow to anger, abounding in love and faithfulness' (Exod. 34:6). Confidence in the LORD's compassion underlies appeals in many of the Psalms (in addition to Psalms 6 and 38, see also Psalms 88 and 102).

2. A Description of Illness (*vv. 2-10*)

It is hard to assess the nature of the illness described here. There are features that suggest a dermatological condition (see vv. 5 and 7). It may have been a form of leprosy, which would also help to explain why the psalmist was so alienated from his friends and acquaintances (v. 11). **For your arrows have pierced me, and your hand has come down upon me** (*v.* 2). The arrows signify divine judgment, while the hand is often a symbol of power in the Old Testament. This verse is an acknowledgment of the sovereign way in which God had dealt with him, penetrating deeply into his heart and life (the same Hebrew verb is represented by 'pierced' and 'has come down'; cf. the use of this verb in Prov. 17:10: 'A rebuke impresses [penetrates deeply] a man of discernment more than a hundred lashes a fool').

Because of your wrath there is no health in my body; my bones have no soundness because of my sin. My guilt has overwhelmed me like a burden too heavy to bear (*vv. 3-4*). There is not always a connection between sin and sickness,

[1] Wilfred G. E. Watson, *Classical Hebrew Poetry: A Guide to the Techniques* (Sheffield: JSOT Press, 1984), p. 199.

but here the psalmist confesses his sin, as he does again later in the psalm (v. 18). Throughout his whole body he is experiencing the consequences of God's judgment upon him. His health is gone (lit. 'no *shalom* in my bones').[2] A comparison with Isaiah 1:6 is in order, as both the expressions 'no health in my body'//'no soundness in it' and the general tenor of the passages are so similar. He feels that he is being engulfed by his sin and its consequences. The word 'burden' is a fitting term to use of sin and guilt, and its use recalls Cain's words: 'My punishment is more than I can bear' (Gen. 4:13).

My wounds fester and are loathsome because of my sinful folly. I am bowed down and brought very low; all day long I go about mourning (*vv. 5-6*). The terms used here to describe the sickness denote the smell and the discharge of wounds, though they could be used as a figurative description of extreme suffering. 'Sinful folly' is a good translation of a Hebrew word that appears most commonly (twenty-two out of twenty-four appearances) in the Book of Proverbs (cf. especially Prov. 24:9). Verse 6 picks up the idea of sin being a burden (v. 4), as the psalmist suggests he is bent over because of his sin. He goes about in mourning constantly. In later Judaism it was customary for someone coming for trial to appear to be mourning. If this was also an earlier custom, it would suggest that the psalmist was recognising his own guilt and that he stood accused before the LORD.

My back is filled with searing pain; there is no health in my body. I am feeble and utterly crushed; I groan in anguish of heart (*vv. 7-8*). His back is ulcerated and fevered, and he repeats his mournful cry of verse 3: 'There is no health in my body.' This was the way in which Isaiah later spoke of the condition of the nation (Isa. 1:6: 'from the sole of your foot to top of your head *there is no soundness* ...'). Physically and psychologically the psalmist is enfeebled

[2] For a good translation that brings out the use of the Hebrew word *shâlôm*, see Calvin Seerveld, *Voicing God's Psalms* (Grand Rapids: Eerdmans, 2005), p. 54: 'There's no shalom in my bones, because of my sins. Yes, my misdeeds have piled up over my head – they weigh down on me like a too heavy weight'.

to an intense degree. The two terms 'feeble' and 'utterly crushed' are practically synonymous, this point being underscored by the verbal construction.[3] He describes his anguished cries by using the verb (Hebrew *shâʿag*) that is normally used of the roaring of a lion. The same verb is used of the LORD roaring (Amos 1:2; Jer. 25:30; Joel 3:16). But here it is the tortured psalmist who cries out in his grief and pain.

All my longings lie open before you, O Lord; my sighing is not hidden from you. My heart pounds, my strength fails me; even the light has gone from my eyes *(vv. 9-10)*. In his sickness and distress the psalmist knew that his whole life was open before the Lord. Nothing could be hidden from him, even all his 'sighings' (*kol-taʾavâtî*). This is the real meaning of the word here, rather than 'longings'. When normal speech is impossible, sometimes only sighings can express emotional and physical anguish. God, who heard the groaning of his people in Egypt (Exod. 2:24), would understand his condition. His heart beats frantically,[4] and all his strength vanishes. The reference to the light going from the eyes is probably to the fact that his vitality had disappeared (cf. the note regarding Moses in Deut. 34:7: 'his eyes were not weak', for the opposite use of the idiom). The last clause in verse 10 has an awkwardness concealed by the NIV translation. Literally it is: 'And the light of my eyes *they* are not with me'. The plural pronoun 'they' should not be made to refer to the singular 'light'. Rather, it probably is intended as a reference to the 'eyes', emphasising their value for the body: 'and the light of my eyes – even them – I lack it'.

---

[3] The two verbs are connected by simple *vav*, not *vav* consecutive. When this occurs 'it repeats on the same time-scale or, it may be, slightly extends the reference of a previous verb, being thus more or less synonymous with it'. *DIHG~S*, p. 103. Cf. also the discussion in *IBHS*, pp. 497-98.

[4] The form of the verb here, *sᵉcharchar*, is a *hapax legomenon*. It appears to be a Peʿalʿal form derived from the root *s-ch-r*. The repetition of the last two consonants of the root is 'used of movements repeated in quick succession' and so yielding a translation like 'palpitate'. See *GKC* §55 d, and D. W. Thomas, '*libbî sᵉcharchar* in Ps. 38', *JTS* XL (1939), pp. 390-91.

3. Forsaken by Friends (*vv. 11-20*)

The following verses go on to describe the sense of desolation that David was experiencing. First of all, his friends left him, and then his enemies derided him. **My friends and companions avoid me because of my wounds; my neighbours stay far away. Those who seek my life set their traps, those who would harm me talk of my ruin; all day long they plot deception** (*vv. 11-12*). His friends (lit. 'those loving me') want to avoid contact with him. The affliction that he is undergoing was too much for them, and so they distance themselves from him. The word 'wounds' is literally 'affliction, smiting' (*néga*ʿ), a word that is used for leprosy in the Old Testament (Lev. 13:2; Deut. 24:8), but also for other sicknesses. It is probably not just the repulsive nature of his illness that caused their alienation, but a realisation that it came from God. The contrast between those near to him, his neighbours, and the fact that they stand far away, is very poignant. From a distance they plot how they can ensnare him, and in conversation they speak about his ruin. The Hebrew poetry is enhanced by the fact that the first four words of the verse all contain the letter *shin*, so that the resulting assonance is striking to the ear.[5] All day long they are ready to plan things that will cause him even greater harm, and do so in deceitful ways.

I am like a deaf man, who cannot hear, like a mute, who cannot open his mouth; I have become like a man who does not hear, whose mouth can offer no reply (*vv. 13-14*). The psalmist rests his case with God, and he makes no attempt to justify himself to his accusers. He pretends he is both deaf and dumb, and he says it in emphatic fashion by repeating the main ideas in verse 14. Verbal forms of the verb 'to hear' (*shâma*ʿ) occur in both verses, as does the word 'his mouth'. He does not offer a response to the accusations of his friends and neighbours. The NIV translation 'reply' is a little too weak, as the

[5] Transliteration shows the assonance, with the use of the letter *qof* in the two opening words adding to the effect: *vay^{e}naq^{e}shû m^{e}vaq^{e}shê nafshî v^{e}dor^{e}shê râʿâtî dibb^{e}rû havvôt*.

Hebrew word used (*tôkachat*) is often employed to designate an argument that is presented in court. The psalmist's trust is in God and he does not need to fill his mouth with arguments.

In the midst of the lament the psalmist shows where his hope really lies. **I wait for you, O LORD; you will answer, O Lord my God** (*v. 15*). He directs his prayer to the LORD, confident that God will respond. By the end of the psalm there is still no recorded answer, but it is part of the nature of true faith to continue in expectant waiting.[6]

For I said, 'Do not let them gloat or exalt themselves over me when my foot slips' (*v. 16*). The Hebrew text of this verse has simply: 'For I said, "Lest they rejoice over me ..."' Something seems to be understood, such as, 'I will take heed of my ways ...' This was probably a prayer which had been prayed earlier, asking for healing lest his condition give his enemies occasion to rejoice. Even when he stumbled they took the opportunity to exalt themselves, priding themselves that they were not in the same position. After so many metaphorical expressions earlier, the psalmist now prays in very concrete terms. The triumph of the enemies would have meant his call for help had failed.

For I am about to fall, and my pain is ever with me. I confess my iniquity; I am troubled by my sin (*vv. 17-18*). It is hard to know to what 'falling' refers. It could be that in his heart he would come to a wrong conclusion about his present condition, and fail to see it in the light of God's word. He seems to even doubt the promise that God will not let the righteous fall (Pss. 15:5; 37:24; 112:6). Mental and physical distress was his constant companion. At the outset of the psalm he had acknowledged his sin (v. 3), and now he does so again. He was disturbed by it, and willingly makes known his condition before God.

Many are those who are my vigorous enemies; those who hate me without reason are numerous. Those who repay my good with evil slander me when I pursue what is good (*vv. 19-20*). The NIV is rather paraphrastic in its rendering of

---

[6] For a discussion on the various Hebrew verbs used regarding 'waiting on the Lord', see J. G. S. S. Thomson, 'Wait on the Lord', pp. 196-98.

the first part of verse 19. A literal translation of the MT is: 'And my enemies [are] alive: they are vast [or possibly, 'powerful')'.[7] While he seems near death, the psalmist's enemies are very much alive, and they have the numbers and power to enforce their will. Instead of 'my enemies [are] alive', one manuscript from Qumran reads 'my enemies without cause' (Hebrew *chinnâm* in place of *cháyyim*), which is an emendation frequently suggested (cf. Ps. 35:19). However, this manuscript may well have made a deliberate change, and it is preferable to stay with the MT. Without any justification the enemies repaid good with evil, and their hatred was inspired only by their own sinfulness.

4. An Appeal for Help (*vv. 21-22*)

The psalm ends with a prayer for speedy help. **O LORD, do not forsake me; be not far from me, O my God. Come quickly to help me, O Lord my Saviour** (*vv. 21-22*). At the centre of his life there is still true faith. No more mention is made of his sickness or of his enemies. He fears abandonment by God, and asks for urgent help to be granted. The final verse is the equivalent of saying, 'Come and save me quickly.' The ideas in both verses are very similar to those in Psalm 22:1, 11, 19. The two concluding words in Hebrew are 'Lord, my salvation', using the noun along with 'Lord' in phrases that are practically the equivalent of titles (cf. Ps. 51:14).

[7] The verb occurring here (*'âtsam*) seems to vary in meaning between the ideas of being numerous and being mighty. See the discussion in *NIDOTTE*, 3, pp. 487-99.

Psalm 39

For the director of music. For Jeduthun. A psalm of David.

There are aspects of this psalm that resemble some of those in the wisdom psalms (see the Introduction). This is especially so in relation to the teaching regarding the transitory nature of human life (vv. 4-6). It is not sickness that brings forth David's plea, but the knowledge that old age and death are approaching. This is a lament from an individual that does not seem to have been directly connected with any formal worship situation. The psalm moves through two parallel phases, which can be set out as follows:

1. Silence before the LORD (vv. *1-3*)
    2. Prayer to the LORD (vv. *4-6*)
        3. Appeal for Help (vv. *7-8*)
4. Silence before the LORD (v. *9*)
    5. Prayer to the LORD (vv. *10-11*)
        6. Appeal for Help (vv. *12-13*)

The name 'Jeduthun' in the title also occurs in the titles of Psalms 62 and 77. He was one of David's chief musicians (1 Chron. 9:16; 16:38, 41-42). It is unclear whether the use of the name is a reference to the musical director ('For the musical director, Jeduthun') or to a tune by this name.

1. Silence before the LORD (*vv. 1-3*)
The psalm opens with the psalmist telling his readers what his thoughts had been. **I said, 'I will watch my ways and keep my tongue from sin; I will put a muzzle on my mouth as long as the wicked are in my presence'** (*v. 1*).

He had wanted to speak, but because of the presence of the wicked he determined he would not. Perhaps he wanted to speak about the prosperity of the wicked or to ask questions about their relative ease in life. Instead, he muzzled himself and prevented himself speaking hasty or angry words that would have been sinful.[1] The NIV rendering 'I will put' follows a suggested emendation to avoid having the same Hebrew verbal form (*'eshm^erâh*) used in successive verses. While the suggested emendation (*'âsîmâh*) may be supported by the LXX (which renders the Hebrew word by *ethemên*), that does not justify the change.

But when I was silent and still, not even saying anything good, my anguish increased. My heart grew hot within me, and as I meditated, the fire burned; then I spoke with my tongue (*vv.* 2-3). His silence created other problems for him, for as he guarded his mouth his inner thoughts overwhelmed him. His anger is described by the terms 'grew hot' and 'burned'. From what follows in the next section it may be that the psalmist's concerns related to growing old and ultimately dying. He was like Jeremiah with a fire in his heart, which could not be contained (Jer. 20:9). Finally, he had to break his silence and speak, and the words 'then I spoke with my tongue' bring a dramatic end to the introductory verses.

2. Prayer to the LORD (*vv.* 4-6)

This section starts with a prayer, includes a description of the fleeting nature of life, and then has three assertions, which all start in Hebrew with the word 'surely' (Hebrew *'ak*). **Show me, O LORD, my life's end and the number of my days; let me know how fleeting is my life** (*v.* 4). The word 'end' is never used of geographical limits but always of either God's judgments,[2] or, as here, of the end of life. The psalmist wants divine instruction regarding the nature of human life. It is only temporary, and short-lived, and he prays that he may understand this. This section is very similar in idea to

---

[1] This is the only time that the word 'muzzle' (*machsôm*) appears in the OT, though the verb occurs in Deuteronomy 25:4 and Ezekiel 39:11.

[2] Cf. Amos 8:2 where there is word play between 'fruit basket' (*káyits*) and 'the end' (*qêts*).

Psalm 90:1-12, where the counting of days is not just numerical but rather an understanding of human life and its frailty.

You have made my days a mere handbreadth; the span of my years is as nothing before you. Each man's life is but a breath. Selah (*v. 5*). The MT places emphasis on this statement by the use of an introductory particle, 'Behold' (*hinnêh*). God's understanding of our lifetime is quite different from our own, for our lifespan is insignificant before him, a mere handbreadth.[3] The word for 'span' occurs in a similar passage in Psalm 89:47. The first of the three assertions introduced by the Hebrew 'surely' comes at the end of the verse: 'surely, each man's life ...'

Man is a mere phantom as he goes to and fro: He bustles about, but only in vain; he heaps up wealth, not knowing who will get it (*v. 6*). The second and third assertions starting with 'surely' come in this verse: 'Surely, like a shadow as man goes to and fro ... Surely, in vain he bustles about.' It is surprising that the word for 'mere phantom' is also the word for 'image' in Genesis 1:26, 27 (*tsélem*). But man is not God; he is only created in his image, and the image-bearer, because of sin, has a limited lifespan before death comes. All his activity is characterised as vanity, nothingness, and even his wealth will be enjoyed by others. The New Testament teaches that we should be content with God's provision, 'for we brought nothing into the world, and we can take nothing out of it' (1 Tim. 6:7).

3. Appeal for Help (*vv. 7-8*)

'But now, Lord, what do I look for? My hope is in you (*v. 7*). The expression 'But now' (*v*[e]*ʿattâh*) is far stronger in Hebrew than in English, for it marks off a new stage in the psalm.[4] It commences with a rhetorical question, to which the answer is given, 'I look expectantly to you'.[5] Both question and answer

---

[3] The word for 'handbreadth' (*téfach*) only occurs in this sort of context. It is clearly a building or architectural term as shown by its other occurrences in the Old Testament and in the documents from Qumran. Cf. *DCH*, III, p. 373.

[4] Cf. the comment in *NIDOTTE*, 4, p. 1031.

[5] For comment on the Hebrew words for 'waiting on the LORD' or 'looking to him', see f.n. 5 for Psalm 25.

suggest the very opposite of despondency and despair. The only hope for the psalmist was with God.

Save me from all my transgressions; do not make me the scorn of fools (*v. 8*). There is a confession implicit in these words. He prays for the forgiveness of his transgressions, no matter how many they are ('all of my transgressions'), including those already mentioned earlier in the psalm. His sinful thoughts and also wrong ideas concerning the meaning of life were part of his confession. Even a fool could note that he was so taken up with his enemies and the passing matters of human existence. He prays that he will be delivered from their reproaches.

4. Silence before the Lord (*v. 9*)

The second phase of the psalm begins here, with the idea of silence in verses 1-3 being taken up again. **I was silent; I would not open my mouth, for you are the one who has done this** (*v. 9*). He repeats from verse 2 the opening reference to his silence. However, there is a change here. Previously he had stopped himself from speaking, but now that he has seen what God has done, with his new insight he is content to stay silent. This is an acknowledgment that God's providence extends to all that happens in his life.

5. Prayer to the Lord (*vv. 10-11*)

Remove your scourge from me; I am overcome by the blow of your hand (*v. 10*). He is conscious of the Lord's rebuke, using the word 'scourge' to describe it (see the same word in Ps. 38:11, and accompanying comment). It is a military figure, and this is continued in the following phrase for the word 'blow' (*tigrâh;* only used here in the Old Testament) comes from a root that is associated with warfare. The distressing situation into which he has come is in fact the blow he has received.

You rebuke and discipline men for their sin; you consume their wealth like a moth – each man is but a breath. Selah (*v. 11*). The scourge from God is a form of rebuke to the psalmist. The biblical pattern is that 'the LORD disciplines those he loves, as a father the son he delights in' (Prov. 3:12, and cf. the use of these words in Hebrews 12:6). David now knows that human wealth can vanish quickly, just as a moth can eat some clothing. The final words of the verse are a repetition of the idea in verse 5, though what was a personal assertion only in that verse is now made applicable to everyone. It applies to all humanity (*kol-ʾâdâm*), and the statement is made even more impressive by the introductory 'surely' (*ʾak*) that the NIV omits: '*Surely* all mankind is a mere breath!' (ESV).

6. Appeal for Help (*vv. 12-13*)

'Hear my prayer, O LORD, listen to my cry for help; be not deaf to my weeping. For I dwell with you as an alien, a stranger, as all my fathers were (*v. 12*). As the psalm ends, there is another cry to God. David pleads with God to receive his prayer, saying, 'Hear ... listen ... be not deaf.' But he feels that he is a stranger in God's presence, even though he addresses God by using his covenant name, LORD. This is different from the idea that we are to live as strangers and pilgrims in this present world (1 Pet. 2:11). It takes its origin from the fact that the Israelites were themselves aliens in the promised land, for it belonged to the LORD (Lev. 25:23; 1 Chron. 29:15). Just as the strangers living among the Israelites depended upon their kindness, so the Israelites themselves depended upon God's mercy. As often, the two words 'alien' (*gêr*) and 'stranger' (*tôshâv*) are used synonymously.

Look away from me, that I may rejoice again before I depart and am no more' (*v. 13*). Normally psalmists ask for God to look upon them. Here the request is that God will *not* look upon him. In the context it must be a plea that God will avert his judgment from the psalmist. David longs to know the joy of the LORD before death comes.

Psalm 40

For the director of music. Of David. A psalm.

There are unusual features about this psalm. It is most uncommon to have a song of thanksgiving (vv. 1-10) followed by a lengthy complaint (vv. 11-17). The psalm moves from a song of joy concerning the past actions of the LORD to a heartfelt cry from the depths of despair. The *magnificat* becomes a most plaintive *de profundis* ('out of the depths').[1] It is also unusual because part of the psalm (vv. 13-17) is substantially repeated as Psalm 70. There are a few other examples of this in the Psalter (14 = 53; 57:7-11 = 108:1-5; 60:5-12 = 108:6-13).

The earlier experiences of the psalmist form the basis for his prayer for the present. He is pleading past mercies as the ground for this present trust in the LORD as his deliverer. Notwithstanding the use of a part in Psalm 70, which may suggest it was originally a separate composition, yet the repetition of words in the two sections of the psalm point to a unified composition.[2] Thus, the word 'thoughts' (*machsh*ᵉ*votechâ*) in verse 6 is paralleled by the use of the verb from which it is derived (*châshav*) in verse 17, and 'I do not *seal* my lips' (v. 9) and 'Do not *withhold* your mercy' in verse 11 are both translations of the same Hebrew verb (*kâlâ'*). It may be that David added the second part when his circumstances changed for the worse. It should also be pointed out that

[1] This description of Psalm 40 has been attributed to Franz Delitzsch but it does not appear in his commentary on the Psalms.

[2] This is the view of A. Cohen, *The Psalms: Hebrew Text and English Translation with an Introduction and Commentary* (London: Soncino Press, 1969), p. 123.

strong links between this psalm and Psalm 35 are evident (cf. 35:4 with 40:14).

1. A Testimony to Grace (*vv. 1-10*)

I waited patiently for the LORD; he turned to me and heard my cry (*v. 1*). This is a testimony by the psalmist. He is relating what happened to him in the past when he cried to the LORD. The rendering 'waited patiently' is probably too passive a translation of the opening words. The verb means to wait expectantly or to hope in the LORD (see on Psalm 37:8-9), and the expression here is an emphatic one.[3] Perhaps a rendering such as, 'I indeed waited expectantly for the LORD' captures something of the meaning. The cry was heard and the LORD answered.[4]

He lifted me out of the slimy pit, out of the mud and mire; he set my feet on a rock and gave me a firm place to stand (*v. 2*). He describes his experience as if it was like being in a pit, or in a cistern such as the one Jeremiah was put into, which had no water, only mud (Jer. 38:6). From his place of distress, with its desolation and danger, God had delivered him. He was rescued and set on a firm foundation.

He put a new song in my mouth, a hymn of praise to our God. Many will see and fear and put their trust in the LORD (*v. 3*). With distress gone, there was a new song in his mouth. In later psalms such as Psalms 96 and 98, the phrase 'a new song' is linked with final, end-time events, as it is in Revelation 5:9 and 14:3. Here it denotes the salvation song that God gave him, as part of the sequence of actions by him ('he turned … he heard … he lifted … he set … he put'). His experiences will be a testimony to many others, who also will come and find refuge with this Saviour.[5] The use of '*our* God' draws attention to the fact that the psalmist was not alone in these experiences (cf. the references to 'the great congregation' in vv. 9-10).

---

[3] The verb preceded by the inf. absol.: *qavvoh qivvîtî*.

[4] For the words such as 'wait for', etc., see f.n. 5 on Psalm 25.

[5] Literature relating to the verb 'trust' (*bâtach*) and other similar verbs is cited in f.n. 5 on Psalm 9.

Blessed is the man who makes the LORD his trust, who does not look to the proud, to those who turn aside to false gods (*v. 4*). The contrast is now drawn between those who set (*sîm*) their trust on the LORD, and those who put their trust in idols. They are commended (for 'blessed', see on Psalm 1:1), for they have not followed the arrogant ones who deviate from the true God to trust in idols. This is the only occurrence of the word translated 'proud' (*râhâv*), but the root appears to denote 'acting aggressively'. The final phrase in the MT adds to the difficulty of translation as it says 'those who turn aside to falsehood'. This may mean 'fraudulent images'[6] (cf. NIV 'false gods'), and this gives some support to the suggestion that the word 'proud' should be understood, not as a reference to people, but to 'pagan idols'.[7]

Many, O LORD my God, are the wonders you have done. The things you planned for us no one can recount to you; were I to speak and tell of them, they would be too many to declare (*v. 5*). What had happened to the psalmist was another 'wonder' done by the LORD. A 'wonder' was a supernatural act of deliverance that God alone could perform (Ps. 72:18: 'who alone does marvellous deeds'). Just as the deliverance of Israel from Egypt was a 'wonder', so also was the recent deliverance of the psalmist. The NIV translation of the middle clause is dubious. The Hebrew verb (*ʿârak*) can often mean 'to set in order' (cf. Ps. 23:5), but it can also be used in the sense of 'compare'. It is best to follow two standard Hebrew dictionaries and accept that the translation involves an exclamation: 'Many, O LORD my God, are the wonders you have done, the things you planned for us. There is none to be compared to you!'[8] No one could recount all the divine acts of salvation, for they were so numerous.[9]

---

[6] As accepted by M. Dahood, *Psalms I:1-50*, p. 243.

[7] Cf. Dahood's translation, ibid., 'who turns not to pagan idols, or to fraudulent images'.

[8] See *BDB*, p. 789; *HALOT*, 2, p. 885.

[9] It is hard to be sure that the final verb (*sâfar*, Pi.) means recount, as the Pi. form can at times have the same meaning as the Qal, namely, 'to count', rather than 'recount', 'declare'.

The section that follows (vv. 6-10) has often been taken as messianic because of its use in Hebrews 10:5-7. However, in the setting here in Psalm 40 the psalm is not primarily messianic, for among other things David confesses his own sinfulness (v. 12). It is taken over and applied to Jesus, who as the greater David fulfils the spirit of these words. The quotation is made from the Greek Septuagint, whose variations from the Hebrew text made its use easier in Hebrews 10. **Sacrifice and offering you did not desire, but my ears you have pierced; burnt offerings and sin offerings you did not require** (*v. 6*). These words should not be interpreted as if they were denying the validity of the Old Testament sacrificial system. Rather they are to be understood, as in 1 Samuel 15:22, as stressing that obedience was more essential than sacrifice. Such practices were ineffective when not accompanied by a humble and obedient spirit. Four of the common sacrifices are designated. The first two are more general terms, while the last two are the terms for the offering completely consumed on the altar and the expiatory offering. The reference to the piercing of his ears is probably to his readiness to hear the word of the LORD and obey it, as the following verse makes plain. The expression itself is difficult, as a literal rendering is: 'You have dug two ears for me'.[10] The Hebrew verb in question (*kârâh*) normally means 'to excavate' or 'dig', but here it seems to be used to speak of the opening of ears so that they are ready to hear.[11]

Then I said, 'Here I am, I have come – it is written about me in the scroll (*v. 7*). The psalmist showed great readiness to respond in personal commitment to what God required. Like Isaiah (Isa. 6:8) David puts himself totally at the disposal of God. If David is speaking as king he may well be referring to what was written about the king in the law of Deuteronomy

---

[10] This is the translation given by P. C. Craigie, *Psalms 1-50*, p. 312.

[11] Craigie is right in suggesting that we are dealing with 'an ancient idiomatic usage of which the precise sense is no longer clear' (Ibid., p. 313). The LXX is followed in Hebrew 10:5: 'you have prepared (*katêrtisô*) a body for me.'

(Deut. 17:14-20). Otherwise, the scroll would refer to all the written demands of God upon him.[12]

I desire to do your will, O my God; your law is within my heart' (*v. 8*). He longs to do God's will, for within his heart he has God's instruction. 'Heart' is the English idiomatic term, whereas Hebrew uses *mê̂ʿeh* ('bowels', 'intestines') as a metaphorical expression to denote human emotions. The Hebrew figure of speech carries over in the New Testament (cf. Phil. 2:1; Col. 3:12). The idea of internal possession of the law is one that takes a significant place in the later Old Testament teaching regarding the new covenant (Jer. 31:33-34; Ezek. 36:26-27).

I proclaim righteousness in the great assembly; I do not seal my lips, as you know, O LORD (*v. 9*). To the assembled worshipping community David proclaims (or the Hebrew could also be translated 'proclaimed', cf. v. 3) what God had done. The verb to 'proclaim' (*bâsar,* Pi.) is often associated with the idea of joyful proclamation (see Ps. 96:2 and Isa. 52:7 and 61:1). Here 'righteousness' (*tsédek*) is probably not so much a characteristic of God but a term to describe his saving activity. It is virtually a synonym for 'salvation'. David puts the idea both positively and negatively: he proclaims the fact, and does not restrain his lips from taking part in such a proclamation.

I do not hide your righteousness in my heart; I speak of your faithfulness and salvation. I do not conceal your love and your truth from the great assembly (*v. 10*). This continues the same ideas as in the previous verse. What is important is the accumulation of covenant terminology, with a cluster of words relating to God's character and works. 'Righteousness' is the key word, and 'faithfulness', 'salvation', 'love', and 'truth' are all ways of giving further explanation to it. Emphasis is placed on his public proclamation by the repetition of the phrase 'the great assembly', with the adjective 'great' (*râv*)

---

[12] The expression used for the written document is 'a scroll of writing' (*mᵉgillat sêfer*). It is an indication that the papyrus or leather document was in scroll form. For the technical Old Testament expressions for writing and written documents, see A. R. Millard, 'Writing', *NIDOTTE,* 4, pp. 1286-95.

emphasising the quantitative aspect of the gathering of the worshipping community.

2. A Prayer for Fresh Mercy (*vv. 11-17*)
Attention now focuses on the present situation. While there is no express reference to the earlier part of the psalm, yet it forms the foundation for the requests that are made. **Do not withhold your mercy from me, O LORD; may your love and your truth always protect me** (*v. 11*). The repetition of the phrase 'your love and your truth' from the previous verse makes plain the interconnection of the two parts of the psalm. God is the protector of his people, and the appeal is made to him to show his love and truth in this way. The appeal is even more direct than our English versions suggest, as the Hebrew text begins, 'You, O LORD, you do not ...' It is possible to render the verse as a statement, expressing confidence in God's mercy, or (like RSV and NIV) as a prayer.

For troubles without number surround me; my sins have overtaken me, and I cannot see. They are more than the hairs of my head, and my heart fails within me (*v. 12*). The abundance of difficulties is overwhelming for the psalmist, and he feels as if his courage has forsaken him. The verb 'troubled' is used in 2 Samuel 22:5 and Jonah 2:5 of floodwaters. His sight is also affected and his vision has become dim because of the immensity of his troubles (cf. Ps. 69:3-4: 'my eyes fail', 'those who hate me without reason outnumber the hairs of my head'). A repetition of a Hebrew verb (*'âtsam*) that has already occurred in verse 6 is disguised by translation into English (v. 6, 'too many'; v. 12, 'more than'). This is a further indication of the unified nature of this psalm with vocabulary linking both parts together.

The section from here to the end of the psalm reappears in the Psalter as Psalm 70, with slight verbal alteration. **Be pleased, O LORD, to save me; O LORD, come quickly to help me** (*v. 13*). David longs for a speedy resolution for his problem by the LORD, but that resolution has to be in accord with his will. 'Be pleased' (*retsêh*) is an echo of the word 'will' (*râtsôn*) in verse 8, and it is used in other prayers as well as this one (see Deut. 33:11, 24).

May all who seek to take my life be put to shame and confusion; may all who desire my ruin be turned back in disgrace (*v. 14*). This verse is very close in wording and meaning to Psalm 35:4 (see the comment). It makes plain that it was not just his sins which troubled him, but the activities of his enemies. His very life was in danger from them.

May those who say to me, 'Aha! Aha!' be appalled at their own shame (*v. 15*). The cry of 'Aha!' is one of human joy (Isa. 44:16), but here it is malicious joy said over the misery of another. This usage, together, with the fact that it is always preceded by the verb 'to say', is the regular one for this expression in the Old Testament.[13] The psalmist wants these enemies to be made desolate. As with other curses in the Psalter, the enemies are not just personal enemies, for David is speaking here as king. It may well be that the enemies were aggressive, neighbouring nations who were ready to attack Israel.

But may all who seek you rejoice and be glad in you; may those who love your salvation always say, 'The LORD be exalted!' (*v. 16*). There is much similarity between this verse and Psalm 35:27. In contrast to the shouts of the enemies, he wants the true worshippers of the LORD ('seek' is often used in this sense) to proclaim his greatness. There is also a contrast between those seeking his life (v. 14) and those seeking the LORD. Nothing can add to God's greatness, but praise is a way of drawing attention to it. Praise for God's salvation is to be a perpetual characteristic of his people.

Yet I am poor and needy; may the Lord think of me. You are my help and my deliverer; O my God, do not delay (*v. 17*). The call to God to 'not delay' balances the call to 'come quickly' in verse 13, and there is still the same reliance upon God as his 'help'. The psalmist pleads for urgent assistance, just as Daniel did using the same words (Dan. 9:19). David

---

[13] This expression (*he'âh*) is sometimes followed by a phrase (see Ps. 35:25), or it may be used as here without anything following. It is part of a group of particles in Hebrew which, like in English, 'use sounds not ordinarily part of language's sound system' (*IBHS*, p. 683).

knows his own weakness and inability,[14] and expresses the desire that God would think and plan for his salvation. To the God to whom he had looked expectantly in the past, he now looks again for help and rescue.

[14] 'Poor and needy' is a standard parallel expression occurring in the Psalms and elsewhere to denote the oppressed righteous believers. Cf. the use of the expression in Job 24:14; Amos 8:4; and Psalms 9:19; 12:5; 70:5; and 74:21.

Psalm 41

For the director of music. A psalm of David.

There are many similarities between this psalm and the ones immediately preceding (Pss. 38-40). In them there is repeated mention of human frailty and sickness, though in each there is confident appeal to God for his mercy and deliverance. A specific link occurs with the preceding psalm in that the opening word here, 'blessed' (Hebrew *'ash^{e}rê*), has already been used in verse 6 of Psalm 40. This psalm begins with a general assertion concerning God's character in relation to the righteous. Then follows a prayer for help, with a repeated cry for mercy (vv. 4 and 10). The psalm ends with a doxology, which also concludes the first book of the Psalter.

1. Confidence in the Lord (*vv. 1-3*)

Blessed is he who has regard for the weak; the Lord delivers him in times of trouble (*v. 1*). The opening word recalls the use of the same word (*'ash^{e}rê*) in the first verse of Psalm 1 (see comment). It is a word used only of humans, whereas the expression 'praise to ...' (*bârûk*) that occurs in verse 13 is only applied to God. The person who looks with favour on the needs of the poor will himself be delivered by the Lord. The verb 'to have regard' (*sâkal,* Hi.) often means to have insight that results in prudent action. The idea of this verse finds its fullest expression in the Sermon on the Mount: 'Blessed are the merciful for they will be shown mercy' (Matt. 5:7).

The Lord will protect him and preserve his life; he will bless him in the land and not surrender him to the desire of his foes (*v. 2*). The theme of the Lord as the keeper of Israel finds fuller development in Psalm 121:7-8. Part of the protection referred to here was preservation in time of serious illness. The phrase 'preserve his life' can also be rendered 'keep him alive'. There are difficulties with the following words. The Hebrew text has: 'he will be blessed in the land and do not *you* give him ...' The NIV follows the Septuagint, the Vulgate, and the Syriac in translating it as active ('he will bless'), but the passive form still yields good sense: 'he will be blessed in the land.' The change to a second person singular form in the final clause is understandable if it is part of the prayer addressed to God: 'May the LORD protect ... and preserve ... and not surrender him into the life of the enemy'.[1] In the good land he will be kept safe (see Ps. 37:22), and his enemies will not see their desire for him fulfilled.

The LORD will sustain him on his sickbed and restore him from his bed of illness (*v. 3*). During illness, strength will be provided by the LORD, with the promise of a radical change to take place. The NIV translation fails to observe the second person singular verb in the final clause ('*you* restore him') and also omits the word 'all' (*kol*) before 'his bed'. The same switch from third to second person occurs as in the previous verse, and while such rapid changes trouble us in English, many can be found in Hebrew poetry. Again, it is best to take the verb here as part of direct address to God: '*you* restore him.' 'All his bed' does not denote his constant lying down, but rather the full extent of his illness. Restoration is possible for those who cry to the LORD for help so that their illness can be turned around. The idea of preservation in the first three verses comes to its climax here. The LORD can so intervene that the situation is totally changed.

2. A Cry for Mercy (*vv. 4-9*)

I said, 'O LORD, have mercy on me; heal me, for I have sinned against you' (*v. 4*). The initial 'I said' may refer to past prayers, though it could also be translated 'I say'. Later in the psalm it becomes clear that he is still sick (v. 10). He makes his plea for

---

[1] 'The life of the enemy' (Hebrew *nefesh ʾoyᵉvâv*) is an idiomatic expression (cf. the very similar expression used in Psalm 27:12: *nefesh tsâray*, 'the desire of my foes'). It means to be placed in the control of the enemy, and thus the LXX 'in the hands of his enemy' is a good translation.

mercy and for healing. God had promised through Moses that he was the healer (Exod. 15:26), and the psalmist claims that promise. With his request comes open confession of his sin. All sin is committed against God, as David acknowledges even more specifically in connection with his sin with Bathsheba (Ps. 51:4: 'against you, you only, have I sinned').

My enemies say of me in malice, 'When will he die and his name perish?' Whenever one comes to see me, he speaks falsely, while his heart gathers slander; then he goes out and spreads it abroad (*vv. 5-6*). His enemies are just waiting for his death to take place, so that they can rejoice over it. To have one's name perish meant that there would be no descendants (Ps. 109:13). The importance of having one's name maintained is seen in the provision for levirate marriage (Deut. 25:5, 6). Even when his enemies visit him in his sickness (and this was a normal practice, cf. 2 Kings 8:29), their intent is evil, and they do not speak truthfully. They gossip about him to others and spread false rumours.

All my enemies whisper together against me; they imagine the worst for me, saying, 'A vile disease has beset him; he will never get up from the place where he lies' (*vv. 7-8*). The word used here for 'whisper' is always used of evil whispering, such as when David's servants whispered about his son's death (2 Sam. 12:19). Though the earlier part of the psalm makes mention of 'enemies' (vv. 2, 4), on this occasion they are called 'haters', though the two words appear practically interchangeable in contexts such as this. It is best to allow the alternation of these verbs to show in English translation (cf. AV, RSV, NASB, ESV). Those who hate the psalmist hope that his disease will be fatal,[2] and that where he lies will become his deathbed. They seem to be thinking that

---

[2] The NIV's 'a vile disease' represents the Hebrew *d*^{e}*var b*^{e}*liyya*^{c}*al*, 'a thing of destructiveness'. The word *b*^{e}*liyya*^{c}*al* is not a proper noun in the Old Testament (cf. the influence of the Vulgate on the AV's use in passages such as in Deut. 13:13 and Judg. 19:22). Though its derivation is not exactly clear, it seems to be an abstract noun meaning 'destructiveness', and 'the sons of Belial are then those whose characters are destructive, harmful, evil' (J. A. Emerton, 'Sheol and the Sons of Belial', pp. 214-18). For further information, see the literature cited in *DCH*, II, pp. 608-09.

his disease is a fitting judgment from God. Hence their actions show that they are not recipients of the ascription 'blessed' as in verse 1 (for the New Testament teaching concerning helping the needy, see James 1:27).

Even my close friend, whom I trusted, he who shared my bread, has lifted up his heel against me (*v. 9*). In this situation even the closest of friends (lit. 'a man of my peace', i.e. with whom I have the friendliest relationship) turns against him. The very friend who shared his food proves to be a traitor to him. The exact phrase, 'to lift up the heel', does not occur elsewhere, but it seems to mark out an aggressive or traitorous action. This is the meaning that is given to the verse when Jesus quotes it of Judas (John 13:18). What was true of David was fulfilled to an even greater degree in Judas' betrayal of Jesus.

3. A Renewed Request (*vv. 10-12*)

But you, O LORD, have mercy on me; raise me up, that I may repay them (*v. 10*). The prayer of verse 4 is now renewed. What he had prayed in the past is fitting for the present, because it represents the urgent cry of a needy sinner. The enemies were saying that he would never get up (v. 8), but the psalmist knows that God is able to lift him up again. He seeks this, not for selfish vengeance upon them, but in order to see God's honour vindicated (see vv. 2-3).

The link with the preceding verse is not made clear in the NIV translation of verse 11, for it fails to translate the first word, 'in this' (*b^{e}zo't*). When the LORD lifts him up, then he will know to a greater extent his love to him. Accordingly he can make the declaration: **I know that you are pleased with me, for my enemy does not triumph over me. In my integrity you uphold me and set me in your presence forever** (*vv. 11-12*). It also follows that if the psalmist is raised up by the LORD, then the enemies would not be able to shout out in triumph. The word translated 'triumph' is often used in situations of great festive joy (cf. 1 Sam. 4:5). No such occasion will be given here, for he can confidently look for God's support. The final phrase is best taken as referring to life in the promised land (v. 2) as

God's servant. Just like Elijah, he shall stand before the LORD (1 Kings 17:1).

4. Doxology (*v. 13*)

Praise be to the LORD, the God of Israel, from everlasting to everlasting. Amen and Amen (*v. 13*). This is the first of the doxologies with which all five books of the Psalter conclude. It is a fitting ascription of praise to the God of Israel. The ascription of 'praise' or 'blessed' to God cannot add to his person, but it tells that he is worthy of praise, and such praise directs attention again to his greatness. The double 'Amen' sets the seal to this declaration.

Book 2

Psalms 42-43

For the director of music. A maskil of the Sons of Korah.

In many Hebrew manuscripts Psalms 42 and 43 are regarded as one psalm. This fact is supported by the observation that Psalm 43 has no title, which is surprising, for all the psalms in Book 2 of the Psalter (with the exception of Psalm 71) have one. Moreover, a question in 42:9b ('Why must I go about mourning, oppressed by the enemy?') is repeated in 43:2b. Also, the two psalms share a common refrain, 'Why are you downcast, O my soul? Why so disturbed within me? Put your hope in God ...' (Pss. 42:5, 11; 43:5). If the two psalms were composed as a single poem, then for liturgical reasons they were separated into two songs.

The transition from Book 1 to Book 2 of the Psalter is marked by the substitution of the word 'God' (*'ᵉlohîm*) for the name 'LORD' (*yhwh*). It is possible that originally 'LORD' stood in the text, and was deliberately changed to 'God', perhaps because in a certain area of ancient Israel and at a specific time the name 'God' was more in use than 'LORD'. While 'LORD' still occurs, it is vastly outnumbered by the occurrences of 'God'.[1]

The 'Sons of Korah' were Levites who had special responsibilities in the temple (1 Chron. 6:22; 2 Chron. 20:19). Korah was the great-grandson of Levi. The 'sons of Korah' performed various roles, including being gate-keepers (1 Chron. 9:19). This was clearly an ancient task as the Chronicler says that 'their fathers had been responsible for guarding the

---

[1] 'God' (*'ᵉlohîm*) occurs only 15 times in Book 1, but 164 times in Book 2. On the other hand, 'LORD' (*yhwh*) appears 272 times in Book 1, but only 30 times in Book 2.

entrance to the dwelling of the LORD'.[2] While they continued this function, under David they also assumed an important role among the musicians and singers, and continued to do so under later kings such as Jehoshaphat. Seven psalms in this second section of the Psalter are attributed to 'the sons of Korah' (Pss. 42–49), while another four occur in the next section (Pss. 84–85, 87-88).

1. Longing for God (*Psalm 42 verses 1-4*)

As the deer pants for streams of water, so my soul pants for you, O God (*v. 1*). Intense longing fills the heart of the psalmist. For some unstated reason he is not able to go and enjoy communal worship. He likens himself, however, to a deer that longs for water. So, from the barrenness of his isolation, he has a similar longing after God.

My soul thirsts for God, for the living God. When can I go and meet with God? (*v. 2*). He repeats his desire for God, and calls him 'the living God'. This phrase is unusual, and it may be connected with the idea that God was the 'living water' (cf. Jer. 2:13; 17:13). It also is a reminder that although other gods may have been worshipped, they had no life in them (Ps. 115:1-8). The psalmist voices his concern as to when he can go and see God's face (NIV 'meet with God'). 'To see the face of God' is the technical expression that the Old Testament uses of appearing before God at the sanctuary (Exod. 23:17; Ps. 84:7).[3] It is an anthropomorphic expression that denotes close fellowship and communion with him.

My tears have been my food day and night, while men say to me all day long, 'Where is your God?' These things I remember as I pour out my soul: how I used to go with the multitude, leading the procession to the house of God, with shouts of joy and thanksgiving among the festive throng (*vv. 3-4*). His enemies taunt him continually,

---

[2] It is hard to be certain which 'dwelling' is referred to in this verse. It could have been the Israelite camp, or, more specifically, the tabernacle.

[3] The MT has the verb 'to see' vocalised as a passive (Ni. *'ērā'eh*). It is best to follow the active reading (Qal *'er'eh*) that is supported by some Hebrew manuscripts, the LXX, and the Targum.

for it seems as if God has deserted him.[4] Nothing in the context enables the reader to determine whether the enemies are from within the covenantal community or from followers of heathen gods. The doubts he had while absent from the sanctuary were aggravated by these unfeeling comments. In his grief his tears flood down his face and seem to become his food. No answer can be given to the question that is put to him. Instead, his memory recalls the happier times when he led the festive crowd going to the sanctuary.[5] The annual pilgrimages like the Passover, the Feast of Weeks, and the Feast of Tabernacles were meant to be happy occasions as the tribes went up 'to praise the name of the LORD' (Ps. 122:4).

2. The Refrain (*vv. 5-6a*)

For the first time the refrain comes in, and it gives thematic unity to this combined psalm, as well as providing another striking poetic feature. **Why are you downcast, O my soul? Why so disturbed within me? Put your hope in God, for I will yet praise him, my Saviour and my God** (*v. 5*). In the midst of his spiritual barrenness and longing for God, the psalmist encourages himself. Why should he be so troubled in spirit if he has God as his Saviour?[6] The query that points to self-doubt gives way to a speedy exhortation. He calls upon himself to wait for God, and expresses the conviction that he is yet going to praise him. The final part of the verse in the NIV involves a change in verse division, moving 'my God'

---

[4] The NIV's 'while men say' represents the MT 'in saying' (*be'emor*). It is possible that this should be altered to *be'omrâm*, 'in their saying', as this form occurs later in v. 11, and is supported by four Hebrew manuscripts and the LXX. Certainly this is the meaning in the context.

[5] The clause 'leading the procession' is difficult because of two factors. First, the word for 'procession' (*sâk*) is a *hapax legomenon*, which, with different vocalisation (*sok*), could mean 'a tent' or 'a booth'. This is the way the LXX took it, using the common word for 'tent' or 'tabernacle' (*skênê*). Secondly, the word translated 'leading' (*'eddaddêm*) also creates a problem. Various emendations have been proposed ('majestic ones', 'exalted one', 'prostrate myself') but none seem more satisfactory than the traditional translation. For some further detail, see *HALOT*, I, p. 241.

[6] The form of the verb translated 'downcast' (*tishtôchachî*) only appears in Psalms 42-43. It has traditionally been taken as derived from *shâchâh*, but it is possible it is from the root *châvâh*, meaning 'to coil'.

from being the first word in verse 6 to being the final word of verse 5. This has some support from Hebrew manuscripts, the LXX and the Syriac version, and is the preferable way to deal with this section. The NIV, however, does not translate the Hebrew word *pânâv* ('his face'). Hence, a translation more like the NKJV is needed: 'I shall yet praise Him for the help of His countenance.' The psalmist earlier had longed to see God's face. Now he knows that God's presence will be his salvation.[7]

3. The Cry of a Troubled Heart (*vv. 6b-10*)

The mood of the psalmist switches back to doubt but he is refreshed by memories of the past. **My soul is downcast within me; therefore I will remember you from the land of Jordan, the heights of Hermon – from Mount Mizar. Deep calls to deep in the roar of your waterfalls; all your waves and breakers have swept over me** (*vv. 6-7*). The geographical expressions here suggest that the psalmist was far off from the sanctuary, perhaps even in exile. He seems to be speaking from the area in which the Jordan River rises, though Mount Mizar (the Hebrew means 'little mountain') is otherwise unknown. Perhaps he is referring to the area from which he himself came, or else the terms he uses amount to a reference to Canaan, the land of promise.[8] The thought of the tumbling waters of the Jordan, such as can still be seen at the waterfall at Banyas, provides the idea of the waves that are presently coming over him. No longer is his mind on the 'living water'

[7] Many translators and commentators want to emend 'his face' to 'my face', as the latter form appears in verse 11 and 43:5. But 'his face' is the more difficult reading and should be preserved. S. Terrien, *The Psalms*, p. 353, points out that the alteration to 'my face' does not provide good sense, whereas 'the psalmist crowns the asseveration of the refrain with the expectation of seeing the divine face in intimate communion'.

[8] Nowhere else does a psalmist designate with precision where he himself lived. This in itself may suggest that another interpretation is necessary. Also, the Massoretic punctuation does not link 'the land of Jordan' closely with 'the heights of Hermon', and that latter expression is an unusual one. In Hebrew it is simply 'the Hermons'. Another interpretation that has a lot of merit is that *chermônîm* is from the root *ch-r-m* and means 'holy places, sanctuaries'. In this case 'Mizar' could be a reference to Mount Sion, as many have argued. The view outlined above is found in N. H. Ridderbos, *De Psalmen* (Kampen: Kok, 3rd ed., n.d.), vol. 2 (Psalm 42–60), pp. 23-24.

that God gives (vv. 1-2), but on his own situation in which he has been engulfed.

By day the LORD directs his love, at night his song is with me – a prayer to the God of my life (*v. 8*). In the midst of his distress he is still able to recall God's graciousness to him. In the daytime God commands his steadfast love (*chésed*); at night time he gives a song,[9] that is turned into a prayer.[10] Many Hebrew manuscripts have 'the living God' instead of 'the God of my life'. There is only one letter different in Hebrew, and certainly 'living God' matches well with the same expression in verse 2.

I say to God my Rock, 'Why have you forgotten me? Why must I go about mourning, oppressed by the enemy?' (*v. 9*) The psalmist feels forsaken, yet he is able to call God his 'Rock' (cf. for the use of this description of God, Pss. 18:2; 31:3; 71:3). The use of this metaphor prepares the way for another similar metaphor ('fortress') in 43:2. No fuller explanation is given of the enemies, yet the use of the word 'oppressed' may well be significant. It is most often used of the enemies of the nation of Israel, who attacked and marauded the land.

My bones suffer mortal agony as my foes taunt me, saying to me all day long, 'Where is your God?' (*v. 10*). Illness plagues him, and he has the added pain of opponents who constantly mock him. His present distress is deepened by the attitude and words of others, for they are suggesting that God is unable to help. The continuous nature of their taunts increases his pain.

3. Refrain (*v. 11*)

Why are you downcast, O my soul? Why so disturbed within me? Put your hope in God, for I will yet praise him, my Saviour and my God (*v. 11*). The refrain of verses 5-6a is taken up again, as he expresses confidence in his God. The confident

---

[9] The word *shîroh*, 'his song', has a rare form of 3 masc. sing. suffix. See *GKC* §91.b, p. 256.

[10] Some Hebrew manuscripts have 'praise' instead of 'prayer'. The difference is in one letter only, and in both the old Hebrew script and the square script these two letters (*hê* and *pê*) are not easily confused. Context also favours retaining *t^e fillâh*, 'prayer'.

call to his God stands in marked contrast to the question that has been flung at the psalmist in verses 3 and 10: 'Where is your God?'

4. A Prayer for Vindication *(Psalm 43, verses 1-4)*
From the mountains of northern Palestine, the scene now moves on to Mount Zion, and the joy of worship there. **Vindicate me, O God, and plead my cause against an ungodly nation; rescue me from deceitful and wicked men** (*v. 1*). Several factors here confirm the impression that the enemies were external ones. They are clearly 'ungodly', an expression that suggests that they are strangers to covenantal love (lit. 'not *châsîd*').[11] His appeal for God to plead his cause is typical of similar passages in the prophets (see, e.g., Micah 6:1; 7:9). He wants deliverance from those who practise deceit and unrighteousness, qualities that must not be characteristic of God's followers (Ps. 119:1-3; Mal. 2:6).

You are God my stronghold. Why have you rejected me? Why must I go about mourning, oppressed by the enemy? (*v.* 2). The psalmist cannot reconcile the truth that God is his stronghold with the fact that he is passing through difficult times and enduring such trouble from his enemies. He wonders why God seems to have rejected him. The second part of the verse repeats a question already asked in Psalm 42:9b.

Send forth your light and your truth, let them guide me; let them bring me to your holy mountain, to the place where you dwell (*v.* 3). He now asks for God's light and God's truth to be his guide, and that they will bring him back to Zion. This, in effect, would be the answer to the question he had asked at the very outset (Ps. 42:2). He wants these two angels ('light' and 'truth') to lead him through the desert and bring him into God's presence.

Then will I go to the altar of God, to God, my joy and my delight. I will praise you with the harp, O God, my God (*v.* 4). He looks ahead and anticipates the joy with which he

---

[11] The Hebrew negative particle *lo'* forms other compounds like 'not *châsîd*'. Cf. 'a no-god', Deuteronomy 32:21; 'a son not wise', Hosea 13:13. These, and other examples, are cited in *DIHG~S*, §116 (d).

will worship his God on Zion. In place of sorrow and grief there will be a fresh realisation of God's character, and he will praise him with the harp.[12] He is the joy and delight of his children, and is worthy of praise from those who can say of him, 'God, my God.'

5. Refrain (*v. 5*)

Why are you downcast, O my soul? Why so disturbed within me? Put your hope in God, for I will yet praise him, my Saviour and my God (*v. 5*). The refrain comes in for the third time, but now the emphasis probably falls on the latter part. The thought of joyful worship at the sanctuary revitalises the psalmist.

[12] For an older discussion on the harp, see Sir John Stainer, *The Music of the Bible, with Some Account of the Development of Modern Musical Instruments from Ancient Types* (London: Novello and Co., 1914), pp. 13-27, and for a more recent discussion, with a good bibliography, Robert H. O'Connell in *NIDOTTE*, 2, pp. 666-67.

Psalm 44

For the director of music. Of the Sons of Korah. A maskil.

It was customary in Israel for a song to be sung to the Lord after victory in battle (see Judges 5). It was also commonplace for a song to be sung *after defeat in battle,* and Psalm 44 is such a song. In this psalm the people and the king cry out to God to arise and help them. The language alternates between singular and plural. The singular passages (vv. 4, 6, 15-16) may well have been the words that the king used, while the remainder of the psalm is an appeal from the army or the nation as a whole. However, it may just be a poetic device, used simply to create greater linguistic variation.

A poem like this should not be compared with a string of pearls simply strung together without formal coherence. Rather, it is more like a building in which the upper parts depend on the lower parts. The psalm is composed of four sections (vv. 1-8, 9-16, 17-22, 23-26). 'But when we look at this division from a formal point of view, we are confronted with something striking: the various sections consist, consecutively, of ten, eight, six, and four poetic lines. This could hardly have occurred by chance. The psalm rises up like a *zikkurat*: and only when the poet has come to the topmost flight does he raise up his prayer to God'.[1]

Repetition also plays a part in this poem. In verse 3 mention is made that the people were not saved (*y-sh-*ʿ) by the sword

[1] N. H. Ridderbos, 'The Psalms: Style-figures and Structure (certain considerations, with special reference to Pss. xxii, xxv, and xlv)', *OTS* XIII, 1963, p. 50. Note: a *zikkurat* (or *ziggurat*) was a Babylonian temple-tower shaped like a pyramid. Each successive storey was smaller than the one below it.

(*chérev*), while these two words are repeated in verse 6. Then in verse 11, the people are said to have been delivered over by God 'like sheep' (*k^{e}tsoʾn*), while in verse 22 the people are considered 'as sheep' (*k^{e}tsoʾn*) to be slaughtered.

Because there is no reference to the destruction of the temple, the psalm is probably from late in the history of Judah, in the time of Hezekiah or Josiah. The language of the psalm has definite similarities to that of Jeremiah (see, e.g., Jer. 11:19; 25:34; 51:40), and that may indicate a date of composition contemporaneous with Jeremiah.

1. Confidence in God's Past Help (*vv. 1-8*)

We have heard with our ears, O God; our fathers have told us what you did in their days, in days long ago (*v. 1*). It was the responsibility of one generation to pass on to the next generation the knowledge of God's actions on behalf of his people. These actions could go back a long way in their history, even 'from days long ago' (*mimê qédem*). Exactly the same phrase is used twice in Isaiah (23:7 and 37:26). They had to 'tell the next generation the praiseworthy deeds of the LORD, his power, and the wonders he has done' (Ps. 78:4). Similarly for the Christian community today, what we receive we are to pass on (1 Cor. 15:1-11; 2 Tim. 2:2).

With your hand you drove out the nations and planted our fathers; you crushed the peoples and made our fathers flourish (*v.* 2). Recognition is made of God's sovereign provision of the land of Canaan for his people. The language used reflects the way in which the Book of Deuteronomy describes the dispossession of Canaan so that Israel could inhabit it (see Deut. 4:38; 11:23; 18:12 and note the usage of the same verb as here, *yârash,* Hi.). God transplanted Israel as a vine (see Ps. 80:8-16) and caused its branches to grow. The NIV rendering at the end of the verse captures the sense well, though it is a very free translation. Literally the Hebrew text has 'you sent them out', i.e. the branches, and this is the same verb (*shâlach,* Pi.) that is used of their growth in Psalm 80:11.

It was not by their sword that they won the land, nor did their arm bring them victory; it was your right hand, your

arm, and the light of your face, for you loved them (*v. 3*). The NIV fails to translate two of the three occurrences of the particle *kî* in this verse. Translating them makes even more forceful the contrast between human weakness and divine power: '*For* not by their own sword did they win the land, nor did their own arm save them, *but* your right hand and your arm, and the light of your face, *for* you loved them' (ESV). This is repeating what Moses had taught the people long before (Deut. 4:34; 7:19; 9:4-6; 11:2; 26:8-9). The victory over the Canaanites was not achieved by human power. It had to be attributed solely to God's intervention on their behalf, based on his love for Israel (Deut. 7:7-9). Reference to 'the light of your face' links in nicely with the reference to God's light in the previous psalm (43:3) and indicates how his loving-kindness lightens all darkness.

You are my King and my God, who decrees victories for Jacob (*v. 4*). Now the king speaks in the first person, and makes a very emphatic declaration. It is quite possible that the first clause should be translated '*Yes*, you are my king', or, '*you alone* are my king'.[2] He confesses that God is both his king and his God. Even the human leader of the people was subject to a higher power. He knew that God alone could bring victory. 'Jacob' became a honourable title for the nation from Numbers 23 onwards, and 'Jacob' is spoken of as the object of God's love (Ps. 47:4; Mal. 1:2).

Through you we push back our enemies; through your name we trample our foes (*v. 5*). The imagery of this verse is taken from the actions of cattle. The victories of the past were like a bull butting its opponents, or trampling on its enemies. Through calling on God's name and seeing his power displayed, Israel's enemies had been subdued before them. This type of imagery was widely used of military activities in the ancient Near East.

Having stated positively the fact that all victories came from the LORD, the psalmist now puts this truth negatively. **I do not trust in my bow, my sword does not bring me victory; but you give us victory over our enemies, you put our adversaries to shame** (*vv. 6-7*). Again, the NIV does not

---

[2] For the grammatical point, see *DIHG~S*, p. 2.

translate two occurrences of the particle *kî* in this verse, and this weakens the contrast: '*For* I do not trust ... *but* you give.' Wielding of human weapons of war did not in itself bring salvation in battle. Horses and chariots, bows and swords, would never save. The nation had to know that they should look only to the Holy One of Israel (Isa. 31:1). To shame an adversary was to deprive him of success.

In God we make our boast all day long, and we will praise your name forever. Selah (*v. 8*). At the end of this historical reflection, the psalm rises to a note of joy. The LXX captures the sense when it renders: 'All day long God is praised'. Grateful thanks had always been the hallmark of a rescued people, and there would ever be acknowledgment of God's name.

2. A Lament in the Face of Defeat (*vv. 9-16*)

A sudden change comes into the psalm at this point (for a similar shift using the same verb, 'you have rejected', see Ps. 89:38). After the initial complaint, the psalmist follows on with five more accusations against God, all involving a verbal clause ('you made us plunder for our enemies', v. 10; 'you gave us up', v. 11; 'you sold your people', v. 12; 'you made us a reproach', v. 13; 'you made us a by-word', v. 14). **But now you have rejected and humbled us; you no longer go out with our armies** (*v. 9*). 'But now' (*'af*), with which it opens, marks the transition to complaint. What looked like a victory song in the early verses of the psalm is altered to a national lament. Defeat had taken place on the battlefield, and the people understood this as a rejection by God. They had been shamed in battle, and sensed that God was no longer with them, as, for example, he had been with David when he went against the Philistines (2 Sam. 5:24).

You made us retreat before the enemy, and our adversaries have plundered us. You gave us up to be devoured like sheep and have scattered us among the nations (*vv.* 10-11). They had been beaten in battle and robbed by their enemies. These were neighbouring nations who were filled with spite against Israel.[3] The Israelites accuse God of giving them up to be slaughtered, and of scattering them among the nations. This could be a reference simply to captives taken in battle (cf. the case of Naaman's wife's Israelite slave, 2 Kings 5:2). Captives were often sold off as slaves, further increasing the dispersion. However, the use of the same verb (*zânach*), as in the warning passage in Leviticus 26:33 regarding exile, suggests that the scattering is part of God's judgment against Israel.

You sold your people for a pittance, gaining nothing from their sale (*v. 12*). So worthless were the people, runs their argument, that God had sold them for nothing. He was willing to part with them for no sale price at all. The imagery of sale of Israel to their enemies is common in the Old Testament, especially of defeats suffered during the period of the judges (cf. Deut. 32:30; Judg. 2:14; 3:8; 4:2; 10:7; 1 Sam. 12:9).

You have made us a reproach to our neighbours, the scorn and derision of those around us. You have made us a byword among the nations; the peoples shake their heads at us (*vv. 13-14*). Among the surrounding nations Israel's name had become a laughing matter. The vocabulary used ('reproach', 'scorn', and 'derision') suggests that the neighbours were taunting and ridiculing her. They even had proverbial sayings making fun of her. They scornfully mimic her, and treat her as if she was nothing. Elsewhere shaking the head is also linked with a scornful attitude (Ps. 64:8).

My disgrace is before me all day long, and my face is covered with shame at the taunts of those who reproach and revile me, because of the enemy, who is bent on revenge (*vv. 15-16*). The reproach was not just a national one. Individuals within Israel could feel it deeply too, and now the psalm speaks in personal terms, 'my disgrace', 'my face'. Also, the taunting was done openly and publicly, for the MT speaks of 'the voice (or 'sound') of the reproacher and the reviler'. The enemy wanted more than just the opportunity to

---

[3] The word used here is not the usual word for enemies but 'our haters' (*m^{e}san^e'ênû*). Its use reinforces the nature of the animosity that Israel was experiencing.

make fun of Israel. Revenge was the ultimate aim, though the reason that lay behind this desire is not given.

3. Questions in Perplexity (*vv. 17-22*)
Testimony is now presented that Israel had not renounced the covenant. **All this happened to us, though we had not forgotten you or been false to your covenant. Our hearts had not turned back; our feet had not strayed from your path** (*vv. 17-18*). These verses bring us to the heart of the problem that the people faced. They knew that God had said that if his people were disobedient he would bring judgment upon them, including defeat before their enemies (Deut. 28:15-68, and especially vv. 25-26 and 49-52). But here they claim that they have not broken the covenant nor turned from the LORD's ways.[4] This is not to be understood as a self-righteous claim, but a general reference of adherence to the covenant.[5] The thought of verse 17 is expanded in verse 18 by reference to 'hearts' and 'feet'. The claim is that inward thoughts have not resulted in outward actions. God's path is the way of truth and life that he has revealed, and 'path' (*'orach*) can be a synonym for 'law' (*tôrâh*; cf. Ps. 119:115).

But you crushed us and made us a haunt for jackals and covered us over with deep darkness (*v. 19*). The people cannot understand how God has permitted them to be overwhelmed by the enemy, who had turned their land into a terrible wilderness (cf. 'haunt of jackals' with the almost identical expression in Jer. 10:22). They are in despair and feel as though deep darkness has descended upon them. The words 'deep darkness' translate the same Hebrew word (*tsalmâvet*) that appears in Psalm 23:4: 'through the valley of *the shadow of death*.'

If we had forgotten the name of our God or spread out our hands to a foreign god, would not God have discovered it, since he knows the secrets of the heart? (*vv. 20-21*). Again the people profess that they have been faithful to the covenant.

---

[4] The preposition 'from', used here independently, is an unusual lengthened form, *minnî*.

[5] H. C. Leupold, *Exposition of the Psalms* (Welwyn: Evangelical Press, 1977), p. 349, has good comments on this section.

Had they been unfaithful, God would have known that, for he is able to dig into the darkest recesses of the heart. The same verb for 'discover' (*châqar*) occurs in Psalm 139:1, 23 and Jeremiah 17:10 of God's activity in searching the human heart. Nothing is hidden from his all-searching eye (see the whole of Ps. 139).

Yet for your sake we face death all day long; we are considered as sheep to be slaughtered (*v. 22*). The current afflictions of the people are not the result of their turning from God. Rather, they are undergoing oppression because of their faithfulness to him. For *his* sake they face constant persecution, and in their enemies' minds they are reckoned simply as sheep destined for slaughter. Paul quotes these words after he has summed up the tribulations which are endured by the people of God (Rom. 8:36). Terms that are used in this psalm of the Old Testament believing community are rightly applied by Paul to the situation of the New Testament church. There is continuity in the experience of believers.

3. A Prayer for Deliverance (*vv. 23-26*)

Awake, O Lord! Why do you sleep? Rouse yourself! Do not reject us forever. Why do you hide your face and forget our misery and oppression? (*vv. 23-24*). While this call to God is similar in some respects to that in Psalm 7:6 (see the commentary), yet there is a difference. Here the people suggest that God is so uncaring of them in their trouble that it is as if he is asleep. In their despair they think they are rejected *forever*. In situations like this the people felt that God's face was hidden from them (Pss. 10:11; 27:9; 88:14; 143:7; Isa. 8:17). 'Misery' (*ʿᵒnî*) is used more often than 'oppression' (*lachats*), which is often connected, as here, with enemies or siege situations.

We are brought down to the dust; our bodies cling to the ground (*v. 25*). This is a description of their present distress, but the significance of the expressions are unclear. It describes either their grief which brings them to a prostrate position in prayer, or else their feeling of being so near death that they are almost in the dust of the grave.

Rise up and help us; redeem us because of your unfailing love (*v. 26*). The people have already claimed that they are loyal to the covenant (v. 17), and have asked God to awake. Now they appeal to him to rise up and provide the help they so desperately need. They ask for the continuance of covenantal love (*chésed,* NIV 'unfailing love'), and for this to be expressed in redemption from their present distress. Similarly Paul goes on to assert the unfailing love of Christ Jesus our Lord (Rom. 8:33-39) after he quotes from verse 22.

Psalm 45

For the director of music. To [the tune of] 'Lilies'.
Of the Sons of Korah. A maskil. A wedding song.

It was probably a royal wedding that inspired the composition of this psalm, and it may well have been used repeatedly at later weddings. The greatest difficulty this assessment has is that verses 6-7 appear to be a direct address to God, not to the human monarch who was his vice-regent. Some would then consider the whole psalm as messianic, in view of the use made of verses 6-7 in Hebrews 1:8-9.[1] Preferable is the view that suggests the eyes of the psalmist were lifted up to see the glory of the Davidic ruler as typifying the kingly rule of the Messiah. Accordingly, he addresses him directly, and while this may see a sudden introduction of a messianic element into the psalm, yet it is not without parallel elsewhere (cf. Isa. 9:6-7 and the context).

In support of this change of subject it can be pointed out that change of addressee in psalms is quite frequent. At times the congregation will address God in the third person ('he'), while direct address to him in the second person ('you') may occur in the same psalm. Thus, here a symmetrical structure for the psalm exists with this pattern:

Addressee: The king (v. 2)
God (vv. 6-7)
The king (v. 8)
The bride (v. 10)
The king (v. 16)[2]

[1] For an exposition of the directly messianic view among older commentators, see E. W. Hengstenberg, *Commentary on the Psalms*, II, pp. 118-26, while for modern ones, see H. C. Leupold, *Exposition of the Psalms*, pp. 351-53.

[2] See the discussion by Craig C. Broyles, *Psalms*, p. 207.

1. Introduction (*v. 1*)

My heart is stirred by a noble theme as I recite my verses for the king; my tongue is the pen of a skilful writer (*v. 1*). No other psalm starts in this fashion. The psalmist tells about the great subject matter with which his poem is concerned. His heart is bubbling over with the good things that his verses contain about *a king* (so the Hebrew text, which lacks the definite article 'the'). His tongue is like a skilled writer such as Ezra (cf. Ezra 7:6, which uses the very same phrase as here).[3]

2. Address to the King (*vv. 2-9*)

You are the most excellent of men and your lips have been anointed with grace, since God has blessed you forever (*v. 2*). The king is extolled for qualities that he possesses and for blessings that he has been given. In the Old Testament men are called 'excellent' or 'beautiful', such as the king here, or Absalom in 2 Samuel 14:25. This term refers to their general perfection.[4] Part of God's gift to the king was loveliness of speech, an indication of his blessing. The word 'forever' does not mean 'for eternity' but 'for as long as you live' (cf. its use regarding Moses in Exod. 19:9, and of a slave in 21:6).

Gird your sword upon your side, O mighty one; clothe yourself with splendour and majesty (*v. 3*). The king is thought of as a mighty warrior who needs to buckle on his sword before battle. The second part of the verse is paraphrased by the NIV, as the Hebrew text says simply, 'your splendour, your majesty.' Preferable is the rendering in the RSV and ESV, 'in your splendour and majesty.' These terms may refer to the king's armour, and if this suggestion is correct they may also point to glorious victories in the past achieved because of this armour.

---

[3] It is preferable to render the Hebrew phrase *sôfêr mâhîr* as 'skilled writer' rather than 'quick writer'. The latter translation depends on *mâhîr* being from the root *m-h-r*, 'to hasten'. However, it is more probably connected with a semitic root meaning 'skilled'. Further information is given in J. Barr, *Comparative Philology and the Text of the Old Testament* (London: SCM Press, 1968), p. 295, and the bibliography listed in *DCH*, V, p. 835.

[4] The verbal form is a rare Pealal of *yâfâh*, and while a *hapax legomenon*, no emendation, such as suggested in *BHS*, is necessary.

In your majesty ride forth victoriously in behalf of truth, humility and righteousness; let your right hand display awesome deeds (*v. 4*). The king is pictured as setting out for battle, riding upon his horse.[5] He makes his way through the ranks of the enemy as the champion of truth, humility, and righteousness.[6] The same imagery appears in Revelation of the rider Faithful and True who comes forth on a white horse (Rev. 19:11). These victories will be seen as the victories of God and so inspire awe. Elsewhere, such as in Psalm 65:5, 'awesome deeds' refers to God's own actions.

Let your sharp arrows pierce the hearts of the king's enemies; let the nations fall beneath your feet (*v. 5*). The NIV and many other translations take the phrase 'the hearts of the king's enemies' from the end of the verse (where it comes in the Hebrew text) and link it with the military success spoken of at the start of the verse. The whole verse is difficult to translate, but the essential message of it is clear. From carvings we know that battlefields were littered with slain bodies, shot by arrows. Victory is sure for the king. The fact that the Hebrew text ends with the word 'king' makes the transition to the next verse easier.

Your throne, O God, will last forever and ever; a sceptre of justice will be the sceptre of your kingdom (*v. 6*). Suddenly the psalmist looks beyond the immediate occupant of the throne of David to the kingly glory of the messianic ruler. This is similar to the way in which Isaiah inserts direct address to Immanuel into a passage that is dealing with the impending Assyrian invasion (Isa. 8:8). The divine ruler is not subject to the possibility that his kingdom will be taken from him.[7] Objections have been raised

---

[5] For an illustration of a king setting out, see the picture of Rameses III of Egypt mounting his chariot to go into battle, Othmar Keel, *The Symbolism of the Biblical World: Ancient Near Eastern Iconography and the Book of Psalms* (London: SPCK, 1978), p. 281.

[6] 'Humility and righteousness' translates *ʿanvâh tsedek*, two nouns placed in apposition. The fact that the MT joins the words together by means of a hyphen called *maqqêf* suggests it was treating them as being in a construct relationship. However, the NIV translation is probably the best way to treat the two words.

[7] My own position on this verse is spelt out more fully in 'The Syntax and Interpretation of Psalm 45:7', John H. Skilton, ed., *The Law and the Prophets: Old Testament Studies Prepared in Honor of Oswald Thompson Allis* (Nutley, NJ: Presbyterian and Reformed Publishing Co., 1974), pp. 337-47.

to the traditional translation and interpretation on syntactical grounds.[8] Thus, it has been claimed that in Hebrew even when the preposition meaning 'like' (k^e) is omitted, though the text may say *a* is *b*, the meaning can be *a* is like *b*.[9] But this claim and its appeal to Psalm 80:11 does not hold up under scrutiny, and hence it cannot be used in support of a translation such as 'Your throne is *like* the throne of God, eternal'.[10] The 'sceptre' stands for the king's rule, and it is depicted as being one of which justice is the hallmark.

In Hebrews 1:8 this verse is quoted in a context that points to the eternal glory of Christ. He is the one who has been given 'the throne of his father David, and he will reign over the house of Jacob for ever; his kingdom will never end' (Luke 1:32-33).

You love righteousness and hate wickedness; therefore God, your God, has set you above your companions by anointing you with the oil of joy (*v. 7*). The person designated as 'God' in the previous verse is now marked off from him by the reference to 'your God'. This passage has to be considered along with other messianic passages in the Old Testament. In the descriptions of the Angel of the LORD he is represented as being God himself, and yet at the same time he is distinguished from God. In verse 6 the king is God, while here in this verse he has been given *by* God an exalted position over his companions. These companions are probably other kings. This king is distinguished from them by the fact that his character is different. He is noted for his love of righteousness and his punishment of evildoers, and consequently God has given him special blessings. The anointing with oil is probably a figurative way of saying that God has blessed him with

---

[8] For summaries of the various views that have and are taken in reference to the translation and interpretation of Psalm 45:6, see Murray J. Harris, 'The Translation of *Elohim* in Psalm 45:7-8', *TB* 35 (1984), pp. 65-89, and Gerard van Groningen, *Messianic Revelation in the Old Testament* (Grand Rapids: Baker Book House, 1990), pp. 362-70.

[9] For this argument, cf. the discussion by J. A. Emerton, 'The Syntactical Problem of Psalm XLV.7', *JSS* 13 (1968), pp. 58-63.

[10] P. C. Craigie, *Psalms 1-50*, p. 337, indicates his support for my discussion on this syntactical question, and upholds the traditional translation, 'Your throne, O God, is for ever and ever.'

happiness. It should not be equated with the anointing at a coronation.

All your robes are fragrant with myrrh and aloes and cassia; from palaces adorned with ivory the music of the strings makes you glad. Daughters of kings are among your honoured women; at your right hand is the royal bride in gold of Ophir (*vv. 8-9*). The scene shifts back to the wedding, and to the robes with which the king is adorned. Myrrh was a fragrant resin and it could be used as a valuable gift (Matt. 2:11). Aloes and cassia are both aromatic resins from the bark of trees. Wealthy homes and royal palaces were decorated with ivory (1 Kings 10:18; 22:39), while ivory could also be used as inlay on furniture (Amos 6:4). Festive music sounds from the palace as the wedding preparations continue.[11] The bride comes adorned in the best gold (cf. Isa. 13:12). Ophir has never been identified with certainty, but it was probably in southern Arabia between Mecca and Medina and was noted for its high-quality gold. The bride is accompanied by women of the royal family as she takes her position at the king's right hand.

3. Address to the Bride (*vv. 10-15*)

Listen, O daughter, consider and give ear: Forget your people and your father's house (*v. 10*). The bride is now addressed and this is shown by the verbal forms and the second person feminine singular suffixes to the nouns. She must give attention to the words of advice, and the command to forget her people and her father's house may imply that she is a foreigner. In the Book of Ruth Naomi speaks of Orpah 'going back to her people and her gods'. Ruth, on the other hand, makes her profession: 'Your people [are] my people and your God [is] my God' (Ruth 1:16).

The king is enthralled by your beauty; honour him, for he is your lord (*v. 11*). The king's attachment to his bride is due to her beauty. The expression 'he is your lord' may indicate that they were already married, as 'lord' is used in this way by Sarah of Abraham (Gen. 18:12; and cf. 1 Pet. 3:6, 'her master', lit. 'lord'). If so, the instruction of the previous verse comes

---

[11] The NIV assumes, and probably rightly, that the Hebrew word *minnî* is a shortened form of *minîm*, 'stringed instruments', as in Psalm 150:4.

after their marriage and reflects the new relationship with her husband's people. She is called on to give homage to him.

The Daughter of Tyre will come with a gift, men of wealth will seek your favour (*v. 12*). The marriage brings a new relationship to surrounding nations, as gifts are brought by their peoples to the new queen. The word 'gift' (*minchâh*) can imply tribute (2 Sam 8:2, 6; 1 Chron. 18:2, 6). Hence the setting of this psalm may be in a period in which Israel exercised rule over surrounding nations. 'Daughter of Tyre' may indicate the people of Tyre, just as 'Daughter of Zion' and 'Daughter of Jerusalem' are used in a similar way.

All glorious is the princess within [her chamber]; her gown is interwoven with gold. In embroidered garments she is led to the king; her virgin companions follow her and are brought to you. They are led in with joy and gladness; they enter the palace of the king (*vv. 13-15*). Address is made again directly to the king concerning his bride (called here 'the daughter of the king') and her companions. It is clear from these two verses that it is not inward beauty of the princess that is being described, but outward adornment in beautiful garments. She is brought to the king accompanied by her maids of honour. They are brought into the royal palace in a festive procession, something similar to a modern bridal party entering the church.

4. Conclusion (*vv. 16-17*)

Your sons will take the place of your fathers; you will make them princes throughout the land. I will perpetuate your memory through all generations; therefore the nations will praise you forever and ever (*vv. 16-17*). The speaker seems to be the psalmist, as he reflects on the enduring dynasty that the king will have. His sons will be given positions of great responsibility, for 'princes' (*sârîm*) are frequently mentioned as being connected with a royal house (see 2 Chron. 21:9; 31:8; Jer. 26:21). This enduring dynasty would be a matter of praise even among the Gentile nations. Behind the words of the psalmist here lies the promises of the Davidic covenant (2 Sam. 7), but ultimately blessing to the nations will be a fulfilment of God's promises to Abraham (Gen. 12:3; 22:18).

Psalm 46

For the director of music. Of the Sons of Korah.
According to alamoth. A song.

The historical circumstances that lie behind the composition of this psalm cannot be established with absolute precision. Jerusalem has been attacked, but God has intervened on behalf of his people and shattered the enemy. Though it has been argued that the historical background is the deliverance from the Assyrian Sennacherib,[1] yet the situation depicted in 2 Chronicles 20 seems to fit best. The Moabites and Ammonites came against Jehoshaphat. Jahaziel at that time encouraged the people: 'Do not be afraid or discouraged because of this vast army. For the battle is not yours, but God's' (v. 15). Here the psalmist sings of victory won by the Lord Almighty, and of that city in which God dwells.

The psalm is divided by the threefold appearance of 'Selah' and the repeated refrain in verses 7 and 11. Verse 8 appears to be the pivotal verse, with the opening statement of the psalm, 'God is our refuge' (v. 1), being matched at the conclusion of the psalm by 'the Lord Almighty is with us' (v. 11). In addition, verse 8 also serves to conclude the first section and then to introduce the second main division.

The title contains the word *ʿᵃlâmôt,* which also appears in 1 Chronicles 15:20 as a musical term. The word itself means 'young women'. Hence, it could refer to the type of voices that were to sing the specified song, perhaps tenor or soprano.

This psalm and the two following ones (Pss. 46-48) share many themes in common with Psalm 87. The land of promise (Canaan) was important, but the place of Jerusalem within

---

[1] See the sustained attempt by N. H. Snaith, *Hymns of the Temple* (London; SCM Press, 1951), pp. 70-77, to argue for that background.

it even more so. The LORD had chosen that 'holy mountain' (Pss. 48:1; 87:1) and when the nations turn to him they will become, as it were, citizens of Jerusalem (Ps. 87:6).

1. A Safe Stronghold (*vv. 1-3*)

God is our refuge and strength, an ever-present help in trouble (*v. 1*). A favourite theme of many of the psalms is the fact that God is the refuge of his people (e.g., 61:3; 62:7-8; 71:7; 142:5). The words 'refuge' (*mach^{a}seh*) and 'strength' (*ʿoz*) are often used in conjunction to depict God's character and his actions on behalf of his people. The confession here is communal (for the Hebrew text has 'for *us*'; and also in vv. 7 and 11). The people acknowledge that when in trouble God is near to help. The translation 'an ever-present help' is a traditional one, but the MT simply says 'in trouble he will be found a help – exceedingly.' The emphasis should rather fall on how great a help the LORD is, rather than trying to describe its continuous nature.

Therefore we will not fear, though the earth give way and the mountains fall into the heart of the sea, though its waters roar and foam and the mountains quake with their surging. Selah (*vv. 2-3*). The troubles they had faced (including the most recent battles) are described as if there was a tremendous upheaval of nature. A mighty earthquake has taken place, but amidst everything the people can say: 'We will not fear.' This is based on what has been asserted about God in verse 1. The sea may be used as a symbol for the world as it is agitated by sinful desires of kings and empires. Insufficient detail is given to locate the psalm in a specific historical context.

There is a river whose streams make glad the city of God, the holy place where the Most High dwells. God is within her, she will not fall; God will help her at break of day (*vv. 4-5*). While the term 'Zion' is not used, the psalmist now describes how secure the people are because God has his dwelling in Jerusalem. In other Old Testament passages we also have the picture of Jerusalem, with water streaming from her (cf. Isa. 33:21). God's sanctuary was in Jerusalem, and as long as the people trusted his provision for them, then his help would never fail. When they despised the softly flowing waters of Siloam, then God would abandon them (Isa. 8:5-8). God 'had pity on his people and his dwelling place' until the people mocked his messengers and ultimately the sanctuary itself was destroyed by the Babylonians (2 Chron. 36:15-19). The psalmist's language about Jerusalem idealises the topographical situation, as no 'river' gladdens the sanctuary. The Kidron only flows for a few weeks in winter, while the spring of Gihon struggles to fill the pool of Siloam.

Nations are in uproar, kingdoms fall; he lifts his voice, the earth melts (*v. 6*). In the midst of turmoil among the nearby nations, God has spoken. Kingdoms 'slip', says the psalmist, using a word he has already used of the mountains (NIV, 'the mountains *fall*,' verse 2). The contrast that is so clear is that God's city will not 'slip' or 'fall' (v. 5). When his voice is heard, the inhabitants of the earth tremble in fear. 'The earth melts' is simply a poetical way of saying that people are terrified.

2. An Affirmation of Confidence (v. 7)

The confession that the people go on to make is that they have God's presence. **The LORD Almighty is with us; the God of Jacob is our fortress. Selah** (*v. 7*). The form of the first clause is reminiscent of 'God is with us', 'Immanuel' (Isa. 7:14; 8:8, 10). Instead of 'God' the psalmist here uses the expression 'the LORD of hosts' (NIV 'the LORD Almighty'; see comment on Psalm 24:10). The covenantal God of the patriarchs is with them as a 'fortress' (*misgâv*). This word signified a fortified height to which one could flee for safety, so symbolising the security of believers in God (cf. its use in 2 Sam. 22:3 and Isa. 33:16). It is definitely a poetic word, being found in the Psalms eleven times out of a total of fifteen in the Old Testament. This is the first occurrence of a refrain that is used again in verse 13 to close the Psalm. It may have been in general use, not just an isolated statement appearing in a context such as this.

3. A Summons from the LORD (*vv. 8-11*)

The invitation goes out to take notice of how God has shattered the enemies that came against his people. **Come and see the works of the LORD, the desolations he has brought on the earth. He makes wars cease to the ends of the earth; he breaks the bow and shatters the spear, he burns the shields with fire** (*vv. 8-9*). The 'works' of God are the distinctive actions he performs, especially in saving and sustaining his people.[2] The word 'desolations' is explained by what follows. He brought peace by destroying the enemies and their weapons. Their military power was broken as if bows and spears were destroyed. In the final clause of verse 9 the NIV renders the Hebrew word 'chariots' by 'shields'. This is following three early translations – the LXX, the Aramaic Targum, and the Latin Vulgate. However, the word 'chariots' makes good sense, especially as we know that chariots were burnt after they were captured (Josh. 11:6, 9).

'Be still, and know that I am God; I will be exalted among the nations, I will be exalted in the earth' (*v. 10*). The call is addressed to the Gentile invaders to withdraw. 'Be still' conveys too much the idea of being quiet, whereas the Hebrew verb means more 'to let alone', 'to abandon'. Because of his actions they should recognise that he is God and submit to his authority. The verb 'know' was used in secular treaties in this sense. He assures them that all nations are going to exalt him, even the whole earth. Quite often this verse is used in encouraging Christians to be calm, but that is a wrong application of it, as it is not addressed to believers but to the Gentile nations.

The LORD Almighty is with us; the God of Jacob is our fortress. Selah (*v. 11*). The refrain from verse 7 is repeated to close the psalm. It is an appropriate way to sum up the gratitude of the people as they again profess their faith in their deliverer.

---

[2] The word used for 'works' (*mifʿalôt*) only occurs three times in the Old Testament (apart from here, in Ps. 66:5 and Prov. 8:22). No indication exists to show that it differs at all from the more common related word, *poʿal*.

Psalm 47

For the director of music. Of the Sons of Korah. A psalm.

Psalms 46 and 47 seem to be positioned together in the Psalter because of their great similarity. Both celebrate God's victories on behalf of his people. This psalm has two calls to praise, followed by explanations. In each case there is a concluding statement. The first one points to God on his throne in Jerusalem (v. 5), while the second one praises him as the universal ruler (v. 9). These explanations are introduced in the Hebrew text in the manner typical of hymns by the presence of 'for' (*kî*) as the introductory word (see comments on Hymns in the Introduction). This is not so apparent from the NIV translation, but is carried over well in the NASB, RSV NKJV, and ESV. In addition to introducing the substance of praise in verses 2 and 7, the word 'for' also prefaces the final declaration of praise in verse 9. The part this word plays in the structure of the psalm is reinforced by the repetition of the words 'king' and 'all the earth' in verses 2 and 7. In fact, the repetition of 'people' (vv. 1, 3, 9), 'king' (vv. 2, 6, 7) and 'earth' (vv. 2, 7, 9) throughout the psalm gives overall unity to it.

1. Call to Praise (*v. 1*)

Clap your hands, all you nations; shout to God with cries of joy (*v. 1*). Clapping hands was a sign of joy, and the call goes out to Gentile nations to share with Israel in praising God. At coronations it was apparently customary to clap the hands and shout, 'Long live the king!' (2 Kings 11:12). Reference to clapping also occurs in a later song of rejoicing over God's kingship in Psalm 98:8.[1] The content of the shouting could be simply that God is king, or expressed in terms such as we have later in this psalm.

2. God's Rule over Israel (*vv. 2-5*)

How awesome is the LORD Most High, the great King over all the earth! (*v. 2*). The nations are asked to rejoice concerning the LORD, for he is 'the great king'. This term was used frequently by Near Eastern rulers (see 2 Kings 18:19 and Isa. 36:4, 13 in reference to the king of Assyria), but here it is appropriated of the even greater king, the LORD Most High.[2] His territory is not restricted as with earthly rulers, but rather it embraces the whole earth.

He subdued nations under us, peoples under our feet. He chose our inheritance for us, the pride of Jacob, whom he loved. Selah (*vv. 3-4*). The song reflects upon the conquest of Canaan by Israel. It was God who acted sovereignly to dispossess other nations and to make them submissive to Israel's rule.[3] Verse 4 is explaining the conquest and allocation of the land of Canaan in terms that echo statements in the Book of Deuteronomy (see especially Deut. 4:37-38). God's love for the patriarchs and for Jacob in particular (see Mal. 1:2) resulted in his giving them as their inheritance the land of Canaan, called here 'the pride of Jacob'. The conjunction of the verbs 'to choose' and 'to love' both here and in Deuteronomy 4:37 stress the sovereign nature of God's relationship with Israel.

God has ascended amid shouts of joy, the LORD amid the sounding of trumpets (*v. 5*). The verb 'ascended' is used because God is thought of having descended when he came to help his people. The same idea appears in Psalm 68:18: 'When you ascended on high, you led captives in your train ...' The

[1] Countries near Israel also practised clapping. For an illustration, see the picture of the Egyptian goddess Mert with hands upraised ready to clap in Othmar Keel, *The Symbolism of the Biblical World*, p. 334.

[2] It is also used of God in Psalms 48:2 and 95:3, and Malachi 1:14. Further comment on its use in Assyrian and extra-biblical sources can be found in M. Cogan and Hayim Tadmor, *II Kings: A New Translation with Introduction and Commentary* (New York: Doubleday & Co., 1988), pp. 230-31.

[3] The verb for 'subdue' is *d-v-r* II, and comment has already been made concerning it in reference to its use in Psalm 18:47.

LORD is pictured as returning to heaven amidst joyful acclaim from his people. The noun used of 'shouts of joy' (*terûʿâh*) links in with the use of the verb from which it comes in verse 1 ('shout'). Blowing of trumpets was specified for certain festive occasions, including New Year (Lev. 23:24; Num. 29:1).

3. Another Call to Praise (*v. 6*)

Sing praises to God, sing praises; sing praises to our King, sing praises (*v. 6*). The second call to praise is notable for its fourfold repetition of the verb 'to sing praises' (*zâmar* Pi.). This adds both emphasis and urgency to the command. The verb is almost exclusively used in the psalms, calling upon individuals and the community to join in praise to God, often in the context of musical accompaniment of song.[4] The people's relationship with God is defined in terms of his lordship over them. They sing to him as their God and as their king.

4. God's Rule over the Nations (*vv. 7-9*)

For God is the king of all the earth; sing to him a psalm of praise. God reigns over the nations; God is seated on his holy throne (*vv. 7-8*). The reason given for this second call to praise is that God's lordship is over all the earth, and this knowledge should result in another psalm of praise. This is the fifth call to praise in two verses, all imperatives from the same verb. The command to praise is followed on this occasion by an object: 'a psalm of praise' (*maskîl*). Apart from its use here, this word appears in the title of thirteen psalms (Pss. 32, 42, 44, 45, 52-55, 74, 78, 88, 89, 142). Hence, the direction could be to sing one of these specific psalms, or, more probably, a song that exemplifies a spirit of wisdom and understanding in accordance with the basic idea of this verb.[5] The Old Testament understands God's kingship to be from eternity (cf. 93:2). From his throne he exercises his rule and judgment over all nations.

---

[4] The verb occurs thirty-nine times in the Psalter, and only four times elsewhere (Judg. 5:3; 2 Sam. 22:50; Isa. 12:5; 1 Chron. 16:9).

[5] The verb is *sâkal*, used seventy-four times of which seventy-two are in the Hi. stem. Quite often it is close in meaning to other Hebrew verbs but it seems frequently to indicate having insight or understanding.

The nobles of the nations assemble as the people of the God of Abraham, for the kings of the earth belong to God; he is greatly exalted (*v. 9*). The word rendered 'nobles' is literally 'willing ones', but the NIV has taken its cue from the parallel word 'kings'.[6] The context here gives a picture of princes of the Gentile nations coming voluntarily and uniting with Jews as 'the people of Abraham'. This is part of the universalistic vision of the psalmists for the ultimate future of God's kingdom (cf. Pss. 67:1-7; 72:8-11). Gentile rulers 'belong to God' in the sense that they have become his servants. The conclusion is that God is indeed 'exalted', using a verbal form connected with 'Most High' (v. 2) and 'has ascended' (v. 5).

[6] The NIV is correct in taking the Hebrew word *mâgên* here as suzerain or king. For discussion on this translation, see M. Dahood, *Psalms I:1–50*, p. 17, and also the entries in *DCH*, III, p. 134 and *TWOT*, 1, p. 169. This also obviates any felt need to emend the MT text from *mâgᵉnê* to *sigᵉnê* as suggested in *BHS*.

Psalm 48

A song. A psalm of the Sons of Korah.

This psalm is clearly connected with Psalms 46 and 47. However, it is much more specific in relation to Mount Zion (called simply 'the city of God' in Psalm 46:4) and to matters relating to worship there. Whereas Psalms 46 and 47 speak more of the LORD's victories, Psalm 48 is a song of rejoicing over Zion and the blessings associated with her. It is notable for the collection of phrases used, especially in verses 1-2, to describe Jerusalem. Praise is offered concerning Jerusalem, 'the city of our God' and 'the city of the Great God', of Zion as 'his holy mountain' and especially of the God of Zion.

1. The God of Zion (*vv. 1-3*)

Great is the LORD, and most worthy of praise, in the city of our God, his holy mountain (*v. 1*). The initial emphasis is not on Zion, but on the God of Zion. The opening invocation sets the theme for the whole psalm as it directs attention to his greatness, and in particular as it is displayed in the symbolism of Mount Zion. The choice of Zion was the LORD's (Ps. 132:13-14), and from the time that David captured it (2 Sam. 5:6-7) it was central to the theology of the Old Testament. In the wider biblical picture Zion became the model for the New Jerusalem, and in Christian hymnology its imagery is taken over for the church (see John Newton's 'Glorious things of thee are spoken, Zion, city of our God').

It is beautiful in its loftiness, the joy of the whole earth. Like the utmost heights of Zaphon is Mount Zion, the city of the Great King (*v. 2*). Mount Zion is not actually the highest peak in the area, yet because of its religious significance it is extolled by the psalmist.[1] He pictures it as a place of joy not just to those who live or worship there, but to the whole earth. Zaphon was a mountain in northern Syria known from Canaanite sources, and it was supposed to be the dwelling place of the god Baal. Zion, though like Zaphon, was distinguished by the fact that it is the dwelling place of 'the great king' (see Ps. 47:2). This is an assertion that though others claimed Zaphon as the holy mountain, the *real* mountain of God where divine revelation occurred was Zion.

God is in her citadels; he has shown himself to be her fortress (*v. 3*). God's presence in Zion was shown by the bringing of the ark of the covenant there, and then by the building of the temple. He had taken up his abode in her palaces, and he had proved to be her defender. God's demonstration of his protection for Zion may have been shown just before this psalm was composed, perhaps in some battle situation such as spoken of in Psalm 46.

2. The Glory of Zion (*vv. 4-8*)

When the kings joined forces, when they advanced together, they saw [her] and were astounded; they fled in terror. Trembling seized them there, pain like that of a woman in labour. You destroyed them like ships of Tarshish shattered by an east wind (*vv. 4-7*). In a manner similar to Psalm 2, this psalm describes a gathering together of foreign kings against the LORD and against his chosen dwelling place, Jerusalem. Coalitions could be formed, but they were soon shattered. What the attackers 'saw' is unclear.[2] It could have been the fortified Zion, or, on the other hand, it could have been some visible appearance of God, a theophany. 'There', where they had that vision, they were frightened and panic seized them.[3] The idea of a woman in travail is a frequent Old Testament

---

[1] Zion rises to 743 metres, 66 metres lower than the Mount of Olives. However, from the south end of the walls of ancient Jerusalem, its inhabitants had to climb about 100 metres to reach the top of Zion.

[2] A similar case of the verb 'to see' without an object occurs in the MT of 1 Kings 19:3 in relation to Elijah: 'And when he *saw*, he arose and ran for his life.'

[3] The same idiom occurs here as appears in its fuller form in verse 10. The initial introductory *k^e* or *ka'^{a}sher* is omitted, while the Hebrew word *kên* ('and' in the NIV translation) points to the consequence: 'they saw *so* they feared.'

illustration of pain and anguish (cf. Isa. 21:3; Jer. 4:31; 49:24). Even if the assembled armies are like the mighty ships that trade to Tarshish (see Jonah 1:3), they will be destroyed as easily as an east wind brings them to a watery grave.[4]

As we have heard, so have we seen in the city of the LORD Almighty, in the city of our God: God makes her secure forever. Selah (*v. 8*). These words sum up the experience of the people. They had heard in the past of the wonderful things that the LORD had done for his people (cf. Ps. 44:1: 'we have heard with our ears, O God'; Ps. 78:3: 'things we have heard and known'). The use of the appellation 'the LORD Almighty' (*yhwh ts^evâ'ôt*) is fitting in a context in which God is depicted as the protector and defender of his people.[5] Now, however, their own eyes had seen his saving power right in the midst of Jerusalem. They thought that this experience would make her safe forever, but God's presence was conditional on their continued obedience.

3. The Words of the Worshippers (*vv. 9-11*)

After their deliverance the people address God directly. **Within your temple, O God, we meditate on your unfailing love. Like your name, O God, your praise reaches to the ends of the earth; your right hand is filled with righteousness** (*vv. 9-10*). When the worshippers assemble in the sanctuary they recognise that it is due to covenant love that they have been saved. They now have fresh evidence of the LORD's steadfast love. The expression of this truth is made using a Hebrew idiom ('as is your name ... so is your praise') that links God's self-revelation of himself ('his name') with the fact that he is therefore worthy of praise.[6] Worship in the temple had significance for the whole world. What had happened was known far and wide, so that the praise of the LORD was co-extensive with knowledge of his actions. Wherever people

---

[4] Tarshish is linked with Sheba, Seba, and Dedan, and hence its location was probably in Arabia or east Africa. Some port on the Red Sea would satisfy the references to it in the Old Testament. See also the comments on Psalm 72:10.

[5] For discussion on 'the LORD Almighty', cf. the comments on Psalm 24:10.

[6] The Hebrew idiom is dealt with in *DIHG~S*, p. 161.

heard about the events in Jerusalem they would praise the mighty actions of God in giving victory to his people.

Mount Zion rejoices, the villages of Judah are glad because of your judgments (*v. 11*). On Mount Zion and throughout the villages of Judah there is gladness on account of the recent victory.[7] That victory was called a filling of God's hand with righteousness in the previous verse, and now it is called his 'judgments'. The demonstrations of power shown in overthrowing Israel's enemies were expressions of God's judgments as he established his kingdom. This verse is very similar to Psalm 97:8.

4. An Invitation to View Zion (*vv. 12-14*)

Walk about Zion, go around her, count her towers, consider well her ramparts, view her citadels, that you may tell of them to the next generation (*vv. 12-13*). An invitation is given to view Jerusalem and to see her fortifications. Clearly this was not to take pride in her simply because of her good defences. She was 'the city of the LORD' (v. 8), and as such she was given divine protection. Passing on to the next generation this truth would continue the transmission of knowledge of the LORD. His praiseworthy deeds could not be hidden from the next generation (Ps. 78:4). Each generation of believers has a responsibility to teach the following one.

For this God is our God for ever and ever; he will be our guide even to the end (*v. 14*). The people make confession of the fact that this God who has saved them is indeed their God. They own him as their personal deliverer, and they know that he will shepherd them to the very end. This last clause continues the imagery of God as a shepherd of his people that is frequent in the Old Testament (cf. Pss. 23:1; 77:20; 80:1; Isa. 40:11; 49:9-10; Ezek. 34:11-12).

---

[7] 'Villages of Judah' is literally 'daughters of Judah', but the plural form as here can have the figurative meaning of 'villages', as in Numbers 21:25; Joshua 15:45; Judges 1:27; and Jeremiah 49:2.

Psalm 49

For the director of music. Of the Sons of Korah. A psalm.

The first series of Korahite psalms (Pss. 42-49) ends with a wisdom psalm (see the Introduction). The overriding thought is that the might of those who are rich but godless is not enduring, for all men, rich and poor, must die (see v. 12). In its general form it is like passages in the books of Job and Proverbs, even using the word 'proverb' (v. 4). The reference in that verse to it being sung is the only time in the Old Testament that mention is made of wisdom teaching being accompanied by music. However, many cultures, not only those in the Near East, combine music and instructional poems.

Whereas in another wisdom psalm, Psalm 37, the solution to the problem of the prosperity of the wicked is that God providentially cares for his own, the solution given here is that there is life beyond the grave for those whom God redeems. After an introduction it provides two answers to the problem, each with its own refrain.

No indication occurs in the psalm relating to its date of composition. The inscription 'To the sons of Korah' and also the contents point to a pre-exilic date. Both form and content are similar to other psalms from the time of David, and it is best attributed to that period.

1. Introduction (*vv. 1-4*)

Hear this, all you peoples; listen, all who live in this world, both low and high, rich and poor alike: My mouth will speak words of wisdom; the utterance from my heart will give understanding (*vv. 1-3*). The call (*shimᵉʿ û zoʾt*) is given to all to listen to the words of wisdom that are going to be spoken.[1] An uncommon Hebrew word is used for 'world' (*chéled*). It not only denotes the physical environment but the whole sphere of transitory life. All classes of society are addressed. The phrase 'low and high' is the translation of an antithetical Hebrew expression (*gam bᵉnê ʾâdâm gam bᵉnê ʾîsh*) that denotes those of low degree contrasted with those of high degree or influence (cf. the use of the same contrast in Ps. 62:9). The promise is that much (or possibly, profound) wisdom[2] and great understanding will be bestowed. The issues of life and death to be addressed are of interest to all.

I will turn my ear to a proverb; with the harp I will expound my riddle (*v. 4*): 'Proverb' and 'riddle' occur here together as they do in Psalm 78:2, Proverbs 1:6, Ezekiel 17:2, and Habakkuk 2:6. They tell of the ways in which wisdom and understanding are going to be conveyed. A 'proverb' could be much longer than the short saying we think of in English, while 'riddle' has a range of usage from the 'riddles' Samson set his Philistine guests (Judg. 14) to the 'hard questions' which the Queen of Sheba asked Solomon (1 Kings 10:1-3). The usage here is nearer the latter in meaning.

2. Transitory Wealth (*vv. 5-12*)

Why should I fear when evil days come, when wicked deceivers surround me – those who trust in their wealth and boast of their great riches? (*vv. 5-6*). The psalmist already knows the answer to his question, and it will be given later on (see v. 15). He is surrounded by evil men who have put their confidence in their wealth, and he wants to set the record straight concerning them, for no amount of money can buy off death. The MT makes the opposition somewhat more pointed by speaking about '*my* wicked deceivers'.[3]

---

[1] For similar calls to 'listen', compare Deuteronomy 32:1; Psalm 50:7; and Micah 1:2.

[2] The promise is that 'wisdoms' (*chokmôt*) will be proclaimed, the use of the plural giving intensification to the singular *chokmâh*. This usage, sometimes called 'the plural of majesty', is covered in *DIHG~S*, p. 19.

[3] The word rendered in the NIV by 'deceivers' (*ʿᵃqêvay*) is problematic. The noun 'heel' (*ʿâqêv*) is well known, but a verb with the same consonants exists and has the meaning 'to deceive'. The word here is probably an adjective from this verb.

No man can redeem the life of another or give to God a ransom for him – the ransom for a life is costly, no payment is ever enough – that he should live on forever and not see decay (*vv. 7-9*). The teaching of these verses is that no one can escape death by paying money. A rich person may live well, and in such a way as to give the impression that he is going to live forever. But there can be no ransom paid to God for him, for such redemption[4] is beyond the ability of men to achieve. Ultimately even the richest person will see decay (lit. 'see the pit'; cf. its use in Ps. 16:10, where it is used in parallelism with 'Sheol', 'the grave').

For all can see that wise men die; the foolish and the senseless alike perish and leave their wealth to others. Their tombs will remain their houses forever, their dwellings for endless generations, though they had named lands after themselves (*vv. 10-11*). The common experience of life is that everyone dies, 'for death is the destiny of every man' (Eccles. 7:2). The reference to 'wise men' and 'foolish' is to the same two groups that Psalm 37 calls 'the righteous' and 'the wicked'. Whatever wealth they have acquired is left to others. The biblical teaching is that we bring nothing into this world and we can take nothing out of it. The real riches consist of 'godliness with contentment', while storing up treasures is achieved by being rich in good deeds and being generous and willing to share (1 Tim. 6:6-7, 17-19). Rich people may build luxurious mansions, trying in this way to perpetuate their memory. Such buildings may last, but they themselves perish, and their eternal home is the grave (Eccles. 12:5).

But man, despite his riches, does not endure; he is like the beasts that perish (*v. 12*). A concluding statement sums up this section of the psalm. Riches cannot bestow eternal life, for man is no different from the animals in this respect. The rich have tried to provide for themselves a lodging place, but they will find no permanent place of abode (the word translated

---

[4] The NIV rendering disguises the fact that the MT speaks of 'redemption' (*pidyôn*), not 'ransom'. The verb 'redeem' (*pâdâh*) has already occurred at the beginning of verse 7, and it appears again in verse 15.

'endure' literally means 'to lodge the night'). The grave will receive both men and animals.

3. Redemption by God (*vv. 13-20*)

The folly of the rich concerning death has been described in the preceding section. Now the teacher goes on to show their folly in life, but he also points to the way in which God can redeem a soul from the grave. **This is the fate of those who trust in themselves, and of their followers, who approve their sayings. Selah** (*v. 13*). Those who have a false confidence,[5] namely in themselves or in their riches, follow a particular way of life (MT, lit. 'their path'). Their followers could either be their descendants or perhaps more likely those who imitate them (Exod. 23:2; 2 Sam. 2:10). They listen to their teachers and adopt their instruction as their own way of life.

Like sheep they are destined for the grave, and death will feed on them. The upright will rule over them in the morning; their forms will decay in the grave, far from their princely mansions (*v. 14*). The Hebrew text of this verse is difficult to translate, as is shown by the variations of it in the English versions, and also by the footnote in the NIV. The proud rich are 'like sheep shipped to Sheol',[6] a translation that attempts to bring out the alliteration in the Hebrew text.[7] They are ready for the slaughter. The grave will swallow them,[8] and the distance between their place of burial and their former mansions will be great. On the other hand, the righteous will come through their suffering and enter a new day. That 'day' is not the morning of the resurrection, but the morning that dawns after the destruction of the ungodly.

---

[5] The MT has 'This is their way, their folly (*kêsel*)'. Elsewhere the word is noted as an evil thing (Eccles. 7:25). To live for this world and what it affords is indeed folly.

[6] The translation is that by Craigie, *Psalms 1-50*, p. 358.

[7] MT *katstso'n lish^{e}'ôl shattû*, with a doubled consonant *ts* being followed by a double *sh*.

[8] The word that the NIV renders as 'decay' (*l^{e}vallôt*) could mean 'for consumption'. This is the interpretation followed by Craigie, *Psalms 1-50*, pp. 356-7, and based on Dahood, *Psalms I: 1–50*, p. 301, and J. C. L. Gibson, *Canaanite Myths and Legends*, pp. 68, 143.

But God will redeem my life from the grave; he will surely take me to himself. Selah (*v. 15*). One man cannot redeem another (see v. 7), but God is able to do so. Resurrection of the body will be God's ultimate redemption of his saints. The use of the verb 'take' (*lâqach*) is important for it is used of the translation of both Enoch (Gen. 5:24) and Elijah (2 Kings 2:5), and here too it seems to be used specifically to denote the way in which God will snatch from the grave. Redemption and bringing into God's own presence are divine works. It is God alone who takes us to glory (Ps. 73:24).

Do not be overawed when a man grows rich, when the splendour of his house increases; for he will take nothing with him when he dies, his splendour will not descend with him (*vv. 16-17*). A word of advice is now offered to all the readers of the psalm. After what has been said already about the position of the rich it is clear that they should not be envied nor feared. Their wealth may be real, but a time comes when they have to leave it behind. Paul expands on this Old Testament teaching in 1 Timothy 6:3-10, noting that 'we brought nothing into the world, and we can take nothing out of it' (v. 7).

Though while he lived he counted himself blessed – and men praise you when you prosper – he will join the generation of his fathers, who will never see the light [of life] (*vv. 18-19*). Two characteristics mark out the unrighteous person. First of all, instead of praising God, he blesses himself. Then, secondly, he enjoys the flattery of other people, who see his prosperity and assess him accordingly. But these experiences will not gain him any lasting benefits, for when he joins the dead there is no prospect of life with God.[9] 'To see the light [of life]' implies resurrection from the dead (cf. Isa. 53:11 and the Servant of the LORD).

A man who has riches without understanding is like the beasts that perish (*v. 20*). The refrain is picked up from verse 12, with the change of 'does not endure' to 'without

[9] At the beginning of verse 19, the verb is *tâwô'*, 'she will go'. If the MT is retained then the feminine form of the verb must have *néfesh*, 'soul', as its antecedent, even though it is rather remote. The other alternative is to follow the LXX and change to the masculine form *yâwô'*, 'he will go.'

understanding'. That change is intentional to stress that riches, when spiritual understanding is absent, make a man no better than the animals that die. The question of verse 5, 'Why should I fear when evil days come?', finds its answer in this verse.

Psalm 50

A psalm of Asaph.

The covenant relationship comes to the fore in this psalm, with it being expressly mentioned in verses 5 and 16. It has strong resemblances to covenant lawsuit passages such as Deuteronomy 32, Isaiah 1, Micah 6, and Jeremiah 2 in which heaven and earth are summoned to listen to God's judgment against his people. It also has strong affinities with Psalm 81, especially in the call to the people to listen, followed by the opening words of the Decalogue (cf. 50:7-8 with 81:8-10). It should also be compared with Psalm 95, where the divine speech is in the first person ('tested *me*', '*I* was angry', '*I* said', '*I* declared'). The psalm may have been written for a ceremony renewing the covenant, such as was carried out every seven years at the Feast of Tabernacles (Deut. 31:10-11). The opening of the psalm, in the form of a theophany, recalls the manner in which God revealed himself at Sinai to his people. The two further sections declare the true meaning of sacrifice (vv. 7-15) and a warning to those who despise the demands of the covenant (vv. 16-23).

This is the first of the psalms that are specifically linked with Asaph, though the other eleven are all in a single block (Pss. 73-83). In 2 Chronicles 29:30 it is noted that King Hezekiah commanded the people 'to praise the Lord with the words of David and of Asaph the seer'. While no group is ever called 'the sons of Asaph' (cf. 'the sons of Korah'), the phrase does occur in the narrative about David's appointment of singers ('some of the sons of Asaph', 'from the sons of Asaph', 1 Chron. 25:1-2). Clearly Asaph was an important figure in the musical history of the tabernacle/temple. Among those who returned from exile were singers who were the descendants of Asaph (Ezra 2:41). He is again linked with David in Nehemiah 12:46 as being part of a line of temple singers.

1. God Comes to Judge (*vv. 1-6*)

The Mighty One, God, the LORD, speaks and summons the earth from the rising of the sun to the place where it sets. From Zion, perfect in beauty, God shines forth (*vv. 1-2*). God is not described by a single title, but by a cluster of them. The words 'the Mighty One' and 'God' seem to draw attention to the position of God as the judge over all, while 'LORD' identifies him as the covenant God of Israel. If the covenant renewal ceremony was carried out at dawn, the significance of the ceremony would be emphasised by the sun's rays striking Zion. He summons the earth, not for judgment, but to witness his accusations against his own people. Because of God's choice of Zion it is regarded as a place of beauty (Ps. 48:1-2), from which the LORD 'shines forth'. This term is used of his shining from Mount Paran (Deut. 33:2) and from between the cherubim (Ps. 80:1). In the Bible God is pictured as dwelling in light (Exod. 13:21-22; Dan. 2:22; 1 Tim. 6:16).

Our God comes and will not be silent; a fire devours before him, and around him a tempest rages (*v. 3*). The description of God's coming is borrowed from the account of the revelation he made of himself at Sinai. God, who is a consuming fire (Deut. 4:24; 9:3), revealed himself by fire at Sinai, where he spoke 'from out of the fire on the mountain' (Deut. 5:4). The people heard his voice 'while the mountain was ablaze with fire' (Deut. 5:22-23). Elijah was later to have a similar revelation of God at Sinai (1 Kings 19:11-12). Theophanies in the Old Testament involved speech as well as a visionary experience. Hence, God's 'coming' is associated with declaration of his will.

He summons the heavens above, and the earth, that he may judge his people: 'Gather to me my consecrated ones, who made a covenant with me by sacrifice' (*vv. 4-5*). The heavens and the earth are summoned to listen to what God has to say to 'his people'. Those who belong to this category are then defined as God's 'consecrated ones' (Hebrew, *chasidîm;* see on Psalm 31:23) and as those who are entering into a covenant by sacrifice. The reference seems to be to the ensuing ceremony which reaffirmed the covenant described in Exodus 24:5-8. The Hebrew text here uses the technical term for making a covenant, 'to cut a covenant' (*kârat berît*), which goes back to the common practice of including some cutting ritual as part of a covenant ceremony. The covenant is declared to be God's covenant (*berîtî,* 'my covenant'), a term expressing the unilateral nature of his covenantal dealings with men.

And the heavens proclaim his righteousness, for God himself is judge. Selah (*v. 6*). The very heavens seem as if they are announcing God's righteousness, as he comes to enter into judgment with his covenant people. What is left indefinite in verse 4 (namely, who is doing the judging) is now clarified. The judge of the people is none other than the God of the covenant himself.

2. The True Sacrifices (*vv. 7-15*)

At this point the change is made to first person singular, as divine speech is addressed to the assembled congregation. **Hear, O my people, and I will speak, O Israel, and I will testify against you: I am God, your God** (*v. 7*). The opening words of the LORD echo the formula that appears frequently in the Book of Deuteronomy (4:1; 6:4; 9:1; 20:3; 27:9), while the words 'I am God, your God' recall the opening words of the Decalogue (Exod. 20:2; Deut. 5:6). God is now ready to provide the evidence against his people. The use of the word 'testify' provides a link with the prophetic ministry of warning the people of their sins (2 Chron. 24:19; Neh. 9:26). Psalm 81:8 is very similar to this verse, though the NIV translation does not make this clear.[1]

[1] When set out in parallel with an alternative translation the similarity becomes apparent:

Psalm 50:7, 'Hear, O my people, ..., O Israel, and I will testify against you.'
Psalm 81:8, 'Hear, O my people, and I will testify against you, O Israel.'

I do not rebuke you for your sacrifices or your burnt offerings, which are ever before me (*v. 8*). There is no intended rejection of sacrifice in itself in the accusation of the Lord. The people were observing the law regarding the offering of sacrifices, and they were constantly coming to the place of sacrifice with the required offerings. What was wrong, as succeeding verses show, was that a wrong spirit motivated them.

I have no need of a bull from your stall or of goats from your pens, for every animal of the forest is mine, and the cattle on a thousand hills. I know every bird in the mountains, and the creatures of the field are mine (*vv. 9-11*). God makes the declaration that he is the creator of all things. Hence, he does not need the small offerings presented to him as sacrifices. All the animals in the world, both wild and domestic, are his possession, so he does not require a few more gifts to supplement his vast empire. The declaration does not say that God will refuse to accept sacrifices. Rather, even if the people do not voluntarily bring one, he will not come and forcefully remove one from their houses (*loʾ ʾeqqach mibbêtᵉkâ*). A young steer was a valuable possession, and would often be kept in a stall forming part of the house. 'Creatures of the field' (*zîz sâday*) is a rare expression, only occurring here and in Psalm 80:13.

If I were hungry I would not tell you, for the world is mine, and all that is in it. Do I eat the flesh of bulls or drink the blood of goats? (*vv. 12-13*). Even within Israel there were false views of God. Some thought that their sacrificial offerings were a form of food for him, as happened in other religions in the Near East (see Deut. 32:38). Here God disabuses them of these ideas, for he is already the owner of the whole world and everything in it (Deut. 10:14; Ps. 24:1). He did not need food of this kind to be provided as his meat and drink.

Sacrifice thank-offerings to God, fulfil your vows to the Most High, and call upon me in the day of trouble; I will deliver you, and you will honour me' (*vv. 14-15*). What was needed was sacrifices offered in a true spirit of thanksgiving. Both 'thank-offerings' and 'vows' were sacrifices in which the worshippers shared in a meal, partaking of what they themselves had brought (Lev. 7:12; 22:29-30). The LORD did not *need* such sacrifices, but they were a means of expressing gratitude to him. A promise is added to the command. In difficult times prayer to God will result in deliverance. He does not need to be bribed by offerings, but will respond readily to the heartfelt cry of his people. Then in turn fresh honour will be given him for his answer.

3. True Obedience to the Law (*vv. 16-23*)
The first part of God's speech was directed against those who were trusting in the formal offering of sacrifices. Now attention is paid to those who, though offering sacrifices, were offending against the standards of God's covenant. **But to the wicked, God says: 'What right have you to recite my laws or take my covenant on your lips? You hate my instruction and cast my words behind you** (*vv. 16-17*). There were those within the covenant community whose life was a lie. They were transgressors, yet outwardly acknowledged their obedience to God's demands. They even recited the covenant regulations, but yet in reality they hated God's discipline (*mûsâr*, NIV 'instruction'). This word 'discipline' in its Old Testament usage suggests the fatherly correction that a son receives (cf. Deut. 11:2-7; Jer. 31:18). The reference to God's 'words' may well be specifically to the Decalogue, which is called 'the Ten Words' in the Hebrew text (Exod. 34:28; Deut. 4:13; 10:4). They were even prepared to reject the core of the covenant. The fact that the transgression was against God himself is stressed by repetition: '*my* statutes, *my* covenant, *my* words.' Paul develops the ideas present here more fully in Romans 2:17-29, where he distinguishes between external observance of the law and internal change of heart. The real Jew is one inwardly (2:29).

When you see a thief, you join with him; you throw in your lot with adulterers. You use your mouth for evil and harness your tongue to deceit. You speak continually against your brother and slander your own mother's son (*vv. 18-20*). The Seventh, Eighth, and Ninth Commandments were openly flouted. Theft and adultery were encouraged,[2] while the sins of the tongue were very evident. The closeness of family relationships did not prevent slander and lying, nor did belonging to a circle of friends. While the NIV translation of the beginning of verse 20 is possible,[3] it is better to take the Hebrew verb 'sit' literally. The imagery, then, is of a circle of friends conversing together with the bonds between them broken by false accusations. While the final word in the verse in the MT (*dofi*) only occurs here in the Old Testament, yet the parallelism in the verse points to a translation like that given in the NIV.[4] The sins of the tongue, as compared with other breaches of the Ten Commandments, take up an important place in the warnings of both the Old Testament and the New Testament (Col. 3:9; James 3:1-12). Just as with physical assault, slander is an attack on the image of God (James 3:9).

These things you have done and I kept silent; you thought I was altogether like you. But I will rebuke you and accuse you to your face (*v. 21*). God's silence was being misunderstood by the people. They were thinking that silence was acquiescence in their sin. This was not the only time in the Old Testament when this took place (see Mal. 2:17 and 3:14-15). One of the greatest mistakes humans can make is to think that God is like themselves. Sinners constantly want to exchange 'the glory of the immortal God for images made to look like mortal man and birds and animals and reptiles' (Rom. 1:23). The earlier assertion that God will not keep silent (*v. 3*) is now both reaffirmed and acted upon, as he rebukes and sets out the case against his people. The verb 'accuse'

---

[2] In the first clause the MT has 'and you were delighted with him' (*vattirets*) while the second clause lacks a verb, 'and with adulterers [is] your portion'. The LXX clearly accepted different vocalisation of the verb, reading it as *vatârâts*, 'and you ran along with him', while it added a verb to the second clause, 'and with adulterers *you set* your portion.' The first change is possible, though it does not alter the meaning to any extent, while the second is probably an attempt to render the phrase into Greek idiom rather than implying that there was an alternative Hebrew text available to the LXX translators.

[3] It is followed by Craigie, *Psalms 1-50*, p. 363, though he recognises that Dahood's rendering, 'you sit speaking,' is quite feasible.

[4] The literal rendering is 'you give fault'.

(*ʿârak*), while basically meaning 'to arrange in order', appears in forensic contexts such as this in the sense of stating one's case in a legal way (Job 13:18; 32:14; Ps. 5:3).

At last God speaks, and he now reproves his erring covenant children. **Consider this, you who forget God, or I will tear you to pieces, with none to rescue: He who sacrifices thank-offerings honours me, and he prepares the way so that I may show him the salvation of God'** (*vv. 22-23*). As many as God loves he rebukes and chastens (Rev. 3:19). Those who forget God and despise his instruction are warned that he will come like a lion and tear them. Amos also uses the analogy of a lion to describe God's activities (Amos 3:8). Saying that there is 'none to rescue' is simply acknowledging that salvation was from God alone. In their usage of this phrase, the psalmists and prophets were probably following on from the words of Deuteronomy 32:39, 'no one delivers from his hand' (cf. in addition to Ps. 50:22, Ps. 71:11 and Isa. 42:22 and 43:13). What God wants is heartfelt worship from his people. The theme of the thanksgiving offerings is picked up again (see verse 14). While other sacrifices could be misunderstood as making God in some way obliged to the offerers, the thank-offerings were a response to grace. This was a way of honouring him, just as God requires of Christian people that they 'continually offer to God a sacrifice of praise – the fruit of lips that confess his name' (Heb. 13:15). As he thus prepares his way aright, he will know indeed that salvation is of God alone.

Psalm 51

To the director of music. A psalm of David. When the prophet Nathan came to him after David had committed adultery with Bathsheba.

This is the second of Luther's 'Pauline Psalms' (see Introduction), which declares the same way of forgiveness proclaimed in the New Testament. Traditionally, this psalm was one of the seven penitential psalms (6, 32, 38, 51, 102, 130, 143), a collection known to Augustine, and mentioned by Cassiodorus (AD *c.* 584). It was often known by its opening word in Latin, *miserere* ('have pity').

The title links it with David, and specifically the incidents concerning his adultery with Bathsheba and his arranging the death of her husband Uriah. This psalm should be read in conjunction with the historical account in 2 Samuel 11:2-12:24. While David received forgiveness from God, he still had to face the consequences of his sin, and this included the death of the child that Bathsheba bore (2 Sam. 12:18). Forgiveness does not free us from responsibility for our actions.

It is a psalm of confession before the LORD and of assurance of his pardon. Redeemed sinners know the reality of God's pardon, and they also share with David in his desire to tell others of the way back to him (see v. 13).

The intensity of David's intercession is marked by the number of imperatives in the text, especially in verses 6-15. The range of requests shows the great variety of different ways that appeal for pardon can take.

The closing verses of this psalm may have been added by a later poet, probably after the fall of Jerusalem in 586 BC, as they imply that the walls of the city have been broken down.[1] If this is so, then these verses form a lament by the community who want the LORD to respond to their need in a way similar to his response to David at his time of great personal need. King and people alike needed God's blessing and could respond with appropriate sacrifices (see vv. 17, 19).

1. A Cry for Mercy (*vv. 1-2*)

David cries for mercy out of the anguish of his heart. **Have mercy on me, O God, according to your unfailing love; according to your great compassion, blot out my transgressions** (*v. 1*). Realising his own great need, he calls for God's gracious act of mercy towards him. This is a prayer that David uses on various other occasions at the beginning of psalms (see Pss. 56, 57, and 86). The basis for his cry is God's unfailing love (Hebrew, *chésed*). This word carries with it the idea of absolute commitment. God had revealed himself to Moses as: 'The LORD, the LORD, the compassionate and gracious God, slow to anger, abounding in love and faithfulness' (Exod. 34:6). He would not go back on that word, and David accordingly pleads for a fresh visitation of mercy for himself. The second part of verse 1 parallels 'great compassion' with 'unfailing love', and 'blot out my transgressions' with 'have mercy'. Because he was conscious of his 'great' sin, he recognises that he needs 'great' compassion. The verb 'blot out' has the idea of wiping a dish clean, or removing something completely.

The next verse repeats the call for mercy but uses other terms: **Wash away all my iniquity and cleanse me from my sin** (*v. 2*). The verb 'wash' is preceded in Hebrew by a form of the verb 'to be many', which some think means that David is praying for repeated cleansings. This goes contrary to the context, which suggests a once-for-all act on God's part, and the verb 'wash' is used elsewhere in the Old Testament for the removal of sin (Isa. 1:16; Jer. 2:22; 4:14). Similarly, the word

---

[1] Cf. Psalm 89:38-51, which appears to be another instance of later words being added to an earlier song. It is clear from the quotations in the historical books that parts of songs were often blended together. See, for example, 1 Chronicles 16:8-36, where sections of Psalms 105, 96, and 107 form the song that David first committed to Asaph and his fellow singers.

'cleanse' is used of a declaration that the priest made over the cleansed leper (Lev. 13:6, 34). Only God can declare the sinner clean.

The cluster of words in these first two verses is remarkable. It contains a rich vocabulary of language relating to sin and forgiveness. To describe his (and our) relationship to God, David uses:

transgression: rebellious actions against authority;
iniquity: what is crooked or bent;
sin: missing the mark;
have mercy: a request that speaks of graciousness beyond expectation;
unfailing love: the term of covenantal commitment;
compassion: the word describing the tenderest love;
blot out: complete removal;
wash away: used of scrubbing clothes and removing all stains;
cleanse: a ritual term for pronouncing someone clean.

2. Confession of Sin (*vv. 3-6*)

David cannot escape from his sin. He says: **For I know my transgressions and my sin is always before me** (*v. 3*; cf. Ps. 32:3, 4). Luther puts this truth in this way: 'My sin plagues me, gives me no rest, no peace; whether I eat or drink, sleep or wake, I am always in terror of God's wrath and judgment.' The psalmist is ready to acknowledge his wayward actions, and he is unable to escape from the consciousness of guilt. For no matter how much he had sinned against others (and specifically against Bathsheba and Uriah), yet the reality of the situation is that his sin was primarily against God.

Against you, you only, have I sinned and done what is evil in your sight (*v. 4a*). This translation brings out well the force of the Hebrew word order here. The primary focus of sin is against God. Though men might have acquitted David, yet he knows that before God he is guilty of adultery and murder. The words that follow, **so that you are proved right when you speak and justified when you judge** (*v. 4b*), have created considerable discussion, because how can God be justified in his speaking? Probably, it is best to think of God being true to his pledged word (see comments on v. 1). He is 'justified' when he hears the cry for mercy and acts in accordance with his covenantal promise. These words are quoted by Paul in Romans 3:4.

David's sin, in this case, is not his first sin, for he has been a sinner from the very beginning. Having looked back to the immediate past, he now focuses on the distant past, even to his birth. As he has owned up to his repeated sins (note the fivefold use of 'my' in vv. 1-3), so he acknowledges the bias in his nature. **Surely** (Hebrew, *hên, behold*) **I was sinful at birth, sinful from the time my mother conceived me** (*v. 5*). He is speaking of the inborn bias that affects all of us by nature. Sin inevitably appears in each new life because it is now part of human nature as a result of Adam's sin ('sin entered the world through one man, and death through sin, and in this way death came to all men', Rom. 5:12). The only one to escape this taint of sin was Jesus (Heb. 4:15), and that was because he was conceived in Mary's womb by the Holy Spirit (Matt. 1:20-21; Luke 1:35-37).[2]

Even as a sinner David knows the standard that God requires. **Surely you desire truth in the inner parts; you teach me wisdom in the inmost place** (*v. 6*). God demands integrity and uprightness, characteristics that David now knew that he lacked. The way of God's wisdom has been forsaken for the way that seems right to a man, but which in the end brings death (Prov. 14:12).

3. Prayer for Forgiveness (*vv. 7-9*)

With deep intensity of heart David prays for cleansing and forgiveness. **Cleanse me with hyssop, and I will be clean; wash me and I will be whiter than snow** (*v. 7*). Hyssop, a common plant, was used at the Passover (Exod. 12:22), and in various procedures carried out by the priests (see Lev. 14:4, 6, 49, 51, 52). Now David asks for God to sprinkle him so that he will become even whiter than snow. This analogy is

---

[2] The *Westminster Shorter Catechism* Q. 16 carefully notes that all mankind descending from Adam 'by ordinary generation' are sinners, thus excluding Jesus.

taken up later in the Old Testament, seemingly in conscious dependence upon this verse. To the sinful people in Isaiah's day, whose hands were full of blood, the LORD says: 'Though your sins are like scarlet, they shall be as white as snow' (Isa. 1:18). In both Psalm 51 and Isaiah 1 it is clear that God's forgiveness can be experienced, provided that true repentance is shown.

To this petition for cleansing David adds: **Let me hear joy and gladness; let the bones you have crushed rejoice** (*v. 8*). Under God's chastening hand, he feels crushed and bruised, and longs for festive joy to be given to him. This is part of God's forgiveness, as his children rejoice in his mercy and love to them. The compound phrase 'joy and gladness' (*sâsôn v^e^simchâh*) occurs thirteen times in the Old Testament,[3] and with the addition of 'gladness' (or another cognate noun such as 'shout of joy', *rinnâh*) it denotes an enthusiastic expression of joy. Isaiah uses the phrase when speaking of great redemptive acts of God (Isa. 35:10; 51:3, 11), while Jeremiah uses it five times (Jer. 7:34; 15:16; 16:9; 25:10; 33:11). The expression, 'crushed bones', represents the ultimate in physical or psychological distress.[4]

Hide your face from my sins and blot out all my iniquity (*v. 9*). At other times in the Old Testament the people cry out to God because he has hidden his face from them (see e.g. Pss. 10:1; 44:24; 88:14; 104:29; Isa. 8:17). Here David desires that God will not look on his sin, covering his eyes, as it were, so that he would not see his evil deeds. The thought of verse 1 ('blot out my transgressions') reappears with the appeal to 'blot out' completely his iniquities. As the following verses show, David recognised that what was needed was a new creative act by God.

---

[3] Of these occurrences all but two of them (Esther 8:16-17: 'gladness and joy') have the order of the words as here. However, the alteration of order with fixed pairs (see Glossary) is not uncommon, without any discernible difference in meaning.

[4] The verbal form *dikkîtâ* in this verse and the participle *nidkeh* in verse 17 come from the root *d-k-h*, but it is unsure whether this is a discrete verbal root or merely a by-form of the root *d-k-'*. The best discussion on this question is in *TDOT*, III, pp. 195-98.

4. A Call for a Renewed Heart (*vv. 10-12*)

Create in me a pure heart, O God, and renew a steadfast spirit within me (v. *10*). The Hebrew verb used for 'create' (*bârâ'*) is exclusively employed in the Old Testament with God as the subject, and here it is paralleled with 'renew'. It is also linked with the word 'steadfast', which comes from a Hebrew word that is often associated with God's creative activity (Ps. 24:2: 'established it upon the waters'; Isa. 45:18). Purification from sin is a work of God alone.

> Not the labours of my hands
> Can fulfil thy laws demands;
> Could my zeal no respite know,
> Could my tears for ever flow,
> All for sin could not atone;
> Thou must save and thou alone.
> (Augustus Toplady, 1740-1778)

When confronted with our sin, there is a feeling that we are to be banished from God's presence because of it. Hence David prays: **Do not cast me from your presence or take your Holy Spirit from me. Restore to me the joy of your salvation and grant me a willing spirit, to sustain me** (*vv. 11-12*). The Holy Spirit was operative in the Old Testament period, though a new phase of the Spirit's ministry began with the death and resurrection of Jesus and the Day of Pentecost. Old Testament believers had the same indwelling Spirit as Christians today, and David pleads that he will not experience the withdrawal of that Spirit. The presence of sin also causes absence of joy, because peace has gone. With the coming of forgiveness there can be a restoration of the joy of salvation. In addition to 'a pure heart' and 'the Holy Spirit' the psalmist also wants 'a willing spirit'. This term carries echoes of freewill offerings such as the voluntary sacrifices that were made, not out of command but as an act of religious devotion.[5]

---

[5] The verb *nâdav* is used to express uncompelled willingness to worship or sacrifice to God. The associated noun *n^edâvâh* describes acts that are free. What is typical of the person who is voluntarily sacrificing or worshipping is denoted by the term used here in Psalm 51:12, *n^edîvâh*.

4. A Thankful Heart (*vv. 13-17*)
The response of a purified sinner is to seek to make known the good news of God's grace, just as Isaiah later offered himself so willingly as the Lord's messenger (Isa. 6:8). The psalmist had a similar experience. **Then I will teach transgressors your ways, and sinners will turn back to you. Save me from bloodguilt, O God, the God who saves me** (*vv. 13-14a*). An experience of redeeming grace creates an urge to tell others of the Lord's forgiveness and a desire to teach them his ways. The ultimate aim is to see other sinners coming back to God in repentance and faith. The verb 'turn back' (Hebrew, *shûv*) is often used of repentance and of a return to God (Isa. 44:22; Hos. 6:1). David has just asked that God will restore to him the joy of salvation (*shûv* Hi.) and now uses the same verb of his action towards other sinners (*shûv* Qal). The one to whom joy has been restored will himself be the means of restoring others to God. David's sin weighs heavily upon him, and he seems to fear especially the result of his murder of Uriah. The word 'bloodguilt' is literally 'bloods', and by comparison with Genesis 4:10 it denotes bloodshed, murder. Rather than thinking of protection of David from vengeance from Uriah's family, it is preferable to see it as a prayer for deliverance from the guilt of his crime, by the God who saves him. In this way the ideas fit in best with the whole context in the psalm.

A forgiven sinner also wants to praise God for what he has done. **And my tongue will sing of your righteousness. O Lord, open my lips, and my mouth will declare your praise** (*vv. 14b-15*). Here David shows the spirit of thanksgiving that filled him after God heard his cry. The word of pardon came through the prophet Nathan who said to him: 'The Lord has taken away your sin' (2 Sam. 12:13b). His desire is that God will open his lips, and that his mouth will be filled with God's righteousness and praise. This commitment to praise is one of the firstfruits of salvation. Under the Mosaic law various sacrifices were appointed, but there was none for premeditated murder. David's action came under the category of sins of a high hand (see Num. 15:30), for he had acted defiantly and in rebellion against God's law.[6]

But even if a sacrifice could be offered, David rightly recognises that the spirit in which it is offered is primarily important. The Old Testament sacrificial system was never meant to operate without consideration of the heart of the offerer. **You do not delight in sacrifice, or I would bring it; you do not take pleasure in burnt offerings. The sacrifices of God are** (or NIV margin, **My sacrifice, O God, is ...**) **a broken spirit; a broken and contrite heart, O God, you will not despise** (*vv. 16-17*). Mere formal ceremony could never result in forgiveness. Rather, there had to be a heart touched by the Holy Spirit, the one who convicts of sin (John 16:8). The NIV margin represents a very slight change in vocalisation of the MT (*zivkî* instead of *zivchê*), but, as no manuscript support is available, it is best retain the MT and hence the translation 'the sacrifices of'. Brokenness in this case is a sign of deep distress of heart over sin. The word 'contrite' is from the same verb used in verse 8, '*crushed* bones', and it would be best to use the word 'crushed' here as well. 'Contrite' is almost exclusively a theological term, whereas the Hebrew verb in question corresponds exactly to both literal and figurative usages of 'crushed'.

5. Prayer for Zion (*vv. 18-19*)

If these words are those of David, he could be acknowledging that his sin has serious consequences for the whole nation, using concrete illustrations ('Zion', 'walls of Jerusalem') to depict spiritual realities. However, it is preferable to view them as words added during the period between the fall of Jerusalem in 586 BC and the commencement of the rebuilding in 536 BC. The community wants the LORD to respond to their need, just as he did when David cried to him out of his grief of heart. **In your good pleasure make Zion prosper; build up the walls of Jerusalem. Then there will be righteous**

[6] An excellent summary of the law relating to 'a high hand' is given by R. K. Harrison, *Numbers*, Wycliffe Bible Commentary (Chicago: Moody Press, 1990), p. 227.

sacrifices, whole burnt offerings to delight you; then bulls will be offered on your altar (*vv. 18-19*). These words show that the preceding reference to sacrifices was not to disparage the whole sacrificial system as such. God had set his choice upon Jerusalem, and the prayer is that God's blessing on, and protection of, his people will continue. Then the people will be able to continue with their sacrifices, and bring offerings with which God will be well pleased. When the rebuilding of the walls of Jerusalem was completed, the fulfillment of this prayer took place: 'And on that day they offered great sacrifices, rejoicing because God had given them great joy. The women and the children also rejoiced. The sound of rejoicing in Jerusalem could be heard far away' (Neh. 12:43).

Psalm 52

For the director of music. A maskil of David. When Doeg the Edomite had gone to Saul and told him: 'David has gone to the house of Ahimelech.'

Psalms 51 and 52, though placed in adjoining positions, are in marked contrast with one another. Psalm 51 deals with David's deep need for God's forgiveness, whereas Psalm 52 contains an extended description of David's enemies, with curses having divine authority being expressed against them. In this respect the psalmist is acting very similarly to the prophets who also proclaimed divine punishment on the ungodly. Though not of the same type as Psalm 49 (a wisdom psalm), yet there are many similarities between the two.

This is one of eight psalms (Pss. 7, 34, 52, 54, 56, 57, 59, 142) whose titles link them with the period in which David was pursued by Saul. The historical note in this title alludes to the incident in David's life when Doeg betrayed the priests who had helped David. When the king's officials were not prepared to kill the priests, Doeg carried out the executions (1 Sam. 22:6-18). Though the title mentions Doeg, it does not necessarily mean that Doeg is the subject of the psalm. It makes better sense to understand it as referring to Saul. The description of the enemy throughout does not match with what is known about Doeg, the servant, but with Saul, 'the mighty man'.[1] While complaining about his enemy at the

---

[1] Older commentators took this position. See, for example, E. W. Hengstenberg, *Psalms*, II, pp. 211-12; J. A. Alexander, *The Psalms Translated and Explained*, p. 236. In more recent times it has been common to reject the superscription as being inaccurate. However, H. C. Leupold, *Exposition of the Psalms*, pp. 409-11, accepts that Saul is in view, a view shared with J. Barton Payne, *TWOT*, 1, p. 210.

beginning of the psalm, by the end the psalmist is expressing confident trust in God.

1. A Complaint against the Evildoer (*vv. 1-4*)

Why do you boast of evil, you mighty man? Why do you boast all day long, you who are a disgrace in the eyes of God? (*v. 1*). It is very unusual to find a psalm that does not begin by addressing God, but this one is first directed to an evil man. He is described as a 'mighty man' or 'noble', and because 'nobles' had the privilege of bearing arms for the king (cf. Ruth 2:1; 1 Sam. 9:1) the term then became applied to warriors or soldiers. It is possible that the word comes near to meaning 'tyrant',[2] though he uses words, not the sword, as his weapon. The last part of the verse is difficult and the NIV translation follows the LXX. The Hebrew text says: 'covenant love (*chésed*) of God all the day', which makes sense in the context and was supported by older commentators.[3] It also gives a striking contrast between the animosity of the mighty man and the abiding love of the LORD. Another possibility is to follow the Syriac version and take this as the Hebrew word *châsîd*, which denotes a loyal covenant servant. It would then be a description of the psalmist: 'Why do you boast all day long against God's loyal servant?'[4]

Your tongue plots destruction; it is like a sharpened razor, you who practise deceit (*v. 2*). The warrior is not described by exploits in battle, but by his ability to use his tongue as his weapon to cause harm. The comparison of the tongue with a sharp razor is not common, whereas linking it with 'deceit' (*r*[e]*miyyâh*) and 'falsehood' (*shéqer*) is (note the use of 'deceit' again in v. 4, and 'falsehood' in v. 5). The phrase, who 'practises deceit', is literally 'one who does deceit' and a good modern English equivalent is 'con-man'.[5] The exact phrase appears again in Psalm 101:7,

---

[2] The cognate word in Arabic has this meaning.

[3] For example, J. A. Alexander, *The Psalms Translated and Explained*, p. 236; F. Delitzsch, *Psalms*, II, pp. 143-44.

[4] For more details and other possibilities, see M. Tate, *Psalms 51-100*, p. 33.

[5] This is the translation of M. Tate, ibid., p. 32. For other synonymous phrases involving the tongue, see Eugene H. Merrill, *NIDOTTE*, 2, p. 821.

while the expression 'a deceitful tongue' occurs twice in Psalm 120, in verses 2 and 3.

You love evil rather than good, falsehood rather than speaking the truth. ***Selah*** (*v.* 3). It adds to the accusation when the psalmist speaks directly to the tongue itself (cf. a similar usage in Ps. 120:2). Deceit and destruction that are the hallmarks of the enemy proceed from a heart that is set on evil ways. The preference for evil is an ingrained characteristic, and thus falsehood takes the place of righteousness (NIV 'truth'). 'Selah' occurs at the end of this verse and also of verse 7. These occurrences conform to a common pattern of dividing psalms into three sections by the use of the Hebrew word *sélâh,* but still do not explain whether it is a musical term or serves some other function (see the comments on 3:3).

You love every harmful word, O you deceitful tongue! (*v. 4*). The repetition of 'you love' at the beginning of two consecutive verses serves to reinforce the directness of the accusations. The words that bring destruction are what he treasures. A 'harmful word' (*bâla*ʿ) is one that devours or swallows (cf. Jer. 51:44, which has the only other instance of this word in the Old Testament).

2. God's Judgment Announced (*v. 5*)

Surely God will bring you down to everlasting ruin: He will snatch you up and tear you from your tent; he will uproot you from the land of the living. ***Selah*** (*v. 5*). The opening word could also be rendered 'therefore', introducing the concept of judgment on those who lead ungodly lives.[6] The contrast is presented of God's righteous judgment, and the words used to describe it suggest the suddenness with which it comes: 'snatch', 'tear', 'uproot'. 'Everlasting ruin' is a rather free rendering of the MT (*lânétsach*), which only indicates everlastingness. A suitable translation is by a phrase like 'for ever', or, if taken as a superlative, a word such as 'utterly' (cf. NLT, 'But God will strike you down once and for all'). The

---

[6] M. Tate, *Psalms 51-100*, pp. 32, 34, correctly notes this usage of the Hebrew word *gam*. See also the range of meanings listed in *DCH*, II, p. 357, including 'therefore'.

reference to the 'tent' does not seem to be to the tabernacle, but rather to the individual dwelling of the unrighteous person. To be taken from the land of the living is synonymous with death (cf. the same phrase used of the Servant of the Lord in Isa. 53:8). Again *Selah* marks the conclusion of another section of the psalm (see comment on verse 3).

3. The Blessing of the Righteous (*vv. 6-9*)

The righteous will see and fear; they will laugh at him, saying, 'Here now is the man who did not make God his stronghold but trusted in his great wealth and grew strong by destroying others!' (*vv. 6-7*). When the righteous see the judgment of God they stand in awe, for in this way God has displayed his righteous wrath. They also understand that this judgment is meant to be an encouragement to them, and so they rejoice in it. Their laughter is not so much derision as joyful recognition of the just nature of God's actions. They point, in effect, to the unrighteous person, 'See there ...' (Hebrew lit. 'behold the man'). If a man fails to make God his refuge, and trusts in his own riches, isn't it right then if he is uprooted? The pride of the unrighteous is displayed in his boasting and his arrogant attacks on others, seeking to destroy them.[7]

But I am like an olive tree flourishing in the house of God; I trust in God's unfailing love for ever and ever (*v. 8*). The same sort of contrast is drawn between the righteous and the wicked as is made in Psalm 1. Whereas the wicked are like trees that will be uprooted, the righteous are like a flourishing olive tree. The comparison with an olive tree is probably because of its long life and its productive nature. The psalmist expresses the constancy of his trust in God's covenantal love,

[7] The MT is difficult in verse 7d, and this explains some variation in English versions (cf. ESV: 'and sought refuge in his own destruction'). The first problem is the verb *yā̂ʿoz*, which could be either from the verb *ʿ-z-z*, 'be strong', or from *ʿûz*, 'to take refuge'. As vocalised, it is the former verb, and the meaning fits the context. The second problem is that the final word could be 'in his desire', but as the word 'destruction' has already occurred in verse 2, it seems best to retain it here. An emendation, followed by the RSV translators ('in his wealth'), is unnecessary.

that trust being in marked contrast to the false trust of the unrighteous in his own wealth (v. 7).[8]

I will praise you forever for what you have done; in your name I will hope, for your name is good. I will praise you in the presence of your saints (*v. 9*). God's actions on behalf of his people call forth praise, and this also involves offering praise in an assembly of God's people. His goodness has been displayed to the psalmist who now wants to acknowledge that fact. With the acknowledgment comes a further expression of confident trust in God's character ('your name'), which has been shown to be both good and loving. Much of the language of this verse was clearly part of the common formulae used in praising God for past actions ('what you have done', cf. Ps. 22:31, 'that he has done [it]'; for 'I will wait for your name, for it is good', cf. Pss. 54:6; 100:5; 106:1; 107:1; 135:3; and 136:1).

[8] The same verb (*bâtach*) is used in both verses.

Psalm 53

For the director of music. According to mahalath.
A maskil of David.

For comments on the comparison between this psalm and Psalm 14, see commentary on Psalm 14. Repetition of the words from other psalms is a regular feature in the Psalter. Thus Psalm 70 is virtually the same as Psalm 40:13-17, while Psalm 108 repeats the words of Psalm 57:7-11 and Psalm 60:5-12. When earlier words are taken up and used again, there is often some variation in the text to accord with the new situation in which it is used. This is definitely so in this case.

Psalm 53 has a longer title than Psalm 14, including two technical terms, *mâchᵃlat* and *maskîl*. The former occurs elsewhere only in the title of Psalm 88, where it may mean 'sickness', 'suffering', but such a meaning is not particularly appropriate for this psalm.[1] It has also been suggested that it may denote a mournful tune of that name, which certainly fits fairly well in both settings. *Maskîl* is probably a skilfully constructed song or tune, though here the presence of the word in verse 2 may have prompted its use in the title.

In the early part of the psalm, in addition to the alteration of the divine name ('God' replaces 'LORD'), 'iniquity' replaces 'deeds' in verse 1. The expression, 'doing abominable iniquity', strengthens the condemnation and also points further to the narrative in Genesis 6:5-12 forming the background for the description here (see comment on Ps. 14:1-2). The NIV appears to regard the changed term as meaning 'ways'. Then in

---

[1] The suggestion that *mâchᵃlat* could mean 'sickness' stems largely from its similarity to the word *machᵃlâh* that means 'sickness' or 'disease'. However, no proof exists that *mâchᵃlat* comes from the root *ch-l-h*.

verse 3 there is a slight change concerning 'all', and in place of 'turned aside' in Psalm 14:3, the verb is 'turned back' (Hebrew *sûg* in place of *sûr*). Sinful man turns away from God and the only restorative for apostates, including Israel, is the grace and power of God (see the use of *sûg* in Ps. 80:17-18).

The more important change is in connection with verses 5-6 in Psalm 14: **There they are overwhelmed with dread, for God is present in the company of the righteous. You evildoers frustrate the plans of the poor, but the LORD is their refuge.** In place of that, Psalm 53:5 has: **There they were, overwhelmed with dread, where there was nothing to dread. God scattered the bones of those who attacked you; you put them to shame, for God despised them.** This verse seems to have been altered to this form to make specific reference to a great historical occasion. The most probable one would have been the destruction of Sennacherib's army by the angel of the LORD (2 Kings 19:35; Isa. 37:36). The meaning would be that God's people were greatly afraid, when there was nothing to fear. The bones of the Assyrian army were scattered on the field, and God had shown how he despised those who were classed with the fools and those who did not know him. For comment on the other verses, see the notes on Psalm 14.

Psalm 54

For the director of music. With stringed instruments. A maskil of David. When the Ziphites had gone to Saul and said, 'Is not David hiding among us?'

The title of this psalm is similar to that of Psalm 52, in that an incident from David's life, when fleeing from Saul, forms its basis (cf. 1 Sam. 23:19; 26:1), though coupled with directions for its use in the tabernacle/temple. The Ziphites seemed to have antipathy to David, perhaps because they did not want a roving band in their territory, led by such a gifted leader. They wanted to be rid of David, and went twice to Saul seeking action against him (1 Sam. 23:19-24; 26:1-5). However, the contents of the psalm do not explain how it ties in with that incident. Its scope is sufficiently wide to allow any persecuted believer to use it as a request for divine intervention.

1. Petition for Deliverance (*vv. 1-3*)

Save me, O God, by your name; vindicate me by your might (*v. 1*). The psalm starts with a reference to God's name, and it ends with praise of it (v. 6). The psalmist calls to God because he knows God's character, and therefore he can confidently cry for help. He seeks deliverance from his present distress, which went beyond the slanderous attacks being made on him. Murder was also part of the scheme (v. 3). The call is to his Saviour and to his Judge. 'Vindicate' (*dîn*) has practically the same meaning as 'judge' (*shâfat*), though it is more common in the poetical books and may well be the more archaic term.[1] It also is used practically exclusively of divine activity, with its occurrence in Ezra 7:25 being the only time it is used of human judges.

[1] This is the view of R. D. Culver in *TWOT*, 1, p. 188, who provides a concise summary of the usage of *dîn*.

Hear my prayer, O God; listen to the words of my mouth (*v.* 2). The opening words of the verse seem to have been a standard way of requesting help: 'Hear my prayer, listen to ...' (Pss. 4:1; 84:8; 143:1). At times, customary expressions take on a new urgency, when circumstances drive us to seek God's immediate help. This prayer is a request for God to hear and answer, with no great difference between the verbs 'hear' (*shâma*ʿ) and 'listen' (*ʾâzan* Hi.), though the latter is predominantly a poetic word.

Strangers are attacking me; ruthless men seek my life – men without regard for God. ***Selah*** (*v.* 3). The word 'strangers' (*zârîm*) is replaced by the word 'proud' (*zêdîm*) in many Hebrew manuscripts and in the Targum. These two words are very similar and the letters *dálet* and *rêsh* can be confused, though in the older form of the Hebrew script they are quite distinct. When this verse reappears in Psalm 86:14 the word is certainly 'proud, arrogant'. These facts explain the variation in some English translations here (cf. NEB 'insolent men'), and though 'proud' fits the context well, the manuscript evidence is not strong enough to compel an emendation here. These violent men are coming against the psalmist with murderous intent. They do not give God the pre-eminence in their lives, and consequently they do not live by his commands (Ps. 119:30). Both terms, 'strangers' and 'violent men', could have been applied to Saul and his men, while the Ziphites could be designated as 'strangers' because of their unneighbourly behaviour.

2. Confidence in God (*vv.* 4-5)

Surely God is my help; the Lord is the one who sustains me. Let evil recoil on those who slander me; in your faithfulness destroy them (*vv.* 4-5). The psalmist turns to the one source of assistance. He certainly knows that the Lord is his only helper.[2] The wish for judgment to come

---

[2] The statement is introduced, as the one in Psalm 52:7, with the word *hinnêh*. While this word normally means 'behold', 'when introducing asseveration or strong affirmation' it can be translated by 'indeed' or 'surely'. See *DCH*, 2, p. 574. An excellent discussion on *hinnêh* can be found in T. O. Lambdin, *Introduction to Biblical Hebrew* (New York: Charles Scribner, 1971), pp. 169-70. A discussion on the role this particle plays in emphasis is in T. Muraoka, *Emphatic Words and Structures in Biblical Hebrew* (Leiden: E. J. Brill, 1985), pp. 137-40.

upon his slanderers has to be understood in the light of the broader question of cursing in the Psalms (see section on the Imprecatory Psalms in the Introduction). Because the slanderers are indeed opponents of God himself, the psalmist prays for their destruction.[3] He knows that God acts in accordance with his faithfulness, and protection to his people is but a tangible expression of it.

3. Spontaneous Thanksgiving (*vv. 6-7*)

I will sacrifice a freewill offering to you; I will praise your name, O LORD, for it is good. For he has delivered me from all my troubles, and my eyes have looked in triumph on my foes (*vv. 5-6*). The offer is made of a voluntary sacrifice. Such a sacrifice could be made at any time by a thankful Israelite (see Lev. 22:18-30; Num. 15:1-10). Praise is to be given to God because he has shown his goodness, expressed in a standard formula (see comment on Ps. 52:9). The psalmist anticipates the LORD's deliverance from all his troubles, and he acquiesces in God's judgment. The final clause has nothing in the MT corresponding to 'in triumph', which is added to many English translations. Without this addition the verse indicates that the psalmist can look on his enemies without any fear or alarm; for he knows that he is protected by God's power.

---

[3] The consonants in the MT for 'let recoil' point to a Qal form of the verb 'to return' (*shûv*), vocalised either as *yâshûv* ('it will return') or *yâshov* ('let it return'), though the Jewish Massoretes vocalised it as *yâshîv* (Hi.).

Psalm 55

For the director of music. With stringed instruments.
A maskil of David.

Older Jewish interpreters linked this psalm with the betrayal of David by his counsellor Ahithophel (2 Sam. 16:15-23; 1 Chron. 27:33). Modern writers have often drawn a comparison between the experience of the psalmist and that of the prophet Jeremiah. He too wished to be far off in a desert (vv. 6-7, cf. Jer. 9:2), he suffered at the hands of his own family (Jer. 12:6), and a fellow priest, Pashur, had him beaten and placed in stocks (Jer. 20:1-2). There is an ancient tradition in the Latin church that the psalmist's experience points to the betrayal of Jesus by Judas.

This is a psalm of complaint, as the writer speaks about the terrors that have come to him (v. 5). He also is suffering from a severe reversal of friendship with one who was previously his close companion (vv. 20-21). In all these experiences, though, he learns how to cast his burden on the LORD (v. 22).

Certainly our Lord's betrayal gives us the highest example of the pattern of suffering described here by the psalmist. It is of great encouragement to us that because Jesus 'suffered when he was tempted, he is able to help those who are being tempted' (Heb. 2:18).

1. A Call for Help (*vv. 1-3*)

The psalm opens with a despairing cry. **Listen to my prayer, O God, do not ignore my plea; hear me and answer me** (*v. 1*). From his distress the psalmist appeals for help. His request, that God should not ignore his plea, recalls the passage in Deuteronomy 22:1-4 where the same verb is used (*ʿâlam*). When a person saw a neighbour's ox or sheep in trouble, they were not to ignore it. Here the psalmist feels as if he is being ignored by God, as if he is unwilling to help. The parallel phrases take the request a stage further, for he wants God not merely to hear but to respond.

My thoughts trouble me and I am distraught at the voice of the enemy, at the stares of the wicked; for they bring down suffering upon me and revile me in their anger (*vv.* 2-3). He not only has trouble from outside himself, but his own thoughts cause him distress. The MT is difficult because three of the phrases involve problematic words, though the NIV captures the general meaning.[1] The psalmist is humiliated, and the sound of the approaching enemy overwhelms him. That enemy is not identified, except by the description of being 'wicked'. What the wicked do to him is the result of hatred and it is intended to cause him distress. This is aggravated by the fact that the wicked bring verbal accusations against him. They act as court adversaries.[2]

2. Anguish of Heart (*vv.* 4-8)

A succession of words descriptive of the deep trouble of his heart flow from the psalmist's mouth. **My heart is in anguish within me; the terrors of death assail me. Fear and trembling have beset me; horror has overwhelmed me** (*vv.* 4-5). He is under intolerable strain as he faces the attacks of his enemy. He even compares himself to a woman in childbirth (NIV 'in anguish'). The fear he has is that death is near at hand, and the

---

[1] The problems of translation and interpretation here are well set out by Marvin Tate, *Psalms 51–100*, p. 51. NIV 'my thoughts' (*sîchî*) is probably a little weak, as this noun generally has the connotation of a spoken complaint. 'Trouble' represents a verbal form *'ârîd*, but it could be derived from several different roots. The LXX rendering *elupêthên*, 'to give pain to someone', is helpful and supports the NIV translation. 'Distraught' renders a verb that is cohortative 1 sing. in form, though again the root is uncertain. However, the LXX helps by using the verb *tarassô*, pass. 'to be disturbed'. This verb is descriptive 'of mental and spiritual agitation and confusion': W. F. Arndt and F. W. Gingrich, *A Greek-Lexicon of the New Testament* (Chicago: University of Chicago Press,1957), p. 813. The word *'âqâh* (NIV 'stares') is a *hapax legomenon*, and the meaning may possibly be from a Semitic root meaning 'to apply pressure'.

[2] The verb here (*sâtan*) is the root from which the noun *sâtân*, 'accuser', comes.

great anxiety he is experiencing produces physical symptoms of trembling and shuddering.[3]

I said, 'Oh, that I had the wings of a dove! I would fly away and be at rest – I would flee far away and stay in the desert. ***Selah.*** **I would hurry to my place of shelter, far from the tempest and storm'** (*vv. 6-8*). Another way of describing his despair is to wish that he was far off in some desert location.[4] He wants to fly like a dove and find a safe dwelling place (NIV 'be at rest'). Some additional word is needed in the opening of verse 7 as the MT has *hinnêh.* NASB has the more traditional 'behold', while the ESV has 'yes, I would flee away'. Lodging in the desert[5] would mean that there would be escape from his persecutors as he would find a hiding place there, while 'place of shelter' or 'haven' is one of the synonyms for 'refuge'.[6] Imagery such as that employed here may well reflect military campaigns in the rocky hills of Judah. Jeremiah uses the same imagery of a place in the desert (Jer. 9:2) and of the dove finding a safe nest (Jer. 48:28). 'Tempest and storm' tell of the reality of his present distress.

3. A Lament over Betrayal (*vv. 9-15*)

The psalmist lodges his complaint with God. **Confuse the wicked, O Lord, confound their speech, for I see violence and strife in the city** (*v. 9*). 'Confuse' is literally 'swallow', and it is used to ask for destruction of the oppressors. The idea of confounding the speech is probably intended to recall what

[3] NIV 'horror' is the translation of a rare word only occurring three times in addition to this verse (Isa. 21:4; Job 7:18. 21:6). Etymology and context suggest a translation such as 'shuddering'. See M. Dahood, 'Hebrew-Ugaritic Lexicography VIII', *Biblica* 51 (1970), pp. 397-98.

[4] The wish is expressed in a common Hebrew form, 'Who will give to me ...' (*mî yittên lî*). Other good examples in the Psalms are found in 14:7 and 53:7. For discussion on this idiom see *DIHG~S*, pp. 185-86, and R. J. Williams, *Hebrew Syntax: An Outline*, 2nd ed. (Toronto: University of Toronto Press, 1984), pp. 21, 91-92.

[5] 'Lodge' represents the Hebrew verb *lîn* which usually means 'to spend the night', but it does seem to have a wider connotation, and so NIV 'stay' is acceptable (cf. the use of this verb in Ruth 1:16 and Prov. 15:31). Marvin Tate, *Psalms 51-100*, p. 52, suggests the translation 'bivouac in the wilderness'.

[6] This word, *miflât*, only occurs here, but the verb from which it comes (*pâlat*, 'escape') is quite frequent.

happened at Babel, when God thwarted the sinful plans of men by confusing their language (Gen. 11:1-9). There is no way of identifying the city, as the Hebrew word (*ʿir*) denotes a settlement with fortifications, irrespective of its size. It is a place where the psalmist had experienced violence and strife.

Day and night they prowl about on its walls; malice and abuse are within it. Destructive forces are at work in the city; threats and lies never leave its streets (*vv. 10-11*). His expressions depict both the character of the city, and the constancy with which the forces of evil show themselves in it. The MT does not identify the subject of the verb 'prowl' (lit. 'go around'). It could be the evildoers, or else, with an ironic twist, 'malice' and 'abuse' are the watchmen on the walls. They are the appointed 'protectors'! 'Abuse' (Hebrew *tok*) is a rare word only occurring four times (in addition to this verse, Pss. 10:7; 72:14; and Prov. 29:13). In this context it is descriptive of a violent, strife-torn city, and since the other instances link it with oppression of the poor, it probably also connotes exploitation of the weak. The city's market area (NIV 'streets') is no longer a place for peaceful trading but distinguished by deceitful practices and danger.

If an enemy were insulting me, I could endure it; if a foe were raising himself against me, I could hide from him. But it is you, a man like myself, my companion, my close friend, with whom I once enjoyed sweet fellowship as we walked with the throng at the house of God (*vv. 12-14*). The opening clauses of verse 12 have problems. The NIV follows the LXX that alters the MT, 'For it is not an enemy that insults me', by a change of one word (MT *loʾ*, 'not', changed to *lû, 'if'*), 'For if an enemy ...' This is not sufficient evidence to warrant emending the MT, and a translation such as, 'For it is not an enemy who taunts me – I could bear [that]', makes good sense.[7] If the opponent was already an enemy, the psalmist could deal with the situation. However, the person is close to him, someone of like mind, though we are not provided

[7] This is the translation by Marvin Tate, *Psalms 51-100*, pp. 50, 52.

with enough information to enable identification of David's friend. Within his own close circle of friends, one proved to be a traitor, and that makes the pain of the incident all the more intense. A friend of equal rank with himself, and with whom he had been closely associated in worship or other festive occasions, had turned against him.[8] It is not 'an enemy' or 'a foe' who was insulting him, but one of his own companions. The tragedy of David's words here is that they apply to his own treachery against Uriah, who is reckoned among David's closest associates (2 Sam. 23:39). In applying the truth of God to others, we must also apply it relentlessly to our own lives.

Let death take my enemies by surprise; let them go down alive to the grave, for evil finds lodging among them (*v. 15*). David asks for God's sudden judgment to come on his enemies.[9] It is not just the one former friend who is spoken about, but a group of enemies ('let them ...'). A sudden shift is made from the singular subject in verses 12-14 to the plural in verse 15. This is a typical occurrence in imprecatory psalms. The reference to going down alive into the grave seems to be an allusion to the incident concerning Korah, Dathan, and Abiram (Num. 16:31-40). Just as those who had treated the LORD with contempt in Moses' day were destroyed, so David wants his enemies (who were also God's enemies) to have a similar fate. The final clause is rendered very freely in the NIV, though a more literal translation such as that in the NASB may

---

[8] I am taking the Hebrew word *sôd* to mean the talk between a group, possibly a group of elders at the gate of the city, or a group on a special worship occasion. It is clearly a word with various nuances, as its twenty-one uses in the MT require twelve different words in the LXX translation. See *TDOT*, II, p. 147.

[9] The opening clause is difficult, though not impossible. The MT has 'Desolations [be] on them' (*yassîmâvet ʿâlêmô*). The Q[e]re reading is *yshy mut*, which is followed by ASV, RSV, NIV, ESV, and other translations ('Let death ...'). However, this presumes that the verb in the Q[e]re form was a defective writing of *yashîʾ* with a final *alef*. I think it is better to retain the MT without emendation. It makes good sense, for, as J. E. Hartley wrote, 'there is no place more desolate than Sheol' (*TWOT*, I, p. 414). A fuller discussion of the suggested emendations is given in Marvin Tate, *Psalms 51-100*, p. 53.

be a better rendering, 'For evil is in their dwelling, in their midst'.[10]

4. Justice with God (*vv. 16-21*)

But I call to God, and the LORD saves me. Evening, morning, and noon I cry out in distress, and he hears my voice (*vv. 16-17*). As is typical in psalms of complaint, David tells of his approach to God in prayer, and his believing trust in him. 'Evening, morning, and noon' are probably not meant to be taken as the only times in the day when he prayed. Rather, these expressions speak of the constancy of his requests to God. His actions stand in sharp contrast to his former friend, this being marked out in the Hebrew text by an emphatic 'And you' at the start of verse 13, and an emphatic 'I' at the commencement of verse 16. He is assured that God both listens to his plea and acts upon it.

He ransoms me unharmed from the battle waged against me, even though many oppose me (*v. 18*). The confidence the psalmist has is that God is his deliverer. 'Ransom' is used here in this general sense of deliverance from trouble. God is able to bring his people into a peaceful situation (NIV 'unharmed'), even when the opponents are so many and their attacks so hostile. The word used for 'battle' (*qerâv*) is a rare poetic word denoting a hostile approach. Though the verbal form 'ransoms' (*pâdâh*) should normally be translated 'he redeemed', it probably indicates here the intention to redeem.[11]

God, who is enthroned forever, will hear them and afflict them, *Selah* **men who never change their ways and have no fear of God** (*v. 19*). It is to the creator God that the psalmist calls, for the NIV 'forever' is an attempt to translate a Hebrew word (*qédem*) which points backwards, not forwards. Hence a translation such

---

[10] Various opinions have been expressed about this clause. Some suggest the final phrase, 'in their midst' should be deleted, but no manuscript evidence supports this, while the LXX clearly upholds it (*en mesô autôn*). The RSV 'their graves' is only achieved by transposing consonants. '[Their] lodging' (*megûrâm*) has also been interpreted in different ways, and this is the only Old Testament occurrence of the word *mâgôr* (See *DCH*, V, p. 133). While other possible translations have been suggested, it seems most probable that it is from the common root *gûr*, 'to sojourn', 'to lodge'.

[11] The perfect of resolve is noted in *IBHS*, p. 489.

as 'enthroned from of old' is preferable.[12] The verse speaks of God as being enthroned from creation itself (cf. the use of *qedem* twice in the same chapter in Deut. 33:15, 'the *ancient* mountains', and 33:27, 'the *eternal* God'). The eternal God is the one who hears not only his people, but who also takes notice of the wicked. They are described using a term that is normally used of changing a garment (Gen. 45:22; Ps. 102:26). Their characteristics are that they do not change from their ungodliness and they lack the fundamental mark of godliness, the fear of God. The position of *Selah* is most unusual, in that it comes in the middle of the verse (for discussion on *Selah,* see comments on Ps. 3:2). If *Selah* was a musical term denoting loud song or music, then it would be fitting for it to point to exuberant praise of the eternal king.

My companion attacks his friends; he violates his covenant. His speech is smooth as butter, yet war is in his heart; his words are more soothing than oil, yet they are drawn swords (*vv. 20-21*). Another aspect of the attack by his so-called friend comes out in these verses. The Hebrew text lacks a subject for the verb, and from the context 'my companion' is added. Even 'his friends' have to bear the brunt of his antagonism.[13] He is in a covenant bond with someone, as covenants were often made between people (cf. the one between David and Jonathan, 1 Sam. 20:16). But this 'friend' has no regard for such solemn commitments. On the surface he speaks smoothly, but underneath he is plotting treachery.[14]

---

[12] The MT has *v^eyoshêv qédem*, 'and sits [from of] old'. The clause is an explanatory one concerning God, who is the subject of the first two verbs in the verse. The introductory 'and' is equivalent to 'and he ...' The verb *yâshav* is often used with God as the subject, and describes his enthronement. A close parallel to the expression here is Psalm 9:11, 'enthroned [in] Zion' (*yoshêv tsiyyôn*).

[13] The expression for 'his friends' is unusual, as the noun *shâlôm* is used in the plural as an adjective, 'his friendly ones'. Probably the expression here is equivalent to *sh^elêmîm 'ittô*, 'his friends' (see this idiomatic expression in Gen. 34:21).

[14] The MT has 'the curds of his mouth are smooth'. Various emendations have been proposed, changing the verb to the singular ('*his* mouth is smooth[er] ...) and altering 'curds of his mouth' to 'than curdled milk'. Examples of proposed emendations can be found in *DCH*, III, p. 242, and V, p. 221. J. J. S. Perowne, *The Psalms*, I, p. 459, while retaining the MT, explained the rare form by comparison to the formation of other Hebrew nouns.

His words are deceptive, for 'war' is in his heart, with the same word (*qᵉrâv*) being used here that has already occurred in verse 18. In stabbing his covenant allies in the back, he violates a sacred bond to which God is witness.

5. A Divine Burden-Bearer (*vv.* 22-23)

Cast your cares on the LORD and he will sustain you; he will never let the righteous fall (*v.* 22). The 'cares' are all that God gives to us, and the invitation is to throw them on the LORD. The word used for 'cares' (*yᵉhâv*) only occurs here, and it seems to mean a matter of concern, or one's circumstances in life. The promise is not that he will carry *them,* but rather that 'he will sustain *you*'. The word 'sustain' is used of the action of Joseph in providing for his family in Egypt (Gen. 45:11), and especially of God's gracious provision for his people in the wilderness (Neh. 9:21). That sustaining mercy will be given to ensure that there is no final disaster awaiting the righteous. The first part of the verse is echoed in the New Testament in 1 Peter 5:7, while the general theme is amplified in Jesus' teaching (Matt. 6:25-34; 10:19; Luke 12:22-31; 21:34).

But you, O God, will bring down the wicked into the pit of corruption; bloodthirsty and deceitful men will not live out half their days. But as for me, I trust in you (*v.* 23). The relationship between the psalmist and his God is what matters most. The words 'But you, O God' and 'But as for me' highlight this. God may indeed deal with the wicked, bringing them to a premature death, though he does not always act in this way.[15] However, the psalmist's trust is in his God. He clearly has cast *his* cares on the LORD; already he enjoys being sustained by him. These final words are a summary of the whole psalm, for throughout the psalmist has expressed his confident trust in God.

---

[15] The expression 'deceitful men will not live out half their days' is literally 'they shall not halve their days', which seems to be saying the opposite. In the context the meaning is clearly that the normal length of life will be shortened by direct divine intervention.

Psalm 56

For the director of music. To [the tune of] 'A Dove on Distant Oaks.' Of David. A miktam. When the Philistines had seized him in Gath.

While 'For the director of music' is common in the Psalms, occurring fifty-five times, the designation 'To [the tune of] "A Dove on Distant Oaks"' appears only in the title of this psalm. Its translation and significance is uncertain.[1] The use of the word *miktam* in the title links Psalms 56-60 together (for explanation of the term see the introduction to Psalm 16).The historical note in the title refers to an incident in David's life when he was seemingly held captive in Gath. The biblical text in 1 Samuel does not actually say he was captured, but the comment, in 1 Samuel 22:1, that he escaped to the cave of Adullam, leaves no doubt about it. The Philistines came from, or via, Crete (referred to as Caphtor in Jer. 47:4 and Amos 9:7), and they settled on the coast of Palestine. Their major cities were Ashdod, Ashkelon, Ekron, Gath, and Gaza. They were troublesome to Israel from the period of the Judges, until David drove them out of the hill country and even attacked Philistia itself (2 Sam. 5:25). During the divided monarchy they were still a problem, and the last mention of them in the Bible is from the post-exilic period (Zech. 9:6).

The psalm moves from appeal in the opening, through lament in the central part, to joyful thanksgiving at the conclusion. The imprecation in verse 7 links it with the two previous psalms that both include imprecations (Pss. 54:5; 55:9, 15, 23). The mood of the psalmist changes from the early declaration 'I fear' (*'îrâ'*, *verse 3*) to 'I will not fear' (*lo' 'îrâ*, v. 11). The repeated refrain in verses 4 and 11 indicates abiding confidence in the Lord, giving to the whole psalm the note of trust.

[1] Good summaries of the various views are contained in Marvin Tate, *Psalms 51–100*, pp. 65-66, and Samuel Terrien, *The Psalms*, p. 431.

1. A Plea for Mercy *(vv. 1-2)*
Be merciful to me, O God, for men hotly pursue me; all day long they press their attack (*v. 1*). This and the following psalm begin with the identical plea, though NIV varies the translation.[2] It occurs frequently in the Psalter (cf. 4:2; 6:2; 27:7; 51:1; 86:3; 123:3). The description of relentless pursuit certainly fits the experience of David. He cries to God because his enemies are breathing down his neck, and he has no relief from their oppression. The NIV renders the final clause very colloquially, while the MT has 'all day long a fighter presses me'. More literal translations are given, for example, by NASB ('Fighting all day long he oppresses me') and ESV ('all day long an attacker oppresses me').

My slanderers pursue me all day long; many are attacking me in their pride (*v. 2*). There is an emphasis, in this psalm, on the role of the enemies in using bitter words against the psalmist (see also verse 5), though he clearly felt in deadly peril (v. 6). The repetition of 'all day long' in successive verses speaks of the feeling that there was no let up in the attacks upon him. The conclusion of the verse has caused considerable discussion going back centuries. The problem is the final word in the MT, *mârôm*. The NIV follows a commonly accepted view that it is a noun, 'height', used adverbially to mean 'haughtily = with pride'. However, the AV translators took it as a divine title, 'O thou most high', a view reinforced by some modern scholars,[3] and which may be coupled with the suggestion that it should be transferred to become the first word in the next verse (cf. NRSV).[4] An exegetical decision is hard to make, though the easiest choice appears to be to follow the NIV translators.

2. Refrain: Trust in God *(vv. 3-4)*
When I am afraid, I will trust in you. In God, whose word I praise, in God I trust; I will not be afraid. What can mortal

---

[2] Quite a few English translations share the NIV's inconsistency in the translation of a Hebrew word (*chonnênî*, 'be merciful to me').The NKJV is consistent in rendering both opening expressions by 'Be merciful to me.'

[3] See especially M. Dahood, *Psalms I:1-50*, pp. 44-45. This view, though reinforced by modern linguistic arguments, goes back to the Aramaic Targum, Aquila, and Jerome.

[4] For a summary of different viewpoints, see *DCH*, V, pp. 483-84.

man do to me? (*vv. 3-4*). Striking alliteration draws attention to the confident assertion in verse 3. The statement opens with the Hebrew word 'day' (*yôm*) used adverbially to indicate 'when'.[5] It is followed by four consecutive words starting with the letter *alef* (represented by ʾ in transliteration); *yôm ʾîrâ ʾanî êlekâ ʾevtach*: 'When I fear, in you I trust.' There is no doubt that David knows fear, but he claims that trust in God robs it of terror.[6] He is afraid, yet not afraid! At the time when he fears, he will trust in God, and at the moment of speaking he is confidently placing his reliance on God's word of promise. Other psalms contain similar references to God's word (cf. 107:20; 130:5), without indication of how that word came to the psalmists. It is possible that a 'word' such as Eli spoke to Hannah could be in mind (1 Sam. 1:17). Verse 4 ends with a challenge to mortal man (Hebrew, *bâsâr*, 'flesh'). Human power is nothing compared to God's might, as King Hezekiah said to his officers when Jerusalem was faced with an attack by King Sennacherib of Assyria (2 Chron. 32:8).

3. Complaints against the Enemies (*vv. 5-9a*)
The evil designs of the enemies are now spelt out in greater detail. **All day long they twist my words; they are always plotting to harm me** (*v. 5*). The words of David were distorted by his enemies, presumably Saul and his supporters. Another possible rendering is 'they injure my cause', as in Hebrew the 'word' (*dâvâr*) can have a wider connotation than is normal in English. All their endeavours are directed with evil intent.

They conspire, they lurk, they watch my steps, eager to take my life (*v. 6*). In every possible way the enemies are seeking to harm the psalmist, even to the extent of taking his life. The first verb may have the idea that they troop together to plot an ambush,[7] and while the second verb can have varied meanings, 'lurk' seems appropriate here. Rather than 'steps', the more literal 'heels' is to be preferred as it fits in with the idea of enemies hiding in ambush. What they may have in

---

[5] *DCH*, IV, pp. 171-72.

[6] For the verb 'trust' (*bâtach*), see comment on Psalm 9:10.

[7] This is how Jerome understood it, and hence rendered it in Latin as *congregabuntur*.

mind is some kind of murder by abuse of the legal system, such as happened in the case of Naboth (1 Kings 21:1-14). They treat the psalmist unjustly and are on the look-out for any opportunity to injure him.

On no account let them escape; in your anger, O God, bring down the nations (*v. 7*). The great variation in the English versions of this verse points to difficulty in understanding the Hebrew text. Some have suggested there was an early copying mistake, because, with the change of one letter, the verb 'escape' (*pâlat*) could be 'requite' (*pâlas*). However, leaving the Hebrew text unchanged can still provide the basis for a translation that forms a question: 'On account of their evil, will there be escape for them?' The answer is clearly 'No', for God will show his anger against the nations.[8] The use of the plural 'nations' suggests that it is the Philistines who are in view. David set himself, after he became king, to subdue the power of the Philistines (2 Sam. 5:17-25; 8:1).[9]

Record my lament; list my tears on your scroll – are they not in your record? Then my enemies will turn back when I call for help (*vv. 8-9a*). David knows that God administers justice in his time, not ours. Hence he asks for a record to be kept of his grief,[10] his request being stated in a very emphatic way. He even asks that his tears be kept in a bottle or wineskin (following the footnote

---

[8] No interrogative particle is used, but in biblical Hebrew a simple *Yes–No* question can be asked without one. Presumably the tone of voice could indicate that it was a question, just as can happen in English (cf. the statement, 'You're going home!' which can often be in effect a question). On the grammatical point in Hebrew, see *DIHG~S*, p. 183; *IBHS*, p. 316 n.1.

[9] The use of the word 'peoples' (*'ammîm*) is unusual in this context, as it most commonly denotes foreign nations attacking Israel. To regard it here as having the narrower meaning of the Philistines makes good sense. Another possibility is to suggest that the appeal 'for a particular judgement is absorbed in the desire for a general judgement of the world' (A. F. Kirkpatrick, *The Book of Psalms*, p. 318).

[10] The word translated 'lament' is the first of three rare words used in verse 9. The AV translation 'wanderings' has been followed by the NASB and NKJV. While it could be from the verb *nûd*, 'to wander', the context suggests a meaning in keeping with 'tears'. *DCH*, V, p. 618 is ambivalent.

reading in the NIV).[11] The verse ends with a question that expects a positive response: 'Yes, they are indeed recorded in God's scroll'.[12] God does not need a written record to remember his people and their needs, but the idea is used in the Old Testament as a reassuring way of speaking of God's knowledge of, and care for, his people (Exod. 32:32; Pss. 69:28; 139:16; Mal. 3:16). The following statement (v. 9a) gives proof of the psalmist's confidence. Whenever he calls to God, asking for his intervention, then the enemies will be put to flight.

4. Refrain: Trust in God *(vv. 9b-11)*

By this I will know that God is for me. In God, whose word I praise, in the Lord, whose word I praise – in God I trust; I will not be afraid. What can man do to me? (*vv. 9b-11*). The essential parts of the refrain of verses 3-4 are repeated here. Instead of the opening reference to trusting in God when he is afraid, the psalmist expresses absolute certainty that God is for him. The introductory 'by this', as well as the verb 'know', draws attention to his conviction that God's actions are proof of his continuing care and justice. The following phrases also differ slightly. The first one ('In God whose word I praise') is given twice,[13] while 'his word' in verse 4 is simply 'word'

---

[11] This is the second difficult word in the verse. The Hebrew word (*no'd*) is used of 'skins of milk' or 'skins of wine'. Because parchment made of skins was used as a writing material, and since the final clause contains the word 'scroll', some have thought that the psalmist is asking for a written record. However, the concept of tears in a skin bottle better suits the expression. The LXX rendering (*enôpion sou*) suggests that the translators were reading the Hebrew as *b^enegd^ekâ*, 'before you', but as the LXX gives a very free translation of the whole verse, this is insufficient evidence to justify any possible emendation.

[12] This word is the third problem in the same verse. Some have suggested that 'record' should be translated as 'bag' to carry on the idiom from the preceding clause. The word used (*sifrâh*) is a *hapax legomenon*, but no convincing argument has been given for not connecting it with the root *s-f-r* already used in the first clause. *CHAL*, p. 260, gives the meaning as '(heavenly memorandum) book'.

[13] The use of refrains in which the second or final occurrence is lengthier than the original is a feature that also occurs in Psalm 99:3, 5 , 9: 'for he is holy … for he is holy … for the Lord our God is holy.'

in verse 10, though in the context no confusion arises as to whose word is being mentioned. Also the repeated phrase has LORD [*yhwh*] instead of God. Verse 11 repeats verse 4b, only altering 'mortal flesh' (*bâśâr*) to 'man' (*'âdâm*). The New Testament passage which presents the same message is Romans 8:28-39, and it may be based on this refrain. Paul starts with the certainty of knowledge ('we know', v. 28), and ends with the ringing affirmation that nothing 'will be able to separate us from the love of God that is in Christ Jesus our Lord' (Rom. 8:39).

5. A Vow of Thanksgiving (*vv. 12-13*)

I am under vows to you, O God; I will present my thank-offerings to you. For you have delivered me from death and my feet from stumbling, that I may walk before God in the light of life (*vv. 12-13*). Seemingly David had made special commitments to God which he now says he will pay. He actually calls them God's vows (MT *nedâreka*, 'your vows'), which strengthens the idea of his obligation to keep them. Both 'vows' and 'thank-offerings' can refer to sacrificial offerings. He looks back on the reality of deliverance from the danger of death, and though his enemies had watched his every step (v. 6), yet God had also delivered his feet from stumbling. The NIV translation should be emended to make this a question as it is in the MT: 'Haven't [you kept] my feet from stumbling?'[14] The identical phrase, 'my feet from stumbling', occurs again in Psalm 116:8, also in a context in which mention is made of vows (Ps. 116:14). The final clause expresses the confidence of walking joyfully before God in his light (cf. Ps. 36:9). The Old Testament expressions relating to God as light come to fulfilment in the Gospel (John 1:3-5). Jesus declared: 'I am the light of the world. Whoever follows me will never walk in darkness, but will have the light of life' (John 8:12). His subsequent debate with the Pharisees added weight to the declaration.

[14] The form of the question is identical to the one at the end of verse 8. They both commence with the interrogative marker (*ha-*) and lack a verb.

Psalm 57

For the director of music. [To the tune of] 'Do not Destroy.' Of David. A miktam. When he had fled from Saul into the cave.

There are close links between Psalms 56 and 57, and the titles locate both psalms in the period of David's flight from Saul. They are similar in style, with both beginning with a cry for mercy and ending on a strong note of thanksgiving. Also, both contain a repeated refrain (56:3-4, 10-11; 57:5, 11). Links also exist among Psalms 57, 58, and 59, in that part of their title is common to all three. In addition, they share the words 'Do Not Destroy' in their titles (as does Psalm 75), and it probably represents the first words of a popular song.

Psalm 57:7-11 is repeated in Psalm 108:1-5. This may suggest that the two parts of Psalm 57 were originally separate compositions. God's covenantal love and faithfulness resound in both sections of the psalm, while the opening verse suggests David's presence at the central worship centre of the covenant, the tabernacle.

1. Lament and Refrain (*vv. 1-5*)

Have mercy on me, O God, have mercy on me, for in you my soul takes refuge. I will take refuge in the shadow of your wings until the disaster has passed (*v. 1*). The psalm begins with a call for God to be merciful, along with a repeated assertion of trust in him. The reference to taking refuge under the shadow of God's wings could be either a general allusion to God's protective care,[1] or it

[1] The same idiom is found in Boaz's reference to Ruth: 'May you be richly rewarded by the Lord, the God of Israel, under whose wings you have come to take refuge' (Ruth 2:12). This description has to be set alongside Ruth's profession of conversion: 'Your people [are] my people, and your God [is] my God' (Ruth 1:16).

could relate to his presence at the tabernacle. In Exodus 25:20 the wings of the cherubim are said to overshadow the cover (the mercy-seat) of the ark of the covenant. Hence it is possible that 'your wings' is a way of saying that the psalmist will go to the tabernacle to meet with his God and to find refuge there until the present distress passes by. The word 'disaster' has been translated 'destructive forces' in 55:11. It is a rare word but the parallels of 'malice' and 'abuse' in that context help to define its meaning. In this context, the psalmist professes confident trust in God's ability to protect him until the present destruction is past.

I cry out to God Most High, to God, who fulfils [his purpose] for me. He sends from heaven and saves me, rebuking those who hotly pursue me; *Selah* God sends his love and his faithfulness (*vv.* 2-3). He calls to 'God Most High',[2] using a double name for God which also occurs in Psalm 78:56 (cf. 'LORD Most High' in Ps. 7:17). The verb 'fulfils' is a rare one, only occurring five times in the whole of the Old Testament, all of them in the Psalms. Here, and in Psalm 138:8, it speaks of the way in which God brings to completion what he undertakes for his saints. The Most High God, the ruler over all, brings blessing to his people while visiting his enemies in judgment. He 'sends' salvation to those who are in deep distress, showing in this way his continuing covenant commitment. He is the God who is 'abounding in love and faithfulness' (Exod. 34:6). 'Selah' appears in the middle of a verse in English versions, but at the conclusion of a clause, not, as in Psalm 55:19, in the middle of a sentence.

I am in the midst of lions; I lie among ravenous beasts – men whose teeth are spears and arrows, whose tongues are sharp swords (*v.* 4). The enemies are described as if they were wild animals. The expressions used ('in the midst of lions', 'I lie among ravenous beasts') suggest the constant hostility with which the enemies attacked, while use of the comparison with spears, arrows, and swords depict their cruelty and their venom. The words 'spears', 'arrows', 'sharp', and 'swords'

---

[2] On the use of the word *'elyôn* ('Most High') as a title for God, see the comments on Psalm 7:17.

all commence with the same letter in Hebrew (*chêt*), the alliteration drawing attention to the danger that confronts the suppliant.

Be exalted, O God, above the heavens; let your glory be over all the earth (*v. 5*). The psalmist knows that God is not an idle onlooker. His words in this verse are both a declaration concerning God's glory and an indirect appeal for his help. He longs for the full expression of God's rule to be manifest, because that would mean that deliverance would come for him. One of the ways in which God gets glory is by displaying his power over his enemies (cf. Exod. 14:4, 17, 18). This invocation is repeated exactly as the final verse of the psalm.

2. Transition – The Wicked Trap Themselves (*v. 6*)

They spread a net for my feet – I was bowed down in distress. They dug a pit in my path – but they have fallen into it themselves. *Selah* (*v. 6*). This verse serves as a bridge between the earlier section of the psalm, with its cry to a faithful God, and the later section with its confident praising of him. The truth is that the wicked often fall prey to their own schemes. They prepare a trap for the righteous, but God so overrules in his providence that they fall into it themselves. The song which follows rejoices in this event, which is not brought about simply by the folly of the wicked, but by the direct intervention of God. 'Selah' marks the end of the second section of the psalm.

3. Thanksgiving and Refrain (*vv. 7-11*)

My heart is steadfast, O God, my heart is steadfast; I will sing and make music (*v. 7*). The Hebrew word rendered 'steadfast' is the same word translated as 'willing' in Psalm 51:12. It could also be rendered 'prepared' or 'set'. Its use here describes the fixed trust that the psalmist has in God, and the repetition emphasises that still further. No indication is given in the text to whom the praise is rendered, but it is clear from the context that it is to be sung to God. Faith and praise are very closely linked together. Both the repetition of phrases and the use of parallel expressions in the verse are characteristic of the whole of the psalm.

Awake, my soul! Awake, harp and lyre! I will awaken the dawn (*v. 8*). The psalmist calls on himself[3] and his instruments to wake up and to prepare for praise. Praise often helps to dispel darkness and despair (cf. the experience of Paul and Silas in gaol, Acts 16:25). Harps and lyres refer to stringed instruments that were used in both formal and informal worship situations, and there is little information to make a distinction between them. Before the dawn signalled a new day, praise would be given to the LORD.

I will praise you, O Lord, among the nations; I will sing of you among the peoples. For great is your love, reaching to the heavens; your faithfulness reaches to the skies (*vv. 9-10*). The gratitude of the psalmist is so great that he wants even the Gentile nations to hear his praise of God, in accordance with God's promise to Abraham (Gen. 12:3). The use of the word 'nations' is not a restricted use of the word to mean 'the Philistines' (as in Ps. 56:7), but in the same way that Psalm 67 uses it. The focus is on the nations of the world, as the context and the use of the word 'peoples' (*'ummîm*) makes clear. The subject matter of David's praise relates to God's covenant love and faithfulness (see v. 3). God has sent his love and faithfulness, and the psalmist wants others to know their dimensions. They cannot be measured for they reach to the heavens.

Be exalted, O God, above the heavens; let your glory be over all the earth (*v. 11*). The statement of verse 5 is used as a refrain to conclude the psalm. It fittingly continues the theme of verse 10 and again focuses on the prayer for the manifestation of God's glory.

---

[3] The word translated 'soul' is *kâwôd,* that often means 'glory'. It can also be used as a means of self-reference, as it is here. For further discussion, see Robert Chisholm in *NIDOTTE,* 2, p. 583.

Psalm 58

For the director of music. [To the tune of] 'Do not Destroy.' Of David. A miktam.

This psalm is directed against prominent officials who misuse their office, and so fail to administer justice rightly. It is unique in that the opening words are not addressed to God but to rulers. After they are charged and a description given of their sin, a sevenfold curse is expressed against them. At the close of the psalm the righteous are depicted as rejoicing in the fact that God, the judge of all the earth, will avenge them. This is one of the imprecatory psalms (see the Introduction) and has close affinity with others in this group, but also with those that deal with the seeming triumph of the wicked (see Pss. 37, 49, 73, and 94).

The psalm is carefully crafted. Verse 1 mentions speaking righteously (NIV 'justly') and judging uprightly. The same two Hebrew roots (*ts-d-k* and *sh-f-t*) appear in the closing verse. A declaration is made concerning the righteous, coupled with the assurance that God is indeed the universal judge. Other repetitions within the psalm are the words 'earth' (vv. 2 and 11) and 'the wicked' (vv. 3 and 11).

1. Leaders Charged (*vv. 1-2*)

Do rulers indeed speak justly? Do you judge uprightly among men? No, in your heart you devise injustice, and your hands mete out violence on the earth (*vv. 1-2*). The various English versions show great variety in verse 1. The problem is the Hebrew word rendered 'rulers' in the NIV. The AV took it as meaning 'congregation', but this has no real basis. The Hebrew word in question (*'ēlem*) is best taken as being the word 'gods' (*'ēlîm*), and having the meaning of 'judges', 'rulers', just as a related Hebrew word (*ʾᵉlôhîm*) has this meaning in Exodus 22:7-8 and Psalm 82:1 (cf. John 10:34-36).[1] The charge is that the rulers neither speak justly nor judge uprightly. The very people who should have represented God's concern for justice instead conjure up evil plans in their hearts, and then act them out. The sequence of 'heart' and then 'hands' is important, for this is the way in which sin works (cf. Jesus' words in Matt. 15:16-20). The close of the psalm shows that the true model for judges is God himself (v. 11).

2. The Sins of the Leaders Described (*vv. 3-5*)

Even from birth the wicked go astray; from the womb they are wayward and speak lies (*v. 3*). While the context is not dealing with universal sinfulness, yet the comparison with David's confession in Psalm 51:5 should be made. What was happening with the judges should not have been thought surprising, because the judges were only displaying their true character. From birth they have been estranged from God and his ways. This is how the Bible constantly pictures sinful men and women. 'They are darkened in their understanding and separated from the life of God because of the ignorance that is in them due to the hardening of their hearts' (Eph. 4:18).

Their venom is like the venom of a snake, like that of a cobra that has stopped its ears, that will not heed the tune of the charmer, however skilful the enchanter may be (*vv. 4-5*). The wicked are compared to a poisonous snake that will not even obey its trainer. It will turn against the person who has carefully trained it and will not listen. The reason for this, as is now known, is that the cobra is deaf, and it only responds to its trainer's movements, not to the sound of the music. Hence the NIV interpretation 'tune' should be replaced with the more literal 'voice'. The final clause in verse 5 employs one of the

---

[1] The translation of *ʾᵉlôhîm* in Exodus 21 and 22 is discussed by J. R. Vannoy, 'The Use of the Word *hâʾᵉlôhîm* in Exodus 21:6 and 22:7, 8', in J. H. Skilton, ed., *The Law and the Prophets: Old Testament Studies in Honor of Oswald T. Allis* (Nutley, NJ: Presbyterian and Reformed, 1974), pp. 225-41. He concludes that the translation 'God' should be retained in Exodus 21:6, but 'judges' used in 22:7, 8.

technical terms for weaving spells,[2] and the ESV captures the meaning well with 'cunning enchanter'. The point here is that wicked rulers are just as insensitive as the cobra, in that they do not hear the cry for justice from the poor and needy.

3. Prayer for Judgment (*vv. 6-9*)

The cry goes out for God to intervene in the situation and bring judgment upon these ungodly people (for curses in the Psalms, see the Introduction). This sevenfold curse is very difficult in the Hebrew text, and this causes the great variety in the English translations of it. The prayer for judgment increases in intensity until it reaches its climax in verse 9. **Break the teeth in their mouths, O God; tear out, O LORD, the fangs of the lions!** (*v. 6*). Instead of being likened to a cobra, the wicked judges are now compared to lions. They are all ready to attack with their teeth, unless God intervenes and breaks them.[3] In the MT the two words for deity frame the content with one beginning the verse (*ʾᵉlohîm*) and the other (*yhwh*) concluding it. This is brought out in translation by the ESV translation: 'O God, break the teeth in their mouths; tear out the fangs of the young lions, O LORD.'

Let them vanish like water that flows away; when they draw the bow, let their arrows be blunted (*v. 7*). Two different comparisons are made to suggest taking away the power of the enemies. The psalmist wants them to become 'like water spilled on the ground, which cannot be recovered' (2 Sam. 14:14). This is symbolism for death. If they do persist in their attacks, then he wants their arrows to be blunted so that they cannot harm him.

Like a slug melting away as it moves along, like a stillborn child, may they not see the sun (*v. 8*). The word rendered 'slug' (*shabbᵉlûl*) only occurs here. It is preferable to take it as parallel to 'stillborn' in the following clause: 'Like the miscarriage that melts away, like the stillborn that never

[2] Cf. the use of the same phrase, *chôvêr chᵃvârîm*, in the list of forbidden Canaanite sorcery practices in Deuteronomy 18:11.

[3] The word translated 'fangs' (*maltᵉʿôt*) only occurs here, though a similar word (*mᵉtalʿâh*) meaning 'tooth' is more common. In the context it is either means the jaws or the teeth of young lions.

sees the sun'.[4] The same imagery is used in Job 3:16 and Ecclesiastes 6:3. The miscarried foetus or the stillborn child never sees the light of day. So the psalmist wishes his wicked enemies to become as if they had never existed.

Before your pots can feel [the heat of] the thorns – whether they be green or dry – the wicked will be swept away (*v. 9*). The NIV footnote rightly says: 'The meaning of the Hebrew for this verse is uncertain.' However, the introductory word 'before' is sometimes used to introduce prophetic speech that is depicting something going to happen (cf. Isa. 7:16; 8:4), while the last clause gives the expectation that God's judgment is going to be final. This is the climax to the whole prayer.

4. Assurance for the Righteous (*vv. 10-11*)

The righteous will be glad when they are avenged, when they bathe their feet in the blood of the wicked (*v. 10*). The righteous delight in justice, and when God vindicates his own people in victory, then they can rejoice all the more. Vengeance belongs to God, and he vindicates them (Deut. 32:35-36; Ps. 94:1-2).[5] Without that vengeance there can be no justice. Bathing feet in blood is a biblical imagery for victory (Ps. 68:23; Isa. 63:1-6; Rev. 14:19-20; 19:13-14).

Then men will say, 'Surely the righteous still are rewarded; surely there is a God who judges the earth' (*v. 11*). Men in general will ultimately make the declaration that the righteous receive the fruit of their lives from the God who judges the whole earth (cf. Ps. 94:2 where God is called 'judge of the earth'). The psalmist is confident that a day is coming when even the heathen will acknowledge this fact. Believers know that God, the righteous judge, is going to reward them at the last day (2 Tim. 4:8) and they must wait patiently for the day of reckoning (James 5:1-11).

---

[4] This is the interpretation of A. A. Anderson, *Psalms 1-72*, p. 433, and is based on a discussion by G. R. Driver that he cites.

[5] For discussion on the biblical concept of God's vengeance, see H. G. L. Peels, *The Vengeance of God: The Meaning of the Root NQM and the Function of the NQM-Texts in the Context of Divine Revelation in the Old Testament* (Leiden: *OTS* 31, 1995), and his summary in *NIDOTTE*, 3, pp. 154-56.

Psalm 59

For the director of music. [To the tune of] 'Do not Destroy.' Of David. A miktam. When Saul had sent men to watch David's house in order to kill him.

Two sets of enemies seem to be in view in this psalm. On the one hand, wicked men within the nation attack the psalmist like a pack of wild dogs (vv. 6 and 14). On the other hand, surrounding nations are in view (vv. 5-8). It seems, then, to be a psalm appealing for help from both local and foreign enemies. The manner of deliverance is expressed in terms of God's judgments falling on the wicked. This puts this psalm into the same category of imprecatory psalms as the previous one (for the imprecatory psalms, see the Introduction).

Within the psalm there are features that are unusual, in that there are repeated refrains (vv. 6 and 14) and repeated affirmations of confident trust in the LORD (vv. 9 and 17). The second time the refrain occurs a change of a single letter alters 'O my Strength, I watch for you' to 'O my Strength, I sing praise to you'.[1] The use of three cognate words also helps to bind the whole psalm together. In verse 3 the evil adversaries are called 'fierce men' (*ʿazîm*), while in the refrain (vv. 9 and 17) God is addressed as 'my strength' (*ʿuzzî*). Also, the psalmist sings to God and uses the expression 'your might' (*ʿuzzekâ*). These three words all come from the word 'strength' or 'power' (*ʿoz*). In addition, the psalm is framed by the use of the same Hebrew root in verse 1 (*sâgav*, 'to protect') and in verse 17 (*misgâv*, 'fortress'). There are some interesting word parallels between this psalm and the

---

[1] In Hebrew the change is from *ʾeshmorâh*, 'I will keep', to *ʾazammêrâh*, 'I will sing praise.'

account in 1 Samuel 19 and 24 of David's flight from Saul (including the reference to wild dogs, cf. vv. 6-7, 14-15, with 1 Sam. 24:14).

1. A Cry for Deliverance, and a Refrain (*vv. 1-10a*)

Deliver me from my enemies, O God; protect me from those who rise up against me (*v. 1*). From the psalmist's heart comes this cry of distress. He longs for the deliverance that comes only from God. The word 'protect' means 'to set on high' or 'defend'. God takes the afflicted and he lifts them up (Ps. 107:41). This is what David asks here, as he acknowledges the fierce opposition he is facing. He appeals for help from his 'enemies', those who 'rise up' against him.

Deliver me from evildoers and save me from bloodthirsty men. See how they lie in wait for me! Fierce men conspire against me for no offence or sin of mine, O LORD (*vv. 2-3*). He repeats his plea for deliverance, and in so doing uses two more terms to describe his opponents ('evildoers', 'bloodthirsty men'). These four terms are all practically synonymous in this context. The people have planned their attacks with military precision,[2] and they are busy stirring up strife against the psalmist. He protests that he has done them no hurt to cause such spite, and the words he uses recall David's words in 1 Samuel 20:1 and 24:11.

I have done no wrong, yet they are ready to attack me. Arise to help me; look on my plight! (*v. 4*). So strong is his protestation of innocence that he uses still another term ('no wrong') to speak of his lack of offence to either God or man.[3] To him it looks as if God is asleep, and therefore he calls on him to stir himself and come to his rescue. The call to God to 'arise' is a standard expression in the Psalter (see comment on 3:7).

O LORD God Almighty, the God of Israel, rouse yourself to punish all the nations; show no mercy to wicked traitors. Selah (*v. 5*). The combination of divine names, 'LORD God

---

[2] The verb translated 'conspire' is *gûr* II, not *gûr* I. See *DCH*, I, p. 336.

[3] The Hebrew has *b*^{e}*lî-ʿâwôn*, a compound expression created from the negative particle *b*^{e}*lî* and a noun: 'without iniquity'. Cf. 'without water' (Job 8:11); 'without clothing' (Job 24:10).

Almighty,' recurs in Psalms 80:4, 19 and 84:8.[4] It points to the power of God, while the addition of 'the God of Israel' is suggestive of his loving concern for his people. The psalmist appeals to God to deal with the nations around Israel and also with those within the nation who are disloyal to God's covenant (cf. Psalm 78:57 for the use of the same verb, *bâgad*, of covenant unfaithfulness). It is rare to have the verb 'show mercy' used negatively, for almost always it is used positively of a plea for God to be gracious. The only other place in the Psalms where it is used negatively is in another imprecatory one ('May no one take pity on his fatherless children', Ps. 109:12).

They return at evening, snarling like dogs, and prowl about the city. See what they spew from their mouths – they spew out swords from their lips, and they say, 'Who can hear us?' (*vv. 6-7*). The opponents are compared with wild dogs, which hunt for their prey around the city at night. They habitually look for ways to attack and, if possible, to destroy him. They speak so sharply that their words are like swords. The expression is unusual, though other psalms speak of the cutting effect of the tongue (Pss. 52:2; 57:4; 64:3). In their arrogance they claim that no one, including God, hears them, or will take any action to curtail their activities.[5]

But you, O LORD, laugh at them; you scoff at all those nations (*v. 8*). This seems to be a standard way of describing God's derision of the ungodly (cf. the use of the same two verbs in Ps. 2:4 and Prov. 1:26). The contrast is very marked. Wicked men express their blasphemies, but God in heaven knows that his rule will be vindicated. His enemies will in the end become his footstool (Ps. 110:1; 1 Cor. 15:24-25).

---

[4] The Hebrew expression is unusual in that it has *ʾ^{e}lohîm ts^{e}vâʾôt*, 'God, hosts' instead of the expected *ʾ^{e}lohê ts^{e}vâʾôt*, 'God of hosts'. Possibly the phrase in the MT is an example of enclitic *mem*, where the letter *mem* was added to words but with no discernible meaning. For explanation of this phenomenon, see *DIHG~S*, pp. 24-25; *IBHS*, pp. 158-60; M. Dahood, *The Psalms III:101–50*, Anchor Bible: Garden City, NY: Doubleday, 1970) pp. 408-09.

[5] 'They say' is not represented in the MT, but a verb of thinking or saying is needed to make sense in the context.

O my Strength, I watch for you; you, O God, are my fortress, my loving God (*vv. 9-10a*). While the enemies coming against David are strong (v. 3, 'fierce'), yet his trust is in even greater strength. The NIV and other translations emend the first word in the MT (*ʿuzzô*) to make it a divine epithet, 'my strength' (*ʿuzzî*).[6] They watch for him (see the title), but he watches for God. He has asked that God will protect him (v. 1), and he now confesses that his place of protection is indeed God himself ('protect' and 'fortress' come from the same Hebrew root). He looks expectantly to his gracious God. In the expression 'my loving God', the word 'loving' represents the Hebrew word *chésed*, and another rendering could be 'my God of covenant love'.

2. A Description of the Enemies and a Refrain (*vv. 10b-17*)

David prays for God's judgments to be made known, not immediately, but progressively, and he wants this to be a testimony to the surrounding nations. **God will go before me and will let me gloat over those who slander me** (*v. 10b*). The NIV translation glosses over a difficulty with the simple translation 'God'. The consonantal text has 'God of his lovingkindness' (*ʾelohê chasdô*), and while this is awkward grammatically, yet it can be regarded as a regular construction.[7] The psalmist knows that God will meet him (cf. the use of the same Hebrew verb in Psalm 21:3, NIV 'welcomed'), and he will allow him to gaze on the victory he is providing. The

[6] This emendation is fairly strongly supported by the Hebrew manuscripts and the early versions. Without emendation it is hard to construe the sentence. The AV adds words to make some sense: '*Because of* his strength ...', and this procedure could be followed with a more modern translation such as 'Because he is so strong'.

[7] By a slight change of vocalisation 'God of' (*ʾelohê*) becomes 'my God' (*ʾelohay*) and this translation is supported by the LXX and a few Hebrew manuscripts. Jewish Massoretes noted in the margin (the Qere reading) that the vocalisation of the second word in the phrase should be changed (*chasdô* altered to *chasdî*). This enables a translation like 'my loving God' (cf. the identical phrase in verse 17). Most English translations opt for one or other of these emendations. The first is followed by the RSV, NASB, NEB, NKJV, and the ESV, while the second is represented in the AV, NASB margin, and ESV margin. REB alters 'God of' to 'my God' but retains the MT of the following word: 'My God, in his unfailing love ...'

demonstration of God's judgment will be satisfying to him as he sees God vindicated (cf. Psalm 54:7).

But do not kill them, O Lord our shield, or my people will forget. In your might make them wander about, and bring them down (*v. 11*). Appeal is made to God[8] that his judgment should not be a speedy one, lest it be over and done with so quickly that the lesson will not be learned by the people. Instead, the prayer is that the people will wander about aimlessly and thus be seen as a living example of God's judgments. Another interpretation of the verse could be that the psalmist is asking that God should not kill his enemies as this would only be a short-term solution to the problem.

For the sins of their mouths, for the words of their lips, let them be caught in their pride. For the curses and lies they utter, consume them in wrath, consume them till they are no more. Then it will be known to the ends of the earth that God rules over Jacob. *Selah* (*vv. 12-13*). The sins of the enemies are again spelt out as involving vicious words of cursing and lying. The idea of being caught by their own pride is rather like the idea of Psalm 57:6. The wicked are often too clever for themselves, and their own sin rebounds on them. The repeated cry of 'consume them' emphasises the prayer for utter destruction of the enemies. The end result will not only be satisfying to the psalmist (v. 10b) but glorifying to God as well. Judgment is a demonstration of his sovereign rule over his people, and this serves as a witness to the ends of the earth.

They return at evening, snarling like dogs, and prowl about the city (*v. 14*). The words of verse 6 are repeated in this fresh description of the characteristics of the enemies. The use of this refrain draws attention to the pack of roaming dogs that are always ready to attack.

They wander about for food and howl if not satisfied (*v. 15*). The imagery of roaming dogs is continued (cf. verse 11). They are always on the lookout for food, and if they do not find it they whine. Some English versions take the verb translated in the NIV as 'howl' (*lûn*) to be the verb 'to spend the night' (see AV margin and RV), but it is best to assume that

[8] For the word 'shield' applied to God, see the note on 3:5.

the verb means 'to murmur', and hence descriptive of the whimpering of hungry dogs.

But I will sing of your strength, in the morning I will sing of your love; for you are my fortress, my refuge in times of trouble (*v. 16*). While the mention of singing is new, all the other ideas are already found earlier in the psalm (for 'strength', see verse 9; for 'love', see verse 10a; for 'fortress', see verse 9). These ideas form the subject matter of song and praise. The psalmist's approach to God in this way stands in marked contrast to the arrogance of his oppressors. The expressions 'in the morning' and 'in the day of' (NIV 'in times of') are parallel and simply denote the constancy with which the psalmist will proclaim God's favour.

O my Strength, I sing praise to you; you, O God, are my fortress, my loving God (*v. 17*). The words of verses 9-10a are picked up as a concluding refrain. The main alteration is the replacement of 'I watch [for you]' (*'eshmorâh*) with 'I sing [to you]' (*'azammêrâh).* In the last two verses of the psalm there are three synonyms in the Hebrew text, all rendered by 'sing' in English (*shîr, rânan* Pi., *zâmar* Pi.). In spite of all his circumstances the psalmist ends on a note of praise, with the very last word in Hebrew being the word *chésed,* 'covenant love'.

Psalm 60

For the director of music. To [the tune of] 'The Lily of the Covenant.' A miktam of David. For teaching. When he fought Aram Naharaim and Aram Zobah, and when Joab returned and struck down twelve thousand Edomites in the Valley of Salt.

The title of the psalm links it with David's victories against Aram Naharaim, Aram Zobah, and Edom (see 2 Sam. 8:1-4, 13; 10:6-19; 1 Chron. 18:1-13; 19:6-19), but the psalm itself is not commemorating any victory. It is a lament of the people when they were defeated and apparently lost some of the southern part of the land. Twice in the psalm they challenge God's rejection of them (see vv. 1 and 10). The difficulty of reconciling God's sure promises to his people with the reality of military defeat and even loss of some of their territory is faced in other psalms as well (see Pss. 44:19-26 and 89:38-51). Part of this psalm (vv. 5-12) is combined with Psalm 57:7-11 to make up Psalm 108.

The title is the longest in the whole psalter. Several of the terms are used elsewhere ('For the director of music' occurs in the title of fifty-five psalms and in Hab. 3:19; 'To [the tune of] "The Lily of the Covenant"' occurs only here though with the plural 'lilies' it is found in the title of Ps. 80; 'miktam' appears in Pss. 16 and 56-60). It is impossible to be certain whether the historical reference is to the same battle(s) as recorded in 2 Samuel 8:13. The number of the slain is different (in 2 Sam. it is 18,000, here it is 12,000) and also the commander is Joab, not David as in 2 Samuel. The latter difference is not of great concern, as victories can be attributed to a king or his commander (1 Sam. 13:3-4).[1]

---

[1] Discussion on the connection between 2 Samuel 8:13 and the title of Psalm 60 is found in commentaries such as Ronald Youngblood, '1, 2 Samuel', *EBC*, vol. 3, p. 908.

1. A Complaint over Rejection (*vv. 1-3*)
You have rejected us, O God, and burst forth upon us; you have been angry – now restore us! (*v. 1*). God's anger is spoken of as the primary cause of the present distress. The people complain that he has made a breach in their defences (NIV 'burst forth'), and they feel that this is a sign that God has rejected them.[2] The same Hebrew verb for 'reject' occurs in other laments (cf. Pss. 44:9, 23; 74:1; 88:14; 89:38; Lam. 3:17). What the people want is action by God to change the situation, for it is beyond their power to remedy it. While the NIV rendering 'restore us' is feasible, yet the verb (*shûv*, Pol.) is used at times of God's action in turning back from executing punishment (see Exod. 32:12; Num. 10:35; 2 Kings 23:26). Hence, a translation such as 'return [from your anger] to us' is also possible.

You have shaken the land and torn it open; mend its fractures, for it is quaking. You have shown your people desperate times; you have given us wine that makes us stagger (*vv. 2-3*). A metaphorical description is given of the trouble as if it was an earthquake that had occurred. Deep fissures have appeared in the land and God is appealed to as the one who alone can heal and restore. The people are going through bitter experiences that have left them dazed as if they were drunk. The use of the word *qâsheh* (NIV, 'desperate times') may well have conjured up recollections of the bitter experiences of Israel in Egypt (cf. its use in Exod. 1:14).

2. Confident of Victory (*v. 4*)
But for those who fear you, you have raised a banner to be unfurled against the bow. *Selah* (*v. 4*). The banner mentioned here is not calling for a military campaign but rather to show where protection is to be found. Against the attacking armies (called here 'the bow'), God is providing a place of refuge for those who fear him. Jeremiah 4:6 illustrates this same use of the word for 'banner', where the signal is for *flight* instead of

---

[2] The Hebrew verb *pârats* can be used of God's punitive action against Israel (Isa. 5:5; Ps. 80:12), just as it can be employed to describe his judgments upon Israel's enemies (2 Sam. 5:20; 1 Chron. 14:11).

fight. The verb 'unfurled' may have been used deliberately as it seems to echo the word 'banner'.[3]

3. An Appeal for Salvation (*vv. 5-8*)

Save us and help us with your right hand, that those you love may be delivered (*v. 5*). In spite of all the troubles, the psalmist still sees the nation as God's people (NIV 'those you love'). He wants God's might to be shown in saving them. The appeal is stated even more urgently than our English versions suggest. He asks: 'Save by your right hand, and answer us!'[4]

God has spoken from his sanctuary: 'In triumph I will parcel out Shechem and measure off the Valley of Succoth (*v. 6*). The assurance which the psalmist has about ultimate victory comes from a declaration which God has made. The word 'sanctuary' in the NIV could also be rendered 'holiness', which would make the expression like that in Psalm 89:35: 'I have sworn by my holiness.' The declaration refers to all the major areas of David's kingdom, both on the west bank of the Jordan and in Transjordania. Occupation of these areas is by the sovereign determination of God. Shechem is north of Jerusalem, near the mountains Ebal and Gerizim. Succoth is east of the Jordan near the brook Jabbok.

Gilead is mine, and Manasseh is mine; Ephraim is my helmet, Judah my sceptre. Moab is my washbasin, upon Edom I toss my sandal; over Philistia I shout in triumph' (*vv. 7-8*). God's sovereignty embraces all the territory occupied by Israel, but also that of the surrounding nations Moab, Edom, and Philistia. Gilead and Manasseh represent the territory captured on the east bank of the Jordan before the main conquest took place. Ephraim and Judah, in turn, represent the territory on the west bank of the Jordan, and they are the LORD's helmet and the commander's staff (for Judah, as the sceptre, see Gen. 49:10 and Num. 24:17). The

---

[3] The word 'banner', *nês*, is followed by the verb *lᵉhitnôsês*, though the verb could be either a denominative verb created from *nês* and meaning 'to rally [around a banner]', or from the verb *nûs* meaning 'to flee'.

[4] The Qᵉre has 'save me', but it is better to follow the Kᵉtiv and read 'save *us*'.

references to Moab, Edom, and Philistia imply that they are totally subservient to God.

4. A Further Complaint over Rejection (*vv. 9-11*)

Who will bring me to the fortified city? Who will lead me to Edom? Is it not you, O God, you who have rejected us and no longer go out with our armies? Give us aid against the enemy, for the help of man is worthless (*vv. 9-11*). In the midst of the seeming alienation from God, the psalmist still knows that help only comes from him. He asks to be brought against a fortified city (possibly an allusion to Tyre, see 2 Sam. 24:7), and for leadership in battle against Edom. In spite of defeats that they had endured, the people recognise that if victory is to come, it will only be by God's leadership in battle. Hence they appeal to God to intervene with divine help. They know that they cannot gain assistance from other human sources, for the strength of man is a delusion (1 Sam. 17:47; Jer. 17:5). In verse 12 the MT has the word 'God' (*'elohîm*) twice, whereas the NIV only translates it once. The double usage gives a further sense of urgency to the prayer for help.

5. A Song of Victory (*v. 12*)

With God we will gain the victory, and he will trample down our enemies (*v. 12*). The psalm begins with God's rejection of his people. It ends with a note of assurance. Strength for battle is the LORD's, and he is able to subdue his enemies, who are also the enemies of his people. God, who had allocated the land to Israel (vv. 6-7), and who controlled the destinies of the surrounding nations (v. 8), is able to bring deliverance to his people.

Psalm 61

For the director of music. With stringed instruments. Of David.

Psalms 60 and 61 share some common features. Both have as their background military situations, with the call to God to provide defence and safety (60:9-12; 61:1-4). They also refer to his people in similar terms (60:4: 'those who fear you'; 61:5: 'those who fear your name'). Both psalms also mention the tabernacle, 60:6 calling it 'his holy place' (*qodshô*), whereas 61:4 uses the common expression of 'tent' (*'ôhel*). While Psalm 60 is specific in its reference to enemies, Psalm 61 alludes to them in non-specific terms. This fact, and the generous use of metaphorical language, makes the psalm applicable to many different situations, and so enhances its usefulness to contemporary believers.

The central plea for help contained in this psalm is typical of many other psalms, yet the prayer for the king (vv. 5-7) raises various questions. Is this psalm composed *by* the king, or is it written by someone else who includes the petition *on behalf of* the king? While no definitive answer can be given to these questions, yet it is most probable that the prayer is on behalf of the king by some other Israelite. Abrupt prayers for the king occur in others psalms as well (cf. Ps. 63:11). The prayer for the king reached its fullest answer in the provision of Christ as the one to whom is given the throne of his father David and who will reign for ever and ever (Luke 1:32-33).

1. A Prayer for Protection (*vv. 1-5*)

Hear my cry, O God; listen to my prayer (*v. 1*). The nature of the distress is not spelled out, but the psalmist asks for God to pay attention to his cry. This word 'cry' is used in the Old

Testament both of cries of joy (cf. Isa. 14:7, NIV 'singing') as well as of cries of sorrow (cf. 1 Kings 8:28). Here it is clearly used of sorrow, as the following verses show. The request is for God to hear, and by implication, to answer his call. The vocabulary, especially the use of synonyms, is typical of cries of distress in the Psalter (cf. among other instances, Ps. 17:1, cry/prayer; Pss. 39:12 and 102:1, prayer/cry for help; Ps. 143:1, prayer/cry for mercy).

From the ends of the earth I call to you, I call as my heart grows faint; lead me to the rock that is higher than I *(v. 2)*. The opening of verse 2 has suggested to some commentators that the psalm was composed when David was fleeing from Saul and therefore when he was literally far away. However, the expression need not be pressed in this geographical way. It may well be expressing the conviction that wherever he is, and in whatever distressing circumstances, he will call on God. In his weakness he calls out, and desires to find a sure place of refuge with his God.[1] In the Old Testament God is often called a rock (*tsûr*, cf. 1 Sam. 2:2), and some personal names also reflect this concept (cf. Zuriel [Num. 3:35, 'my Rock is El']; Zurishaddai [Num. 1:6, 'my Rock is Shaddai']). The thought is the same as Psalm 27:5, 'he will ... set me high upon a rock', though there is no need to follow the LXX here and render 'you lifted me up on a rock' which conforms the text closer to that earlier psalm.

For you have been my refuge, a strong tower against the foe (*v. 3*). The psalmist looks back at past deliverances, and he makes these the basis for confidence for the future. He had found in God a true shelter when he was attacked by enemies.[2] The phrase 'a strong tower' (*migdal ʿoz*) occurs in other places in the Old Testament (Judg. 9:51; Prov. 18:10) as well as in documents from Qumran.[3] It can be regarded

---

[1] The NIV inserts a second 'I call' that does not appear in the MT. This is unnecessary as the phrase can be rendered 'when my heart grows faint (or, is faint)'.

[2] The MT has simply 'a foe', not 'the foe'. This suggests the psalmist was not thinking of a specific event, but rather indicating that whenever a threat appeared he had a secure place of refuge.

[3] *DCH*, V, p. 131.

as a compound noun,[4] and may even warrant the translation 'impregnable tower'.

I long to dwell in your tent forever and take refuge in the shelter of your wings. ***Selah*** (*v.* 4). Refuge may well have been found at the tabernacle in Jerusalem (see, in addition to this verse, Isa. 14:32). This was an extension of the custom that in certain circumstances a fleeing criminal could find safety by seizing the horns of the altar (1 Kings 1:50). To take refuge under God's wings may be an allusion to the wings of the cherubim over the ark of the covenant, or else as a general allusion to the protective care of God which resembled a bird's care of its young. Isaiah 14:32 utilises the idea of finding refuge under the wings of the LORD to make the point that diplomacy will never save. What is required is finding safety with the LORD (for other passages using the same idiom, see also Ruth 2:12; Pss. 17:8; 36:7; 57:1; and 91:4). The use of the verb 'to take refuge' (*châsâh*) reinforces the idea already made in the previous verse with the occurrence of the derived noun 'refuge' (*machseh*).

In times of past distress the psalmist had made vows to God, and his prayers had been answered. **You have heard my vows, O God; you have given me the heritage of those who fear your name** (*v.* 5). The 'heritage' normally refers to the life in the promised land, which was a possession belonging to those who fear the LORD (Ps. 25:12-14). In more general terms, 'heritage' refers to the benefits of covenant life. The idea is carried over in the New Testament in the words of Jesus: 'Blessed are the meek, for they will inherit the earth' (Matt. 5:5).

2. A Prayer for the King (*vv.* 6-7)

Increase the days of the king's life, his years for many generations. May he be enthroned in God's presence forever; appoint your love and faithfulness to protect him (*vv.* 6-7). The focus switches from personal petition to a prayer

---

[4] As Dahood, *The Psalms II: 51-100*, p. 85, takes the words as a composite noun, arguing that composite words in Ugaritic 'are sufficient to indicate that Hebrew lexicographers have underestimated their number in the OT'. He renders it 'towered fortress'.

for the divinely established monarchy. To ask for 'days' for the king is equivalent to requesting prosperity for him, and this is strengthened by reference to 'years' and 'generations'.[5] The psalmist wants the king to remain for ever,[6] supported and upheld by God's love and faithfulness. The Davidic dynasty had been promised an enduring existence (cf. Ps. 89:36), and ultimately Christ would come of this line. The Aramaic Targum on this psalm (dating from post-Christian times) refers to 'the King Messiah', showing how Jewish understanding of this psalm interpreted it after the seeming end of the Davidic line. The second part of verse 7 is awkward for two reasons. First, the verb 'appoint' (*man*) is omitted in two manuscripts and by Jerome, but that is not sufficient reason to delete it. It appears to be an abbreviated imperative from the verb 'to appoint' (*mânâh*).[7] Secondly, the verb 'to protect' is strictly an imperfect form, 'they will protect', and it lacks the expected 'and' before it. However, it makes good sense to see it as designating the consequence of God's appointment of 'love and faithfulness' as the king's guardian angels.[8]

3. A Vow to God (*v. 8*)

Then will I ever sing praise to your name and fulfil my vows day after day (*v. 8*). The subject in the closing verse is again the psalmist himself. The psalm, which begins with an appeal for help, closes on a note of confidence. Praise shall constantly be made to God's name, and vows will be fulfilled as an expression of gratitude. The emphasis is on continual

---

[5] The literal rendering of the MT is 'days on the days of the king you will add'. This idiom with the preposition *ʿal,* used in the sense of 'in addition to', is also found in Deuteronomy 19:9 with the same verb (*yâsaf,* Hi.). The form of the verb is imperfect in Hebrew ('you will increase'), but in the context the NIV translation ('Increase') can be defended, even though it is not absolutely required.

[6] The use of the verb 'sit' in the sense of 'sit enthroned' is well attested in regal contexts. Many of the references are given in *TDOT,* VI, pp. 430-31, and in *DCH,* IV, p. 318.

[7] This was noted long ago by F. Delitzsch, *Psalms,* I, p. 204, who cites other similar abbreviated imperatives (*has, nas, tsav*).

[8] *DIHG~S,* p. 107, notes this passage as an example where the *vav* is sometimes omitted in a clause indicating purpose or consequence.

praise, rather than eternal praise. This is made clear by the parallelism between 'ever sing' and 'day after day' (Hebrew, *yôm yôm*, lit. 'day, day'). The vows have previously been referred to as having been heard by God (*v.* 5); now there is an additional commitment to keep them.

Psalm 62

For the director of music. For Jeduthun.[1] *A psalm of David.*

This psalm is unusual in that it does not contain prayer or address to God. However, it does contain repeated assertions concerning his character, especially as saviour and defender. In this respect it is similar to the preceding psalm in the range of metaphors it uses to depict God's might. He is called 'a rock' (*tsûr*), 'a fortress' (*misgâv*), 'my mighty rock' (*tsûr ʿuzzî*), and 'my refuge' (*machsî*). These metaphors reach a climax with the declaration in verse 11 that 'might belongs to God' (*kî ʿoz lêʾlohîm*, NIV 'that you, O God, are mighty'). Another link with Psalm 61 is the fact that both psalms make reference to God's covenantal love (*chésed*) near their conclusion (61:7; 62:12).

There is a refrain in verses 1-2 and 5-6, though this comes at the beginning of sections, rather than at the end of them as is more common. The term *Selah* appears twice (vv. 4 and 8), and in these cases it does seem to designate an end of a specific division of the psalm. Six times in the psalm the same Hebrew particle occurs (*ʾack*), always at the beginning of verses. It is very noticeable in the refrain, where in the NIV it is rendered 'alone' in verses 1-2 and 5-6.

Another striking feature of the psalm is the alternation that occurs regarding who is being addressed. In verses 1-2 the psalmist is talking with himself, a conversation amplified in verses 5-7. He also has some opponents in mind in verses 3-4,

---

[1] The word 'Jeduthun' appears in the titles of three psalms (39, 62, and 77). While it may be a reference to a man by that name whom David appointed to be the director of music at the temple (1 Chron. 16:41-42), yet here and in Psalm 77 the fact that it is preceded by the preposition *ʿal* ('according to') suggests that is the name of a tune.

and the shift to the plural in verses 8-10 ('*our* refuge') implies that he is addressing an assembly of God's people. At the end of the psalm, after ascribing strength to God (v. 11), he directly addresses the Lord (v. 12).

1. Confidence in God (*vv. 1-4*)

My soul finds rest in God alone; my salvation comes from him. He alone is my rock and my salvation; he is my fortress, I will never be shaken (*vv. 1-2*). The concept of rest in the Lord is found in other psalms as well (see 37:7; 131:2; and cf. Lam. 3:26). It denotes a quiet waiting for salvation that comes exclusively from him. The word 'rest' (*dûmiyâh*) is actually from a Hebrew root that means 'to be silent' (*dâmâh* III). The psalmist waits silently and in confidence before his Saviour, and he mounts up expressions to point to his utter confidence in God. He is a rock and fortress, able to give sure defence to those who trust in him. The promise was given that God would never let the righteous be shaken (Ps. 55:22; NIV 'never fall'). The psalmist appropriates that promise for himself and rests in that knowledge.

How long will you assault a man? Would all of you throw him down – this leaning wall, this tottering fence? They fully intend to topple him from his lofty place; they take delight in lies. With their mouths they bless, but in their hearts they curse. ***Selah*** (*vv. 3-4*). From speaking of his refuge in God, the psalmist turns to the enemies who have been coming against him and addresses them directly. There is much similarity to the words and situation in Psalms 4:2 and 5:9. The words 'how long' imply that they have been opposing him for some time. They are attacking him as if he is a rickety fence, which can be pushed over easily.[2] Even though he is a person who occupies a high position in society, the plan is to remove him. They want to remove him from his lofty place and to bring him low. Hypocrisy is involved, as outwardly these people speak words of encouragement, but inwardly they curse. It

---

[2] This may be a way of speaking of his weakness, or even of the way in which his enemies view him, 'a pushover' (following J. H. Stek in the NIV *Study Bible*, [Grand Rapids: Zondervan, 1985], p. 848).

is significant that the word 'heart' is not used of these people. Instead the expression 'in their inside' (*b^e^qérev*) is employed, as though they had no heart. Later in the psalm the righteous are described as those 'with hearts' (v. 8).

2. Salvation in God Alone (*vv. 5-8*)

Find rest, O my soul, in God alone; my hope comes from him. He alone is my rock and my salvation; he is my fortress, I will not be shaken (*vv. 5-6*). The refrain of verses 1-2 recurs with slight alterations. 'My soul finds rest' gives way to an imperative, 'Find rest', while 'salvation' in verse 1 is replaced by 'hope' in verse 5. The final word of the Hebrew text in verse 2 is omitted in verse 6, and this accounts for the variation in the NIV: 'I will *never* be shaken,' compared with 'I will not be shaken'. The new section starts with a familiar affirmation that salvation is found in God alone.

My salvation and my honour depend on God; he is my mighty rock, my refuge (*v. 7*). This verse carries on the theme of the refrain, repeating some of the terms already used of God ('salvation', 'rock'). The opening descriptive terms ('salvation' and 'honour') are linked by the conjunction 'and'. This combined phrase asserts the single idea, 'my glorious salvation'.[3] It is an assertion that the psalmist's whole hope is to be found in God alone, and the accumulation of so many expressions forms a tremendous climax to his reaffirmation of trust in his sure refuge.

Trust in him at all times, O people; pour out your hearts to him, for God is our refuge. ***Selah*** (*v. 8*). An assurance of salvation for himself impels a call to others to share in the same experience of God. He wants the people as a whole to trust God at all times, for he is their refuge as well as his (cf. 'my refuge' in v. 7 with 'our refuge' here). The verb 'pour out', while a common verb, appears only rarely in

---

[3] This is following the suggestion by Marvin Tate, *Psalms 51-100*, p. 118, who also draws attention to the chiasm in the verse:

on God
    my salvation and my honour
    my mighty rock, my refuge
in God.

this expression, 'pour out your hearts' (see Lam. 2:19, 'pour out your heart like water'). It seems to imply prayer to God, openly acknowledging all the needs of the heart and life.

3. A Call to Trust in God, not Man (*vv. 9-12*)

Lowborn men are but a breath, the highborn are but a lie; if weighed on a balance, they are nothing; together they are only a breath (*v. 9*). The last division of this psalm is introduced by a statement that speaks of the futility of trusting in men, whether rich or poor. It follows the positive call to trust in God in verse 8 and the negative call of verse 10 not to trust in riches. The Hebrew text uses two different words for man (*'îsh* and *'âdâm*), represented in the NIV by 'lowborn men' and 'the highborn'.[4] It does not matter what status or wealth a person has, for he is nothing[5] and he provides no lasting support.

Do not trust in extortion or take pride in stolen goods; though your riches increase, do not set your heart on them (*v. 10*). To the sins of lies and cursing, mentioned in verse 4, are added extortion and robbery. Those who have enriched themselves in this way may think that they have acquired lasting wealth and power. However, the psalmist rightly instructs his readers not to trust in these things. The verb 'take pride' (*hâvâl*) is another use of the same Hebrew root from which 'breath' (*hével*) comes. It conveys the idea of acting vainly.[6] 1 Timothy 6:17 could be a commentary on this section of the psalm: 'Command those who are rich in this present

---

[4] The same antithetical expression (*b^enê 'âdâm b^enê 'îsh*), denoting those of low degree contrasted with those of high degree, has already been used in Psalm 49:2. It is used as a term for all humanity.

[5] Twice the Hebrew word *hével* occurs in this verse. It signifies 'a breath of air', and is placed in parallel with *kâzâv*, 'a lie', that has already been used in verse 4.

[6] The translation of the Hebrew word *hével* is not easy. It has been made more difficult because of the English word 'vanity'. It comes from the Latin word ('vanitas') that Jerome used in the Latin Vulgate Bible, taking a concrete Hebrew word and translating it by an abstract term. Contextual translation is required. Good discussions of the word will be found in Tremper Longman III, *The Book of Ecclesiastes* (NICOT; Grand Rapids: Eerdmans, 1998), pp. 61-65, and Roy B. Zuck, ed., *Reflecting with Solomon: Selected Studies on the Book of Ecclesiastes* (Grand Rapids: Baker Book House, 1994), pp. 224-25, 227-31.

world not to be arrogant nor to put their hope in wealth, which is so uncertain, but to put their hope in God, who richly provides us with everything for our enjoyment.'

One thing God has spoken, two things have I heard: that you, O God, are strong, and that you, O Lord, are loving. Surely you will reward each person according to what he has done (*vv. 11-12*). These concluding verses provide the basis for the disparagement of trusting in men given in the preceding verses. Verse 11 opens with a numerical saying of which the Old Testament has several examples (Prov. 6:16-19; 30:18-31). However, here there is no precise enumeration such as in Proverbs 6, for *three,* not *two,* statements follow. Rather than follow the NIV ('two things'), it is preferable to take the Hebrew numerals as meaning 'once, twice', in a similar way to the English use of 'two or three' to indicate an indefinite number.[7] The affirmation of God's strength and his covenantal love may have come through a recital of his great deeds for his people (cf. Ps. 136). The opening assertions of the psalm are now repeated in an alternative form. Rest and salvation are found alone with God who is both strong and loving. The concluding statement gives the subsidiary truth that God deals justly with his creatures, a truth reaffirmed several times in the New Testament (Rom. 2:6; 1 Cor. 3:8; 2 Tim. 4:14; Rev. 22:12).

---

[7] This usage is noted in *DIHG~S,* p. 48. The interpretation ('Once God spoke, twice that I heard it') was held in the nineteenth century by J. A. Alexander, *The Psalms Translated and Explained,* p. 270, and more recently by Marvin Tate, *Psalms 51-100,* p. 119, and Samuel Terrien, *The Psalms,* pp. 457, 459. I am assuming that the word *zû* following 'twice' is not the demonstrative 'this', but the relative 'that'.

Psalm 63

A psalm of David. When he was in the Desert of Judah.

The desire for God, which this psalm expresses, is similar to that in Psalms 42-43 and 84. While it contains some elements similar to the psalms of complaint, yet it is better seen as a song of rejoicing in God. Since it contains references to 'early' (v. 1; the AV, NKJV, and the NEB follow the Latin text in this regard) and to 'night' (v. 6), this psalm was used as a morning prayer from early Christian times.[1] The title sets the psalm in a period when David was a fugitive, and because of the reference to 'the king' in verse 11, the period is probably that of Absalom's rebellion rather than that of Saul's persecution.

Clear links exist between this psalm and the previous one. Words such as 'strength' (62:7, 11), 'glory' (62:7; 63:2), and 'covenant love' (62:12; 63:3) appear in each. Links also exist with Psalm 61, for in addition to the thought of 'covenant love' (61:7; 63:3), mention of the 'king' is prominent in both psalms (61:6; 63:11). The three psalms are tied together by confident trust in God and expressions of commitment to him.

In another respect, however, a contrast exists between Psalm 62 and Psalm 63. In the former the psalmist speaks of God in the third person ('he', 'him'), only changing to direct address in the final verse: '... you, O Lord, are loving.' In this psalm the direct address commences from the outset and continues through to the end of verse 8, while the final verses refer in the third person to God (cf. 'God's name' in v. 11). The abundant use of the personal pronouns 'I' and 'you' highlights

[1] The LXX also takes the reference to 'watches' in verse 7 as being the morning by its rendering *en tois orthrois*, 'in the mornings'.

the closeness of the relationship between the psalmist and his God. The repetition of 'I' and 'my' point to the personal nature of the appeals, while the use of 'you' or 'your' direct attention to his source of help and salvation.

1. Longing for God (*vv. 1-5*)

The psalm begins with a confession of absolute confidence in God. **O God, you are my God, earnestly I seek you; my soul thirsts for you, my body longs for you, in a dry and weary land where there is no water** (*v. 1*). Faith always lays hold of the personal relationship with the living God. The verb rendered 'seek' (*shâchar*) may come from a noun meaning 'dawn' (*shachar*), and because of this connection many versions have translated it by 'to seek early'. In the other usages of this verb in the Old Testament the idea of seeking God *early* is not present, and hence the NIV translation ('earnestly seek') seems close to the mark. As in Psalm 42:1-2, the psalmist compares himself to dry land which longs for water, and so does his soul long for his God.[2] The same thought appears in Psalm 143:6: 'My souls thirsts for you like a parched land.' The expression of longing for God is heightened by the parallel statements 'my soul thirsts for you, my body longs for you', even though the verb translated 'longs' only occurs here.[3] Gregory of Nazianzus (*c.* 330-389) expressed it well: 'God thirsts, to be thirsted for' (*Deus sitit, sitiri*). He longs to see his people ardently desiring him.

I have seen you in the sanctuary and beheld your power and your glory. Because your love is better than life, my lips will glorify you (*vv. 2-3*). The NIV does not translate the opening word of this verse (*kên*), which has long been a

---

[2] The Hebrew noun 'land' (*'érets*), being feminine, should be followed by feminine adjectives, but while 'dry' (*tsiyyâh*) is feminine, 'weary' (*'âyêf*) is masculine. This usage reflects the priority of the masculine gender in biblical Hebrew. For general comment on this, see *IBHS*, pp. 108-09, and for this particular example, p. 258.

[3] The verb is *k-m-h*, and the translation of it must depend on the context here. The parallelism is very clear in the Hebrew text: *tsâmᵉ'âh lᵉkâ nafshî/ kâmah lᵉkâ bᵉsârî*. The root may also appear in the personal name Chimham in 2 Samuel 19:37, 38, 40, and in the place name Geruth Chimham in Jeremiah 41:17.

discussion point.[4] Past experience of God vitalises his present relationship. He looks back to times when, at the tabernacle, he has had a vision of God. This could have been similar to Isaiah's vision (Isa. 6:1-3). The thought of 'seeing God' is used elsewhere as a metaphor for worshipping him at the tabernacle/temple (Pss. 11:7; 17:15). The content of the vision is summed up in the words: 'your power', 'your glory', 'your love'. 'Your power' may be a reference to the ark of the covenant, as the word 'power' (Hebrew, *ʿoz*) is used virtually as a synonym for 'the ark'.[5] The love that the psalmist has already experienced is preferable to any kind of life without God's favour, and it causes the psalmist to sing his praise. The verb translated 'glorify' is normally used of praising God for his mighty acts of triumph (Pss. 106:47; 117:1; 145:4; 147:12), and the NIV uses a variety of English verbs to convey the meaning ('glory', 'extol', 'commend').

I will praise you as long as I live, and in your name I will lift up my hands. My soul will be satisfied as with the richest of foods; with singing lips my mouth will praise you (*vv. 4-5*). Constant praise of the Lord is his pledge, as he directs his prayer to him. The lifting up of the hands was an outward expression of the uplifted heart (Pss. 28:2; 141:2; 1 Tim. 2:8). The fact that it was the palms or open hands that are referred to may suggest waiting on God in order to receive his blessings. He has indeed received abundantly, being filled with 'the richest of foods' (lit. 'marrow and fat'). The language may be borrowed from the ritual of sacrifice, but the fat of sacrifices was never eaten (see Lev. 3:16-17). The idea is that God's presence is

---

[4] J. J. S. Perowne, *The Psalms*, I, pp. 509-10, has a note setting out five different attempts to explain the word. His own view is that it means 'so' in the sense that it is referring back to the expressions of longing for God's presence. This is the way that the AV and NASB take it ('thus') and the RSV, NRSV, and the ESV ('so'). A similar usage of the Hebrew word is found in Psalm 127:2.

[5] This is discussed by G. Henton Davies, 'The Ark in the Psalms', in F. F. Bruce, ed., *Promise and Fulfilment: Essays Presented to Professor S. H. Hooke in celebration of his ninetieth birthday 21st January 1964* (Edinburgh: T. & T. Clark, 1964), pp. 51-61. The actual Hebrew word for 'ark' (*ʾărôn*) only occurs in the Psalter in Psalm 132:8.

like the richest of foods, and a satisfied heart will overflow in praise. The psalmist's whole being will be engaged in adoration and thanksgiving ('my soul', vv. 1 and 5; 'my body', v. 1; 'my lips', vv. 3 and 5; 'my hands', v. 4). For Christians today the New Testament direction is that through Jesus we 'continually offer to God a sacrifice of praise – the fruit of lips that confess his name' (Heb. 13:15).

2. Confidence in God's Protection *(vv. 6-10)*

On my bed I remember you; I think of you through the watches of the night (*v. 6*). The thought of verse 1 is expanded to describe a longing for God even during the hours of darkness. In Old Testament times, for civic and military purposes, the night was divided into three watches. The word 'remember' is used in the sense of 'meditate', as it parallels another Hebrew word (*hâgâh,* NIV 'think of') which is used elsewhere of meditation (see Ps. 1:2).[6]

Because you are my help, I sing in the shadow of your wings (*v. 7*). 'Help' in this context means 'deliverance'. Assurance of divine protection gives ground for joyful songs. 'Sing' (*rânan,* Pi.) picks up the element of joyful song already mentioned in verse 5, where a noun from this same root has been used (*sifᵉtê rᵉnânôtî,* NIV 'singing lips'). Many other believers have passed through similar experiences to the psalmist, including Paul and Silas (Acts 16:25). 'Shadow of your wings' refers in general to God's protective care of his servant (see comment on Ps. 57:1).

My soul clings to you; your right hand upholds me (*v. 8*). God had invited his covenant people to cling to him (see especially Deut. 10:20; 11:22; 13:4; 30:20; Josh. 22:5; 23:8), and the psalmist acknowledges that he is responding in this way. He is a loyal servant who is walking in God's way and fearing him. Consequently he is held in the sure grip of his God (for the same thought and using the same verb [*tâmak*], see Ps. 41:12 and Isa. 41:10). The promise in the gospel is of a

---

[6] The same parallelism involving *zâkar* and *hâgâh* appears again in Psalm 143:5. For other passages where *zâkar* has a broader meaning than just 'remember', see *DCH*, III, p. 108.

Saviour who holds his people so that no one can snatch them out of his hand (John 10:28).

They who seek my life will be destroyed; they will go down to the depths of the earth. They will be given over to the sword and become food for jackals (*vv. 9-10*). Ultimate vindication lay ahead of the psalmist, when his enemies will come under divine judgment. Those who now seek his life will find that their own lives will be taken. The language of verse 10 describes a military battle and its aftermath, with dead bodies being left in the field as carrion for wild animals.

3. Joy in God (*v. 11*)

But the king will rejoice in God; all who swear by God's name will praise him, while the mouths of liars will be silenced. The psalm ends on a note of joyful confidence. David refers to himself as 'the king', for even when fleeing from Jerusalem he still knows that he is the divinely appointed king. In his rejoicing he will be joined by 'all who swear by God's name' (Hebrew, 'by him'). This is a reference to the practice of taking oaths in God's name (Deut. 6:13; 10:20; 1 Kings 8:31). In the MT no object follows the verb 'praise'. Either 'him' can be inserted as the NIV does, or else an alternative choice of verb that does not need an object can be used (e.g. 'boast'). The liars are those enemies whose destruction has just been described (vv. 8-9). Their voices will be stilled, while those of the faithful will rise in joyful song.

Psalm 64

For the director of music. A psalm of David.

Once more evident links occur with the preceding psalms. Both Psalms 63 and 64 end on the same note of praise and with the same verbs ('rejoice', *sâmach*; 'praise', *hâlal*, Hitp.). While Psalm 63 is expressive of confidence in God who protects and covers his saints, Psalms 61, 62, and 64 all use either the verb 'to trust' (*mâchâh*) or the derived noun, 'refuge' (*machseh*) to describe the relationship with God (see 61:3, 4; 62:8; 64:10).

Many of David's psalms of complaint are similar in tone to this one. They tell of enemies who wound with words, though they are not named. There is a sharp contrast in this psalm between two kinds of attacks. On the one hand, the enemies attack with their deadly arrows (v. 3), but on the other hand God attacks them with his arrows (v. 7). What is striking is the fact that both sections, dealing with the enemies' attacks and God's response, use almost identical language in Hebrew.[1]

evildoers (v. 3, Hebrew, root *p-ʿ-l*)	God's doing (v. 9, Hebrew, root *p-ʿ-l*)
their tongue (v. 3)	their tongue (v. 8a)
arrows (v. 3b)	his arrow (v. 7a)
suddenly (v. 4b)	suddenly (v. 7b)
without fear (v. 4b)	everyone will fear (v. 9a)
who can see (v. 5b)	all who see (v. 8b)
heart (v. 6b)	upright in heart (v. 10b)

This pattern serves to emphasise the fact that the evil actions of the enemies are repaid to them by God, a theme that is

[1] This is set out well by Konrad Schaefer, *Psalms* (Collegeville: Liturgical Press, 2001), p. 155.

dealt with in Psalms 7:6 and 37:14-15 (see the commentary on these passages).

The psalm rises to its climax in the final verse, with the thought of God's protective care of his people, and the resultant praise that the upright render to him. This praise is not just from a few who have observed what has happened, but from 'all mankind'. The thought that all will see the great works of God and many will find salvation in him, is developed further in both the Psalms and the prophets (Pss. 67:7; 98:1-3; Isa. 45:20-25).

1. The Opening Call to God *(v. 1)*

Hear me, O God, as I voice my complaint; protect my life from the threat of the enemy *(v. 1)*. From a troubled heart the psalmist cries out to God. The more common form of request is 'Hear my prayer' (cf. 4:1; 39:12; 54:2; 84:8), though 'Hear my voice' also occurs elsewhere in the Psalms (cf. 27:7; 119:149), and the two expressions are practically synonymous. He prays for protection 'from the threat (lit. 'fear') of the enemy', for he knows that God has the power to keep his people safe. His love and faithfulness will ever protect them (see the same verb in Ps. 61:7, another link with the preceding psalms).

2. The Description of the Enemies *(vv. 2-6)*

Hide me from the conspiracy of the wicked, from that noisy crowd of evildoers. They sharpen their tongues like swords and aim their words like deadly arrows *(vv. 2-3)*. The battle is not fought with physical weapons but with sharp words that wound as if they are swords or arrows. The tongue is 'restless evil, full of deadly poison' (James 3:8). These bitter words (Hebrew, *mar*, 'bitter', 'poisonous') come after the wicked have taken counsel together, and from this noisy crowd there come attacks from which the psalmist needs God's protection.[2] God is able to keep the psalmist and hide him from mortal enemies (see Ps. 17:8-9).

[2] NIV's 'noisy crowd' translates *rigshâh*, a word that only occurs here in the OT. In the context this seems close to the mark, as it continues and probably surpasses the idea of evildoers taking counsel together. The rabble are out to take their revenge.

They shoot from ambush at the innocent man; they shoot at him suddenly, without fear (*v.* 4). The enemies act in deceptive ways in that they wait in hiding places (NIV 'ambush').[3] From these they launch their attacks without warning, and they do so brazenly. The psalmist again protests his innocence, not in the sense of sinlessness, but in that he is clear in conscience before God, an upright man (Hebrew, *tâm*). The word occurs thirteen times in the Old Testament, many of these in reference to Job (see, e.g., Job 1:8; 2:3).

They encourage each other in evil plans, they talk about hiding their snares; they say, 'Who will see them?' They plot injustice and say, 'We have devised a perfect plan!' Surely the mind and heart of man are cunning (*vv.* 5-6). The threat of the enemy is further defined.[4] Those who are plotting evil against the psalmist take mutual encouragement in their schemes. They plan 'an evil matter' (*dâvâr raʿ*), a phrase that matches the earlier expression 'a deadly matter' (*dâvâr mar)* in verse 2. The enemies also boast that this is hidden from others, and that they have devised the ideal plot. This displays the innate sinfulness of mankind. In addition, it is a triumphal expression that betrays the pride that sinners take in their own wickedness. The final statement in verse 6, 'Surely the mind and heart of man are cunning', is best taken as an expression of the psalmist, and should be marked off in some way, perhaps with parentheses: ('The inward nature and the human heart – how deep they are!')[5] It should be set beside

---

[3] The word 'ambush' (*mistâr*) is from the same root as the verb 'hide' (*sâtar*) in verse 2.

[4] The translation of the first part of verse 7 is difficult for several reasons: 1. Three words from the same Hebrew root (*ch-f-s*) appear: the verbal form 'they plot' (*yachpᵉsû*), the noun 'plot' (*chêpes*), and the participle 'searched out', 'plotted' (*mᵉchupâs*). 2. The noun *ʿôlot* is most probably the plural of *ʿavlâh*, 'perversity'. 3. The verbal form *tamᵉnû* could be the qal pf. 1 pl. of *t-m-m*, with it being an unusual form instead of the expected *tammônû*, as was suggested by *GKC* §67.e. Alternatively, it could be from the root *t-m-n*, 'to hide', that has already been used in verse 5 (though the initial letter of this verb is *tet*, not *tav*). In view of the uncertainty, the NIV is an acceptable attempt at translation. Tate, *The Psalms 51-100*, p. 131, goes so far as to say that 'no translation should be treated with confidence'.

[5] This is Tate's translation, ibid., p. 130.

that of Psalm 14:3, as a description of the depth of human sinfulness: 'All have turned aside, they have together become corrupt; there is no one who does good, not even one.'

3. God's Impending Judgment (*vv. 7-9*)
But God will shoot them with arrows; suddenly they will be struck down. He will turn their own tongues against them and bring them to ruin; all who see them will shake their heads in scorn (*vv. 7-8*). Earlier the psalmist has spoken of the suddenness with which the enemies shoot at him (v. 4). Now he says it is God who is going to shoot suddenly! This is a presentation of the teaching given elsewhere in the Psalms that the sins of people often turn back against themselves (Pss. 37:14-15; 54:5; 59:12). The NIV is paraphrastic in verse 8. The MT has: 'They will make him stumble, their tongue [being] against them; all who see them will nod their heads' (or, 'will flee from them').[6] A more literal translation than the NIV is: 'And they are confounded, their tongue comes upon themselves, all their admirers flee away'.[7] Despite the uncertainty the general message is clear. God will bring judgment upon these wicked people, and this will be greeted with the recognition by others that this is indeed a just penalty for them. What form the judgment will take is not specified.

All mankind will fear; they will proclaim the works of God and ponder what he has done (*v. 9*). Those who once showed no fear (see v. 4) will now, along with everyone, show fear. God's judgment will be seen by men in general and cause them to acknowledge the fitness of what has happened. Those who were doers of evil (*poʿ*ᵃ*lê ʾâven*, v. 2) will discover that what God has done (*poʿal* ᵉ*lohîm*) has made their plans ineffective. Being an eyewitness of God's mighty hand at work should cause men to 'know that the LORD is God; besides him

---

[6] The translation differs according to the view taken on the verb in question. Standard dictionaries take varied positions as to whether the verb is *nâdad* Hitp., 'to flee', or *nûd* Hitp., 'to shake the head'.

[7] This is the translation of E. W. Hengstenberg, *Commentary on the Psalms*, II, p. 308, and similar translations can be found in J. A. Alexander, *The Psalms Translated and Explained*, p. 284; F. Delitzsch, *The Psalms*, II, p. 220; and A. F. Kirkpatrick, *The Psalms*, p. 359.

there is no other' (Deut. 4:35). True acknowledgment of God's actions should lead to proclamation to others of his actions, and meditation on the wonder of his works.

4. A Call to Rejoice (*v. 10*)

Let the righteous rejoice in the LORD and take refuge in him; let all the upright in heart praise him! (*v. 10*). The righteous should take encouragement for the future from the promise of God's judgment. We are not to take revenge ourselves on enemies, but to 'leave room for God's wrath, for it is written: "It is mine to avenge; I will repay," says the Lord' (Rom. 12:19). Meanwhile, those who belong to the LORD take refuge in him and extol his name in praise and adoration. Quiet confidence in him has to replace fear of scheming enemies. The contrast between the wicked and the righteous is made clear – the former have pursued their evil plots, while the latter have displayed uprightness of heart.[8]

[8] R. Davidson, *The Vitality of Worship: A Commentary on the Book of Psalms*, Grand Rapids: Eerdmans, 1998), p. 202, makes a link between this psalm and Psalm 1, pointing also to Paul's words in Philippians 4:4-9 which call for rejoicing, but then describe the character of the righteous (vv. 8-9).

Psalm 65

For the director of music. A psalm of David. A song.

This psalm is the first of a quartet of psalms that share common themes. While mention is made of the temple in Jerusalem (65:4; 66:13; 68:24, 29), yet the note of universalism pervades them (65:2, 5; 66:1, 4, 8; 67:3-5; 68:28-33). These songs constitute a call to the nations to acknowledge the God of Israel as the mighty saviour and to join in praise to him.

While the latter part of this psalm could easily be called simply a harvest song, yet the clear framework of the psalm shows that it had a much wider setting. Its structure is clear. It begins with a declaration that God is the one who answers prayer, and then shows three ways in which this prayer is answered. There is a meeting with God in his temple (v. 4), a revelation of his power in the created world (vv. 5-8), and finally attention is drawn to the bounty of God in providing so liberally for his creatures (vv. 9-13). There are no indications in the psalm of any specific setting for its use. Hence, it can be assumed to be a thanksgiving song appropriate on many occasions throughout the year.[1]

1. A Prayer-Hearing God (*vv. 1-4*)

Praise awaits you, O God, in Zion; to you our vows will be fulfilled (*v. 1*). The opening phrase is difficult, for literally it says, 'To you, praise is silence.' The AV margin notes that literally its rendering 'waiteth' is 'silent', while the NIV margin

[1] Craig Broyles, *Psalms*, pp. 266-67, argues that the psalm points to various specific times throughout the agricultural year (Feast of Tabernacles, Feast of Unleavened Bread, Day of Atonement). The phraseology in the psalm is too indefinite to allow precise identification to take place.

says: 'Or, *befits*; the meaning of the Hebrew for this word is uncertain'.[2] Perhaps the picture is a personification of praise that waits to be stirred up by the worshippers (cf. Ps. 57:8, and see the comments on Ps. 62-1-2). Most English versions follow the AV in suggesting the meaning is that praise waits for God. The psalmist seems to be concentrating on Jerusalem[3] and the temple (see v. 4) as the places where praise is specially dedicated to God, though the following verse shows that he is not restricting it to these locations. The vows could have been made during a time of trouble, or else may reflect a promise to God at the time of planting of the crops.

O you who hear prayer, to you all men will come (*v.* 2). The psalmist is confident that men everywhere will see evidences of God's goodness, and they will turn to him. The words imply that they will come to him as the prayer-hearing God, and make their requests. 'All flesh' (NIV 'all men') elsewhere denotes all mankind (see Ps. 145:21, NIV 'every living creature'). The choice of 'all *flesh*' (*kol bâsâr*) throws emphasis on the frailty of humans as they make their approach to the mighty God (cf. the contrast in Isaiah 31:3 between God/spirit and men/flesh).

When we were overwhelmed by sins, you forgave our transgressions (*v.* 3). In the past the psalmist and his people were in a position in which there seemed to be no answer to the problem of their sin and guilt. The NIV rendering of verse 3 emends the MT, altering 'various kinds of iniquities have overwhelmed *me*' to 'overwhelmed *us*'.[4] However, the MT can be explained without this change. The psalmist thinks first of his own sins in all their variety,[5] and then says to God:

---

[2] The early versions, such as the LXX, interpret the word rendered 'silence' as 'fitting', 'what is due'. This needs an emendation of the MT text so that the word is from *dâmâh*, 'to be like'. Modern versions that adopt this approach include the RSV, JB, REB, and the ESV.

[3] The LXX makes the location of Zion explicit by adding 'in Jerusalem' at the end of the verse.

[4] The alteration involves changing the MT *mennî*, 'from me', to *mennû*, 'from us', which does appear in some Hebrew manuscripts.

[5] The Hebrew expression is *div^erê ʿ^avonot*, lit. 'words (or, deeds) of iniquities'. It is a very unusual phrase, and I am taking it as meaning the many kinds of iniquities that the psalmist had committed.

'Our sins – you atone for them!' Where sin abounded, grace abounded all the more (Rom. 5:20)! God provided atonement for their sins, just as he did when he declared to Isaiah: 'Your guilt is taken away and your sin atoned for' (Isa. 6:7).[6]

Blessed are those you choose and bring near to live in your courts! We are filled with the good things of your house, of your holy temple (*v. 4*). How blessed is the person on whom God sets his love (cf. the use of the verb 'choose' of Israel in Deut. 7:7, and of the choice of Zion in Ps. 132:13), and whom he invites into his sanctuary! The emphasis is on God's work – '*you* choose', '*you* bring near'. This is the answer to the questions of Psalms 15:1 and 24:3. Because of God's free grace, he atones for the sins of the penitent and brings them into close and abiding fellowship with himself. What is received at the sanctuary is not only material blessings (i.e. a share in the fellowship offerings), but also the spiritual blessings that are given in full measure to forgiven sinners. The expression 'the good things' (*tûv*) is a collective one denoting the fullness of blessings that God provides.

2. A Creator God (*vv. 5-8*)

You answer us with awesome deeds of righteousness, O God our Saviour, the hope of all the ends of the earth and of the farthest seas, who formed the mountains by your power, having armed yourself with strength, who stilled the roaring of the seas, the roaring of their waves, and the turmoil of the nations (*vv. 5-7*). The great creator God answers the prayers of his people by deeds that inspire awe. The phrase 'awesome deeds' can refer to the events of the Exodus (see Exod. 34:10; Deut. 10:21; and Ps. 106:21-22), but here it refers to some more recent demonstrations of God's saving power. The thought of 'deeds of righteousness' is similar to the use of the word 'righteousness' (*tsédek*) in Isaiah in particular to denote 'victory' or 'triumph' (Isa. 41:2, 10; 46:13; 51:5-6). Here God has shown his saving power on behalf of his people. Three things are then said about this Saviour. First, he is the object of the hope of all the world. Even those of the farthest seas will come

---

[6] The same Hebrew verb *kâfar*, Pi., 'to atone', is used in both Isaiah 6:7 and here in verse 5.

to trust in him. The psalms show us that the missionary vision flowing from Genesis 12:3 was very real for some Old Testament believers (cf. Ps. 67 also). Secondly, he is the creator of the mighty mountains, which stresses how powerful he is as Saviour. Thirdly, he is the controller of his world, in that he stills both the roaring of the mighty oceans and also the turmoils of human society.

Those living far away fear your wonders; where morning dawns and evening fades you call forth songs of joy (*v. 8*). The vision of the psalmist is still on the ends of the earth. Even to the remotest place, knowledge of God's wonders will reach, and there people will come to fear him. The word 'wonders' is literally 'signs', which most commonly points to miraculous acts of God's power such as the plagues at the time of the Exodus (Exod. 7:3; Deut. 4:34). 'Morning' and 'evening' are used here to denote 'east' and 'west'. All over the world God is going to call forth songs of joy from creation itself, a theme developed later in the Psalter (see 96:11-13; 97:1, 6; and 98:4-9).[7]

3. A Bountiful God (*vv. 9-13*)

The switch to the third section of the psalm takes place here. The subject is the fruitfulness that God grants to the land. Because of his gracious providence, there is bountiful provision for his world. **You care for the land and water it; you enrich it abundantly. The streams of God are filled with water to provide the people with grain, for so you have ordained it. You drench its furrows and level its ridges; you soften it with showers and bless its crops** (*vv. 9-10*). While this part could be a harvest song, yet its use is far wider, as it appears to be stating general principles.[8] One of the promises of God to the children of Israel was that the land of

---

[7] Craig Broyles, *Psalms*, p. 271, is right in pointing out that whereas the NIV translates the final verb without an object, it should have 'the going forth of the morning' (east) and 'the evening' ('west') as the object, so that the picture is of creation, not only its inhabitants, rejoicing.

[8] It is difficult to decide on the best tenses for the English translation of verses 10-13. Some want to see verses 10-12a as being in the past, while verses 12b-13 are in the present. Others want to take some of the verbs as imperatives – 'drench', 'soak', 'bless'. I agree with the NIV translators that the passage is describing God's characteristic actions towards his creation.

Canaan was going to be a land 'that drinks rain from heaven. It is a land the LORD your God cares for; the eyes of the LORD your God are continually on it from the beginning of the year to its end' (Deut. 11:11-12). Here that promise is put into poetic language. 'The streams of God' may be equivalent to the expression 'the floodgates of the heavens' (Gen. 7:11; 8:2). The preparation of the land (see NIV margin) is described in greater detail in verse 10. The early rains prepare the ground for sowing, while later rains in mid-winter soften it and allow the crops to grow.

You crown the year with your bounty, and your carts overflow with abundance (*v. 11*). The climax of the whole process is that God gives the harvest, he provides the bounty (*tôvâh,* lit. 'goodness'; cf. its use in Pss. 31:19 and 68:10). The NIV presents one interpretation of the second half of the verse. God is pictured driving through the land in his chariots, which are so richly laden that they drop some of their abundance. However, the word rendered 'carts' is a rare word, and it is preferable to take it as meaning 'pastures' as in Psalm 23:3, as this fits the context admirably.[9]

The grasslands of the desert overflow; the hills are clothed with gladness. The meadows are covered with flocks and the valleys are mantled with grain; they shout for joy and sing (*vv. 12-13*). Nature herself is personified, as in Psalms 96:11-12 and 98:7-8 and Isaiah 44:23 and 49:13. She sings for joy at the bountiful harvest that God has given. Even the deserts will blossom, overflowing with new growth. Grasslands, hills, meadows, and valleys have all experienced his bountiful provision, and together they rejoice at such evidence of his love and care.

---

[9] The difficulty of translating this word is highlighted by the fact that the *DCH*, V, pp. 379-80 gives four possibilities for it. One of these is followed in the NLT ('even the hard pathways overflow') and this also makes good sense in the context, as it forms a parallel with the expression 'grasslands of the desert' in the next verse.

Psalm 66

For the director of music. A song. A psalm.

There are obvious links between Psalms 65 and 66. Both have the vision of all the earth praising God (65:2, 8; 66:1, 4), and specific reference to his awesome deeds in both is a further connecting idea (65:5; 66:3). No precise historical setting can be given for Psalm 66. It seems to be a song of thanksgiving after some victory by the nation, such as when Sennacherib of Assyria was defeated (2 Kings 19:35-36). The sudden switch from the use of the first person plural in verses 1-12 to the first person singular in verses 13-20 has suggested to many that two earlier psalms were joined together. However, the 'I' of verses 13-20 could be the king speaking on behalf of the people, or a personification of the nation as an individual (cf. a similar situation in Lam. 1). The latter suggestion, though, seems unacceptable, as the speaker appears to be a real person who can appeal to his fellow-believers (v. 16). Also, the content of verses 13-20 flow on from the historical references in verses 8-12.[1] The use of similar phrases, 'Come and see' (*l^{e}kû ûr^{e}ʾû*, v. 5), and 'Come and hear' (*l^{e}kû shim^{e}ʿû*, v. 16) link the two major sections of the psalm together.

1. Universal Praise of the King (*vv. 1-4*)
Shout with joy to God, all the earth! Sing to the glory of his name; make his praise glorious! (*vv. 1-2*). The opening call is repeated in Psalms 98:4 and 100:1 (with the substitution of 'Lord' for 'God'). A series of imperatives ('shout', 'sing',

[1] The personification view was advanced, among others, by E. W. Hengstenberg, *Commentary on the Psalms*, II, pp. 328-29, and followed by J. A. Alexander, *The Psalms Translated and Explained*, p. 280.

'make') call for praise to be given in song to God. Because of his greatness, glory is to be ascribed to his name. His character surpasses all others, and while human praise does not add to his glory, it is rightful recognition of his majesty and kingly rule.

Say to God, 'How awesome are your deeds! So great is your power that your enemies cringe before you. All the earth bows down to you; they sing praise to you, they sing praise to your name.' *Selah* (*vv.* 3-4). When the people look on God's actions, both those in the distant past and those more recently, they acknowledge that they are demonstrations of his great power. Onlookers stand in awe of them, and enemies will submit before him. The Hebrew word translated 'cringe' (*kâchash*) is not a common word, and it has an unusually large range of meanings. Basically it seems to mean 'deny' or 'deceive' and this may well lie behind this and other similar passages in which 'cringe' or 'submit' seems best in English (Deut. 33:29; Pss. 18:44; 81:15). This would suggest that the submission takes place, but without true belief on the part of the enemies. It is only feigned submission. In verse 4 the thought is probably that *in the future* all the earth will worship the Lord, rather than that it is doing so now. It is a picture of universal adoration and praise as the nations bow in worship before him. Ultimately all God's enemies will bow in subjection to him (Phil. 2:10-11; 1 Cor. 15:25), and they will worship him (Rev. 15:4).

2. Praise for God's Deliverances (*vv. 5-12*)

Come and see what God has done, how awesome his works in man's behalf! (*v. 5*). The invitation goes out (presumably to 'all the earth') to take notice of God's works, with this expression being practically the same as that in Psalm 46:8. In particular, his awesome deeds as he intervened on behalf of his people, are to be the object of admiration and awe. The two following verses illustrate this by appealing to the events of the Exodus.

He turned the sea into dry land, they passed through the waters on foot – come, let us rejoice in him. He rules

forever by his power, his eyes watch the nations – let not the rebellious rise up against him. Selah (*vv. 6-7*). Part of God's miraculous provision for his people was that he dried up the Red Sea. 'The waters' is 'river' in Hebrew, but nowhere is this particular word used of the Jordan. Hence, rather than see here a reference to the Red Sea *and* the Jordan, it is better to take it as alluding to the former only. The clause, 'Come, let us rejoice in him,' has been interpreted as an invitation to join in praise, but it is best to take it as a past tense.[2] The NIV 'come' translates the Hebrew word *shâm,* which normally means 'there', but at times it can mean 'then'.[3] The expression points to the rendering of praise to God for what he did at the time of the Exodus. While this may include the Song of the Sea (Exod. 15:1-18), it is a general comment on the response of the people to God's intervention on their behalf. The recollection of past divine actions is meant to form the basis of continuing praise. The reference to God's kingly rule in verse 7 is interesting, because the Song of the Sea concludes with the words: 'The LORD will reign for ever and ever' (Exod. 15:18). It is as if the psalmist is making a conscious allusion to the Book of Exodus. God's eyes are on all the nations, for he oversees all and yet overlooks none. The warning follows that the rebellious person should not vaunt himself against such a sovereign. The first of two occurrences of 'Selah' in this psalm indicates a break at the end of verse 7.

Praise our God, O peoples, let the sound of his praise be heard; he has preserved our lives and kept our feet from slipping (*vv. 8-9*). Attention switches to more recent displays of God's power, and the nations are again asked to participate in praise of what God has done. Whatever the precise details were of the recent events, it was a difficult time for the people, for their lives were in danger. God had preserved them, and he had been their keeper. When the verb 'slip' is used with 'foot' or 'feet', it denotes slipping in a time of trouble. The Lord is the one who is immovable and who gives stability to

---

[2] Though the form of the verb here is cohortative, 'let us rejoice', yet it can be translated as a past indicative, 'we rejoiced'. See *DIHG~S,* p. 83, rem. 3.

[3] *IBHS,* p. 658. Another example in the psalms occurs in Psalm 36:12.

believers (Pss. 30:6; 62:2; 112:6). He holds his children so that their feet do not slip (Pss. 17:5; 94:18).

For you, O God, tested us; you refined us like silver. You brought us into prison and laid burdens on our backs (*vv. 10-11*). The experiences the people had just undergone were intended by God to purify them. This may have meant refining the people so that the ungodly among the nation were removed (Jer. 6:29), or that the people were better prepared for service. The idea of refining of metals becomes a common Old Testament metaphor for the testing and refining of God's people (Pss. 17:3; 26:2; Isa. 1:25; Zech. 13:9). The word translated 'prison' may mean a net or a fortress, and so it serves as a metaphor for imprisonment. The word 'burdens' only occurs here in the Old Testament, and seems to indicate the afflictions associated with prison.

You let men ride over our heads; we went through fire and water, but you brought us to a place of abundance (*v. 12*). The imagery is of conquered people being forced to lie down and to be trampled underfoot, a practice widely attested in the ancient Near East. 'Fire and water' speak of the great dangers that the people endured (cf. Isa. 43:2), before they were finally brought through them and into God's generous provision. The ancient translations of the Old Testament (Greek LXX, Latin Vulgate, and the Aramaic Targum) all render the last phrase 'place of liberty' (*r^{e}vâyâh*), which fits well with the picture of prison in verse 11. However, the comparison with its use in Psalm 23:5 ('my cup *overflows*') suggests that it is used here to express God's overflowing goodness to them, perhaps with the idea in mind of the provision of the land flowing with milk and honey.

3. Personal Thanksgiving (*vv. 13-20*)

I will come to your temple with burnt offerings and fulfil my vows to you – vows my lips promised and my mouth spoke when I was in trouble (*vv. 13-14*). During times of troubles vows were made to God. Some of these could be like the sinful vow Jephthah made when he went to fight the Ammonites (Judg. 11:30-40; the same verb 'promised' (*pâtsâh*) is used in

vv. 35-36 as here in Ps. 66). What had been spoken to God as a promise by the king (cf. Ps. 65:1 for reference to vows) is now to be paid. Vows were made for a variety of reasons, including, as here, for deliverance in a time of trouble. Usually thanksgiving offerings were partially consumed on the altar and the remainder was used in a communal meal. In this case the whole offering is dedicated to the LORD, which indicates a sombre mood on the part of the people as they reflect on the gravity of the danger through which they have come.

I will sacrifice fat animals to you and an offering of rams; I will offer bulls and goats. Selah (*v. 15*). The variety of animals offered in sacrifice helps to emphasise the spirit of thanksgiving. Not content with one kind, the psalmist pledges himself to present several kinds as a reflection of his total dedication to the LORD. The word used for 'offering' (*q^{e}toret*) is strictly 'smoke' or 'incense', but it is also employed in a more general way for offerings.[4] 'Selah' introduces another pause before the final song of thanksgiving.

Come and listen, all you who fear God; let me tell you what he has done for me. I cried out to him with my mouth; his praise was on my tongue (*vv. 16-17*). The final section of the psalm starts with a double command: 'Come; listen.' While it is conceivable that 'all you who fear God' is a reference to the God-fearing Gentiles (cf. the use of the term God-fearers in the New Testament, Acts 2:5), yet in the context it is more likely that devout believers within Israel are intended. The psalmist gives his own personal testimony concerning the things God has done for him. With his mouth he both called to God, and with it he extolled him. The same lips that prayed were ready to praise. The final clause, 'his praise was on my tongue', translates the MT that says 'praise was *under* my tongue'. The word 'praise' (*rômam*) is a *hapax legomenon,* and is often emended. It appears to be an unusual form from a common Hebrew root (*rûm*) that is used to express 'exaltation' or 'praise'. The idiom, 'under the tongue', may be similar to the English one, 'on the tip of the tongue'. The point is that the

[4] L. C. Allen, *Psalms 101-150* (Waco: Word Books, 1983), p. 272, n. 2.b, discusses the meaning of the word.

psalmist experienced a speedy response from God and he was ready immediately to give him praise.

If I had cherished sin in my heart, the Lord would not have listened; but God has surely listened and heard my voice in prayer (*vv. 18-19*). The verb 'listen' binds verses 16-19 together. 'Come, *listen,*' says the psalmist, for 'God has surely *listened.*' He proclaims his innocence before God, announcing the truth that if a person looks with satisfaction on his sin (the Hebrew text says 'if I had *looked* on'), then God will not hear him. It is to the godly man who does God's will that the LORD will listen (John 9:31; cf. 1 John 3:21-22).

Praise be to God, who has not rejected my prayer or withheld his love from me! (*v. 20*). The concluding verse is an expression of adoration of God. It probably goes back to Exodus 18:10, when Jethro, on hearing of what had happened to Israel, said: 'Praise be to the LORD, who rescued you from the hand of the Egyptians and of Pharaoh …' The psalmist praises the Lord for answering prayer and for bestowing covenant love upon him. God has not proved false to his own declared character (Exod. 34:6-7). He who was Israel's God ('*our* God', verse 8) is also the God of the individual believer ('*my* prayer', verse 20).

Psalm 67

For the director of music. With stringed instruments.
A psalm. A song.

Psalms 65-67 are all linked together because of their universalism. The expression 'all [the ends of] the earth' occurs in each one (65:5; 66:4; 67:7). The link with Psalm 66 is even more patent, as it ends with the phrase 'blessed be God' (*bârûch ʾᵉlohîm*), while Psalm 67 begins and ends with the thought of God's blessing on his people ('may he bless us', *vîvârᵉkênû*, v. 1, and 'may God bless us', *yᵉvârᵉkênû*, vv. 6 and 7).

This psalm goes further than the previous ones as it includes a prayer for double blessing – first on Israel, and then on the Gentiles. The repetition of the refrain in verses 3 and 5 highlights the vision of the Gentiles sharing in the saving mercy of God, and it also divides the psalm into three parts. The beginning and the end invoke God's blessing (vv. 1-2 and 6-7), while in verses 3-5 God is addressed directly. Such a switch in address is not unusual in Hebrew poetry.

1. A Prayer for Blessing (*vv. 1-3*)

May God be gracious to us and bless us and make his face shine upon us, *Selah* that your ways may be known on earth, your salvation among all nations (*vv. 1-2*). The opening verse is an echo of the priestly benediction of Numbers 6:24-26. This is one of six occurrences of this expression in the psalms (the others are in 31:16; 80:3, 7, 19; 119:135). The use of well-known words forms a link with the past history of Israel as the psalmist seeks a fresh demonstration of God's mercy upon the people. 'Selah' comes at a most unusual place, though it may well be positioned to emphasise the opening petition.[1] What follows is a desire for Israel's saving knowledge of God and his ways to be manifest to all nations. The thought here may be similar to Isaiah 43:10-13, where Israel is declared to be a witness that the LORD is God, and that there is no saviour apart from him. After being blessed, Israel becomes a blessing to the nations.[2]

May the peoples praise you, O God; may all the peoples praise you (*v. 3*). The desire of verses 1-2 is now turned into a direct prayer, which is repeated exactly in verse 5. Knowledge of God should flow into acknowledgment and praise of him. Hence, the psalmist prays that when the nations have come into knowledge of the one true God, they lift their voices in thankful song.[3] The reference to 'all the peoples' comes at the end of the clause in Hebrew and accentuates the thought: 'May the peoples praise you – all of them!'

2. A Prayer for the Nations (*vv. 4-5*)

May the nations be glad and sing for joy, for you rule the peoples justly and guide the nations of the earth. *Selah* (*v. 4*). The thought of the preceding verses is taken a step further with the idea of exuberant praise being given by the nations. God's saving power (v. 2) is also seen in his just rule, for there is a standard of equity that governs his acts of judgment.[4] Though in operation now, this rule will come to full expression at the return of Christ, when he 'will judge the

---

[1] A number of commentators suggest moving 'Selah' to the end of the verse. However, the Hebrew manuscripts uniformly have it in its present position, and the LXX is testimony to this being so at the time when it was translated.

[2] The word here for 'nations' is *gôyîm*. While it is sometimes used of Israel (Deut. 4:6; Josh. 3:17), yet much more often it is used of the Gentile nations. Two other Hebrew words for 'nation' occur in this same psalm, *ʿam* and *lᵉʾum*, all virtually interchangeable in a context like this.

[3] The verb translated 'praise' is not one of the usual ones (*h-l-l, z-m-r, sh-v-ch*) but *y-d-h*, that has more the meaning of 'acknowledge' or 'thank'.

[4] The word for 'justly' is *mîshôr*, which has the basic meaning of a 'plain' or 'flat land', but takes on a wider meaning of what is 'right' or 'just'. It is also used in Isaiah 11:4 conjoined with the verb 'to judge' (*shâfat*) as here in this verse (cf. Ps. 72:12-14).

world in righteousness and the peoples with equity' (Ps. 98:9). Just as God leads his own people, so the prayer is that he will bring blessing and salvation to the Gentiles. The Christian's prayer is:

> Let Zion's time of favour come;
> O bring the tribes of Israel home;
> And let our wondering eyes behold
> Gentiles and Jews in Jesus' fold.
>
> Almighty God, Thy grace proclaim
> In every clime of every name;
> Let adverse powers before Thee fall,
> And crown the Saviour Lord of all.
> (William Shrubsole, 1759-1829)

May the peoples praise you, O God; may all the peoples praise you (*v. 5*). The use of the recurring refrain (see comment on v. 3) serves to draw attention to the theme of universal praise that dominates throughout this psalm. The vision is of a world falling down in praise to God the Saviour. Ultimately the Lord Jesus will be the object of praise as depicted in Revelation 5:12: 'Worthy is the Lamb, who was slain, to receive power and wealth and wisdom and strength, and honour and glory and praise!'

3. A Prayer for Universal Blessing (vv. 6-7)

Then the land will yield its harvest, and God, our God, will bless us. God will bless us, and all the ends of the earth will fear him (*vv. 6-7*). One of the opening petitions is made the focal point of these final verses. The psalmist is confident that God, whom faith claims as 'our God', will indeed bless his people with abundant harvest in the land he has given them.[5] The wording of the first clause is almost exactly the same as Leviticus 26:4. Material and spiritual blessings seem to be joined together, for blessing of Israel is linked with the idea that the ends of the earth will come to fear the Lord. The

---

[5] While the Hebrew word *'érets* is translated as 'earth' earlier in the psalm (vv. 2 and 4), yet here when the reference is to 'our God', 'land' is necessary.

opening and close of the psalm strike the same note. Blessing of Israel brings God's knowledge to the nations so that they will revere him. Through the fall of Israel riches indeed came to the Gentiles, and how much greater riches will the ingathering of Israel bring (Rom. 11:11-12)!

Psalm 68

For the director of music. Of David. A psalm. A song.

There is no more triumphant song in the whole of the Psalter than Psalm 68. It begins with an echo of Moses' prayer when the ark of the covenant led the people in the wilderness (Num. 10:35). It moves on to a description of the journey from Sinai to the promised land, with the procession of the ark into Jerusalem in David's time. This was seen as God's coming there. It closes with a song of praise to the Lord who rules over all the kingdoms of the earth.

There are many textual difficulties in this psalm, including the fact that fifteen words or expressions in it occur nowhere else in the Old Testament. At times a sudden change of ideas occurs that is difficult to fit into the overall unity of the psalm. The emphasis on God is maintained throughout, and a great variety of names for God is employed (*ʾᵉlohîm*, 23×; *ʾᵃdonay*, 6×; *ʾēl*, 2×; and *shaddai, Yahweh, Yâh, Yahweh ʾᵃdonay*, and *Yahweh ʾᵉlohîm* once each). In the centre of the psalm (vv. 19-20) a cluster of references to God is an emphatic declaration concerning his saving activity. Alternation in the use of the third and second person forms which is seen in Psalms 66 and 67 appears here also ('May God arise … God sets the lonely in families … You went out … The Lord announced the word … When you ascended on high … Praise be to the Lord … Your procession has come into view … Summon your power, O God … Sing to God, O kingdoms of the earth … You are awesome, O God … Praise be to God!').

1. A Prayer for the Coming of the Lord (*vv. 1-6*)
May God arise, may his enemies be scattered; may his foes flee before him. As smoke is blown away by the wind, may

you blow them away; as wax melts before the fire, may the wicked perish before God (*vv. 1-2*). The call to God is given in the language that Moses used whenever the ark set out: 'Rise up, O LORD! May your enemies be scattered; may your foes flee before you' (Num. 10:35). This processional hymn starts with the request for God's intervention on behalf of his people, just as he intervened in times past. The enemies are compared to smoke and wax to illustrate how feeble they are to stand against the power of the LORD. Four verbs are used to describe the reaction of the wicked to God's presence – 'scatter', 'flee', 'blown away', and 'perish'. As the metaphors change, a varied picture is given of God's ability to overcome his enemies.

But may the righteous be glad and rejoice before God; may they be happy and joyful (*v. 3*). Whereas the wicked flee before God (v. 1), the righteous are joyful before him. The initial 'but' marks the sharp contrast that is going to be stated.[1] Just as four terms were used of the wicked's reaction, so here four terms are employed to describe the way in which the godly respond – 'be glad', 'rejoice', 'be happy', 'joyful'. Relationship with God determines conduct in his presence. At the final coming of the LORD, the wicked will be shut out from his presence, while the righteous believers will glorify him in that day (2 Thess. 1:9-10).

Sing to God, sing praise to his name, extol him who rides on the clouds – his name is the LORD – and rejoice before him (*v. 4*). The invitation is to sing to God, whose name is the LORD. In the Hebrew text the word 'LORD' is an abbreviated form of the divine name (*Yâh*), and it occurs most commonly in poetic passages such as this, in names like Elijah or Uzziah, and in the expression 'Hallelujah' ('Praise the LORD!'). Another three words relating to praise appear in this verse ('sing', 'sing praise', 'extol him'). The last of these (*sâlal*) is quite common, but with the meaning of building a highway. Because it comes here in parallel with two well-known verbs denoting praise (*shîr* and *zâmar*, Pi.) the context requires a translation

---

[1] 'But' is represented by the conjunction (*v^e*), which is used here in an adversative way, and the normal word order in such cases (conjunction + subject) is followed. For this usage, see *IBHS*, p. 129, 8.3b.

that carries on this idea. It is quite possible that a verb that originally meant 'to lift up [stones]' could be extended to mean 'lift up a song'.[2] The translation of the description of the LORD as the one 'who rides on the clouds' is difficult. It is better to follow the NIV footnote, 'who rides through the deserts', which then would agree with verses 7-8. The ESV also accepts this interpretation.[3]

A father to the fatherless, a defender of widows, is God in his holy dwelling. God sets the lonely in families, he leads forth the prisoners with singing; but the rebellious live in a sun-scorched land (*vv. 5-6*). Though God is so powerful, yet he has a concern for the needy. The three groups most likely to suffer injustice were the orphans, the widows and the strangers (Deut. 10:18-19; 24:17). Here, and in Psalm 146:9, the fatherless and the widows are said to be the special objects of God's interest. It is unclear whether God's holy dwelling is heaven or the temple. The strangers and other lonely ones are brought under his protection, while even the foreign prisoners (the word usually means this, cf. Ps. 69:33; Isa. 14:17; and Zech. 9:11) experience his redemption, and consequently his joy. The rebellious within Israel, however, have none of this joy, and they are depicted as if they live in a barren place.

2. From the Exodus to Jerusalem (*vv. 7-18*)

A poetic description is now given of the way in which God led his people through the wilderness to Canaan (vv. 7-10), his gift

---

[2] I discuss the root and its derivatives in *NIDOTTE*, 3, pp. 264-67. No noun from the root *s-l-l* means 'praise'. They are all related to road building or construction of siege ramps. Articles relating to this root are listed in *DCH*, VI, p. 834. For this passage *CHAL*, p. 257, offers the translation 'prepare a road (while singing)'.

[3] The Hebrew word in question is *ʿ*ᵃ*rāvôt*, 'wildernesses'. While it can refer to specific geographical areas (see its use for the rift valley along the Jordan in Num. 22:1 and Josh. 4:13; and for the shore area south-west of the Dead Sea in 1 Sam. 23:24 and Isa. 51:3), it also designates, in general, sparsely vegetated areas (as in Isa. 33:9 and Jer. 51:43). The translation 'clouds' derives from equating it with the Ugaritic epithet for Baal, 'rider of the clouds' (*rkb ʿrpt*). This assumes that the Hebrew consonant *b* has replaced the Ugaritic *p*. The *DCH*, VI, pp. 552-53, gives it as meaning 'steppe, desert', and then tentatively points to the possibility that it means 'cloud'.

to them of the land (vv. 11-14), and how he then took up his abode on Mount Zion (vv. 15-18). There is a change from the use of the third person to direct address to God himself.

When you went out before your people, O God, when you marched through the wasteland, – *Selah* – the earth shook, the heavens poured down rain, before God, the One of Sinai, before God, the God of Israel (*vv. 7-8*). This account of the Exodus draws upon the Song of Deborah (Judg. 5:4-5). God went ahead of his people (Exod. 13:21), after the events at the Red Sea had demonstrated his great power. The reference to 'wastelands' uses a word (*y^eshîmôn*) that can denote a specific area, either in the Negev (1 Sam. 23:19, 24; 26:1, 3) or in Transjordan (Num. 21:20; 23:28). It can also have a wider meaning much like the regular word for 'desert' (*midbâr*), as is shown by the use of these two words in parallel (cf. Isa. 43:19, 20). Earthquake and storm were symbolic of God's presence and power. He was the one who had displayed his greatness at Sinai when he entered into a covenant with his people Israel.[4] The use of 'Selah' here and in verses 19 and 32 in the middle of a stanza appears to give special emphasis to the preceding expression.

You gave abundant showers, O God; you refreshed your weary inheritance. Your people settled in it, and from your bounty, O God, you provided for the poor (*vv. 9-10*). The land of Canaan was a gracious provision of God for his people. He gave them a land 'that drinks rain from heaven' (Deut. 11:11). Several of the phrases in verse 9 are difficult to translate. NIV 'gave' is a verb (*nûf*) that may mean 'sprinkle' or 'deliver in large measure', the latter matching the context well.[5] 'Abundant showers' (*géshem n^edâvâh*) uses the regular word for 'rain' but qualifies it with an adjective that is often used of the freewill offerings or contributions for building the tabernacle and the temple (Exod. 35:29;

---

[4] NIV's 'the One of Sinai' is the translation of *zeh sînai*, lit. 'this Sinai'. When compared with other expressions like *zeh ʿonî*, 'this poor one' (Ps. 34:6), the NIV translation makes good sense. It is the equivalent of 'the God of Sinai'.

[5] *DCH*, V, pp. 645-47, lists six homonyms for *nûf*, preferring the alternatives given above for this passage.

2 Chron. 31:14; Ezra 1:4). It denotes 'rain of generosity', hence 'abundant rain'. 'Refresh' (*kûn*, Pol.) conveys the idea of sustaining God's 'inheritance' (*nachalâh*), one of the distinctive terms for the gift of the land. It is described as being 'weary' (*nil'âh*), a land impoverished because of drought.[6] The beginning of verse 10 is rather cryptic, and both the early versions and modern translations differ widely. The opening word (*chayyâh*) is normally used to denote animals, not humans. The LXX understood it to mean 'living creatures' (*ta zôa sou*, cf. Revelation 4:6-9), though the context demands a reference to people. Hence, the NIV translation 'your people', or 'your troop' fits the passage.[7] The mention of the 'poor' is significant, for this word (*'onî*) is translated as 'afflicted' in other places, and it is used to describe the condition of Israel in Egypt (see Exod. 3:7, 17 [NIV 'misery']). While these verses draw attention to material blessings in Canaan, most probably they also speak of all the bountiful and varied ways in which God blessed Israel.

The Lord announced the word, and great was the company of those who proclaimed it: 'Kings and armies flee in haste; in the camps men divide the plunder. Even while you sleep among the campfires, the wings of [my] dove are sheathed with silver, its feathers with shining gold' (*vv. 11-13*). Comparison with other translations shows how difficult all translators have found these and the following verses.[8] There seem to be allusions to Deborah's Song (Judg. 5), but perhaps also to other songs not recorded in Scripture. The general picture is that God gave his message concerning the conquest of Canaan, and the women proclaimed it ('those who proclaimed it' is

---

[6] The Hebrew phrase is 'your inheritance and weary' (*nachalâtekâ venil'âh*), a grammatical construction (*hendiadys*) in which the one idea is presented in two expressions. Cf. the English phrase, 'with might and main'.

[7] *DCH*, III, pp. 207-09, gives four possible meanings for *chayyâh*, and prefers the translation of the clause as 'Your dwelling place, they dwelt in it'. Some Hebrew manuscripts have a different verb, 'they return' (*yâshûvû*), but the LXX translators clearly read it as the verb 'to dwell' (*katoikousin*).

[8] Very helpful notes on verses 12-13 can be found in VanGemeren, 'Psalms', p. 448, and in *NIDOTTE*, 2, pp. 269-70.

feminine in Hebrew). The verb used (*bâsar*, Pi.), while it can be neutral, yet significantly is used to depict the servant of the LORD's mission of proclaiming 'good news' (Isa. 61:1; cf. also Isa. 40:9 in connection with proclamation of salvation). Armies were forced to flee before Israel (the RSV stays close to the Hebrew, and depicts the vividness of the action, 'they flee, they flee'!), leaving their spoils behind them. 'In the camps' is a possible interpretation of an obscure phrase (*n*[e]*vat báyit*),[9] though, since the following verb (*t*[e]*challêq*, 'she divides') is feminine singular, another interpretation is preferable. This expression may be rendered 'the beauty of the house' and be a collective expression for 'the women'.[10] 'In the campfires' lacks credible support. The word rendered 'campfires' (*sh*[e]*fatâyim*) only appears here and in Ezekiel 40:43 in the Old Testament, and some consider it means 'pack saddles'.[11] The verse is best taken as describing the women who wait at home and then are given spoils won in battle. The exact nature and significance of the 'dove' is unclear. It may have been some special cultic object taken after victory over Canaanites.

When the Almighty scattered the kings in the land, it was like snow fallen on Zalmon (*v. 14*). Similarly, this verse is perplexing, because we cannot be sure of the location of Zalmon, nor of the significance of the snow. It could mean that God sent a snowstorm to rout the enemy forces at Zalmon. This could be a location either near Shechem (see Judg. 9:48), or on the east bank of the Jordan, as suggested by the mention of Bashan in the next verse. An alternative interpretation is that the bleached bones of fallen warriors looked like snow on the hillside.

The mountains of Bashan are majestic mountains; rugged are the mountains of Bashan. Why gaze in envy, O rugged mountains, at the mountain where God chooses to reign, where the LORD himself will dwell forever? (*vv. 15-16*). God did not choose the highest of mountains within the land of

---

[9] For the various possible translations, see M. Tate, *Psalms 51–100*, p.164-65.

[10] This interpretation is the one preferred by Tate, ibid., pp. 160, 165.

[11] So *KB*, p. 1006.

promise. Rather, he chose Zion (see Ps. 132:13-18).[12] Bashan may well have been Mount Hermon, and it represented what was powerful and rich (Deut. 32:14; Amos 4:1; Ps. 22:12).[13] It is rebuked for being envious of Zion, which is the seat of God's kingdom. Zion was the mountain of God's inheritance, and from there the LORD would reign (Exod. 15:17-18).

The chariots of God are tens of thousands and thousands of thousands; the Lord [has come] from Sinai into his sanctuary. When you ascended on high, you led captives in your train; you received gifts from men, even from the rebellious – that you, O LORD God, might dwell there (*vv. 17-18*). On the march into Canaan God is accompanied by his mighty forces. The expressions for the numbers are unusual (lit. 'two countless hosts, thousands of repetition'), but NIV captures well the general sense.[14] These are his heavenly servants (Deut. 33:2; 2 Kings 6:15-17). Jesus could have called for such heavenly assistants and his Father would have sent more than twelve legions of angels (Matt. 26:53). The revelation at Sinai was a revelation of God's holiness (Hebrew has 'in holiness', which the NIV interprets to mean 'in the holy place', 'in the sanctuary'). This revelation left the people fearful (Deut. 5:23-27). God's holiness was shown in so many incidents on the way to Canaan. When Zion was finally reached it was like a victory procession, with captives being led there, along with their tribute gifts (2 Sam. 8:11; 1 Kings 4:21). Verse 18 is quoted by Paul with some variation in Ephesians 4:8, and in particular he has 'he *gave* gifts to men' in place of 'he *took* gifts'. The exegetical problem in Ephesians has been noted as far back as the early church fathers, with Chrysostom (AD 345-407) commenting that the words 'took' and 'gave' convey the same meaning. Many explanations have

---

[12] The verb used here for 'choose' is *châmad,* which often means 'desire'. However, in Isaiah 1:29 it is paralleled with *bâchar,* the much more common verb meaning 'choose'.

[13] The NIV rendering 'majestic mountains' is probably correct, though the MT has *har ᵓᵉlohîm,* 'the hill of God'. The use of a divine name in connection with a noun is a Hebrew way of giving a superlative sense. For details on this usage, see *DIHG~S,* p. 46, rem. 5; *IBHS,* p. 268, including bibliography in f.n. 26.

[14] The word 'repetition' (*shin'ân*) is a *hapax legomenon,* and presumably it is a by-form from the verb *shânâh,* 'to repeat'.

been offered for the change.[15] The parallel with God's action in taking the Levites and giving them back to Israel as a gift (see Num. 8 and 18) fits well the context in Ephesians. Paul's stress lies on the fact of Christ's ascension and his bestowal of gifts on his people, just as the psalm goes on to speak of the blessings that God dispenses (vv. 19-30).

3. Praise for the Saviour *(vv. 19-23)*

The account of the triumphal procession is broken off (not resumed until v. 24) for an ascription of praise to the Saviour. **Praise be to the Lord, to God our Saviour, who daily bears our burdens.** ***Selah*** *(v. 19)*. Recollection of God's great acts of deliverance and redemption call forth a song of praise. He is extolled as the Saviour and as the burden bearer. The wonderful thing is that the mighty God stoops to his people, and daily carries their burdens (or possibly it could be rendered, 'who daily carries *us*', i.e. like a shepherd).[16] The New Testament still encourages us to cast all our anxiety on the Lord because he cares for us (1 Pet. 5:7).

Our God is a God who saves; from the Sovereign LORD comes escape from death *(v. 20)*. A more literal translation is 'Our God is a God of *deliverances,* to the Sovereign LORD belong *escapes* from death'. The plurals may be used deliberately, as Calvin suggested, to show that although numerous threats of death may come against us, yet God has innumerable ways of delivering us.[17] The emphasis is on the bounteous provision that God makes for his people, in displaying his abundant grace and power in deliverance.

Surely God will crush the heads of his enemies, the hairy crowns of those who go on in their sins *(v. 21)*. The reverse is also certain. God is pledged to destroy those who oppose

---

[15] An excellent summary of the various viewpoints can be found in Peter O'Brien, *The Letter to the Ephesians,* pp. 288-93. Two important journal articles are G. V. Smith, 'Paul's Use of Psalm 68:18 in Ephesians', *JETS* 18 (1975), pp. 181-89, and R. A. Taylor, 'The Use of Psalm 68:18 in Ephesians 4:8 in Light of the Ancient Versions', *BS* 148 (1991), pp. 319-36.

[16] Daily' is represented in the MT, not by the common word *yômâm,* but by the repetition of the word 'day', *yôm yôm*. It, and similar forms (*yôm vâyôm* and *yôm b^{e}yôm*), signify 'day after day'.

[17] John Calvin, *A Commentary on the Psalms of David,* II, p. 210.

him. The same verb 'to crush' is used in Psalm 110:5-6 of God's activity in judging kings and rulers. 'The hairy crowns' seem to refer to the pride of the enemies as they go on in their sinful ways.

The Lord says, 'I will bring them from Bashan; I will bring them from the depths of the sea, that you may plunge your feet in the blood of your foes, while the tongues of your dogs have their share' (*vv. 22-23*). In the Hebrew text the object of the verb 'bring' in verse 22 is not expressed.[18] While it could be 'you', i.e. the people of Israel, yet the context suggests it is 'them', i.e. the enemies. No place is so remote that God's enemies can find a hiding place from him. Both from inaccessible places on land (Bashan, east of the Jordan) and sea (the depths) God will bring his enemies for judgment. The graphic imagery of battle may be too strong for modern Westerners, but it certainly is in agreement with other Old Testament descriptions, including the account of the deaths of Ahab and Jezebel (1 Kings 21:19; 22:38; 2 Kings 9:36). The reference to dogs licking the blood may have been a proverbial expression for retribution.

4. Praise of God in the Congregation (*vv. 24-27*)

Your procession has come into view, O God, the procession of my God and King into the sanctuary (*v. 24*). Attention comes back to the procession after victory in battle.[19] Whereas previously God was called 'our God', the psalmist now speaks in more personal terms still, calling him '*my* God and King'. The procession continues until it arrives in the sanctuary, already mentioned earlier in verse 17. True faith appropriates this type of language as it responds to the close relationship with God. New Testament parallels are

---

[18] The verb is actually 'bring back' (*shûv*, Hi.). Though it is used more often of the return of Israel to Palestine, yet here the context requires 'the enemies' to be the subject.

[19] The NIV translation of the opening clause is rather free but captures the sense. The MT has simply 'they saw' (*râ'û*), an impersonal use of the 3rd pers. pl. form of the verb. No need exists for emendation in order to agree with the LXX, 'they were seen'.

Thomas's words, '*My* Lord and *my* God' (John 20:28), and Paul's, 'the Son of God, who loved *me* and gave himself for *me*' (Gal. 2:20).

In front are the singers, after them the musicians; with them are the maidens playing tambourines (*v. 25*). This scene recalls what happened after the deliverance at the Red Sea, when Miriam led the women in singing and dancing (Exod. 15:19-21). The singers and musicians are going before the main procession, rejoicing in the deliverances that resemble the Exodus. The NIV translation suggests that the maidens are simply 'with' the singers and musicians. The MT requires the translation 'in the midst of girls [playing] tambourines'.

Praise God in the great congregation; praise the LORD in the assembly of Israel (*v. 26*). Either these words form what the women said in praise, or else they are a call to everyone to extol him in the midst of the congregation of Israel. Israel was made up of many companies (NIV 'great congregation'), which all stemmed from the one source, 'the fountain of Israel' (following the Hebrew text).[20]

There is the little tribe of Benjamin, leading them, there the great throng of Judah's princes, and there the princes of Zebulun and of Naphtali (*v. 27*). The four tribes mentioned seem to represent the whole of Israel. North and south are together, as they were at the time of the conquest. Even in the New Testament these tribes were important, as our Lord and some of his apostles came from Judah, while Paul, 'the least of the apostles' (1 Cor. 15:9), came from Benjamin (Phil. 3:5). Various suggestions have been made as to why Paul draws attention to his Benjamite background, but it is probably simply to make the point that he was truly an authentic Jew.[21]

---

[20] The evidence is not conclusive that the word *mâqôr* should be rendered 'assembly' or 'convocation'. No need exists here, or in Proverbs 18:4, for this translation, the two passages claimed as supporting the alteration (see *DCH*, V, p. 466). 'Source' or 'well-spring' fits well in this context: '[You who are] from the source of Israel' (so Marvin Tate, *Psalms 51-100*, pp. 161, 167-68).

[21] A good survey of the various interpretations of Paul's use of the phrase 'from the tribe of Benjamin' is given by W. Hendriksen, *A Commentary on the Epistle of Paul to the Philippians* (London: Banner of Truth, 1963), pp. 156-58.

The remainder of the apostles were from the territory of Zebulun and Naphtali.

5. Praise of God in all the World (*vv. 28-35*)

Summon your power, O God; show us your strength, O God, as you have done before. Because of your temple at Jerusalem kings will bring you gifts (*vv. 28*-29). The NIV interpretation is that God is enthroned, and now he is asked for a fresh demonstration of his great power. The problem is that the MT has '*Your* God has commanded *your* strength' (NKJV, following the AV, NASB; the ESV margin has 'Your God has commanded your power').The reference is to the way in which God had in the past strengthened his people. The psalmist goes on to request a fresh demonstration of God's power, seen in the Exodus and in many later deliverances (v. 20). However, now the demonstration is to all the kingdoms of the earth, and foreign kings will come to do homage before the Lord in Jerusalem. The eschatological picture here is amplified in the Book of Revelation. Into the New Jerusalem, which has the Lord God Almighty and the Lamb as its temple, 'the kings of the earth will bring their splendour' (Rev. 21:24).

Rebuke the beast among the reeds, the herd of bulls among the calves of the nations. Humbled, may it bring bars of silver. Scatter the nations who delight in war. Envoys will come from Egypt; Cush will submit herself to God (*vv. 30-31*). 'The beast' is probably an allusion to an historical enemy, most probably Egypt. Elsewhere Leviathan (apparently either the crocodile or the hippopotamus) stands for Egypt (Ps. 74:14; Isa. 27:1). 'The herd of bulls' (*ʿᵃdat ʾâbbîrîm*) is probably intended as a reference to the leaders or kings,[22] while the calves seem to be less powerful nations who follow their leaders.[23] The second half of verse 30 is uncertain. The verb 'humbled'

---

[22] Cf. the expression 'a band of ruthless men' (*ʿᵃdat ʿârîtsîm*) in Psalm 86:14.

[23] The expression 'among the calves of the people' (*bᵉʿeglê ʿammîm*) is very unusual, and it is difficult to ascertain its significance. To translate it 'calf-people' (see M. E. Tate, *Psalms 51-100*, p. 168) does not elucidate it any further. I am presuming that it depicts smaller nations that follow leaders, just as calves follow a bull.

(*mitrappês*) may come from a root meaning 'to make oneself polluted by trampling' and hence be equivalent to humbling oneself.[24] 'May it bring bars of silver' is one interpretation of the following words, though the RSV rendering 'those who lust for silver' is probably closer to the mark.[25] Nations that delight in war find that God's hand comes against them, and they are dispersed. Egypt will come[26] and do homage to the Lord by sending ambassadors.[27] This is part of the prophetical picture of the events on the great day of the LORD (Isa. 19:18-25). Even ancient foes of Israel such as Egypt will come in submission, while her tributary Cush (upper Egypt or Ethiopia) will also display her allegiance (cf. Isa. 45:14).

Sing to God, O kingdoms of the earth, sing praise to the Lord, Selah – to him who rides the ancient skies above, who thunders with mighty voice (*vv. 32-33*). A song of rejoicing is needed from all the kingdoms of the earth as a fitting acknowledgment of the universal sway of God. 'Selah', inserted in the middle of the stanza, stresses this call. The song itself is an expansion of verse 4, using again two of the verbs already employed (*shîr* and *zâmar*, Pi.). The thought of riding through the skies is probably based on Deuteronomy 33:26, while 'the ancient skies' (*sh*[e]*mê qédem*) recalls Moses' assertion that 'to the LORD your God belong the heavens, even the highest heavens' (Deut. 10:14). The heavens are ancient in the sense that no one knows their beginning. God is pictured as riding through them like a king in his chariot traversing his territory. The God of eternity, who had already made his proclamation (see v. 12), now speaks in mighty power (cf. Ps. 29:3-5).

---

[24] See the discussion of this word by Bruce Waltke, *Proverbs 1-15*, p. 333, f.n. 53.

[25] The RSV takes the verb to be *râtsâh*, 'to be pleased with'.

[26] The verb for 'come' is *'âtâh*, found only in poetical passages in Hebrew, but much more common in Aramaic. It appears in the standard formula, 'Come, O Lord' (*maran-atha*, 1 Cor. 16:22).

[27] The word for 'ambassadors' (*chashmannîm*) only occurs here in the MT. If we follow the LXX translation of *presbeis*, 'envoys', this does not preclude the possibility that such envoys were marked out by the wearing of red cloth, as W. F. Albright suggested. See M. E. Tate, *Psalms 51-100*, p. 169, f.n. 32.a.

Proclaim the power of God, whose majesty is over Israel, whose power is in the skies. You are awesome, O God, in your sanctuary; the God of Israel gives power and strength to his people. Praise be to God! (*vv. 34-35*). The wording here seems to continue echoing Deuteronomy 33:26. God's majesty is displayed in two ways. First, he shows his power in creation and providence, as he rules over the earth and skies. Secondly, his majesty is seen in a special way as it is revealed to his people Israel. The psalmist addresses God directly, declaring that he is there in the midst of them in the sanctuary or holy place ('from *your* sanctuary'), and he is to be feared (*nôrâ'*). The great God condescends to meet his people, and as they worship him he imparts strength to them. Then a switch back to the third person takes place in the final declarations. Earlier the psalmist has spoken a doxology on behalf of Israel (v. 19). Now he concludes with one that is to be spoken both by Israel and by the kingdoms of the world: 'Praise be to God!' The psalm concludes on the note of fulness of praise being ascribed to Israel's God. The New Testament points to a day when the kingdoms of this world will become the kingdoms of our Lord and of his Christ (Rev. 11:15).

Psalm 69

For the director of music. To [the tune of] 'Lilies.' Of David.

This is one of the most quoted psalms in the New Testament. The following list shows how widely it is utilised: verse 4 (John 15:25); verse 9 (John 2:17); verse 21 (Matt. 27:34, 48); verses 22-24 (Rom. 11:9-10); verse 24 (Rev. 16:1); verse 25 (Acts 1:20). The psalm deals with sin and its consequences, and the extended use of it in the New Testament shows that even Christians today cannot evade the issues it raises. There is no separation of sin from the sinner in the Bible, in the way in which people often wish to divorce a sinner (who is loved) from his sin (which is hated). This is another psalm that has many curses in it (see Introduction), but the very fact that Jesus takes part of it on his lips should cause us to look carefully at it. Originally it referred to the bitter experiences of David, and then typically it is applied to Christ. The similarities between David's experience and those of Jesus are not exhausted by the quotations. The mockery mentioned in verse 12 is reflected in the mockery of Jesus recorded in Matthew 27:27-30, while the offer of vinegar to drink (v. 21) has its parallel in the wine mixed with myrrh that the soldiers offered to Jesus (Mark 15:23).

Interesting connections also exist between Psalm 69 and Psalm 40, so much so that they have been called 'twin-Psalms'.[1] The description of need as sinking into water or mire occurs in both psalms (69:2 and 40:2), while the expression 'more than the hairs of my head' also appears in both (69:4 and 40:12). Very similar statements are made about

[1] The phrase is that of F. Delitzsch, *Psalms*, I, p. 275.

ceremonial acts (69:31 and 40:6) and the indication is given that the righteous will extol the Lord's deeds (69:32 and 40:16). No dependence can be shown, but certainly the vocabulary indicates that expressions common in Israel were being used in both psalms. The link between Psalms 40 and 69 is made explicit by the fact that Psalm 70 is composed of a slightly altered version of Psalm 40:13-17.

1. A Personal Cry (*vv. 1-4*)
Save me, O God, for the waters have come up to my neck. I sink in the miry depths, where there is no foothold. I have come into the deep waters; the floods engulf me (*vv. 1-2*). The psalm commences with a general cry, and it is not until a few verses later that the nature of his need is specified. The psalmist compares himself to a drowning man, who is desperately trying to keep his head above the water. Sudden floods in Palestine made very realistic the idea of water reaching up to the neck (see Isa. 8:8). Though the MT simply says 'water up to neck' the context requires '*my* neck', a translation that goes back as far as the LXX.[2]

I am worn out calling for help; my throat is parched. My eyes fail, looking for my God (*v. 3*). The psalmist's distress has been going on for some time, for he is wearied by his attempts to attract God's attention. His throat is sore and, as he waits for God to intervene, his eyes are like those of a sick person who has wept copiously.[3]

Those who hate me without reason outnumber the hairs of my head; many are my enemies without cause, those who seek to destroy me. I am forced to restore what I did not steal (*v. 4*). This verse presents difficulties of translation and interpretation. The first two clauses are clearly parallel:

> '[More] numerous than the hairs of my head [are] those who hate me without cause'

---

[2] I am taking the Hebrew word *néfesh* as meaning 'neck'. For the wide range uses of this word in the Old Testament, see *DCH*, V, pp. 724-34.

[3] The word for 'looking [for God]' (*yâchal*, Pi.) conveys the idea of 'expectant waiting', and hence of 'hoping'. Cf. its use in Psalm 31:24.

'[More] numerous [are] my destroyers [than] those who are my enemies without reason'

The verbs are to be taken as synonyms (*râvâh*//*ʿâtsam*),[4] while the final phrases are also synonymous, having exactly the same Hebrew construction.[5] The full parallelism breaks down in reference to the middle words ('from the hairs of my head', 'my destroyers'). Emendation has been proposed by various scholars so that 'my destroyers' becomes 'my locks', so matching the reference to hair.[6] But the MT makes sense in that his enemies, without any legitimate reason, are dedicated to his destruction. This first part of the verse is quoted partially in John 15:25 when Jesus is speaking about the world's hatred of his disciples. The final clause declares that there is no truth in the false accusation that he is stealing from others. It may well be a proverbial saying in question form: 'What I did not steal must I now restore?'[7]

2. An Explanation of His Suffering (*vv. 5-12*)

You know my folly, O God; my guilt is not hidden from you (*v. 5*). Before going on to describe further his suffering, the psalmist makes an open confession to God. He has done foolish things in God's sight,[8] and he knows that he cannot hold anything back from him. His very nature is under the scrutiny of God (Ps. 139:15). Later in the psalm (v. 26) mention

---

[4] It is correct that the verb *ʿâtsam* can refer to strength, but the context here is about the large number of foes, not their physical capabilities.

[5] Both have a Hebrew participle + an adverb: 'my haters without cause' (*sonᵉʾay chinnâm*) and 'my enemies without reason' (*ʾoyᵉvay shéqer*). For these constructions, see *DIHG~S*, pp. 41-42. They have the same word order: verb + prepositional phrase + subject.

[6] See, e.g., M. Dahood, *Psalms II:51–100*, p. 157. However, no manuscript support can be cited, and apart from the Syriac, which has 'from my bones', the early versions support the MT.

[7] This is an interpretation suggested by M. E. Tate, *Psalms 51–100*, p. 189, n. 5. c.

[8] The expression 'my folly' (*ʾivvaltî*) is preceded by *lᵉ*. This is an example of the use of *lᵉ* in a non-prepositional way. Here it serves a function rather like *ʾêt* to mark a direct object of a transitive verb. For discussion of this usage, see *DIHG~S*, pp. 108, 115-18, and *IBHS*, p. 165.

is made of God's 'wounding', probably a reference to the consequences of his sin spoken of here.

May those who hope in you not be disgraced because of me, O Lord, the LORD Almighty; may those who seek you not be put to shame because of me, O God of Israel (*v. 6*). The cluster of names for God is highly appropriate in this setting. Appeal to him as LORD Almighty (i.e. over all things) is made, yet he is also the covenant God of Israel who is near his people to help them in times such as this. The thought of not being disgraced has already been presented in Psalm 25:3, and the two roots denoting disgrace or shame (*bûsh* and *k-l-m*) occur several times in parallel in other psalms (cf. Pss. 44:15; 70:2; 71:13; 109:28-29). The psalmist does not want those who are truly God's (lit. 'your hopers' and 'your seekers') to suffer because of anything he does.

For I endure scorn for your sake, and shame covers my face. I am a stranger to my brothers, an alien to my own mother's sons; for zeal for your house consumes me, and the insults of those who insult you fall on me (*vv. 7-9*). It is not for his own sake that the psalmist suffers reproach or mocking (lit. 'carrying reproach', *nâsâh cherpâh*). The description adds to the use of the verb 'put to shame' (*kâlam*) in the previous verse by the employment now of the related noun 'shame' (*k[e]limmâh*). He is cut off from his closest family members for God's sake (cf. the communal acknowledgment of suffering for God's sake in Ps. 44:22). He is so identified with the temple, for which he has the deepest longing, that he becomes the object of taunting from God's enemies. The manner in which the longing for the temple is displayed is not stated. The NIV rendering, 'the insults of those who insult you', fails to bring out the fact that the Hebrew root for 'insults' and 'insult' (with verb and noun from the same root being used together) has already been employed in verse 7. As the theme of reproach is central to this psalm, consistency of translation helps focus on this aspect. The word 'reproach' (*cherpâh*) occurs in verses 7, 9, 10, 19, 20, for which the NIV has 'scorn(ed)' in all but verse 9, where it uses 'insults'. The first part of verse 9 is quoted in

John 2:17 in reference to Jesus' cleansing of the temple. What Jesus did was evidence of consuming zeal for God's house.

When I weep and fast, I must endure scorn; when I put on sackcloth, people make sport of me. Those who sit at the gate mock me, and I am the song of the drunkards (*vv. 10-12*). The taunting is made more bitter by being directed at him when he is clearly in mourning. Even when it is evident that he is suffering, he has to endure reproach. Instead of joining him in his expressions of grief, his enemies 'make fun of him'.[9] Just as people gather in a town mall today, in ancient Israel they gathered at the city gate (Ruth 4:1-4; 2 Sam. 15:2). The assembled community, as they gossip together, talk disparagingly of the afflicted sufferer, while even the drunkards join in with rowdy songs. When he longs for the worship of the temple (v. 9), all he hears is a totally different kind of singing.

3. A Prayer for Help (*vv. 13-18*)

But I pray to you, O LORD, in the time of your favour; in your great love, O God, answer me with your sure salvation (*v. 13*). Out of his pressing need, the psalmist makes his cry to God. He knows, that in God's good and favourable time, help will come for him. The expression 'time of favour' (*'êt râtsôn*) points to the anticipated activity of God that involves his gracious deliverance (cf. the same use in Isa. 49:8). There seems to be an echo here and in the following verses of Exodus 34:6, where God declared his own character as 'abounding in love and faithfulness'. Because of God's revelation of himself, the psalmist can appeal for a sure answer.

Rescue me from the mire, do not let me sink; deliver me from those who hate me, from the deep waters. Do not let the floodwaters engulf me or the depths swallow me up or the pit close its mouth over me (*vv. 14-15*). Reference to 'mire' (*tîṭ*) recalls the opening of Psalm 40: 'He lifted me out of the

[9] The expression is lit. 'I became a *mâshâl* to them'. This word *mâshâl* has a range of meanings, from 'pithy saying' through to 'parable'. Sometimes, as here, the word is used when there is an intention to make the hearer or reader pass judgment on himself/herself. Cf. also its use in Isaiah 14:4, where the NIV has 'taunt'.

slimy pit, out of the mud and mire' (v. 2). The imagery of flood waters is still to the fore (cf. the opening verses), with the word for 'floodwaters' (*shibbolet*) being repeated from verse 2.[10] The picture is of grievous trouble surrounding him, possibly even death, for the word 'pit' (*b^{e}'êr*) seems to be a synonym for 'Sheol', 'the grave'. He appeals with great intensity for God to intervene and save him.

Answer me, O LORD, out of the goodness of your love; in your great mercy turn to me (*v. 16*). It is for covenant mercy that the psalmist prays, as he picks up the theme of verse 13 and rephrases it. The same expression, 'out of the goodness of your love' (*kî tôv chasdékâ*) occurs in Psalm 109:21, and there too it is associated with the appeal, 'Rescue me' (*nâtsal*, Hi. imper.), as here in verse 14. The use of the phrase, 'in your great mercy', recalls its use in David's appeal for forgiveness in Psalm 51:1: 'According to your great mercy blot out my transgressions.' He wants God to let his gaze be set on him, and so see his need and send deliverance.

Do not hide your face from your servant; answer me quickly, for I am in trouble (*v. 17*). The opening petition is an appeal to God not to withdraw his favour. It became almost a standard expression for seeking God's forgiveness or forbearance (see the use of it in Pss. 27:9; 102:2; 119:19; and 143:7). Someone in a covenantal relationship with God, like the psalmist, could plead as a servant. The use of this term 'servant' recognises that relationship and uses it as a basis for prayer. Speedy help is needed, and divine assistance is the only way of escape from trouble.

---

[10] Two homonyms exist in biblical Hebrew. *Shibbolet* I means 'an ear of grain', while *shibbolet* II is used in contexts such as this to indicate 'a stream' or 'a flood'. In both verse 2 and verse 14 *shibbolet* is used with the verb *shâtaf*, 'flood, overflow'. Good discussion on these homonyms, with accompanying bibliography, can be found in *NIDOTTE*, 4, pp. 30-32. The word *shibbolet* was pronounced differently by the Israelites east of the Jordan than by those in Canaan, who gave the initial letter a softer 's' sound and hence said *sibbolet*. In Judges 12:1-6 the men of Ephraim were marked out by their pronunciation of this word, and from this passage 'Shibboleth' came into English to denote a peculiarity of speech or the catchword of a group.

Come near and rescue me; redeem me because of my foes (*v. 18*). In this psalm many different expressions are used as the psalmist pleads with his God. He has already said 'save' (*yâsha*ʿ, Hi.), 'answer' (*ʿânâh*), and 'rescue' (*nâtsal*, Hi.). Now he adds 'come near' (*qârav*, Hi.), 'rescue' (*gâʾal*, a different word than that in v. 14), and 'redeem' (*pâdâh*). The multiplicity of terms adds intensity to his requests, but there is little advantage in trying to distinguish sharply among them.[11]

4. The Psalmist's Enemies (*vv. 19-21*)

You know how I am scorned, disgraced and shamed; all my enemies are before you. Scorn has broken my heart and has left me helpless; I looked for sympathy, but there was none, for comforters, but I found none. They put gall in my food and gave me vinegar for my thirst (*vv. 19-21*). The psalmist makes his renewed appeal to God, repeating the account of his experience of derision and shame (see v. 7). The description is intensified by the repetition of 'scorn/reproach' (2×) and 'shame', and the introduction of 'helpless' (*ʾânûsh*).[12] Those whom he expected to provide comfort failed to stand by him, and he waited in vain for them to offer support. Another addition here is the reference to gall and vinegar in verse 21. 'Gall' (*roʾsh*) was derived from a poisonous herb, and the word may be a Babylonian name for a specific plant. The idea is that the comforters went so far as to betray him by application of poison to his food. In his agony Jesus was offered wine mixed with gall, but he refused to drink it (Matt. 27:34), as it

---

[11] This applies particularly to any attempt to distinguish sharply between 'rescue' (*gâʾal*) and 'redeem' (*pâdâh*). Both verbs mean 'redeem', as is shown by the fact that the same range of Greek words are used in the LXX to translate them. In this passage the LXX uses 'redeem' (*lutróomai*) for the first one, and 'rescue' (*rúomai*) for the second. For discussion on these two Hebrew verbs, see B. B. Warfield, *The Person and Work of Christ* (Philadelphia: Presbyterian and Reformed Publishing Company, 1950), pp. 429-75, and Leon Morris, *The Apostolic Preaching of the Cross* (London: Tyndale Press, 1955), pp. 9-17.

[12] This is the only occurrence of this verb in the Old Testament. The NIV translation seems close, especially when *DCH*, V, p. 648, is very indeterminate, offering several possibilities: 'be sick', 'incurable', or 'tremble'.

could have affected his self-control at this crucial stage of his suffering. He did not want his senses dulled as he offered up himself as a sacrifice for the sins of his people (Heb. 7:27).

5. A Call for God's Judgment (*vv. 22-28*)

May the table set before them become a snare; may it become retribution and a trap. May their eyes be darkened so they cannot see, and their backs be bent forever (*vv. 22-23*). The psalmist appeals for God's direct intervention in the situation, and for his judgment to be visited on his enemies (for the wider problem presented by these passages, see the Introduction). Those who had tried to poison him will find their own table will become a trap for them. The NIV marginal note on verse 22 follows the Aramaic Targum, which suggests that instead of 'retribution' the Hebrew word should be read as meaning 'peace offerings'.[13] This provides a good parallel with 'table' in the first part of the verse. Verse 23 refers to physical changes that would be a sign of God's disfavour. The psalmist has undergone physical changes (cf. v. 3), and now he prays that the health of his enemies will be affected. He wants them to be afflicted with blindness, and their loins to be trembling.

Pour out your wrath on them; let your fierce anger overtake them. May their place be deserted; let there be no one to dwell in their tents (*vv. 24-25*). The petitions continue to ask for the reversal of all the good things of life. In place of mercy the request is for wrath; in place of joyful family life a deserted dwelling place. Peter quotes the words of verse 25 in reference to the reward that Judas Iscariot received for his wickedness (Acts 1:18-20). He illustrated the same antagonism

[13] The word that gives the difficulty is *shᵉlômîm*, the plural of *shâlôm*, 'peace'. The only other time the plural occurs is in Jeremiah 13:19. The LXX points to a translation like 'recompense' or 'vengeance', while the Syriac probably supports this. The AV understood it as referring to 'welfare', an interpretation followed in the NKJV, 'well-being'. The evidence does not point strongly in one direction, and so I prefer to take it as being the plural of *shélem*, this in my judgment best suiting the context. Cf. RSV 'their sacrificial feasts'. More detail can be found in the note in M. E. Tate, *Psalms 51-100*, p. 190, n. 23.a.

that had been displayed by the psalmist's enemies, and he came under a similar judgment.[14]

For they persecute those you wound and talk about the pain of those you hurt. Charge them with crime upon crime; do not let them share in your salvation (*vv. 26-27*). The opening words of verse 26 are simply 'For you', which do not fit easily with the words that follow: 'whom you have struck, they persecute'. Likely, after the opening words, 'As for you', the psalmist breaks off to speak about those like himself who have been wounded by God: 'As for you – they persecute whomever you have struck'.[15] The psalmist was willing to accept God's chastisements, but when he was under the afflicting hand of God, enemies visited him with even greater hurts. The talking about him was clearly a form of mockery (cf. v. 12), as they rejoiced over his suffering. He asks that they be given what they deserve – punishment corresponding to their sins, and exclusion from God's saving activity. This means additional guilt (the lit. translation is 'Give them iniquity upon iniquity'), and absence of any vindication by God.

May they be blotted out of the book of life and not be listed with the righteous (*v. 28*). The idea of the book of life comes from Exodus 32:32, where Moses prays that if God does not forgive his people, then let his name be blotted out of God's book. For the wicked, the request of the psalmist is that they perish, and that their names not be written alongside those of the righteous. The same concept of a book appears also in Daniel 12:1 and Revelation 3:5; 13:8; 17:8; and 20:15. Clearly this is an anthropomorphic expression, as God does not need a written list of the names of his people.

---

[14] The NIV marks off Acts 1:18-20 as a parenthesis, implying, probably correctly that the words are not part of Peter's speech, but form a commentary by Luke, the author of Acts. The primary references of the two psalms quoted (Pss. 69 and 109) were connected to enemies of David, but as Judas' character matched the enemies in those psalms, the words are applied to him. For commentary on the passage in Acts, see F. F. Bruce, *The Acts of the Apostles: The Greek Text with Introduction and Commentary*, 3rd ed., (Leicester: Apollos, 1990), pp. 109-10.

[15] This is the explanation offered by M. E. Tate, *Psalms 51-100*, pp. 188, 190-91.

6. A Song of Praise (*vv. 29-33*)

I am in pain and distress; may your salvation, O God, protect me (*v. 29*). The focus now shifts back to the psalmist himself a little more emphatically than the NIV rendering suggests: '*But as for me,* I am afflicted ...' He is concerned, not only for the punishment of evil enemies, but for his own salvation. The verb 'to protect' (*sâgav*, Pi.) has the idea of setting on high, and therefore of putting in a position of safety.

I will praise God's name in song and glorify him with thanksgiving. This will please the LORD more than an ox, more than a bull with its horns and hoofs (*vv. 30-31*). In anticipation of God's salvation the psalmist declares his intention of praising him in song. The 'thanksgiving' could be a sacrifice (cf. Lev. 7:12; 22:29) which formed a thank-offering, or a song of praise, which seems to be the meaning here. Such heart-felt praise is more acceptable to God than the mere offering of animal sacrifice, even if it was complete with horns and hoofs! Like Psalm 51:16-17, there is recognition that the sacrificial system did not work automatically. The heart of the worshipper was also very important.

The poor will see and be glad – you who seek God, may your hearts live! (*v. 32*). When the humble (defined further by the expression 'who seek God') see what is happening and hear this praise, they too will rejoice. An individual response will translate into a communal one. In turn the worshippers will find that reviving comes through this experience of seeing and acknowledging the salvation of the LORD. The expression 'May your hearts live' is equivalent to saying 'Do not lose heart'.

The LORD hears the needy and does not despise his captive people (*v. 33*). This is the statement of an abiding truth. It is characteristic of God that he listens to the cry of the needy. The 'needy' are shown elsewhere in the Psalms to be those whose distress is caused by their enemies, but whose trust is in the LORD. 'His captive people' is a rendering of the Hebrew 'his bound ones', which is either a reference to binding in sin before the LORD brings release, or else to those who are bound in service to him as devoted captives.

7. Universal Adoration (*vv. 34-36*)

Let heaven and earth praise him, the seas and all that move in them, for God will save Zion and rebuild the cities of Judah. Then people will settle there and possess it; the children of his servants will inherit it, and those who love his name will dwell there (*vv. 34-36*). Earlier (in verse 2) the waters were engulfing the psalmist. Now they are subdued. Along with all of inanimate nature they should praise the Lord, for he makes himself known as the saviour of his people. Earlier in the psalm there has not been any mention of the need of the nation, or of distress that has come upon Zion and Judah. While it is possible that the psalmist's great need was but a microcosm of the need of the nation as a whole, these verses may well be an addition to adapt the psalm for use at a time much later than that of David. Reference is made to Judah, not Israel. This ending would fit in with the period of Hezekiah (see 2 Kings 18-20; 2 Chron. 29-32), or with the Babylonian exile, if the captives were being encouraged to look for the restoration of Zion (see Jer. 30:18-31:14; cf. Ps. 51:18). God is able to provide help for Zion, and to bring his people back to settle again in the land. The lesson is clear from this psalm that, even in times of great distress, the eye of faith has to look to the full demonstration of God's restoring mercy. There is 'a home of righteousness' awaiting the people of God (2 Pet. 3:13).

Psalm 70

For the director of music. Of David. A petition.

This sung prayer is almost the same as Psalm 40:13-17 (see the fuller comments on that psalm). There are, however, several variations. The first two terms of the title are the same as those in Psalm 40, but the word 'psalm' is replaced here by 'petition' (*l*ᵉ*hazkîr*).[1] There are also changes in respect to the use of the divine name, but not in a uniform manner, for twice *ʾ*ᵉ*lohîm* replaces *yhwh* (LORD), but then LORD is used in place of both *ʾ*ᵃ*donay* and *ʾ*ᵉ*lohîm* and retained in verse 1b. Other changes include the absence of 'be pleased' (v. 1), the absence of 'to take' (v. 2), the change of 'be appalled' to 'turn back' (v. 3), and the alteration of 'think on me' to 'come quickly to me' (v. 5). These verses may have been taken over from Psalm 40 and used at some time of great distress. The fact that the Aramaic Targum has 'Make haste to deliver *us*' in verse 1 points to a use of the psalm with an application to the nation as a whole. The changes of cognate nouns ('salvation' and 'help') could have been for dialectal reasons.

No indication is given in the text as to why this part of Psalm 40 has been repeated here in a slightly altered fashion. A psalm that was composed for another occasion has been adapted for a new set of circumstances.

---

[1] As a term used in the titles of Psalms, *l*ᵉ*hazkîr* only occurs here and in Psalm 38. It could relate to singing while bringing an *ʾazkârâh*, 'a token offering', a word that occurs in Leviticus and Numbers to denote a handful taken from a grain offering (Lev. 2:2, 9, 16). See *DCH*, I, p.169, and note the variety of meanings listed in *CHAL*, p. 8.

Psalm 70 forms a bridge between Psalms 69 and 71. Corresponding ideas occur in Psalms 70 and 71.[2] In this second book of the Psalter, where nearly every psalm has a title, the absence of one for Psalm 71 suggests that it may be reckoned as almost a continuation of Psalm 70. In this way these two psalms correspond essentially to the way in which Psalms 42 and 43 function as a single unit.

Hasten, O God, to save me; O LORD, come quickly to help me (*v. 1*). The opening word in Psalm 40:14, 'be pleased' (*retsêh*) is omitted. This makes the commencement of the psalm more abrupt. The LXX translators realised the problem that now 'to save me' lacked a prior verb, and so they added the first clause to the title, 'that the Lord may save me'.

May those who seek my life be put to shame and confusion; may all who desire my ruin be turned back in disgrace (*v. 2*). Two changes are made to the text. The word 'together' has been omitted after 'May they be put to shame and confusion', and 'to snatch away' at the end of the first colon has also been omitted.

May those who say to me, 'Aha! Aha!' turn back because of their shame (*v. 3*). 'Turn back' (*yâshûvû*) replaces 'be appalled/made desolate' (*yâshommû*) in Psalm 40:15, a somewhat softer expression. Also, 'to me', is not represented in the MT of this verse, and hence the translation should only be 'who say, "Aha! Aha!"'

But may all who seek you rejoice and be glad in you; may those who love your salvation always say, 'Let God be exalted!' (*v. 4*). In addition to the alteration of the divine name ('God' for 'LORD'), 'and' is put before 'say', and one word for 'salvation' (*teshuʿâ*) is replaced by another from the same root and with identical meaning (*yeshûʿâ*).

Yet I am poor and needy; come quickly to me, O God. You are my help and my deliverer; O LORD, do not delay (*v. 5*). In this final verse there are several changes as compared with Psalm 40. Instead of 'O Lord, take account of me', Psalm 70

[2] Cf. 70:1, 5 with 71:12; 70:2 with 71:13, 24; 70:4 with 71:6, 8, 14-16, 24. Also, 71:24 expresses confidence in the Lord in a way that is the fulfilment of the request of 70:1.

has 'O God, hasten to me', repeating the cry for speedy intervention already used in verse 1. Then, like the change for the words for 'salvation' in verse 4, one word for 'help' (ʿ*ezrâh*) is replaced by another from the same root (ʿ*êzer*).

Psalm 71

This is a psalm of old age (see vv. 9 and 18), written by a believer who, even near the end of life, is still being tormented by enemies. There is no heading to help set the psalm in a particular historical setting, or to note any ascription of authorship. It is to be taken as being linked inseparably with Psalm 70 (see comments on that psalm), and forms part of a trilogy of psalms (Pss. 69-71). These three psalms have many themes in common – the need of the psalmist, the cry for rescue, the declaration of praise to God the redeemer. God's righteousness is again to the forefront, while the psalmist's shame is mentioned at the beginning (v. 1), in the middle (v. 13), and at the end (v. 24). Like the previous two psalms, this one ends on a strong note of praise.

Persecution is a fact of life for committed believers (2 Tim. 3:12), and there is no stage of life when they are exempt from it. Here the psalmist blends together phrases from other psalms, which shows how deeply ingrained in his mind and heart were the words of other singers of Israel. Yet the psalm is a song of hope, as he looks expectantly to the Lord.

1. A Confident Prayer (*vv. 1-4*)

In you, O Lord, I have taken refuge; let me never be put to shame. Rescue me and deliver me in your righteousness; turn your ear to me and save me. Be my rock of refuge, to which I can always go; give the command to save me, for you are my rock and my fortress. Deliver me, O my God,

from the hand of the wicked, from the grasp of evil and cruel men (*vv. 1-4*). These opening verses are very similar to the start of Psalm 31 (see commentary on that psalm). They express the sure confidence that his abiding refuge ever since his youth (see v. 5) has been the LORD. He continues to appeal to God to be attentive to his cry and to save him in his present trouble. The NIV translation 'rock of refuge' (*tsûr mâʿôz*) in verse 3 follows a few Hebrew manuscripts and makes this verse conform to Psalm 31:2. However, it is better to retain the reading in the majority of manuscripts, 'rock of *habitation*' (*tsûr mâʿôn*).[1] Clearly, from early times, Israel had thought of the LORD as being the dwelling place of his people (see Moses' words in Ps. 90:1). Even in his old age the psalmist is still surrounded by wicked men, from whose grip he seeks release. Whereas Psalm 31:4 refers to deliverance from a snare, here the thought is release 'from the grasp of evil (*meʿavvêl*, Pi. ptc.) and cruel men' (*chômêts*, Qal ptc.), using two rare words to create the parallel with 'from the hand of the wicked'. Words like 'rescue', 'deliver', and 'save' stress the urgency of the situation, and the need for God's speedy intervention.

2. A Declaration of Praise (*vv. 5-8*)

For you have been my hope, O Sovereign LORD, my confidence since my youth. From birth I have relied on you; you brought me forth from my mother's womb. I will ever praise you (*vv. 5-6*). Several times Jeremiah calls God 'the hope of Israel' (Jer. 14:8; 17:13), which is one reason why it has been suggested that he may be the author of this psalm. The words also seem to echo Psalm 22:9-10. The psalmist's confidence in the LORD is no newly found trust, but one which goes back to the very commencement of his life. Right from birth when

[1] The number of other differences between Psalms 71 and 31 suggest that the alteration of 'habitation' to 'refuge' is deliberate. While the first verse is identical in both psalms, Psalm 71 is not just a duplication of the earlier song. Some other phrases are repeated ('Turn to me your ear', 'Be my rock of ...', 'For you are my rock and my fortress'), while certain words occur in both (such as 'righteousness', 'rescue', 'deliver', 'save'). However, the changes look like deliberate alteration and expansion.

he was taken from his mother's womb,[2] he has set his hope on the LORD. Hence, it is not his own faith that is the object of his praise, but the grace of God that he has known since childhood. Constant praise is a way of indicating his response to God's keeping power.

I have become like a portent to many, but you are my strong refuge. My mouth is filled with your praise, declaring your splendour all day long (*vv. 7-8*). To many of his contemporaries he has become a sign or wonder. The word 'portent' (*môfêt*) is used in the section of Deuteronomy dealing with the curses that will come on Israel because of disobedience, and it is in parallel with the more common word 'sign' (*ʾôt*, Deut. 28:46). Here it seems to indicate that the psalmist feels himself to be the object of God's chastisement, so that he becomes an example to others. However, in spite of this, he does not hesitate to commit himself to his sure place of refuge. He picks up on the thought of praise already mentioned in verse 6, with stress on how continual was his adoration (v. 6, 'ever praise'; v. 8, 'all day long'). God's splendour or glory was what he wanted to proclaim constantly.

3. Prayer in Old Age (*vv. 9-13*)

Do not cast me away when I am old; do not forsake me when my strength is gone. For my enemies speak against me; those who wait to kill me conspire together (*vv. 9-10*). From reflection upon his commitment to the LORD from his youth, the psalmist now turns to his present old age.[3] In his increasing weakness he pleads that God will not cast him off (the same expression as David uses in Ps. 51:11). 'Casting off' is the equivalent of being abandoned. Even at this stage of his earthly pilgrimage there are those who plot against him,

---

[2] The translation 'you brought me forth' (*gôzî*) certainly fits the context, though the derivation of the verb is uncertain. It is best taken as the Qal part. of *gâzâh* and means 'the one who severed me [from the womb]'. Various emendations have been proposed but they lack manuscript confirmation. See *DCH*, II, p. 339.

[3] The word for 'old age' (*ziqnâh*) only occurs six times in the Old Testament, two of which are in this psalm (vv. 9, 18). It points more to bodily weakness, rather than to great age. The suffix 'my' is not added, as often it is omitted if the context supplies it. See *DIHG~S*, pp. 4-5.

watching to see if they can take his life.[4] Evil men combine together as they plan their attacks on believers (cf. Ps. 83:3).

They say, 'God has forsaken him; pursue him and seize him, for no one will rescue him' (*v. 11*). The opening words, 'they say', picks up on the use of the same verb in the previous verse (NIV 'speak'), and then gives the content of what they say.[5] Similar speeches of enemies are given in Psalm 3:2 and 41:6. One of the hardest taunts for believers to face is the one that in their distress God has forsaken them. But the reality is that God will not forsake his faithful ones (Ps. 37:28), and so the taunt is a lie. While the enemies claim that there is no deliverer, the psalmist knows full well that this is untrue, as the following petitions show.

Be not far from me, O God; come quickly, O my God, to help me (*v. 12*). This verse seems to be an echo of Psalms 22:11, 19; 38:21-22; 40:13; and 70:1. It is a help in times of distress to use words that others have used before us in their urgent situations. Others have passed the same way and have made their plea for speedy assistance. The change from 'O God' to 'O my God' in the second clause stresses the covenantal relationship between the needy servant and the powerful deliverer.

May my accusers perish in shame; may those who want to harm me be covered with scorn and disgrace (*v. 13*). These words are close to Psalms 35:4, 26; 40:15; 70:3, and 109:29.[6] His appeal is for God to vindicate him and he awaits divine judgment upon his enemies.

---

[4] The expression 'those who wait to kill me' is literally 'the watchers of my soul'. The thought of 'waiting to kill' is implied in the context, especially with the use of the verb 'to take counsel' (cf. Ps. 2:2).

[5] 'They say' is a translation of *lê'mor* ('to say, saying'). It often occurs in Hebrew prose following a finite form of the same verb, 'say, saying ...' but rarely in poetry. In prose passages it is frequently omitted in English translation, and could be here without any alteration of meaning as the inverted commas mark the speech content.

[6] All of these passages use either the verb *kâlam* (Ni. 'be ashamed') or the related noun *k^elimmâh* ('shame', 'disgrace'). They also use similar constructions to denote the enemies: 'seekers of my life' (35:4), 'gloaters over my distress' (35:26), 'seekers of my life' (40:14; 70:2), 'my accusers' (109:29), and 'condemners of his soul' (109:31). This common phraseology suggests a standard way of denoting enemies in petitionary prayers.

4. Confidence in Old Age (*vv. 14-18*)
But as for me, I will always have hope; I will praise you more and more. My mouth will tell of your righteousness, of your salvation all day long, though I know not its measure (*vv. 14-15*). The contrast is very clear between the fate of the enemies and the future of the psalmist.[7] He is confident that even in his old age he will proclaim God's salvation, and do so to an increasing degree. 'Righteousness' is used in the sense of God's saving acts, as is shown by the parallel 'salvation'. The word 'measure' (*s^eforôt*) is connected to the Hebrew word for 'tell' (*sâfar*, Pi.), and it only occurs here in the whole of the Old Testament. It probably means he is unable to count the 'number' of God's saving acts.[8]

I will come and proclaim your mighty acts, O Sovereign LORD; I will proclaim your righteousness, yours alone. Since my youth, O God, you have taught me, and to this day I declare your marvellous deeds (*vv. 16-17*). The opening clause of verse 16 has given difficulty, as the variety in English versions shows. The AV rendering. 'I will go in the strength of the LORD God' is hard to sustain, as the 'strength' (*g^evurôt*) is the LORD's, not the speaker's.[9] The NIV rendering is also without support, for it inserts 'and proclaim' without any textual evidence. An attractive possibility is that the verb 'come' (*bô'*) can mean to commence or begin an action. This makes good sense here as the psalmist is asserting that he will begin with the mighty acts of the LORD.[10] Several words are used to describe God's actions. The psalmist will make mention of

---

[7] The contrast is marked in the Hebrew text by the way the verse opens: 'But I continually, I will hope ...' The NIV translation captures the meaning, as does the NLT: 'But I will keep on hoping ...'

[8] Because of the rarity of this word it is difficult to make a decision regarding its meaning. Another suggested translation is 'the art of writing': 'My mouth shall declare your victories, your salvation all the day, for I do not know the art of writing.' However, that hardly fits the context for the psalmist *is* writing. See the various possibilities listed in *DCH*, VI, pp. 193-94.

[9] The suffix 'your' attached to 'righteousness' also applies to 'mighty acts'.

[10] For this interpretation, see *DCH*, II, p. 102; G. R. Driver, 'Hebrew Notes', *VT* 1 (1951), p. 249.

those actions which are God's alone,[11] his royal power which has been displayed in victories. He is also declared to be a God of faithfulness who does things that are beyond human capability (*niflâʾôt*, 'marvellous deeds'; cf. its use in Pss. 72:18 and 86:10). All that he has learned of the LORD's actions on behalf of his people forms part of his songs of praise. This learning has been from his early days right up to the present, for God not only teaches his people in general but individuals like the psalmist also.

Even when I am old and grey, do not forsake me, O God, till I declare your power to the next generation, your might to all who are to come (*v. 18*). As he nears the end of life the psalmist still wants to declare to the coming generation the great things that God has done. Not only the nation but he himself has experienced the power of God (Hebrew, *zᵉrôʿᵃkâ*, 'your arm'), and this forms a further testimony to God's saving might. Having already prayed that God would not abandon him (v. 9), he again prays for his sustaining presence and help.

5. A Confident Song (*vv. 19-24*)

Your righteousness reaches to the skies, O God, you who have done great things. Who, O God, is like you? (*v. 19*). The psalm moves to a conclusion with a strong note of confidence. The early part of this verse echoes Psalm 36:5-6, while the rhetorical question, 'Who is like you?', is paralleled in Psalm 89:8. Both the latter passage and this verse in Psalm 71 may be echoing the words of the Song of the Sea in Exodus 15:11. 'To do great things' is a standard expression for demonstrations of God's power. The whole verse is an emphatic assertion of the fact that God's righteousness is beyond human comprehension, and that no one can be compared to the LORD.

Though you have made me see troubles, many and bitter, you will restore my life again; from the depths of the earth you will again bring me up (*v. 20*). Just as the psalmist has declared that God's righteousness extends to the heavens, he now speaks of the experiences he and others have been

---

[11] 'Make mention' is the translation of the Hebrew verb *zâkar* Hi. that means 'to cause to be remembered', hence mention in praise.

through.[12] The experiences of the individual blend into those of the nation. They have seen many distressing situations (perhaps even the exile) when they seemed as good as dead (cf. Ps. 30:3). From the grave or the depths of the earth they can appeal to God to restore them again.[13] This is a confessional response by the believing community, which, having been afflicted, can cry for restoration. The psalmist is sure that God will not forsake them, and this must always remain the confidence of believers.

Though troubles assail and danger affright,
Though friends should all fail and foes unite,
Yet one thing secures us, whatever betide,
The Scripture assures us the Lord will provide.

No strength of our own or goodness we claim;
Yet, since we have known the Saviour's great Name,
In this our strong tower for safety we hide,
The Lord is our power, the Lord will provide.

(John Newton, 1725-1807)

You will increase my honour and comfort me once again (*v. 21*). The psalmist switches to speak of his own condition, and he appeals for restoration to a place of dignity. He wants to know the comforting presence of his God once again.[14]

I will praise you with the harp for your faithfulness, O my God; I will sing praise to you with the lyre, O Holy One of

---

[12] While in the NIV the objects of the verbs are singular in this verse ('you have made *me* see troubles', 'you will restore *my* life again', 'you will again bring *me* up'), the K^e^tiv reading in the MT definitely has plural objects for the first two, while many manuscripts, the Targum, and Jerome have a plural for the third one as well.

[13] The idea of 'again' is conveyed twice by the use of the Hebrew verb *shûv*, which by itself normally means 'return', 'go back'. Hebrew lacks the adverbs that occur in English and other European languages. Instead it often uses two verbs, whereas these other languages use a verb + an adverb. Information on this Hebrew usage can be found in *IBHS*, pp. 75-76, 656; *DIHG~S*, p. 139; with good examples listed in *BDB*, p. 998.

[14] 'Again' represents the Hebrew verb *sâvav*, 'to turn', used here in the same way as *shûv* was in the previous verse.

Israel. My lips will shout for joy when I sing praise to you – I, whom you have redeemed (*vv. 22-23*). The NIV translation fails to render the very first word in verse 22 (*gam*). While it often means 'also', in some situations it signifies 'therefore' as here and in Psalm 52:5 (see comment on that verse).[15] God's faithfulness and holiness form the subject of praise. The expression 'Holy One of Israel' is most frequently used as a title for God in the prophecy of Isaiah (see, e.g., Isa. 1:4; 5:19, 24; 29:19; 47:4; 60:14).[16] God's holiness is seen in the way in which he redeems his people, and it will always be mentioned in the songs of the redeemed (cf. Exod. 15:11; Rev. 15:3-4).

My tongue will tell of your righteous acts all day long, for those who wanted to harm me have been put to shame and confusion (*v. 24*). The Hebrew text opens with the word *gam* (see comment on v. 22). The NIV omits it, while many translations render it by 'and' or 'also'. However, rendering it 'therefore' makes good sense in the context. Praise follows redemption. The psalmist knows, too, that God will not desert him. The judgment of God upon his enemies is a demonstration of his righteousness, and as such it forms the subject of his continuous song of praise.

---

[15] This same usage can be seen in prophetic passages (such as Isa. 66:4, Ezek. 16:43 and Mal. 2:9) where *gam* = *lâkên*.

[16] 'Holy one of Israel' (*q^e dôsh yisrâêl*) occurs twenty-nine times in the Book of Isaiah, and only six times elsewhere. Three of these other occurrences are in the Psalms (71:22; 78:41; 89:18).

Psalm 72

Of Solomon.

Jesus shall reign where'er the sun
Does his successive journeys run;
His kingdom stretch from shore to shore,
Till moons shall wax and wane no more.

With these words Isaac Watts (1674-1748) captured the spirit of this psalm. The promises that are given concerning the king go far beyond anything that could be promised to an ordinary descendant of David. The psalm is devoted to celebration of the Davidic kingship, seeking gifts for him that are going also to come upon his people. Thus, for example, endowed with righteousness (v. 1), he will be able to judge righteously (v. 2). The vision presented of the Davidic king far transcends any other description. *All* kings are going to bow before him (v. 11), and the extension of his kingdom is described in terms identical to the messianic passage in Zechariah 9:9-13. Early Jewish thinking took the same viewpoint, as the Targum adds after the word 'king' in verse 1, 'Messiah'. The background of the psalm is the covenant with David in 2 Samuel 7, but the vision is of the ultimate Davidic ruler, Jesus Christ. The Hebrew title is ambiguous, as it can mean either 'by Solomon', or 'for Solomon'.

1. A Prayer for the King (*vv. 1-4*)
Endow the king with your justice, O God, the royal son with your righteousness (*v. 1*). In terms of the covenant with David, the Davidic king was adopted as God's son (2 Sam. 7:14; cf. also Ps. 89:26-27). Hence he can be called either 'the king' or 'the

son of the king' (NIV 'the royal son'). The initial appeal here is for the gift of righteous rule to him, so that his administration will reflect the very character of God himself.

He will judge your people in righteousness, your afflicted ones with justice. The mountains will bring prosperity to the people, the hills the fruit of righteousness (*vv.* 2-3). The idea expressed in verse 1 is carried over into these following verses. The endowment with justice and righteousness will enable the king to rule well. Clearly here and elsewhere (cf. Exod. 22:25) 'your people' (*ʿammᵉkâ*) and 'your afflicted ones' (*ʿᵃniyyekâ*) are synonymous, for 'the afflicted' (*ʿᵃniyyîm*) are the LORD's people in a special relationship with him.[1] The effective and just rule of the king is stated poetically in the thought that there will be a harvest of peace[2] and righteousness, so that even the mountain ranges will produce the crops that denote prosperity (cf. a similar poetic usage in Joel 3:18).

He will defend the afflicted among the people and save the children of the needy; he will crush the oppressor (*v.* 4). None of the oppressed need to fear during the reign of this king, for they will be defended by him. He will bring vindication to them, and so the thought of verse 2 is enlarged to embody the promise that the defenceless are his special care. The oppressors will find that they are treated in the way in which they themselves treated others, a principle which the New Testament reasserts (James 2:13).

2. An Enduring Kingship (*vv.* 5-7)

He will endure as long as the sun, as long as the moon, through all generations (*v.* 5). In contrast to other dynasties, the promise to David was that his kingdom was going to endure (2 Sam. 7:11b-16), expressed here in comparison with

---

[1] The significance of 'the afflicted' is also shown by the fact that the opposite in biblical terms is not the rich but the wicked. Full discussion on the term is provided by W. J. Dumbrell, *NIDOTTE*, 3, pp. 454-64.

[2] While the word 'peace' (*shalom*) is used, it has its wider meaning here and in verse 7 of 'well-being', 'prosperity'. The English word 'peace' tends to have negative connotations (absence of war or conflict), whereas in Hebrew it is positive. The biblical and modern Hebrew way of enquiring about the well-being of someone is asking whether they have *shalom* (Cf. Gen. 43:27, lit. 'Does your aged father [have] peace?').

the sun and moon. The promise was repeated several times in the Old Testament (Pss. 89:28-29; 132:11-12; Isa. 9:7), and it was renewed in the words of Gabriel to Mary, as he announced the coming birth of Jesus (Luke 1:31-33).

He will be like rain falling on a mown field, like showers watering the earth. In his days the righteous will flourish; prosperity will abound till the moon is no more (*vv. 6-7*). The opening of verse 6 picks up an idea from David's last words in 2 Samuel 23:3-4: 'when one rules over men in righteousness, ... he is like ... the brightness after rain that brings the grass from the earth.' The prosperity, under the Davidic house, is likened to the effect of rain that stimulates further the growth of newly mown grass. The righteous will have conditions in which they will flourish (for the same expression see Ps. 92:12 and Prov. 11:28), and this will continue until the end of time.

3. A Universal Kingdom (*vv. 8-11*)

He will rule from sea to sea and from the River to the ends of the earth (*v. 8*). The extent of the kingdom of the messianic ruler is stated in terms of the promise to Abraham. It was during the Davidic/Solomonic empire that the boundaries of 'the promised land' reached their fullest extent (1 Kings 4:21, 24). However, there is one notable change here compared with the earlier Old Testament references to the land. The boundary does not extend up to the [Euphrates] River,[3] but from it outwards! No longer will it be the restricted territory allotted as the promised land, but it will consist of a universal kingdom. Psalm 72:8 cannot be considered on its own, as almost identical language is used in Zechariah 9:10: 'I will take away the chariots from Ephraim and the war-horses from Jerusalem, and the battle-bow will be broken. He will proclaim peace to the nations. His rule will extend from sea to sea and from the River to the ends of the earth.' Both in that

---

[3] Hebrew has an amazing number of words denoting 'river', the one used here (*p^erât*) designating only the Euphrates. Cf. the NLT of this verse: 'May he reign from sea to sea, and from the Euphrates River to the ends of the earth'.

passage and here in Psalm 72 the contexts are dealing with eschatological events.[4]

The desert tribes will bow before him and his enemies will lick the dust. The kings of Tarshish and of distant shores will bring tribute to him; the kings of Sheba and Seba will present him gifts (*vv. 9-10*). From far-off places people will acknowledge the rule of Messiah, and his enemies will be brought to own his authority over them. 'To bow before' and 'to lick the dust' are synonymous expressions of submission (see Isa. 49:23). The places mentioned (Tarshish, Sheba, and Seba)[5] represent the distant nations, with their rulers coming to present their tribute as a sign of allegiance to this universal king. The New Testament speaks of a day coming when Jesus will have destroyed all other dominions and powers, and all his enemies will be placed under his feet (1 Cor. 15:24-25).

All kings will bow down to him and all nations will serve him (*v. 11*). Though this and the previous verses express the idea of submission in terms alluding to Solomon's kingdom, yet the final fulfilment of this promise will be when Jesus, as the Lamb, overcomes because he is Lord of lords and King of kings (Rev. 17:14; 19:16).

4. Concern for Righteousness and Justice (*vv. 12-14*)

For he will deliver the needy who cry out, the afflicted who have no one to help. He will take pity on the weak and the needy and save the needy from death (*vv. 12-13*). Earlier in verses 2-4 the psalmist spoke about the king's support for those who needed his special care. Now he returns to this theme, with the assurance that he will act in mercy to those who are oppressed. In contrast to other Near Eastern kingdoms, the

---

[4] Cf. the use made of the Zechariah passage in Matthew 21:5, with the opening words being taken from Isaiah. The sort of language used of the kingdom extension 'is extravagant unless heard in an eschatological key', as Christopher Wright expresses it. See *NIDOTTE*, 1, p. 521.

[5] Several references to Tarshish in the Old Testament link it with the sea, but it is unclear whether this is the Mediterranean or the Red Sea (or even the coast of Africa). Sheba was probably located in south-eastern Arabia, while Seba could be near it, or else just another name for Sheba. This would mean taking the 'and' linking the two words here as meaning 'that is'. Cf. *DCH*, II, p. 597 and the literature cited on p. 641; also, *IBHS*, pp. 652-53.

Davidic throne was established in love, and the Davidic king was 'one who in judging seeks justice and speeds the cause of righteousness' (Isa. 16:5).

He will rescue them from oppression and violence, for precious is their blood in his sight (*v. 14*). It was part of the promise to David that the wicked would not oppress any more (2 Sam. 7:10). This verse picks up that theme, declaring that when subjects are faced with violence, the king will rescue them (Hebrew, lit. 'will redeem'). The Hebrew word used for redeem (*gâ'al*) often denotes the action of a kinsman in redeeming his kin from difficulty or danger (cf. its use in Ruth 4, where it refers to the redeeming of the land which belonged to Naomi). In the king's sight, the life of even these afflicted ones is very special (cf. the almost identical phrase used of God in Ps. 116:15).

5. Universal Blessing (*vv. 15-17*)

An even more direct reference to the covenant with Abraham occurs in these closing verses, with the psalm ending with a prayer for the fulfilment of that covenant. **Long may he live! May gold from Sheba be given to him. May people ever pray for him and bless him all day long** (*v. 15*). The prayer for the continuing existence of the dynasty is put in terms of the normal salutation of a new king (cf. 1 Sam. 10:24; 2 Sam. 16:16; 1 Kings 1:25, 34).[6] Just as the Queen of Sheba brought gifts to Solomon, including gold (1 Kings 10:10), so the psalmist pictures further tribute being presented to the Davidic king. In addition, prayer is made for his welfare and praise given to him for the prosperity he brings.

Let grain abound throughout the land; on the tops of the hills may it sway. Let its fruit flourish like Lebanon; let it thrive like the grass of the field (*v. 16*). The picture of prosperity is painted in terms of abundant crops, even to the very tops of the mountains! Just as Lebanon was noted for its bountiful forests, so may the land yield an abundant harvest.

---

[6] The form of the prayer is simply 'and let him live' (*vîchî*), but this verb (*châyâh*) quite often has the sense of continuing in life, remaining alive (*BDB*, p. 311), and hence the English phrase 'Long may he live' is quite appropriate as a translation.

The covenantal blessings that promised abundant crops and herds (Deut. 28:3-6) will find their fulfilment through the messianic king.

May his name endure forever; may it continue as long as the sun. All nations will be blessed through him, and they will call him blessed (*v. 17*). An enduring kingship was going to bring blessing to many more countries than just Israel. In fact, the promise of the covenant with Abraham (Gen. 12:2-3) was going to find its fulfilment through the messianic kingship of Jesus, when the nations would receive the blessing of the Spirit (Gal. 3:14). It is curious that the 'name' is not expressly mentioned either in this verse or verse 19 ('his glorious name'), yet the allusion to the blessing through Abraham seems the obvious reference point.[7] The allusion goes back to what the LORD said to Abraham as recorded in Genesis 12:3 and in Genesis 22:17, and to Isaac in Genesis 26:4. Through the king's/messiah's government the Abrahamic covenant will find fulfilment. What is especially significant here is the link that is made between the Abrahamic and Davidic covenants.[8]

6. Concluding Benediction (*vv. 18-20)*

Praise be to the LORD God, the God of Israel, who alone does marvellous deeds. Praise be to his glorious name forever; may the whole earth be filled with his glory. Amen and Amen (*vv. 18-19*). Like all the five books of the Psalter, this second one concludes with a doxology. The covenant God of Israel is indeed the only one able to do 'marvellous' deeds (see the comment on Ps. 71:17). His name is worthy of praise because of the glory of his actions in redeeming and keeping his people. The desire for the whole earth to be filled with God's glory is an echo of Numbers 14:21. To that desire the people respond with a double 'Amen'. 'Amen' is frequently

---

[7] The form of the verb 'to bless' in this passage is Hitpael imperfect (*yibar*e*kû*). This follows the use of the same form in Genesis 22:18. One of the advantages of opting for a reflexive or reciprocal meaning for this verbal form here is that it provides a concrete significance to the use of Abraham's name. The meaning will be that people invoke a blessing on themselves. 'May we be blessed just as Abraham was blessed!'

[8] Craig Broyles, *Psalms*, p. 298, makes this point well.

used after prayers and hymns of praise (see 1 Chron. 16:36; Neh. 8:6; Pss. 41:13 and 106:48).

This concludes the prayers of David son of Jesse (*v. 20*). This note does not refer to the whole Psalter, for there are later Davidic psalms (cf. Pss. 86, 108-110, 138-145). It appears to have been added to the collection, that precedes, to mark it off from the psalms of Asaph which follow (Pss. 73-83).

MENTOR
Matthew
A MENTOR COMMENTARY
Volume 1: Chapters 1-13
Knox Chamblin

MENTOR
Matthew
A MENTOR COMMENTARY
Volume 2: Chapters 14-28
Knox Chamblin

Matthew

Volume 1 (chapters 1-13)
Volume 2 (chapters 14–28)

A Mentor Commentary

Knox Chamblin

This thoughtful and thorough commentary on the First Gospel comes from a scholar who has obviously spent many years at the feet of Matthew the teacher, and even more importantly, at the feet of the One to whom Matthew bears witness.

Jonathan Pennington,
Associate Professor of New Testament Interpretation,
The Southern Baptist Theological Seminary, Louisville, Kentucky

What, you might say, am I to do with 2 volumes and 1,400 pages on Matthew? Well, what should you do if given two million pounds? Spend it, of course–but not all at once. So with Chamblin's Matthew. Preach an Advent series – and use Chamblin on chapters 1–2; then preach from the Old Testament and come back to the Sermon on the Mount – and use Chamblin on chapters 5–7; then map out a series on Matthew's passion narrative – and use Chamblin on chapters 26–28. I'm not a hypocrite – I'm using him on Matthew 13 even as I write this!

Dale Ralph Davis,
Well respected author and Bible expositor

Knox Chamblin taught for thirty-four years in Jackson, Mississippi, first at Belhaven College, then at Reformed Theological Seminary until retirement in 2001.

Volume 1 ISBN 978-1-84550-364-2
Volume 2 ISBN 978-1-84550-379-6

Ezra & Nehemiah

A MENTOR COMMENTARY

Tiberius Rata

Ezra & Nehemiah

A Mentor Commentary

Tiberius Rata

Tiberius Rata combines exegetical skill, knowledge of the ancient world, and a pastor's heart in this volume. His explanations of the text are clear, forceful, yet concise. This work will assist the church in understanding its call to godly service to Christ and will motivate its readers to re-consecrate their lives and possessions to the work of the Kingdom.

Kenneth A. Matthews,
Professor of Divinity, Beeson Divinity School, Birmingham, Alabama

Reasoned, researched, and concise, Rata's commentary on Ezra and Nehemiah opens a window on the historical setting for these significant books of the Old Testament. This volume ably addresses the interests of laymen and pastors alike as they study the biblical text of the two books.

William D. Barrick,
Professor of Old Testament, The Master's Seminary, Sun Valley, California

Tiberius Rata's work should be warmly received by pastors and teachers. His commentary is clear and to the point, yet he discusses some problems at length, furnishing thoughtfulness and insight for solutions. His viewpoint is solidly orthodox and reverent. His high view of Scripture and of the God of Scripture is reflected throughout the work. His work demonstrates competent scholarship and conveys a pastor's heart-the work of a pastor scholar. His outlines and comments are helpful for understanding the flow ofthe historical narrative and are suggestive for sermon preparation.

Russel Fuller,
Professor of Old Testament Interpretation,
The Southern Baptist Theological Seminary, Louisville, Kentucky

Tiberius Rata is the chair of the Biblical Studies Department and professor of Old Testament Studies at Grace College and Theological Seminary, Winona Lake, Indiana.

ISBN 978-1-84550-571-4

Galatians

A MENTOR COMMENTARY

David McWilliams

Galatians

A Mentor Commentary

David McWilliams

...addresses interpretive issues with clarity and cogent discernment, and he engages recent misperceptions of Paul's central concern—which is not merely sociological or ecclesiastical, but soteriological (How may guilty sinners be reconciled to their holy Creator?)—all the while keeping in view the aim of preaching this good news of sovereign grace.

Dennis E. Johnson,
Professor of Practical Theology,
Westminster Seminary in California, Escondido, California

Timely, lucid, and reliable, this is an excellent commentary for preachers, Bible study leaders and others. David McWilliams admirably succeeds in his aim for brevitas and claritas, the two qualities in commentators that Calvin most commended. He distils a great deal of scholarship into uncluttered and readable prose. Paul's message in Galatians has rarely been so urgently needed as today, when justification only by faith is under attack from many sides. McWilliams explains it with judicious care.

Robert Letham,
Senior Tutor, Systematic & Historical Theology,
Wales Evangelical School of Theology, Brigend, Wales

Having had the opportunity of reading this clear and gracefully written book during its production, I commend it most highly. Certainly it is one pastors ought to consider adding to theirs libraries.

Richard Gaffin,
Professor of Biblical and Systematic Theology, Emeritus,
Westminster Theological Seminary, Philadelphia, Pennsylvania

David McWilliams has been the senior pastor at Covenant Presbyterian Church, Lakeland, Florida for 20 years.

ISBN 978-1-84550-452-6

MENTOR

Lamentations

A MENTOR COMMENTARY

John L. Mackay

Lamentations

A Mentor Commentary

John L. MacKay

The five chapters of Lamentations may be easily overlooked. Not only is it brief, but it is also sandwiched between the two giants of Old Testament prophecy, Jeremiah and Ezekiel. Lamentations also deals with realities which we rather wish were not discussed – consequently the book is little studied. However, although there much here to challenge faith, there is much that builds it up. Lamentations was not written in the first instance to serve as warning to others, or to even keep alive the present memory of past suffering, it is the present that dominates the thought of the book.

And in that present are overiding thoughts – 'has God left us?'; 'Have we blown our chance as God's covenant people?' 'Is there a way forward towards the restoration?'

A popular view today is that Lamentations is a dreary book with nothing to say to today's society. The reality is that it could not be more relevant, more authentic.

Mentor combines a high view of Scripture with access to the latest academic theological research. This unique combinations allows the reader to see what recent scholarly research has discovered without losing sight of Scripture.

John L. Mackay is the Principal of the Free Church College, Edinburgh and internationally known as an Old Testament scholar. He is also in demand for church retreats where his skill in the practical exposition and application of doctrine are well respected.

ISBN 978-1-84550-363-5

Christian Focus Publications

publishes books for all ages

Our mission statement –
STAYING FAITHFUL
In dependence upon God we seek to impact the world through literature faithful to His infallible Word, the Bible. Our aim is to ensure that the Lord Jesus Christ is presented as the only hope to obtain forgiveness of sin, live a useful life and look forward to heaven with Him.

REACHING OUT
Christ's last command requires us to reach out to our world with His gospel. We seek to help fulfill that by publishing books that point people towards Jesus and help them develop a Christ-like maturity. We aim to equip all levels of readers for life, work, ministry and mission.

Books in our adult range are published in three imprints.

Christian Focus contains popular works including biographies, commentaries, basic doctrine and Christian living. Our children's books are also published in this imprint.

Mentor focuses on books written at a level suitable for Bible College and seminary students, pastors, and other serious readers. The imprint includes commentaries, doctrinal studies, examination of current issues and church history.

Christian Heritage contains classic writings from the past.

Christian Focus Publications, Ltd
Geanies House, Fearn, Ross-shire,
IV20 1TW, Scotland, United Kingdom
www.christianfocus.com

Psalms

Volume 2

Allan Harman's commentary is the fruit of a lifetime's study of the Psalter and provides a well-informed, reliable guide to the vast literature on the subject. The extensive introduction is itself worth its weight in gold while the Scripture text is opened up in a clear, careful and devout way.

Philip H Eveson,
Former principal of London Theological Seminary and lecturer in Old Testament exegesis, theology and preaching

Harman's Commentary on the Psalms is a solid exposition of the Psalms. The focus is on the original meaning of the psalms with clear explanations of the message of each psalm through an analysis of structure, key words, and the flow of the psalm. And yet, the meaning of the psalms for God's people today is also emphasized by showing important connections to the New Testament. The reader will discover the rich treasures in the Psalms through the use of this commentary.

Richard P. Belcher, Jr.
Professor of Old Testament, Reformed Theological Seminary, Charlotte, North Carolina

Allan Harman writes as a Christian scholar, with academic precision and devotional warmth. The unique character of this commentary is undoubtedly due to the method of its preparation (revealed in the author's "Foreword"). After completing careful exegesis of each Psalm, Allan brought the fruits of his study into the service of family worship in his own home. The result is a commentary that is both academically solid and devotionally rich. This commentary will be a worthy resource for the pastor and student in the study as well as the layman seeking personal edification.

Michael LeFebvre
Pastor, Christ Church Reformed Presbyterian Church, Indianapolis, Indiana

Psalms

Volume 2

Psalms 73-150

A Mentor Commentary

Allan Harman

To Mairi

Allan Harman is Research Professor of Old Testament at the Presbyterian Theological College in Melbourne, Australia. He has taught graduate courses at Ontario Theological Seminary, Toronto and Reformed Theological Seminary, Jackson, Mississippi.

ISBN 978-1-84550-738-1

(Volume 1 ISBN 978-1-84550-737-4)

10 9 8 7 6 5 4 3 2 1

Published in 2011
in the
Mentor Imprint
by
Christian Focus Publications,
Geanies House, Fearn, Tain,
Ross-shire, IV20 1TW, Great Britain
www.christianfocus.com

Cover design by Daniel van Straaten
Printed and bound by MPG Books, UK

Contents

BOOK 5

Abbreviations

ASV	*American Standard Version.*
AV	*Authorised (King James) Version.*
BASOR	*Bulletin of the American Schools of Oriental Research.*
BBR	*Bulletin for Biblical Research.*
BDB	Brown, Driver, and Briggs, *eds., A Hebrew and English Lexicon of the Old Testament.* (Oxford: Clarendon Press, 1975 reprint).
BHS	*Biblia Hebraica Stuttgartensia (Stuttgart: Deutsche Bibelstiftung, 1967/77).*
Bib	*Biblica.*
BS	*Bibliotheca Sacra.*
c.	Latin, around, about.
CJT	*Canadian Journal of Theology.*
CHAL	*A Concise Hebrew and Aramaic Lexicon of the Old Testament (Grand Rapids: Eerdmans, 1988).*
DCH	*Dictionary of Classical Hebrew,* ed. David J.A. Clines, 7 vols. (Sheffield: Sheffield Academic Press, 1993-)
DIHG~S	J. C. L. Gibson, *Davidson's Introductory Hebrew Grammar~ Syntax,* 4th ed. (Edinburgh: T. & T. Clark, 1994).
DOTT	*Documents from Old Testament Times.*
EBC	*Expositor's Bible Commentary.*
ESV	*English Standard Version.* Wheaton: Good News Publishers, 2001.
EQ	*Evangelical Quarterly.*
ET	*Expository Times.*
GKC	*Gesenius' Hebrew Grammar,* 2nd ed., Gesenius, Kautzsch, Cowley eds. (Oxford: Clarendon Press), 1966.
HALOT	*The Hebrew and Aramaic Lexicon of the Old Testament* (Leiden: Brill, 2000).
Heb.	Hebrew.
IBHS	*An Introduction to Biblical Hebrew Syntax,* Bruce K. Waltke and M. O'Connor (Winona Lake: Eisenbrauns, 1990).
IBS	*Irish Biblical Studies.*
IDB	*Interpreter's Dictionary of the Bible,* 4 vols. (Nashville: Abingdon Press, 1962).
ISBE	*International Standard Bible Encyclopaedia.* 4 vols. (Grand Rapids: Eerdmans, 1979).
JANES	*Journal of the Ancient Near Eastern Society.*
JB	*Jerusalem Bible.*
JBL	*Journal of Biblical Literature.*
JETS	*Journal of the Evangelical Theological Society.*
JNSL	*Journal of North West Semitic Languages.*
JSOT	*Journal for the Study of the Old Testament.*

JSS — *Journal of Semitic Studies.*
JTS — *Journal of Theological Studies.*
lit. — literally.
LXX — The Septuagint, the oldest and most important Greek translation of the Old Testament made in Egypt about 250 BC.
mg. — margin.
MT — Massoretic text, the Hebrew text of the Old Testament that became recognised as authoritative after the fall of Jerusalem in 70 AD.
NASB — *New American Standard Bible*: Updated Edition. Anaheim, CA: Foundation Publications, 1997.
NEB — *The New English Bible*. New York: Oxford University Press, 1976.
NICOT — *New International Commentary on the Old Testament.*
NIDOTTE — *New International Dictionary of Old Testament Theology and Exegesis*, ed. Willem A. VanGemeren, 5 vols. (Grand Rapids: Zondervan, 1997).
NIV — *New International Version*. Colorado Springs: International Bible Society, 1984.
NKJV — *New King James Version*. Nashville: Thomas Nelson, 1982.
NLT — *New Living Translation*. Wheaton: Tyndale House, 1996.
NRSV — *New Revised Standard Version*. Nashville: Thomas Nelson, 1989.
OTS — *Oudtestamentische Studiën.*
part. — participle.
pass. — passive.
PEQ — *Palestine Exploration Quarterly.*
PTR — *Princeton Theological Review.*
REB — *The Revised English Bible*. Oxford University Press, 1989.
RSV — *Revised Standard Version.*
RTR — *Reformed Theological Review.*
RV — *Revised Version.*
SJT — *Scottish Journal of Theology.*
TB — *Tyndale Bulletin.*
TS — *Theological Studies.*
TDOT — *Theological Dictionary of the Old Testament*, 15 vols. (Grand Rapids: Zondervan, 1997).
TWOT — *Theological Wordbook of the Old Testament*, 2 vols. (Chicago: Moody Press, 1980).
VT — *Vetus Testamentum.*
WTJ — *Westminster Theological Journal.*
× — The number of occurrences of a word in a particular verse or section is marked by this multiplication sign, e.g. 2×.
ZAW — *Zeitschrift für die alttestamentliche Wissenschaft.*
ZPEB — *Zondervan Pictorial Encyclopedia of the Bible*, 5 vols. (Grand Rapids: Zondervan Publishing House, 1975).

Glossary

acrostic	In an acrostic poem the first letter of each verse or stanza follows an alphabetic sequence.
Dead Sea Scrolls	About 800 scrolls containing all or part of Old Testament books discovered at or near Qumran, on the north-western side of the Dead Sea.
fixed pair	The term 'fixed pair' refers to words that regularly occur in parallel expressions in Hebrew, e.g., head/skull, earth/dust, mouth/lip.
ellipsis (or, gapping)	This occurs when a normal element of a sentence is missing and has to be understood from the context.
hapax legomenon	A word occurring only once (pl. *hapax legomena*).
hendiadys	lit. 'one through two [words]', the presentation of one idea by two expressions, e.g., 'with might and main'.
homonym	A word having the same sound as another, but with a different meaning and origin. In the text, these Hebrew words are marked by the addition of a Roman numeral as listed in the *Dictionary of Classical Hebrew*, e.g., *rav* II.
inclusio	A literary device by which a repeated theme both introduces and concludes a passage, so marking it as a separate section.
K^{e}tiv	A massoretic marginal note to the Hebrew text meaning 'that which is written' (see also Q^{e}re).
maqqef	A short horizontal stroke linking two Hebrew words.

Massoretes	Groups of Jewish scholars (AD 600-1000) who produced the final form of the OT text, adding the vocalisation, accents, and various notations.
Q^{e}re	A massoretic marginal note to the Hebrew text meaning 'that which is to be read' (in place of 'that which is written', the K^{e}tiv).
Qumran	See above, 'Dead Sea Scrolls'.
targum	An Aramaic translation or paraphrase of some part of the Old Testament. They were oral at first but were later written. The earliest examples (found at Qumran) are from the second century BC.
theophany	A visible appearance of God.
Vulgate	The Latin version of the Bible produced by Jerome in the period AD 380-405, which became the official Bible of the Roman Catholic Church at the Council of Trent in 1546.

Notes on Hebrew

Verbal Themes

Qal	Qal
Ni.	Nif'al
Pi.	Pi'el
Pu.	Pu'al
Hi.	Hif'il
Ho.	Hof'al
Hitp.	Hitpa'el

Grammatical Expressions

absol. inf. — Absolute infinitive: a verbal form normally placed before another form of the verb in order to emphasise it.

cognate accusative — The use of a noun as the object of a verb which comes from the same root, e.g., 'They dreaded [with] dread' (Ps. 14:5).

coh. — cohortative: indirect imperative forms in the 1st person singular and plural, e.g., 'Let me (us) send'.

constr. — construct: a noun, usually in a shortened form, placed before another noun and with a close semantic relation to it, covering all the nuances of the English *of*.

enclitic *mem* — A final *mem* added to words in poetry. This is a rare survival of an archaic form that has no obvious function.

imper. — imperative

imperfect — A verbal conjugation in Hebrew that identifies a situation as fluid or in motion.

inf. — infinitive

interrogative marker	The use of h^a prefixed to a sentence to change it into a question.
jussive	3rd person forms of the indirect imperative, e.g., 'Let him (them) send'.
m.	masculine
part.	participle
pass.	passive
perfect	A verbal conjugation in Hebrew that identifies a situation as static or at rest.
pers.	person
pl.	plural
vav consecutive	The use of the conjunction *vav* ('and') and a verbal form to indicate a simple action that has arisen out of something that has gone before.

Transliteration of Consonants

alef	ʾ
gimel	g
dalet	d
he	h
vav	v
zayin	z
chet	ch (as in German *ich*, or Scottish *loch*)
tet	t
yod	y
kaf	k
lamed	l
mem	m
nun	n
samek	s
ayin	ʿ
peh	p/f

tsadeh	ts
qof	q
resh	r
sin	s
shin	sh
taw	t

Note:

1. Long vowels are marked with a circumflex, e.g. *â, ê, î, ô, û*.
2. Hebrew words are normally accented on the final syllable. However, there is a group of nouns in which the stress is placed on the first of a pair of vowels, resulting in next-to-last syllable stress. This is marked by the use of an acute, e.g. *régel* (foot). The acute is also used with a small number of other nouns that do not have the stress on the final syllable, e.g. *shâmáyim* (heavens).

Book 3

Psalm 73

A psalm of Asaph.

This third book of the Psalter starts with a group of psalms attributed to Asaph (Pss. 73-83). He was a descendant of Gershon, son of Levi (cf. 1 Chron. 6:39-42), and he was one of the leaders of music whom David appointed (1 Chron. 15:16-17; 2 Chron. 5:12).[1] Communal psalms of complaint dominate this section of the Psalter (cf. Pss. 74, 79, 80, 83). If the introductory psalms are left out of the reckoning (Pss. 1 and 2) and also the doxological ones at the end (Pss. 146-150), then Psalm 73 is positioned exactly at the middle of the complete book. This fact, however, may just be accidental, not by the design of the compiler(s).[2]

Psalm 73 is close in style to Psalms 37 and 49, in that it struggles with the problem of why wicked people seem to prosper as compared with the righteous. Only when the psalmist went to worship did he understand what was to be the final destiny of the wicked (vv. 16-17). The psalm is carefully crafted, with the association of the word 'good' (*tôv*) with God appearing at the beginning and end (vv. 1 and 28).[3] Also, three key verses in the psalm are introduced by the Hebrew word *ʾak,* translated consistently in the NIV by 'surely' (vv. 1, 13, 18). Four times, too, a verse begins with

[1] For fuller discussion on 'the sons of Asaph', see the introduction to Psalm 50.

[2] The whole question of the structure of the Psalter is discussed in the Introduction.

[3] This is a poetic device in which the poem is framed between repeated phrases, or, as in this psalm, identical individual words. For discussion on this device, termed an envelope figure, see Wilfred G. E. Watson, *Classical Hebrew Poetry: A Guide to its Techniques* (Sheffield: JSOT Press, 1984), pp. 282-87.

'And I' (Heb. *va'ₐnî*) with the NIV translating it as, 'But as for me …' in verses 2 and 28, 'I was …' in verse 22, and 'Yet I am …' in verse 23.

1. Complaint to God (*vv. 1-3*)
The psalm opens with a declaration of God's relationship to his people. He is in covenant friendship with them. **Surely God is good to Israel, to those who are pure in heart** (*v. 1*). The opening word (Heb. *'ak*) allows the psalm to begin on a note of certainty. There can be no doubt about God's goodness to his people Israel, who are further defined as the 'pure in heart'.[4] Here and in Psalm 24:4 this phrase describes those with a single mind towards God, though the same word can be used of God's commands (Ps. 19:8, NIV 'radiant').

But as for me, my feet had almost slipped; I had nearly lost my foothold. For I envied the arrogant when I saw the prosperity of the wicked (*vv. 2-3*). Though he knew well the truth expressed in the opening verse, the psalmist gave way to doubt. The expression at the beginning of verse 2, 'But as for me' (*va'ₐnî*), is very emphatic. Although the truth of God's goodness was so real, yet when he saw the prosperity (lit. 'peace')[5] of the wicked, he began to be jealous of them. Along with many other saints, his observation that the wicked seem to do so well led him to doubt God's goodness.

2. The Character of the Godless (*vv. 4-12*)
They have no struggles; their bodies are healthy and strong. They are free from the burdens common to man; they are not plagued by human ills (*vv. 4-5*). Appearances often deceive. It seems at first to the psalmist that the wicked never suffer sickness. The NIV rendering is rather free, though it conveys the general meaning. The literal transla-

---

[4] Many commentators and translations (cf. RSV, NEB, NRSV) chose to change 'to Israel' (*lᵉyisrâ'êl*) into 'to the upright to[wards] God' (*lᵉyâshâr 'el*). This emendation retains the consonantal text and provides an attractive parallel to 'pure in heart'. However, no manuscript evidence can be cited to support it. Hence, the traditional rendering of the AV and many later translations (RV, NASB, NKJV, NLT) should be maintained.

[5] Cf. the note on Psalm 72:3 for the meaning of 'peace' in Heb.

tion of verse 4 is, 'there are no fetters in their death, and fat are their bodies'.[6] Also, the assertion is that they are immune to the troubles that often afflict others. The full reality of the situation only dawns on him later in the psalm (see vv. 16-20). He has yet to learn that affliction is not necessarily a sign of God's disfavour (see John 9:1-3; Heb. 12:7-11).

Therefore pride is their necklace; they clothe themselves with violence. From their callous hearts comes iniquity; the evil conceits of their minds know no limits (*vv. 6-7*). The arrogant deck themselves with their pride, as if it was jewellery to be displayed around their necks. Their boastful attitudes lead to violent actions, because they think that they can 'get away with it'. Many different translations of verse 7 have been made, some depending on emendation of the MT. Literally it can be translated, 'Their eye bulges from fatness; the imaginations of [their] heart overflow.' 'From fatness' appears to mean 'from fatness of heart', the noun 'heart' only appearing in the second clause. Instead of 'their eye' some Hebrew manuscripts and the LXX have 'their iniquity'. It is best to retain the MT and accept that we have archaic Hebrew idioms here, of which we lack enough other examples to be absolutely certain of the meaning. The NIV translation certainly gives the general sense.[7] The reminder is given here that it is from the heart that all evil springs (Matt. 12:34-35; 15:16-20), and the schemes that sinful minds can think up, are endless.

They scoff, and speak with malice; in their arrogance they threaten oppression. Their mouths lay claim to heaven, and their tongues take possession of the earth

---

[6] Two words in this verse are *hapax legomena*, 'fetters' (*chartsubôt*) and 'body' (*'ûl*). The early versions do not help a great deal (a good survey can be found in J. J. S. Perowne, *The Book of Psalms*, (London: George Bell & Sons, 1886), II, p. 17). Various attempts have been made to alter the text. Cf. particularly Marvin Tate, *Psalms 51-100* (Dallas: Word Books, 1990), p. 228, n. 4.a, who says that a change to something like the translation achieved by the RSV ('For they have no pangs; their bodies are sound and sleek') preserves the consonantal text and provides good parallelism. However, the MT is not unintelligible.

[7] For other freer translations, cf. REB or ESV. The NLT gets the meaning of the verse right, though conveys it using an idiom that is unlikely to be known to all English readers and is probably ephemeral: 'These fat cats have everything their hearts could ever wish for!'

(*vv. 8-9*). The description of arrogance and pride in the wicked continues. As proud boasters they threaten others. They daringly talk as if they are God himself, and thus the whole world is theirs.[8] Here we recognise attitudes and outward expressions of minds that dismiss God. Paul amplified the theme in Romans 1:28-32 (see especially v. 30). Another Old Testament wisdom passage reminds us that God resists the proud (Prov. 3:34), a statement that is quoted twice in the New Testament (James 4:6; 1 Pet. 5:5).

Therefore their people turn to them and drink up waters in abundance. They say, 'How can God know? Does the Most High have knowledge?' This is what the wicked are like – always carefree, they increase in wealth (*vv. 10-12*). Verse 10 is difficult to translate (see NIV footnote), but its meaning determines the explanation of the following verses. The NIV text makes good sense, except that it requires 'his people' to be retained instead of 'their people', this probably being a reference to God's people.[9] The people who are attracted to and who follow such proud boasters turn to them, and try and share in their success. They soak up 'the waters of abundance', i.e., the prosperity of the wicked.[10] They mock at the idea of a God who has knowledge of their activities, and they act as if they will never have to give an account of their actions. Like the rich fool of whom Jesus speaks in his parabolic teaching (Luke 12:13-21), they hoard wealth for themselves, little expecting ever having to answer to God. Taking life easy – eating, drinking, and merry-making – conflicts with our calling to trust in the Lord.

3. A Personal Response(*vv. 13-20*)

Surely in vain have I kept my heart pure; in vain have I washed my hands in innocence (*v. 13*). After speaking in the third person up to this point, the focus now changes to the

---

[8] 'Lay claim' is literally 'set'. The boasters are usurping divine prerogatives.

[9] The MT 'his people' (*'ammô*) is to be retained, while 'turn to them' assumes that the Q^{e}re reading ('turn', *yâshûv*) is correct, indicating a turning away from God to the prosperity of the wicked.

[10] 'Soak up' translates a verb *mâtsâh* that has the idea of draining or wringing out (cf. its use in Lev. 1:15; Judg. 6:38; and Isa. 51:17).

first person – 'I', 'me', and 'my' are the dominating pronouns in the remainder of the psalm. The same certainty with which the song commenced (v. 1) is repeated here, as the psalmist openly admits that he has been troubled before with doubts. He has tried to live uprightly and he has avoided the overtly sinful actions of the wicked that he has just described. The idea of washing one's hands in innocence (cf. the same phrase in Ps. 26:6) probably comes from Exodus 30:17-21, where Aaron and his sons were commanded to wash their hands and feet before they did service at the altar. But now, in spite of complying with the law's requirements, doubt grips his heart. Has it all been for no real purpose?

All day long I have been plagued; I have been punished every morning. If I had said, 'I will speak thus,' I would have betrayed your children (*vv. 14-15*). Compared with the wicked, the psalmist has known constant affliction and punishment at the Lord's hand. He has felt no respite, and so was tempted to express his doubts to the believing community. He knows that if he yielded he would have caused other believers to stumble. It would have been treachery on his part. What one believer does and says may have a profound effect upon the believing community as a whole.

When I tried to understand all this, it was oppressive to me till I entered the sanctuary of God; then I understood their final destiny (*vv. 16-17*). Trying to work out life's problems without God's help is futile.[11] It was a matter of grief and pain to the psalmist until he went to worship, probably at a local altar.[12] There he suddenly came to a fresh understanding of the ultimate end facing the wicked. This could have been through some specific revelation, or through

---

[11] The second part of verse 16 is lit. 'it was trouble in my eyes', but the NIV captures the sense well.

[12] The Heb. text has '*sanctuaries* of God'. The plural also occurs in the MT of Psalm 68:35, where some Heb. manuscripts have the singular. In this verse in Psalm 73 the LXX and Syriac both translate it as singular. It can be taken in both passages as a plural of extension or amplification (cf. *GKC*, §124; *IBHS*, p. 120). Alternatively, it can be regarded as denoting an indefinite singular, 'one of the sanctuaries of God', which makes good sense here (see *GKC*, §124o). It is clear that many altars existed, not just the sanctuary in Jerusalem (cf. 1 Kings 19:10, 14).

his purposeful meditation on God's great goodness (cf. v. 1). God often resolves our perplexities when we think deeply about his revealed character. Present experiences must always be evaluated in the light of God's final judgment (2 Cor. 5:10).

Surely you place them on slippery ground; you cast them down to ruin. How suddenly are they destroyed, completely swept away by terrors! As a dream when one awakes, so when you arise, O Lord, you will despise them as fantasies (*vv. 18-20*). For the third time in the psalm a statement begins with 'surely' (*'ak*). Here the certainty relates to how God will deal with the wicked. Apparent security and prosperity cannot help in the day of judgment, because a house built on sand will fall with a great crash (Matt. 7:24-27). Spiritual cultivation of heart and life is needed lest the sudden coming of the Lord finds one unprepared (Mark 13:36).[13] Quite frequently the sudden intervention of God in judgment is described in the Psalms as if he awakens from sleep (35:23; 44:23; 59:4; 78:65). 'Fantasies' here mean mere vanities, unrealities, like the image-gods so common in the neighbouring cultures of ancient Israel.

4. A Confession (*vv. 21-22*)

When my heart was grieved and my spirit embittered, I was senseless and ignorant; I was a brute beast before you (*vv. 21-22*). As he looks back on his misunderstanding, the psalmist humbly acknowledges the great mistake he had made. The language is highly poetic but there is no doubt as to its meaning.[14] His wrong attitude had been an affront to God. As for himself (with an emphatic personal pronoun being used at the commencement of v. 22),[15] he had nearly fallen in to unbelief. He had shown no more spiritual knowledge of God's providential dealings than an animal. True understanding eluded him until he entered God's presence. Spiri-

[13] There is a play on words at the beginning of verses 18 and 19. 'Surely' (*'ak*) and 'how' (*'êk*) are similar in writing and in speech.

[14] The lit. translation of verse 21 is: 'My heart is bitter, and [as to] my kidneys, I was pierced.' The language, though rare, depicts how deep the psalmist's jealousy was towards the prosperous.

[15] The verse commences with 'and I' (*va'ănî*).

tual truths are imparted by a direct and gracious work of God (1 Cor. 2:13-16).

5. An Affirmation of Faith (*vv. 23-28*)

Yet I am always with you; you hold me by my right hand (*v. 23*). The turning point in the psalm was reached earlier (v. 17), so now the profession of trust and confidence in God duly follows. Again, the psalmist draws attention to himself at the opening of the verse using the same emphatic personal pronoun as in the previous verse. We read of a powerful recognition of the relationship between the psalmist and his God. Despite his feelings in times of doubt, the truth remains that God has not deserted him. To be held by the right hand is a vivid way of expressing the help that God constantly gives his children (cf. Isa. 41:10, 13; 42:6).

You guide me with your counsel, and afterward you will take me into glory (*v. 24*). What is affirmed is guidance in life, and presence with God after death, for in the context 'afterward' refers back to the 'destiny' that is coming for the wicked (v. 17). As in Psalm 49:15 (see the comment on that verse), the verb used for 'take' (*lâqach*) probably has connotations of God taking the psalmist as he did Enoch (Gen. 5:24) or Elijah (2 Kings 2:5). In the MT 'glory' is not preceded by a preposition, which is not at all unusual in poetry. The LXX took it to mean 'with glory' (*meta doxês*) which may be preferable as the Hebrew word does not seem to be used elsewhere to denote 'heaven'.[16] While the thought of the individual believer's heavenly dwelling comes into clearer focus in the New Testament, yet passages such as this show that it was a reality for Old Testament saints as well.

Whom have I in heaven but you? And earth has nothing I desire besides you. My flesh and my heart may fail, but God is the strength of my heart and my portion forever (*vv. 25-26*). The psalm draws to a close on the note

---

[16] This is pointed out by A. Cohen, *The Psalms* (London: Soncino Press, 1969), p. 235. In Christian circles 'glory' is often used as equivalent to heaven. In the Old Testament 'glory' is used repeatedly of the manifestation of God's presence especially at the tabernacle, and so linking it with God's action in taking believers to himself is a quite appropriate extension of that idea.

of triumphant confidence in God. What other saviour and sustainer exists besides the Lord? 'But you' is not represented in the MT, but it is certainly implied by 'besides you'.[17] In earth and heaven his desire is only for his God. Even though his physical and mental powers fail, yet God remains his 'strength' (Heb. 'rock', *tsûr*). Just as he was Levi's portion (Deut. 10:9), so he was to all believers. The psalmist has seen that other earthly treasures fail, but that there is eternal blessing in God's presence.

Fading is the worldling's pleasure,
All his boasted pomp and show;
Solid joys and lasting treasure
None but Zion's children know.
(John Newton 1725-1807)

Those who are far from you will perish; you destroy all who are unfaithful to you. But as for me, it is good to be near God. I have made the Sovereign LORD my refuge; I will tell of all your deeds (*vv. 27-28*). Unbelievers are far from God, and their continued unbelief keeps them there. It is only through the blood of Christ that those who are far away can be brought near (Eph. 2:13). The word rendered 'unfaithful' (*zônâh*) is the technical term for the prostitute, but it is used in this psalm and elsewhere (see, e.g., Lev. 20:6) to describe any form of departure from God and his standards. The final contrast of the psalm is in the last verse, which begins with the same emphatic 'and I' that occurred in verses 22 and 23. The psalmist returns to his opening theme (v. 1) and reasserts in personal terms how wonderful it is to be within God's saving mercy. He has found his lasting shelter, saying that he has fixed in the sovereign LORD his refuge (cf. the similar idea using the same Heb. root *ch-s-h* in Ps. 2:12). This is the highest good, and therefore he desires to tell others of all that God has done.

---

[17] M. Dahood, *Psalms II: 51–100*, (New York: Doubleday, 1974), p. 195, suggests that 'besides you' (*'imm^{e}kâ*) serves as a kind of swivel or hinge, serving both the preceding and the following phrases.

Psalm 74

A maskil of Asaph.

The devastation caused by the destruction of Jerusalem by the Babylonians in 586 BC left a deep impression on the faithful believers. They mourned the loss of the temple, the absence of prophets, and the seeming rejection of the covenant. Jeremiah, prior to the exile, had warned the people not to think that the temple was inviolate. Repetition of the phrase, 'This is the temple of the LORD,' was not going to protect it (Jer. 7:4).

This psalm is probably by a later member of the sons of Asaph. It follows one called 'a song' (*mizmôr*), and, like Psalm 78, it is entitled 'a maskil'.[1] This word may come from a Hebrew verb (*s-k-l*) that means 'to be wise' or 'to instruct', which would fit well the nature of both Psalms 74 and 78 as they are both didactic songs. Psalm 74 comes from after the destruction of the temple, when it appeared that the distress had, or was going to, last 'for ever'. It has many similarities to the conclusion of Psalm 89 and to the Book of Lamentations (cf. passages such as Lam. 2:2, 7). It should also be compared for its covenantal orientation with Daniel's prayer (Dan. 9:4-19).

The tension in the minds of believers was very real. They were trying to reconcile how the destruction of Jerusalem and the temple, and the subsequent Babylonian captivity, could be reconciled with God's choice of both Israel and Mount Zion. Commitment to the LORD and his covenant had to be accompanied by genuine and heartfelt obedience to its demands.

---

[1] An interesting link between Psalms 73 and 74 exists in the common use of a very rare Heb. word (*m^{e}shô'âh*) meaning 'a ruin' or 'a desolate place'. See Psalms 73:18 and 74:3.

1. An Appeal to God (*vv. 1-2*)
Why have you rejected us for ever, O God? Why does your anger smoulder against the sheep of your pasture? Remember the people you purchased of old, the tribe of your inheritance, whom you redeemed – Mount Zion, where you dwelt (*vv.* 1-2). Even though the fall of Jerusalem may have happened a comparatively short time before, yet to the psalmist it seems as if it has been forever. To feel 'rejected' (*zânach*) is common in psalms of complaint (see 43:2; 44:9, 23; 60:1,10; 77:7; 88:14; 89:38; 108:11), even for those who claim to be the flock of God.[2] His plea is that God will remember the congregation he purchased long ago at the time of the Exodus.[3] The two verbs 'purchase' (*pâdâh*) and 'redeem' (*gâʾal*) are used together in Exodus 15:13, 16, and in the same Song of the Sea there is reference to Israel being planted on the mountain of God's inheritance (Exod. 15:17, *b^{e}har nach^{a}lât^{e}kâ*). The language reflects that association of 'inheritance' and the 'mountain' where God dwells.

2. A Destroyed Temple (*vv. 3-8*)
Historical accounts of the destruction of Jerusalem and its temple, by the Babylonians, are given in 2 Kings 25:8-17 and 2 Chronicles 36:17-19. Here the poet describes the devastation wrought on the conquered city, and pleads for God to intervene. **Turn your steps toward these everlasting ruins, all this destruction the enemy has brought on the sanctuary. Your foes roared in the place where you met with us; they set up their standards as signs** (*vv. 3-4*). The sanctuary was invaded and the Babylonians marked their conquest by setting up their military standards there. The verb 'to roar' (*shâʾag*) can be used both of enemies who roar like a lion against their

---

[2] It is exiled Judah who is speaking in this psalm, but she can legitimately lay claim to be the true 'Israel', the nation purchased by God as his possession. The foundation of the appeal is that Israel is God's flock, an important Old Testament concept.

[3] The NIV 'people' is the rendering of one of the Heb. words for 'congregation' (*ʿêdâh*), and is virtually synonymous with the other common word for congregation, *qâhâl*. A good summary of the OT usage of *ʿêdâh* is given in *TWOT*, I, p. 388. The translation 'congregation' should be retained here in Psalm 74:2.

foes (as here), and the LORD who roars back in judgment (see especially, Amos 1:2; 3:4). At the very place where God met with his people, there the Babylonians set up their standards[4] and committed atrocities, including murder (2 Chron. 36:17).

They behaved like men wielding axes to cut through a thicket of trees. They smashed all the carved panelling with their axes and hatchets. They burned your sanctuary to the ground; they defiled the dwelling place of your Name (*vv. 5-7*). The great variety of English translations shows how difficult is the Hebrew in verse 5.[5] The general picture seems to be that the Babylonians came in wielding axes like the ones that are used to fell trees.[6] The Most Holy Place had cedar panelling (1 Kings 6:16) and it was attacked as if it were a clump of trees to be felled. That destruction was completed by the burning of the temple (2 Kings 25:9; 2 Chron. 36:19). This was an act of defilement of the place where God had recorded his name. Isaiah explains that this was not only an act of the Babylonians but God himself defiled his own inheritance because his people broke his laws (Isa. 47:6, 'desecrated').

They said in their hearts, 'We will crush them completely!' They burned every place where God was worshipped in the land (*v. 8*). The Babylonians under Nebuzaradan were determined to crush rebellious Israel. They made up their minds as to the plan of attack,[7] and carried it out with overwhelming force. It is hard to know if the reference to burning is meant to apply just to the temple (the singular of the 'place where God was worshipped' is used in v. 4 of the temple). More probably it refers to other worship centres such as had existed in Elijah's time (1 Kings 19:10, 14), and

---

[4] The Heb. word used here is a common word for a 'sign' (*'ôt*). While it is more often used of the LORD's actions on behalf his people, in Numbers 2:2 it is used for a standard or flag.

[5] Cf. the way in which the NEB attempts a translation that it calls 'probable', but adds 'unintelligible'. The ESV says: 'The meaning of the Hebrew is uncertain.'

[6] An alternative translation is to replace 'wielding' with 'as an entrance': 'They chopped down the entrance like woodcutters in a forest' (NLT).

[7] For the expression, 'to say in one's heart', cf. Psalm 10:11, where the NIV translates more idiomatically by 'he says to himself.'

which had arisen again after Josiah's attempt to centralise the worship in Jerusalem.

3. A Cry for Help (*vv. 9-11*)

We are given no miraculous signs; no prophets are left, and none of us knows how long this will be (*v. 9*). The only 'signs' that the people see are the military standards of the Babylonians (v. 4; the same word is used in Hebrew for 'standards' and 'signs'). They are without the valuable ministry of prophets to teach and guide them (cf. Lam. 2:9, 'her prophets no longer find visions from the LORD'). Jeremiah had been taken to Egypt (Jer. 43:6-7), and no information is available to indicate whether Ezekiel was still prophesying. The likely scenario is that the composer of this psalm was still in the land, perhaps in hiding. Those left must have been perplexed, but if they had listened to Jeremiah, they would not have had to ask the question, 'How long?' (see his declaration, Jer. 25:11).

How long will the enemy mock you, O God? Will the foe revile your name forever? Why do you hold back your hand, your right hand? Take it from the folds of your garment and destroy them! (*vv. 10-11*). The devastation of Jerusalem and the people (by exile) is viewed as an affront to God. The people still cannot understand why God does not intervene and alter the whole situation. The mockery mentioned here should be compared with that of the Assyrians when Jerusalem was besieged (2 Kings 18:28-35). The people think God is withholding his aid and want him to demonstrate his power and destroy his, and their, enemy.[8] This prayer should be compared with that of Daniel, who after confessing that God's righteous judgments had come on the people, pleads for God's favour on the desolate sanctuary, the city, and the people: 'For your sake, O my God, do not delay' (Dan. 9:17-19).

---

[8] This verse has occasioned much discussion, which is reviewed in an extensive note by Marvin Tate, *Psalms 51-100*, p. 243, 11.a. The NIV is rather free in rendering 'take it from the folds of your garment and destroy them' as the MT has 'from the midst of your bosom destroy.' 'Your bosom' (*chêq^ekâ*) is the Q^ere reading, while the K^etiv is 'your decree' (*chôq^ekâ*) which does not seem to fit in the context. Though the verb (*kâlâh*, Pi. imper.) lacks an object, the construction is the same as in Psalm 59:13.

4. The Record of the Past (*vv. 12-17*)
Suddenly the psalmist recalls great events of the past, in which God's power had been displayed. **But you, O God, are my king from of old; you bring salvation upon the earth. It was you who split open the sea by your power; you broke the heads of the monster in the waters. It was you who crushed the heads of Leviathan and gave him as food to the creatures of the desert** (*vv. 12-14*). Whereas in other Near Eastern religions, praise was reserved for what *men* had done for the gods, in Israel praise was given for what *God* had done for his people. The switch from third person to first person (*malkî*, 'my king') expresses the covenantal relationship in very personal terms, while the psalmist still speaks as the representative of his people. God had secured their salvation from slavery, dividing the waters of the Red Sea and crushing the power of the Egyptian forces, which are called here 'the monster' and 'Leviathan'. 'Monster(s)' (*tannînîm*) not only indicates various animals and sea creatures, but also (in a figurative sense) God's powerful enemies (for other uses regarding Egypt see Isa. 51:9; Ezek. 29:3 and 32:2; and in reference to Babylon, see Jer. 51:34). 'Leviathan' was probably the crocodile, and therefore a natural symbol in this poetic passage to describe the Egyptian soldiers.[9]

It was you who opened up springs and streams; you dried up the ever flowing rivers (*v. 15*). The first part of this verse is a reference to the incident when water came from the rock at Massah (Exod. 17:6), while the second part recalls what happened to the Jordan River when Israel needed to cross into Canaan. The same verb 'dried up' (*yâvash*) is used twice in Joshua to describe what God did to the Jordan (Josh. 4:23; 5:1).

The day is yours, and yours also the night; you established the sun and moon. It was you who set all the boundaries of the earth; you made both summer and winter (*vv. 16-17*). The same God had done even greater things when he created the world. Hence, it was not surprising that he was able to control

---

[9] 'Leviathan' was used in Canaanite mythology of an associate of the sea-god Yam. It occurs five times in the Old Testament (Job 3:8; 41:1 [Heb. 40:25]; Pss. 74:13-14; 104:26; Isa. 27:1) without borrowing all its mythological implications from Canaanite use.

the waters, the day and night, the heavenly bodies, the earth, and the seasons of the year.[10] This expresses in poetic form the basic truth of Genesis 1 regarding creation, which is enlarged further in Psalm 104.

5. A Covenantal Plea (*vv. 18-23*)

Remember how the enemy has mocked you, O LORD, how foolish people have reviled your name. Do not hand over the life of your dove to wild beasts; do not forget the lives of your afflicted people forever (*vv. 18-19*). The psalmist now returns to his immediate concerns after his recollection of the power of his God. He uses the same verbs ('mocked', 'reviled') as he already has in verse 10, as he asks God to remember how his holy name has been blasphemed. Wild beasts are near, and he does not want God's dove (Israel) handed over to them for final dispatch.[11] He pleads with God to bear in mind his afflicted people – 'Don't leave us in this state forever', with that final word appearing here for the third time in the psalm (see vv. 1 and 10).

Have regard for your covenant, because haunts of violence fill the dark places of the land. Do not let the oppressed retreat in disgrace; may the poor and needy praise your name (*vv. 20-21*). Appeal is made to the abiding covenantal relationship. Judah in exile was not divorced, only separated temporarily from the LORD (see Isa. 50:1; 54:4-8).[12] The reference to 'your covenant' is probably to that made at Sinai, as the historical references in verses 13-15 concern the exodus and entry into Canaan. The 'dark places of the

---

[10] The NIV 'sun and moon' translates the MT 'lightbearer and sun', *mâ'ôr vâshêmesh*). The word 'lightbearer' is used in Genesis 1:14-16 to include the 'sun' and 'moon', but here the normal word for 'moon' (*yârêach*) does not occur. Perhaps the translation should be 'you established the lightbearers, even the sun.'

[11] The reference to 'your dove' (*tôrekâ*) was misinterpreted by all the ancient versions. Some (like the Targum, Symmachus, and Jerome) thought that it was 'your law' (*tôrâtekâ*), while others (LXX, Syriac, Arabic, Ethiopic) rendered it 'give thanks to you' (*tôdekâ*). These variations are not surprising seeing that the reference is so unusual. The comment above takes 'dove' to be an endearing name for Israel/Judah.

[12] Cf. the same usage in verse 1 of Judah in exile being identified as the true 'Israel'.

land' are also mentioned in Psalm 88:6 and Lamentations 3:6, denoting the hidden dens of violent men. The psalmist wants God to look with favour upon the land, and ensure that the present injustices stop. When that happens, even those now most oppressed (' the poor and needy'), will be able to rejoice in his praise (cf. the use of this description of believers in Pss. 40:17 and 70:5).

Rise up, O God, and defend your cause; remember how fools mock you all day long. Do not ignore the clamour of your adversaries, the uproar of your enemies, which rises continually (*vv. 22-23*). Another term is used in asking for God's intervention ('rise up'; see the comment on Ps. 7:6, where the same expression is used). 'Defend your cause' (*rîv*) is a technical covenantal expression that is used by the prophets when they speak of God having a legal case against his people (Jer. 2:9; 50:34).[13] Here it is used of God's cause, which is also the people's cause. The enemies are not just Israel's enemies – they are God's enemies! The reference to 'fools' picks up on what has already been said about them in verse 18. The final plea is for the turmoil and uproar caused by these enemies to be noted by God and to stir him to action. These enemies do not let up – they 'mock all day long' (v. 22) and their uproar is continuous (v. 23). The people had yet to learn that only when sin was confessed and repentance followed, would God restore them. Nehemiah grasped the point (Neh. 9:31) – in God's great mercy he did not put an end to them, or abandon them.

---

[13] Good discussions on *rîv* are found in *TWOT*, 2, pp. 845-46, and *NIDOTTE*, 3, pp. 1105-06.

Psalm 75

For the director of music. [To the tune of] 'Do Not Destroy'.
A psalm of Asaph. A song.

Psalms 74 and 75 are linked thematically by the thought of God's judgment. The divine king is also the divine judge. At the end of the previous psalm the appeal has been made for God to rise up and defend his own cause (Ps. 74:22-23). In this psalm the theme of judgment occurs, especially in verses 2-8, where it is made plain that the scope of that judgment is universal. The character of the righteous and the godless are set over against one another (v. 10), and the vindication of one results in the humiliation of the other (v. 7). There is no certain indication within the psalm of the historical setting, though the use of 'Do Not Destroy' in the title suggests it was composed in a period of impending danger for God's people.[1] The most probable date is the Assyrian siege of 701 BC. The language of this psalm borrows from earlier songs, especially the song of Hannah (1 Sam. 2:1-10).

Changes in person throughout the psalm are indications of shifts in focus. The people speak at the outset (v. 1, '*We* give thanks to you'), while divine speech follows in verses 2-5 ('*I* choose'). Then description in the third person of God's role as judge follows in verses 6-8 ('But it is God who judges'), with first person being resumed in verses 9-10.

1. Praise to the God who is Near (*v. 1*)

We give thanks to you, O God, we give thanks, for your Name is near; men tell of your wonderful deeds (*v. 1*). The opening song of praise is related to both the sense of the immediate pres-

[1] The title of the tune, 'Do not destroy', occurs also in Psalms 57-59.

ence of God with the people and to the knowledge that he has acted on their behalf in a mighty way in the past. The syntax of the sentence is awkward, as a literal translation of the second part of the verse is, 'and your name is near; they will recount'.[2] One of the simplest solutions is to take 'your wonderful deeds' as the subject of the verb 'tell' (*sippᵉrû*, Pi. 3 pers. pl.), and this yields the translation, 'We give thanks to you, O God, we give thanks, your name is near; your wonderful deeds declare it.' 'Name' here is used in a way similar to Exodus 23:20-21, where the LORD declared that his name was in the angel who was being sent before the children of Israel. 'Name' is simply the revelation of God's character. 'The Name of the LORD' occurs as a title for God in Isaiah 30:27. Knowledge of God's past deeds on their behalf brings reassurance to the people in their present distress.

2. God Speaks in Judgment (*vv.* 2-5)

You say, 'I choose the appointed time; it is I who judge uprightly. When the earth and all its people quake, it is I who hold its pillars firm.' ***Selah*** (*vv.* 2-3). God speaks decisively to his people of the fact that he will intervene at his chosen time.[3] He is the divine judge who calls all people to account. Lest his people think that they have been able to save themselves he waits until the very foundations of the earth shake. 'It is I' is emphatic, drawing attention to God's intervention, not theirs.

To the arrogant I say, 'Boast no more,' and to the wicked, 'Do not lift up your horns. Do not lift your horns against heaven; do not speak with outstretched neck' (*vv.* 4-5). A different form of reassurance is given to the proud. They need to realise that they can try and exalt themselves against God, but all their pride and boasting will come to nought. 'Horn' is often used in the Psalms to denote power or strength (cf. Pss. 18:2; 89:17, 24), while 'outstretched neck' speaks of pride or arrogance. God's declaration is directed to the wicked, seeking the cessation of their boastful displays.

---

[2] For the variety of suggestions on how to translate this verse, see Marvin Tate, *Psalms 51-100*, p. 256.

[3] The NIV inserts 'You say' to make it plain that what follows is divine speech. Similar passages can be found in Psalms 2:6 and 50:5, in both of which the NIV simply uses inverted commas.

3. The Psalmist Confirms God's Judgment (*vv. 6-8*)
No one from the east or the west or from the desert can exalt a man. But it is God who judges: He brings one down, he exalts another (*vv. 6-7*). The variety of translations, both ancient and modern, of verse 6 show that there is a difficulty. The first part of verse 6 mentions 'east' and 'west', using two out of several terms common in Old Testament Hebrew for these points of the compass.[4] It is possible to translate the last clause of the verse as 'from the desert to the mountains', or perhaps better still, 'from the desert of the mountains'.[5] If the first of these alternatives is chosen, then this would be an assertion that no one from north or south, east or west, can usurp the place of God. If the second alternative is preferred, then it refers to the southern part of Palestine and the mountains of Arabia. In this case, no complete listing of the points of the compass occurs, but the general point is that no human help can come from any direction at all. As verse 7 emphasises, it is God alone who is the judge and deliverer, and he acts sovereignly to bring either judgment or deliverance.

In the hand of the LORD is a cup full of foaming wine mixed with spices; he pours it out, and all the wicked of the earth drink it down to its very dregs (*v. 8*). 'Cup' stands for God's judgment (as does 'wine' in Ps. 60:3), and he is pictured as putting the cup to the lips of the wicked until they drink it to the last dregs. The prophets repeatedly use the same imagery for the concept of God's wrath (Isa. 51:17-23; Jer. 25:27; 49:12; Hab. 2:15-16).

4. A Final Song of Thanksgiving (*vv. 9-10*)
As for me, I will declare this forever; I will sing praise to the God of Jacob. I will cut off the horns of all the wicked, but the

---

[4] The word for 'east' (*môtsâ'*) only occurs here, but the word for 'west' (*ma'ărâv*) appears 14×. For information on Hebrew words for points of the compass, see *ISBE*, 3, p. 615, and *IDB*, 3, pp. 608-09.

[5] The Heb. is *mimmidbar hârîm*. The word 'desert' (*midbar*) is construct in form, 'desert of' (cf. Exod. 19:1), while *hârîm* is the regular pl. of *hâr*, 'mountain'. The alternative translations, like NIV, assume that *hârîm* is the Hi. inf. constr. of the verb *rûm*, 'to lift up'. Several Hebrew manuscripts have the absol. form of the noun (*midbâr*), and this is necessary if the NIV rendering is to be adopted.

horns of the righteous will be lifted up (*vv. 9-10*). The song of praise that began the psalm is repeated at the close, though now it is not the communal ('we') but the personal ('I'). It may well be the king who uttered these words. In contrast to the arrogant oppressors ('But I ...'), the psalmist will constantly sing praise to his God. It is surprising the number of times in the Psalter that God is called 'the God of Jacob' (20:1; 24:6; 46:7; 76:6; 81:1, 4; 84:8; 94:7; 114:7; 132:2, 5; 146:5). This is either to recall the special relationship between God and Jacob, or else a reminder that he is still the God of Jacob's descendants. The psalmist thinks of himself as sharing in the execution of God's judgment on the wicked, but he knows that at the same time the righteous are going to be exalted. For us today the principle remains valid that 'whoever exalts himself will be humbled' (Matt. 23:12).

Psalm 76

For the director of music. With stringed instruments.
A psalm of Asaph. A song.

Psalms 75 and 76 fit together as a unit, for while Psalm 75 looks forward to the coming of God's judgment, this psalm rejoices in the fact that it has come. The actual occasion is not mentioned in the psalm. However, the LXX adds to the title, 'concerning the Assyrian', suggesting the defeat of Sennacherib and his forces in 701 BC as recorded in 2 Kings 19 and Isaiah 37. Verses 6-7 and 11-12 could relate to this unusual victory, but nothing allows definitive identification. Similarities exist with Psalms 46 and 48, so that historical victories become the model for the endtime events when God will indeed triumph over his enemies. This psalm is also significant because of the way in which it emphasises God's character – he 'is known' (v. 1), 'resplendent with light' (v. 4), 'majestic' (v. 4), 'to be feared' (v. 7; cf. also v. 12).[1] The double use of *Selah* at the end of verses 3 and 9 marks the natural division in the psalm.

1. God and His People (*vv. 1-3*)

In Judah God is known; his name is great in Israel. His tent is in Salem, his dwelling place in Zion (*vv. 1-2*). Here God and his people are linked in a special way. Among his own people he has revealed himself and he is present at the sanctuary. 'Judah' and 'Israel' are used in parallel to describe the whole nation. Moreover, the ark of the covenant has been housed in Salem (short for 'Jerusalem'), so that Zion, where the temple stood, can be viewed as God's dwelling place. The

[1] A good note on these descriptive terms is found in R. Davidson, *The Vitality of the Psalms: A Commentary on the Book of Psalms* (Grand Rapids: Eerdmans, 1998), pp. 244-45.

use of 'Salem' (*shâlêm*) may be deliberate in order to highlight its meaning of 'secure', 'at peace' (from the same root as *shâlôm*).[2]

There he broke the flashing arrows, the shields and the swords, the weapons of war. *Selah* (*v. 3*). It was at Jerusalem that God brought peace to his people, by destroying the weapons of war that were formerly used against them. 'There' (*shâmmâh*), in Jerusalem, where his name is great, he showed his power by overcoming the attackers. This same motif of destroying enemies' weapons is used elsewhere in the Old Testament in contexts stressing God's superiority over the nations (Ps. 46:8-10; Isa. 9:5; Hosea 2:18).

2. God Victorious (*vv. 4-10*)

You are resplendent with light, more majestic than mountains rich with game. Valiant men lie plundered, they sleep their last sleep; not one of the warriors can lift his hands. At your rebuke, O God of Jacob, both horse and chariot lie still (*vv. 4-6*). The poem switches to direct speech to God, reverting back to the third person at the end (vv. 11-12). These verses certainly match the idea that the victory was over the Assyrians. On the mountains where the Assyrians planned to make Jerusalem their prey, they became the prey themselves. God had appeared in his glory, and he had destroyed the attackers (cf. 2 Kings 19:35).[3] The connection with that event is strengthened by the fact that God had made a promise concerning Assyria: 'I will crush the Assyrian in my land; on my mountains I will trample him down' (Isa. 14:25). The picture is of slain warriors no longer able to use their limbs to wield weapons of war.

---

[2] The identification of Salem with Jerusalem goes back to Josephus (*Ant.* 1.180). Alternative proposals can be found in the *IBD*, 3, p. 1370, and *ISBE*, 3, p. 1000.

[3] 'Resplendent' is the translation of a Heb. participle, *nâ'ôr*, from the root *'ôr*, 'to be light'. Several modern translations (cf. NEB) reflect the assumption that the consonants of the word have been interchanged and that it should be 'feared' (*nôrâ'*, from the root *yârê'*). However, while the LXX renders it as 'illumine', this is simply accepting that the verb is *'ôr*, but making it a causative form (*tâ'îr*).

Their sleep is final.[4] The reference to 'the God of Jacob' links this psalm with the previous one (see Ps. 75:9).

You alone are to be feared. Who can stand before you when you are angry? (*v. 7*). Before God, his people must stand in awe (cf. Isa. 8:13). The NIV addition of 'alone' does not represent any Hebrew word in the text, but it is certainly the intention of the clause to assert the truth of God's uniqueness. He alone is awesome (*nôrâ'*). Human might fades into insignificance before his presence, and without divine provision, no one can stand in his holy place (Ps. 24:3). The phrase 'when you are angry' is literally 'from the time of your anger' (*mê'az 'appekâ*). While similar to the phrase 'the strength of your anger' (*'oz 'appekâ,* Ps. 90:11), no alteration to the text is justified.

From heaven you pronounced judgment, and the land feared and was quiet – when you, O God, rose up to judge, to save all the afflicted of the land. ***Selah*** (*vv. 8-9*). The victory is viewed as a heavenly judgment that brings silence to the earth. The expression that God rises to judge is often used in martial contexts such as this. It can be used to denote preparation for battle (Judg. 7:15) or victory. The description here ties together the themes of judgment and salvation. On the one hand, God's action is judgment, while on the other it is salvation. Such redemptive judgment comes to its greatest expression in the cross of Calvary, where God's judgment and mercy meet. Humble believers, who have endured the bitter opposition of kings of the earth (v. 12), find deliverance in God alone. 'Selah' marks the end of the second section of the psalm.

3. A Final Call to Worship (*vv. 11-12*)

Surely your wrath against men brings you praise, and the survivors of your wrath are restrained (*v. 10*). This verse is very condensed in the Hebrew text and various ways of understanding it are possible. The NIV translation is rather free at this point, especially with the interpretation that it is God's wrath that is in view. A fairly literal translation is probably

---

[4] The MT has 'they slept their sleep', but the context makes it plain that death is the meaning of the expression.

best: 'Surely the wrath of man brings you praise, and you will gird yourself with the remainder of wrath.' This means that in the end man's anger against God will bring praise to God. Even the final outburst of that anger will serve as a garment or ornament for his glory.

Make vows to the LORD your God and fulfil them; let all the neighbouring lands bring gifts to the One to be feared (*v. 11*). Because of God's intervention on behalf of his people, the call goes out to Israel to pay homage to him. The NIV's 'let all the neighbouring lands' is an attempt to explain a phrase that means 'all who are about him'. The whole verse seems to look back to Deuteronomy 23:21, which specifies that if a vow was made to God, then the person who vowed had to pay it expeditiously. Those 'about him' must be those of Israel, not neighbouring peoples. It is only of Israel that it is said that they were around the tabernacle (Num. 2:2). 'Those about him' must be the subject of the first two verbs. 'Vow and fulfil (or, pay)' simply means 'pay what you owed'. The final clause points to Gentile rulers bringing their gifts to the God of Israel. The exact expression 'they bring gifts' (*yôvîlû shây*) is only used twice elsewhere in the Old Testament (Ps. 68:29; Isa. 18:7), both of which describe Gentile kings bringing offerings to the LORD. The origin of the word 'gifts' (*shây*) is unknown. What happened to Israel was inevitably noted by surrounding nations (Deut. 4:6-8), and after God's deliverance of Hezekiah many did bring gifts to Jerusalem (2 Chron. 32:20-23).

He breaks the spirit of rulers; he is feared by the kings of the earth (*v. 12*). God is able to take the life of rulers, using the analogy of pruning of vines.[5] Not only within Israel is he the object of fear, but foreign rulers are called on to treat him with awe. Events in Israel and Judah were intended to be a lesson for other nations as well. The theme of fear of God occupies a central (*nôrâ'*, v. 7) and concluding place in this psalm (*môrâ'*, v. 11; *nôrâ'*, v. 12).

---

[5] The verb used (*bâtsar*) is especially employed for pruning or cutting of vines.

Psalm 77

For the director of music. To Jeduthun. Of Asaph. A psalm.

This psalm is the heartfelt cry of an individual to God, though there is nothing in the text to link it with any specific incident or date. What is remarkable is the change in tone as the writer recalls the LORD's powerful deeds, especially those connected with redeeming his people from Egypt. God did mighty deeds for them (v. 14), and he redeemed the descendants of Jacob and Joseph (v. 15). The events of the Exodus are explicitly linked with the leadership of Israel vested in Moses and Aaron (v. 20). The poet's own troubles recede into the background as he remembers this great redemption. The occurrences of 'Selah' again indicate the separate divisions of this poem.

1. Appeal in Distress (*vv. 1-3*)

I cried out to God for help; I cried out to God to hear me (*v. 1*). The urgency of his request is shown by the repetition of his appeal. Literally it is simply, 'my voice to God … my voice to God'. The words 'for help' in the NIV represent a verb (*tsâʾaq*) that normally indicates a cry for help, or an appeal for injustice to be rectified. The final words 'to hear me' (*veha'azîn ʾêlây*) are literally 'and he heard me', but other translations are also possible. 'And he will hear me' suits the context well, though it could also be an appeal for God to act: 'Let him hear me!'[1] Instead of becoming preoccupied with his own feelings, the psalmist turns his attention to the only true source of help. Just how deep his distress was becomes clear later in the psalm (see especially vv. 7-9).

[1] This is following the suggestion in *DIHG~S*, p. 75 that the verbal form here is a substitute for a cohortative.

When I was in distress, I sought the LORD; at night I stretched out untiring hands and my soul refused to be comforted. I remembered you, O God, and I groaned; I mused, and my spirit grew faint. *Selah* (*vv.* 2-3). The opening words are of frequent occurrence in the Psalms to describe a great variety of distressful situations (see, for example, the same phrase in 20:1; 50:15; 102:2), while 'to seek the LORD' is also a common Old Testament expression. Often it means 'to seek with care', and the end in view is to gain knowledge or insight into a particular problem. In distress the psalmist prayed with hands outstretched in typical Oriental fashion, and he had found no help in human comforters.[2] The words in this opening section have to be set against the change that comes as he meditates on the past actions of God. Clearly this forms the basis of his comfort that becomes stronger as the psalm progresses. While he felt keenly his present position, being extremely distressed in spirit, this meditation was the beginning of encouragement for him, as it ultimately gave new hope.

2. Remembering God's Mercies (*vv.* 4-9)
You kept my eyes from closing; I was too troubled to speak. I thought about the former days, the years of long ago; I remembered my songs in the night. My heart mused and my spirit inquired (*vv.* 4-6). At night he could not sleep, as God kept his eyelids open.[3] The psalmist's perplexity was so great that he could not even utter words. All he could do was to let thoughts and memories of long ago flood through his mind. The same verb 'thought'

---

[2] The idiom is unusual as 'untiring' is actually a verb that normally means 'poured out' (*niggᵉrâh*) and occurs with 'eye' or 'water' as the subject. The difficulty has long been recognised (as far back as the Aramaic targum), and translations such as the RV and REB follow this and emend the text to 'eye' and 'tears' respectively. An older note on the verse can be found in A. F. Kirkpatrick, *The Book of Psalms*, (Cambridge: CUP, 1903), p. 458, and a modern one in M. Tate, *Psalms 51-100*, (Word Biblical Commentary: Dallas: Word Books, 1990), p. 269. The odd translation in the AV ('*my sore* ran in the night') follows a medieval Jewish commentator, Rashi, in taking 'hand' to mean 'blow' or 'wound'.

[3] The word translated 'eyelid' (*shᵉmurâh*) only occurs here in the Old Testament, and derives from the verb 'to guard' (*shâmar*).

(*châshav*) occurs when Malachi is commending those who feared the LORD and 'thought' on his name (Mal. 3:16). In the past the psalmist had recalled songs in the night, which seemed to help him sleep; however, at present this is no longer the case. Rather, his mind is full of questions about God's present dealings with his people.

'Will the LORD reject us forever? Will he never show his favour again? Has his unfailing love vanished forever? Has his promise failed for all time? Has God forgotten to be merciful? Has he in anger withheld his compassion?' ***Selah*** (*vv. 7-9*). In tone the many questions he asks are like those in Psalm 85:5-6. It is striking that he looks beyond his personal distress, and mourns for the community as a whole ('Will the LORD reject *us*?'). He asks why God's forgiving grace is not shown to the people, nor his covenantal love (*chasdô*, 'unfailing love') maintained towards them. If God was true to his word (*'ómer*, 'word' or 'promise', v. 8; cf. God's own declaration of his nature in Exod. 34:6-7), then why was he not again showing his mercy and grace?[4] The final verse of this section continues the series of questions, focusing on God's grace and compassion.[5] The psalmist is going to answer his own perplexity in the following section of the psalm.

3. Recollection of God's Mercies (*vv. 10-12*)

Then I thought, 'To this I will appeal: the years of the right hand of the Most High' (*v. 10*). These questions just asked, all require the answer, 'No!' In the midst of his sleeplessness and overwhelmed by grief, he suddenly realises that God has not

[4] Verse 9 is composed of two parallel clauses, with the question marker (h^a-) occurring only with the first, but the context requires a second question. The first verb 'vanished' (*'âpês*) is not common, but the second one, 'failed' or 'ended' (*gâmar*), is even rarer. While it is possible that the subject of 'ended' could be 'he' or 'the LORD' (see *DCH*, II, p. 365), yet the parallelism supports the NIV rendering.

[5] The two questions in verse 9 show a common pattern, in that the first one is introduced by h^a-, while the alternative question is marked by the particle *'im*. The grammatical point is covered in *DIHG~S*, p. 184, §153.

altered.[6] This could well be a question that he poses: 'Has the right hand of the Most High changed?'[7] 'Hand' or 'right hand' became practically a substitute expression for 'God' in the Old Testament (Pss. 20:6; 139:10; Isa. 41:10). The use of the name 'Most High' recalls the use of this title for God by Abraham (Gen. 14:22) after a notable victory.

The psalmist suddenly becomes aware that the past history of Israel should give him the answers to his present perplexities. **I will remember the deeds of the LORD; yes, I will remember your miracles of long ago. I will meditate on all your works and consider all your mighty deeds** (*vv. 11-12*). He finds encouragement in God's mighty works for his people in the past. These wonderful acts were things that only God could do (see on Pss. 71:17; 72:18). Different synonyms (NIV 'deeds', 'miracles', 'works'; 'mighty deeds') are used to describe God's actions and portray the variety of ways in which he has acted towards and on behalf of his people. Meditation on God's deeds on behalf of his people (both in biblical history and since) should always be an encouragement for the believing community.

4. Confidence from Great Redemptive Deeds (*vv. 13-20*).
Your ways, O God, are holy. What god is so great as our God? You are the God who performs miracles; you display your power among the peoples (*vv. 13-14*). The contemplation of God's past deeds brings out this declaration of the nature of his actions. These actions of God also reflect his holiness. The question, 'What god is so great as our God?' recalls the statements to the same effect in Exodus 15:11, Deuteronomy 7:21 and 10:17, and

---

[6] The basis of this statement is an alternative translation of two words in the MT. Instead of reading the verb 'appeal', it is probable that the word is a noun with 1 pers. sing. suffix, 'my grief'. Also, instead of taking the Heb. word *sh*[e]*nôt* as 'years', it is more likely that it is the verb *shânâh*, 'to change' or 'alter'. Cf. ESV footnote: 'This is my grief: that the right hand of the Most High has changed.'

[7] This would then be a question that does not have any particle to mark it as such, but depended on the tone of voice. For this usage, consult *DIHG~S*, p. 183, §153 (a).

Psalm 95:3. God is indeed a miracle-working God,[8] whose wonders are a demonstration both of his power and his love (see Ps. 31:21, God performs 'marvels of love'). They were intended not only for his own people, but also as a display among the surrounding nations. Even the Gentiles would have to say: 'The LORD has done great things for them' (Ps. 126:2b).

With your mighty arm you redeemed your people, the descendants of Jacob and Joseph. ***Selah*** (*v. 15*). God's 'arm' is a way of describing his power. It occurs frequently in Deuteronomy either by itself (Deut. 3:24; 7:8; 9:26) or along with the word 'hand' as a way of speaking of God's power in redeeming his people from Egypt (Deut. 4:34; 5:15; 11:2; 26:8; cf. the use of 'right hand' in v. 10). 'Jacob' is used to designate the whole nation, to which is added 'Joseph', as a way of designating the ten northern tribes. Here it is a synonym for 'Israel', the whole nation (as in Obad. 18; see also the conjunction of 'Israel' 2×, 'Jacob' and 'Judah' in Ps. 114:1-2).

The waters saw you, O God, the waters saw you and writhed; the very depths were convulsed (*v. 16*). The psalmist expresses in poetic language what happened when God intervened to let his people cross the Red Sea. Frequently in the Old Testament similar heightened descriptions are given in poetry of the events of the Exodus (Exod. 15:8; Ps. 114:3-5). Here, not only are the waters in turmoil, but they are in travail. A similar idiomatic use of the verb 'writhe' (*chîl*) occurs in Ps. 97:4: 'The earth sees and *trembles*.'

The clouds poured down water, the skies resounded with thunder; your arrows flashed back and forth. Your thunder was heard in the whirlwind, your lightning lit up the world; the earth trembled and quaked (*vv. 17-18*). No mention is made in the Book of Exodus of a thunderstorm or an earthquake at the time the children of Israel crossed the Red Sea. When God showed his glory and majesty at that time, he displayed his

---

[8] I have used this phrase, 'a miracle-working God', to try and bring out a subtle aspect of the Heb. vocalisation. The MT does not have 'one doing wonders', but *'osêh péle'*, where the two words are so linked that they practically form a compound word, 'miracle-working'. The same phenomenon occurs in Exodus 15:11: 'Who is like you, ... a miracle-worker?'

control over creation so that the flashes of lightning seemed to be his arrows. Verse 18 is a continuation of the description of the earth in turmoil, and the same verb (*râgaz*) reappears (v. 16 NIV 'convulsed'; v. 18 'trembled'). For the Canaanites Baal was the storm God, but the Israelites knew that their redeemer was the God of great power and wonders. Not surprisingly, when he came as redeemer, the Lord Jesus showed his control of all creation (Mark 4:35-41).

Your path led through the sea, your way through the mighty waters, though your footprints were not seen. You led your people like a flock by the hand of Moses and Aaron (*vv. 19-20*). God guided the children of Israel by a pillar of cloud by day and a pillar of fire by night (Exod. 13:21-22). They did not *see* God himself, just as Moses did not see him when he revealed to him his glory (Exod. 33:18–34:9). Hence in poetic terms, God's 'footprints were not seen'. God was the great shepherd who guided his own flock (Pss. 78:52: 80:1), using Moses and Aaron as the great leaders. Isaiah 63:11-14 also describes the role of Moses as the shepherd who brought God's flock out of Egypt. The psalm may seem to come to an abrupt end, but the implications of past history would be clear. The God who saved his people in such a wonderful way could do so yet again.

Psalm 78

A maskil of Asaph

While the opening of this psalm resembles the wisdom psalms (Pss. 37, 49, and 73) and also has strong affinities in style with the opening chapters of the Book of Proverbs, its main purpose is really to give a recital of the great historical events in Israel's history. In particular, it concentrates on events that confirm God's covenantal dealings with his people, and in so doing acts as a call to faithfulness on the part of its readers and hearers in later generations. Whereas other Near Eastern peoples praised their human leaders, Israel praised God who had done so many wonderful things for her. The mention of David (vv. 70-72) links this psalm with Psalm 77, which ended by referring to Moses and Aaron, earlier leaders of God's people. Not only is the Exodus theme common to both, but the vocabulary used reveals strong links between these two psalms.[1] The term 'Ephraim' is used to designate 'Israel', as it was the dominant tribe of the northern kingdom. Hosea and Isaiah both do the same, and it is likely that this psalm comes from the same period as that in which these prophets were ministering.

Another link exists with the previous and the two subsequent psalms. At the end of this psalm, mention of

---

[1] This shared vocabulary includes God's 'might' or power', *'oz* (77:14; 78:26; cf. also the use of a related, but rare word of the same meaning, *'ezûz*, in 78:4), 'right hand', *yâmîn* (77:10; 78:54), and the divine title 'Most High', *'elyôn* (77:10; 78:17, 35, 56). Both psalms also focus on the wonderful deeds of the LORD, using words from the same Heb. root (*p-l-'*) to describe his actions (77:12, 14; 78:4, 11, 32).

David's role as the shepherd king brings it to a close. God took him 'from tending sheep ... to be shepherd of his people Israel' (v. 71). David was acting in a role already seen in the way Moses and Aaron cared for the flock (Ps. 77:20). Then, in Psalm 79:13 the praying community in address to God call themselves 'your people, the sheep of your pasture', while the following psalm opens with an appeal to the 'Shepherd of Israel' who leads 'Joseph like a flock' (Ps. 80:1). This imagery is very powerful and pervades much of the Old Testament.[2]

The pattern of the psalm is quite symmetrical. It has an introduction that gives the purpose. Then follows the major part (vv. 17-64), flanked at beginning and end by a stanza that highlights the sin of Ephraim (vv. 9-16) and the final one (vv. 65-72) that focuses on God's salvation and his choice of David and Jerusalem. The overall pattern can be shown in this way:

1. Introductory call to pass on this teaching (vv. 1-8)
    2. Accusations against Ephraim (vv. 9-16)
    3. First Cycle: The History of Rebellion (vv. 17-39)
        3.1 Recollection of wilderness experiences (vv. 17-31)
        3.2 Judgment and mercy (vv. 32-39)
    4. Second Cycle: The History of Rebellion (vv. 40-64)
        4.1 Recollection of wilderness experiences (vv. 40-55)
        4.2 Judgment and mercy (vv. 56-64)
    5. Promises to Judah and Jerusalem (vv. 65-72)

Introductory call – listen vv. 1-8						
	Against Ephraim vv. 9-16					Promises to Judah vv. 65-72
		Wilderness experiences vv. 17-31	Judgment and mercy vv. 32-39	Wilderness experiences vv. 40-55	Judgment and mercy vv. 56-64	

[2] A very helpful discussion on the theological significance of the 'flock' can be found in *NIDOTTE*, 3, pp. 729-31.

1. Introductory Call to Pass on this Teaching (*vv. 1-8*)
O my people, hear my teaching; listen to the words of my mouth (*v. 1*). One of the great responsibilities of parents and elders in Israel was to pass on the knowledge of the LORD to successive generations (see especially Deut. 6:4-9; 11:18-21; 29:29). The same responsibilities continue for Christians both in regard to children (Eph. 6:4) and adults (1 Tim. 4:11-14; Titus 2:1-15). The Hebrew text places stress on the aspect of hearing: 'Give ear, my people, [to] my teaching; incline your ears to the words of my mouth.' The call is couched in standardised language, with an initial invitation followed by a parallel clause.[3] The New Testament emphasises that faith comes by hearing the message, and the message is heard through the word of Christ (Rom. 10:17).

I will open my mouth in parables, I will utter hidden things, things from of old – what we have heard and known, what our fathers have told us (*vv. 2-3*). The Hebrew word translated here by 'parables' (*mâshâl*) has a somewhat different connotation than our English word 'parable'. It is used far more extensively than just for short sayings of general truth. It often appears either as a longer teaching passage (see Proverbs 1:8-19) or, as here, when the actions of an individual or a group are made a public example to others. Three times prophets are called on to lift up a *mâshâl* (Isa. 14:4; Micah 2:4; Hab. 2:6), just as it is employed of the object lessons used by Balaam (Num. 23:7; 24:3, 15, 20, 21, 23). The reader or hearer has to come to a judgment on himself or his situation, a principle that comes to fullest expression in the parables of Jesus.[4] The word for 'hidden things' (*chîdôt*) seems to have a similar meaning here. The lessons from Israel's history, which have been passed

---

[3] The imperative 'hear' (*ha'ᵃzînâh*) is a distinctly poetic word, and is normally used in parallel with other expressions such as 'hear' (*shâma'*), or 'give heed' (*qâshav*, Hi.), or synonymous ones to that in this verse, 'incline your ear' (*hattû 'ozneᵉkem*). Most of the parallels with 'hear' are listed in *DCH*, I, pp. 169-70.

[4] See the discussion, A. S. Herbert, 'The "Parable" (*Māŝal*) in the Old Testament', *SJT* 7 (1955), pp. 180-96.

down from generation to generation, had to be passed on to children and grandchildren.

We will not hide them from their children; we will tell the next generation the praiseworthy deeds of the LORD, his power, and the wonders he has done (*v. 4*). These object lessons from history were not to be concealed, but rather revealed! Covenantal history was a record of what God had done for his people, and the power and wonderful deeds that he had demonstrated were worthy of praise and adoration. The word 'hide' (*kâchad,* Pi.) conveys the idea of refusing to make something known. The truth about the past had to be told to successive generations.

He decreed statutes for Jacob and established the law in Israel, which he commanded our forefathers to teach their children, so the next generation would know them, even the children yet to be born, and they in turn would tell their children (*vv. 5-6*). The basic demands of God expressed in the covenantal responsibilities were to be taught generation after generation (Exod. 10:2; 12:26-27; Deut. 6:6-9, 20-22; 11:19-21). The process of educating later generations was specified by the LORD. The gap between the generations was to be bridged by instruction, so that there would be continuity in transmission of the statutes and laws of the LORD. Various expressions are used to designate those who would need teaching – 'their sons' (vv. 4 and 6), 'the coming generation' (vv. 4 and 6), and 'unborn children' (v. 6). Continuity of physical life had to be matched with continuing spiritual instruction.

Then they would put their trust in God and would not forget his deeds but would keep his commands. They would not be like their forefathers – a stubborn and rebellious generation, whose hearts were not loyal to God, whose spirits were not faithful to him (*vv. 7-8*). This transmission was intended to be something more than just knowledge of the past. It was to bring each generation to personal confidence in God, so that from the heart they would revere and obey him. An unusual word is employed for 'trust' (*késel*) that is elsewhere used in the sense of 'foolishness' or 'absurdity'. Probably the idea was of stubbornly holding on to God.[5] In particular, this would avoid the problem that arose with the wilderness generation, which is often characterised, as here, as being stubborn and rebellious (Deut. 9:6-7, 13, 24; 31:27; 32:5, 20; Acts 2:40). There is the constant danger that a head knowledge of biblical history will replace a heart relationship with God, and the obedience which stems from love to him.

2. Accusations against Ephraim *(vv. 9-16)*

The central part of the psalm begins with reference to the northern kingdom of Israel, here called Ephraim after its most dominant tribe. The closing part of the psalm focuses by contrast on the southern kingdom of Judah, for God 'did not choose the tribe of Ephraim; but he chose the tribe of Judah, Mount Zion, which he loved' (vv. 67-68). **The men of Ephraim, though armed with bows, turned back on the day of battle; they did not keep God's covenant and refused to live by his law** *(vv. 9-10)*. There is no record or specific mention of the tribe of Ephraim being cowardly in battle.[6] The reference seems rather to be a general one of disloyalty to God and the requirements of his covenant. From its very beginning around 931 BC the northern kingdom was marked by a rejection of covenantal obligations, and the alterations which Jeroboam I felt free to make in patterns of worship were evidence of this (1 Kings 12:25-33). Ultimately the northern kingdom fell in 722 BC because its people rejected God's 'decrees and the covenant he had made with their fathers and the warnings he had given them' (2 Kings 17:15). They refused to live by God's laws (lit. 'in his law they refused to walk').

---

[5] The Hebrew expression here, 'to put trust in God' (*sîm bêʾlohîm kesel*), has practically the same meaning as 'to make the LORD my refuge' (*shît baʾdonây yhwh machsî*, Ps. 73:28). The Heb. idioms are very similar.

[6] The word used here for 'battle' (*qᵉrâv*) is rare, only occurring eight times in the Old Testament, three of which are in the Psalter (in addition to this verse, Pss. 55:18 and 144:1). Its meaning, however, is clear because it is used in Job 38:23 and Psalm 144:1 as a synonym of the very frequent word *milchâmâh*.

They forgot what he had done, the wonders he had shown them. He did miracles in the sight of their fathers in the land of Egypt, in the region of Zoan (*vv. 11-12*). Before Israel even entered Canaan, God had warned about the dangers of forgetfulness (see especially Deut. 8) and indicated the covenantal curses that would come upon a disobedient people (Lev. 26:14-39; Deut. 28:15-68). The psalmist recalls events that should have reminded Ephraim of God's grace and power, and these memories should have helped to keep them faithful to the LORD. He begins with the demonstration of divine power shown in the miracles that took place in Egypt, mentioning specifically Zoan, a city in the north-east of the Nile delta. The poetic description employs three words that are virtually synonymous to denote the saving actions of God (in the MT, 'his deeds', 'his wonders', 'he performed wonders').[7] Fuller details are given later of the various plagues (see vv. 44-51).

He divided the sea and led them through; he made the water stand firm like a wall. He guided them with the cloud by day and with light from the fire all night (*vv. 13-14*). There were further miracles as Israel was led out of Egypt, and a summary is given of the miraculous way in which God brought his people through the Red Sea. He divided the sea and set the waters in a heap.[8] Constant guidance was provided by the cloud and by the fire (Exod. 13:21-22), so that Israel was never without direction and protection from the Lord. The language, especially the use of the verb 'guided' (*nâchâh*, Hi.), suggests deliberate allusion to passages like Exodus 13:17, 21, and 15:13.

---

[7] The first of these, 'deeds' (*ʿâlîlôt*), is cognate to the word 'deeds' (*maʿᵃlâlîm*) already used in verse 7. It is frequently used of God's righteous deeds as compared with the wicked actions of men (cf. Isa. 12:4). The second, 'wonders' (*niflâʾôt*), was used in verse 4, and comes from the same Heb. root (*p-l-ʾ*) as the third word, 'wonder' (*péleʾ*). This combination of words descriptive of God's work draws attention to the fact that his redemptive deeds were demonstrations of divine power, events outside human ability to perform.

[8] Instead of 'heap' (*nêd*) the LXX has 'leather bottle' (*askon* = *nod*), but the verb 'set' (*nâtsav*, Hi.) suggests that 'heap' or 'wall' is the correct translation.

He split the rocks in the desert and gave them water as abundant as the seas; he brought streams out of a rocky crag and made water flow down like rivers (*vv. 15-16*). The reference is to the incident recorded in Exodus 17:1-7. In addition to this passage other poets and prophets celebrate the same provision that God made for his people (see Pss. 105:41; 114:8; Isa. 48:21). The verb used of splitting the rock (*bâqaʿ*) has already occurred in verse 13 of dividing the water.[9] The poetic language emphasises the miracle involved – not just a trickle of water but 'streams' (*nôzᵉlîm*; cf. the use of the verb from the same root in Isa. 48:21, 'water *gushed* out').

3. First Cycle: The History of Rebellion (*vv. 17-39*)

3.1 Recollection of wilderness experiences (*vv. 17-31*)

Mentioning the provision of water clearly recalled for the poet the way in which Israel rebelled against the LORD, and doubtless he expected his readers to bring the same episodes to mind. **But they continued to sin against him, rebelling in the desert against the Most High. They wilfully put God to the test by demanding the food they craved. They spoke against God, saying, 'Can God spread a table in the desert? When he struck the rock, water gushed out, and streams flowed abundantly. But can he also give us food? Can he supply meat for his people?'** (*vv. 17-20*). Even redeemed Israel was noted for a spirit of constant grumbling against the LORD and his provision for them. They 'rebelled' against their God, the majestic and exalted God (cf. the use of the term 'the Most High' in other psalms such as 18:13; 73:11; 77:10; and 83:18). The contrast between God's gracious provision and the sinful behaviour of Israel is often brought out in this psalm by the use of 'he' and 'they'. 'To rebel' against God is a technical term (*mârâh*), used almost exclusively of the action of Israel against God (forty out of forty-five times in the Old Testament). It is

[9] The difference between the two uses is that in verse 13 the Qal form of the verb is used, whereas in verse 15 the Pi'el occurs. While *IBHS*, p. 363, cites this as contrasting the meaning of the two verbal forms (v. 13 'split'; v. 15 'split up'), this is hard to sustain, especially as Isaiah 48:21, 'and he split the rock', has the Qal form, not the Pi'el.

used particularly of what happened in the wilderness, and it occurs four times in this psalm (vv. 8, 17, 40, 56). At times the rebellion was merely oral complaint (as at Massah), but here and at other times the people were challenging God to provide special food to meet their tastes. The psalmist seems to be combining the two incidents of Exodus 16:2-3 and Numbers 11:4-6.

When the LORD heard them, he was very angry; his fire broke out against Jacob, and his wrath rose against Israel, for they did not believe in God or trust in his deliverance (*vv. 21-22*). God's response was one of anger against his people, and some of them died because of fire that he sent at Taberah (Num. 11:1-3). As a result of Moses' intercession the rest of the people were spared. The reference to not believing in God seems to be an echo of Exodus 14:31 ('the people feared the LORD and put their trust [lit. 'believed'] in him and in Moses his servant'). At the outset of their wilderness wanderings they believed in the LORD, but soon they reached the opposite position of distrust both in himself and his saving power.

Yet he gave a command to the skies above and opened the doors of the heavens; he rained down manna for the people to eat, he gave them the grain of heaven. Men ate the bread of angels; he sent them all the food they could eat (*vv. 23-25*). In spite of the unbelief of the people, God provided for them, sending down manna as if it was being poured out of the open doors of heaven (for this expression, cf. Gen. 7:11; 2 Kings 7:2; and Mal. 3:10). Elsewhere the manna is called 'bread of heaven' (Exod. 16:4; Ps. 105:40; John 6:31-32) while Paul calls it 'spiritual food' (1 Cor. 10:3). The fact that it was divine provision is emphasised by calling it 'the bread of angels',[10] and the provision was so liberal that their hunger was completely satisfied.

---

[10] 'Bread of angels' (*léchem ʾabbîrîm*) is a *hapax legomenon,* here matching 'grain of heaven' (*dᵉgan shâmayim*) as a description of God's provision of food for Israel. It is only here in the Old Testament that *ʾabbîrîm* means 'angels', but this interpretation goes back to the LXX (*arton angellôn*) and seems plausible, especially as a similar phrase ('mighty ones') is used in parallel with 'angels' in Psalm 103:20.

He let loose the east wind from the heavens and led forth the south wind by his power. He rained meat down on them like dust, flying birds like sand on the seashore (*vv. 26-27*). As with the dual historical reference to the provision of water in verse 20, so here both the accounts in Exodus 16:2-3 and Numbers 11:31-32 of the provision of food seem to be in mind. While the account in Numbers of the giving of the quail as a source of meat supply mentions that a wind from the sea blew them in (Num. 11:31), it does not specify the wind directions as here. If the quail were migrating at this time, then the south wind would bring them north and the east wind would direct them across to where Israel was encamped. The use of dust and sand as similes is used to focus attention on the bounty of God's provision. No count could be made of the number of quails.

He made them come down inside their camp, all around their tents. They ate till they had more than enough, for he had given them what they craved (*vv. 28-29*). The quails were brought right to where Israel was encamped, inside the camp (Exod. 16:13) and round about it (Num. 11:31).[11] What they lusted after, they received in abundance, even to the point where they loathed it. The use of the word 'craved' (Heb., *ta'ᵃvah*) alludes to the place name Kibroth Hattaavah, 'graves of craving' (Num. 11:34).

But before they turned from the food they craved, even while it was still in their mouths, God's anger rose against them; he put to death the sturdiest among them, cutting down the young men of Israel (*vv. 30-31*). The psalmist returns to the theme of God's anger (see v. 21) and shows how that anger manifested itself. While they were still pleased with God's provision (Heb., 'they were not estranged from their desire') and had it in their mouths, God struck down the strongest of the young men, so that 'their bodies were scattered over the desert' (1 Cor. 10:5). This verse is clearly dependent on Numbers 11:33.

---

[11] The MT has '*his* camps', but while it is possible to understand it as a reference to God's camp, yet the NIV rendering '*their* camp' is better, especially as it is easier to explain the plural 'camps'.

3.2 Judgment and Mercy (*vv. 32-39*)

Experience of God in both gracious provision and demonstration of wrath did not change the Israelites. The poet summarises the repeated acts of God in dealing with his people, as he showed both goodness and severity to them. In every generation the believing child of God can look back on life and say:

> With mercy and with judgment
> my web of time He wove,
> And aye the dews of sorrow
> Were lustred by His love;
> I'll bless the hand that guided,
> I'll bless the heart that planned,
> When throned where glory dwelleth
> In Immanuel's land.
> (Anne Ross Cousin 1824-1906)

In spite of all this, they kept on sinning; in spite of his wonders, they did not believe. So he ended their days in futility and their years in terror (*vv. 32-33*). Probably the rebellion of the people after the return of the spies is chiefly in view (cf. v. 32b with Num. 14:11). Even God's mighty acts of grace and power (*niflâ'ôt;* see comment on verses 11-12 and footnote 5) could not convince them to trust him. Judgment was pronounced against all the men of twenty years of age and upward who had grumbled against the LORD (Num. 14:26-38). Those who had spread the disparaging report about the land of Canaan died of a plague (v. 37), so ending their days in futility and terror (terms descriptive of the brevity and uncertainty of life).

Whenever God slew them, they would seek him; they eagerly turned to him again. They remembered that God was their Rock, that God Most High was their Redeemer (*vv. 34-35*). The cycle of events summarised here was typical of the period of the judges in particular (see the fuller description of the period in Judg. 2:6-23). God's judgment upon the people brought them to a realisation of their need of mercy, and so they sought him in their affliction.

Temporary forgetfulness was replaced by memory of the fact that God was both their refuge and their redeemer. To call God 'their Rock' recalls an ancient title for the God of Israel (cf. Deut. 32:4, 15, 18, 31), while the use of the title 'their redeemer' points back to God's actions in freeing his people from slavery in Egypt (cf. the use of 'redeem' in Exod. 6:6 and 15:13).

But then they would flatter him with their mouths, lying to him with their tongues; their hearts were not loyal to him, they were not faithful to his covenant (*vv. 36-37*). These verses suggest that the people were deceitful, making promises that they had no intention of keeping, or else rash promises that they were unable to fulfil. Their turning to God was not from the heart, but only an expression with their lips (cf. Isa. 29:13; Jer. 12:2). Unfaithfulness to covenantal commitments was characteristic of them, a point which has already been made earlier in the psalm (see v. 10). Verse 37 also forms a parallel with verse 8, in that the same two verbs are used in both (*kûn,* Ni. 'to be secure', Hi. 'to make firm', and *ʾâmên,* Ni. 'to have stability').[12]

Yet he was merciful; he forgave their iniquities and did not destroy them. Time after time he restrained his anger and did not stir up his full wrath. He remembered that they were but flesh, a passing breeze that does not return (*vv. 38-39*). In spite of all the repeated sin of Israel, God still displayed his character as the compassionate God (Exod. 34:6; Num. 14:18; Deut. 4:31). He made atonement for their sin by the provision of a substitute.[13] The stress, as in other passages such as Psalm 85:2-3, is on forgiveness that depends, not upon human ability, but on divine grace. Hence, he did not completely destroy them all, holding back his anger so that

---

[12] Another form of the verb *ʾâmên* has been used in verse 32, as the Hi. form means 'to believe' in the sense of trusting that something is reliable.

[13] The verb is *kâfar,* Pi. and means to 'make expiation for', or 'to effect ransom for someone' (see *DCH,* IV, pp. 455-56). The usage here with the verb being followed by a direct object, 'iniquity' (*ʿâwôn*), forms one of the occurrences of this verb indicating that God himself can provide forgiveness and remove his wrath. For other similar passages, see Deuteronomy 32:43; Psalms 65:3; 79:9; and Ezekiel 16:63.

the people were not exposed to the full demonstration of his wrath. Making atonement for sin is equated with the removal of divine anger. This act on God's part happened repeatedly.[14] He knew the frailty of his people, and his understanding of their weakness awakened his compassion for them. The thought of verse 39 is developed more fully in Psalm 103:14-16.

4. Second Cycle: The History of Rebellion (*vv. 40-64*)

4.1 Recollection of Wilderness Experiences (*vv. 40-55*)

The second descriptive cycle of the events in the wilderness occupies this section of the psalm. The poet traces the history of Israel from the plagues of Egypt until entry into the land of Canaan. **How often they rebelled against him in the desert and grieved him in the wasteland! Again and again they put God to the test; they vexed the Holy One of Israel** (*vv. 40-41*). Rebellion against their covenant God was not just an isolated incident but something repeated over and over again (for the technical expression 'to rebel', see the comment on v. 17). Isaiah uses the same language of Israel rebelling and grieving the Holy Spirit (Isa. 63:10). In spite of a clear instruction not to put God to the test as at Massah (Deut. 6:16) Israel did so, and this is emphasised in this historical song by mention of it three times (vv. 18, 41, 56). The Hebrew word for 'vexed' (*tâvâh*) occurs only here in the Old Testament, but there is no doubt as to its meaning in the context as it stands parallel with 'they tested'.[15]

They did not remember his power – the day he redeemed them from the oppressor, the day he displayed his miraculous signs in Egypt, his wonders in the region of Zoan (*vv. 42-43*). At times Israel could remember the LORD (see v. 35), but at other times the people were utterly forgetful of his great love and power shown to them. There may be the suggestion that this forgetfulness was a deliberate neglect of the LORD. He had promised to stretch out his hand against Egypt (Exod. 3:20), and did so, yet Israel forgot

---

[14] The Heb. idiom is 'he multiplied to turn back his anger', i.e. he time and time again restrained his anger.

[15] The LXX, the earliest translation of the Heb. Old Testament, renders it *paroxynô*, 'provoke'.

'his power' (Heb. 'his hand'). The redeemer of Israel had shown his 'signs' (*'otôt,* cf. Exod. 4:9, 28, 30) and 'wonders' (*môf^e^tîm,* cf. Deut. 29:3; 34:11), and even these miraculous demonstrations were not recalled. This is the first time in the Psalter that the combination of 'signs and wonders' occurs. It is used again in Psalm 135:9, but it is frequent elsewhere (Exod. 7:3; Deut. 4:34; 6:22; 7:19).

He turned their rivers to blood; they could not drink from their streams. He sent swarms of flies that devoured them, and frogs that devastated them. He gave their crops to the grasshopper, their produce to the locust. He destroyed their vines with hail and their sycamore-figs with sleet. He gave over their cattle to the hail, their livestock to bolts of lightning. He unleashed against them his hot anger, his wrath, indignation and hostility – a band of destroying angels. He prepared a path for his anger; he did not spare them from death but gave them over to the plague. He struck down all the firstborn of Egypt, the firstfruits of manhood in the tents of Ham (*vv. 44-51*). Several of the plagues are mentioned, though not in chronological order.

first plague:	river of blood (v. 44)
fourth plague:	flies (v. 45a)
second plague:	frogs (v. 45b)
eighth plague:	locusts (v. 46)
seventh plague:	hail and lightning (v. 47)
fifth plague:	death of animals (v. 48)
tenth plague:	death of the firstborn (vv. 50-51)

These plagues were to convince Pharaoh and his people to let the Israelites go. They culminated in the final plague, the death of the firstborn, and it is that final judgment which receives the emphasis here (vv. 49-51). Four terms are used to describe God's attitude to the Egyptians ('hot anger', 'wrath', 'indignation', 'hostility'), and they are likened to a band of angels bringing calamities. God's anger was not restrained, and it resulted in the death of Egypt's firstborn. Elsewhere in the Psalms, Egypt is called 'the land of Ham' (105:23, 27; 106:22), and the expression 'the tents of Ham' that occurs in verse 51 seems to be identical in meaning, even though this is its only occurrence in the Old Testament. These Psalter passages are simply noting the descent of Egypt from Ham (Gen. 10:6).

But he brought his people out like a flock; he led them like sheep through the desert. He guided them safely, so they were unafraid; but the sea engulfed their enemies (*vv. 52-53*). In describing the Exodus from Egypt the poet uses one of the terms that is often used in the Book of Exodus of the journeyings of Israel (*nâsa'*, Exod. 14:15; 16:1; 17:1), here in a causative form as in Exodus 15:22.[16] He pictures Israel as a flock of sheep or goats (the Hebrew term, *'êder*, refers to small animals) being led and cared for by God. The same imagery is also found in Psalms 74:1 and 80:1. Whereas the Egyptians were seized with panic, Israel had no reason to be afraid because God's saving power was shown in their deliverance (Exod. 14:13). Judgment came on the pursuing Egyptians and the sea covered them (NIV 'engulfed', the same word as in Exod. 15:10).

Thus he brought them to the border of his holy land, to the hill country his right hand had taken. He drove out nations before them and allotted their lands to them as an inheritance; he settled the tribes of Israel in their homes (*vv. 54-55*). Some commentators have taken the reference to the territory in verse 54 to be to the holy mountain, i.e. Zion, but the NIV translation makes excellent sense.[17] God brought Israel to the eastern border of Canaan, the land of his choice and the land separated off for Israel's use, and hence 'holy land' (*g^{e}vûl qodshô*, lit. 'the border of his holiness'). Then the hill country was taken, and after entry into Canaan the other nations were driven out and the tribes were allotted their territory. The victory was the LORD's ('the

[16] The same two verbs in verse 52 (*nâsa'*, 'he brought out', and *nâhag*, Pi., 'he led'), have already been used in verse 26 of God's actions in bringing the quails for food. God is depicted, by the use of the same language, as controlling the forces of nature and the actions of men.

[17] The territory is described as being *har-zeh*, where *zeh* is not the demonstrative adjective 'this' but used as a relative: 'the hill [country] which ...' The usage is noted in *DIHG~S*, p. 7, §6, Rem. 4.

nations *I* conquered', Josh. 23:4) and he allotted to them their inheritance (Ps. 105:11).

4.2 Judgment and Mercy (*vv. 56-64*)

But they put God to the test and rebelled against the Most High; they did not keep his statutes. Like their fathers they were disloyal and faithless, as unreliable as a faulty bow (*vv. 56-57*). Once more the refrain of putting God to the test and rebelling against him is added (cf. vv. 8, 17, and 40). Possession of the 'holy land' did not change the character of the people, and they were no different to their forefathers. The book of Judges and the early chapters of 1 Samuel provide many illustrations of disloyalty and faithlessness. The illustration of a faulty bow that disappoints the user is also used by Hosea of the waywardness of the northern kingdom (Hosea 7:16).

They angered him with their high places; they aroused his jealousy with their idols. When God heard them, he was very angry; he rejected Israel completely (*vv. 58-59*). Often the people resorted to Canaanite sites of sacrifice, or else built new altars on local hills. These led to the introduction of pagan practices into their worship, including idols. Because these challenged God's exclusive claims, his jealousy was provoked. When he heard their prayers to such idols, he was angry and gave them over to their enemies. This must be the meaning of 'rejected completely' in this verse, as God never utterly abandoned his people, including the ten northern tribes. As the verb means 'to reject' (*mâ'as*) and is accompanied by the adverb indicating 'greatly' (*m*e*'od*), an alternative translation is preferable, such as 'he vehemently repudiated'.[18]

He abandoned the tabernacle of Shiloh, the tent he had set up among men. He sent [the ark of] his might into captivity, his splendour into the hands of the enemy (*vv. 60-61*). What God did abandon was Shiloh, the place where the ark was located from the time of Joshua (Josh. 18:1) until it was destroyed by the Philistines, seemingly at the time when God allowed them to capture the ark (1 Sam. 4:1-11; Jer. 7:12). In Psalm 132:8 the ark is called 'the ark of your

[18] This is the translation offered by M. E. Tate, *Psalms 51-100*, p. 280.

might' (*'arôn 'uzzekâ*), while here 'his might' (*'uzzô*) and 'his splendour' (*tif'artô*) are used to describe it. The ark was a visible indication of God's strength and glory. The two words, 'might' and 'beauty', come together again in Psalm 96:6 (NIV, 'splendour and majesty').

He gave his people over to the sword; he was very angry with his inheritance. Fire consumed their young men, and their maidens had no wedding songs; their priests were put to the sword, and their widows could not weep (*vv. 62-64*). The judgment of destruction by the sword was one of the curses predicted if Israel was disobedient to the demands of the covenant (Lev. 26:25, 33). When the ark was captured, Israel was indeed put to the sword, losing 30,000 soldiers (see 1 Sam. 4:10). The fact that God's anger was directed against 'his people', 'his inheritance', emphasises how greatly he was provoked by the sin of Israel. The young men in particular were killed in battle, and therefore many young women were unable to find husbands. The reference to priests dying is probably an allusion to what happened to the sons of the priest Eli, when the ark was taken (1 Sam. 4:11, 17). Likewise the reference to widows is especially to the wife of Phinehas who died in childbirth after hearing of the death of her husband and father-in-law (1 Sam. 4:18-22). As she was dying she named her son, 'Ichabod' ('no glory', or, 'where is the glory?').

5. Promises to Judah and Jerusalem (*vv. 65-72*)

The concluding section of the psalm balances the earlier one dealing with Ephraim (vv. 9-16) by showing how God had chosen Judah (not Ephraim), Zion (not Shiloh), and David (not Saul) to fulfil his purposes. **Then the Lord awoke as from sleep, as a man wakes from the stupor of wine** (*v. 65*). In comparison with previous periods, the time of David was a wonderful manifestation of God's action on behalf of his people. It was as if the sleeping warrior woke up and intervened on their behalf. It is possible to translate the second part of the verse, 'as a man shouts [or, 'is stimulated by'] from wine', which would give a better parallel with 'wakes' (see RSV,

NKJV, and ESV). Certainly the NIV rendering 'wakes' is without foundation, and it obscures the fact that the verb (*rânan*, Hitp.) is always used of singing or moaning. Perhaps it depicts the moaning of a person awakening from sleep induced by wine, and so is similar to the usage of this verb to indicate sad shouting in Psalm 84:2 and Lamentations 2:19.[19]

He beat back his enemies; he put them to everlasting shame (*v. 66*). While there are no details given of these victories, the context suggests that the reference is to those of David, and possibly also to those of Samuel and Saul. In addition, the word 'enemies' (*tsârâv*, lit. 'his oppressors') points to the Philistines, so that the victories would be those of 2 Samuel 5 onwards. Saul was only able to secure partial victory over the Philistines, whereas an unified nation under the leadership of David was able to crush them so that they were never again a major power in the region. This verse uses the same language as does 2 Samuel 8:1 to describe the defeat of the Philistines (Ps. 78:66: *vayak tsârâv*, 'and he smote his oppressors'; 2 Sam. 8:1: *vayak Dâvid 'et-p^elishtîm*, 'and David smote the Philistines').[20]

Then he rejected the tents of Joseph, he did not choose the tribe of Ephraim; but he chose the tribe of Judah, Mount Zion, which he loved. He built his sanctuary like the heights, like the earth that he established forever (*vv. 67-69*). The contrast is very pronounced: 'He *did not choose* … but he *chose*'. God's choice was not the tribe of Ephraim (called here 'the tents of Joseph') but the tribe of Judah (cf. the initial promise concerning Judah in Gen. 49:10). The verb used of God's election of Judah (*bâchar*, 'he chose') is one of the main verbs employed in the Old Testament to denote God's special relationship with his covenant people. Just as God chose Judah, so likewise his

---

[19] Tremper Longman III has an excellent summary discussion of this verb in *NIDOTTE*, 3, pp. 1128-32.

[20] Good discussions on David's relationships with the Philistines can be found in David Payne, *Kingdoms of the Lord: A History of the Hebrew Kingdoms from Saul to the Fall of Jerusalem* (Exeter: Paternoster Press, 1981), pp. 135-39, and E. H. Merrill, *Kingdom of Priests: A History of Old Testament Israel* (Grand Rapids: Baker Book House, 1988), pp. 236-38.

choice was not Shiloh (cf. v. 60), but Mount Zion.[21] The ark of the covenant was brought to Zion (2 Sam. 6:1-19) and there the temple was built (1 Kings 6:1-38).[22] It seemed as secure as the earth itself. The description of it as being 'forever' has to be understood in the sense of lasting into the distant future, not lasting eternally. Because of the sins of the people, Zion was to be captured and the sanctuary destroyed at the time of the exile (cf. the way Ps. 74:3-8 describes that destruction).

He chose David his servant and took him from the sheep pens; from tending the sheep he brought him to be the shepherd of his people Jacob, of Israel his inheritance. And David shepherded them with integrity of heart; with skilful hands he led them (*vv. 70-72*). The historical narrative of the appointment of David draws attention to the fact that he was tending the sheep when the call came to him to be the shepherd of Israel (1 Sam. 16:11-13). When the elders of the northern tribes came to Hebron to anoint David king over Israel, they referred to God's promise to him: 'You will shepherd my people Israel' (2 Sam. 5:2). He was God's choice (the same verb as used of the nation and Zion in v. 68), and in that sense a man after God's own heart (1 Sam. 13:14). While the sanctuary in Jerusalem was important, yet the most important sign of God's presence with Israel was David, the chosen king. In general, he carried out his role with uprightness and knowledge,[23] except in particular for the incident regarding Bathsheba and Uriah. David the

---

[21] The verb 'chose' is used later in the Psalter to describe both God's choice of a people for himself (Ps. 135:4) and of Zion as the place for his sanctuary (Ps. 132:13).

[22] The word used for sanctuary (*miqdâsh*) comes from the root meaning 'to be holy' (*q-d-sh*), and it is one of the words the Old Testament uses for the tabernacle and temple. It was a holy or sacred place because it was where God dwelt among his people (Exod. 25:8).

[23] The phrases used of David (*tom l*^{e}*vâv* and *t*^{e}*vûnâh*) denote respectively someone who had integrity of character and aptitude for the task. The MT has '*like* integrity of heart' (*k*^{e}*tom l*^{e}*vâvô*) but many manuscripts have '*with* integrity of heart' (*b*^{e}*tom l*^{e}*vâvô*), while instead of 'with *aptitudes* of his hands' many Heb. manuscripts and the LXX have '*with aptitude of* his hands' (*bit*^{e}*vûnât kappâv*). Even if these readings are accepted, no real change takes place in the meaning. While the last verse lacks 'David' as the subject of the verbs, the NIV translators correctly inserted it.

shepherd of Israel became the hope of the Old Testament prophets (Ezek. 34:23; 37:24; Mic. 5:4), and in Jesus that hope was fulfilled (Matt. 2:6; Rev. 7:17).

Psalm 79

A psalm of Asaph.

The setting of this psalm seems to be the period just after the fall of Jerusalem in 586 BC, and hence it shares many themes with Psalm 74. The exiles, now banished from the land, had seen so much destruction wrought by the Babylonians. They now reflect on this, and particularly on the underlying hatred towards the LORD and his people. The appeal to God is for pardon and deliverance. They, as the flock of God (v. 13), want to be able to praise the LORD forever. The theme of God's flock links this psalm both with the two preceding and the one following (77:20; 78:70-72; 80:1).[1]

The basis of appeal to God is that Israel belongs to him, something that is stressed throughout by the repeated use of the pronoun 'your': 'your inheritance', 'your holy temple', 'your servants', 'your saints', 'your people', 'your pasture' (vv. 1-2, 13). Another post-exilic prayer, recorded in Daniel 9:4-19, shows many similarities, especially as the climax of Daniel's prayer is an appeal for God to act because of his name and for his own sake (cf. Ps. 79:9 with Dan. 9:17-19).

1. A National Lament *(vv. 1-4)*

O God, the nations have invaded your inheritance; they have defiled your holy temple, they have reduced Jerusalem to rubble (*v. 1*). The mention of God's inheritance provides a link with the close of the preceding psalm (Ps. 78:71). But the contrast is very marked. There, it is a

[1] See the introductory comment on Psalm 78 and footnote 1 on that psalm.

positive message of the choice of David and the establishment of the sanctuary on Mount Zion, while here, it is of Jerusalem devastated. The sanctuary is called 'your holy temple' (*hêkal qodsh^{e}kâ*). This phrase and other similar ones ('temple of his holiness', and 'holy place of your temple') all draw attention to the fact that the tabernacle/temple was intended to be a revelation of God's holiness.[2] Even though the destruction of Israel's cities was threatened long before by Moses (Deut. 28:52), yet when it came the people were shattered by it. The invaders had no thought that the land was God's inheritance, nor that the temple was sacred. They came against Judah, destroyed the temple (cf. the description in Ps. 74:4-7), and made Jerusalem just a heap of stones.

They have given the dead bodies of your servants as food to the birds of the air, the flesh of your saints to the beasts of the earth. They have poured out blood like water all around Jerusalem, and there is no one to bury the dead (*vv. 2-3*). In spite of what had happened to Jerusalem, the psalmist still knows that God has not completely cast off his people. In his prayer he calls them 'your servants', 'your saints'. One of the threats if Israel disobeyed was that dead bodies would be food for the birds of the air. The language here is very close to Deuteronomy 28:26.[3] The historical accounts record the massive loss of life at the time of the fall of Jerusalem (see especially 2 Chron. 36:17). The reference to the bodies being left unburied as food for the birds of the air may also be an echo of Jeremiah's description of the death of the covenant breakers (Jer. 34:17-20).

We are objects of reproach to our neighbours, of scorn and derision to those around us (*v. 4*). This verse is almost

---

[2] For 'temple of your holiness' (*hêkal qodsh^{e}kâ*) see Psalms 5:7; 79:1; 138:2; Jonah 2:4, 7; 'temple of his holiness' (*hêkal qodshô*) see Psalm 11:4; Micah 1:2; Habakkuk 2:20; 'holy place of your temple' (*q^{e}dosh hêkâlekâ*) see Psalm 65:4.

[3] Deuteronomy 28:26 has 'and your dead body shall be for food for all the birds of heaven' (*vehây^{e}tâh nivlât^{e}kâ l^{e}ma'^{a}kâl l^{e}kol-'ôf hashshâmáyim*), while Psalm 79:2 has 'They have given the dead bodies of your servants as food to the birds of the heaven' (*nat^{e}nû 'et-nivlat '^{a}vâdekâ ma'^{a}kâl le'ôf hashshâmáyim*).

identical to Psalm 44:13. Instead of fulfilling a missionary function to the surrounding nations, Israel had become a laughing stock. They cast scorn on her, ridiculing her as her slain inhabitants lie unburied, and others are taken away into exile. Another link with Daniel 9 (see introductory comments to this psalm) exists in this verse, as the phrase 'a reproach ... to our neighbours' is practically the same as that in Daniel 9:16, 'for a reproach to all our neighbours.'

2. A Prayer for Forgiveness (*vv. 5-8*)

How long, O LORD? Will you be angry forever? How long will your jealousy burn like fire? (*v. 5*). The question 'How long?' marks the start of the prayer, and it also suggests confidence in the LORD. The psalmist knew that God was not going to leave them forever in their present distress. The closest parallel is Psalm 89:46. God was a jealous husband of Israel (Exod. 20:5), and the psalmist is appealing for an end to this period of anger.

Pour out your wrath on the nations that do not acknowledge you, on the kingdoms that do not call on your name; for they have devoured Jacob and destroyed his homeland (*vv. 6-7*). The threat of the covenantal curse against unfaithful Israel also involved turning that curse on the persecuting enemies (Deut. 30:7). The psalmist is not pleading for a cessation of God's wrath, but rather the redirection of it against the ungodly Gentiles. Of the prophets, Jeremiah and Ezekiel both speak of the way in which God is going to turn his jealous wrath against the nations (Jer. 50:9-16; Ezek. 36:5-7), while Jeremiah 10:25 is virtually identical with these two verses. The psalmist calls on God to honour his commitment, and he uses words taken almost exactly from Jeremiah 10:25. The prayer is an appeal for God's justice to be manifest, for the nation has been consumed and his dwelling place devastated. The use of a word normally meaning 'pastures' (*nâvâh*) for 'homeland' may be a deliberate extension of the idea of Israel being God's flock (cf. its use in 'shepherd' passages such as Ps. 23:2 and Amos 1:2).

Do not hold against us the sins of the fathers; may your mercy come quickly to meet us, for we are in desperate need (*v. 8*). The psalmist acknowledges that it was 'former sins' that had caused the exile.[4] This is a reference to the sins of those just prior to the exile (2 Kings 24:3 mentions particularly the sins of Manasseh). He beseeches God to show divine compassion to his afflicted people, not holding against them (lit. not remembering) any longer the sins of a previous generation.

3. A Prayer for Help (*vv. 9-11*)
Help us, O God our Saviour, for the glory of your name; deliver us and forgive our sins for your name's sake (*v. 9*). While 'the fathers' had sinned, so also had those in exile. Hence the request for forgiveness, though the appeal is not for their sake. The only basis the psalmist could plead was that it would be for God's honour and for *his* name's sake (cf. Dan. 9:19; see introductory comment on this psalm). He knew that the only source of deliverance would be from the one he calls 'our Saviour'.

Why should the nations say, 'Where is their God?' Before our eyes, make known among the nations that you avenge the outpoured blood of your servants. May the groans of the prisoners come before you; by the strength of your arm preserve those condemned to die (*vv. 10-11*). If God did not intervene, then the outcome would be that the heathen nations would make derisive comments about Israel's God. Instead of glory being given to him, his name would be a reproach. While the exile was a judgment on Israel, yet the psalmist wants to see those who carried out the massacres of the people punished, and for this to happen so that exiled

---

[4] The NIV 'sins of the fathers' is a common translation of the Heb. phrase *ʿᵃwônot riʾshonîm*, but *ri'shonîm* is an adjective usually meaning 'former'. It can, in some contexts, refer to former persons (Lev. 26:40; Deut. 19:14). Perhaps it is an abbreviation of the longer expression found in Jeremiah 11:10, 'the iniquities of their fathers who were at the first' (*ʿᵃwônot ʿawôtâm hâriʾshonîm*). Whatever explanation of the precise phrase is preferred, the reference is back to the pre-exilic sins that had angered God.

Israel can witness it.[5] The exiles are called 'prisoners', though in fact they were not in prisons as such. They were compelled to stay in Babylonia, and any attempt on their part to return home would result in death. The attitude to the gloating enemies expressed in this psalm is consistent with the view taken elsewhere in the exilic literature of the Old Testament, that renewed divine mercy to Israel would be expressed in divine vengeance on those enemies (cf. especially the way this is dealt with in Lam. 1:21-22; 3:58-66; and 4:21-22).

4. A Vow of Praise (*vv. 12-13*)

Pay back into the laps of our neighbours seven times the reproach they have hurled at you, O Lord. Then we your people, the sheep of your pasture, will praise you forever; from generation to generation we will recount your praise (*vv. 12-13*). This appeal for judgment on the enemies of Israel does not stem from a sense of personal vindictiveness. The psalmist wants payment made in full measure to them (symbolised by the use of the number seven) because of what they had done *to God*.[6] They had reviled him, and if the surrounding nations met their just reward, then Israel would in contrast praise the Lord's name forever. Recovery of the prisoners would become a topic to be recounted from generation to generation. God's flock would rejoice in the memory of what their shepherd had done for them. The thought is very similar to Psalm 78:5-6.

---

[5] 'Those condemned to die' translates the Heb. 'sons of death' (*b^e^nê temûtâh*). The phrase only occurs twice, here and in another song from the exile, Psalm 102:20. The word 'death' (*temûtâh*) is not attested other than in these passages, but the general consensus is that it is related to the common word for 'death', *mût*. The phrase could mean what the NIV translators accepted, 'those condemned to die', or simply be a general reference to the fate of the exiles. Most of them were going to die, alienated from the land covenanted to them.

[6] This point is also made emphatically in Psalm 5:9-10 where the psalmist asks that the wicked be made to bear their own guilt, and then says: 'For they have rebelled against *you*.'

Psalm 80

For the director of music. To [the tune of] ' The Lilies of the Covenant.' Of Asaph. A psalm.

The references in this song suggest that it came from the northern kingdom of Israel, or else the author lived in the kingdom of Judah but had a very deep interest in the north. The mention of God dwelling between the cherubim (v. 1) points to the psalm originating in Jerusalem where the true sanctuary was still located. It certainly comes from a time later than the division of the kingdom following the death of Solomon, and may be from about the time of the attacks by Assyria that culminated in the fall of Samaria in 722 BC. The Septuagint version has the addition of the words 'concerning the Assyrian' in the title, which lends some support to this suggestion.[1] It comes from a time of disaster for the nation, when foreign invaders had trampled down the country. Appeal is made on the basis of God's past help, and the assurance that Israel was a transplanted vine occupying the land of God's appointment. A psalm such as this confirms that in spite of the division of the kingdom into Israel (the ten northern tribes) and Judah (Judah and Simeon), God had a concern for both. He did not abandon Israel, but, by sending messengers such as Hosea and Amos, confirmed his continuing concern for the northern tribes.

---

[1] The biblical text points to the presence of northerners in Judah. When Hezekiah reinstituted the Passover those who brought tithes to the Lord are described as 'the men of *Israel* and Judah who lived in the towns of Judah' (2 Chron. 31:6). Micah 1:9 suggests that the sins of Israel have come to Judah, while Micah 1:13 points to the presence of an Israelite sanctuary at Lachish so that 'the transgressions of *Israel*' were found there. Archaeology confirms that a rapid increase in population took place in Judah after the Assyrian invasion, as many fled for safety to the south.

1. An Appeal for Help (*vv. 1-3*)

Hear us, O Shepherd of Israel, you who lead Joseph like a flock; you who sit enthroned between the cherubim, shine forth before Ephraim, Benjamin and Manasseh. Awaken your might; come and save us (*vv. 1-2*). The title used here for God goes back to Genesis 48:15, where Jacob says: 'The God before whom my fathers Abraham and Isaac walked, *the God who has been my Shepherd* all my life to this day, the Angel who has delivered me from all harm – may he bless these boys.' This continues the motif of shepherd/flock already found in Psalms 74:1; 77:20; 78:52, 71-72; 79:13. 'Joseph' is used as a convenient designation of the ten northern tribes that formed the nation of Israel, with the tribes named after Joseph's sons (Ephraim and Manasseh). The tribe of 'Benjamin' is used as a parallel expression in verse 2.[2] The appeal is to the God of power who sits enthroned between the cherubim (cf. 1 Sam. 4:4; 2 Sam. 6:2; 2 Kings 19:15). The idea is probably more than simply that God is enthroned above the mercy seat. He is seated on his heavenly throne. From there he is asked to come and execute judgment and lead his people as of old, restoring them to their former position.

Restore us, O God; make your face shine upon us, that we may be saved (*v. 3*). For the first time the threefold refrain used in the psalm occurs (see also v. 7 and 19). The prayer is expressed in terms of the Aaronic blessing (Num. 6:25). God's face is pictured as being hidden from them, and now fulfilment of the blessing is requested. If that happens, then they will be delivered according to their request.

2. A Lament over Punishment (*vv. 4-7*)

O LORD God Almighty, how long will your anger smoulder against the prayers of your people? You have fed them with the

[2] Benjamin must have belonged with the northern tribes, and thus been part of Israel, for only one tribe, Judah (and Simeon which was incorporated with it), constituted the southern kingdom (1 Kings 12:20). However, it seems that a part of Benjamin must have been attached to Judah, as its territory bordered on Jerusalem. For the evidence supporting this view, see E. W. Hengstenberg, *Commentary on the Psalms*, (Edinburgh: T. & T. Clark, 1869), III, pp. 9-11. His position was followed by J. A. Alexander, *The Psalms Translated and Explained*, (Edinburgh: Andrew Elliott and James Thin, 1864; republished by Zondervan, n.d.) pp. 341-42.

bread of tears; you have made them drink tears by the bowlful (*vv. 4-5*). The psalmist recognises that the afflictions which the people are undergoing have been caused by God's anger, and he appeals to him as 'Lord God Almighty'.[3] The historical account of the fall of the northern kingdom stresses this aspect of the provocation of God (2 Kings 17:17-18). The anger is said to be against the prayers of the people because of the seeming lack of response on God's part to the cries of the people. Their prayers were unavailing. Trouble and sorrow are pictured as being their daily food, so that tears substitute for bread and drink.

You have made us a source of contention to our neighbours, and our enemies mock us. Restore us, O God Almighty; make your face shine upon us, that we may be saved (*vv. 6-7*). God was using the surrounding nations to bring judgment upon his own people. Perhaps the mocking was in the form of the question, 'Where is your God?' (cf. the similar theme in Ps. 42:3, 10). In their situation of strife the people repeat the prayer that has already been used (see v. 3) but with an increasing intensity, replacing the simple 'God' (*ʾᵉlohîm*) with 'God Almighty' (*ʾᵉlohîm tsᵉvâʾôt*), and so closing another stanza. The only way that their condition can change is for God to shine with favour on them.

3. Prayer for the Transplanted Vine (*vv. 8-15*)

You brought a vine out of Egypt; you drove out the nations and planted it. You cleared the ground for it, and it took root and filled the land. The mountains were covered with its shade, the mighty cedars with its branches. It sent out its boughs to the Sea, its shoots as far as the River (*vv. 8-11*). The Exodus from Egypt and the conquest of Canaan are described poetically in terms of a vine being transplanted (cf. Gen. 49:22; Isa. 5:1-7; Hosea 14:7; and Jer. 2:21 for use of the imagery of the vine). Verses 8-9 stress that the events were sovereign acts of God ('*you* brought ... *you* drove out ... *you* planted it ... *you* cleared the ground'). When the vine was planted in Canaan, it then established itself and grew so that it covered the territory

---

[3] For comment on this title, used here, in verse 19, and in Psalm 84:8, see the comments on Psalm 59:5.

that had been promised to Abraham (Gen. 15:18-21; 17:8; for later descriptions of the borders of Israel see Exod. 23:31; Josh. 1:3-4; and 1 Kings 4:21, 24). The vine covered Canaan. It reached north to the mountains (of Lebanon) so that the mighty cedars were covered by its branches.[4] Westward it reached the (Mediterranean) Sea, and on the north-east it reached as far as the (Euphrates) River.[5]

Why have you broken down its walls so that all who pass by pick its grapes? Boars from the forest ravage it and the creatures of the field feed on it (*vv. 12-13*). Continuing with the analogy of the vine, the psalmist speaks of the way in which the defences of Israel have been broken down so that the land has been exposed to the invaders. The fruit of the vine is being taken by others who have no right to it.[6] The boar was an unclean animal (Deut. 14:8), and destructive, and therefore it was a suitable description for Israel's enemies.[7] The final clause carries on the idea of the way in which wild animals would be able to graze where once enclosed fields had been carefully tended.[8] The meaning is clear: God has handed over defenceless Israel into the enemies' power.

---

[4] The MT has 'cedars of God' (*ʾarzê-ʾēl*) but this is probably a kind of superlative. See comment on Psalm 36:6.

[5] Whereas in Psalm 72:8 a special word for the Euphrates is used (*pᵉrât*), here a very general word (*nâhâr*) is used, though in the context there is no doubt as to which river is meant.

[6] 'Those who pass by' is too neutral a translation, as M. E. Tate, *Psalms 51-100*, p. 307, notes. In the context something stronger is needed, in keeping with the description of hostile incursions. Perhaps a term like 'invaders' comes close.

[7] There is an oddity in the MT in that in the word 'forest' (*yaʿar*) the middle consonant *ayin* is suspended, i.e. written higher than the other letters. This is one of four occurrences in the MT of this phenomenon. While the Talmud explains this as being a way of noting the middle letter in the Hebrew Book of Psalms, it may just have been that *ayin*, one of the larger letters, may have been mistaken for a suspended letter. Modern comment on the suspended letters can be found in Page H. Kelley, Daniel S. Mynatt, and Timothy G. Crawford, *The Masorah of Biblia Hebraica Stuttgartensia*, (Grand Rapids: Eerdmans, 1998), p. 35.

[8] The word translated 'creatures' (*zîz*) only occurs here and in Psalm 50:11. In both passages some Heb. manuscripts have a similar word (*zîv*) that means 'splendour'. The parallel clause, 'Boars from the forest ravage it', and the use of the verb 'to graze' (*râʿâh*), both suggest that 'creatures' or 'moving thing' (*DCH*, III, p. 101) is as close as can be determined in light of present knowledge.

Return to us, O God Almighty! Look down from heaven and see! Watch over this vine, the root your right hand has planted, the son you have raised up for yourself (*vv. 14-15*). The appeal is for a visitation of God to remedy the situation, using words that are similar to the refrains of verses 4 and 7. 'Watch over' translates a Hebrew verb (*pâqad*) that means 'to visit'. The establishment of Israel in Canaan was a divine activity. It was a demonstration of his power, described here in the anthropomorphic expression, 'the root your right hand has planted'.[9] Such a visitation can either be in judgment or (as here) to bring about a beneficial result (cf. Ruth 1:6: 'come to the aid of'; Jer. 15:15: 'care for'). While 'son' is a term used elsewhere of Israel (Exod. 4:22-23; Hosea 11:1), yet it can also be used of a branch, which makes good sense here especially seeing it is used in parallel to 'root'. The psalmist pleads with the divine gardener to come and take care of his own precious plant that he placed in the garden of Canaan. God had raised it up for his own purposes and for his own glory.

4. Restore Us, O Lord (*vv. 16-19*)

The psalm ends with a further plea for restoration, along with an assurance of renewed commitment to the LORD. **Your vine is cut down, it is burned with fire; at your rebuke your people perish. Let your hand rest on the man at your right hand, the son of man you have raised up for yourself** (*vv. 16-17*). The request is for judgment upon those who have devastated the vine, and at the same time help for the afflicted people. The NIV interprets verse 16b to be a reference to Israel ('your people'), but the Hebrew text does not specify the subject of the rebuke. Verse 16 can be translated, 'They burned it (i.e. the vine); it is burned with fire. May they perish at your rebuke.' This would then be an appeal to destroy the enemies who have burned the vine with fire. To have God's hand resting on Israel would be a sign of his favour. The language of the verse makes it clear that 'man' and 'son of man' are references to the

[9] 'Root' (*kannâh*) is a *hapax legomenon*, and some word like it, or 'stock', is needed in the context which describes planting. Emendations have been proposed, but they are not convincing. Cf. *DCH*, IV, pp. 434-45.

'root'/'son' of verse 15 (cf. also the use of the phrase 'you have raised up for yourself' in both verses).[10]

Then we will not turn away from you; revive us, and we will call on your name (*v. 18*). The pledge is given on behalf of the people as a whole that they will never again turn away from God, i.e. become apostates and renounce their covenantal obligations.[11] The Hebrew word translated 'call' (*qârâ'*) can also mean to proclaim (see Exod. 33:19; 34:6; Deut. 32:3). If renewed life is given to Israel by God, then the people will proclaim his sovereign acts and gracious character. Later, the concept of renewal of life became a way of describing God's actions in restoring the exiles to Palestine (see especially Ezekiel's use of this verb in 37:5, 6, 9,10, 14).

Restore us, O LORD God Almighty; make your face shine upon us, that we may be saved (*v. 19*). For the third time the refrain comes in, this time to close the psalm. The amplifying use of divine names in the refrain seems to be deliberate, as the psalm mounts to a climax: 'God' (v. 3); 'God Almighty' (v. 14); 'LORD God Almighty' (v. 19). The characteristics of God as expressed in his names are used as a ground for the answer to this prayer. If God shows himself favourable to his people, then the outcome will be their salvation.

---

[10] The MT has 'the man *of* your right hand', not '*at* your right hand'. As the man of God's right hand (the stock) has been planted and raised up by God, it can thus be said to be *at* God's right hand.

[11] While 'turn away' is the translation of the verb *sûg*, this verb is normally accompanied by the preposition *'âchor*, 'back[wards]'. The preposition is not employed here but the meaning is clearly the same as the fuller expression, *sûg 'âchôr*.

Psalm 81

For the director of music. According to gittith. *Of Asaph.*

This psalm has much in common with Psalm 50, especially because of the covenantal theme that pervades it. The reference to *'gittith'* is probably to an instrument or tune (see the introductory comments on Ps. 8). Likewise, it is a psalm of Asaph. It seems to depict a ritual in Israel which was kept by divine decree (vv. 4-5), and which was connected with the covenant. It is unclear which festival is in view, but the use of the expression 'on the day of our Feast' suggests one of the pilgrimage festivals (Passover, Feast of Weeks, or Tabernacles). The reference to deliverance out of Egypt gives credence to the view that the Passover is the intended feast.

The psalm consists of two dissimilar parts. Verses 1-5 are a song of praise dedicated to, or performed at, a specific feast. On the other hand, verses 6-16 are a declaration by God himself, reminding his people that he is the only God. In order to recall them from idolatry, he repeats the opening words of the Decalogue setting out the almighty redeemer's claims. He declares he is 'the Lord your God' (v. 10) who demands exclusive worship: 'You shall have no foreign god among you' (v. 9). The style and content of this second section of the psalm is very like the way in which prophetic calls were made (Isa. 7:13-14; Jer. 7:2-8; Hosea 4:1; Amos 3:1-7).

1. A Call to Praise (*vv. 1-2*)

The opening call is for all the people to sing a joyful song to the Lord. **Sing for joy to God our strength; shout aloud to the God of Jacob** (*v. 1*). The festivals were meant to be joyous occasions, and so the psalmist calls on the people to worship the LORD in a spirit of thanksgiving. The terms in which God is described are typical for the Psalter. God was the strength of his people (cf. 18:1; 28:7), and he was the God of Jacob (cf. 20:1; 46:7, 11; 132:2). The two verbs used here (*rânan* and *rûʿa*) are virtually indistinguishable in meaning in passages such as this.[1]

Begin the music, strike the tambourine, play the melodious harp and lyre (*v.* 2). At the time of the institution of the Passover (Exod. 12), there is no mention of singing. However, the instruments mentioned here are also listed in later references to the worship at the temple (2 Chron. 5:12; 29:25). The musical accompaniment of the Passover in times of Hezekiah and Josiah was probably the regular practice for much of the Old Testament period (2 Chron. 30:21-22; 35:15).

2. An Appointed Feast (*vv. 3-5*)

The call to the feast now goes out to the Levites. **Sound the ram's horn at the New Moon, and when the moon is full, on the day of our Feast; this is a decree for Israel, an ordinance of the God of Jacob** (*vv. 3-4*). The word translated 'New Moon' (*chôdesh*) can also mean 'month', and it is probably better to assume that the psalmist mentions first the month, and then the specific part of it, 'when the moon is full.' The word 'feast' (Heb. *chag*, cf. Arabic *haj*) is used of various festival occasions (Exod. 23:15-16; 34:18-22; Deut. 16:16; 2 Chron. 8:13), and specifically of the Passover (Exod. 12:14; Num. 28:17). Reference is then made to the historical origins of this feast. It was not simply a social custom but a divine prescription, with 'decree' and 'ordinance' being used in parallel. In a context such as this, it is impossible to draw any sharp distinction between them.[2] The first clause in verse 4 draws specific attention to the statute that God had given,[3] while the second one

---

[1] Tremper Longman III points out that when these verbs are used in parallel *rânan* occurs first, perhaps indicating it was the more frequently used of the two. See his comments in *NIDOTTE*, 3, p. 1082.

[2] Discussion on the various words used in the Psalter for God's revelation is found in W. VanGemeren, 'The Psalms', *The Expositor's Bible Commentary* (Grand Rapids: Zondervan, 1991, 5, pp. 184-87.

[3] The MT has: 'For a statute to Israel it (*hûʾ*)', where the pronoun is best taken as a demonstrative, 'this'.

points to it being an ordinance of 'the God of Jacob' (cf. use of the title in v. 1).[4]

He established it as a statute for Joseph when he went out against Egypt (*v. 5a*). The word rendered 'statute' or 'testimony' (*ʿêdût*) is used as a synonym for 'covenant' (cf. 'the tablets of the testimony', Exod. 31:18; 32:15; 34:29). If the subject of the whole sentence is 'God', then the reference will be to his actions against Egypt at the time of the Exodus. Should the subject of the sentence be taken as Israel, then the idea is simply that the Passover was established when Israel left Egypt (this is possible, but it requires taking a Heb. preposition, *ʿal*, in an unusual sense).[5]

The words that follow, **where we heard a language we did not understand** (*v. 5b*), are difficult. NIV follows most English translations in taking the verbs as plurals, and making them refer to the past tense. However, the verbs in Hebrew are in the first person singular ('I do not know', 'I hear [a voice]'), and are best taken as referring to the present time. It is a statement of wonder at the LORD's words that are to come, and thus forms a transition between the opening verses and verses 6-16. The psalmist declares: *I hear [something] unlike any language with which I am acquainted.* The NASB comes close to this, but takes the verbs as past tense ('I heard ... I did not know').

3. A Divine Word of Deliverance (*vv. 6-7*)

The divine word focuses first of all on the actual deliverance at the time of the Exodus. **He says, 'I removed the burden from their shoulders; their hands were set free from the basket. In your distress you called and I rescued you, I answered you out of a thundercloud; I tested you at the waters of Meribah'. *Selah*** (*vv. 6-7*). The opening words 'He

---

[4] In Heb. it is 'an ordinance belonging to (l^e) the God of Jacob' (*mishpât lê'lohê yaʿ^{a}qov*). This is probably a case where the preposition l^e is used with a possessive meaning. Cf. R. J. Williams, *Hebrew Syntax: An Outline*, 2nd ed. (Toronto: University of Toronto Press), p. 48, § 270.

[5] This requires *ʿal* to have an ablative meaning in certain contexts. Other passages would include Job 29:7; Psalm 4:7; Proverbs 25:22; and Daniel 2:1. *IBHS*, p. 218, notes that in this verse the preposition *ʿal* has 'a rare separative sense'.

says' does not represent any word(s) in the MT. The NIV adds them to indicate that what follows is direct speech, but most versions simply mark it with inverted commas.[6] What is most interesting is the way that the people are addressed. While it is a much later generation of Israel, yet they are regarded as being part of the community at the time of the Exodus: *You called, and I rescued you; I answered you out of a thundercloud; I tested you at the waters of Meribah.*

This is carrying out the pattern which Moses set in Deuteronomy 5:2-3, where he identified all his hearers as being part of the believing community at the time of the covenant-making at Mount Sinai. So now the people stand in the same relation to God as their forefathers did long ago. The same language of relief from a burden is repeated in Isaiah 10:27, where the Assyrian is going to have his burden removed from Israel's shoulders. This is a definite reference back to the experience of Israel in Egypt as 10:24 makes clear. The first person verbs lay emphasis on the divine actions in the rescue of Israel from her Egyptian bondage: '*I* removed', '*I* rescued', '*I* answered', '*I* tested.'

4. The Decalogue Reasserted (*vv. 8-10*)

The word of the LORD that comes to the people at this festival time is a reminder of the initial covenant relationship established at Sinai. **Hear, O my people, and I will warn you – if you would but listen to me, O Israel! You shall have no foreign god among you; you shall not bow down to an alien god. I am the LORD your God, who brought you up out of Egypt. Open wide your mouth and I will fill it** (*vv. 8-10*). The LORD's words to Israel in Deuteronomy 4:1 and 6:4 are echoed in this call to hear. God brings an accusation against his people and longs that they would heed him. The word that comes to Israel is put in terms of the opening of the Ten Commandments, reminding them in this way that it is the covenant God of Israel who is still speaking to his

---

[6] Many commentators and versions want to change the pronouns in the MT of verse 6 from 3rd pers. sing. (lit. 'his shoulder', 'his hands') to 2nd pers.: 'I relieved *your* shoulder of the burden; *your* hands were freed from the basket' (NRSV). This is unnecessary as Heb. often has a sudden switch in persons (cf. Pss. 44; 84; 85).

covenant people. The LORD reasserts his own relationship as the redeemer God of the Exodus and the one who claims from his people an exclusive worship. Verse 9 is a paraphrase of the first two commandments. In place of the Decalogue's 'You shall have no *other* gods before me', the psalmist substitutes 'You shall not have no *foreign god* (*'êl zâr*) among you.' No basic difference in meaning exists, as the phrase speaks of illegitimate gods using 'foreign' (*zâr*), which is often paralleled with another word meaning 'alien' or 'foreign' (*nokrî*). At this festival the people are invited to open their mouths and God would fill them. This would show their inability to meet their own needs, and accordingly that they are waiting for God's provision.

5. A Rebellious People (*vv. 11-16*)

The festival is also a time to accuse the people as a whole of their erring ways. **But my people would not listen to me; Israel would not submit to me. So I gave them over to their stubborn hearts to follow their own devices** (*vv. 11-12*). The contrast between verse 8 and verse 11 is most marked. Israel was called to 'hear' or 'listen carefully', but now comes the reminder that in the past Israel did not listen. There was a basic and enduring unwillingness to yield to the LORD.[7] In turn, he gave them up (*shâlach*, Pi., a verb used elsewhere of letting captives go, or giving over to sin) to their own stubborn desires. This is always the greatest of God's judgments against his people (Ps. 78:29-31). However, the LORD's concern was still there for them (cf. Heb. 12:6).

If my people would but listen to me, if Israel would follow my ways, how quickly would I subdue their enemies and turn my hand against their foes! Those who hate the LORD would cringe before him, and their punishment would last forever (*vv. 13-15*). Again the LORD repeats his strong appeal for his people to follow his ways. In the future he longs for them to be an obedient people, walking in his paths. If they respond, then he promises to deal speedily with the enemies

---

[7] The expression is: 'And Israel was not willing (*'âvâh*) to me', i.e. 'Israel would not accede to me' (so, *DCH*, I, p. 102).

who oppress them. This earnest desire of God is seen in its ultimate expression in the words of Jesus concerning Jerusalem (Matt. 23:37-39). The final part of verse 15 is ambiguous in the Hebrew text. It simply says 'their time (*'ittâm*) will last for ever'. This can be interpreted either positively or negatively. The fact that the suffix is 3rd person plural ('*their* time'), and thus does not agree with the immediately preceding 'cringe before *him*', suggests that the commonly accepted negative interpretation needs rethinking. 'Their' refers back to the children of Israel in verses 11-14: 'their stubborn hearts', 'their own devices', 'their foes'. Hence, the meaning is that in spite of the foes, Israel will stand for ever, a reassuring word to endorse the principle given in 2 Samuel 7:24: 'You have established your people Israel as your very own for ever.'

The final verse sets before them the prospect of rich blessing. **But you would be fed with the finest of the wheat; with honey from the rock I would satisfy you** (*v. 16*). The promise is given in terms that echo Deuteronomy 32:13-14, and in language that speaks of supernatural provision for their needs. Perhaps 'wheat' and 'honey' represent the basic needs and the more luxurious foods, a composite picture of abundant prosperity. The New Testament promise goes even further, and believers have the assurance that 'God will meet all your needs according to his glorious riches in Christ Jesus' (Phil. 4:19).

Psalm 82

Psalm of Asaph.

God always had deep interest in justice in Israel, and warnings were often given concerning its perversion at the hands of sinful rulers (Exod. 22:27; Deut. 10:17-18; Pss. 10:14, 18; 58:1-11; Mal. 3:5). The repetition of 'God' (*'elohîm*) and the verb 'judge' (*shâfat*) is a distinctive feature and reflects the keynote that God is the righteous judge. Psalm 82 is like other psalms of Asaph in which the judgment of the nation is in view (Pss. 75; 81). This applies to the form of the psalm, the representation of God as judge, and the introduction of God as the speaker. Here as elsewhere, 'gods' is a Hebrew term applied to human rulers (Exod. 21:6; 22:8-9),[1] and Jesus' use of the passage supports this interpretation (John 10:36). This is a much more satisfactory explanation than attempting to make it refer to angels.

Another quite prevalent view is that some sort of heavenly council is intended in verse 1. This interpretation is similar to that which considers Isaiah 6:8, in using the plural 'we', is designating God and the seraphim. Such views are out of keeping with the rest of biblical revelation in that nowhere is God depicted as deliberating with his creatures to determine a course of action.

1. Judge of Judges (*v. 1*)

God presides in the great assembly; he gives judgment among the 'gods': (*v. 1*). The language is that of the courtroom. God takes his place as judge (cf. Isa. 3:13-14a) in the

---

[1] See the comment on Psalm 58:1 and footnote.

assembly of his people. The word 'assembly' is often used by itself, though some qualifier can be added to make plain the intention (cf. a swarm of bees in Judg. 14:8; a multitude of bulls in Ps. 68:30). Its most frequent use, however, is in the books of Exodus, Leviticus, and Deuteronomy to designate the assembly of God's people. This could be the meaning here, or, alternatively, the 'great assembly' could be just a gathering of judicial officials who are summoned before God. The NIV 'the great assembly' (*ʿᵃdat-ʾēl*) is another passage in which the divine name (here *ʾēl*) is employed as a kind of superlative.[2]

2. The Character of the Judges (*vv. 2-4*)
'How long will you defend the unjust and show partiality to the wicked?' *Selah* (*v.* 2). God now speaks against corrupt judges in a manner often found in the prophetic witness against false judges. Perversion of justice is no new thing. The implication of the question is that it has been practised in the past, and the query is made as to how long it is to continue.

'Defend the cause of the weak and fatherless; maintain the rights of the poor and oppressed. Rescue the weak and needy; deliver them from the hand of the wicked' (*vv.* 3-4). Judges had the responsibility to see to it that the weak and downtrodden had justice administered fairly for them. The most vulnerable and underprivileged group in the community should have been able to expect help (see the comments on Pss. 10:14 and 68:5-6, and cf. Isa. 1:16-17). Just as God was the one who rescued and delivered, so the judges are commanded to imitate him and to free the needy from the power of the wicked. These two verses have symmetry in Hebrew that serves to highlight the message. They begin with a command ('defend the cause', 'deliver'), followed by parallel phrases repeating the word 'weak' (*dal*), and each end with another command ('maintain the rights', 'deliver').[3]

---

[2] For this usage, see the comment on Psalm 36:6 and footnote.
[3] The Heb. phrases are: *shifᵉtû-dal vᵉyâtôm ... hatsdîqû*
pallᵉtû-dal vᵉʾevyôn ... hatstsîlû.

3. The Frailty of Human Rulers (*vv.* 5-7)

'They know nothing, they understand nothing. They walk about in darkness; all the foundations of the earth are shaken' (*v.* 5). God gives a description of human judges. They lack the very qualities that should have been paramount in their work as rulers. Like Solomon, they should have asked for 'a discerning heart' and for the ability 'to distinguish between right and wrong' (1 Kings 3:9).[4] Instead of walking in the light, they themselves were walking in darkness and ignorance. The conclusion of the verse sums up the consequences of all this – the whole moral order is rotten to its roots.

'I said, 'You are 'gods'; you are all sons of the Most High.' But you will die like mere men; you will fall like every other ruler' (*vv.* 6-7). God makes an emphatic declaration concerning the rulers, 'I said, "You [are] gods".' In Hebrew the statement is even more notable because of the alliteration. Each of the four words begins with the letter *alef*, the first letter in the Hebrew alphabet (*ʾanî ʾamartî ʾelohîm ʾattem*). They are occupying an office in which they represent God and therefore are to administer his laws. Hence, they can be called 'gods' and 'sons of the Most High'. Jesus appeals to this verse in John 10:34-36 in his debate with the Jews over their accusation of blasphemy against him. Jesus' argument is of the 'how much more' variety. If the psalm applied this term 'god' to men, how much more may it be applied to one whom the Father set apart and sent into the world (John 10:36)? Verse 7 begins in Hebrew with a word which points to marked contrast – 'on the contrary!' Though called 'gods' the judges are mere men, and like all other rulers they will ultimately die. Though the word for 'man' here is a common one (*'âdâm*), yet the contrast in the verse justifies the translation 'mere men'.

4. An Appeal to the Great Judge (*v.* 8)

Rise up, O God, judge the earth, for all the nations are your inheritance (*v.* 8). The conclusion of the psalm is an appeal by the psalmist for God himself to act as the judge. The psalm that began on the note of God as judge (v. 1) ends on the same

---

[4] The same Heb. verb for 'discern' (*bîn*) is used in both passages.

note. As in other psalms (see 94:1-3; 96:1-6; 98:9) there is the recognition that God is the supreme ruler, and when human rulers fail, the prayer is that God will speedily deliver justice to all. The New Testament assurance is that God 'has set a day when he will judge the world with justice by the man [the Lord Jesus] whom he has appointed' (Acts 17:31). At the last great day, all will appear before the judgment seat of Christ (2 Cor. 5:10).

Psalm 83

A song. A psalm of Asaph.

Even with the explicit references to the enemies in verses 6-8 it is difficult to find an event that matches exactly with the details given in this psalm. The nearest identification appears to be the attack on Judah during the reign of Jehoshaphat as recorded in 2 Chronicles 20. The same nations are in view, with the Edomites, Moabites, and Ammonites as the leaders. According to verses 4 and 12 the intention of the enemies was to destroy Judah, which agrees with 2 Chronicles 20:11. The problem remains, however, of finding a time when *all* these nations were allied together against Judah. The date has to be pre-exilic, as Amalek (v. 7) is never mentioned in the post-exilic literature. The remaining Amalekites were destroyed by the Simeonites (1 Chron. 4:43). Similarly the mention of Assyria points to the same period.

When faced with a powerful coalition of armies, the psalmist prays that the Most High will again demonstrate his saving power. A short prayer begins the psalm (v. 1), followed by a complaint about the many nations that have conspired to blot out the name of Israel forever (vv. 2-8). The final section (vv. 9-18) is an appeal to God for his intervention. He is called 'the Most High' (*ʿelyôn,* verse 18), a divine title used already in the preceding psalm (Ps. 82:6), and thus forming a link between these two songs.

1. A Call for God's Help (*v. 1*)

O God, do not keep silent; be not quiet, O God, be not still (*v. 1*). As far as the people are concerned, their greatest danger does not lie with the enemies. It is that God will remain a silent onlooker in this time of danger and distress. While the appeal to God is put in negative terms, yet the call is for him to speak and to be moved to help. The actual expression 'Do not keep silent' only occurs here and in Isaiah 62:7, though the following one, 'Be not quiet', is frequently used (for examples, see Pss. 28:1; 35:22; 39:12). While these two expressions relate to speech, the final one is a call for action on God's part. The implication is that God cannot remain indifferent to the cry of his people (note v. 3, 'against *your* people').

2. A Complaint about the Enemies (*vv. 2-8*)
See how your enemies are astir, how your foes rear their heads. With cunning they conspire against your people; they plot against those you cherish (*vv. 2-3*). The psalmist calls on God to take notice of what the enemies are doing. 'Rearing the heads' may well be more a description of pride and boldness than conveying the idea of readiness to strike. The use of the word 'cunning' (*sôd*) suggests a secret agreement was reached by the enemies as they plotted their attack. The verb from which the noun comes is used in Psalm 2:2 of crafty plotting by enemies against the LORD's anointed one. The psalmist does not regard them as Judah's enemies, but as God's enemies. Also, he does not call Judah 'my people' but '*your* people', 'those *you* cherish'. His prayer is governed by the Godward direction of his thinking.

'Come,' they say, 'let us destroy them as a nation, that the name of Israel be remembered no more'(*v. 4*). The plan of the enemies is very simple. They just want Israel utterly destroyed as a nation, so that in time to come people will not even recollect that Israel had ever existed. Destruction of the people and possession of their territory (see v. 12) was their aim. The use of the term 'Israel', even though this psalm is from the period when only Judah still existed, is not a problem, as the southern kingdom was the true continuation of the total nation of Israel.

With one mind they plot together; they form an alliance against you – the tents of Edom and the Ishmaelites, of Moab and the Hagrites, Gebal, Ammon and Amalek, Philistia,

with the people of Tyre. Even Assyria has joined them to lend strength to the descendants of Lot. ***Selah*** *(vv. 5-8)*. There is unity among the enemies, and they confirm this by entering into a treaty (the same Hebrew word *b^erit* is used of a treaty as is used elsewhere of the covenant between God and his people). The attack is coming from every quarter. First, the nations on the south and east are mentioned (Edom, Ishmaelites, Moab, and the Hagrites). Then those on the north-west (Gebal), followed by those on the east (Ammon and Amalek), the south-west (the Philistines), and then again those on the north-west (Tyre). The Hagrites were a nomadic tribe living east of Gilead (1 Chron. 5:10). Gebal has often been taken to be the hill country in the north of Edom, but the NIV footnote, which identifies it with the modern Byblos in Lebanon, is more probable. The modern Arabic name for Byblos is Jebail. Even distant Assyria, seemingly just emerging as a major power, has joined the alliance, linking up with distant relatives of Israel, the Moabites and Ammonites, Lot's descendants (see Gen. 19:36-38).

3. Prayer for God's Judgment on the Enemies *(vv. 9-18)*
As he prays for God's judgment on the coalition of forces arrayed against Israel, the psalmist recalls God's great victories in the past, especially in the time of the Judges. He selects two notable battles, the victory over the Canaanites recorded in Judges 4–5 and the victory of Gideon over the Midianites in Judges 7–8. The fact that only the enemy kings are named, not the judges, highlights the fact that God was the deliverer.

Do to them as you did to Midian, as you did to Sisera and Jabin at the river Kishon, who perished at Endor and became like refuse on the ground *(vv. 9-10)*. The prayer is for a similar victory of the Lord to come as when victory over the Midianites was achieved by Gideon (Judg. 7), or when Sisera and Jabin were destroyed (Judg. 4). In the latter passage there is no mention of Endor, yet the location fits the description of Mount Tabor in Judges 4, and Endor was situated at the foot of Mount Tabor. The river Kishon occurs several times in connection with the victory won by Deborah and Barak

(Judg. 4:7, 13; 5:21). The same appeal to this mighty victory of the Lord is made elsewhere in the Old Testament (Isa. 9:4; Hab. 3:7).

Make their nobles like Oreb and Zeeb, all their princes like Zebah and Zalmunna, who said, 'Let us take possession of the pasturelands of God' (*vv. 11-12*). According to Judges 7:25, Oreb and Zeeb were the commanders of the Midianite army, while Zebah and Zalmunna were the kings. The aim of the Midianite attack was to dispossess the Israelites and seize the land of Canaan. The phrase, 'the pasturelands of God', draws attention to Canaan as territory over which God had control, and who had ceded rights over it to Israel. The psalmist prays that the present attackers may suffer the same fate as the Midianite leaders long before.

Make them like tumbleweed, O my God, like chaff before the wind (*v. 13*). The picture is of the tumbleweed (so-called because of its wheel-shaped stem) being driven before the wind.[1] The request is for the divine warrior to chase these enemies in a like manner.

As fire consumes the forest or a flame sets the mountains ablaze, so pursue them with your tempest and terrify them with your storm (*vv. 14-15*). The thought of God's fiery judgment being like a forest blaze is developed further in Isaiah 10:16-19. Here the psalmist joins to it the idea of God bringing the storm clouds of his wrath (see also Ps. 68:4). The word 'tempest' (*sûfâh*) is used elsewhere in the Old Testament for a visible manifestation of God (cf. Job 38:1; 40:6). Here, as in Isaiah 29:6, it is used as a symbol of God's judgment. He relentlessly purses the enemies and out of the thunderstorm he terrifies them.

Cover their faces with shame so that men will seek your name, O LORD (*v. 16*). The request here is for the enemies to be shown their true place and position in God's sight. The word for 'shame' (*qâlôn*) is a poetic word that often stands as the opposite of 'honour'. The request is for something more

---

[1] The word for 'tumbleweed' (*galgal*) comes from the Heb. root *g-l-l* that means 'to turn'. Other words from this root include 'wheel' (*galgal*) and Gilgal (*gilgâl*), the site of a stone circle, the name of several sites in Palestine (see *DCH*, II, p. 348).

than simply degrading enemies before God and men. Rather, the aim is that they will then come to seek God for themselves.

May they ever be ashamed and dismayed; may they perish in disgrace. Let them know that you, whose name is the LORD – that you alone are the Most High over all the earth (*vv. 17-18*). The shame and disgrace that the psalmist seeks for the enemies is not inward feelings but outward position and standing. The aim of this judicial dealing with the enemies is that they will be brought to an acknowledgment of the sovereignty of God over the whole world. This is parallel to King Hezekiah's request that God would save Judah from the hand of Sennacherib 'so that all kingdoms on earth may know that you, alone, O LORD, are God' (Isa. 37:16). In the midst of a call to judgment, the psalmist is thinking of the enemies being constrained to 'know' God just as his people do. He wants the display of God's justice to end in conversion of Israel's (and God's) enemies.

Psalm 84

For the director of music. According to gittith.
Of the Sons of Korah. A psalm.

The general mood of this psalm is closest to the longing for God's presence expressed in Psalms 42–43. No exact date can be placed on it, but the reference to the king in verse 9 ('your anointed one') suggests a date prior to the exile. There is no reason, however, to link it explicitly with David's life. The use of the term '*gittith*' also occurs in the titles of Psalms 8 and 81 (for comment on the term, see the introductory comments on Ps. 8).

This song seems to have been used in connection with a pilgrimage to Jerusalem, most probably the Feast of Tabernacles (see the reference to 'autumn rains' in verse 6). It may well have been composed by a priest who lived far away from the sanctuary, but used by pilgrims to Jerusalem as they came to the entry of the temple. There they would sing of their intense desire to be in the LORD's house, and of the blessing on those who constantly worship at the sanctuary.

This psalm is the first of the second group of psalms that are attributed to the sons of Korah (Pss. 84; 85; 87; 88). In David's time the sons of Korah were among those whom he put in charge of the music of the sanctuary (1 Chron. 6:31-48).

1. Longing for God's House (*vv. 1-4*)

How lovely is your dwelling place, O LORD Almighty! My soul yearns, even faints, for the courts of the LORD; my heart and my flesh cry out for the living God (*vv. 1-2*). The word 'lovely' normally means 'loved', but perhaps both ideas are involved: 'How loved and lovely is your dwelling place!' The term 'dwelling place' is commonly used of the tabernacle, but here the plural is used (lit. 'your dwelling places'). This aligns with the same usage in Psalm 43:3. Perhaps the plural has in mind the various parts of the temple. In this psalm a variety of other terms are used to refer to the building in question: 'courts of the LORD' (v. 2); 'your house' (v. 4); 'your courts'; and 'the house of my God' (v. 10). It is best to take the references as being to the temple. The psalmist is spiritually hungry for the presence of God, so that his intense desire makes him grow pale and it consumes him. His whole being ('heart' and 'flesh') sings for joy to the living God (cf. the same term in Ps. 42:2), who is also the mighty LORD of hosts.

Even the sparrow has found a home, and the swallow a nest for herself, where she may have her young – a place near your altar, O LORD Almighty, my King and my God (*v. 3*). The psalmist even envies the small birds that have been able to get so near to the altar. They have found a snug home for themselves in the sanctuary of God. This is where he longs to be also. The NIV translation is rather free in the middle of the verse. The NRSV is preferable: 'Even the sparrow finds a home, and the swallow a nest for herself, where she may lay her young, at your altars, O LORD of hosts, my King and my God.' The impassioned nature of the plea is elevated further by the fact that only one verb appears in verse 3 ('she may set'). The description of the altar is followed by a cluster of terms that describe the great God whose altar it is, and the God with whom the psalmist is in such a personal relationship ('*my* King', '*my* God').

Blessed are those who dwell in your house; they are ever praising you. *Selah* (*v. 4*). Those who spiritually make God's presence their dwelling place know his favour and blessing. 'Dwell' has the idea of constantly abiding somewhere (cf. its use in Pss. 15:1; 23:6; and 61:4). Those who know what it is to abide with God, praise him for all the blessings he gives. 'Selah' marks the end of the first section of the psalm.

2. Blessed Pilgrims (*vv. 5-7*)

Blessed are those whose strength is in you, who have set their hearts on pilgrimage (*v. 5*). How happy are those who have found that the LORD is their deliverer, and who want to go on a pilgrimage to Jerusalem! 'Set their hearts on' is literally 'in whose hearts are [the] highways', i.e. the pathways which led to Zion. The devout Israelites were always thinking about going up to the festive occasions.[1]

As they pass through the Valley of Baca, they make it a place of springs; the autumn rains also cover it with pools. They go from strength to strength, till each appears before God in Zion (*vv. 6-7*). The picture is of a wilderness journey which becomes a place of springs (or, as in NIV footnote, 'blessings').[2] 'Baca' is unknown as a locality in Israel, so it may just be used to denote dry and difficult territory (it may possibly mean 'weeping').[3] It is possible that there is a play on the two meanings, so that the Valley of Baca (the dry place) becomes the Valley of Baca (the place of weeping).[4] The experiences of the pilgrims resemble the provision God made in the wilderness for his people as they journeyed to Canaan (Deut. 8:1-20; Pss. 78:15-16; 114:8). In spite of the hardships on the way, the pilgrims find that God abundantly meets their needs until, with increasing strength, they reach their destination.

3. A Prayer for the King (*vv. 8-9*)

Hear my prayer, O LORD God Almighty; listen to me, O God of Jacob. *Selah* (*v. 8*). No hint is given of the situation that calls forth this prayer. Some tragedy has struck the people and the

---

[1] As the English translations show, the expression 'in whose hearts are [the] highways (*m^esillôt*)' can have several different interpretations. 'Highways' comes from the root *s-l-l* that means 'to raise up', and it is used both of building roads and ramps (cf. the comments on Ps. 68:5). M. Dahood, *Psalms II: 51–100*, p. 281, considers that the word can mean 'high praise' ('your extolments'). This explanation is also listed in *DCH*, V, p. 366, though very tentatively. It is doubtful if this one occurrence carries a different meaning from the other appearances of the word.

[2] Two Heb. words, 'blessing' and 'pond, pool', share the same vowels, but differ in vocalisation ('blessing', *b^erâkâh*; 'pond', *b^erêkâh*). Here the plural form (*b^erâkôt*) seems to point to the word being 'blessings'.

[3] The words Baca and the verb 'to weep' share the same consonants, but the consonants differ in that Baca ends in an *alef* (Baca, *bâkâ'*), while 'to weep' ends in *hê* (*bâkâh*).

[4] So Marvin Tate, *Psalms 51-100*, pp. 353-54.

psalmist addresses the great God who is able to deliver, just as he delivered Jacob of old. The expression 'God of Jacob' is common in the Psalms (see 20:1; 24:6 [in an abbreviated form]; 46:7, 11; 75:9; 76:6; 81:1). The appeals used here ('hear my prayer' and 'listen to me') are frequent in the Psalms and are often used in conjunction (cf. 143:1).

Look upon our shield, O God; look with favour on your anointed one (*v. 9*). God himself is the shield of his people (see v. 11), just as he proclaimed himself long before to Abraham (Gen. 15:1). The same expression is also applied to the king, who as the LORD's 'anointed one' is also the 'shield' (Heb., *magên*) or protector of the people.[5] In Carthage in North Africa a related Semitic word was used of the generals (*mâgôn*), translated into Latin as *imperator (leader, commander)*. The king was to be to the people what God promised of himself.

4. The Source of Blessing (*vv. 10-11*)

Better is one day in your courts than a thousand elsewhere; I would rather be a doorkeeper in the house of my God than dwell in the tents of the wicked (*v. 10*). The psalmist traces the source of blessing to its true fountain. He considers *one* day spent in God's presence as better than *a thousand* elsewhere. The second part of the verse expands the thought and gives a variation on the same idea. The word 'doorkeeper' (*histôfêf*) suggests too strongly the thought of being an official servant at the temple. The Hebrew word occurs only here in the Old Testament, and it merely indicates 'standing or lying at the threshold'. To be on the very fringe of the temple was far better than any secure dwelling among the wicked.

For the LORD God is a sun and shield; the LORD bestows favour and honour; no good thing does he withhold from those whose walk is blameless (*v. 11*). The opening word ('for') places emphasis on what follows ('*truly*, the LORD God …'). Nowhere else in the Old Testament is God called directly a 'sun'. It seems to be similar to calling him a 'light' (Ps. 27:1). He is both the source of happiness and joy for his people, as well as being their protector ('shield'). Moreover, he gives

---

[5] Cf. the use of the expression 'shield' in Psalms 3:3 and 5:12.

abundantly to those who are upright in their lives, bestowing saving mercy on them (Heb. 'grace and glory', *chên v^e^kâvôd;* NIV 'favour').

5. Concluding Blessing (*v. 12*).

O LORD Almighty, blessed is the man who trusts in you (*v. 12*). The final blessing of the psalm (for the others, see vv. 4 and 5) announces the good news that anyone who trusts in the LORD will be blessed by him. A similar expression occurs in Psalm 40:4. With this concluding statement the psalm ties together its whole content, and it reinforces the point that true blessing belongs only to those who have committed themselves in believing trust to the LORD.

Psalm 85

For the director of music. Of the Sons of Korah. A psalm.

In this communal lament there is no precise indication of the occasion that prompted it. The absence of references to the king and temple suggest that it comes from the period of the return from exile. If that is so, then the reference in verse 12 may well be to the drought that God brought on his people in the time of Haggai (Hag. 1:5-11). The key ideas in the psalm are shown by the repetition of words which relate to the covenantal relationship: *return/restore* (Heb. verb *shûv* in vv. 1, 3, 4, 6, 8); the covenant terms *peace* (*shâlôm* in v. 8), *unfailing love* (*chésed* in v. 10), *faithfulness* (*'ᵉmet* in vv. 10-11), and *righteousness* (*tsédek* vv. 11 and 12); *land* (*'érets* in vv. 1 and 12); *saviour/salvation* (*yéshaʿ*) (vv. 4, 7, 9). The reference to 'land' is significant. Not only does the psalmist say that it is God's land ('*your* land', v. 1), but he also claims it for the restored community as well ('*our* land', v. 12). These were not mutually exclusive assertions, for God gave Canaan to his 'son' Israel as an inheritance (Deut. 15:4; 25:19).[1]

1. A Confession of Faith (*vv. 1-3*)

You showed favour to your land, O Lord; you restored the fortunes of Jacob. You forgave the iniquity of your people and covered all their sins. *Selah* (*vv. 1-2*). The psalmist recalls God's graciousness to his people and land in the past. The expression 'restore the fortunes' can also be translated 'bring back from captivity' (see NIV text and notes on Jer. 29:14 and

[1] I have discussed the concept of 'land' in the Old Testament in my commentary on Deuteronomy in the Focus series: *Deuteronomy: The Commands of a Covenant God*, (Fearn: Christian Focus, 2007), pp. 15-24.

Ps. 126:1).[2] God had heard and answered the urgent prayers of the people in exile, typified by Daniel's staccato pleas: 'O Lord, listen! O Lord, forgive! O Lord, hear and act! For your sake, O my God, do not delay, because your city and your people bear your Name' (Dan. 9:19). The reference to Jacob is an alternative way of describing the nation of Israel. The psalmist uses common expressions (cf. the almost identical ones in Ps. 32:1) to describe the reality of forgiveness.

You set aside all your wrath and turned from your fierce anger (v. 3). God had made it plain that he was angry with his people for all their sins, and so he sent them into exile (see 2 Kings 17: 18; 2 Chron. 36:16-21). Now the psalmist rejoices in the fact that this righteous anger has been replaced by tender favour. The verb 'set aside' (*'âsaf*) is used quite often in the sense of removing or taking something away.[3] Proof of God's forgiveness was seen in the return from exile, as Israel's sin had been paid for (Isa. 40:2).

2. A Cry for Salvation (*vv. 4-7*)

Restore us again, O God our Saviour, and put away your displeasure toward us (*v. 4*). It is the immediate situation that the psalmist now brings into focus. Since God was merciful before, the psalmist seeks a fresh demonstration of God's mercy towards the people in their present need. The way in which the prayer is expressed implies confession of sin as the psalmist pleads for a removal of God's wrath. No great difference can be discerned between 'displeasure' (*ka'as*) and the word 'wrath' (*'af*) in the previous verse.

Will you be angry with us forever? Will you prolong your anger through all generations? Will you not revive us again, that your people may rejoice in you? (*vv. 5-6*). Similar requests are found in other psalms (see 79:5; 80:4; 89:46) as the people long for the cessation of God's wrath. From the latter part of this

---

[2] Contexts in which this expression is used demand something more to be understood than just a change in fortune. As in Psalm 126:1, the psalmist here is appealing to the objective actions of God, and hence a translation like 'You restored the captivity of Jacob' is needed. See my discussion on the expression in 'The Setting and Interpretation of Psalm 126', *RTR* 44, 3 (1985), pp. 74-80.

[3] The range of objects with this verb when it means 'take away', 'remove', is set out in *DCH*, I, p. 347.

psalm there is no doubt that the psalmist knew that this anger was not going to be displayed forever against the people. A time was coming when God's favour would be upon them, and then the people would be glad in the LORD. The word 'revive' (*châyâh*, Pi.) may have connotations for us that the Hebrew verb does not suggest. The meaning is close to 'preserve alive', 'maintain life'.

Show us your unfailing love, O LORD, and grant us your salvation (*v. 7*). What the psalmist wants is a fresh display of covenantal love (Heb., *chésed*), which is equated here with 'salvation' (*yêsha*ʿ). His appeal in verse 4 was to the 'Saviour' (lit. 'the God of my salvation', *ʾelohê yishʿênû*). Now he looks for 'salvation' from him in the sense of deliverance from the present troubles.

3. God's Word to His People (*vv. 8-13*)

I will listen to what God the LORD will say; he promises peace to his people, his saints – but let them not return to folly (*v. 8*). Here is the confidence for the future. The psalmist knows that God's word for his people is one of 'peace'. Perhaps the Aaronic blessing is in mind (Num. 6:22-26) with its assurance of peace. The promise of peace is renewed in a special way in the gospel, for Jesus, who is our peace (Eph. 2:14), is able to give his own lasting peace to his followers (John 14:27). It is in this way that peace and mercy flow to the Israel of God (Gal. 6:16). The accompanying warning given here is still applicable. Possession of God's peace is dependent upon not straying from his ways and returning to folly (cf. John 14:26-27; Matt. 28:20).

Surely his salvation is near those who fear him, that his glory may dwell in our land (*v. 9*). This verse puts in another way what has just been said in the previous verse. The psalmist had earlier asked for God's salvation (v. 7), and now he affirms the truth that those who fear the LORD, 'his saints', indeed experience God's saving power. Through Isaiah God had promised that his salvation would draw near to his people (Isa. 46:13; 51:5). Just as the glory of the LORD had dwelt on Mount Sinai (Exod. 24:16-17), so it would take up abiding residence in the land.

Love and faithfulness meet together; righteousness and peace kiss each other. Faithfulness springs forth from the

earth, and righteousness looks down from heaven (*vv. 10-11*). The psalmist personifies God's favour to his people, and he presents a picture of 'love', 'faithfulness', 'righteousness', and 'peace' meeting and embracing one another. The combination of 'love' and 'faithfulness' (*rav-chésed v*[e]*'emet*) goes back to God's self-revelation in Exodus 34:6, where he declared himself as 'abounding in love and faithfulness'. It is because God's faithfulness manifests itself in salvation that it is often linked with 'love', and also because these two attributes of God lead to peace with him, it is expressly associated with his peace (cf. *shâlôm ve'*[e]*met,* Isa. 39:8; Jer. 33:6). 'Faithfulness' (*'emet*) springs up like a flourishing plant, while 'righteousness' (*tsédek*) oversees affairs among men (cf. similar ideas in Isa. 45:8). These four blessings are essential aspects of God's kingdom. Paul confirms this when he says that 'the kingdom of God is not a matter of eating and drinking, but of righteousness, peace, and joy in the Holy Spirit' (Rom. 14:17). Likewise, he reinforces the general point of the psalmist's declaration by saying of God: 'If we are faithless, he will remain faithful, for he cannot disown himself' (2 Tim. 2:13).

The LORD will indeed give what is good, and our land will yield its harvest. Righteousness goes before him and prepares the way for his steps (*vv. 12-13*). If the LORD brought an end to the drought, then the land would again produce bountiful crops. Renewed tokens of his favour would show the abiding nature of his love.

> All good gifts around us
> are sent from heaven above;
> Then thank the Lord, O thank the Lord,
> for all his love.
> (Mathius Claudius 1740-1815)

Righteousness is regarded as a person who goes before the LORD and prepares for his intervention on behalf of his people. The coming of the LORD is often pictured as being preceded by preparation (Isa. 40:3-5; Mal. 3:1; Matt. 3:1-12). Here the messenger going before him is his saving righteousness. The victory of the LORD will be followed by his coming in glory (see v. 9).

Psalm 86

A prayer of David.

In Book Three of the Psalter this is the only psalm attributed to David. The term 'servant' (*'eved*), used both at the beginning (v. 2) and the end of the psalm (v. 16), points to the royal status of David who was called by God 'my servant' (2 Sam. 7:5; see also this description used of him in the title of Ps. 18). The nature of the distress that lies behind this plea is not stated. It could be the plotting of those within his kingdom, or else nations surrounding Israel who seek his downfall.

The psalm is composed in a symmetrical manner. It has five stanzas, with the first and last having four verses, and the others each having three verses. It opens with a request, 'Hear, O LORD, and answer me' (v. 1) and ends with another request, 'Give me a sign of your goodness' (v. 17). The other remarkable feature of Psalm 86 is that every verse is an echo of another part of the Old Testament. Well-known Scripture has been moulded into a new song. Memorised Bible passages should always be a basis for private and corporate prayer.

1. A Servant's Prayer (*vv. 1-4*)

Hear, O LORD, and answer me, for I am poor and needy (*v. 1*). While the phrase 'poor and needy' is a common one (Pss. 35:10; 37:14; 109:16, 22), yet its use here stems from a sense of great urgency. The psalmist's condition is the basis of his request,[1] and the combined phrase appears most often, as here, in an appeal from an individual. He confesses his deep personal need

[1] 'For' represents the Heb. particle *kî* that occurs nine times throughout this psalm (vv. 1, 2, 3, 4, 5, 7, 10, 13, and 17, all which the NIV translates except for the one at the commencement of v. 5).

(cf. the words of Ps. 40:17 = Ps. 70:5), and asks his sovereign LORD to listen to his plea. The unusual place for the pronoun 'I' (*'ânî*) at the very end of the verse in the MT serves to draw further attention to the pitiable condition of the petitioner.

Guard my life, for I am devoted to you. You are my God; save your servant who trusts in you (*v. 2*). The appeal is based on a relationship between the psalmist and his God. He is a servant who has a covenantal commitment to his master. The phrase 'devoted to you' (Heb. *châsîd*) is translated in the NIV by a variety of expressions: 'godly' (Pss. 4:3; 12:1); 'saints' (Pss. 30:4; 52:9; 79:2); 'consecrated ones' (Ps. 50:5); 'faithful people' (Ps. 89:19). The variety of expression is needed in English, but in all the contexts the focus is on devotion to the covenantal God. The psalmist makes that profession,[2] and in acknowledging also that he is God's servant, he appeals for protection. The NIV smoothes over the word order in the second part of the verse, and though it has often been suggested that the words 'You are my God' should be transferred to the beginning of the next verse (cf. the NRSV), no manuscript evidence supports this.[3]

Have mercy on me, O Lord, for I call to you all day long. Bring joy to your servant, for to you, O Lord, I lift up my soul (*vv. 3-4*). He pleads for mercy (cf. Ps. 57:1) and indicates how constantly his approach is being made to his God. The opposite of sorrow is joy, and so he asks that God will make his servant rejoice as his prayer is answered. 'To lift up the soul' is a synonym for praying to God (Pss. 25:1; 143:8).

---

[2] The phrase 'for I am devoted to you' has exactly the same word order as 'for I am poor and needy' in verse 1, in that the pronoun 'I' comes at the end of the clause. Cf. the word order and how this draws attention to the condition/status of the psalmist: *kî 'ânî v^e'evyôn 'ânî* ('for poor and needy [am] I'; *kî châsîd'ânî* ('for devoted to you [am] I').

[3] The lit. rendering is 'Save your servant – you are my God – the one trusting in you'. The difficulty is the position of the central affirmation. It certainly puts into juxtaposition the relationship of servant/God, but breaks up the sequence of thought. This is a case of interrupted syntax that is found elsewhere as well. See Psalm 87:4. The ESV translation is good: 'Save your servant who trusts in you. You are my God'. Alternatively, Marvin Tate's translation works on the premise that the verb 'Save' applies to both clauses: 'Save your servant, O You my god, (save) this one who trusts in you' (see Marvin Tate, *Psalms 51-100*, p. 374).

2. A Gracious God *(vv. 5-7)*

You are forgiving and good, O Lord, abounding in love to all who call to you (*v. 5*). In this next section, like so many other Old Testament passages, the language of Exodus 34:6-7 is clearly behind the words used by the psalmist. The reason why the psalmist can approach God so confidently, '*for* (*kî*) you are good and forgiving', is knowledge of God's own self-revelation.[4] The verb translated 'forgiving' is only used in the Old Testament with God as the subject. He is able to blot out sin, and all who call upon him in their sinfulness and need find him 'abounding in love' (Heb. *rav chésed*), a phrase based on Exodus 34:6 (cf. its use again in v. 15, and in Ps. 103:8).

Hear my prayer, O LORD; listen to my cry for mercy. In the day of my trouble I will call to you, for you will answer me (*vv. 6-7*). With confidence the psalmist approaches a merciful God with his plea for mercy. The word '[cry for] mercy' (*tach^{a}nûn*) comes from a verb (*chânan*), and in the Book of Psalms it normally appears, as here, with the word for 'voice' or 'cry' (*qôl*; cf. 28:2; 31:22; 116:1; 130:2; 140:6).[5] The form of the noun here is plural (*tach^{a}nûnôt*), this being the only time this form occurs. Its rarity suggests that it has been used deliberately to emphasise either the repeated nature of the pleas or the entreaties coming from a position of weakness.[6] Such a supplication is an expression of a loyal servant's trust in his Lord. The day of his trouble is the present distress he is experiencing, and he knows that in such a situation he must call for help. He is also assured that out of his love and mercy God will answer his prayer.

3. The Only God *(vv. 8-10)*

Among the gods there is none like you, O Lord; no deeds can compare with yours (*v. 8*). The Old Testament repeatedly makes

[4] The NIV omits the translation of *kî* ('for') and also inexplicably reverses the order of the words 'good and forgiving'. Almost all other versions retain the word order of the MT. The earlier printings of the NIV had the correct order but instead of 'good' had 'kind': 'You are kind and forgiving, O Lord.'

[5] *Chânan* in the Qal means 'be gracious', and in the Hifil 'plead for grace'.

[6] This is the explanation given by E. W. Hengstenberg, *Commentary on the Psalms*, III, p. 105. Delitzsch also takes note of the plural form and translates the phrase by 'importunate supplications'. See his *Psalms*, (Edinburgh: T. & T. Clark, 1874), III, p. 13.

exclusive claims regarding God. This one is an echo of passages such as Exodus 15:11, Deuteronomy 3:24, and Psalm 35:10. The living God is vastly different from the dead idols that the surrounding nations worshipped (Ps. 115:5-7). The New Testament reaffirms that people must turn from 'worthless things to the living God, who made heaven and earth and sea and everything in them' (Acts 14:15; see also 1 Thess. 1:9 and Heb. 9:14).

All the nations you have made will come and worship before you, O Lord; they will bring glory to your name (*v. 9*). From the preceding statement of the uniqueness of God, the psalmist draws the conclusion that all the nations will come and worship him. This is part of the eschatological vision of the Old Testament, and the closest parallel to it elsewhere in the Bible is Revelation 15:4. In both passages the thought of the uniqueness of the living God leads on to a declaration that the nations are going to bow in submission before him. The thought of bringing glory to God's name occurs also in Psalm 96:8 with the call to 'ascribe to the LORD the glory due to his name'.

For you are great and do marvellous deeds; you alone are God (*v. 10*). Extolling the greatness of God is another way of stressing his uniqueness. Moreover, he does things that no one else can do (cf. the comments on Pss. 71:17 and 72:18), for he works wonders (NIV 'marvellous deeds'). This is because these acts are not within human power. They are demonstrations of divine power. The expression 'do marvellous deeds' (*ʿôseh niflâʾôt*) is a standard one to describe God's exclusive activities in creation and redemption,[7] while the combination of the assertion of God's greatness and his ability to perform superhuman acts is also a regular occurrence (cf. in addition to this passage Pss. 96:3-4; 106:21-22; and Neh. 9:17). The bold declaration, 'You are God alone', is parallel in meaning to 2 Kings 19:15, 19//Isaiah 37:16, 20, Nehemiah 9:6, and Psalm 83:18.[8] The language used in verses 8-10 was part of the liturgy of praise in Israel.

---

[7] The conjunction of the verb 'do' (*ʿâsâh*) and either *péleʾ* or *niflâʾôt* occurs many times in the Psalter. Cf. 40:5; 72:18; 78:4, 12; 86:10; 98:1; 105:5; 136:4.

[8] The nearest parallel is 2 Kings 19:15//Isaiah 37:16. Cf. *ʾâttâh-hûʾ hâʾᵉlohîm lᵉvadᵉkâ* in these passages as compared with *ʾâttâh ʾᵉlohîm lᵉvadᵉkâ* here.

4. A Prayer of Thanksgiving (*vv. 11-13*)

Teach me your way, O LORD, and I will walk in your truth; give me an undivided heart, that I may fear your name (*v. 11*). The psalmist wants further instruction from the LORD, and gives a commitment to continue to be guided by his truth. The opening words are identical with Psalm 27:11, while the thought of walking in truth is very close to Psalm 26:3. Psalm 25:4-5 is another passage that contains the same concepts. 'An undivided heart' indicates complete loyalty, and leads a person to revere God's character.

I will praise you, O Lord my God, with all my heart; I will glorify your name forever. For great is your love toward me; you have delivered me from the depths of the grave (*vv. 12-13*). As part of his commitment the psalmist pledges himself to praise God with singleness of heart. There is no apparent difference here between 'praise' and 'glorify'. What has been said about the nations (v. 9) is now taken up in a personal way, with the pronouns emphasising both the experience of God's love and the responsive heart that wants to praise him (cf. '*I* will praise'; 'with all *my* heart'; '*I* will glorify'; 'love toward *me*'; 'you have delivered *me*'). The first part of verse 12 is practically the same as Psalm 9:1, while the opening part of verse 13 appears elsewhere in the Book of Psalms (cf. 57:10; 108:4). The psalmist has been brought to death's door,[9] but God's deliverance of him becomes the subject of his praise.

5. The Prayer Renewed (*vv. 14-17*)

The closing verses of the psalm return to the theme of its opening, and the petition is renewed for God's intervention in a dangerous situation. **The arrogant are attacking me, O God; a band of ruthless men seeks my life – men without regard for you** (*v. 14*). The only description of the enemies is that given in this verse, and it is so general that they cannot be identified with any certainty. The word 'arrogant' (*zêdîm*) is used of people who proudly go their rebellious and wilful ways. They are a group of men who cause terror and seek innocent lives, without giving thought to

---

[9] The MT has 'the deepest she'ol'. For a note on *sh^{e}'ol* see the comments on Psalm 6:4, and footnote.

God and his demands. This is expressed in the MT by the words, 'And the congregation of the arrogant seek my life and they do not set you before them.' The positive expression using this same idiom is found in Psalm 16:8: 'I have set the LORD always before me.' The whole verse is very nearly the same as Psalm 54:3.

But you, O Lord, are a compassionate and gracious God, slow to anger, abounding in love and faithfulness (*v. 15*). These words echo verse 5, but once more it is the declaration of Exodus 34:6 that lies behind the psalmist's words. No greater appeal could be made in proclaiming the character of God than to use the very words that God used of himself. They seem to have had a place in the hearts and language of Old Testament believers as a kind of credal statement (Num. 14:18; 2 Chron. 30:9; Neh. 9:17; Pss. 103:8; 111:4; 116:5; Joel 2:13; Jonah 4:2).

Turn to me and have mercy on me; grant your strength to your servant and save the son of your maidservant. Give me a sign of your goodness, that my enemies may see it and be put to shame, for you, O LORD, have helped me and comforted me (*vv. 16-17*). The urgent need of the psalmist is for God's compassion to be shown to him. He confesses his relationship with his God – he is a servant, the son of a female servant, and therefore bound in perpetual service to his master.[10] The language of servanthood is used in both Old and New Testaments to denote the bond between a devout believer and the Lord (for the New Testament see the opening of Paul's letters [Rom. 1:1; Phil. 1:1; Titus 1:1] and passages such as Eph. 6:6 and 2 Tim. 2:24). The final request is for the LORD to be victorious over his and the psalmist's enemies. The LORD's goodness will be shown by relieving his distress and bringing him deliverance. He wants this proof of God's goodness to him, 'a sign' that all will be well. The contrast between the opening and the close of the psalm is most emphatic – 'I', 'I', 'I' (vv. 1-2); 'you', 'you' (vv. 15, 17). The plaintive repetition of 'I' gives way to declaration and appeal to God himself.

---

[10] The NIV marginal note, 'save your faithful son', depends upon following Mitchell Dahood's revocalisation of the last word of verse 16 from *'âmâh*, 'female servant', to *'emet*, 'true', 'reliable'. It is stretching the argument somewhat to claim that this is in keeping with the stress on fidelity back in verse 11. The earliest translation, the LXX, renders it 'Save the son of your handmaid'. Dahood's view is found in his *Psalms II: 51-100*, p. 296.

Psalm 87

Of the Sons of Korah. A psalm. A song.

While this psalm has much in common with other songs relating to Zion (see Pss. 46; 48; 76; 125; 129; and 137), yet it goes beyond them in picturing inhabitants of Gentile nations being incorporated among the citizens of Zion. This could be understood as a widespread conversion of people from the nations mentioned in the Psalm, who were representative of those nations long hostile to Israel. However, it can also be understood as a declaration of God to these nations (see NIV footnote, verse 4) that he has recorded the names of all his people – 'those who acknowledge me' – wherever they may be and he regards them as belonging to Zion.

The teaching of this psalm has its parallels in prophetic passages that also depict a conversion of Gentiles, sometimes giving the picture of their pilgrimage to Jerusalem (Isa. 2:2-4; Micah 4:1-5).[1] The earlier prophets speak of restoration; the later prophets speak of hope for the future. Psalms such as this share this expectation and have a global horizon.

1. Praise of Zion (*vv. 1-3*)

He has set his foundation on the holy mountain; the LORD loves the gates of Zion more than all the dwellings of Jacob (*vv. 1-2*). The Old Testament asserts that the choice of Zion (i.e. Jerusalem) was made by God (Ps. 132:13; Isa. 14:32). That is why it was called 'the city of the LORD Almighty' (Ps. 48:8). This choice of Jerusalem was an expression of the LORD's love, and consequently Zion was preferred more than any other

[1] I have discussed this passage in my commentary, *Isaiah: A Covenant to be Kept for the Sake of the Church,* (Fearn: Christian Focus, 2005), pp. 47-48.

town. As the MT has '*hills* of holiness' (*harrê qodesh*) it is best to retain this in translation, even though it seems practically equivalent to the singular, 'hill of holiness' (Ps. 15:1; Isa. 27:13; Zech. 8:3). If the plural has wider significance it would be to the fact that Zion is just one of the mountains in the vicinity of Jerusalem. 'Jacob' is used here as a synonym for Israel, as it was the name by which Israel was earlier known (Gen. 32:28).

Glorious things are said of you, O city of God: ***Selah*** (*v. 3*). The psalmist has heard or read statements of others about Zion, and in this psalm he summarises these 'glorious things'.[2] The expression 'of you' is ambiguous in Hebrew, as it could also be translated 'in you'. If that rendering is preferred, the meaning will be that in Zion itself prophecies concerning Zion are uttered. 'The city of God' is the location as well as the theme of prophetic announcements.

2. Enrolled in Zion (*vv. 4-6*)

I will record Rahab and Babylon among those who acknowledge me – Philistia too, and Tyre, along with Cush – and I will say, 'This one was born in Zion' (*v. 4*). It is probably best to take the places mentioned as being directly addressed by God ('I will record [you] O Rahab, O Babylon').[3] God acknowledges that he has his own people in all the Gentile nations near to Israel, with the nations mentioned being representative of the wider Gentile world. 'Rahab' is a poetic name for Egypt (Isa. 30:7; 51:9), and comes from a Hebrew root that means 'to behave proudly'.[4] Among these nations God has his own people who are regarded as if they were born in Zion. A clear link exists between the thought here and

---

[2] The syntax is unusual as the plural subject, 'glorious things' (*nikbâdôt*), is followed by a singular verb, 'is spoken' (*m*[e]*dubbar*), though other similar examples can be cited. Cf. Psalms 66:3 and 119:137 and Isaiah 16:8. Probably the 'glorious things' are reckoned as a single entity.

[3] This is a case of interrupted Heb. syntax. Cf. Psalm 86:2 for another example. The opening verb (*zâkar*, Hi.) is causative, 'I will cause to remember', or, 'I will mention'. The NIV translators have added the words, 'I will say', to smooth out the syntax, but they are not represented in the MT.

[4] No connection exists between Rahab here and Rahab the harlot in Joshua 2, as the spelling, though the same in English, is different in Heb.

what is expressed in the previous psalm regarding the nations coming to bow to the Lord (Ps. 86:9).

Indeed, of Zion it will be said, 'This one and that one were born in her, and the Most High himself will establish her.' The LORD will write in the register of the peoples: 'This one was born in Zion.' ***Selah*** (*vv.* 5-6). No matter where true believers live, they are regarded as being enrolled among the citizens of Zion, the city that God sustains (Ps. 48:8).[5] The idea of a register or book is simply a way of saying that God knows those who are his and not one of them will perish (see, for the Old Testament, Exod. 32:32 and Pss. 69:28 and 139:16; for the New Testament, Rev. 17:8 and 21:27). Not only has God chosen Zion, but he will sustain her as well. This same teaching is found in Psalms 46:5 and 48:8, where the verb in the latter ('establish her', *y^ekônnehâ*) is identical with that here. These verses may well contain a note of warning to the nations too. If God has noted who his people truly are, then he will hold accountable those who harm them (cf. Isa. 14:28-32).

As they make music they will sing, 'All my fountains are in you' (*v.* 7). This verse is separated off from the earlier verses by the 'Selah' that comes at the close of verse 6. It brings the psalm to an abrupt conclusion, and with terse brevity that makes interpretation difficult.[6] It is unclear who are the singer(s), and who is referred to by the words 'in you'.[7] In the context it is best to accept that this is a description of the great

---

[5] 'This one and that one' is a translation of the Heb. 'man and man' (*'îsh v^e'îsh*), a Heb. way of using the same two singular nouns to express diversity. This usage is noted in *IBHS*, p. 116.

[6] A. F. Kirkpatrick, *The Book of Psalms*, p. 523, even wondered whether this verse was 'a liturgical direction to sing the anthem, "All my fountains are in thee" at the end of the psalm, as an expression of the joy of Zion's citizens.' A. Cohen, *The Psalms*, p. 284 comes close to this with his suggestion that 'All my fountains are in you' may be 'the opening words of a song'.

[7] For fuller discussion of the difficulties and proposed solutions, see Marvin Tate, *Psalms 51-100*, p. 387, and T. Booij, 'Some Observations on Psalm lxxxvii', *VT* 37 (1987), pp. 16-25. The LXX is completely different: 'How delighted will all those be whose dwelling is with you!' It conveys the thought of feeling at home with God, but it cannot be matched up with the MT. Aquila, followed by the Vulgate, translates the MT.

crowd of enrolled citizens of Zion rejoicing in the fact that their source of salvation is in Zion and especially in Zion's God. The whole community of believers is looked on as a unified group ('*my* fountains'). Irrespective of their country of origin they have found that salvation flows from God's fountain (cf. Ps. 36:9 and Isa. 12:3). When John Newton (1725-1807) wrote the hymn 'Glorious things of thee are spoken, Zion city of our God', he rightly saw the ingathering of Gentiles in gospel times foreshadowed in this psalm. Christians today can say with him:

> Saviour, if of Zion's city
> I, through grace, a member am,
> Let the world deride or pity,
> I will glory in Thy name.
> Fading is the worldling's pleasure,
> All his boasted pomp and show;
> Solid joys and lasting treasure
> None but Zion's children know.

Psalm 88

A song. A psalm of the Sons of Korah. For the director of music. According to mahalath leannoth. A maskil of Heman the Ezrahite.

This is probably the saddest song in the whole of the Psalter, even sadder in the Hebrew text than in English because it ends with the word 'darkness' (*machshâk*).[1] It could be an individual appeal for help, or else a communal one from the time of the exile. The Aramaic Targum and also the Syriac version indicate that this is how their translators understood the content of the psalm. The title is unusual, for the first part is a mirror of that prefixed to Psalm 87, while the second part seems to be the title of the tune (*mâch*^{a}*lat l*^{eʿ}*annot*) with an ascription of it to 'Heman the Ezrahite'. The difficulty is that several men by the name of Heman are mentioned elsewhere in the Old Testament (see 1 Kings. 4:31; 1 Chron. 15:17, 19). However, in 1 Chronicles 6:33 (Heb. 18) mention is made of Heman being among the Levitical singers. Both in this case and the title of the next psalm, Psalm 89, the linking of Heman, Ethan, and the Korahites is not mentioned anywhere else. The term 'Ezrahite' is also ambiguous, for it could mean either 'of the family of Ezrah' or 'the native-born'.[2]

The psalms of lamentation, of which this is a notable member, are important as they show the emotional depths to

---

[1] The choice of this word rather than the much more common *choshek* may well be deliberate. The latter appears over 80x in the Old Testament, whereas *machshâk* only occurs 7×, all in poetry. Both are from the same Heb. root (*ch-sh-k*), but *machshâk* may add emphasis to the uniqueness of the psalmist's situation.

[2] The suggestion that the term 'Ezrahite' could mean 'the native-born' or 'member of a pre-Israelite family' was made by W. F. Albright, *Archaeology and the Religion of Israel* (Baltimore: John Hopkins University Press, 1956), pp. 127, 210, and it has been followed by Mitchell Dahood, *Psalms II: 51–100*, p. 302.

which even believers can descend. Just as Elijah was broken by the experiences culminating in the events of Carmel and regarded himself a failure (1 Kings 19:4: 'It is enough, O LORD, take away my life, for I am no better than my fathers'), so other believers passed through similar troughs. It should not be thought surprising that there are many connections between this psalm and the Book of Job, both in regard to the physical and psychological conditions described and the expressions used.[3]

1. An Appeal for Help (*vv. 1-2*)

The opening of the psalm shows that even in the midst of his despair, the psalmist can turn to his saviour. His personal problems become even more acute for him because of his trust in the covenantal love of the LORD (v. 11). **O LORD, the God who saves me, day and night I cry out before you. May my prayer come before you; turn your ear to my cry** (*vv. 1-2*). Out of his sorrow and distress he cries to his covenantal LORD, acknowledging that his salvation comes from him alone. Constantly he makes his prayer to him,[4] and pleads for a ready hearing for his cry for help. Probably the verb 'cry out' (*tsâʿaq*) does double-duty: 'By day I cry out; by night [I cry out] before you.' 'Turn your ear' is a common mode of appeal for help' (cf. its use in Pss. 17:6; 31:2; 71:2; and 116:2). A situation similar to the one in the psalm may be behind Henry Francis Lyte's words:

> Abide with me: fast falls the eventide;
> The darkness deepens; Lord, with me abide;
> When other helpers fail, and comforts flee,
> Help of the helpless, O abide with me.

---

[3] F. Delitzsch, *Commentary on the Psalms*, III, p. 23, has a note on the connections between this psalm and the Book of Job.

[4] Emendation has been proposed of verse 1, so that it would read as in the RSV: 'O LORD, my God, I call for help by day; I cry out in the night before thee.' The NRSV even omits 'day': 'O LORD, God of my salvation, when, at night, I cry out in your presence', while 'God of my salvation' is following the LXX. No Heb. manuscript evidence supports this change.

2. Living on the Edge of the Grave (*vv. 3-5*)

For my soul is full of trouble and my life draws near the grave. I am counted among those who go down to the pit; I am like a man without strength (*vv. 3-4*). There is no precise indication of what peril the psalmist is facing. It could be illness that brings him near to death, or some other situation that places him in serious danger. The use of 'soul' and 'life' cannot be pressed to denote different aspects, as they are clearly just parallel terms. The psalmist is reckoned along with those whose bodies are placed in the grave, like a man whose strength has gone completely.

I am set apart with the dead, like the slain who lie in the grave, whom you remember no more, who are cut off from your care (*v. 5*). The psalmist pictures himself lying in the grave, 'set apart with the dead'. The Hebrew text has 'freed from the dead' (*chofshî*),[5] which seems to mean released from the normal responsibilities of life. He is like those who are now in the grave, having been killed by battle wounds or dead because of famine. He speaks from the standpoint of this life when he describes them as being outside God's care. The Hebrew expression for this is that they are cut off from his hand, using 'hand' to denote God's power and protective care (cf. the later use of 'God's good hand' for his protection of the returning exiles, Ezra 7:9; 8:22; Neh. 2:18). The statements in this verse are not to be taken as denial of life after death or of God's eternal care of his children.

3. God's Heavy Hand (*vv. 6-9a*)

You have put me in the lowest pit, in the darkest depths. Your wrath lies heavily upon me; you have overwhelmed me with all your waves. *Selah* (*vv. 6-7*). The psalmist feels forsaken by man and by God. He accuses God directly of causing his present position ('*You* have put me', v. 6; '*you* have made me repulsive', v. 8). He cannot explain why it has happened, yet knows that God's hand has been at work. His distress is all the greater because his grief has been caused by the saviour to whom he appeals (v. 1). The picture of waves breaking over him is used to describe the flood of troubles that have come upon him.

---

[5] This word, which occurs 16×, is normally used of release from slavery.

You have taken from me my closest friends and have made me repulsive to them. I am confined and cannot escape; my eyes are dim with grief (*vv. 8-9a*). Isolation from his companions follows. While he is not actually afflicted with leprosy, yet he reckons himself like a leper and feels socially hemmed in by the restrictions placed upon him. He is shunned by his former companions and constant weeping has affected his eyesight (cf. Ps. 6:7 for similar ideas). He languishes because of his affliction.

4. A Cry of the Heart (*vv. 9b-12*)

I call to you, O LORD, every day; I spread out my hands to you (v. *9b*). The psalmist's prayer is the same day by day.[6] Even though he cannot explain his present distress, he makes his constant appeal to his covenantal LORD. His gestures are those of someone imploring help, as he stretches out his hand. The expression used here is not a common one, only occurring with this meaning in this verse. It is denoting a posture in prayer, and may be similar in meaning to 'lifting up the hands' (see Ps. 28:2).

Do you show your wonders to the dead? Do those who are dead rise up and praise you? *Selah* Is your love declared in the grave, your faithfulness in Destruction? Are your wonders known in the place of darkness, or your righteous deeds in the land of oblivion? (*vv. 10-12*). With a series of questions the psalmist draws attention to the condition of those who perish, and whom he considers he will soon be joining. He uses two different terms for the dead (*mêtîm* and *refā'îm*)[7] and a variety of expressions to describe their location – 'the

---

[6] The Heb. phrase for 'every day' is *b^ekol-yôm*, about which there is some ambiguity. The difficulty is that it could mean 'all the day' as well as 'day by day', 'every day', and some Heb. dictionaries quote both meanings. Cf. *CHAL*, p. 131. However, when the article appears, 'all *the* day' (*kol-hayyôm*), it seems to be designating a particular day, whereas when the article is absent, as here, the meaning is 'every day'. Cf. the use of *kol-hayyôm* later in this psalm in verse 17.

[7] This is the only occurrence in the Psalms of *refā'îm*, whose etymology is uncertain. A link with a cognate Ugaritic word may exist, but its meaning has to be determined by its contextual use in the OT. It appears in parallel with death/dead in Proverbs 2:18 and Isaiah 26:14, 19. In this psalm it is also in parallelism with 'dead' and simply denotes 'dead ones'. See the discussion by R. Laird Harris, *TWOT*, 2, p. 858.

grave', 'Destruction', 'the place of darkness', and 'the land of oblivion'. 'Destruction' is *ʾavaddôn* in Hebrew, and it is used in transliteration in Revelation 9:11 as a name for the devil. The psalmist also uses a variety of expressions to describe God's gracious acts on behalf of his people – 'wonders' (vv. 10 and 12), 'love' (v. 11), 'faithfulness' (v. 11), and 'righteous deeds' (v. 12). It is amongst the living that there are such divine manifestations of mercy and power.

5. Another Call for Help *(vv. 13-14)*

But I cry to you for help, O LORD; in the morning my prayer comes before you. Why, O LORD, do you reject me and hide your face from me? (*vv. 13-14*). One of the conventional times for prayer was in the morning. The Hebrew text emphasises the one praying and the one to whom he prays: 'But *I – to you* I cry for help.' While the afflicted psalmist cannot understand his present experiences, he still knows that his only possible source of help is the LORD. He hangs on desperately to the truth that God alone can deal with his situation. Relief is not yet in sight, and he still feels rejected by his God.

6. Lifelong Gloom *(vv. 15-18)*

From my youth I have been afflicted and close to death; I have suffered your terrors and am in despair (*v. 15*). The litany of trouble continues, and the opening words 'afflicted [was] I' (*ʿonî ʾanî*) sound very similar and draw further attention to the abject devastation the psalmist feels. His experiences are not new, for he confesses that he has lived with the shadow of death looming over him from youthful days. He has had a difficult life, whether from sickness or another reason. His condition brings him to the point of losing all hope, confessing that he is helpless.[8]

Your wrath has swept over me; your terrors have destroyed me. All day long they surround me like a flood; they have completely engulfed me. You have taken my companions and loved ones from me; the darkness is my closest friend

[8] The verb 'I am in despair' (*ʾâpûnâh*) is a *hapax legomenon*, and its root is uncertain. The NIV rendering fits the context.

(*vv. 16-18*). These closing verses of the psalm do not introduce any new ideas, but reiterate what has already been announced (see in particular verses 6-9). The psalmist traces his troubles back to God himself, accusing him of separating him from all his companions and loved ones. The only friend he has is darkness itself, with the word 'darkness' being the final word.[9] Yet we must balance this conclusion with the opening of the psalm. Isolated from human help, he is still able to call God his saviour. That is where his true hope lies. In days when there is no light the believer has to walk, trusting in his God (Isa. 50:10), and say:

When darkness seems to veil His face
I rest on His unchanging grace;
In every high and stormy gale,
My anchor holds within the veil.

His oath, His covenant, and blood,
Support me in the whelming flood;
When all around my soul gives way,
He then is all my hope and stay.
(Edward Mote 1797-1874)

[9] See the introductory comments to this psalm.

Psalm 89

A maskil of Ethan the Ezrahite.

The central theme of this psalm is the covenant God made with David, promising a throne for his dynasty forever. Once David brought the ark of the covenant to Jerusalem no other site was ever suggested for its location. The king's throne and the ark were adjacent to one another, and the enduring nature of their location in Judah stood in marked contrast to the instability shown by the northern tribes (Israel) regarding their capital and centre of worship. While David initially wanted to build a house (i.e. a temple) for God (2 Sam. 7:1-2), it was God who built a house (i.e. a dynasty) for him (2 Sam. 7:11-16). The word 'house' (*báyit*) can mean both a literal building and also a house in the sense of a dynasty (cf. our English phrase, 'the house of Windsor').

The promises that God made to David involved Solomon as the temple builder, whose kingdom was going to endure (2 Sam. 7:13). The language of adoption is used of Solomon, with God promising that he would be his father, and that Solomon would be his son (2 Sam. 7:14). This is the personalising of the covenantal promise, 'I will take you as my own people, and I will be your God' (Exod. 6:7). David realised how far-reaching this would be when he responded to God's promises: 'Who am I, O sovereign Lord, and what is my family, that you have brought me this far? And as if this were not enough in your sight, O sovereign LORD, you have also spoken about the future of the house of your servant. This is the charter by which man is directed, O sovereign LORD?'

(2 Sam. 7:18-19).[1] David's recognition that a descendant of his would be called God's son and have everlasting dominion is confirmed by his words in his last prayer (2 Sam. 23:1-7).

It is very clear that this covenant had a great impact on the thinking of God's people, and it is expounded in various other psalms as well (see Pss. 21; 61; 72; 132). The prophecy of a Wonderful Counsellor draws upon it (Isa. 9:6-7), while the message of the coming birth of Jesus is announced in terms of the covenant with David (Luke 1:30-33).

A marked change in the psalm occurs at the end of verse 37. The rejoicing over God's covenant is replaced by a section in which the covenant is deemed to be broken, and God is charged with allowing enemies to triumph over his people. This section is best taken as a later reflection on the covenant when some disastrous events had overtaken Judah. The most feasible suggestion is that it dates from the time when Nebuchadnezzar attacked Jerusalem in 597 BC, and Jehoiachin was taken into exile (2 Kings 24:8-17).

1. Great is the LORD's Faithfulness (*vv. 1-4*)

I will sing of the LORD's great love forever; with my mouth I will make your faithfulness known through all generations (*v. 1*). The dominant theme of the first part of this psalm is the love and faithfulness of the LORD. The words 'love' (*chésed*) and 'faithfulness' (*ʾemûnâh*) each occur seven times (allowing for an alternative, though related word, for 'faithfulness', *ʾemet*, in v. 14). When used together they form a compound expression – 'love-and-faithfulness'. This is the foundation of the covenantal relationship that is described in the following verses. It was the subject of the psalmist's song as he declares his intention of continuing to proclaim the covenantal mercies of the LORD.

---

[1] I am following the interpretation of David's response given by Walter Kaiser Jr., 'The Blessing of David: The Charter for Humanity', in John H. Skilton, ed., *The Law and the Prophets: Old Testament Studies in Honor of Oswald T. Allis* (Nutley, NJ: Presbyterian and Reformed Publishing Co., 1974), pp. 337-47. This position can also be found in Kaiser's *Toward an Old Testament Theology* (Grand Rapids: Zondervan, 1978), pp. 149-64. It is also endorsed by W. J. Dumbrell, *Covenant and Creation: An Old Testament Covenant Theology* (Exeter: Paternoster Press, 1984), pp. 151-52.

I will declare that your love stands firm forever, that you established your faithfulness in heaven itself (*v.* 2). There is difficulty in linking up verses 2-3 with the opening verse. It is best to take the commencement of this verse as referring to past time ('For I have said', AV, NKJ, NASB; 'For I said', ESV; 'I said', NEB), indicating that the psalmist had earlier made a declaration concerning God's love-and-faithfulness. The introductory 'for' (*kî*) is needed as well, as it provides the link with the opening verse, though omitted in the NIV. The declaration was to the effect that God had settled the matter of his covenantal mercy in heaven itself, and its endurance did not therefore depend upon actions of men. It would 'stand firm' (Heb. literally, 'be built', *yibbâneh,* a word very important in the covenant passage in 2 Samuel 7).

You said, 'I have made a covenant with my chosen one, I have sworn to David my servant, "I will establish your line forever and make your throne firm through all generations."' ***Selah*** (*vv.* 3-4). The words, 'You said', are not in the Hebrew text, but their insertion makes clear that the words that follow are God's words. God had entered into a covenantal bond with David, even though the word 'covenant' (*b^{e}rît*) does not occur in 2 Samuel 7. However, the ingredients of covenant are there, and this is confirmed by passages such as this, as well as 2 Samuel 23:5 and Psalm 132:11-12. David was indeed the LORD's servant (2 Sam. 7:5, 8, 26; Ps. 132:10) and chosen one (Ps. 78:70). An essential part of the covenant was the choice of David's family to form the continuing royal line.[2] Accordingly, the Davidic throne was to last throughout all generations (2 Sam. 7:16; Isa. 9:7), and ultimately it found its fulfilment in the person of Jesus (Luke 1:32). There is no mention in 2 Samuel 7 of God swearing an oath, but the reference to it here and Psalm 132:11 confirms that the arrangement was indeed a covenant.

---

[2] The Heb. verb to 'choose' (*bâchar*) is used negatively concerning the fact that the LORD did not choose David's brothers (1 Sam. 16:8-10) but chose David, a fact that he later acknowledges (2 Sam. 6:21). Here the noun for 'chosen' is *bâchîr* whereas later in the psalm *bâchûr* occurs (v. 20). The former is a noun formed from the root *b–ch-r,* while the latter is a pass. part. No discernible difference in meaning exists between the two words.

2. The Majesty of God (*vv. 5-18*)
At first glance it may seem that this section is a digression from the main theme of the psalm. What it does, however, is to emphasise the character of God which certifies that the covenant will be maintained. **The heavens praise your wonders, O LORD, your faithfulness too, in the assembly of the holy ones** (*v. 5*). God's glories are manifest in all the heavens, and his angels join together in a gathering to praise his faithfulness. The word 'wonders' – here the Hebrew has the singular, *péle'* – is used elsewhere of the miraculous acts of God in creation and especially in redemption.[3] It is a term used to describe his sovereign lordship over events (Ps. 78:11-12). Both inanimate creation and angelic beings (lit. 'in a congregation of holy ones') join in praise of God's mighty acts.

For who in the skies above can compare with the LORD? Who is like the LORD among the heavenly beings? In the council of the holy ones God is greatly feared; he is more awesome than all who surround him. O LORD God Almighty, who is like you? You are mighty, O LORD, and your faithfulness surrounds you (*vv. 6-8*). These verses draw attention to the uniqueness of God. The questions that are asked find their answer in the response, 'You are mighty, O LORD.' There is no one else who can be compared with him, for his awesome character sets him apart from all of his creation, including his holy ones. The phrase 'heavenly beings' is literally 'sons of God', an expression used also in Psalm 29:1 (NIV, 'mighty ones') of the angelic host (see the comment on that verse). 'The council of the holy ones' seems to equate with 'a congregation of holy ones' in verse 5. God's character separates him from his creatures, for he is more to be feared than any of them. The expression 'You are mighty, O LORD' represents only two words in Hebrew (*ch^{a}sîn yâh*). The first of these occurs only here, while *yâh* is simply a shortened form of the divine name *yhwh*.[4] Perhaps there are

---

[3] Cf. the comment on Psalm 77:12-13.

[4] *Yâh* is a shortened form and definitely a poetic word, occurring about 50 times, as compared with over 6,800 occurrences of the full form. It also appears in the call to praise, *hall^{e}lû-yâh*, 'praise (2 pers. pl. masc.)*Yâh*' or 'praise the LORD'.

echoes here from the great song of redemption in Exodus 15 (see especially v. 11).

You rule over the surging sea; when its waves mount up, you still them. You crushed Rahab like one of the slain; with your strong arm you scattered your enemies (*vv. 9-10*). God's mighty power as seen in the creation is described as though it was a battle against other great forces. The sea is personified as 'Rahab' (Job 26:12; Isa. 51:9), and here it may be the same as Leviathan (Ps. 74:14). All the powers of creation are under God's control, and he orders the seas in accordance with his will. Like slain warriors the waters are subdued before him.

The heavens are yours, and yours also the earth; you founded the world and all that is in it. You created the north and the south; Tabor and Hermon sing for joy at your name. Your arm is endued with power; your hand is strong, your right hand exalted (*vv. 11-13*). The whole of creation came into being by God's command, and so 'the earth is the Lord's, and everything in it' (Ps. 24:1; cf. also Ps. 50:12). The mighty mountains give praise to God's greatness and help to proclaim his character. The fact that 'north' and 'south' are used in parallel to 'Tabor' and 'Hermon' suggest that two other mountains may be intended, though no clear identification can be given for them. Mount Tabor was the site of Deborah's victory (Judg. 4:12, 14), while Mount Hermon was symbolic of physical majesty.[5] All of nature sings for joy, and as a testimony to the fact that it has been made by God's power. The anthropomorphic expressions in verse 13 ('arm', 'hand', 'right hand') simply draw attention to God's power displayed in his creative work.

Righteousness and justice are the foundation of your throne; love and faithfulness go before you (*v. 14*). God's rule is marked out by righteousness and justice. These form the basis on which his kingship operates (cf. Ps. 97:2b for an almost identical expression). The twin pair of love-and-faithfulness appear to precede all of God's works. They are like angels that go before him to proclaim his coming.

---

[5] Since these two mountains are on either side of the Jordan River, they may be used to indicate 'east' and 'west'. However, no other similar use of these two mountains as direction markers is found.

Blessed are those who have learned to acclaim you, who walk in the light of your presence, O LORD. They rejoice in your name all day long; they exult in your righteousness (*vv. 15-16*). The psalmist now moves on to describe the kind of God upon whose promises Israel depends. Those who trust in the LORD are able to proclaim their knowledge of him, and they do so with a joyful or festive shout.[6] Their daily lives are lived in the knowledge of God's favour to them (for 'the light of your presence', cf. the Aaronic blessing in Num. 6:24-26, and Pss. 4:6 and 44:3). God's self-revelation of himself (his 'name') becomes a ground of unceasing joy for his people, and the demonstration of his saving power an object of their praise. The NIV takes the final verb in verse 16 (*yârûmû*) to mean 'exult', 'praise'. Its normal meaning is 'to be on high', 'to be exalted'. While it has been argued that it can also mean 'exult',[7] it makes good sense to understand it to mean 'to be raised up' and so have the upper hand. 'Righteousness' can mean 'victory', 'triumph' (cf. its use in Isa. 41:2) and hence the idea is that through God's victorious actions his people will also be conquerors.

For you are their glory and strength, and by your favour you exalt our horn. Indeed, our shield belongs to the LORD, our king to the Holy One of Israel (*vv. 17-18*). God is the ornament or glory of his people, just as Israel is said to be God's 'glory' (*tif'eret*; see the Heb. text of Isa. 46:13; 62:3; and Jer. 13:11; 33:9). Moreover, he is their strength, which he renews according to his gracious will. Rather than understanding this strength as being the support God gives to each individual believer, 'horn' may be parallel to 'shield' and 'king'. Elsewhere the term 'shield' is used to describe kings in general (Ps. 47:9) and specifically the king of Israel (Ps. 84:9, and see comment on that verse). Israel's king is regarded as a vice-regent of God himself, who is called here 'the Holy One of Israel'. This term for God becomes a favourite with Isaiah, who uses it twenty-six times, while it is only used six times elsewhere in the Old Testament.

---

[6] The MT says, 'Blessed are *the people* who know the joyful shout', words that are used in many Jewish communities on New Year's Day after the trumpet (the *shofar*) has sounded. Some communities use verses 15-18.

[7] See Mitchell Dahood, *Psalms I: 1–50*, p. 77.

3. The Covenant with David (*vv. 19-37*)
This section of the psalm is a long poetic description of the covenant that God made with David (see 2 Sam. 7). It details God's choice of David and the promises given to him, as well as affirming the enduring love which was expressed in this covenant. **Once you spoke in a vision, to your faithful people you said: 'I have bestowed strength on a warrior; I have exalted a young man from among the people. I have found David my servant; with my sacred oil I have anointed him** (*vv. 19-20*). The opening word 'once', or better 'then',[8] refers back to the occasion when the covenant was proclaimed. The narrative in 2 Samuel 7 refers to this vision (2 Sam. 7:17), though it does not say expressly that the revelation was for the faithful people (Heb., *the chªsîdîm*, cf. the comment on Ps. 31:23). It becomes clear in David's response that the message has implications for Israel as a whole and the non-Jewish world as well (2 Sam. 7:18-29; see the introductory comments to this psalm). The psalmist looks back to the earlier choice of David by God, and the fact that this was *his* choice is more explicit than the NIV may suggest. The term 'young man' is actually 'a chosen one' (*bâchûr*),[9] and his anointing by Samuel (1 Sam. 16:1-13) was based on that prior action of God. To be from 'among the people' was a requirement for the king (Deut. 17:15). God calls David 'my servant' here and elsewhere (cf. the titles of Pss. 18 and 36), using a term reserved for those men in a special relationship with him. That God's hand was in the matter was demonstrated by the fact that after his anointing the Spirit of the LORD came upon him with power (1 Sam. 16:13).

My hand will sustain him; surely my arm will strengthen him. No enemy will subject him to tribute;

---

[8] The word *'az* is an adverb meaning 'then', 'at that time' and while it has some variation in meaning, *DCH*, I, p. 167, lists this verse under the entry 'then, at that time'.

[9] The matter is confusing in that there seems to be two words, written and pronounced identically. The first one is the pass. part. of the verb 'choose', and hence the translation of this form is 'chosen [one]'. The second is a noun meaning 'young man', which can be distinguished at times because it is contrasted with *zâkên*, 'old', 'the oldest'.

no wicked man will oppress him. I will crush his foes before him and strike down his adversaries (*vv. 21-23*). The divine promise is that support will be given to David, so that his kingdom will be secure. This is a poetic description of what is stated in 2 Samuel 7:10-11. The closest parallel is between 'wicked people will not oppress them anymore' (2 Sam. 7:10) and the words here, 'no wicked man will oppress him'.[10] David is to be given victory over his opponents, who are described by various terms: 'enemy', 'wicked man', and 'foe'. The consequence of God's promise is that the rest the land already had will be assured for the future.

My faithful love will be with him, and through my name his horn will be exalted. I will set his hand over the sea, his right hand over the rivers (*vv. 24-25*). The assurance regarding God's love-and-faithfulness given earlier in the psalm (see especially verses 1-3) is now stated as God's own declaration to David. Constant support for David comes from the LORD, and his strength will be maintained by him. The expression 'to exalt one's horn' denotes putting someone in a position of triumph (cf. Hannah's words, 'He will give strength to his king and exalt the horn of his anointed', 1 Sam. 2:10). The promise of verse 25 could be to the borders of the promised land as they were reached under the empire of David and Solomon, or more probably to the extent of the messianic kingdom, without even the definiteness expressed in Psalm 72:8. There is no need to try and specify which rivers are intended. The ultimate messianic kingdom ruled over by Christ, the greater son of David, will be universal in extent.

He will call out to me, 'You are my Father, my God, the Rock my Saviour.' I will also appoint him my firstborn, the most exalted of the kings of the earth (*vv. 26-27*). The

---

[10] The expression used for 'wicked man' is 'son of injustice' (*ben-ʿavlâh*) with the plural form 'sons of wickedness' occurring in 2 Samuel 7:10. Probably the expression is similar in meaning to the phrase 'son of Belial' (*ben-bᵉliyyʿal*) in Deuteronomy 13:13, which refers to a worthless man, or one given over to destructiveness. See my comment on the latter phrase in *Deuteronomy: The Commands of a Covenant God*, pp. 157-58.

promise to David puts in individual terms what was the core of God's covenant with his people: 'I am your God, and you shall be my people.' This is now expressed in the affectionate language of a child speaking to his father.[11] David will call out to God, 'My Father', and designate him as his God, Rock, and Saviour. The highest of privileges will be given to David, for as the firstborn he has royal honours, and no other earthly king could rise to his position. The language here is taken over and used of the Lord Jesus in Revelation 1:4-5: 'Grace and peace to you ... from Jesus Christ, who is the faithful witness, the firstborn from the dead, and the ruler of the kings of the earth.'

I will maintain my love to him forever, and my covenant with him will never fail. I will establish his line forever, his throne as long as the heavens endure (*vv. 28-29*). The enduring nature of God's covenant with David is an expression of mercy and grace. Repeatedly the Old Testament reminds readers that God will not go back on his covenantal word to David (see Ps. 132:11-18). Part of the promise is that his family (lit. 'his seed') will continue, and that possession of the throne by them is just as certain as the enduring nature of the heavens (for fuller expression of this idea, see vv. 36, 37). David's dynasty did reign for centuries, but the eternal fulfilment of the promise is to be found in Jesus Christ (John 12:34; Rom. 1:2-4; Rev. 22:16).

If his sons forsake my law and do not follow my statutes, if they violate my decrees and fail to keep my commands, I will punish their sin with the rod, their iniquity with flogging; but I will not take my love from him, nor will I ever betray my faithfulness. I will not violate my covenant or alter what my lips have uttered (*vv. 30-34*). These words are a paraphrase of 2 Samuel 7:14-15. Nathan indicated to David that the sins of individual kings are going to be punished, but he promises that the Davidic family will continue. God is going to act as a father in chastising his sons, and so punishment will follow

---

[11] Father–son relationships were used in extra-biblical covenants and also in non-theological covenants in the Old Testament. For example, Ahaz made a treaty with Assyria, and so he refers to himself as a son of Tiglath Pileser; 'I am your servant and your vassal' (lit. 'and your son', *ûvinᵉkâ*), 2 Kings 16:7.

breach of his laws. Chastisement is part of the father/son relationship (Heb. 12:7-11). However, a wonderful contrast is brought out by the repetition of the word 'violate' (*châlal*, Pi.) in verses 31 and 34. Individual kings might violate God's laws, but God will never violate his covenant! He will never go back on his word (Num. 23:19). The combination of love-and-faithfulness comes in again in verse 33. The security of the covenant is dependent on God's own gracious character.

Once for all, I have sworn by my holiness – and I will not lie to David – that his line will continue forever and his throne endure before me like the sun; it will be established forever like the moon, the faithful witness in the sky.' *Selah* (*vv. 35-37*). The psalmist returns to the theme of God's oath (see comment on v. 3). God's promise to David was: 'Your house and your kingdom will endure forever before me; your throne will be established for ever' (2 Sam. 7:16). Because there is no one greater than God, he swears by his own character (cf. the same thing in reference to his oath to Abraham, Heb. 6:13). This was done 'once and for all', not just on some individual occasion in the past.[12] Though the oath was a positive affirmation of David's line, the negative element was there as well – God committed himself not to deceive his servant David.[13] The thought of verses 36-37 is an expansion of verse 29. The enduring Davidic family and its royal position are as sure as the sun and moon.

4. Faith in a Time of Trial (*vv. 38-51*)

There is a sudden shift in the psalm at this point. The psalmist takes up the present position of the people and of the Davidic family, and pleads for them on the basis of God's covenantal promises. How is it possible that God could seemingly renounce his covenant? The setting seems to be the time of the Babylonian attack on Jerusalem in 597 BC when the youthful king Jehoiachin was taken away captive to Babylon (see

---

[12] The numeral *'achat* ('one') is used here in an adverbial manner, 'once (and for all) I have sworn'. For this usage, see *IBHS*, p. 275.

[13] An oath need not have a special oath formula; but after it, or a statement that indicates an oath, a negative clause is introduced by the particle *'im* as here. For discussion of the Heb. form for oaths, see *DIHG~S*, pp. 186-87.

2 Kings 24:8-17). **But you have rejected, you have spurned, you have been very angry with your anointed one. You have renounced the covenant with your servant and have defiled his crown in the dust** (*vv. 38-39*). The emphasis is on what God has done, for the psalmist rightly sees his hand in the events surrounding the Babylonian invasion. The shift from the stress on the covenant to the present distress of the people is marked by the emphatic opening to this section: 'But *you*' (*v*e*'attâh*). The psalmist rightly sees God's hand in the events that have happened. The capture of Jerusalem and of the king are an expression of his wrath. The king is referred to as the 'anointed one' (*mâshîach*), as is confirmed by other passages in which 'king' and 'anointed one' are in parallel (cf. Ps. 18:50/ 2 Sam. 22:51). The covenant seems to be broken, though the Old Testament points to a continuity of the covenant in spite of a temporary separation between God and his people (see, e.g. Isa. 50:1-2; 54:4-8). The rejection of the Davidic king is as if the crown had been thrown away into the dust (cf. a similar expression in Lam. 5:16).

You have broken through all his walls and reduced his strongholds to ruins. All who pass by have plundered him; he has become the scorn of his neighbours (*vv. 40-41*). The language used in these verses gives a picture of the overthrow of Judah by the Babylonians. The defences have been breached, and neighbouring countries have been able to take what they wanted (cf. the similar language of Ps. 80:12-13). God's people have become an object of derision because they seem to have been abandoned by their God (cf. also Ps. 44:13-14).

You have exalted the right hand of his foes; you have made all his enemies rejoice. You have turned back the edge of his sword and have not supported him in battle (*vv. 42-43*). Victory over Judah was granted by God to the nation's enemies, and so they rejoice in their success. The warriors of Judah might as well have been fighting with blunt swords, and there was no divine aid when the final assault came against Jerusalem. God's help had been withheld from his people, for he had earlier spoken through Isaiah to King

Hezekiah of the Babylonian invasion (2 Kings 20:16-18). The message had a pointed introduction ('Behold!') that drew attention to the significant event, but the following words, 'days are coming ...', added to the force of the message because of their indefiniteness.[14]

You have put an end to his splendour and cast his throne to the ground. You have cut short the days of his youth; you have covered him with a mantle of shame. *Selah* (*vv. 44-45*). The king has been humiliated by being removed from his place of authority. Casting the throne to the ground is synonymous with defiling the crown in the dust (v. 39). The reference to 'the days of his youth' supports the interpretation that the psalm comes from the period of Jehoiachin's captivity in Babylon. He was eighteen years old when he became king, and he only reigned for three months (2 Kings 24:8). It was a disgrace for a king to be taken away with all his family and attendants. The final picture that the historical record gives of him is that he ate regularly in Babylon at the king's table all the days of his life (2 Kings 25:29-30). This is not a picture of hope but a recognition that the Davidic monarchy was at an end.[15]

How long, O LORD? Will you hide yourself forever? How long will your wrath burn like fire? Remember how fleeting is my life. For what futility you have created all men! What man can live and not see death, or save himself from the power of the grave? *Selah* (*vv. 46-48*). The psalmist questions God regarding the length of time his favour is going to be turned away from his people. The prayer, 'How long, O LORD?', is an expression of boldness on the part of psalmists as in their perplexity they cried to God (cf. the comments on Ps. 6:3). They knew that the basis of these requests was the continuing covenantal relationship. When God is angry with

---

[14] I have discussed this in my commentary, *Isaiah: A Covenant to be Kept for the Sake of the Church*, p. 263.

[15] Cf. the words of W. J. Dumbrell: 'One cannot help feeling that the epilogue to the second book of Kings, in which the Davidic representative Jehoiachin is treated as a puppet figure, eating as Saul's survivor Mephibosheth did in David's time (2 Sam. 9:13) at an overlord's table (and this time at a pagan table!) eloquently expresses in a picture of total dependency the final historical demise of the Davidic monarchy' (*Covenant and Creation: An Old Testament Covenantal Theology*, p. 162).

his people he is said to hide himself (Pss. 27:9; 30:7; Isa. 8:17; 45:15). The question, 'How long will your wrath burn like fire?' is a repetition, with slight variation, of Psalm 79:5. The psalmist speaks as the representative of his community, and wonders how short is his lifespan.[16] He and all men must die, but will God's wrath against his people be displayed *forever*? No one is able to escape from death, not even a man at the height of his powers (the Heb. word for 'man' in verse 48 is not the usual word, but a special word, *géver*, denoting man in his strength).

O Lord, where is your former great love, which in your faithfulness you swore to David? (*v. 49*). In the final verses of the psalm the argument alters. Whereas the psalmist has been pleading on the basis of the shortness of human life, he now pleads that what is happening is bringing dishonour on God himself. He bases his cry on God's covenantal oath that had been made to David (see vv. 3, 35), which was a demonstration of love-and-faithfulness. He goes right back to the note on which the psalm commenced. One question of translation affects the interpretation of this verse. The NIV translation 'your former great love' is an attempt to render the plural phrase in the MT 'your former *loves*' (*chasâdékâ hâri'shonîm*). It is quite true that sometimes in Hebrew plurals are used to express an intensification of the singular, and this is clearly how the NIV translators took the plural.[17] Alternatively, the plural could denote 'acts of mercy', 'deeds of love'.[18]

Remember, Lord, how your servant has been mocked, how I bear in my heart the taunts of all the nations, the taunts with which your enemies have mocked, O LORD, with which they have mocked every step of your anointed

---

[16] 'Remember how fleeting is my life' is a good translation though the Heb. syntax is difficult and various emendations have been proposed. The literal translation is: 'Remember, I, what is it the duration of life?' (*zekor 'anî meh-châled*). As Delitzsch pointed out long ago, this is probably the same phrase that occurs in Psalm 39:4 with the more normal word order, *meh-châled 'anî*, 'how transient I am' (NASB). See his *Commentary on the Psalms*, III, p. 44.

[17] This usage is covered in *DIHG~S*, p. 19.

[18] Cf. *DCH*, III, p. 278. See also other passages where the plural is used, such as Genesis 32:11; Isaiah 55:3; 2 Chronicles 6:42 and Lamentations 3:22.

one (*vv. 50-51*). These words may well reflect the shouting of the crowds as Jehoiachin and others were taken away into captivity (the Heb. text has the plural 'servants').[19] The land may well have been full of strangers from 'all the nations', or else the psalmist is thinking of the way the surrounding nations were mocking the Jews.[20] 'Anointed one' picks up from the earlier reference to the king in verse 38. A defeated and captive king did not escape the jeers of enemies as he was led off to Babylon.

5. Concluding Doxology (*v. 52*)

Praise be to the LORD forever! Amen and Amen (v. 52). This doxology, while it comes at the end of this psalm, is really placed here to conclude the third book of the Psalter. This is the shortest of all the concluding doxologies, but it contains the essential thrust of them all – an ascription of praise to the covenantal LORD, with the affirmation of a double 'Amen'.

---

[19] It is hard to judge the textual question here, as twenty-four Heb. manuscripts and the Syriac version have the singular 'servant'. However, the LXX translators clearly had the plural before them: 'Where, O Lord, are your ancient mercies?' On balance, the plural, 'your servants', should be accepted as the reading.

[20] The phrase is unusual, 'all the many people' (*kol-rabbîm ʿammîm*). Marvin Tate, *Psalms 51–100*, p. 423, suggests that it is roughly parallel to 'all the many nations' (*kol goyîm rabbîm*) in Ezekiel 31:6, thus indicating 'the many different peoples'.

Book 4

Psalm 90

A prayer of Moses, the man of God

This is the oldest psalm in the whole collection, the only one that the title designates as 'a prayer of Moses'.[1] In language it has many resemblances to the books attributed to Moses (the Pentateuch), especially to the book of Deuteronomy. It is a solemn statement of the eternity of God in contrast to the brevity of human life. The emphasis on his sovereignty stands over against the futility of human existence spoken of in Psalm 89:48. The repetition of the question, 'How long?', in Psalm 89:46 and Psalm 90:13 also provides a link between these psalms. As the fourth book of the Psalter (Pss. 90-106) begins, the picture is painted of how sinful man looks when viewed in the light of God's awesome presence. The wilderness experiences of Israel elicited this prayerful response.

The main point of the psalm is reached in verse 12: 'Teach us to number our days aright, that we may gain a heart of wisdom.' Wisdom in the Old Testament is not just theoretical knowledge and understanding, but rather the ability to apply that God-given knowledge to the practical affairs of life. 'The fear of the LORD' was the response of faith to God. It also provided understanding of man and society that gave cohesion and meaning to life. With the passing of days and years, Moses prays for himself and the people as a whole that they will understand the frailty of human life and set their hearts on true wisdom.

The paraphrase of this psalm by Isaac Watts (1674-1748) has been widely used and greatly loved.

---

[1] In Deuteronomy 31:30 Moses recites a song, but it is the one the LORD had given to him and Aaron (Deut. 31:19-22).

O God, our help in ages past,
Our hope for years to come,
Our shelter from the stormy blast,
And our eternal home.

1. An Eternal Refuge (*vv. 1-2*)
Moses reflects on the past, and recognises that the Lord has been his people's dwelling place. He begins by making a direct affirmation to him. **Lord, you have been our dwelling place throughout all generations. Before the mountains were born or you brought forth the earth and the world, from everlasting to everlasting you are God** (*vv. 1-2*). God is called here the dwelling place, using a word that is applied elsewhere to God's heavenly dwelling place (Deut. 26:15; Ps. 26:8). The idea of refuge seems heightened here and in Psalm 91:9 by the idea of God being our home, with all the comfort and personal security that mere refuge might lack, where both 'dwelling place' and 'refuge' occur together. The Greek translation (LXX) was probably paraphrasing when it used the word 'refuge', and some Hebrew manuscripts also follow this reading (in Hebrew, having *mâʿôz* for *mâʿôn*). Moses uses the general word for 'Lord' (*ʾadonây*), whereas in verse 13 he uses the covenant name 'LORD' (*yahweh*). Because he is eternal, God does not change from human generation to generation. Before the mountains came into existence, or the earth and the world were formed, God was there.

2. Man's Mortality (*vv. 3-6*)
Man's very nature is such that he came from the earth and he returns to it (Gen. 3:19). **You turn men back to dust, saying, 'Return to dust, O sons of men'** (*v. 3*). The NIV has inserted the second occurrence of 'to dust', and this is probably a correct interpretation of the meaning of God's words.[2] In verse 8 reference is made to sin, which makes an allusion to the curse on man, pronounced after the Fall, all the more likely. As

[2] This is the only occurrence of *dakkâʾ* in the sense of 'dust', though it appears several times as an adjective, 'crushed, contrite' (cf. Ps. 34:18; Isa. 57:15).

human beings work with the soil it is a reminder to them both of their origin and their destiny.

For a thousand years in your sight are like a day that has just gone by, or like a watch in the night (*v. 4*). The point of this verse is to contrast the Lord's unchanging presence with the fleeting time which man spends on this earth. It is so brief compared with the Lord's perspective on time. The reference to a thousand years seems to be back to those like Methuselah who lived almost that long. In God's sight this is like a day, or even just like a watch in the night (a third part of the night). 2 Peter 3:8 quotes and amplifies this verse when it says: 'With the Lord a day is like a thousand years, and a thousand years are like a day.'

You sweep men away in the sleep of death; they are like the new grass of the morning – though in the morning it springs up new, by evening it is dry and withered (*vv. 5-6*). How short is man's life on the earth! It is only like grass, which springs up in the morning but by night-time it has changed (twice the Heb. verb for 'change', *châlaf*, is used in the verse; cf. its use in Isa. 40:31, where it indicates exchanging weakness for strength). Similar imagery for man's life is found in Psalm 103:15-16 where again grass is used as the illustration, along with reference to God remembering that we are dust. The reference to vegetation highlights a well-known difficulty in the opening part of verse 5, as the ideas do not seem to blend easily. The first verb (*z^eramtâm*, NIV 'sweep away') has been interpreted variously, as has its suffix ('them'), while 'sleep' has often been taken as 'the sleep [of death]'. The NIV rendering of the verb and suffix is quite acceptable, but the next phrase should be separated from it: 'You sweep men away; they are [in] sleep'.[3] The reference to sleep should not be understood as 'death' but

[3] This is following the accents in the MT. The accentuation system is somewhat analogous to our punctuation marks. It helped in reading or chanting of the text and should also be viewed as 'an early and reliable witness to a correct interpretation of the text' (*IBHS*, p. 30). For a good summary of the textual work on the Hebrew text from AD 135 to AD 1000, see Ellis R. Brotzman, *Old Testament Textual Criticism: A Practical Introduction* (Grand Rapids: Baker Book House, 1994), pp. 47-55.

rather as a fleeting morning sleep.[4] The point here is that human existence is so transitory, especially when viewed in the light of God's power and eternal existence.

3. God's Wrath (*vv. 7-10*)

There were many demonstrations of God's wrath against his people in Moses' day, and against Moses himself (Deut. 1:37; 4:21). His testimony is: **We are consumed by your anger and terrified by your indignation** (*v. 7*). Even against his own people, God shows his wrath, for he cannot bear to see sin in their lives. Both verbs (*kâlâh*, 'consume', and *bâhâl*, 'terrify') appear in passages dealing with the suddenness and the severity of God's judgments.

Nor can secret sins be hidden from his sight. **You have set our iniquities before you, our secret sins in the light of your presence** (*v. 8*). Israel was very prone to wander from the LORD's paths, but this waywardness did not go unnoticed. While the Hebrew word *ʿâwôn* is often translated, as here, by 'iniquity', yet one of its primary meanings, as shown by contextual evidence in the Old Testament, is to 'err from the road'.[5] Everything stands open in the eyes of the Lord, so that no sin is hidden from him. Elsewhere 'the light of your face' denotes God's favour (Ps. 89:15), but here a similar expression denotes the all-searching eye of God.

> Eastward, westward, still you guide me,
> From your grip I cannot stray;
> Nor will darkness hide me from you:
> Night to you is clear as day.
> (*The Book of Praises*, Ps. 139)

---

[4] 'The sleep of death' is simply *shênâh* in Hebrew. Because of its similarity to the word for 'year' (*shânâh*), the early versions took it as 'year', and an emendation to *shânâh shânâh*, 'year after year', has been proposed. While various suggestions have been made concerning several aspects of verse 5, none are convincing, and it is best to retain the translation 'sleep'.

[5] See the discussion by Ronald Youngblood, 'A New Look at Three Old Testament Roots for "Sin",' in Gary A. Tuttle, ed., *Biblical and Near Eastern Studies: Essays in Honor of William Sanford LaSor* (Grand Rapids: Eerdmans, 1978), p. 204.

All our days pass away under your wrath; we finish our years with a moan. The length of our days is seventy years – or eighty, if we have strength; yet their span is but trouble and sorrow, for they quickly pass, and we fly away (*vv. 9-10*). Moses expresses his overall view on the waywardness of the people, who had experienced God's anger against them, so that even at the end there is just the expression of 'a moan' or 'a sigh' (the word *hegeh* is connected with 'meditate', *hâgâh,* in Psalm 1:1). A lifespan is seventy or eighty years, but however long it is, it is full of trouble and sorrow. Those years speed by so quickly, and are soon gone.[6] Behind the words of these verses is the realisation that in life we make so many mistakes and achieve so little.

4. True Wisdom (*vv. 11-12*)

Who knows the power of your anger? For your wrath is as great as the fear that is due you. Teach us to number our days aright, that we may gain a heart of wisdom (*vv. 11-12*). The form of the question ('Who knows the power of your anger?) is one which is used especially in the book of Ecclesiastes (see 2:19; 3:21; 6:12; 8:1), and it serves to highlight the subject about which it asks. It is the equivalent of 'no one knows'. The answer is expressed in a very condensed way in Hebrew (lit. 'like your fear [is] your wrath'). The only way to prevent ourselves from offending against God is to acknowledge his anger against sin and to seek to fear him. The prayer of Moses is that he and the people as a whole would be able to assess their days and use them aright. The only way to true knowledge is to have God as our instructor. Here, 'to number' means something far more than mere arithmetic. It is a spiritual approach to our human life, and especially to our fleeting earthly existence. The end result of such numbering is that we are able to bring to God as an offering, a heart of wisdom (the same verb translated 'gain' is used of Cain and Abel's offerings in Gen. 4:4).

---

[6] The verb 'quickly pass' (*gûz*) only occurs here and in Numbers 11:31 (of the quails), while 'quickly' is a noun (*chîsh*) that is a *hapax legomenon,* though the meaning seems clear from the twenty times that the verbal form (*chûsh*) is used.

5. Pray for Blessing (*vv. 13-17*)

Relent, O Lord! How long will it be? Have compassion on your servants. Satisfy us in the morning with your unfailing love, that we may sing for joy and be glad all our days (*vv. 13-14*). Just as God so often asked his people to repent, so now Moses prays that he will do so himself. He pleads for unmerited love to be shown to God's covenant servants. He asks that each morning God will give them a reminder of his steadfast love (*chésed*), so that joy and gladness may abound.

Make us glad for as many days as you have afflicted us, for as many years as we have seen trouble (*v. 15*). In comparison to the years of trouble, he now wants to have as many years of joy in turn. The plea is for compensation in the form of joy, and the number of such joyful days to agree with the number of the days of affliction. The idea of thanks for affliction occurs also in other psalms (e.g., 119:75).[7]

May your deeds be shown to your servants, your splendour to their children. May the favour of the Lord our God rest upon us; establish the work of our hands for us – yes, establish the work of our hands (*vv. 16-17*). The final prayers of this psalm relate to the demonstration of God's power not just in the present, but for future generations as well ('to their children'). God's mighty deeds are a demonstration of his glory, using a word (*hâdâr*) that is employed to describe God's magnificence. In our prayers we need similarly to focus on future needs, and to think of a succession of believing generations. If God's favour rested on the people, then their work would see lasting results – they will have counted their days aright. So intense is his request that the psalm finishes with this repeated prayer.

[7] The Hebrew words 'days of' (*y^{e}môt*) and 'years of' (*shânôt*) are unusual, as they are used in place of the regular forms, *y^{e}mê* and *sh^{e}nê*. Both the words here in Psalm 90:15 occur together in Deuteronomy 32:7, and while *y^{e}môt* does not occur outside these two passages, the appearance of *sh^{e}nê* in Deuteronomy 32:7 marks its first appearance as a poetic plural form.

Psalm 91

This psalm has no title, something it shares in common with most of the psalms in this, the fourth, book of the Psalter (Pss. 90-106). The Greek translation (the LXX) ascribes it to David, but no support exists for this in Hebrew manuscripts. Links exist between this psalm and both Psalm 90 and Psalm 92 suggesting that its position here in the Psalter is deliberate.[1] It follows the request for God's favour with which Psalm 90 ends. Psalm 91 contains a multifaceted promise of God to believers in verses 14-16, and then it is followed by their response in Psalm 92. The major part of Psalm 91 is similar in style to the wisdom literature, and therefore it is best classified as a wisdom psalm (see the Introduction). The general statements of the psalm find dramatic confirmation in the LORD's words with which the psalm closes.

Changes between first person singular ('I', 'me', 'my'), second person singular ('you', 'your') and third person singular ('he', 'his', 'him') forms occur throughout the psalm. This led the Targum to postulate that the psalm was a dialogue between David and Solomon. It has David beginning at verse 2, Solomon responding in verse 9, and God entering the discussion at verse 10. While some commentators have followed this approach, others have tried by emendation to ease the apparent difficulty, especially by changing 'I said' (*ʾomar*) in verse 2 to 'he said' (*yôʾmar*). Neither of these approaches solve all the apparent difficulty, and it is best to

[1] Both Psalms 90 and 91 seem to echo the song in Deuteronomy 32. For suggested parallels between Psalm 91 and Deuteronomy 32, see A. F. Kirkpatrick, *The Book of Psalms*, p. 554.

recognise that Hebrew poetry changes persons far more than we are accustomed to do in English poetry. Psalm 121 forms an instructive parallel, where first person ('I', 'my') in verses 1-2 is changed to second person ('you', 'your') in verses 3-8.

1. Sure Refuge with the LORD (*vv. 1-10*)

He who dwells in the shelter of the Most High will rest in the shadow of the Almighty (*v. 1*). The opening verse of Psalm 91 uses names of God that go back to the patriarchs, and this may be one of the reasons why the Psalm of Moses (Ps. 90) is immediately followed by this psalm. 'The Most High' (*ʿelyôn*) as a name for God is first used in Genesis 14:18-20, while 'the Almighty' (*shadday*) was a title which God used when he revealed himself to Abraham, Isaac, and Jacob (Gen. 17:1; 28:3; 35:11).[2] The psalm opens with a statement (possibly by one of the priests) concerning the sure place of refuge to be found with God. He is a hiding place (*sêter*, NIV 'shelter'), and under the shadow of the wings of the cherubim there is safety (see comments on Ps. 61:4).

I will say of the LORD, 'He is my refuge and my fortress, my God, in whom I trust' (*v. 2*). The words with which this verse begins point back to the statement in verse 1, but now the psalmist makes a personal affirmation. He himself has found shelter with the LORD, and he describes that experience by using synonyms, 'my refuge' (*machsî*) and 'my fortress' (*meᵉtsûdâtî*). He boldly claims the great blessing that he has indeed found security with his God.

Surely he will save you from the fowler's snare and from the deadly pestilence. He will cover you with his feathers, and under his wings you will find refuge; his faithfulness will be your shield and rampart (*vv. 3-4*). The unseen danger from enemies is described by language referring to the bird catcher, imagery that is used elsewhere in the Psalms in a similar way (Ps. 124:7). Likewise, deadly pestilence was an occurrence that called forth prayer to God for safety (1 Kings 8:37). In such situations the protective care of God

[2] Only twice in the Psalter is the title 'the Almighty' used, here and in Psalm 68:14.

would be given, and believers would be hidden (speaking metaphorically) under his wings (Ps. 17:8; Matt. 23:37). The same idiom for safe protection is used in Boaz's description of Ruth's faith ('under whose wings you have taken refuge', Ruth 2:12).[3] God's faithfulness to his covenantal promises would serve like a shield to protect them.

You will not fear the terror of night, nor the arrow that flies by day, nor the pestilence that stalks in the darkness, nor the plague that destroys at midday (*vv. 5-6*). These verses take up the ideas of verse 3 and enlarge on them, concentrating on physical danger in verse 5 and sickness in verse 6. Attacks from enemies, either by day or by night, are not to be feared if the LORD is protecting his people. Similarly, sudden plagues of disease should not cause terror, even though they reach epidemic proportions. However, not all believers enjoy this assurance of God's protective care in times of danger. His word is their stay and on it they must rest, rather than on their own emotions.

A thousand may fall at your side, ten thousand at your right hand, but it will not come near you. You will only observe with your eyes and see the punishment of the wicked (*vv. 7-8*). The use of a thousand and ten thousand in parallel phrases is typical of Hebrew poetry (Judg. 20:10; 1 Sam. 18:7; Ps. 144:13). The combined phrase points to a great magnitude without precise definition of the exact number.[4] No matter how many fall to enemy attacks or to disease, yet the speaker assures his listeners that God will keep them safe. They will be spectators of God's judgments on the wicked, rather than being themselves participants.

If you make the Most High your dwelling – even the LORD, who is my refuge – then no harm will befall you, no disaster will come near your tent (*vv. 9-10*). These verses form a parallel with verses 1-2, and so form a frame around

---

[3] The Hebrew idiom is exactly the same in Psalm 91:4 and Ruth 2:12: *châsâh tachat k^e^nâpayim*. The idiom only occurs in these two passages, though a similar idiom ('to seek refuge in the shadow/shelter of [the LORD's] wings') is found in Psalms 57:1 and 61:4. The thought may well be based on Exodus 19:4 and Deuteronomy 32:11.

[4] For this and other higher numbers, see *IBHS*, pp. 281-83.

verses 3-8. The use of 'dwelling' (*mā'ôn*) links up also with the opening verse of Psalm 90. Verse 9 is difficult to translate and interpret mainly because of the shift in persons: 'you' (m.s.), 'my refuge', 'you make' (lit. 'set'), 'your dwelling'. The NIV rendering follows a long history of English translation, but taking the first phrase in Hebrew as a parenthesis ('even the LORD, who is my refuge') forms a very harsh construction.[5] The problem is that the reader expects '*your* refuge' to correspond to 'your dwelling', not '*my* refuge'. Without emending the Hebrew text, which many want to do,[6] the best solution is to begin with a declaration: 'Indeed, you are my refuge'.[7] Probably the REB translation is the best: 'Surely you are my refuge. You have made the Most High your dwelling place; no disaster will befall you, no calamity touch your home.' Anyone who could say, 'The LORD is my refuge,' has found a place of safety, and can rest in the thought that nothing happens outside his will. God knows all the circumstances of his children and directs them for their good.

2. God's Gracious Care (*vv. 10-13*)

For he will command his angels concerning you to guard you in all your ways; they will lift you up in their hands, so that you will not strike your foot against a stone. You will tread upon the lion and the cobra; you will trample the great lion and the serpent (*vv. 11-13*). Satan used the words of verses 11-12 as he tempted Jesus, trying to get him to act rashly. However, Jesus responded by quoting Deuteronomy 6:16: 'Do not test the LORD your God' (Matt. 4:5-7; Luke 4:9-12). In the context here their connection with verse 9 is plain. Protecting care is promised to those who make the LORD their refuge. The metaphor concerning protection by the angels is probably taken from Exodus 19:4 and 23:20. The LORD, who carried Israel out of Egypt on eagles' wings, is still able to ensure that his people do not stumble (Ps. 121:3). God

---

[5] This 'harsh' construction is the expression used by J. J. S. Perowne, *The Book of Psalms*, II, p. 174, and is followed by A. F. Kirkpatrick, *The Book of Psalms*, p. 557.

[6] Cf. the RSV and NRSV, while the NASB, NKJV, and ESV all follow the traditional rendering of the AV.

[7] This is the solution of Marvin Tate, *Psalms 51-100*, pp. 446-48, and is the position taken by Perowne and Kirkpatrick (see previous note).

will guard from all kinds of dangers, representative examples of which are cited in verse 13. No need exists to try and explain the distinctive character of the various animal and serpent threats mentioned. Illustrations of victories over lions are cited in Old Testament history (Samson, Judg. 14:5-6; David, 1 Sam. 17:34-35; Daniel, Dan. 6:21-23). Jesus repeated the promise in this verse as he sent out his disciples (Luke 10:19).

3. God's Word of Promise (*vv. 14-16*)

'Because he loves me,' says the LORD, 'I will rescue him; I will protect him, for he acknowledges my name (*v. 14*). The closing verses of the psalm are given in the form of a prophetic oracle, with God announcing through the speaker that he will keep safely those who acknowledge him.[8] The verb to 'love' used here (Heb., *châshaq*) is not the most common Hebrew verb for 'love'. It denotes deep and passionate attachment, and is used of God's attitude to Israel (Deut. 7:7; 10:15). If anyone has a genuine love for God, then God promises to keep and guard him. To acknowledge his name implies understanding the revelation that God has given of himself and demonstrating one's commitment to it (cf. the phrase 'those who love your name' in Ps. 5:11).

He will call upon me, and I will answer him; I will be with him in trouble, I will deliver him and honour him. With long life will I satisfy him and show him my salvation' (*vv. 15-16*). The main idea of these verses is similar to Psalm 50:15, 23. The assurance is given in this prophetic word that there will be a ready response by the LORD whenever there is a call to him in troublous times. He will intervene and bring deliverance. 'Honour' comes when others see how graciously the LORD has acted. In contrast to those visited by death (see vv. 7-8), the person whose prayer is answered will be preserved alive. The Hebrew of verse 16 is a little less definite than the NIV makes it. The idea is that as long as he lives, God will provide food and so satisfy him (cf. Exod. 16:8 and Ps. 132:15 for the use of this verse 'satisfy'). God both preserves life and also provides daily spiritual and physical food. His 'salvation' is the outworking of his purposes of mercy.

---

[8] The NIV 'says the LORD' has no counterpart in the Hebrew text, though the declaration in verses 14-16 does appear to be divine.

Psalm 92

A psalm. A song. For the Sabbath day.

No other psalm shares this designation as a psalm intended for use on the Sabbath. We know from the Jewish Mishnah (*Tamid* 7:4), that this psalm was sung by the Levites in the temple. The Greek translation (LXX) allots other psalms so that there is one for each day of the week. The schedule was: first day, Psalm 24; then (2) Psalm 48; (3) Psalm 82; (4) Psalm 94; (5) Psalm 81; (6) Psalm 93. Neither in the title nor in the content of the psalm is there any indication why it was chosen for the Sabbath. The reference to creation (vv. 4-5) may be the clue, however, as the Sabbath came as the climax of creation (Gen. 1:1–2:4). The psalm celebrates the righteous rule of God and also the ultimate prosperity of the righteous. A personal experience of salvation (v. 4) is taken as a guarantee of fuller redemption from the LORD. His enemies will be vanquished and the righteous will be able to sing in praise of their Rock (v. 15). The final eschatological Sabbath will be accompanied with praise for God's completed redemption (Heb. 4:1-10).

Some have thought that this psalm was intended for temple worship in the pre-exilic time. While the mention of music and musical instruments (vv. 2-3) may point in that direction, the fact that God is praised 'at night' suggests that the song was intended for personal worship. While that does not conclusively exclude temple worship, yet as it points to the time after sunset, it probably is indicating worship when the temple would be closed.

1. Praise to the LORD (*vv. 1-3*)

It is good to praise the LORD and make music to your name, O Most High, to proclaim your love in the morning and your

faithfulness at night, to the music of the ten-stringed lyre and the melody of the harp (*vv. 1-3*). The opening declaration concerning the nature of praise to the LORD is not so much that praise makes us feel 'good', but that it is fitting that we should praise God. 'Good' is what is in accordance with his will (cf. the use of 'good' in the creation account in Gen. 1), and rightly he calls for praise from his creatures. He is addressed here as 'Most High' (*ʿelyôn*), a epithet for God that points to his majesty (see comment on Ps. 7:17). Praise is due especially to God for his love-and-faithfulness, because his character calls forth adoration.[1] This is to be done morning and night. The word for 'night' is actually plural, 'nights' (*lêlôt*), which points to the fact that the praise was carried on constantly. The 'harp' and the 'lyre' are frequently mentioned in the Psalms, and it is difficult for us to distinguish between these two stringed instruments. It is possible (because of their use in parallel expressions) that the two words refer to the same instrument. The rippling sound of both can evoke joy.

2. Joy in God's Actions (*vv. 4-5*)

For you make me glad by your deeds, O LORD; I sing for joy at the works of your hands. How great are your works, O LORD, how profound your thoughts! (*vv. 4-5*). The prayer of Psalm 90:14-16 has been answered, and now there can be joy over God's saving actions. The declaration in verse 4 is neatly balanced, beginning and ending with verbs of praise (*sâmach* and *rânan*). Similarly, two different but parallel expressions describe God's mighty actions. The 'deeds' and 'works' of the LORD are his actions in delivering the psalmist from the evil designs of his enemies (see vv. 9-11). Contemplation of what God has done calls forth exclamations of wonder at his deeds, and at the depth of his thoughts (MT lit., 'your thoughts are very deep'). Both of these ideas feature elsewhere in the Scripture (great deeds, Pss. 40:5; 77:12; 106:2; deep thoughts, Isa. 40:13, 28; 55:9; Rom. 11:33).

---

[1] On the combination of the Hebrew words *chésed* ('love') and *ʾemûnâh* ('faithfulness'), see comments on Psalm 89:1.

3. God's Exaltation over His Enemies (*vv. 6-9*)

The senseless man does not know, fools do not understand, that though the wicked spring up like grass and all evildoers flourish, they will be forever destroyed (*vv. 6-7*). The 'enemies' who are going to be destroyed (see v. 9) are described as lacking in spiritual understanding and insight (cf. Paul's words in 1 Cor. 2:6-16). They are like animals, in that they share the same inability to understand God's purposes and they refuse to accept his grace (for the other four Old Testament occurrences of 'senseless', see Pss. 49:10; 73:22; Prov. 12:1; 30:2; for 'fool', see the comment on Ps. 14:1). Such people do not realise that God's eye is on the wicked, and though they may seem to flourish, yet God has appointed an inevitable end for them. The analogy of vegetation, particularly grass, that grows quickly but also perishes quickly is a favourite one in the Old Testament (Pss. 1:3-5; 102:4, 11; 103:15-16; Isa. 37:27).

But you, O Lord, are exalted forever. For surely your enemies, O Lord, surely your enemies will perish; all evildoers will be scattered (*vv. 8-9*). By contrast, God is eternal and remains forever as the exalted king and ruler.[2] This theme, that the Lord is the majestic conqueror, will be developed in the psalms that follow (Pss. 93–100). The contrast is marked by the opening words ('*But you* …') and by the phrases 'forever destroyed' and 'exalted forever'. As eternal king God rules over all, and that ensures that his enemies must ultimately be destroyed. The precarious position of the wicked is stressed by drawing attention to them in the repetition of 'for surely your enemies' in verse 9.[3] They will be like a defeated army, fleeing from God's presence (see Ps. 68:2). Paul develops this theme in 1 Corinthians 15 as he speaks of Christ destroying

---

[2] The Hebrew word translated 'exalted' (*mârôm*) may in some contexts be a divine title, 'the Exalted One', but no compelling reason exists to translate it in this way here. Cf. *DCH*, V, pp. 483-84. One of the older commentators, J. A. Alexander, *The Psalms Translated and Explained*, pp. 387-88, explained *mârôm* as the divine title 'Most High'.

[3] In Hebrew the subject of the verb 'perish' is contained in the repeated phrase (*kî hinnêh 'oyᵉvekâ*). The repetition should be noted in English translations. Cf. ESV: 'For behold, your enemies … for behold, your enemies …'

all dominion, authority and power, and then delivering the kingdom to God the Father (1 Cor. 15:24-25).

4. God's Exaltation of the Psalmist (*vv. 10-11*)
You have exalted my horn like that of a wild ox; fine oils have been poured upon me (*v. 10*). As a result of the way in which God has dealt with his enemies, the psalmist realises that he has been blessed by God. He has received special favours from him. This is expressed by the combination of the verb 'exalt' (*rûm*) and the word 'horn' (*qeren*), an idiomatic way in Hebrew of describing elevation in position. The idea of fine oils may not seem to be connected readily with the horns of the wild ox. Probably the connection in thought is because horns were used to hold oil used for anointing (cf. 1 Sam. 16:1, 13).

My eyes have seen the defeat of my adversaries; my ears have heard the rout of my wicked foes (*v. 11*). The psalmist has seen for himself how God has overcome their joint enemies. The language is cryptic, and almost all English translations have to add words (like, 'defeat of', and 'the rout of', in the NIV).[4] 'Adversaries' is based on an emendation. It is unnecessary as the Hebrew word has the idea of 'watchers', i.e. those who wait in ambush or watch insidiously.[5] Likewise, 'my wicked foes' is a rendering of the MT, 'the enemies who rise against me'. The psalmist does not gloat over this, though it is a thing of joy for him. The news about their overthrow is a happy message that he has heard.

5. The Prosperity of the Righteous (*vv. 12-15*)
The righteous will flourish like a palm tree, they will grow like a cedar of Lebanon; planted in the house of the LORD, they will flourish in the courts of our God (*vv. 12-13*). The distinction between the wicked and the righteous is now made plain. Whereas the wicked are going to be destroyed

---

[4] Cf. the similar interpretation in the REB: 'I look on my enemies, ruin, I hear the downfall of my wicked foes.'

[5] The MT has *b^eshûray*, from the verb *shûr* I, 'to gaze at', while the common emendation followed by NIV is *b^eshôreray*, seemingly a Polel participle (without the prefixed *mem*) meaning 'foe' or 'enemy'. The latter form appears six times in the Psalms (5:8; 27:11; 54:5; 56:2; 59:10; 92:11).

or be scattered, the righteous person will have a sure future, planted by the LORD in his own house. The palm tree and the cedar of Lebanon are used here as the symbols of the righteous. The palm is one of the most stately trees of the Near East, being widely used especially for shade and food. The cedar of Lebanon was a massive tree with a vigorous root system and strong timber, and hence it too could be used as a metaphor for a person's or a nation's character in God's sight (Pss. 72:16; 104:16; Song of Songs 4:8, 11, 15; Jer. 18:14; Hosea 14:5, 6, 7, 8).

They will still bear fruit in old age, they will stay fresh and green, proclaiming, 'The LORD is upright; he is my Rock, and there is no wickedness in him' (*vv. 14-15*). Such persons will last, and even in old age they will still be fruitful. They are God's planting and they know his tender care. Right to the end of their lives they will proclaim the character of their God. The content of the proclamation is an echo of Deuteronomy 32:4. The idea of God's sure strength is linked in both passages with the idea that there is no unrighteousness in him. He is the righteous rock who also brings judgment to the wicked, as the psalmist has already declared (see vv. 7, 9, 11; and cf. Hab. 1:12). The rock imagery is frequent in the Psalms in passages like this describing the security that believers have in God (Pss. 18:2; 28:1; 62:2; 71:3; 91:2).

Psalm 93

This is the first of a group of psalms (93-100) that speak of the reign of the heavenly king who is far superior to any earthly monarch, and rules supreme over the whole world. There is no power of nature or of men that can challenge him. The content of these psalms is very similar to Psalm 47, which is another song rejoicing in God's kingship. While it is often suggested that this group of psalms were composed for some special religious ceremony in which the kingship of the LORD featured prominently, there is no indication of this within the psalms. They form a united confession concerning God's lordship and the extent of his kingdom. As far back as the Greek translation (the LXX) Psalm 93 was designated as the song to be used on the eve of the Sabbath.[1] This practice became part of later Jewish liturgy.[2] The connection with the Sabbath was probably made because of the twin themes of creation and God's rule.

Attempts have been made to find the background for this psalm (and others such as 47 and 96-99) in a yearly enthronement festival. However, no evidence can be produced to support this theory.[3] Instead, the Old Testament points to *human* kingship being announced as early as the Abrahamic period, while the eternal reign *of the LORD* is proclaimed in song after

---

[1] 'The full title in the LXX is: 'For the day preceding the Sabbath, when the land was inhabited. A song of praise by David.'

[2] *Rosh HaShanah* 31a.

[3] For discussion on this theory, see E. J. Young, 'Appendix III: The Festival of Enthronement', *The Book of Isaiah: The English Text, with Introduction, Exposition, and Notes, Volume I Chapters I-XVIII* (Grand Rapids: Eerdmans, 1965), pp. 494-99; and *Volume III Chapters XL-LXVI*, pp. 550-52.

the Exodus from Egypt (Exod. 15:18). In psalms such as this one, the eternal and sovereign reign of God is stressed. From eternity, he exercises rule over the universe, and no other, whether so-called deity or human, can deny his authority.

1. God's Rule over the World (*vv. 1-2*)

The LORD reigns, he is robed in majesty; the LORD is robed in majesty and is armed with strength. The world is firmly established; it cannot be moved (*v. 1*). God's kingship predates time. The nation 'Israel' was of recent origin, whereas her God had been king before the creation of the world. He is a majestic God, whose glory is visible. Just as ancient kings were robed in garments suitable to their position, so the LORD is regarded as being dressed in majesty and strength. The verb translated 'armed' (*'âzar,* Pi.) is often associated with being girded for battle, and so here the picture is of God as the divine warrior.[4] Because the LORD is the world's creator, it stands firm forever. These words ('The world … cannot be moved') are repeated in Psalm 96:10.[5]

Your throne was established long ago; you are from all eternity (*v.* 2). After commencing with an assertion in the third person, the psalmist now switches to direct address: 'your throne was established …' Just as the world was 'established' (v. 1), so was God's throne, using the same verb for both (*kûn*). God did not need to assume kingship like an earthly ruler, for his throne has been established from all eternity. This basic fact is repeated throughout this group of psalms, as well as elsewhere in the Old Testament (Zech. 14:9).

2. God's Rule over the Waters (*vv. 3-4*)

The seas have lifted up, O LORD, the seas have lifted up their voice; the seas have lifted up their pounding waves. Mightier than the thunder of the great waters, mightier

---

[4] For discussion on this point, see Tremper Longman III, *NIDOTTE*, 4, pp. 545-49.

[5] In the MT verse 1b is introduced by the particle *'af,* but the NIV does not translate it. It gives additional force to the statement and should be translated. Cf. NKJV: 'Surely the world is established, so that it cannot be moved,' and ESV: 'Yes, the world is established: it shall never be moved.'

than the breakers of the sea – the LORD on high is mighty (*vv. 3-4*). It is a graphic picture which the psalmist draws. The mighty waves of the sea displayed their might, but the LORD's voice spoke authoritatively and order resulted (Gen. 1:6-10; Pss. 33:7-9; 104:7-9). The threefold repetition of 'the seas have lifted up' highlights the terrifying power of mighty seas, as do the synonyms 'pounding waves', 'great waters', and 'breakers of the sea'. But over them reigns the LORD, who is vastly superior to them. He reigns from his throne 'on high',[6] and just as he was able to calm the waters by his word (Pss. 33:7; 104:7; Job 38:11), so he will subdue all enemies who rise against him.

3. God's Rule over His People (*v. 5*)

Your statutes stand firm; holiness adorns your house for endless days, O LORD (*v. 5*). God's rule is also expressed in another way. He is the sovereign over his covenantal people, and he gave them statutes that are directives to govern their lives. These statutes are trustworthy (Ps. 19:7) and exceptionally firm (the Heb. text here has 'very firm'; see RSV, NRSV, NASB, NKJV, and ESV, which all translate the word *m*ᵉ*ʾod*, 'very'). The king is also characterised by holiness, and yet he condescends to make his dwelling with his people. The thought of God's holiness is repeated in three other psalms in this group (96:9; 98:1, 9; 99:3, 5, 9). The tabernacle was a constant reminder to Israel of God's presence that he had set among them (Deut. 12:5, 11). The ultimate realisation of the principle of God's presence with his people will be seen in the heavenly dwelling. Into that holy city nothing sinful or unclean shall ever enter in, because it will be the full expression of God's holiness (Rev. 21:22-27).

---

6 See Psalm 92:8 for the use of this same word 'high' (*mârôm*).

Psalm 94

Within the group of kingship psalms (93-100), this psalm is unique. It is an appeal to the 'Judge of the earth' (v. 2) to deal with the wicked and to recompense them for their actions. It is related to the other kingship psalms in that the appeal to the Lord as the God of vengeance recognises that he is the great judge and king. From the context it is clear that those who are oppressing the widow, the alien, and the fatherless are within Israel itself. The afflicted make appeal to God to overturn the injustices perpetrated on them. No indication is given of the time when it was composed, and it blends national interests (vv. 1-15) with individual concerns (vv. 16-23).

The Jewish Mishnah indicates that this psalm was sung on the fourth day of the week (Wednesday),[1] and this is confirmed in the titles added to the Greek and Latin versions.[2] In this connection, it is noteworthy that it shares the same general theme as Psalm 82, the psalm designated for Tuesday. Both psalms are dealing with the vulnerable in society, and the treatment they receive from the hands of the arrogant wicked. Both psalms also have an appeal to God for speedy action: 'Rise up, O God, judge the earth' (Ps. 82:8); 'Rise up, O Judge of the earth: pay back to the proud what they deserve' (Ps. 94:2).

1. Appeal to the Judge *(vv. 1-3)*

O Lord, the God who avenges, O God who avenges, shine forth. Rise up, O Judge of the earth; pay back to the proud

[1] *Tamid* 7.2.

[2] The LXX has 'A psalm of/for David, for the fourth day of the week'.

what they deserve (*vv. 1-2*). The strident plea of the psalmist centres on the repeated call to the 'God who avenges'. This description of God is synonymous with the following phrase, 'the Judge of all the earth' (cf. Gen. 18:25). He is the God who carries out his just punishment and who puts right wrongs that have occurred.[3] 'Shine forth' is used in other passages of the majesty of God's presence being revealed (Deut. 33:2; Pss. 50:2; 80:1).[4] 'The proud' are those who arrogantly carry out their own plans at the expense of others, exalting themselves above God and men.

How long will the wicked, O LORD, how long will the wicked be jubilant? (*v. 3*). The repeated 'how long?' gives further urgency to the plea. These proud boasters gloat over their success, and they seem so sure that their actions will never be challenged. The ideas of pride and boasting are brought together by the use of the verb 'jubilant' (*ʿ-l-z*).[5]

2. Description of the Wicked (*vv. 4-7*)

This section of the psalm gives a more detailed description of the wicked than verses 1-3. **They pour out arrogant words; all the evildoers are full of boasting** (*v. 4*). The wicked are more than doers of wrong actions; they boast constantly of themselves, letting these boasts gush forth. The verb 'pour out' is only used once of water (Prov. 18:4), whereas it frequently denotes speaking folly (Ps. 59:7; Prov. 15:2, 28; Eccles. 10:1). This shows their real character; they delight in their wrong doing and are proud of it.[6]

---

[3] The English expression 'avenges' is too negative as a translation, for the Hebrew verb *n-q-m* and its associated nouns, *nâqâm* and *nᵉqâmâh*, relate to the positive concepts of lawfulness and justice. For discussion on this point, see H. G. L. Peels in *NIDOTTE*, 3, pp. 154-56, and W. A. VanGemeren, *'The Psalms'*, p. 610.

[4] The NIV takes the verb as an imperative, 'Shine forth' (*hôfiʿâh*), rather than as a perfect, 'He shined forth' (*hôfiyaʿ*). The best parallel is Psalm 80:1, where the imperative occurs. On textual grounds, supported by the early versions, the NIV is probably correct.

[5] Enough occurrences of *ʿ-l-z* in the MT suggest that two verbs may be in view, one denoting 'exult' and the other 'to be proud'. Cf. the verbal entries and the associated nouns in *DCH*, VI, pp. 419-20.

[6] The verb is *ʾâmar*, Hitp. It only occurs here and in Isaiah 61:6 in this form, though the context shows what parallel meaning is required for the second verb.

They crush your people, O LORD; they oppress your inheritance (*v. 5*). Their attitude to God's people also shows their attitude to God himself. Instead of honouring them, they inflict great pain. The basis for this plea is the fact that Israel stood in a special relationship with the LORD – she was indeed his chosen 'inheritance' (*nachᵃlâh*).[7] To 'crush' and 'oppress' are verbs that describe the actions taken against an enemy.

They slay the widow and the alien; they murder the fatherless. They say, 'The LORD does not see; the God of Jacob pays no heed' (*vv. 6-7*). The actions of the wicked go beyond oppression and persecution. They try to take the life of some of God's people, especially those who are less able to defend themselves. Those who are powerless are the very ones God himself will defend (Pss. 10:14; 68:5; 146:9). The biggest mistake the wicked make is to think that God takes no notice of what they do. They think that they can get away with their evil acts. The name, 'the God of Jacob', is relatively common in the Psalter (46:7, 11; 75:9; 76:6; 81:1; 84:8).

3. The Wicked Rebuked (*vv. 8-11*)

The wicked make a great mistake if they continue to think and act as they have done, and now a rebuke is given to them. **Take heed, you senseless ones among the people; you fools, when will you become wise?** (*v. 8*). The way in which the wicked are addressed ('senseless ones', 'fools') suggests that their actions show that they are making wrong moral decisions in life. They are living like animals (the Heb. word *baʿar*, 'senseless', is connected with *beʿîr*, a word meaning 'animals'), and so a word of instruction is given to them.[8] The fact that those addressed are from 'among the people', i.e. from within Israel, is significant. Of all people they should have had better understanding and not needed this instruction. 'Take heed' (*bîn*) and 'become wise' (*sâkal*, Hi.) are often used together, both coming from the language relating to wisdom.

---

[7] The expression 'the LORD's inheritance' only occurs four times, but on many occasions, as here, a possessive suffix ('my', 'your', 'his') describes the relationship with the LORD. For discussion on this usage, see Christopher J. H. Wright, *NIDOTTE*, 3, pp. 77-81.

[8] The opening clause contains alliteration that makes it more notable: *bînû boʿᵃrîm bâʿam.*

Does he who implanted the ear not hear? Does he who formed the eye not see? Does he who disciplines nations not punish? Does he who teaches man lack knowledge? (*vv. 9-10*). One thing the fool does not understand is that because God is the creator he knows all that is taking place in his world. He gave men their ears and their eyes. He also controls nations by disciplining them by punishment, while, as the source of all knowledge, he gives instruction to his creatures. In the Hebrew, verse 10 has only one question, with the second half of the verse describing more fully from where knowledge comes: 'Does he who disciplines nations not punish, [even] he who teaches men knowledge?'[9]

The LORD knows the thoughts of man; he knows that they are futile (*v. 11*). God sees through humans, and he understands that they themselves are only short-lived. 'Futile' (*hével*) is best taken here in this sense, as its use is similar to that in other Psalter passages and in Job where it refers to the brevity and uncertainty of human life (Job 7:16; Pss. 39:5, 6; 62:9; 78:33). Its use stresses the contrast between the powerful creator and his frail creatures.

4. Justice for God's People (*vv. 12-15*)

Blessed is the man you discipline, O LORD, the man you teach from your law; you grant him relief from days of trouble, till a pit is dug for the wicked (*vv. 12-13*). The psalmist picks up the words 'discipline' and 'teach' which he has already used in verse 10. Now he applies them to the way in which God directs the lives of the righteous. 'LORD' (*yâh*) is the abbreviated form of the divine name (see comment on Ps. 68:4). He gives instruction that explains the meaning of life, and this teaching stands in good stead in the days of trouble. Those who receive this teaching are indeed 'blessed', and they are able to understand the final fate of the wicked.

For the LORD will not reject his people; he will never forsake his inheritance (*v. 14*). Even though the wicked crush God's inheritance (see v. 5), yet that inheritance is safe. As

---

[9] This is the interpretation given by J. J. S. Perowne, *The Book of Psalms*, II, p. 187.

Samuel said to the covenant people in his day: 'For the sake of his great name the LORD will not reject his people, because the LORD was pleased to make you his own' (1 Sam. 12:22). God will never abandon his children, but will sustain them even in the midst of oppression. Paul may well be echoing this verse in Romans 11:1-2.

Judgment will again be founded on righteousness, and all the upright in heart will follow it (*v. 15*). The powerful creator (see vv. 9-11) is also the righteous judge, and judgment that may not have been practised for a time will be restored. The verb used here (*shûv*) not just denotes being founded but rather conveys the idea of restoration. Those whose trust is in the LORD will follow his righteous ways. Other interpretations of this verse have been suggested, but it seems best to understand 'follow *it*' as referring back to 'righteousness'.[10]

5. Confidence in the LORD (*vv. 16-19*)

Who will rise up for me against the wicked? Who will take a stand for me against evildoers? Unless the LORD had given me help, I would soon have dwelt in the silence of death (*vv. 16-17*). In the face of opposition from the wicked the psalmist knows where his help really lies. 'Rise up' and 'take a stand' are equivalent to saying 'help'. It soon becomes clear that there is no other helper but the LORD (Ps. 124:1-2). Without his aid the wicked will succeed in silencing the psalmist who will lie silent in the grave.[11]

When I said, 'My foot is slipping,' your love, O LORD, supported me. When anxiety was great within me, your consolation brought joy to my soul (*vv. 18-19*). The psalmist had thought at some stage that he was going to be put to death, and so slip into the grave. But at that very moment he knew the sustaining power of God's love, and his deep distress was turned into great joy. In his heart he experienced the reassurance of God's gracious presence.

---

[10] Some of the proposals are given by Marvin Tate, *Psalms 51-100*, p. 485. The Greek translation (the LXX) adds at the end of this verse *diapsalma* = *selâh*, but no Heb. ms. supports this.

[11] 'The silence of death' is a translation of the Hebrew word *dûmâh*. It occurs here and in Psalm 115:17 as parallel to 'death'.

6. The Righteous Judge (*vv.* 20-23)
The final verses of the psalm acknowledge that the only source of true judgment is with God alone. **Can a corrupt throne be allied with you – one that brings on misery by its decrees? They band together against the righteous and condemn the innocent to death** (*vv.* 20-21). There can be no alliance between corrupt rulers and God. Those who set up themselves in a seat of power in order to pursue their sinful ways need not think that they can work along with God. Such a combination does not produce anything but toil and travail. The concern of this type of ruler is to oppose the righteous and to bring death and destruction to the good and the innocent.

But the LORD has become my fortress, and my God the rock in whom I take refuge. He will repay them for their sins and destroy them for their wickedness; the LORD our God will destroy them (*vv.* 22-23). The psalmist has found a sure refuge with the LORD, who alone is the righteous judge. He calls God his 'fortress' (*misgâv*). This is the same word which occurs in Psalm 46:7, 11, and as there it signifies a fortified height to which one could flee for safety. The addition of 'rock' (*tsûr*) and 'refuge' (*machᵃseh*) strengthens the idea of how safe he felt in God's care.[12] The psalm opened with the call to God to avenge. It closes with the assurance that God will vindicate and ultimately the wicked will be destroyed. The repetition of the expression, 'He will destroy them' (*yatsmîtêm*), emphasises how absolute destruction will be. The Christian's hope remains the same. God will avenge the blood of his servants, and then his redeemed people will say: 'Hallelujah! For our Lord God Almighty reigns' (Rev. 19:6).

---

[12] While 'refuge' (*machᵃseh*) does occur by itself, yet more often it appears in a combined phrase along with 'strength' (*ʿoz*; Pss. 46:1; 62:7; 71:7; Prov. 14:26), or 'rock' (*tsûr*; Ps. 94:22; Job 24:8), or 'fortress' (*mᵉtsûdâh*; Ps. 91:2). The greatest cluster of terms for 'refuge/shelter/support' occurs in Psalm 62. See verses 1-2, 'my salvation', 'my rock', 'my salvation', 'my fortress', and verses 5-8, 'my hope', 'my rock', 'my salvation', 'my honour', 'my rock of strength', 'my refuge', 'our refuge'.

Psalm 95

While the main focus of this psalm is not on kingship, yet there is mention of God's kingship (v. 3) within the setting of its twin themes of creation and redemption. Hence, it is appropriately placed in the context of the kingship psalms (Pss. 93-100), all of which may have been composed by temple servants and used in the worship there. One significant factor is that the psalm views Israel's God as the supreme ruler over the whole universe. In the Near East this perception stood in stark contrast to the localised nature of other gods, who were the deities of particular peoples living in a certain geographical area. Israel's assertion of the universal rule of God was a challenge to pagan faiths.

This psalm consists of two sections each beginning with a call to God's people ('Come', vv. 1 and 6).[1] Each is also followed by the reasons for joining in the celebration (vv. 2-4, 7a).[2] The second section amplifies the call by using the wilderness experiences. Israel was fed by God since the people were 'the sheep of his pasture', a term descriptive of the covenantal relationship between God and Israel (cf. its use in other psalms such as 74:1, 79:13, 100:3, and in prophetical passages such as Jer. 23:1, 25:36 and Ezek. 34:31).The mention of God's judgment in the past reinforces the call to obey him in the present (vv. 7b-11).

---

[1] The two calls are translated identically in English, even though they use different verbs in Hebrew (*hâlak* in verse 1, *bô'* in verse 6).

[2] In the Hebrew text the reason is marked by *kî*, 'for', at the commencement of verses 3 and 7.

The section is quoted in Hebrews 3:7-11 when the subject of unbelief is being considered. This great psalm has inspired many hymns for Christian worship.[3]

1. Come Sing for Joy (*vv. 1-5*)

Come, let us sing for joy to the LORD; let us shout aloud to the Rock of our salvation. Let us come before him with thanksgiving and extol him with music and song (*vv. 1-2*). The psalmist gives a strong call to the assembly of Israel for hearty praise to the LORD in song. The undated setting was worship in the temple, and the call was probably given by a priest or a Levite. In the preceding psalm God is also called 'the Rock' (94:22; see also 18:2 and 89:26). 'To come before the LORD' means to appear at the sanctuary, and there the people are to sing to him in praise and adoration.

For the LORD is the great God, the great King above all gods (*v. 3*). The compelling reason for the call to praise is the greatness of the LORD. That is the supreme motive for songs of adoration, and it is amplified in the following verses. The LORD is exalted above all things and all other beings. There is no god that can be compared with him. The expression, 'the great King above all gods', is very similar to 'the great King over all the earth' (Ps. 47:2). It is an expression of his superiority over all of his creation, even over the so-called gods of the nations. Mention of such gods does not assume their existence. They are only the figments of the imagination.

In his hand are the depths of the earth, and the mountain peaks belong to him. The sea is his, for he made it, and his hands formed the dry land (*vv. 4-5*). These verses draw attention to some of the awesome features of the world in which we live – the deepest recesses of the earth, the highest mountains, the mighty seas, the continents – in order to show the control that the LORD has over his creation. The verbs 'made' (*'âsâh*) and 'formed' (*yâtsar*) are regularly used of God's creative activity.[4]

---

[3] Two of the modern hymns based on this psalm are 'Let us sing to the God of salvation' by Richard Bewes, and 'Come, sing praises to the Lord above' by Michael Perry.

[4] The two verbs are not exactly synonyms, for *yâtsar* is used more of specific objects of God's design and care – such as man (Gen. 2:7); the servant of the LORD (Isa. 49:5, 8); and the spirit within man (Zech. 12:1).

He's the King above the mountains high,
the sea is His, the land and sky
subterranean depths that man defy
are in the hollow of His hand.
(Michael Perry 1942-)

2. Come Bow Down in Worship *(vv. 6-11)*

Come, let us bow down in worship, let us kneel before the LORD our Maker; for he is our God and we are the people of his pasture, the flock under his care (*vv. 6-7*). The second call to the worshippers is to acknowledge the LORD as their maker. The call itself is defined further by the words that follow. In Hebrew there are three verbs: 'bow down', 'bow the knees', and 'kneel'. While the words may give some indication of the posture in prayer, the real emphasis is on the attitude towards the LORD. The call is to come in reverence before him because of the relationship, initiated by God, between him and his people. He by grace is their God and they are his flock (Ps. 100:3: 'we are his people, the sheep of his pasture'). Just as kings are called 'shepherds' of their people, so are their kingdoms called 'pastures' (Jer. 25:36; 49:20). The final expression, 'the flock under his care' (lit., 'flock(s) of his hand') is simply parallel to the preceding one, 'the people of his pasture'.[5]

Today, if you hear his voice, do not harden your hearts as you did at Meribah, as you did that day at Massah in the desert, where your fathers tested and tried me, though they had seen what I did (*vv. 6-9*). At a ceremony the leader would speak these words to the worshippers and call them to fresh obedience to the LORD. The switch to first person speech ('tested and tried *me*') happens in other cases where the spokesman of God is actually speaking (Isa. 3:1-4). The response that God desires from his flock is starkly different from that which the people gave at the incidents at Meribah and Massah (Exod. 17:7; Num. 20:13). Despite knowing so

[5] The similarity to Psalm 79:13, 'and we your people, flocks of your pasture', was pointed out by David Howard, *The Structure of Psalms 93-100* (Winona Lake: Eisenbrauns, 1997), pp. 77-78. Comparison of these two verses also shows that emendation here, as frequently proposed, is unnecessary.

much about God's power, the people then challenged him. The experiences of their fathers at the Red Sea and the miraculous food supply which they received should have convinced each generation to trust the LORD and to be obedient to him.

For forty years I was angry with that generation; I said, 'They are a people whose hearts go astray, and they have not known my ways' (*v. 10*). All the disobedience of Israel came to a climax when the people refused to carry out the conquest of Canaan, and wanted to return to Egypt (Num. 14:1-4). Only after Moses pled with God on behalf of the people were they forgiven (Num. 14:13-25), but they were condemned to stay in the wilderness for forty years (Num. 14:34). God's declaration about the people paraphrases his words in Numbers 14:11.

So I declared on oath in my anger, 'They shall never enter my rest' (*v. 11*). The oath is given in Numbers 14:23-35 where it is said that the people will never enter into *the land*, with a summary statement in Deut. 1:34-36. However, the promise was repeatedly given of *rest* in the land of Canaan (see especially Deuteronomy 3:20; 12:9-10; 25:19), and so 'rest' (*m*[e]*nûkâh*) could easily serve as a synonym for 'land [of Canaan]'. The epistle to the Hebrews draws upon this psalm when dealing with the subject of the entry of believers into the eschatological rest (Heb. 3:7–4:13). The writer points out that just as rest awaited the church in the wilderness, so rest still awaits New Testament believers. It is only through Jesus that believers come into possession of rest and look forward to the ultimate Sabbath of rest in heaven (Heb. 4:8-10). In Hebrews, 'rest' is identical with 'the heavenly country' sought by believers, 'the lasting city which is to come' (Heb. 13:14; cf. 11:16).

Psalm 96

Psalms 96-99 form a small group within the wider section of Psalms 93-100. They have many words and ideas in common, and they may well have been composed by the same author. This psalm appears in a slightly altered form in 1 Chronicles 16:23-33 in connection with the bringing of the ark of the covenant to Jerusalem. There it is combined with parts of Psalms 105 and 106.[1] The new use of these psalms explains the textual variations in 1 Chronicles 16 as compared with the originals, and also how the composer of the medley could simply use the beginning of Psalm 105, and the beginning and end of Psalm 106.

The psalm divides into two parts, both introduced by commands to sing praise to God: 'Sing ... sing ... sing' (vv. 1-2) as compared with 'ascribe ... ascribe ... ascribe' (vv. 7-8). In each case the commands are followed by celebration of God's greatness and power. This praise is not just to take place within Israel but among the Gentile nations as well (v. 10). Psalm 96 is a call to all nations to praise the LORD, and forms part of the missionary outlook of the Old Testament. It is an anticipation of the worldwide mission of the Christian church (Matt. 28:16-20). Early Christians saw the significance of the

[1] 1 Chronicles 16:8-36 is an adaptation of parts of the three psalms to fit the new occasion. Some English versions misunderstand the MT in 1 Chronicles 16:7, inserting, as NIV does, the words 'this psalm', which are totally lacking in the Hebrew. The point is that David 'first appointed' the Levites to their musical role, not that this psalm was actually sung as the ark of the covenant arrived in Jerusalem. Neither Psalm 96 nor 1 Chronicles 16:8-36 can be used to alter the text in the other, as they have to be regarded as separate compositions.

psalm, and the old Latin version in verse 10 has: 'Say among the nations, the Lord reigns *from the cross*.'

1. A Call to Praise (*vv. 1-3*)

Like the adjacent psalms, this one opens with a call to all the world to sing praises to the LORD. This, and many other expressions, are similar to parts of Isaiah 40-66 (see for the opening words, Isaiah 42:10). There is often a close link between the psalmists and the prophets. **Sing to the LORD a new song; sing to the LORD, all the earth. Sing to the LORD, praise his name; proclaim his salvation day after day** (*vv. 1-2*). The call to praise is repeated three times: 'Sing (*shîrû*) ... sing (*shîrû*) ... sing' (*shîrû*), emphasising the exuberant feelings of the psalmist. The term 'a new song' can indicate simply the freshness of the song (see comment on Ps. 33:2-3), or, as here, it can indicate an eschatological or end-time song (see Rev. 5:9; 14:3). This fits in with the whole tenor of the psalm, which points to the final reign of the LORD as king and judge. Universal praise is to be made to him, and there is to be constant proclamation of his saving grace. In the final clauses, two different verbs are used to repeat the same theme (NIV 'praise', *bârak*, Pi. and NIV 'proclaim', *bâsar*, Pi.), though here no real distinction can be made between them.

Declare his glory among the nations, his marvellous deeds among all peoples (*v. 3*). God's amazing salvation is to be proclaimed to people everywhere. The combination 'declare his marvellous deeds' is a standard expression in the Psalter (see comment on 9:1, and cf. also 26:7; 40:5; 75:1; 98:1). His saving acts on behalf of his people are to be made known to Jew and Gentile. This is an anticipation of the New Testament proclamation that 'salvation is found in no-one else, for there is no other name under heaven given to men by which we must be saved' (Acts 4:12).

2. The Majesty of the LORD (*vv. 4-6*)

A fuller explanation is now given why God should be praised universally. **For great is the LORD and most worthy of praise; he is to be feared above all gods. For all the gods of the**

nations are idols, but the LORD made the heavens (*vv.* 4-5). The expression 'Great is the Lord' was clearly a regular way of ascribing honour to God (see the same phrase in Pss. 48:1; 96:1; 145:3). Belief in God is repeatedly linked with confession of him in praise, for faith and joyful acknowledgment hang together (Rom. 10:8-11). While other 'gods' are referred to, yet their existence is denied in verse 5. The psalmist puns on the Hebrew word for God (*'elôhîm*), saying that the heathen gods are only worthless idols or nobodies (*'elîlîm*). They are put to shame before the sovereign God (Ps. 97:7; Isa. 19:1). They are not real, and therefore do not have power like the God who made the heavens.

Splendour and majesty are before him; strength and glory are in his sanctuary (*v.* 6). 'Splendour and majesty' (*hôd vehâdâr*) commonly occur together in the Psalms in description of God (21:5; 45:3; 104:1; 111:3), while 'strength and glory' (*'oz vetif'eret*) occur in Psalm 78:61 in reference to the ark (NIV 'might', 'splendour'). It is difficult to decide whether 'sanctuary' refers to God's heavenly dwelling or to the temple. The overall thought of the psalm suggests the former, though in the context of a temple song the latter can hardly be excluded.

3. A Call to Worship (*vv.* 7-9)

In parallel with the opening verses, another call goes out to the nations to worship the LORD. **Ascribe to the LORD, O families of nations, ascribe to the LORD glory and strength. Ascribe to the LORD the glory due his name; bring an offering and come into his courts**(*vv.* 7-8). The threefold use of 'ascribe' (*hâvû*) in these verses parallels the threefold 'sing' in verses 1-2.[2] They form a command to everyone from all nations to acknowledge the LORD and to offer to him such ascription of praise that recognises and promotes the glory of his person. This praise

---

[2] This verb (*yâhav*, imper. 2 pl. m. *hâvû*), while used in a general sense for 'come!', has its important theological meaning in passages denoting giving glory to the LORD. See, in addition to this verse, Deuteronomy 32:3, Psalm 29:1-2, and 1 Chronicles 16:28-29. These passages are a call to acknowledge the LORD as supreme king, and to give him the glory that corresponds to his majesty.

must be more than mere words; suitable attitudes and actions are required as well. In the New Testament the call becomes: 'Repent, for the kingdom of heaven is near' (Matt. 3:1-6), while the allusion to the promise given to Abraham of blessing to the nations ('O families of nations', see Gen. 12:3 and 22:18) finds fulfilment in the redeeming work of Jesus (Gal. 3:10-14).

Worship the LORD in the splendour of his holiness; tremble before him, all the earth (*v. 9*). In ascribing glory to the LORD, his creatures acknowledge his greatness by bowing before him. If the footnote in the NIV is followed ('with the splendour of his holiness') it would imply coming before him with garments that are ritually clean (Lev. 11:24-28). The verb 'tremble' is the counterpart of 'fear' in verse 4. Today God demands the offering up of our bodies as living sacrifices, holy and pleasing to him (Rom. 12:1). Likewise the church is to be presented to him without stain or blemish, but holy and blameless (Eph. 5:27).

4. Joy to the World (*vv. 10-13*)

Just as verses 4-6 explained the reason for the call to sing to the LORD a new song, so these verses explain the reason for the call to ascribe glory to the LORD. **Say among the nations, 'The LORD reigns.' The world is firmly established, it cannot be moved; he will judge the peoples with equity** (*v. 10*). The basic reason is that the LORD is the king over all since he is the creator of the world. It stands firm because of his decree (Ps. 33:8-11), and from all eternity his throne has been established. All mankind is subject to his equitable judgment. The New Testament reaffirms this principle, making it explicit that God will judge the world through the Lord Jesus, raising him from the dead as proof of this (Acts 17:31).

Let the heavens rejoice, let the earth be glad; let the sea resound, and all that is in it; let the fields be jubilant, and everything in them. Then all the trees of the forest will sing for joy; they will sing before the LORD, for he comes, he comes to judge the earth. He will judge the world in righteousness and the peoples in his truth (*vv. 11-13*). When the LORD comes in judgment at the end of time, then all the universe will rejoice before him. The whole of nature will sing for joy when it is 'liberated from its bondage to decay and brought into the glorious freedom of the children of God' (Rom. 8:21). The repetition of both the phrase 'he comes' (*kî vâ'*), and the fact that he is coming to judge, emphasise the certainty and the nature of that coming. Just as the triple occurrence of the verb 'ascribe' (vv. 7-8) parallels the triple use of 'sing' in verses 1-2, so also the double use of 'for' (*kî*) corresponds to the earlier use in verses 4-5. In both sections of the psalm this use of 'for' introduces the motive for praise. God will come to bring justice to the ungodly and deliverance to his saints. The prospect is that Gentiles will also be among those for whom he comes in righteousness and truth. The New Testament picture is of every creature in heaven and earth at the last day singing:

> 'To him who sits on the
> throne and to the Lamb
> be praise and honour and
> glory and power,
> for ever and ever!' (Rev. 5:13)

Psalm 97

This psalm commences with the declaration of the LORD's kingship that it shares with the opening verses of Psalms 93 and 99. Verse 7 forms a pivotal verse around which the whole psalm revolves, a poetic device frequently used in the Psalter (cf. 6:6; 42:8; 48:8; 71:14; 113:5). The NIV, and also other English versions, accurately show the parallel between the commencement of these two sections. The verbs in both 1 and 8 are identical, appearing in a typical chiastic pattern:

Verse 1	'Be glad (*tâgêl*) … and rejoice (*yism^{e}chû*)'
Verse 8	'Rejoices (*vatismach*) … and are glad (*vatâgêl*)'

This parallelism ties the whole psalm together by means of a common theme.

The opening section is a call to the nations (including those around the Mediterranean) to acknowledge the greatness of the LORD, while the closing section is a call to Zion to rejoice in the LORD and in his righteous rule. The message of verse 7 is that idol worshippers and even their idols must bow before his sovereignty. Israel and the Gentile nations are both to confess that they have seen and acknowledge the glory of the great king.

No indication is given of the time of composition. The Hebrew text does not have a title, but the LXX has 'Of David, when his land was restored'. Some have thought that the reference in verse 8 to 'the daughters of Judah' (*b^{e}nôt y^{e}hûdâh*, NIV 'villages of Judah') also points to a time after the return from exile, but the phrase is very indefinite. It is more likely that the song was composed some time after the division of the kingdom following Solomon's death.

1. Let Distant Shores Rejoice (*vv. 1-6*)

The LORD reigns, let the earth be glad; let the distant shores rejoice (*v. 1*). The opening declaration concerning the LORD's kingship is followed by a call for the earth to be glad and the distant shores to rejoice. All the inhabitants of the world are to be joyful in the knowledge that the LORD reigns. A fitting response to the eternal reign of God is worship and adoration (see Rev. 11:15; 15:3-4; 19:6). The word translated 'shores' is also used of islands, which explains the variation in other translations (see AV, NKJV). It is practically a technical term for 'Gentiles', and here serves to draw attention to the universal nature of God's kingship.[1]

Clouds and thick darkness surround him; righteousness and justice are the foundation of his throne. Fire goes before him and consumes his foes on every side. His lightning lights up the world; the earth sees and trembles (*vv. 2-4*). The description of God's rule echoes language in other passages that speak of the majesty of God's appearance (cf. Exod. 20:18-21; Deut. 5:22-26). His glory is such that it is veiled from human sight lest it dazzle the eyes. His glory when seen is likened to lightning flashes which both serve as a source of light and also bring terror with them. His enemies perish before his presence (Ps. 68:1-2). Amidst this description there is also a reaffirmation of the foundations of God's kingly rule. His kingship is characterised by the fact that he does not reign like a human ruler in self-interest and with perversion of justice. Instead, his rule is noted for its righteousness and its fair administration.

The mountains melt like wax before the LORD, before the Lord of all the earth. The heavens proclaim his righteousness, and all the peoples see his glory (*vv. 5-6*). Even the mighty mountains, which symbolise all that is stable and

[1] The Hebrew word *ʾî* (pl. *ʾiyyîm*) means 'coast' or 'island'. It is used thirty-eight times in the Old Testament, seventeen of these being in Isaiah. Certainly the word includes Greece and other Mediterranean countries.

enduring, cannot stand before the LORD. The repetition of 'before the LORD' (cf. the repetition of 'he comes' in Ps. 96:13) probably occurs to highlight his majesty and kingly rule over the universe. Undergirding the whole moral order in the universe is the righteousness of God, and his general revelation declares this fact (Ps. 19:1). The world of creation and providence proclaims its dependence upon God's character for its continuing existence. All men have a knowledge of God because they still bear his image, even though it is marred by sin. Though they try and suppress this knowledge, they are left without excuse before him (Rom. 1:20).

2. A Call to Worship *(v. 7)*

All who worship images are put to shame, those who boast in idols – worship him, all you gods! (*v. 7*). The thought of this verse is the central aspect of the psalm. Idol worshippers are called upon to renounce their allegiance to their present 'gods' and to confess the true God and King as their master. No man-made idol has the power to save those who worship it (Isa. 44:17). All who trust in what are nobodies will ultimately realise their folly.[2] The consistent teaching of the Old Testament is that trusting in idols brings shame and disgrace (Isa. 1:29; 42:17).[3] The psalmist makes it clear that even these so-called 'gods' are really subject to the one true God. Before him they must prostrate themselves.

3. Let Zion Rejoice *(vv. 8-12)*

Zion hears and rejoices and the villages of Judah are glad because of your judgments, O LORD. For you, O LORD, are the Most High over all the earth; you are exalted far above all gods (*vv. 8-9*). God's own people hear again the declaration, 'The LORD reigns', and they are glad. The fact that God's judgments are acts of deliverance on behalf of his

---

[2] For comment on the pun, using the words *ʾᵉlôhîm* and *ʾᵉlîlîm,* see Psalm 96:5.

[3] This sense of horror over idolatry explains the transmutation of the names of Saul's sons, Ish*baal* (a man of Baal) and Mephi*baal* (a word of Baal) becoming Ishbosheth (a man of shame) and Mephi*bosheth* (a word of shame). See 2 Samuel 2:8; 9:6.

people brings joy in the settlements throughout the land. The word translated 'villages' is actually the plural 'daughters' (*b^e nôt*), but it is used quite often of villages that are regarded as daughters of larger towns.[4] The people acknowledge again that God is so exalted above all his creation, and none of the idols can compete with his position (for comment on 'the Most High' [*ʿelyôn*], see Ps. 7:17).

Let those who love the LORD hate evil, for he guards the lives of his faithful ones and delivers them from the hand of the wicked (*v. 10*). God's people are called on to show both love and hatred – love for God himself, but hatred towards evil. The description of those who are in a close relationship with God as those who love him is also found concerning Abraham (Isa. 41:8, 'friend', Heb. 'the one who loves me'). Protective care surrounds God's 'friends', and he vindicates and delivers them from those who conspire against himself as well as against them.

Light is shed upon the righteous and joy on the upright in heart. Rejoice in the LORD, you who are righteous, and praise his holy name (*vv. 11-12*). The rule of God is described here and elsewhere in terms of light and joy (cf. the combination of light and joy in Isa. 58 and 60). 'Shed upon' is literally 'sown', which may indicate something strewn in the path of the righteous.[5] The expression used here to describe them ('the upright in heart') is frequently used in this way in the Book of Psalms. The call to 'rejoice' links both with the last word in the Hebrew text of verse 11 ('joy') and also with the call in verse 1 for the distant shore to 'rejoice'. 'Name' is literally 'memorial', but clearly, as in Exodus 3:15, it is a synonym for 'name', though twice in the Psalms (111:4; 145:7) it refers to the recitation of God's wonderful deeds. Here something of this meaning would be quite in keeping with the context.

---

[4] Cf. the entry in *DCH*, II, p. 282, with many examples cited.

[5] The word for 'sow' is *zâraʿ*. A few Hebrew manuscripts and some of the early versions read a different verb with one consonantal change, *zârach*, 'to shine'. While 'shine' fits the context, the evidence is not sufficiently strong to support any alteration. Since 'sow' elsewhere has a fairly wide range of use (cf. sow peace, Zech. 8:12; sow righteousness, Prov. 11:18), there can be little objection to sowing happiness here.

Psalm 98

A psalm.

There is much similarity between Psalms 96 and 98, especially in relation to the manner in which they commence and finish. In spite of the fact that Psalm 98 does not contain the words 'The LORD reigns', yet it fits in well with the other kingship psalms in this group (Pss. 93-99). The expression 'the LORD, the king' (*hammelek yhwh*) at the end of verse 6 is virtually a synonymous statement.

Psalm 98 shows a marked progression in the main theme, as the call to sing to the LORD is progressively widened. First, the congregation is called upon to sing to the LORD, then all the peoples of the earth, and finally, all of creation. The reason for such universal praise is the salvation that God has made known. This may well be understood as an accumulation of various acts of deliverance wrought by him rather than just a single one such as the return from exile in Babylon. Just as a sequence of verbs is used to issue the call to praise ('sing', 'shout for joy', 'burst into song', 'make music', 'sing for joy'), so another sequence of verbs is used to describe God's actions ('done [marvellous things]', 'saved', 'made known', 'revealed', 'remembered', 'comes', 'will judge'). There is clearly a focus too on the final coming of the Lord, when the Lord Jesus will return to gather his people and to judge the whole world (Matt. 25:31-46). Isaac Watts captured the spirit of Psalm 98 with his words:

> Joy to the world! The Lord is come;
> let earth receive her King.
> let ev'ry heart prepare Him room,
> and heaven and nature sing:

and heaven and nature sing:
and heaven and nature sing.

1. Israel – Sing to the LORD (*vv. 1-3*)

Sing to the LORD a new song, for he has done marvellous things; his right hand and his holy arm have worked salvation for him (*v. 1*). In words identical to the opening of Psalm 96 (see the commentary), the call goes forth to the congregation of Israel to respond to the LORD's goodness with a new song. As in Psalm 96, 'a new song' is one with eschatological overtones, an end-time song. The reason for the invitation to praise (marked in Hebrew by the word *kî*, 'for') is that the LORD has performed acts that are unmistakably divine ('marvellous things' often has this meaning; see the comment on Ps. 71:17), and which are explained in verses 2-3. 'Right hand' and 'holy arm' are indications of the LORD's might, so that he has brought about the salvation without anyone else's intervention (Isa. 59:16; 63:5).

The LORD has made his salvation known and revealed his righteousness to the nations. He has remembered his love and his faithfulness to the house of Israel; all the ends of the earth have seen the salvation of our God (*vv. 2-3*). In continuing to express the reason why praise is necessary, the psalmist begins and ends these verses with the idea of God's salvation ('his salvation', v. 2; 'the salvation of our God', v. 3). When God acts in salvation that is a demonstration of his righteousness, and it is done openly so that it forms a self-revelation to the nations. In this way God proclaims to the nations his essential character and his saving power. No mention is made here of the fact that when God does bring salvation it so often is accompanied by judgment to the nations. Towards Israel God acted with covenant faithfulness and he took appropriate action to deliver his people. When he 'remembers' he saves his people (Exod. 2:24) or preserves them (Lev. 26:44-45).[1] This had been done openly, and so this salvation

---

[1] No real difference exists between the Hebrew expressions 'he remembered his covenant' (*zâkar ʾet-bᵉrîtô*) and 'he remembered his steadfast love' (*zâkar chasdô*). Both speak of the LORD's utter faithfulness in fulfilling his covenant promises. For further comment, see P. Kalluveettil, *Declaration and Covenant: A Comprehensive Review of Covenant Formulae from the Old Testament and the Ancient Near East* (Rome: Biblical Institute Press, 1982), p. 48.

was apparent to the world at large (cf. the reference in Ps. 26:2 regarding the Gentile nations recognising the 'great things' done by the LORD). In this way God had proclaimed his saving power.

2. The Nations – Shout for Joy (*vv. 4-6*)
It is not only Israel who is called on to rejoice in the LORD, but the [Gentile] nations as well. The opening words of verse 4 are the same as Psalm 66:1 (cf. also Ps. 47:1). **Shout for joy to the LORD, all the earth, burst into jubilant song with music; make music to the LORD with the harp, with the harp and the sound of singing, with trumpets and the blast of the ram's horn – shout for joy before the LORD, the King** (*vv. 4-6*). The Hebrew text uses a cluster of commands to the nations, and in so doing highlights the praise that is expected from them. They are to 'shout for joy' (twice), 'burst forth into song', 'shout for joy', and 'make music' (twice). The NIV text renders them quite idiomatically into English, though the smoothness of the translation loses something of the forcefulness that the repeated commands have in Hebrew. The closing words of verse 6 point to the motive that is to lie behind their praise. The nations are to own the covenant LORD of Israel as their God and King. This, then, is really a call for conversion of the nations, and a commitment to the living God.

3. The World – Sing for Joy (*vv. 7-9*)
The final stage of the psalm brings the whole world in on the song of praise. **Let the sea resound, and everything in it, the world, and all who live in it. Let the rivers clap their hands, let the mountains sing together for joy; let them sing before the LORD, for he comes to judge the earth. He will judge the world in righteousness and the peoples with equity** (*vv. 7-9*). The whole of creation is to be part of this chorus, as well as all the inhabitants (the second part of verse 7 is identical with the second part of Ps. 24:1). Nature is personified, and rejoices in the coming of the LORD as judge of the earth. The description of the LORD's coming is almost identical to Psalm 96:13. To 'judge' involves deliverance for his people and destruction for his enemies. At the last great appearing of the LORD he

will deal with all in accordance with his righteousness and uprightness. The revelation of his righteousness in the past (v. 2) foreshadowed a yet greater demonstration in the future (v. 9). When the redeemed in heaven sing the song of Moses and the song of the Lamb, they will confess:

> Great and marvellous are your deeds,
> Lord God Almighty.
> Just and true are your ways,
> King of the ages (Rev. 15:3).

Psalm 99

Along with Psalms 93 and 97, Psalm 99 commences with the explicit affirmation of the LORD's kingship: 'The LORD reigns' (*yhwh mâlâk*), which is further strengthened by the addition of the thought that he 'sits enthroned between the cherubim'. This reference, which directs attention to the ark of the covenant, suggests the poem was composed some time in the pre-exilic period. It is clear that the psalmist did not regard this kingship as of recent origin, for he appeals to the relationship which God had with his people in the times of Moses, Aaron, and Samuel, though without mentioning specific acts of deliverance.

The psalm shows signs of careful composition, with the word 'LORD' occurring seven times (symbolically pointing to completeness), as well as a sevenfold occurrence of Hebrew personal pronouns referring to him. There is also a threefold division in the psalm, marked out by the refrain 'he is holy' in verses 3 and 5, expanded to the fuller expression 'for the LORD our God is holy' in the final verse. Such a threefold liturgical phrase was probably a standard feature of worship (Isa. 6:3; Rev. 4:8).

1. The Exalted LORD (*vv. 1-3*)

The LORD reigns, let the nations tremble; he sits enthroned between the cherubim, let the earth shake. Great is the LORD in Zion; he is exalted over all the nations (*vv. 1-2*). The LORD is the king over Israel (he is enthroned between the cherubim, and he is exalted in Zion). This is a reference to the fact that he met with his people at the mercy seat in the tabernacle. Yet he is far greater than that, for he is king of the nations and they are called to tremble in awe before him. This verb 'tremble' (*râgaz*) is used in the Old Testament both for trembling before the judgment of God (Isa. 64:2; Joel 2:1), and also of the response to God's gracious actions (Jer. 33:9). In this psalm both aspects are present. As the nations bow before the holy and righteous king, they are reminded of his gracious character in forgiving sin (v. 8). Verse 2 is very similar in thought and wording to Psalm 48:1, where Jerusalem is referred to as 'the city of our God'.

Let them praise your great and awesome name – he is holy (*v. 3*). The nations are not only to tremble but to praise, a thought that is also present in Psalm 48:1 ('most worthy of praise'). God is indeed great and holy (Deut. 7:21), and the nations should acknowledge that fact and bow before him in reverence. There is a sudden shift from the second person ('*your* great and awesome name') to the third person ('*he* is holy'). The expression, 'he is holy', seems to be one used in a worship situation, as a declaration stemming from God's own declaration, 'I am holy' (Lev. 11:44; 19:2; 20:26; 21:8).

2. The Righteous LORD (*vv. 4-5*)

The King is mighty, he loves justice – you have established equity; in Jacob you have done what is just and right (*v. 4*). This verse begins with a declaration about God ('The King is mighty, he loves justice'), and then addresses him directly in the second person ('*You* have established equity'). Though God is mighty, and shows that in his kingly rule, yet he always acts in accordance with his own character, and so does what is right and good. He acts rightly because that is his nature (Ps. 4:1; Ezra 9:15). It is *his* rule that is in view, not that of the Davidic family. The period when this rule began for Israel as a nation (called here by the alternate name 'Jacob') was when the covenant was made at Sinai.

Exalt the LORD our God and worship at his footstool; he is holy (*v. 5*). For the temple worshippers the call is to lift up the name of their God in praise and adoration. The place where this is to be done is the LORD's 'footstool'. Most probably this means the cover of the ark of the covenant, 'the place of atonement' (1 Chron. 28:2, 11). When God is on his heavenly throne, metaphorically his earthly footstool becomes the tabernacle. In verse 9 this is simply called 'his holy mountain', i.e. Sinai. The motive behind this worship is that God is holy, repeating the declaration from verse 3.

3. The Forgiving LORD (*vv. 6-9*)

Moses and Aaron were among his priests, Samuel was among those who called on his name; they called on the LORD and he answered them (*v. 6*). God provided priestly servants who interceded for the people (Exod. 32:11-13), and who taught them the way of the LORD (Mal. 2:4-6). Moses carried out various priestly functions (Exod. 24:6, 8; 40:22-27), while Samuel prayed on behalf of Israel (1 Sam. 7:9; 12:16-18). Their prayers were effective, in that God responded to them. The promise is given elsewhere that God responds to those who call to him (Ps. 145:18).

He spoke to them from the pillar of cloud; they kept his statutes and the decrees he gave them. O LORD our God, you answered them; you were to Israel a forgiving God, though you punished their misdeeds (*vv. 7-8*). A summary statement is given of the manner in which God answered their prayers. While the reference to 'the pillar of cloud' points directly to the experience of Moses and Aaron (see Exod. 33:9 and Num. 12:5-6), yet that of Samuel may also be included, as he was called by God at the sanctuary, where God's ark was situated (1 Sam. 3:3). However imperfectly the decrees that God gave were kept in Israel, yet it was to his people specifically that they were given. Israel did not escape punishment for her sins, but mercy was shown so often to a wayward people by a forgiving God. The one whom the poet calls 'our God' repeatedly forgave his people's sins (Ps. 103:11-13; Dan. 9:9).

Exalt the LORD our God and worship at his holy mountain, for the LORD our God is holy (*v. 9*). The psalm closes with an expanded version of verse 5. The relationship between the LORD and his people is emphasised by the double occurrence of the phrase 'the LORD *our* God', in addition to its double use already (cf. vv. 5 and 8). In place of worship at 'his footstool', the people are called to God's 'holy mountain' (i.e. Zion). The addition of the words 'the LORD our God', which come last in the Hebrew text, throw emphasis on the relationship which the worshippers had with the holy God. Though so different in character from his sinful people, yet he was indeed their God. Since the coming of Jesus true worship is offered wherever believers 'worship the Father in spirit and in truth'.

Psalm 100

A psalm. For giving thanks.

The final psalm in this section (Pss. 93-100) is a triumphal song of praise to the LORD. The second part of the title (*l^e^tôdâh*) occurs only here, and it has suggested to some that the psalm was composed to accompany the presentation of a thank-offering to the LORD (Lev. 7:11-15). Though the Hebrew word *tôdâh* can refer to such a sacrifice (2 Chron. 29:31), there is no indication that this was the specific purpose of this psalm. In fact, verses 2 and 4 suggest vocal praise, not sacrificial offering.[1] The LXX rendering of the title, 'a psalm for thanksgiving' (*psalmos eis exomologêsin*), also supports this view.

A strong link exists between Psalms 95 and 100, with several phrases being very similar (cf. 95:1-2 with 100:1-2, and 95:7 with 100:3). A close connection also exists between Psalms 99 and 100. In Psalm 99 mention is made of the LORD's rule over all the nations (*v.* 2), but also of his special relationship with Israel (*vv.* 6-8). Here in Psalm 100, while all the earth is called upon to worship the LORD, the position of Israel as his flock is emphasised (*v.* 3).

In the early church Psalm 100 was used for morning prayer, while throughout the history of the Christian church it has often been used by the assembled people of God as they engage in communal worship before the LORD. It is commonly referred to as 'the Old Hundredth', after the name of the stately tune to which it is often sung. This tune was composed

[1] Some commentators have understood the phrase *l^e^tôdâh* to mean 'with a thanksgiving [sacrifice]', but this is not shown by the preposition *le* ('to', or 'for'). If 'with' had been intended, then another preposition, probably *'al*, would be expected.

by Louis Bourgeois and first appeared in the French Genevan Psalter of 1551.

1. A Call to Worship (*vv. 1-3*)

Shout for joy to the LORD, all the earth (*v. 1*). These opening words are identical to Psalm 98:4a. All the earth should respond to this call when they see what the LORD has done for his people. It is in effect a missionary invitation, for the psalmist wants everyone, Jew and Gentile, to rejoice before the King.

Worship the LORD with gladness; come before him with joyful songs (*v. 2*). The Hebrew word rendered 'worship' (*'âvad*) has a range of meaning, which extends from acting as a servant or slave (Ezek. 29:18), or functioning as subjects of a ruler (Jer. 27:7; 28:14), to serving the LORD (Exod. 23:25). Serving the LORD 'with gladness' (*b^esimchâh*) was the response expected of Israel (Deut. 28:47). The Gentile nations are called to give their allegiance to the covenantal God of Israel ('the LORD'), and to join in joyful worship of him.

Know that the LORD is God. It is he who made us, and we are his; we are his people, the sheep of his pasture (*v. 3*). Following the call to worship comes a declaration regarding Israel's covenantal status. To 'know' God is to confess him, making open acknowledgment that he, the LORD, is the only God. An alternative rendering would be, 'Acknowledge that the LORD alone is God.' The nations should know that it is the LORD who formed the Israelites into a nation for himself, and that nation belongs to him. For 'and we are his', there is an alternative translation, 'and not we ourselves'. It comes from an ambiguity in the Hebrew text because two Hebrew words share the same pronunciation but differ in both their written form and meaning (Heb. *lô*; it can mean either 'not' [*lo'*], or 'belonging to him', 'his' [*lô*]).[2] The thought of Israel

[2] The MT has 'not we [ourselves]', and this was followed by the LXX and the Latin Vulgate. While Psalms 79:13 and 95:7 have 'we' linked with 'people', yet the Hebrew manuscript evidence supports the MT over against the Q^ere reading, 'and belonging to him'. In the context the stress is on the fact that Israel was not self-created, but made by the LORD and hence he had proprietary rights over her. Cf. the comments of E. W. Hengstenberg, *Commentary on the Psalms*, III, p. 201.

as the LORD's flock has already been presented in Psalm 95:7. This concept is developed further in the New Testament with the teaching concerning Jesus as the shepherd (John 10:2; Heb. 13:20; 1 Pet. 2:25), with a special people (Titus 2:14) whom he has purchased as his servants (1 Cor. 6:20; 7:21-23).

2. A Call to Thanksgiving (*vv. 4-5*)

Enter his gates with thanksgiving and his courts with praise; give thanks to him and praise his name (*v. 4*). Those entering the temple and presenting themselves in its courtyards are encouraged to come with joyful thanksgiving before the LORD. Clearly this was a song sung either by priests or worshippers as they entered into the precincts of the temple. The mention of 'thanksgiving' ties in with the expression in the title, 'with thanksgiving' (it is the same word in Hebrew). The final expression is literally 'bless his name' (*bâr^{a}kû sh^{e}mô*), drawing attention to the fact that the worshippers are to have the LORD himself as their focal point. His self-revelation as the redeemer of his covenant people calls forth praise. Some church buildings have a brass plate in their foyer with the Latin inscription: '*Ad majorem Dei gloriam*' ('To the greater glory of God'). This captures the central point in this call.

For the LORD is good and his love endures forever; his faithfulness continues through all generations (*v. 5*). These words may well have been the confession that worshippers in Israel made when they came to the sanctuary. As in the first part of this psalm, reference to the covenant relationship follows the call to praise (v. 3). God's 'goodness' (*tôv*) is a summary expression for the things promised in the covenant (see the comments on Pss. 23:6 and 34:8). His covenantal love and faithfulness never fail, and they are praised by generation after generation (Pss. 89:1-2; 106:1; 107:1). The idea and terminology here become the opening call of Psalm 136:1: 'Give thanks to the LORD, for he is good. His love endures for ever'.[3]

---

[3] Comparison of the Hebrew text shows how close they are:
Ps. 100:4-5 *hôdû lô … kî tôv … l^{e}ʿôlâm chasdô.*
Ps. 136:1 *hôdû lyhwh kî tôv kî l^{e}ʿôlâm chasdô.*

Psalm 101

Of David. A psalm.

Another minor collection of psalms within the whole book commences with Psalm 101 and extends as far as Psalm 110. It is arranged symmetrically, with the first five psalms dealing with the king, an individual prayer, praise of the LORD's great love, creation, and Israel's redemption. The following five psalms deal with the same topics in reverse order. The following diagram shows the pattern:

Psalm 101 — Psalm 110
Psalm 102 — Psalm 109
Psalm 103 — Psalm 108
Psalm 104 — Psalm 107
Psalm 105 Psalm 106

The outer psalms in this diagram (101 and 110) are concerned with kingship, while the innermost ones (105 and 106) recite Israel's history. The group forms a mini-Psalter within the Psalter, following a group of psalms (Pss. 92-100) that are largely devoted to kingship, while preceding a collection of Hallelujah psalms (Pss. 111-118). These groups, both in themselves and in respect to their position in the Psalter, clearly draw attention to editorial decisions in the framing of the whole book.

In this psalm the king (presumably David, according to the title) is the speaker. He is settled in Jerusalem, which is called in verse 8 'the city of the LORD'. Probably the psalm comes from the period following David's bringing the ark of the covenant to Jerusalem. He sings of his commitment to the LORD, his wish that his rule will reflect the Lord's righteousness, and his desire that all unrighteous people will be removed from his city. The ideal king pictured here only found fulfilment in David's greater son, the Lord Jesus Christ.

1. The Standards for the King (*vv. 1-3*)
I will sing of your love and justice; to you, O LORD, I will sing praise (*v. 1*). The opening verse captures the theme of the whole psalm. What the king desired for the nation was merely an expression of the righteous rule of God himself. Hence he sings of two of the major features that characterise God's rule, love, and justice, and while the Hebrew text does not have the possessive pronoun 'your', yet that insertion clarifies the meaning. This conjunction of 'love' (*chésed*) and 'justice' (*mishpât*) occurs elsewhere (Ps. 89:14).

I will be careful to lead a blameless life – when will you come to me? (*v. 2a*). The patriarch Abraham was called to walk with God and to be blameless (Gen. 17:1). Here the psalmist commits himself to live by God's standard of blamelessness (perhaps 'upright' is closer to the idea). His question, 'When will you come to me?', expresses his longing for God's help in keeping his resolve. It is a recognition of his inability to fulfil his commitment without divine assistance.

I will walk in my house with blameless heart. I will set before my eyes no vile thing. The deeds of faithless men I hate; they will not cling to me. Men of perverse heart shall be far from me; I will have nothing to do with evil (*vv. 2b-4*). The LORD's words to Solomon after the building of the temple help us in determining the meaning of walking with a 'blameless heart' (*b^{e}tom lêvâv*). Solomon was told by the LORD: 'As for you, if you walk before me in integrity of heart (*b^{e}tom lêvâv*) ... I will establish your royal throne over Israel for ever' (1 Kings 9:4-5). It was doing all that the LORD commanded and observing his decrees and laws. Frequently the Old Testament links heart and eyes together in relation to conduct (Eccles. 2:10; Jer. 22:17). Influences both from within ('heart') and from without ('eyes') determine actions. The psalmist pledges himself to have nothing to do with those whose minds are set on evil. The opposite of an upright heart is a 'perverse heart' (*lêvâv ʿiqqêsh*). Those who have such a heart are contrasted to those who are blameless (2 Sam. 22:26-27; Ps. 18:26). Such rebellious people will not be his companions.

2. Righteous Rule in the LORD's City (*vv. 5-8*)
Whoever slanders his neighbour in secret, him will I put to silence; whoever has haughty eyes and a proud heart, him will I not endure (*v. 5*). Slander is treated so seriously because it could involve false testimony that could threaten the life of another person (Lev. 19:16). 'Haughty eyes' (*g^e^vah ʿênáyim*) occurs only here in the Old Testament, but there is a similar expression in Psalm 18:27, 'eyes that are haughty' (*ʾênáyim râmôt*). 'A proud heart' is literally 'broad of heart' (*r^e^chav lêvâv*), but in the context this is a reference to arrogance. The king will not tolerate such people. He has an obligation to discipline those who live by their own rules and violate the rights of others.

My eyes will be on the faithful in the land, that they may dwell with me; he whose walk is blameless will minister to me. No one who practises deceit will dwell in my house; no one who speaks falsely will stand in my presence (*vv. 6-7*). A further pledge is given that the faithful will be encouraged as they support the king. Those who are blameless (see comment on v. 2)[1] will act as the king's servants, while the treacherous will be excluded from his presence. The expressions 'before me' and 'in my house' may well mean the royal court and even the whole land (see 'in the land' in vv. 6 and 8).

Every morning I will put to silence all the wicked in the land; I will cut off every evildoer from the city of the LORD (*v. 8*). It seems to have been the custom for the king to hear cases every morning (2 Sam. 15:2; Jer. 21:12). The judge shall not allow the wicked to prevail, for they shall be without

---

[1] The same idiom is used in both verses, 'walking in the way of uprightness' (*holêk b^e^dérek tâmîm*).

excuse.[2] Here the king promises to remove the wicked from the land and from the city of the LORD. Elsewhere Jerusalem is called the city of God (Pss. 46:4-5; 48:1; 87:1-3). This ideal of a purified land will ultimately come to fulfilment in the New Jerusalem, when no one 'who does what is shameful or deceitful' will be allowed to enter in, 'but only those whose names are written in the Lamb's book of life' (Rev. 21:27).

[2] The verb used here for 'put to silence' is *tsâmat*, which has already been used in verse 5 (NIV, 'I put to silence'). It is a poetic word occurring nine times in the Old Testament, and all but one of its twelve appearances are in the Psalms.

Psalm 102

A prayer of an afflicted man. When he is faint and pours out his lament before the Lord.

The title of this psalm is very unusual, as no other psalm has one like it. The various words, however, are all known from other psalms.[1] No author is named, and there is no link with any precise historical circumstances. We are not even told the details of the affliction, though from the content of the psalm they seem to relate both to individual and to national troubles. Most probably the psalm comes from the time of the exile in Babylon (compare the reference to Zion in vv. 13, 16, 21 with the way in which Lam. 5:17-18 refers to the desolate city). The date of composition is some time into the exile but before the return to Jerusalem took place in 537 BC. Zion lies in ruins (v. 13) with the poet acknowledging that God's wrath has been outpoured against him (v. 10). It is clearly the prayer of an individual, but because the petitions also relate to the nation, it is likely that it was a member of the Davidic royal house who composed it while in exile. The general nature of the psalm is reflected in the title, and it is not surprising that it has been used as one of the traditional penitential psalms.

1. A Cry for Help (*vv. 1-2*)

Hear my prayer, O Lord; let my cry for help come to you. Do not hide your face from me when I am in distress. Turn your ear to me; when I call, answer me quickly (*vv. 1-2*). The psalmist's serious plight produces a flood of requests

[1] For 'faint' (*'âṭaf*), see Psalm 61:2; for 'pours out' (*shâfak*), see Psalm 62:8; for 'lament' (*sîak*), see Psalm 142:2, and note also the presence of the verb 'pour out' (*shâfak*) in this verse also.

to the LORD. He uses expressions that occur in other psalms, which suggests that psalmists often employed well-known forms of prayer in appealing to God (for similar prayers, see Pss. 18:6; 56:9; 69:17). It is not just formal prayer though, for the urgency and anguish of his requests breaks through here and throughout the psalm. He pleads for God to pay attention to his prayer and to answer it quickly.

2. A Miserable Situation (*vv. 3-11*)

After the initial appeal the psalmist convincingly describes his distress. **For my days vanish like smoke; my bones burn like glowing embers. My heart is blighted and withered like grass; I forget to eat my food. Because of my loud groaning I am reduced to skin and bones** (*vv. 3-5*). The sufferer uses a variety of metaphors to depict his condition. He compares his life to smoke and grass (see also v. 11), which both disappear so quickly.[2] The bitterness of his soul might have physical causes. He may be describing burning fever that has him in its grip. On the other hand he may be comparing his sense of being forsaken by God to a physical illness. Food loses its priority in life as distress increases, and absence of nourishment increases physical weakness, and he is now only skin and bones.

I am like a desert owl, like an owl among the ruins. I lie awake; I have become like a bird alone on a roof (*vv. 6-7*). The owls are introduced because they are unclean birds (Lev. 11:17; Deut. 14:16), and they often live in isolated places (other versions including the AV have 'pelican' for the first bird, but this is unlikely as the pelicans are water

---

[2] Two textual problems occur in verse 3. The text in *BHS* has 'in smoke' (*b*^{eʿ}*âshân*) whereas many manuscripts have 'like smoke' (*k*^{eʿ}*âshân*). NIV adopts this reading so that 'like smoke' and 'like grass' (v. 5) are parallel phrases. However, Psalm 37:20 has the same idiom as here (*kâlû b*^{eʿ}*âshân*, 'they disappear in smoke'), and hence no emendation is necessary. At the end of verse 3 the MT has 'burns like a furnace' (*k*^{e}*mô-qêd nichârû*). This seems like an oddity in the manuscript used by *BHS*, as a word *qêd* is not otherwise attested in Hebrew. The NIV and other modern translations accept that instead the reading should be *k*^{e}*môqêd*, 'like glowing embers'.

birds).[3] The psalmist feels his isolation, just as if he is one of these birds perched on a lonely rooftop.

All day long my enemies taunt me; those who rail against me use my name as a curse (*v. 8*). In addition to physical suffering he is enduring the torment of verbal abuse.[4] His enemies even use his name in cursing. There is a case in Genesis 48:20 of names used in blessing ('May God make you like Ephraim and Manasseh'). Here the psalmist's name and condition have become such that they are a byword, able to be used in connection with curses.[5]

For I eat ashes as my food and mingle my drink with tears because of your great wrath, for you have taken me up and thrown me aside (*vv. 9-10*). People sat in ashes when in mourning (cf. Job 2:8 and Jonah 3:6), and to say that tears become drink is simply to emphasise how deep the grief really is (Pss. 42:3; 80:5). There is also the recognition that God is dealing in his great wrath (Heb. has *zaʿam*^{e}*kâ v*^{e}*qitspekâ*, 'your wrath and your anger') with the psalmist and with the nation.[6]

My days are like the evening shadow; I wither away like grass (*v. 11*). The reversion to the ideas of verses 3-4 shows turmoil of mind. His life is coming to an end, and he pictures it as a day that it coming to a close. The idiom used is that his days are like 'the shadow when it lengthens' (*k*^{e}*tsêl nâtûy*), and here and elsewhere it denotes late afternoon or early evening (cf. its use in Judg. 19:8 and Ps. 109:23).[7] He feels that his life is about to vanish completely.

---

[3] One of the best discussions is Burton Goddard, 'Birds of the Bible', *The Encyclopedia of Christianity*', ed. Jay Green (Marshallton, DE: National Foundation for Christian Education), II, pp. 80-104. He indicates that while the two mentioned in this verse (NIV, 'owl' and 'desert owl') are possibly owls, 'the identifications are obviously guesswork' (p. 97).

[4] The verb 'taunt' is an acceptable translation, but 'rail against me' is doubtful. The vocalisation suggested in *BHS* is *m*^{e}*hôl*^{a}*lay*, 'those who make a fool of me'. The LXX and Syriac reflect a Hebrew form *m*^{e}*hal*^{e}*lay*, 'those who praise me'.

[5] The MT says 'They swear by me'. This seems to indicate swearing using the psalmist's name: 'May God do to me/you, as he has done to this man'.

[6] NIV is correct in translating the combined phrase by 'great wrath'. For this usage, see *IBHS*, p. 70.

[7] The verbal form used is a passive participle of the verb *nâtâh*, 'to stretch out'. No one English word can translate it in its various occurrences. *NIDOTTE*, 3, p. 91, lists fourteen different renderings of it in the NIV translation of the Psalms.

3. Confidence in the LORD (*vv. 12-17*)

But you, O LORD, sit enthroned forever; your renown endures through all generations (*v. 12*). But over against the frailty and brevity of human life stands God's eternal kingship. His fame is permanent, not temporary. The vision of the destitute psalmist turns from his own condition to the reality that the LORD indeed reigns as king. The contrast is marked very strongly by the words, 'But you ...' [8]

You will arise and have compassion on Zion, for it is time to show favour to her; the appointed time has come. For her stones are dear to your servants; her very dust moves them to pity (*vv. 13-14*). It is clear that the psalmist is not only mournful concerning his own condition, but his concern is also for afflicted Zion. Possibly he has in mind some word from one of the prophets concerning a visitation of the LORD to Zion. 'To have compassion' is a technical expression denoting the favour a master owes to his bonded servant, and the presence of 'your servants' in verse 14 confirms that this is a borrowing of covenantal concepts.[9] This will be 'the time to show favour', 'the appointed time', when God comes to deliver his people. The double reference regarding the time, while unusual, is in keeping with the double reference to the LORD's coming in Psalm 96:13 when the same verb (*bôʾ*, 'come') is used. The argument of verse 14 is that if the people treasure Zion so much, how much more concern does God have for the city that bears his name (Dan. 9:18-19)?

The nations will fear the name of the LORD, all the kings of the earth will revere your glory (*v. 15*). God's saving actions will result in universal recognition, as the Gentiles come to fear him.[10] This had been true of the Exodus from Egypt, and it was to be true again at the time of the return from exile in Babylon. When the restoration to Palestine took place the nations said:

---

[8] This is a very clear example of how biblical Hebrew marks off a contrasting statement. Cf. the *vᵉʿattâh* here with *vᵉʿattâh hûʾ* in verse 27, and also with 'but Noah' (Gen. 6:8) and 'but I' (Ps. 2:6).

[9] Leslie C. Allen, *Psalms 101-150*, (Waco: Word Books, 1983), p. 9, 14a.

[10] Some manuscripts read 'and they will see' (*vᵉyirᵉʾû*) instead of 'and they will fear' (*vᵉyîrᵉʾû*). However, the LXX, 'And they shall fear the name of the Lord', supports the MT.

'The LORD has done great things for them' (Ps. 126:2). God's greatest act of salvation is in Jesus Christ, and it is through his atoning life, death, and resurrection that the most extensive acknowledgment is going to come. Every eye will see him, and every knee will bow to him (Rev. 1:7; Phil. 2:10).

For the LORD will rebuild Zion and appear in his glory. He will respond to the prayer of the destitute; he will not despise their plea (*vv. 16-17*). The psalmist declares his confidence that God will respond to the pleas of his people and come in majestic power to restore Jerusalem. When his destitute people cry from the heart, he will answer.[11] His rebuilding of Zion will be a demonstration of his mighty power. What actually happened when Jerusalem was restored in the late sixth century BC was only a foreshadowing of the ultimate city of God. When the heavenly Jerusalem is revealed it will shine with the glory of God (Rev. 21:11).

4. The Sure Promises of God (*vv. 18-22*)

The assurances that the psalmist has just uttered are to be recorded for the sake of coming generations. **Let this be written for a future generation, that a people not yet created may praise the LORD: 'The LORD looked down from his sanctuary on high, from heaven he viewed the earth, to hear the groans of the prisoners and release those condemned to death'** (*vv. 18-20*). This is the only reference in the Book of Psalms to the recording of God's great deeds in a scroll or book. Just as God heard the cry of his people in Egypt (Exod. 2:23-25), so he will hear again. The psalmist rests in the confidence that God will respond to the groans of the exiled people, who are called here 'the prisoners' (see the comment on Ps. 79:11) and 'those condemned to death'.[12] They themselves clearly felt that they were condemned to die far from their own land (Ezek. 37:1-14). The great King will look down from his dwelling place and take

---

[11] The word translated 'destitute' (*ʿarʿar*) only occurs here. The LXX renders it by *tapeinos*, 'lowly', 'humble'. It is probably connected with the verb (*ʿârar*), 'to strip bare'. This is the position taken in *DCH*, VI, p. 565.

[12] The expressions for both 'the groans of the prisoners' (*ʾenqat ʾâsîr*) and 'those condemned to death' (*bᵉnê tᵉmûtâh*, lit. 'sons of death') occur only here and in Psalm 79:11. See comment on that verse for further information.

action to release those in captivity.[13] The thought of verses 19-20 is heightened by the poetic style, with assonance involving four words which all contain the *sh* sound.[14]

So the name of the LORD will be declared in Zion and his praise in Jerusalem when the peoples and the kingdoms assemble to worship the LORD (*vv. 21-22*). The picture is of a great gathering in restored Jerusalem when those who are converted from the Gentiles will take part in praising the name of the LORD. This is what the prophets declared will take place (see Isa. 2:2-4; Micah 4:1-3), and it is part of the vision of the end times which the prophets and psalmists share.[15] The ingathering that started on the Day of Pentecost (Acts 2) will lead eventually to an assembly before the throne of God of those 'from every nation, tribe, people and language' (Rev. 7:9).

5. A Renewed Complaint (*vv. 23-28*)

In the course of my life he broke my strength; he cut short my days (*v. 23*). The thought of the psalmist reverts to the personal complaints he has brought earlier (see vv. 3-11), and reflects upon the past.[16] He sees God's hand at work, taking away his vigour[17] and limiting the length of his earthly life, and he then recalls what he had said concerning this.

---

[13] The word used for 'release' is the verb *pâtach,* Pi. Its more normal meaning is 'to open', but both Qal and Pi'el forms can be used of the release of prisoners. See *DCH,* VI, pp. 802, 804.

[14] These words are: *hishqîf* ('he looked down'); *qodshô* ('his holy place'); *mishshâmáyim* ('from heaven'); *shêm* ('name'). The word *shêm* has already occurred in verse 15, and reappears in verse 21.

[15] I have commented more fully on this eschatological vision of Isaiah 2:2-4 and Micah 4:1-3 in *Isaiah: A Covenant to be Kept for the Sake of the Church,* pp. 47-48.

[16] The NIV translation, 'in the course of my life', is an attempt to translate a Hebrew phrase 'in the way' (*baddérek*), perhaps being influenced by 'in the midst of my days' in the following verse. Quite a few translations take this to mean 'in the middle of my life' (cf. ESV, NRSV, 'in midcourse'). Another possibility is that it refers to the journey ('the way') the psalmist and others took when they went into captivity.

[17] The MT has 'his strength' (*kochô*), whereas some manuscripts have 'my strength' (*kochî*). The LXX rendered it by *ischuos autou* ('his strength'). The Massoretes indicated that 'my strength' should be the reading. This makes good sense too, because if 'his strength' were retained, it would be the subject of the verb, but no object would be stated.

So I said: 'Do not take me away, O my God, in the midst of my days; your years go on through all generations (*v. 24*). He remembers his plea to God that his life would not be cut short. In his earlier lament he had compared his life to smoke (v. 3) and grass (vv. 4 and 11). His request is motivated, not just from a desire to live longer, but to see God's glory revealed in Israel's restoration. The verb 'to take away' (*ʿâlâh,* Hi.) is unusual, and it normally means 'to take up', not 'take away'. The best parallel is the reference to Elijah's death in 2 Kings 2:1. The poet wants removal from life in a manner similar to God's taking of Elijah. Then he proceeds immediately, without having received an answer, to draw comfort from the thought that God is ever the same. He acknowledges how different God's existence is compared with mankind, for he is eternal (cf. v. 12).

In the beginning you laid the foundations of the earth, and the heavens are the work of your hands. They will perish, but you remain; they will all wear out like a garment. Like clothing you will change them and they will be discarded. But you remain the same, and your years will never end (*vv. 25-27*). The eternal God created the heavens and the earth, but he is so different to his creation. The words 'But you' at the beginning of verse 27 are very emphatic in Hebrew (*vᵉʿattâh hûʾ*; cf. the footnote on v. 12). While he remains the same throughout all time, the creation perishes. Just like old clothing, the heavens and the earth will pass away. In Hebrews 1:10-12 the words of verses 25-27, here spoken of the LORD himself, are taken over and in a powerful argument applied to Jesus. The New Testament writers, having applied the title 'Lord' (Greek, *kurios*) to Jesus, had no difficulty in applying to him other passages in the Old Testament addressed to God.[18]

The children of your servants will live in your presence; their descendants will be established before you' (*v. 28*). God's eternal nature is the ultimate security for his people. The promise is given that the descendants of the present

[18] The quotation is from the LXX and it includes the vocative 'Lord' (*kurie*) that is not in the MT. No known Hebrew manuscript contains this word, so either it was in a manuscript used by the LXX translators, or it is an insertion here without manuscript support.

believers will continue in God's presence and care. While the initial reference of the phrase 'live in your presence' alludes to life in the land of Palestine after the exile, yet the wider application of the principle is found in the New Testament. God, who commences a work in the hearts and lives of his children, carries on that work until the day of Christ Jesus (Phil. 1:6). As the author of their salvation, the Lord Jesus is able to bring many sons to glory where they shall live in his presence (Heb. 2:10).

Psalm 103

Of David.

This psalm emphasises the love and compassion of Israel's covenant-keeping God. It begins and ends on the note of praise, with a double call in verses 1-2, and a fourfold call in verses 20-22. The core of the psalm is a recital of personal benefits received (vv. 3-5) and of the LORD's compassion to his people Israel (vv. 6-19). With clarity almost comparable to the New Testament, this psalm proclaims the greatness of God's love for his people and his gracious removal of their sins – though the method of such removal remains unrevealed.

Clear connections occur between this psalm and both Psalms 102 and 104. Thoughts from the previous psalm relating to God's eternity are taken up (102:12, 25-27 with 103:17), as are expressions comparing fleeting human life to grass that withers and dies (102:3-4, 11, 23 with 103:15-16). Both Psalms 103 and 104 are framed by the call to praise the LORD, with identical language being used (103:1, 22 with 104:1, 35). The only difference is that 'Hallelujah' is added at the end of Psalm 104. Whatever the difference in subject matter between these psalms, they are grouped together in Book 4 because of similarities. Many connections also are apparent between this psalm and Isaiah 40-66.

1. Let My Soul Praise the LORD (*vv. 1-2*)

Praise the LORD, O my soul; all my inmost being, praise his holy name. Praise the LORD, O my soul, and forget not all his benefits (*vv. 1-2*). The psalmist puts his whole being into a powerful chorus of praise to his God. The word translated 'praise' is literally 'bless' (*bârak*, Pi.), a word used in the Old Testament to express thanks and gratitude. It is commonly used, as here, of God, and calls attention to his loving and faithful character. Both Psalms 103 and 104 commence with this self-exhortation. The 'name' of God refers to his character, and especially those aspects that are going to be recited in the following verses. One of the characteristics of God's people is that they love his name (Ps. 5:11). The psalmist wants his whole being to unite in this chorus of praise to his God. Twice he refers to himself using the word 'soul' (*nefesh*), once using a word that is virtually a synonym (*qerev*).[1]

2. Praise for Personal Blessing (*vv. 3-5*)

who forgives all your sins and heals all your diseases, who redeems your life from the pit and crowns you with love and compassion, who satisfies your desires with good things so that your youth is renewed like the eagle's (*vv. 3-5*). The psalmist recites first the various blessings he personally has received from the LORD. He does so using five participles ('forgives', 'heals', 'redeems', 'crowns', 'satisfies') that point to the ongoing nature of God's actions.[2] The pronoun 'your' refers back to 'my soul', and therefore it is equivalent to speaking about 'my sins' and 'my diseases'. The word translated 'forgives' (*solêach*) is never used of people forgiving one another, but it is used exclusively of God in the Old Testament, for it describes his gracious action in pardoning sinners. Here its parallel is 'heal' (*rofêh*), which can be used in the figurative sense of healing spiritual diseases (Ps. 147:3; Isa. 53:5). However, in this context it refers to healing from illnesses that almost brought the psalmist down to the grave. God redeems

[1] The word *qerev* means 'inside', but when used in parallel with either 'heart' (*lêv*, Jer. 9:8) or 'soul' (*nefesh*, here in Ps. 103:1 or Isa. 26:9) it indicates a person, a self.

[2] The participle in Hebrew is timeless, but takes its tense from the context. 'They describe continuous action in the time of the context, which may be either past, present, or future': Page H. Kelley, *Biblical Hebrew: An Introductory Grammar* (Grand Rapids: Eerdmans, 1992), p. 200. A similar statement can be found in T. O. Lambdin, *Introduction to Biblical Hebrew* (New York: Charles Scribner, 1971), p. 19.

(*gôêl*) from death,[3] and restores to a royal position. The translation 'crowns you' is possible, but the only unambiguous text with this meaning is Song of Solomon 3:11. Here and elsewhere it seems to indicate more 'to surround', and hence it can be translated 'surrounds you with love and compassion'.[4] So invigorated is the psalmist that he feels as though he has the fresh strength of an eagle (cf. the same figure in Isa. 40:31). Covenant life should be an experience of God who 'forgives', 'heals', 'redeems', 'crowns', and 'satisfies'. The cluster of terms highlights the graciousness of God.

3. Praise for National Blessing (*vv. 6-19*)
This section of the psalm opens and closes with declarations concerning God's reign and its character. **The LORD works righteousness and justice for all the oppressed** (*v. 6*). Turning away from his own situation and his own individual experiences, the psalmist speaks of the way in which the LORD supports the oppressed. The word used here for 'oppressed' (*'ashûqîm*) often has the connotation of 'extortion' or 'despoilation'. Towards the most needy in society – the widow, the orphan, the poor, the sojourner – God commits himself as their defender. He performs righteous and saving deeds, which are often at the same time judgments upon the godless.

He made known his ways to Moses, his deeds to the people of Israel (*v. 7*). Following a verse that speaks of God's righteousness and justice, it is most likely that the reference here is to the revelation of God's personal qualities, character, and manner of operating which he showed to Moses. Particularly after the incident with the golden calf, God, in response to Moses' request to be taught his ways (Exod. 33:13), granted him a fresh revelation of his glory (Exod. 34:6-7). Those ways

---

[3] The verb used here for 'redeem' (*ga'al*) is most frequent in Exodus–Deuteronomy. In contrast to another verb 'to redeem' (*pâdâh*), which comes from the realm of commerce, this verb is from the sphere of family relationships. That explains why it is so frequent in the book of Ruth (Ruth 4:4 3×; 4:6 2×). The active participle, *gô'êl*, serves as a noun, often with a suffix ('my redeemer', 'your redeemer', 'his redeemer', 'their redeemer').

[4] This is the translation of Robert Day in *NIDOTTE*, 3, p. 384.

involved maintaining his covenant love but also not letting the wicked go unpunished. The following verses spell out the content of that revelation.

The LORD is compassionate and gracious, slow to anger, abounding in love. He will not always accuse, nor will he harbour his anger forever; he does not treat us as our sins deserve or repay us according to our iniquities (*vv. 8-10*). Verse 8 is almost an exact quotation from Exodus 34:6. It summarises the character of the covenant God of Israel – deeply merciful, not quick to anger, abundant in steadfast love. These characteristics are spelt out in the following verses. 'To accuse' (*rîv*) is a technical term that means to bring a charge against an erring covenant servant. In spite of the sins of his people, God stretches out his hands to them in mercy. In his grace he gives them what they do not deserve – unmerited favour![5] The gospel proclaims that God, who is rich in mercy, makes us alive in Christ even when we were dead in transgressions (Eph. 2:4). God acts the same in both Testaments.

For as high as the heavens are above the earth, so great is his love for those who fear him; as far as the east is from the west, so far has he removed our transgressions from us (*vv. 11-12*). Two illustrations are given to demonstrate the greatness of God's mercy. The immeasurable distances between heaven and earth and between east and west are used to draw attention to the measureless nature of God's love for his people. His forgiving grace is infinite towards 'those who fear him', a term descriptive of true believers (see on Ps. 34:7). The phrase 'removed our transgressions' may have in mind the procedure on the Day of Atonement, when a goat, symbolically bearing the people's sin, was led away into the wilderness (Lev. 16:20-22). Such a procedure taught the people the reality of sins being removed. In the New Testament it becomes clear that forgiveness comes through the shed blood of Christ on the cross.

---

[5] The word 'repay' (*gâmal*) can be used to speak of rendering either good or evil to someone. Here it has the idea of recompense for iniquities committed. Sin brings its own reward.

Marvellous grace of our loving Lord,
grace that exceeds our sin and our guilt!
Yonder on Calvary's mount outpoured,
there where the blood of the Lamb was spilt.
(Julia H. Johnston 1849-1919)

As a father has compassion on his children, so the LORD has compassion on those who fear him; for he knows how we are formed, he remembers that we are dust (*vv. 13-14*). God's love is not indiscriminate, for he has compassion on 'his children', on those who fear him (cf. the use of the identical phrase in v. 11). At the time of the Exodus the people of Israel were adopted as God's children, becoming a holy nation. The New Testament takes over this language of the church (1 Pet. 2:9-10). In the fullness of time Jesus came to lay down his life for his sheep (John 10:11, 14-15), purchasing his church with his own blood (Acts 20:28). The frailty of human beings is also a cause for God's compassion, for he knows that we are but creatures, made from the dust. The way in which this statement is introduced needs a slightly emended translation to bring out its force: 'for he, he knows …' The verb used for 'create' (*yâtsar*) is often employed of God's creative activity, especially in the book of Isaiah (22:11; 27:11; 29:16; 37:26), while Isaiah also uses it of God's action in forming Israel into a nation (43:1, 7, 21; 44:2, 21, 24).

As for man, his days are like grass, he flourishes like a flower of the field; the wind blows over it and it is gone, and its place remembers it no more (*vv. 15-16*). Not only is man a creature, but he is also frail, and his time on earth is temporary. These ideas are emphasised by the use of a word for 'man' (*'enôsh*) that quite often connotes man's transience and frailty. The imagery here is used elsewhere in the Old Testament of the fleeting nature of a person's life (Pss. 90:5-6; 92:7; Isa. 51:12), while at other times 'flower of the field' is a similar comparison (Job 14:2; Isa. 40:6-7). The wind blows the grass away, and where it was remains unrecognised.[6]

[6] The verb here (*nâkar*, Hi.) is not the equivalent of 'remember' (*zâkar*). It is more 'to recognise'. It indicates that there is nothing left where the grass had been to remind of its existence.

But from everlasting to everlasting the LORD's love is with those who fear him, and his righteousness with their children's children – with those who keep his covenant and remember to obey his precepts (*vv. 17-18*). The contrast is so marked. Man, like grass, perishes, whereas the eternal God's covenant love and righteousness last forever. God's 'love' (*chésed*) is permanently towards his children, and even if the mountains move, yet his 'love' and his 'covenanted peace' (*b^{e}rît sh^{e}lômî*) remain (Isa. 54:10). To those who fear him, his character is displayed in the same way generation after generation. The nature of 'those who fear him' is defined by obedience to their covenant obligations.[7] They have to 'keep his covenant and remember to obey his precepts'. In contexts such as this no real distinction can be made between 'keep' and 'remember'.[8] Outward allegiance to the covenant was quite insufficient. What was needed was obedience from the heart (Rom. 2:25-29). 'Circumcision is nothing and uncircumcision is nothing. Keeping God's commands is what counts' (1 Cor. 7:19). The sign of belonging to the truth is love with action (1 John 3:18-19).

The LORD has established his throne in heaven, and his kingdom rules over all (*v. 19*). This declaration concludes this section of the psalm. From his heavenly throne the LORD exercises his rule over all his creation, a truth already expressed in Psalms 9:4, 7; 11:4; 47:8; and 93:2, and is enunciated again in Psalm 123:1. He has a kingdom that is everlasting, and his authority and power extend to all generations (Ps. 145:13). What was said of his activity in verse 6 is dependent on the nature of his kingly rule.

4. Let All Creation Praise the LORD (*vv. 20-22*)

The psalm comes to a close with a fourfold call to praise, ending with a repetition of the opening words of the psalm.

---

[7] Almost exactly the same terminology is used of God keeping the covenant, and his people keeping it. Cf. Deuteronomy 7:9, where the LORD is said to 'keep the covenant and the love' (*$habb^{e}$rît v^{e}hachésed*) while the recipients of his love are those who 'love him and keep his commandments' (*l^{e}'oh^{a}bâv $\hat{u}l^{e}$$shom^{e}$rê mitsvotâv*).

[8] The same applies to the change from 'remember' (*zâkôr*) to 'keep' (*shâmôr*) in the sabbath command in the two passages containing the Decalogue (Exod. 20:8 and Deut. 5:12).

Praise the LORD, you his angels, you mighty ones who do his bidding, who obey his word (*v. 20*). Angelic multitudes are called on to extol the LORD. The angels are his messengers, often sent to perform some specific task committed to them. They are his 'mighty ones' (Rev. 10:1-3), obedient to his requests, faithful in fulfilling his commands.

Praise the LORD, all his heavenly hosts, you his servants who do his will (*v. 21*). The word 'hosts' can have various meanings in the Old Testament.[9] It is used of the heavenly bodies, as well as of the armies of Israel. In this context it is best to think of it as being a description of the heavenly bodies. Whereas the angels do God's bidding (v. 20), the sun, moon, and stars simply fulfil his will in bringing to completion whatever he pleases.

Praise the LORD, all his works everywhere in his dominion. Praise the LORD, O my soul (*v. 22*). The call to praise is broadened further to include all of creation (Pss. 96:11; 148:1-12). Everything within his realm is to acknowledge the LORD and give him praise. The whole creation is to be a choir, joining in exaltation of its maker. The psalmist reverts to a personal focus with the closing call, as he takes us again to where he began in verse 1, and thus ties the whole psalm together with the repetition of his opening words.

---

[9] See the comment on the expression 'hosts' in Psalm 24:10. Here, a difference exists in the form of the word, as instead of the normal feminine plural, *ts^{e}vâ'ôt*, the masculine plural is used (*ts^{e}vâ'âv*, 'his hosts'). This may have been done deliberately to signify that the reference is not to 'angels', but rather to inanimate creation.

Psalm 104

Nowhere else in the Psalter is there such a long hymn in praise of the creator and creation. There is the short creation song in Psalm 8 and slightly longer ones in Psalms 33 and 145, but in this psalm there is an extensive poetic description of creation that matches the narrative of creation in Genesis 1. The parallels with the days of creation can be shown in this way:

Day 1 : verse 2a
Day 2: verses 2b-4
Day 3: verses 5-9
Day 4: verses 14-16
Day 5 : verses 17, 25-26
Day 6: verses 18, 23

Verse 30 brings the account to a climax, with reference to the creative power of the Spirit of God. Then follows a concluding song of praise, exalting the God of creation. Some of the expressions used also suggest that Job 38-41 (especially 38:3-30) and Proverbs 8:22-31 were in mind as well as Genesis 1.

The traditional interpretation has been that Psalm 104 is a creation song. More recently some have claimed that verses 6-9 refer to the Flood.[1] At first sight this view may seem to have some merit, since some striking similarities exist between expressions here and the flood narrative in Genesis (cf. the

---

[1] For example, see John C. Whitcomb, Jr., and Henry M. Morris, *The Genesis Flood: The Biblical Record and Its Scientific Implications* (Nutley, NJ: Presbyterian and Reformed, 1961), pp. 77, 122, 267, 269.

description of the waters standing above the mountains in Ps. 104:6 and the account in Gen. 7:19). However, it is hard to see why a short passage dealing with the Noachian flood would be inserted into a song about creation. Also, the link between Psalm 104 and Genesis 7-9 is not nearly as significant as the links with Job and Proverbs noted above. The poet is expressing his joy and admiration of God's handiwork as he views the majesty of creation and that leads him to sing the glory of the creator.

1. A Call to Praise (*v. 1*)

Praise the LORD, O my soul. O LORD my God, you are very great; you are clothed with splendour and majesty (*v. 1*). The creation song opens with the same call to praise that occurs at the beginning and at the end of Psalm 103. The call is to 'bless' God (see the comment on Ps. 103:1). God's person and character are not changed or increased by praise, but attention is appropriately drawn to them. It is an expression of adoration, acknowledging the perfection and wonder of his person. Here God is addressed as a great king, whose creation surrounds him like royal robes.

2. The Splendour of God (*vv. 2-4*)

He wraps himself in light as with a garment; he stretches out the heavens like a tent and lays the beams of his upper chambers on their waters. He makes the clouds his chariot and rides on the wings of the wind. He makes winds his messengers, flames of fire his servants (*vv. 2-4*). The first two days of creation are described, with the focus being on the creator rather than the creation. God not only commanded light to shine, but no one has seen him who 'lives in unapproachable light' (1 Tim. 6:16). He is light, in whom there is no darkness at all (1 John 1:5). The heavens form a habitation for the king, with the firmament being described as a canopy or tent (cf. the similar description in Isa. 40:22). His palace is formed above the waters of the firmament, and as sovereign he controls the clouds, the winds, and the flames of fire (lightning). God not only has his created angelic messengers (Ps. 103:20-22), but the natural elements like wind and lightning also do his bidding (see v. 4, 'messengers', NIV footnote 'angels').

3. The Creator Forms the Earth (*vv. 5-9*)

Day three of creation is described in this section of the psalm, which has strong parallels in Job 38:4-30 and Proverbs 8:22-31. All three mention the laying of the foundations of the earth and the decree of God by which the boundaries were set for the oceans. **He set the earth on its foundations; it can never be moved. You covered it with the deep as with a garment; the waters stood above the mountains** (*vv. 5-6*). The psalmist sings of creation as the foundation that God laid in his creative work. The building is secure because of the work of the almighty creator, and hence it stands forever (Ps. 93:1). At that stage in creation the dry land had not yet appeared. It is possible that the bronze sea in Solomon's temple was meant to serve as a symbolic representation of this primeval sea (1 Kings 7:23-26; 2 Kings 25:13).

But at your rebuke the waters fled, at the sound of your thunder they took to flight; they flowed over the mountains, they went down into the valleys, to the place you assigned for them. You set a boundary they cannot cross; never again will they cover the earth (*vv. 7-9*). The poetic account continues by describing the separation of the waters from dry land (Gen. 1:9-10). God had only to speak and the waters obeyed him (Ps. 33:6-9). The waters are pictured as being some mighty foe, which by the word of the LORD are put to flight. As they receded, the dry land was revealed, and this happened by the decision and power of God. Everything that took place was under his complete control.

4. The Creator's Provision of Food (*vv. 10-18*)

The sequence of creation is interrupted in verses 10-13 by reference to God's providential care of his world. **He makes springs pour water into the ravines; it flows between the mountains. They give water to all the beasts of the field; the wild donkeys quench their thirst. The birds of the air nest**

by the waters; they sing among the branches. He waters the mountains from his upper chambers; the earth is satisfied by the fruit of his work (*vv. 10-13*). The thought of the waters in verses 7-9 continues in these verses, as the psalmist proceeds to draw attention to the creator's way of sustaining his world. He gives water from beneath the ground that creates streams that flow down the valleys between the mountains.[2] All the wild animals get nourishment from it. Likewise, birds can nest by the waters and sing joyfully in the trees growing beside them. In addition to springs of water God gives rain from above. He is the source of the rain from heaven that descends upon the mountains and refreshes the earth. The description may well echo Moses' words concerning the land of Israel in Deuteronomy 11:11-12a: 'a land of mountains and valleys that drinks rain from heaven. It is a land the LORD your God cares for.'

He makes grass grow for the cattle, and plants for man to cultivate – bringing forth food from the earth: wine that gladdens the heart of man, oil to make his face shine, and bread that sustains his heart. The trees of the LORD are well watered, the cedars of Lebanon that he planted (*vv. 14-16*). The third day involved the creation of plant life that was intended to sustain the life of cattle and of man. The psalmist concentrates on the bounty of God's provision, so that all the main needs of an eastern banquet (wine, oil, and bread) are mentioned as part of God's gifts for man. These products stem from the basic crops of grapes, olives, and wheat. Of the trees, the cedars of Lebanon are singled out because their majestic appearance points in a special way to their creator, and since he planted them they are called 'the trees of the LORD'.

There the birds make their nests; the stork has its home in the pine trees. The high mountains belong to the wild goats; the crags are a refuge for the coney (*vv. 17-18*). Provision has been made for the birds and wild animals as well. The birds nest in the trees, while the mountains form a natural home for wild goats and coneys (not a rabbit but a type of rock badger).

---

[2] The NIV translation, 'it flows', needs to be changed to the plural, 'they flow' (*yᵉhallêkûn*).

These are but a selective sample of the range of animal and bird life sustained by God's care. Lebanon was famous for its trees and for the wealth of its bird and animal life, and so its riches are used to illustrate the bounty that God has provided in his world. Our response has to be:

> This is my Father's world,
> and to my list'ning ears
> all nature sings,
> and round me rings the music of the spheres.
> This is my Father's world;
> I rest me in the thought of rocks and trees,
> of skies and seas,
> His hand the wonders wrought.
> (Maltbie D. Babcock 1858-1901)

5. The Creator's Rule over the Seasons (*vv. 19-23*)

Now the fourth day of creation comes into focus. **The moon marks off the seasons, and the sun knows when to go down. You bring darkness, it becomes night, and all the beasts of the forest prowl** (*vv. 19-20*). The rhythmic flow of the seasons is a result of God's appointment of the sun, moon, and stars. They were set in the expanse of the sky to 'serve as signs to marks seasons, and days, and years' (Gen. 1:14). The heavenly bodies were God's gift, not to be worshipped (Deut. 4:19) but recognised as rulers that configured the various time frames within which man operates.[3] There is an orderliness about creation which is there by God's design, and both men and animals regulate their activities according to the fluctuation of day and night and the various seasons of the year.

The lions roar for their prey and seek their food from God. The sun rises, and they steal away; they return and lie down in their dens. Then man goes out to his work, to his labour until evening (*vv. 21-23*). The lion, the lord of the night, is used to represent the movements that take place

[3] Cf. the astute comment of Derek Kidner regarding the mention of lightbearers in Genesis 1:14: 'In these few simple sentences the lie is given to the superstition as old as Babylon and as modern as a newspaper-horoscope' (*Genesis: An Introduction and Commentary,* [London:Tyndale Press, 1967], p. 49).

in the animal world. They prowl by night, and at dawn lie down again in their dens.[4] Man, the lord of the day, then goes out to his work, fulfilling the divine pattern for human life (Gen. 2:15; Exod. 20:9). 'Work' (*poʿal*) and 'labour' (*ʿavodâh*) are synonymous terms used to describe the task which man, God's servant, is called on to fulfil. Just as God worked, and then rested, so man is appointed to imitate him.

5. The Creator's Rule over Earth and Sea (*vv. 24-26*)

How many are your works, O LORD! In wisdom you made them all; the earth is full of your creatures (*v. 24*). Before going on further to speak of the sea, the psalmist pauses to praise God for his manifold works. The opening words are an exclamation, which, in drawing attention to God's works, in effect are a statement of praise of them. This clause is similar in form and intent to Psalm 8:1: 'How majestic is your name in all the earth!' Several Old Testament passages in addition to this one draw attention to the manifestation of God's wisdom in creation (Ps. 136:5; Prov. 3:19; Jer. 10:12). The variation between English translations of the last word in the verse (either 'your creatures', or, 'your possessions') is due to uncertainty as to the Hebrew root from which it comes (cf. its use in the next psalm, where the translation as 'possessions' is necessary, Ps. 105:21).[5]

There is the sea, vast and spacious, teeming with creatures beyond number – living things both large and small. There the ships go to and fro, and the leviathan, which you formed to frolic there (*vv. 25-26*). On the fifth day of creation God formed the ocean life (Gen. 1:20-21), including the large sea creatures such as dolphins and whales. The term 'leviathan' was known in the ancient Near East as a reference to a mythological monster of creation, and it appears five times in the Old Testament (Job 3:8; 41:1 [Heb. 40:25]; Pss. 74:13-14; 104:26; Isa. 27:1). These passages do not carry over the mythological implications from Canaanite use. 'Leviathan' is

---

[4] The NIV expands on the MT by adding the words 'they return'. This is entirely unsupported and the addition is unnecessary.

[5] For discussion on this point, see *NIDOTTE*, 3, p. 941.

always under God's control, and here the psalmist refers to it as God's pet, frolicking in the oceans and joining the ships as they travel backwards and forwards.

6. The Creator's Rule over Life (*vv. 27-30*)

The sixth day of creation comes into focus at this point, with emphasis being placed on God's gracious provision for mankind and for animals (Gen. 1:28-30). **These all look to you to give them their food at the proper time. When you give it to them, they gather it up; when you open your hand, they are satisfied with good things** (*vv. 27-28*). The closest parallel to this passage is Psalm 145:13b-16, in which there is similar reference to expectant waiting on God until he opens his hand and provides liberally for his creatures. Much of the language is also common to the two passages (cf. 'look'; 'their food at the proper time'; 'you open your hand'; 'they are satisfied'). His creation flourishes seeing he looks with favour upon it, and he gives bountifully in order to sustain it.

When you hide your face they are terrified; when you take away their breath, they die and return to the dust. When you send your Spirit, they are created, and you renew the face of the earth (*vv. 29-30*). All of life is dependent on God. His Spirit is the source of that life, and by his sovereign act creation takes place. If that Spirit is withdrawn, then creatures die and return to the dust. Perhaps Job 34:14-15 was in the mind of the psalmist as he penned these words. Normally the 'hiding' of God's face describes anger (Ps. 13:1), but here it refers to the withdrawal of his sustaining power.

6. A Final Song of Adoration (*vv. 31-35*)

May the glory of the LORD endure forever; may the LORD rejoice in his works – he who looks at the earth, and it trembles, who touches the mountains, and they smoke (*vv. 31-32*). Clearly 'the glory of the LORD' here is the creation which displays his wisdom and power (Ps. 19:1). Just as God looked over the initial creation and pronounced it 'very good' (Gen. 1:31), so he rejoices in all his providential care of the world. His relationship with creation is such that he is in complete control of it, so that even a look or a touch can alter it. His power is such that he could blot out what he had created.

I will sing to the LORD all my life; I will sing praise to my God as long as I live. May my meditation be pleasing to him, as I rejoice in the LORD (*vv. 33-34*). Not only does God rejoice, but the psalmist does as well. He makes a vow that as long as his earthly life continues he will praise God, and rejoice in the work of his hands. The opening words of verse 33 are repeated with a slight change in Psalm 146:2 ('I will praise the LORD' being substituted for 'I will sing to the LORD') while the remainder of the verse is quoted exactly. The 'meditation' is what has already preceded in the psalm itself. Response to the display of God's mighty power should always be one of praise and adoration.

But may sinners vanish from the earth and the wicked be no more. Praise the LORD, O my soul. Praise the LORD (*v. 35*). All that mars God's creation is the presence of sin. So the psalmist prays for the removal of sinners, for they have no rightful place amidst the beauty of purity of God's creation. Even creation longs for its own liberation (Rom. 8:19-22), and in the new heaven and the new earth there will be no more sin (Rev. 21:27). This creation song ends on the same note of praise with which it began, to which is added a 'Hallelujah!' (NIV 'Praise the LORD').

> O Lord my God, when I in awesome wonder
> consider all the works Thy hand hath made,
> I see the stars, I hear the mighty thunder,
> Thy power throughout the universe displayed;
> Then sings my soul, my Saviour God to Thee:
> How great Thou art, how great Thou art!
> (Stuart K. Hine 1899-1989)

Psalm 105

Two major historical psalms, 105 and 106, trace the history of Israel from God's covenant with Abraham through to later periods in Canaan. The theme of the utter faithfulness of God in the first of these psalms stands in marked contrast to that of the unfaithfulness of the people in the second. This is one of the major teaching aspects of the historical psalms (see the Introduction). Psalm 105 is unique in that it concentrates on the Abrahamic covenant, and that covenant provides the framework for the whole psalm.[1] After an introduction composed of seven verses, the main body of the psalm, rehearsing the history of Israel from the patriarchs through the desert experiences, is framed by two sets of verses dealing with the Abrahamic covenant (vv. 8-11, 42-45). The structure then is as follows:

1. Introductory Praise (vv. 1-7)
   2. The Covenant with Abraham (vv. 8-11)
      3. Covenant History (vv. 12-41)
   4.The Covenant with Abraham (vv. 42-45a)
5. Concluding Praise (vv. 45b).

Two further introductory comments are needed. First, in this psalm there are clusters of covenantal language, such as 'Abraham, his servant', 'sons of Jacob, his chosen ones', 'he remembers his covenant', 'the covenant he cut with Abraham',

[1] Thus the comment by Dillard and Longman, *An Introduction to the Old Testament* (Grand Rapids: Zonderman, 1994), p. 228, that covenant is the major theme only in Psalms 89 and 132 should be modified to include Psalm 105.

'an everlasting covenant', and 'his holy promise'. Secondly, the first fifteen verses of this psalm, along with Psalm 96 and Psalm 106:1, 47-48, make up 1 Chronicles 16:8-36, in the context of David's bringing the ark of the covenant to Jerusalem. The use of this part of Psalm 105 points to the continuing significance of the Abrahamic covenant for the post-exilic community.

1. Introductory Praise (*vv. 1-7*)

Give thanks to the LORD, call on his name; make known among the nations what he has done (*v. 1*). The opening words set the tone for the succeeding commands. They are a call to praise the LORD, and may well be an echo of Isaiah 12:4b, as the first half of the verse is exactly the same. From the context 'to call on the name of the Lord' means here proclamation of God's name, rather than invoking his name in prayer. In praising the LORD the psalmist wants his listeners to tell of the things that he has done (called in the following verses 'wonderful acts', 'wonders', and 'miracles'). The psalm is devoted to the implications of the Abrahamic covenant, and immediately the reader is confronted with its worldwide implications. The Gentile nations are to hear about God's wonderful deeds.

Sing to him, sing praise to him; tell of all his wonderful acts. Glory in his holy name; let the hearts of those who seek the LORD rejoice (*vv. 2-3*). The series of commands continues, with emphasis on making known God's saving actions on behalf of his people. The NIV translation 'tell' is too strong, as the Hebrew verb (*sîach*) has more the connotation of meditation or reflection. Better is the NASB margin: 'Meditate on all His wonders'.[2] God's name (i.e. his character) is shown in what he has done, and, therefore, praise is an appropriate response. The command at the beginning of verse 3 (NIV 'glory') points to exultation or boasting in the LORD.[3] Those who come to worship him should approach his presence with joyfulness.

---

[2] For discussion on this verb, see *NIDOTTE*, 4, pp. 1234-35.

[3] The verbal form is *hâlal*, Hi., and it occurs eight times in the Psalms: 34:2; 49:6; 52:1; 63:11; 64:10; 97:7; 105:3; 106:5. The NIV is very inconsistent in its renderings, using 'boast' (3×), 'praise' (2×), 'glorify', 'glory', and 'giving praise'. The preference should be 'praise' or 'boast', as using 'glory' suggests the presence of a different verb.

Look to the LORD and his strength; seek his face always. Remember the wonders he has done, his miracles, and the judgments he pronounced, O descendants of Abraham his servant, O sons of Jacob, his chosen ones (*vv. 4-6*). The focus of worship is the LORD himself and his mighty power. Strength is an essential characteristic of God (Pss. 62:11; 63:2), and that strength is displayed in his saving actions on behalf of his people.[4] This seeking the LORD was not just to be on the present occasion, but it was to be a constant characteristic of their devotion to him. The psalmist calls his listeners (described by a variety of terms in verse 6) to remember how that power has been shown, especially at the time of the Exodus from Egypt. God had performed actions that only he could do (for 'wonders', see Pss. 71:17 and 72:18), and he had passed sentence on Pharaoh and his people (Exod. 6:6; 7:4; 12:12).

He is the LORD our God; his judgments are in all the earth (*v. 7*). The Exodus is further recalled by the use of the covenant name for God (the LORD) that was so closely linked with the whole experience of redemption from Egypt (Exod. 3:13-15). This confessional statement acknowledges that the covenantal LORD is indeed the God of his people. He had revealed himself to Moses as the LORD (*yhwh*), but he was also the God of Abraham. His judgments are open for all to see, and what had happened in Egypt was known to all the surrounding nations.

2. The Covenant with Abraham (*vv. 8-11*)

He remembers his covenant forever, the word he commanded, for a thousand generations, the covenant he made with Abraham, the oath he swore to Isaac (*vv. 8-9*). Abraham and Jacob have already been mentioned (v. 6), and the foundational covenant bond made with them is reasserted in this historical song. The people have to be encouraged to remember God's great deeds (v. 5), but God keeps his covenant pledge without the need for help in recalling it. To say that

[4] The NIV's translation 'look for' and 'seek' represent paired Hebrew verbs (*dârash* and *bâqash*, Pi.) that are virtually synonymous. Sometimes the order is *dârash-bâqash* (Judg. 6:29; Ps.105:4; Ezek. 34:6); at other times it is *bâqash-dârash* (Deut. 4:29; Ps. 38:12).

God 'remembers his covenant' means that he keeps his word of promise and fulfils the conditions he has placed on himself. His intentions contained in the covenantal promises come to fulfilment.[5] The term 'oath' is used in the Old Testament in contexts such as this as virtually the equivalent of 'covenant'. This, however, is the only place in the Psalter where the two are equated. Such an oath was not needed by God himself (who is unchangeable), but it was a blessing to his servants as a confirmation of his purposes (the oath to Abraham [Gen. 22:16] was repeated to Isaac [Gen. 26:3-5]). It was to last 'for a thousand generations', an expression not necessarily meaning 'for ever' but for countless generations to come (see Deut. 5:10; 7:9).

He confirmed it to Jacob as a decree, to Israel as an everlasting covenant: 'To you I will give the land of Canaan as the portion you will inherit' (*vv. 10-11*). Furthermore, the same covenant commitment was made to Jacob (Gen. 28:13-15). While the terminology used here is unusual, yet it reinforces the point that the covenant with Jacob was not a new one but rather a reaffirmation of the Abrahamic covenant.[6] The content of that covenant is narrowed down to one of its main features, the promise of land.[7] From the descriptions given of the land, the promise of 'the land of Canaan' meant the whole of Palestine (cf. the descriptions of the land in Gen. 15:18-19; Num. 34:1-12; Josh. 1:4; Ps. 80:8-11).[8] It was a decree in the sense that it was an enduring provision that God made for his covenantal people.

---

[5] The covenantal terminology employed in these verses is important. The psalmist uses the technical expression to originate a covenant (*kârat b^erît*), which, along with the expression 'his covenant' (*b^erîtô*), points to the unilateral nature of such divine covenants.

[6] Two aspects of the terminology are unusual. First, the word for 'confirm' is a *hapax legomenon* (*'âmad*, Hi., lit. 'to cause to stand'), but it appears to be synonymous with the more usual expression (*hêqîm b^erît*; cf. Gen. 6:18). Secondly, the word 'decree' (*choq*) is not common when used by itself, but it is regularly used in sequences with other terms denoting covenant stipulations, such as 'words', 'law', 'judgment', 'testimony', and 'commandment'.

[7] No indication is given that this comprises all the promises to Abraham, for verse 24 indicates that a large family was also part of the covenant commitment.

[8] I have discussed the concept of the land (including its content) in *Deuteronomy: The Commands of a Covenant God*, pp. 15-24.

3. Covenant History (*vv. 12-41*)
From here to the end of verse 41 there is a summary of the way in which God acted on behalf of his people, caring for them and redeeming them from slavery in Egypt. **When they were but few in number, few indeed, and strangers in it, they wandered from nation to nation, from one kingdom to another** (*vv. 12-13*). At the early stage of their history, God's people were only a small number and they were without any definite territory of their own. They migrated to and from Egypt, and even within Palestine they were only 'strangers' (*gârîm,* i.e. they did not have rights of permanent residents, but were resident aliens).

He allowed no one to oppress them; for their sake he rebuked kings: 'Do not touch my anointed ones; do my prophets no harm' (vv. 14-15). God's protective care was shown to the patriarchs. He even rebuked kings such as Pharaoh (Gen. 12:17) and Abimelech of Gerar (Gen. 20:7). The term 'anointed ones' (*m^{e}shîchîm*) is synonymous with 'chosen ones' (*b^{e}chîrîm,* v. 6), while 'prophets' (*n^{e}vîʾîm*) is a general term applied here to Abraham, Isaac, and Jacob. Abraham is the only one of the three specifically called a 'prophet' in the Old Testament (Gen. 20:7), but all three were called by God and were recipients of his covenant revelation. As such their lives were to be regarded as sacred.

He called down famine on the land and destroyed all their supplies of food; and he sent a man before them – Joseph, sold as a slave. They bruised his feet with shackles, his neck was put in irons, till what he foretold came to pass, till the word of the LORD proved him true. The king sent and released him, the ruler of peoples set him free. He made him master of his household, ruler over all he possessed, to instruct his princes as he pleased and teach his elders wisdom (*vv. 16-22*). These verses provide a summary of Genesis 37, 39-41, showing how God prepared the way for his people by bringing Joseph down to Egypt and having him appointed to a prominent position. He arrived in Egypt as a slave, sold by his own brothers (Gen. 37:28-36), yet this was part of God's plan to save lives (Gen. 45:5). The description that is given of his captivity is a poetic one, using the imagery of a later period ('his feet in shackles, his neck was put in irons'). In his dreams that he related to his brothers (Gen. 37:5-11) and in his interpretation of the dreams of his fellow prisoners (Gen. 40:5-23; 41:12) Joseph spoke prophetically. Ultimately this revelation from God was proved true when things came to pass as Joseph had said. He was released from prison and appointed as second-in-charge in Egypt (Gen. 41:41-46), having Pharaoh's princes under his control. One significant aspect of this account that is not brought out in the NIV translation is the play on the idea of binding. Joseph, whose own neck had been bound (lit. 'iron came into his soul', verse 18), was given authority to 'bind' (*le'esor*: NIV 'to instruct')[9] Pharaoh's princes according as he desired (Heb. *benafshô*).[10]

Then Israel entered Egypt; Jacob lived as an alien in the land of Ham. The LORD made his people very fruitful; he made them too numerous for their foes (*vv. 23-24*). Verse 23 picks up the theme of the famine, introduced in verse 16, but interrupted by the account of Joseph's slavery. Jacob was amazed when he heard that Joseph was the ruler of Egypt, but eventually agreed to go and live in Egypt with all his family (Gen. 45:25–46:7; from the statement in Gen. 10:6, Egypt is called 'the land of Ham' here and in verse 27, and also in Ps. 106:22; in Ps. 78:51 the expression 'the tents of Ham' is used). During a stay of some centuries there, Israel increased in numbers and consequently became a problem for the Egyptians (Exod. 1:7-14).

whose hearts he turned to hate his people, to conspire against his servants. He sent Moses his servant, and Aaron, whom he had chosen. They performed his miraculous signs among them, his wonders in the land of Ham. He sent darkness and made the land dark – for had they not rebelled against his words? He turned their waters into blood, causing their fish to die (vv. 25-27). English translations disguise the

---

[9] The NIV follows the LXX, Syriac, and Jerome in taking the verb as 'instruct' rather than 'bind'.

[10] The Hebrew word *néfesh* can have a wide range of meaning, from 'soul' or 'mind' to 'neck', 'person', and, as here, 'will' or 'desire'. *DCH*, V, pp. 724-34 lists twelve possible meanings for it.

fact that these verses form a chiastic pattern that is clearly evident in the Hebrew text. It can be diagrammed as follows:

A. He *turned* their hearts (v. 25)
  B. He *sent* Moses and Aaron (v. 26)
    C. They *performed* his signs and miracles (v. 27)
  B[1]. He *sent* darkness (v. 28)
A[1]. He *turned* their waters into blood (v. 29)

God's hand directed the Egyptians' actions so that ultimately even their sinful acts against Israel served his sovereign purposes. Calling Moses God's servant is an echo of Exodus 14:31, while the appointment of Aaron as Moses' prophet and as God's 'chosen' one is given in Exodus 7:1. As in Psalm 78, the plagues are not mentioned in chronological order. Rather, the poet highlights the final two plagues (darkness and death of the firstborn) by placing the other plagues between them. Also, two of them (the plague on livestock and the plague of boils) are omitted. Verses 27-36 are a summary of Exodus 7:14–11:10. They serve as a reminder of how important were the signs and wonders which God performed at the time of the Exodus. They were demonstrations of divine power that Israel never forgot, for Israel was God's firstborn son (Exod. 4:22) who was redeemed from slavery in Egypt by his mighty arm.

Their land teemed with frogs, which went up into the bedrooms of their rulers. He spoke, and there came swarms of flies, and gnats throughout their country. He turned their rain into hail, with lightning throughout their land; he struck down their vines and fig trees and shattered the trees of their country. He spoke, and the locusts came, grasshoppers without number; they ate up every green thing in their land, ate up the produce of their soil. Then he struck down all the firstborn in their land, the firstfruits of all their manhood (*vv. 28-36*). Summary statements are given of the following plagues: the second (frogs); the fourth (flies) and the third (gnats); the seventh (hail); the eighth (locusts); with the account culminating in the tenth and final plague (death of the firstborn). The language concerning the final plague is very similar to Psalm 78:51, including the reference to 'the firstfruits of their offspring', a phrase that goes back to the blessing of Reuben in Genesis 49:3.

He brought out Israel, laden with silver and gold, and from among their tribes no one faltered. Egypt was glad when they left, because dread of Israel had fallen on them. He spread out a cloud as a covering, and a fire to give light at night. They asked, and he brought them quail and satisfied them with the bread of heaven. He opened the rock, and water gushed out; like a river it flowed in the desert (*vv. 37-41*). After the preceding description of Israel's time in Egypt, the poet summarises the actual Exodus experience. He uses one of the standard Old Testament expressions ('brought out') to describe how it happened. God intervened on behalf of his people and he led them out, and this intervention included making the Egyptians favourably disposed towards Israel (Exod. 12:33-36). Initially the Egyptians were glad to see Israel go, but they then realised that they had lost their work force and so pursued them (Exod. 14:5-9). God sustained and protected his people, so that during the daytime they had the cloud as a covering, and at night they had fire. He also provided food and drink for them in the wilderness. All these experiences confirmed the supernatural nature of the Exodus and God's gracious care of them.

4. Concluding Praise (*vv. 42-45*)

The psalm concludes with reference again to the covenant with Abraham. **For he remembered his holy promise given to his servant Abraham** (*v. 42*). The content of verses 8-9 is summarised, using again the expression 'word' (Heb. *dâvâr*, NIV 'promise') which functions both here and in verse 8 as a synonym for 'covenant'. 'Word' can refer to a particular stipulation of a covenant, or can be used for the covenant itself (cf. its use to refer to the Decalogue, 'the ten words', as the Heb. text calls it).[11]

He brought out his people with rejoicing, his chosen ones with shouts of joy; he gave them the lands of the

---

[11] In Hosea 10:4, 'speaking words' is parallel to 'making a covenant', while in Hag. 2:5 'word' (*dâvâr*) occurs alongside the verb for 'making a covenant' (*kârat*).

nations, and they fell heir to what others had toiled for – that they might keep his precepts and observe his laws. Praise the LORD (*vv.* 42-45). These statements tie together the election of Abraham and the redemptive deliverance of Israel from Egypt in the same way as Deuteronomy 7:8: 'But it was because the LORD loved you and kept the oath he swore to your forefathers that he brought you out with a mighty hand and redeemed you from the power of Pharaoh king of Egypt'. The psalm concludes with reference again to the covenant with Abraham. The Exodus was a fulfilment of what God had promised him long before (Gen. 15:13-14), and Israel entered into possession of a land complete with houses, wells, and vineyards that others had laboured to provide (Deut. 6:10-12). The response of the people had to be shown by more than joy. They were instructed to obey all the decrees of the LORD and to fear him (Deut. 6:24-25). The covenant carried responsibilities that the people had to honour, as they conformed their lives to God's demands and thus learned the holiness of his ways. The psalm that began with a call to praise ends with a 'Hallelujah', a feature it shares with Psalms 104 and 106.

Psalm 106

Psalm 106 follows on very fittingly from Psalm 105, but also contrasts with it. Both are historical in approach, as they draw attention to the greatness of God in history, and so supplement Psalm 104 which deals with God's greatness in nature. Yet Psalm 106 concentrates on the sins of Israel rather than on divine deliverance. In this regard it is closer to Psalm 78 in its treatment of Israel's history. Whereas Psalm 105 ends on the note of obedience to God's laws, Psalm 106 shows how often the people had rebelled against him and failed to observe his precepts.

The language of Psalm 106 is similar to the confessional prayers found in Nehemiah 9 and Daniel 9. This is one of the pointers to the fact that Psalms 105 and 106 appear to come from the time of the Babylonian exile. Verses 44-46 point to a time when there was some amelioration in their circumstances, while verse 47 suggests that they were still scattered in Babylon and elsewhere. The similarity with Daniel 9 has suggested to some that this psalm may well be a poetical paraphrase of that confession, either by Daniel or a contemporary.[1] The call for all the people to say 'Amen' (v. 48), suggests a use in corporate worship on return from the exile.

Along with Psalm 105:1-15 and the whole of Psalm 96, verses 1 and 47-48 of this psalm make up the composition found in 1 Chronicles 16:8-36 (see the introductory com-

---

[1] This suggestion can be found in J. A. Alexander, *The Psalms Translated and Explained*, p. 436.

ments on these psalms).[2] Some differences exist between Psalm 106 and 1 Chronicles 16, including the alteration of 'O LORD our God' to 'O God our saviour', the insertion of 'and save us' after 'and gather us', and instead of 'and say' it has 'and said'. Words from this psalm also occur in the New Testament. Paul, in describing the universal sinfulness of mankind (Rom. 1:18-31), draws on the language of Psalm 106:23-28.[3]

1. Praise and Prayer (*vv. 1-5*)

Praise the LORD. Give thanks to the LORD, for he is good; his love endures forever. Who can proclaim the mighty acts of the LORD or fully declare his praise? (*vv. 1-2*). It is appropriate that the further recital of the mighty acts of the LORD should start with the call, 'Praise the LORD' (Heb. *Halleluyah*). For Israel, recollection of past history was closely connected with praise, for the people were bringing to remembrance what God had done for his people. Here the call is to extol the goodness of their covenant God,[4] and recognise yet again how enduring is his mercy. The question in verse 2 suggests that no one is able fully to make known all the deeds of the great warrior king. Human achievements pale into insignificance beside his mighty acts.

Blessed are they who maintain justice, who constantly do what is right (*v. 3*). Those who serve this great king should show the same characteristics as he displays when it comes to matters of justice in the land. The pronouncement of a blessing upon them (for 'blessed' see the comment on Ps. 1:1) is really an encouragement for all to act in this way.

Remember me, O LORD, when you show favour to your people, come to my aid when you save them, that I may

---

[2] Ps. 106:1, 'Praise the LORD. Give thanks to the LORD, for he is good; his love endures forever', occurs in other psalms as well (cf. Pss. 107:1; 136:1). Because 1 Chronicles 16 utilises the conclusion of Psalm 106, it has been assumed that it also uses the opening verse as well, though there is no way to prove this.

[3] For discussion on this NT use of Psalm 106, see L. C. Allen, 'The OT in Romans 1-8', *Vox Evangelica* 3 (1964), pp. 28-29.

[4] For the ascription of goodness to God, see comments on Psalms 23:6, 25:8, and 34:8.

enjoy the prosperity of your chosen ones, that I may share in the joy of your nation and join your inheritance in giving praise (*vv.* 4-5). The appeal for God to 'remember' has the idea of paying special attention to needs. There is no inconsistency between the psalmist calling on the whole community in verses 1-3 and his personal petitions in these verses. What he requests is that he may share in the communal blessings of God's people when the LORD visits them and brings deliverance, and so be a partaker in their joy.[5] He sees himself as part of the covenant family, and he wants to share with all of God's 'chosen ones' in the joyful acknowledgment of his saving power.[6] The expressions, 'your people', 'your chosen ones', 'your nation', and 'your inheritance', all refer to Israel, God's special people. Even in exile Israel was still special in the LORD's eyes (cf. Isa. 54:1-10).

2. The Rebellion of Israel (*vv. 6-43*)

The major part of the psalm is taken up with historical review of Israel's history. First, events surrounding the Exodus, and especially what happened at the Red Sea, are recounted (vv. 6-12), followed by narration of Israel's rebellions during the wilderness wanderings (vv. 13-33). Israel's disobedience in Canaan is summarised (vv. 34-39), while the closing section (vv. 40-43) speaks of God's sovereign judgments against his rebellious people.

a) *At the Red Sea (vv. 6-12)*

We have sinned, even as our fathers did; we have done wrong and acted wickedly. When our fathers were in Egypt, they gave no thought to your miracles; they did not remember your many kindnesses, and they rebelled by the sea, the Red Sea (*vv.* 6-7). As with other recitals of history,

---

[5] The MT has 'to rejoice in the rejoicing of your nation'. English avoids such cognate accusative constructions and hence some phrase like 'greatly rejoice' is to be preferred.

[6] While the Hebrew text uses the word 'nation' (*gôy*) in reference to Israel, a term normally reserved for the Gentiles, yet here it is clearly in parallel with the earlier use of the common description of Israel as God's *ʿam*. Cf. A. Cody, 'When is the Chosen People Called a *gôy*?' *VT* 14 (1964), p. 2.

there is a confession of sin at the outset (cf. Dan. 9:4-6). The psalmist links those of his day with those who sinned in Egypt (the Heb. text says, 'We sinned *with* our fathers'). He and others of his generation are regarded as sharing in the rebellion of Israel of old, and as continuing that rebellion. The three verbs ('sinned', 'done wrong', and 'acted wickedly') are all used by Solomon in his prayer at the dedication of the temple (1 Kings 8:47), and probably formed part of the regular vocabulary of confession of sin.[7] Together, the three verbs give a comprehensive view of sin – it involves wandering from God's way, it includes perverse behaviour, and it is passionate about following unjust ways. Two important points are made here about Israel at the time of the Exodus. First, the nation was rebellious from its very foundation, even despising God's miracles and rebelling by the Red Sea soon after the crossing. Secondly, the wonder of God's grace is displayed in that he redeemed such a sinful, rebellious people.

Yet he saved them for his name's sake, to make his mighty power known (*v. 8*). In biblical thought salvation is always an initiative of God and it is for his name's sake (cf. Daniel's prayer, Dan. 9:19). It was in spite of their sins that the Israelites were delivered from Egypt, in order that God's promise to Abraham would be fulfilled (Gen. 15:13-15). Salvation from bondage and sin is always a demonstration of God's great power.

He rebuked the Red Sea, and it dried up; he led them through the depths as through a desert. He saved them from the hand of the foe; from the hand of the enemy he redeemed them. The waters covered their adversaries; not one of them survived (*vv. 9-11*). These verses summarise in song Exodus 13:17–14:29. What God did for Israel ('*he* rebuked … *he* led them … *he* saved them…*he* redeemed') is the subject of continuous praise. He controlled the forces of nature to deliver his people and to bring judgment on the Egyptians. Israel came through the Red Sea on dry land, but the pursuing Egyptians were engulfed by the returning water. The language

---

[7] 1 Kings 8:47 appears to be the basis for the use in Psalm 106:6 and Daniel 9:4. While there are slight differences, the same three verbs (*châtâ*', '*âvâh, râsha*') are used in the three passages, and always in the same order.

used here points to the theological significance of the Exodus – it was a saving act of God that involved redemption ('he *saved* them . . . he *redeemed* them').

Then they believed his promises and sang his praise (*v. 12*). This verse summarises Exodus 14:30–15:21. The display of the LORD's power convinced the Israelites to put their trust in him and in Moses his servant (Exod. 14:31). They confessed their 'Amen' to what God had said.[8] The song with which Moses and the Israelites praised God (Exod. 15:1-18) was a hymn of triumph, celebrating *his* victory over the Egyptians. The LORD, the mighty warrior, had vanquished the enemy and therefore the people sang, 'Who is like you – majestic in holiness, awesome in glory, working wonders?'(Exod. 15:11).

b) *During the Wilderness Wanderings (vv. 13-33)*

But they soon forgot what he had done and did not wait for his counsel. In the desert they gave in to their craving; in the wasteland they put God to the test. So he gave them what they asked for, but sent a wasting disease upon them (*vv. 13-15*). The cyclic experiences of Israel continued soon after the deliverance at the Red Sea. Sin in Egypt, salvation at the Red Sea, and then sin again in the desert! The psalmist links together some of the experiences of the people soon after the crossing of the Red Sea (Exod. 15:22-25; 16:1–17:7) with the later incident when, because they ate food without due preparation, they were punished with a severe plague (Num. 11:31-34; Ps. 78:28-31).[9] Each incident illustrated the people's unbelief and their desire to go their own sinful way.

---

[8] The Hebrew verb for 'believe' (*'âmên*, Hi.) may be a verbal form derived from the word 'Amen' (*'âmên*). If so, it may carry both the meaning of 'believe in', and also 'declare "Amen".' It makes good sense here in a recital of covenant history to understand the expression to mean 'they declared "Amen" to his word'. See the discussion by Meredith Kline, 'Abram's Amen', *WTJ* 31 (1968-69), pp. 1-11.

[9] The word used for 'wasting disease' (*râtsôn*), in addition to its use in reference to judgment inflicted on Israel in the wilderness, is also used by Isaiah to depict God's judgment on Assyria (Isa. 10:16), probably the disease that came upon the well-fed and proud Assyrians as recorded in 2 Kings 19:35.

In the camp they grew envious of Moses and of Aaron, who was consecrated to the LORD. The earth opened up and swallowed Dathan; it buried the company of Abiram. Fire blazed among their followers; a flame consumed the wicked (*vv. 16-18*). Many envied the special relationship which Moses had with the LORD. Miriam and Aaron spoke against him (Num. 12:1-15). Aaron also occupied a special position (in Heb. he is called 'the LORD's holy one'), and to challenge his authority was to challenge the LORD's authority. Korah, Dathan, and Abiram led another 250 prominent leaders in challenging the exclusive roles to which Moses and Aaron had been called by God (Num. 16:1-50). The earth opened and Korah, Dathan, and Abiram were swallowed up, and the 250 men were consumed by fire sent by the LORD. As in Deuteronomy 11:6 there is no mention of Korah here. Perhaps part of the explanation is that the first punishment fell on non-Levites, Dathan and Abiram, while the second punishment fell upon the Levites led by Korah, whose sons were not killed (Num. 26:11).

At Horeb they made a calf and worshipped an idol cast from metal. They exchanged their Glory for an image of a bull, which eats grass. They forgot the God who saved them, who had done great things in Egypt, miracles in the land of Ham and awesome deeds by the Red Sea. So he said he would destroy them – had not Moses, his chosen one, stood in the breach before him to keep his wrath from destroying them (*vv. 19-23*). Whereas verses 16-18 are concerned with indirect attack upon the LORD, these verses recount a direct one. While Moses was still on Mount Sinai, the people sinned by making a golden calf. The summary here does not mention that it was a golden calf, but in Exodus 32:24, 31 that is explicit. Aaron even claimed that he had thrown the gold into the fire and out came the calf (Exod. 32:24)! The sin was an attempt to replace God with an idol, and one that represented a grass-eating creature! It almost led to the destruction of the nation of Israel (see Exod. 32:9-10). God is called 'their Glory', i.e. their glorious one, and Paul echoes this language in Romans 1:23. They had soon forgotten all the miracles[10] in Egypt (called by its poetic name, 'the land of Ham', cf. Ps. 105:23; Ps. 78:51 has 'the tents of Ham') and at the Red Sea. Moses acted as a mediator and his intercession resulted in the substitution of a plague for total destruction (Exod. 32:31-35). 'To stand in the breach' is military language, used of a soldier willing to give his life for others by defending the gap in the wall (see Ezek. 22:30).

Then they despised the pleasant land; they did not believe his promise. They grumbled in their tents and did not obey the LORD. So he swore to them with uplifted hand that he would make them fall in the desert, make their descendants fall among the nations and scatter them throughout the lands (*vv. 24-27*). These verses should be compared with the narrative in Deuteronomy 1:21-33 and Numbers 13:25-14:45. Many of the expressions are borrowed from the Pentateuch.[11] One of the great promises to Abraham was of a land for his descendants (Gen. 15:18-19; 17:8). But when, a little over a year after leaving Egypt, they reached the southernmost portion of Canaan, and heard the report of the spies who went to survey it, the people rebelled and wanted to return to Egypt (Num. 13:1-14:9). They rejected God's promise,[12] and despised 'the pleasant land' (described by the same Hebrew phrase in Jer. 3:19; 12:10; Zech. 7:14; cf. Dan. 8:9; 11:16, 41 'the Beautiful [Land]'). The penalty was an oath by God[13] that that generation would die in the wilderness (Num. 14:28-32), and likewise that the generation of the exile would be scattered among the nations (part of the covenantal curse, Lev. 26:33-35; Deut. 28:64-68). A very similar statement appears in Ezekiel 20:33: 'Also with uplifted hand I swore

---

[10] The language typically describes God's redemptive work using the terms 'great deeds', 'miracles', and 'awesome deeds'.

[11] Cf. 'despised', Num. 14:31; 'grumbled in their tents', Deut. 1:27; 'with uplifted hand', Exod. 6:8; Deut. 32:40; 'made them fall', Num. 14:29, 32.

[12] The language here (lit. 'they did not believe his word') is the negative form of the expression in verse 12. See comment.

[13] The Heb. expression is 'and he lifted his hand to them'. This was a gesture associated with making an oath, and so NIV rightly expands it, 'So he swore to them with uplifted hand'. A similar idiom (substituting the verb *rûm* Hi., for *nâsâʾ*) appears in Abram's words to the king of Sodom in Gen. 14:22.

to them in the desert that I would disperse them among the nations and scatter them among the countries'.[14]

They yoked themselves to the Baal of Peor and ate sacrifices offered to lifeless gods; they provoked the LORD to anger by their wicked deeds, and a plague broke out among them. But Phinehas stood up and intervened, and the plague was checked. This was credited to him as righteousness for endless generations to come (*vv. 28-31*). The incident at Shittim to which the poet refers in these verses is recorded in Numbers 25, and the opening expression in verse 28 echoes that account (the verb 'yoked', *tsâmad,* occurs in Num. 25:3, 5). Not only was there sexual immorality with Moabite women, but, as is also made plain here, a breach of the covenant with the LORD by worshipping other gods (see Num. 25:2-3). Some commentators have considered that instead of 'sacrifices to lifeless gods' (*ziv*ᵉ*chê mêtîm*) the Hebrew expression means 'sacrifices *for* the dead'. However, it appears to be a comment on 'sacrifices to their gods' (*ziv*ᵉ*chê* ʾᵉ*lohêhen*) (Num. 25:2). Phinehas, the grandson of Moses, killed an Israelite, who had brought to his family a Midianite woman. By Phinehas' action the plague which God had sent stopped. What he did was in marked contrast with the wickedness of his uncles, Nadab and Abihu (see Lev. 10:1-5). Just as Abraham's faith was credited to him as righteousness (Gen. 15:6), so this act was credited to Phinehas. God entered into a covenant of peace with him by which he and his descendants were given a lasting priesthood (Num. 25:10-13; Mal. 2:4-6).

By the waters of Meribah they angered the LORD, and trouble came to Moses because of them; for they rebelled against the Spirit of God, and rash words came from Moses' lips (*vv. 32-33*). Two incidents involving provision of water, in both of which the people tested God, seem to be joined together here (Exod. 17:1-7; Num. 20:1-13). The blending of

---

[14] The one main difference is that Ezek. 20:23 has *l*ᵉ*hâfîts,* 'to scatter', whereas Ps. 106:26-27 twice uses *l*ᵉ*hâffîl,* 'to make them fall'. While the Syriac version and the Targum change the second occurrence in Ps. 106:27 to conform with Ezek. 20:23, there is insufficient reason to suggest emendation (cf. RSV, '*disperse* their descendants among the nations, scattering them over the lands').

these two incidents also occurs in Deuteronomy 1:37, and there as in Deuteronomy 3:26 the point is made that God was angry with Moses on account of the people (here, 'because of them'). The Hebrew text of these verses literally says: 'And they angered by the waters of Meribah, and trouble came to Moses because of them; for they rebelled against his spirit, and rash words came from his lips' (see NIV footnote).[15] However, comparison with Isaiah 63:10 ('Yet they rebelled and grieved his Holy Spirit') confirms the interpretation embodied in the NIV rendering (cf. also the use in Ps. 78:40 of the same verb 'to rebel'). Moses' rash words were those recorded in Numbers 20:10, as he spoke out of his anger and years of frustration with the people.

c) *In Canaan (vv. 34-39)*

They did not destroy the peoples as the LORD had commanded them, but they mingled with the nations and adopted their customs. They worshipped their idols, which became a snare to them. They sacrificed their sons and their daughters to demons. They shed innocent blood, the blood of their sons and daughters, whom they sacrificed to the idols of Canaan, and the land was desecrated by their blood. They defiled themselves by what they did; by their deeds they prostituted themselves (*vv. 34-39*). These verses give a concise picture of the long years of rebellion which the people showed after they came into Canaan. What actually happened was in direct contradiction of the instructions that had been given (see especially Deut. 7:1-6; 12:1-9, 29-32), and the biblical text records the disobedience (Judg. 1:21; 2:3, 17; 3:5-6).

---

[15] In verse 32 an object has to be provided for the verb 'they angered', and most English versions agree with the NIV that it is a reference to the LORD. Greater variation is shown in verse 33 because of the verb (*him^{e}rû*) and its object (*'et-rûchô*). While the vast majority of Heb. manuscripts have 'they rebelled against his spirit', two manuscripts have 'they made his spirit bitter' (*hêmêrû*). The LXX, the Syriac, and Jerome support this rendering, which is why so many English versions have followed it (cf. RSV, NRSV, NEB, ESV). However, the parallelism in the two verses suggests that the LORD is spoken of in the first clause of each, and Moses in the second clause. Thus, 'they angered [the LORD]' is matched by 'his spirit' (i.e. the LORD's), with 'trouble came to Moses' being matched by 'rash words came from his lips' (i.e. Moses' lips).

The Israelites intermarried with those outside the covenant, and soon they became ensnared in their practices – idolatry, human sacrifice, murder. They even dedicated their children to false gods.[16] Both the people and the land were rendered unclean by these actions. The language of prostitution is used in the Old Testament to describe both Israel's departure from God's moral standards (Isa. 1:21) and the nation forsaking the LORD by entering into marriage with other gods (Ezek. 16:32-36). The concept of harlotry against God dominates Hosea's presentation of Israel's breach of the covenant obligations.

d) *God's Sovereign Judgments (vv. 40-43)*

Therefore the LORD was angry with his people and abhorred his inheritance. He handed them over to the nations, and their foes ruled over them. Their enemies oppressed them and subjected them to their power. Many times he delivered them, but they were bent on rebellion and they wasted away in their sin (*vv. 40-43*). Here the poet gives a shortened account of God's reaction to the sins of his people over centuries of life in the promised land (for a longer description, see 2 Kings 17:7-23).[17] He showed his anger with his people, by allowing surrounding nations to invade and oppress them. The word for 'subjected' (*kâna*ʿ, Ni.) forms a word play with the word for Canaan (*k*ᵉ*nâ*ʿ*n*) used in verse 38, though there is no direct etymological link between them. Repeated divine deliverances did not alter the sinful bent of the people; they persisted in their rebellion.[18] The end result was predicable

[16] In verse 37 the false gods are called *shêdîm*, a word that may be connected with an Assyrian word *shêdû* meaning 'demons'. But here, and in the only other place it is used in the OT (Deut. 32:17), *shêdîm* seems just to be equivalent to 'false gods' or 'idols of Canaan' (v. 38).

[17] The particular expression used here for God's wrath (*chârâh* ʾ*af b*ᵉ) is not common in the Psalms or the prophetical books. It is more usual in narrative. Its use here, however, may be another reflection of dependence on the Book of Numbers, for it is used in Num. 11:1 of God's anger when the people complained about their hardship in the wilderness.

[18] The Heb. text says 'and they rebelled [against him] in their counsel'. The verb (*mârâh*, Hi.) was already used in verse 33, while 'in their counsel' is similar to the phrase 'they walked in counsels' in Jer. 7:24. It points to the emphatic opposition of their purposes to God's purposes and ways.

– humiliation for them, as they 'wasted away in their sin'. This was one of the predicted outcomes of rebellion against the LORD, as they wasted away in the lands of their enemies (Lev. 26:39). Right through from the days of the judges to the Babylonian exile the curses of the covenant were applied to sinful Israel.

3. The Blessings of the Covenant(*vv. 44-47*)
But he took note of their distress when he heard their cry; for their sake he remembered his covenant and out of his great love he relented (*vv. 44-45*). At times of great distress for his people, God is said to note (Heb. 'and he saw', *vayyar'*) their condition. The language relating to God's reaction is similar to descriptions of other occasions when he expressed great concern for them (cf. Exod. 2:23; 3:7; 1 Sam. 9:16; 2 Chron. 20:6-12). Just as God had pledged sanctions against his erring inheritance, so he had promised that he would remember his covenant (Lev. 26:42, 45; cf. also Ps. 105:8, 42). 'To remember his covenant' means to implement it, which he did by showing abundant covenantal mercy.

He caused them to be pitied by all who held them captive. Save us, O LORD our God, and gather us from the nations, that we may give thanks to your holy name and glory in your praise (*vv. 46-47*). The use of language relating to 'pity' draws attention to the promises made in similar terms of what would happen when the people repented of their sins (see 1 Kings 8:50; 2 Chron. 30:9; Jer. 42:12). This means that the reference here to captivity specifically refers to the Babylonian exile, because this language is not used of any other captivity. Recalling those promises, the dispersed community prays for God to gather them from among the Gentile nations where they have been scattered. Such restoration would result in triumphant praise of God's mercy.

4. Concluding Doxology (*v. 48*)
Praise be to the LORD, the God of Israel, from everlasting to everlasting. Let all the people say, 'Amen!' Praise the LORD (*v. 48*). The psalm, and also book 4 of the Psalter, ends with

this doxology (cf. 1 Chron. 16:36). The first part of it ('Praise be to the LORD, the God of Israel, from everlasting to everlasting') was most probably an original part of the psalm, while the second part ('Let all the people say, "Amen!" Praise the LORD') is an adaptation of the statement of 1 Chronicles 16:36, that after David's psalm of thanks, 'then all the people said "Amen" and "Praise the LORD".' It forms a fitting conclusion to book 4, and matches the doxologies in Psalms 41:13, 72:19, and 89:52.

Book 5

Psalm 107

There are strong links between Psalms 105, 106, and 107. They all include the words, 'Give thanks to the Lord', in their introductions, and they share the same historical perspective. From one aspect, Psalm 107 gives the Lord's response to the prayer of Psalm 106:47, 'Save us, O Lord our God, and gather us from the nations.' It recounts how in four kinds of adversity the Lord had delivered those who cried to him: from hunger and thirst (vv. 4-9), from prison (vv. 10-16), from sickness (vv. 17-22), and from storm at sea (vv. 23-32). Each of these stanzas has the same basic form: an account of the distress, the cry to the Lord and his deliverance,[1] and then a summons to praise him for his covenant love (Hebrew *chésed;* see on 36:5). Each of these is also followed by a refrain: 'Let them give thanks to the Lord for his unfailing love and his wonderful deeds for men' (vv. 8, 15, 21, 31). The two stanzas that follow these are more general, showing how the Lord delivered in various ways (vv. 33-42). The introductory call to praise and the concluding admonition tie together the whole structure of the psalm into a testimony to the Lord's redeeming grace.

This psalm comes from after the return from the Babylonian captivity (see vv. 2-3; and compare verse 1 with

[1] The cries for help (vv. 6, 13, 19, 28) are also in the form of standardised statements. The first and fourth (vv. 6 and 28) use the verb *tsâʿaq,* whereas in verses 13 and 19 a different, but similar sounding verb (*zâʿaq*) appears. On the first and fourth occasions, the deliverance is described using different verbs (in v. 6, 'he delivered them' [*yatstsîlêm*]; in v. 28, 'he brought them out' [*yôtsîʾêm*]). In verses 13 and 19 the same verb is used: 'he saved them' (*yôshîʿêm*).

Jeremiah 33:11), and may even be from the time of Nehemiah (c. 444-432 BC). The fact that Book 5 contains psalms attributed to David (Pss. 138-145) is not a problem, as the composition of a particular book was not contemporaneous with the writing of the songs. Hence, some psalms in each of the five books may antedate the collection by considerable periods of time.

Though Psalm 107 is closely connected to Psalms 105 and 106, yet it was chosen to commence the final section of the Psalter as a whole. This can possibly be explained as an attempt to provide suitable psalms to form the seam between Books 4 and 5. However, it represents a conscious choice on the part of an editor to ignore the close connection between Psalms 106 and 107 and to use Psalm 107 as the opening of the final book. Various possible explanations have been offered, yet it remains unclear why the fourth book did not end with Psalms 104-107, or why, alternatively, they were not the first collection in Book 5.

1. Invitation to Praise (*vv. 1-3*)

Give thanks to the LORD, for he is good; his love endures forever (*v. 1*). These words, which have already been used at the beginning of Psalm 106 (see comment), form the command to the assembled community of Israel (for the identical words, see also Ps. 136:1). They, and especially those who have come back from captivity, are called to extol the goodness and mercy of the LORD (cf. the combination of 'goodness' and 'mercy' in Ps. 23:6).

Let the redeemed of the LORD say this – those he redeemed from the hand of the foe, those he gathered from the lands, from east and west, from north and south (*vv. 2-3*). The return from captivity was clearly an act of God, a redemption that he had promised to the exiles (Isa. 51:9-11). The word for 'redeemed' (*ge'ûlîm*) comes from the verb 'redeem' (*gâ'al*) used of God's deliverance of Israel from Egypt (Exod. 6:6; 15:13) and then of his redemption of exiled Israel from Babylon (cf. its use in Pss. 74:2; 77:15; 78:35; 106:10).[2] God delivered his

[2] For wider discussion of the Old Testament use of *gâ'al*, see Leon Morris, *The Apostolic Preaching of the Cross* (London: Tyndale Press, 1955), pp. 12-15.

people and gathered the dispersed of Israel from all points of the compass. However, large numbers remained in Babylon and contributed greatly to later Judaism. Instead of 'south' (*yâmîn*) the Hebrew text has 'from the sea' (*miyyâm*, i.e. the Mediterranean). As 'west' has already been mentioned, NIV and many other versions take the Hebrew word to mean 'south' (one letter in Hebrew makes the difference). But exactly the same phrase occurs in Isaiah 49:12, 'from north and from the sea' (*mitstsâfôn ûmiyyâm*) which suggests that emendation is unnecessary. Also, other passages can be cited where there is incomplete reference to the points of the compass (see Ps. 75:6).

2. Deliverance from Hunger and Thirst (*vv. 4-9*)

Some wandered in desert wastelands, finding no way to a city where they could settle. They were hungry and thirsty, and their lives ebbed away (*vv. 4-5*). The first description of distress is the hunger and thirst of those travelling through the desert. Those who came out of Egypt experienced first hand the problems of life in the desert, and while living in Palestine the people knew the reality of major deserts to the south and east. These had to be crossed by traders, as well as by many of the returning exiles. The Hebrew words used for the expression 'a city where they could settle', *ʿîr môshâv*, indicates an inhabited city (see its use again in v. 7; *môshâv* in modern Hebrew means a smallholder's co-operative settlement). Those in this new exodus experienced many of the same difficulties that had confronted Israel of old. They felt their strength was being sapped from them.

Then they cried out to the LORD in their trouble, and he delivered them from their distress. He led them by a straight way to a city where they could settle (*vv. 6-7*). The standardised account of their prayer to God and of his response (cf. for almost the same words, vv. 13, 19, and 28) is followed by a fuller description of God's special provision for them in their need. This is the first occurrence of the fourfold description of appeal to God for help (see the comment on the introduction to this psalm). The wanderers, who could not find where to dwell (v. 4), were led to a place, where in addition to shelter, there was food and drink, thus giving security to human existence.

Let them give thanks to the LORD for his unfailing love and his wonderful deeds for men, for he satisfies the thirsty and fills the hungry with good things (*vv. 8-9*). The psalmist bids the congregation (or readers) to praise the LORD for his love (Heb., *chésed*) and for 'his wonderful deeds' (see on Ps. 72:18). Just as God had fed Israel in the wilderness, so he met the needs of the returning exiles. A supply of food and drink was divine provision for the hungry and thirsty. The same refrain (v. 8) occurs again in verses 15, 21, and 31, in each case including the same reason for praise.

3. Deliverance from Prison (*vv. 10-16*)

Hunger and thirst were not the only situations of distress that the people faced. There were others, including imprisonment. **Some sat in darkness and the deepest gloom, prisoners suffering in iron chains, for they had rebelled against the words of God and despised the counsel of the Most High. So he subjected them to bitter labour; they stumbled, and there was no one to help** (*vv. 10-12*). One of the punishments that God inflicted on the people because of their rebellion was imprisonment in foreign countries. The people's distress is described in vivid language, 'darkness and shadow of death' (*chôshek v^etsalmâvet*). This phrase seems to have been a standard expression for 'deep darkness',[3] and being in darkness is used elsewhere of prisoners (Isa. 42:7; 49:9). The final clause in verse 10 was a regular way of describing both the form and the nature of imprisonment (lit. 'prisoners of affliction and iron'; cf. Job 36:8 and Ps. 105:18). The use of

---

[3] The phrase occurs twice in this context (vv. 10 and 14), and in Job 3:5; 10:21; 34:22. For the traditional rendering 'shadow of death' for *tsalmâvet*, see the comment on Psalm 23:4, and the article by D. W. Thomas, '*ṣlmwt* in the Old Testament', *JSS* 7 (1977), pp. 191-200. For a wider discussion, see also D. L. Block, 'Beyond the Grave: Ezekiel's Vision of Death and Afterlife', *BBR* 2 (1992), pp. 113-41.

'rebel' and 'despise' in parallel strengthens the idea of how Israel refused to listen to the divine commands.[4] Instead of cherishing the words of the Most High, they treated them lightly, even the threats of exile and imprisonment (Lev. 26:33; Deut. 28:47-48). They landed in situations where there was no human help in their predicament. The expressions used here could include other distressing situations, such as sickness, in addition to imprisonment.

Then they cried to the LORD in their trouble, and he saved them from their distress. He brought them out of the darkness and the deepest gloom and broke away their chains (*vv. 13-14*). The amazing thing about this statement is that it is describing God's deliverance from a situation which was a result of the people's own sin. He sent them into bondage, but, in accordance with his promise (Lev. 26:40-45), when they humbled themselves and cried to him, God answered in mercy. A different but similar sounding verb for 'cry' (*zâʿaq* instead of *tsâʿaq*) appears here, this being part of the poetic pattern of verses 4-32, while the deliverance is described by using 'save' (*yâshaʿ*, Hi.) instead of 'deliver' (*nâtsal*, Hi.; see introductory comments to this psalm). The description of their deliverance ('out of darkness and the deepest gloom') carries on from verse 10, reinforcing the point that even in the blackest of circumstances, God's grace and power prevailed.

Let them give thanks to the LORD for his unfailing love and his wonderful deeds for men, for he breaks down gates of bronze and cuts through bars of iron (*vv. 15-16*). The refrain calls again for praise, this time for the wonderful deliverance from captivity, especially that in Babylon. Part of the work of Cyrus as God's appointed deliverer of his people was to 'break down gates of bronze and cut through bars of iron' (Isa. 45:2). The language of verse 16 echoes this description in praising God for his release of the prisoners in Babylon.

---

[4] The verb 'despise' (*nâʾats*) is often used, as here, with another synonym. See its use with 'hate' (Prov. 5:12), 'forsake' (Isa. 1:4), 'reject' (Isa. 5:24), and 'scorn' (Ps. 74:10).

4. Deliverance from Sickness (*vv. 17-22*)
The sins of the people also caused physical illnesses, and from them God also delivered. **Some became fools through their rebellious ways and suffered affliction because of their iniquities. They loathed all food and drew near the gates of death** (*vv. 17-18*). Another of the covenantal curses was the threat of divinely imposed illness (Lev. 26:16, 25; Deut. 28:20-22, 35, 58-61). Those who suffered these illnesses are called 'fools' (*ʾᵉvîlîm*), not because they were mentally stupid, but because their life was marked by insolence towards God (cf. the contrast between someone who has the fear of the LORD and the fool who despises instruction, Prov. 1:7).[5] The verb translated 'suffered affliction' is reflexive in form (*ʿânâh*, Hitp.) and this should be expressed in the translation. The point is that they brought their suffering upon themselves, and so it can be rendered: 'And because of their iniquities, bring affliction on themselves'.[6] Their illnesses were so serious that they lost all appetite and waited for death to receive them, which is viewed as a city with gates.

Then they cried to the LORD in their trouble, and he saved them from their distress. He sent forth his word and healed them; he rescued them from the grave (*vv. 19-20*). The recurring formula introduces the recovery that God commanded, and the verbs here ('cry' and save') are the same as in verse 13 (see comment on that verse, and the introductory comments on this psalm). God spoke the word, and they were restored, so being rescued from death.[7]

Let them give thanks to the LORD for his unfailing love and his wonderful deeds for men. Let them sacrifice thank

---

[5] Instead of 'some became fools', the LXX has *antelabeto*, which suggests a Hebrew reading *ʾᵃzârâm*, 'he helped them'. However, no Hebrew manuscript has such a text, neither does any textual evidence support emending the word 'fools' (*ʾᵉvîlîm*) to 'languishing' (*ʾumlâlîm*) or 'sick' (*chôlîm*).

[6] I am following the comments of J. J. S. Perowne, *The Book of Psalms*, II, p. 278.

[7] The word translated 'from the grave' is 'from their pits'. Various emendations have been suggested, but the fact that the identical form occurs in Lamentations 4:20 puts its validity beyond question. See L. C. Allen, *Psalms 101-150*, p. 59, and Delbert R. Hillers, *Lamentations: a new Translation with Introduction and Commentary* (New York: Doubleday & Co., 1972), p. 85.

offerings and tell of his works with songs of joy (*vv. 21-22*).[8] The refrain calls for praise for this further evidence of God's unfailing love, and for tangible acts to show how deep their gratitude was. This call and the next one (v. 31) both specify the form that the praise is to take. Jeremiah 33:11 depicts the joy which was characteristic of the return from exile, while Psalm 126:1-2, in telling of the exuberance of the returnees, uses the same word as here for their 'joy' (*rinnâh*).

5. Deliverance from Perils at Sea (*vv. 23-32*)

The fourth situation of distress was danger at sea. **Others went out on the sea in ships; they were merchants on the mighty waters. They saw the works of the LORD, his wonderful deeds in the deep. For he spoke and stirred up a tempest that lifted high the waves. They mounted up to the heavens and went down to the depths; in their peril their courage melted away. They reeled and staggered like drunken men; they were at their wits' end** (*vv. 23-27*). While Israel was not noted for being a sea-faring nation, yet she had traders who ventured far in search of precious goods. In Solomon's time, in particular, there was a very active sea-going trade (see 1 Kings 9:26-28; 10:22; 2 Chron. 8:17-18). Those who sailed on the seas acknowledged that the mighty storms were brought about by the word of the LORD,[9] even when they were terrified by the power of nature. They came to a place where their own skills could aid them no more ('were at their wits' end', Hebrew literally, 'and all their wisdom was swallowed up').

Then they cried out to the LORD in their trouble, and he brought them out of their distress. He stilled the storm to a

---

[8] Verses 21-26, and verse 40, in the MT are marked with an upturned letter *n* (an inverted *nun*). No satisfactory explanation of this has been advanced. For discussion, see Page H. Kelley, Daniel S. Mynatt, and Timothy G. Crawford, *The Masorah of Biblia Hebraica Stuttgartensia*, pp. 34-35.

[9] The expression 'for he spoke and stirred up a tempest' may well be an echo of Psalm 33:9 in reference to the creative word of God: 'for he spoke (*'âmar*), and it came to be; he commanded, and it stood [firm] (*vayya'ᵃmod*)'. Both of these verbs are used here in Psalm 107:25. He who spoke and so brought the world into being, can also speak and control nature. He is a God of creation *and* providence.

whisper; the waves of the sea were hushed. They were glad when it grew calm, and he guided them to their desired haven (*vv. 28-30*). For the fourth time the same description is given of their prayer to God and their deliverance. Here the poet reverts to the verb 'cried' used in verse 6, though instead of 'he delivered them', he says that God 'brought them out'. This latter expression is often used of the Exodus from Egypt (Exod. 3:10; 13:3; 20:2), but it was also a fitting expression to use of the exodus from Babylon (Isa. 42:7; 49:22; Ezek. 20:41; 34:13). In this case the deliverance took the form of calming the stormy seas so that they were able at last to reach the harbour for which they were heading. The LORD of nature had the power to control the wild storm, just as the Lord Jesus was able to still the storm on the Sea of Galilee (Mark 4:35-41).

Let them give thanks to the LORD for his unfailing love and his wonderful deeds for men. Let them exalt him in the assembly of the people and praise him in the council of the elders (*vv. 31-32*). The final occurrence of the refrain calls on the people in public assembly and before their leaders to acknowledge what God has done for them. The words here are identical to those in verse 8. The people's praise had to have a communal aspect to it, as they testified to this demonstration of the LORD's wonderful love. If the psalm comes from the post-exilic period, then the assemblies will be the precursors to the formal synagogue, and the 'elders' will be the heads of families.

6. Preservation in the Land (*vv. 33-38*)

A general description follows of periods of devastation for the land and then renewed blessings as God again gave them abundant harvests. **He turned rivers into a desert, flowing springs into thirsty ground, and fruitful land into a salt waste, because of the wickedness of those who lived there** (*vv. 33-34*). As a consequence of the sins of the people, God sent reversal of fortunes to the land of Palestine. Covenantal curses were inflicted on disobedient Israel, and the narrative description of them in passages such as Leviticus 26:34-35 and Deuteronomy 28:38-42 is here turned into poetry. Instead of Palestine being a land of milk and honey, it was visited by drought and famine, becoming a salt waste almost like Sodom and Gomorrah (Gen. 19:1-29).[10] Both the judgment of salt and being made like those two cities were explicitly set out in Deuteronomy 29:23 when the covenant was being renewed prior to entry into Canaan. The main point here is that God has complete control over nature, and his power extends to 'rivers', 'springs', and 'fruitful land'. Famines like those in the days of Elijah and Elisha may be in view (cf. 1 Kings 17:1-16 and 2 Kings 8:1-2).

He turned the desert into pools of water and the parched ground into flowing springs; there he brought the hungry to live, and they founded a city where they could settle. They sowed fields and planted vineyards that yielded a fruitful harvest; he blessed them, and their numbers greatly increased, and he did not let their herds diminish (*vv. 35-38*). The opposite reversal could take place just as quickly, and the language used is similar to Isaiah 35:6-7, 41:18, and 43:19-20. 'The desert' and 'the parched ground' could become respectively 'flowing springs' and 'a city where they could settle'.[11] The point is that sedentary life could resume as a result of the Lord's blessing the people and the land. The hungry now had abundance, and they themselves and the cattle increased greatly. This was a fulfilment of some of the promises made to the exiles (Isa. 49:19-20; 54:1-3).

7. Protection in Calamity (*vv. 39-42*)

The final section of historical recollection deals with the devastation caused by invasion. **Then their numbers decreased, and they were humbled by oppression, calamity and sorrow; he who pours contempt on nobles made them wander in a trackless waste** (*vv. 39-40*). Part of God's punishment of his people for their sins was to allow invasion to take place. They had to face attacks from powerful armies like those of the Syrians (2 Kings 6:24-25), the Assyrians (2 Kings 17:3-6; 18:13-15), and

---

[10] The word for 'salt waste' (*m^{e}lêchâh*) is rare, only occurring here and in Job 39:6 and Jeremiah 17:6. The verb from which it comes, *mâlach*, is also rare, but the word 'salt' (*mélach*) occurs nine times in the phrase 'sea of salt' (*yâm hammélach*), i.e. the Dead Sea, and five times in the expression 'the valley of salt' (*gê' mélach*).

[11] This phrase (*'îr môshâv*) has occurred twice already in this psalm in verses 4 and 7.

the Babylonians (2 Kings 25:1-26). Such attacks brought much devastation to the land, and they were particularly humbling to the nation's leaders. It is probably the last two kings of Judah – Jehoiachin and Zedekiah – who are particularly in mind (see 2 Kings 24:8-25:7). Verse 40 is a borrowing from Job 12:21a and 24b without any alteration. 'Trackless' represents a Hebrew phrase, 'a no-way' (*lô'-dârek*).[12]

But he lifted the needy out of their affliction and increased their families like flocks. The upright see and rejoice, but all the wicked shut their mouths (*vv. 41-42*). Even such disasters were reversed by God when he heard the cry of the people and freed them from their distress. 'The needy' renders the Hebrew word for 'poor' (*'evyôn*), which is often used in the wider sense (as here) of those who require divine assistance. Again the size of the population increased,[13] and both good and evil people within the land knew what had happened. The first clause in verse 42 is based on Job 22:19, while the second depends on Job 5:16.[14] The good saw it, and were glad. The evil saw it, and, recognising God's hand in the matter, were silenced.

8. A Call to the Wise (*v. 43*)

Whoever is wise, let him heed these things and consider the great love of the LORD (*v. 43*). The poet ends his composition in a manner reminiscent of the end of Hosea's prophecy (Hosea 14:9). Both finish with the question, 'Who is wise?', directing attention to the teaching function of what has just preceded. 'These things' could refer to verses 33-42, or more probably to the whole of verses 4-42. The psalm, which commenced with an assertion of the covenant mercy of the LORD (*chasdô*, 'his mercy', v. 1), ends with a call to contemplate his great deeds and to reflect upon that mercy (*chasdê yhwh*, 'the great love of the LORD').[15]

---

[12] For this usage, see *GKC* §152u.

[13] The Hebrew has: 'and he set families like a flock.' This seems to be an idiomatic way of saying that the number in Israel grew so that the people resembled large flocks of sheep or goats. Cf. the similar usage in Job 21:11.

[14] The use of Job 5:16 is interesting as the context there is very similar to the final section of Psalm 107, including the use of 'the needy' (cf. Ps. 107:41 with Job 5:15).

[15] This use of the plural of 'love' (*chésed*) to denote 'great love' is a Hebrew way of expressing intensification of the singular. Cf. *DIHG~S*, p. 19.

Psalm 108

A song. A psalm of David.

This psalm is composed of parts of two other psalms. Psalm 57:7-11 and Psalm 60:5-12 are combined, and there is no indication in the biblical text why this was done. Verses 1-5 are drawn from Psalm 57, while verses 6-13 reflect Psalm 60. There are some slight variations as compared with the original psalms, but none of major significance.[1] The use of Psalm 57 fits admirably in this new context, especially as it carries on the theme of God's love with which Psalm 107 finished (cf. 107:43 with 108:4).[2] For comments, see those on Psalms 57 and 60.

It has to be remembered, however, that Psalm 108 is not two separate songs. Rather, it is a single new composition, put together by a compiler for some specific purpose. Probably the background of it is some renewed hostility by neighbouring countries towards the post-exilic community in Palestine. Edom was certainly a problem (Mal. 1:2-5), but, in using these psalms, restored Israel was asserting that it was through their God alone that they could have the victory (v. 13).

My heart is steadfast, O God; I will sing and make music with all my soul. Awake, harp and lyre! I will awaken the dawn. I will praise you, O Lord, among the nations; I will

---

[1] For details of the variations, see H. C. Leupold, *Exposition of the Psalms*, (Welwyn: Evangelical Press, 1977), p. 762, or L. C. Allen, *Psalms 101-150*, pp. 66-67.

[2] The Hebrew idiom differs in these verses in drawing attention to the LORD's great love. However, no discernible difference in meaning exists between 'the great love of the LORD' (*chasdê yhwh*) and 'great is your love' (*gâdôl … chasdekâ*).

sing of you among the peoples. For great is your love, higher than the heavens; your faithfulness reaches to the skies. Be exalted, O God, above the heavens, and let your glory be over all the earth. Save us and help us with your right hand, that those you love may be delivered. God has spoken from his sanctuary: 'In triumph I will parcel out Shechem and measure off the Valley of Succoth. Gilead is mine, Manasseh is mine; Ephraim is my helmet, Judah my sceptre. Moab is my washbasin, upon Edom I toss my sandal; over Philistia I shout in triumph.' Who will bring me to the fortified city? Who will lead me to Edom? Is it not you, O God, you who have rejected us and no longer go out with our armies? Give us aid against the enemy, for the help of man is worthless. With God we will gain the victory, and he will trample down our enemies (*vv. 1-13*).

Psalm 109

For the director of music. Of David. A psalm.

This is a prayer by one who calls himself the LORD's servant (v. 28). He appeals to his sovereign to intervene in his situation since he is under attack by his accusers. Some have thought that verses 6-19 are the speech of accusers against the psalmist, to which he responds in verses 20-31. This view is represented in the NRSV (and NIV margin), placing the words in verses 6-19 in inverted commas, and inserting 'They say' before them, even though these words are not in the Hebrew text. But it is much more in keeping with the content of the psalm to think of the psalmist referring at first to the accuser in the singular, and then elsewhere in the psalm in the plural. Perhaps it is best to think of a band of accusers, with the prominent leader being singled out for special attention. His animosity has inspired others to express their hatred against the psalmist.

The background of the expressions used in this psalm is found in the covenant curses (Deut. 27:15-26; 28:15-46). The request is for punishment to fit the crime. The use of the Hebrew expressions for accusing (vv. 4, 6, 20, 29) and judging (v. 7), with the accuser and the defender both being at the right hand (vv. 6 and 31), are all part of vocabulary that shows that the focus is on judicial redress.

There are three main petitions in the psalm (vv. 1-5, 21, and 26-29), interspersed by a long section involving curses against the [main] accuser (vv. 6-20), a description of the poor and needy suppliant (vv. 22-25), and a final song of praise to the LORD. The Hebrew form that characterises a wish ('May such and such happen') dominates throughout ('may' occurs nineteen times in the NIV text). For a discussion of the wider issues raised by the curses in this psalm, see the Introduction.

1. An Urgent Cry (*vv. 1-5*)
O God, whom I praise, do not remain silent, for wicked and deceitful men have opened their mouths against me; they have spoken against me with lying tongues (*vv. 1-2*). The psalmist's prayer is directed to the divine judge, from whom he wants a ready response. 'Praise' in this context has the idea of public acknowledgment that God is his defender. To remain silent would show an attitude of unconcern for his welfare (for the use of the same expression, cf. Ps. 35:22), whereas the opposite would be a declaration of his innocence. The accusers had been spreading false reports about the psalmist, acting with malicious intent towards him.

With words of hatred they surround me; they attack me without cause. In return for my friendship they accuse me, but I am a man of prayer. They repay me evil for good, and hatred for my friendship (*vv. 3-5*). The fuller description of the accusations being made against the psalmist provide a contrast between his character and that of his enemies. The verb rendered 'accuse' (*sâtan*) is only used six times in the Old Testament, always with the connotation of verbal accusations.[1] He is devoted to prayer (the Hebrew simply says, *va'ᵃnî tᵉfillâh*, 'but I am prayer'),[2] while they attack without due reason and even repay good with evil. He maintains his innocence in the situation, trying to hold friendly relationships with others who only respond with hatred and bitterness.[3]

---

[1] The verb occurs again in verse 20, while the noun from this root, *sâtân*, 'accuser', appears in verse 6.

[2] This construction is an extension of the Hebrew practice of placing two nouns in apposition to one another, the second noun specifying the common relationship. 'I [am] prayer' is a clause without a verb, having just a subject (the pronoun 'I') and a predicate ('prayer'). For other examples, see the discussion in *DIHG~S*, p. 42, §40.

[3] The NIV rightly translates the verbs in verses 3-5 by present tenses in English, even though there is a sequence of perfect, *vav* consecutive imperfect, imperfect, and *vav* consecutive imperfect forms. Cf. *DIHG~S*, pp. 62-63.

2. Appeal for Divine Justice (*vv. 6-15*)

Appoint an evil man to oppose him; let an accuser stand at his right hand (*v. 6*). His first call is for someone to be appointed to bring his enemy to the bar of God's justice. He calls him an accuser (Heb., *sâtân*), a meaning that the Hebrew word uniformly has in the Old Testament. To stand at the right hand was apparently the position that the accuser took in court trials (cf. Zech. 3:1), but also where the defender stood (cf. v. 31).[4]

When he is tried, let him be found guilty, and may his prayers condemn him. May his days be few; may another take his place of leadership. May his children be fatherless and his wife a widow. May his children be wandering beggars; may they be driven from their ruined homes (*vv. 7-10*). For his enemy the psalmist seeks the judicial death penalty. The one who has been causing him so much trouble was either a leader in the nation or the leader of a band of men seeking his destruction. Even if such a one pleads for a different verdict, his prayers must go unanswered.[5] The verdict sought is a premature end to the opponent's life and his replacement in office by another. The words of verse 8 are quoted in Acts 1:20 in reference to the appointment of another apostle to take Judas' place. The ultimate verdict will not only affect the enemy, but his wife and children will also suffer. This is an expression of the principle stated in the Second Commandment whereby God punishes the children to the third and fourth generation of those who hate him (Exod. 20:5). Verse 10 has caused difficulty for translators and interpreters. A literal translation is: 'May his children wander

---

[4] One difference in usage is that the verb is followed by the preposition *ʿal* in verse 6 where the accuser stands at the right hand, whereas in verse 31 the preposition is *l*[e] when the defender takes up that position. The latter usage also occurs in Psalm 110:1, which may suggest that the variation in prepositional use reflects a consistent pattern, though the occurrences are too few to be definite.

[5] The NIV rendering 'may his prayers condemn him' represents an attempt to translate 'and his prayer(s) to sin'. While the Hebrew, *lach*[a]*tâʾâh*, 'to sin', could mean 'to guilt', yet it may be better to follow W. VanGemeren and take the word to mean 'miss', yielding a translation, 'may his prayer be a miss' (*'The Psalms'*, p. 691).

about and beg; may they seek from their ruins.' Two verbs are used in parallel, 'beg'[6] (*shâ'al*, Pi.) and 'ask' (*bâqash*, Pi.), and both are used elsewhere with 'bread' as the object (Ps. 37:25; Lam. 4:4). It is best to understand 'bread' as the object here – 'may they beg [for bread], may they seek [for bread] from their ruins.' The ESV translation is probably the best of the modern versions: 'May his children wander about and beg, seeking food far from the ruins they inhabit.' It is unnecessary to follow the LXX, as NIV does, and change the verb from 'seek' to 'be driven out'.[7]

May a creditor seize all he has; may strangers plunder the fruits of his labour. May no one extend kindness to him or take pity on his fatherless children. May his descendants be cut off, their names blotted out from the next generation (*vv. 11-13*). The ideas here must be understood against the background of the family structure in ancient Israel. A very close bond existed between parents and children, with several generations often being part of the same household. The life of each family member was closely linked with all the others, and what affected one affected all. Hence, the family survivors will be deprived of any wealth that might otherwise be available for them. Those from outside the family will profit from the work that has been put into business or property. Creditors had extensive powers (see 2 Kings 4:1) and they will take their share of the estate. Pity would normally have been expected for orphan children, but the psalmist asks that it be withheld in this case.[8] To be childless was regarded as a disgrace in Israel, and so to have names blotted out meant the extinction of the family line.

May the iniquity of his fathers be remembered before the LORD; may the sin of his mother never be blotted out.

---

[6] The verb translated 'beg' is the frequentive form (Pi.) of the verb *shâ'al* 'to ask'. It represents, not an intensification of the idea of asking, but rather repetitive action. Cf. R. J. Williams, *Hebrew Syntax*, pp. 27-28.

[7] The LXX has *ekblêthêtôsan* which would correspond to the Hebrew passive form *yᵉgorᵉshû*, but no Hebrew manuscript has this reading.

[8] The expression is 'not to prolong kindness (*chésed*) to him'. This is one of the usages of *chésed* involving a human-to-human relationship. Each person in Israel had a moral obligation to help the weak and the needy, and 'kindness' was the ideal attribute for everyone.

May their sins always remain before the LORD, that he may cut off the memory of them from the earth (*vv. 14-15*). The whole family of the enemy is regarded as being involved in his sins, and therefore they are to share in his punishment. The iniquities of the fathers and the sins of the mother are tied in with the offences committed by this individual whom the psalmist wants called to account. The use of the verb 'cut off' in verse 13 and 15 echoes language of the covenant (Gen. 17:14), and suggests that the enemy has to be seen as a covenant rebel upon whom God's curse is coming. With covenant disobedience the promises of long and prosperous life in the land of promise are reversed (Lev. 26:9; Deut. 6:2, 18, 24; 7:12-15).

3. The Character of the Enemy (*vv. 16-20*)

For he never thought of doing a kindness, but hounded to death the poor and the needy and the brokenhearted (*v. 16*). The enemy has been notorious for ill-treating the destitute and even bringing about the death of those who should have been protected and nourished. Towards them he showed no commitment of love and mercy, denying even the basic responsibilities of protection and care. Once again 'kindness' (*chésed*) is a characteristic expected of everyone (see comment on v. 12).

He loved to pronounce a curse – may it come on him; he found no pleasure in blessing – may it be far from him. He wore cursing as his garment; it entered into his body like water, into his bones like oil. May it be like a cloak wrapped about him, like a belt tied forever around him (*vv. 17-19*). In place of kindness the enemy substituted evil desires, which he expressed in terms of a cursing procedure. The words of verse 18 may reflect some practice in which there was a ritual involving water and oil. Perhaps they were poured over the body to demonstrate the way in which the curse was supposed to enter right into the bones. The curse was thought to surround the person so that it was like a garment held tight around the body by a belt.

May this be the LORD's payment to my accusers, to those who speak evil of me (*v. 20*). Instead of reading this verse as a continuation of the curse, it should be translated as a statement concerning God's judgment upon the enemy: 'This is my accusers' reward from the LORD.' The psalmist is innocent, and he is sure that God is going to redirect the curses back on the accuser himself. The change from the singular 'my accuser' to the plural 'my accusers' is carried on through to the end of the psalm.

4. An Urgent Prayer for Help (*vv. 21-29*)

But you, O Sovereign LORD, deal well with me for your name's sake; out of the goodness of your love, deliver me (*v. 21*). The opening words of the prayer (*vᵉʿattâh*, 'But you') are very emphatic, contrasting the evil character of the accuser with the gracious character of the prayer-hearing God. David wants action from the LORD, not for his own sake, but for God's sake (cf. the final petitions of Daniel's prayer in Dan. 9:17-19, which include, 'O Lord, look with favour on your desolate sanctuary ... For your sake, O Lord, hear and act! For your sake, O my God, do not delay, because your city and your people bear your Name'). He regards God's character as being on trial, and knows that the righteous judge is his only source of deliverance. God will act in accordance with his own character.

For I am poor and needy, and my heart is wounded within me. I fade away like an evening shadow; I am shaken off like a locust. My knees give way from fasting; my body is thin and gaunt. I am an object of scorn to my accusers; when they see me, they shake their heads (*vv. 22-25*). David claims that he is 'poor and needy', an expression which has already been used (see v. 16) and which denotes his depth of need at this time (cf. the use of the same phrase in Pss. 70:5 and 86:1). The expression 'my heart is wounded within me' suggests a deliberate wordplay, as 'wounded' (*châlal*) sounds very like 'curse' (*qelâlâh*) in verses 17 and 18. The psalmist has a broken heart, while his accuser is characterised by cursing.[9] His strength is gone, and he is about to

[9] The existence of wordplay would also help to explain why such an unusual expression is used. The verb 'wounded' (*châlal*) only occurs here with the subject 'my heart' (*lêv*). *BHS* suggests reading a passive verbal form *cholal*, 'is pierced', while others have drawn attention to a very similar clause in Psalm 55:4 but with a different verb, *chîl*, 'to writhe'. The MT tradition is too strong to support a change to another verb.

fade away. He uses a variety of expressions to convey the idea that he has no power of his own, with his body so weak and helpless. His accusers[10] know the reality of his position, and so they mock him in his weakness and frailty. They think that his end is in sight for him.

Help me, O LORD my God; save me in accordance with your love. Let them know that it is your hand, that you, O Lord, have done it (*vv. 26-27*). To the previous cries of 'deal well' and 'deliver' (v. 21), the psalmist now adds, 'help me' and 'save me'. All of these point to his consciousness that only with the LORD is there any hope of relief from his distress. He knows that salvation will be a demonstration of divine mercy. When that deliverance does come he wants his accusers to know that it is solely the LORD's action. Salvation is always of the LORD.

They may curse, but you will bless; when they attack they will be put to shame, but your servant will rejoice. My accusers will be clothed with disgrace and wrapped in shame as in a cloak (*vv. 28-29*). As this section of the psalm concludes, many of the ideas that have already been introduced are reinforced. David is confident that though the enemies may curse, yet God will bless. This is a clear allusion to God's words to Abraham in Genesis 12:3: 'I will bless those who bless you, and whoever curses you I will curse, and all peoples on earth will be blessed through you.' The outcome will be that he, as God's devoted servant, will be joyful while his opponents will suffer disgrace, as if they were wrapping themselves up in garments to depict their shame.

5. A Vow of Praise (*vv. 30-31*)

With my mouth I will greatly extol the LORD; in the great throng I will praise him. For he stands at the right hand of the needy one, to save his life from those who condemn him (*vv. 30-31*). As with many other songs of complaint, this particular one, though starting with the grave situation of the psalmist, ends on a note of praise. When gathered with the worshipping assembly of Israel, David pledges that he will

---

[10] The MT has simply 'and I was a reproach to them', but clearly the NIV is correct in inserting 'I am an object of scorn to *my accusers*'.

sing praise to the LORD. The expression 'in the great throng I will praise him' (*b^e^tôk rabbîm ʾ^a^hal^e^lennû*) seems to be another way of describing the 'congregation' (*qâhâl*).[11] The reason for this praise is that the LORD is at his right hand as his defender, not as his accuser (cf. v. 6). At the judgment, he will have one to stand there and deliver him from his accusers.

[11] The closest parallel is Psalm 22:22, 'in the congregation I will praise you' (*b^e^tôk rabbîm ʾ^a^hal^e^lekâ*).

Psalm 110

Of David. A psalm.

No psalm is more frequently quoted or referred to in the New Testament than this one. Jesus used it (Matt. 22:43-45; Mark 12:36-37; Luke 20:42-44) and Peter appealed to it on the day of Pentecost (Acts 2:34-36). The author of the Book of Hebrews also draws heavily upon it (Heb. 1:13; 5:6-10; 7:11-28). There is no indication of the setting or time of the psalm. It may have had its origin at the time of Solomon's enthronement, but David is looking prophetically (2 Sam. 23:2) to his greater future son, the Messiah. Even in pre-Christian times it was regarded as messianic by the Jews, and Jesus, by his use of it, silenced his opponents: 'No one could say a word in reply, and from that day on no one dared to ask him any more questions' (Matt. 22:46).

Difficulties face all translators of this psalm, as is made evident by the variations between translations but also by the marginal readings they contain. The RSV and NRSV have three such variant readings, while the ESV has four. The literature relating to this psalm is very extensive,[1] and the variety of interpretations are many. What the context in Psalm 110 and the New Testament application both assert is that the psalmist is writing about a person who is both king and priest, something that never occurred in the Old Testament. The

[1] Cf. the literature listed in L. C. Allen, *Psalms 101-150*, pp. 78-79, and the more recent list in Samuel Terrien, *The Psalms: Strophic Structure and Theological Commentary* (Grand Rapids: Eerdmans, 2003), pp. 749-51. Two very helpful discussions by Maarten J. Paul should also be added: 'Melchizedek', *NIDOTTE*, 4, pp. 934-36, and 'The order of Melchizedek (Ps. 110:4 and Heb. 7:3)', *WTJ* 49 (1987), pp. 195-211.

Testaments also agree that the promised son of David would not be a Levitical priest but one after the order of Melchizedek. Priesthood would be his, not by ancestry, but by divine oath.

The psalm is structured around two prophetic oracles (vv. 1 and 4), and these are the verses from the psalm that are quoted in the New Testament. A prophet speaks, and makes declarations concerning the messianic priest-king. The psalm has this pattern:

1. A Divine Promise:	'Sit at my right hand' (v. 1)
Explanation:	A sceptre from Zion (v. 2a)
	Rule over enemies (v. 2b)
	A willing people (v. 3)
2. A Divine Oath:	'You are a priest for ever' (v. 4)
Explanation:	God's ready help (v. 5a)
	Victory over the nations (vv. 5b,6)
	Confidence in the LORD (v. 7)

1. A Divine Promise *(vv. 1-3)*

The LORD says to my Lord: 'Sit at my right hand until I make your enemies a footstool for your feet' (*v. 1*). There are three persons involved in this verse – the LORD God, the psalmist/prophet, and the one he calls 'my Lord'. The psalmist is David, a fact endorsed both by the Lord Jesus (Mark 12:36) and the apostle Peter (Acts 2:34).[2] The manner of introducing this statement ('the LORD says', Hebrew *n*^{e}*'um yhwh*) resembles that of the prophets. It occurs only here in the Psalms, but it is very common in Jeremiah (167 times), Ezekiel (83 times), Isaiah (23 times), and Amos (21 times). As Israel never had a priest-king (see later discussion on v. 4), these words cannot apply to an ordinary descendant of David. Rather, David is calling the future priest-king *his* sovereign lord. The prophetic word points to the exaltation of God's Messiah to his right hand (the position of honour beside the king, see Ps. 45:9 and 1 Kings 2:19). He is to take his seat there until his enemies are

[2] The comments on authorship by Derek Kidner, *Psalms 73-150: A Commentary on Books iii-v of the Psalms* (London: Inter-Varsity Press, 1975), pp. 391-92, are very apposite.

in subjection to him.[3] As Peter pointed out in his Pentecost sermon, this refers to Jesus, who is 'exalted to the right hand of God' (Acts 2:33).

The LORD will extend your mighty sceptre from Zion; you will rule in the midst of your enemies. Your troops will be willing on your day of battle. Arrayed in holy majesty, from the womb of the dawn you will receive the dew of your youth (*vv. 2-3*). These verses contain three explanatory comments. First, his rule will extend outwards from Zion, which was not only David's city but the LORD's dwelling place (Ps. 132:13). The dominion of the messianic ruler will be from the promised land outwards to the ends of the earth (Ps. 72:8; see comments on that psalm). Secondly, though his enemies will take their stand against him, yet he will exercise his kingly rule over them. It is quite feasible to take this as a command, '*Rule* in the midst of your enemies', but, if so, it is a strong prediction to be fulfilled in the future.[4] The same verb is used in Psalm 72:8, and is used elsewhere in passages speaking of compulsory submission, not ruling over a peaceful situation. Thirdly, his people, the covenant people, will show willingness to serve him. Just as freewill gifts to the LORD were used to build the tabernacle (and Moses had to restrain the people's generosity, Exod. 36:2-7), so in the day of battle the LORD's people will give themselves willingly to the task. In particular, covenant youth will follow him ready for the battle. They will be arrayed in priestly attire for participation in a holy war (cf. the similar description in Rev. 19:14: 'The armies of heaven were following him, riding on white horses and *dressed in fine linen, white and clean*'). They are likened to the refreshing dew that comes at dawn (see NIV footnote).[5]

---

[3] For near eastern illustrations of enemies forming the footstool, see Othmar Keel, *The Symbolism of the Biblical World: Ancient Near Eastern Iconography and the Book of Psalms,* (London: SPCK, 1978), pp. 252-56.

[4] The grammatical point is that an imperative (*rᵉdêh,* 'rule') may be used to convey the idea of a promise or prediction to be fulfilled in the future. See *GKC,* §110c; *IBHS,* p. 572; *DIHG~S,* p. 81.

[5] This is a very difficult verse, concerning which I have given my interpretation above. More detailed notes on the Hebrew text are found in L. C. Allen, *Psalms 101-150,* pp. 79-81, with discussion of various suggested alterations.

2. A Divine Oath *(vv. 4-7)*

The LORD has sworn and will not change his mind: 'You are a priest forever, in the order of Melchizedek' (*v.* 4). Now there is a divine pledge by way of an oath. The LORD binds himself unchangeably as he addresses the priest/king. He declares that the king is also an eternal priest (see also Zech. 6:13: 'he will be clothed with majesty and sit and rule on his throne. And he will be a priest on his throne').[6] This could not be said of any human priest or king. It is given added emphasis by the reference to him being of the order of Melchizedek,[7] who was king of Salem and priest of the Most High God (Gen. 14:18-20). Just as Melchizedek was a priest/king, having his priesthood directly from God, so Jesus received a permanent priesthood through this oath by God (see the full New Testament explanation in Heb. 7:1-28). One of David's descendants was to be a priest, not after the order of Levi (which would have meant he obtained his office by right), but by divine appointment as was the case with Melchizedek.

The Lord is at your right hand; he will crush kings on the day of his wrath. He will judge the nations, heaping up the dead and crushing the rulers of the whole earth. He will drink from a brook beside the way; therefore he will lift up his head (*vv.* 5-7). Just as three points of explanation are given of the Messiah's kingship (vv. 2-3), so now three points of explanation follow about his priesthood. First, he is assured of God's ready help, with 'at the right hand' here indicating divine protection (v. 5a; cf. Pss. 16:8; 121:5).[8] Secondly, he will

---

[6] It is clear that the argument regarding the priest goes beyond the idea of eternal priesthood. The same expression 'forever' (*l*[eʿ]*ôlâm*) is used of the Aaronic priesthood (Exod. 29:9; see also Num. 25:13 and 1 Sam. 2:30). Both Psalm 110 and Hebrews 7 point to hereditary rights being the major consideration.

[7] A very unusual expression is used for 'in the order of' (*ʿal-divrâtî*). It only occurs in three other Old Testament passages (Job 5:8 [without the preposition]; Eccles. 3:18; 7:14). All the ancient translations of this verse give something like 'according to', because of', and this is supported in *DCH*, II, p. 412.

[8] The phrase here, 'at your right hand' (*ʿal-y*[e]*mînekâ*), differs from the one in verse 1, 'sit at my right hand' (*shêv lîmînî*). In verse 1 *the priest/king* sits at the right hand, i.e. in a position of honour. Here *the lord* is at the right hand to help.

be victorious over his enemies in the day when God's wrath is shown against the rebellious nations (vv. 5b-6; cf. Ps. 2:5). The verb 'crush' (*mâchats*) is used twice (vv. 5-6), so emphasising the nature of God's action against them. Those actions are likened to a battlefield, as enemies are totally crushed (cf. Rev. 19:11-16). Thirdly, he will have such confidence that the victory is secure that he will stop to refresh himself at the brook before pressing on to final victory (v. 7). He will be reinvigorated in the task, with his head lifted up as a sign of his exhilaration and confidence that victory is secure.[9] The writer to the Hebrews draws the practical implications from this teaching concerning Jesus' priesthood, that he is able to give eternal salvation to all who obey him (Heb. 5:9) and to save completely all who come to God through him (Heb. 7:25).

[9] The NIV margin, 'the one who grants succession will set him in authority', rests on suggested alteration of the MT.

Psalm 111

Psalms 111-118 consist of a group of Hallelujah songs, so-called because they emphasise praise, as is shown by the Hebrew word *hall^{e}luyah* occurring so frequently. It is only absent in Psalms 114 and 118. Psalms 111 and 112 form a pair to commence the group. They are similar in structure, in that in each the main body of the song expounds the opening idea, and then the closing verse brings the main focus to a fitting conclusion. They are also similar, being acrostic poems, which (contrary to the normal pattern) start *each short half-verse* with the consecutive letter of the Hebrew alphabet.[1] The initial 'Praise the LORD' (Hebrew, *hall^{e}luyah*) stands outside the acrostic pattern. The two psalms also are twins, in that phrases occurring in Psalm 111 are repeated in Psalm 112. For example, in 111:3 the expression occurs 'and his righteousness stands [NIV 'endures'] forever' (*v^{e}tsidqâtô ʿomédet lâʿad*). This is repeated in 112:3 and again in verse 9 with the 'and' (*v^{e}*) omitted so that it fits the acrostic pattern. The same Hebrew idiom ('stands forever') is also used in verse 10 with 'his praise' (*t^{e}hillâtô*) as the subject. Reference to the gracious character of God in 111:4 finds its parallel expression in man being called 'gracious and compassionate and righteous' in 112:4.

The main theme of the psalm is praise for the LORD's works by those who fear him, with the credal statement of Exodus 34:6 providing the main basis. This is not surprising as the psalm contains two references to the covenant. The Hebrew word

---

[1] The Hebrew alphabet has twenty-two letters. Both the Hebrew and the English text have only ten verses, but the last two verses each have three lines beginning with a different letter of the alphabet. The same is true of Psalm 112.

'covenant' (*b^erit*) only occurs twenty-one times in the Psalter, as compared with 286 uses of it in the whole Old Testament. Here, in the one psalm, the word appears twice (vv. 5 and 9), with the affirmations that God remembers his covenant forever, and that he has ordained it forever. Almost certainly it is the Sinai covenant that is in view, as the context refers to the Exodus events (cf. 'his wonders', 'his works', 'redemption', 'his precepts') along with the echo of God's self-declaration of his character, 'the LORD is gracious and compassionate' (*channûn v^erachûm yhwh*, v. 4, and cf. Exod. 34:6, *'êl rachûm v^echannûn*).

1. Public Praise of the LORD (*v. 1*)

Praise the LORD. I will extol the LORD with all my heart in the council of the upright and in the assembly (*v. 1*). An exclamation of praise forms the opening and the closing of this psalm. The unnamed psalmist pledges himself, with fullest devotion, to confess the LORD both in the general assembly of the people and also in a smaller group. This latter group, called here 'the council of the upright', was probably a band of trusted friends who shared the same fear of the LORD.[2]

2. Praise for the Redeemer (*vv. 2-9*)

Great are the works of the LORD; they are pondered by all who delight in them. Glorious and majestic are his deeds, and his righteousness endures forever (*vv. 2-3*). The works of the LORD are great because they are demonstrations of his intrinsic power. They display his greatness as they manifest his unique character, especially as the redeemer of his people. Those who are redeemed by him reflect deeply upon his actions,[3] as they carefully consider those things that are to them

[2] The word 'council' (*sôd*) occurs in other contexts where it can denote a group of youths (Jer. 6:11), the assembly of the holy ones (Ps. 89:7), or, as here, of the company of the upright. These 'upright men' (*y^eshârîm*) are equated with the 'righteous' (Ps. 33:1).

[3] The NIV 'pondered' is a translation of the Hebrew verb *dârash*. The passive plural participle used here, *d^erûshîm*, never occurs anywhere else. It probably conveys the idea of the LORD's deeds being 'worth studying'. This is the opinion of L. C. Allen, *Psalms 101-150*, p. 88. See also the entry in *DCH*, II, p. 474: 'seek with interest, be intent on, study, interpret'.

a delight (cf. the use of the same word in Ps. 1:2). Just as Psalm 104:1 declares that creation is a display of God's 'splendour and majesty', so likewise are God's actions in redemption 'glorious and majestic' (in Hebrew the words are the same in both psalms: *hôd vᵉhâdâr*).[4] The word 'righteousness' (*tsedâqâh*) in the Old Testament often means more than just uprightness. As here, it often denotes God's saving activity on behalf of his people and in accordance with his covenant promises (see v. 5).

He has caused his wonders to be remembered; the LORD is gracious and compassionate. He provides food for those who fear him; he remembers his covenant forever (*vv. 4-5*). In various ways, but especially in the appointment of the annual Passover celebration, God provided for recollecting and pondering the great facts of the redemption from Egypt. The recitation of the historical psalms (such as Pss. 78; 105; 106; 136) also kept the Exodus events in mind, as did the ceremonial presentation of the firstfruits (Deut. 26: 1-11). The people were always to assert from the credal declaration in Exodus 34:6 that the LORD is 'gracious and compassionate' (the fact that these adjectives occur in reverse here is because the poet needed this order to fit his acrostic pattern). The LORD is also praised because he provides food for his people, so fulfilling covenant promises. The worshipping community is referred to as 'those who fear him', whose needs of food and protection are met (Pss. 33:18-19; 34:9). The word 'covenant' (as distinct from the concept) is not common in the Psalms, yet it occurs twice in this same psalm.

He has shown his people the power of his works, giving them the lands of other nations. The works of his hands are faithful and just; all his precepts are trustworthy. They are steadfast for ever and ever, done in faithfulness and uprightness (*vv. 6-8*). God did not act in secret. He made promises concerning his future actions, and then after the events themselves had happened, he provided explanations

---

[4] The combination *hôd vᵉhâdâr* forms a fixed pair, always appearing in this order on its seven occurrences: Psalms 21:5; 45:3; 96:6 (= 1 Chron. 16:26); 104:1; 111:3; Job 40:10. The word *hôd* is unique to Hebrew, no related root having been found in other Semitic languages.

of what had occurred. This was so in relation to the gift of the land of Canaan to Israel, and not one of all God's good promises ever failed (Josh. 23:14). The 'lands of other nations' is more literally 'the inheritance of the Gentiles' (*nach[a]lat gôyîm*), using the term 'inheritance' that is so frequently used of Israel's possession of Canaan. What had been the inheritance of the Gentiles became, through God's actions, Israel's inheritance (Ps. 105:10-11). Those actions were certain because, according to the declaration in Exodus 34:6, he was a God 'abounding in love and faithfulness'. All his requirements for his people ('precepts', *piqqûdîm,* a word used most commonly in Ps. 119) are sure and reliable. God's precepts are a reflection of his truth and uprightness. These characteristics add to those already invoked in verse 4.

He provided redemption for his people; he ordained his covenant forever – holy and awesome is his name (*v. 9*). God not only fed his people, but he did something far more wonderful. Part of the commitment of God's covenant with Abraham was the promise of redemption from Egypt (Gen. 15:13-16), a promise reaffirmed to Moses (Exod. 3:7-10, 16-17). In later Old Testament prophecy (Isa. 42:6-7; 49:8; 55:3-5; Jer. 31:31-34) and in New Testament fulfilment (Matt. 26:28; Luke 22:20) redemption remained central to the covenant idea. The declaration regarding the covenant uses the same expression to denote its continuance as was used already in verse 5 (*l[e]'ôlâm b[e]rîtô*). The covenant God, the redeemer of his people, also showed his character in what he did in providing redemption. He was seen as holy (Exod. 3:5-6; Deut. 5:23-27) and awesome (Deut. 10:17).

3. A Summary of True Wisdom (*v. 10*)

The fear of the LORD is the beginning of wisdom; all who follow his precepts have good understanding. To him belongs eternal praise (*v. 10*). The conclusion drawn from all the wonderful works of the LORD is that reverence for him is fundamental for wise living. The God who is *awesome* (*nôrâ'*, v. 9) is to be *feared* (*yir'at yhwh*; the Hebrew for the two words 'awesome' and 'fear' come from the same root, *yârê'*). This special fear is practical. It is related to everyday living, and in particular, it is shown by obedience to God's precepts (see commentary on 34:8-14).[5] The expression here, 'the fear of the LORD is the beginning of wisdom', is paralleled in other wisdom passages (cf. Job 28:28; Prov. 1:7; 9:10; 15:33). It is significant that it comes here in a context about covenant, since the wisdom writers understood 'the fear of the LORD' in covenantal terms.[6] The psalm that began on a note of praise, *hallᵉlûyâh* (v. 1), comes to a close with the declaration that God's praise (*tᵉhillâtô*, 'his praise') stands firm forever. This is more pointed in Hebrew than in English, for the word 'praise' (*tᵉhillâh*) comes from the same root as the verb *hallᵉlû*.

---

[5] For detailed discussion on the concept, see the important, though technical, article by Henri Blocher, 'The Fear of the Lord as the "Principle" of Wisdom', *TB* 28 (1977), pp. 3-28.

[6] See the discussion on this point in Graeme Goldsworthy, *Gospel and Wisdom* (Paternoster Press, 1987), pp. 65-72.

Psalm 112

For the director of music. A psalm of David.

Psalm 111 praises God for his work and character, and Psalm 112 complements it by recognising the work and character of the godly man. It takes up the idea of the fear of the Lord (Ps. 111:10) and develops it by describing the way of life of the righteous man. The content of the psalm shows great similarity with that of Psalm 1, though the contrast with the wicked is not developed as much. The structure of this psalm is the same as the previous one, and it shares the same acrostic pattern, with verses 1-8 each having two lines beginning with different letters while verses 9-10 have three. Moreover, eleven terms or phrases used in Psalm 111 are also used in it, seven of them having been used of God in the previous one are now used of the righteous person. The following table sets these out (in each case the Hebrew word used is the same, though the NIV translation varies).

Psalm 111	**Psalm 112**
The Lord's Qualities	The Qualities of the Godly Man
righteous (3)	*righteous* (3, 6, 9)
gracious and compassionate (4)	*gracious and compassionate* (4)
just (7)	*justice* (5)
remembers (5)	*remembered* (6)
steadfast (8)	*secure* (8)
provides (Hebrew *gave,* 5)	*gifts* (Hebrew *he gave,* 9)
forever (5, 8, 9)	*forever* (6)

1. The Blessing of Fearing the Lord *(v. 1)*

Praise the Lord. Blessed is the man who fears the Lord, who finds great delight in his commands *(v. 1)*. The familiar 'Hallelujah' commences the psalm and sets the tone, before a description is given of the true God-fearer. The language is reminiscent of Psalm 1:1-2, though the idea is developed in line with Psalm 111. Fear of the LORD calls forth the proclamation of a blessing on such a person, whose main distinguishing mark is his delight in God's requirements. Reverence for God and joy in him flows into obedience to him.

2. The Description of the Righteous (*vv. 2-9*)

His children will be mighty in the land; the generation of the upright will be blessed. Wealth and riches are in his house, and his righteousness endures forever (*vv.* 2-3). The children of the righteous also enjoy blessings. In general, they will be privileged (the Hebrew word *gibbôr*, 'mighty', indicates nobility, who had the right of carrying arms in defence of the king),[1] and as long as they maintain the character of the 'upright' they will be pronounced 'blessed'. 'Wealth and riches' stand for prosperity,[2] while what was said of God's righteousness in Psalm 111:3 is now said of the God-fearer. God's faithfulness to his covenant ensures that there is continuity in his care for his people.

Even in darkness light dawns for the upright, for the gracious and compassionate and righteous man (*v.* 4). The language of this verse may well be drawn from Isaiah 60:2, in which passage Isaiah pictures the world in darkness whereas Jerusalem is lit by the LORD's glory (cf. also Isa. 9:1 and the quotation of it in Matt. 4:15-16 in reference to Jesus' ministry). What this verse means is that in times of trouble ('in darkness'), God sends his salvation, called here by the figure of speech, 'light'. Psalm 97:11 expresses the idea in similar language: 'Light is shed upon the righteous and

---

[1] The NIV recognises that the translation of *gibbôr* has to be wider than the traditional 'warrior'. Cf. the way in which it renders it by 'a man of standing' in Ruth 2:1 and 1 Samuel 9:1.

[2] 'Wealth' (*hôn*) is the poetic equivalent of the prose word *r*^{e}*kûsh* that indicates 'goods' or 'substance'. It appears here and in Proverbs 8:18 with the word 'riches' (*ʿosher*), and in Proverbs 10:15 and 18:11 with the cognate word 'rich', 'wealthy' (*ʿâshîr*).

joy in the upright in heart.' Those who are godly share in the very characteristics of God himself, and as they receive God's mercy, they show similar compassion to others.[3]

Good will come to him who is generous and lends freely, who conducts his affairs with justice (*v. 5*). 'Good' in a statement such as this is equivalent to 'blessed' (in Hebrew the phrases are parallel: 'blessed is the man ... good is the man').[4] To be 'generous' is willingly to offer assistance when others need what one has available. The same phrase, 'generous and lends freely', is used in Psalm 37:26 (cf. the use of similar phrase, 'gives generously', in v. 21 of the same psalm). The type of person described acts justly, just as he is again an imitator of God in this respect (Ps. 111:7).

Surely he will never be shaken; a righteous man will be remembered forever. He will have no fear of bad news; his heart is steadfast, trusting in the LORD. His heart is secure, he will have no fear; in the end he will look in triumph on his foes (*vv. 6-8*). During his lifetime the righteous man will remain immovable, while in death he will be remembered and his memory will be a blessing (Prov. 10:7). He will not be perturbed if there is bad news, because his confidence has been placed in the LORD. A close similarity exists with Isaiah 26:3: 'You will keep in perfect peace him whose mind is steadfast, because he trusts in you'.[5] Bad news may sadden, but the righteous man maintains his godly composure in the face of adversity. As for the wicked, he is sure that he will see them receiving their rightful punishment (cf. v. 4 and Ps. 91:8). The NIV rendering of verse 8 rightly accepts that the Hebrew

---

[3] The Hebrew grammar is awkward in that the words 'gracious', 'compassionate', and 'righteous' are singular, whereas the word 'upright' in the preceding clause is plural. While 'light' is singular, it is difficult to see how these characteristics could apply to it. The acrostic pattern placed constraints on the poet, and so these words were put side by side without any marker to indicate their reference point.

[4] The definite article is omitted in both expressions because in each case 'man' is defined by the attributes that follow.

[5] The verbs 'secure' (*sâmak*) and 'trust' (*bâtach*) are common to both Psalm 112:7-8 and Isaiah 26:3.

'will look on his foes' implies looking exultantly over vanquished foes.[6]

He has scattered abroad his gifts to the poor, his righteousness endures forever; his horn will be lifted high in honour (*v. 9*). This is a reiteration of verse 5. The righteous man scatters his gifts abroad, just as freely as someone sowing seed, and so meets the needs of the poor. This is a practical demonstration of his righteous character. Such behaviour does not go unnoticed by God, who lifts a person like this into a position of honour. Even the giving of a cup of cold water in Jesus' name will not be unrewarded (Mark 9:41).

3. The Contrast with the Wicked (*v. 10*)

The wicked man will see and be vexed, he will gnash his teeth and waste away; the longings of the wicked will come to nothing (*v. 10*). The closing verse offers the reverse picture. The wicked person is the very opposite of the righteous. He knows neither graciousness nor compassion, and his attitude to life is totally different. He will be angry, yet his hatred will not lead to any productive result. Instead, he will show his frustration by grinding his teeth, but this will in no wise prevent his disappearance from the scene. Whatever his longings are, including the destruction of the righteous, they will fail to come to pass. Lacking the blessing of God, he will simply perish.

---

[6] NIV 'in the end' represents the Hebrew *ʿad-ʾᵃsher* (lit. 'unto which'). Here, and in Psalm 110:1, *ʿad* expresses a relative limit 'beyond which the action or state described in the principal clause still continues': *GKC* §164f. This explains why L. C. Allen, *Psalms 101-150*, p. 94, renders the clause 'as he awaits looking at his foes with gratification'.

Psalm 113

With Psalms 114-118, this psalm formed part of the so-called 'Egyptian Hallel' ('Egyptian Praise'), which in Jewish usage was sung at the time of the major religious festivals (Passover, Feast of Weeks, Tabernacles). The reference to 'Egyptian' stems from the fact that the first Passover was celebrated in Egypt (Exod. 12:21-30). At the commencement of the Passover service Psalms 113 and 114 were sung, while Psalms 115-118 were used at the conclusion (cf. Matt. 26:30; Mark 14:26).[1]

The early part of this psalm draws attention to God. The word 'LORD' (*yhwh*) appears six times in the first five verses (not including the abbreviated form *yâh* in the opening call to praise). While on the one hand Psalm 113 is a hymn of praise to the exalted God, it is also a declaration concerning his care for the lowly. God manifests his power and grace in stooping to choose the foolish, weak, and lowly things of the world (1 Cor. 1:26-29), taking those who were alienated from him by their sins and exalting them to be seated with Christ in the heavenly realms (Eph. 2:1-7).

1. A Call to Universal Praise (*vv. 1-3*)

Praise the LORD. Praise, O servants of the LORD, praise the name of the LORD (*v. 1*). This hymn opens and closes with a 'Hallelujah'. The use of the expression 'servants' appears to have become a standard description of the whole worshipping community in the period following the return from exile

[1] For further details on Jewish usage of this group of psalms, see F. Delitzsch, *Psalms*, III, pp. 202-03.

(cf. its use in Ezra 5:11 and Nehemiah 1:10). Those servants are now asked to join in communal praise as the LORD's name is extolled.

Let the name of the LORD be praised, both now and for evermore. From the rising of the sun to the place where it sets, the name of the LORD is to be praised (*vv. 2-3*). The call is for such praise to be perpetual and universal, so that there is reference to both time and space. The repetition of the phrase 'the name of the LORD' is typical of this kind of call to praise (Ps. 96:1-2). The expression 'from the rising of the sun to the place where it sets' also occurs in Psalm 50:1 and in Malachi 1:11, with a similar phrase occurring twice in Isaiah (45:6; 59:19).[2] Its use points to the union of Jew and Gentile in worship of the true God, for it can hardly refer only to dispersed Jews. The fuller realisation of this vision only came with the ministry of Jesus and the proclamation of the gospel throughout the world. The ministry of Jesus and his disciples prior to his death was essentially to Jews only. Our Lord instructed his disciples, 'Do not go among the Gentiles or enter any town of the Samaritans. Go rather to the lost sheep of Israel' (Matt. 10:6). Only with the atoning death of Christ could his 'other sheep' (John 10:16) be brought in, and all kinds of people be drawn to him (John 12:32).[3]

2. The Universal LORD (*vv. 4-6*)

The LORD is exalted over all the nations, his glory above the heavens (*v. 4*). This explains the call to universal worship in the preceding verse. The LORD is sovereign over all the nations, not just over Israel his special people. His infinite kingship is also displayed by the fact that his glory is above the heavens, drawing attention to his rule over the whole of creation. This is a reassertion of what is stated in Psalms 8:1 and 57:5, 11.

---

[2] For the eschatological interpretation of this group of passages, see Joyce Baldwin, 'Malachi 1:11 and the Worship of the Nations in the Old Testament', *TB* 23 (1972), pp. 117-24.

[3] I have discussed the change in mission marked by the death of Jesus in 'Missions in the Thought of Jesus', *EQ* XLI, 3 (July-September, 1969), pp. 131-42.

Who is like the LORD our God, the One who sits enthroned on high, who stoops down to look on the heavens and the earth? (*vv. 5-6*). As so often in the Old Testament, a rhetorical question is used to highlight the main point, and also to imply that the response will be negative (for other examples, cf. Exod. 15:11; 1 Sam. 4:8; Ps. 89:6; Isa. 40:18).[4] No one is like the exalted One who sits enthroned on high.[5] The gracious condescension of God is a thing that amazes, but it is taught in both Old (Ps. 138:6) and New Testaments (Phil. 2:5-8). The exalted God stoops to meet his created order with mercy.

3. Practical Illustrations (*vv. 6-9*)

He raises the poor from the dust and lifts the needy from the ash heap; he seats them with princes, with the princes of their people. He settles the barren woman in her home as a happy mother of children. Praise the LORD (*vv. 7-9*). The psalmist illustrates the general truth that he has just stated by pointing to ways in which God shows his concern for the lowly. Verses 7-8 are taken almost word for word from Hannah's song (1 Sam. 2:8). God reverses the situation of the poor, so that instead of living the life of beggars they dine with nobility. One of the greatest tragedies for a married woman in Israel was to be childless, because this meant that she would be desolate in old age, without anyone to help her. God was able to answer Hannah's prayer for a child, and when her son was born she called him 'Samuel', saying, 'Because I asked the LORD for him' (1 Sam. 1:20). The concluding 'Hallelujah' provides a fitting conclusion to a triumphal hymn in praise of the majestic and gracious God.

---

[4] For the grammatical point concerning rhetorical questions, see *DIHG~S*, pp. 7-8.

[5] The Hebrew expressions translated 'the One who sits enthroned on high' and 'who stoops down' are actually Hif'il forms, *hammagbîhî* and *hammashpîlî*. The ending on these words is a genitive one, a fact noted by M. Dahood, *Psalms III: 101-150*, (New York: Doubleday, 1974), pp. 131, 480-81, but also much earlier by J. J. S. Perowne, *The Book of Psalms*, II, p. 324. The same phenomenon occurs also later in the psalm with the Hi. participles in verses 7-9. The listener to the Hebrew psalm is struck by the repetition of the same ending *-î* five times in verses 5-9.

Psalm 114

In the midst of a group of psalms linked by usage with the Passover, comes this one with specific reference to the Exodus and the conquest of Canaan. The previous psalm has extolled the majesty of God, and now that is illustrated in the control he had over creation at the time of the Exodus.[1] The psalm gives a very condensed account and telescopes events together that happened many years apart. It uses vivid poetic imagery to show how the creator used the forces of nature to achieve his purpose.

It is constructed from four equally balanced stanzas, which are also crafted into a chiastic pattern:

A vv. 1-2 – God's presence at the sanctuary – Israel, Jacob, Judah
    B vv. 3-4 – the [Red] Sea, the Jordan, mountains and hills
    B[1] vv. 5-6 – the [Red] Sea, the Jordan, mountains and hills
A[1] vv. 7-8 – the presence of the Lord, the God of Jacob. [2]

No precise time of composition can be given, though the reference to Judah (v. 2) has suggested to some that it comes from the period after the division of the kingdom. However, a time after the exile would not be a problem, as this psalm (among many others) could have been a message of encouragement following the return to Palestine.

---

[1] The LXX takes the 'Hallelujah' that ends Psalm 113 as the opening of Psalm 114. Certainly this creates four psalms in succession that all commence in the same way, but the MT does not know this construction. However, the absence of an antecedent to the pronominal references in verse 2 ('his sanctuary', 'his dominion') has encouraged some commentators to follow the LXX.

[2] This is the position of Konrad Schaefer, *Psalms*, (Collegeville: Liturgical Press, 2001), p. 282.

1. The Significance of the Exodus (*vv. 1-2*)
When Israel came out of Egypt, the house of Jacob from a people of foreign tongue, Judah became God's sanctuary, Israel his dominion (*vv. 1-2*). This simple opening description states the fact of the Exodus. Its form (lit. 'in the going-out of Israel from Egypt') was almost a standard expression (cf. its use in Deut. 4:45-46; 23:4; 24:9; 25:17; and Josh. 2:10; 5:4-5). Israel/Jacob had lived in Egypt among a people of 'foreign tongue' (*ʿam loʿêz*). This phrase occurs nowhere else in the Old Testament, but it appears to mean that the Egyptians spoke a language that was unintelligible to the Israelites. They heard what was for them a stammering tongue. Presumably the Israelites learned sufficient Egyptian so that there was communication between them and their masters. From that foreign environment God delivered them, and the whole nation of twelve tribes (Judah/Israel) became his sanctuary. Other interpretations are that the sanctuary could be the promised land itself (see Exod. 15:17), or else the tabernacle/temple. In view of the use of the word 'dominion', the first suggestion is most probable, as Israel was God's special treasure, his kingdom of priests (Exod. 19:6).

2. A Poetic Description of the Exodus (*vv. 3-4*)
The sea looked and fled, the Jordan turned back; the mountains skipped like rams, the hills like lambs (*vv. 3-4*). The crossing of the Red Sea and of the Jordan River are brought together as if there were a single event. This may occur elsewhere (Ps. 66:6), though in that passage 'the waters' may just be an alternative way of describing the Red Sea. The prose description of the two crossings is found in Exodus 14:21-22 and Joshua 3:14-17 respectively. The rivers are personified, and so are described as seeing the approach of God and running away. Likewise the mountains (especially Mount Sinai) trembled before God's presence. The whole imagery is intended to bring to mind the formidable events of the Exodus (cf. Exod. 19:18) and conquest that were due to God's invincible power.

3. Questions Needing No Answer (*vv. 5-6*)
Why was it, O sea, that you fled, O Jordan, that you turned back, you mountains, that you skipped like rams, you hills, like lambs? (*vv. 5-6*). Four rhetorical questions emphasise the point that has just been made in the previous stanza and prepare for the call to the earth that is to follow in verses 7-8. The natural world is personified so that questions can be directed to it. These verses echo the words already used in verses 3-4, with verse 6 being almost identical to verse 4.[3] They also anticipate the climax in the closing verses.

4. The God of Present Blessing (*vv. 7-8*)
Tremble, O earth, at the presence of the Lord, at the presence of the God of Jacob, who turned the rock into a pool, the hard rock into springs of water (*vv. 7-8*). The climax is reached in this stanza. 'The Lord' who controls nature is also 'the God of Jacob', the covenantal God of his people. Up to this point it has been implied that the reference was being made to God, but now it becomes explicit. He is referred to as 'the Lord' (*'âdôn*). The repetition of 'at the presence of' is a reminder that before such a God the earth can only quake as his power is shown. Two experiences of great power are recalled (Exod. 17:6; Num. 20:11), one soon after leaving Egypt, the other when coming close to the promised land. That God is still one who 'turns' (as it is expressed in Hebrew) rocks into water, which is a reassurance of his continuing protective care of his people. It is no wonder that the earth is called on to respond to his divine power.

---

[3] The only change is that the verb 'skip' is a perfect form in verse 4 (*râqᵉdû*) and imperfect in verse 6 (*tirqᵉdû*), but with no difference in meaning.

Psalm 115

Many of the ancient translations of the Psalms (Greek, Latin, Syriac, Arabic, and Ethiopic) and a few Hebrew manuscripts join together Psalms 114 and 115. However, there is no good reason for this, as the content of the two psalms is quite different. This psalm is a song, probably prepared and used in the temple worship after the return from exile, which extols the person and character of the God of Israel in contrast to the worthless idols of the Gentile nations. Verses 3-8 appear in very similar form in Psalm 135:6, 15-18. Within the psalm there is alternation between second and third persons, which suggests that it was intended for antiphonal voices, with congregation and priest(s) sharing in the song or recitation.

The use of repetition throughout the psalm is also typical of liturgical use (cf. Pss. 96:1; 103:20-22; 118:2-4; 135:1; 136:1-3). This starts at the very outset ('Not to us, O LORD, not to us', v. 1) and continues throughout. Verses 9-11 contain a threefold call to trust in the LORD that is phrased in almost identical terms except for the different subject.[1] This triplet is then followed by the fourfold blessing in verses 12-13. Actually, 'blessing' occurs six times (vv. 12-18), while the divine name (either *yhwh*, or its shortened form *yâh*) appears eight times. The idea of trusting is also both repeated and contrasted, for the opposite of trusting in idols (v. 8) is trusting in the LORD, who is a helper and shield (vv. 9-11).

[1] The only other difference is that the subject 'Israel' requires the singular imperative (*b^etach*) rather than the plural imperative (*bit^echû*).

1. An Ascription of Exclusive Praise (*v. 1*))

Not to us, O LORD, not to us but to your name be the glory, because of your love and faithfulness (*v. 1*). The psalm commences with a statement that is both an affirmation and a denial. It denies that any glory is due to the community of Israel because such glory belongs to the LORD alone. If the psalm comes from the post-exilic period, as is most probable, the expressions here would fit in well with statements of both Ezekiel and Daniel (Ezek. 20:9; 36:21-23; Dan. 9:18-19). God had fulfilled his words of promise to his people, and shown yet once again his love and faithfulness in restoring them to Palestine. The introduction at the outset of covenantal language (*chésed*, 'love'; *ʾemet*, 'faithfulness') is not surprising in the midst of a group of psalms whose focus is redemption from Egypt.

2. The Futility of Idol Worship (*vv. 2-8*)

At various times in her history Israel was challenged regarding the reality of her God (2 Kings 18:31-35; Pss. 42:3; 79:10). At the time of the exile the Gentile nations were mocking the Israelites regarding God's ability to help his people. **Why do the nations say, 'Where is their God?'** (*v. 2*). The question they were asking seemed to them to highlight the predicament of the Israelites, yet it failed to reckon with the fact that the God of Israel was the only living and true God. The form of the question is identical with Psalm 79:10, except that here a little particle of taunt or entreaty (*nâʾ*) is added. This does not translate as 'now' (cf. AV, NASB) but rather, if required at all in English, as 'pray', 'please'.[2]

Our God is in heaven; he does whatever pleases him (*v. 3*). The English versions almost uniformly fail to recognise that the Hebrew of this verse commences with the conjunction *vav*, which has to serve a wide range of functions.[3] This serves here to mark the contrast between the claims of the Gentiles

---

[2] Cf. L. C. Allen, *Psalms 101-150*, p. 106: 'Where, pray, is their God?'; and the note in W. VanGemeren, 'The Psalms', p. 721.

[3] Hebrew lacks many of the adversatives that English possesses, such as 'but', 'nevertheless', and 'however'. In many contexts, it has to make do with *vav*.

and the reality: '*But* our God is in heaven'.[4] The people assert again the existence of a God in heaven who fulfils his sovereign will.

> Not unto us, O Lord of heav'n,
> but unto Your Name be glory given;
> in love and truth Lord, You fulfil
> the counsels of Your sovereign will.
> Though nations fail Your pow'r to own,
> yet Lord, You reign, and You alone.
> (*Trinity Hymnal*, 1961)

Gentiles probably mocked Jews because they had no image of their God. This assertion points to God being in heaven, and therefore invisible. From his throne he does what pleases him, i.e. he has both freedom and power to fulfil his will. The same words 'he does whatever pleases him' occur also in Psalm 135:6, though the scope of his activity is described more fully as being 'in the heavens and on earth, in the seas and all their depths'.

But their idols are silver and gold, made by the hands of men. They have mouths, but cannot speak, eyes, but they cannot see; they have ears, but cannot hear, noses, but they cannot smell; they have hands, but cannot feel, feet, but they cannot walk; nor can they utter a sound with their throats (*vv. 4-7*). The summary statement of Deuteronomy 4:28 is expanded here, and these verses are most probably the basis of Psalm 135:15-18. Over against the sovereign God whom Israel worshipped, the idols of the Gentiles are impotent and lifeless. They might have all the visible parts similar to a human body, but they have no ability to respond to human needs. They are simply the work of men's hands. Isaiah in even fuller fashion mocks the folly of those who think they can create their own gods (Isa. 44:9-20).

Those who make them will be like them, and so will all who trust in them (*v. 8*). The people who create and worship such idols of silver and gold will be just as ineffective as those

[4] Discussion on this use of the conjunction *vav* can be found in *IBHS*, pp. 650-51, and *DIHG~S*, pp. 172-73.

gods themselves. They may mock worshippers of the true God, yet they are trusting in their own futile creations that can offer no help at all. The principle that the Bible asserts is that idol worshippers are similar to their very objects of veneration. Isaiah says that idol worshippers are 'empty' (*tohû*), using the same word that describes the idols themselves (cf. Isa. 44:9 with 1 Sam. 12:21).

3. A Call to Trust in the LORD (*vv. 9-11*)

O house of Israel, trust in the LORD – he is their help and shield. O house of Aaron, trust in the LORD – he is their help and shield. You who fear him, trust in the LORD – he is their help and shield (*vv. 9-11*). The false trust just spoken about in verse 8 must be replaced by confidence in the living God. The use of the three phrases 'house of Israel', 'house of Aaron', and 'you who fear him', also occurs in Psalms 118:2-4 and 135:19-20 (with the addition of 'house of Levi'). The involvement of the 'house of Aaron' is particularly fitting for the period after the exile, when the priests had to assume a very prominent role and were the principal teachers of the people (Mal. 2:5-6). 'You who fear him' could be a reference to the whole worshipping community, or else it could refer to the proselytes who had come to trust in the God of Israel (cf. the New Testament use of the term 'god-fearers' for Gentiles who had converted to Judaism: Acts 10:2; 16:14; 17:4, 17). The call is for all these groups to renounce any allegiance to idols and to trust in the LORD. The expression 'help and shield' is used also in Psalm 33:20 (see comment there).

4. A Confession of Trust (*vv. 12-13*)

The LORD remembers us and will bless us: He will bless the house of Israel, he will bless the house of Aaron, he will bless those who fear the LORD – small and great alike (*vv. 12-13*). In response to the call to trust, the people now respond with fresh commitment to the LORD. The recurring 'he will bless' offers assurance of the continuity of God's love and faithfulness to all the groups already mentioned in verses 9-11. Added assurance is given by saying that God 'remembers' them. This means that God recalls his promises and acts upon them to all who trust in him. It is part of the covenantal language of the Old Testament in relation to God's faithfulness (Gen. 8:1; 19:29; 30:22; Exod. 2:24). Social class or wealth make no difference when it comes to God's blessing. 'Small and great alike' are only distinguished by the presence (or lack) of faith in God.

5. The Priestly Blessing (*vv. 14-15*)

May the LORD make you increase, both you and your children. May you be blessed by the LORD, the Maker of heaven and earth (*vv. 14-15*). After the return from exile Israel's numbers were very small. Part of the blessing of God for obedience was the increase in children (Deut. 28:4). The words used here may well echo the prayer that Moses uttered just before Israel crossed the Jordan into the land of Canaan: 'May the LORD, the God of your fathers, increase you a thousand times and bless you as he has promised!' (Deut. 1:11). Those making this request can be confident that the blessing will be realised because the one to whom the prayer is addressed is indeed 'the Maker of heaven and earth'. This is a standard description, used repeatedly of the living God (Pss. 121:2; 124:8; 134:3; 146:6).

6. The Congregational Confession (*vv. 16-18*)

The highest heavens belong to the LORD, but the earth he has given to man (*v. 16*). The community of Israel join in a response that magnifies the God they worship. While he is the God of heaven,[5] yet he has allocated the earth to humanity. 'He did not create it to be empty, but formed it to be inhabited' (Isa. 45:18). Humans have been given special responsibility for the earth, over which they rule as God's vice-regents (Gen. 1:28-30). It has been put in their trust.

---

[5] The NIV 'The highest heavens belong to the LORD' is an attempt to translate the Hebrew *hashshâmáyim shâmáyim layhwh*, by understanding the construction to be a superlative expression. However, the grammar points rather to a translation such as 'The heavens are the LORD's heavens' (NRSV, ESV).

It is not the dead who praise the LORD, those who go down to silence; it is we who extol the LORD, both now and for evermore. Praise the LORD (*vv. 17-18*). Part of the responsibility of living people is to praise the LORD. Those in the grave do not engage in praise. While there may well be more references to life after death in the Old Testament than has often been thought,[6] yet the fuller teaching on it is given in the New Testament. Believers at death are immediately present with the Lord. The point here at the end of this psalm is that it is not corpses but living people who render thanksgiving to the LORD. Hence the community encourages themselves to do this continually: 'it is *we* who extol the LORD'. They immediately do so with the exclamation: 'Hallelujah!'

[6] The discussion by Elmer Smick, 'The Bearing of New Philological Data on the Subjects of Resurrection and Immortality in the Old Testament', *WTJ* 31 (1968-69), pp. 12-21, is important as an evangelical assessment of some of the more radical suggestions put forward by Mitchell Dahood.

Psalm 116

An unnamed psalmist cries out here in thanksgiving for his personal deliverance. The exact circumstances of his trouble are not indicated, but it is clear that he had been through deep waters, and he now wishes to express his heartfelt praise to God his Saviour. There are many ways in which this psalm is reminiscent of King Hezekiah's thanksgiving after his recovery from his illness (Isa. 38). The psalm appears to come from later in the Old Testament period, as it uses phrases that we know from other earlier Psalms (especially Pss. 18, 27, 31, and 56). Also, the language, because of the presence of Aramaic forms or usage, has suggested to some that the psalm is from just before the fall of Jerusalem in 586 BC, or from the early exilic period.[1]

Just as the Greek and Latin versions join Psalms 114 and 115 together, so they split Psalm 116 into two (vv. 1-9 and 10-19). In neither case is there justification for such division. The content of Psalm 116 points to a common author, with the theme of death appearing in verses 3, 8, and 15, along with praise to the LORD for the deliverance he has provided. 'Call[ed] on the name of the LORD' is also common to both parts (vv. 4, 13, 17), while 'you have freed me from my chains' (v. 16) describes the deliverance requested earlier in the psalm (v. 4).

---

[1] This argument has to be handled carefully, as Aramaic was in widespread use in the region before the exile, and Aramaic forms are not necessarily proof of late authorship. Mitchell Dahood, *Psalms III: 101-150*, p. 145, asserts strongly that the language and syntax point to a date of composition much earlier than the post-exilic period.

1. A Cry Heard (*vv. 1-4*)
I love the LORD, for he heard my voice; he heard my cry for mercy (*v. 1*). This translation of the NIV is possible, but the position of the word 'LORD' is debatable. The preferred and more literal rendering is, 'I love, for the LORD heard the voice of my supplications'. Twice more in the psalm verbs are used without an object ('call' in v. 2; 'believed' in v. 10). The unusual expression may well draw attention to the intensity of the love that he felt for the LORD, just as John the apostle declared, '*We love,* because he first loved us' (1 John 4:19). All through this psalm the covenantal name for God (Heb. *yhwh,* 'LORD') is used, and later the psalmist declares that he is a true covenantal servant (see v. 16).

Because he turned his ear to me, I will call on him as long as I live (*v. 2*). 'To turn the ear' is a common Old Testament expression for giving heed to what is said, or listening to a prayer (cf. its usage elsewhere in the Psalms, where it is normally the imperative, 'turn your ear to me': 17:6; 31:2; 71:2; 86:1; 88:2; 102:2). Because the LORD had responded to his prayer the psalmist pledges lifelong appeal to him as his deliverer.[2] The pattern is set here for other believers to follow:

> I love the Lord; he heard my cries
> And pitied every groan.
> Long as I live, when troubles rise
> I'll hasten to his throne.

The cords of death entangled me, the anguish of the grave came upon me; I was overcome by trouble and sorrow. Then I called on the name of the LORD; 'O LORD, save me!' (*vv. 3-4*). Some great sickness or danger had confronted the psalmist and he felt near to the grave. The combination of various expressions for the danger emphasises how pressing a danger it was. However, he tells how at that

---

[2] The NIV's 'as long as I live' is the translation of the MT's *b^eyâmay,* 'in my days'. To explain this word, F. Delitzsch, *Psalms,* III, p. 216, appeals to Isaiah 39:8, but this is not a real parallel. While the expression is certainly unusual, yet the NIV translation is probably correct.

time he cried to the LORD, and asked for deliverance. The verb translated 'save me', is literally, 'cause me to escape' (*mall^{e}tâh*), which directs attention again to the acute nature of his grief and trouble. He was entangled in death's cords, which has as its parallel 'the anguish of the grave' (lit. 'the straits of Sheol').[3]

2. God's Character Reaffirmed (*vv. 5-7*)

The LORD is gracious and righteous; our God is full of compassion (*v. 5*). The psalmist does not say that God answered him, but instead he fixes attention on his God. A fresh experience of God's mercy calls for a fresh declaration regarding his character. By the word of Scripture and again through personal experience the psalmist knows that God is merciful and righteous. He has already spoken of his cry for mercy (v. 1) and now says that God is indeed merciful, for he has listened and answered! In Hebrew, the words 'my cry for mercy' (*tach^{a}nûnây*, v. 1) and 'gracious' (*channûn*, v. 5) come from the same root (*ch-n-n*).The linking together of God's attributes of mercy and compassion is frequent in the Old Testament (Exod. 34:6; 2 Chron. 30:9; Neh. 9:17, 31; Ps. 103:8).

The LORD protects the simplehearted; when I was in great need, he saved me. Be at rest once more, O my soul, for the LORD has been good to you (*vv. 6-7*). The expression 'simple-hearted' (*petâ'im*) does not imply lack of understanding but just that these people are resting on the LORD and his promises. The psalmist was a simple-hearted person when in humility he called on the LORD, and he was saved. The Hebrew word used here (*y^{e}hôshî'a*) reminds us of the name *Joshua*, which means 'saviour', both coming from the same root. With the trouble behind him, the psalmist can encourage himself to take his rest, for the LORD has dealt with him as one of his children. The needy child has met with gracious, parental care, and there is

---

[3] The Hebrew word for 'anguish' is actually a plural construct form, *m^{e}tsârê*, from a late Hebrew word *mêtsâr*, that only occurs here and in Psalm 118:5 and Lamentations 1:3.

abundant rest for the soul trusting in him (this is brought out in Hebrew by the use of plural noun, 'be at *rests*').[4]

3. Thanks for God's Mercy *(vv. 8-19)*

For you, O LORD, have delivered my soul from death, my eyes from tears, my feet from stumbling, that I may walk before the LORD in the land of the living (*vv. 8-9*). Now the psalmist returns to his past need. He had been looking death in the face, but God had delivered him.[5] He uses yet another synonym (*chálats,* Pi., 'plunder', 'take out') to describe his release (cf. 'cause to escape', v. 4; 'save', v. 6; 'deliver', v. 8). The outcome of his experience was that he was still alive, and living his life in the presence of his God. These verses seems to be a deliberate use of Psalm 56:13, and this would also explain the change here to the second person singular (*'you,* O LORD').[6] It may well be that Psalm 27:13 is in mind: 'I am still confident of this: I will see the goodness of the LORD in the land of the living'. In both psalms 'land of the living' is just a poetic description of being alive.[7]

I believed; therefore I said, 'I am greatly afflicted'. And in my dismay I said, 'All men are liars' (*vv. 10-11*). At this point the Greek (LXX) translation starts a new psalm, probably as part of the need to restore the 150 psalms (see the Introduction). There is, however, no exegetical reason for this. While the words 'I believed' correspond to 'I love' in verse 1, yet there is no reason to break the psalm into two (see the introductory

---

[4] The word for 'rest' (*m^e^nûkâh*) is quite common, but only here does the masculine plural form appear. The use of the plural appears to stress the fulness of rest found with the LORD.

[5] The NIV adds the words 'O LORD', which, though implied, are not in the MT.

[6] The two passages are very close in wording. The first clause ('For you have delivered my soul from death') is identical, while the second is added here ('my eye from tears'). The third is essentially the same in meaning in both psalms (56:13: 'Have [you] not [delivered] my feet from stumbling?'; 116:8: '[you have delivered] my foot from stumbling'). The fourth clause is very similar (56:13: 'to walk before God in the light of life'; 116:9: 'I will walk before the LORD in the lands of the living').

[7] Psalm 27:13 has the singular '*land* of the living'. The change here to the plural '*lands* of the living' is a common poetic usage of the plural to indicate multiplicity. See *IHBS,* p. 120; *DIHG~S,* p. 19.

comments on this psalm). Both the verbs 'love' and 'believe' normally take a direct object in Hebrew, but that is lacking in both instances. It is best to take 'believe' in the sense of 'have faith'. He has just declared in what he has faith – 'that I may walk before the LORD in the land of the living' (v. 9).[8] The first part of verse 10 is quoted from the Greek (LXX) translation by Paul in 2 Corinthians 4:13 as he faced a similar situation to the psalmist. Even in the depths of despair, the psalmist never lost hope in God. Men may have been giving him false advice, and he knew them well enough to declare them to be liars. But God was ever faithful and worthy of his trust.[9]

How can I repay the LORD for all his goodness to me? I will lift up the cup of salvation and call on the name of the LORD (*vv. 12-13*). Recalling his deliverance, the psalmist asks what would be a fitting acknowledgment to the LORD.[10] The use of the expression 'all his goodness' links the question directly with the latter part of verse 7, as the noun 'goodness' (*tagmûl*) is derived from the verb 'be good' (*gâmal*).[11] 'The cup of salvation' could be a general reference to experiencing the saving blessings that God gives his children, or it could refer to a specific festival occasion. The latter may well be in view, because of the reference to vows, and to the fact that the psalmist was going to be in the house of the LORD in Jerusalem (see v. 19). Some have seen the expression 'the cup of salvation' as a reference to one of the cups used in the Passover (1 Cor. 10:16). There is perhaps support for this idea,

---

[8] This interpretation was given by A. F. Kirkpatrick, *The Book of Psalms*, p. 690, including taking 'I believed' absolutely. *DCH*, I, p. 360, lists this as one of five examples of this meaning of the verb.

[9] One of the fullest notes on the Hebrew of this verse is that by J. J. S. Perowne, *The Book of Psalms*, II, pp. 336-37.

[10] The phrase 'all his goodnesses' is actually the object of the verb 'repay', so the NIV 'for' is unnecessary. The translation can be: 'How shall I repay all the LORD's goodnesses to me?'

[11] This is the only occurrence of the noun 'goodness' (*tagmûl*) in the Old Testament. It is plural in form ('goodnesses'), and while the attached suffix 'his' has often been noted as an Aramaic form (cf. *BDB*, p. 168; *GKC* §91 l), yet it may well be a Phoenician third person masculine suffix -*î* that appears in Hebrew poetry. For this explanation, see M. Dahood, *Psalms III: 101-150*, p. 149.

since this is one of the psalms used by the Jews at the time of the Passover celebration, and it was probably one of the psalms that Jesus and his disciples sang after the first Lord's Supper (Matt. 26:30). 'And call upon the name of the LORD' is repeated exactly as it is at the beginning of verse 4.

I will fulfil my vows to the LORD in the presence of all his people (*v. 14*). The psalmist uses the standard language for keeping what was promised by a vow to the LORD.[12] A vow was a verbal promise to God (Num. 30:1-4) that had to be performed (Deut. 23:21), and in most cases it involved the offering of a promised gift for a sacrifice. This meant that it was done publicly in the presence of the congregation (see vv. 17-19).[13]

Precious in the sight of the LORD is the death of his saints (*v. 15*). This can hardly mean that God is pleased when his people die. In the context it means more that God will never be uncaring when his people come near to death. Their blood is precious in his sight (Ps. 72:14).[14]

O LORD, truly I am your servant; I am your servant, the son of your maidservant; you have freed me from my chains (*v. 16*). The psalmist expresses himself now in covenantal language. To say, 'I am your servant', was a statement of submission and loyalty (cf. Ahaz' words, 2 Kings 16:7). He makes it to the covenantal LORD, and repeats it in asserting

---

[12] The verb is 'pay', 'fulfil' (*shâlêm* Pi.), the usual verb used when payment of a vow is involved (Deut. 23:21; Pss. 22:25; 66:13; Prov. 7:14).

[13] The form of the preposition 'in the presence of' (*neged*) is unusual (*negᵉdâh*), occurring only here and in verse 18. Also, it is followed by *-nâ'*, which is normally a particle accompanying commands or requests, similar to the English 'please' in such contexts. Insufficient grammatical evidence exists to make a definitive judgment on the lengthened form of the preposition or the presence of *-nâ'*. For some possible explanations, see *GKC*, p. 308, fn. 1; M. Dahood, *Psalms III: 101-150*, p. 149; L. C. Allen, *Psalms 101*-150, p. 113; *IBHS*, pp. 578-79; T. O. Lambdin, *Introduction to Biblical Hebrew*, (New York: Charles Scribner, 1971), pp. 170-71. The AV and NKJV both translate *-nâ'* by 'now', while the NASB makes it express a wish: 'Oh *may it be* in the presence of all His people ...'

[14] The word 'death' appears in a feminine form (*hammâvᵉtâh*) that does not occur anywhere else. The addition of the long *-âh* ending, when viewed with *negᵉdâh* in the previous verse, may point to a dialect of Hebrew that favoured this ending in poetry.

that he is the son of woman who was likewise devoted to her LORD. He has been freed from his chains, an expression broad enough to be used of a variety of pressing situations.[15]

I will sacrifice a thank-offering to you and call on the name of the LORD. I will fulfil my vows to the LORD in the presence of all his people, in the courts of the house of the LORD – in your midst, O Jerusalem. Praise the LORD (*vv. 17-19*). The regulations regarding offering of sacrifices of thanksgiving and also sacrifices to fulfil vows are set out in Leviticus 7:11-21. The psalmist will not only make the offering, but he will also call on the name of the LORD (the phrase is repeated from verse 13). This could mean that he will pray, but 'call' (*qârâ'*) in Hebrew can also mean, 'call out', 'proclaim'. The latter meaning fits better here, as it agrees also with Psalm 22:25 in that public proclamation or confession was part of thanksgiving. Verses 18-19 describe both to whom the sacrifices were to be presented but also the place of offering. Using the words of verse 14, the psalmist adds to them to indicate that his vows would be fulfilled in the courts of the temple in Jerusalem. There he would have the opportunity of sitting with others to eat of the cakes that would be presented. A communal meal was a fitting way to rejoice before the LORD. The final 'Hallelujah', 'Praise the LORD', is not at all surprising.

---

15 Once more a grammatical oddity occurs, as the object of the verb (*môsêrây*, 'my chains') is marked by the use of the preposition *l*^{e}, a usage common in Aramaic but not in Hebrew. *DIHG~S*, pp. 117-18 notes this non-prepositional usage of *l*^{e}. For the Aramaic practice of marking the object of a verb with *l*^{e}, see F. Rosenthal, *A Grammar of Biblical Aramaic*, 2nd revised printing (Wiesbaden: Otto Harassowitz, 1963), p. 56, and Alger F. Johns, *A Short Grammar of Biblical Aramaic*, revised edition (Berrien Springs: Andrews University Press, 1972), p. 11.

Psalm 117

This shortest of all the psalms is a missionary call. Stemming from experience of God's steadfast love the psalmist looks to the Gentile nations to come and rejoice with Israel. This prospect of Gentile incorporation into God's kingdom was part of the vision of Old Testament psalmists and prophets. It was only the coming and death of Christ that opened the way for universal mission.[1] Luther commented on the brevity of this psalm and said that it was short so that everyone could grasp its meaning. It speaks of abundant mercy. In response to it a loud 'Hallelujah' is needed. The psalm is an excellent example of a hymn of praise, as it commences with a call to the nations, tells the reason for praise, and then repeats the call again (for these hymns, see Introduction).

1. A Missionary Call (*v. 1*)

Praise the Lord, all you nations; extol him, all you peoples. The psalmist issues a call to the Gentile nations to join in the Lord's praise. Even those regarded by Jews as *gôyîm* are invited to participate in worship and adoration of the Lord.[2] In effect this is a call to experience the saving power of God, and to know him just as believing Israel did. 'Praise' and 'extol' are close in meaning, while 'peoples' matches 'nations'.[3] Paul uses this verse along with other Old Testament quotations to

---

[1] See comments on Psalm 113:2-3.

[2] While *gôyîm* normally refers to non-Jews, it can on occasions be used of Israel. Cf. the discussion in *TWOT*, I, pp. 326-27.

[3] An unusual word is used for 'peoples' (*'ummîm*), though it sounds very like the much more common word *'ammîm*.

show that it was God's intention that the Gospel would result in the Gentiles glorifying God for his mercy (Rom. 15:8-12).

2. An Explanation *(v. 2a-b)*

For great is his love towards us and the faithfulness of the LORD endures for ever. A double explanation is provided of the reason behind the call to praise. First, the psalmist says God's covenant love (*chasdô*) has been great to us. Secondly, he knows that God's complete faithfulness (*'emet*) is one of his enduring characteristics. These two, covenant love and faithfulness, go hand in hand, as they do in Psalm 89:1-2.

3. Another Hallelujah *(v. 2c)*

Praise the LORD. The psalmist practises what he preaches. Having called on the Gentiles to 'praise the LORD', he does so himself. The initial call is now put into direct address, an ascription of praise to the one who is worthy of all honour. The chorus of 'Hallelujah' will sound out fully in heaven: 'Hallelujah! Salvation and glory and power belong to our God' (Rev. 19:1).

Psalm 118

Various interpretations have been given of this psalm. The different approaches stem from the fact that it combines personal and communal elements, and its content involves both imagery of battle and of the temple. The most satisfactory background for the psalm is a time when the LORD had given victory to his people, like when Jehoshaphat and his army defeated the combined forces of Moab and Ammon (see 2 Chron. 20:1-30, especially 20-23, 27-28). The tone of the psalm suggests that it is a song of national thanksgiving.

After the opening praise, the victorious warrior rejoices in God's salvation, while in the latter part of the psalm the people as a whole join in the praise. The use of this psalm as part of the praise at the end of the Passover was most fitting (see the introduction to Ps. 113). It has connections in language with the Song of Moses (Exod. 15), and it may have formed part of the hymn that Jesus and his disciples used after the institution of the Lord's Supper (Matt. 26:30).

Many phrases in the psalm are echoes of other psalter contexts. In particular, the assertion of the enduring nature of covenantal love (*kî l^{e}ʿôlâm chasdô*: 'for his love endures for ever') at both the beginning and end points to the centrality of this truth in Israel's faith (cf. its use both in other psalms such as Pss. 100:5, 106:1, 107:1, and as a refrain twenty-six times in Ps. 136). Its use on major religious occasions confirms this fact (see comment on v. 1).

1. Enduring Love (*vv. 1-4*)

Give thanks to the LORD, for he is good; his love endures forever (*v. 1*). The opening and closing verses of the psalm are part of the terminology of praise that appears in almost identical form in Psalms 105-107, 136, 1 Chronicles 16:8, 34, and 2 Chronicles 20:21. The fact that God is good is shared with other passages in the Psalter (such as 25:8 and 73:1). At a time of personal and national rejoicing, the use of the covenantal title of God (*LORD*) and the theme of covenant love direct attention to the object of praise. Once more the mercy of God has been experienced by king and people.

Let Israel say: 'His love endures forever.' Let the house of Aaron say: 'His love endures forever.' Let those who fear the LORD say: 'His love endures forever' (*vv. 2-4*). The triplet, 'Israel', 'house of Aaron', and 'those who fear the LORD', recalls the same usage in Psalm 115:9-13. These comprehensive titles are used so that none in the covenant nation are excluded from the call to affirm yet again the wonder of God's grace to them. While the subjects are different in these verses, the content of praise remains the same.

2. A Song of Deliverance (*vv. 5-21*)

In my anguish I cried to the LORD, and he answered by setting me free. The LORD is with me; I will not be afraid. What can man do to me? The LORD is with me; he is my helper. I will look in triumph on my enemies (*vv. 5-7*). The poet, who may be the king, reflects upon what happened when he was in distress. The terms he uses suggest some military situations, probably being besieged by opposing armies. He declares that divine intervention resulted in him being brought into open space (*bammerchâv*). Out of a siege situation he was delivered, and therefore he can declare that because the LORD is with him, his fear is banished. The repetition of 'The LORD is with me' is one of many such repetitions throughout the psalm. They serve to enhance the poetic effect and to draw attention to the thought being expressed. To claim that the LORD is his helper also points to a battle situation, as 'helper' (*ʿozer*) often has a military connotation. Since he has such divine assistance the psalmist knows that he can look in triumph on his enemies. Psalm 54 forms a fitting parallel, containing both the idea of God as the helper (54:4) and looking in triumph on enemies (54:7). The words of verses 6-7 are quoted in Hebrews 13:6 as an encouragement to contentment. The joyful thanksgiving of the Old Testament believers is made the pattern for Christians. The answer to the question, 'What can man do to me?' is to be found in Paul's words: 'If God is for us, who can be against us?' (Rom. 8:31).

It is better to take refuge in the LORD than to trust in man. It is better to take refuge in the LORD than to trust in princes (*vv. 8-9*). These two verses are identical apart from the final phrase in each. Both prophets and psalmists warn of the folly of looking to the strength of man for help, instead of looking to the LORD (Ps. 33:16-19; Isa. 30:1-5). The combined expression is a forceful way of emphasising how good it is to put one's trust in the living God.

All the nations surrounded me, but in the name of the LORD I cut them off. They surrounded me on every side, but in the name of the LORD I cut them off. They swarmed around me like bees, but they died out as quickly as burning thorns; in the name of the LORD I cut them off (*vv. 10-12*). These verses display repetitive language to describe the way the speaker, the king, triumphed over the enemies with God's help. The verb surround (*sâvav*), which in a military context means 'surround' or 'hem in', occurs four times, while the expression 'I cut them off' appears three times.[1] When Israel was surrounded by neighbouring nations who were attacking like bees (for the use of bees to depict an attacking army, see Deut. 1:44; and Isa. 7:18-19), the king was able to overcome them in the name of the LORD. 'The name of the LORD' stands for his character, which was displayed in the victories he gave his people over their enemies. The king recognises that victory only comes through trusting the LORD and his power. The

---

[1] 'I cut them off' translates a verb with a suffix, *ʾamîlam*. This seems to be the verb *mûl* which normally means 'circumcise', but nowhere else does it appear in the causative (Hi.) form. It could be that this verb is used to signify 'cut off', or else, as listed in *DCH*, V, p. 173, it is as another verb, *mûl* II, that means 'fend off', 'drive away'.

language of verse 12 suggests a sharp attack by the enemies, but swift victory for Israel.

I was pushed back and about to fall, but the LORD helped me. The LORD is my strength and my song; he has become my salvation (*vv. 13-14*). The king recounts how he was retreating and about to fall (i.e. be killed in battle) when the LORD intervened.[2] Verse 14 is drawn from Exodus 15:2, which appears to have become a song of praise used in situations such as this (see also Isa. 12:2, where the additional divine name *yhwh* is added). Each new act of God's salvation can bring forth the same response as the people made to the deliverance from Egypt.

Shouts of joy and victory resound in the tents of the righteous: 'The LORD's right hand has done mighty things! The LORD's right hand is lifted high; the LORD's right hand has done mighty things!' (*vv. 15-16*). Communal joy marks the victory that the LORD has brought. The term 'the tents' most probably means the permanent dwellings of the righteous (cf. Ps. 91:10), though it has also been suggested that it means the temporary accommodation erected in Jerusalem for the great festival occasions. The godly part of the nation extol the actions of the LORD's right hand (*yâmîn*). Again, the triumphal song after the Exodus provides the language used by the people many centuries later (see Exod. 15:6). 'Right hand' points to the LORD's might, for he has brought about the victory, and the triple use of 'right hand' in these two verses draws special attention to God's power. The divine warrior has conquered! (for similar use of this expression, see Pss. 89:13; 98:1).

I will not die but live, and will proclaim what the LORD has done. The LORD has chastened me severely, but he has not given me over to death (*vv. 17-18*). The king has survived the battle, and now pledges to declare to others what the LORD has done. The expression here, 'what the LORD has done' (*maʿ*ª*sê yâh*), is a standard one for God's sovereign actions that were demonstrations of divine power (see the use of 'marvellous' in

---

[2] The verb 'to fall' (*nâfal*) is used with a variety of military connotations. I have discussed this in *NIDOTTE*, 3, p. 130.

v. 23). It is the living who praise him, not those who go down to the grave (Ps. 115:17-18). Even fatherly acts of discipline are praiseworthy.[3] God disciplines with justice (Jer. 30:11), and the New Testament develops the idea to say that the purpose of discipline is that we may share in God's holiness (Heb. 12:10). The psalmist was spared death, and lives to testify to God's mercy.

Open for me the gates of righteousness; I will enter and give thanks to the LORD. This is the gate of the LORD through which the righteous may enter. I will give you thanks, for you answered me; you have become my salvation (*vv. 19-21*). The victorious procession arrives back at Jerusalem, and the king calls for the city gates to be thrown wide open to receive the grateful worshippers. They come with joyfulness to celebrate at the sanctuary and to give thanks for answered prayer. In time of battle God heard the cries of his people, and he answered by giving deliverance or salvation. The righteous person will enter the presence of God knowing his requirements (Pss. 15:2-5; 24:3-6), and realising that on his appearance there 'he will receive blessing from the LORD and vindication from God his Saviour' (Ps. 24:5).

3. Communal Praise of God's Mercy (*vv. 22-27*)

The stone the builders rejected has become the capstone; the LORD has done this, and it is marvellous in our eyes (*vv. 22-23*). As the people sing of God's mercy, they use words that may well have been a proverbial saying. A stone that was spurned by builders turns out to be the main stone over a doorway. The initial reference here is to the king, who was despised by the leaders of the invading armies. However, the words have been taken over in several places in the New Testament. Jesus uses them following his parable of the tenants to reinforce the point that the kingdom is being taken away

---

[3] The words 'chastened me severely' are a translation of a verb and its cognate complement (*yassor yissᵉrannî*). This use of what is an infinitive absolute in Hebrew (*yassor*) is the most characteristic use of this form. However, translation of it by an adverb, such as 'severely' in this passage, may be unnecessarily strong. On this grammatical point, see *DIHG~S*, pp. 123-24.

from the Jewish people (Matt. 21:42; Mark 12:10; Luke 20:17). It is also applied to the rejection of Jesus (Acts 4:11) and to the fact that he has become the foundation stone of God's new building, the church (Eph. 2:20; 1 Pet. 2:7). Coupled with it in this psalm is an affirmation that the victory achieved has been the work of the LORD alone, and that is a thing of wonder in the eyes of the people.

This is the day the LORD has made; let us rejoice and be glad in it (*v. 24*). The day of the LORD's victory becomes a day of rejoicing for the people. This verse continues the theme that has already been noted in verses 15-17. Response to God's salvation comes in the form of jubilant song, a characteristic of the New Testament as well (cf. the songs in Revelation that are linked to salvation, 5:11-14; 7:9-17; 15:1-4).

O LORD, save us; O LORD, grant us success. Blessed is he who comes in the name of the LORD. From the house of the LORD we bless you (*vv. 25-26*). The rejoicing prompts the people to cry out, 'Save us' (Heb., *hôshî̔âh nâ̓*, cf. *Hosanna* in Matt. 21:9 and Mark 11:9-10, when the crowds in Jerusalem greet Jesus with the words of these verses). Originally this was a cry for help (Ps. 28:9) or for mercy (2 Sam. 14:4), but was later used in praise as a declaration that the LORD has saved. The great Jewish commentary on the Old Testament from around AD 200 (the Mishnah) records that these words were used by the priests after the offering of sacrifices at the time of the Feast of Tabernacles. Blessing is pronounced on the king who has won the victory in the name of the LORD (see vv. 10-12). It is unclear if the king is also the one being blessed from the house of the LORD. This is because the *you* is plural (see NIV footnote). The plural may have been used as a mark of respect for the king (the royal *we*), or it could refer to the army collectively on return with him from battle.

The LORD is God, and he has made his light shine upon us. With boughs in hand, join in the festal procession up to the horns of the altar (*vv. 26-27*). The people again acknowledge that their Saviour, the LORD, is indeed their God. He has brought light from the midst of their darkness in a time of national distress. 'To make light shine' is an allusion to the words of the Aaronic blessing (Num. 6:25). The following expression is difficult to translate (cf. the NIV text and footnote), though the general meaning is clear enough. In addition to songs of joy, the people also came with appropriate outward manifestations of their response to God's mercy, probably bringing sacrificial thank offerings to the altar. This would be in accordance with the principle that no one should approach God with an empty hand (Exod. 23:15; Deut. 16:16-17).

4. A Renewed Confession (*v. 28*)

You are my God, and I will give you thanks; you are my God, and I will exalt you (*v. 28*). As the individual speaker earlier in the psalm is the king, it is best to assume that he now reaffirms his relationship with his God. Trust in him inevitably leads to praise and adoration. Whenever there is a declaration that 'Salvation belongs to our God', there is also reverence and worship (Rev. 7:9-12).

5. Enduring Love (*v. 29*)

Give thanks to the LORD, for he is good; his love endures forever (*v. 29*). The final words of the psalm are identical with the opening words, so that the whole response of king and people is framed by this declaration of the enduring nature of God's goodness and love.

Psalm 119

This psalm stands out in the whole collection of psalms for several striking reasons.

1. It is an acrostic poem, based on all the letters of the Hebrew alphabet in consecutive order and so is divided into twenty-two stanzas. All the verses of each stanza begin with the same letter of the Hebrew alphabet. The fact that it has eight verses in each stanza makes it the longest psalm of all. The occurrence of the divine name 'LORD' twenty-two times is probably intentional, matching the number of stanzas. The effect of the acrostic is striking both to the eye and to the ear when read and heard.[1] No carry over of this practice into English usage can be deemed satisfactory.[2]

2. It is a poem that rejoices in the fact that God has revealed himself to his people. He has spoken, and the unnamed psalmist shows intense devotion to the word of God. The

---

[1] An inherent difficulty in Hebrew of employing an acrostic based on the alphabet is that not all the letters occur with the same frequency (cf. in English the very few words that start with 'x'). For example, the letter *vav* only commences three or four nouns. The author of Psalm 119 uses it eight times, all of which are the conjunction 'and' (see 119:41-48). Similarly 'and' appears in the acrostics in Psalms 9-10, 111, 112, 119, and 145, but it is lacking completely in 25 and 34. This paucity of words beginning with a certain letter added to the difficulty of employing the acrostic form.

[2] Cf. the attempt by Edward M. Sugden, *The Psalms of David: Translated into English* (Melbourne: MacMillan & Co., 1924), to carry over the acrostics into English translation, and, especially for Psalm 119, pp. 163-73, results in a very stilted and artificial rendering. Poetic features of one language are very difficult to reproduce in another.

focus of attention throughout is on God, either by direct address or by the use of the pronoun 'your': '*your* righteous laws', '*your* word', '*your* commands'. The acrostic pattern and the repetitiveness of the main ideas may seem quite foreign to modern readers, but the poet uses the features of Hebrew poetry with great skill to express his utter devotion to the word of God. That word provides his hope, but it also forms his guide to life.

3. A range of Hebrew terms is used to describe God's revelation: law, statutes, covenant stipulations, precepts, commandments, laws, decrees, word, promise.[3] Their use is distributed throughout the twenty-two stanzas, so that all these eight terms appear in six stanzas, and never fewer than six in any one stanza. There are just a few variant expressions, such as 'ways' in verses 3 and 15 (different words in Hebrew) and 'faithfulness' in verse 90. It is only in verses 84 and 122 that no synonym occurs at all. There is no regular pattern to their use, either in regard to the number of times they occur in a stanza or the order in which they appear.

4. The psalm does not fit neatly into any particular category, because it embraces distinctive features of many types. It contains hymnic elements, but at the same time there are many verses that deal with sorrow and grief. It conveys confident trust in the LORD, but also appeals for help in times of danger and distress.

5. The two other psalms that are closest to this one are Psalms 1 and 19. The first of these shows the commitment of a believer to the law of the LORD, while the second in praising God's revelation uses six of the same synonyms that appear in Psalm 119. While those two earlier psalms contain the same theme, they cannot match the development of it in all its breadth and fullness in this psalm.

---

[3] A helpful discussion of these terms is to be found in John P. Milton, *The Psalms* (Rock Island, IL: Augustana Book Concern, 1954), pp. 101-06.

6. There is a strong affinity between this psalm and earlier portions of the Old Testament, with many expressions closely following passages in books such as Deuteronomy. For example, in the opening section of the psalm the words of verse 2 echo those of Deuteronomy 4:29, while the command of Moses in Deuteronomy 6:6-9 regarding the word of God is fulfilled in the psalmist's experience. For him the word of God was a living reality in his life.

7. While there does not seem to be any progressive development of the theme in the psalm, yet in most stanzas a major aspect is in focus. The choice of the acrostic pattern, while striking in its own way, limits the development of ideas in a structural way leading to a climax. It must be noted, too, that the first three verses (119:1-3) and the last three (119:174-76) seem to have been inserted to express fitting introductory and closing themes.

Aleph (*vv. 1-8*)

Blessed are they whose ways are blameless, who walk according to the law of the LORD. Blessed are they who keep his statutes and seek him with all their heart. They do nothing wrong; they walk in his ways (*vv. 1-3*). These opening verses set the scene for the whole psalm. They resemble closely both the content and the form of Psalm 1. They employ terms that are going to be spoken of again and again, yet without defining them. The word used for 'law' (Heb., *tôrâh*) has a broad meaning, pointing to any instruction that God has given his people (see comment on Ps. 1:1), while 'statutes' points to covenant stipulations. Just as Psalm 1 speaks of the blessedness of those who meditate on the law of the LORD, so Psalm 119 commences with an ascription of blessedness to those whose life follows the paths set out by the LORD in his word. The psalmist is not asserting sinless perfection for believers (as the following verses make plain), but a commitment to the revealed truth of God, and an obedient submission to his demands. The NIV does not attempt to translate the first word (*'af*) in the Hebrew text of verse 3. It is an adverb that coordinates two sentences, and here can carry the idea of 'also' (cf. the translations of this verse in the NASB and NKJV).[4]

You have laid down precepts that are to be fully obeyed (*v. 4*). The first words of direct address to God in the psalm are a declaration that God has spoken and that his precepts relate to practice. 'You have laid down' is more literally 'You have commanded' (*tsivvîtâh*), a translation preserved in AV, RSV, NASB, and ESV. The way to life is the way of obedience (Deut. 30:15-16). The call to discipleship under the gospel remains a call to implicit obedience (John 14:23-24; 15:9, 14).

Oh, that my ways were steadfast in obeying your decrees! Then I would not be put to shame when I consider all your commands (*vv. 5-6*). The psalmist's desire is that his life will be dedicated to the covenant directives that God has given his people (for the use of the term 'decrees', see Deut. 6:2; 28:15, 45; 30:10, 16). This may in fact echo the wish which God himself had expressed concerning his people: 'Oh, that their hearts would be inclined to fear me and keep all my commands always' (Deut. 5:29). The wish is expressed using an unusual particle (*'achªlê*, 'would that') but its only other appearance, in 2 Kings 5:3, confirms its meaning.[5] 'To consider commands' means to pay attention to them.[6] If that is done, then the outcome will be that the psalmist's hopes will not be disappointed and he will suffer no shame because of his commitment to God's directives.

I will praise you with an upright heart as I learn your righteous laws. I will obey your decrees; do not utterly forsake me (*vv. 7-8*). God's laws are righteous, something which Psalm 19:9 has already asserted, and which this psalm repeatedly claims (vv. 62, 75, 106, 123, 138, 144, 160, 164, 172).

---

[4] This adverb is weaker in meaning than *gam*, and though often it is not much stronger than the conjunction *vᵉ*, 'and', 'but', 'then', yet it marks a connection between statements.

[5] The derivation of this word is unknown, though it may have a connection with the interjection *'ach*, 'alas'.

[6] The verb translated 'consider' (*nâvat*, Hi.) means 'look at' in the sense of 'regard', 'consider', and has as synonyms *sâkal*, Hi. ('consider'), *shâma'* ('hear') and *râtsâh* ('accept').

Just as God himself is righteous (Ps. 119:137), so are his laws. The confidence already expressed that obedience results in lack of shame leads to the praise of God by those whose hearts are set on him and his ways. The final verse in the section is really an appeal for help. It is a confession that without God's presence and aid, his decrees cannot be kept. It is exactly the same as the appeal in Psalms 27:9, 38:21 and 71:18, except that the adverb 'very', 'extremely' (*m^{e}ʾod*) is added.

Beth (*vv. 9-16*)

How can a young man keep his way pure? By living according to your word (*v. 9*). The content of the question does not necessarily mean that the psalmist was himself a young man.[7] He is speaking in a manner used by wisdom teachers in the Psalms and in Proverbs in particular (Ps. 34:11-14; Prov. 1–7). This must have been a regular teaching device. He answers his question by directing attention to the role God's word plays in restraining one from sin. Purity is impossible unless God's word is observed (cf. the various synonyms for 'word' used in the following verses). The answer to the question (lit. 'to keep according to your word') is simply a summary of repeated instructions in Deuteronomy concerning keeping God's commands (see, for example, 6:17; 10:13; 11:8; 27:1; 30:10).

I seek you with all my heart; do not let me stray from your commands. I have hidden your word in my heart that I might not sin against you (*vv. 10-11*). The psalmist identifies himself with those upon whom he has already pronounced a blessing in verse 2 (the same Hebrew verb for 'seek', *dârash,* is used in both verses). His commitment is whole-hearted, and he has treasured up God's word in his heart in order to be kept in the ways of righteousness. 'Word' in this instance

---

[7] F. Delitzsch, *Psalms,* III, p. 243, argued that this verse, taken in conjunction with verses 99-100, shows that the author of Psalm 119 was a young man who finds himself in a situation where he is derided and oppressed. That inference does not follow. Rather, the internal evidence within the psalm points to the poet being someone with experience of life who looks back and seeks to give instruction to young people. In this way it is similar to the counsel of Ecclesiastes 12:1: 'Remember your Creator in the days of your youth.'

is a Hebrew word (*ʾimrâh*) that is often rightly translated as 'promise' on many other occurrences.[8] To hide God's word in the heart is more than just being able to recite from memory. It is living in accord with the directives that he has given. To stop listening to that instruction causes one to 'stray from the words of knowledge' (Prov. 19:27). Hence he appeals to God to keep him faithful.

Praise be to you, O LORD; teach me your decrees. With my lips I recount all the laws that come from your mouth (*vv. 12-13*). Before asking for further teaching the psalmist extols his God (Heb., 'Blessed are you, O LORD'), which is a prelude to the joy he expresses in the final verses of this section. Recounting the laws could mean simply meditating on them, and in that way saying them over and over, one after another. However, it may point to something more formal, such as the recitation of the covenant stipulations (Ps. 50:16). When the priests were reading the law as appointed by God (Deut. 31:9-13), the people may well have joined in the recitation, just as they do in Christian churches when the Ten Commandments or Apostle's Creed are said. The reference to words that come from God's mouth recall passages such as Deuteronomy 8:3 where the assertion is 'that man does not live by bread alone, but man lives by every word (Heb., 'by all') that comes from the mouth of the LORD.' To say that the word(s) come from the LORD's mouth is simply emphasising the divine origin of the revelation.

I rejoice in following your statutes as one rejoices in great riches. I meditate on your precepts and consider your ways. I delight in your decrees; I will not neglect your word (*vv. 14-16*). The spiritual and emotional response to God's law is one of joy, just as when a great treasure has been found. God's ordinances are more precious than 'much pure gold' (Ps. 19:10), 'than thousands of pieces of silver and gold' (Ps. 119:72) or 'great spoil' (Ps. 119:162). The idea of meditating on God's word is quite frequent throughout this

---

[8] Biblical Hebrew has no word corresponding to the English word 'promise'. Instead it uses terms such as the verbs to 'speak' (*dâvar*, or *ʾâmar*) or to 'swear' (*shâvaʿ*) and nouns denoting speech (e.g. as here, *dâvâr*/*ʾimrâh*). The English phrase 'the promised land' is 'the sworn land' in Hebrew.

psalm, and the word used here (*sîach*) also occurs in verses 23, 27, 48, 78, and 148. It refers mainly to rehearsing aloud things relating to God – his works, his precepts, his wonders, his promises. The parallel to this is 'consider (*nâvat,* Hi.) your ways', which picks up the phrase 'when I consider (*nâvat,* Hi.) all your commands' in verse 6, a repetitive style that is very characteristic of this psalm. Delight in God leads the psalmist to pledge that he will not become forgetful in relation to what God has spoken.

Gimel (*vv. 17-24*)

Do good to your servant, and I will live; I will obey your word (*v. 17*). A plea for gracious dealing from God opens this section. The expression 'do good' (*g^e^mol*) has a wide range of meaning in the Old Testament, but it is used in connection with weaning of children and (as here) of acting generously to someone (cf. its use in Pss. 13:6; 103:10; 116:7). Life with God's blessing is assured to those who are recipients of his favour (Lev. 18:5; Deut. 6:24). God's care ensures life and as a grateful response the psalmist promises obedience. The expression 'I will obey your word' (Heb., *v^e^'eshm^e^râh d^e^vârekâ*) is the same idiom already used in verse 9.

Open my eyes that I may see wonderful things in your law. I am a stranger on earth; do not hide your commands from me (*vv. 18-19*). God's law contains many precious things that require spiritual illumination. Without it, these things remain hidden, and cannot form part of meditation (see v. 27, where the same Hebrew word, *nifl^e^'ôt,* is translated 'wonders').[9] 'See' translates the same Hebrew verb (*nâvat,* Hi.) already used in verses 6 and 15, and instead of changing to a different English verb here, it is preferable to retain 'consider' (see note on v. 6). Confessing he is a 'stranger on earth' does two things. First, it identifies the psalmist with his people, who experienced being strangers and exiles both in Egypt and Babylon. Secondly, it suggests that he has not a real home here on earth. He is not a citizen who feels he belongs to the kingdoms of this world. The New Testament develops this further with the reminder that we are strangers and

[9] See the note on *nifl^e^'ôt* in the comment on Psalm 9:1.

pilgrims on this earth (1 Pet. 2:11), whose real citizenship is in heaven (Phil. 3:20).

My soul is consumed with longing for your laws at all times. You rebuke the arrogant, who are cursed and who stray from your commands (*vv. 20-21*). The contrast between the righteous and the unrighteous is brought out in these verses. The one always loves God's laws with deep and intense longing. The other despises them, refusing to obey their demands. God uses strong admonitions against the arrogant, who as rebels are cursed, and so deprived of his blessing. They are characterised by their pride and their wilful disobedience of God's commands.

Remove from me scorn and contempt, for I keep your statutes. Though rulers sit together and slander me, your servant will meditate on your decrees. Your statutes are my delight; they are my counsellors (*vv. 22-24*). For the first time in this psalm there is reference to the troubles that have come to the psalmist because of his attitude to God's word. He wants to be insulated from attitudes of reproach and contempt that are directed to the righteous.[10] His relationship to God is that of a servant ('your servant', in vv 17 and 23), who takes great pleasure in what God has revealed, making it his meditation and his guide.[11] However, this also brings conflict with others, especially those who hold a leadership position in society, who pour reproach on him and who misrepresent him.[12] While appealing to God to change his circumstances, the psalmist shows no movement away from his devotion to his statutes. These remain his 'delight', an attitude he is going to repeat in

---

[10] The word 'remove' (*gal*) is an imperative from the verb 'to reveal', 'uncover' (*gâlâh*) that has already occurred in verse 18. It has often been suggested that the vocalisation should be changed to *gol*, 'roll away', but if scorn and contempt are viewed as garments, then the retention of the Massoretic vocalisation is quite appropriate. *CHAL*, p. 60, lists as one of the meanings of this verb '(have to) go away, disappear'. See also the note in M. Dahood, *Psalms III: 101-150*, p. 176.

[11] This is another occurrence of one of the verbs 'to meditate' (*sîach*) used in this psalm. Cf. the note on verse 15.

[12] The word 'rulers' (*sârîm*) does not refer to Israelite kings, but more to leaders such as city officials or clan leaders. For examples of its usage, see *NIDOTTE*, 3, p. 1295.

verses 77, 92, 143, and 174. Like Asaph, he is guided by the counsel of the LORD (Ps. 73:24).

Daleth (*vv. 25-32*)

The difficulties of composing a poem using an acrostic pattern come out in this section in Hebrew. Four of the verses start with the same Hebrew noun (*dérek*, 'the way of …'), one starts with the plural of this word, while two start with the same verb (*dâvaq*, 'to cling to'). **I am laid low in the dust; preserve my life according to your word. I recounted my ways and you answered me; teach me your decrees** (*vv. 25-26*). The psalmist concentrates on his difficulties in this section, and he prays for the strength and consolation that come from God's word. His situation is desperate, almost bringing him to the grave (cf. the use of 'dust' in Ps. 30:9 in parallel with 'pit'). The Hebrew text says that his soul clings to the dust, a graphic description of how close he feels to the grave. However, he knows 'that man does not live on bread alone but on every word which comes from the mouth of the LORD' (Deut. 8:3). Hence his appeal to God to keep him alive, for he knows that he has answered him in the past. His present appeal is on the basis of past deliverances, and now he wants further divine instruction.

Let me understand the teaching of your precepts; then I will meditate on your wonders (*v. 27*). A sharp contrast exists between the psalmist's ways and God's ways (Heb., 'my ways', v. 26; 'the way of your precepts', v. 27).[13] He previously recounted his ways, and now he wants to understand the path that God's precepts set out for him. Fuller knowledge of them will lead to thoughtful appreciation of the wonders they contain. Both the law (v. 19) and the precepts point to God's wondrous deeds, the deeds of grace and power displayed in saving his people.

My soul is weary with sorrow; strengthen me according to your word. Keep me from deceitful ways; be gracious to

---

[13] The phrase, 'the way of your precepts' (*dérek pikûdekâ*), is the first of four phrases in this section which all begin in Hebrew with 'the way of …' This is a common use of 'way' in a metaphorical sense to describe a manner of life. Many illustrations of it are given in *DCH*, II, pp. 468-69. The other occurrences here are in verses 29, 30, and 32.

me through your law. I have chosen the way of truth; I have set my heart on your laws (*vv. 28-30*). God's word ministers to those in grief, not only when there is a loss of a family member, but when difficult circumstances cause pain and vexation. This is the only occurrence of the word 'sorrow' (*tûgâh*) in the Psalter, and the association here with the verb 'to be weary' (*dâlaf*) suggests the idea of the soul being brought to extreme weakness through sorrow. The request for 'strengthening' (Heb., *qûm*, Pi.) does not seem very different from the oft repeated 'preserve my life'.[14] Deceit on the part of others should not lead to similar behaviour on the part of a believer. Strength and comfort from God through his word confirm the resolve to shun the evil ways of the tormentors. The NIV translation, 'be gracious to me through your law', disguises the fact that in Hebrew the verb 'be gracious' (*chânan*) takes two objects – 'me' and 'your law'. The ASV and NRSV are better: 'Graciously teach me your law'.[15] The psalmist sets himself to follow single-mindedly 'the way of truth' (Hebrew, 'the way of faithfulness'), and acknowledges that his heart is fixed on God's judgments.[16] The parallelism of 'way of truth' and 'statutes' (NIV 'laws') suggests that life in the covenant is in mind.[17]

I hold fast to your statutes, O LORD; do not let me be put to shame. I run in the path of your commands, for you have set my heart free (*vv. 31-32*). The expressions of dedication to the LORD continue seeing that his heart has been enlarged to give increased understanding (NIV 'set free'; lit. 'you have

[14] The verb 'keep alive' (*châyâh*, Pi.) is frequently used throughout this psalm (vv. 25, 37, 40, 50, 88, 93, 107, 149, 154, 156, 159). In this form the verb can have a variety of meaning, such as 'keep alive' and 'cause to live, revive' (see *DCH*, III, p. 206). Its use points to the LORD as the giver and sustainer of life, and also the one who can revive the soul. The older translations rendered it by 'quicken', while the NIV is consistent in using 'preserves [my] life'.

[15] Cf. the use of this same verb in Genesis 33:5 with two objects: 'They are the children whom God has graciously given your servant.' This verb carries the idea of acting graciously, but the verb associated with it will vary in English translations. For example, in Genesis 33:5 the verb 'give' is required, while here in Psalm 119:29 a verb such as 'teach' or 'instruct' is necessary.

[16] The expression is elliptical. The text simply says '[On] your judgments I set …', so something like 'heart' is required to complete the idea. The fuller idiom with a different verb, *sâm libbô*, 'he set his heart', occurs. Cf. Isaiah 41:22.

[17] This point is made by E. H. Merrill in *NIDOTTE*, 1, p. 991.

enlarged my heart'). The New Testament uses the same idiom (2 Cor. 6:11). He clings to God's statutes ('hold fast' represents the same verb as used in v. 25, 'clings to the dust'), and sets himself to follow the way set out in them. 'Run' does not appear to have any idea here of urgent action but rather of resolute adherence to the set path (cf. Prov. 4:10-12). The thought of being put to shame, first introduced in verse 6, is taken up again. Hopes will be not disappointed if there is such confident trust in the LORD and his word.

He (*vv. 33-40*)

In these eight verses the main plea is for further instruction from the LORD, and preservation in his pathways. Every verse contains an imperative – 'teach', 'give understanding', and so on. **Teach me, O LORD, to follow your decrees; then I will keep them to the end** (*v. 33*). The request is modelled closely on the prayer, 'Teach me your ways', which occurs in Psalms 27:11 and 86:11. The verb 'teach' (*yârâh III,* Hi.), when used in the Psalms, always has as its object the word 'way' (*dérek;* here the Hebrew has 'the way of your decrees').[18] The verb in itself does not indicate anything about the method of instruction. The translation 'to the end' is taken from the early Greek and Aramaic renderings of this verse. However, in Hebrew the final word of the verse (*ʿêqev*) is one that often indicates the consequence of something, or a reward, and it is best to preserve this interpretation (see also v. 112). What pleases the LORD is regarded by the psalmist as in itself a satisfying reward.

Give me understanding, and I will keep your law and obey it with all my heart. Direct me in the path of your commands, for there I find delight (*vv. 34-35*). The thought of the previous verse is continued, with the psalmist confessing the pleasure he has in following the demands of God's law. He recognises that he needs spiritual understanding that comes

---

[18] Cf. its use also in Psalms 25:8, 12; 27:11; 32:8; 86:11; 119:102. It usually takes two objects, teaching someone something. In meaning this verb does not seem different from 'learn' (*lâmad,* Pi.) and 'make to know' (*yâdaʿ*, Hi.). Of these two verbs, *yâdaʿ* does not occur in Psalm 119, while *lâmad* is used seven times with the same object ('decrees'; vv. 12, 26, 64, 68, 124, 135, 171).

from God alone, using the identical Hebrew expression already used in verse 27 (*h^{a}vînênî*: NIV 'Let me understand'). Also, he seeks directions for life,[19] which, when lived in obedience to God, is very pleasurable. When the psalmist has received spiritual teaching, he promises to act upon it and to give ready obedience to the law. Isaac Watts (1674-1748) put verse 35 into verse:

> Make me to walk in Thy commands;
> Tis a delightful road;
> Nor let my head, or heart, or hands,
> Offend against my God.

Turn my heart toward your statutes and not toward selfish gain. Turn my eyes away from worthless things; preserve my life according to your word (*vv. 36-37*). The combination of heart and eyes is common in the Old Testament (Num. 15:39; Job 31:7; Jer. 22:17; Ps. 101:2-5). The heart is regarded as controlling the whole direction of life, while the mention of eyes suggests the external influences that affect behaviour. The psalmist wants a heart motivated by devotion to God's statutes, not by the thought of getting material rewards. He knows that looking at such things can tempt, and so asks for his eyes to be averted from alluring vanities. Again, the plea is for preservation (see comment on v. 25 and footnote). The NIV margin notes that a textual problem exists with the last word of verse 37. The MT has 'in your way' (*bid^{e}râkekâ*), whereas two manuscripts have 'with your word' (*bid^{e}vârekâ*). The variant reading, which is followed by the NIV, seems to stem from a desire to conform this verse to the expression in verse 25 ('according to your word'). The MT should be retained, and it means that God gives life to those walking in his ways.[20]

---

[19] The verb 'direct' is from the root (*d-r-k*) from which the word 'way' (*dérek*) comes. That its meaning is close to 'teach', 'make learn', and 'cause to know' is shown by the way these four verbs are used interchangeably in Psalm 25:4-14.

[20] This is the position taken by L. C. Allen, *Psalms 101-150*, p. 127, and supported by W. VanGemeren, 'The Psalms', p. 744.

Fulfil your promise to your servant, so that you may be feared. Take away the disgrace I dread, for your laws are good. How I long for your precepts! Preserve my life in your righteousness (*vv. 38-40*). The psalmist now asks for God's word (*ʾimrâh*) to be fulfilled towards him, and, as so often throughout this psalm, mention is made of God's gracious promises which provide the basis of his confidence. Each fulfilment of a promise brings further encouragement, and directs attention back to God himself. Action taken in accordance with his word gives new reason to revere and adore the living God. Devotion to God and his word often brings reproach, and the psalmist prays for release from such attitudes from his enemies. His heart is set on God's precepts and he knows that God's saving power (his righteousness) is able to keep. The New Testament amplifies this, pointing to the words of prophecy that have been fulfilled in the salvation which has come through Christ. This means that we can be kept 'by God's power until the coming of the salvation that is ready to be revealed in the last time' (1 Pet. 1:5).

Waw (*vv. 41-48*)

Each verse in this section begins with the letter *waw*,[21] which is used to form the conjunction 'and' in Hebrew. The Hebrew constructions used indicate that all the verses are tied together so that a common theme runs through them all. They consist of a prayer that God's word will remain with the psalmist and then he will be able to answer those who mock him, and also testify before kings.

May your unfailing love come to me, O LORD, your salvation according to your promise; then I will answer the one who taunts me, for I trust in your word (*vv. 41-42*). The psalmist is still concerned because of the persecution for the truth that he is enduring. He relies upon the sure word of promise which he has been given as his stay, and knows that God will deliver him in accordance with his covenant love

[21] *Waw* is the traditional pronunciation of the sixth letter of the Hebrew alphabet, but as modern Hebrew pronounces it *vav*, this is often now followed, as throughout this commentary.

(Heb., *chésed*). This Hebrew word is virtually a summary of what the LORD covenanted to do for his people. It appears here for the first time in this psalm, but is used several times in later sections (see vv. 64, 76, 88, 124, 149, 159). The answer to those who taunt him will take the form of God's intervention and salvation. The psalmist's confidence is firmly fixed in God's revelation of himself by his word. Only here is this expression of trust used in Psalm 119, though it is frequent in other psalter passages.[22]

Do not snatch the word of truth from my mouth, for I have put my hope in your laws. I will always obey your law, for ever and ever. I will walk about in freedom, for I have sought out your precepts (*vv. 43-45*). Having God's word in one's heart always is necessary in the life of a believer (see vv. 11-13). The psalmist is probably thinking of the quiet murmuring of this word during meditation and desires that that word will never be removed from him. The connection with the preceding verses can be seen more clearly if the opening of verse 43 is rightly translated, 'so do not remove the word of truth'. The NIV does not attempt to translate two Hebrew words in verse 43 (*ʿad-m*^{e}*ʾod*) that most other versions give as 'utterly' (cf. AV, NKJV, RSV, ESV): 'Take not your word *utterly* from my mouth.' While the syntax is unusual and difficult, yet the Hebrew manuscript tradition is so strong that an attempt to translate it must be made. In the context, a translation such as 'utterly' seems quite appropriate.[23] There may seem to be some contradiction between obeying God's law and walking in freedom, but coming into whole-hearted devotion and service to God sets one's heart free (v. 32) to give lifelong attention to his demands. The last clause of verse 45 is repeated exactly in verse 94.

I will speak of your statutes before kings and will not be put to shame, for I delight in your commands because

---

[22] The Hebrew idiom is 'trust in' (*bâtach b*^{e}), which appears to be no different from *bâtach l*^{e} (Isa. 36:9), *bâtach ʾel* (Ps. 31:6), or *bâtach ʿal* (Ps. 31:14). A very full list of examples can be found in *DCH*, II, pp. 140-41.

[23] As *ʿad-meʾod* occurs elsewhere with a noun or verb indicating some intensification, here adding the adverb 'utterly' seems quite appropriate. A good summary of this use of *ʿad-meʾod* can be found in *NIDOTTE*, 2, p. 826.

I love them. I lift up my hands to your commands, which I love, and I meditate on your decrees (*vv. 46-48*). Once again the psalmist makes reference to his official role, for he has responsibility to speak before kings (as mentioned here) and before rulers (vv. 23 and 161). As the priests were teachers of the law (Mal. 2:4-6), it is probable that he himself occupied such a position in the post-exilic period. He knows that he will not be shamed, a conviction stated here in exactly the same form as in verse 6 (*lo' 'êwôsh*). His attitude is one of constant pleasure in God's commands, reaching out for them with his hands. This expression is unusual, but as the lifting up of hands is mentioned in connection with praise (Pss. 28:2; 63:4; 134:2; 141:2), it probably means that he praises the commands that he loves.[24]

Zayin (*vv. 49-56*)

Just as the letter *waw* does not commence many words in Hebrew, so also the letter *zayin*. Three of the verses of this section begin with the verb 'remember' (*zâkar*) and two with the word 'this' (*zo't*). **Remember your word to your servant, for you have given me hope. My comfort in my suffering is this: Your promise preserves my life** (*vv. 49-50*). As he reflects upon his experiences, the psalmist knows that he rests upon the word that God has spoken. This is a recurrent theme throughout Psalm 119 (see vv. 43, 81, 114, 147). His confidence does not rest on his own plans, but on God's revealed purposes (which remain the sure basis for believing hope, Rom. 8:28-30). The verb 'hope' (*yâchal*, Pi.) is very much a poetic word in the Old Testament and points to enduring and expectant hope. It occurs in verse 49 and four other places in this psalm (vv. 74, 81, 114, 147), always with 'your word(s)' as the object. In his

---

[24] Appeal is sometimes made to Lamentations 3:41 in reference to lifting up the hands. The NIV renders it: 'Let us lift up our hearts and our hands.' However, that verse has its own difficulties, including the double use of the preposition 'to' (*'el*) and also the presence of the very similar word 'God' (*'êl*). Iain Provan, *Lamentations* (The New Century Bible: London: Marshall Pickering, 1991), pp. 100-01, defends the MT and suggests that the Hebrew can mean either that the hearts were lifted up *upon* their hands (so LXX and Syr.), or that their hearts were lifted up *as well as* hands (Vulg.).

present suffering (i.e., persecution) he is assured by certain promises, and, as expressed earlier (see vv. 25 and 37), God's revelation sustained him.

The arrogant mock me without restraint, but I do not turn from your law. I remember your ancient laws, O LORD, and I find comfort in them (vv. 51-52). Adherence to God's ways provokes opposition, but the taunts of proud scoffers fail to make the psalmist deviate from adherence to God's law.[25] He recalls that this law is not new revelation. Rather it is from of old (*mêʿ ôlâm*).[26] God's law was given from creation onwards, and at Mount Sinai it was put into a special form when God entered into a covenant with the nation of Israel. Prophets and priests can appeal for remembrance of the decrees and laws which God gave for all Israel (Mal. 4:4). The expression 'find comfort' comes from a reflexive verb in Hebrew (*nâcham,* Hitp.), which suggests that the psalmist comforts himself as he contemplates these ancient laws. This reinforces what is said in verse 50 (the word used there for 'comfort', *nechâmâh,* derives from the verb here).

Indignation grips me because of the wicked, who have forsaken your law (*v. 53*). This verse expresses another aspect of relationship to the law. Love to God and his commandments has as its complement very strong feelings against those who refuse to submit to his demands (cf. the way in which Paul was greatly distressed by the idolatry of the Athenians, Acts 17:16). 'The wicked' are not Gentiles, but those within Israel who, though knowing the law, have wilfully chosen to reject its claims.

Your decrees are the theme of my song wherever I lodge. In the night I remember your name, O LORD, and I will keep your law. This has been my practice: I obey your precepts (*vv. 54-56*). After the business of daytime activities, the

---

[25] The NIV 'without restraint' translates the same Hebrew phrase (*ʿad-m^{e}ʾod*) that occurred in verse 43 (see comment). As in verse 43, 'utterly' gets closest to the meaning. Cf. NASB, NRSV, ESV.

[26] The phrase can refer to God or his attributes that are 'from eternity' (Pss. 25:6; 93:2), but it is also used for events like the Exodus from Egypt (Mal. 3:4). Here the giving of the law at Sinai is the most obvious interpretation.

night provides an opportunity for meditation and for praise (the MT has the plural 'songs', which should be retained in translation). Several other psalms refer to night-time songs (Pss. 42:8; 77:6; 92:1-3). The term 'wherever I lodge' links in with the reference in verse 19 to being a pilgrim on the earth ('stranger' and 'wherever I lodge' come from the same Hebrew root, *gûr*). Throughout his earthly life the psalmist is committed to doing what he has promised, and so guards the stipulations of the Lord. He shows by his obedience that he belongs to him. This principle was reasserted by the Lord Jesus (John 14:15).

Heth (*vv. 57-64*)

You are my portion, O Lord; I have promised to obey your words (*v. 57*). The word 'portion' (*chêleq*) could imply that the psalmist was himself a Levite. It is the word used of the share that the various tribes received of the land of Canaan. No territory was allotted to the Levites, and the special provision made for their maintenance meant that the Lord was their portion (Num. 18:20; Deut. 10:9). However, the word took on a wider meaning as it was used to describe the relationship between God and his people (Pss. 16:5; 73:26), and this is probably its sense here.[27] Obedience is the response to God's gracious provision, and the expression 'to keep your words' (*lishmor d^evârekâ*) is synonymous with other similar expressions ('to keep your statutes', v 5; 'to keep according to your word', v. 9; 'to keep your commandments', v. 60; 'to keep your righteous laws', v. 106).

I have sought your face with all my heart; be gracious to me according to your promise. I have considered my ways and have turned my steps to your statutes (*vv. 58-59*). The intensity of feeling for the Lord is brought out, both by the verb used ('sought', *châlâh*, Pi.) and again by reference to the fact that his whole being was behind his entreaty.

---

[27] Because this word 'portion' had spiritual implications, it was repeatedly used as a component in Hebrew personal names, e.g. Hilkiah ('Yah is my portion'). Cf. also Helek (Josh. 17:2) and Helkai (Neh. 12:15).

The verb has been considered by some to denote a literal stroking of the face of an image, but no evidence exists for such a practice. The phrase 'with all my heart' shows that an inward attitude was the important factor.[28] The plea for mercy is grounded on the promise that had been given.[29] The NIV rendering of verse 59 suggests a past time of reflection and resolve. It may, though, refer to the constant attitude of the psalmist: 'Whenever I consider my ways, I turn my feet ...' This is an assertion that the covenantal directives form a constant guide to the psalmist, whose plans for life are directed by adherence to revealed truth.

I will hasten and not delay to obey your commands. Though the wicked bind me with ropes, I will not forget your law (*vv. 60-61*). The promised obedience is not deferred, but is yielded with immediate readiness. The verb 'hasten' (*chûsh*) is often used by psalmists pleading for God's immediate help (Pss. 22:19; 38:22; 40:13; 70:1, 5; 71:12; 141:1), but it can also be used to indicate readiness to act. All the scheming of enemies will not distract from giving attention to God's law. 'Binding with ropes' is not just literal oppression, but any form of scheming that restricts or impedes. The declaration 'I will not forget your law' parallels 'I will not delay to obey your commands' in the previous verse, and these expressions form part of a cluster of synonymous phrases in this psalm.[30]

At midnight I rise to give you thanks for your righteous laws. I am a friend to all who fear you, to all

---

[28] While many dictionaries list this verb as connected with *châlâh*, 'to be or become sick', it is much more probable that it is a completely different verb whose derivation is unknown. It occurs sixteen times in the Old Testament, always with the expression 'the face of' (*p^enê*) and means 'entreat', 'seek the favour of'. Many of these occurrences have a plural subject ('priests', Mal. 1:9; 'official emissaries', Zech. 7:2), but this is the only time an individual worshipper is the subject.

[29] The verb 'be gracious' (*chânan*, Qal) is often used in another stem (Hitp.) to mean 'entreat'; combination of these two verbs here seems to reflect this link.

[30] Cf. 'forget your words', 119:16, 139; 'forget your law', 119:61, 109, 153; 'forget your decrees', 119:83; 'forget your precepts', 119:93, 141; 'forget your commandments', 119:176.

who follow your precepts (*vv. 62-63*). The thought of songs in the night (see comment on v. 55) is taken up again. The identical phrase, 'righteous laws', has already occurred in v. 7. Walking in the ways of the LORD means sharing companionship together, just like those in Malachi's day who 'talked with each other, and the LORD listened and heard' (Mal. 3:16). The concept of 'the fear of the LORD' appears in Psalms 34:8-14 and 111:10 (see comment on those sections). Common allegiance to the LORD brings with it a fellowship of joint devotion and service.

The earth is filled with your love, O LORD; teach me your decrees (*v. 64*). God's love extends in one sense to the whole of creation, made by his skill and maintained by his faithfulness. The earth and its fulness belongs to him, as do its inhabitants (Ps. 24:1). The word 'filled' (*mâl*^{e}*ʾâh*) is the verb from which the noun 'fulness' (*m*^{e}*lôʾ*) in Psalm 24:1 comes. God has an everlasting covenant between himself and all living creatures (Gen. 9:16). For guidance and salvation more is needed than merely the knowledge of God we obtain from the natural world. Instruction in God's own revelation is often spoken of in this psalm, with the particular phrase used here ('teach me your decrees') appearing seven times (vv. 12, 26, 64, 68, 124, 135, 171).

Teth (*vv. 65-72*)

The thought of what is good dominates this section. The Hebrew adjective (*tôv*) occurs four times, a related noun once (*tûv*), and the verb 'to do good' (*mêṭîv*, Hi. participle) also appears once. **Do good to your servant according to your word, O LORD** (*v. 65*). This opening verse summarises the teaching of the section as a whole. The appeal is for God to act in fulfilment of his word and deal graciously with his servant. Solomon's words may be in mind, when he assured the people at the time of the dedication of the temple that not one word had failed of all the good that the LORD had promised his people (1 Kings 8:56). God will continue to act in complete faithfulness to his word. The words 'Do good' (*ʿâsîtâ tôv*) and 'your servant' (*ʿavd*^{e}*kâ*) are both covenant expressions, denoting the relationship with the LORD and the covenant promises he had made.[31]

Teach me knowledge and good judgment, for I believe in your commands (*v. 66*). The request for teaching is given in a variant form from the one already noted (see comment on v. 64), though with practically identical meaning. The word 'judgment' translates a Hebrew word (*ta*ʿ*am*) that can mean 'discernment' or 'behaviour' (cf. its use in 1 Sam. 21:14 of David's change of conduct before Achish). This meaning fits well here, for the psalmist is requesting instruction in knowledge and good behavioural patterns, while confessing that he agrees in his heart with God's commands. He has confident trust in them.[32]

Before I was afflicted I went astray, but now I obey your word. You are good, and what you do is good; teach me your decrees (*vv. 67-68*). The psalmist acknowledges that previously he had known what it was to err, but coming through a period of affliction (most probably the persecution and oppression he had faced) he is acting as an obedient servant. Arising out of his experience of God he can praise him both for his character and for the way he displays it in his actions. Keeping God's word is synonymous in meaning with keeping his decrees (vv. 5, 8), his word (vv. 9, 17, 57, 101), his law (vv. 44, 55, 136), his commandments (v. 60), and his precepts (vv. 63, 134, 168).

Though the arrogant have smeared me with lies, I keep your precepts with all my heart. Their hearts are callous and unfeeling, but I delight in your law (*vv. 69-70*). He gives further details concerning his enemies, whose hearts are callous and unfeeling (Heb. lit. 'insensitive as fat', *tâfash kachêlev*). They, with overbearing pride, desire to oppress him (cf. the previous references to them in vv. 51 and 61). They slander him, but even that does not cause him to change his attitude to God's law. He still takes great pleasure in it and

---

[31] Cf. the note on Psalm 23:6, and also the similar expression in Psalm 86:17: 'Give me a sign of your goodness' (ʿ*ᵃsêh* ʿ*immî* ʾ*ôt lᵉtôvâh*).

[32] Paul's prayer for the Philippians, that their love 'may abound more and more in knowledge and depth of insight' (Phil. 1:9), may be an echo of verse 66.

follows it. Though another verb is used here for 'keep' as compared with previous expressions in this psalm (using *nâtsar* in place of *shâmar*), there is no alteration in meaning.

It was good for me to be afflicted so that I might learn your decrees. The law from your mouth is more precious to me than thousands of pieces of silver and gold (*vv. 71-72*). The period of affliction turned the heart of the psalmist more and more to God's law. What he says in verse 71 complements his appeal for divine instruction in verse 68 ('teach me your decrees'). His estimation continues to be that it is more valuable to him than large sums of money (see the similar references in vv. 14, 127, and 162).[33] Spiritual values override worldly riches.

Yodh (*vv. 73-80*)

Your hands made me and formed me; give me understanding to learn your commands (*v. 73*). The psalmist looks to his creator for spiritual insight so that he may learn his commands. Just as he came into existence by God's power, so he needs to rely on him for illumination. The same combination of the verbs 'made' (*ʿâsâh*) and 'formed' (*kûn*, Polal) occurs in the Song of Moses; 'Is he [the LORD] not your Father, your Creator, who *made* you and *formed* you?' (Deut. 32:6).

May those who fear you rejoice when they see me, for I have put my hope in your word. I know, O LORD, that your laws are righteous, and in faithfulness you have afflicted me. May your unfailing love be my comfort, according to your promise to your servant (*vv. 74-76*). Those who fear the LORD have already been mentioned as the friends of the psalmist (v. 63). He longs for them to be encouraged by his example of trusting the LORD. Earlier he has noted that it was the LORD who brought him to that place of trust (see v. 49). He continues to speak of his afflictions, but does so without any accusations against God for them. On the contrary, he confesses that God's decisions (Heb., *mishpâtîm*) concerning him are righteous, and that he has acted in

[33] Practically all English translations, including the NIV, disguise the fact that verses 71 and 72 begin identically in Hebrew: *tôv-lî*, 'it is good for me ...'

faithfulness.[34] God remains absolutely true to his promises. The Song of Moses may also be behind the thought of verse 75 (cf. Deut. 32:4). The psalmist rests on God's word to him, finding that in his affliction the promises contain the assurance of covenant love. The cluster of covenant words ('your laws', 'your unfailing love', 'your promise', 'your servant') again focuses on the bond between the LORD and his devoted followers. The way in which the prayer is formed in Hebrew (using the particle *nâʾ*) suggests that it follows on from what he has just said about the nature of God's laws in the previous verse.[35]

Let your compassion come to me that I may live, for your law is my delight (*v. 77*). The preceding prayer is reinforced by a further request for mercy. It is practically synonymous with the first petition in verse 17: 'Do good to your servant and I will live.' While the reference to delighting in the law is different from that in verse 70, the meaning is practically the same.[36] The Hebrew verb 'delight in' (*shâʿaʿ*) and the noun from it, 'delights', (*shâʿashûʿîm*) are definitely poetical words, and the verb occurs three times in Psalm 119 (vv. 16, 47, and 70), with the noun appearing five times (vv. 24, 77, 92, 143, 174). All these occurrences have reference to God's word, and the noun always comes in contexts where oppression or distress is in view. This may be done to indicate how persecution intensifies the preciousness of God's revelation.

May the arrogant be put to shame for wronging me without cause; but I will meditate on your precepts. May those who fear you turn to me, those who understand your statutes. May my heart be blameless toward your decrees, that I may not be put to shame (*vv. 78-80*). The attitude of two groups in his society are so different towards the psalmist. On the one hand, the arrogant persecutors have no desire for God's ways (see vv. 21, 51, and 69 for

---

[34] The noun 'faithfulness' (*ʾemûnâh*) is used in verse 75 to indicate the manner of God's action, a usage that is common in poetry whereas Hebrew prose employs a preposition with the noun. Cf. *ʾemûnâh ʿinnîtânî* here with *beʾemûnâh hêm ʿosîm* in 2 Kings 12:15. For this adverbial use of a noun, see *DIHG~S*, p. 145.

[35] This is in accordance with the explanation of this word given by T. O. Lambdin, *Introduction to Biblical Hebrew*, p. 170.

[36] In verse 70 the psalmist says: 'For [in] your law I delight', whereas here he says 'For your law is my delight' (with a plural in Hebrew, 'delights', to express intensification of the idea).

previous references to these oppressors). They act falsely towards him,[37] trying to shame him, but this simply makes him engage in meditation on God's precepts. On the other hand, those who fear the LORD share in fellowship with him, joining in a common understanding of the covenantal stipulations (*ʿêdôt*). To pray for a blameless heart (v. 80) is to ask for a God-given devotion to his statutes. If this is given, then the psalmist knows that he will suffer no shame because of his commitment to God's directives. The psalmist wants his oppressors to know shame, while he, with his heart set on God's truth, will not suffer shame.

Kaph (vv. 81-88)

The first half of the psalm concludes with this stanza. Like the final stanza of the psalm (vv. 169-176), it is more of a prayer for help rather than just a description of need. With questions like 'When will you …?' and 'How long …?', it resembles in tone the appeals for help such as Psalm 13. **My soul faints with longing for your salvation, but I have put my hope in your word. My eyes fail, looking for your promise; I say, 'When will you comfort me?'** (*vv. 81-82*). The felt weakness of the psalmist is depicted by the phrases 'my soul *faints*' and 'my eyes *fail*' (in Hebrew these two verbs are the same, *kâlâh*). Though deliverance is slow in coming, yet his trust remains in God's word. The expression used here (*lid^{e}vâr^{e}kâ yichaltî*) is identical with that in verses 74 and 114. Similar expressions occur in verses 43 and 49. The psalmist thinks he is near death, and his eyes fail because of weeping. However, as in many laments, his confidence is still in the promises God has given, and he can ask, 'When?'

Though I am like a wineskin in the smoke, I do not forget your decrees. How long must your servant wait? When will you punish my persecutors? (*vv. 83-84*). The effect of his trouble is that he feels like a wineskin, dried up and shrivelled because it has been hung over a fire. His afflictions have left their mark on him, and he feels that he is near the end of his life (see v. 87). He

[37] The Hebrew grammar here is exactly the same as in verse 69 (see comment). The Hebrew has: 'For they wrong me without cause.' The word *shéqer* is a noun meaning 'falsehood' or 'deception'. Here it functions as an adverb, 'without reason', or 'without cause'. Another example with this word can be seen in Psalm 35:19.

wonders how long it will be before his God intervenes (Heb. lit., 'How many are the days of your servant?'). It is justice that he wants for his persecutors. However, in spite of his circumstances he clings to God's word and will not let it slip from him. Verses 84 and 121 are the only ones in the whole of Psalm 119 that do not have either a direct reference to God's word, or an indirect one (see vv. 90 and 132).

The arrogant dig pitfalls for me, contrary to your law. All your commands are trustworthy; help me, for men persecute me without cause (*vv. 85-86*). His enemies fail to live according to God's law, and in their rebellion against its demands they try and bring the psalmist to his end. 'Pitfalls' could have the meaning of 'traps', 'snares', but it may even have the stronger meaning of 'graves'. Total destruction was their aim. They persecute without any valid reason,[38] but given their hostility to God's law, anyone loving it would become a natural target for them.

They almost wiped me from the earth, but I have not forsaken your precepts. Preserve my life according to your love, and I will obey the statutes of your mouth (*vv. 87-88*). In spite of the persecution that almost took his life, the psalmist is still committed to God's precepts. 'Not forsaken' is just another way of expressing 'not forgotten' (see v. 83). In the midst of all his troubles God's covenant love stands firm, and if the psalmist's life is continued, he owns that he will obey what God has spoken. He repeats the cry for preservation that has already been made several times earlier in the psalm (see vv. 25, 37, 40). It appears several times later as well (see vv. 107, 149, 154, 156, 159).

Lamedh (*vv. 89-96*)

This stanza concentrates on the enduring nature of God's word.[39]

Your word, O LORD, is eternal; it stands firm in the heavens. Your faithfulness continues through all generations; you established the earth, and it endures (*vv. 89-90*). Just as God is eternal, so is

[38] For comment on the phrase 'without cause' (*shéqer*), see on verse 78.

[39] All the verses in this section commence with the Hebrew letter *lamed* (*l*). It is not a letter that frequently appears at the beginning of words (only a quarter of the number as compared with the next letter *mem*). Seven of the verses begin with the preposition *l^e*, 'to' or 'for', while the remaining one commences with *lûlê*, 'if not'.

his revelation and his faithfulness (see Ps. 89:1-2, and cf. Jesus' words in Mark 13:31). It was by God's word that the heavens were created (Ps. 33:9), and they remain as a testimony to that fact, as well as to his faithfulness in sustaining them. Creation is a witness to the power of God's word, and generation after generation have a testimony, for nature confirms God's steadfastness.

Your laws endure to this day, for all things serve you (*v. 91*). The laws that govern creation are inherent, for the whole of creation has God as its maker and he established the principles on which it operates. Creation is not to be worshipped as though it was divine, for all parts of creation are but servants who do his bidding (cf. Gen. 1:14-18 which shows that the heavenly bodies are God's servants, while Deut. 4:15-19 forbids the worship of creation).

If your law had not been my delight, I would have perished in my affliction. I will never forget your precepts, for by them you have preserved my life (*vv. 92-93*). The psalmist reflects on the encouragement and support that came to him from God's laws. By God's word he has been preserved (cf. v. 88), and those statutes that he delighted in (cf. the same or similar expressions in vv. 24, 77, 143, 174) have been his stay in times of affliction (see the comments on v. 77 regarding the link between delight(s) and affliction). The pledge never to forget them is a repetition of one already given several times in this psalm (see vv. 16, 61, 83).

Save me, for I am yours; I have sought out your precepts. The wicked are waiting to destroy me, but I will ponder your statutes (*vv. 94-95*). In Hebrew the emphasis falls on the psalmist's relationship with God: '*I am yours;* save me.' As a consequence, he directs prayer to *his* God, and asks for preservation in the midst of present dangers (Ps. 54:1). His enemies are intent on his total destruction, but he trusts in his Saviour to deliver him. He knows what God's word promises, and he makes that his meditation. The expressions 'seek out your precepts' and 'ponder your statutes' are virtually synonymous, with the former one identical with verse 45b.

To all perfection I see a limit; but your commands are boundless (*v. 96*). As he looks around him, the psalmist sees the limitations of earthly things, as everything fits within the boundaries that God has allotted.[40] On the other hand, God's commands are limitless, and there are riches in them that can never be exhausted. God's law transcends all that we can observe in creation.

Mem (*vv. 97-104*)[41]

Oh, how I love your law! I meditate on it all day long (*v. 97*). The central theme of this psalm is summed up by this exclamation. Twice already the psalmist has declared his love for God's *commandments* (vv. 47, 48) and he returns to this later on (v. 127). Now for the first time he says he loves God's *law*, but this statement is going to be repeated (vv. 113, 163), along with affirmation of love for God's *statutes* (v. 119) and *precepts* (v. 159). Constant meditation on God's revelation provides wisdom that cannot be found elsewhere, and this wisdom exceeds that of enemies, teachers, and elders, as the following verses explain.

Your commands make me wiser than my enemies, for they are ever with me. I have more insight than all my teachers, for I meditate on your statutes. I have more understanding than the elders, for I obey your precepts (*vv. 98-100*). These verses make comparisons with other sources of wisdom. The enemies, though they show great skill in devising plots, lack access to the enduring word of God. On the other hand, the psalmist's experience is that wisdom comes from God's commands, which are ever his.[42] The NIV's expression, 'they are ever with me', is

---

[40] The word translated 'perfection' (*tiklâh*) only occurs here. A pun may be intended, with the poet saying that he has seen an 'end' (*qêts*) of all 'completeness' (*tiklâh*).

[41] Of the eight verses in this section, six start with the preposition *mi-* ('from'), with the remaining two commencing with *mâh-* ('how').

[42] Two grammatical problems occur in verse 98. The first is that the verb 'make me wiser' is singular whereas the subject 'your commands' is plural. The second is that the subject in the second clause (NIV, 'they') is actually singular, 'it' (*hî'*). One Hebrew manuscript has the singular 'your command', with which the LXX is in agreement (*tên entolên sou*). This appears, though, to be a deliberate attempt to make the grammar conform to normal practice. However, 'commands' seems to be used here as a summary of 'law', and hence the singular is used appropriately. Analagous cases can be seen in 2 Samuel 22:23 and 2 Kings 17:22.

somewhat weak, as the Hebrew text has 'they are eternally mine' (*leʿôlâm hîʾ lî*). Teachers may have considerable worldly wisdom, but they have not been instructed through meditation on God's statutes (cf. the use of the verb 'meditate' in v. 97, and the noun 'meditation' here). Senior members of the community may have wealth of experience behind them, but still not have as much spiritual insight as someone who obeys God's precepts. The clause in 100b, 'for I obey your precepts', is an exact repetition of verse 56b.

I have kept my feet from every evil path so that I might obey your word. I have not departed from your laws, for you yourself have taught me (*vv. 101-102*). Progression takes place in the psalmist's references to wisdom. He is wiser than his enemies (v. 98), wiser than his teachers (v. 99), wiser than his seniors (v. 100). Now he asserts that real knowledge comes from God himself and this enables the psalmist to shun every evil way (vv. 101-102). The emphasis falls on the source of the psalmist's wisdom; it is from God: '*You yourself* have taught me.' God's laws have instructed him according to his earlier request for teaching (see v. 33). Obedience keeps him from walking in sinful ways, and ensures that he does not turn aside from the pathway of obedience.

How sweet are your words to my taste, sweeter than honey to my mouth! I gain understanding from your precepts; therefore I hate every wrong path (*vv. 103-104*). Just as God's words have been compared to great riches (see v. 72, and cf. v. 127), so now the comparison is made with the sweetest thing imaginable. As the mouth loves the taste of honey, so the psalmist expresses his delight in God's words (cf. the same analogy in Ps. 19:10). They are extremely pleasurable to him, providing him with instruction that gives him joy in truth and hatred of false ways. Fear of the Lord brings with it a hatred of false paths.

Nun (*vv. 105-112*)

Your word is a lamp to my feet and a light for my path (*v. 105*). The idea that God's word gives light appears elsewhere in the Old Testament (Prov. 6:23). It acknowledges that without God's teaching and direction we walk in darkness, for the way of the wicked is both dark and slippery (Ps. 35:6). The highest expression of the idea comes in the words of Jesus in John 8:12: 'I am the light of the world. Whoever follows me will never walk in darkness, but will have the light of life.'

I have taken an oath and confirmed it, that I will follow your righteous laws. I have suffered much; preserve my life, O LORD, according to your word (*vv. 106-107*). Because covenants normally involved a solemn oath, the expression 'to take an oath' could be identical with 'to make a covenant'. Thus, even when deceived by the Gibeonites into making a covenant with them, the Israelites refer to that covenant by saying: 'We have *sworn* to them ...' (Josh. 9:19; cf. also Neh. 10:29).[43] The psalmist had not only entered into covenant with the LORD, but he had confirmed it at some later stage, pledging obedience to God's righteous demands.[44] Such attachment to the LORD brought intense suffering on him, and so he once more pleads for preservation in the midst of his trials (see on v. 88).

Accept, O LORD, the willing praise of my mouth, and teach me your laws. Though I constantly take my life in my hands, I will not forget your law. The wicked have set a snare for me, but I have not strayed from your precepts (*vv. 108-110*). Even when under persecution the psalmist has learned to live joyfully, maintaining his adherence to God's precepts. He wants to give a voluntary offering of praise to the LORD,[45] while requesting further teaching.[46] Constant danger

---

[43] Discussions on the use of the verb *shâvaʿ* ('to swear an oath') and the noun *sheᵉvûʿâh* ('oath') in connection with covenant can be found in *ISBE*, 3, pp. 572-74, and *TWOT*, 2, pp. 899-901.

[44] The technical term for confirming a covenant (*qûm*, Hi.) is used here. For discussion on this usage, see W. J. Dumbrell, *Covenant and Creation*, pp. 24-26.

[45] The word 'willing' (*nᵉdâvâh*) is normally used of sacrifices that were offered spontaneously (Lev. 7:16). Here 'freewill offerings of my mouth' are praises given from a devoted heart.

[46] The NIV rendering of the Hebrew *mishpâtekâ* by 'your laws' is inconsistent, as normally it uses 'your commandments' for this expression (cf. vv. 86, 96, and 98). Elsewhere in this psalm the verb 'teach' (*lâmad*, Pi.) has a different object, especially 'decrees', (vv. 12, 26, 68, 124, 135, 171) without any discernible difference in meaning.

to his life, as he continues to confess the LORD, has not caused him to deviate into other pathways.[47] He lives dangerously, facing traps laid for him by his enemies, yet desires more instruction to guide and strengthen him. His pledge is that he will not stray from God's precepts.[48]

Your statutes are my heritage forever; they are the joy of my heart. My heart is set on keeping your decrees to the very end (*vv. 111-112*). As part of his spiritual inheritance, the psalmist has received God's statutes. He uses an expression that is normally used of inheritance in the land of Canaan (*nâchaltî*). Israel forfeited her right to it, but the godly Israelite had a perpetual inheritance in God's law. Outward troubles do not take away his inward joy, as he confirms his resolve to observe the directions for life he has received from God. The expression 'to the very end' renders a Hebrew word (*ʿêqev*) that often indicates the consequence of something, or a reward. As in verse 33 it is best to maintain this interpretation and so translate: 'My heart is set on keeping your decrees: the reward is lasting'.[49] Hence, what the psalmist is saying is that there is constant spiritual delight or blessing in keeping God's decrees.

Samekh (*vv. 113-120*)

I hate double-minded men, but I love your law (*v. 113*). In contrast to the evildoers, the psalmist reaffirms his own relationship to God. He contrasts his commitment of love to God's law with those who vacillate in their acceptance of its demands. The Hebrew word translated 'double-minded' (*sêʿêf*, pl. *sêʿafîm*) occurs only here, and by derivation and use points to those who lack single-minded devotion to God.[50]

---

[47] The Hebrew idiom 'to take or put one's life in one's hands' means to expose oneself to mortal danger. For other examples of this usage, see Judges 12:3, 1 Samuel 19:5, and Job 13:14.

[48] Cf. the use of the same verb 'to stray' (*tâʿâh*) in the final verse of this psalm: 'I like a lost sheep went astray' (*tâʿîtî*).

[49] Of the modern English translations the NEB is the best: 'I am resolved to fulfil your statutes; they are a reward that never fails.'

[50] The word was variously translated in the old versions. The LXX rendered it by 'transgressors', while the Latin Vulgate had 'wicked'. An extensive note on it is found in *NIDOTTE*, 3, p. 276. A noun from the same root appears in 1 Kings 18:21: 'Why do you halt between two *opinions*?'

Such a person 'should not think that he will receive anything from the Lord; he is a double-minded man, unstable in all his ways' (James 1:7-8).

You are my refuge and my shield; I have put my hope in your word. Away from me, you evildoers, that I may keep the commands of my God! (*vv. 114-115*). In God the psalmist has a sure hiding place, bringing together two terms to describe him that are favourites with the psalmists (for Heb., *sêter*, 'refuge' or 'shelter', see Pss. 27:5; 31:20; 32:7 [NIV 'hiding place']; 61:4; and 91:1; for Heb., *mâgên*, 'shield', see Pss. 3:3; 28:7; 33:20; and 84:11). Towards God's law he shows continuous love and hope, using an expression that appears in identical form four times in Psalm 119 (*lid*^{e}*vâr*^{e}*kâ yichâltî*; 'I have put my hope in your word'; verses 74, 81, 114, 147 [Q^{e}re]).[51] He wants no influence of evildoers to distract him from obedience to the law's claims. Verses 113 and 114 are directed to God, but verse 115 is directed to the evildoers, with the express desire that they remove themselves far from him. **Sustain me according to your promise, and I will live; do not let my hopes be dashed. Uphold me, and I will be delivered; I will always have regard for your decrees** (*vv. 116-117*). To be kept by the power of God is a promise given in both Old and New Testaments (Ps. 37:17, 24; Isa. 26:3; 1 Pet. 1:5). Hence the prayer for God's continued help and support in the midst of trials. Answer to these prayers will mean life and salvation, without any cause for hope in God to be disappointed. The NIV translation 'Do not let my hopes be dashed' is a very good and idiomatic way of expressing what more literally can be rendered 'Let me not be put to shame in my hope' (ESV). God's intervention on the psalmist's side means continuation in life (v. 116), or being saved as verse 117 expresses it (*v*^{e}*ʾivvâshêʿâh*). The Hebrew verb translated 'have regard' (*shâʿâh*) is usually used of looking expectantly to someone, or looking with approval and favour. It is an apt word for the attitude of the psalmist to God's decrees.

[51] Another expression, almost identical in meaning, is used in verse 49: 'the word on which you have made me hope'.

You reject all who stray from your decrees, for their deceitfulness is in vain. All the wicked of the earth you discard like dross; therefore I love your statutes (*vv. 118-119*). The language used here of the wicked reminds of that in Psalm 1:4-5. Rebellious sinners, who deviate from divine precepts, are going to be cast aside similar to how dross is removed during the refining process. Deceit brings no security for them. The only way to ensure spiritual progress and absence of judgment is to love the Lord and to love his commands. Whoever has Jesus' commands and obeys them shows that he loves him, and anyone who so loves Jesus will be loved by the Father also (John 14:21).

My flesh trembles in fear of you; I stand in awe of your laws (*v. 120*). The concluding expressions in this stanza speak of reverence towards God and his laws. 'My flesh', just like 'my soul', can be another way of referring to one's self. It is not the fear of judgment, but the devout attitude and feelings towards God that dominate a believing heart. Where there is perfect love, there is absence of fear (1 John 4:18).

Ayin (*vv. 121-128*)[52]

In a stanza in which prayer for deliverance is most prominent, there is also a threefold reference to the fact that the psalmist is God's servant (see vv. 122, 124-125). He makes his appeal as a devoted member of the covenant community. **I have done what is righteous and just; do not leave me to my oppressors** (*v. 121*). The psalmist asserts that his present troubles are not because of his own wilful desertion of God's ways. He has acted uprightly, and so he pleads for deliverance, and his attitude shows that this is not a statement stemming from self-righteousness. This and verse 84 are the only ones in the whole of Psalm 119 that do not have either a direct reference to God's word, or an indirect one (see vv. 90 and 132).

---

[52] In this section the letter *ayin* was difficult to fit into the acrostic pattern. Two verses begin with the same phrase 'therefore' (*'al-kên*), with two others starting with different forms of the verb 'to do' (*'âsâh*).

Ensure your servant's well-being; let not the arrogant oppress me (*v. 122*). The opening expression is noteworthy, because the Hebrew verb used (*'ârav*) has the idea of taking responsibility for someone else. For example, Judah assured his father that he would guarantee Benjamin's safety if he went down to Egypt (Gen. 43:9). Here the servant appeals to his sovereign master to protect him and take responsibility for his safety. He wants to be shown the blessings promised to covenant servants (lit. 'stand surety for the good of your servant').[53] This is the fifth and final reference to 'the arrogant' (*zêdîm*) in this psalm, and indicates again how the psalmist longed to be free from oppressive enemies.[54]

My eyes fail, looking for your salvation, looking for your righteous promise. Deal with your servant according to your love and teach me your decrees. I am your servant; give me discernment that I may understand your statutes (*vv. 123-125*). Faith clings to the promises of God, even when his intervention is delayed and there is no speedy deliverance. The construction at the beginning of verse 123 is the same as in verse 82 (lit. 'my eyes fail for …'), and in both cases the NIV rightly inserts 'looking'. The psalmist knows that God will continue to act in accordance with his promise and his covenant commitments. 'Deal with your servant' is literally 'do with your servant', which may be an ellipsis for 'do good with your servant' as in verse 65. In facing continued opposition and oppression, the psalmist requests further teaching and enlightenment in relation to God's decrees. A teachable spirit is a mark of godliness, and the psalmist over and over again asks both for instruction (vv. 12, 26, 64, 66, 71, 73, 108, 135, 171) and for spiritual illumination (vv. 27, 34, 73, 144, 169).

It is time for you to act, O LORD; your law is being broken. Because I love your commands more than gold, more than pure gold, and because I consider all your precepts right, I hate every wrong path (*vv. 126-128*). The reference to the law 'being broken' (*pârar*, Hi.) is a technical term used for

---

[53] For the covenantal significance of the Hebrew word 'good' (*tôv*), see the note on Psalm 23:6. The Jewish Talmud understood 'good' to be a reference to 'the law'. See *Berakot* 5a.

[54] The earlier references to 'the proud' are in verses 51, 69, 78, and 85.

breaches of the covenant (Isa. 24:5; 33:8; Jer. 11:10; 31:32). The oppression being carried out against the psalmist is being done by covenant breakers, who have turned to paths that he abhors. He asks for speedy help so that God's honour will be upheld.[55] On his part he again refers to the preciousness of God's commands (see the earlier references in vv. 14, 57, 72, and 111, and the later one in v. 162), heightening the comparison by using the word for 'pure gold' (*paz*). Such gold was at that time the most valuable metal, and hence referring to it is a fitting way to describe the priceless worth of God's law. The final verse in this section has unusual Hebrew grammar with the word for 'all' (*kol*) occurring three times. It begins: 'Therefore all the commands of all ...' In this psalm normally the term 'law' or its synonyms have a divine suffix. The LXX and Jerome both insert it here: 'to all your commands I direct myself', but no Hebrew manuscript has this reading.[56] In the light of present knowledge, the NIV seems close to the mark.

Pe (*vv. 129-136*)

Your statutes are wonderful; therefore I obey them. The unfolding of your words gives light; it gives understanding to the simple. I open my mouth and pant, longing for your commands (*vv. 129-131*). Further praise of God's word begins with the use of the word 'wonderful' (*pele'*). It is a word exclusively used of God's actions or words, and marks out what cannot be produced by human effort (cf. the comments on Ps. 77:11, 14). Here its use extols both the origin and the glory of God's truth. Recognition of the nature of God's revelation (brought about

---

[55] The Hebrew text has *lyhwh*, which often means 'for Yhwh', but this is probably a good illustration of the vocative *lamed*, 'O LORD', and the NIV takes it this way. For support, see M. Dahood, *Psalms III: 101-150*, p. 407, and *IBHS*, p. 211-12. The contrary opinion is expressed by P. D. Miller, 'Vocative Lamed in the Psalter', *Ugarit-Forschungen* 11 (1979), pp. 617-37.

[56] It is possible to come near this by altering the division of words and taking the consonant *lamed* as an emphatic: 'All your precepts I consider truly right.' For this position, see M. Dahood, *Psalms III: 101-150*, p. 187, and L. C. Allen, *Psalms 101-150*, p. 138. It is worth consulting the older commentators such as J. J. S. Perowne, *The Book of Psalms*, II, p. 368, and J. A. Alexander, *The Psalms Translated and Explained*, p. 500, who writes: 'The construction here is very foreign from our idiom, and by no means easily translated into it.'

by the Holy Spirit's work) produces conviction as to its authority over our lives. When the teaching of God's word is unfolded to us (the Hebrew says 'the *opening* of your words'), then it is like light shining on our way (cf. v. 105). All who lack spiritual knowledge are included in the class called 'the simple' (see Ps. 19:7). As he reflects on the nature of God's word, the psalmist speaks of his intense desire for it, resembling himself to a panting animal longing for water.

Turn to me and have mercy on me, as you always do to those who love your name. Direct my footsteps according to your word; let no sin rule over me (*vv. 132-133*). Knowledge of God's habitual manner of acting ('you always do', Hebrew *mishpât*) forms the basis of the appeal for mercy. Because God's faithfulness is great, his compassions never fail (Lam. 3:22-23). 'Those who love your name' is one of the ways of describing faithful believers (cf. Ps. 69:36; and 'those who love your salvation' in Psalm 70:4). The psalmist wants his footsteps to be set surely according to God's word of promise, and in this way sin will not be able to tyrannise him. The verb 'rule' (*shâlat*) has this connotation of exercising dominion in a tyrannical way (cf. its use in Neh. 5:15).

Redeem me from the oppression of men, that I may obey your precepts. Make your face shine upon your servant and teach me your decrees (*vv. 134-135*). Once more the oppression the psalmist is facing presses in upon him, and he asks for deliverance from it. This oppression constrains him,[57] and militates against his freedom to keep God's laws. The prayer of verse 135 is given in terms of the Aaronic benediction (Num. 6:24-26; cf. also Pss. 31:16; and 80:3, 7, 19).

Streams of tears flow from my eyes, for your law is not obeyed (*v. 136*). Previously the psalmist has described his indignation when God's law is forsaken (v. 53). Now he pictures the depth of his grief when he sees others abandoning God's demands. His tears become a flood, just like the anonymous author of Lamentations as he grieved over the destruction of his people (Lam. 3:48).

---

[57] This is the only occurrence of the noun 'oppression' (*ʿoshek*) in this psalm, though two verbal forms appear in verses 121 and 122.

Tsadhe (*vv. 137-144*)

The important thought of God and his righteous laws dominate this section, with the Hebrew words for right/ righteous occurring five times in eight verses. Three of these cognate words are used to commence verses, as they all have *tsadhe* as the initial consonant (*tsâdîk*, *ts*^{e}*dâqâh*, and *tsédek*). **Righteous are you, O LORD, and your laws are right. The statutes you have laid down are righteous; they are fully trustworthy** (*vv. 137-138*). God's character is reflected in the laws he gives. In contexts such as this, 'righteous' (*tsâdîk*) has the idea of utter faithfulness, for the synonyms used with it are 'trustworthy' and 'true'. The divine king has laid down his statutes, which accord both with his nature and with his plans for the well-being of his creatures. The expression 'trustworthy statutes' repeats the parallel and synonymous phrase 'trustworthy commands' (v. 86), with heightening by the addition of 'very' or 'fully' (Heb., *m*^{e}*ʾod*).

My zeal wears me out, for my enemies ignore your words. Your promises have been thoroughly tested, and your servant loves them (*vv. 139-140*). 'Zeal' (*qinʾâh*) is practically equivalent here to 'anger' (cf. 'indignation' in v. 53). Whereas the psalmist often prays that he will not forget God's law (see vv. 16, 61, 83, 93, 109, 141, 153, 176), this is the very thing that occurs with his enemies ('ignore' is Hebrew *shâkach*, 'forget'). In all his troubles the psalmist has been able to rely on God's word, and he finds it absolutely trustworthy. It is like a precious metal that has come through the refining process unscathed. In verses 121 to 128 the psalmist has already confessed that he is in a servant/master relationship with God, and now he acknowledges this again, and confirms his love for God's word. Several times up to this point in the psalm, declarations have been made of love for God's 'commands' (see vv. 47, 48) and for his 'law' (vv. 97, 113). Now a declaration of love for God's word joins these earlier affirmations.

Though I am lowly and despised, I do not forget your precepts. Your righteousness is everlasting and your law is true. Trouble and distress have come upon me, but your commands are my delight (*vv. 141-143*). Though others may treat him as insignificant,[58] the psalmist commits himself to maintain his adherence to God's laws. While his enemies 'forget' God's word (v. 139), he will 'not forget' God's precepts (the same verb, *shâkach,* is used in both cases). The NIV rendering 'Your righteousness is everlasting' disguises the fact that the MT has two cognate words in the same clause, 'righteousness' (*tsᵉdâqâh*) and 'righteous' (*tsédek*). Preferable is either the ESV ('Your righteousness is righteous forever') or the NRSV ('Your righteousness is an everlasting righteousness'). The second part of verse 142 is an affirmation of the reliability of God's law, since it reflects his own character,[59] and it may lie behind Jesus' words in John 17:17; 'Your word is truth.' In the midst of difficulties, in which he is confronted with trouble and distress, he takes pleasure in God's commands, as he has already declared several times (the same verb, 'delight', is used in vv. 16, 47, 70; its related noun occurs in vv. 24, 77, 92, 143, and 174).

Your statutes are forever right; give me understanding that I may live (*v. 144*). The thought of verse 138 is amplified by reference to the enduring nature of God's righteous statutes. They are not the fickle decrees of a human king, but the lasting ordinances of the eternal God. The opening statement can also be rendered, 'Your statutes are righteous forever,' which brings out how close a parallel it forms with the opening of verse 142. Spiritual insight into the meaning of God's statutes provides wisdom that guides through life.

Qoph (*vv. 145-152*)[60]

I call with all my heart; answer me, O LORD, and I will obey your decrees. I call out to you; save me and I will keep

---

[58] The word rendered 'lowly' (*tsâʿîr*) can mean 'small', i.e. 'young', but it often has the idea of being 'insignificant', 'unimportant'.

[59] Similar statements are made about God's word (v. 43), his commandments (v. 151), and his words (v. 160).

[60] In this section a restricted number of words are used to make up the acrostic pattern. The verb 'call' (*qârâ'*) appears twice, the verb 'go before' (*qâdam,* Pi.) twice and the cognate noun 'long ago' (*qédem*) once, and the cognate verb 'draw near' (*qârav*) and adjective 'near' (*qârôv*) once each.

your statutes (*vv. 145*). Prayerfulness is one of the marks of a believer. As this psalm moves towards its conclusion, the direct prayers to God increase. The opening of this stanza is very similar to the first verse of Psalm 4: 'Answer me when I call to you, O my righteous God.' Following a stanza extolling the righteousness of God, the psalmist cries to him, and he longs for an answer that will bring deliverance to him. Response to the requests 'Answer me' and 'Save me' will produce the same result. The commitment made in the second part of both these verses has already been made repeatedly earlier in the psalm (for the use of Heb., *nâtsar*, 'obey', see vv. 22, 33, 34, 56, 69, 100, 115, 129: for Hebrew *shâmar*, 'keep', see vv. 5, 8, 17, 34, 44, 55, 57, 60, 67, 88, 101, 106, 134). It is prompted by devotion to God and it is the response of a heart dedicated to his service. Jesus reinforced the principle when he taught that love to him must be demonstrated by obedience to his commands (John 14:15, 21; 15:10, 12).

I rise before dawn and cry for help; I have put my hope in your word. My eyes stay open through the watches of the night, that I may meditate on your promises (*vv. 147-148*). The psalmist pleads with such urgency that he either gets up early or stays awake in the night. The Hebrew verb (*qâdam*, Pi.) used at the beginning of both verses means to come before something else in time, but it is awkward to use similar translations in both clauses.[61] However, this can be done by rendering: 'Before morning twilight ... Before the night watches'.[62] The New Testament application of the principle comes in the parable of the persistent widow (Luke 18:1-8), when Jesus asks his disciples the questions: 'And will not God bring justice for his chosen ones, who cry out to him day and night? Will he keep putting them off?' (v. 7). Meditation on, and trust in, God's promises are a necessary foundation of believing prayer. The expression 'I have put my hope in your word' occurs in identical form four times in this psalm (see comment on v. 114).

---

[61] This was recognised by J. J. S. Perowne, *The Book of Psalms*, II, p. 364, who tried to translate by: 'I was before-hand with the dawn ... Mine eyes were before-hand with the night watches.'

[62] This is the translation of L. C. Allen, *Psalms 101-150*, p. 132.

Hear my voice in accordance with your love; preserve my life, O LORD, according to your laws (*v. 149*). Covenant mercy is promised, so the psalmist pleads for an attentive hearing to his prayer. 'Voice' (*qôl*) is used here, as often in the Psalms, in phrases that indicate it is a voice raised in prayer or supplication. This is made clear by the addition of the request: 'Hear!' The plea for preservation appears again, to be repeated in identical form in verse 156.

Those who devise wicked schemes are near, but they are far from your law. Yet you are near, O LORD, and all your commands are true (*vv. 150-151*). The contrasts drawn are most marked. While the enemies are near, yet they are far from God's law. While they are near, the LORD is nearer still, ready to help and to provide deliverance. The attitudes and actions of the enemies show that they are far removed from following the ways of the LORD. The testimony of the psalmist is that the God of truth is indeed near, as he is 'to all who call on him, to all who call on him in truth' (Ps. 145:18). The final clause in verse 151 is synonymous with the conclusion of verse 142.

Long ago I learned from your statutes that you established them to last forever (*v. 152*). Recent experiences have not brought the psalmist into knowledge of God's statutes. That knowledge came to him long ago and he relies upon the statutes because he knows that they are part of God's enduring revelation. As Jesus expressed it: 'Until heaven and earth disappear, not the smallest letter, not the least stroke of a pen, will by any means disappear from the Law until everything is accomplished' (Matt. 5:18).

Resh (*vv. 153-160*)

Look upon my suffering and deliver me, for I have not forgotten your law. Defend my cause and redeem me; preserve my life according to your promise. Salvation is far from the wicked, for they do not seek out your decrees (*vv. 153-155*). An afflicted but loyal servant prays for God to look with compassion on him. Unlike the wicked, who do not enquire into God's decrees, he has set his heart on them and has kept them in his mind. He reinforces what he has already said in verse 141 ('I do not forget your precepts') by affirming that he is not forgetful of God's law. The words 'Defend my cause and redeem me' constitute legal terminology, with God being represented as the advocate who comes to aid the accused (see comments on Ps. 74:22). The verbs 'defend' (Hebrew *rîv*) and 'redeem' (Hebrew *gâ'al*) come together in other Old Testament passages (e.g., Jer. 50:34),[63] and the translation could rightly be 'Defend ... and vindicate me'. The plea for preservation dominates this section of the psalm, with two further similar petitions in verses 156 and 159. No such deliverance will be given by God to those who wilfully transgress his laws. Such people forget his words (v. 139) and make no attempt to study (Heb., *dârash*) his statutes.

Your compassion is great, O LORD; preserve my life according to your laws (*v. 156*). What so often sustains believers is confidence in the abounding compassion of God (cf. David's words to Gad in 1 Chron. 21:13). That is seen in acts on their behalf that display his mercy. The psalmist knows that it is the never-failing compassion of the LORD that will keep him alive.

Many are the foes who persecute me, but I have not turned from your statutes. I look on the faithless with loathing, for they do not obey your word (*vv. 157-158*). The contrast between the psalmist and his enemies is again emphasised (see vv. 84, 86, and 150). Unlike him, they are characterised by departure from God's laws and an unwillingness to be subject to them. 'The faithless' (*bog^{e}dîm*) is a description of those who prove false to the LORD (Ps. 78:57; Jer. 9:2), acting treacherously, and breaching their covenant obligations. Though faced with a multitude of such enemies, the psalmist does not deviate from the way of righteousness. His attitude towards their manner of life is one of revulsion, as they are not subservient to God's word (cf. Paul's words in 2 Thess. 1:8 regarding those

---

[63] In Jeremiah 50:34 God is declared to be the 'redeemer' (*gô'êl*) of Judah and Israel, and the sense is given greater emphasis by the addition of a clause using the verb *rîv* in two forms and with the cognate noun *rîvâh*: *rîv yârîv 'et-rîvâm* ('he will vigorously defend their cause'). Assonance and alliteration in Hebrew make the statement even more memorable.

'who do not know God and do not obey the gospel of our Lord Jesus Christ').

See how I love your precepts; preserve my life, O LORD, according to your love. All your words are true; all your righteous laws are eternal (*vv. 159-160*). The viewpoint put in a negative way in the preceding verses is now stated positively. There is heartfelt devotion to God's precepts (see similar expressions of love to God's commandments [vv. 47, 48, 127], God's law [vv. 97, 113, 163), and God's statutes [v. 167]). The totality of God's words (Heb., 'the head of your words', i.e. the sum of them, as in Ps. 139:17) is absolutely sure, for all his words are trustworthy (vv. 86, 138), true (vv. 142, 151, 160) and eternal (vv. 89, 111, 142, 144, 152).

Sin and Shin (*vv. 161-168*)[64]

Rulers persecute me without cause, but my heart trembles at your word (*v. 161*). Earlier in this psalm (vv. 23 and 46), reference was made to the relationship that the psalmist had to rulers and kings (see comments on these verses). Even though they derided him, the psalmist is prepared to declare God's statutes to them. He does not stand in awe of them, for his heart is devoted to God's word. The idea of a trembling heart is probably explained by Proverbs 28:14, where fearing God is contrasted to hardening the heart.

I rejoice in your promise like one who finds great spoil. I hate and abhor falsehood but I love your law (*vv. 162-163*). The inestimable value of God's word is likened to the taking of spoil in battle (Hebrew *shâlâl,* cf. the name of Isaiah's second son, Maher-Shalal-Hash-Baz, 'quick to the spoil, hasting to the plunder', Isa. 8:1). This links in with earlier references to the treasure found in God's law (see vv. 14, 72, and 111). The psalmist's attitude to falsehood and deception is that he hates and abominates them. On the other hand, his devotion to God's law expresses itself again as love for it (see the comment on v. 97).

---

[64] *Sin* and *Shin* were originally one letter, and when Hebrew is written without vowels they are represented by the one sign. When vowels are used, a dot is placed at the top of the left hand of the letter to indicate *sin,* and a dot over the top of the right hand to indicate *shin.*

Seven times a day I praise you for your righteous laws. Great peace have they who love your law, and nothing can make them stumble. I wait for your salvation, O LORD, and I follow your commands (*vv. 164-166*). 'Seven times' expresses completeness. The psalmist is asserting that he praises God's law all the day. In addition to showing mercy to those who love his law (v. 132), God gives them 'peace' (*shâlôm*). This is much more than mere absence of hostility or strife. It is a gift to those who are blessed, guarded, and treated graciously by the LORD (Num. 6:24-26). It signifies an unimpaired relationship with him, which comes now through the Prince of Peace (Isa. 9:6) who himself is our peace (Eph. 2:14). Those who truly love God's law, in their devotion to him, have the best preservative against stumbling.[65] This devotion is also exhibited in patient waiting for God's deliverance (cf. Jacob's very similar words, 'I look for your deliverance', Gen. 49:18),[66] and a commitment to do his will.

I obey your statutes, for I love them greatly. I obey your precepts and your statutes, for all my ways are known to you (*vv. 167-168*). The section concludes with a double declaration of obedience to God's laws and statutes, and a further expression of love for them (cf. v. 119). The final verse is unusual in that it contains two of the synonyms for God's word in the same verse. The concluding declaration is a statement that confirms what the psalmist has just said. His daily conduct, which is well known to God, shows his love for, and obedience to, God's laws.

Taw (*vv. 169-176*)

Just as the first half of the psalm concludes with a stanza crying for help (*vv. 81-88*), so the second half of the psalm ends in a similar manner. All but one of the verses has direct appeal to God. The psalmist's great need and his confidence

---

[65] The LXX rendered the last clause in verse 165 by *ouk estin autois skandalon*, 'and there is no stumbling block to them'. Cf. 1 John 2:10: *skandalon ouk estin en autô*, 'and there is no stumbling block in him.'

[66] The verb translated 'wait for' (*sâvar*, Pi.) is not a common verb. In fact, it is the least common of all the verbs denoting hope or expectation. It does not seem to be any different in meaning from the more common *yâchal* or *qâvâh*.

in the Lord's word dominate his thoughts. **May my cry come before you, O Lord; give me understanding according to your word. May my supplication come before you; deliver me according to your promise** (*vv. 169-170*). The approach to God is defined as 'my cry' (*rinnâtî*) and 'my supplication' (*t^{e}chinnâtî*). The first of these terms describes a ringing cry of either joy (Isa. 14:7) or sorrow (1 Kings 8:28). From the context it is clearly the latter here. The second term always means either mercy, or a cry for mercy. The psalmist longs for God to listen to his prayer, and to respond in grace. He needs further help in appreciating God's word and the way it ministers to him in his need. Right throughout the psalm this appeal for spiritual understanding has been made (see vv. 27, 34, 73, 125, 130, 144, 169) and now it is repeated near its close. He also renews his call for deliverance and bases it on God's own word of promise.

May my lips overflow with praise, for you teach me your decrees. May my tongue sing of your word, for all your commands are righteous (*vv. 171-172*). The fitting response to mercy is praise, and so the psalmist asks that joyful song will be given to him. He expects God to answer his cry, and so he can look forward to his own subsequent praise. The NIV 'sing' is the translation of a Hebrew verb (*ʿânâh*) that normally means 'to answer'. It fits the context well if it is understood as 'repeat' or 'echo'. In the midst of all his experiences he still knows that God's commands are just, and that he needs further instruction concerning them. No matter how long a person has been a believer, the request for further teaching will always be appropriate (cf. Paul's words in Phil. 3:10).

May your hand be ready to help me, for I have chosen your precepts. I long for your salvation, O Lord, and your law is my delight (*vv. 173-174*). 'Hand' is a synonym for 'power' (as in Deut. 32:39 and Isa. 28:2). The appeal is for a demonstration of divine action in rescuing him from his trouble. Near the end of his life Moses put before Israel the alternatives of life and death, encouraging the people to choose life. This was defined in terms of loving the Lord, walking in his ways, and keeping his commands, decrees and laws (Deut. 30:15-16).

Here the psalmist speaks of his commitment of choice. He is following the ways of the LORD and as the psalm draws to a close he reaffirms his delight in the law (cf. for the use of the verb 'delight in' vv. 16, 47, and 70, and the noun 'delight' used here, vv. 24, 77, 92, and 143).

Let me live that I may praise you, and may your laws sustain me. I have strayed like a lost sheep. Seek your servant, for I have not forgotten your commands (*vv. 175-176*). The theme of praise is continued. As God preserves, then the psalmist will extol him in praise and adoration.[67] The final words of this psalm are highly significant. Though throughout professing deep love and devotion to God's commands, the psalmist complains that he has been like a lost sheep. This cannot be understood in the same sense as in Jesus' parable of the lost sheep (Luke 15:1-7), for here the 'lost sheep' is someone who loves God and does not forget his commands. It must be a reference to the psalmist's helplessness in the face of persecution, and even the feeling that he is perishing.[68] The words 'I have strayed' are a confession, though, and hence the element of sin on his part comes into the picture as well (cf. Isaiah's confession: 'We all, like lost sheep, have gone astray', Isa. 53:6, where the same Hebrew verb, *tâʿâh,* is used). He is still a servant, and therefore asks to be found by his good and gracious shepherd. The beautiful imagery of God as the shepherd (cf. Ps. 23; Isa. 40:11; Ezek. 34:11-16) is taken up by Jesus, who declares that he is the good shepherd (John 10:11, 14), while he also uses the picture of wandering sheep to teach God's concern for the lost (Luke 15:4-7).

---

[67] 'Sustain' is the same verb (*ʿâzar*) already used in verse 173, though translated there by 'help'.

[68] The participle of the verb translated 'lost' (*'ovêd*) can also mean 'about to perish', as in Deuteronomy 26:5, where the reference to Jacob can either mean 'a wandering Aramean', or 'an Aramean about to die'. See my discussion on this passage in my commentary on *Deuteronomy*, pp. 231-32.

Psalm 120

A song of ascents.

This psalm begins a group that share an unusual title. The word 'ascents' (Hebrew *maʿalôt*) comes from the verb 'to go up' (*ʿâlâh*), and the most plausible meaning in this context is that it refers to going up to Jerusalem.[1] This could either be the return of the exiles from Babylon in the second half of the sixth century BC, or, more probably, the annual journey of pilgrims for the great festivals (Passover, Weeks, and Tabernacles). Because of the presence of harvest imagery in several of the psalms (see 126:5-6; 127:2; 128:2; 129:6-8; 132:15), it is likely that the songs were intended for use at the Feast of Tabernacles.[2]

The fifteen psalms in this collection seem to be divided into two sections of seven psalms each, with Psalm 127 (attributed to Solomon) forming the central pivot.[3] There is remarkable symmetry in that each of these groups of seven contain the divine name twenty-four times, with each of the sub-groups (120-23; 124-26; 128-31; 132-34) containing it twelve times. This is far too systematic to be an accidental feature.

Psalm 120 follows on from the idea of the wandering sheep mentioned in Psalm 119:176. Here the psalmist is like a sheep among wolves in his own country, and this sets the

---

[1] In modern Hebrew, the noun *ʿaliyyâh* from this verb means 'pilgrimage' (especially to Jerusalem), or, very commonly, 'immigration (to Israel)'.

[2] For a recent good discussion on the Songs of Ascents and their place in the fifth book of the Psalter, see C. Hassell Bullock, *Encountering the Psalms: A Literary and Theological Introduction* (Grand Rapids: Baker Academic, 2001), pp. 79-82.

[3] This was pointed out in the nineteenth century by E. W. Hengstenberg, *Commentary on the Psalms*, III, pp. 409-10, with support from J. A. Alexander, *The Psalms Translated and Explained*, p. 506.

scene for the pilgrimage from a hostile home environment to the joys and blessings of worship in Jerusalem. It gives the background of the following songs of pilgrimage, and shows how gladly a pilgrim set out for Jerusalem and how heartily he must have prayed for the peace of Jerusalem and all who love her (Ps. 122:6-7).[4]

1. Remembrance of Past Experiences (*v. 1*)

I call on the LORD in my distress, and he answers me (*v. 1*). The psalm opens, not with the immediate situation confronting the psalmist, but with recollection of former help provided by the LORD. He had repeatedly gone to him in the past and his cry had brought a speedy response. The remembrance of former help is the encouragement to direct prayer to God again.

His love in time past
Forbids me to think
He'll leave me at last
In trouble to sink.
(John Newton 1725-1807)

2. The Cry of Distress (*vv. 2-4*)

The opening words of this section specify the present need. **Save me, O LORD, from lying lips and from deceitful tongues** (*v. 2*). The psalmist appeals for divine deliverance, even though the actual circumstances prompting his cry are not recorded.[5] If the psalm is from the post-exilic period, the situation may well have been like that faced by the returning exiles, who had to contend with the slander of the Samaritans (Ezra 4:1-24; Neh. 4:1-14; 6:5-14). Christians have to follow the pattern of our Lord. He was called a glutton and a drunkard, and yet he did not respond in like manner (1 Pet. 2:23).

---

[4] The concept of 'peace' (Hebrew *shâlôm*) is intrinsic to the whole group, with the word occurring in 120:7; 122:6; 125:5; 128:6.

[5] NIV is rather inconsistent with its translation of the Hebrew verb 'to deliver' (*nâtsal*, Hi.). In Psalm 119:170 it is rendered 'deliver', but here it has 'save'. Other versions such as NASB, ESV, and NRSV are more consistent.

What will he do to you, and what more besides, O deceitful tongue? (*v. 3*). This is an indirect appeal to God to bring judgment on the slanderer, with the question being asked of the tongue itself. It is phrased in terms similar to Hebrew oaths such as 'May God do so to you, and more also' (1 Sam. 3:17; 20:13). The appeal is for God to deal with the situation, though the actual penalty is not expressed. Perhaps there was some accompanying action that indicated the nature of the penalty.

He will punish you with a warrior's sharp arrows, with burning coals of the broom tree (*v. 4*). Here the punishment is specified. The answer seems to have in mind the descriptions given elsewhere of the lying tongue. In the Old Testament it is called a sharp sword (Ps. 57:4), and a deadly arrow (Jer. 9:8), while later the New Testament calls it a member set on fire by hell (James 3:6). The expected punishment will be a fitting response, for it will match the offence. The broom tree had very hard wood and therefore produced coals that were long-lasting. The act of judgment will be more deadly that the slanderer's own words.

3. A Foreigner in His Own Land (*vv. 5-7*)

Woe to me that I dwell in Meshech, that I live among the tents of Kedar! (*v. 5*). Meshech and Kedar were not geographically close. Meshech was named after a son of Japheth (Gen. 10:2), and it refers to Eastern Anatolia (modern day Turkey). Kedar was one of Ishmael's sons and father of the tribe that bore his name (Gen. 25:13). It refers to Bedouin Arabs who lived south-east of Damascus. So acute was the psalmist's distress that he felt as if he was living among barbarians! He was a foreigner in his own land!

Too long have I lived among those who hate peace. I am a man of peace; but when I speak, they are for war (*vv. 6-7*). The contrast between the two groups in his society is brought out by these verses. Light and darkness are incompatible. When the psalmist talks about peace, the reply he gets is in terms of war. The Hebrew says tersely, 'I [for] peace … they for war'. While the cry for help in verse 2 is not repeated again, yet it echoes to the end of the psalm. There is clearly an intense longing for deliverance to come from the LORD.

Psalm 121

A song of ascents.

This psalm's setting seems to show the idea of ascent to Jerusalem. Of all the psalms in this group this is the only one that has the particular designation in Hebrew, 'a song *for* the ascents', although the NIV and almost all English versions do not translate it any differently. Bearing in mind the content of the psalm, this distinctive title perhaps marked it out for special use on the journey to Jerusalem.[1]

A significant theme of this psalm is the fact that the LORD is the keeper, with various forms of the Hebrew verb 'to keep' (*shâmar*) appearing five times in verses 3-8. The thought builds up from the description of the LORD as 'my help' in verse 1, which is repeated in verse 2, and then amplified in the later verses under the motif of the LORD as 'the keeper'.

The shift from first person in verses 1 and 2 ('*I* will lift'; '*my* help') to second person singular in verses 3-8 ('*your* foot'; '*your* shade'; '*your* life') has been explained in various ways. While it could be within a single heart (see Pss. 42-43), it is more probable that after the opening statements by the psalmist, an unidentified voice responds in verses 3-8.[2]

---

[1] Commentators and others have often wanted to change the title to 'the ascents' (*hamm'alôt*) so that it is identical with that in all the other songs in this group. But the MT has the more difficult reading, as Dahood points out (*Psalms III: 101-150*, p. 200). He finds a solution for the expression in this title by taking the initial *lamed* (*la*) as part of a genitive construction, and so arrives at the same translation as the English versions, 'a song of ascents' (ibid.).

[2] More elaborate explanations have been given of how the psalm could have been used by a group of pilgrims in which both individuals and then all the pilgrims take part responsively. As the background is unknown, the simple solutions are preferable.

The words of the psalm, though, have brought comfort and inspiration to many as it has been sung by the Christians throughout the centuries. The Scottish metrical version of this psalm has some powerful expressions, and its use has brought widespread appreciation of it.

1. The Psalmist's Help (*vv. 1-2*)

I lift up my eyes to the hills – where does my help come from? My help comes from the LORD, the Maker of heaven and earth. As the pilgrim comes within sight of his destination he sees the hills surrounding Jerusalem. To many these hills gave a feeling of confidence. But the psalmist then asks from where does his help *really* come? His answer is emphatic. The covenant God of Israel is his keeper, whose creative power as 'Maker of heaven and earth' (*ʿoseh shâmáyim vâʾârets*) is a surety of his ability to help his people. This phrase (or, [who] 'made the heavens and the earth'] was clearly a standard one in Hebrew poetry (cf. Pss. 115:15; 124:8; 134:3; 146:6; Isa. 37:16). The Maker of all things is able to stoop down to meet the needs of his people, and in both Old and New Testaments appeal to this ability is repeatedly made (note Isaiah's acknowledgment of the creator God and his power to help, Isa. 40:12-17; 42:5; 45:11-12; and for the New Testament, see Acts 4:24).

2. The Psalmist's Safety (*vv. 3-4*)

He will not let your foot slip – he who watches over you will not slumber; indeed, he who watches over Israel will neither slumber nor sleep. Will the singing pilgrim now stumble at this stage of the journey? Assuredly not, for he has a guard who does not sleep, and with emphasis he says that his feet will not be allowed to slip (cf. Ps. 17:5). This expression probably encompasses the idea that God is alert to any of the dangers of the journey. 'Indeed' (*hinnêh*) calls attention to the emphatic statement that follows,[3] while 'slumber' and 'sleep'

---

[3] An excellent discussion on the use of *hinnêh* can be found in T. O. Lambdin, *Introduction to Biblical Hebrew*, pp. 169-170. For other passages where this usage occurs, see the listing in *DCH*, II, p. 574.

seem to be synonyms. How different the true God was from Baal! Elijah on Carmel could taunt Baal's prophets that he was asleep (1 Kings 18:27).

3. The Psalmist's Protection (*vv. 5-6*)

The LORD watches over you – the LORD is your shade at your right hand; the sun will not harm you by day, nor the moon by night (*vv. 5-6*). The LORD was not just the keeper of all Israel, but in speech to a single speaker he could be spoken of as 'your keeper'. Calling him 'shade' is probably a shortened form of the expression 'the shadow of your wings' (Pss. 17:8; 36:7; 57:1; 63:7; Isa. 25:4; 51:16). The 'right hand' suggests the position of the defender or protector (Pss. 73:23; 77:10; 110:5), and the psalmist knows that his God is as near to him as that. By day and by night he would be kept safe from any harm, 'sun' and 'moon' expressing the totality of daily life. Sunstroke was familiar in the Middle East, while the Greek and Latin words for insanity come from the word for the moon, and from the latter we have borrowed our English word 'lunatic'.[4]

4. The Psalmist's Preservation (*vv. 7-8*)

The LORD will keep you from all harm – he will watch over your life; the LORD will watch over your coming and going both now and forevermore. The song closes by picturing Jehovah as an eternal keeper. In the midst of a sinful and dangerous world he is able to keep us from falling (Jude 24). God will guard amidst all the varied experiences of life ('your coming and going'), and ultimately he will bring his called ones to glory (Rom. 8:30). As present day pilgrims we rejoice that Israel's keeper and ours is still the living and true God. He continues to fulfil this role towards his people. May our prayer then be:

---

[4] The bad effects attributed to the moon were possibly connected with the idea in the Near East that the sun and moon had divine powers. Sicknesses caused by sleeping out under the moon were probably not from the moon's light, but rather from the mists that came on a clear night after a hot day.

Through each perplexing path of life
Our wand'ring footsteps guide;
Give us each day our daily bread,
And raiment fit provide.

O spread thy cov'ring wings around,
Till all our wand'rings cease,
And at our Father's lov'd abode
Our souls arrive in peace.
(Philip Doddridge 1701-1751)

Psalm 122

A song of ascents. Of David.

Three of the pilgrim psalms are ascribed to David, this one and Psalms 124 and 131. David's connection with Jerusalem – his capture of it, his building programme, and bringing the ark of the covenant there – make the expressions here all the more relevant if David is the author of this song. Expressions used in the psalm point to the Davidic period. These include the reference to the Davidic family as 'David's house' (v. 5), for David established a house in place of Saul's house (2 Sam. 3:1) and God promised its perpetuity (2 Sam. 7:16). In his final words David referred to the relationship of his house and God, who had made an everlasting covenant with him (2 Sam. 23:5). The use of the name 'Israel' in verse 4 for the whole people points to a time before the division of the kingdom, as does mention of the pilgrimage of all the tribes to Jerusalem (v. 3).

Later generations could take up the refrain and use it of their joyful arrival in Jerusalem and express their prayer for her prosperity. Moreover, throughout church history this psalm has been sung as believers sensed rightly that 'Zion' and 'Jerusalem' stand in the Bible not just for the whole of Israel, but for the entire people of God. They can rejoice that, through grace, they are members of Zion's city, and look forward with expectancy to the ultimate city of God, the New Jerusalem.

1. Joy in Jerusalem (*vv. 1-2*)

I rejoiced with those who said to me, 'Let us go to the house of the LORD.' Our feet are standing in your gates, O Jerusalem

(*vv. 1-2*). The first two verses are introductory, and set the scene for the development of the theme in the two following stanzas. David recalls his heartfelt joy when neighbours gave the invitation – 'Come to God's house!' Whenever they said this he responded gladly. These two characteristics displayed here, love for worship of God and for the fellowship of his people, marked out God's people in both old covenant and new covenant times (Heb. 10:25), and should do so still. The second verse suggests that the pilgrims have already arrived in Jerusalem. The trials of the journey are over, and all is joy at their arrival within the gates they longed to see.[1] The name 'Jerusalem' means foundation of peace (see the play of words later in the psalm in v. 6).

2. Esteem for Jerusalem (*vv. 3-5*)

Jerusalem is built like a city that is closely compacted together. That is where the tribes go up, the tribes of the LORD, to praise the name of the LORD according to the statute given to Israel (*vv. 3-4*). For those coming from distant parts of Israel, the sight of Jerusalem must have been overwhelming. It was not just a conglomeration of buildings, but a compact, well-ordered city – the national capital.[2] Also, it was a symbol of the unity of the nation, as all the tribes of the LORD went up there on the special festive occasions to the place he had chosen as a dwelling for his name (Deut. 16:1-17).[3] The main purpose was to praise the name of the LORD, for the great feasts

---

[1] The Hebrew construction of the first clause in verse 2 consists of a participle of the verb 'stand', together with the verb 'to be', with the subject 'our feet': *ʿomᵉdot hâyû raglênû*. This type of combination often indicates 'the state in which a person (or thing) is found … The reference is usually to the past. . . .' Hence, 'our feet have been standing'. *DIHG~S*, p. 138.

[2] The Hebrew text has *she* as the relative (joined to the following word) both here and in the next verse. This is in place of the usual *ʾᵃsher*. However, this is not an indication of late date for the composition of this psalm as *she* occurs in early poetry. Cf. *DIHG~S*, p. 12, where it is stated that *she* is not restricted to late passages, with the older statement in *BDB*, p. 979, that in usage *she* is 'limited to late Heb., and passages with N. Palest. colouring'. The use of this particle several times in the Songs of Ascent (122:3, 4; 123:2; 124:1, 2, 6; 129:6, 7; 133:2, 3) forms a distinctive linguistic feature.

[3] I have discussed this passage and its implications in my commentary, *Deuteronomy*, pp. 147-48.

like Passover, the Feast of Weeks, and the Feast of Tabernacles, were meant to be times of rejoicing in the presence of the LORD.

There the thrones for judgment stand, the thrones of the house of David (*v. 5*). Jerusalem was also the centre of civic life, to which people came to have decisions made by the king whenever they had complaints. The system did not always work perfectly, for we know how Absalom, David's son, took advantage of it in order to gain a following for himself (2 Sam. 15:1-6).

3. Concern for Jerusalem (*vv. 6-9*)

Pray for the peace of Jerusalem: 'May those who love you be secure. May there be peace within your walls and security within your citadels' (*vv. 6-7*). The call to prayer involves a play on the name Jerusalem. 'Jerusalem' has in it a form of the Hebrew word 'Shalom', which means 'peace'. The word-play (and also the play on the same sounds in Hebrew) can be brought out approximately by translating, 'Ask for the shalom of *Yerushâláyim*' ('Ask for the peace of the foundation of peace').[4] The psalmist also wants the blessing of security for all the inhabitants of Jerusalem. From the time of David's capture of Jerusalem (2 Sam. 5:6-10), it occupied a central place in the thinking of the people of Israel. Thus in the exile Daniel pleads with God: 'Turn away your anger and your wrath from Jerusalem, *your city, your holy hill*' (Dan. 9:16).

For the sake of my brothers and friends, I will say, 'Peace be within you.' For the sake of the house of the LORD our God, I will seek your prosperity (*vv. 8-9*). Not only is the nation as a whole in view, but also the psalmist's close friends as well. He realises that blessing for them depends on the prosperity of Jerusalem. In particular the house of God was so important that he longs for the continued prosperity of the city itself. The deep feelings of the people towards the temple were shown when they lament over its destruction (Ps. 74:3-8; Isa. 64:11; Lam. 2:6-7).

---

[4] The Hebrew has *sha'alû shelôm yerûshâlâyim*.

Psalm 123

A song of ascents.

This short psalm has many similarities with Psalm 120. Both start with reference to the source of help and both speak of the reproach of ungodly neighbours. Whereas Psalm 120 focuses on God's ability to rescue, this one concentrates on his grace. The psalmist looks beyond earthly things to the heavenly throne and makes his appeal for mercy. It is one of the characteristics of the Songs of Ascent that meditation on God's ways and works is prominent, while petition occupies a lesser place. However, there is no mistaking the urgency of the repeated cry of verse 3.

The psalm commences in the singular ('*I* lift *my* eyes', v. 1), but immediately switches to the plural and maintains it throughout ('*our* eyes ... *our* God ... have mercy on *us* ... *we* have endured much contempt ... *we* have endured much ridicule'). The first verse is probably the personal expression of the leader of the worship, but he proceeds then to speak on behalf of the whole worshipping community.

1. Our Attitude to God in Prayer (*v. 1*)

I lift up my eyes to you, to you whose throne is in heaven (*v. 1*). The attitude of the psalmist is one of reverence for God. He comes in prayer to lift his eyes to the LORD, as real believers always do (Ps. 25:15). The difference between himself and his God is emphasised by recognising that he is enthroned in the heavens as the all-powerful creator of all things. The assertion that God's throne is in the heaven has already been made in Psalms 9:4, 103:19 and 113:5.[1] Our Lord Jesus taught his disciples to address God as 'Father', but to also say, 'who is in heaven' (Matt. 6:9). As we come to God we must say with John Newton (1725-1807):

> Approach my soul the mercy seat,
> Where Jesus answers prayer,
> There humbly fall before his feet,
> For none can perish there.

2. Our Expectancy (*v.* 2)

As the eyes of slaves look to the hand of their master, as the eyes of a maid look to the hand of her mistress, so our eyes look to the LORD our God, till he shows us his mercy (*v.* 2). In the Eastern countries servants are often directed by hand signals. Hence they have to be very attentive to their master's wishes. This has been the common interpretation of this verse, but in comparison with other passages and as suggested by the context, the idea is rather of expectantly waiting for food (cf. Pss. 104:27-28; 145:15-16).[2] Similarly the attitude of the believing individual and community has to be one of expectancy towards the LORD. God, who will not despise the cry of the afflicted (Ps. 102:17), will answer in grace to his children. The promise is that God will supply all the needs of his children 'according to his glorious riches in Christ Jesus (Phil. 4:19)'.

3. Our Need (*vv.* 3-4)

Have mercy on us, O LORD, have mercy on us, for we have endured much contempt. We have endured much ridicule from the proud, much contempt from the arrogant (*vv.* 3-4). The climax of the psalm is this repeated call for mercy, as in

---

[1] The form of the Hebrew word translated 'whose throne' (*hayyoshᵉvî*, lit. 'who sits') is unusual. The final vowel (-*î*) is probably an old genitive ending, while the definite article (*ha*-) serves as a relative pronoun. Cf. M. Dahood, *Psalms III: 101-150*, pp. 208-09.

[2] Among the older commentators this view was espoused by A. F. Kirkpatrick, *The Book of Psalms*, p. 743, and among the modern ones by L. C. Allen, *Psalms 101-150*, pp. 160-61.

Psalm 57:1. The assurance that God's mercy would indeed come (see v. 1) is now turned into impassioned prayer. The psalmist is living in an hostile environment. He has been exposed to ridicule from the proud and the arrogant, whose bitter words must have wounded him so deeply. From men the psalmist cannot expect mercy, so he turns to his God who alone could show true mercy. Out of his deep need he cries to him.

Psalm 124

A song of ascents. Of David.

Though the title in many Hebrew manuscripts attributes the psalm to David, yet it is lacking in some of them and also in the earliest manuscripts of the LXX. If it is David's, it probably comes from an early period in his reign, and it reflects the severe pressure put on his kingdom by the Philistines. At Baal Perazim he said, 'The Lord has broken out against my enemies before me' (2 Sam. 5:20). However, the psalm may well be from after the exile as the people rejoice in God's preservation of them. This would explain why the ideas are expressed in communal terms: 'Israel', 'against *us*', 'did not give *us*', '*we* have escaped', '*our* help'.

The lack of specific allusions has made this psalm applicable in many different situations. Because it does not give the details that led to this thanksgiving song it is appropriate for use in a variety of settings. Throughout the centuries Christians have, therefore, taken over this triumphant song of praise when God's arm has been stretched out to deliver them.

1. The Affirmation of the Lord's Help (vv. 1-2)

If the Lord had not been on our side – let Israel say – if the Lord had not been on our side when men attacked us *(vv. 1-2)*. The double use of 'if' (*lûlê*) is only hypothetical, for there is no doubt at all that their covenant God has been with them. Probably the better translation would be 'except that', or, 'unless'.[1] The call is for Israel to make a declaration concerning God's deliverance, but the words to be used are

[1] So *DCH*, IV, p. 530.

omitted in this verse. It is possible that verse 8 provides them: 'Let Israel say ... Our help is in the name of the LORD, the Maker of heaven and earth'. The fact that by God's grace they were rescued from the brink of ruin, now calls for praise from their hearts and lips.

2. Illustrations (*vv. 3-5*)

When their anger flared against us, they would have swallowed us alive; the flood would have engulfed us, the torrent would have swept over us, the raging waters would have swept us away (*vv. 3-5*). In order to make much more graphic the sense of deliverance, the psalmist uses two illustrations. The first one (v. 3) deals with the way in which their enemies had sought the complete destruction of the nation. The extreme peril in which the nation was placed is made even more vivid by suggesting that the monster attacking would only need one bite to take them. The second illustration (vv. 4-5) relates to sudden floods that are a familiar feature of life in the Near East. A dry wadi can become a raging stream within minutes.[2] The picture of destruction caused by a sudden flood is used to depict the sudden attacks made on Israel by arrogant enemies (cf. Isa. 8:5-8 of the impending Assyrian invasion). Both illustrations point to attacks that were intended to bring total destruction on the nation.

3. Escape Provided (*vv. 6-7*)

The failure of such sudden and severe attacks is the cause for a song of praise and thankfulness. **Praise be to the LORD, who has not let us be torn by their teeth** (*v. 6*). The right response to the experience through which they had passed is, 'Praise (or 'Blessed', *bârûch*) be to the LORD.' This expression often occurs in the psalms when there is remembrance of what God has done for his people (cf. Pss. 28:6; 31:21; 66:20; 144:1). The terrifying monster had not devoured them, because God had not given them over as prey!

[2] The best illustration from modern times is the raging torrent (3 metres deep) that swept into the canyon (1.5 km long) leading into the ancient city of Petra in Jordan in 1963. Twenty-two pilgrims on their way to view it were drowned.

We have escaped like a bird out of the fowler's snare; the snare has been broken, and we have escaped (*v. 7*). The metaphor is changed, as Israel is compared to a bird escaping out of a trap. The climax is reached in the words, 'the snare has been broken'. God had destroyed the trap, no less terrifying than gaping jaws, set for his people (likened to a defenceless little bird). They were able to escape, the double use of the verb 'escape' (*mâlat*) stressing how real their deliverance was. These words have been applicable in many situations in the course of church history, when God's grace and power have been shown to his people facing severe opposition and persecution.

4. A Profession of Trust (*v. 8*)

Our help is in the name of the LORD, the Maker of heaven and earth (*v. 8*). As suggested earlier, this may be the refrain that Israel is called on to sing (see v. 1). While the intervening verses have been speaking about the past (vv. 2-7), now sight is set on the future and a profession of confidence in the covenant God of Israel is made. God had revealed his 'name' or 'character', and this includes his power that is evident in his work as creator. The Maker of heaven and earth has the ability and power to be the constant helper of his people. Our confidence in our own strength or achievement must be replaced by boasting in the name of our God (Ps. 20:7). Past present, future – he remains the helper, and into the hands of a faithful creator we must entrust our souls (1 Pet. 4:19). It is not surprising that the Reformed churches, among others, have so often used the words of this verse as the opening confession in their worship services.

Psalm 125

A song of ascents.

The pilgrims now meditate on Jerusalem's position – surrounded by mountains – and draw a lesson of faith. As the psalm is probably from the post-exilic period, this picture of Zion/Jerusalem may not only present the view of it obtained by pilgrims, but also may be the one that was seen by the returning exiles. The pilgrims contrast the ways of the righteous and those of the wicked. The same contrast is made in prophetical passages such as Isaiah 3:10-11, and is repeated in the New Testament by the Lord Jesus himself (see Matt. 7:13-14 and 25:31-46). The reference to 'peace' (*shâlôm*) in the final verse maintains a focus that began back in Psalm 120:7. It was emphasised in Psalm 122 by the frequent use of 'Jerusalem' or *shâlôm* (vv. 2, 3, 6, 7, 8), and now concludes this song with a petition (v. 5) that appears to be a concise form of the priestly benediction (Num. 6:26).

1. The Song of Confidence (*vv. 1-2*)

The psalm opens with an assertion regarding the character of God's people. **Those who trust in the Lord are like Mount Zion, which cannot be shaken but endures forever** (*v. 1*). Faith is one of the major themes of the psalms, and here we have the description of the abiding characteristic of God's people. They are not only saved by faith, but they should live by faith! This trust marks out the individual believer, but it should also characterise the church as a whole. The Lord's believing saints are compared to Mount Zion, with the point of comparison being its immovability.

As the mountains surround Jerusalem, so the LORD surrounds his people, both now and for evermore (*v. 2*). Now the psalmist speaks of the natural fortification that Jerusalem has, and he makes this an illustration of the protection that the LORD affords his people. Just as the mountains encircle Jerusalem, so the LORD encircles his people for all times. The reference to 'his people' clearly applies to their standing as the covenantal people of God. Just as Zion will endure, so will the people of God because he holds them safe forever (cf. the teaching of Jesus [John 10:28]; and of Paul [Phil. 1:6]).

2. The Promise (*v. 3*)

The sceptre of the wicked will not remain over the land allotted to the righteous, for then the righteous might use their hands to do evil (*v. 3*). This is a difficult verse, though the general import of it is clear. The sceptre refers to the rule that conquerors exercise over lands that they occupy. This may refer to the exile, when God allowed other peoples temporarily to take over Judean territory. However, God had set a limit to their rule, and the foreign sceptre would not be permitted to stay indefinitely over it. As a fact of history, the post-exilic period had little of the glory of the Davidic/Solomonic empire. The returnees were few in number compared with those who had become exiles, and the territory resumed was only a small fraction of the land initially occupied. The second part of the verse could mean that if the rule of the wicked were to continue for any great length of time, then the righteous might begin to envy them and turn their own hands to evil.

3. The Prayer (*v. 4*)

Following a promise, now comes a prayer. **Do good, O LORD, to those who are good, to those who are upright in heart.** God often gives or reaffirms a promise which then prompts his people to pray. The word 'good' has covenantal overtones, for it is used of the things which were promised under God's covenant (see on Ps. 23:6; and also, for example, 1 Sam. 25:30 and 2 Sam. 7:28). The psalmist pleads for covenanted mercies to God's people who are also described as the upright in heart.

This is a prophetic declaration that God only truly blesses those who have this type of character.

4. The Warning (*v. 5*)
The psalmist now brings in the other side of the two ways. **But to those who turn to crooked ways the LORD will banish with the evildoers** (*v. 5a*). Those who set themselves on things which are opposed to God will ultimately find that they themselves are led away by God (see our Lord's words in Matt. 25:31-46). Evildoers will not dominate for ever, because a day is coming when God's power over them will prevail (cf. Ps. 37:13: 'his day [i.e. the wicked man's day] is coming').

The final declaration concerns the Israel of God. **Peace be upon Israel** (*v. 5b*). What a blessing it is to belong to Israel, especially when Israel enjoys the blessing of God! For the Hebrew people 'peace' (*shâlôm*) denoted prosperity and health, the enjoyment of the richest of God's blessing (cf. the similar prayer in Gal. 6:16). The Aaronic benediction (Num. 6:24-26) was often on the minds of devout Israelites, and this is probably a condensed version of it (cf. the identical phrase in Ps. 128:6).

Psalm 126

A song of ascents.

There can be no doubt that the experience in exile was an extremely bitter one for the Jewish people (cf. Ps. 137). But restoration to home brought intense joy. While the people could not sing in Babylon (Ps. 137:1-6), when they were brought back to Judah they sang 'songs of joy' (v. 2). This psalm expresses something of the wonder of what God had done for his people. There are many similarities between this psalm and Psalm 85, and the prophecy of Joel. As in Psalm 85 this song has the same two aspects in view – past restoration and an appeal for further deliverance. It was included among 'the songs of ascent' because Jerusalem/Zion is the focus.[1]

1. The Joy of Restoration to Zion (*vv. 1-2a*)

When the LORD brought back the captives to Zion, we were like men who dreamed. Our mouths were filled with laughter, our tongues with songs of joy (*vv. 1-2a*). Following the decree of Cyrus in 537 BC, some of the exiles in Babylon returned to Palestine. The foundation of the second temple was laid with intermingling of weeping and joy (Ezra 3:13). God had raised up Cyrus for this very purpose (see Isa. 44:24–45:7), and through him brought about the return. Many modern English versions take the opening expression to be a more general one implying restoration of fortunes (cf. RSV, NRSV ESV, NIV margin), rather than to the return from exile. However, there are good

[1] In explaining the meaning of this psalm, I am drawing upon aspects of my discussion in 'The Setting and Interpretation of Psalm 126', *RTR* 44 (1985), pp. 74-80.

reasons to retain 'brought back',[2] but the phrase must be 'the captives of Zion' (*shîvat tsiyyôn*). The text does not say '*to* Zion'. No preposition comes before 'Zion', so the phrase 'captives of Zion' must be the object. The closest parallels to this are found in Isaiah 49-52 where the exiles in Babylon are referred to as 'Zion' (Isa. 49:14; 51:3) or 'the captive daughter of Zion' (Isa. 52:2). The reference to dreaming may describe the amazement of the people at what had happened, or, more probably, to their condition while still in Babylon. They dreamed of a return, stimulated by earlier prophecies regarding such a prospect, and by those of their fellow exile, Ezekiel (Ezek. 36:24; 37:1-14). The effect was that the sorrow and gloom of exile were replaced by laughter and song. This is in agreement with prophetic descriptions of how the restoration would take place (Isa. 49:8-13; 52:8-10).

2. Announcement to the Nations (*vv. 2b-3*)

Then it was said among the nations, 'The LORD has done great things for them.' The LORD has done great things for us, and we are filled with joy (*vv. 2b-3*). In addition to what happened to Israel, the return also had an effect on the surrounding nations. Isaiah had spoken of God's people being his witnesses (Isa. 43:10-13; 44:8). The nations were now proclaiming what had happened to Israel. The explanation was: 'The LORD has dealt magnificently with them'.[3] This same profession was made by those returning, who from personal experience testified to the redeeming power of God. The manifestation of God's saving power in the Exodus from Egypt and the return from exile were preparatory of a far greater display in the coming and work of Jesus.

3. The Prayer (*v. 4*)

Restore our fortunes, O LORD, like streams in the Negev (*v. 4*). There seems to be a gap in time between the initial restoration and the situation in which the psalm is written.

---

[2] Ibid., pp. 75-76.

[3] The expression in Hebrew is *higdîl yhwh laʿᵃsot,* which only occurs here and in Joel 2:20, 21.

This could be the period following the restoration in 536 BC up to the completion of the temple in 516 BC, or the longer period before the reforms of Ezra and Nehemiah in the following century (458 BC/444 BC).[4] The psalmist asks for the fuller restoration to take place for captive Israel, so that there will be a further ingathering of those still scattered in exile. The second half of the verse contains a reference to a well-known phenomenon – streams in the Negev (the southern part of Israel). This reference draws attention to the suddenness with which the further return could take place, and the blessing that would follow – just like the wilderness blossoming after refreshing rains (cf. Isa. 35:1).

4. The Assurance (*vv. 5-6*)

Those who sow in tears will reap with songs of joy. He who goes out weeping, carrying seed to sow, will return with songs of joy, carrying sheaves with him (*vv. 5-6*). The psalmist is confident of the outcome, and he speaks of the time of exile and restoration as sowing and harvest. He looks back on former tears that have been replaced by joy. These words have the ring of a proverbial saying about them, not dissimilar to Jesus' words in John 4:36-38, which may be an echo of this psalm. The period of sorrowful sowing is over. What is anticipated now is the joy of harvest. As the psalm began, so it ends with the note of joy.

---

[4] I discuss this more fully in 'The Setting and Interpretation of Psalm 126', pp. 77-79.

Psalm 127

A song of ascents. Of Solomon.

From the opening words of this psalm in Latin, the city of Edinburgh, Scotland, has derived its motto (*Nisi Dominus frustra,* 'without the Lord it is in vain'). That use of part of the psalm picks up its main point. No human activity or work for the kingdom of God will be fruitful, unless God blesses with his presence and help. In German, a rhyming couplet expresses this truth: *An Gottes Segen ist alles gelegen,* 'Everything depends on God's blessing.' The three main activities mentioned in the psalm are building, security, and raising a family. The ascription to Solomon is notable, for he failed in the very things which the psalm emphasises. Part of his building programme was unwise (1 Kings 9:10, 15-19), his marriages were a denial of God's covenant with Israel (1 Kings 11:1-6), and his kingdom ended in division (1 Kings 11:4-13).

1. Building without the Lord (*vv. 1-2*)

Unless the Lord builds the house, its builders labour in vain. Unless the Lord watches over the city, the watchmen stand guard in vain (*v. 1*). The first two activities with which the phrase 'in vain' is used are building a house and guarding a town.[1] Both were common activities requiring considerable effort, often done with self-confidence, but without the Lord's help that work is pointless. A pun exists, in that the Hebrew word 'builders' (*bônîm*) is very similar to the word 'sons' (*bânîm*) in verse 3.

[1] Some have thought that 'house' here is a reference to the temple, but as the context is concerned with daily life in Israel, it has to be understood of any family home.

In vain you rise early and stay up late, toiling for food to eat – for he grants sleep to those he loves (*v.* 2). The third illustration is that of a 'workaholic'. He gets up early and goes to bed late. This idea is conveyed in concise phrases; 'hasting to get up, retarding to sit [down]'. After all that time and effort he knows sorrow, not joy. 'Toiling for food' involves the word *ʿatsâvîm*, 'toils', sorrows', which suggests a connection with the curse in Genesis 3:16-17 where the word occurs twice and a related noun once: 'I will greatly increase your *pains* in childbearing; with *pain* you will give birth to children ... Through *painful toil* you will eat of it all the days of your life.' The last clause, 'for he grants sleep to those he loves', is awkward, since it seems to imply that while the 'workaholic' is labouring hard, the godly believers are not working but are asleep. This is contradicted by other parts of the Bible (Prov. 6:9-11; 31:27). Better is the suggestion that what is being expressed is that while many look to gain from their own hard labours, believers can rest secure in the knowledge that as God gives them sleep he is working out his blessings on them.[2]

2. Building a Family (*vv.* 3-5)

The focus now changes to another sort of house. This change is marked out in the Hebrew text by the use of a word (*hinnêh*) at the start of the verse, which arrests attention: 'Take notice!'[3] **Sons are a heritage from the LORD, children a reward from him** (*v.* 3). The building of a family is ultimately the gift of the LORD himself, as those who adopt children know better than most. God is the creator and sustainer of life, and the coming of children is to be seen as something he bestows upon parents.[4]

---

[2] Another difficulty about verse 2 is that the word for 'sleep' (*shênâʾ*) is not the normal word, but has a final *alef* in place of *he*. The usual form is *shênâh*. For further discussion, see J. A. Emerton, 'The Meaning of *senaʾ* in Psalm 127:2', *VT* 24 (1974), pp. 15-31.

[3] NIV does not translate this word but it serves an important function and should appear in English translations. Cf. ESV 'behold'. The RSV preserved the 'lo' that appeared in the AV, while the NRSV inserts 'indeed'.

[4] NIV 'children' is a translation of the Hebrew *p^erî habbéten*, 'the fruit of the womb'.

Like arrows in the hands of a warrior are sons born in one's youth. Blessed is the man whose quiver is full of them. They will not be put to shame when they contend with their enemies in the gate (*vv.* 4-5). Children bring responsibilities upon the parents, but in turn they become active in the life of the family. Their gifts and abilities serve the needs of the whole family. The illustration here is from Near Eastern society, with the thought of the children providing protection in time of trouble and old age. A full quiver would help to defend the family when it was under attack (for the use of 'blessed', *'ash^{e}rê,* see comment on Ps. 1:1).

Psalm 128

A song of ascents.

This psalm is similar to the previous one in that it is a wisdom psalm, setting out in particular the blessings of the family. Brief reference to civic life also comes in verse 5. The way in which it commences ('Blessed are ...') is the same as Psalm 1 (see comment on Ps. 1:1 for this introductory formula). The family is the basic unit of society, and the emphasis on hearth and home in passages such as this displays the biblical concept that family units are the building blocks of community life. The ending ('Peace be upon Israel', v. 6b) may have been composed for use by a priest as a blessing on families gathered in Jerusalem for the annual festivals. The repetition of mention of fearing God (vv. 1 and 4) shows that the focus is on godly living and divine blessing.

1. The Blessing of Family Life (*vv. 1-4*)

Blessed are all who fear the Lord, who walk in his ways. You will eat the fruit of your labour; blessings and prosperity will be yours (*vv. 1-2*). The godly person can be described in various ways. Here two qualities are brought to the fore – fear of the Lord,[1] and walking in his ways. Where true reverence towards the Lord exists, there will also be a life of obedient attention to his ways. Those who walk according to the law of the Lord are indeed blessed (Ps. 119:1). Part of that blessing is receiving the enjoyment of eating the fruits of their labour. The word 'blessings' (lit. 'your blessings', *ʾashᵉrekâ*) may be a deliberate echo of Deuteronomy 33:29: 'Blessed are you,

[1] For explanation of the expression 'the fear of the Lord', see comments on Psalm 15:4.

O Israel! (*'ash^ereka yisrâ'êl*) Who is like you, a people saved by the LORD?' It is also significant that the promise of eating their own crops is the very opposite of what was threatened to disobedient Israel (Lev. 26:16; Deut. 28:33). Instead of a curse, obedient Israel receives blessing.

Your wife will be like a fruitful vine within your house; your sons will be like olive shoots around your table. Thus is the man blessed who fears the LORD (*vv. 3-4*). Another aspect of the blessing is a happy home life. Wife and children are also gifts of God. As compared with the husband who was mainly involved with food production, the wife was engaged in domestic duties.[2] The use of vine and olive tree as illustrations is probably because both were so central to daily life in Israel, and both were well known for the fact that they live for a long time. Happy and continuing family life is something that God bestows. The psalmist returns to his opening thought to conclude the picture, drawing attention again in so doing to the inevitable connection between blessing and fearing the LORD. The NIV omits any translation of the Hebrew word *hinnêh* at the beginning of verse 4 (see comment on Ps. 127:3), but it is needed to draw attention to the following statement: 'Take notice, this is how a man is blessed …'

2. The Benediction (*vv. 5-6*)

May the LORD bless you from Zion all the days of your life; may you see the prosperity of Jerusalem, and may you live to see your children's children. Peace be upon Israel (*vv. 5-6*). These words appear to be a benediction pronounced on a God-fearing worshipper in Jerusalem. He has come on pilgrimage, and now the priest prays for the LORD's blessings to flow to him from Zion. Once the ark of the covenant was brought there, it was thereafter spoken of as the place of blessing

---

[2] The Hebrew text simply says that the wife is 'in the sides of your house' (*beyark^etê vêtekâ*). This expression is used elsewhere of the inner parts of some area, such as the depths of a cave (1 Sam. 24:3), or a ship (Jon. 1:5). It is probably no different in meaning from 'in the house', and should not be pressed to suggest the secluded aspect of a wife's life.

(Pss. 3:4; 20:2).[3] An earlier Song of Ascents has spoken of the peace and prosperity of Jerusalem (Ps. 122:6-9). Part of the joy of the devout Israelite was seeing the continuing prosperity of Jerusalem, and also of living long in the promised land. The prayer already used at the end of Psalm 125 is again employed to conclude this psalm. God's blessing extended from individuals to families, and then to the whole nation of Israel. We should not think these repetitions trite, but indicative of confidence in basic aspects of the faith, both Hebrew and Christian.

---

[3] The devotion towards Jerusalem during the exilic period is set out graphically in Psalm 137:1-9, and in Daniel's prayer concerning the city of Jerusalem and the sanctuary (Dan. 9: 17-19).

Psalm 129

A song of ascents.

The tone of this psalm marks it off from the ones that immediately precede (Pss. 124-128). While they speak of the many blessings that God has given to Israel, this psalm asks for the withholding of blessing. No precise setting is given for it, but the reference to deliverance in verse 4 suggests that it comes from after the return from exile in Babylon. There are strong resemblances between this psalm and Psalm 124, not least in the repetition that occurs in the first two verses of each, and the use of the phrase 'Let Israel now say'. It is a song of confidence, in which Israel as a nation sings of release from oppression, and in which she prays for judgment on her enemies.

1. Freedom from Oppression (*vv. 1-4*)

They have greatly oppressed me from my youth – let Israel say – they have greatly oppressed me from my youth, but they have not gained the victory over me (*vv. 1-2*). Israel is asked to think back over her past history, even to her 'youth' in Egypt. Just as she was in slavery then, so she endured many years of domination by enemies during the course of her 'adult' years. The opening statement reinforces how conscious Israel was of long years of oppression. However, it is a victory song that Israel is to sing, because these enemies have not achieved their goals. She is still alive and free![1]

[1] The NIV 'they have not gained the victory' is a translation of *lo' yâkelû*. Normally the verb *yâkol* means 'to be able', but in this and other instances it is best translated 'prevail [against]', 'overcome'. See *DCH*, IV, pp. 212-13.

Ploughmen have ploughed my back and made their furrows long. But the LORD is righteous; he has cut me free from the cords of the wicked (*vv. 3-4*). While harsh treatment of prisoners of war, including drawing farming implements over their backs, may have taken place (cf. Amos 1:3), yet the expression in verse 3 is best interpreted figuratively. The imagery of farming is used to illustrate both the sufferings of Israel and her eventual release from captivity. The 'ploughmen' are the soldiers who have attacked her, and her 'back', scarred with long furrows, is the whole period of history during which she was at the mercy of her attackers. Freedom has come because the LORD has cut her free from her cords, just as when a yoke is taken off the neck of an animal. God acts in accordance with both his nature and his promises and vindicates his people. The last great yoke has been taken away, and a restored Israel rejoices in God's deliverance.

2. Judgment on the Oppressors (*vv. 5-8*)

May all who hate Zion be turned back in shame (*v. 5*). It is characteristic of the enemies that they hate everything that Zion represents – God's presence, the covenant blessings, the believing community. The prayer is that they will come to a position where their evil plans are thwarted and they are disgraced in the eyes of others. Just as Israel knew the shame of exile, so will the enemies know confusion and disillusionment.

May they be like grass on the roof, which withers before it can grow; with it the reaper cannot fill his hands, nor the one who gathers fill his arms (*vv. 6-7*). The farming analogy is maintained. Grass may grow on a roof, but because of lack of soil it soon withers.[2] No one can reap a harvest from crops

[2] The clause 'which withers before it can grow up' has two difficulties. The relative *she* introduces it, but the following word (*qadmat*) appears in a different usage than normal. It seems to be a construct form of *qadmâh*, but instead of meaning 'origin' or 'former condition' it is here used as a conjunction, 'before'. Possibly it is a borrowing from Aramaic, which does have a preposition *qadmat*. The other difficulty is the verb 'grow up' (*shâlaf*) which normally means 'draw out'. *BDB*, p. 1025 tentatively suggests an extension of this idea to 'shoot up', and this still remains the best suggestion, as this is what the context demands. A play on words exists between 'withers' (*yâvêsh*) and 'be ashamed' (*yêvoshû*) in the previous verse.

self-grown in such a place. The psalmist wants to see the lives of Zion's enemies as unproductive, and their end as certain.

May those who pass by not say, 'The blessing of the LORD be upon you; we bless you in the name of the LORD' *(v. 8)*. There cannot be simultaneous blessing and cursing. No one should invoke God's blessing on those whose hearts are so opposed to him and his kingdom. While they continue to hate Zion (see v. 5), the only course of action is to withhold pronouncing any blessing on them. This is not a case of reciprocal blessings (cf. Ruth 2:4), for the whole statement is put into the mouths of those who are passing by.

Psalm 130

A song of ascents.

This is a song from the depths of despair, and it forms the sixth of the penitential psalms (Pss. 6, 32, 38, 51, 102, 130, 143). In the history of the Christian church it has often been known by its opening words in Latin, *De profundis*, 'out of the depths'. Martin Luther classified it as Pauline in character, and composed an evangelical hymn based on it (*Aus tiefer Not schrei ich zu dir*, 'From deepest woes I cry to you'). It is far more than just a cry for help, for it also contains the assurance of the abundant mercy of God that is able to blot out our sins and iniquities. The closest parallels to the wording of this psalm are found in Psalm 86.[1] The background situation was very similar for both psalms, though the closing verse of Psalm 130 goes beyond the thought of Psalm 86.

The date of this psalm is most probably post-exilic as it contains expressions that come from that period. In verse 2 the appeal to God is in a form only appearing elsewhere in 2 Chronicles 6:40; 'Let your ears be attentive to ...': *tihyenâh ʾoznekâ qashshuwôt l*ᵉ). While the root from which 'attentive' comes (*q-sh-v*) is fairly common, yet this adjective (*qashshuv*) and another similar one (*qashshâv*, Neh. 1:6, 11) are clearly words from late Hebrew. Similarly the word 'forgiveness' (*s*ᵉ*lîchâh)* in verse 3 only occurs here and in Daniel 9:9 and Nehemiah 9:17. All three of these occurrences come in passages in which there is confession of sin, but with it the assurance of God's pardoning mercy.

---

[1] For a note setting out the similarities in the Hebrew text of Psalms 86 and 130, see F. Delitzsch, *Commentary on the Psalms*, II, p. 302.

1. The Psalmist's Condition (*vv. 1-2*)

Out of the depths I cry to you, O LORD; O Lord, hear my voice. Let your ears be attentive to my cry for mercy (*vv. 1-2*). The opening words set the tone for the whole psalm. The expression 'out of the depths' is not a common one in the Psalms. When it does occur it denotes a situation of deep distress (cf. Ps. 69:2, 14), and in these and the two other passages in which it is used (Isa. 51:10; Ezek. 27:34) it is clear that it refers to depths of the sea. It is paralleled in English by the expression 'to be in deep waters'. When in a situation of utter calamity, and conscious of the gulf between himself and God that his sin has caused, the psalmist appeals to the LORD for mercy. The urgency of his situation is shown by the repetition of his requests using a variety of expressions (*I cry ... hear my voice ... Let your ears ...*).

2. Assurance of Forgiveness (*vv. 3-4*)

If you, O LORD, kept a record of sins, O Lord, who could stand? But with you there is forgiveness; therefore you are feared (*vv. 3-4*). The impossibility of a sinner such as himself standing his ground in the presence of a holy God causes the psalmist to ask the question in verse 3. The verb 'keep' (*shâmar*) has here the more specialised sense of 'regard' or 'give heed to' iniquities, and so the NIV translation captures the meaning well. The psalmist knows that none are righteous before God (Ps. 143:2), and that includes himself. God forgives and remembers sin no more for his own name's sake (Isa. 43:25), and forgiven sinners are aware of the reverence due to him for his grace and mercy. Receiving mercy increases our sense of awe and reverence in God's holy presence.

3. Patient Waiting (*vv. 5-6*)

I wait for the LORD, my soul waits, and in his word I put my hope (*v. 5*). This is a declaration of certain trust in the LORD. Twice the verb for 'wait for' (*qâvâh,* Pi.) is used and once the verb 'to hope' (*yâchal,* Hi.). These verbs are very close together in meaning, and convey the idea of expectant waiting.[2] The

[2] A very good summary of the Old Testament teaching on hope can be found in *NIDOTTE,* 3, pp. 894-95.

psalmist is not waiting in case God should be gracious. On the contrary, he has clearly received forgiveness, and now continues in the sure confidence that God, while remaining just, is able to blot out iniquities (Rom. 3:26). Upon God's own word he places his complete reliance (cf. the similar language in Ps. 119:49).

My soul waits for the Lord more than watchmen wait for the morning, more than watchmen wait for the morning (*v. 6*). This is a powerful picture of eagerness, patience, and confidence – the dawn always comes.[3] The city watchmen looked expectantly for the glimmers of light marking the start of another day. Their longing, however, is not as great as that of the psalmist and others whose trust is in the forgiving God.

4. God's Mercy to Israel (*vv. 7-8*)

O Israel, put your hope in the LORD, for with the LORD is unfailing love and with him is full redemption (*v. 7*). Having experienced God's forgiveness himself, the psalmist appeals to Israel as a whole to trust in the LORD. He wants them to do what he has already declared of himself (see v. 5, 'and in him I put my hope', using here the same Hebrew verb). With the LORD, and with him alone, is steadfast love (Heb., *chésed*), and the full measure of redeeming grace is only found with him. The word 'redemption' (*p[e]dût*) only occurs here and in Psalm 111:9, though the root is common (see the very next verse).[4]

He himself will redeem Israel from all their sins (*v. 8*). While the Hebrew verb 'redeem' (*pâdâh*) occurs over sixty times, yet this is the only place in the Old Testament in which it is used along with 'sin'. 'Redemption' is understood in spiritual terms, and Paul rightly uses the language of this verse when describing the work that Jesus did for his people

---

[3] The Hebrew is more cryptic than the English versions, as no verb for 'waiting' is used. It simply says: 'My soul to the Lord more than watchers for the morning, watchers for the morning.' To convey the force of the Hebrew in English, however, the insertion of the double 'waits for' is necessary.

[4] No adjective occurs with it, but 'full redemption' (NIV) or 'plentiful redemption' (ASV) are based on the verb governing it: '[he] multiplies redemption'.

– 'who gave himself for us to redeem us from all wickedness' (Titus 2:14). In New Testament terms, redemption flows from God's free grace (Rom. 3:23-25: Eph. 1:7), and forgiveness is based on Jesus' atoning sacrifice for sin (1 John 2:2). Ultimately redemption depends upon belonging by faith to the true Israel of God, for 'neither circumcision nor uncircumcision means anything, what counts is a new creation' (Gal. 6:15).

Psalm 131

A song of ascents. Of David.

Following Psalm 130, this short song carries on the idea of trust in the LORD, with which that psalm finished (cf. 130:7 with 131:3). It describes the character of the humble worshipper who does not seek illumination in matters that belong only to God, nor tries to exalt himself into a position that belongs to God alone. The psalmist also reveals a spirit of contentment with his position in life. The fact that the dangers are from prosperity points to a period in Israel's history in which the nation was experiencing vigorous economic life. Some time in the Davidic kingdom would suit well (cf. the ascription of the psalm to David).

My heart is not proud, O LORD, my eyes are not haughty; I do not concern myself with great matters or things too wonderful for me (*v. 1*). The psalmist denies that he is motivated by pride, arrogance, or ambition as he comes before the LORD. When it comes to his manner of life, he does not concern himself (lit. 'I do not walk in …')[1] with matters which are beyond him, and his focus is not on seeking great things. As the Hebrew word translated 'things too wonderful' is often used of God's great deeds (see Pss. 71:17; 72:18), the idea may be that he does not attempt to elevate himself into a Godlike position. No human efforts, whether in battle or business, can be a substitute for divine acts of power.

---

[1] The verb is *hâlak,* Pi., though the Qal and Hi. themes are used with similar meaning of men and women living out their days. The verb occurs over 1500 times in the Old Testament, and several hundred of these have a figurative meaning. For other examples of the Pi. forms to compare with that here, see the listing in *DCH,* II, p. 556.

But I have stilled and quieted my soul; like a weaned child with its mother, like a weaned child is my soul within me (*v.* 2). In quiet confidence the psalmist rests on the LORD. The thought of a weaned child is ambiguous. It could mean a child who was prematurely weaned, and therefore was restless because of lack of milk. More probably, it refers to a weaned child who is still resting contentedly on its mother's breast.[2] In a similar way, the trusting soul is depicted as being quiet and submissive in the presence of the LORD.

O Israel, put your hope in the LORD both now and for evermore (*v.* 3). The call to Israel in the preceding psalm is now repeated exactly (Ps. 130:7), but with the addition of the phrase 'now and for evermore'.[3] Just as David is resting in the LORD, so should everyone in Israel do at all times. Hoping in the LORD is not a momentary act, but an abiding experience.

---

[2] The MT has a double occurrence of the word 'on', though two different vocalisations appear (*'alê* and *'âlay*). Rather than translating it as 'within', the usual meaning of 'on' fits the context. L. C. Allen, *Psalms 101-150*, p. 197, has a full note, agreeing with an article of G. Quell (published in 1967). However, two nineteenth century commentators, J. A. Alexander, *The Psalms Translated and Explained*, p. 523, and J. J. S. Perowne, *The Book of Psalms*, II, p. 408, both advanced this explanation.

[3] There is no word corresponding to 'both' in the Hebrew text, and it is not needed. Cf. the ASV rendering, 'from this time forth and for evermore', and the NRSV, 'from this time on and forevermore.'

Psalm 132

A song of ascents.

Two psalms, Psalms 89 and 132, put into poetic form the covenant God made with David (2 Sam. 7 = 1 Chron. 17). They expressly call the relationship a covenant (see 89:3, 28, 34; 132:12), even though the historical passages do not use this term. In this they are in agreement with 2 Samuel 23:5 and Isaiah 55:3. Verses 8-10 of this psalm are quoted in 2 Chronicles 6:41-42 in connection with the dedication of the temple in Jerusalem. The psalm is a prayer for God to show his favour to the king who sits on David's throne. The language and ideas of the psalm point to a date of composition early in the period of the monarchy.

The Davidic covenant focused attention on the family from whom the Messiah was eventually to come (cf. Rom. 1:3, with the declaration that Christ Jesus 'as to his human nature was a descendant of David').[1] The choice of the Davidic family was linked also with the choice of Zion/Jerusalem. While the first of these concepts led to the abiding hope of God's provision of a messiah, the second led to a false sense of security. Zion was so elevated in the minds of many in Judah that they thought that they were safe because of their association with it. The prophet Jeremiah had to warn the people that though they might chant repeatedly, 'This is the temple of the Lord', without a change in their ways they would be removed from the land (Jer. 7:4). Covenant privilege demanded covenant obedience.

---

[1] For comment on this covenant, see also the introduction to Psalm 89.

1. Remember! (*v. 1*)

O LORD, remember David and all the hardships he endured (*v. 1*). An individual or the congregation pray for the Davidic king, and especially ask that God will remember all the hardships that David endured as a result of his oath. The word 'remember' (*z^{e}kôr*) may be significant as it is used in covenant settings where God 'pays attention to' his promises.[2] For example, he remembered his covenant and delivered his people from Egypt (Exod. 2:24, *vayizkor $^{\text{'}e}$lohîm 'et b^{e}rîtô*), and he later remembered them in preserving them (Lev. 26:44-45). This idea fits in well at this point. The troubles or hardships[3] that David endured were not the outward ones but rather the inward ones of distress that the ark and the covenant were separated, and that the ark did not have a permanent resting place.

2. David's Oath (*vv. 2-5*)

In the historical narrative in Samuel and Chronicles there is no express mention of an oath on David's part, though it is implied. Now it is made explicit that there were reciprocal oaths made by David and God. **He swore an oath to the LORD and made a vow to the Mighty One of Jacob: 'I will not enter my house or go to my bed – I will allow no sleep to my eyes, no slumber to my eyelids, till I find a place for the LORD, a dwelling for the Mighty One of Jacob'** (*vv. 2-5*). When David saw the blessing which had come to Obed-Edom because of the presence of the ark of the covenant (2 Sam. 6:12), he set about bringing the ark to Jerusalem and establishing

[2] J. A. Alexander, *The Psalms Translated and Explained*, p. 523, pointed out that the AV rendering, 'LORD, remember David, and all his afflictions', omits a preposition (*l^{e}*) and inserts a conjunction, 'and'. However, the preposition is not needed in translation as the Hebrew idiom is *zâkar l^{e}* (cf. Pss. 98:3; 106:45; 119:49), in which the preposition simply marks out the object (cf. the other similar cases listed in *DIHG~S*, p. 109). The idiom means to remember for the benefit of someone (*DCH*, III, p. 107). On the second point Alexander was strictly correct, though the two objects of the verb (David, his afflictions) are best conjoined by the conjunction 'and'.

[3] Many English versions follow the AV in the rendering 'hardships', but the word in question (*'unnôtô*) is not a plural noun but the Pu. inf. of *'ânâh*, 'his being afflicted'. Perhaps 'his trouble' is the best rendering.

a permanent home for it there. Twice in these verses the phrase 'the Mighty One of Jacob' occurs. This goes back to Genesis 49:24, where Jacob used this expression in invoking a blessing on his son Joseph. It is clearly synonymous with 'the Mighty One of Israel' (Isa. 1:24). David made the solemn pledge that he would not rest until he found a suitable resting place for the ark of his God.[4]

3. An Invitation to Worship (*vv. 6-9*)

Many translations and commentaries assume that the reference to what was heard is to the ark (see the second footnote on v. 6 in the NIV). However, the Hebrew suffixed pronoun 'it' (*hâ*) is feminine, whereas the word 'ark' (*'ᵃrôn*) is masculine. More probably, therefore, the call to worship that follows is what was heard. **We heard it in Ephrathah, we came upon it in the fields of Jaar** (*v. 6*). Both the place names here need some explanation. The ark is said to have returned from the Philistines to stay for twenty years at Kiriath Jearim ('town of the woodlands', 1 Sam. 6:21–7:2). David took the ark from Baalah of Judah to bring it to Jerusalem (2 Sam. 6:2; see NIV footnote). Here 'Ephrathah' is used of the region around Bethlehem from which David came (Ruth 4:11; Micah 5:2), while 'fields of Jaar' is just another way of describing Kiriath Jearim ('Jearim' is the Heb., plural of 'Jaar'). Ephrat was the second wife of Caleb (1 Chron. 2:18-20), and so gave her name to her descendants around the region of Bethlehem.

'Let us go to his dwelling place; let us worship at his footstool – arise, O LORD, and come to your resting place, you and the ark of your might. May your priests be clothed with righteousness; may your saints sing for joy' (*vv. 7-9*). The picture is presented of the people in David's home region encouraging one another to go to Jerusalem and worship. The location of the ark was God's 'dwelling place' (*v. 7*), God's 'resting place' (*v. 8*). After all its travels it had finally come to its permanent home, and there the ark formed a footstool for

[4] The Hebrew word for 'a dwelling' is the plural of *mishkân*, a common term for the 'tabernacle'. The plural form is used here and in verse 7, and this is paralleled in other psalms when reference is to the temple complex (see 43:3; 46:4; 84:1).

the LORD (cf. Ps. 99:5). It is called 'the ark of your might' (*ʾarôn ʿuzzekâ*) because it represented the very presence of the God of power. Both priests and people were to be united in worship and to reflect the saving righteousness of God.

4. Don't Reject! (*v. 10*)
For the sake of David your servant, do not reject your anointed one (*v. 10*). The first half of the psalm is completed with this further reference to David, which ties in with the opening verse. The appeal is made on the basis of David's covenant relationship with the LORD. There are many references to David as the LORD's servant in the historical books, in Psalm 89:20, and in the titles to Psalms 18 and 36. Those kings following him were regarded as being the LORD's anointed ones. The parallel to 'remember' in verse 1 is now 'do not reject' (*ʾal tâshêv*), which means 'continue to look with favour' (cf. Ps. 84:9). The divine promise was that God would never take away his covenant love from the Davidic family (Ps. 89:33-37).

5. The LORD's Oath (*vv. 11-12*)
While the first half of the psalm is devoted to David's oath, attention in the second half is on the LORD's oath. **The LORD swore an oath to David, a sure oath that he will not revoke: 'One of your own descendants I will place on your throne – if your sons keep my covenant and the statutes I teach them, then their sons will sit on your throne for ever and ever'** (*vv. 11-12*). The relationship with David was confirmed by a divine oath, by which it was indicated that the covenant originated with God, not David. He calls it 'my covenant' (*beritî*). The words here are not quoted exactly from 2 Samuel 7 or 1 Chronicles 17, but they summarise the promises given to David, which were also repeated to Solomon after the building of the temple and the royal palace (1 Kings 9:3-5; 2 Chron. 7:17-18). In speaking to Solomon, God said that he covenanted with his father David (2 Chron. 7:18), and Psalm 89 makes mention of the swearing of an oath (vv. 3, 35). The promise of hereditary kingship for the Davidic family and its fulfilment in the succession of

Davidic rulers marks out the kingly line in Judah.[5] It contrasts so sharply with the non-hereditary succession in the northern, and rebellious, kingdom of Israel. The relationship was a binding covenant on the Davidic family, but ruling over a kingdom in Israel was conditional upon obedience to the LORD's statutes. The threat stated to Solomon was that if the people were disobedient then exile was ahead (see 1 Kings 9:6-9; 2 Chron. 7:17-22). Disaster for the people did not mean the setting aside of the covenant with David, for the sure mercies to David continued (Isa. 55:3).

5. Chosen Zion (*vv. 13-16*)
For the LORD has chosen Zion, he has desired it for his dwelling: 'This is my resting place for ever and ever; here I will sit enthroned, for I have desired it – I will bless her with abundant provisions; her poor will I satisfy with food. I will clothe her priests with salvation, and her saints will ever sing for joy (*vv. 13-16*). Just as God chose Israel to be his people (Deut. 7:7), so he also chose Zion as the place where he would make his name dwell (Deut. 12:11; Ps. 2:6). As far back in Israel's history as the Song of the Sea (Exod. 15:17-18), reference is made to God bringing Israel to his own mountain, the place where he would establish his sanctuary. This was fulfilled centuries later by the building of the temple. The prayer of the people (v. 8) is followed by assurance that Zion is indeed God's choice. Miraculous signs marked out that choice – fire from heaven on the altar of burnt offering set up by David on Araunah's threshing floor (1 Chron. 21:26) and the fire from heaven and the glory cloud at the dedication of the temple (2 Chron. 7:1). David's desire for a permanent habitation for the ark in Jerusalem and God's own desire coincided. The Hebrew word for 'resting place' is used of the temporary resting place that God sought for his people (Num. 10:33), but also of the rest he provided for them in the land of Canaan and particularly in connection with Jerusalem

---

[5] The NIV 'descendants' is the translation of the Hebrew 'fruit of your body' (*mippᵉrî bitnekâ*). The Hebrew word *béten* usually means a woman's 'womb', but it can also be used of a man's body. See *DCH*, II, pp. 141-42.

(1 Kings 8:56). As the great king he is enthroned in Zion, and consequently he promises abundant provisions to his people, including bountiful blessings even for the poor (cf. Deut. 15:4). The prayer of verse 9 is answered in even fuller terms than the request, as verse 16 shows. The desire for 'righteousness' (*tsédek*) is answered by the promise of 'salvation' (*yeshaʿ*), while the saints will not just 'sing for joy' but 'shout aloud for joy' (Hebrew, *rannên yᵉrannênû*, using two parts of the same verb to provide emphasis: '*really* shout for joy'). Christians have even greater cause for such joyous expression.

6. God's Reassurance to David (*vv. 17-18*)

'Here I will make a horn grow for David and set up a lamp for my anointed one. I will clothe his enemies with shame, but the crown on his head will be resplendent' (*vv. 17-18*). The requests of verses 1 and 10 are brought to a climactic conclusion, for from Zion comes Israel's hope.[6] Frequently in the Old Testament 'horn' (*qéren*) is used to symbolise strength or vigour (cf. Pss. 18:2; 75:4-5, and see NIV footnote here), while in David's sons he would have a continually burning lamp never to be snuffed out (see David's prayer in Ps. 18:28, and the LORD's words to Jeroboam in 1 Kings 11:36). The promise to David was of a continuing succession of kings, with the Lord Jesus ultimately being given the throne of David (Luke 1:31-33). The final verse reiterates this idea by contrasting the treatment given to the priests (vv. 9 and 16) with a different sort of clothing for the enemies of God's people. 'Shame' (*bôshet*) will take the place of 'salvation' for them, while the Davidic family will not only grow but blossom.

---

[6] It is difficult to know why the NIV translators used 'here', for the Hebrew word at the commencement of verse 17 is *shâm* which means 'there'. It simply points back to Zion (v. 13).

Psalm 133

A song of ascents. Of David.

A suitable setting for this psalm would be the period after David became king not only of Judah but also of Israel (see 2 Sam. 5:1-5). Its original application to the joyful unity of the twelve tribes comprising Israel and Judah would be further enhanced as it was used in the annual pilgrimage to Jerusalem. As the tribes went up to Jerusalem and the proclamation of peace was made concerning it (see Ps. 122), the use of this psalm reinforced the sense of unity among the people and recalled for them the blessings of the LORD here and in eternity.

1. The Privilege of Unity (*v. 1*)

How good and pleasant it is when brothers live together in unity! (*v. 1*). In Hebrew the verse begins with a word that draws attention to the statement that follows (Heb. *hinnêh*, 'behold', 'take notice'). This word serves as a marker for the reader in order to highlight the exclamation that follows. Unity in the family is extolled as a very precious thing. The two qualities attributed to it stress its intrinsic goodness (*tôv*)[1] and how delightful it is (*nāʿîm*).[2] Friction among individuals and tribal groups is highlighted in the Old Testament narrative, but the ideal was of harmonious living. Brothers were meant to live together.[3]

---

[1] The use of 'good' recalls the repeated use of this adjective of creation in Genesis 1:10, 12, 18, 21, 25, 31.

[2] *Nāʿîm* only occurs in poetry, though the verb (*nāʿam*) is widely distributed throughout the Old Testament.

[3] The NIV does not translate one word in the verse: 'How good and pleasant it is when brothers live in unity *also* (*gam*) together!' There is no reason to omit the translation of *gam*. It can be an emphasising particle as

2. Application (*vv.* 2-3)

It is like precious oil poured on the head, running down the beard, running down on Aaron's beard, down upon the collar of his robes. It is as if the dew of Hermon were falling on Mount Zion. For there the Lord bestows his blessing, even life for evermore (*vv.* 2-3). Two illustrations follow the opening statement. The first is that the oil used in anointing the high priest runs down his head, on to his beard, and even on the collar of his robes.So symbolically the tribes are pervaded with one holy anointing of brotherly love. The second illustration concerns the dew of Hermon that is pictured as reaching even to Mount Zion. Probably the idea is that the same moisture affects Hermon in the north as touches Zion in the south. God provides the refreshing dew for the whole land. Mention of Zion leads to the thought that it is the place where God meets in a special way with his people and bestows his blessings, which are summed up in the idea of abiding life that is found with him. Similarly, believers today have a unity in Christ as they make their way to Mount Zion, the city of the living God (Heb. 12:22-24; 13:14-16).

---

well, and this usage fits here in Psalm 133 where the phrase *gam-yâchad* indicates the full harmony that is meant to exist between brothers. They *indeed* dwell *together*.

[4] The Hebrew text uses the same participle (*yorêd*) of the verb 'run down' three times: the oil *runs down* the beard, *runs down* Aaron's beard, and the dew *runs down* onto Mount Zion. Such exuberance should characterise brotherly life together.

Psalm 134

A song of ascents.

The fifteen pilgrim songs end on a note of blessing. They conclude with the pilgrims asking the Lord's ministers to bless him (vv. 1-2), and then in turn asking for blessing from the Lord in Zion. It is an 'Amen' to the whole group. Just as the short Psalm 117 concludes a collection of 'Hallelujah' psalms (Pss. 111-117), so this one brings the pilgrim songs to a fitting conclusion.

1. Praise to the Lord (*vv. 1-2*).

Praise the Lord, all you servants of the Lord who minister by night in the house of the Lord (*v. 1*). The command to praise is directed to the Lord's servants, which is explained by the next phrase with its reference to priestly ministry in the temple. Part of the work of the Levites was 'to carry the ark of the covenant of the Lord, to stand before the Lord to minister and to pronounce blessings in his name' (Deut. 10:8). There was clearly an evening ministry in the temple, but details about it are uncertain. 1 Chronicles 9:33 records that the singers were relieved of menial duties 'because they were responsible for the work day and night' (cf. Isa. 30:29).

Lift up your hands in the sanctuary and praise the Lord (*v. 2*). Lifting up of hands represented outwardly an inward attitude of prayer, perhaps of waiting expectantly to receive from the Lord (see comment on Ps. 28:2). The New Testament carries over this terminology when Paul says that he wants 'men everywhere to lift up holy hands in prayer, without anger or disputing' (1 Tim. 2:8). In the holy place of the temple praise should ascend from the lips of the priests.[1]

2. Blessing from the Lord (*v. 3*)

May the Lord, the Maker of heaven and earth, bless you from Zion (*v. 3*). The use of the phrase 'the Maker of heaven and earth' is important. It recalls Genesis 1, where God blesses his creation, and was a standard expression in Hebrew poetry (see comment on Ps. 121:2). The prayer is that the creator will continue to bless and to empower his servants. The expression 'bless you' is an echo of the Aaronic blessing (Num. 6:22), while 'bless you from Zion' has already occurred in Psalm 128:5.[2] Now in the New Testament era the emphasis is not on the temple but on Jesus. Our blessings come through him from the heavenly Jerusalem (Heb. 12:22-24).

---

[1] The Hebrew text has simply 'Lift your hands holiness'. While this could mean 'in holiness', yet the usage elsewhere and the context here suggests that 'holiness' (*qódesh*) is a synonym for the sanctuary. See Psalm 20:2, where 'from the sanctuary' is parallel to 'from Zion'.

[2] The fact that the singular 'you' is indicated (*yᵉvârekâ*) may be a reference to the whole congregation, or else it is an individualising expression applicable to everyone in the congregation.

Psalm 135

The anonymous author of this psalm was clearly very familiar with other parts of the Old Testament, and especially with other psalms. It is an expansion of the preceding psalm, and is complemented by the following one. The similarity with Psalm 136 comes out especially in some of the historical statements:

Psalm 135	**Psalm 136**
He struck down the firstborn of Egypt (v. 8)	to him who struck down the firstborn of Egypt (v. 10)
He struck down many nations and killed mighty kings (v. 10)	who struck down great kings … and killed mighty kings (vv. 17-18)
Sihon king of the Amorites, Og king of Bashan (v. 11)	Sihon king of the Amorites … and Og king of Bashan (vv. 19-20)
And he gave their land as an inheritance to his people Israel (v. 12)	And gave their land as an inheritance … an inheritance to his servant Israel (v. 21)

Much of the thought and language resembles Psalm 115, including the threefold call to the houses of Israel and Aaron and to those who fear the Lord, expanded here to include also the house of Levi. The praise of the Lord fixes attention on his character (contrasted with the inability of idols to help their worshippers), and on his great acts of salvation for Israel. Redemption forms the central theme of the psalm.

1. Israel's Praise (*vv. 1-4*)

Praise the LORD. Praise the name of the LORD; praise him, you servants of the LORD, you who minister in the house of the LORD, in the courts of the house of our God (*vv. 1-2*). The psalm opens and closes with a 'Hallelujah' (NIV 'Praise the LORD'). These are part of stanzas with which the psalm begins and ends, so that invitations to praise enclose its central message. The call is to those who minister at the sanctuary (the priests and Levites) to praise the LORD's name. The description of the LORD's servants as those who minister in his house is repeated from the previous psalm (Ps. 134:1). The setting seems to be in the time after the exile, which is also indicated by the mosaic of earlier Scripture portions integrated into this psalm.

Praise the LORD, for the LORD is good; sing praise to his name, for that is pleasant. For the LORD has chosen Jacob to be his own, Israel to be his treasured possession (*vv. 3-4*). The main reason for praise is simply the LORD's goodness (for earlier statements of similar import in the Psalms, see 25:8; 34:8; 73:1; 86:5; and 100:5). Later in the psalm mention is made of specific ways in which that goodness was demonstrated. The phrase 'for that is pleasant' (*kî naʿîm*) is ambiguous, since in Hebrew the subject could be God: 'for he is pleasant (i.e. beautiful; cf. RSV 'sing to his name, for he is gracious!'). However, comparison with Psalm 54:6 and Psalm 147:1 supports the NIV interpretation. It was an act of grace for God to choose Israel (Deut. 7:7-8), and to take her to be his treasured possession (Exod. 19:5). The Hebrew word rendered 'special possession' (*s^egullâh*) is a rare word, only occurring eight times in the Old Testament. It denotes how special and treasured God's people are in his sight (cf. 1 Chron. 29:3 where it is used of special treasure belonging to the king).[1]

[1] Of the other passages in which it is used, Deuteronomy 7:6, 14:2, and 26:18 are almost identical expressions, as is Malachi 3:17.

It is noteworthy that it appears here along with the idea of God's choice of Israel ('for Jacob he *chose*', *bâchar*), as it does in Deuteronomy 7:6. Titus 2:14 and 1 Peter 2:9 are two New Testament passages that build on this Old Testament idea.

2. Praise of the Creator (*vv. 5-7*)

I know that the LORD is great, that our Lord is greater than all gods (*v. 5*). Preceding a later description of the lifeless idols (vv. 15-17) comes a declaration concerning the living God. He is beyond comparison with any man-made gods. This verse is probably based on Exodus 18:11: 'Now I know that the LORD is greater than all other gods'.[2] The same declaration was made by David just after God made a covenant with him (2 Sam. 7:22). The Hebrew word 'great' (*gâdôl*) is combined at times with the divine name to form personal names (e.g. Gedaliah, 'the LORD is great').

The LORD does whatever pleases him, in the heavens and on the earth, in the seas and all their depths. He makes clouds rise from the ends of the earth; he sends lightning with the rain and brings out the wind from his storehouses (*vv. 6-7*). God is sovereign in his universe, being able to do whatever he takes delight in. The almost identical expression has been used already in Psalm 115:3. The expanse of the heavens or the depths of the seas are equally at his disposal, for he is their creator. All the forces of nature are part of his plan, and he is able to use wind, rain, and lightning to fulfil his purposes. They are servants, not powers in their own right, as many Near Eastern religions believed.

I know the Lord is high in state,
above all gods our God is great;
the Lord performs what He decrees,
in heaven and earth, in depths and seas.
He makes the moisture to ascend
in clouds from

[2] Here the pronoun 'I' ('*ănî*) is added, giving the expression the idea of strong personal conviction: 'For I, I know that the LORD is great', or more colloquially, 'As for myself, I know that the LORD is great'. Cf. also the similar expression in Psalm 138:5: 'for the glory of the LORD is great'.

earth's remotest end;
the lightnings flash at His command;
he holds the cyclone in His hand.
(*The Psalter*, 1912)

3. Redeeming Grace (*vv. 8-12*)

Whenever the psalmists and prophets start to speak of sovereign grace, they invariably point to the redemption from Egypt. **He struck down the firstborn of Egypt, the firstborn of men and animals. He sent his signs and wonders into your midst, O Egypt, against Pharaoh and all his servants** (*vv. 8-9*). Not only Israel, but Egypt is also reminded of what happened at the time of the Exodus. Both then and at the more recent return from exile, God 'was appalled that there was no one to intervene, so his own arm worked salvation for him, and his own righteousness sustained him' (Isa. 59:16). References to smiting the firstborn[3] and sending plagues form a very abbreviated summary of what is recorded in Exodus 7–14, but yet they highlight the way in which God sovereignly acted on his people's behalf. 'Signs and wonders' (*'otôt ûmofᵉtîm*) describe the character of the plagues in Egypt, for they were demonstrations of God's power (see the similar references in Pss. 78:43 and 105:27; cf. Exod. 4:9, 28, 30 and Deut. 29:3).

He struck down many nations and killed mighty kings – Sihon king of the Amorites, Og king of Bashan and all the kings of Canaan – and he gave their land as an inheritance, an inheritance to his people Israel (*vv. 10-12*). These verses summarise the accounts of the defeat of Sihon and Og (Num. 21:21-35) and the occupation of the land of Canaan (Josh. 1-21). It was only by God's power that strong enemies were overcome, and Israel's possession of the land was his gift. Even before the occupation of Canaan, Moses reminded Israel that their own efforts were not going to achieve possession of cities, houses, wells, and vineyards (Deut. 6:10-12). The land was an inheritance gift from the LORD (Deut. 4:21; 4:38; 12:9; and many other passages throughout Deuteronomy). Part

[3] The language here is based on Exodus 12:29: 'At midnight the LORD struck down all the firstborn in Egypt.'

of Israel's song was praise for fulfilment of the promise to Abraham of a land for his seed (cf. Pss. 78, 105, 106, 136).

Your name, O LORD, endures forever, your renown, O LORD, through all generations. For the LORD will vindicate his people and have compassion on his servants (*vv. 13-14*). God's 'name' is the character he displays in his actions. This is brought to his remembrance (*zikrᵉkâ,* NIV 'your renown') by successive generations. The language of verse 13 goes back to God's declaration to Moses: 'This is my name forever, the name by which I am to be remembered from generation to generation' (Exod. 3:15). The psalmist here is either directly echoing that statement, or picking up the language from a passage such as Psalm 102:12. Over both Israel and the nations God exercises government, and he is able to uphold his own people and to maintain his own name in the face of hostile attacks. Verse 14 is drawn from Deuteronomy 32:36, in a passage that looks beyond the punishment of the exile to a time when God will extend mercy to his covenant people. Hebrews 10:30 could be a quotation either from this psalm or from Deuteronomy, as the two passages are identical.

4. The Futility of Idol Worship (*vv. 15-18*)

The idols of the nations are silver and gold, made by the hands of men. They have mouths, but cannot speak, eyes, but they cannot see; they have ears, but cannot hear, nor is there breath in their mouths. Those who make them will be like them, and so will all who trust in them (*vv. 15-18*). These verses are almost identical to Psalm 115:4-6, 8 (see the commentary on those verses). The differences are minor verbal ones (such as different verbs for hearing being used, Ps. 115 using *shâmaʿ*, whereas Ps. 135 has *ʾâzan,* Hi.), the omission of reference to hands and feet, and the substitution of 'nor is there breath in their mouths' for 'noses, but they cannot smell'. Once again the emphasis falls on how powerless the heathen idols really are.

5. A Renewed Call to Praise (*vv. 19-21*)

O house of Israel, praise the LORD; O house of Aaron, praise the LORD; O house of Levi, praise the LORD; you who fear him,

praise the LORD (*vv. 19-20*)**.** While the call to the houses of Israel and Aaron and to the God-fearers resembles Psalm 115:9-11 (see also the threefold call in Ps. 118:2-4), yet the form of the call is closer to the conclusion of Psalm 103:20-22. In both Psalm 103 and Psalm 135, the call is to 'praise the LORD' (Heb., *bârak*, 'bless'), which indicates that the worshippers are being encouraged to express thanksgiving and adoration. There is also mention of the 'house of Levi', probably because the psalm comes from a temple setting, where the Levites would be ministering (see vv. 1-2). The assembled congregation and officiating priests are to give united praise to the LORD. 'Those that fear him' is a typical description of God's people, one that is often used in the Psalter (cf., e.g., 22:23; 85:9; 103:13; 115:13; 118:4; 128:1).

Praise be to the LORD from Zion, to him who dwells in Jerusalem. Praise the LORD (*v. 21*). The temple in Jerusalem was the visible token of God's presence with his people. From there he blessed them (see Ps. 128:5), and in turn they ascribe praise to him. Praise is to flow out from Jerusalem. The ultimate fulfilment of this was the spread of the gospel from Jerusalem, to Judea and Samaria, and then to the ends of the earth (Acts 1:8). The initial 'Hallelujah' in verse 1 finds its counterpart in the concluding phrase. After so much evidence of God's power and grace, an ascription of praise forms a fitting conclusion.

Psalm 136

There is no other psalm like this one in the whole Psalter, with a refrain occurring in every verse. It is very probable that a Levitical song leader led the historical recital, and that the worshippers responded with the refrain (2 Chron. 7:3, 6; 20:21). The same refrain, 'for his love endures for ever' (*kî* l^{e}*'ôlâm chasdô*), occurs in Psalms 106:1, 107:1, and 118:1, 29.

This psalm continues the joint themes of Psalm 135 of God as creator and redeemer. Many of the expressions it uses parallel those that occur in the previous psalm (see introduction to Ps. 135). Both psalms commemorate the way in which the LORD brought his people out of Egypt and gave them possession of the promised land. The fact that it was the LORD alone who did this (cf. v. 4) is made clear by there being no mention at all of Joshua and the Israelite army. Naming specific instances of God's great deeds for his people is unnecessary, as generic expressions like 'great wonders' serve as pointers to all of God's redemptive deeds.[1]

1. A Call to Praise (*vv. 1-3*)

Give thanks to the LORD, for he is good.
His love endures forever.
Give thanks to the God of gods.
His love endures forever.

---

[1] 'Great wonders' (*niflâ'ôt* g^{e}*dolot*) is unique, though 'For you are great, and do marvellous deeds' (Ps. 86:10) is very close, using both the adjective 'great' (*gâdôl*) and the plural participle 'wonders' (*niflâ'ôt*). The NIV translation is inconsistent, using both 'wonders' and 'marvellous deeds'.

Give thanks to the Lord of lords:
His love endures forever (*vv.* 1-3).

Each of the opening verses have an identical call to praise, except that the object of the verb is varied: 'LORD', 'God of gods', 'Lord of lords'. The reason for praise is the LORD's goodness and covenant love. Both these terms ground the praise in the realm of covenant, for God's goodness is a way of expressing the blessings of the covenant (see on 34:8), while his love is the commitment of covenant faithfulness (see on 36:5). The varied terms for God seem to be used to draw attention to his uniqueness, and therefore to his claim for exclusive praise.

2. Praise for Creation (*vv. 4-9*)

to him who alone does great wonders,
His love endures forever.
who by his understanding made the heavens,
His love endures forever.
who spread out the earth upon the waters,
His love endures forever.
who made the great lights –
His love endures forever.
the sun to govern the day,
His love endures forever.
the moon and stars to govern the night;
His love endures forever (*vv. 4-9*).

Creation forms the basis for the recounting of the great historical happenings for Israel, and it is the first of the many wonders that God performed. The fact that no one else can do this is clear, for *he alone* (*l^evadô*) has such power at his disposal.[2] It is also a display of God's wisdom (cf. Prov. 3:19; Jer. 10:12). 'Spreading out the earth upon the waters' is an echo of Genesis 1:6-8, with the Hebrew word for 'firmament' (*râqîaʿ*) coming from the same root

---

[2] Deuteronomy 4:35 is basic for the later Old Testament declarations of God's uniqueness. It states the truth using another form of the same preposition, 'beside him' (*mil^evadô*). The same idea can be expressed, as Isaiah so often does, either by using *zûlat* (Ps. 18:31; Isa. 26:13; Isa. 45:5), or *ʾên ʿôd* (Isa. 45:5).

as the word translated 'spreading out' (*râqaʿ*). The English word 'firmament' is simply a borrowing from Latin (*firmamentum*) to try and express the idea of the expanse of the sky. Isaiah 42:5 re-echoes the same language. The formation of the sun, moon and stars is summarised in verses 7-9, with direct links with Genesis 1:16. Their function is to give light and to regulate time by ruling over the day and night.

3. Praise for the Exodus (*vv. 10-15*)
to him who struck down the firstborn of Egypt
His love endures forever.
and brought Israel out from among them
His love endures forever.
with a mighty hand and outstretched arm;
His love endures forever (*vv. 10-12*).

The exact language of Exodus 12:12, 23, 27, 29 is used in verse 10 to describe the last of the plagues of Egypt, while verse 11 reminds that it was only by the power of God that Israel was brought out from bondage and slavery in Egypt. 'Brought out' is one of the commonest expressions in Deuteronomy to describe the Exodus (cf. Deut. 1:27; 4:20; 4:37; 5:6; 16:1; 26:8; 29:25), and it is often linked with 'a mighty hand and an outstretched arm' to indicate the manner in which the Exodus took place (cf. Deut. 5:15; 7:8; 9:29; 26:8). The redemption of Israel from Egypt was solely a wonder of God's doing. Though that redemption involved death to the firstborn in Egypt (and later to kings, cf. verse 17), it was also a demonstration of covenant love (*chésed*) towards Israel, as the refrain once more asserts.

to him who divided the Red Sea asunder
His love endures forever.
and brought Israel through the midst of it,
His love endures forever.
but swept Pharaoh and his army into the Red Sea;
His love endures forever (*vv. 13-15*).

These verses summarise Exodus 14:21-31. The crossing of the Red Sea was salvation for the Israelites, but judgment for the pursuing Egyptian army. The one action of God had two entirely different consequences. The waters were divided, and Israel went through on dry land, but the LORD swept the Egyptians into the sea. Such a demonstration of divine power caused the Israelites to fear and to put their trust in God and in Moses his servant (Exod. 14:31). The New Testament regards the wilderness experiences as being part of our history as Christians, and from them we must learn spiritual lessons (Rom. 15:4; 1 Cor. 10:1-13).

4. Praise for the Wilderness Experiences (*v. 16*)
to him who led his people through the desert,
His love endures forever (*v. 16*).

It was not only at the time of the Exodus that God displayed his power. During the wilderness experiences he gave his people divine protection and divine sustenance. He was the great shepherd who led his people like a flock and guided them to safety (Ps. 78:52-53). The psalmists seem to have borrowed expressions from Deuteronomy (Deut. 8:2; 8:15; 29:5) and the prophets describe in similar terms the wilderness experiences (Isa. 48:21; Jer. 2:6; Amos 2:10).

5. Praise for the Conquest (*vv. 17-22*)
who struck down great kings,
His love endures forever,
and killed mighty kings –
His love endures forever.
Sihon king of the Amorites
His love endures forever.
and Og king of Bashan –
His love endures forever (*vv. 17-20*).

In coming towards Canaan the Israelites had to cross hostile territory east of the Dead Sea. Neither Sihon king of the Amorites nor Og king of Bashan would allow undisputed passage, and after defeat at the hand of the Israelites their lands were taken. The historical accounts are given in Numbers 21:21-35 and Deuteronomy 2:24-3:11. The sin of the Amorites (Gen. 15:16) had finally reached full measure. The territory of Sihon and Og provided land for two and a half of the tribes – Gad, Reuben, and half of Manasseh.

and gave their land as an inheritance,
His love endures forever,
an inheritance to his servant Israel;
His love endures forever (*vv.* 21-22).

The basic promise of the land of Canaan given to Abraham (Gen. 12:7), was reaffirmed at the time of the Exodus and called an inheritance for Israel (Exod. 32:13). When Israel occupied Canaan it was distributed as an inheritance by lot (Num. 33:54), so that God settled 'the tribes of Israel in their homes' (Ps. 78:55). An important consequence of this was that Israel was a sojourner under God's protection (Lev. 25:23), and the land belonged to him. Individual Israelites were God's servants, but the nation as a whole could also be called by God, 'my servant' (cf. also Isa. 41:8; 44:1, 2).

6. Renewed Call to Praise (*vv.* 23-26)
The concluding verses serve to summarise the psalm as a whole, and perhaps they express the repeated experience of Israel from the time of the conquest to the exile.

to the One who remembered us in our low estate
His love endures forever,
and freed us from our enemies,
His love endures forever.
and who gives food to every creature.
His love endures forever (*vv.* 23-25).

God did not forsake his covenant commitments but remembered his people (on the use of 'remember', see the comment on Ps. 132:1). 'Low estate' (*shêfel,* or elsewhere more commonly the verb *shâfêl*)[3] is an Old Testament term for 'abasement' or 'humiliation', and it could describe times like domination by surrounding peoples during the period of the judges or some of the later periods including the abject humiliation of the exile. The twin themes of creation and redemption are brought together again in verses 24-25. God was the deliverer, but he was also the one who provided for all flesh in accordance with his promise to Noah (the use of the phrase 'all flesh' [NIV 'every creature'] ties Gen. 9:11, 15-17 and Ps. 136:25 together).

Give thanks to the God of heaven.
His love endures forever *(v. 26).*

The final verse picks up the opening song of praise (vv. 1-3), and reiterates it in summary fashion with one slight alteration. The mode of address to God becomes 'the God of heaven'. Nowhere else in the psalms does this title occur, and it was a designation for God that came into greater prominence in the period after the exile (Ezra 1:2; 6:10; 7:12, 21; Neh. 1:4; Dan. 2:18).

[3] Cf. the use of the related word *shᵉfêlâh* to describe the lowland between the Philistine plain and the mountains which was first recognised as a technical term by George Adam Smith, *The Historical Geography of the Holy Land*, 4th ed. (London: Hodder & Stoughton, 1904), pp. 201-36. For more recent discussion, see Denis Baly, *Geography of the Bible*, rev. ed. (London: Lutterworth Press, 1974), pp. 140-43.

Psalm 137

The reality of the bitterness of exile in Babylon is recalled by a psalmist who has recently returned home. To have undergone the horrors of the destruction of Jerusalem at the hands of Babylonians and Edomites, and then the cruelties of deportation, were experiences that deeply affected the people. There was a concern not only for themselves but for Zion and all that it represented. Even in a prayer of confession such as Daniel's (Dan. 9:4-19), with its acknowledgment of the rightness of God's judgment, there is the request that God would look with favour on his desolate sanctuary and see the desolation of the city which bore his name (vv. 17-18). In this psalm the singer reveals that same deep love of Zion as he recalls the distress of alienation from all that was dear to him.

The latter part of the psalm (vv. 7-9) contains curses against Edom and Babylon. These must be viewed from the perspective of the covenant.[1] Though no reference to a judicial procedure appears in Psalm 137, yet the background passages in Hosea and Isaiah do contain judicial sentences against enemies (see the exposition below). Psalmists and prophets speak similar language when expressing God's judgment on Israel's oppressors.

1. Sorrow in Babylon (*vv. 1-3*)

By the rivers of Babylon we sat and wept when we remembered Zion (*v. 1*). The Tigris and Euphrates Rivers

[1] In my exposition of this psalm I am following what I wrote in 'The Continuity of Covenant Curses in the Imprecations of the Psalter', *RTR* 54, 2 (1995), pp. 65-72.

and a series of irrigation canals provided the source of life in Babylonia. Being in exile was not harsh or close imprisonment for the Jewish people, yet to be separated from Zion deeply affected the faithful believers. Sitting was not a sign of ease or comfort. It was the posture of mourners (Isa. 47:1, 5), and tears were shed as they thought about all that was lost in the destruction of Jerusalem.

There on the poplars we hung our harps, for there our captors asked us for songs, our tormentors demanded songs of joy; they said, 'Sing us one of the songs of Zion!' (*vv.* 2-3). The Babylonian captors wanted to hear them sing some of the songs for which the Jewish people were renowned.[2] How could they sing joyful songs and entertain their tormentors 'there' – the place of captivity and mourning? At such times 'the joyful harp is silent' (Isa. 24:8), and the poplars were a convenient spot on which to hang the harps and so show their refusal to take part in entertainment.

2. Commitment to Zion/Jerusalem (*vv.* 4-6)

How can we sing the songs of the LORD while in a foreign land? (*v.* 4). This question should not be taken to mean that the Jews never sang at all when away from their own land. In the context here it clearly means that they could not take part in a concert to entertain their captors while in a foreign land (*ʾadmat nêkâr,* lit. 'land of foreignness'). The songs of Zion were not meant to be used in such settings.

If I forget you, O Jerusalem, may my right hand forget [its skill]. May my tongue cling to the roof of my mouth if I do not remember you, if I do not consider Jerusalem my highest joy (*vv.* 5-6). The place of Jerusalem in the affection of the faithful exiles comes out in these verses. The same attitude is taken in the book of Lamentations, as the author of that book weeps for the desolate Jerusalem (Lam. 1:16; 2:11). As

---

[2] The Hebrew text has 'words of song' (*divᵉrê-shîr*). In quoting the captors, the psalmist says they requested 'a song of Zion' (*shîr tsiyôn*), also called 'a song of the LORD' (*shîr-yhwh*) in the following verse. The early versions took these references to be to 'songs', and this is the way practically all the English translations understand it. The expressions can be regarded as collectives, 'songs', 'song book'.

God had chosen Zion (Pss. 78:68; 132:13), so then his believing people remembered it as the place of his dwelling with them and longed passionately for return to it. The psalmist calls down a curse upon himself if he is ever unfaithful to the promises concerning Jerusalem. He would prefer his right hand to wither (and so prevent him playing the harp), and his tongue to stick to the roof of his mouth so that he can no longer sing if he is ever untrue to Jerusalem.[3] It is his highest joy because of its association with God.

3. God's Curse on Edom and Babylon (*vv. 7-9*)

Remember, O LORD, what the Edomites did on the day Jerusalem fell. 'Tear it down,' they cried, 'tear it down to its foundations!' (*v.* 7) The Edomites were descendants of Esau (see Deut. 2:4-5). Earlier in the Old Testament there is comparative friendliness between Israel and Edom, but later bitter hostility developed (see the curses expressed against Edom in Amos 1:11-12; Jer. 49:7-22; Obad. 1-21; and Mal. 1:2-5). While Edom was only a minor power, it had aided Babylon at the time of Jerusalem's fall. The Edomites had looted the city and killed fugitives trying to escape (Obad. 11-14; Ezek. 25:12-14; 35:5-15). The psalmist calls upon God to remember against them their evil actions.[4] Not only did they want to see Jerusalem razed to the ground, but the very foundations of God's rule obliterated. The call for God's judgment on Edom is spelt out more fully in the book of Obadiah.

O Daughter of Babylon, doomed to destruction, happy is he who repays you for what you have done to us – he

---

[3] The clause 'May my right hand forget' has evoked considerable discussion. Some suggest that there is a play on the meanings of the verb 'forget' (*shâkach*), which has its normal meaning in verse 5a, but an alternative meaning 'wither away' in verse 5b: 'If I *forget* ... may my right hand *wither away*'. No convincing proof can be cited to confirm this. Another suggestion is that the consonants of the verb have been rearranged (*shâkach* becoming *kâshach*). For this view, see *NIDOTTE*, 2, p. 733. As the LXX and Jerome understood both verbs to mean 'forget', it is best to retain this translation and insert an object with the second occurrence, 'its skill'.

[4] The Hebrew idiom is 'remember against' (*zâkar l^e*). This can mean either 'remember for the benefit of someone' (Pss. 132:1; 136:23), or 'remember against'. See *DCH*, III, p. 107.

who seizes your infants and dashes them against the rocks (*vv. 8-9*). Judgment is expressed against Babylon.[5] Two important facts help us in understanding this curse. First, the language here echoes that of Isaiah 13:16, and recalls the judicial sentence already pronounced by Isaiah against Babylon, the great enemy of Zion (see especially Isa. 13:1-14:23; 21:1-10; cf. the similar language used in Hosea 13:16 about Samaria). Secondly, many of the biblical and extra-biblical treaties contain curses relating to absence of off-spring or the cutting off of succeeding generations (Pss. 55:23; 69:25; 109:8-9, 13). When these facts are combined, they suggest that the psalmist is echoing well-known prophecies already given against Babylon and (using the language of brutal warfare of that time) asking for the destruction of Babylon as a nation. If her children were cut off, then her days as a nation would be numbered. The final enemy of God's people is called 'Babylon' in the book of Revelation, and with joy her overthrow is greeted (Rev. 18:1-19:4).

---

[5] 'Daughter of Babylon' is similar to other expressions using 'daughter': 'daughter of Zion' (Isa. 1:8); 'daughter of Tyre' (Ps. 45:12); 'daughter of Edom' (Lam. 4:21). It is a personification of Babylon itself.

Psalm 138

Of David.

This psalm is the first of the final group of psalms (Pss. 138-145) ascribed to David. The difficulties mentioned in the psalm (see vv. 3 and 7) seem to be more than personal incidents. They reflect some major national situation in which God intervened to rescue his own people Israel. Thus this psalm has features in common with David's song of thanksgiving (Ps. 18), though much shorter and more direct. It is both a song of praise and an expression of confident trust. The opening verses are typical of thanksgiving songs in that a cluster of terms are employed to describe the psalmist's adoration of God ('… praise … sing praise … bow down … praise'). Verses 1-2 are also balanced later in the psalm by verses 4-6.[1]

Verses 1-2	**Verses 4-6**
for (kî) praise (yâdâh)	*kings . . . praise (yâdâh)*
your name	LORD
your word ('imrâh)	*the words of your mouth ('imrîm)*
for (kî) you have exalted (gâdal, Hi.)	*for (kî) great (gâdôl) is the glory*

1. Praise for Deliverance (*vv. 1-3*)
I will praise you, O Lord, with all my heart; before the 'gods' I will sing your praise (*v. 1*). The psalmist rejoices in what the Lord has done for him.[2] The reference to all the heart may well be a deliberate recollection of Deuteronomy 6:5. Here as

---

[1] This is pointed out by Konrad Schaefer, *Psalms,* p. 324.

[2] 'O Lord' is not in the Hebrew text, but clearly some identification is needed of whom reference is made by the words 'I will praise *you*.'

elsewhere, 'gods' is a Hebrew term applied to human rulers (Exod. 21:6; 22:8-9; Ps. 82:1), and therefore synonymous with 'kings' in verse 4.[3]

I will bow down toward your holy temple and will praise your name for your love and your faithfulness, for you have exalted above all things your name and your word (*v.* 2). Prostration in worship, whether for private prayer or at the sanctuary, was common. The verb 'bow down' is often accompanied by another verb, here being amplified by 'praise'.[4] The mention of the temple does not compel a dating of the psalm after the building of the first temple, far less after the building of the post-exilic temple. The Hebrew term for temple (*hêkâl*) is applied to the tent that was God's house before the temple was built (1 Sam. 1:9; 3:3), and in Psalm 27:4-5 it is used along with house (*báyit*), booth (*sukkâh*), and tent (*'óhel*) to describe the temporary dwelling place for the ark of the covenant. The king will prostrate himself in adoration before God, and in particular will praise his covenant love and faithfulness. In providing deliverance for him and for his people, God has demonstrated above all else his abiding character and his commitment to his promises. God's name and word are dominant over everything.[5]

When I called, you answered me; you made me bold and stout-hearted (*v.* 3). On the day of deliverance, a cry for help was heard and answered. The idiom here for address to God (*b^eyôm qârâ'tî*, lit. 'in the day I called') is frequently used in the Psalter (for examples, see 56:9; 86:7; 102:2). God responded to the need of his servant the king and of his people. In the face of attackers he was encouraged and helped. Elsewhere David claims God as his 'strength' (Ps. 27:5). Here he confesses that God has imparted strength to him (NIV 'made me … stout-hearted').

---

[3] For discussion on 'gods', see the comments on Psalm 58:1.

[4] This unusual verb (*histach^avâh*) is probably derived from a root *châvâh* rather than from *shâchâh* as traditionally thought. See *NIDOTTE*, 2, p. 42.

[5] The last clause in this verse is awkward, for the MT has, 'for you have magnified your word above all your name.' The NIV rendering is following a long tradition in English translations that goes back at least to the Prayer Book Version (1662), and which was based on Sebastian Münster (1488-1552) whose Latin translation was, *Magnificasti supra omnia nomen tuum et eloquium tuum*. Other views are summarised by L. C. Allen, *Psalms 101-150*, p. 244.

2. A Prayer for Gentile Rulers (*vv. 4-5*)
May all the kings of the earth praise you, O LORD, when they hear the words of your mouth. May they sing of the ways of the LORD, for the glory of the LORD is great (*vv. 4-5*). David's prayer is for the conversion of the kings (and presumably their subjects) when they hear his testimony (cf. his desire to praise God among the nations in Ps. 18:49). What they will hear will be the promises that God has made to Israel, the disclosure of his gracious purposes for those who trust in him. The ways of the LORD are the instructions he has given to guide his children and so direct their steps (Ps. 25:8-12). Gentile kings and nations will join in praise for these loving and faithful ways, which in themselves testify that God is righteous (Ps. 145:17) and which show his supreme glory. No great difference exists between 'for the glory of the LORD is great' and the similar expression in Psalm 135:5: 'for the LORD is great'.

3. Confidence in God's Keeping Power (*vv. 6-8*)
Though the LORD is on high, he looks upon the lowly, but the proud he knows from afar. Though I walk in the midst of trouble, you preserve my life; you stretch out your hand against the anger of my foes, with your right hand you save me (*vv. 6-7*). The God of glory stoops to look with favour on the lowly (*shâfâl*; cf. 136:23, 'who remembered us in our low estate'), while at the same time he notes from afar (possibly meaning, 'from heaven') the character of the proud. These he mocks, but to the lowly he gives grace (Prov. 3:34). The psalmist knows that, in his dangerous situations, he has been protected by God, with God's hand being turned towards him in saving power. However, that same hand is turned to oppose his hateful enemies.

The LORD will fulfil [his purpose] for me; your love, O LORD, endures forever – do not abandon the works of your hands (*v. 8*). The verb 'fulfil' (Hebrew *gâmar*) is a rare word, but, as in Psalm 57:2, it seems to refer to God's purpose or will being completed, and hence the NIV addition of the words 'his purpose' brings out the meaning well. Part of that purpose is that covenant love is maintained for all time (see the refrain in Ps. 136, 'his love endures forever'). The final prayer is that God's people will not be abandoned. This interpretation of 'the works of your hands' is supported by reference to Isaiah 60:21 and 64:8.

Psalm 139

For the director of music. Of David. A psalm.

The content of this psalm is intensely personal. Its main theme is the way in which God knows all about his creatures. Nowhere can we hide from him, and darkness itself is not able to cover us or our actions from his all-seeing eye. After the first eighteen verses, there is a sudden shift, for then we are confronted with a section invoking curses on the psalmist's (and God's) enemies. This is clearly an integral part of the psalm, for the concluding prayer (vv. 23-24) repeats the ideas and language of verses 1-3. If we want to join in that final prayer, we must understand the content of the psalm and pray in the same spirit as the psalmist.

The psalm contains a profound awareness of the solemnity of asking God to search us – not just the outward life but the inward soul as well. We are known before and after birth, and nothing can be hidden from him. The nearest biblical passages to this occur in the Book of Job.

1. The All-Seeing God (*vv. 1-6*)

O Lord, you have searched me and you know me. You know when I sit and when I rise; you perceive my thoughts from afar (*vv. 1-2*). Every detail of our lives is open before God. The language of human digging and searching is applied to God to show how deep and personal is his knowledge of each one of us. Irrespective of our immediate situation, he knows us absolutely, and even the inmost recesses of our minds are like an open book before him.[1] The presence of the personal pronoun 'you' (*'attâh*) at the start of verse 2 is probably for emphasis: 'you indeed', or 'you alone'.

You discern my going out and my lying down; you are familiar with all my ways. Before a word is on my tongue you know it completely, O LORD (*vv. 3-4*). The whole of the psalmist's life, summarised by the expressions 'going out' and 'lying down', is open before God. Our very thoughts are perceived by God before we even speak a word. As becomes evident later in the psalm, the psalmist's enemies are clearly in his mind as he speaks about God's knowledge of his situation. He is addressing God as the ruler of the world and the divine judge.

You hem me in – behind and before; you have laid your hand upon me. Such knowledge is too wonderful for me, too lofty for me to attain (*vv. 5-6*). There is no escape from God's presence. If the psalmist goes forward, God is there. If he goes backward, he still meets with him. God's hand reaches out to keep him within grasp. While the verb 'hem in' (*tsûr*) can have a hostile intent ('besiege'), yet here, as elsewhere, it denotes God's protective care. God is not only all-knowing (omniscient) but also everywhere present (omnipresent), and his knowledge is beyond human understanding. It is called here 'wonder' knowledge, using a Hebrew expression that regularly denotes actions that by their very nature are beyond human ability (cf. its use in Pss 71:17; 72:18; and 86:10; NIV 'marvellous deeds'). We can truly know God because he reveals himself to us, but we cannot know him exhaustively. That type of knowledge is his alone, and that is what the psalmist means when he says: 'I cannot [attain] to it.'

2. The Inescapable God (*vv. 7-12*)

Where can I go from your Spirit? Where can I flee from your presence? (*v. 7*). These rhetorical questions introduce several possibilities of where the psalmist could seem to go to escape

---

[1] 'My thoughts' (*rē̂'î*) involves a rare word (*rêa'*) that only occurs here and in verse 17. It is probably an Aramaic word related to *ra'yôn* in Daniel 2:29; 4:16; 5:6, 10; and 7:28. Aramaic influence is also present in the use of *l^e* to mark 'my thoughts' as the object of the verb 'you perceive'. For this grammatical usage, see the note on Psalm 116:16.

from God. There is no implication that escape from God is possible. Rather, the point is being made, as in Jeremiah 23:24, that there is nowhere one can go to evade God.

If I go up to the heavens, you are there; if I make my bed in the depths, you are there. If I rise on the wings of the dawn, if I settle on the far side of the sea, even there your hand will guide me, your right hand will hold me fast (*vv. 8-9*). Nowhere in all of creation provides a hiding place from God. The extremities are used to signify the totality of the universe (for similar language, see Job 11:7-9; Amos 9:1-4). Height and depth, east ('the wings of the dawn') and west (*yâm*, 'the sea', i.e. the Mediterranean), embrace all that exists. Wherever one may go, God's hand is able to reach and to control the unfolding of events. Clearly 'to hold fast' (*'âchaz*) denotes the same kind of protective care indicated by 'hem in' (v. 5; cf. also the use of the same verb in Ps. 73:23, 'you hold me by my right hand').

If I say, 'Surely the darkness will hide me and the light become night around me,' even the darkness will not be dark to you; the night will shine like the day, for darkness is as light to you (*vv. 11-12*). Another illustration is given. If distance (height/depth, east/west) will not let one escape from God, perhaps darkness will provide a suitable cover. The answer comes that day and night are alike to God. The final sentence is very brief in Hebrew: 'like the darkness, like the light' (the idiom has come over into English, 'like father, like son'). Darkness lets no one escape from God's superintendence.

3. The Creator God (*vv. 13-18*)

For you created my inmost being; you knit me together in my mother's womb. I praise you because I am fearfully and wonderfully made; your works are wonderful, I know that full well (*vv. 13-14*). In describing his creation the psalmist uses an unusual verb for create (*qânâh*). It only occurs five times in this sense in the Old Testament,[2] rather than the more

[2] The other passages are Genesis 14:19, 22; Deuteronomy 32:6; Psalm 78:54; and Proverbs 8:22. Psalm 78:54 is another possible occurrence. See *TWOT*, II, p. 208

common verb (*bârâ'*) of Genesis 1:1 and many other places. Abram used it when speaking to Melchizedek and the king of Sodom, when he called God, '*Creator* of heaven and earth' (Gen. 14:19, 22). From conception we are God's creation, with a body carefully constructed and woven together. Hence, when the psalmist considers himself, he stands amazed at this creative work. The use of the words 'wonderfully' and 'wonderful' draw attention to the divine activity that brought him into existence (cf. the comments on Pss. 71:17 and 72:18 for the use of this Hebrew word).

My frame was not hidden from you when I was made in the secret place. When I was woven together in the depths of the earth, your eyes saw my unformed body. All the days ordained for me were written in your book before one of them came to be (*vv. 15-16*). His life was open before God even from before birth. The womb is called 'the secret place' and 'the depths of the earth', because it shares with those areas the idea of separation from the normal realm of life. It is dark and hidden from human vision, but quite open to God's sight. The length of life is sovereignly determined by God, and with foreknowledge he knows the life history as if it was written beforehand. God does not need a written record, but the idea of a book is used in the Old Testament as a reassuring way of speaking of God's knowledge of, and care for, his people (Exod. 32:32; Pss. 56:8; 69:28; Mal. 3:16). These thoughts are very comforting to a believer, who sings:

> Whate'er my God ordains is right;
> Here shall my stand be taken;
> Though sorrow, need, or death be mine,
> Yet I am not forsaken;
> My Father's care is round me there:
> He holds me that I shall not fall,
> And so to Him I leave it all.
>
> (Samuel Rodigast 1649-1708)

How precious to me are your thoughts, O God! How vast is the sum of them! Were I to count them, they would outnumber the grains of sand. When I awake, I am still with you (*vv. 17-18*). God's 'thoughts' are his interest in, and concern for, the psalmist (cf. comment on v. 2). They are precious or valuable simply because they come from the inexhaustible depths of God's wisdom.[3] If the attempt is made to count them, then it is just like counting grains of sand. If such counting brings on sleep, then on waking the psalmist still finds his mind is preoccupied with his God.[4] He is still taken up with him (cf. the similar expression in Ps. 73:23, 'I am still with you'). This is rich meditation.

4. The Avenging God (*vv. 19-22*)

The psalm takes a sudden change at this point. From gratitude the tone changes to judgment and curse, as the situation of the psalmist's (and God's) enemies is addressed. **If only you would slay the wicked, O God! Away from me, you bloodthirsty men! They speak of you with evil intent; your adversaries misuse your name** (*vv. 19-20*). The psalmist appeals to God to intervene and remove his enemies.[5] The character of the wicked is noted as being blood-thirsty, and malicious and blasphemous in speech. The last clause is ambiguous, because the Hebrew text says: 'lifted up in vain – your cities.' The NIV (along with most English versions) considers that 'cities' should be read as 'adversaries' (only one letter is different in Hebrew),[6] and that 'lifted up in

---

[3] The word for 'sum' is *ro'sh,* which normally means 'head'. In Numbers 5:7 it refers to the sum of money to be paid, while in Psalm 119:160 it is the sum of the LORD's words. Here the totality of his thoughts are in view.

[4] 'I awake' has often been interpreted as a reference to the resurrection, but no mention of death has occurred in this psalm. This view was based on the Targum and Symmachus. Revocalisation to *h*ᵃ*qitstsotî,* 'I come to an end', has been proposed but it has no manuscript support.

[5] Two unusual words occur in this verse. The word for 'God' (*'elôâh*) appears in some of the oldest poetry in the Old Testament (Deut. 32:15, 17), and is frequent in the debates in the Book of Job (forty-one times). Three times it is used in the Psalter (Pss. 50:22; 114:7; 139:19). The word 'slay' (*qâtal*), though well known to students of Hebrew because of its use as a paradigm verb, is actually only used three times in the Old Testament (Job 13:15; 24:14; Ps. 139:19). It is used six times in the Aramaic passages in Daniel.

[6] The NIV translation, 'your adversaries', can be supported by reference to the use in Daniel 4:19 of *'ârâk,* 'your adversaries'. The word *'âr* may well be an Aramaic word and not the Hebrew word meaning 'city'. Cf. possible Aramaic influence noted in verses 2 and 19.

vain' is an echo of the Third Commandment. The adversaries misuse God's name, either by using it blasphemously, or by bringing reproach on it by their false way of life.[7]

Do I not hate those who hate you, O LORD, and abhor those who rise up against you? I have nothing but hatred for them; I count them my enemies (*vv. 21-22*). These verses show clearly that the cry for vengeance on enemies is not out of personal vindictiveness. As in Psalm 5:8-10 (see comment) the enemies are God's enemies. Here the psalmist is pledging his loyalty to the LORD in a manner customary in the ancient Near East. In the international treaties of the Near East a party entering into an alliance was obliged to treat the other party's enemies as his enemies. The principle was, as an ancient Hittite treaty put it: 'With my friend you shall be friend, and with my enemy you shall be enemy'.[8] God himself had promised in the Book of the Covenant: 'I will be an enemy to your enemies and I will oppose those who oppose you' (Exod. 23:22). For the wider issues raised by cursing in the Psalms, see the Introduction.

5. The Guiding God (*vv. 23-24*)

Search me, O God, and know my heart; test me and know my anxious thoughts. See if there is any offensive way in me, and lead me in the way everlasting (*vv. 23-24*). The concluding thoughts echo the opening of the psalm. The psalmist exposes himself to the all-seeing eye of God and is prepared for his thoughts to be tested by him. He contrasts two ways – the offensive way and the everlasting way. He shuns the former and prays for his footsteps to be guided in the latter. 'The way everlasting' (*dérek ʿôlâm*) may be a reference backward, rather than forward. It is in the old way, revealed to Abraham, Isaac, and Jacob, and in which they walked, that the psalmist wants to be led. If he goes in that way, then he will be kept and continue in God's presence eternally.

---

[7] I understand the Third Commandment to direct life to be lived without hypocrisy or sham. Its focus is more on action than words. A believer has to bear the name of the LORD, i.e. his character. I have set out this explanation in 'The Interpretation of the Third Commandment', *RTR* 47 (1988), pp. 1-7.

[8] Treaty of Suppiluliumias and Aziras of Amurru (ii) 10.

Psalm 140

For the director of music. A psalm of David.

While this appeal for help describes the attacks made on the psalmist, it shows how faith holds on to God in the hour of trial. The latter part of verse 3 is quoted by Paul in Romans 3:13 as part of the list of Old Testament quotations which point to universal sinfulness. The use of *Selah* in this psalm is very balanced, occurring after each of the first three stanzas (see the note on *Selah* in the comment on Ps. 3:2). The fourth stanza (vv. 9-11) is followed immediately by a double-verse conclusion (vv. 12-13). The translation and interpretation of the psalm are made more difficult because it contains several words that are found nowhere else in the Old Testament. Comparison with Psalms 54 and 64 is helpful, because they are generally similar in content, and all three psalms end on the same note. The enemies are both individuals and groups, though the individual ones are probably to be construed as collective references. The flow of thought throughout suggests that conclusion.

1. A Plea for Help (*vv. 1-3*)

Rescue me, O Lord, from evil men; protect me from men of violence, who devise evil plans in their hearts and stir up war every day (*vv. 1-2*). The psalmist used the word 'rescue' (*châlats*, Pi.), which occurs quite often describing God's rescue of his people from distress (see, e.g., Pss. 6:4; 18:19; 34:7; 50:15; and 81:7). The wicked act in secret to make their plans, and then carry out their premeditated evil. With hostile intent they come against the psalmist, who needs divine protection in such circumstances. He lives in a situation of perpetual warfare. The psalmist is speaking about enemies *within* Israel, who conjure up many acts of evil in their hearts. Like another psalmist (Ps. 120:7) he knows that even when he speaks peace, the enemies are bent on war.

They make their tongues as sharp as a serpent's; the poison of vipers is on their lips. ***Selah*** (*v. 3*). This verse is a combination of the ideas of Psalms 64:3 and 58:4. The tongues of the wicked are as sharp and as venomous as those of snakes. The effect of the words is heightened by onomatopoeia, as the repetition of the *sh* sound three times is an imitation of the hissing sound of serpents.[1]

2. A Prayer for Protection (*vv. 4-5*)

Keep me, O LORD, from the hands of the wicked; protect me from men of violence who plan to trip my feet (*v. 4*). The opposition of the enemies is not only verbal. It also takes the form of physical violence. The initial plea of verse 1 is extended in this verse to emphasise the nature of the enemies. 'Protect me from men of violence' is an exact repetition, while the final clause defines further the enemies' activities. They set snares for the psalmist, attempting to trap him and cause him to stumble.

Proud men have hidden a snare for me; they have spread out the cords of their net and have set traps for me along my path. ***Selah*** (*v. 5*). The adjective 'proud' (*gê'îm*) or its synonyms are used both negatively and positively in the Old Testament. It can be used of God's pride or excellency (cf. the name of the spy from the tribe of Gad, Geuel [*ge'ûêl*], which means 'God is majestic', Num. 13:15). However, the majority usage is of a negative character, of people who are arrogant and presumptuous. Here it describes those whose ultimate source of confidence is themselves, not God. The metaphors from hunting continue as the psalmist speaks of the attacks that have been made upon him. Psalm 10:2-11 contains the same imagery and some of the same language (such as 'arrogance', which comes from the same Hebrew root as 'proud' here).

[1] Mitchell Dahood, *Psalms III: 101-150*, p. 301, has pointed this out. The Hebrew is *shân[a]nû l[e]shônâm k[e]mô-nâchâsh*.

3. A Profession of Trust (*vv. 6-8*)

O LORD, I say to you, 'You are my God.' Hear, O LORD, my cry for mercy (*v. 6*). As is typical in appeals for help, there is a strong assertion of confidence in the LORD. The psalmist professes his close relationship with him, and uses that as the basis for his plea. The similar plea for God to listen occurs in the following psalm (Ps. 141:1). Crying for mercy is a recognition of the need for God's forgiving grace.[2]

O Sovereign LORD, my strong deliverer, who shields my head in the day of battle – do not grant the wicked their desires, O LORD; do not let their plans succeed, or they will become proud. *Selah* (*vv. 7-8*). The LORD is the protector of his servants, shielding them from the deadly blows of the enemies. They have their designs set on destruction, and it is only God who can intervene to thwart them. The Hebrew word for 'plans' (*zâmâm*) occurs nowhere else in the Old Testament, but its meaning here appears similar to related words in Psalms 26:10 and 37:7 ('wicked schemes'). The psalmist does not wish these plans to be promoted.[3] The final clause of verse 8 is difficult. The Hebrew text simply says, 'they lift up' (*yârûmû*), which the NIV interprets as lifting up in pride or arrogance. Other modern translations (see RSV, GNB, REB) link it with the next verse. The NIV interpretation makes good sense in the context.

4. A Prayer for Vindication (*vv. 9-11*)

Let the heads of those who surround me be covered with the trouble their lips have caused. Let burning coals fall upon them; may they be thrown into the fire, into miry pits, never to rise (*vv. 9-10*). The context shows that this is not a personal vendetta of the psalmist against his enemies. He is a loyal covenant servant (see v. 6) who wants God to vindicate him by turning the evil of the enemies back upon themselves. The prayer is for judgment to be carried out on them of such

---

[2] The noun 'cry for mercy' always occurs in the plural (*tach*^{a}*nûnîm*), and in six of its seven occurrences in the Psalms it occurs with 'voice', as it does here.

[3] This seems to be the meaning of this rare verb, *pûq* II. See *BDB*, p. 809; *DCH*, VI, p. 669.

severity (likened to 'burning coals', 'fire', and 'miry pits') that it will be final ('never to rise'). Their cutting words and traps made for others will rebound on themselves and such punitive action will be unanswerable (Ps. 36:12).

Let slanderers not be established in the land; may disaster hunt down men of violence (*v. 11*). Some of the attacks are not physical but verbal (see v. 3), and his prayer is that such slanderers will not find a secure place in the land. They have been the hunters (vv. 4-5), and now the prayer is that their own plans will recoil on them. What they have planned for others will be inflicted on these men of violence. This is the third occurrence of the idea, though the phrase here is singular, 'man of violence', not plural as in verses 1 and 4.

5. Confidence in God's Judgment (*vv. 12-13*)

I know that the LORD secures justice for the poor and upholds the cause of the needy. Surely the righteous will praise your name and the upright will live before you (*vv. 12-13*). As with Psalms 54 and 64, this one ends on a note of joyful triumph. These verses stand parallel to verses 6-7, with first person verbs commencing both sections ('I say', 'I know'). The psalmist rests assured that the LORD will see that the rights of the poor and needy are maintained. That confidence translates into the expectation that when victory comes for the upright, they will rejoice that their lives have been spared. There will be confession then that divine grace has overcome all the enemies and that God's name is to be exalted because of his wondrous victory. The characterisation of the godly as 'righteous/upright' is typical language in the Psalter. They shall indeed dwell in the presence of God.[4]

---

[4] The NIV rendering of 'live' for the verb *yêsh^{e}vû* is an unnecessary change, for 'dwell' has rich connotations of abiding in God's presence. Cf. Psalms 15:1 and 91:1.

Psalm 141

A psalm of David.

Psalms 140 and 141 are closely related in language and tone. This psalm is also an appeal for help, and it displays the same confidence in the Lord. Both psalms contain many references to parts of the body: hands, mouth, lips, heart, head, bones, eyes. This vivid language provides imagery that reinforces the thought patterns. After the temple was rebuilt following the return from exile, this psalm became part of the liturgy, being chanted as the evening candles were lit. The practice of using this psalm in this way carried over into the life of the early church, though John Chrysostom (AD 345-407) commented that it was sung without the obscure parts of it being understood. The use of rare Hebrew words increases the difficulty of translation and interpretation. While uncertainties remain, yet the main thrust of the appeal and its expression of trust in the Lord are clear.

1. Appeal for Help (*vv. 1-2*)

O Lord, I call to you; come quickly to me. Hear my voice when I call to you (*v. 1*). The language is typical of appeals for help (Pss. 70:1; 86:1).[1] The request is for speedy intervention by the Lord and ready response to the psalmist's cry.

May my prayer be set before you like incense; may the lifting up of my hands be like the evening sacrifice (*v.* 2). The language of the sacrificial system is used to give expression to the prayer for acceptance. It is reading too much into the words to suggest that the idea is that prayer replaces sacrifice.

---

[1] See comment on Psalm 140:6.

The psalmist wants his prayer to be accepted by God just as the incense and evening sacrifice are.

2. Prayer for Wisdom (*vv. 3-5c*)

Set a guard over my mouth, O LORD; keep watch over the door of my lips. Let not my heart be drawn to what is evil, to take part in wicked deeds with men who are evildoers; let me not eat of their delicacies (*vv. 3-4*). In the previous psalm mention is made of the slander of wicked men (Ps. 140:3). Now it is the action of wicked men that is in view.[2] The psalmist pleads that he will not share in such use of the tongue. If God guards his mouth, then no evil words will come from it. The New Testament teaches that our speech can both 'bless our Lord and Father', and also 'curse people made in the likeness of God' (James 3:9). Such behaviour should not be found among God's children. In addition, the psalmist asks that his thoughts and his actions will be kept pure. He does not want to associate with evildoers, not even as much as to partake of their hospitality. It may be that the psalmist is thinking particularly of their ill-gotten gains that enable them to purchase such delicacies. By his thoughts, words, and deeds he must be marked off from those who are intrinsically evil.

Let a righteous man strike me – it is a kindness; let him rebuke me – it is oil on my head. My head will not refuse it (*v. 5a-c*). At this point the language of the psalm becomes much more difficult and many variations occur in translations. The exegesis behind the NIV rendering of this verse goes back a long way, and can be found in several commentaries.[3] The psalmist is willing to be rebuked by a good man, for such rebuke is to be regarded as 'wounds from a friend' (Prov. 27:6; also Prov. 17:10). When this happens it is an expression of

---

[2] The plural 'men' is here *'îshîm* instead of the usual form *nâshîm*. This same plural form is also found in Isaiah 53:3 and Proverbs 8:4.

[3] For example, cf. J. A. Alexander, *The Psalms Translated and Explained*, p. 545; E. W. Hengstenberg, *Commentary on the Psalms*, III, p. 513; F. Delitzsch, *Commentary on the Psalms*, II, p. 364; J. J. S. Perowne, *The Book of Psalms*, II, pp. 452-53.

true kindness (Heb., *chésed*), a sign of the strength of the bond between two people. Instead of inflicting harm on him, it is as soothing as oil on the head (cf. Ps. 23:5),[4] and will not be refused.[5]

3. A Prayer for Vindication (*vv. 5d-7*)

Yet my prayer is ever against the deeds of evildoers; their rulers will be thrown down from the cliffs, and the wicked will learn that my words were well spoken. [They will say,] 'As one ploughs and breaks up the earth, so our bones have been scattered at the mouth of the grave' (*vv. 5d-7*). In consecutive psalms prayers for vindication occur (140:9-11; 141:5d-7). On this occasion the prayer is directed against both the evildoers and their rulers.[6] The latter are singled out because they have allowed evil to triumph in society. The desire is for them to come to a cruel end. When that happens, the wicked will make a pronouncement, using what appears to be a proverbial saying. The idea behind verse 7 is that a farmer when ploughing turns up much that is underneath and leaves it on the surface. So the bones of the rulers will have no permanent burial place but will lie scattered over the ground.

5. Prayer for Deliverance (*vv. 8-10*)

But my eyes are fixed on you, O Sovereign LORD; in you I take refuge – do not give me over to death (*v. 8*). The psalm ends with further prayer but also with an assertion of the psalmist's settled conviction of heart and mind. His hope is in his

---

[4] The Hebrew text has *shémen ro'sh*. While *ro'sh* often means 'head', it can also mean 'choicest' (see this usage in Ps. 137:6), and L. C. Allen, *Psalms 101-150*, pp. 269, 271, prefers this meaning here.

[5] The verb (*yânî*) appears to be from *nâvâ'* (see *DCH*, V, p. 634), and the NIV is following this derivation.

[6] The Hebrew text of these verses is difficult, partly because the subjects are unclear. In verse 5d '*their* evil deeds' does not specify who is intended, while in verse 6, '*they* will be cast down' and '*they* will learn', need some identification if the English translation is going to be meaningful. The NIV rendering attempts to smooth out the text, adds the words 'They will say' at the beginning of verse 7, and overall is an acceptable version of the Hebrew.

God, to whom he looks with expectancy and in whom he finds shelter. In the face of danger from wicked men he asks for preservation in life (Heb., 'do not empty my life').[7]

Keep me from the snares they have laid for me, from the traps set by evildoers. Let the wicked fall into their own nets, while I pass by in safety (*vv. 9-10*). The concluding requests are for safety in the face of the enemies' plots, and for the enemies to be ensnared by their own schemes. This is a reassertion of what is enunciated in Psalms 9:15-16 and 57:6 (see comment).

---

[7] The verb appears to be *ʿârâh* Pi., in the sense of 'pour out', 'lay bare one's life'.

Psalm 142

A maskil of David. When he was in the cave. A prayer.

There are many repeated expressions throughout this psalm, which give intensity to the psalmist's loneliness and grief. The title locates it in the period when David was fleeing from Saul, with the cave most probably being Adullam (1 Sam. 22:1) rather than Engedi (1 Sam. 24:1-22). As the final part of a trilogy of psalms, its theme continues that of Psalms 140 and 141. In the midst of distress there is confession of sure trust in the LORD, and acknowledgment that he knows the whole circumstances in which his servant is placed. The opening verses (1-3a) are intensely personal, as the psalmist pours out his soul in complaint to the LORD. The switch to confident trust is marked by the words '*But you* know my way' (v. 3a). Powerful enemies oppose him, but the LORD is able to set him free, a deliverance over which the righteous will rejoice (v. 7).

1. A Cry for Help (*vv. 1-4*)

I cry aloud to the LORD; I lift up my voice to the LORD for mercy. I pour out my complaint before him; before him I tell my trouble (*vv. 1-2*). The psalmist adopts formal language to state his initial requests, language such as would be used in addressing a superior like a king. There is parallelism in the Hebrew not brought out in English translations:

> '[With] my voice to the LORD I cry out;
> [with] my voice to the LORD I make supplication'.

This emphasises both the nature of his requests, and the one to whom he looks for help. The typical language of laments is continued in verse 2 (cf. Pss. 42:2; 62:8), as mention is made of his complaints in his distress. Complaint is an appropriate element in worship as believers acknowledge in this way God's superintendence of their lives.[1]

When my spirit grows faint within me, it is you who know my way. In the path where I walk men have hidden a snare for me (*v. 3*). To speak of the spirit growing faint describes a condition when outward circumstances overwhelm a person (Ps. 77:3; Isa. 57:16). David knows that his enemies have plotted against him and laid a snare for him to trip over (cf. the use of 'snare' in Pss. 140:5 and 141:9). But in spite of his distress he recognises that his ways are known to his God. This shift to second person speech ('it is you') highlights his deep personal relationship with the LORD, who understands his way. 'Way' (*n^e^tîvâh*) probably means 'way out of my distress'. It is not the common word for 'way', occurring twenty-one times in the Old Testament, and only here and in Psalm 119:105 in the Psalter. However, it is not very different in meaning from two other Hebrew words for 'way' (*dérek* and *ʾórach*), as is shown especially by the fact that *ʾórach* is used here in the parallel phrase ('in *the path* where I walk'). Where it does differ is that it means more a lifestyle, a pattern of behaviour.[2]

Look to my right and see; no one is concerned for me. I have no refuge; no one cares for my life (*v. 4*). There is no contradiction between this and the previous verse. God truly knows his way (v. 3). The psalmist now uses the typical language of prayer in which appeal is made to God often likening him to a human being (anthropomorphism). When he looks to his right, the place of the helper is vacant (Pss. 109:31; 121:5). No one takes note of his situation except the LORD,[3] who abides when other helpers fail. Any source of

---

[1] Verse 2 is couched in a typical poetic style, with a chiastic pattern and balanced formation: *ʾeshpok lefânâv sîchî*, 'I pour out before him my complaint'; *tsârâtî lefânâv ʾaggîd*, 'My trouble before him I tell'.

[2] E. H. Merrill has a good discussion of these synonyms in *NIDOTTE*, 3, pp. 202-03.

[3] The verb that the NIV translates as 'concerned' is *nâkar*, Hi. It has as one of its meanings 'pay attention to' (see *DCH*, V, p. 693).

help known to him has disappeared,[4] and no one seeks his good.

2. A Cry from the Heart (*vv.* 5-7)

I cry to you, O LORD; I say, 'You are my refuge, my portion in the land of the living' (*v.* 5). Just as the psalm began with a repeated call ('I cry aloud … I lift up my voice'), so the second section commences with a double expression of need and confidence ('I cry … I say'). Among men David found no place of refuge (Heb., *mânôs*, v. 4), but he knows that he has a place of shelter (Heb. *machseh*) in the LORD. To make this confession to the LORD is recognition of his own insecurity and helplessness. 'My portion' is a borrowing of the language relating to God's provision for the Levites (see the comment on Ps. 16:5).

Listen to my cry, for I am in desperate need; rescue me from those who pursue me, for they are too strong for me. Set me free from my prison, that I may praise your name. Then the righteous will gather about me because of your goodness to me (*vv.* 6-7). The urgency of the situation is plain from the series of cries: 'Listen … rescue … set me free'. The psalmist has been brought very low (Heb., *dallôtî meo'd*), and cries out for rescue from his persecutors. 'The prison' (*masgêr*) is not one in our modern sense, but rather it is a metaphor for loneliness and despair.[5] If God does act in response to the prayer, then praise will follow. Though presently separated from fellow believers, deliverance will bring renewed fellowship with them and united praise. In contrast to the enemies, God will act in tender love towards his afflicted servant.[6]

---

[4] The NIV 'I have no refuge' is the translation of the Hebrew *'âvad mânôs mimmennî*, 'Refuge has perished from me.' Other versions are closer to the Hebrew idiom: NASB, mg., 'Escape has perished from me'; NKJV, 'Refuge has failed me'; ESV, 'No refuge remains to me'.

[5] Cf. its only other Old Testament usages in Isaiah 24:22 and 42:7.

[6] The final verb is *gâmal* which can have a wide range of meaning. Because it is used of a mother's love for her infant child, the traditional English rendering in this psalm, 'has dealt bountifully', is close to the mark. Cf. this interpretation in AV, NASB, NKJV, ESV. The REB renders 'when you give me my due reward', picking up on another use of the verb to denote paying recompense. This understanding of the verse, however, does not seem very likely.

Psalm 143

A psalm of David.

This is the last of Luther's 'Pauline Psalms' (see Introduction), and also the last of the penitential psalms (see the introductory comment on Ps. 6). It is not surprising in the least that the apostle Paul should twice echo this psalm (Rom. 3:20; Gal. 2:16), and in both cases add the explanatory words that justification in God's sight is not by observing the law. This is an implication from what the psalm says about God's judgment, for verse 2a is recognition that if God does judge according to works, then the psalmist will be condemned. The psalm puts the emphasis on grace and faith, and Paul rightly sees that and uses it when expounding the gospel.

The psalm is divided into two sections, with *Selah* in verse 6 marking the division. In the first six verses the psalmist describes his situation and makes his appeal. In the second section of six verses he presents his prayer to God for speedy deliverance. The psalm contains some of the most beautiful language of confident trust in God's mercy to be found anywhere in the Old Testament.

1. An Initial Prayer for Mercy (*vv. 1-2*)

O Lord, hear my prayer, listen to my cry for mercy; in your faithfulness and righteousness come to my relief (*v. 1*). As in many of the later verses, this opening verse has similarities with other passages in the psalms. These similarities are great with two similar appeals in nearby psalms (see 140:6, 'hear ... my cry for mercy; and 141:1,

'Listen to my voice').[1] There was clearly a deep knowledge of other biblical passages that could be utilised in prayer (see the introductory comment on Ps. 86). The opening petitions resemble Psalms 28:2; 39:12; and 54:2, while mention of 'faithfulness and righteousness' recalls the character of the covenant God of Israel (Exod. 34:6). The NIV correctly paraphrases the Hebrew 'answer me' with the words 'come to my relief'.

Do not bring your servant into judgment, for no one living is righteous before you (*v.* 2). David knows that he will be condemned if he is judged on his own behaviour and character. Not a single person is able to maintain a righteous standing with God by their own works. Paul quotes the second part of this verse twice in his epistles (Rom. 3:20; Gal. 2:16).[2] This Old Testament teaching is amplified in the New Testament where we are taught that God 'saved us, not because of righteous things we had done, but because of his mercy' (Titus 3:5). Augustus Toplady (1740-1778) described accurately this biblical understanding of salvation:

> Not the labour of my hands
> Can fulfil thy laws demands;
> Could my zeal no respite know,
> Could my tears for ever flow,
> All for sin could not atone:
> Thou must save and thou alone.
> ('Rock of Ages')

2. Present Distress and Past Mercy (*vv.* 3-6)

The enemy pursues me, he crushes me to the ground; he makes me dwell in darkness like those long dead. So my spirit grows faint within me; my heart within me is

---

[1] The imperative *ha'ᵃzînâh* (*'âzan*, Hi.) is translated differently by the NIV in Psalms 140:6 and 141:1 ('hear') as compared with Psalm 143:1 ('listen'). Throughout the Psalter as a whole it uses 'listen' much more than 'hear' as the translation. It is preferable to use the same translation in all passages where this imperative occurs.

[2] In both passages Paul adds the words, 'not by works of the law' (*ex ergôn nomou*). While these words do not occur in Psalm 143:2, yet they correctly interpret its meaning.

dismayed (*vv. 3-4*). The persecution the psalmist is enduring has as its aim his ultimate destruction. 'Darkness' (*machshâk*) is a synonym for the grave.[3] The second part of verse 3 ('he makes ... long dead') appears in almost identical form in Lamentations 3:6, while the first part of verse 4 is an almost exact repetition of Psalm 142:3a. Constant persecution has had its effect, and the psalmist is at the point of utter despair.

I remember the days of long ago; I meditate on all your works and consider what your hands have done (*v. 5*). In circumstances like these, what brings hope is reflection on the past actions of the LORD. The words and ideas of this verse are very similar to Psalm 77:11-12 (see commentary). Meditation on God's wonderful activity in the past gives confidence for the present.

I spread out my hands to you; my soul thirsts for you like a parched land. *Selah* (*v. 6*). Encouraged by the past, the psalmist stretches out his hands as he prays to God (for similar expressions, see Pss. 28:2; 44:20; 88:9; and Lamentations 1:17). Just as the dry ground longs for refreshing rain, so his soul thirsts for God (cf. the similar expressions of longing for God in Psalms 42:1-2 and 63:1).

4. Prayer for Deliverance (*vv. 7-10*)

Answer me quickly, O LORD; my spirit fails. Do not hide your face from me or I will be like those who go down to the pit (*v. 7*). Speedy help is required, for the seeming absence of God from the situation causes the soul to pine away. When God appears to be absent, this is referred to as a hiding of his face (Pss. 30:7; 44:24; 88:14). Frequently, as here, the plea to him is not to hide his face (Pss. 27:9; 69:17; 102:2; 143:7). The state of death is often described as going down to the pit (Pss. 28:1; 88:4, 6).

Let the morning bring me word of your unfailing love, for I have put my trust in you. Show me the way I should go, for to you I lift up my soul (*v. 8*). The covenant servant has his heart firmly fixed on God ('I have put my trust', the

[3] It is a poetical word used only seven times (Isa. 29:15; 42:16; Pss. 74:20; 88:6, 18; 143:3; Lam. 3:6). In Psalm 88:6-7 it is parallel with 'grave' (*qéver*).

expression of settled conviction; see comment on Ps. 9:10), and he pleads for covenant mercy (Heb. *chésed*) to be shown towards him. The same connection of the verb 'to trust' (*bâtach*) with covenant mercy occurs also in Psalms 13:5 and 52:8. The darkness of the night is to be replaced with the light of God's favour in the morning. The servant who lifts up his heart in devotion and praise to his God, also asks for guidance in the way of righteousness, a request that is repeated in another form in verse 10. These verses are very similar to Psalm 25:1-2, 4.

Rescue me from my enemies, O LORD, for I hide myself in you. Teach me to do your will, for you are my God; may your good Spirit lead me on level ground (*vv. 9-10*). Verse 9 opens with a familiar appeal for deliverance from enemies.[4] The request for deliverance is followed by a difficult phrase. The Hebrew text says, 'to you I covered' (*'êlekâ kissitî*),[5] which the NIV interprets as 'I hide myself.' While many suggestions have been made, and English translations differ widely, the NIV translates it according to the context, for an expression of trust is what is expected.[6] The section closes with a further request for teaching, putting the prayer of verse 8a in another form. Submission to God's will is required, so that life without dangers can be likened to level ground (*'érets mîshôr*; cf. the almost identical Hebrew expression, *'érets hammîshôr*, used in Deut. 4:43, 'the desert plateau'). A physical term is here given a spiritual application. The term 'good Spirit' is also used elsewhere of the Holy Spirit (Neh. 9:20).

---

[4] This is a standard expression (cf. its use in 18:17; 59:1), which is often varied by using different objects: 'from the sword' (22:20); 'from evildoers' (59:2); 'from the hand of the wicked' (82:4); 'my soul' (86:13; 120:2).

[5] The expression is very unusual and it is not difficult to see why it has caused problems for very early translators right through to the modern period. The verb (*kâshâh*, Pi.) normally has an object expressed, and in addition this is the only time it appears with the preposition 'to' (*'el*). It is possible that the change to *'el* instead of the more common *'al* is just the known phenomenon of prepositional interchange.

[6] For further discussion, but without definitive solutions, see J. J. S. Perowne, *The Book of Psalms*, II, pp. 462-63; L. C. Allen, *Psalms 101-150*, p. 281; A. A. Anderson, *The Book of Psalms II* (London: Marshall, Morgan & Scott, 1972), p. 929.

4. Concluding Summary Prayer (*vv. 11-12*)

For your name's sake, O LORD, preserve my life; in your righteousness, bring me out of trouble. In your unfailing love, silence my enemies; destroy all my foes, for I am your servant (*vv. 11-12*). The concluding verses re-echo the opening of the psalm. While the psalmist again acknowledges that he is the LORD's servant, yet he knows that he cannot appeal for help for his own sake. It must be for God's sake that salvation is given, for he always acts in accordance with his covenant commitment (Heb., *chésed*, NIV 'unfailing love'). A servant's foes were also the foes of his covenant overlord, and so David asks God, who always acts in accordance with his righteousness, to destroy completely the psalmist's enemies. The final acknowledgment of covenant status, 'I am your servant' (*kî ʾᵃnî ʿavdekâ*) is identical to the statement in Psalm 116:16 (see comment).

Psalm 144

Of David.

There are many similarities between this psalm and David's song when God delivered him from the hand of Saul (Ps. 18). Strong echoes of other psalms also appear, but the closing verses are unlike any other passage in the Psalter. The earlier part (vv. 1-10) consists of the king's personal prayer for help, asking for deliverance from the deadly sword. After a transitional verse (v. 11), the concluding section seeks blessings on the people as a whole. While the change at verse 12 is quite marked, yet the NIV translation correctly notes the connection between the two parts of the psalm: 'Deliver and rescue me ... *Then* our sons in their youth will be like well-nurtured plants'.

After two psalms that are dominated by prayers (Pss. 142, 143), this psalm forms a bridge with the theme of praise that occurs in Psalm 145, a theme that is carried through with the hallelujah psalms that complete the whole collection (Pss. 146-150). The ascription of praise at the opening of Psalm 144, 'Blessed be the LORD, my Rock', finds its response in the opening of Psalm 145, 'I will exalt you, my God the King.'

1. A Song of Praise (*vv. 1-4*)

Praise be to the LORD my Rock, who trains my hands for war, my fingers for battle (*v. 1*). The opening exclamation of praise is a slight expansion of Psalm 18:46, while the second part echoes Psalm 18:34a. The king knows that his security is found in the LORD alone, and if victory comes in battle it is due to his assistance.

He is my loving God and my fortress, my stronghold and my deliverer, my shield, in whom I take refuge, who subdues peoples under me (*v. 2*). The accumulation of titles for God is very similar to Psalm 18:2, except for the first one. 'My loving God' is an attempt to translate an unique title for God (Heb., *chasdi,* 'my steadfast love'). The expression is probably an abbreviation of the fuller phrase (Heb., *ᵓᵉlohê chasdi,* 'God of my steadfast love', or 'my God of covenant love') which occurs in Psalm 59:10, 17. The titles highlight the character of God as the mighty saviour, who defends the king and gives him victory over surrounding nations.

O LORD, what is man that you care for him, the son of man that you think of him? Man is like a breath; his days are like a fleeting shadow (*vv.* 3-4). The question is very similar to that in Psalm 8:4 ('What is man that you are mindful of him, the son of man that you care for him?'), while the answer ('Man is like a breath; his days are like a fleeting shadow', v. 4) summarises the thought of Psalm 39:4-5. Man's lifespan is so short, and this must be accepted patiently. Also, if man's existence is of such a fleeting nature, then how much does he need the LORD's help?

2. Prayer for Deliverance (*vv. 5-8*)

Part your heavens, O LORD, and come down; touch the mountains, so that they smoke. Send forth lightning and scatter [the enemies]; shoot your arrows and rout them (*vv.* 5-6). What is described in Psalm 18 (see especially verses 9-14) as God's actions on behalf of David are now made the subject of prayer. Another appearance of God like at Mount Sinai (Exod. 20:18-19; Deut. 5:22-27) is sought. The bolts of lightning are regarded as God's arrows (see the same usage in Pss. 18:14, 77:17; and Hab. 3:11). The requests include 'scatter them' and 'rout them', which the NIV rightly interprets as directed against the enemies (cf. the same usage in Psalm 18:14: 'and scattered them').

Reach down your hand from on high; deliver me and rescue me from the mighty waters, from the hands of foreigners whose mouths are full of lies, whose right hands are deceitful (*vv.* 7-8). The series of direct requests continues. The staccato effect of these prayers stresses the urgency of the need. The psalmist wants God to condescend to him in his trouble, as he faces the might of armies around him. When the foreign leaders lift their right hands to make an oath (Deut. 32:40), they either swear falsely or else fail to keep their word. They make a pledge, but it is intended only to bring advantage to them in battle.

3. A Song of Thanksgiving (*vv. 9-10*)

I will sing a new song to you, O God; on the ten-stringed lyre I will make music to you, to the One who gives victory to kings, who delivers his servant David from the deadly sword (*vv. 9-10*). David's response is to sing 'a new song', using this expression in the same way as in Psalms 33:3, 40:3, 96:1 and 98:1. The new song is in praise of God's saving action that has delivered David from the threat of death. He names himself here as in Psalm 18:50, drawing attention also to his role as a servant who exercises kingly rule by divine appointment (see the use of the phrase 'the servant of the LORD' in the title of Ps. 18). Victory in battle could be commemorated by a musical procession, and the ten-stringed lyre may well have been a modified form of the instrument that could be carried and played by a single person.

4. A Renewed Prayer (*v. 11*)

Deliver me and rescue me from the hands of foreigners whose mouths are full of lies, whose right hands are deceitful (*v. 11*). This verse serves two purposes. It repeats the prayer of verses 7-8 (abbreviating it by omitting 'from on high' and 'from the mighty waters') in order to stress the urgency of his cry. It also serves to provide a link with the following verses, for if the prayer is answered, then peace and prosperity will follow for the nation.

5. God's Blessing of the Nation (*vv. 12-15*)

Then our sons in their youth will be like well-nurtured plants, and our daughters will be like pillars carved to adorn a palace (*v. 12*). God's deliverance from the threat of enemy attack will result in security for the people. Sons and daughters will be nurtured in a secure environment where they will be able to grow and develop. The grace and beauty of the daughters are compared to carved pillars, since it was often the practice in the Near East to have pillars carved in the shape of young women.

Our barns will be filled with every kind of provision. Our sheep will increase by thousands, by tens of thousands in our fields; our oxen will draw heavy loads. There will be no breaching of walls, no going into captivity, no cry of distress in our streets (*vv. 13-14*). God's blessing will result in abundant harvests and a great increase in flocks and herds.[1] The language reflects the covenant promise of blessing contained in passages such as Deuteronomy 28:1-14. Part of that promise was security against attack from enemies (Lev. 26:6; Deut. 28:7), here stated as the defensive walls not being breached, no exile, and none of the turmoil of battle in the city streets that leads to lamentation.

Blessed are the people of whom this is true; blessed are the people whose God is the LORD (*v. 15*). The final statement is a summary of the privileged position of Israel. The people whom God chose for his inheritance could indeed be pronounced 'Blessed' (Ps. 33:12)! An abiding covenantal relationship with the LORD results in sustained blessings for his people, though the greatest blessing of all is being able to call him our God. For the Christian, material blessings cannot compare with the privilege of being able, by the work of the Holy Spirit, to say in truth that 'Jesus is Lord' (1 Cor. 12:3).

---

[1] 'Every kind of provision' (*mizzan 'el-zan*) employs the Aramaic word for 'portion' or 'kind', *zan*, instead of the more common Hebrew *mîn*. This word also comes in 2 Chronicles 16:14, suggesting that it is a late usage, and may well be a Persian loan-word.

Psalm 145

A psalm of praise. Of David.

The final section of Davidic psalms (Pss. 138-145) is concluded by a song that extols the universal kingship of God and his gracious and just provision for all his creatures. This emphasis on the scope of God's mercy is brought out in the NIV translation by the repeated use of 'all' (see vv. 9, 10, 12, 13, 14, 15, 17, 18, 20). The psalm is an alphabetic acrostic, though in most Hebrew manuscripts the strophe commencing with the Hebrew letter *nun* is missing (v. 13b). However, as the NIV footnote on verse 13 records, one Hebrew manuscript contains it, as do the Dead Sea Scrolls and early translations such as the Syriac and Greek. Some other later versions, including Scottish Gaelic, have also included it. The psalm, after an initial song of praise (vv. 1-2), contains four sections, with a final expression of praise to conclude (v. 21). The scope of praise is broadened from the beginning to the end. In verses 1-2 the poet expresses praise to *his* God and vows to extol his name for ever and ever. In the final verse, not only does he continue praise, but he wants *every creature* to praise God's name for ever and ever.[1] Among all the psalms with titles, this is the only one that uses the word 'praise' (Heb., *tᵉhillâh*), which word also reappears in the final verse ('in praise of the LORD', *tᵉhillat yhwh*).

---

[1] The final words of verses 1 and 2, 'for ever and ever' (*leʿôlâm vâʿed*), are repeated exactly at the end of verse 21. The continuity of God's kingdom is stressed in other ways as well in the psalm, including the thought of successive generations (vv. 4 and 13) and of it being an everlasting kingdom (v. 13).

1. Praise to the King (*vv. 1-2*)

I will exalt you, my God the King; I will praise your name for ever and ever. Every day I will praise you and extol your name for ever and ever (*vv. 1-2*). The language which opens this song of praise concerning the great king and his kingdom is very similar to Psalms 30:1 and 34:1, 3. At times when God was praised by his people, language such as that in these psalms (and David's doxology in 1 Chron. 29:10-13) provided a reservoir from which appropriate expressions could be drawn. The pledge is given of constant praise that will be rendered to the King, and there is no apparent difference in meaning between 'exalt' (*rûm*, Hi.), 'praise' (*bârak*, Pi.), and 'extol' (*hâlal*, Pi.). Other versions, including the ESV, keep a little closer to the Hebrew in translating these three verbs as 'extol', 'bless', and 'praise'.

2. The Splendour of God's Majesty (*vv. 3-7*)

Great is the LORD and most worthy of praise; his greatness no one can fathom (*v. 3*). Again, there is borrowed language here. The first half of the verse echoes Psalms 48:1 and 96:4, while the second part ('his greatness no one can fathom') is modelled on Job 5:9; 9:10 and Isaiah 40:28. The psalmist draws attention to the way in which God is distinguished from his creatures. His greatness is such that it does not come within human scrutiny, for he transcends all of his creation. No one is able to penetrate his depths of knowledge.

One generation will commend your works to another; they will tell of your mighty acts. They will speak of the glorious splendour of your majesty, and I will meditate on your wonderful works (*vv. 4-5*). God's 'works' and 'mighty acts' are the subject of repeated praise, generation after generation. It was part of the responsibility of parents and elders to teach successive generations about the great deeds of the LORD (cf. Deut. 6:4-9; and see the comments on Psalm 78:1-8). As the people meditated upon what the LORD had done they would be moved to praise the wonder of his actions in creation and redemption.[2] The cluster of terms referring to God's person and works emphasises his exalted position and his great power.

They will tell of the power of your awesome works, and I will proclaim your great deeds. They will celebrate your abundant goodness and joyfully sing of your righteousness (*vv. 6-7*). The description of God's actions mount up – 'awesome works', 'great deeds', 'abundant goodness',[3] 'righteousness'. These expressions, and those in the preceding verses, are not meant to be carefully distinguished from one another, but their cumulative effect is to draw attention to the overwhelming power and majesty of God's actions. To celebrate God's goodness is clearly to take part in praiseful worship, as the parallel, 'and joyfully sing of your righteousness', indicates.

3. The Glory of God's Kingdom (*vv. 8-13a*)

The LORD is gracious and compassionate, slow to anger and rich in love. The LORD is good to all; he has compassion on all he has made (*vv. 8-9*). God's own declaration of his character (Exod. 34:6) once more forms the basis for praise (see the comments on Pss. 86:5 and 103:8). The word 'gracious' (*channûn*) comes first in the Hebrew text in order to fit the acrostic pattern. Towards all his creation the LORD shows himself as the God of abundant love and compassion. Once again the language of this passage is full of covenantal associations.

All you have made will praise you, O LORD; your saints will extol you. They will tell of the glory of your kingdom and speak of your might, so that all men may know of your

---

[2] NIV 'they will speak' depends on an alteration of the Hebrew text from 'and the words of' (*v^ediverê*) to 'they will speak' (*y^edabbêrû*). While this makes good sense, yet there is no support from the Hebrew manuscripts, though the LXX (*lalêsousin*) may reflect such a text, or else be an interpretation of the extant text. Perhaps *v^ediverê* is best understood as meaning 'the matters of' and hence the rendering: 'Of the glorious splendour of your majesty and the matters of your wonderful works, I will meditate.'

[3] The Hebrew is unusual because the adjective 'much' or 'great' (*râv*) comes *before* the expression 'your goodness' (*tûv^ekâ*). The two words are connected by a hyphen and probably they form a compound noun, 'much-goodness'.

mighty acts and the glorious splendour of your kingdom (*vv. 10-12*). Both human beings and inanimate creation are depicted as rendering praise to God. There is no essential difference between 'they will tell of your mighty acts' (v. 4) and 'they will speak of your might' (v. 11). 'Kingdom' here conveys the idea of the universal reign of God over all of creation. The 'saints' (for this term see the comment on Ps. 30:4) have the task of proclaiming the greatness of God and the glorious nature of his kingdom. The purpose of this proclamation has a missionary intent, in that all men may come to know how gracious and condescending God is. In teaching his disciples, Jesus applied the principle of God's care of the birds to show how much more his providential care extends to his believing followers (Matt. 6:25-34).

Your kingdom is an everlasting kingdom, and your dominion endures through all generations (*v. 13a*). This assertion puts in other words the declaration in the Song of the Sea: 'The LORD will reign for ever and ever' (Exod. 15:18), and similar words occur in Daniel 4:3 and 4:34. Unlike earthly kingdoms, God's kingdom is not temporary but eternal. That is why generation after generation can testify to his mighty acts (v. 4).

4. The Gracious Care of the LORD (*vv. 13b-16*)

The LORD is faithful to all his promises and loving toward all he has made (*v. 13b*).[4] Towards his creation the LORD shows utter dependability. His words stand sure, and having made a commitment he upholds his creation and in this way demonstrates his faithfulness. The word 'loving' is a Hebrew word (*châsîd*) used here of God, whereas it more commonly is used of his loyal covenant servants (see the comments on Pss. 4:3; 12:1; 18:25; and 31:23).

The LORD upholds all those who fall and lifts up all who are bowed down (*v. 14*). This is a statement of the general

---

[4] See the comments in the introduction to this psalm regarding this verse. English versions differ in their treatment of it. The AV, NASB, and NKJV all omit it entirely. The RSV, NIV, ESV, and NRSV all include it but with an appropriate footnote. While verse 13b may not be part of the original text, the teaching it contains is in accord with the Old Testament doctrine of God.

and repeated actions of the LORD.[5] He sustains those who are stumbling (Pss. 37:17, 24; 54:4; 119:116) and restores those bowed down in distress or by humiliation (Ps. 18:6).

The eyes of all look to you, and you give them their food at the proper time. You open your hand and satisfy the desires of every living thing (*vv. 15-16*). The language and ideas are very close to Psalm 104:27-28 (see the comment). Both men and animals are fed from the hands of a gracious creator who, as the heavenly Father, cares even for those who neither sow nor reap (Matt. 6:26).

5. The LORD's Providence (*vv. 17-20*)

The LORD is righteous in all his ways and loving toward all he has made. The LORD is near to all who call on him, to all who call on him in truth (*vv. 17-18*). In the manner in which he operates the LORD always deals in accordance with the norms he has set. He is gracious and righteous (Ps. 116:5), and his laws are right (Ps. 119:137). Verse 17b is the repetition of verse 13b.[6] While those far off from the LORD will not know his ready response to their cry (Isa. 29:13), yet to those who call in truth he is ready to respond by drawing near to help. He whose commands are true is ever near (Ps. 119:151).

He fulfils the desires of those who fear him; he hears their cry and saves them. The LORD watches over all who love him, but all the wicked he will destroy (*vv. 19-20*). The LORD's people are described by two terms also used elsewhere in the Psalms. They are 'those who fear him' (22:23; 25:12, 14; 33:18; 119:63) and those 'who love him' (5:11; 97:10; 119:132). Love and reverence for the LORD are fully compatible. Here the 'desire' is not for food (cf. v. 16) but for salvation from danger or distress. While the wicked are brought to destruction, the LORD preserves his own people (Hebrew *shâmar*, the same verb as in Ps. 121:7-8). As in verse 14, the participial form

---

[5] The two participles in this verse, 'upholds' (*sômêk*) and 'lifts up' (*zôqêf*), are used to express the notion of continuous action. See *IBHS*, p. 626, and *DIHG~S*, p. 133.

[6] This may help to explain the presence of the same words in verse 13b. It is possible that a scribe deliberately chose these words from later in the psalm to complete the acrostic pattern.

('watches over', *shômêr*) conveys the idea of continuous action. In contrast, the wicked will be destroyed by decisive divine action.

6. Praise to the LORD (*v. 21*)

My mouth will speak in praise of the LORD. Let every creature praise his holy name for ever and ever (*v. 21*). The opening call to praise is resumed (vv. 1-2), but carried a stage further. Not only will the psalmist engage in praise, but he calls on all creatures to share in it. 'Every creature' (Heb., *kol-bâsâr*, 'all flesh') may refer only to humans (Ps. 65:2), but the similar phrase 'everything that has breath' (*kol-n*[e]*shâmâh*) describes humans and animals in Psalm 150:6. Probably the NIV translation is correct, and therefore the psalm ends with an invitation to all living things to join in perpetual praise to the LORD.

Psalm 146

The final group of psalms (146-150) have a common feature. They all commence and finish with the expression 'Praise the Lord' (Heb., *hall^elûyâh*). For this reason they were called the 'Hallel' psalms (cf. the comment on Ps. 113 for reference to the group of psalms called the 'Egyptian Hallel'). Along with Psalm 145 they were used in later Jewish practice in the morning worship in the synagogue. They bring the whole Book of Psalms to a close on a note of triumphant praise. Psalm 146 is a typical hymn of praise, with opening and closing calls to praise enclosing a description of the ways in which the creator and King helps the needy. In the Greek and Latin versions, both Psalms 146 and 147 are ascribed to Haggai and Zechariah. The language of the psalm suggests that it comes from after the exile, but there is no express statement to confirm this.

1. A Call to Praise (*vv. 1-2*)

Praise the Lord. Praise the Lord, O my soul. I will praise the Lord all my life; I will sing praise to my God as long as I live (*vv. 1-2*). After the initial communal call to praise (it is plural in form), the hymn continues with the psalmist encouraging himself to praise the Lord. He then makes a vow to do so all through life,[1] so that this song is only one expression of the praise that he offers. Verse 2 is identical with Psalm 104:33, except that 'I will sing to the Lord' is replaced

[1] The Hebrew for 'all my life' is *b^eʿôdî*. The adverb *ʿôd* is preceded by the preposition *b^e* ('in'), and has a 1st person singular suffix appended. The phrase is used in the sense 'while I have being'. Cf. the similar use in Psalm 104:33.

by 'I will praise the LORD'. While he refers to God repeatedly as 'the LORD' (eleven times in this short psalm), yet he also calls him 'my God'. It is from personal faith that he commits himself to a life lived to praise his creator and deliverer.

2. A Call to Trust in the Lord (*vv. 3-9*)

Before describing God as the great helper the psalmist sets a contrast by issuing a warning against putting trust in men. **Do not put your trust in princes, in mortal men, who cannot save. When their spirit departs, they return to the ground; on that very day their plans come to nothing** (*vv. 3-4*). The theme of refusing to depend on mere men or military might is common in the psalms (see, for example, Pss. 44:4-8 and 118:6-12). Human leaders are only mortal, and no salvation can be found in them. Their mortality is shown by the fact that when death comes they return to the earth and their plans never reach fruition. The word for 'plans' (*'eshtonot*) only occurs here, but comes from a verb that means 'devise', 'keep in mind'.[2]

Blessed is he whose help is the God of Jacob, whose hope is in the LORD his God, the Maker of heaven and earth, the sea, and everything in them – the LORD, who remains faithful forever (*vv. 5-6*). The psalmist sings of the happy condition of those who have trusted instead in the LORD (for comment on 'blessed', see Ps. 1:1). The God of the patriarch Jacob is equated with the covenant LORD of Israel. This title, 'the God of Jacob', is quite common in the Psalter (Pss. 20:1; 46:7, 11; 75:9; 76:6; 81:1; 84:8; cf. also Isaiah's term, 'The mighty one of Jacob,' in Isa. 49:26 and 60:16). As in Psalm 121:1, reference to 'help' brings the reassurance that the real helper is the creator of heaven and earth. First, the almighty creator has the ability to help his people because everything in heaven, earth and sea was made by him (for the phrase 'Maker of heaven and earth', see Pss. 115:15 and 121:2). Secondly, he is a God who will not fail to keep his covenanted word (Heb., 'who keeps truth for ever'). Whoever trusts in this God is eternally blessed!

---

[2] *DCH*, VI, p. 624.

He upholds the cause of the oppressed and gives food to the hungry. The LORD sets prisoners free, the LORD gives sight to the blind, the LORD lifts up those who are bowed down, the LORD loves the righteous. The LORD watches over the alien and sustains the fatherless and the widow, but he frustrates the ways of the wicked (*vv. 7-8*). In the Hebrew text a series of participles explains further about the maker of heaven and earth. He 'upholds ... and gives ... sets prisoners free ... gives sight ... lifts up ... loves ... watches over'. Many of the expressions used occur in other psalms, such as the opening of verse 7 that abbreviates Psalm 103:6. Both the content and the order of the phrases have similarities with Psalm 107. The reference to lifting up the bowed down occurs in this form in the Old Testament only here and in Psalm 145:14. While translated similarly in the NIV, the two final statements ('sustains ... frustrates') contain different verbal forms in Hebrew as compared with 'watches over'.[3] These statements complete the description by stating two opposing facts. Towards the most needy in society the LORD shows compassion, but he makes crooked the ways of the wicked.

3. A Final Call to Praise (*v. 10*).

The LORD reigns forever, your God, O Zion, for all generations. Praise the LORD (*v. 10*). As the poet renews the call to praise, he echoes the words of Exodus 15:18: 'The LORD reigns forever.' His address is to Zion/Jerusalem, reminding her that God is the everlasting King who has chosen to dwell with his people (see Ps. 132:14-15). God's reign is not of limited duration, but lasts 'throughout all generations'.[4] That fact should bring reassurance to those whose hope is in the LORD (v. 5), and produce from them a response to the final call: 'Praise the LORD' (Heb., *hallᵉlûyâh*).

---

[3] A participle (*shomêr*, 'watches over') is followed by two prefix conjugation forms (*yᵉʿôdêd*, 'sustains', and *yeʿavvêt*, 'frustrates'). This example illustrates well the usage of both participle and prefix conjugation (imperfect) in describing habitual action, with tense to be determined from the context. See T. O. Lambdin, *Introduction to Biblical Hebrew*, pp. 19 and 100.

[4] The expression 'throughout all generations' (lit. 'to generation and generation', *lᵉdor vâdor*) is a standard one for perpetuity.

Psalm 147

While the LXX divides this psalm into two (vv. 1-11 are Psalm 146; vv. 11-20 are Psalm 147), its unity is apparent from the parallelism throughout the sections and the way in which the opening and close form a frame for the central content of the psalm. The dependence on earlier parts of the Old Testament (especially Deut. 4 and Pss. 33, 104) and the reference to the return of the exiles suggest it was a song composed in the post-exilic period. The most probable occasion for its composition would have been the dedication of the rebuilt walls of Jerusalem (Neh. 12:27-43). Such a joyous time would have been most appropriate for a song calling for praise to the LORD for his great love and favour to Israel. The psalm is composed of three sections, all commencing either with description of how beautiful praise is ('How good it is to sing praises', v. 1) or imperatives calling for praise ('sing', v. 7; 'extol' and 'praise', v. 12).

1. Praise to the Great Creator (*vv. 1-6*)

Praise the LORD. How good it is to sing praises to our God, how pleasant and fitting to praise him! (*v. 1*). The opening call to praise is followed by exclamations that speak of the worth of such praise. It is 'good' (*tôv*), 'pleasant' (*nâʿîm*),[1] and 'fitting' (*nâʾvâh*). There is a cumulative impact created by these adjectives. From the declaration that praise is good, the psalmist moves on to the idea that praise is pleasant, before

[1] The RSV and NRSV strangely apply the adjective *nâʿîm* to God; 'for he is gracious'. In the context it is the praise that is declared to be 'pleasant'.

the closing term 'fitting' or 'appropriate' is applied to it.[2] While there is some similarity with Psalm 33:1-2, yet the closest parallel to this opening is Psalm 135:3. It is quite possible to take the Hebrew here as an emphatic statement: 'It is *indeed* good to sing praises ...' Praise is an appropriate response, but it is also a joyful thing.

The LORD builds up Jerusalem; he gathers the exiles of Israel. He heals the broken hearted and binds up their wounds (*vv.* 2-3). The setting of the psalm is the period after the return from exile. One of the terms for the exiles is used (*nid*ᵉ*chê yisrâ'êl*), reinforcing the promise of Deuteronomy 30:4 that if the exiles repented, God would gather them and bring them back to Palestine.[3] What happened when the exiles were permitted to return home, and subsequently to rebuild Jerusalem was the LORD's work (Ps. 126:2-3). Here the psalmist looks at this as a continuing work of healing ('heals ... binds') as the LORD deals in grace with grief-stricken and afflicted exiles (see Ps. 137).

He determines the number of the stars and calls them each by name. Great is our Lord and mighty in power; his understanding has no limit. The LORD sustains the humble but casts the wicked to the ground (*vv.* 4-6). Encouragement comes to the people with the thought that the restorer of Israel is none other than the God of creation. Even the stars are his, and he knows them individually. His providential work in sustaining his creation is evidence of his might and his wisdom. One of the implications of this is that God therefore is easily able to intervene on behalf of his people in order to 'sustain' them (the same verb is used as in Ps. 146:9). Seeing that he knows so much about things like stars that he gives them names, how much more does he care for his hurting people. He also acts in judgment to destroy the wicked, bringing them down to the grave.

---

[2] It is possible that the word translated 'fitting' (*nâ'vâh*) is actually a verbal form that means 'to glorify [with praise]'. Cf. the discussion by J. D. Shenkel, 'An Interpretation of Psalm 93:5', *Bib* 46 (1965), pp. 401-16.

[3] Cf. the use of this expression for the 'exiles' in other passages such as Isaiah 11:12; 56:8; Jeremiah 16:15; and Micah 4:6.

2. Praise to the Great Provider (*vv. 7-11*)

Sing to the LORD with thanksgiving; make music to our God on the harp (*v. 7*). The opening word 'sing' is literally 'respond', 'answer' (*'ânâh*), but the parallel verb 'make music' (*zâmar*, Pi.) confirms its meaning. In Hebrew this is the same verb as the NIV translates by 'sing praises' in verse 1. Praise is an excellent way of proclaiming the greatness of God. It is a thanksgiving or a confession to others of what we know of him. Here the mention of 'harp' links such praise with musical accompaniment.[4]

He covers the sky with clouds; he supplies the earth with rain and makes grass grow on the hills. He provides food for the cattle and for the young ravens when they call (*vv. 8-9*). The creator is not only concerned with the stars (v. 4), but also with the needs of cattle and birds that he made. He easily provides the rain, which in turn helps to produce the food for both domestic and wild animals. This is teaching that has already been given in slightly different form in passages such as Psalms 104:13, 21 and 145:16.

His pleasure is not in the strength of the horse, nor his delight in the legs of a man; the LORD delights in those who fear him, who put their hope in his unfailing love (*vv. 10-11*). Human strength, even military might, is no substitute for divine power. This lesson was stressed in passages such as Isaiah 31:1 and Psalm 20:7 (see comment). God does not delight in what men can achieve.[5] Rather, he delights in those who recognise their own weakness, and then trust in his steadfast love (Heb., *chésed*). Those who fear him (with the reverence of a child, not that of a slave; see Pss. 25:12; 34:9) have confidence in his ability to meet their needs.

---

[4] The idiom here (*zammêr b^e*) is used both for location of the praise, and also for the instrument being employed (lyre, Ps. 71:22; harp, Ps. 33:2; tambourine, Ps. 149:3; voice, Ps. 98:5).

[5] V. 10 is an excellent example of nicely balanced parallelism, with the verb in the first part being *châfêts* ('delight'), and in the second clause *râtsâh* ('take pleasure'). Also, both clauses commence with the negative particle 'not' (*lo'*), and are followed by construct phrases ('in the might of the horse' and 'in the legs of man').

3. Praise to Zion's God (*vv. 12-20*)

Extol the LORD, O Jerusalem; praise your God, O Zion, for he strengthens the bars of your gates and blesses your people within you (*vv. 12-13*). Zion/Jerusalem is addressed directly, picking up mention of her from verse 2. She is commanded to praise her God. Instead of the verbs 'sing' and 'make music' (see v. 7), this section commences with alternative verbs, 'extol' (*shâvach*, Pi.) and 'praise' (*hâlal*, Pi.), though no marked difference in meaning is discernible. The reasons for this command are then given. God provides for the defences of the city, and he gives his blessings to her inhabitants (lit. 'your sons'). Strengthening of defences may be a reference to some specific historical occasion that cannot now be identified.

He grants peace to your borders and satisfies you with the finest of wheat (*v. 14*). The people have rest from battle. The Hebrew word 'peace' (*shâlôm*) can convey both the ideas of absence of warfare and also prosperity (cf. its use in a question to ask for the welfare of someone, *h^ashâlôm ʾ^avîkem hazzâqên*, 'How is your aged father?' Gen. 43:27). Conveying the double meaning is possible with a translation like 'grants your borders prosperity and security'.[6] God gives his people abundant crops so that their hunger is satisfied with the best wheat. The same expression occurs in Psalm 81:16, and both occurrences may be dependent on Deuteronomy 32:14 ('the finest kernels of wheat').

He sends his command to the earth; his word runs swiftly. He spreads the snow like wool and scatters the frost like ashes. He hurls down his hail like pebbles. Who can withstand his icy blast? He sends his word and melts them; he stirs up his breezes, and the waters flow (*vv. 15-18*). God's word is likened to a messenger swiftly carrying out his commands. Though the wording is different, the meaning is the same as in Psalm 33:9: 'For he spoke, and it came to be; he commanded, and it stood firm.' The divine word carries with it divine power (cf. Jesus' word to the paralytic, 'Stretch out your hand,' in Matt. 12:13). To the earlier reference to clouds

---

[6] This is following the suggestion of L. C. Allen, *Psalms 101-150*, pp. 305-06.

and rain (v. 8) is now added snow, frost, and hail. Such wintry weather is a demonstration of God's power, before which no human can stand. But when God sends his further word, the warm breeze comes and the snow and ice melt.

He has revealed his word to Jacob, his laws and decrees to Israel (*v. 19*). God's greatest gift was, however, another 'word', which involved revelation of his will for his people. He had revealed his authoritative pronouncements and his judicial ordinances.[7] The nation whom he had made for himself was guided by the laws he gave, so that successive generations might fear him and have long life in the land of Canaan (Deut. 4:40; 6:1-2).

He has done this for no other nation; they do not know his laws. Praise the LORD (*v. 20*). Israel's position was unique. No other nation could claim the privilege enjoyed by Israel of righteous decrees and laws. This should have provoked envy when other nations saw how near God was to his people (Deut. 4:5-8). Both law and gospel come only from divine revelation (Gal. 1:11-12). After recital of all these works of the LORD, the final call fittingly is a repetition of the initial one. Consideration of God's actions in creation and redemption should lead to further praise, denoted here by a final *hall[e]lûyâh*.

---

[7] It is unclear whether the NIV translates the two Hebrew words (*chuqqîm* and *mishpâtîm*) denoting God's revelation differently than elsewhere, or whether it simply reverses the order in which they come in the Hebrew text. It would have been preferable to retain the Hebrew order here: 'his decrees and laws'.

Psalm 148

As part of the Psalter's grand climax of praise, Psalm 148 celebrates the honour of the king of creation. Heavenly bodies and earthly creatures are called to extol him. At least from the time of Hilary of Poitiers in the early church (*c.* AD 315-367), many have seen this psalm as a prophetic picture of the praise which will given to God when creation itself is freed from its present bondage (Rom. 8:18-21). However, the psalm itself does not suggest an eschatological setting. Rather, it is directed to heaven and earth – including angels, men, and animals – as a call to extol the name of the LORD, and is similar to Psalms 33, 103, and 104. The language of Nehemiah 9:5-6 is expanded here.

The key to understanding the psalm comes from the concluding stanza (vv. 13-14). The motivation to praise is not simply the wonder of creation. Rather it is the saving acts of God exercised on Israel's behalf. This comparison of redemptive deeds to God's mighty acts in creation is frequent in the Old Testament (see, in addition to these verses, Pss. 65:5-8; 74:12-17; 89:9-18; and Isa. 27:1; 40:6-14, 21-31; 51:9-11). The covenant community ('his saints') are to praise God both for the created universe and for his gracious and saving provision for it.

Many hymns have been inspired by the words of Psalm 148. 'All creatures of our God and King' (William Henry Draper 1855-1933) draws upon much earlier words by Francis of Assisi (1182-1226). However, for congregational singing, the rendering in the Scottish Metrical Version (1650) has rightly been a favourite:

The Lord of heaven confess,
On high his glory raise.
Him let all angels bless,
Him all his armies praise.
Him glorify
Sun, moon and stars;
Ye higher spheres,
And cloudy sky.

1. God's Praise in the Heavens (*vv. 1-6*)

Praise the LORD. Praise the LORD from the heavens, praise him in the heights above. Praise him, all his angels, praise him, all his heavenly hosts. Praise him, sun and moon, praise him, all you shining stars (*vv. 1-3*). A repeated call to praise commences this song exalting God and his works. Whereas the previous psalm varied the verbs for 'praise', this one uses the same one twelve times (*hâlal,* Pi.). The closest parallel to these opening words is found in the concluding verses of Psalm 103. All creatures in the heavens are commanded to praise the LORD. These extend from his angelic messengers to the sun, moon, and stars. No part of the heavens is exempt from giving praise.

Praise him, you highest heavens and you waters above the skies. Let them praise the name of the LORD, for he commanded and they were created. He set them in place for ever and ever; he gave a decree that will never pass away (*vv. 4-6*). The highest heavens[1] and the waters above (Gen. 1:7; 7:11; Ps. 29:10) are to share in praise. In the imagery of the Old Testament, God waters the earth from this reservoir (Ps. 104:13). The motivation for the praise is the decisive way in which they were created. God 'spoke and it came to be; he commanded, and it stood firm' (Ps. 33:9b).[2] He brought all things into being, and set them in their place (the same verb

[1] The Hebrew text has 'the heavens of heavens' (*sh^emê hashshâmayim*). This phrase is used in passages where it is said expressly that 'the highest heavens' are God's creation (Neh. 9:6) and hence belong to him (Deut. 10:14), and he cannot be contained within them (1 Kings 8:27).

[2] The Greek LXX carried the allusion to Psalm 33:9b further by adding verse 9a: 'For he spoke, and they were made'. Whereas Psalm 33:9a has, 'For he commanded and *it stood*', this psalm has, 'And *they were created.*'

is used here in Hebrew as in Gen. 1:17). The phrase 'for ever and ever' (*lā'ad l*[e]*'ôlâm*) only occurs here and in Psalm 111:8, but with no apparent difference in meaning from other similar expressions.[3] The final part of verse 6, instead of the interpretation given by the NIV, may mean that creation cannot transgress the bounds set by God.[4]

2. God's Praise on Earth (*vv. 7-12*)

Praise the LORD from the earth, you great sea creatures and all ocean depths, lightning and hail, snow and clouds, stormy winds that do his bidding, you mountains and all hills, fruit trees and all cedars, wild animals and all cattle, small creatures and flying birds, kings of the earth and all nations, you princes and all rulers on earth, young men and maidens, old men and children (*vv. 7-12*). In general, these verses follow the order of creation in Genesis 1, coming to a climax with the references to mankind. Everything on the earth – vegetable, animal, and human – must join in the chorus of praise. Just as God commanded and everything came into being (v. 5), so does his 'word' (*d*[e]*vārô*, NIV 'bidding') control the operations of nature. The fact that all of creation is called on to praise the LORD points to the fact that no part of creation is independent of the creator. In distinction from many other peoples in the Near East, Israel, by divine instruction, was not to worship animals or the heavenly bodies (cf. the prohibitions of Deut. 4:15-31).

3. God's Praise from His People (*vv. 13-14*)

Let them praise the name of the LORD, for his name alone is exalted; his splendour is above the earth and the heavens (*v. 13*). Creation is testimony to the power and craftsmanship of God. The opening words are identical with those in verse 5a, and just as that statement is followed by the motivation to

[3] The Hebrew words *'ad* ('perpetuity', 'eternity') and *'ôlâm* ('everlastingness') occur in a variety of compound expressions, and whichever word comes first does not seem to affect the meaning. Cf. the usage of *l*[e]*'ôlâm va'ad* and *'ôlâm va'ad*. See *TWOT*, 2, p. 645, and *DCH*, VI, pp. 267-69 and 304-05.

[4] For this view, see E. W. Hengstenberg, *Commentary on the Psalms*, III, p. 551, and J. A. Alexander, *The Psalms Translated and Explained*, p. 560.

praise ('for he commanded and they were created'), so in this verse ('for his name alone is exalted'). This motivation is probably derived from Isaiah 2:11, 17, in a description of the Day of the LORD.[5] When creation is viewed, God's 'eternal power and divine nature' (Rom. 1:20) are evident, and so his name is exalted. That 'his splendour is above the earth and the heavens' means that the creator's splendour far exceeds that of the creation.

He has raised up for his people a horn, the praise of all his saints, of Israel, the people close to his heart. Praise the LORD (*v. 14*). Elsewhere in the Psalms the term 'horn' is used of the king (Ps. 132:17), and it makes the best sense to take it in this way here also.[6] The provision of the Davidic family is rightly seen as God's creative act. Three terms are used to describe God's people. Firstly, they are called 'saints' (see on Ps. 30:4). Secondly, he calls the people 'Israel', and thirdly, he refers to them as 'the people close to his heart' (*ʿam-qᵉrovô*).[7] This latter expression is not common, though it does occur in Leviticus 10:3 ('those who approach me'). It serves as a convenient expression to denote the special relationship between God and his people. The final call to praise rounds off the majestic song of adoration.

---

[5] In Isaiah 2:11, 17 the phrase is *vᵉnisgâv yhwh lᵉvadô* ('and the LORD alone will be exalted'), while here it is *kî nisgâv shᵉmô lᵉvadô* ('for his name alone is exalted'). I have discussed the Isaianic references in *Isaiah: A Covenant to be Kept for the Sake of the Church*, pp. 51-52.

[6] Some have taken 'horn' to be a reference to the strength of God's people, though 'a praise *to* all his saints' (as the Hebrew text has) does not seem to suggest that the 'horn' and the 'saints' are identical.

[7] The expression is 'a people close to him'. The NIV, while not an exact translation, certainly captures its meaning well.

Psalm 149

This may be the response to the call for praise of the LORD's name in the previous psalm (Ps. 148:13). While the praise elements of this psalm are by no means unusual, yet the coupling of praise (vv. 1-5) with cursing (vv. 6-9) is unique in the Psalter. The nearest parallel would be the tender compassion of Deuteronomy 7 (see especially vv. 7-9) alongside the judgment of God on those who hate him, both in Israel and in Canaan (vv. 1-6, 9-10). It is best to understand the joy of the people being directed first to their present position. They have already experienced God's saving mercy both in reality and in future promise. Then the psalmist points to an eschatological day when foreign powers are going to be subjected to God's judgment, when he looses 'the fatal lightning of His terrible swift sword'. It is significant that the meting out of this judgment is by the saints (cf. Jesus' words in Matt. 19:28 about his followers judging the twelve tribes of Israel). Present and future are linked together by God's written decree (v. 9).

1. A Call to Praise *(v. 1)*

Praise the LORD. Sing to the LORD a new song, his praise in the assembly of the saints (*v. 1*). The command to praise comes with the instruction regarding its content. The song to be sung is 'a new song'. As in Psalm 96:1 (see the comment), or Isaiah 42:10,[1] this means more than just a newly composed

[1] See my comment in *Isaiah: A Covenant to be Kept for the Sake of the Church*, pp. 289-90.

song. The phrase carries eschatological overtones concerning the final judgment, which explains its use in the Book of Revelation (5:9; 14:3). The praise is to be communal, as the worshipping people of God gather together. 'Saints' is one of the many synonyms for God's people in this psalm (cf. 'people of Zion', v. 2; 'his people' and 'the humble', v. 4; 'the saints', v. 5).

2. Rejoicing in the LORD (*vv. 2-5*)

Let Israel rejoice in their Maker; let the people of Zion be glad in their King. Let them praise his name with dancing and make music to him with tambourine and harp (*vv. 1-2*). Saving acts of mercy lie behind the spiritual joy of the people. He who formed Israel into a nation is extolled as their maker (Pss. 95:6; 100:3),[2] but also as their sovereign, their King (cf. the reference to the 'horn' [king] in the previous psalm, 148:14). As the subjects experience the saving power of their King, they lift up his name in exuberant song, using instruments such as tambourine and harp to magnify their praise. It is uncertain whether instruments like the tambourine were permitted in the temple worship. If not, then this praise is some occasion outside the sacred precincts. The tambourine is elsewhere linked with dancing (Exod. 15:20; 1 Sam. 18:6; Ps. 150:4).

For the LORD takes delight in his people; he crowns the humble with salvation. Let the saints rejoice in this honour and sing for joy on their beds (*vv. 4-5*). God's pleasure in those who fear him (Ps. 147:11) is expressed again. Two more synonyms are added for the company of believers: 'his people' and 'the humble'. The wonder of God's grace is seen in the fact that he brings to himself those who are not his people and that he makes them 'sons of the living God' (Hosea 1:8-10;

---

[2] The Hebrew text has 'Let Israel rejoice in his *makers*' (*yismach yisrâ'êl b*ᵉ*ʿosâv*). This usage of the plural, 'makers', should be compared with Isaiah 54:5 where two similar plurals are used, 'your makers' (*ʿosayik*) and 'your husbands' (*boʿᵃlayik*). I have discussed this usage in *Isaiah: A Covenant to be Kept for the Sake of the Church*, p. 370. It may be an assimilation to the word *ʾᵉlôhîm*, which looks like a Hebrew plural form, but when used of Israel's God always takes a singular verb. Alternatively, it could be the so-called plural of majesty (see the discussions in *DIHG~S*, p. 19, and *IBHS*, pp. 122-23).

Rom. 9:25-26). He grants salvation to the humble,[3] another link in thought with Psalm 147 (see v. 6). The saints are called on in verse 5 to respond joyfully to this expression of salvation. Nights of sorrow are to be replaced with nights of song. The reference to 'beds' confirms the view taken above that the praise here is something outside of the temple worship. The couch drenched with tears (Ps. 6:6) is to be exchanged for songs in the night (Pss. 42:8; 77:6).[4]

3. Rejoicing in Hope (*vv. 6-9*)

May the praise of God be in their mouths and a double-edged sword in their hands, to inflict vengeance on the nations and punishment on the peoples, to bind their kings with fetters, their nobles with shackles of iron, to carry out the sentence written against them. This is the glory of all his saints. Praise the LORD (*vv. 6-9*). The contrast between the two main parts of the psalm is very sharp, but it stems from the two classes of people being described. In verses 1-5 it is the people of God who are in view. Here it is another people (Hebrew uses different words for 'people(s)' in vv. 4 and 7), who do not acknowledge the lordship of Israel's God, and who have a sentence of judgment carried out against them. The written sentence (*mishpât kâtûv*) could be one like that given in Isaiah 65:6-7 (cf. also the reference in Ps. 139:16 to God's book in which were written the psalmist's days). Vengeance is not man's prerogative but God's (Deut. 32:35, 41; cf. the use of this passage in Rom. 12:19 and Heb. 10:30). It is the expression of his character as the just and holy God. The prophets and the psalmists shared a common view that God's vengeance

---

[3] The Hebrew text says that the LORD 'crowns' (*pâ'ar*, Pi.) the pious humble with salvation. This verb, in this theme, only occurs six times in the Old Testament, and here and in Isaiah 55:5 the objects are humans, while in the four other instances (Isa. 60:7, 9, 13; Ezra 7:27) the reference is to the temple. The derived nouns, *p^e'êr* ('turban'), *tif'ârâh* and *tif'eret* (both meaning 'beauty') are much more common.

[4] Many commentators have found the reference to shouting for joy upon their beds difficult, and consequently have proposed various alterations (see L. C. Allen, *Psalms 101-150*, p. 318 for these). However, meditation on beds was practised (Ps. 63:6), and no convincing objection can be brought against the idea of singing on beds.

will prepare for a new Zion (see Isaiah 34:8; 61:2-3), and that all obstacles will be removed. Thus, the picture here is of end-time judgment in which God's people will participate (1 Cor. 6:1-3). At the present, God's people conquer through the sword of the Spirit (Eph. 6:12, 17; Heb. 4:12). The saints have a position of peculiar honour (v. 5) that will be seen especially at the last great judgment day. A final call to praise brings the assembled saints back to their present task.

Psalm 150

It is very likely that this psalm was composed as the concluding doxology of the whole Psalter. Whereas the earlier books that comprise the Psalter end with briefer doxologies (Pss. 41:13; 72:18-19; 89:52; 106:48), the final book ends with a complete psalm that constitutes the climax of praise. Thirteen times the command is given to 'praise the LORD' (Heb., *hall^{e}luyâh*). Just as Psalm 1 forms an appropriate introduction, so Psalm 150 brings to a close the whole collection (see the introduction to Ps. 1). While the psalms traverse all the varied moods of human life, this closing one draws the songbook of Israel to a conclusion on the note of overwhelming praise of God in his worthiness. It sums up the whole psalter by declaring where praise is to be given (v. 1), its content (v. 2), its manner (vv. 3-5), and, finally, its extent (v. 6). This is the grand finale to the songs of Zion.

1. Praise in Earth and Heaven (*vv. 1-2*)

Praise the LORD. Praise God in his sanctuary; praise him in his mighty heavens. Praise him for his acts of power; praise him for his surpassing greatness (*vv. 1-2*). The opening of the psalm asks for praise in earth and in heaven. There seems to be a deliberate use of 'sanctuary' (*qodesh*) to refer to the earthly dwelling place of God, while the following clause calls for heavenly choirs to sing God's praise (Hebrew, 'in the firmament of his strength'). Heaven and earth are to unite in joyful adoration, singing of the demonstrations of his great might (*big^{e}vûrotâv*, 'his mighty deeds', as in Pss. 20:6; 66:7; 71:16) and majestic power (*k^{e}rov gudelô*, 'according to the abundance of his greatness'). Doubtless both creation and redemption are in view.

2. Praise with a Complete Orchestra (*vv. 3-5*)

Praise him with the sounding of the trumpet, praise him with the harp and lyre, praise him with tambourine and dancing, praise him with the strings and flute, praise him with the clash of cymbals, praise him with resounding cymbals (*vv. 3-5*). The call to praise is repeated with the trumpet (*shôfâr*) being first mentioned. It was not only a common musical instrument, but it was also used as a signal for times such as new moon and new year and also to inaugurate the year of jubilee (Lev. 25:9). This initial reference to musical accompaniment in verse 3 is soon enlarged, as the psalmist proceeds to enumerate the other instruments, using doubled phrases to do so. This stylistic feature adds to the feeling of movement towards a climax. The whole orchestra is involved, ranging from the shepherd's pipe (*'ûgâv*) to the loud percussion instruments (*tof*, 'tambourine'; *tselts[e]lîm*, 'cymbals'). Mention is also made of dancing, which features elsewhere as a joyful response to God's saving power (Ps. 149:3; Jer. 31:4, 13).

3. Praise from All Creatures (*v. 6*)

Let everything that has breath praise the LORD. Praise the LORD (*v. 6*). The last verse in the Book of Psalms ends with a call to all creatures to give praise to the LORD. The preceding commands are implicitly directed to Israel, as the naming of the instruments shows. Now the direction is widened to embrace not only humans but all of God's creatures who breathe. While the Hebrew expression here (*n[e]shâmâh*) particularly denotes humans, yet it is used more widely of all living creatures (Gen. 7:21-22). Praising God as long as breath lasts suggests that praise and life are to be inseparately linked together. This final command to praise in the Psalter has its echo in a vision in the Book of Revelation. John says: 'Then I heard every creature in heaven and on earth and under the earth and on the sea, and all that is in them, singing: "To him who sits on the thone and to the Lamb be praise and honour and glory and power, for ever and ever!"' (Rev. 5:13). The concluding psalm ends fittingly with a final 'Praise the LORD!', 'Hallelujah!'

Scripture Index

Exodus (cont.)

Leviticus

Numbers

Jeremiah

Subject Index

A

B

C

D

E

F

G

H

I

J

S

T

U

W

Y

Z

FOCUS • ON • THE • BIBLE

PSALMS: 1 – 89

THE LORD SAVES

ERIC LANE

Psalms 1-89: The Lord Saves
Psalms 90-150: The Lord Reigns

Focus on the Bible Commentaries

Eric Lane

A Psalm is basically a poem set to music, and sung. This sets the book of Psalms apart from other Scripture. You will find other Psalms and songs scattered throughout Scripture – some are also used for worship – but they tend to be part of a narrative. Because people think of the Psalms purely as a 'song book' they have tended to overlook them as a place to look for teaching – even considered them as a less important part of the Bible.

Yet, for many centuries the Psalms would have been the most familiar part of Scripture to people who had no access to books. They are not only an integral part of the shared experience of the church but they also communicate God's guidance to this world, unfurl his character and encourage his people.

The range of subjects covered is staggering! They extol God's greatness and invite repentance, express commitment to his covenants and adherence to his law – and look forward to the coming Messianic kingdom. The style is predominantly praise but includes prayers, complaints – and even curses! Many were composed as liturgy, to be sung by God's people together, others are private and personal – yet have still found a place as shared worship in the church.

Eric trained to be a minister in the Church of England where he remained for 7 years. He was then called to be the minister of an Independent Evangelical Church where he pastored for 30 further years until his retirement.

Psalms 1-89 ISBN 978-1-84550-180-8
Psalms 90-150 ISBN 978-1-84550-202-7

FOCUS • ON • THE • BIBLE

ISAIAH

A COVENANT TO BE KEPT
FOR THE SAKE OF THE CHURCH

'Allan Harman's 'Isaiah' has made me wish wholeheartedly that I could start all over again. The detailed interpretative work is superb.'
Alec Motyer

ALLAN HARMAN

Isaiah

A Covenant to be kept for the sake of the Church

Allan Harman

Too often modern commentaries become a discussion between commentators rather than an exploration of what the text has to say to contemporary readers. Allan Harman's methods follow those of Leon Morris and Allan McRae in that he devotes most of his energy to discovering what God is saying through his prophet, rather than what we are saying amongst ourselves.

Outstanding. What I mean by that is that he has been able to do the work of a first class exegete, yet make it understandable to a wide audience. As I train my theological students in the prophets of the Bible I will send them to this book immediately.

John Currid,
Carl McMurray Professor of Old Testament,
Reformed Theological Seminary, Charlotte, North Carolina

With Allan Harman's 'Isaiah' *before me, I know what the saying means that 'even a cat can look at the queen'! His work has made me wish wholeheartedly that I could start all over again. The detailed interpretative work is superb, and Harman's defence of the unity of Isaiah is robust (to say the least), and, in my view, unanswerable. I thrill to a commentator whose prime aim is to understand and explain the Hebrew Text, not just to distil the opinions of others. Thank God for this book - and its author.*

Alec Motyer,
Well known Bible expositor and commentary writer

ISBN 978-1-84550-053-5

FOCUS • ON • THE • BIBLE

DEUTERONOMY

THE COMMANDS OF A COVENANT GOD

ALLAN HARMAN

Deuteronomy

Commands of a Covenant God

Allan Harman

'Deuteronomy' is a misnomer, it means 'the second law'. The name is taken from Deuteronomy 17:18 where the expression really means having a copy of the law. Deuteronomy is therefore not a second, different, law but a renewal of the covenant made on Mount Sinai. For a people on the brink of entering their promised land Deuteronomy confirmed God's gracious promises as they prepared for new horizons and adventures.

He keeps the connectedness of the text before us and yet can dash off to capture a Hebrew participle or suffix, pilfer a bit of Near Eastern background, or serve up the succinct result of a word study – all to light up a passage."

Dale Ralph Davis,
Well respected author and Bible expositor

Allan Harman's exposition is as clear as crystal... This is a work of fine scholarship lightly worn.

Geoffrey Grogan,
Late Principal Emeritus of Glasgow Bible College and well-respected author

ISBN 978-1-84550-268-3

MICHAEL LEFEBVRE

SINGING THE SONGS OF JESUS

REVISITING THE PSALMS

Singing the Songs of Jesus

Revisiting the Psalms

Michael Lefebvre

"This book powerfully reminds us that the church has for too long ignored a vibrant source of devotion-the song book of Jesus... we can't afford to neglect this divinely inspired song book that God has given us."

Donald W. Sweeting,
President & Professor of Church History,
Reformed Theological Seminary, Orlando, Florida

Speaking to God in words that He has chosen, with the breadth and depth of topics He has revealed, instead of singing about Him, would enrich our worship. Yes, it will prove a learning experience for our congregations, but the dimensional richness the Psalms afford would be well worth the effort.

John D. Hannah,
Distinguished Professor of Historical Theology,
Dallas Theological Seminary, Dallas, Texas

The Psalms accurately reflect our spiritual health. The more I am 'at home' in singing the Psalms, the spiritually fitter I am. Uniquely in the Bible, the Psalms both speak to us – Luther derived much of his theology from the Psalter, – and also speak for us. They are the God-given words with which we can address both our Heavenly Father and each other. Michael LeFebvre's book is both scholarly and readable, and provides a wonderful incentive to 'Sing the Psalms, again'.

Jonathan Fletcher,
Vicar of Emmanuel Church, Wimbledon, London

Michael Lefebvre is pastor of Christ Church Reformed Presbyterian Church, Indianapolis, Indiana

ISBN 978-1-84550-600-1

Christian Focus Publications

publishes books for all ages

Our mission statement –
STAYING FAITHFUL
In dependence upon God we seek to impact the world through literature faithful to His infallible Word, the Bible. Our aim is to ensure that the Lord Jesus Christ is presented as the only hope to obtain forgiveness of sin, live a useful life and look forward to heaven with Him.

REACHING OUT
Christ's last command requires us to reach out to our world with His gospel. We seek to help fulfill that by publishing books that point people towards Jesus and help them develop a Christ-like maturity. We aim to equip all levels of readers for life, work, ministry and mission.

Books in our adult range are published in three imprints.

Christian Focus contains popular works including biographies, commentaries, basic doctrine and Christian living. Our children's books are also published in this imprint.

Mentor focuses on books written at a level suitable for Bible College and seminary students, pastors, and other serious readers. The imprint includes commentaries, doctrinal studies, examination of current issues and church history.

Christian Heritage contains classic writings from the past.

Christian Focus Publications, Ltd
Geanies House, Fearn, Ross-shire,
IV20 1TW, Scotland, United Kingdom
www.christianfocus.com